ZONDERVAN

KING JAMES
VERSION
COMMENTARY

NEW TESTAMENT

GENERAL EDITORS

Edward Hindson, MA, ThM, ThD, DPhil · Assistant Chancellor, Dean of the Institute of Biblical Studies and Distinguished Professor of Religion at Liberty University, Lynchburg, Virginia. Author or editor of forty books, including the Gold Medallion–winning *Knowing Jesus Study Bible* (Zondervan) and the *Zondervan KJV Study Bible*. He has also served as a visiting lecturer at Oxford University and the Harvard Divinity School and is a Life Fellow of the International Biographical Association, Cambridge, England.

Daniel Mitchell, ThM, STM, ThD · Dean and Professor of Theological Studies at Liberty Theological Seminary, Lynchburg, Virginia. Author of commentaries on First and Second Corinthians (AMG Publishers). He was a general editor of the *King James Study Bible* (Thomas Nelson) and consulting editor of the *Zondervan KJV Study Bible*. He has also taught at Western Seminary (Portland, Oregon), Tyndale Theological Seminary (Amsterdam, Holland), and ABECAR Institute in Sao Paulo, Brazil.

AUTHORS AND CONTRIBUTORS

Barth Campbell, MA, PhD · Late Professor of New Testament Studies, Simpson University, Redding, California

Mal Couch, MA, ThM, PhD · Founder and former President, Tyndale Theological Seminary, Fort Worth, Texas

Steven Ger, ThM, PhD · President, Sojourner Ministries, Garland, Texas

Harvey Hartman, ThM, ThD · Professor of Biblical Studies, Liberty University, Lynchburg, Virginia

Ronald Hawkins, MDiv, DMin, EdD · Vice Provost and Professor of Counseling and Practical Theology, Liberty University, Lynchburg, Virginia

Fred Smith, MDiv, PhD · Associate Professor of Biblical Studies and Theology, Liberty Theological Seminary, Lynchburg, Virginia

Jon Venema, MDiv, PhD · Associate Professor of New Testament Literature and Languages, Western Theological Seminary, Portland, Oregon

Gary Yates, ThM, PhD · Associate Professor of Biblical Studies, Liberty Theological Seminary, Lynchburg, Virginia

ACKNOWLEDGMENTS

The two-volume *Zondervan King James Bible Commentary* is based upon the original study notes in the *Zondervan KJV Study Bible*.

ZONDERVAN
KING JAMES VERSION ⌒ COMMENTARY

New Testament

EDWARD E. HINDSON
General Editor

& DANIEL R. MITCHELL
General Editor

ZONDERVAN
ZONDERVAN.com/
AUTHORTRACKER
follow your favorite authors

ZONDERVAN

Zondervan King James Version Commentary — New Testament
Copyright © 2010 by Zondervan

Requests for information should be addressed to:

Zondervan, *Grand Rapids, Michigan 49530*

Library of Congress Cataloging-in-Publication Data

Zondervan King James Version commentary : New Testament / Edward E. Hindson, Daniel R. Mitchell,
   general editors.
         p. cm.
      Includes bibliographical references and index.
      ISBN 978-0-310-25150-7 (hardcover, printed)
      1. Bible. N. T. English—Versions—Authorized. 2. Bible. N.T.—Commentaries. I. Hindson, Edward E.
II. Mitchell, Daniel R.
   BS2086.Z66 2010
   225.7 — dc22   2010019093

Maps by International Mapping. Copyright © 2010 by Zondervan. All rights reserved.

Any Internet addresses (websites, blogs, etc.) and telephone numbers printed in this book are offered as a
resource. They are not intended in any way to be or imply an endorsement by Zondervan, nor does Zondervan vouch for the content of these sites and numbers for the life of this book.

Cover design: Angela Eberlein
Cover photography: Jeremy Woodhouse, Getty Images
Interior design: Ben Fetterley

Printed in the United States of America

10 11 12 13 14 15 16 /DCI/ 26 25 24 23 22 21 20 19 18 17 16 15 14 13 12 11 10 9 8 7 6 5 4 3 2 1

CONTENTS

PREFACE

The message of the Bible represents the timeless truth of God. As each generation seeks to apply that truth to its specific context, an up-to-date commentary needs to be created for them. The editors and authors of the *Zondervan King James Bible Commentary* have endeavored to do just that. This team of scholars represents conservative evangelical scholarship at its best. We have approached the time-honored text of the King James Version with humility and respect as we explore its meaning and message for our generation.

The King James text used in this commentary follows that of the *Zondervan KJV Study Bible* (2002), which is based upon the final revision of fifteen different printings of the King James Version from 1611 to 1769 by F. H. A. Scrivener in 1873. The Scrivener edition of the King James Version sought to standardize the marginal notes, explanatory comments, italicized type, punctuation, spelling, and capitalization of the various editions of the King James Version, resulting in the most highly regarded edition of the Authorized Version, known as the *Cambridge Paragraph Bible*, edited by Dr. Scrivener in 1873.

Understanding the meaning of the Bible is a challenge that faces every reader of the biblical text. Explaining the meaning of that text to the average reader is then the challenge of every expository commentator. In the biblical story of Philip and the Ethiopian eunuch, who was reading the book of Isaiah, Philip asked him if he understood what he was reading. The eunuch replied, "How can I except some man should guide me?" (Acts 8:31). That is exactly what the editors and authors of this unique two-volume commentary have endeavored to do.

We have assembled a team of biblical scholars from a variety of backgrounds to comment on the sixty-six books of the biblical canon. Their comments are intended to provide the reader with clear explanations of both antiquated English terms of the King James text (e.g., "letteth" in 2 Thess. 2:7) and Hebrew, Aramaic, and Greek words from the original languages of the Bible (e.g., Greek, *harpazo* in 1 Thess. 4:17). They have also focused their comments on the intended meaning of the original authors, providing linguistic, historical, and archaeological insights that illuminate our understanding of the biblical text (e.g., the kinsman-redeemer in Ruth 2:20; 4:4).

We acknowledge that we are fallible humans attempting to explain the infallible truths of God's Word. Therefore, we have approached this challenge with sincere respect for the Scriptures and personal devotion to God, who is the ultimate author of its inspired message both to our generation and to every generation that has been blessed by its life-changing truths. The psalmist reminds us, "His truth endureth to all generations" (Ps. 117:2). Jesus said, "And ye shall know the truth and the truth shall make you free" (John 8:32). Thus, our comments are intended both to explain the meaning of the biblical text and to apply its truths to our lives. Therefore, the *Zondervan King James Bible Commentary* is both expository and practical, designed for use by pastors and lay readers alike.

The New Testament has guided the Christian church for over two thousand years. This one testament is composed of twenty-seven books, penned by godly men through the inspiration of the Holy Spirit. It tells of the life of Jesus Christ, His atoning death for our sins, His miraculous resurrection, His ascension to heaven, and the promise of His second coming. It also tells the story of the birth and growth of the church and the people and principles that shaped its early history. The New Testament concludes with the book of Revelation pointing ahead to the glorious return of Christ.

Without the New Testament, the message of the Bible would be incomplete. The Old Testament points ahead to the coming Messiah, the King of Israel and the Savior of the world. In commenting on the Hebrew Scriptures, Jesus said, "All things must be fulfilled which were written in the Law of Moses, and in the prophets, and in the psalms, concerning me" (Luke 24:44). But the Old Testament ends without His arrival. All of its ceremonies, pictures, types, and prophecies are left awaiting the coming of the "Lamb of God, which taketh away the sin of the world" (John 1:29).

Jesus Christ is the greatest person who has ever lived. There have been great men and women whose lives have made an impact while they were here on earth. But the greatest of them does not hold a candle to the blazing brilliance of His life. His person, character, wisdom, love, and grace leap off the pages of the New Testament into the hearts of all who believe in Him. It is our sincere hope that you will come to know Him better and live for Him more effectively as our comments enlighten your mind and challenge your soul.

Edward Hindson

Daniel Mitchell

THE GOSPEL ACCORDING TO ST. MATTHEW

INTRODUCTION

Author

The early church fathers were unanimous in holding that Matthew, one of the twelve apostles, was the author of this gospel. In addition, every early manuscript of Matthew that has been preserved attributes the gospel to him. No one in the early church ever suggested that anyone else was the author. Matthew is quoted by Ignatius as early as AD 110 and is quoted by various church fathers more often than Mark or Luke.

The results of modern critical studies, however, in particular those that stress Matthew's alleged dependence on Mark for a substantial part of his gospel, have caused some biblical scholars to abandon Matthean authorship. Why, they ask, would Matthew, an eyewitness to the events of the Lord's life, depend so heavily on Mark's account? The best answer seems to be that he agreed with it and wanted to show that the apostolic testimony to Christ was not divided. In addition, writers often seek an outline to help them in their work, even when they are familiar with the subject. Mark offered a convenient and accurate framework for Matthew's work.

Matthew, whose name means "gift of the Lord," was a tax collector who left his work to follow Jesus (see 9:9–13). In Mark and Luke, he is called by his other name, Levi, and Mark also mentioned that he was "the son of Alpheus" (Mark 2:14). As a tax official, he had to be intelligent and literate, and thus capable of precisely recording the events of Jesus' life. Matthew frequently mentioned money and had an interest in large figures (see 18:24; 25:15).

Date and Place of Composition

The Jewish nature of Matthew's gospel may suggest that it was written in the Holy Land, though many think it may have originated in Syrian Antioch. Some have argued, on the basis of its Jewish characteristics, that it was written in the early church period, possibly the early part of AD 50, when the church was largely Jewish and the gospel was preached to Jews only (see Acts 11:19). Those who have concluded that both Matthew and Luke drew extensively from Mark's gospel, however, date it later—after the gospel of Mark had been in circulation for some time (see chart, *Zondervan KJV Study Bible,*

p. 1349). Accordingly, some feel that Matthew would have been written in the late 50s or in the 60s. Others, who assume that Mark was written between 65 and 70, place Matthew in the 70s or even later.

Recipients

Since his gospel was written in Greek, Matthew's readers were obviously Greek-speaking. They also seem to have been Jews. Many elements point to Jewish readership: Matthew's concern with the fulfillment of the Old Testament (his quotations from and allusions to the Old Testament are more numerous than that of any other gospel writer); his tracing of Jesus' descent from Abraham (1:1–17); his lack of explanation of Jewish customs (especially in contrast to Mark); his use of Jewish terminology (e.g., "the kingdom of heaven"; see discussion on 3:2) and "Father in heaven," in which "heaven" reveals the Jewish reverential reluctance to use the name of God); his emphasis on Jesus' role as the "Son of David" (1:1; 9:27; 12:23; 15:22; 20:30–31; 21:9, 15; 22:41–45). This does not mean, however, that Matthew restricted his gospel to Jews. He recorded the coming of the wise men (non-Jews) to worship the infant Jesus (2:1–12), as well as Jesus' statement that "the field is the world" (13:38). He also gave a full statement of the Great Commission (28:18–20). These passages show that, although Matthew's gospel is Jewish, it has a universal outlook.

Theme and Theological Message

Matthew's main purpose was to prove to his Jewish readers that Jesus was their Messiah. He did this primarily by showing how Jesus, in His life and ministry, fulfilled the Old Testament Scriptures. Although all the gospel writers quoted the Old Testament, Matthew included nine additional proof texts (1:22–23; 2:15; 2:17–18; 2:23; 4:14–16; 8:17; 12:17–21; 13:35; 27:9–10) to drive home his basic theme: Jesus is the fulfillment of the Old Testament predictions of the Messiah. Matthew even saw the history of God's people in the Old Testament recapitulated in some aspects of Jesus' life (see, e.g., his quotation of Hos. 11:1 in 2:15). To accomplish his purpose, Matthew also emphasized Jesus' Davidic lineage (see "Recipients," above).

Literary Features

The way the material is arranged reveals an artistic touch. The whole gospel is woven around six great discourses: (1) chapters 5–7; (2) chapter 10; (3) chapter 13; (4) chapter 18; (5) chapter 23; and (6) chapters 24–25. That this is deliberate is clear from the refrain that concludes each discourse: "When Jesus had ended these sayings," or a similar phrase (7:28; 11:1; 13:53; 19:1; 26:1). The narrative sections, in each case, appropriately lead up to the discourses. The gospel has a fitting prologue (chaps. 1–2) and a challenging epilogue (28:16–20).

Matthew begins as "The book of the generation of Jesus Christ" (1:1), much as Genesis begins each of its ten main sections with "the generations of …" (see discussion on Gen. 2:4). Jewish readers would have noticed the similarity immediately. Matthew cited Jesus' royal lineage and supernatural birth (chaps. 1–2), followed by His qualifications through His baptism and temptation (chaps. 3–4). Then he gave Jesus' basic message (chaps.

5–7), followed by a grouping of miracles (chaps. 8–10). After describing Christ's rejection (chaps. 11–12), Matthew recorded Jesus' parables that showed a different direction from the immediate kingdom He had been announcing for the Jews. The climax of Matthew is found in the passion story, which makes up much of the rest of the book.

Outline

    I. The Birth and Early Years of Jesus (chaps. 1–2)
       A. His Genealogy (1:1–17)
       B. His Birth (1:18–2:12)
       C. His Sojourn in Egypt (2:13–23)
    II. The Beginnings of Jesus' Ministry (3:1–4:11)
       A. His Forerunner (3:1–12)
       B. His Baptism (3:13–17)
       C. His Temptation (4:1–11)
   III. Jesus' Ministry in Galilee (4:12–14:12)
       A. The Beginning of the Galilean Campaign (4:12–25)
       B. The Sermon on the Mount (chaps. 5–7)
       C. A Collection of Miracles (chaps. 8–9)
       D. The Commissioning of the Twelve Apostles (chap. 10)
       E. Ministry throughout Galilee (chaps. 11–12)
       F. The Parables of the Kingdom (chap. 13)
       G. Herod's Reaction to Jesus' Ministry (14:1–12)
   IV. Jesus' Withdrawals from Galilee (14:13–17:20)
       A. To the Eastern Shore of the Sea of Galilee (14:13–15:20)
       B. To Phoenicia (15:21–28)
       C. To the Decapolis (15:29–16:12)
       D. To Caesarea Philippi (16:13–17:21)
    V. Jesus' Last Ministry in Galilee (17:22–18:35)
       A. Jesus Foretells His Death (17:22–23)
       B. Temple Tax (17:24–27)
       C. Discourse on Life in the Kingdom (chap. 18)
   VI. Jesus' Ministry in Judea and Perea (chaps. 19–20)
       A. Teaching concerning Divorce (19:1–12)
       B. Teaching concerning Little Children (19:13–15)
       C. The Rich Young Man (19:16–30)
       D. The Parable of the Laborers in the Vineyard (20:1–16)
       E. Jesus Prophesies His Coming Death Again (20:17–19)
       F. A Mother's Request (20:20–28)
       G. Restoration of Sight at Jericho (20:29–34)
  VII. Passion Week (chaps. 21–27)
       A. The Triumphal Entry (21:1–11)
       B. The Cleansing of the Temple (21:12–17)
       C. The Last Controversies with the Jewish Leaders (21:18–22:46)
       D. The Denunciation of the Scribes and Pharisees (23:1–36)

Bibliography

Blomberg, Craig L. *Matthew*. The New American Commentary 22. Nashville: Broadman & Holman, 1992.

Gundry, Robert H. *Matthew: A Commentary on His Literary and Theological Art*. Grand Rapids, MI: Eerdmans, 1982.

Hendriksen, William. *Gospel of Matthew*. Grand Rapids, MI: Baker Academic, 1974.

Hindson, Edward, and James Borland. *Matthew: God with Us*. Chattanooga: AMG, 2005.

MacArthur, John F. *Matthew*. 4 vols. The MacArthur New Testament Commentary. Chicago: Moody Press, 1985–89.

Walvoord, John F. *Matthew: Thy Kingdom Come*. Chicago: Moody Press, 1974.

EXPOSITION

I. The Birth and Early Years of Jesus (chaps. 1–2)

A. His Genealogy (1:1–17)

1:1–17. Matthew's gospel begins by connecting Jesus to the promised messianic line in the Old Testament. For a comparison of Matthew's genealogy with Luke's, see discussion on Luke 3:23–38. The types of people mentioned in this genealogy reveal the broad scope of those who make up the people of God as well as the genealogy of Jesus.

1:1. The son of David. A messianic title (see discussion on 9:27) found several times in this gospel

(in 1:20, however, it is not a messianic title). **The son of Abraham.** Because Matthew was writing to Jews, it was important to identify Jesus in this way.

1:2–5. By including four women (contrary to custom) in his genealogy, Matthew may have been indicating, at the very outset of his gospel, that God's activity is not limited to men or to the people of Israel. The four women are: **Thamar** (v. 3; see Genesis 38), **Rachab** (v. 5; see Joshua 2), **Ruth**, and Bathsheba, "her that had been the wife of Urias" (1:6). At least three of these women were Gentiles (Tamar, Rahab, and Ruth). Bathsheba was probably an Israelite (see 1 Chron. 3:5) but was closely associated with the Hittites because of Uriah, her Hittite husband. **Aminadab** (v. 4). Aaron's father-in-law (see Exod. 6:23).

1:6. Because quite a long time had elapsed between Rahab and **David** (v. 6) and because of Matthew's desire for systematic organization (see discussion on 1:17), many of the generations between these two ancestors were assumed, but not listed, by Matthew.

1:7–15. Joram begat (v. 8). Matthew calls Joram the father of Ozias, but from 2 Chronicles 21:4–26:23 it is clear that, again (see discussion on 1:6), several generations were assumed (Ahaziah, Joash, and Amaziah) and that "begat" is used in the sense of "became the forefather of." **Josias begat** (v. 11). Similarly, Josias is presented as the father of Jechonias (i.e., Jehoiachin), whereas he was actually the father of Jehoiakim and the grandfather of Jehoiachin (see 2 Chron. 36:1–9). For **Salathiel begat** (v. 12), see discussion on 1 Chronicles 3:19.

1:16. Matthew did not say that **Joseph** was the father of Jesus, only that he was **the husband of Mary** and that Jesus was born of her. In this genealogy, Matthew showed that although Jesus was not the physical son of Joseph, He was his legal son and therefore a descendant of David. By not being Joseph's son, Jesus avoided the curse on Jechonias's descendants (see Jer. 22:30).

1:17. Fourteen generations … fourteen … fourteen. These divisions reflect two characteristics of Matthew's gospel: (1) an apparent fondness for numbers and (2) a concern for systematic arrangement. The number fourteen may have been chosen because it is twice seven (the number of completeness) and/or because it is the numerical value of the name David (see *KJV Study Bible* note on Rev. 13:17). For the practice of telescoping genealogies to achieve the desired number of names, see 1 Chronicles, Introduction: "Genealogies."

B. His Birth (1:18–2:12)

1:18. Mary was espoused to Joseph. There were no sexual relations during a Jewish betrothal period,

but it was a much more binding relationship than a modern engagement and could be broken only by divorce (see 1:19). In Deuteronomy 22:24, a betrothed woman is called a "wife," though the preceding verse speaks of her as being "betrothed unto a husband." Matthew used the terms "husband" (1:19) and "wife" (1:24) of Joseph and Mary before their betrothal was consummated.

1:19. Just. To Jews, this meant being zealous in keeping the law. **Put her away privily.** Joseph was considering signing the necessary legal papers for a divorce but not having Mary judged publicly and stoned (see Deut. 22:23–24).

1:20. In a dream. This phrase occurs five times in the first two chapters of Matthew (here; 2:12–13, 19, 22) and indicates the means the Lord used for speaking to Joseph. **Thou Son of David** was perhaps a hint that the message of the angel related to the expected Messiah. **Take unto thee Mary thy wife.** Joseph and Mary were legally bound to each other but were not yet living together as husband and wife. **That which is conceived in her is of the Holy Ghost**. This agrees perfectly with the announcement to Mary (see Luke 1:35), except that the latter was more specific (see discussion on Luke 1:26–35).

1:21. JESUS … shall save. The name Jesus is the Greek form of Joshua, which means "the LORD saves."

1:22. That it might be fulfilled. Sixteen times (here; 2:15, 17, 23; 3:15; 4:14; 5:18; 8:17; 12:17; 13:14, 35; 21:4; 24:34; 26:56; 27:9, 35) Matthew spoke of the Old Testament being "fulfilled," that is, of events in New Testament times that were prophesied in the Old Testament—a powerful testimony to the divine origin of Scripture and its accuracy even in small details. In the fulfillments, we also see the writer's concern for linking the gospel with the Old Testament. Matthew, writing especially for the Jews, demonstrated how Jesus fulfilled numerous prophecies.

1:23. See discussion on Isaiah 7:14. This is the first of at least forty-seven quotations, most of them messianic, that Matthew cited from the Old Testament (see marginal notes throughout Matthew). **A virgin** refers to Mary, the mother of Jesus. Quoting

Isaiah 7:14, Matthew used the Greek *parthenos* to translate the Hebrew *'almah* precisely as a "virgin" in the technical sense. His usage of "fulfilled" in 1:22 clearly indicates that he believed the Isaiah passage prophesied the virginal conception of Jesus. **Emmanuel** means "God with us" and is used as a title of Jesus' divinity.

1:24 – 25. And knew her not till she brought forth her firstborn son (v. 25). Matthew and Luke both made it clear that Jesus was born of a virgin (see Luke 1:26 – 35). Although this doctrine is often ridiculed, it is an important part of the evangelical faith.

2:1. Bethlehem of Judea. A village about five miles south of Jerusalem. Matthew recorded nothing of the events in Nazareth (see Luke 1:26 – 56). Possibly wanting to emphasize Jesus' Davidic background, he began with the events that happened in David's city. It is called "Bethlehem of Judea," not to distinguish it from the town of the same name about seven miles northwest of Nazareth, but to emphasize that Jesus came from the tribe and territory that produced the line of Davidic kings. That Jews expected the Messiah to be born in Bethlehem and to be from David's family is clear from John 7:42. **Herod the king.** Herod the Great (37 – 4 BC), to be distinguished from the other Herods in the Bible (see chart, *KJV Study Bible*, p. 1355). Herod was a non-Jew, an Idumean, who was appointed king of Judea by the Roman senate in 40 BC and gained control only by military conquest by 37 BC. Like many other rulers of the day, he was ruthless. Herod murdered one of his wives, three of his sons, a mother-in-law, a brother-in-law, an uncle, and many others — not to mention the babies in Bethlehem (see 2:16). His reign was also noted for splendor, as seen in the many theaters, amphitheaters, monuments, pagan altars, fortresses, and other buildings he erected or refurbished — including the greatest work of all, the rebuilding of the temple in Jerusalem, begun in 19 BC and finished sixty-eight years after his death. **Wise men.** Perhaps they were from Persia or southern Arabia, both of which are east of the Holy Land. **Jerusalem.** Since they were looking for the "King of the Jews" (v. 2), they naturally came to the Jewish

capital city (see Map 10 at the end of the *KJV Study Bible*).

2:2. King of the Jews. Indicates the wise men were Gentiles. Matthew showed that people of all nations acknowledged Jesus as "King of the Jews" and came to worship Him as Lord. **Star.** Probably not an ordinary star, planet, or comet, though some scholars have identified it with the conjunction of Jupiter and Saturn. It must have been a supernatural object that looked like a star but that could actually move along and lead the wise men. It eventually led them to the proper house (see 2:9).

2:3 – 6. Chief priests (v. 4). Sadducees (see discussion on 3:7) who were in charge of worship at the temple in Jerusalem. The chief priests included the ruling high priest, Caiaphas; the former high priest, Annas; and the high priestly families. **Scribes.** The Jewish scholars of the day, professionally trained in the development, teaching, and application of Old Testament law. Their authority was strictly human and traditional. **Thou Bethlehem** (v. 6). This prophecy from Micah 5:2 had been given seven centuries earlier.

2:7 – 12. Child (v. 9). Contrary to tradition, the wise men did not visit Jesus at the manger on the night of His birth, as did the shepherds. They came some months later and visited Him in His **house** (v. 11). **The young child with Mary his mother.** Every time the child Jesus and His mother are mentioned together, He is mentioned first (here, 2:13 – 14, 20 – 21). **Gold, and frankincense, and myrrh** (for "myrrh," see discussion on Gen. 37:25). The three gifts perhaps gave rise to the legend that there were three wise men. The Bible does not indicate the number of the magi, however, and they were almost certainly not kings.

C. His Sojourn in Egypt (2:13 – 23)

2:13 – 15. Matthew saw the history of Israel (God's children) recapitulated in the life of Jesus (God's unique Son). **Into Egypt** (v. 13). Just as Israel as an infant nation went down into Egypt, so the child Jesus went there. **Out of Egypt have I called my son** (v. 15). As Israel was led by God out of Egypt, so also was Jesus. This quotation from Hosea 11:1 originally referred to God's calling the nation of Israel out of Egypt in the time of Moses, but Matthew, under the inspiration of the Spirit, applied it also to Jesus. How long Jesus and His parents were in Egypt is not known. **The death of Herod**. In 4 BC.

2:16. Slew all the children … two years old and under. The number killed has often been exaggerated as being in the thousands. In so small a village as Bethlehem, however (even with the surrounding area included), the number was probably not large—though the act, of course, was no less brutal.

2:17–18. See discussion on Jeremiah 31:15.

2:19–23. Archelaus (v. 22). This son of Herod the Great ruled over Judea and Samaria for only ten years (4 BC–AD 6). He was unusually cruel and tyrannical and so was deposed by Rome. Judea then became part of the Roman province of Syria, administered by prefects appointed by the emperor. **Galilee**. The northern part of the Holy Land in Jesus' day.

Nazareth (v. 23). A rather obscure town, nowhere mentioned in the Old Testament. It was Jesus' hometown (see 21:11; 26:71; Luke 2:39; 4:16–24; John 1:45–46). **He shall be called a Nazarene**. These exact words are not found in the Old Testament and probably refer to several Old Testament prefigurations and prophecies (note the plural, **prophets**) that the Messiah would be despised (e.g., Ps. 22:6; Isa. 53:3), for in Jesus' day, "Nazarene" was virtually a synonym for "despised" (see John 1:45–46). Some hold that in speaking of Jesus as a "Nazarene," Matthew was referring primarily to the word "Branch" (Hebrew, *neṣer*) in Isaiah 11:1.

II. The Beginnings of Jesus' Ministry (3:1–4:11)

A. His Forerunner (3:1–12)

3:1. John the Baptist. The forerunner of Jesus, born circa 7 BC to Zacharias, a priest, and his wife Elisabeth (see Luke 1:5–80). **The wilderness of Judea**. An area that stretched some twenty miles from the Jerusalem-Bethlehem plateau down to the Jordan River and the Dead Sea, perhaps the same region where John lived (see Luke 1:80). The people of

Qumran (often associated with the Dead Sea Scrolls) lived in this area too.

3:2. Repent. Make a radical change in one's life as a whole. **The kingdom of heaven**. A phrase found only in Matthew, where it occurs thirty-two times (see Introduction: "Recipients"). Mark and Luke referred to "the kingdom of God," a term Matthew used only four times (see *KJV Study Bible* note on Mark 11:30). The kingdom of heaven is the rule of God and is both a present reality and a future hope. The idea of God's kingdom is central to Jesus' teaching and is mentioned fifty times in Matthew alone.

3:3. All three Synoptic Gospels quote Isaiah 40:3 (Luke quotes two additional verses) and apply it to John the Baptist. **Make his paths straight**. Equivalent to "Prepare ye the way of the Lord" (see discussion on Luke 3:4). The preparation was to be moral and spiritual.

3:4–6. A leathern girdle (v. 4). Used to bind up the loose outer garments. **Locusts and wild honey**. A man living in the wilderness did not hesitate to eat insects, and locusts were among the clean foods (see Lev. 11:21–22). John's simple food, clothing, and lifestyle were a visual protest against self-indulgence. For **Jordan** (v. 6), see discussion on Mark 1:5.

3:7. The Pharisees and Sadducees. The Pharisees (see discussions on Mark 2:16; Luke 5:17) were a legalistic and separatist group who strictly, but often hypocritically, kept the law of Moses and the unwritten "tradition of the elders" (Matt. 15:2). The Sadducees (see discussions on Mark 12:18; Luke 20:27; Acts 4:1) were more worldly and politically minded, and were theologically unorthodox—among other things denying the resurrection, angels, and spirits (see Acts 23:8). For **his baptism**, see discussion on Mark 1:4. **The wrath to come**. The arrival of the Messiah will bring repentance or judgment.

3:8–10. We have Abraham to our father (v. 9; see John 8:39). Salvation does not come as a birthright (even for the Jews) but through faith in Christ (see Rom. 2:28–29; Gal. 3:7, 9, 29). **These stones**. John may have pointed to the stones in the Jordan River. **Children unto Abraham**. The true people of God are not limited to the physical descendants of

Abraham (see Rom. 9:6). **The axe is laid unto the root of the trees** (v. 10). Judgment is near.

3:11. With water unto repentance. John's baptism presupposed repentance, and he would not baptize the Pharisees and Sadducees because they failed to give any evidence of repentance (see 3:7–8). **With the Holy Ghost, and with fire.** Demonstrated in a dramatic way at Pentecost (see Acts 1:5, 8; 2:1–13; 11:16), though here "fire" may refer to judgment to come (see 3:12). The outpouring of the Holy Spirit on all God's people was promised in Joel 2:28–29.

3:12. Fan. Or "winnowing fork" (for the process of winnowing, see discussion on Ruth 1:22). Here this implement is figurative for the day of judgment at Christ's second coming. The Old Testament prophets and the New Testament writers sometimes compressed the first and second comings of Christ so that they seem to be one event.

B. His Baptism (3:13–17)

3:13–15. This occasion marked the beginning of Christ's messianic ministry. There were several reasons for His baptism: (1) Jesus' baptism **fulfil[led] all righteousness** (v. 15), indicating that He was consecrated to God and officially approved by Him, as especially shown in the descent of the Holy Spirit (see 3:16) and the words of the Father (see 3:17; Ps. 2:7; Isa. 42:1). All God's righteous requirements for the Messiah were fully met in Jesus. (2) At Jesus' baptism, John publicly announced the arrival of the Messiah and the inception of His ministry (see John 1:31–34). (3) By His baptism, Jesus completely identified Himself with man's sin and failure (though He Himself needed no repentance or cleansing from sin) and became our substitute (see 2 Cor. 5:21). (4) His baptism was an example to His followers.

3:16–17. All three persons of the Trinity are clearly seen here. This alone is not a proof of the Trinity, but an intimation of it. We prove the Trinity by showing there are three eternal persons, each of whom has the attributes of deity, yet there is only one God.

The Spirit of God (v. 16). The Holy Spirit came upon Jesus, not to overcome sin (for He was sinless), but to equip Him (see discussion on Judg. 3:10) for His work as the divine-human Messiah. **Like a dove**. Either in the form of a dove or in a descent like a dove (see discussion on Mark 1:10).

A voice from heaven (v. 17). The voice (1) authenticated Jesus' unique sonship and echoes Psalm 2:7 ("Thou art my Son"), (2) identified Jesus with the suffering servant of Isaiah 42:1 ("whom I uphold"), and (3) offered the Father's support of Jesus in His mission (**in whom I am well pleased**). This word from the Father must have tremendously encouraged Jesus at the very outset of His earthly ministry. The idea of "I am well pleased" is not that the Father was well pleased with what Jesus had done. It was not an evaluation of Jesus' past performance. Similarly, it was not an evaluation of what the Father knew Jesus would do. Instead, it is a statement of God's eternal pleasure in the Son. He is at all times pleased with the Son simply because He is the Son.

C. His Temptation (4:1–11)

4:1–11. The significance of Jesus' temptations, especially because they occurred at the outset of His public ministry, seems best understood in terms of the kind of Messiah He was to be. He would not accomplish His mission by using His supernatural power for His own needs (first temptation), by using His power to win a large following with miracles or magic (second temptation), or by compromising with Satan (third temptation). Jesus had no inward desire or inclination to sin, for these in themselves are sin (see Matt. 5:22, 28). Because He was God, He did not sin in any way, whether by action, word, or inner desire (see 2 Cor. 5:21; Heb. 7:26; 1 Peter 2:22; 1 John 3:5); yet His temptation was real, not merely symbolic. Jesus "was in all points tempted like as we are, yet without sin" (Heb. 4:15). The Tempter confronted Him with a real opportunity to sin. Although Jesus was the Son of God, He defeated Satan by using a weapon that everyone has at his or her disposal: the sword of the Spirit, which is the Word of God (see Eph. 6:17). He met all three temptations with Scriptural truth (vv. 4, 7, 10) from Deuteronomy. Jesus was able to withstand temptation because He knew and relied on God's Word.

4:1. Led up of the Spirit … to be tempted. This testing of Jesus (the Greek verb translated "tempted" can also be rendered "tested"), which was divinely intended, has as its primary background Deuteronomy 8:1 – 5, from which Jesus also quoted in His first reply to the Devil (see Matt. 4:4; Deut. 8:3). There Moses recalled how the Lord led the Israelites in the wilderness forty years "to humble thee, and to prove thee, to know what was in thine heart, whether thou wouldest keep his commandments, or no" (Deut. 8:2). Here at the beginning of His ministry, Jesus was subjected to a similar test and showed Himself to be the true Israelite who "live(s) by … every word that proceedeth out of the mouth of the Lord" (Matt. 4:4; Deut. 8:3). Whereas Adam failed the great test and plunged the whole race into sin (see Genesis 3), Jesus was faithful and thus demonstrated His qualification to become the Savior of all who receive Him. It was, moreover, important that Jesus be tempted (tested) as are "His brethren," the Israelites and all of God's children, "that he might be a merciful and faithful high priest" (Heb. 2:17) and thus be "able to succour them that are tempted" (Heb. 2:18; see Heb. 4:15 – 16). Finally, as the one who remained faithful in temptation, He became the model for all believers when they are tempted. **Tempted of the devil.** God surely tests His people, but it is the Devil who tempts to evil (see discussion on Gen. 22:1; see also 1 John 3:8; Rev. 2:9 – 10; 12:9 – 10). Like the Hebrew for "Satan," the Greek for "devil" means "accuser" or "slanderer." The Devil is a personal being, not a mere force or influence. He is the leader of the hosts of darkness and is the great archenemy of God.

4:2. Forty days and forty nights. The number recalls the experiences of Moses (see Exod. 24:18; 34:28) and Elijah (see 1 Kings 19:8), as well as the forty years of Israel's temptation (testing) in the wilderness (see Deut. 8:2 – 3).

4:3. If thou be the Son of God. Meaning, "since you are." The Devil was not casting doubt on Jesus' divine sonship but was tempting Him to use His su-

pernatural powers as the Son of God for His own ends.

4:4. Just as God gave the Israelites manna in a supernatural way (see Deut. 8:3), so also man must rely on God for spiritual feeding. Jesus relied on His Father, not on His own miracle-working power, for provision of food.

4:5 – 11. For **up into the holy city** (v. 5), see discussion on Luke 4:2. **A pinnacle of the temple** (see discussion on Luke 4:9). The temple, including the entire temple area, had been rebuilt by Herod the Great (see discussion on 2:1; see also John 2:20). The courtyard had been greatly enlarged, to about 330 by 500 yards. To accomplish this, a huge platform had been erected to compensate for the sharp falling off of the land to the southeast. An enormous retaining wall made of massive stones was built to support the platform. Today the drop from the pinnacle area is large. It was even more pronounced in Jesus' day. On the platform stood the temple, with its porches and courtyards flanked by beautiful colonnades. For **Satan** (v. 10), see discussion on 4:1.

III. Jesus' Ministry in Galilee (4:12 – 14:12)

A. The Beginning of the Galilean Campaign (4:12 – 25)

4:12. John was cast into prison. Jesus took this occasion to move to Galilee, there to begin His public preaching and teaching ministry (see Mark 1:14 and discussion on Luke 3:20). The reason for John's imprisonment is given in 14:3 – 4.

4:13. Capernaum. Although not mentioned in the Old Testament, Capernaum was evidently a sizable town in Jesus' day. Peter's house there became Jesus' base of operations during His extended ministry in Galilee (see Mark 2:1; 9:33). A fifth-century basilica now stands over the supposed site of Peter's house, and a fourth-century synagogue is located just several hundred feet from it.

4:14 – 16. Another messianic prophecy from Isaiah. **The people … saw great light** (v. 16). Matthew never quoted Jesus saying, "I am the light of the world" (John 8:12), but clearly had this in mind here. The "great light" is Jesus Himself. To be in the presence of Jesus is to be in the presence of light, that is, the truth of God. Jesus is Himself the revelation of God and is the embodiment of truth. Of course, this is manifested best in His teachings and in His deeds, which reveal the character, will, and purposes of God. When Jesus came into an area, everyone saw and heard the truth about God. Jesus spent most of His public ministry in **the land of Zabulon, and the land of Nephthalim** (v. 15), which is north and west of the Sea of Galilee. Indeed, among these people, light had certainly **sprung up** (v. 16).

4:17. From that time. These words indicate an important turning point in the life of Jesus and occur three times in Matthew's gospel (see also 16:21; 26:16). Some think these words mark the three main sections of the book. **Repent**. Jesus began His public ministry with the same message as that of John the Baptist (see 3:2). The people were called to repent because God's reign was drawing near in the person and ministry of Jesus Christ. Repentance is more than a change of mind or feeling sorry for one's sins. It is a radical and deliberate change that affects not only one's mind and emotions but also the will. The Bible knows nothing of a repentance that does not bear fruit in deeds and words. Always be suspicious of a "repentance" that is nothing more than warm feelings or an acceptance of a new set of ideas. For **the kingdom of heaven**, see discussion on 3:2.

4:18. For **the sea of Galilee**, see discussion on Mark 1:16. **Net**. A circular casting net used either from a boat or while standing in shallow water.

4:19. Fishers of men. Evangelism was at the heart of Jesus' call to His disciples. As He came to "save his people from their sins" (1:21), so He calls others to the ministry of proclaiming His salvation. Evangelism was the business of Jesus and the business of His disciples. He called them so that they might bring the lost to Him, the only hope of a lost world.

4:20. See discussions on Mark 1:17–18.

4:21. Mending their nets. Washing, mending, and hanging the nets up to dry in preparation for the next day's work.

4:22. Left the ship and their father, and followed him. Some treat this passage as if Jesus were here giving us an object lesson on "leaving all to follow Him." While this is not likely, the parallel is certainly apt. As James and John left their preoccupation with making a living and the cares of this world to follow Jesus, so must every Christian make following Christ a priority. As these two left the entanglement of fishing nets, so must believers leave the entanglement of this world's cares to follow the Lord. This does not mean that secular employment is not part of God's plan for most believers. There is evidence that the disciples retained access to a boat and fishing equipment and used them on occasion even after the resurrection (see John 21:3–8). The question for believers today is one of priorities: are Jesus and His call first and foremost in one's life? Is the believer willing to be interrupted in the midst of life's cares to follow Him?

4:23. Teaching ... preaching ... and healing. Jesus' threefold ministry. The **synagogues** (see discussion on Mark 1:21) provided a place for Him to teach on the Sabbath. During the week, He preached to larger crowds in the open air. For **gospel**, see discussion on Mark 1:1.

4:24. Syria. The area north of Galilee and between Damascus and the Mediterranean Sea. **Lunatick**. In Greek, this word originally meant "moonstruck" and reflected the ancient idea that the moon could affect behavior. **Palsy**. The Greek word used here, *paralytikos*, has come directly into English, "paralytic." Greek physicians were among the best in ancient times, and many of our medical terms come from their language.

4:25. Decapolis. A league of free cities (Decapolis means "the ten cities") characterized by high Greek culture. All but one, Scythopolis (Beth Shan), were east of the Sea of Galilee and the Jordan River. The league stretched from a point northeast of the Sea of Galilee southward to Philadelphia (modern Amman).

B. The Sermon on the Mount (chaps. 5–7)

5:1–7:29. The Sermon on the Mount is the first of six great discourses in Matthew (chaps. 5–7; 10; 13; 18; 23; 24–25). It contains three types of material: (1) beatitudes, that is, declarations of blessed-ness (5:1–12), (2) ethical admonitions (5:13–20; 6:1–7:23), and (3) contrasts between Jesus' ethical teaching and Jewish legalistic traditions (5:21–48). The Sermon ends with a short parable stressing the importance of practicing what had just been taught (7:24–27) and the crowds' amazement at the authority with which Jesus spoke (7:28–29).

Opinion differs as to whether the Sermon on the Mount is a summary of what Jesus taught on one occasion or a compilation of teachings presented on numerous occasions. Matthew may have taken a single sermon and expanded it with other relevant teachings of Jesus. Thirty-four of the verses in Matthew's Sermon on the Mount occur in Luke in contexts other than the apparently parallel Sermon on the Plain (Luke 6:17–49; see discussion on Luke 6:20–49). Most likely, this account is a summary of what Jesus usually taught everywhere He went, with some variations due to time constraints and the situation.

Following the opening, the sermon develops one organizing theme: "Except your righteousness shall exceed the righteousness of the scribes and Pharisees, ye shall in no case enter into the kingdom of heaven" (5:20). Much of the sermon consists of examples of the traditional teaching of the Pharisees contrasted with a higher ethic, a righteousness exceeding that of the scribes and Pharisees. Jesus called His hearers to genuine faith in God, encouraging secret giving and private prayer rather than public demonstrations, as well as prayer made in simple faith that does not require "vain repetitions" and "much speaking" (6:3–7). In both cases, He challenged his hearers to believe that God really does hear prayer and that He rewards those who pray and who do good. Those who truly believe that God will reward them do not need to do these things publicly, thereby earning the praise of men as reward. Again, this points to a righteousness that "exceed(s) the righteousness of the scribes and Pharisees" (5:20) since it proceeds out of genuine faith in God Himself.

The Sermon on the Mount's call to moral and ethical living is so high that some have dismissed it as being completely unrealistic or have projected its

fulfillment to the future kingdom. There is no doubt, however, that Jesus (and Matthew) gave the sermon as a standard for all Christians, realizing that its demands cannot be met in our own power. It is also true that Jesus occasionally used hyperbole to make His point (see, e.g., discussion on 5:29–30).

5:1. A mountain. The exact location is uncertain. It may have been the gently sloping hillside at the northwest corner of the Sea of Galilee, not far from Capernaum. Matthew may have recorded this incident with the giving of the Mosaic law on Mount Sinai in mind. The parallel may be incidental, but for Matthew's mostly Jewish audience, it may not have gone unnoticed. **When he was set.** It was the custom for Jewish rabbis to be seated while teaching (see Mark 4:1; 9:35; Luke 4:20; 5:3; John 8:2). **Disciples.** Literally, "learners." Since at the end of the sermon the crowd expressed amazement at Jesus' teaching (see 7:28), "disciples" may here be used in a broader sense than the Twelve. Or perhaps the sermon is addressed to the Twelve with the crowds also listening.

5:2–5. Blessed (v. 3). The word means more than "happy," because happiness is an emotion often dependent on outward circumstances. "Blessed" here refers to the ultimate well-being and distinctive spiritual joy of those who share in the salvation of the kingdom of God (see *KJV Study Bible* notes on Ps. 1:1; Rev. 1:3). **The poor in spirit.** In contrast to the spiritually proud and self-sufficient. **Theirs is the kingdom of heaven.** The kingdom is not something one earns. It is more a gift than a recompense. This beatitude should also be seen in light of Jesus' call to private prayer and private giving (see 6:3–7). The proud and self-sufficient do not pray because they need God, and they do not give because they care about the needs of others. Jesus was promising that "the poor in spirit," who know they need God and who are sensitive to the needs of others, will find grace in response to their faith. **Meek** (v. 5). This beatitude is taken from Psalm 37:11 and refers not so much to an attitude toward people as to a disposition before God, namely, humility. **The earth.** The new Promised Land (see Rev. 21:1). This is not a promise that "good people always win" in this age.

5:6 – 12. Heart (v. 8). The center of one's being, including mind, will, and emotions (see *KJV Study Bible* note on Ps. 4:7). **Peacemakers** (v. 9). Those who promote peace, as far as it depends on them (see Rom. 12:18). **They shall be called the children of God** because, in promoting peace, they reflect the character of their heavenly Father. **Theirs is the kingdom of heaven** (v. 10). A present reality as well as a future hope.

5:13 – 15. Salt (v. 13). Used for flavoring and preserving. **Lost his savour.** Most of the salt used in Israel came from the Dead Sea and was full of impurities, which caused it to lose some of its flavor. **Candle** (v. 15). In Jesus' day, people used small clay lamps that burned olive oil drawn up by a wick (see *KJV Study Bible* note on Exod. 25:37). **Bushel.** A basket that held about eight quarts of ground meal or flour.

5:16. Father which is in heaven. Matthew used the term "Father which is in heaven" or "heavenly Father" nineteen times, Mark twice, Luke once, and John not at all. Matthew apparently wanted to distinguish between God the Father and earthly fathers, something that may have been important to Jewish readers, as it was to those who heard Jesus originally.

5:17. The law. The first five books of the Jewish Scriptures (our Old Testament). **The prophets.** Not only the Latter Prophets — the Major Prophets (Isaiah, Jeremiah, and Ezekiel) and the twelve Minor Prophets (which the Jews grouped together as "the Book of the Twelve") — but also the so-called Former Prophets (Joshua, Judges, Samuel, and Kings). Taken together, "the law" and "the prophets" designates the entire Old Testament, including the Writings, the third section of the Hebrew Bible (see 13:35, where Matthew used "which was spoken by the prophet" to introduce a quotation from the Writings [Ps. 78:2]). **Fulfil.** Jesus fulfilled the law in the sense that He gave it its full meaning. He emphasized its deep, underlying principles and total commitment to it rather than mere external acknowledgment and obedience.

5:18 – 20. Jesus was speaking not against observing all the requirements of the law but against hypocritical, Pharisaical legalism. Such legalism was not the keeping of all details of the law but the hollow sham of keeping laws externally, to gain merit before God, while breaking them inwardly. It was following the letter of the law while ignoring its spirit. Here is the heart of the sermon. Jesus enjoined genuine, heartfelt obedience to the law and never called people to disobedience. The issue is not license versus legalism, but legalism versus righteousness arising from faith in God and His goodness. Here Jesus repudiated the Pharisees' interpretation of the law and their view of righteousness by works. He preached a righteousness that comes only through faith in Him and His work. In the verses that follow (5:18 – 37), He gave six examples of Pharisaical externalism.

Jot (v. 18). One word in Greek, *iōta,* which we use when we say, "It doesn't make one iota of difference." It is the nearest Greek equivalent to the Hebrew *yodh,* the smallest letter of the Hebrew alphabet (see Ps. 119:73 title). **Tittle.** The Greek word means "horn" and was used to designate the slight embellishment or extension of certain letters of the Hebrew alphabet (somewhat like the bottom of a *j*).

5:21. Ye have heard that it was said. The contrast that Jesus set up (here, 5:27, 31, 33, 38, 43) was not between the Old Testament and His teaching (He has just established the validity of the Old Testament law). Rather, it was between externalistic interpretation of the rabbinic tradition on the one hand and Jesus' correct interpretation of the law on the other. **Kill.** This word, used in Exodus 20:13, specifically means "murder."

5:22. Raca. This word may be related to the Aramaic word for "empty" and means "Empty-head!" For **council,** see discussion on Mark 14:55. **Hell.** The Greek word is *geenna,* which derives its name from a deep ravine south of Jerusalem, the "Valley of (the Sons of) Hinnom" (Hebrew, *ge hinnom*). During the reigns of the wicked Ahaz and Manasseh, human sacrifices to the Ammonite god Molech were offered there. Josiah desecrated the valley because of the pagan worship there (see 2 Kings 23:10; Jer. 7:31 – 32; 19:6). It became a sort of perpetually burning city dump and later became a figure for the place of final punishment.

5:23–26. Two illustrations of dealing with anger by means of reconciliation. **Farthing** (v. 26). The smallest Roman copper coin.

5:27–28. Looketh on a woman to lust after her (v. 28). Not a passing glance but a willful, calculated stare that arouses sexual desire. According to Jesus, this is a form of adultery even if it is only **in [one's] heart**. By extension, looking at any form of pornography violates this standard as well.

5:29–30. Here Jesus used hyperbole. He was not teaching self-mutilation, for even a blind man can lust. The point is that we should deal with sin as drastically as necessary. For **hell** (v. 30), see discussion on 5:22.

5:31–32. For **saving for the cause of fornication** (v. 32), see discussion on 19:3. Neither Mark 10:11–12 nor Luke 16:18 mentions this exception.

5:33–37. The Old Testament allowed oaths except those that profaned the name of God. Jesus would do away with all oaths, in favor of always speaking the truth.

5:38. For **an eye for an eye**, see KJV Study Bible notes on Exod. 21:23–25; Lev. 24:20.

5:39. Resist. Here it probably means in a court of law. **Smite.** The Greek verb used here means "slap with the back of the hand." It was more of an insult than an act of violence. The point is that it is better to be insulted, even twice, than to take the matter to court. This is an application of "Blessed are the meek" (5:5). One who responds with genuine meekness to an insult does so from the perspective that God is in control and will exact justice. This also is an application of "Blessed are the peacemakers" (5:9). Often one who insults another deliberately and repeatedly will give up if there is no response.

5:40. Coat. An undergarment. **Cloke.** A loose outer garment. Jesus wants His followers to be more eager to meet the needs of others than to hold on to worldly goods, which can be replaced. Believers should be to the world an example of sacrificial giving, of giving more than the minimum, and should give eagerly rather than grudgingly. Those who trust God to meet their needs can be eager and cheerful about meeting the needs of others.

5:41. Compel. The Greek verb comes from a Persian word meaning "press into service" and is used in 27:32, where the Roman soldiers pressed Simon into service to carry Jesus' cross. This is another application of the principle of eagerness to give, this time of one's time and energy rather than just material goods. Christians, of all people, should be the most accepting of interruptions in their plans, as another's need is an opportunity to minister and to show forth grace. The latter is why Jesus said, **go with him twain.** When Christians do more than is asked or compelled, they are an example of grace, of unmerited favor, in the way they relate to others. They are also an example of Paul's injunction that "each esteem other better than themselves" (Phil. 2:3).

5:42. This is probably not a general requirement to give to everyone who asks but rather a mandate to give to the poor (see Deut. 15:7–11; Ps. 112:5, 9).

5:43. Hate thine enemy. Words not found anywhere in the Old Testament. Hatred for one's enemies, however, was an accepted part of the Jewish ethic at that time (see KJV Study Bible note on Lev. 19:18).

5:44. Pray. Prayer is one of the practical ways love expresses itself (see Job 42:8–10). When we pray for our **enemies**, it forces us to focus on their benefit. The act becomes performative in our hearts in that as we seek the Lord for their good, our attitude toward them is transformed.

5:45. That ye may be the children of your Father which is in heaven. Loving one's enemy does not make one a son of the heavenly Father. It does make that relationship manifest in reality. **On the just and on the unjust.** God shows His love to people without distinction.

5:46–47. Publicans (v. 46). Or "tax collectors," local men employed to collect taxes for Roman tax contractors. Because they worked for Rome and often demanded unreasonable payments, the tax collectors gained a bad reputation and were generally hated and considered traitors.

5:48. Be ye therefore perfect. Christ set up the high ideal of perfect love (see 5:43–47). While we cannot fully attain this ideal in this life, it is, however, God's high standard for us.

6:1. Alms. Or "righteousness." This verse introduces the discussion of three acts of righteousness: (1) giving (6:2–4), (2) praying (6:5–15), and (3) fasting (6:16–18). **Reward of your Father**. Spiritual growth and maturity, or perhaps a heavenly reward of some kind. Jesus' point was that these good works are to be done out of faith in God and His goodness. If we seek earthly recognition or reward, it may be because we do not really have faith that God will reward us or that He really hears and sees what we do.

6:2–4. Sound a trumpet before thee (v. 2). Perhaps a reference to the noise that coins made as they were thrown into the temple treasury. Or the phrase may be used figuratively to mean "make a big show of it." **Hypocrites**. The Greek word means "playactor." Matthew used the word thirteen times (Mark, twice; Luke, three times). Here it refers to those who fake being pious. **They have their reward**. The honor they receive from people is all the reward they will get. **Let not thy left hand know what thy right hand doeth** (v. 3). Not to be taken literally but as a way of emphasizing that one should not call attention to one's giving. Self-glorification is always a present danger.

6:5–15. Closet (v. 6). The Greek word means "storeroom." Unlike most of the rooms in the house, it had a door that could be shut. **Use not vain repetitions, as the heathen do** (v. 7). Jesus was not necessarily condemning all long prayers but rather was condemning meaningless verbiage in prayer. God is not impressed when we ask for something in florid words, nor when we repeat ourselves over and over in the same prayer. He responds to faith, not performance. **Debts** (v. 12). Moral debts, that is, sins (see discussion on Luke 11:4).

6:16–18. For **fast** (v. 16), see discussions on Mark 2:18 and Luke 18:12. **Anoint thine head, and wash thy face** (v. 17). Jews put ashes on their heads when they fasted, but Jesus told them to maintain their regular appearance. Fasting should not be done in an ostentatious way. One should fast to seek God, not to be thought "spiritual" by others.

6:19–21. The dangers of riches are often mentioned in the New Testament (e.g., 6:24; 13:22;

19:22; Mark 10:17–30; Luke 12:16–21; 1 Tim. 6:9–10, 17–19; Heb. 13:5), but nowhere are riches condemned in and of themselves. What Jesus condemned here was greed and hoarding of money. There are more important things than wealth, and believers ought to seek spiritual treasures over worldly riches. Greed betrays a heart attitude that says this world's riches are of ultimate importance, and hoarding demonstrates a lack of faith that God will provide. None of this is to be taken to mean that Christians should not plan for retirement or save for "a rainy day." Believers are to be wise in financial affairs but focus their hearts' attention on the things of God and trust Him to take care of their needs, both for today and for the future.

Moth and rust (v. 19). Representative of all agents and processes that destroy worldly possessions. **Break through and steal**. Houses in the Holy Land had walls made of mud bricks and could be broken into easily.

Treasures in heaven (v. 20). Anything done in this life that has eternal value. The phrase is the equivalent of being "rich towards God" (Luke 12:21). In this context, it probably more specifically refers to using one's material wealth for good causes.

6:22–23. See discussions on Luke 11:33–36.

6:24–34. See discussion on Luke 12:27–28. **Lilies** (v. 28). Here represents flowers generally. **Cast into the oven** (v. 30). Grass was commonly used to heat the clay ovens of the Holy Land.

7:1–2. The Christian is not to judge hypocritically or self-righteously, as can be seen from the context (7:5). The same thought is expressed in 23:13–39 (see also Rom. 2:1). This is not meant to be a prohibition against discerning persons' characters and motives. The standard, however, is God and His Word, not ourselves, and we must not set ourselves up as the final arbiter but rather point to God's Word as the "judge" in every case. In fact, to obey Christ's commands in this chapter, we must first evaluate a person's character—whether he is a "dog" (see 7:6) or a false prophet (see 7:15), or whether his life shows fruit (see 7:16). Scripture repeatedly exhorts believers to evaluate carefully and choose between good and bad people and things (whether they are sexually immoral, 1 Cor. 5:9; "dogs," Phil. 3:2; "false prophets," 1 John 4:1; or masquerading as "an angel of light," 2 Cor. 11:14). The Christian is to "prove all things" (1 Thess. 5:21).

7:3–6. Mote … beam (v. 3). An example of Jesus' use of hyperbole in His teachings (see 19:24, where Jesus spoke of a camel going through the eye of a needle). Its purpose is to drive home a point. Everyone has known people who talk about the sins of others, when bigger sins, often of similar kind, may be found in their own lives. Jesus here warned His followers to be aware of this possibility and to examine themselves first. A believer's words will have more credibility when he has first dealt with the issue in his own life and can share out of his own struggles. Then he can **see clearly** (v. 5) in ways that one who is still in the sin cannot. **Dogs** (v. 6). The unclean dogs of the street were held in low esteem. Teaching should be given in accordance with the spiritual capacity of the learners.

7:7–12. Asketh … seeketh … knocketh (v. 8). Greek present imperatives are used here, indicating constant asking, seeking, and knocking. Persistent prayer is being emphasized.

Whatsoever ye would that men should do to you, do ye even so to them (v. 12). The so-called Golden Rule is found in negative form in rabbinic Judaism and also in Hinduism, Buddhism, and Confucianism. It occurred in various forms in Greek and Roman ethical teaching. Jesus stated it in positive form. It summarizes the sermon's theme of loving others in every possible way (see 5:7, 9, 23–24, 40–48), in faith that God will take care of our own needs if we trust Him. A believer can consider others' needs and preferences as much as she would want her own considered because she has confidence that God is considering her as much or more than she is considering others. For **the law and the prophets**, see discussion on 5:17.

7:13–14. The strait gate (v. 13). The gate that leads into the kingdom of heaven. It is synonymous with **life** (v. 14). **Destruction** (v. 13). Separation from God in hell. Jesus left no room here for any

such foolishness as the ideas that all religions lead to heaven or that one need only be sincere to enter the kingdom. God has made the way **narrow** (v. 14). Only Christ can save. There is no other way, and believers are not necessarily arrogant when they bear witness to that fact.

7:15. False prophets. People who have not been sent by God but claim that they have been (see 24:24; Jer. 23:16–22 and discussions). This verse is an apt warning in light of 7:13–14. Believers are to beware of anyone who preaches another gospel or who offers salvation by any means other than by grace through faith in Jesus Christ (see Gal. 1:8–9).

7:16–20. Here the Lord used an analogy. A tree is known by its fruit, by what it produces. Likewise, whether a prophet is true or false can be known by the results he produces. As men do not gather fruit from trees that produce **thorns, or … thistles** (v. 16), so also we should not seek truth from those who preach false doctrine. This passage also emphasizes that God's main concern is with truth. False doctrine very often comes couched in attractive packages. Even Satan quoted the Bible when he sought to lead Christ away from His mission (see 4:3–11). Today, false teaching may come with glitzy packaging or point to numbers and dollars as an indicator of "God's blessing." Here Jesus reminded believers not to be fooled by externals. The same Lord who prayed that His followers "might be sanctified through the truth" (John 17:19) here warned His followers to discern whether a teaching is true or false, by examining the fruit it produces.

7:21–27. This is the invitation section of the Sermon on the Mount. Jesus invited His hearers to apply to their lives the truths He had taught.

7:21–23. Lord (v. 21). A title that sometimes means only "sir" or "master." Here, however, it seems to mean more than that, since Jesus is the one who makes the final decision about a person's eternal destiny. For **the kingdom of heaven**, see discussion on 3:2.

That day (v. 22). The day of judgment (see Mal. 3:17–18). **Prophesied**. In the New Testament, this verb primarily means to give a message from God, not necessarily to predict. **Devils**. Or "demons" (see discussion on Mark 1:23).

I never knew you (v. 23). Jesus made it clear that the issue was not what they had done but whom they knew. The one who does not know Christ, or whom Christ does not know, has no hope regardless of good works, even good works done in His name. Conversely, the implication is that the one who does know Christ, or whom Christ knows, has assurance of salvation apart from works. Jesus said that the one **that doeth the will of my Father** (v. 21) will enter the kingdom of heaven, but this is not a commendation of works salvation. The whole thrust of the Sermon on the Mount is that believers should put their faith in God. It is faith, not works, that saves. Faith, then, is "the will" of God the Father.

7:24–27. Jesus again used analogy to make a teaching vivid. Some who hear His words will act on them—that is, live a life of faith in God and His goodness and care, which will show forth in their attitudes and actions—and some will not. Those who act on Christ's words are like the **wise man, which built his house upon a rock** (v. 24), and those who do not act on His words are like the **foolish man, which built his house upon the sand** (v. 26). The "rock" here is God's Word, what Jesus revealed in this sermon. He who builds on that foundation will withstand the storms. It is not pushing the analogy too far to see these storms as the trials that life sends, the temptations to sin and to trust in men rather than in God. The one who builds on a foundation of "sand" will face the same trials but will not be able to stand up against them.

7:28–29. The people were astonished (v. 28). The reaction of the people came because they had never heard teaching that was so direct. They were used to teaching that quoted different rabbis and often seemed to "referee" between them. Jesus' teaching went straight to the Scripture and was given with divine **authority** (v. 29; see discussion on 2:4).

C. A Collection of Miracles (chaps. 8–9)

8:1–2. Leper (v. 2). The Greek word was used for various diseases affecting the skin, not necessar-

ily leprosy (see Leviticus 13–14 and *KJV Study Bible* note on Lev. 13:2). For **Lord**, see discussion on 7:21. **Make me clean**. Leprosy made a person ceremonially unclean as well as physically afflicted (see discussion on Luke 5:12–16).

8:3–4. Tell no man (v. 4; see 9:30; 12:16; Mark 1:44; 5:43; 7:36; Luke 8:56). Perhaps for several reasons: (1) Jesus did not want to be considered just a miracle worker, (2) He did not want His teaching ministry hindered by too much publicity being given to His healing miracles, and (3) He did not want His death to come prematurely, that is, before He had finished His ministry. For **shew thyself to the priest**, see discussion on Luke 5:14. **Them**. Refers to the priests.

8:5–13. Although the incident in John 4:43–54 is similar, it probably is a separate episode in the life of Jesus.

8:5–8. For **Capernaum** (v. 5), see discussion on 4:13. **Centurion**. A Roman military officer in charge of a hundred soldiers. In Luke's account (Luke 7:1–5), Jewish elders and friends of the centurion came to Jesus on his behalf, but Matthew did not mention these intermediaries. He may have had in mind his intention to show the universality of the gospel to his Jewish readers. Since the centurion's faith is in view here, and since he caused the meeting between his friends and Jesus, it is proper to say that the centurion came to Him. A parallel situation is the flogging of Jesus by Pilate. Pilate himself obviously did not carry out the act but ordered the Roman soldiers under him; "he had Jesus scourged" (27:26; lit., "he flogged Jesus").

I am not worthy that thou shouldest come under my roof (v. 8). In Greek, the words "I am not worthy" are the same as those used by John the Baptist in 3:11 ("I am not worthy"). The entire statement reveals how highly the centurion regarded Jesus. Or perhaps his response reflects his sense of moral guilt in the presence of Jesus. Clearly, Jesus had become known to this man as someone who lived an exemplary life, in line with the principles He set forth in the Sermon on the Mount (chaps. 5–7). Apparently, the purity of Jesus' life was well known from early on, which may help explain why no one was able to bring charges of any substance against Him at His trial (see Mark 14:55–59).

8:11–12. The universality of the gospel is one of Matthew's themes (see Introduction: "Recipients"). In these verses, Jesus was saying that many will be in the kingdom who are not of Israel, while many others will be left out who thought they were in. **Many shall . . . sit down . . . in the kingdom of heaven** (v. 11). This may be a reference to the eschatological messianic banquet, which symbolizes the blessings of an intimate relationship with God (see Isa. 25:6–9). **The children of the kingdom** (v. 12). Jews who thought their Judaism was an inherited passport for entrance into the kingdom (see 3:9–10 and discussion on 3:9). **Outer darkness** is a reference to judgment. **Weeping and gnashing of teeth** indicates that the "outer darkness" will be a place of conscious sorrow, not a matter of annihilation for those who are condemned.

8:13. In this instance, Jesus healed without going into the presence of the one who was sick. Jesus healed by the power of God. He did not need spells or incantations or potions. He responded to the centurion's faith, **and his servant was healed**. So also one need only trust Him for salvation and for daily needs. Believers are in His care, and His power sustains them and fulfills His promises to them.

8:14–17. This act of healing took place, not in public, but in the intimacy of the home of a disciple. It was followed by a public service in the evening, during which many more people were healed and evil spirits were cast out. Perhaps the leper Jesus had healed earlier (see 8:1–4) had not followed His injunction not to tell anyone. Clearly, Jesus had by this time developed a reputation as one who could heal, and many of the sick were coming to Him.

His wife's mother (v. 14). Peter was married (see 1 Cor. 9:5; Mark 1:30; Luke 4:38). **Bare our sicknesses** (v. 17). The quote is from Isaiah 53:4.

8:18–22. The other side (v. 18). The east side. The Sea of Galilee is about twelve miles long and eight miles wide. Two men came to Jesus, wanting to follow Him, but were turned away. The first, a **scribe**

(v. 19; see discussion on 2:4), was unwilling to make the necessary sacrifices and risks involved in a life of faith. The second man placed family obligations ahead of discipleship. The parallel account in Luke 9:57–62 states that a third would-be disciple also approached Jesus. For reasons unknown, Matthew chose to describe only two men. For **the Son of man** (v. 20), see discussion on Mark 2:10.

Let the dead bury their dead (v. 22). Let the spiritually dead bury the physically dead. The time of Jesus' ministry was short and demanded full attention and commitment. This statement stresses the radical demands of Jesus' discipleship, since Jews placed great importance on the duty of children to bury their parents. In no way does Jesus place low priority on the family, and no one should treat their family shabbily. A Christian life involves new priorities, however, and those who would live a life of faith must put Jesus first in all things and let Him work out every other circumstance of life.

8:23–9:38. This section shows different reactions to Jesus. First there are reactions that sprang from a lack of faith. The disciples panicked in the storm on the lake and marveled that nature obeys Christ (8:23–27). The Gerasenes, rather than marveling that God was in their midst, demonstrated by His power over the demons, invited Him to leave (8:28–34). Then the scribes who witnessed a demonstration of His deity, accused Him of blasphemy rather than believing His claim to be God (9:1–8). The Pharisees' expectations were overturned when Jesus dined with sinners (9:9–13). Next there are a series of healings in response to the faith of the persons involved (9:18–31). The contrast between the lack of faith or refusal to believe on the part of so many and the eager, expectant faith of a few is hard to miss. In addition, Jesus overturned the expectations of the established rulers by His behavior and claims. It is not the job of the Lord, or of His church, to maintain the status quo or to confirm people in their current situations. Rather, it is to meet human needs in the context of calling people to repentance and faith and to a lifestyle that is consistent with the revealed will of God. This long section is well seen in light of that mission. The different reactions to Jesus ranged from outright rejection, surprise, accusations, all the way to overcoming faith. These reactions to the gospel are typical of those one may expect in any age.

8:23–27. For **great tempest** (v. 24), see discussion on Mark 4:37. **But he was asleep**. This is a picture of exhaustion. If the events immediately preceding this section were typical of Jesus' ministry, well might He have been tired. It causes one to note the humanity of the Lord. Being fully man, He was capable of tiredness and other weaknesses of the body, such as hunger (see Matt 4:2) and thirst (see John 19:28), yet being fully God, He was able to command the forces of nature. **Even the winds and the sea obey him** (v. 27; see discussion on Mark 4:38). Early in His ministry, Jesus revealed His true identity to the disciples little by little. They had seen Him heal people as He commanded sickness to leave, and they had seen Him cast out demons (see 8:6). Now they saw great forces of nature obey His word. God is the Creator, and He is in command of His creation. These incidents reveal the deity of Christ, but the disciples at this point could still **marvelled [at] What manner of man** He was.

8:28. The country of the Gergesenes. The region around the city of Gergesa, in the hills to the east of the Sea of Galilee. Mark and Luke identify the region by the city of Gadara, located about six miles southeast of the sea. **Two possessed with devils**. Mark and Luke mention only one Gadarene/Gergesene demoniac (see Mark 5:2; Luke 8:27 and discussion).

8:29. The time. The time of their judgment. The demons were fearful of being sent into eternal punishment, that is, "into the deep" (see discussions on Mark 5:10; Luke 8:31).

8:30. A herd of many swine. Large numbers of Gentiles lived in Galilee. Normally, Jews did not raise pigs, since they were considered the most "unclean" of all animals.

8:31–32. Though Jesus seemingly consented to the demons' request, the pigs carried the demons into the depths of the sea—perhaps symbolic of the Abyss (see Luke 8:31 and discussion). The biblical accounts here and in Mark and Luke make it clear that Jesus was encountering a supernatural spiritual reality. This was not merely a man with emotional problems, whom Jesus healed while accommodating the superstitions of the people. Nor was this a case of the man's screams scaring the pigs. They had heard him, no doubt, for many days. The demonic spirits were quite real. Too often Christians today explain away matters in the Bible that challenge modern secularistic assumptions. The call from God is to "repent and believe," not "ignore and explain away."

8:33–34. They besought him that he would depart (v. 34). The townspeople may have been more concerned about their financial loss than about the deliverance of the miserable demon-possessed man. Certainly, they valued their peace and prosperity over the meeting of real human needs. Jesus has a way of upsetting expectations, of opening unexpected doors, and of challenging people beyond their comfort zones. As long as He remains the meek and mild moral philosopher whom all can admire, He is welcomed. When the Lord gets down to the serious business of changing lives and overturning expectations, He is too often shunned and pushed away. So it was here.

9:1. Passed over. The northern end of the Sea of Galilee. **His own city**. Capernaum (see discussion on 4:13).

9:2. Their faith. The faith of the men who carried him as well as the faith of the paralytic. Jesus focused first on the man's deepest need: forgiveness of sins. He also had in mind the lesson for His disciples and for the Pharisees who were present. By forgiving the man's sins, Jesus implicitly claimed to be God. It is often His implicit claims, the ones in which He assumes He is God and acts on that assumption, that are the most startling. In other places, He made explicit claims, such as, "I and my Father are one" (John 10:30). However, these implicit claims, coming as they did in the course of ministry and as teaching opportunities, are also worthy of study. Here the implication to deity lies in the fact that He did what only God can do: forgive sins. Once again Jesus upset the expectations of the religious establishment, in the course of meeting someone's need. The reaction, which Jesus surely expected, was swift in coming.

9:3. The Pharisees who were present recognized Jesus' implicit claim at once. They might have acknowledged that here indeed was "God with us," but instead they rejected His claim and accused Him "in [their] hearts" (v. 4). Here the term **blasphemeth** includes usurping God's prerogative to forgive sins (see discussion on Mark 2:7). The Pharisees' charge again stemmed from Jesus' implicit claim to be God. The Pharisees assumed that Jesus was only a man, and a man's claims to be God diminish God, making Him out to be something less than He is.

9:4–8. Jesus had read their thoughts, and He replied. Of course it is **easier, to say** (v. 5) that someone's sins are forgiven than it is to heal someone, and Jesus acknowledged this (see *KJV Study Bible* notes on Mark 2:9–10; 14:64). Jesus healed the paralytic to prove that He could also do the harder work, forgiving sins. Through His power to heal, He showed that He has also the power to forgive sins. Once again, Jesus met a physical need, but as always, His focus remained on the deeper spiritual need. The man's healing demonstrated that his spiritual need had been met, and even more important for the Lord's teaching and revealing purpose, it demonstrated that Jesus is God and has the authority that God alone has. For **the Son of man** (v. 6), see discussion on Mark 2:10.

9:9–13. Here is an instance of Jesus acting in a way that overturned the expectations of social respectability. He ate with those whom most people avoided. This passage challenges one to take the gospel to those who are not respectable. Some people do this more easily than others. It is often society's outcasts who are the most eager for grace, for a second chance. Those who have known rejection and scorn respond most joyfully to acceptance and love. They are more likely than others to see their need and the value of being accepted unconditionally in the love of God.

9:9. One would do well to study all of the times Jesus said **Follow me** in the Gospels (here; 4:19; 9:9; 16:24; 19:21; the parallels in the other gospels and

additional occurrences recorded in them). **Matthew.** This disciple is called Levi in the parallel accounts in Mark and Luke (but see also Mark 3:18; Luke 6:15; Acts 1:13). For **the receipt of custom**, see discussion on Mark 2:14. For **he arose, and followed him**, see discussion on Luke 5:28.

9:10–12. For **publicans** (v. 10), see discussions on 5:46 and Mark 2:16. For **sinners**, see discussion on Mark 2:15. For **Pharisees** (v. 11), see discussion on Mark 2:16. Jesus was not saying here that the Pharisees were spiritually healthy; far from it. They, however, did not see their need.

9:13. I am not come to call the righteous, but sinners to repentance. Jesus knew the Pharisees had a false righteousness, and it would not be wrong to see a touch of irony in His words here. In addition, Jesus knew that it is difficult to call to repentance those who see themselves as having no need of it (see discussion on Mark 2:17). One cannot preach repentance to those who do not see themselves as sinners. The Pharisees would have to wait for another time to be called to repentance.

9:14–17. For **the disciples of John** (v. 14), see discussions on Mark 2:18 and Luke 5:33. For **fast**, see discussions on Mark 2:18 and Luke 5:33. For **the bridegroom** (v. 15), see discussions on Mark 2:19–20.

New bottles (v. 17). Or "new wineskins." In ancient times, goatskins were used to hold wine. As the fresh grape juice fermented, the wine would expand, and the new wineskin would stretch. A used skin, already stretched, would break. Jesus brings a newness that cannot be confined within the old forms. New ways of understanding the Messiah's role and the power and purposes of God are required. It is well to note, however, that Jesus did not preach new doctrines or the abandonment of God's moral teachings. Jesus left no room for such an option. He had already said that the Law will not pass away and that He had not come to destroy it (see 5:17–18). Jesus' statements about **new wine** and "new wineskins" have to do with fulfilling truth, not replacing it, and with deepening people's understanding of God's plan, not changing it utterly.

9:18. A certain ruler. From Mark and Luke, we know that the official was Jairus (see *KJV Study Bible* note on Mark 5:22). The amazing thing here is that the man expressed full confidence that Jesus could raise his daughter to life. That confidence was well placed, a contrast with the disciples' amazement that the forces of nature obey Jesus (see 8:27).

9:20–22. An issue of blood twelve years (v. 20; see *KJV Study Bible* notes on Lev. 15:25; Mark 5:25, 28). This woman demonstrated great faith and great humility. Unlike Jairus, she could not approach boldly, but she did approach. This account, embedded in the account of the healing of Jairus's daughter, demonstrates the extent to which faith alone is all one needs to approach the Lord. Whether bold faith or timid faith, it is sufficient. The Lord responds to faith, not to public demonstrations of righteousness. Both Jairus and this woman would have their needs met, for both demonstrated faith in the Lord Jesus Christ, though in very different ways.

For **Daughter** (v. 22), see discussion on Luke 8:48. **Made thee whole** (see discussion on Mark 5:34). Her faith, born of desperation, was honored by the Lord. While she sought anonymity, the Lord called her out of the crowd, not to embarrass her, but to commend her faith. It is never the intention of God to minister impersonally. His power is not like the power of an electrical battery or the force of gravity. It is the outworking of His personal intention to do good and meet needs. Rather than let her be healed with no personal attention, Jesus offered her a word of comfort and encouragement, along with physical healing. He also desired that her healing would be a testimony, that all would know that it had come by God's power and was no accident.

9:23–26. Minstrels (v. 23). Musicians hired to play in mourning ceremonies. **People making a noise**. Mourners hired to wail and lament. For **not dead, but sleepeth** (v. 24), see discussion on Luke 8:52.

The people were put forth (v. 25). Jesus had often healed in public places, along roadsides and in the midst of crowds. Here He had the people put out of the room, possibly so that the child would not wake up in a room full of official mourners, which might have been traumatic. Once again this is a demonstration of the Lord's sensitivity to people's needs and His pastoral concern for them.

9:27. Blind men. Isaiah prophesied the healing of the blind in the messianic age (see Isa. 35:5). **Son of David**. A popular Jewish title for the coming Messiah (see, e.g., 12:23; 20:30; 21:9; 22:41–45; see also discussion on 1:1). Again people are expressing their faith in Jesus. These men recognized who Jesus was, based on what He had just done for the woman with an issue of blood and for Jairus's daughter (8:18–26).

9:28. When he was come into the house. Why, in this instance, Jesus waited until they were in the house is unknown. He questioned whether the men's faith was genuine, and it may be that He wanted them to examine their faith before He healed them. Often the Lord will delay His answer to prayers so that one's faith may be tested and strengthened.

9:29. Jesus rewarded the men's faith by healing them. They had faith that He would heal them, and He did so **According to [their] faith**, that is, in line with their faith and what they sought. Their faith was rewarded specifically, as they had come to Him with a specific need and request. The Lord will bless according to one's faith, that is, in line with what one believes and as specifically as one believes. Christians should learn to ask God for specific things, not for "blessings" in general. He will reward "according to" the faith that one brings Him.

9:30–31. Here again Jesus charged the men not to tell anyone, but they disobeyed and **spread abroad** (v. 31) the news of their healing (see discussions on 8:4 and 16:20).

9:32. Dumb man. Isaiah prophesied that the mute would talk in the messianic age (see Isa. 35:6).

9:33–34. In this case, the man's infirmity was caused not by a physical problem but by an evil spirit that specialized in making people unable to speak. When Jesus had **cast out** (v. 33) this spirit, **the dumb spake**.

While **the multitudes marvelled** (v. 33), the Pharisees charged that Jesus' power over demons came from **the prince of the devils** (see discussion on 10:25). Here is the beginnings of tension between the public acceptance of Jesus and the official rejection of His ministry. While this tension is implied earlier in Matthew's gospel, here the multitude's reaction is directly contrasted with the Pharisees' "official" rejection. Later on, the Pharisees would be delayed in their plans to arrest Him because "they feared the multitude" (21:46; see Mark 12:12, Luke 20:19).

9:35. For **synagogues**, see discussion on Mark 1:21. For **the gospel**, see discussion on Mark 1:1.

9:36–38. When he saw the multitudes (v. 36), Jesus felt **compassion** for those seeking help and direction in life. As "the good shepherd" (John 10:11), He cared for the **sheep** and wanted to bring them under His care and protection. Even here, His focus was on the condition of their souls. In verses 37–38, Jesus used an agricultural metaphor to make the point that evangelism is a priority. Here the people are the grain or the fruit ready to be taken in, and the need for laborers to work the harvest is great. He had promised His disciples earlier that they would be "fishers of men" (4:19), and His heartbeat for evangelism remained undiminished. The need was not physical care, but spiritual care. Compassion led Jesus to evangelism and to His prayer for more evangelists.

D. The Commissioning of the Twelve Apostles (chap. 10)

10:1–42. In this chapter, Jesus sent the Twelve out on their first preaching mission. Before doing so, He instructed them on some practical matters related to ministry. Some of the instructions related to the apostles' immediate mission, but others were clearly intended for their extended ministry after His death and resurrection. All of His instructions should be seen in light of the call to live a life of faith and to trust God in all circumstances.

The heart of the chapter (v. 16–23) is a discussion of the opposition that the disciples would face from three sources: difficult people they might witness to (vv. 14–16), official governmental sources (vv. 17–20), and family members (v. 21). Jesus'

admonitions, while different for each of the three situations, were in line with His exhortations to live by faith, in obedience to His teachings, putting Him first always.

10:1. In preparation for their preaching mission, the Lord gave His apostles certain powers that, up to this point, He had been exercising. They had seen Him preach, teach, heal, and cast out unclean spirits. They had gained a clear idea of how these things fit into the overall ministry. Jesus never did anything as a stunt, nor to draw a crowd. He always sought to respond to people's faith, meet their needs, and point them to repentance and righteousness through faith. His disciples, now aware of His priorities, were ready to minister in His name. In ministry, one must do God's work, in God's way, with His priorities in mind, or it is not legitimate ministry. As with the disciples, believers' preparation for ministry comes from getting to know God and His Word, until they have His priorities and heartbeat within themselves.

10:2–4. See discussions on Luke 6:14–16. **Apostles** (v. 2). This is the only occurrence of this word in Matthew's gospel. The word is in fact rare in the Gospels and more common in the Epistles. Its basic meaning is "one who is sent" as a representative or ambassador. It can denote a messenger or a missionary of the church (as in 2 Cor. 8:23) but is usually used as a title for the Twelve and for Paul (see discussion on Mark 6:30).

10:5–7. Go not (v. 5). The good news about the kingdom was first to be proclaimed to Jews only. After His death and resurrection, Jesus commanded that the message be taken to all nations (see 28:19; 21:43). Also, the apostles may yet have lacked the maturity, and certainly the experience, to minister effectively in different cultures. It may have been best to start them out "close to home" in a sense, until they had built up confidence and had learned a few things that come only with direct experience. **Samaritans.** A mixed-blood race resulting from the intermarriage of Israelites left behind when the people of the northern kingdom were exiled and Gentiles brought into the land by the Assyrians (see 2 Kings 17:24). Bitter hostility existed between Jews and Samaritans in Jesus' day (see John 4:9). For **The kingdom of heaven** (v. 7), see discussion on 3:2.

10:8 – 13. Lepers (v. 8). The Greek word for "leprosy" was used for various diseases affecting the skin, not necessarily leprosy (see *KJV Study Bible* note on Lev. 13:2). The last half of verse 8 belongs with verses 9 and 10. The gospel is given freely, and the disciples had received their calling freely from the Lord. If they had charged a fee, it would have detracted from their message. They were to take no provisions, trusting God to supply for them. This way their faith in God would be evident. They were working for the Lord, and **the workman is worthy of his meat** (v. 10). The Lord pays for what He orders and would supply their needs. God's people are often eager to give when they see a godly minister doing God's work in God's way. Jesus challenged the apostles to live such a life and see God work (see discussions on Mark 6:8 – 9). They were to trust God for a **worthy** (v. 11) person who would give them lodging and food. **Salute it** (v. 12). The Jews' greeting then, even as now, was *shalom*, meaning "peace."

10:14 – 16. Here is Jesus' first advice on how to handle opposition. The first type of opposition He addressed was opposition from difficult people. **Shake off the dust of your feet.** A symbolic act that the Pharisees practiced when they left an "unclean" Gentile area. Here it represented an act of solemn warning to those who rejected God's message (see discussions on Luke 9:5; Acts 13:51; see also Acts 18:6).

10:15. Those who rejected the preaching of the gospel would fare worse than **Sodom and Gomorrha** (see Gen. 19:23 – 29). This is quite a warning. Truly, when people are given additional light, refusing it brings additional judgment. This is a warning to all who have heard the gospel of God's grace and refused it.

10:16. As sheep in the midst of wolves. It is interesting that Jesus used this analogy in the context of their doing ministry in Israel. The spiritual condition of the nation must have been poor, even after the revival under John the Baptist's preaching.

Jesus used another unusual analogy: **be ... wise as serpents.** The comparison to serpents may seem odd

at first, as serpents are usually associated with evil. The context, however, governs the comparison here. Consider that a serpent will slither away to avoid conflict if at all possible. Rarely does a snake bite unless it is cornered. Jesus was telling them to avoid conflict, to depart as a serpent would to avoid conflict, and to be **harmless as doves.** Jesus was encouraging an attitude that would result in their being wise for their own protection, without being combative. This fits with His teaching to turn the other cheek (5:39) and is in the same context as the admonition to let their peace return to them if they were rejected (10:13). In other words, they were not to force the message on anyone, and if they met with active and possibly violent rejection, they were to move on rather than start an argument or a fight.

10:17 – 20. The second type of opposition the Lord addressed was that from official governmental sources. Here the context broadens. It is unlikely that the apostles faced much of this type of opposition on their first preaching tour, but later as opposition arose, especially after Christ's resurrection and ascension, this increasingly became the situation the apostles faced. Jesus told them to beware of officials who might cause them trouble. **Councils** (v. 17). The lower courts, connected with local synagogues, that tried less serious cases and flogged those found guilty. For **synagogues,** see discussions on Mark 1:21 and Luke 21:12.

Ye shall be brought before governors and kings (v. 18). It was unlikely that this would happen on the disciples' first preaching tour, but Jesus took advantage of a teachable moment to warn them of future persecution and what to expect and what to do.

Take no thought how or what ye shall speak (v. 19; see Luke 21:14 – 15). This is not to be used by preachers as an excuse for lack of sermon preparation. The context is that of a courtroom situation, in which the disciples might be tried for the preaching of the gospel, not a church service. One cannot change the context without violating the intent of the Scriptures. In a courtroom setting, where the Christian is not in charge and may not know what questions will be asked, a special level of dependence on the Spirit is necessary, and here Jesus promised that such faith will not go unrewarded. An example of this in action might be Acts 6:8–7:60. When Stephen was arrested and asked to testify, he delivered a brilliant sermon apparently spontaneously, as the Spirit led him.

10:21. The third type of opposition Jesus addressed was opposition from family members. The governing context here is not limited to this particular preaching mission; Jesus was speaking of the apostles' ministry in general. The apostles were being sent out "as sheep in the midst of wolves" (10:16) and could expect persecution of all three types in the course of their ministry.

10:22. For **he that endureth to the end shall be saved**, see *KJV Study Bible* note on Mark 13:13.

10:23. This is a more direct statement of the admonition to "be … wise as serpents" (10:16), that is, to flee from places where they were rejected. Here Jesus explicitly told them to go to **another** city in such cases. Jesus' statement about all **the cities of Israel** is best seen, in light of the wider context of His remarks here, as a promise that there will always be places to minister. The gospel being rejected in one place does not mean there is nowhere to keep on preaching. One should just move on and find another place.

10:24–25. Jesus, again thinking in terms of their total ministry, reminded the apostles that the servant is no greater than the master. If the **master** (v. 24) suffers something, **the servant** can expect no less. These words would have more meaning for the Twelve after the crucifixion of Christ, when they would face persecution, which happened rather quickly in Jerusalem (see Acts 4:1–22; 5:17–41). **Beelzebub** (v. 25). Satan, the ruler of demons (see 12:24). The Hebrew epithet Baal-Zebub ("lord of flies") is a parody on and mockery of the Hebrew name Baal-Zebul ("Exalted Baal" or "Prince Baal"; see discussion on Judg. 10:6).

10:26–33. Here Jesus offered the apostles words of comfort. They were not to fear what anyone might do to their bodies but were to speak boldly what He had taught them. In other words, they should withdraw in situations where oppositions arose, but not

out of fear. Rather than engaging in useless fights, they were to move on quickly to more fertile ground. They were not to be fearful, however, for men can **kill the body, but are not able to kill the soul** (v. 28), the true self. Body and soul are closely related in this life but are separated at death and then reunited at the resurrection (see 2 Cor. 5:1–10; Phil. 1:23–24). **Fear him**. God. He alone determines the final destiny of us all. For **hell**, see discussion on 5:22.

10:34–37. Jesus again addressed opposition from family members. Sometimes this is more difficult for believers than official persecution. **I came not to send peace, but a sword** (v. 34). At first glance, this saying seems like a contradiction of Isaiah 9:6 ("Prince of Peace"), Luke 2:14 ("on earth peace among men"), and John 14:27 ("Peace I leave with you"). It is true that Christ came to bring peace — peace between the believer and God, and peace among men. Yet the inevitable result of Christ's coming is conflict — between Christ and the Antichrist, between light and darkness, between God's children and the Devil's children. This conflict can occur even between members of the same family (vv. 35–36). Believers must always be aware that their highest loyalty is to Jesus Christ. They cannot allow opposition from family to turn them away from their task any more than they allow official opposition to do so.

10:38. His cross. The first mention of the cross in Matthew's gospel. The cross was an instrument of death and here symbolizes the necessity of total commitment, even unto death, on the part of Jesus' disciples (see discussion on Mark 8:34).

10:39. Jesus made this statement in the context of sacrificing all for Him. Many people try to "find their lives" by seeking what will make them happy or fulfilled in this world. Jesus turned this upside down. The life that does not focus on the self is the most satisfying. It is in a life of service that one finds the greatest happiness, and thus **findeth his life**. The highest and greatest service is that rendered to Christ, and therefore the way to find one's life is to **lose it** in service to Him. Jesus was telling the apostles that the loss of their "life" in terms of reputation, relationships, personal freedom, and even physical well-being, was worth it, for no believer ever truly regrets the time, energy, and sacrifice expended for the glory of the Lord.

10:40 – 42. During times of persecution, hospitality is especially important, and providing help to God's people during such times can be dangerous. Jesus indicated that those who provide it and show kindness to God's people will receive a reward.

E. Ministry throughout Galilee (chaps. 11 – 12)

11:1. While the twelve apostles were carrying out their first mission, Jesus continued His ministry in Galilee. This verse actually ends the material in chapter 10. Often the chapter divisions in the Bible do not follow the real divisions in the narrative. Verse 1 ends the account of Jesus sending out the Twelve. Verse 2 begins a new narrative.

11:2 – 3. John had heard … [of] the works of Christ (v. 2), the works of teaching and healing recounted in the previous chapters. John apparently had some doubts, even though he had heard of what Christ was doing. One would think that the works would have confirmed John's knowledge of who Jesus was, something John had borne witness to at Jesus' baptism (see John 1:29). Perhaps these doubts arose because Jesus had not freed him from prison (see Gundry, *Matthew*, p. 182). So often one sees God's works only in terms of personal need or advantage. John was in prison, and the one miracle Jesus had not worked, was freeing him. God has His own plans and purposes, and rescuing one believer may or may not fit that plan. He may have a higher purpose that one does not see. **He that should come** (v. 3). The Messiah. For **look for another**, see discussion on Luke 7:19 – 20.

11:4 – 5. Shew John again those things (v. 4). Jesus' reference to the **blind … lame … lepers** (v. 5; see discussion on 8:2) are allusions to the signs that Isaiah said would point to the Messiah (see Isa. 29:18 – 21; 35:5 – 6; 61:1). Jesus was reminding John that He was indeed the Messiah because He was doing what Isaiah prophesied the Messiah would do. John was encouraged to believe because of this. Christians' task today is to continue to believe, for

He is still at work in the world. One need only to see again the things that He is doing and rejoice in them. **The poor have the gospel preached to them** (see discussion on Luke 7:22). Jesus' ministry to the poor was also evidence of His divine mission. He was concerned about those most in need of God's grace.

11:6. Whosoever shall not be offended (see discussion on Luke 7:23). This may have been directed at John himself. God had left John in prison, while Jesus' ministry increased. Jesus may have been implying that the success of another's ministry should not cause John to be jealous. Nor should John claim any special point of privilege with Jesus; that is, he should not be offended if Jesus' ministry did not include rescuing him. It may also be a more general statement. All who rejoice in what Christ is doing shall be blessed, but those who reject Him and are offended by His offer of salvation (and they are many, even to this day) shall miss the blessing.

11:7 – 30. Jesus preached this sermon in several cities right after the encounter with two of John's disciples. Jesus introduced the ministry of John the Baptist and reminded the hearers that they had all gone out to hear him (vv. 7 – 15). He then stated the point of the message, that just hearing the Word preached is not enough (vv. 16 – 19). The hearer must do something with what he has heard. The tone is one of anger with people who heard the message but only criticized or ignored it. Reinforcing the main point, Jesus called for judgment upon the cities that had heard the Word preached and had not repented (vv. 21 – 24). He concluded with a public prayer and an invitation (vv. 25 – 30). Overall, this sermon is reminiscent of the prophetic messages in the Old Testament, where the prophet called down woe and judgment on the people for their sins but ended with a promise of restoration and grace (see, e.g., Isaiah, Ezekiel, Amos, Obadiah).

11:7 – 10. This passage introduces the sermon. The formula **What went ye out into the wilderness to see?** (vv. 7 – 9) is repeated three times. Each time Jesus answered His own question, each time more specifically and pointedly, thereby building his hearers' interest in the message. One imagines His voice rising each time He repeated the question and His hearers leaning forward with just a little more expectation. His first response to the question was, **A reed shaken with the wind?** (v. 7), but of course the people would not go into the wilderness for that, as it would hardly be worth the trip. His second response was, **A man clothed in soft raiment?** (v. 8). Everyone knew, as Jesus pointed out, that such people are found not in wilderness areas but in palaces. In His third response, Jesus got to the real answer: **A prophet? yea … and more than a prophet** (v. 9). The people had gone out to hear John the Baptist preach, for there had not been a prophet in Israel for many years. In this sermon, Jesus would upbraid the people for not repenting upon hearing the preaching of John (and later of Jesus), and here He set the stage. They had gone out to hear a prophet but had not done what the prophet said to do. Jesus explained what He meant when He called John "more than a prophet." John was the **messenger** (v. 10) sent to **prepare** (the) **way** for the Messiah. The people had not repented upon hearing John's preaching and were not ready for the preaching of Jesus. He could offer them the kingdom, but it would fall on deaf ears, dulled by the effects of sin and by the effect of rejecting the message.

11:11. He that is least in the kingdom … is greater than he (John the Baptist). Given John's influence and notoriety, Jesus' statement must have seemed surprising. After all, John was a noted prophet who had influenced thousands. The key to the meaning of this is found in 18:4: "Whosoever … shall humble himself as this little child." Such a person, though "least," is regarded by God as even greater than John the Baptist. This should also be seen in light of Jesus' statement that "he that is greatest among you shall be your servant" (23:11).

11:12. Suffereth violence. The Greek here carries a passive sense. In this context, the passive meaning is "suffers violent attacks." The verse emphasizes the ongoing persecution of God's people and opposition to God's Word.

11:13. The prophets and the law. The entire Old Testament **prophesied** the coming of the kingdom.

These prophecies were available for all the people to hear. John's message had not been new, but was one prophets had given time and again. Their message had been rejected and in John's preaching found rejection one more time, before the coming of Christ. John represented the end of the old economy.

11:14. This is Elias. A reference to Malachi 4:5, which prophesied the reappearance of Elijah before the day of the Lord. Some of the people remembered the prophecy and asked John the Baptist, "Art thou Elias?" He answered, "I am not" (John 1:21). John was not literally the reincarnation of Elijah, but he did fulfill the function and role of the prophet (see Matt. 17:10–13; discussion on Luke 1:17). In other words, Elijah was a prophetic type of John.

11:15. He that hath ears to hear, let him hear. Jesus used this oratorical device to alert the listener that He was saying something important. He used the same device elsewhere (see 13:9, 43, Luke 14:35), always to warn the listener that what He is saying was important.

11:16–19. These verses present Jesus' main point: the people had heard the prophecies, both in the reading of Scripture and in the preaching of John, and it had fallen on deaf ears.

11:16–17. Drawing an analogy, Jesus said the people were **like unto children sitting in the markets** (v. 16; see discussion on Luke 7:31–34). In the markets, children would call to one another with little set rhymes or calls. Those who had heard John and Jesus preach had not responded to the message. **Piped** (v. 17). As if providing music at a wedding. **Mourned.** As if providing music at a funeral. Here Jesus was perhaps likening the latter to John's ministry and the former to His own ministry. In any case, the people of Jesus' **generation** (v. 16) were like children who did not respond to the music in that they did not respond to the preaching of God's Word.

11:18–19. Instead of repenting, the people griped about the lifestyles of both men. **John came neither eating nor drinking** (v. 18), and the people did not like it, saying he had a devil. **The Son of man** (see discussion on Mark 2:10) **came eating and drinking** (v. 19), and they did not like that either.

Rather than responding to the message, people found fault with the messenger. This may stand as a warning to believers today. One may not like the preacher's hairstyle or clothing, and his delivery may not be as entertaining as the former pastor's, but the important matter is the content of the message. Believers should never let the incidentals get in the way of the main point, which is to take the message to heart and live it out in their lives. **Wisdom is justified of her children**. This apparently means that God (wisdom) had sent both John and Jesus in specific roles and that this would be vindicated by the lasting works of both men (see discussion on Luke 7:35).

11:20. Then began he to upbraid the cities. This is a turning point in the message. Jesus here made the point very specific, mentioning by name the cities where He had preached, and perhaps even where He was preaching at this time. In each case, He emphasized that they should have repented at the preaching of the Word but had not.

11:21–22. Chorazin (v. 21). Mentioned in the Bible only twice (here and in Luke 10:13), Chorazin was near the Sea of Galilee, probably about two miles north of Capernaum. **Bethsaida**. On the northeast shore of the Sea of Galilee. Philip the tetrarch rebuilt Bethsaida and named it "Julias," after Julia, daughter of Caesar Augustus. **Tyre and Sidon** (v. 22). Cities on the Phoenician coast north of the Holy Land. **Sackcloth** (v. 21). Here a sign of repentance (see discussion on Gen. 37:34; Rev. 6:12). **Ashes**. Also a sign of repentance. Jesus' point was that these cities would have repented had they seen the signs that Jesus had performed in Chorazin and Bethsaida. How much more would these cities be held accountable, if Tyre and Sidon had already met judgment. Truly, all are accountable for the light they are given. If we are given more, we are more liable to judgment if we do not repent.

11:23–24. The mighty works that Jesus had done in **Capernaum** (v. 23; see discussion on Luke 10:15) would have brought **Sodom** to repentance, and God would have spared the city. It is interesting to note that God knows not only what will happen

but also what would have happened. One cannot say, however, that God did not give Sodom adequate warning. Paul indicates (Rom. 1:18–32) that sinners have sufficient knowledge of God to lead them to repentance, if they do not deliberately refuse it.

11:25–30. Jesus ended the sermon with a prayer and an invitation.

11:25–26. These verses give the content of the prayer. **These things** (v. 25). Probably including an understanding of Jesus' mission and certainly including the matters Jesus had just preached on (11:7–24), the need for repentance and faith in response to the preaching of God's Word. In this context, **the wise and prudent** are the teachers of the law and the Pharisees, and **babes** are the humble followers of Jesus, those who responded with childlike faith to the call to repentance and faith. This echoes Paul's statement in 1 Corinthians 1:26–27 that "not many wise men after the flesh ... are called" to faith, for "God hath chosen the foolish things of the world to confound the wise; and God hath chosen the weak things of the world to confound the things which are mighty." Jesus was thankful perhaps because God's way of salvation does not demand that people have great learning or intelligence. No one is disqualified. Knowing every point of doctrine is not a requirement for salvation. All that is needed is simple faith, to trust God and what He has said in His Word. No one has to pass a test to "qualify" for salvation. There is no secret wisdom that only the initiates can have. The truth is available to whosoever will believe it. Therefore, those cities that had not repented could not plead doctrinal ignorance or a lack of qualified rabbis to interpret the message for them.

11:27. No man knoweth the Son, but the Father; neither knoweth any man the Father, save the Son. Here Jesus used "knoweth" in the sense of knowing who He is and what His secret counsels are. Only the Son knows the Father this intimately and vice versa.

11:28. This is the sermon's invitation. Jesus ended His message with a word of comfort and an offer of grace. **Come unto me** is a call to repentance. Many had rejected Him, questioning His teaching and lifestyle (see 11:19). Others had rejected His preaching, as they had rejected John's. Here Jesus called them to a change of mind and heart. Instead of setting themselves up against Jesus and criticizing His message, they could respond to His call and come to Him in simple faith as a child, in humble dependence on Him. **All ye that labour and are heavy laden** here means all those who sought to make themselves righteous on their own, as the Pharisees had taught. Though the Lord certainly offers encouragement and comfort to those who are discouraged in the Lord's work or who have lost their zeal, here He was offering salvation to those who had labored under legalism.

11:29–30. Take my yoke upon you (v. 29) is in contrast to the yoke of the law, or legalism, which is a theme found elsewhere in the New Testament (see Acts 15:10; Gal. 5:1). **For my yoke is easy, and my burden is light** (v. 30). Jesus contrasted His offer of free grace with the yoke of legalism. This invitation may be seen as a stark contrast to the message it accompanies. The reason is clear, however, upon reflection. The message of repentance is a harsh message, promising judgment on those who turn their backs on God. At the same time, however, the message offers hope to those who do repent.

12:1–50. In chapter 12, the conflict between Jesus and the Pharisees begins to come to a head. Jesus' Sabbath-breaking activities raised their ire, and they began to accuse Him falsely and question Him while seeking an opportunity to destroy Him. Their opposition at this point begins to show signs of an organized effort, which would lead to their official rejection of Jesus as the Messiah.

12:1–14. This section contains two accounts in which the Pharisees challenged Jesus about activities He and the disciples did on the Sabbath. In the first account (vv. 1–8), the disciples picked grain and ate it as they walked through a field. In the second account (vv. 9–14), Jesus healed a man on the Sabbath. The reason the Pharisees challenged Him on this matter becomes clearer in light of Middle Eastern history at that time. The Greeks had conquered the area over three hundred years earlier and had imported Greek culture, language, and architecture

into the area. Some Jewish people had adopted Greek ways, much to the chagrin of those who sought to preserve tradition. The Pharisees were among those who sought to purify Israel from Greek influence. One thing that distinguished the Jewish people from the surrounding cultures was their observance of the Sabbath. Keeping the Sabbath was a very public expression of one's Jewishness and commitment to the law of Moses. When Jesus or His disciples even seemed to break the Sabbath, it upset the Pharisees, for they saw it as a compromise of Jewish culture. In His remarks, Jesus revealed their lack of understanding of the Scriptures in the first account and their hypocrisy in the second, and in both instances, He showed that the main point was not Sabbath-keeping but rather doing the will of God from the heart.

12:1–8. This is the chapter's first account of the Pharisees' reaction to a seeming violation of the Sabbath.

12:1–2. The corn (i.e., "kernel"; v. 1). "Corn" does not mean what most people think of as corn today, which was unknown in Israel. These were fields of wheat or barley; the latter was eaten by poorer people. **Pluck the ears of corn**. They pulled off some of the wheat. This was not illegal, even though the disciples did not own the field; the Old Testament law specifically stated that people passing a field were allowed to do this (see Deut. 23:25). The problem was that they were doing it on the Sabbath. To the **Pharisees** (v. 2; see discussion on Mark 2:16), that was harvesting, which is a work activity. For **that which is not lawful to do upon the sabbath**, see discussion on Mark 2:24.

12:3–4. Jesus' reply seems at first to be unrelated to the Pharisees' reaction. He directed their attention to **what David did** (v. 3; see discussions on Mark 2:25–26). David and his men on one occasion **did eat the shewbread** (v. 4). Each Sabbath, twelve fresh loaves of bread were to be set on a table in the Holy Place (see Exod. 25:30; Lev. 24:5–9). The old loaves were eaten by the priests. The "hot bread" replaced the old bread every Sabbath day (see 1 Sam. 21:6). David was not breaking the Sabbath by doing this, but Jesus' remarks had an underlying point: David's men were hungry, and meeting their need took precedence over the strict letter of the law. It would not have been God's will for the bread to sit there, while hungry men looked on, unable to touch it due to a ritual restriction. In the same way, Jesus' disciples were hungry, and the Sabbath should not interfere with their meeting their need for food.

12:5. Jesus offered another example, one more directly related to the Pharisees' concern. Without guilt, **the priests in the temple profane the Sabbath** by doing work associated with the sacrifices on the Sabbath day.

12:6. Jesus' point seems to be that He is **greater than the temple**, and in His presence, His disciples may do as He wills without blame. Jesus was thus bearing witness to His deity. People sometimes raise the question whether Jesus ever claimed to be God. He did so explicitly in many places (see Matt. 22:44–45; 24:30–31; 26:63–66; Mark 14:61–64; Luke 22:67–71; John 8:58; 10:30–33; 11:25–26; 14:1–6; 17:4–5; 18:37), but perhaps more convincing are His claims that are based on the assumption that He is God. This was one of those occasions. Jesus' statement makes no sense at all unless He really is God. He made no effort here, or anywhere else, to prove that He is God but rather assumed it and made the statement on that basis. By doing so, He once again challenged the Pharisees to accept Him for who He is. As in the previous chapter (11:20–24), this was an invitation to repentance, but the Pharisees rejected it.

12:7. Jesus alluded to several Old Testament passages where the Lord makes it clear that matters of the heart (compassion and **mercy**) are more important than the ritual of the law. His point was that God wants the hungry to eat and will not forbid it on the basis of adherence to ritual and that service to God is more important than adherence to ritual. This verse makes clear an area where repentance on the part of the Pharisees was necessary.

12:8. The Son of man is Lord even of the sabbath day (see discussion on Luke 6:5). This is a summary statement that points up especially the application of Jesus' second example.

12:9–14. This is the chapter's second account of "Sabbath-breaking." Jesus had developed a reputation as someone who could heal the sick. The Pharisees were aware of this but were more focused on the matter of working on the Sabbath than on meeting the man's need or on the fact that Jesus' healings were miracles. They challenged Him, not on whether He could perform miracles. At this point, they assumed that He could. Their challenge was strictly related to whether He would heal on the Sabbath. That they could ask Him this question and not recognize that these healings were miraculous and pointed to Jesus' deity shows how spiritually dull these men were.

12:9. For **synagogue**, see discussion on Mark 1:21.

12:10. Is it lawful to heal on the sabbath days? The rabbis prohibited healing on the Sabbath, unless it was feared that the victim would die before the next day. Obviously, the man with the withered hand was in no danger of this.

12:11–12. Jesus challenged the Pharisees on a point that showed their hypocrisy. That **a man** (v. 12) is worth more than **a sheep** is obvious, and to do good to a man is better than to do good to a sheep. If it is lawful to do good to a sheep on the Sabbath, then it must be lawful to do good to a man on the Sabbath. Jesus was saying that nothing in the will of God should ever prohibit someone from doing good. One is never excused on the basis of ritual from doing what is right.

12:13. Stretch forth thine hand. And he stretched it forth. That the man did what Jesus asked shows a connection between faith and Jesus' healing power. The man did not say, "I can't; I'm paralyzed." He stretched out his hand by faith and was healed.

12:14. The Pharisees reacted to the healing, not by marveling over the miracle, though they had seen it, nor by recognizing the deity of Christ and submitting to Him, but by redoubling their resolve to **destroy him.** Such is the power of sin in one's life; it blinds people to God's truth.

12:15. Jesus **withdrew** because His time had not yet come. He needed to continue to minister until the time was right.

12:16. For **not make him known**, see discussions on 8:4; 16:20.

12:17–21. Another fulfillment passage (see discussion on 1:22). This one is from Isaiah's first servant song (42:1–4) and is the longest Old Testament quotation in Matthew's gospel. It summarizes the quiet ministry of the Lord's servant, who will bring justice and hope to the nations.

12:17–18. My servant (v. 18). Jesus is called God's servant only here and in Acts 3:13 (see discussion there), 26; 4:27, 30. **My beloved, in whom my soul is well pleased** echoes the statement made at Jesus' baptism (see discussion on 3:17).

12:19. He shall not strive, nor cry specifically points out that Jesus' ministry was carried out without fanfare, though multitudes followed Him. More than once, including in 12:16, Jesus is seen forbidding people to whom He ministered to speak about Him. This is in contrast to His words in Matthew 28:19–20, which are in a different context.

12:20. Jesus mends broken lives (see 12:15; John 4:4–42; 8:3–11). Here is shown the extraordinary tenderness and care of the Lord, with imagery of **bruised** plants and **smoking flax** lamp wicks making the picture more vivid in the reader's mind.

12:21. In his name shall the Gentiles trust. Here again Matthew quoted a verse showing his original readers that the significance of the gospel goes beyond just the nation of Israel.

12:22–37. This section begins with an account of Jesus casting out a demon spirit, for which the Pharisees criticized Him more sharply than ever. Chapter 12 steps up the tension between Jesus and the Pharisees, something seen in each incident recorded. This section concludes with Jesus refuting the claims of the Pharisees and setting forth the issue of genuine faith.

12:22–23. Is not this the son of David? (v. 23; see discussion on 9:27). The people now began to recognize that Jesus was the Messiah. This is in sharp contrast to the Pharisees' reaction (see 12:24).

12:24. The Pharisees attributed Jesus' power to **cast out devils**, or demons, to Satan. This was the most serious charge they had brought against Him

so far. Jesus' response (12:25–37) left no room for doubt as to where He saw these Pharisees standing. For **Beelzebub**, see discussion on 10:25.

12:25–27. Jesus began by giving the general principle by which He would refute them. A **kingdom** (or "household") **divided against itself shall not stand** (v. 25). He then made the direct application. He could not be working by the power of **Satan** (v. 26), for He was working against Satan. If He was doing a work that led the people to recognize His messiahship (see "the son of David," 12:23), then He could not be doing a work empowered by Satan.

Jesus then turned the tables on the Pharisees. Apparently, some of them had been involved in a ministry of casting out demons. If Jesus cast out demons by the power of Satan, **by whom [did they] cast them out?** (v. 27). They had to either say they were in league with Satan or repudiate their own criticism of Jesus. Of course, they did neither one.

12:28–29. Jesus made it clear that He **cast out devils by the Spirit of God** (v. 28). This becomes important in 12:32. For **the kingdom of God**, see discussion on 3:2. The Pharisees were in the position of having the kingdom in their midst in the person and work of the Messiah, and they did not recognize it. Having attributed the power of the kingdom to Satan, they were now under even greater condemnation. Jesus had to **first bind the strong man** (v. 29) by the power of the Spirit of God. That is, He had to break the power Satan had gained in people's lives before they could be taken back from him and brought unto the Lord.

12:30. Here Jesus offered a significant statement related to one's attitude and actions toward Him. The first part of the verse deals with attitude: **He that is not with me is against me.** Either one identifies with Jesus or one opposes Him. Obviously, these Pharisees were against Him. This verse has significance for the matter of the exclusivity of Christ, the truth that there is only one way to heaven, and in no way can one say that "all religions lead to God." Also, nothing in the context bars the use of this verse in an evangelistic context. It leaves no room for fence-sitters. One is either with Jesus or against Him. There is no middle ground. In this context, the Pharisees were definitely against Him, but then so is the person who makes no decision or who believes he will "decide later." This passage makes it very clear that anyone who hears the gospel walks away either "with Jesus" or "against Him."

The second part of the verse deals with actions: **he that gathereth not with me scattereth abroad**. This relates directly to evangelism. Jesus had earlier used fishing as a paradigm, calling His disciples to be "fishers of men" (4:19). Here the idea of harvest is in view, an analogy Jesus also used elsewhere for evangelism (see John 4:35). Jesus reminded His hearers that one is either bringing people to the kingdom of heaven or one is sending them away from it. Again, there is no neutral ground. This applies to evangelism today. Either one is winning souls for Christ or one is sending people away from the gospel.

12:31–32. These two verses have caused much trouble in the hearts of believers. This is because they are so often taken out of context. Jesus here pronounced a specific condemnation on these Pharisees. Since His power to cast out demons comes from the Holy Spirit, and they had said it comes from Satan, they had spoken, not against Jesus, but against the Spirit.

12:31. Blasphemy against the Holy Ghost shall not be forgiven. The context (see 12:24, 28, 32) suggests that the "unpardonable sin" was attributing to Satan Christ's authenticating miracles done in the power of the Holy Spirit (see discussion on Mark 3:29).

12:32. To avoid any misunderstanding, Jesus restated the matter in slightly different words, but to the same effect. It was one thing to accuse Jesus of being a Sabbath-breaker, but quite another to attribute to Satan the work of the Spirit.

12:33–37. This section is a general commentary on the fact that an evil heart will produce evil words. The application to what the Pharisees had just said (see 12:24) is clear. They had spoken evil words because their hearts were evil. In fact, they had seen Jesus do a number of miracles, and they had heard His teaching. The multitudes had begun to sense who Jesus really was. The Pharisees had rejected Him, thus showing how far from God they really were, even though outwardly they looked like godly men.

12:33. To further his point, Jesus made a comparison between people and trees. This is one of a number of instances in the New Testament where what a person's life produces is likened to **fruit**. Fruit is what a **tree** produces. By implication, evil words are what evil people produce, and good words are what good people produce. It is not enough just to look at the tree; one must try the fruit. In the same way, it is not enough just to see a man saying prayers and keeping the outward forms of the law. One must examine what his life produces. As an evil tree produces evil fruit, so an evil heart produces evil words, and by implication, evil deeds as well. All of this is based on much of what Jesus said in the Sermon on the Mount about the nature of genuine righteousness. His statement here presupposed that the hearers understood that teaching and would interpret His words in light of it.

12:34. Jesus compared the Pharisees to **vipers**, poisonous snakes. As the viper uses its mouth to inject poison, so these Pharisees had used their mouths to inject spiritual poison into their hearers. How could they, **being evil**, do otherwise? They could only produce what was in their hearts. As a viper produces poison, so the Pharisees produced evil words.

12:35–37. Jesus made the application clearly in these verses. Verse 35 states the point of 11:33–34. Verse 36 contains a warning. Words should be spoken carefully, with attention to the motive. Verse 37 makes it clear that one's **words** reveal the content of one's heart. Judgment will be based on one's words, for they reveal what is inside.

12:38. The Pharisees wanted to see a spectacular miracle, preferably in the sky (see Luke 11:16), as **a sign** that Jesus was the Messiah. Instead, Jesus cited them a "sign" from history (see discussion on Luke 11:29).

12:39. Adulterous. Referring to spiritual, not physical, adultery, in the sense that their generation had become unfaithful to its spiritual husband

(God). Jesus promised only **the sign of the prophet Jonas**. What He meant is made clear in 12:40–42.

12:40. Three days and three nights (see discussion on Luke 24:46). Including at least part of the first day and part of the third day, a common Jewish reckoning of time. **The whale's belly**. The Greek word means "sea creature," that is, a huge fish or marine mammal (see discussion on Jonah 1:17). Jesus drew an analogy between Jonah's time inside the fish and His own coming death and resurrection. The sign, the indicator that Jesus is who He says He is, would be the resurrection. It would vindicate His ministry and point unmistakably to God's acceptance of His death on the cross as payment for sins.

12:41–42. The men of Nineveh shall rise in judgment (v. 41). They repented of their sins (see Jonah 3:5–10), and who better to condemn those who did not repent? Jesus is the one who is **a greater than Jonas** (v. 41) and **a greater than Solomon** (v. 42; see discussion on Luke 11:31–32). Those who had heard Jesus preach had even more reason to repent than Nineveh, for they had heard the message directly from God. **The queen of the south**. In 1 Kings 10:1, she is called "the queen of Sheba," a country in southwest Arabia, now called Yemen.

12:43–50. This passage appears at first glance to be unconnected to the context of the preceding passage, but actually it fits well. Jesus' disciples are His "family" in the sense that they are "with Him" as the Pharisees were not.

12:43–45. See discussion on Luke 11:24.

12:46–49. For **his mother and his brethren**, see discussion on Luke 8:19–20.

12:50. For **whosoever shall do the will of my Father**, see discussion on Mark 3:35.

F. The Parables of the Kingdom (chap. 13)

13:1–58. The first twelve chapters of Matthew emphasize Jesus' presentation of Himself as the King of the Jews. Chapter 13 represents a major shift. It now became apparent that the Jewish leaders would reject the kingdom. The parables in this chapter serve to explain and illustrate the events of chapters 9–12. The disciples had seen a variety of reactions to

Jesus' message. The Pharisees had moved from vague dislike to open opposition (12:14). Some among the multitudes had begun to realize that Jesus was more than just a prophet (9:27; 12:22–23). Some of the cities, however, had rejected Him completely (12:41–42). To His disciples, it must have seemed incomprehensible that anyone would reject Jesus and His message, which they had come to love. The parable of the sower demonstrates that people will have different reactions to the Word of God, and the parable of the wheat and the tares demonstrates that some will not respond to God's Word.

13:1. The same day connects these parables to the material in chapter 12. The parables should be interpreted in light of those events.

13:2. And sat. Sitting was the usual position for Jewish teachers (see 5:1; Luke 5:3; John 8:2).

13:3–9. For the interpretation of this parable, see 13:18–23.

13:3. Parables. The word "parable" comes from the Greek *parabolē*, which means "a placing beside," thus a comparison or an illustration. Its most common use in the New Testament is for the illustrative stories that Jesus drew from nature and human life. The Synoptic Gospels contain about thirty of these stories (see discussions on Mark 4:2; Luke 8:4). John's gospel contains no parables but uses other figures of speech. For **to sow**, see discussion on Luke 8:5. It is reasonable to assume that Jesus spoke other parables on this occasion as well, but the ones Matthew chose to reproduce here are illustrative both of Jesus' teaching and of the reactions to the word His disciples had witnessed among the people. Parables of the Kingdom—Matthew 13

1. Sower and Seed 13:3–9; 18–23
2. Wheat and Tares 13:24–30; 36–43
3. Mustard Seed 13:31–32
4. Leaven (Yeast) 13:33
5. Hidden Treasure 13:44
6. Pearl of Great Price 13:45–46
7. Net 13:47–50

13:4. Each of the places where the **seeds** (v. 4) fell represents a different type of hearer of God's Word (see discussion on Mark 4:3–9), as Jesus explained in 13:18–23. For the seed that **fell by the way side**, see 13:19 and discussion.

13:5–6. Stony places (v. 5). Not ground covered with small stones, but shallow soil on top of solid rock (see discussion on Luke 8:6). Seed in such a situation will spring up quickly, as will seed in other places, but the plants cannot take **root** (v. 6). Jesus' hearers lived close to the soil. They knew well the loss that a failed crop meant and the importance of prepared soil for success. Their lives depended directly on proper planting of each year's crop.

13:7. Some fell among thorns. The seed fell on a place where seeds of thorny plants were already in the soil. The thorny plants grew along with the good plants and won out, as weeds often will.

13:8–9. An hundredfold (v. 8). Again, an agricultural people knew well that one part of a field might yield more than another and that well-prepared soil, **good ground**, was the best guarantee of any harvest at all (see discussion on Luke 8:8). For **Who hath ears to hear, let him hear** (v. 9), see discussion on 11:15.

13:10. Why speakest thou unto them in parables? Since they themselves understood only some of the parables, **the disciples** (see discussion on Luke 8:9) knew that the people, who were less familiar with Jesus' teaching, might not understand. Jesus' answer confirmed their suspicion and explained it.

13:11. The mysteries of the kingdom of heaven (see discussions on Mark 4:11; Luke 8:10). These "mysteries," or "secrets," were not revealed in the Old Testament. They are unique to the New Testament and reveal new information about Christ's earthly rule.

13:12. Whosoever hath refers to those who have faith in Christ, as opposed to those who do not believe, **whosoever hath not.** Those who believe live by faith and gain even more, whereas those who do not believe miss out on God's blessings altogether. **From him shall be taken away** refers to those who refuse to believe in Jesus as the Messiah. By rejecting the King, they reject the blessings of His kingdom.

13:13–14. These verses expand on what Jesus said in 13:12 and apply it to His teaching session of that day. Jesus spoke **in parables** (v. 13) because of the spiritual dullness of the people (see discussion on Luke 8:4). For **they seeing see not**, see *KJV Study Bible* note on Mark 4:12; discussion on Luke 8:10. Once again Matthew pointed to an Old Testament **prophecy** (v. 14) that was fulfilled here (see Isa. 6:9–10). Jesus' life and ministry, for Matthew, was a matter of fulfilling prophecy, which confirmed His Messiahship.

13:15. Lest at any time they should see ... and hear ... and should be converted means that many had closed their eyes and ears to avoid being converted. The idea here is not that God does not want people to hear and understand. God wills that all men should repent (see Acts 17:30), but when people refuse the truth, "lest at any time they should see ... and hear ...," God will not force them. Jesus used parables so that those eager for the truth will explore and discover it, while those who want to avoid it can do so.

13:16–17. Jesus affirmed the rightness of seeking spiritual truth. The disciples were receiving the fuller revelation that the prophets had not received.

13:18. Hear ye therefore the parable of the sower. Jesus seldom interpreted His parables, but here He did.

13:19. Jesus explained that the soil is the hearer. **The wicked one** is the Devil, who snatches away spiritual truth that is not understood. This is why the Word of God never penetrates so many people who hear it. The Devil takes it away by distracting the hearer with the pleasures of sin or by reminding the hearer of other priorities. If the Devil gets us focused on immediate wants, we will not be thinking about eternal truths. **The way side** refers to the walking path beside the field. In other words, when the **seed** of God's Word falls on a hard heart, that person has no response or receptivity to it, so the Devil snatches it away, as though the person never heard it in the first place.

13:20–21. Stony places (v. 20) refers to shallow or rocky ground that has insufficient soil. **Anon with joy** refers to shallow and emotional responses to the gospel that do not last but wither away. **Persecution** (v. 21) causes those whose profession of faith is not real to turn away from following Christ. Some people believe that coming to Christ means all of their problems go away. When this does not happen, they become disappointed and drop out. This verse may be used as a reminder to believers that even after they have received the Word of God, that is, after they have been saved, troubles may still come.

13:22. The seed that falls "by the way side" (13:19) never takes root. Such a person hears the truth but never believes it, having other priorities in life. The seed that falls "into stony places" (13:20) produces much joy in the listener, but it is only a temporary emotional response. The seed that falls **among the thorns** is soon choked out by **the care**(s) **of this world**. The person hears and receives **the word** and claims to believe the gospel but is soon distracted with worldly matters and material goods.

13:23. Regarding the seed that falls into **good ground**, Jesus described a threefold process: the person **heareth the word**, he **understandeth it**, and it **beareth fruit**. These three responses must all be present for one to be a genuine disciple. Hearing the Word includes reading it. In Jesus' day, most people could not read, and the Word of God was most often heard in the synagogues and memorized. Understanding God's Word involves meditating on it, asking questions and finding answers, memorizing it, and imagining it lived out in one's life. The Word bears fruit when it is applied to one's life. In the New Testament, the word "fruit" is used in various ways. Usually it involves living the Christian life, in the sense of obedience to God's Word. In Galatians 5:22–23, however, Paul used it to describe the kinds of virtues the Spirit produces in one's life. Theologians debate which of these responses to the gospel actually produces saving faith, but only the final one produces spiritual fruit.

13:24–30. This is the parable of the wheat and tares. Jesus again wanted His disciples to see that while some people respond to the preaching of God's Word, not all will. Since much of the opposition in the preceding chapter came from the Pharisees, Jesus may have had them in mind here. As tares look like the wheat during the growing season and are hard to

separate out, so also the Pharisees "looked" spiritual even though theirs was only a surface spirituality, not a matter of the heart. For the interpretation of this parable, see 13:36–43.

13:24. The kingdom of heaven is likened unto. This phrase introduces six of the seven parables in this chapter (all but the parable of the sower).

13:25–30. Tares (v. 25). Probably darnel, which looks very much like wheat while it is young but can later be distinguished. The **field** (v. 27) is "the world" (13:38). Thus, the people of the kingdom live side by side with the people of the Evil One. It is wise not to press the analogy too far. While a farmer might have trouble distinguishing wheat from darnel, God does not have any trouble distinguishing His own from the lost people of the world. As the wheat and the tares were mixed together, so also God's people live in the world with the lost. God does not separate them out, until the time for harvest. The point of this parable is that some people will initially profess to be believers, but later it will be clear that they are not.

13:31–33. These two short parables, that of the mustard seed (vv. 31–32) and the leaven (v. 33), are meant to counterbalance the parables of the sower and of the wheat and tares. The disciples could have easily become discouraged. They had just seen evidence that there would be opposition to the message they loved so well, and Jesus had just related two parables confirming that not everyone will respond to the Word of God. If not everyone will respond to the Word positively, why bother with preaching at all? Sometimes we have an all-or-nothing attitude about things we care about. When Christians witness and meet with opposition or indifference, it is easy to give up in discouragement. Jesus therefore wanted the disciples to realize that while God's plan in this world may have a small beginning, it will be influential in significant ways. The mustard seed and the leaven, though small and easily overlooked, do make a difference. God's Word may produce little fruit among a group of hearers, but that fruit will have a lasting effect. Preaching impacts eternity.

13:31–32. Although the kingdom will seem to have an insignificant beginning, it will eventually spread throughout the world. **The least of all seeds ... the greatest among herbs** (v. 32). The **mustard seed** (v. 31) is not the smallest seed known today, but it was the smallest seed used by farmers and gardeners in the Holy Land, and under favorable conditions, the plant could reach some ten feet in height. **A tree ... the branches thereof** (v. 32). This could be an allusion to Daniel 4:21, suggesting that the kingdom of heaven will expand to world dominion and that people from all nations will find rest in it (see Dan. 2:35, 44 – 45; 7:27; Rev. 11:15), or it could picture evil coming into the kingdom, since "the fowls" in 13:4 is interpreted as "the wicked one" in 13:19.

13:33. In the Bible, **leaven** usually symbolizes that which is evil or unclean (see discussion on Mark 8:15). Here it could picture evil, or possibly it is a symbol for growth. As leaven permeates a batch of dough, so **The kingdom of heaven** spreads through a person's life. Alternatively, the leaven may signify the growth of the kingdom by the inner working of the Holy Spirit (using God's Word).

13:34. This summary statement introduces a bridge to Jesus' interpretation of the parable of the tares.

13:35. Spoken by the prophet. The quotation is from Psalm 78, a psalm ascribed to Asaph, who, according to 2 Chronicles 29:30, was a "seer" (prophet). Matthew's determination to show that the ministry of Jesus fulfilled Old Testament prophecy is again seen here. This statement could have been left out without changing the sense of this chapter. One can only imagine that Matthew included it because of his emphasis on fulfilled prophecy.

13:36. Here is an example of what Jesus meant by "good ground" (13:23). The disciples remembered what Jesus said and now they sought to understand it. One reasonably expects that they intended to apply it in their lives and ministry as well. All believers should do the same and should not become discouraged if people do not respond to their witness for Christ.

13:37 – 39. For **the Son of man** (v. 37), see discussion on Mark 2:10. Jesus answered their request and interpreted the parable of the tares. The parable

is something of an allegory, in which each element is a symbol of something else. Readers of the Gospels should be careful, however; not every parable may be interpreted in this way. That Jesus offered an interpretation of this parable and that of the sower should alert readers to the fact that these two are different from most of His parables.

In the parable of the tares, **the reapers are the angels** (v. 39). They are the ones who will **harvest** the crop; that is, they will gather those who have been saved. Jesus said essentially the same thing in Matthew 24:31, where he said that angels will gather believers at the end of the age. **The enemy** is Satan, who seeks to pervert the Word and work of God in our lives.

13:40 – 43. Here we see a promise of judgment. **A furnace of fire** (v. 42) is often mentioned in connection with the final judgment in apocalyptic literature (see Rev. 19:20; 20:14). Notice that the fire of the parable (see 13:30) is clearly said to be **fire** (v. 40) in Christ's interpretation. **Wailing and gnashing of teeth** (v. 42) occurs six times in Matthew's gospel (8:12; here; 13:50; 22:13; 24:51; 25:30) and nowhere else in the New Testament. It is important to note that it is in the furnace that there will be the wailing and gnashing of teeth. In no way may this be seen as annihilation of the wicked. This is conscious and continuous punishment for sin. Hell is always treated in Scripture as a reality and as a place of continual punishment, not a place of cessation.

13:44 – 46. These two parables, that of the hidden treasure (v. 44) and the pearl of great price (v. 45 – 46), teach the same truth: The kingdom is of such great value that one should be willing to give up all he has to gain it. Jesus was not implying that one can purchase the kingdom with money or good deeds. He was emphasizing that those who had rejected His preaching had missed something very valuable, something that would have been worth giving up anything else, including worldly goods or prestige, to have.

13:44. Treasure hid in a field (v. 44). In ancient times, it was common to hide treasure in the ground since there was no widespread equivalent of modern bank vaults for the safekeeping of funds, though there were "exchangers" (see 25:27 and discussion). Sometimes one unexpectedly stumbles across the gospel message, without searching for it, as with the treasure in this parable.

13:45–46. Seeking goodly pearls (v. 45). The pearl was found after a diligent search, in contrast to the treasure. Either way, whether one stumbles across the gospel or discovers it after a long search for truth, it is of inestimable value.

13:47–51. The parable of the **net** (v. 47) teaches the same general lesson as the parable of the tares: There will be a final separation of the righteous and the wicked. The parable of the tares also emphasizes that we are not to try to make such a separation now and that this is entirely the Lord's business (see 13:28–30, 41–42). The Lord used this fishing analogy to illustrate the same truth, perhaps because some of the disciples were fishermen. This demonstrates His intention to make His teaching interesting and relevant to the audience, without compromising the message. At the end of this, Jesus confirmed that His disciples had **understood** (v. 51) the parable.

13:52. Every scribe. This verse may seem odd, but Jesus was speaking to His disciples, not to scribes. The key may be that the disciples had understood the parables. Having been instructed in spiritual matters, they had an abundance to share.

13:53. This verse concludes a teaching section and introduces a narrative section (compare 7:28–29).

13:54–57. In a sense, this passage returns to the theme of some not receiving the Word in their hearts. The key is that He was in **his own country**, Galilee, and Nazareth (v. 54; see discussion on 2:23), the town He called home, where He grew up. For **he taught them in their synagogue**, see discussion on Mark 1:21. Those who have done it know that some of the most difficult preaching comes when a preacher returns to the church of his childhood.

The carpenter's son (v. 55). The word translated "carpenter" could mean "stonemason" (see discussion on Mark 6:3). Joseph may or may not have been living at the time of this incident. **Brethren.** Sons born to Joseph and Mary after the virgin birth of Jesus (see discussion on Luke 8:19–20). Essentially, the people were saying, "Hey, we know this man. He is nothing special." It is part of human nature to regard someone from out of town as an automatic "expert" while overlooking or not taking seriously the local person. Many in Jesus' audience probably remembered Him as a child. It is difficult to see someone you knew as a child behaving as one with authority. The Lord understands human nature on this matter, which is why He calls some to be evangelists or missionaries. The "expert" from out of town can preach the same message the local pastor has preached for years and get results where before there were none, simply because he is from out of town.

13:58. Unbelief. The close relationship between faith and miracles is stressed in Matthew's gospel (see 8:10, 13; 9:2, 22, 28–29).

G. Herod's Reaction to Jesus' Ministry (14:1–12)

14:1. Tetrarch. The ruler of a fourth part of a region. **Herod** (Herod Antipas) was one of several sons of Herod the Great. When Herod the Great died, his kingdom was divided among three of his sons (see charts, *KJV Study Bible*, pp. 1355, 1451). Herod Antipas ruled over Galilee and Perea (4 BC–AD 39). Matthew correctly referred to him as "tetrarch" here, as Luke regularly did (Luke 3:19; 9:7; Acts 13:1). In 14:9, however, Matthew called him "king," as Mark also did (Mark 6:14), because that was his popular title among the Galileans as well as in Rome.

14:2. John the Baptist ... is risen from the dead (see discussion on Mark 6:16). This curious assumption on Herod's part is explained in the parenthetical section that follows (14:3–12). Matthew gave much attention to this incident, most likely in light of his Jewish readers (see Introduction, "Recipients"). John the Baptist's ministry had a long-lasting impact on all of Judea and beyond. Many years after his beheading, Paul found some disciples of John the Baptist at Ephesus (see Acts 19:1–7). Matthew apparently believed it was necessary to explain to his readers what had happened to John and why he was not active in the church in the years following the day of Pentecost.

This incident also displays yet another reaction to Jesus' ministry. That Herod would come up with this explanation shows human depravity and credulity. How often have we encountered people who are ready to believe anything rather than humble themselves and repent before the Lord. Herod would believe in the resurrection of John the Baptist before he would believe the message of Christ. Haunted by his sin and guilt, he would believe a fantasy before he would bow before a gracious and loving God.

14:3. Herodias was a granddaughter of Herod the Great. Her first husband was her uncle Herod Philip I (Herod the Great had two sons named Philip), who lived in Rome. While a guest in their home, Herod Antipas had persuaded Herodias to leave her husband for him. Marriage to one's brother's wife while the brother was still living was forbidden by the Mosaic law (see Lev. 18:16). Philip I was the son of Herod the Great and Mariamne, the daughter of Simon the high priest, and was thus a half-brother of Herod Antipas, born to Malthace (see chart, *Zondervan KJV Study Bible*, p. 1355).

14:4–5. John the Baptist was a man of conviction unintimidated by worldly authority and willing to preach the truth, even if it is unpopular with his audience. John held up Herod's life to the unfailing plumb line of God's Word and found Herod wanting. Would that more of God's people would confront the world with the truth of God. Compromise, for the sake of one's life or for the sake of respectability, is displeasing to the Lord. The contrast between the fearless man of God and the fearful sinner is hard to miss in these two verses. Herod was a man who **feared the multitude** (v. 5) and could not act because he feared the opinion of men. This had kept him from doing a greater evil, until the events in 14:6–12, and he should have been as fearless in doing good as he was fearful in doing evil.

14:6–7. The daughter of Herodias (v. 6). Salome, according to Josephus. She later married her granduncle Philip II (a son of Herod the Great), who ruled the northern territories (see Luke 3:1). At this time, Salome was a young woman of marriageable age. Her dance was undoubtedly lascivious, and the perfor-

mance pleased both Herod and his guests. Under the influence of her charms, Herod made a rash promise. Perhaps he underestimated her, thinking that as a mere child, she would ask for trinkets or for wealth, which he had in abundance. He never anticipated that she would ask what he feared to do most.

14:8. Charger. A flat wooden dish on which meat was served. Salome was **instructed [by] her mother** to request **John Baptist's head.** Perhaps her mother, knowing Herod's probable reaction, also goaded her to dance. Her mother may have expressed her hatred for John in the past and told Salome that if she ever got the chance, she should make this request. It is interesting that Salome requested John's head; surely she would have wanted other things more. Perhaps her mother had threatened her if, given the opportunity, she requested something else.

14:9. Herod, a man driven by his lusts and by guilt and fear, nevertheless could be morally scrupulous at certain points, which is why he granted her request, **for the oath's sake.** The Bible presents fallen humanity in all of its complexity. People can commit serious sins and yet be scrupulous regarding other sins. In addition, this verse shows again how Herod was driven by public opinion. He granted her request also because of **them which sat with him at meat,** that is, his guests. He would not go back on his word for fear of what those around him would think. Both his having spared John previously and his decision to behead him were thus driven, in part, by fear of what people would think. Would that we all would heed this warning and be driven by what God thinks rather than by the opinions of others.

14:10–11. Herod fulfilled her request immediately.

14:12. Jesus was told of John's beheading. This verse connects the section to what follows.

IV. Jesus' Withdrawals from Galilee (14:13–17:20)

A. To the Eastern Shore of the Sea of Galilee (14:13–15:20)

14:13–21. This incident, the feeding of the five thousand, is recorded in all four gospels (see Mark 6:33–44; Luke 9:10–17; John 6:1–15 and discussions). It must have made quite an impression on the disciples. In all four accounts, the event is recorded as a miracle, leaving no room to see it as anything else. Some have tried to say that the people were shamed into sharing their food and that this is how everyone got fed, but if that had been the case, the story would have been recorded that way somewhere, and the accounts we have would vary far more widely than they do. As it is, the variations between the four accounts can be harmonized and in no way indicate that the Bible is in error in any detail. Nor do the variations justify the notion that this account is fabricated in any way. What is recorded is what happened. A noteworthy miracle took place, one that the disciples never forgot.

14:13–14. Jesus **departed** (v. 13) because of the beheading of John. Jesus' ministry was not yet complete, and He did not want to be in danger at this time. He thus went to a remote location, yet even there, He attracted crowds. That they were far from the city, and therefore from food supplies, sets the scene for the miracle that follows.

14:15–16. Jesus wanted to test the faith of the disciples. He prompted them to do what He knew they could not do on their own. They needed to trust Him for what was to follow. Many times God will ask of believers what may seem impossible, and which, in their own resources, is impossible. We should remember that when He leads us into a ministry, He will provide the resources for success. All we need to do is obey Him.

14:17–19. Here the lack of resources on the part of the disciples is made clear, as well as their obedience to the Lord. With no fanfare, Jesus accepted the little food they had and used it to bless the people. He gave the food to the disciples, who gave it to **the multitude**. Other gospels reveal that the source of what food the disciples did have was a small boy's lunch, but that detail did not concern Matthew. It is hard to read this passage without seeing a parallel to ministry in general. We offer to God what we have. He blesses it and commands us to share of our spiritual resources with the people to whom He calls us to minister. This is not an allegory, as it is a historical incident, but the parallel is clear and is at least a part of the significance of this passage.

14:20–21. There was more than enough food for everyone. God is not limited by personal resources. All He asks for is availability and obedience, and He will take care of the rest. **Beside women and children** (v. 21). Matthew alone noted this. He was writing to the Jews, who did not permit women and children to eat with men in public. The women and children were thus in a place by themselves.

14:22. Constrained. The Greek word used here is strong. It means "to compel" and suggests a crisis. John recorded that after the miracle of the loaves and fish, the crowds "would come and take him by force, to make him a king" (John 6:15). This involved a complete misunderstanding of Jesus' mission. The disciples may have been caught up in the enthusiasm and needed to be removed from the area quickly (see 16:5–12). Also, Jesus may have wanted to set the scene for the miracle of His walking on water. Jesus **sent the multitudes away** after He sent the disciples away. Apparently, He had more in mind than just telling the people goodbye and leaving immediately. He probably preached to them one more time and left them with words of encouragement and exhortation. Perhaps He spoke to them in small groups according to where they lived, with specific exhortations, before dismissing them.

14:23. To pray. Matthew recorded Jesus praying fewer times than Luke recorded, who emphasized Jesus' humanity. Besides here, Matthew showed Jesus praying in Gethsemane (cf. 26:36–46) and on the cross (27:46). Jesus also thanked the Father for the provision both for the five thousand (14:19) and for the four thousand (15:36). Jesus certainly needed spiritual strength at this time; He had just completed a strenous time of ministry, and many needs had been brought to Him during the course of the day.

14:24. This verse sets the scene for the miracle of Jesus walking on the sea. The disciples were in a stormy sea, in the night. It was perhaps frightening even for the skilled boatmen among them, and well might they have thought they saw "a spirit" (14:36) coming to them on the water.

14:25. The fourth watch. 3:00–6:00 a.m. According to Roman reckoning, the night was divided into four watches: (1) 6:00–9:00 p.m., (2) 9:00 p.m.–midnight, (3) midnight–3:00 a.m., and (4) 3:00–6:00 a.m. (see *KJV Study Bible* note on Mark 13:35). The Jews had only three watches during the night: (1) sunset–10:00 p.m., (2) 10:00 p.m.–2:00 a.m., and (3) 2:00 a.m.–sunrise (see Judg. 7:19; 1 Sam. 11:11). For **walking on the sea**, see discussion on Mark 6:48.

14:26–27. As noted in 14:24, it was a dark, stormy night. The disciples did not recognize Jesus immediately and would not have expected to have seen Him coming in that way in any case. Jesus **spake unto them** (v. 27) a word of comfort.

14:28–31. This passage describes Peter walking on the water. It is a favorite passage for preaching, as it is a vivid example of genuine faith and of faith that yet falls short. Apparently, Peter either did not recognize Jesus' face due to the darkness or was not sure it was really Him, for he said, **Lord, if it be thou** (v. 28). His request to come out onto the water is startling. It is often, and perhaps rightly, seen as an example of Peter's impetuosity, his tendency to speak before thinking. Having made the challenge, Peter had no choice but to step out of the boat at the Lord's bidding. Peter was fine until **he saw the wind boysterous** (v. 30), then, shifting his focus away from the Lord, he suddenly and naturally became **afraid** and began **to sink**. It is no misuse of this passage to point out that Peter looked at the circumstances rather than at the Savior, and thus his faith failed. He prayed the shortest prayer in all of the Bible, **Lord, save me**, and Jesus did so. They returned to the boat together. One should be careful when preaching this passage, however. Matthew's purpose was to show that Jesus is the Messiah, not to give an illustration of faith. The passage can be used in that way, as long as one keeps in mind Matthew's real purpose, which is made clear in the next two verses.

14:32–33. When Peter and Jesus returned to the ship, **the wind ceased** (v. 32), meaning that the storm ended immediately. The disciples had witnessed, in a fairly short period of time, several miracles. Jesus had healed the people (14:14), had fed five thousand of them miraculously, had walked on water, and had enabled Peter to do the same. Then He stilled the storm. He had shown power over nature and power to supernaturally meet needs. The disciples **worshipped him** (v. 33), recognizing that He is **the Son of God**. This was Matthew's point. Only God could do the things Jesus had done in the space of the last twenty-four hours.

14:34–36. These verses briefly explain what Jesus did once on the other side of the sea and demonstrate His growing popularity. He had been healing since early in His ministry, and the leaders of the community quickly spread the word of His arrival. People were healed merely by **touch[ing] the hem of his garment** (v. 36; see discussion on Mark 5:28), which was symbolic of their faith in Him. Jesus often challenged those whom He healed about their faith (see, e.g., Matt. 9:22; 15:28), and there is no warrant to assume that faith was not central here as well. Jesus' healing ministry made clear that His power came from God. He was no conjurer or caster of spells. His power came from God, and He needed no aids to heal.

Gennesaret (v. 34). Either the narrow plain, about four miles long and less than two miles wide, on the west side of the Sea of Galilee near the north end (north of Magdala), or a town in the plain. The plain, fertile and well watered, was considered a garden spot of the Holy Land.

15:1–20. This passage illustrates a familiar pattern. An incident raised a particular question, and Jesus took the opportunity to teach on the matter. Here Matthew recorded another instance of opposition to Christ on the part of the Pharisees, along with some scribes (vv. 1–2). Jesus answered them with a specific challenge on the matter they had brought up (vv. 3–9), and then He called the multitudes to Himself and taught them a more general principle based on the same incident (vv. 10–20).

15:1–2. These **scribes and Pharisees ... were of Jerusalem** (v. 1). Matthew noted this since he was beginning to point the narrative toward the showdown in Jerusalem, at the trial of Jesus. His ministry had now attracted attention as far away as Jerusalem, and opposition to Him from official sources came from there as well. **The tradition of the elders** (v. 2). After the Babylonian captivity, the Jewish rabbis began to make meticulous rules and regulations governing the daily life of the people. These were interpretations and applications of the law of Moses, handed down from generation to generation. In Jesus' day, this "tradition of the elders" was in oral form. It was not until circa AD 200 that it was put into writing in the Mishnah. The Pharisees complained that the disciples **wash not their hands** (see Mark 7:1–4). Their objection had to do with an outward observance. By eating with unwashed hands, the disciples were possibly putting into themselves something that was not pure. This became the touchstone of Jesus' teaching to the multitude (see 15:10–11).

15:3–6. In responding to their objection, Jesus began by issuing the Pharisees and scribes a counterchallenge, asking why they had substituted for the written law a man-made **tradition** (v. 3), one that many had taken advantage of to the detriment of their parents. Jesus was admittedly answering a question with a question, but in doing so, He revealed the hypocrisy of His questioners. He cited the commandment about honoring one's parents (v. 4) and then their tradition that set aside the clear commandment (vv. 5–6; see discussions on Mark 7:10–11, 13). The Pharisees had no answer. They had raised a point of strict observance to ceremonial law, and Jesus countered with a point on which they were setting aside a law that involved important family relationships. No one could argue that the point on which they had challenged Jesus was more important than taking care of family, and clearly these leaders were making an issue of something that was small in comparison to their own teaching, which also violated the strict letter of the law.

15:7–9. Jesus then condemned the Pharisees as **hypocrites** (v. 7) and cited Isaiah's prophecy against those who honor the Lord outwardly **with their lips; but their heart is far from me** (v. 8; Isa. 29:13). Their worship was **vain** (v. 9); that is, it was empty of any value and did neither them nor the Lord any

good. This condemnation relates to Jesus' teaching to the multitude (see 15:10–11). God is concerned not with what is on the outside but with what is in the heart. Going through the motions of worship or obeying laws that relate only to the physical side of life does not mean much if one's heart is not in it.

15:10–11. Jesus **called the multitude** (v. 10) and told them that what **cometh out of the mouth** (v. 11), or out of one's heart, is what **defileth a man**. What goes in does not defile. In other words, what a person has in her heart, not what she eats, determines her character. Outward observance of the ceremonial law is easy and proves nothing about the heart. The heart attitude, which comes out in the way one treats others, demonstrates whether one is righteous or defiled. This harks back to the Sermon on the Mount, in which Jesus pointed out in different ways how the heart attitude, not the actions, demonstrate true righteousness. Here again the people were challenged to seek a righteousness that "shall exceed the righteousness of the scribes and Pharisees" (Matt. 5:20).

15:12–14. Jesus' disciples were concerned that Jesus had **offended** (v. 12) the authorities, perhaps because this incident occurred so soon after the beheading of John. Jesus' reply seems not to relate directly to their concern, but He was showing them that the Pharisees were on the wrong side of the question. God would take care of the problem in His own time. **Every plant, which my heavenly Father hath not planted** (v. 13) may be understood in two ways. (1) It may refer to the false teaching of the Pharisees, harking back to the parable of the sower. In this case, Jesus was saying that the false teaching would not take root in the people's hearts. (2) It may refer to the Pharisees themselves, harking back to the parable of the tares. In this case, Jesus was saying that the scribes and Pharisees, as false teachers, would be rooted out by God. Either way, Jesus wanted His disciples to know that the truth He preached would prevail and that they should not be concerned that some opposed it. Jesus did not deal specifically with the possible consequences to Himself for upsetting the Pharisees, but His teaching made it clear that His mission was to teach the truth and let God take care of error, in whatever form.

15:15–20. Jesus, in response to Peter's request, explained to the disciples clearly that what is in the heart is most important. Outward things do not defile. He used the example of eating food. Even "unclean" food is eliminated by the body. To make sure He was understood concerning what comes out of the heart, Jesus presented a sin list. The list, which includes not only things forbidden in the Ten Commandments but also **evil thoughts** (v. 19), harks back to matters He discussed in the Sermon on the Mount. His point was that the outward keeping of the commandments is no good if the heart is not right.

B. To Phoenicia (15:21–28)

15:21. For **Tyre**, see discussion on Mark 7:24. **Sidon.** About twenty-five miles north of Tyre. Matthew did not say why Jesus went to minister in this region.

15:22. A woman of Canaan. This term is found many times in the Old Testament but only here in the New Testament. In New Testament times, there was no country known as Canaan. Some think this was the Semitic manner of referring to the people of Phoenicia at the time. Mark wrote, "The woman was a Greek, a Syrophenician" (Mark 7:26). This woman knew that Jesus was the **Son of David** and apparently knew why that was important. She also was aware that Jesus cast out demons.

15:23. Jesus' response appears cold, but He wanted to test the woman's faith. The disciples wanted Him to **Send her away.**

15:24. Here Jesus gave an answer that Matthew's Jewish readers would have readily understood. Jesus told the woman that His mission was to the Jewish people, **the lost sheep of the house of Israel.** Jesus had every intention of meeting her need, but His focus in ministry at this time was the Jewish people. Matthew used this incident, however, to remind his readers that the gospel has a universal aspect as well. By contrasting Jesus' statement regarding the focus of His mission with His subsequent action, Matthew was able both to confirm his readers' understanding of Israel's position as the chosen people of God and to challenge them with the wider ministry of the church as it would develop over time.

15:25–26. The children's bread (v. 26). That belonging to "the lost sheep of the house of Israel" (15:24). **Dogs.** The Greek says "little dogs," meaning a pet dog in the home. Jesus' point was that the gospel was to be given first to Jews.

15:27–28. Truth, Lord (v. 27; see *KJV Study Bible* note on Mark 7:28). The woman understood Jesus' implication and was willing to settle for **crumbs.** Twice she called Him "Lord" in this passage. The Greek for this title can mean something close to "sir," but in light of the nature of her request and the fact that she called Him "Son of David" (15:22), it is not unreasonable to assume that she understood at least His messianic role, though not necessarily His deity.

Jesus left the region immediately after this event, and it is reasonable to suppose that He believed that His work there was now finished. This incident could have been left out of Matthew's account with no loss of continuity. That he recorded it was most likely due to his desire to show his readers the universal nature of the gospel.

C. To the Decapolis (15:29–16:12)

15:29–39. See Mark 7:31–8:10 and discussions.

15:29–31. Jesus **departed** (v. 29) and ministered near **the sea of Galilee.** The **multitudes came** (v. 30), bringing the sick, **and he healed them.** Because of the healings, **they glorifed the God of Israel** (v. 31). Jesus' miracles always pointed to God. They were never done just for their own sake. Jesus taught many things just by doing these miracles of healing: the compassion of God, the grace of God, the need for faith, and the perfect will of God, among others.

15:32–38. The feeding of the five thousand is recorded in all four gospels, but the feeding of the four thousand is only found in Matthew and Mark. In the feeding of the five thousand, twelve baskets were filled with leftovers, which Jesus possibly gave to the twelve apostles, though some think He gave them to the little boy. The **seven baskets** (v. 37) mentioned here were possibly larger baskets.

15:39. Magdala. The home of Mary Magdalene. Mark 8:10 has "Dalmanutha."

16:1–4. This incident marks a turning point in Jesus' interaction with the Pharisees. For one thing, the Saducees joined in the effort to trap Jesus. The Pharisees and Saducees were rivals over some matters of Old Testament interpretation relating to the supernatural, but they were now working together to discredit Jesus. Another mark of a turning point is how they sought to trap Jesus. Whereas previously the Pharisees had asked for a sign (see 12:38), now they asked for **a sign from heaven** (v. 1). They sought something spectacular and more directly supernatural, a heavenly affirmation of His ministry (see discussion on Mark 8:11). It is hardly credible that they actually believed Jesus could or would do this. They wanted to expose Him as a fraud when He either refused or failed. Apparently, they were aware that the multitudes recognized Jesus as the Messiah. In the past, the Pharisees had challenged Jesus on matters related to Sabbath-breaking and the interpretation of the law; now they challenged the central point of His ministry at this stage: His messiahship. Jesus did not provide them with "a sign from heaven" but instead rebuked them for being able to forecast the weather but unable to **discern the signs of the times** (v. 3). He also rebuked them for seeking a sign at all and promised them only **the sign of the prophet Jonas** (v. 4). This is the second time that Jesus pointed to Jonah in reply to a request for a sign (see 12:39–40). He offered no explanation, unlike the previous occasion, but one may assume that He had the same point in mind. The sign that He would give would be His own resurrection (see discussion on Luke 11:30). That would be proof and vindication of His ministry, His messiahship, and His right to rule on the throne of David forever.

16:5–6. This is another situation in which Jesus took advantage of a teaching opportunity. The disciples **had forgotten to take bread** (v. 5) with them for the journey. For **the leaven of the Pharisees and of the Sadducees**, see 16:12; see also discussions on 3:7; Mark 2:16; 8:15; 12:18.

16:7–12. The disciples' discussion reveals that they were clueless as to what Jesus meant (v. 7). He explained the matter directly, pointing to the feeding of **the five thousand** (v. 9) and the feeding of **the four thousand** (v. 10) and reminding them of the abundance of the leftovers. When they were with Jesus, they had no need to worry about food, for He could supply all they needed. Jesus had something much more important in mind here, however. Matthew ended with a short commentary on what the disciples now **understood** (v. 12), that Jesus was warning them about **the doctrine of the Pharisees and the Sadducees**. Matthew often explained the meaning of Jesus' words (see 17:13).

Christians today might well heed this warning. So often believers are led astray because they like the personality of the minister or they enjoy the music program of a church. All of these things are good, but believers must be careful that they do not sacrifice truth on the altar of entertainment and good feelings. Christian faith is faith in the truth about Jesus Christ — His life, death, and resurrection — and its significance for salvation. It is faith in the truths revealed in God's Word. Considerations other than truth should not guide one's choices in matters of faith and practice.

D. To Caesarea Philippi (16:13–17:21)

16:13. Cesarea Philippi. To be distinguished from the magnificent city of Caesarea Maritima, which Herod the Great built on the coast of the Mediterranean. Caesarea Philippi, rebuilt by Herod's son Philip (who named it after Tiberius Caesar and himself), was twenty-five miles north of the Sea of Galilee, near the slopes of Mount Hermon. Originally it was called Paneas (the ancient name survives today as Banias) in honor of the Greek god Pan, whose shrine was located there. The region was especially pagan. It is interesting to note that Jesus took His Jewish disciples to this very Gentile place to announce the establishment of His church, which would include both Jews and Gentiles.

Jesus asked His disciples about the peoples' understanding of His identity. For **the Son of man**, see discussion on Mark 2:10. His purpose was to set up the revelation of the truth concerning who He is. Sometimes one must clear up misconceptions before stating the truth.

16:14–15. Perhaps in the moment of stating out loud, for the first time, some of what they had heard, the disciples saw that none of these answers made any sense, but His messiahship did. The answers the disciples gave included the one that Herod had earlier believed, that Jesus was John the Baptist resurrected from the dead. Jesus followed up with a question that required them to make a decision. Good preaching and teaching should always aim for a decision. The disciples could have debated the relative merits of different theories all day long, but it was time for them to recognize and state the truth.

16:16. It was Peter who spoke, but his confession may be understood as reflecting the understanding of all the disciples. **Christ**, or "Messiah" (also in 16:20). Both mean "the Anointed One." The Old Testament equivalent ("Messiah") is used of anyone who was anointed with the holy oil, such as the priests and kings of Israel (see, e.g., Exod. 29:7, 21; 1 Sam. 10:1, 6; 16:13; 2 Sam. 1:14, 16). The word carries the idea of being chosen by God, consecrated to His service, and endued with His power to accomplish the assigned task. Toward the end of the Old Testament period, the word assumed a special meaning. It denoted the ideal king anointed and empowered by God to rescue His people from their enemies and establish His righteous kingdom (see Dan. 9:25–26). The ideas that clustered around the title "Messiah" tended to be political and national in nature. Probably for that reason, Jesus seldom used the term. He did, however, on occasion acknowledge Himself as Messiah (see Mark 8:27–30; 14:61–63; John 4:25–26).

16:17. Jesus pointed out that Peter had come to this knowledge not by human means but by revelation. Others had come up with answers to His identity that made no sense, such as that he was John the Baptist or Elijah. This is because human reasoning cannot get to divine truth. Christians today might well recognize that it is by submitting to the teaching of God's Word, illumined by the Spirit, that one will come to the knowledge of the truth. Human wisdom leads to a dead end. Submission to God's Word under the teaching of God's Spirit leads to life.

16:18. Peter … rock … church. In the Greek, "Peter" is *Petros* ("detached stone") and "rock" is *petra* ("bedrock"). Several interpretations have been given to these words. The "bedrock" on which the church is built is (1) Christ; (2) Peter's confession of faith in Jesus as the Messiah (16:16); (3) Christ's teachings—one of the great emphases of Matthew's gospel; (4) Peter himself, understood in terms of his role on the day of Pentecost (see Acts 2) and in the Cornelius incident (see Acts 10) and his leadership among the apostles. The best answer is that it refers to Peter's confession, which is expressive of the disciples' faith and hence the apostles' doctrine. The rock on which the church is built is the confession that Jesus Christ is Lord, that He is the "chosen one," chosen to die for the sins of the world and chosen to reign. Ephesians 2:20 indicates that the church is "built upon the foundation of the apostles and prophets." This perhaps means that it is built on the foundation of the Old Testament and the preaching of the apostles, that is, on the Word of God in the Old and New Testaments. In the Gospels, the word **church** (Greek, *ekklēsia*; "called out" or "assembly") is used only by Matthew (here and twice in 18:17). In the Septuagint, it is used for the congregation of Israel. In Greek circles of Jesus' day, it indicated the assembly of a city's free, voting citizens (see Acts 19:32, 39, 41). Matthew's use of "church" need not be understood as a later addition. Jesus could very well have used the word here, or an Aramaic word that could well be translated this way. Jesus meant that He would gather His people, "assemble" them, around the truth of His identity and mission. **Hell.** The English word here translates the Greek name for the place of departed spirits, Hades, generally equivalent to the Hebrew *sheol* (see discussion on Gen. 37:35). **The gates of hell** refers to the kingdom of Satan (i.e., all forces opposed to Christ and His kingdom). It has been noted, however, that gates are not an offensive weapon; they are for defense. Believers need to take the initiative. Too often Christians lament that the forces of evil seem to be winning in the world, when they should be on the offensive, presenting truth and bringing people to Christ.

16:19. Keys. Perhaps Peter used these keys on the day of Pentecost (see Acts 2), when he announced that the door of the kingdom was unlocked to Jews and proselytes, and later when he acknowledged that it was also opened to Gentiles (see Acts 10). **Bind … loose.** Not authority to determine, but rather to announce guilt or innocence (see 18:18 and the context there; see also Acts 5:3, 9). In other words, Peter could carry on his ministry of evangelism because God had already opened doors of mercy in heaven.

16:20. That they should tell no man. Because of the false concepts of the Jews, who looked for an exclusively national and political Messiah, Jesus told His disciples not to publicize Peter's confession, lest it precipitate a revolution against Rome (see discussion on 8:4).

16:21 – 22. Began … to shew unto his disciples (v. 21). The beginning of a new emphasis in Jesus' ministry. Instead of teaching the crowds in parables, He concentrated on preparing the disciples for His coming suffering and death. The disciples' recognition of His identity certainly was the factor in opening this chapter in His ministry. **That he must … be killed.** This was Jesus' first prophecy of His death. Peter understandably sought to stop Him from making these comments. No one likes to hear that a loved one will have to suffer, and it is natural to always hope for and expect the best.

16:23. Satan is a loanword from Hebrew, meaning "adversary" or "accuser," and Jesus may have meant it only in that sense, rather than accusing Peter of being in league with the Devil. Peter's offense was that he was looking at the matter from a purely human standpoint. He was Jesus' "adversary" in that the cross was the plan of God, and Peter should not oppose what God had ordained. It may be that Peter's opposition went beyond merely private words with Jesus and that he had been laying plans with the other disciples to keep Jesus away from Jerusalem.

16:24. Take up his cross (see discussion on 10:38; *KJV Study Bible* note on Mark 8:34). Coming right on the heels of His statements regarding His coming death, these words had real significance. Jesus was pointing out to His disciples that they had to be ready to suffer if they were to follow one who was ordained to suffer.

16:25. This verse lays out a general principle. **Save his life** implies someone seeking ways to make his own life comfortable, good, and pleasant. Everyone wants a pleasant and happy life, one that is fulfilling. Unfortunately, most people seek it directly by trying to make themselves happy. The principle here is that such an effort will fail. The proof is seen by looking around at most Americans today. America has been defined as 305 million people desperately trying to make themselves happy. A better route is for one to **lose his life** for the sake of the Lord; then he **shall find it.** That is, if someone sacrifices their own goals, dreams, and happiness for the sake of following Christ, the end result will be a happier, more fulfilling life. In general, a life lived unselfishly will be happier than a life lived for oneself. Specifically, in this context, Jesus was pointing out that someone who dies for Christ and the gospel has lost nothing. He or she will find blessing in eternity. Jesus was making an extreme application of the general principle here, one that Matthew may have felt a need to record for the encouragement of his readers who may have faced just such a possibility.

16:26. Jesus reiterated the reason for the principle. What good is it to **gain the whole world**, that is, every physical pleasure, if in the end it means one will **lose his own soul**?

16:27. For **the Son of man**, see discussion on Mark 2:10. **Shall come.** Refers to the parousia, the eschatological coming of Christ. When Christ returns, those who have suffered for Him will be rewarded. Those who sought this world's pleasures will receive no reward and will know then that they traded away what was truly worthwhile for something worthless.

16:28. There are two main interpretations of this verse: (1) It is a prophecy of the transfiguration, which happened a week later (see 17:1) and which demonstrated that Jesus will return in His Father's glory (see 16:27; discussion on 2 Peter 1:16). (2) It refers to the Son of Man's authority and kingly reign in His post-resurrection church. Some of His disciples would witness and even participate in this, as described in the book of Acts. The context seems to favor the first view.

17:1–9. The transfiguration was: (1) a revelation of the glory of the Son of God, a glory now hidden but to be fully revealed when He returns; (2) a confirmation of the difficult teaching given to the disciples at Caesarea Philippi (see 16:13–20); and (3) a beneficial experience for the disciples, who were discouraged after having been reminded so recently of Jesus' impending suffering and death (see 16:21). See discussions on Mark 9:2–13; Luke 9:28–36.

17:1. After six days. Mark also has "after six days" (Mark 9:2), counting just the days between Peter's confession and the transfiguration, whereas Luke, counting all the days involved, wrote, "about an eight days after" (Luke 9:28). **Peter, James, and John.** These three disciples had an especially close relationship with Jesus (see 26:37; Mark 5:37). **High mountain.** Its identity is unknown, although the reference to Caesarea Philippi (16:13) may suggest that it was Mount Hermon, which was just northeast of Caesarea Philippi (see discussion on Luke 9:28). **Apart.** Luke added "to pray" (Luke 9:28).

17:2. Was transfigured. His appearance changed. The three disciples saw Jesus in His glorified state (see John 17:5; 2 Peter 1:17).

17:3. Moses and Elias (i.e., "Elijah"; see discussion on Luke 9:30). Moses appeared as the representative of the old covenant (the law) and the promise of salvation, which was soon to be fulfilled in the death of Jesus. Elijah appeared as the appointed restorer of all things and as the representative of the prophets (see Mal. 4:5–6; Mark 9:11–13). Luke 9:31 says that they talked about Christ's death.

17:4. Peter was not thinking but rather was speaking out of his excitement. For **three tabernacles,** see *KJV Study Bible* note on Mark 9:5; discussion on Luke 9:33.

17:5. Them. Jesus, Moses, and Elijah. **This is my beloved Son, in whom I am well pleased.** The same words spoken from heaven at Jesus' baptism (3:17). No mere man, but the very Son of God, was transfigured.

17:6. Sore afraid. Primarily with a sense of awe at the presence and majesty of God.

17:7–9. They came down from the mountain (v. 9), the disciples certainly being excited and perhaps a little shaken by the experience. Jesus forbade them to speak of the incident, however, until after the resurrection.

17:10–11. The traditional eschatology of the teachers of the law, based on Malachi 4:5–6, held that Elijah must appear before the coming of the Messiah. The disciples reasoned that if Jesus really was the Messiah, as the transfiguration proved Him to be, why had not Elijah appeared?

17:12. Elias is come already. John the Baptist was Elias in the sense that he prophesied in the spirit and manner of Elijah, against great wickedness. **Likewise.** As John the Baptist was not recognized but was killed, so Jesus would be rejected and killed.

17:13. The disciples understood what Jesus meant (see discussion on 16:12). This also echoed the teaching He had given them in chapter 16 about His coming suffering and death.

17:14–18. The child was possessed by a demon, and the disciples were unable to deal with it. The man seemed to be unaware that the child's lunacy was caused by a demon, since he sought only a **cure** (v. 16) rather than to have it "cast out." Oftentimes we do not know what we really need, but when we come to our Lord with our petitions, He answers our real need, not our specific request.

How long ...? (v. 17). Here Jesus was rebuking not the child's father but rather His disciples. It may be understood as a gentle rebuke for their lack of faith (see 17:20). Jesus cast out the demon, **and the child was cured** (v. 18). Where the disciples had struggled, Jesus accomplished the task easily.

17:19–21. The ease with which Jesus dealt with the demon impressed the disciples, and they asked Him, **Why could not we cast him out?** (v. 19). Jesus' answer pointed to their need for faith. For **mustard seed** (v. 20), see discussion on 13:31–32. **Say unto**

this mountain, Remove hence to yonder place. A proverbial statement meaning to remove great difficulties (see Isa. 54:10; 1 Cor. 13:2). Jesus ended with the statement that **this kind goeth not out but by prayer and fasting** (v. 21). Two things may be learned from this. (1) Prayer and fasting increase faith. It was the disciples' lack of faith that hindered them, and prayer and fasting would have given them success, so faith increases with prayer and fasting. (2) There are different kinds of demons. One should not make too much of this, but the inference from this Scripture is at least interesting. It should also serve as a warning to Christians who think the area of demons and exorcism is one they want to explore. It is more complex than one can imagine and requires more faith than most Christians have. It is best left alone.

V. Jesus' Last Ministry in Galilee (17:22–18:35)

A. Jesus Foretells His Death (17:22–23)

17:22–23. For the second time, Jesus tells His disciples of His coming death, the first time having been in 16:21. Jesus, however, at least alluded to it when He mentioned the Son of Man being raised from the dead in 17:9. Here He was much more explicit: **The Son of Man shall be betrayed** (v. 22), **they shall kill him** (v. 23), and on **the third day he shall be raised again**. Earlier the disciples had reacted with fear and rejection of this message, probably under the leadership of Peter. Now, perhaps because of the transfiguration and Jesus' rebuke, Peter made no move. The disciples **were exceeding sorry**. It may be that the specificity of Jesus' words account for the different reaction.

B. Temple Tax (17:24–27)

17:24. Tribute money. The annual temple tax was required of every male twenty years of age and older (see Exod. 30:13; 2 Chron. 24:9; Neh. 10:32). It was literally a double drachma, worth approximately two days' wages, and was used for the upkeep of the temple. Perhaps the leaders were again trying to find some way to accuse Jesus.

17:25. Peter, being loyal, answered **Yes** and then went to Jesus. Jesus gently pointed out that He did not owe the tax. He is the Son. He was exempt from the tax, as one of the **kings … children**.

17:26–27. Then are the children free (v. 26). Jesus would pay the tax, not because He owed it, but because it would prevent offense. Likewise, Christians should never use their standing with the Lord to offend others. They should be willing to make any sacrifice, to give up any "right," if doing so will prevent them from being a stumbling block to the gospel. Jesus might have asserted His privilege as the Son, but such an assertion would have looked egotistical and like an effort just to avoid making a minor tax payment. How much better to simply pay the tax, offend no one, and gain a hearing for the message. Jesus' manner of paying the tax, however, involved a miraculous event. Peter was to go fishing, and **the fish that first cometh up** (v. 27) would have in its mouth enough money to pay the tax for both of them.

C. Discourse on Life in the Kingdom (chap. 18)

18:1. The disciples brought a question to Jesus: **Who is the greatest in the kingdom …?** (see discussion on Luke 9:46). This was not a proper question, as the kingdom is not about self-exaltation. Their question showed a positive note as well, however. The disciples, under the influence of Jesus' teaching, were taking the kingdom of God seriously, as a reality on which they were now willing to plan. This question opens a section of teaching that extends into chapter 20. Jesus used a variety of means to teach that the kingdom is not about self-exaltation but rather about humility, service, and sacrifice. Rewards in the kingdom are not given out on the same basis as in this world, and the "path to the top" is very different from the self-centered, backbiting world that the disciples knew in their day and that still prevails in our time.

18:2–4. Jesus did not upbraid the disciples for their poor understanding but instead used the opportunity to teach them further about the nature of the kingdom. He told them that they must be **as little children** (v. 3). They must trust God, as a child trusts adult authorities, and they must be humble rather than exalted. The kingdom is not about exalting oneself but rather about humbling oneself. Jesus had taught them in the Sermon on the Mount to turn the other cheek and to go beyond whatever someone might request of them. These actions require an attitude of humility as well as trust in the sovereignty of God. One who trusts God to care for his needs can give his coat to another, and one who trusts God to bring about justice in His own time can turn the other cheek. Jesus reinforced His prior teaching with the illustration of being childlike. He called the one who **shall humble himself ... the greatest in the kingdom of heaven** (v. 4). This is hyperbole and reinforces the point that Christ's followers are to value humility as much as the world values self-exaltation.

18:5 – 6. Jesus said that to **receive [a] child in [His] name** (v. 5) is to receive Him. This is an affirmation of children's ministry but also a promise that Jesus notes and blesses kindnesses bestowed in His name. He followed this promise, however, with a warning about **offend[ing] one of these little ones which believe in me** (v. 6). "Offend" is contrasted with "receive" in this context. The idea is that one who points a child away from Jesus and toward sin will suffer grave consequences, whereas one who receives a child "in [Jesus'] name," that is, pointing the child toward Christ and His teaching, will be blessed. In His warning, Jesus again, as He often did, used a vivid image drawn from agriculture to make His point. **A millstone** is literally "a millstone of a donkey," that is, a millstone turned by a donkey. This type of millstone was far larger and heavier than the small millstones (see 24:41) that women used each morning in their homes.

18:7. This is a general statement about **offences**, bridging between what Jesus had just said about offending children (18:5 – 6) and the comments about the one who offends in verses 8 – 9.

18:8 – 9. "That man by whom the offence cometh" (18:7) is here **thy hand or thy foot** (v. 8) or **thine eye** (v. 9). If it is so bad for a whole man who brings an offense that it were better if "he were drowned" (18:6), then losing one part of the body should seem small by comparison. Jesus was not being literal but wanted to impress on His disciples the need to be serious about repentance of sin (see discussion on 5:29 – 30).

18:10. Their angels. Guardian angels are not exclusively for children but are for God's people in general (see Ps. 34:7; 91:11; Heb. 1:14). **Do always behold** means that they have constant access to God.

18:11. Here Jesus' statement appears to refer specifically to saving children, following immediately upon the context of 18:1 – 10. "Little ones" (v. 10) may have application to any child of God, however, making the application of this verse universal. His mission is to save lost people in general. It ties in to 18:14 because Jesus does the will of His Father. Put together, this whole passage means that God does not want His children to stumble or perish, and Jesus wants to save them. "Their angels" (18:10) are thus always in the presence of God in heaven, ready to do His will on their behalf. Anyone who hinders their spiritual life is therefore justly condemned.

18:12 – 14. The parable of the lost sheep is also found in Luke 15:3 – 7. There it applies to unbelievers, here to believers. Jesus used the same parable to teach different truths in different situations. On **sheep** (vv. 12 – 13), see discussion on Luke 15:4.

18:15 – 20. This is the well-known "Matthew 18 passage" on church discipline. It outlines specific steps to take when one is offended by a Christian brother. This passage deals specifically with an offense between church members. Often it is applied to a believer who is caught in sin generally. It may certainly be applied that way, as the steps outlined here are workable for that situation as well, but the context is of an offense between two people. The larger context includes the preceding passage, where Jesus condemned those who might offend the "little ones" of the kingdom.

18:15 – 17. Here **brother** (v. 15) refers not to a biological brother but to a fellow believer. When dealing with an offense between believers, the first step is to approach the brother privately. This is important in case there has been a misunderstanding. In fact, people rarely offend others deliberately. If the misunderstanding can be cleared up privately, often no one is embarrassed. **Hear thee** means simply to agree to reconcile.

The second step is to approach the brother with a small group. This allows for **witnesses** (v. 16) that the offense has taken place. It also underlines for the errant brother the seriousness with which the grieved party takes the matter. A larger group would be intimidating and would expand too greatly the circle of those who know about the offense.

The third and final step is to **tell it unto the church** (v. 17), meaning the local congregation. Here and 16:18 are the only two places where the Gospels speak of the "church." If the offending brother does not listen to the church on the matter, he is to be shunned as **a heathen**, which to the Jews meant any non-Jewish person, **and a publican**, whom they saw as something of a traitor to Israel (see discussion on 5:46). This verse establishes one basis for excommunication.

18:18. In context, the idea here is that someone who rejects the church's verdict and is shunned by the church will forfeit any blessing from God until he repents (see discussion on 16:19).

18:19–20. These verses teach that when the church is assembled, the mind of Christ is available to them. It affirms that believers together can seek the will of God confidently. Specifically, they can move on matters of church discipline with confidence, assuming that they really **are gathered together in [Jesus'] name** (v. 20). This does not sanction actions taken by divisive factions in the church or by those who seek to impose their own will on the congregation. If, however, the church is assembled with a clear sense that they are on the Lord's business and sincerely pray, seeking His will, they can be confident of His guidance.

18:21. Peter came to Jesus with this question in light of the teaching He had just given. Peter may have been wondering whether he should go through the steps Jesus had just outlined (18:15–17) if the

same brother repeated the same offense. When Peter asked about forgiving **seven times**, he was using the number of perfection. In other words, "Should I forgive him as many times as he sins against me, if he repents?"

18:22. Seventy times seven, or "seventy-seven times." In either case, the sense is "times without number" or "as many times as necessary." Jesus was agreeing with Peter but intensifying it so that there would be no question that grace and forgiveness are to be extended to the repentant brother as often as necessary.

18:23–35. This parable explains why forgiveness should be so freely extended. In **the kingdom of heaven** (v. 23; see discussion on 3:2), forgiveness has been freely received and should be just as freely given. Believers have been forgiven much. In light of how much we have offended God, any offense done to us is a small matter. Jesus was not teaching here that an unforgiving heart leads to loss of salvation. With parables, it does not pay to push the analogy too far. Jesus intended only to teach that those who have been forgiven much should, in turn, forgive much. (For the practice of selling into slavery, see Exod. 21:2; Lev. 25:39; 2 Kings 4:1; Neh. 5:5; Isa. 50:1.)

From your hearts forgive (v. 35) is the one main teaching of the parable. One who does not have a forgiving heart will not enjoy fellowship with God. The one who lets bitterness and a hard heart spring up within may be saved but will not enjoy the benefits and blessings thereof, being instead in bondage once again to the power of sin. "From your hearts forgive" is another allusion to the Sermon on the Mount, in which Jesus taught that true obedience is more than just outward actions. It comes from the heart, if one's righteousness is to "exceed the righteousness of the scribes and Pharisees" (5:20).

VI. Jesus' Ministry in Judea and Perea (chaps. 19–20)

A. Teaching concerning Divorce (19:1–12)

19:1–2. Jesus had finished these sayings (v. 1) is one of Matthew's markers of a transition (see Introduction, "Literary Features"). Jesus went to **the**

coasts of Judea beyond Jordan, which is the east side (known later as Transjordan or Perea and today simply as Jordan), and began ministering there (see discussion on Luke 13:22).

19:3. For **Pharisees**, see discussion on Mark 2:16. **For every cause**. This last part of the Pharisees' question is not in the parallel passage in Mark (Mark 10:2). Matthew included it possibly because he was writing to the Jews, who were aware of the dispute between the schools of Shammai and Hillel over the interpretation of Deuteronomy 24:1–4. Shammai held that "some uncleanness" (Deut. 24:1) meant "immorality" (see Matt. 19:9), the only allowable cause for divorce. Hillel (ca. 60 BC–AD 20) emphasized the preceding clause, "she find no favour in his eyes" (Deut. 24:1). He would allow a man to divorce his wife if she did anything he disliked, even if she burned his food while cooking it. Jesus clearly took the side of Shammai (see Matt. 19:9), but only after first pointing back to God's original ideal for marriage in Genesis 1:27; 2:24.

19:4–9. This is the famous passage in Matthew that lays out the prohibition on divorce except in cases of infidelity (v. 9). The Pharisees again sought to test Jesus, trying to find fault with His teaching so that He might be condemned as a heretic, and Jesus once again confounded their efforts. He did this by going beyond the law of Moses to the creation and showing that God's plan from the beginning did not include divorce.

19:5–6. Jesus quoted from the creation account in the book of Genesis. One inference one can draw from this is that the Genesis account of creation is to be treated seriously. It is not an allegory, nor is it a myth. Here Jesus treated it as truth, something that was to be taken seriously in His day and something on which to base one's life decisions. Would that the Old Testament were treated in that way today.

19:7–8. The Pharisees questioned Jesus about the law of Moses' permission for divorce. Jesus' answer reveals an important point about interpreting the Old Testament law. The law was adapted to a sinful world and its conditions. Divorce was permitted because people's hearts were hardened. God's original plan for marriage should guide us, not a loophole created by conditions of the fall. One may infer that other regulations were treated similarly. For example, the regulation that requires one to return someone's ox if he sees it out running loose (Exod. 23:4) was not permission to allow one's ox to run loose, knowing it would be returned. It was a concession to a less than ideal situation. In the same way, Moses' prescription for divorce was not permission to divorce for any reason whatever. It was a concession to reality. Jesus affirmed this and upheld the ideal.

19:9. Here is the specific statement on divorce. Marriage is a permanent relationship and not severable, **except it be for fornication**. The marriage relationship has been severed already in cases of infidelity, and divorce is permitted. Jesus did not say that divorce is required. In light of the ideal that Jesus had already emphasized, it is best if the marriage can be reconciled and the relationship restored.

19:10–12. See 1 Corinthians 7:7–8, 26, 32–35. The disciples came to a conclusion: **it is not good to marry** (v. 10). Not everyone can accept this teaching, **this saying** (v. 11), because it is not meant for everyone. Jesus then gave three examples of persons for whom it is meant. **Made themselves eunuchs for the kingdom of heaven's sake** (v. 12). Those who have voluntarily adopted a celibate lifestyle to give themselves more completely to God's work. Under certain circumstances, celibacy is recommended in Scripture (see 1 Cor. 7:25–38), but it is never presented as superior to marriage.

B. Teaching concerning Little Children (19:13–15)

19:13–15. Jesus is once again associated with **little children** (vv. 13–14). He reiterated the teaching given in 8:1–14, saying **For of such is** (see discussions on Mark 10:14–15) **the kingdom of heaven** (v. 14; see discussion on 3:2).

C. The Rich Young Man (19:16–30)

19:16–22. This is the story of the rich young man who came to Jesus, wanting eternal life. Jesus used the opportunity to challenge him to live out the meaning of grace. He rejected the challenge.

19:16. For **one came**, see discussion on Mark 10:17. **What good thing shall I do …?** The rich man was thinking in terms of righteousness by works. Jesus had to correct this misunderstanding before answering the question more fully. **Eternal life**. This is the first use of this expression in Matthew's gospel (see 19:29; 25:46). In John, it occurs much more frequently, often taking the place of the term "the kingdom of God [or heaven]," used in the Synoptics, which treat the following three expressions as synonymous: (1) "eternal life" (here; Mark 10:17; Luke 18:18), (2) "enter into the kingdom of heaven [or God]" (Matt. 19:23; Mark 10:24; Luke 18:24), and (3) "be saved" (Matt. 19:25; Mark 10:26; Luke 18:26).

19:17–19. If thou wilt enter into life, keep the commandments (v. 17). To "enter into life" is the same as to "have eternal life" (9:16). One should "keep the commandments," not to establish one's merit before God, but as an expression of true faith. The Bible always teaches that salvation is a gift of God's grace received through faith (see Eph. 2:8). **There is none good but one**. Jesus was not denying His own deity. He may have been challenging the man to see Him as more than just a "Good Master" (19:16). He was also teaching him a lesson about the source of goodness. This man wanted to be "good" so as to qualify for heaven. The only goodness that will count is that which comes from God. The good is not something to be done as meritorious in itself. God alone is good, and all other goodness derives from Him—even the keeping of the commandments, which Jesus proceeded to enumerate (vv. 18–20).

19:20. All these things have I kept (see discussion on Mark 10:20). On the basis of performance, this man had been exemplary.

19:21. Perfect (Greek, *teleios*; "goal," "end"). His goal was eternal life, but wealth and lack of commitment stood in his way. **Go and sell that thou hast.** Jesus was not prescribing a salvation by works. This young man had much wealth, and it is likely that he or his family had earned it. Now he wanted to earn eternal life as well. It may be that Jesus saw an opportunity here to teach him something about grace

by immersing him in it. Eternal life comes by grace, not by works. It is unmerited; it is not a reward for good performance. Jesus challenged the young man to do something that would involve grace. If he gave to the poor what they had not earned, perhaps he would see that God is gracious and gives eternal life to those who have not earned it. As long as he saw blessing and reward as something earned, not something that one receives by grace, he could not see the truth about eternal life. There is no "right" to God's blessing, no "right" to eternal life. God is gracious and gives it to us, not as a reward for doing the right things, but out of His own mercy toward us as sinners. It may be also that Jesus wanted to see the fruits of repentance in the man. He had done "good works" in the sense of keeping the commandments. Now he needed to show forth righteousness from the heart.

19:22. The young man did not accept Jesus' challenge. For **he went away sorrowful**, see discussion on Mark 10:22.

19:23. Jesus offered a commentary for His disciples on what had just taken place, as He had done previously. He was not saying that it is impossible for rich people to be saved, nor that every rich person must sell all that they have. The problem is one of self-reliance. The young man with whom Jesus had just spoken was used to relying on his own resources rather than on God. Rich people often see less need for faith on a daily basis. This is why it is hard for them to **enter into the kingdom of heaven** (see discussion on 3:2).

19:24–25. A camel to go through the eye of a needle (v. 24; see discussion on Mark 10:25). This may well be an example of humor or sarcasm. Obviously, it is hyperbole. The disciples responded as we might, not seeing the hyperbole, and asked the obvious question: **Who then can be saved?** (v. 25).

19:26. Jesus' answer leaves open the possibility that rich people can indeed be saved. It is **impossible** for anyone to save themselves, but God can save anyone (see discussion on Mark 10:27). No one is beyond the reach of God's grace; one need only repent and turn to Christ in simple faith.

19:27 – 28. Peter spoke up, as was his habit. He pointed out that the disciples had **forsaken all, and followed thee** (v. 27), just what Jesus had commanded the rich young man to do (see 19:21), and asked about their reward. For **Verily I say unto you** (v. 28), see discussion on Mark 3:28. For **the Son of man**, see discussion on Mark 2:10. **Judging.** Governing or ruling. The twelve disciples will someday rule with Christ in His literal millennial kingdom on this earth (see Acts 1:6; compare the Old Testament "judge"; see Judges, Introduction: "Title").

19:29. Jesus then gave a promise for all who follow Christ. They shall not suffer loss in the long run, but of all they give up, they **shall receive an hundredfold**. Mark added, along "with persecutions" (Mark 10:30; see discussion there). In addition, they **shall inherit everlasting life.**

19:30. Here Jesus referred back to His teaching about the kingdom in chapter 18. It is not those who are powerful in the worldly sense who will be great in the kingdom. Earthly fame and wealth are no indication of God's eternal blessing. Just as one must "become as little children" (18:3), so also it is important to remember that many who are unknown in this world will be great in the kingdom. There will be Sunday school teachers who are first because of their faithfulness through many years, while noted preachers and evangelists may find themselves at the back of the line. Jesus was not saying to turn down a significant ministry if the doors open. Accept whatever opportunities God gives you to be an influence for Christ, but recognize that greatness is not measured by earthly success. His statement is meant to encourage humility, regardless of position, not to artificially minimize one's influence for the Lord.

D. The Parable of the Laborers in the Vineyard (20:1 – 16)

20:1 – 16. This parable is unique to Matthew. It may emphasize the sovereign graciousness and generosity of God extended to "latecomers" (the poor and the outcasts of society) into God's kingdom. It is not wrong to see this also as referring to those who trust Christ late in life. Deathbed conversions can be legitimate, and those people are just as saved as the ones who trusted Christ as a small child and served Him for a lifetime. Jesus offered this parable in answer to Peter's question about rewards (see 19:27). Believers are simply to serve and leave the rewards to God. Finally, it points out that all who enter the kingdom do so by grace and are rewarded by God's grace, not on the basis of merit.

20:1 – 7. A penny (v. 2). This coin, the denarius, was the usual daily wage of a common laborer. A Roman soldier also received one denarius a day. This was not a large wage, but neither was the **householder** (v. 1) taking unfair advantage of the workers. **The third hour** (v. 3). 9:00 a.m. The householder offered the same wage to those hired at this time. **The sixth and ninth hour** (v. 5). Noon and 3:00 p.m. respectively. **The eleventh hour** (v. 6). 5:00 p.m.

20:8 – 10. When even was come (v. 8). Because farmworkers were poor, the law of Moses required that they be paid at the end of each day (see Lev. 19:13; Deut. 24:14 – 15). They were all paid a full day's wages, even those who served a short while. In this respect, the householder was generous.

20:11 – 14. Those who had agreed to the wage that morning supposed they would get more, but it was not to be so. They had agreed to a set wage and could expect no more.

20:15. Is thine eye evil …? The evil eye apparently was associated with jealousy and envy (see 1 Sam. 18:9). Sometimes this parable, especially this verse, is used to justify employers who are stingy with wages. The parable is not about that and should not be used in this way. In fact, the householder was generous, paying those who had worked little the same wage as those who had worked much. If anything, the parable might be seen as justifying generosity, but again the point has nothing to do with economics, labor relations, and wages. The parable should not be put to service in that way.

20:16. This is the summary statement. In this parable, **the last** were **first** in that they got the same reward as the others. So shall it be in the kingdom of heaven.

E. Jesus Prophesies His Coming Death Again (20:17–19)

20:17–19. Once again Jesus emphasized that when they reached **Jerusalem** (v. 18), He would be **condemn[ed] … to death**. This is the third time Matthew recorded Jesus saying this (see 16:21; 17:22–23; see also Mark 10:32–34; Luke 18:31–33 and discussions). It may be that Matthew used this as a literary device to build the dramatic tension. One may suppose that Jesus may have emphasized this prophecy on numerous occasions. Matthew recorded those that fit his needs, or perhaps the ones that stood out for him most vividly.

And shall deliver him to the Gentiles to mock, and to scourge, and to crucify him (v. 19). This is an additional statement in this third prophecy of the passion. Jesus would not be killed by the Jews, which would have been by stoning, but would be crucified by the Romans. All three instances when Jesus foretold His death included the resurrection on **the third day** (see 16:21; 17:23).

F. A Mother's Request (20:20–28)

20:20. The mother of Zebedee's children. In Mark, "James and John, the sons of Zebedee" (Mark 10:35), asked the question, yet there is no contradiction. The three joined in making the petition. She was a typical mother, wanting the best for her sons.

20:21. For **What wilt thou?** see discussion on Mark 10:35. For **sit, the one on thy right hand, and the other on the left**, see discussion on Mark 10:37. The mother certainly asked for something big, on their behalf and apparently with their approval. This demonstrates that the disciples, or at least these two, did not fully grasp Jesus' teachings in the previous two chapters. Jesus had emphasized over and over that humility is a virtue, that the last shall be first, that the least in the kingdom will be the greatest, that His disciples must become as little children—and now He was faced with this. Jesus betrayed no impatience, though His answer was certainly pointed.

20:22. Jesus pointed out that He would have to suffer (see 26:39). Could they be honored with Him if they did not go through what He would? He

called it **to drink of the cup** (see discussion on Mark 10:38), a figure of speech meaning "to undergo" or "to experience" (the same figure of speech is used for divine wrath or judgment in Jer. 25:15; Ezek. 23:32; Hab. 2:16; Rev. 14:10; 16:19; 18:6). The two disciples answered, **We are able**.

20:23. Jesus promised that they would indeed suffer but said that, even so, the place of honor **is not mine to give** (see discussion on Mark 10:40). His **Father** alone has the right to make that determination. It may be thought that Jesus had gotten them to make the commitment, "to drink of the cup that I shall drink of" (v. 22), with the implication of the reward for it, and then had withdrawn the reward. Actually, His point was that those who are not willing to suffer cannot expect rewards, but that is the minimum requirement. The Father still is the one who determines what and how much each believer will be rewarded. There is no possibility of "striking a deal" for a specific reward for a specific sacrifice. Still, there will be degrees of reward in heaven. The servant is not greater than his Master, and those who avoid the tough commitment of discipleship can expect less than those who give up all to follow the Master.

20:24. The reaction of the other disciples was normal, but the jealousy was still sin (see discussion on Mark 10:41).

20:25–27. It shall not be so among you (v. 26; see discussions on Mark 10:42–45). Jesus contrasted the way the world promotes and rewards people with the way it will be in the kingdom. Again, this is the same principle Jesus had been at some pains to teach in the preceding chapters.

20:28. Jesus pointed to Himself as an example of what He had tried to teach the disciples. He **came not to be ministered unto, but to minister**, as a servant of our need, not to exalt Himself over us. His disciples needed to take the same attitude toward one another and toward life, as servants, not "climbers." Jesus came to **give his life a ransom**. The word "ransom" was often used for the price paid to redeem a slave. Similarly, Christ paid the ransom price of His own life to free us from the slavery of sin.

The preposition **for** emphasizes the substitutionary nature of Christ's death. **Many.** Christ "gave himself a ransom for all" (1 Tim. 2:6). Salvation is offered to all, but only the "many," those who receive Christ, obtain it (see discussion on Mark 10:45).

G. Restoration of Sight at Jericho (20:29–34)

20:29. For **Jericho,** see discussion on Mark 10:46. Jesus was nearing Jerusalem, heading toward His passion.

20:30. Two blind men. The other Synoptics mention only one (see discussion on Luke 18:35). **Son of David** is a messianic title (see discussion on 9:27).

20:31–34. Jesus healed them. This incident looks like a parenthesis. It does not obviously tie in to Jesus' statement in verses 25–28. A closer look, however, reveals that Jesus was illustrating with His actions what He had just said. He "came not to be ministered unto, but to minister" (20:28). A seemingly chance meeting on the roadway provided an opportunity for Him to allow an interruption in His schedule to become a priority. The disciples saw their Lord and Master putting the needs of two strangers ahead of His itinerary toward Jerusalem, reinforcing the teaching that His kingdom is not about privilege and position but about service and humility.

VII. Passion Week (chaps. 21–27)

A. The Triumphal Entry (21:1–11)

21:1–11. This is Christ's triumphal entry into Jerusalem. It had been prophesied in Daniel (Dan. 9:25), something Matthew did not mention. The striking feature is the extent to which Jesus' fame had spread among the multitudes. Matthew indicated at numerous points that the multitudes had begun to recognize Jesus' true identity and referred to Him in messianic terms. Here it all came together as crowds thronged the roads into Jerusalem, calling Him the Son of David.

21:1. Bethphage means "house of figs." Bethphage is not mentioned in the Old Testament, and in the New Testament only in connection with the triumphal entry. In the Talmud, it is spoken of as being near Jerusalem. For **the mount of Olives,** see discussion on Mark 11:1.

21:2. An ass. The donkey was symbolic of humility, peace, and Davidic royalty (see discussions on Zech. 9:9; Luke 19:30). For **colt,** see discussions on Mark 11:2–3 and Luke 19:30.

21:3. For **Lord,** see discussion on Luke 19:31. Perhaps Jesus had made a prior arrangement. More likely, His words were prophetic. Jesus knew supernaturally that a donkey would be there.

21:4–5. Here Matthew cited a prophetic passage, Zechariah 9:9, that was fulfilled in this incident.

21:6–7. Brought the ass, and the colt (v. 7). Mark 11:2 and Luke 19:30 records that Jesus rode the colt. Typically, a mother donkey follows her offspring closely. Matthew mentions two animals, while the other gospels have only one (see discussion on Luke 19:30). This is a matter of detail, and since the other gospels do not deny that there was a colt as well, there is no contradiction.

21:8. The **great multitude spread their garments in the way.** This was an act of royal homage (see 2 Kings 9:13). The people recognized Jesus as the messianic successor to David. It may be that this incident helped to seal the Pharisees' resolve to remove Him. Their power and position was so much tied to the approval of Rome that any seeming challenger to Roman authority could not be tolerated. It is ironic that the Pharisees, wanting to preserve "pure" Judaism, felt so dependent on Rome for the right to do so.

Anytime Jesus and His Word invade the world, things will be upset. He is in the business of challenging assumptions about life, about what is important, and about one's own self-importance. Anytime following Christ seems to get in the way of one's own agenda, that believer needs to check whether he has gotten away from God's will. The teachings of Christ are meant to challenge one's assumptions. The Pharisees were not willing to have their world upset in any way. Christians should be more open than the Pharisees were. Believers should read God's Word expecting to be challenged and should be ready to change their lives to conform to what it says.

21:9. These are three separate quotations, not necessarily spoken at the same time. **Hosanna** (see

KJV Study Bible note on Jer. 31:7) means both prayer and praise. For **Son of David**, see discussion on 9:27. **Hosanna in the highest**, that is, "May those in heaven sing 'Hosanna'" (see Ps. 148:1–2; Luke 2:14).

21:10–11. Jesus' entry into the city set matters astir. Many in the city apparently did not know who He was, but the multitudes who had come to Jerusalem for Passover knew and spread the word.

B. The Cleansing of the Temple (21:12–17)

21:12–17. In the Synoptic Gospels, the cleansing of the temple occurs during the last week of Jesus' ministry; in John, it takes place during the first few months (see John 2:12–16). Two explanations are possible: (1) there were two cleansings, one at the beginning and the other at the end of Jesus' public ministry; (2) there was only one cleansing, which took place during Passion Week but which John placed at the beginning of his account for theological reasons—to show that God's judgment was operative through the Messiah from the outset of His ministry. Different details are present in the two accounts (the selling of cattle and sheep in John 2:14, the whip in John 2:15, and the statements of Jesus in Matt. 21:13; John 2:16). From Matthew's and Luke's accounts, one might assume that the cleansing of the temple took place on Sunday, following the so-called triumphal entry (21:1–11). But Mark 11:15–19 clearly indicates that it was on Monday. Matthew often compressed narratives. This does not violate biblical inerrancy and is a literary device to save space. It is much as one might say, "We were in Canada on the fifth, doing some fishing early this month." They may have been in Canada two or three days before they actually started fishing, on the seventh, but they arrived on the fifth. No one would say that the abbreviated statement is false. In the same way, no one should say that Matthew contradicts the other Synoptic Gospels.

The temple (v. 12). The buying and selling took place in the large outer court of the Gentiles, which covered several acres (see discussions on Mark 11:15 and Luke 19:45). For **the house of prayer** (v. 13), see discussion on Mark 11:17. **Bethany** (v. 17). A village on the eastern slope of the Mount of Olives, about two miles from Jerusalem and the final station on the road from Jericho to Jerusalem.

C. The Last Controversies with the Jewish Leaders (21:18–22:46)

21:18–22. This is another example of a compressed narrative (see discussion on 21:12–17). Mark 11:12–14, 20–25 places the cursing of the fig tree on Monday morning and the disciples' finding it withered on Tuesday morning. In Matthew's account, the tree withered as soon as Jesus cursed it, emphasizing the immediacy of judgment. For the theological meaning of this event, see discussions on Mark 11:12–14; 20–26.

21:18. City. Jerusalem.

21:19–20. Jesus often used "visual aids" in His teaching. Recall that earlier He had called a child into the midst of the disciples to make a point about the kingdom of heaven (see 18:1–6). Here coming upon **a fig tree** (v. 19) provided a teachable moment regarding the judgment that was to come for Israel's rejection of Christ.

21:21. For **say unto this mountain, Be thou removed**, see discussion on 17:20.

21:22. Jesus' point was about prayer. He does not want people to literally move mountains around, but He does want people to pray boldly for things that will glorify God.

21:23. The **chief priests** (see discussions on 2:4; Luke 19:47) and elders asked Jesus, **By what authority doest thou these things?** (see discussions on Mark 11:28 and Luke 20:2).

21:24–27. Jesus answered their question with a question: **from heaven, or of men?** (v. 25; see *KJV Study Bible* note on Mark 11:30; discussion on Luke 20:4). Jesus was not being evasive. He wanted them to see that His ministry, like John's, called into question the assumptions on which they had built their lives and teaching. If they were not willing to accept John's ministry as valid, they would not accept His. It was the chief priests, in fact, who were evasive here. They attempted to "not decide" on the question. Under the circumstances, Jesus was under no obligation to answer their question.

Well might one take warning from this passage. Jesus always calls people to a decision about Him. No one can say, "I don't want to decide." Not to decide is to decide. You can either choose to embrace Christ and trust Him or choose not to. **We cannot tell** (v. 27) was not an answer that put off a decision until later; it was a rejection of Christ and His authority (the matter they were challenging Him on in the first place). Once they had rejected His authority, there was no point in Him telling them where His authority came from.

21:28–32. This parable, that of the **two sons** (v. 28), points to the fact that those who do not repent can expect nothing from God. The less desirable elements of society had repented upon hearing John's preaching, but the more "respectable" elements had not. The former had thus done the will of the Father, while the latter, who "looked" more spiritual, were in reality out of God's will. Christian faith is about turning from sin, whether it is notorious sin or "respectable" sin. One cannot look to his position in the community or how others regard him and derive from that that he is in right relationship with God. The issue is whether one has repented and turned to Christ. **The publicans and the harlots** (v. 31) who had repented had more favor in God's sight than hard-working, respectable people who had not, and so it is today.

21:33–46. See discussions on Mark 12:1–12 and Luke 20:9–18.

21:33–44. This is the parable of the husbandmen. It illustrated how Israel repeatedly rejected the word of God and the prophets who preached it. Now the Son Himself is in their midst and He too is being rejected by them. **Tower** (v. 33). For guarding the vineyard, especially when the grapes ripened, and for shelter. The rabbis specified that it was to be a raised wooden platform, fifteen feet high and six feet square. The **husbandmen** (v. 33) represent the Jews, or their leaders. The **servants** (v. 34) represent the Old Testament prophets, many of whom were killed. The **son** (v. 37) represents Christ, whom the religious leaders condemned to death. **They will reverence my son**. The **householder** (v. 33) represents

God. He sent His Son to the world, and the Son also was rejected by Israel.

21:38–40. Let us seize on his inheritance (v. 38). Here is another case in which one must not push the analogy too far in interpreting the parables. Of course, the Jewish leaders could not have taken Christ's position in heaven much less over the church. In purely earthly terms, however, they believed that eliminating Jesus Christ would protect their position over the people and with Rome. Verse 40 may thus be seen as a warning to these leaders that God was still in control, and they should see things from heaven's perspective, something they were too shortsighted to do.

21:41. Other husbandmen. These are the Gentiles, to whom Paul turned when the Jews, for the most part, rejected the gospel (see Acts 13:46; 18:6). By the second century, the church was composed almost entirely of Gentiles.

21:42–43. Jesus pointed to Himself as **The stone which the builders rejected** (v. 42). This image is used elsewhere in the New Testament. Mark and Luke both recorded this saying of Jesus (see Mark 12:10; Luke 20:17). Peter used it in Acts and again in his first epistle (see Acts 4:11; 1 Peter 2:7). It must have made an impression on him when he heard it on this occasion, especially in light of the events that followed.

21:44. For **shall be broken**, see discussion on Luke 20:18.

21:45. Chief priests. Once again the leadership had been shown as in a mirror their own inner selves. Rather than repent, however, they became even more determined to destroy Jesus (see discussions on 2:4; Luke 19:47). For **Pharisees**, see discussions on 3:7; Mark 2:16; Luke 5:17. For **parables**, see discussions on 13:3; Mark 4:2; Luke 8:4.

22:1–14. The main point of this parable, that of the marriage dinner, relates to the Jews' rejection of the kingdom and the opening of God's grace to the Gentiles. Secondarily, it may refer to Jesus' teaching that the harlots and publicans would enter the kingdom before the chief priests (see 21:31–32).

22:1–2. It is not wrong to see the **king** (v. 2) as God the Father and Jesus as **his son**. In light of the overall point of the parable, it is probably reading too much into it to see **the wedding** as an allusion to the marriage of Christ to His bride, the church. That image is found in Scripture but is not intended here.

22:3–5. The refusal of the invited guests to come to the wedding symbolizes the Jews' rejection of the kingdom.

22:6. This is where the analogy between a wedding and the kingdom of God breaks down. The reaction of the invited guests, **the remnant**, would be rather harsh if this were a literal wedding. The allusion is to the Jews' rejection of Jesus and His message. The identity of the remnant is merely internal to the parable. They are the ones who had not gone off to work their fields or run their businesses (see 22:5). Jesus was not making a distinction between different members of the Jewish community, though it is tempting to see the remnant as a reference to the chief priests and Pharisees. Nothing in this parable or in history warrants that identification, however.

22:7. Burnt up their city. This was a common military practice; here it is possibly an allusion to the coming destruction of Jerusalem in AD 70. In terms of the parable, the king's reaction seems rather severe. Again, Jesus was looking beyond the parable itself, most likely to events that would take place in a few decades.

22:8–12. Had not on a wedding garment (v. 11). It has been conjectured that it may have been the custom for the host to provide the guests with wedding garments. This would have been necessary for the guests at this feast in particular, for they were brought in directly from the streets (vv. 9–10). The man's failure to avail himself of a wedding garment was therefore an insult to the host, who had provided the garments.

Jesus was not saying that some will get into the kingdom unworthily and will be later cast out. He was merely taking the opportunity to teach another truth, that those who are truly admitted to the kingdom of heaven will be there not by virtue of their own righteousness but by virtue of another. Here the garments represent righteousness. The wedding guests had on clothes that were not their usual every-

day wear; so also the redeemed will have a righteousness that is not their own. The man at the wedding without a wedding garment just serves to point out that no one gets into heaven on the basis of their own righteousness.

22:13. Gnashing of teeth (see discussion on 13:42) again goes beyond the scope of the parable. It is hardly credible that merely not being at a wedding that no one cared to attend anyway would be the occasion of much sorrow. Obviously, Jesus was looking beyond the bounds of the parable and alluding to final judgment.

Two images of hell are found in Scripture: fire and **outer darkness**. These are not contradictory. Darkness emphasizes exclusion from the presence of God, and fire emphasizes pain. Both, however, point to conscious experience of judgment rather than to annihilation. In addition, both types of imagery should be given equal weight in formulating a doctrine of hell. One should not use the outer darkness imagery here as an excuse to minimize the fact that judgment will involve real pain and suffering.

22:14. This is a proverbial summary of the parable's meaning. God invites **many** (likely "all" in view of the Semitic usage of "many") to be part of His kingdom, but only a **few are chosen** by Him, that is, those who wear the proper garment of Christ's righteousness.

22:15–17. The Pharisees were ardent nationalists, opposed to Roman rule, while **the Herodians** (v. 16), as their name indicates, supported the Roman rule of the Herods. At this point, however, the Pharisees enlisted the help of the Herodians to trap Jesus in His words. After trying to put Him off guard with flattery, they sprang their question: **Is it lawful to give tribute unto Caesar, or not?** (v. 17). If He said no, the Herodians would report Him to the Roman governor, and He would be executed for treason. If He said yes, the Pharisees would denounce Him to the people as disloyal to His nation.

22:18–19. Jesus perceived their wickedness (v. 18). Their attempted trap did not fool Him at all. Jesus called them what they were, **hypocrites**. They had said that He taught "the way of God in truth"

(22:16), which indeed He did. They did not believe it, however. They were hypocrites for pretending to. Their question was an intended trap, but Jesus turned it into a teachable moment. **Penny** (v. 19). The denarius, the common Roman coin of that day (see discussion on 20:2). On one side was a portrait of Emperor Tiberius, and on the other was the Latin inscription, "Tiberius Caesar Augustus, son of the divine Augustus." The coin was issued by Tiberius and was used for paying tax to him.

22:20–22. Jesus answered the Pharisees' question with a question: **Whose is this image and superscription?** (v. 20). The question forced them to admit that, whatever their opinion of Roman rule, the nation was under Caesar's jurisdiction. The fact could not be denied. Then Jesus gave a wise answer: **Render therefore unto Caesar the things which are Caesar's; and unto God the things that are God's** (v. 21). Jesus accomplished more than one thing with this statement. First, He threw the ball back into their court. It is a principle of Old Testament law that it is proper to render to everyone what they are due. The law knew nothing of cheating anyone out of what was rightfully theirs. Jesus underscored this principle. In the existing situation, they were under Roman governance and should render to the authorities what was properly due them, while being obedient to God. Doing so was in no way a contradiction of the law but rather a requirement. The matter was altogether separate from the matter of whether Rome *should* rule over Palestine. Second, Jesus underscored the proper role of civil government. There is a realm in which government, apart from religious authorities, plays a proper role. Israel had known nothing of this in its history until Rome conquered them. Even the Babylonians had not separated religious and civil authority. Jesus here opened a door to a new way for God's people to conceive of their relationship to government. Third, Jesus distinguished clearly between Caesar and God, implicitly protesting against the false and idolatrous claims made on the coins (see discussions on 22:19; Mark 12:17). Only God should receive worship, not the emperor; but the emperor should receive what is actually due him. Finally, Jesus handed his question-

ers the dilemma of determining exactly what they should "render … unto Caesar." He did not say exactly how much or what was proper. He thus pointed them back to the law and to their own consciences for the real answer to their question. In all, it was a brilliant answer, which seemed to commit Jesus to nothing either way but which actually placed Him squarely in line with the law and with His own teaching in the Sermon on the Mount that true righteousness comes from one's heart, not just from following a set of rules and precepts. In light of all of this, it is little wonder that **they marvelled, and left him** (v. 22).

22:23. The Sadducees, which say that there is no resurrection. The Sadducees were a group committed only to the Pentateuch as the Word of God. They also rejected the supernatural as an active force in the world. Like skeptics today, they loved to come up with "Bible difficulties" to taunt believers. Here they believed that they had found one that Jesus could not answer, but they were shortly proven wrong. The context of their question about the practice of levirate marriage was purely hypothetical and was intended to undermine the doctrine of the resurrection.

22:24–28. Moses said. The Pentateuch had special authority for the Sadducees (see discussion on Mark 12:18). The reference (Deut. 25:5–6) is to the levirate law (from Latin *levir*, "brother-in-law"), which was given to protect the widow and guarantee continuance of the family line.

22:29–30. Biblical questions can often be resolved when one looks at a Scripture in context. The levirate law was given not to create confusion in heaven but to guarantee that widows' needs would be met on earth. Jesus pointed out that **the resurrection** (v. 30) will offer a different context for life than what is experienced on earth. Laws that apply now may not in that age. Their question was irrelevant.

22:31–32. Jesus turned to the Sadducees' real problem. They had asked a question about the resurrection when they did not believe in the resurrection. Jesus wanted to get to the root of their unbelief and deal with that, not with the details that flowed from it. When a skeptic raises a question, often something more basic is behind it. The important thing is to get to the foundational matter with which the skeptic has a problem.

These verses demonstrate the importance of good, careful exegesis. Jesus quoted, **I am the God of Abraham … Issac, and … Jacob** (v. 32; Exod. 3:6). His comment on this quote pointed to the present tense of the verb: **God is not God of the dead, but of the living.** It is important that one examine each word of Scripture carefully, including verb tenses. One must not build doctrine on "pretty close" to what Scripture says but must rather follow the Lord's example and build on *exactly* what the Scripture says. This has implications for inspiration as well. God did not simply inspire the general ideas He wanted to communicate and leave the words up to the authors. Every word and every tense and case is inspired and must be taken seriously as one ponders the meaning of Scripture.

22:33. Now **the multitude**, rather than the leadership (see 22:22), **were astonished at his doctrine.** Matthew continued to subtly emphasize the idea presented at the beginning of this chapter, that the "less respectable" elements of society were more open to His teaching than the religious establishment.

22:34. Here **the Pharisees** (see discussions on 3:7, Mark 2:16; Luke 5:17) made one more attempt to trap Jesus.

22:35–36. The Pharisees' question was, as far as it goes, a fair one, but it had a trap. If Jesus chose any one commandment, He could be accused of diminishing the others.

22:37–39. Jesus' answer is brilliant. In one statement, He managed to quote the Old Testament while showing that the two commandments He cited cover "all the law and the prophets" (22:40). The key word in both commandments is **love** (vv. 37, 39). The Greek verb is not *phileō*, which expresses friendly affection, but *agapaō*, the commitment of devotion that is directed by the will. **With all thy heart … soul, and … mind** (v. 37) means with one's whole being. The Hebrew of Deuteronomy 6:5 has "heart … soul, and … might," but some manuscripts of the Septuagint (the Greek translation of the Old Testament) add "mind." Jesus combined all four terms in Mark 12:30. Jesus was again pointing to the inner attitude.

True obedience comes from one's heart, soul, and mind. It is not strictly an outward show.

22:40. All the law and the prophets. The entire Old Testament (see discussion on 5:17). Note that Jesus mentioned both the Law and the Prophets here. He was speaking to Pharisees, who accepted all of the Old Testament as inspired.

22:41–46. See discussions on Mark 12:35–37; Luke 20:44–47. Here Jesus became the questioner. His goal was not to "tempt" the Pharisees, as they had tried to do to Him (see 22:35). He wanted not want to trap them but to teach them. He did so by presenting them with a conundrum.

22:41–42. Jesus began by asking an easy question about the Messiah: **whose son is he?** (v. 42). This was easy enough for the Pharisees to answer: **The Son of David.**

22:43–45. Then Jesus quoted from the Psalms, where David called Christ **Lord** (v. 44; Ps. 110:1). Jesus' question pointed out that the Messiah is both a descendant of David and yet recognized as divine. By implication, the Pharisees were in the wrong for not recognizing that Jesus is both the son of David and the Son of God. He should thus be recognized as Messiah but revered as Lord. His authority should not be questioned, as the priests, the Pharisees, and the Sadducees did throughout this chapter and the previous one.

22:46. The Pharisees missed the point completely, but they recognized that they had met their match in matters of understanding Scripture, and **neither durst any man from that day forth ask him any more questions.** People who will not recognize Jesus as Lord and yet cannot disprove His claim, often just give up all together and walk away from Him. No man can be Jesus' master, in that no man can argue against His authority on spiritual matters. In the end, one must trust Him as Lord or walk away. There is no middle ground.

D. The Denunciation of the Scribes and Pharisees (23:1–36)

23:1–2. Jesus spoke to **the multitude** (v. 1), most likely those who had just marveled at His response to the Pharisees (see 22:33), and to **his disciples**, who had heard it as well, since the substance of His teaching was a warning to them not to do as **the scribes and the Pharisees** (v. 2) did. **Sit in Moses' seat**. They were the authorized successors of Moses as teachers of the law.

23:3. Jesus warned His listeners to do as the scribes and the Pharisees said, for they were in authority. To the extent that they taught the law of Moses rightly, they were to be followed. Jesus never said that it was good to break the law, though ever since the Sermon on the Mount, He had been trying to get the people to see that the law must be rightly understood and followed from the heart, not just as an outward show.

23:4 – 5. Jesus' major contention with the scribes and the Pharisees was that they were hypocrites, teaching what they themselves did not obey. Jesus did not want His followers doing the same thing. Jesus said also that the Pharisees **make broad their phylacteries** (v. 5). These small boxes, worn on forehead and arm, contained four Old Testament passages (Exod. 13:1 – 10; 13:11 – 16; Deut. 6:4 – 9; 11:13 – 21). Jesus would have had them live up to these passages rather than just wear them. They also **enlarge the borders of their garments**. Both of these actions had to do with making themselves look religious and moral before men, while their hearts were far from God.

23:6 – 7. The chief seats in the synagogues (v. 6; see discussion on Mark 12:39). Whereas 22:4 – 5 dealt with actions the scribes and Pharisees performed to make themselves look religious and moral, these verses point to the consequences they sought from those actions, that is, public honor.

23:8 – 9. Jesus here applies this to His hearers. What He had just described the scribes and Pharisees were doing was exactly what the people should not do. They should not seek to be honored as holy and wise. They should be content to actually be holy and wise. The warning is against seeking titles of honor to foster pride. Obviously, one should avoid unreasonable literalism in applying such commands. A title should be regarded as just that. One can be

proud of refusing to use a title just as much as one can be proud of having one. The heart attitude again is what is important here.

23:10 – 12. Jesus returned to a theme He had touched on before. The disciples were not to exalt themselves. They had one **Master** (v. 10) and were under His authority. It is important to note something that the disciples did not see at the time but that became clear to them later. Jesus, as God, humbled Himself when He became a man (see Phil. 2:5 – 11). He took a lower spot than the one to which He was entitled, so that our great need might be met. If we call Him Lord, can we exalt ourselves higher than He who went to the cross, who suffered and died, who gave His own life for us? Are we greater than He? Why then should we jockey for position when we are under one who humbled Himself so thoroughly?

23:13 – 39. This is a long sermon. It actually ends at verse 33, but verses 34 – 39 form something of an epilogue. The sermon is structured around the sevenfold repetition of the phrase **woe unto you, scribes and Pharisees, hypocrites!** (vv. 13, 14, 15, 23, 25, 27, 29). Each time, Jesus followed this phrase with an indictment of sins they had committed, usually related to hypocrisy.

23:13. This is the first **woe**. Here Jesus pronounced a general statement of what was wrong with the scribes and Pharisees spiritually. They were not right with God; that is, they did not **go in**, nor did they **suffer … them that are entering to go in** to the kingdom of heaven. Examples of these errors are given in 23:14 – 15. They were spiritually wrong, and they led others astray.

23:14. This is the second **Woe**. Here their spiritual condition is laid out. They were greedy, taking **widow's houses** (i.e., their livelihood) in offerings, and they were hypocrites, **for a pretence mak[ing] long prayer**. God is not impressed with prayers that are not sincere. In the Sermon on the Mount, Jesus had warned His disciples that they should not pray long prayers, expecting to be heard for their many words, and He had warned them not to make prayer a public show (see 6:5 – 8). The condemnation here is in line with that teaching. Jesus promised these hypocrites a **greater damnation** (than the unrighteous, apparently, who were not so public in trying to appear righteous).

23:15. This is the third **Woe**. It is the second part of the spiritual problem Jesus raised in 23:13. The scribes and Pharisees led others astray. Jesus did not criticize them for their evangelistic zeal; He objected to its results. The converts wound up "out-Phariseeing" the Pharisees, and that meant the converts became even **more the child[ren] of hell** (i.e., bound for hell) than their teachers were (for "hell," see discussions on 5:22; Luke 12:5).

23:16–22. Here the word **Woe** (v. 16) does not follow the sermon's formula but is merely for emphasis, as this is a longer section. In this passage, Jesus gave a lengthy example of how the scribes and Pharisees were leading their converts astray. They made **the gold of the temple** more valuable than **the temple** (v. 17) itself, and **the gift** (v. 19) of more value than **the altar that sanctifieth the gift**. In both cases, Jesus was upset that they had perverted the truth. A sacrifice is just an animal until it is put on the altar, that is, given to God. That makes the animal something more. The altar sets apart (**sanctifieth**) what is placed on it and thus is more valuable. Similarly, gold is valuable, but the temple that it gilds is more valuable. The reason gold was used on the temple at all was a measure of the temple's value and the value of the One who dwelt there. The point is that God is of more value than any earthly thing, and thus what is given to God gains value. This may be applied, in a distant way, to believers today in that they should not focus on incidentals in church life. The color of the carpet or the brand of microphone is not as important as the God who is worshiped by means of them.

23:23. This is the fourth **Woe**. Jesus did not criticize the observance of the minutiae of the law (He said, **these ought ye to have done**), but He did criticize the hypocrisy often involved (see discussion on 5:18–20). It is wrong to do little things and leave big things undone. Jesus wanted the Pharisees to know that they should not think they were spiritual because they did little outward things, because true spiritual life must come from within. Jesus contrasted outward activity with **judgment, mercy, and faith**. The scribes and Pharisees had an outward righteousness, but for the kingdom, it is necessary that "your righteousness shall exceed the righteousness of the scribes and Pharisees" (5:20), as Jesus had said in the Sermon on the Mount.

23:24. Strain at a gnat. A strict Pharisee would carefully strain his drinking water through a cloth to be sure he did not swallow a gnat, the smallest of unclean animals. Figuratively, however, he would swallow a camel—one of the largest animals. This exaggeration is not meant to be taken literally. The Pharisees had done what was not important and left off what was important.

23:25. This is the fifth **Woe**. Once again Jesus issued a general statement of what the scribes and Pharisees did, focusing on their pretense to religiosity.

23:26. Here Jesus turned to application, once again pointing out that the scribes and Pharisees needed to focus on their inner life and motivation rather than on outward appearance. It amounts to a call for them to practice a righteousness that "exceed[s] the righteousness of the scribes and Pharisees" (5:20).

23:27. This is the sixth **Woe**. Here Jesus used a different analogy. Instead of likening the scribes and Pharisees to unclean cups (see 23:25–26), He likened them to tombs or **whited sepulchres**. A person who stepped on a grave became ceremonially unclean (see Num. 19:16), so graves were whitewashed to make them easily visible, especially at night. They appeared clean and beautiful on the outside, but they were dirty and rotten on the inside. Jesus may have wanted to emphasize their spiritual deadness.

23:28. Here Jesus made the meaning of 23:27 clear.

23:29. This is the seventh and last **Woe**. The scribes and Pharisees were guilty of honoring spiritual leaders of the past and yet not following their teachings. This relates to the theme of doing little things while ignoring the weightier matters.

23:30–32. Their claim that they would have honored the prophets who were stoned in their fathers' day confirmed the hypocrisy of the scribes and Pharisees. They were guilty of the same sins as their fathers, who had stoned the prophets. Their own sins confirmed that they were children of these men. Jesus may have even been looking toward the cross at this point. These men were the ones who would turn Him over for condemnation.

23:33. This verse ends the sermon proper. Jesus pronounced judgment on the scribes and Pharisees: **how can ye escape the damnation of hell?** (see discussions on 5:22; Luke 12:5). Calling them **serpents** and **vipers** is a colorful way of saying that they were evil, as the serpent in the garden had been, and dangerous, as vipers injecting spiritual poison into those whom they taught. It was better to shun them than to admire them.

23:34–38. This passage forms something of an epilogue to the sermon. Here Jesus apparently was addressing the city of Jerusalem and its people. The reference to their killing the ones He had sent to them, however, harks back to the accusations against the scribes and Pharisees and their fathers. It is important to remember that the previous woes were spoken to the multitude and to His disciples (23:1), not directly to a group of scribes and Pharisees. It was altogether appropriate for Jesus to end His sermon with a personal word for His listeners, having just given them quite a negative bombast about their teachers. They had been led astray by the false teachings of the Jewish leaders and were the object of Jesus' concern here for that reason.

23:35. Abel unto … Zacharias (i.e., Zechariah). The murder of Abel is recorded in Genesis 4:8 and that of Zechariah, son (probably grandson) of Jehoiada, in 2 Chronicles 24:20–22. Chronicles is placed at the end of the Old Testament in the Hebrew arrangement of the books. The expression is similar to the Christian saying "from Genesis to Revelation." Jesus was summing up the history of martyrdom in the Old Testament.

23:36. This may be a reference to the coming siege and destruction of Jerusalem in AD 70. Jesus prophesied here that the city would suffer what prophets had suffered in the past.

E. Prophecy concerning Jerusalem (23:37–39)

23:37–39. See discussions on Luke 13:34–35. Jesus expressed tender emotions for the people and expressed His sorrow over their rejection of Him. He knew that His time was drawing near and that He would soon face death and resurrection, and the city would face a harsh judgment not many decades hence. This passage is a window into the tender heart of God, who loves His people even in the face of rejection.

F. Olivet Discourse (chaps. 24–25)

24:1–25:46. These two chapters present the Olivet Discourse, which is the sixth and last of the great discourses in Matthew's gospel (see Introduction, "Literary Features"; discussions on 5:1–7:29; Mark 13:1–37). Jesus in these chapters discussed with his disciples signs of the end of this age (chap. 24), gave them parables of the kingdom (25:1–30), and told them about the judgment that will take place when He returns (25:31–46).

24:1–51. Chapters 24 and 25 are the Olivet Discourse. This relates the second coming of Christ and the Great Tribulation which precedes it. 24:4–14, however, relate to the church age. It tells of how even in "apocalyptic times," times of war and famine and earthquakes (vv. 6–8), the end is not yet. Jesus warns his disciples not to be deceived by these "signs," for no one knows the day or the hour (24:42) of His coming. Even the events surrounding the destruction of the temple (24:15–16), about which the disciples asked in 24:3, are not yet a sign of the end, which will not happen until the gospel is preached in all the world (24:14). Then follows a series of signs and events directly related to the coming of Christ (24:15–41) and a call to be ready (24:42–51). Chapter 25 continues the appeal to be ready for His coming (25:1–30) and also contains a statement about the judgment of the nations (25:31–46).

24:1. Jesus went out, and departed from the temple. Jesus' denunciation of the Scribes and Pharisees apparently had taken place within the temple complex. His disciples now wanted to **shew him the buildings of the temple.** This temple, built by Herod the Great, was a much more elaborate structure than the one built by Solomon. The disciples were rather in awe of it. They would soon discover, however, that Jesus was far less impressed with the works of men than they were and that He knew these buildings would not last for long.

24:2. There shall not be left here one stone upon another (see discussion on Mark 13:1). Fulfilled literally in AD 70, when the Romans under Titus completely destroyed Jerusalem and the temple buildings. Stones were even pried apart to collect the gold leaf that melted from the roof when the temple was set on fire. **Thrown down**. Excavations in 1968 uncovered large numbers of these stones, toppled from the walls by the invaders. Jesus was piquing their interest with this statement. He knew that they would be provoked into asking questions about it and was ready to answer.

24:3. The mount of Olives. A ridge a little more than a mile long, beyond the Kidron Valley east of Jerusalem and rising about two hundred feet above the city (see discussion on Mark 11:1). Here the disciples **came unto him privately** to ask about His statement that the temple would be destroyed (see 24:2). Well did they know that such matters were best not discussed within the city, nor in the presence of others generally. They asked Jesus three questions: **when shall these things be? and what shall be the sign of thy coming, and of the end of the world?** Jesus dealt with these three questions but did not distinguish them sharply. It appears, however, that the description of the end of the age is discussed in 24:4–14, the destruction of Jerusalem in 24:15–22 (see Luke 21:20), and Christ's second coming in 24:23–31.

24:4–5. Jesus warned His disciples, **Take heed that no man deceive you** (v. 4). Jesus knew that much confusion would reign on matters related to the end times. His first concern was the coming of false messiahs. He meant people claiming to be the Messiah, not even necessarily people claiming to be Jesus Himself. Such messianic claims may be understood as claiming to be the Savior sent from God. For **Christ** (v. 5), see discussion on 16:16.

24:6–8. Wars (v. 6), **famines … and earthquakes** (v. 7) are apocalyptic events, especially when they come together. Jesus said that when these things

occur, **the end is not yet** (v. 6). They are merely signs that the end is coming.

Jesus repeated the point, calling these events **the beginning of sorrows** (v. 8). The rabbis, as well as the prophets, spoke of "birth pangs," that is, sufferings, that would precede the coming of the Messiah and lead into "the time of Jacob's trouble" (Jer. 30:7).

24:9. Jesus prophesied that His followers will suffer persecution and that it will increase as the end draws near. The persecution of Christians around the world has increased dramatically in the last century. This will apparently continue as the time of the end draws near.

24:10. Here Jesus was not focusing on the disciples' relationships with one another or with the world. Instead, He was speaking of a general societal breakdown as family, business, and social relationships come apart. There has been a dramatic increase in this in the West over the past generation.

24:11. False religions and heresies will increase in the last days.

24:12. Iniquity and a lack of love are linked here, as they are in life. People who are given over to sin cannot love sacrificially and purely. When the focus is on satisfying the lower urges, one cannot express the higher emotions. People who love their own bellies cannot love their neighbors.

24:13. Jesus ended the depressing picture of the end times with a word of encouragement: **He that shall endure unto the end … shall be saved**. He was not saying that one must survive the end times or be lost. He meant that anyone who is saved can endure whatever troubles the world goes through at that time. All of Jesus' words in 24:4–13 describe events that will characterize the world prior to the rapture of the church.

24:14. This is a promise. It looks forward to the Great Commission (28:19–20) and to its fulfillment before the end of the age. The **gospel of the kingdom** is the gospel of the death, burial, and resurrection of Christ (see Mark 16:15; Acts 20:24; 1 Cor. 1:17; 15:1–4; Eph. 1:13; Col. 1:5).

24:15. Here Jesus began to answer the disciples' question regarding the destruction of the temple.

His answer has apocalyptic implications as well. **The abomination of desolation** is the detestable thing causing the desolation of the Holy Place. The primary reference in Daniel (9:27; 11:31; 12:11) was to 168 BC, when Antiochus Epiphanes erected a pagan altar to Zeus on the sacred altar in the temple of Jerusalem. There are two more stages in the progressive fulfillment of the prophecies in Daniel and Matthew: (1) the Roman destruction of the temple in AD 70 and (2) the setting up of an image of the Antichrist in Jerusalem (see 2 Thess. 2:4; Rev. 13:14–15; see also discussions on Dan. 9:25–27; 11:31). This is not, then, a single event but a series of similar events. Jesus thus answered their specific question about the destruction of the temple while discussing their other questions regarding His second coming and the end of the world.

24:16. The mountains. The Transjordan mountains, where Pella was located. Christians in Jerusalem fled to that area during the Roman siege shortly before AD 70. A similar fleeing will occur during the future great tribulation period (identified with Daniel's Seventieth Week, see Dan. 9:27; discussion on Rev. 12:6, 14).

24:17–18. Take his clothes (v. 18). This is not to be understood as saying that it will be all right to return for other things. The point is that events will happen quickly, and it will be time to flee, leaving behind everything.

24:19. Jesus again emphasized that life will be difficult when these events occur and that being able to move quickly will be important (see discussion on Mark 13:17).

24:20. For **in the winter**, see discussion on Mark 13:18. **Neither on the sabbath.** Matthew alone included this, because he was writing to Jews, who were forbidden to travel more than about half a mile on the Sabbath. Verses 15–19 of this chapter paint a picture of a time of trouble and hardship in which people will need to have their wits about them and be very mobile to survive. Indeed, when Jerusalem was besieged in AD 70, it was a very difficult time for those who had not already left the city. So will it be in the time of the end.

24:21–22. Great tribulation (v. 21). Josephus, the Jewish historian who was there, described the destruction of Jerusalem in almost identical language. The phrase **no nor ever shall be**, however, places this reference in the distant future. The Holocaust during World War II was far more devastating for the Jewish people than the event of AD 70, yet ultimately their greatest suffering will come during the great tribulation of the future (see Dan. 12:1). This statement thus marks the transition to Jesus' second coming, which He took up in 24:23. Verse 22 anticipates that subject, speaking of the level of disaster the people will experience. **Except those days should be shortened** (v. 22) speaks directly of the days of the destruction of Jerusalem, and **no flesh** means none of the Jewish people living there. The statement looks forward to the future great tribulation, however, when it will be fulfilled ultimately. Some hold that this means that the tribulation will be of such intensity that if allowed to continue, everyone would be destroyed. These days will be shortened **for the elect's sake**, that is, for the people of God, including some Jews and Gentiles. "The elect" are not the same as the "flesh" mentioned. Jesus' point was that it is better for the people of God if the entire human race is not wiped out.

24:23–31. Jesus here focuses on the specific question about His second coming posed by the disciples in verse 3. He has treated it in verses 4–22, along with other issues. From here to the end of chapter 25, only the second coming is in view.

24:23–26. Jesus warned His disciples, and by extension, those who have come after, not to believe anyone who says that He, or another messiah, is in a certain place. Even if someone is able to do miracles, it does not establish their claim. This implies that there will always be miracle workers, especially at the end of the age. God's people should not be led astray by such events. Jesus performed miracles but emphasized His teaching ministry. Believers are to be set apart by the truth (see John 17:17), believing it and looking for His coming, rather than following any miracle worker who comes along.

24:27. As the lightning cometh out of the east, and shineth even unto the west; so shall also the

coming of the Son of man be. Jesus was not saying that His coming will be accompanied by flashes of light, though it may well be. His point was that just as lightning is obvious and easily observed, so also will His coming be obvious and easily observed. This refers to His triumphal return to earth at the end of the great tribulation. People will have no need to say, "Look, He is here" or "He is over there." His coming will be so obvious that it will be hard to ignore — like a flash of lightning.

24:28. There will the eagles be gathered together. The coming of Christ will be as obvious as the gathering of vultures around a carcass (see discussion on Luke 17:37, where the saying is used in a slightly different sense).

24:29. See discussion on Mark 13:25. This is a reference to the end of **the tribulation**, when Christ will appear (see Rev. 19:11). Disturbances in the heavens are often used in apocalyptic literature to describe the magnitude and significance of this event, which will bring an end to history.

24:30. For **Son of man**, see discussion on Mark 2:10. This verse describes the Christ's second coming. **Then shall all the tribes of the earth mourn**. The second coming is usually associated with fear or with rejoicing. Many will mourn, for they will see that they have wasted their lives in sin and debauchery and now face judgment. There will be more mourning than rejoicing on that day for those who have rejected Christ as their Messiah and King.

24:31. This description ends with the gathering of God's people to Himself, which will begin the millennial reign of Christ on earth (see Rev. 20:1–6).

24:32–33. Here Jesus called His disciples to apply the message. As they could tell the times and seasons by what was happening in nature, so also they should be able to discern the time of His return. The natural disasters and persecutions that will increase just before the tribulation should not be a cause of concern for believers. They should read the signs and know that God is in control of events and will win in the end.

24:34. For **Verily I say unto you**, see discussion on Mark 3:28. For **This generation**, see discussions on Mark 13:30; Luke 21:32.

24:35. Jesus' **words** will last until all these things have happened, and even then, they will still be true. The events preceding and during the tribulation will not eradicate His Word. Even in those dark days, people will come to faith, having heard the Word of Christ preached.

24:36. Knoweth no man (see discussion on Mark 13:32). Having told His disciples to watch for the signs of His return, Jesus saw the need to warn them about date setting. They could see the signs, but guessing the date was foolish. He was saying, to put it simply, "Do not waste your time guessing the time, because I could come at any time!"

24:37–39. These verses are often misunderstood. Jesus was not saying here that the wickedness of the world will be as bad as in Noah's day, though other Scriptures teach that it certainly will be that bad or worse (see 1 Tim. 3:1–5). His point was that the coming of the Lord will be sudden and unexpected. In Noah's day, people were **eating and drinking** (v. 38); that is, they were going about their daily lives, and **marrying and giving in marriage**, that is, planning for the future. Then **the flood came, and took them all away** (v. 39). They were in the midst of life's business, and then the end came. Likewise, no believer can say, "I know Jesus is not coming soon, for I am getting married next year. He would not lead us to get married and plan a life together if He were coming back." Jesus was saying that this is precisely what will happen. His return will cut across all the business of life as it is happening and will stop everything.

24:40–42. Jesus gave two examples of people going about their business, working side by side; **the one shall be taken, and the other left** (vv. 40–41). Scripture knows nothing of the idea of people gathering at some place to await the Lord's coming. He will come in the midst of life's activities, and He will come suddenly and dramatically.

24:43–44. Jesus used an illustration to reiterate His point. This may be the source of Paul's saying that the Lord will come "as a thief in the night" (1 Thess 5:2). Although Paul was not present on this occasion, he surely heard the teaching. Peter used the same phrase (2 Peter 3:10), undoubtedly thinking back to this incident, and had likely shared the allusion with Paul.

24:45 – 51. Jesus used a parable to warn His disciples to be alert and faithful. The ending of this parable is perhaps to be understood as a warning to the scribes and Pharisees and to all false teachers. Jesus was not saying here that His people will be lost forever if they are not looking for the Lord's return at the exact moment when it happens. **There shall be weeping and gnashing of teeth** (v. 51; see discussion on 13:42). That these people are not among the saved is made clear in 25:1 – 13.

25:1 – 30. Here Jesus told His disciples two parables, that of the ten virgins (25:1 – 13) and the talents (25:14 – 30), to further instruct them about the kingdom of God.

25:1 – 13. This is the parable of the ten virgins. The point of the parable is that some people will be ready when Christ returns, and others will not. Some will be admitted to the kingdom, and others will not. The Bible knows nothing of universalism, the belief that all people will ultimately be saved. Throughout Scripture, there is a sharp division between those who belong to God and those who do not.

25:1. Jesus said that at that time, the rapture, **the kingdom of heaven [will] be likened unto ten virgins**. These virgins were bridesmaids, responsible for preparing the bride to meet the bridegroom. Notice, there was only one bride. The ten virgins were the attendants at the wedding; they were not the bride. Many commentators therefore view them as survivors of the tribulation, of whom some were saved and some were not. The **lamps** refers to torches that consisted of long poles with oil-drenched rags at the top. (Small clay lamps would have been of little use in an outdoor procession.)

25:2. The division is between **wise** and **foolish** virgins. Jesus would not say that wisdom gets people into heaven; that happens by faith. For His purposes in the parable, however, wisdom and foolishness separates them, and His point is about separation, not about wisdom and foolishness.

25:3. Took no oil. Olive oil would have been used. In that day, other kinds of lamp oil were un-

available or very expensive. The oil seems to represent the Holy Spirit.

25:4 – 5. The **wise** (v. 4) virgins brought additional oil for their lamps. All slept, awaiting **the bridegroom** (v. 5).

25:6. At midnight came **a cry** announcing the arrival of **the bridegroom**. Here is the parallel to the second coming of Christ, or more specifically, the rapture. Jesus' point was that it will happen suddenly. No one should delay trusting Christ, for He might come at any time. Only a foolish person would "plan" a deathbed conversion, hoping to enjoy the pleasures of sin and then repent at the end of life. The Lord may return before that time, and all should be ready.

25:7. Trimmed their lamps. The charred ends of the rags were cut off, and oil was added.

25:8. The **foolish** virgins requested oil from the others. They wanted to join the wedding party on the basis of what others had, not on the basis of what they themselves had. Likewise, some people think they can be numbered among the people of God without faith in their own hearts. Many people depend on their parents' faith, or their cultural heritage, or perhaps their membership in an exciting dynamic church. The Lord will not accept any of this. One cannot be saved on the faith of others. It will not help him in that day. One's faith must be his own. Even if this parable is interpreted in ways that see the oil as representative of the Holy Spirit, a common understanding in the Old Testament, the point remains that only those who, by faith, have become Christians (and thus received the Spirit) are saved, not those who are merely associated with people who have faith.

25:9. There be not enough. Torches required large amounts of oil to keep burning, and the oil had to be replenished about every fifteen minutes. Jesus was not teaching selfishness here, only that one must have one's own faith to be saved. As with previous parables, it is best not to push the parable beyond what Jesus intended.

25:10 – 12. It is not likely that the bridesmaids would have been shut out at a real wedding, but this illustrated Jesus' point that some will not be admitted into heaven.

25:13. Watch. This is the application of the parable. Christians are to be alert for His coming. Ones does not know **the day nor the hour** of His return. Christ's coming is always imminent; therefore, one must be ready.

25:14–30. This is the parable of the talents. Having just related a parable showing that one must be saved to enter the kingdom, Jesus directed this parable toward those who are saved. The point of the parable is that there will be degrees of reward in the kingdom.

25:14. The **man travelling into a far country** is Jesus Christ Himself. He was soon to leave His disciples but will return one day. He does not leave believers empty-handed but equips them for ministry. This is represented by the man giving **his own servants … his goods**.

25:15. The term **talents** was first used for a unit of weight (about seventy-five pounds), then for a unit of coinage (see discussion on Luke 19:13). The present-day use of "talent" to indicate an ability or gift is derived from this parable, since the servants received five, two, or just one talent, **to every man according to his several ability**. This is a reminder that not every Christian is gifted in the same way or to the same degree. Some have more, and others less. Believers are not to try to outdo one another in ministry. Jesus had earlier forbidden any competition, calling believers to serve one another rather than seek position. Each believer, however, is called to use whatever he or she is given to the Lord's glory (represented in this parable by the profits derived from the talents).

25:16–18. Each servant did something different with what he was given. The first two servants were able to double what they were given, while the third simply **hid** (v. 18) his talent and did nothing with it.

25:19–23. After a long time the lord of those servants cometh (v. 19). This is one of the few biblical references to the fact that a long time will elapse before Christ returns. The first two servants received a reward for what they had produced. The reward

appears to involve greater responsibility (25:21, 23), but one should not push the analogy too far. There may be work in heaven, though the Bible indicates that it will be a place of worship and celebration. The servants perhaps receive a promotion rather than are wearied with a heavier load.

25:24–28. This passage deals with the servant who hid his talent. He explained that he had hidden his talent because he **was afraid** (v. 25). Again, one should not push the analogy too far. Jesus is not unjust, and believers' service should come from love and loyalty, not from fear and despair. The story demands that the servant have a motive, and one should leave his motive there in the story. It is incidental to Jesus' main point, that His servants will be rewarded on the basis of the quality of their service. This servant was not commended and in fact lost what he had been given. Jesus was not saying that those who are poor servants will lose their salvation. Again, the story has a direction of its own. He was saying that poor servants will lose what reward they might have had.

25:27. The Greek for **the exchangers** comes from *trapeza* ("table"), a word seen on the front of banks in Greece today. Bankers sat at small tables and changed money (see 21:12). The Greek for **usury** was first used in the sense of offspring, interest being the "offspring" of invested money. Even a minimal service would have been more acceptable than nothing at all. It would not be wrong to see this parable in terms of earthly service and earthly reward. Jesus' point was about heavenly rewards, but in fact, faithful preachers or teachers of God's Word will often see their ministry grow and become a wider blessing. A ministry that remains small is no indication of a lack of God's blessing, however, since the main point is about rewards that will be given when Jesus returns. Jesus wants all to be faithful in service, whether one's ministry is large or small. The real rewards will be given out when Christ returns.

25:28. In an earthly sense, if a believer is unfaithful to the ministry God has given him, it may well be given to another.

25:29–30. This is the main point of the parable. Being ready for Christ's coming involves more than playing it safe and doing little or nothing. It demands the kind of service that will bring glory to God regardless of the size of one's ministry. The principle that from the one who **hath not shall be taken away even that which he hath** relates to service and usefulness in ministry, not to salvation. Jesus was not saying that some Christians will be cast into hell.

25:31–46. This section describes the judgment that will take place when Christ returns. Just when the judgment will take place is difficult to determine, as much of chapters 23–24 deal with various parts of the end times but not always chronologically. The two most widely accepted interpretations of this judgment are: (1) It will occur at the beginning of Christ's earthly millennial kingdom (vv. 31, 34), and its purpose will be to determine who will be allowed to enter the kingdom (v. 34). The criterion for judgment will be the kind of treatment shown to the Jewish people ("these my brethren," v. 40) during the preceding great tribulation period (vv. 35–40, 42–45). Ultimately, how a person treats the Jewish people will reveal whether or not he is saved (vv. 41, 46). (2) The judgment will occur at the great white throne at the end of the age (see Rev. 20:11–15), and its purpose will be to determine who will be allowed to enter Christ's eternal kingdom and who will be consigned to eternal punishment in hell (vv. 34, 46). The basis for judgment will be whether love is shown to God's people—true believers of every type (see 1 John 3:14–15).

25:31–33. Before him shall be gathered all nations (v. 32). The word "nations" is *ethnē* and here properly means ethnic groups. All people will be judged as individuals. Entrance to God's kingdom is based not on one's relationship with a certain country but rather on one's relationship with Jesus Christ.

25:34–40. Rewards in the kingdom of heaven will be given to those who serve without thought of reward. There is no hint of merit here, for God gives out of grace, not debt.

25:41–46. Clearly, the division in this judgment is between the saved and the unsaved. This is not a judgment for reward, as in the parable of the talents. Again, the Bible makes it clear that punishment of the wicked is real and conscious and permanent. **Everlasting punishment** (v. 46) implies that it is a punishment that never ends. It must therefore be conscious and more than mere annihilation.

G. Jesus' Betrayal Plotted (26:1–16)

26:1–16. In this passage, Matthew did something that is often seen on television, but he did it with words. Many times, a few short scenes will set the mood and establish a framework for what is coming. The scenes, in different places but happening one close upon another, will treat one aspect of the story from different angles, showing the viewer how events taking place perhaps simultaneously relate to one theme. Similarly, here Matthew presented four scenes of events related to the death of Christ, which is the major concern of the next few chapters. In scene 1, Jesus tells His disciples of His coming death (vv. 1–2). Scene 2 takes place in the palace of the high priest, where the decision is finally made to kill Him (vv. 3–5). This fades into scene 3: in Bethany, where Jesus is anointed with expensive ointment in anticipation of His burial (vv. 6–13). Scene 4 apparently takes place back in Jerusalem: Judas agrees to betray Jesus to the chief priests for thirty pieces of silver (vv. 14–16). These four quick scenes set the stage for the narrative of Christ's crucifixion. The reader is brought back from concerns about the end times and the judgment (see chaps. 24–25) to the present reality from the perspective of the narrative, that Jesus' crucifixion was just about to happen, and is prepared emotionally for the drama to follow. The rapid succession of these four scenes, unusual in Matthew, serves to quicken the pace and builds anticipation and concern in the reader's mind.

26:1–2. Scene 1: Jesus prepared His disciples for His death. **Ye know** (v. 2). For some time, Jesus had been speaking of His death. The time had now come. For **passover**, see discussion on Mark 14:1. For **Son of man**, see discussion on Mark 2:10.

26:3–5. Scene 2: in the high priest's palace. The decision to kill Jesus, which had been discussed on previous occasions, was made. **The chief priests, and the scribes, and the elders of the people** (v. 3) refers to the clerical and lay leadership of the Sanhedrin (see discussion on 2:4). **Caiaphas** was the high priest in AD 18–36 and the son-in-law of Annas (see John 18:13), a former high priest, who served AD 6–15. **And consulted that they might take Jesus … and kill him** (v. 4). They were no longer considering whether they would do it; they were merely determining the details. The passage might be read that they "consulted in order that they might take Jesus."

An uproar among the people (v. 5). Hundreds of thousands of Jewish pilgrims came to Jerusalem for Passover, and riots were not unknown. The religious leaders (see 26:3) knew that many people admired Jesus. They thus decided to avoid doing the deed on the **feast day** itself. Doing it during that week, however, did not pose a problem for them.

26:6–13. Scene 3: in Bethany. A seemingly celebratory fellowship occasion turned into a teachable moment for Jesus to again emphasize His coming death (see discussion on John 12:1–11).

26:6. For **Bethany**, see discussion on 21:17. **Simon the leper** is mentioned elsewhere only in Mark 14:3, though Simon was a common Jewish name in the first century. He was probably a well-known victim of leprosy who had been healed by Jesus.

26:7. Alabaster box. Most "alabaster" of ancient times was actually marble (see *KJV Study Bible* note on Mark 14:3). The anointing of Jesus happened during dinner, which likely was a festive occasion. Simon probably did not often have so many or so notable guests.

26:8–9. The disciples reacted with **indignation, saying, To what purpose is this waste?** (v. 8). Their concern was that the ointment might have been sold and the money given to the poor. This was certainly true, but something more important was going on.

26:10. Jesus rebuked the disciples and described the woman's actions as **good**. In Greek, the word has an aesthetic as well as an ethical meaning.

26:11. Ye have the poor always with you is often cited as an excuse for doing nothing for them. Jesus was not teaching that poverty is an eternal problem and thus no efforts should be made to alleviate it. His point was one of priority. It is good to help the poor, and one should do so at every opportunity. Jesus is more important, however, because He is God. Sometimes doing good works can get in the way of glorifying Jesus. Many churches have lost their focus on Jesus because a particular cause, however noble and good, took over. There are those who would rather save the whales than save the lost. This verse should serve as a reminder that good works gain their value only in relationship to glorifying Jesus Christ.

26:12–13. Jesus used the occasion to point to His death. The woman's motive is not known or what she knew of what was about to happen to Him. **She did it for my burial** (v. 12). Jesus was not saying that this was her intention, only that it had that effect. He had been anointed and would soon be buried, and Jesus connected the two events. His statement in verse 13 has been fulfilled in that the story is recorded in Scripture and is thus told wherever the gospel is preached. One can only wonder what effect His remarks had on the occasion. The disciples never really grasped what His talk of death, burial, and resurrection really meant until the events took place. They must have wondered why He now mentioned the matter again. One can imagine a puzzled and perhaps troubled silence, followed by a slow resumption of conversation. The reader is not privy to this, however, as Matthew portrayed one more quick scene before beginning his narrative proper.

26:14–16. Scene 4: the setting is most likely in Jerusalem, perhaps only hours later, or the next day. For **Judas Iscariot** (v. 14), see discussion on Mark 3:19. Judas agreed to betray Jesus **for thirty pieces of silver** (v. 15). Equivalent to 120 denarii, this was quite a sum of money. Laborers customarily received one denarius for a day's work (see 20:1–16). Judas then began to seek an **opportunity to betray him** (v. 16). At this point, Judas did not know enough of the schedule for the next few days to be sure of just when and where he would have such an opportunity. This sets up the background and atmosphere for what lies ahead. The reader's attention, riveted on the future in chapters 24–25, is now focused on the dramatic events about to unfold.

H. The Last Supper (26:17–35)

26:17. The first day of the feast of unleavened bread. The fourteenth of Nisan (March–April), it was also called the preparation of the Passover. The Passover meal was eaten the evening of the fourteenth after sunset, and therefore technically on the fifteenth, since the Jewish day ended at sunset. The Feast of Unleavened Bread lasted seven days, Nisan 15–21 (see Lev. 23:5–6), but in the time of Christ, the entire period, Nisan 14–21, was referred to under that name (see discussion on Mark 14:12).

26:18–30. These verses clearly indicate that Jesus ate the Passover meal with His disciples the night before His crucifixion. For more information on the Lord's Supper, see discussions on Mark 14:22–24.

26:18. My time is a reference to Jesus' crucifixion.

26:19. For **Made ready the passover**, see discussion on Mark 14:15.

26:20. For **sat down**, see discussion on Mark 14:18.

26:21. Verily I say unto you (see discussion on Mark 3:28). Jesus knew who would betray Him.

26:22–23. Naturally, the disciples were startled that one of their own would betray Jesus and were **exceeding sorrowful** (v. 22). The idea is not so much that they grieved but that they were distressed. Jesus answered their question indirectly, saying that it was **He that dippeth his hand with me in the dish** (v. 23). It was the custom, still practiced by some in the Middle East, to take a piece of bread or a piece of meat wrapped in bread and dip it into a bowl of sauce (made of stewed fruit) on the table. **Shall betray me**. In that culture, as among Arabs today, to eat with a person was tantamount to saying, "I am your friend and will not hurt you." This fact made Judas's deed all the more despicable (see Ps. 41:9). The disciples did not turn on Judas to stop him during the meal, and it is possible that more than one of them actually used the same dish of fruit sauce as Jesus. It could be that He simply meant, "It is one of you here at this table." Either way, the disciples were still unclear as to who exactly Jesus meant. This was necessary, for they might have tried to stop Judas, thus interfering with the plan of God.

26:24. Jesus pronounced a particularly sad evaluation of Judas's life at this point. He acknowledged that, in accordance with God's plan, He would be killed but still recognized that Judas would be held responsible for his deed. This verse serves notice that even though God directs the affairs of men, one is still responsible for one's actions. For **as it is written of him**, see discussion on Mark 14:21. For **Son of man**, see discussion on Mark 2:10.

26:25. Master, is it I? Judas's question is pointed out especially. He had already made plans to betray Jesus and was covering his tracks by asking the same question as the other disciples (see 26:22). Jesus replied, **Thou hast said**, letting Judas know that He knew what he was about to.

26:26. Jesus took bread. This would have been flat bread (unleavened), something like today's matzoh or perhaps pita bread. **And blessed it** here most likely means that He gave thanks for it (see discussions on Mark 14:22–24). Afterward, He **brake it, and gave it to the disciples, and said, Take, eat; this is my body**. The context makes it clear that He meant the bread represents His body. As bread, broken and consumed, gives physical life, so also His body, broken on the cross, gives spiritual life everlasting. He wanted the disciples to remember the source of their spiritual life as they consumed the source of physical life.

26:27–28. Jesus gave thanks for **the cup** (v. 27) and passed it to the disciples as well. The red color of wine is reminiscent of blood. He wanted them to remember that their sins are forgiven because His **blood** (v. 28) was shed. **The new testament** is a reference to the promise in Jeremiah 31:31–33, where the Lord promised a new covenant with His people. As Old Testament covenants were often sealed with a sacrifice, so the new covenant was sealed by the sacrifice of Jesus Christ on the cross.

26:29. This is a reference to the coming wedding supper of the Lamb, when Jesus and His church will celebrate together in the kingdom.

26:30. Hymn. The Passover fellowship concluded with the second half of the Hallel Psalms (Psalms 115–118).

26:31. All ye shall be offended. Not Peter only, but all the eleven (Judas had previously withdrawn, see John 13:30). The meaning of the words "be offended" is seen in Peter's denial (see 26:69–75) and in the terrified flight of the other disciples (see 26:56). For **I will smite the shepherd**, see discussion on Zechariah 13:7.

26:32. Jesus knew that the resurrection would happen and, based on that knowledge, discussed a future meeting with the disciples. One of Jesus' strongest claims to deity lies not so much in His specific claims as in statements He made based on the assumption that He is God. This was one of those occasions. For **into Galilee**, see 28:10, 16–20; Mark 16:7; John 21:1–23.

26:33. Peter, always quick to speak rather than to reflect, here denied that he would ever be offended. It is odd that Peter, who had confessed earlier that Jesus is "the Son of the living God" (16:16) would find himself, in effect, disagreeing with God. Often the Word of God will challenge believers' assumptions about themselves and their commitments. Rather than spasmodically disagree, as Peter did here, it would be better to reflect on what God has said and see what faults may lie within. This verse is a reminder that God's Word should challenge believers to examine their values and the depth of their commitment.

26:34–35. Before the cock crow (v. 34) may refer to the third of the Roman watches into which the night was divided (see discussion on 14:25; see also Mark 13:35), or it may simply refer to early morning, when the rooster crows. Jesus prophesied that Peter would deny Him, but Peter remained adamant that he would not, and the disciples joined him in this. They were to find that their hasty words, spoken in the relative safety of the upper room, would soon be tested in real life. Often God will test a believer's commitments and convictions in real-life situations, and often one fails. As Peter discovered (John 21:16–17), the mercy of God provides forgiveness and a fresh chance. Sometimes the testing comes on a small scale. How often have believers prayed saying, "Lord, I will go anywhere, suffer any hardship for you!" only to make excuses later in the week when asked to help in the nursery or to teach a class.

I. Garden of Gethsemane (26:36–56)

26:36. Gethsemane means "oil press," a place for squeezing the oil from olives. A garden or orchard on the lower slopes of the Mount of Olives, Gethsemane was one of Jesus' favorite places (see Luke 22:39; John 18:2).

26:37. Peter and the two sons of Zebedee. The latter were James and John. These three disciples seem to have been especially close to Jesus (see Mark 5:37; discussion on Acts 3:1). They were the only disciples to accompany Jesus into Jairus's house and to the Mount of Transfiguration.

26:38–39. Jesus did not die serenely, as many martyrs have. He was no mere martyr; He was the Lamb of God bearing the penalty of the sins of the entire human race. The wrath of God was turned loose on Him. Only this can adequately explain what took place at Gethsemane. **This cup** (v. 39) is a symbol of deep sorrow and suffering. Here it refers to His Father's face being turned away from Him when He who had no sin was made sin (i.e., a sin offering) for us (see 27:46; 2 Cor. 5:21).

26:40–41. The disciples still had no clue as to what was about to happen. They had just had a meal, and in the cool of the night, they fell asleep. Jesus' words were not so much a rebuke as encouragement (see discussion on Mark 14:38).

26:42–44. Jesus prayed a second time, again found the disciples asleep, then prayed a third time. His Father's answer apparently was no, for the events proceeded.

26:45. For **Son of man**, see discussion on Mark 2:10.

26:46. It seems odd that Jesus would say **Rise, let us be going** right after telling the disciples to "Sleep on" (25:45). It may be that He almost immediately saw the party coming to arrest Him.

26:47. For **a great multitude with swords and staves**, see *KJV Study Bible* note on Mark 14:43. For **The chief priests and elders**, see discussions on 2:4; 26:3. The party apparently was much larger than was needed, but those who oppose God's people often overreact.

26:48. For **Whomsoever I shall kiss**, see discussion on Luke 22:47.

26:49. Master is the Hebrew word for "(my) teacher." **Kissed him.** The same word is used of the father's kissing of the prodigal son, indicating affection. **He** refers to Judas (see discussions on Mark 14:45 and Luke 22:47).

26:50. It is a mark of God's mercy that even in the moment of betrayal, Jesus called Judas **Friend.**

26:51. One of them which were with Jesus refers to Peter (see John 18:10). **A servant of the high priest's** refers to Malchus (see John 18:10).

26:52. Here Jesus applied what He had said in the Sermon on the Mount about turning the other cheek. In this situation, it was proper to submit to the authorities. Jesus was not giving a general condemnation of war at all times in all places but rather was teaching personal submission to authority and turning the other cheek when opposed.

26:53. Legions. A Roman legion had six thousand soldiers. One is struck by the fact that Jesus, though arrested, tried, and convicted, seems never to have been out of control of the situation. They did not take His life; He gave it up. He was not killed; He died. He was not taken; He gave Himself up.

26:54. The scriptures be fulfilled. In view of 26:56, this is probably a reference to Zechariah 13:7.

26:55–56. Jesus pointed out to those who had come to arrest Him that they could have taken Him at any time. Again, His attitude was one of submission, not resistance. It was not so much that they took Him as it was that he went. **Then all the disciples forsook him, and fled** (v. 56). In the upper room, Jesus had told the disciples, "All ye shall be offended because of me this night" (26:31), and here they flee in terror.

J. Trial before Caiaphas (26:57–68)

26:57–68. Jesus' trial consisted of two stages: the religious trial held under Caiaphas (here) and the civil trial held under Pontius Pilate (27:1–2, 11–26). For a summary of the two stages, see *KJV Study Bible* note on Mark 14:53–15:15.

26:57–58. The disciples were scattered, but **Peter followed** (v. 58) from a distance **to see the end.** This was not idle curiosity on his part, nor was it morbid.

It was a measure of the devotion with which he held his Lord. He would soon be tested and found wanting. This is not to say, however, that Peter had no love, devotion, or commitment, only that the Lord knew better than he did the level to which he possessed these traits.

26:59. The council (see discussion on Mark 14:55). It is interesting that in carrying out a trial that they knew was a sham, they were meticulous in matters of procedure. How often when one is guilty of major sin that one focuses on minor points of scruple.

26:60–61. I am able to destroy the temple of God (v. 61) evidently was an intentional distortion of Jesus' words (see John 2:19).

26:62. Jesus answered not His accusers. Again, He was "turning the other cheek" as He had taught His disciples. It would not do for Him to get into a verbal battle with His accusers.

26:63. Jesus held his peace. He refused to answer the question of 26:62. **I adjure thee.** When the high priest used this form, however, Jesus was legally obliged to reply. For **Christ,** see discussion on 16:16.

26:64. Jesus obeyed the law in the matter and replied with the truth. He described His second coming as well, emphasizing that though He was in their hands now, His power would be manifest at the right time.

26:65. Rent his clothes. Ordinarily the high priest was forbidden by law to do this (see Lev. 10:6; 21:10), but this was considered a highly unusual circumstance. The high priest interpreted Jesus' answer in 26:64 as blasphemy (see discussion on Mark 14:64).

26:66. The verdict was given: **He is guilty of death.**

26:67–68. Mark reported that they blindfolded Jesus (Mark 14:65), which explains the mocking command, **Prophesy…Who is he that smote thee?** (v. 68).

K. Peter's Denial (26:69–75)

26:69–72. Peter, being outside, was questioned, and his association with Jesus was pointed out. Twice he denied it.

26:73. A third time Peter was approached and questioned. **Thy speech be[t]rayeth thee**. Peter had a decidedly Galilean accent, which was conspicuous in Jerusalem.

26:74. Curse … and swear. We are not told what Peter said, but the third time when he denied knowing Jesus, **the cock crew**. There is no indication that these people were threatening in any way. The authorities had the one they wanted, Jesus, and would have taken little interest even if the crowd had pointed Peter out to them. The women certainly could have offered no threat. Peter was in no apparent danger if he had admitted his relationship with Jesus. His denials only piqued the interest of the group, who were sure he was one of them. Perhaps they only wanted an insider's details of life and ministry with Jesus. Peter, blinded by fear, could not see past his own perception of danger.

26:75. And Peter remembered the word of Jesus, who had prophesied this very event. Peter, now confronted with the reality of his lack of commitment and of the rashness of his words the night before, **went out, and wept bitterly**.

L. Judas's Death (27:1–10)

Chapter 27 deals primarily with Jesus' trial before Pilate and the crucifixion. After setting the scene for the trial (vv. 1–2), however, Matthew reported what happened to Judas after he had betrayed Jesus (vv. 3–10).

27:1–2. When the morning was come (v. 1). The Sanhedrin could not have a legal session at night, so at daybreak, a special meeting was held to make the death sentence (see 26:66) official (see discussion on Mark 15:1). **Delivered him to Pontius Pilate** (v. 2). The Roman government had deprived the Sanhedrin of the right to carry out capital punishment, except in the case of a foreigner who invaded the sacred precincts of the temple. Jesus therefore had to be handed over to Pilate for execution. For additional information about Pilate, see discussion on Mark 15:1.

27:3–10. See Acts 1:16–19. This is a parenthesis in the narrative, but an important one. Judas had disappeared except for a brief scene in the garden of Gethsemane, after his meeting with the chief priests earlier in the week. Matthew tied up the loose end by telling what happened to Judas, preventing the reader from wondering about this rather than focusing on the narrative. Also, it appears that Judas approached the chief priests and elders sometime on the morning of the crucifixion, so the incident happened at this point chronologically.

27:4. The callousness of these leaders is shown in that Judas admitted his sin, and they offered him no counsel or solace, only scorn.

27:5. For **hanged himself**, see discussion on Acts 1:18.

27:6–10. The potter's field (vv. 7, 10) may have been purchased some days later, but since Matthew's purpose was to tie up the story, he related it here. **The field of blood** (v. 8). Compare "The valley of slaughter" in Jeremiah 19:6. **Jeremie** (v. 9). The quotation seems to be a combination of Zechariah 11:12–13 and Jeremiah 19:1–13 (or perhaps Jer. 18:2–12 or 32:6–9), but Matthew attributed it to the major prophet Jeremiah, just as Mark (1:2–3) quoted a combination of Malachi 3:1 and Isaiah 40:3 but attributed it to the major prophet Isaiah.

M. Trial before Pilate (27:11–26)

27:11–12. Thou sayest (v. 11). Jesus answered Pilate's direct question but **answered nothing** (v. 12) to the charges brought by His accusers.

27:13–14. Pilate **marvelled** (v. 14), probably because Jesus was calm in the face of false accusations and that He did not get into a shouting match with them. A guilty man will often rant against his accusers. Pilate was astute enough to recognize an innocent man when one appeared in his court.

27:15. The governor was wont to release unto the people a prisoner. A custom of which nothing is known outside the Gospels. It was probably never mentioned because it was incidental to the activities of the Passover week. The Jewish leaders normally did not ask for a notorious or dangerous prisoner to be released, which also minimized the importance of the custom. On this occasion, it was quite different.

27:16 – 18. A notable prisoner, called Barabbas (v. 16). Barabbas had taken part in a rebellion (see Luke 23:19; John 18:40), presumably against the Romans, and would have been a folk hero among the Jews. Why Pilate offered the choice of him or Jesus is unclear. Was he the only prisoner Pilate had? This is unlikely. Was he unpopular? If so, Pilate may have hoped that the contrast would lead the people to ask for Jesus, whom he by now surely knew was popular with the multitudes.

27:19. This incident is found only in Matthew's gospel. It forms something of an interruption of the narrative, but it heightens the drama and emphasizes that Pilate knew that Jesus was innocent.

27:20 – 23. If manipulating the situation was Pilate's intent, it failed. **The chief priests and elders persuaded the multitude that they should ask Barabbas** (v. 20). Apparently, the same crowd that had hailed Jesus on the first day of the week now called for His crucifixion. It may be that the crowd was "handpicked" by the chief priests and elders and was not representative of the majority. Certainly, all the people could not have been in one place at this time.

27:24. This is the origin of the saying "I wash my hands of the situation."

27:25. His blood be on us. The bloodthirsty crowd gave a chilling response, which has often been used to justify the persecution of the Jewish people. It should be noted, however, that it was not God but the people themselves who uttered these words. There is no evidence here that God granted their request. In addition, this crowd was certainly not all the Jewish people alive at the time. Had Jesus' fate been submitted to a vote across all of Judea and Galilee, it is doubtful that He would have been convicted.

27:26. Scourged. Roman floggings were so brutal that sometimes the victim died before crucifixion (see discussion on Mark 15:15).

N. The Soldiers Mock Jesus (27:27 – 32)

27:27. The common hall. The governor's official residence in Jerusalem was the "Pretorium" (Mark 15:16; see discussion there).

27:28 – 31. A scarlet robe (v. 28). The outer cloak of a Roman soldier. For **a crown of thorns** (v. 29), see discussion on Mark 15:17. **Reed** (v. 29). A mock scepter. None of this was likely an official part of the sentence. The soldiers apparently took advantage of the time it took for the preparations for the crucifixion to mistreat Him.

27:32. Cyrene. A city in North Africa on the Mediterranean Sea about seven hundred miles west of Jerusalem. For **Simon … to bear his cross**, see discussion on Mark 15:21.

O. The Crucifixion (27:33 – 56)

27:33. For **Golgotha**, see discussion on Mark 15:22.

27:34. Mingled with gall. Tradition says that the women of Jerusalem customarily furnished this painkilling narcotic to prisoners who were crucified. Jesus refused to drink it because He wanted to be fully conscious until His death (see 27:50).

27:35. For **crucified**, see *KJV Study Bible* note on Mark 15:24. **Casting lots** is explained more precisely in John 19:23 – 24.

27:36 – 37. See discussion on Mark 15:26.

27:38. For **two thieves**, see discussion on Mark 15:27.

27:39 – 43. It is ironic that the people called Him to **save** (v. 40) Himself, when it was by being there that He saved us. The leaders also mocked Him, saying **let him now come down from the cross, and we will believe him** (v. 42). In fact, had He not gone to the cross, believing in Him would have done no good.

27:44. Luke recorded that one of these thieves repented. Matthew omitted this detail, but the two accounts are easily harmonized.

27:45. From the sixth hour … unto the ninth hour. From noon until 3:00 p.m.

27:46 – 49. ELI, ELI, LAMA SABACHTHANI? (v. 46) is a mixture of Aramaic and Hebrew, translated by Matthew for his readers (see discussion on Mark 15:34). Some mistook this for a call to **Elias** (Elijah; v. 49). It may be that the crowd knew little of Aramaic, one of the languages commonly spoken in the Holy Land in Jesus' day, as many were visiting Jerusalem for the feast and may have spoken mostly Greek (see discussion on Mark 15:35).

27:50–51. The vail is the inner curtain that separated the Holy Place from the Most Holy Place. The tearing of the curtain signified Christ's making it possible for believers to go directly into God's presence (see Heb. 9:1–14; 10:14–22).

27:52–53. This incident is found only in Matthew's gospel. These **saints** (v. 52) were a witness to Christ's victory over death.

27:54. The Son of God. It cannot be determined whether **the centurion** (see discussion on 8:5) made a fully Christian confession or was only acknowledging that, since the gods had so obviously acted to vindicate this judicial victim, Jesus must have been one especially favored by them (the Greek can also be translated "a son"). In view of the ridicule voiced by "they that passed by" (27:39–40), however, it seems probable that Matthew intended the former (see discussion on Luke 23:47).

27:55–56. These women were involved in Jesus' burial, and among them were the witnesses to the risen Christ on Sunday morning (see discussion on Mark 15:40).

P. The Burial (27:57–66)

27:57. Arimathea. A village in the hill country of Ephraim, about twenty miles northwest of Jerusalem.

27:58. For **begged the body of Jesus**, see discussion on Luke 23:52.

27:59–60. Others helped Joseph with the burial. He caused it to happen but did not do the preparations alone (see discussion on Mark 15:46).

27:61. These women probably helped with the burial and certainly knew exactly where the tomb was. No one can assert with any credibility that these women went to the wrong tomb on Easter Sunday.

27:62–64. This meeting indicates that Jesus' opponents had a good idea of what He had taught His disciples. They knew that He had not spoken of the literal temple when He said "in three days I will build it again" (16:21), yet this was the statement that provided motivation for the trial against Him.

27:65–66. Ye have a watch (v. 65), most likely made up of Roman soldiers (see 28:4, 11–12).

VIII. The Risen Christ (chap. 28)

A. The Empty Tomb (28:1–10)

28:1. For **the first day of the week**, see discussion on Luke 24:1. **The other Mary.** The wife of Clopas (see 27:56; John 19:25).

28:2. A great earthquake. Only Matthew recorded this earthquake and the one at Jesus' death (27:51, 54). It is clear from the parallel accounts (Mark 16:2–6; Luke 24:1–7; John 20:1) that the events of 28:2–4 occurred before the women arrived at the tomb. The earthquakes, at His death and at the tomb, may have served to emphasize the apolcalyptic aspect of these events. Jesus was, in His death, opening up heaven to all who believe. His death set in motion the events that will culminate in the great tribulation and the millennium and was thus accompanied by apocalyptic signs.

28:3–4. His countenance was like lightning (v. 3) describes the angel that rolled away the stone (see 28:2) and is most likely a reference to brightness. The angel probably had a glow from within. Well might **the keepers … shake** (v. 4) in the presence of such a creature. **Became as dead men** may mean that they fainted or were so afraid that they were unable to move.

28:5–7. The angel announced the risen Christ and reminded the women of His words when He told the disciples He would meet them in **Galilee** (v. 7) after the resurrection (see 26:32).

28:8–10. Fear and great joy (v. 8). These two emotions can certainly go together. The women were fearful most likely because of the unexpectedness of the events and joyful because their Lord was alive. **As they went to tell his disciples … Jesus met them** (v. 9). They **worshipped him**, now recognizing His deity. Jesus reminded them again that He would meet the disciples in **Galilee** (v. 10).

B. The Authorities Cover Up What Really Happened (28:11–15)

28:11–15. Only Matthew related the posting of the guard (see 27:62–66), and here he followed up by telling of their report. The chief priests and elders bribed the soldiers and gave them a false story to report. Apparently, the story still circulated when Matthew wrote this account, which is why he took time to treat its origin here.

C. The Great Commission (28:16–20)

28:16–17. The eleven (v. 16). Judas had committed suicide (see 27:5). For **had appointed**, see 28:10. Meeting Jesus in Galilee as He had instructed them (see 26:32), the disciples **worshipped him**. This is the second time in a few verses that Jesus was worshiped. It stands as a proof of His deity, for when others in the Bible are worshiped (Paul in Acts 14:11–15 and an angel in Rev. 19:10; 22:8), they refuse it and point to the true God. The counterexample is Herod in Acts 12:22, and he was killed for taking to himself the honor due to God. **But some doubted**. They saw the risen Christ, but even with all He had taught them concerning His death and resurrection, it was so miraculous that some were still hesitant to believe, though the record in Acts clearly indicates that they eventually did.

28:18–20. This is the Great Commission. It forms the biblical basis for missions and evangelism.

28:18. Here is the power of missions: Jesus has **All power ... in heaven and in earth**. Missions is not a human endeavor; it takes place under the anointing and empowerment of God Himself.

28:19. The goal of missions is to **teach all nations**. The idea is to make disciples. The commission of Christ's followers is not just to tell the story and move on but to create faith communities — churches — where living out the Christian life becomes the basis of the evangelization of the world. Here also is the universal scope of missions: "all nations." No one is to be excluded from hearing the gospel. Matthew's readers needed the reminder that the gospel was to be taken to the Gentiles (compare 10:5–6). Also, the scope of Christ's Great Commission shows that although it was spoken to the eleven, it was meant for the entire church, in all ages, until He returns. **Baptizing them**. This is the proper activity of the ministry: to build the church, by "baptizing them" (the new disciples) and forming them into communities of faith that worship and study together to evangelize the world with the gospel. This baptism is a sign of their identification with and commitment to Christ (see discussions on Acts 2:38; Rom. 6:3–4). **In the name of the Father, and of the Son, and of the Holy Ghost**. Christ is associated with the other persons of deity in the Trinity. Christians are to baptize new disciples "in the name of the Father, and of the Son, and of the Holy [Spirit]." The elliptical clause in the Greek text clearly distinguishes each member of the Trinity. There is only one God whom we are to worship, and it is this God, the Three in One, and no other.

28:20. I am with you alway. Matthew ended his gospel with the reassuring and empowering words of the One who came to earth to be "God with us" (1:23). **Even unto the end of the world**. Again, this demonstrates that the Great Commission applies to the church at all times until Christ returns.

THE GOSPEL ACCORDING TO ST. MARK

INTRODUCTION

Author

A title "According to Mark" appears with the second gospel in the oldest manuscripts of the New Testament, which originate from the end of the first century, many years after the gospel of Mark had been written. Since there is no direct internal evidence of authorship for the second gospel, the title represents early and valuable external evidence regarding the identity of the writer. The information that the title furnishes is highly reliable since an early Christian author writing a gospel under an assumed name (pseudonymously) would likely have chosen a more prominent name (such as that of an apostle). Mark is, therefore, the probable author. The title "The Gospel according to St. Mark" in the KJV reflects that certainty.

The unanimous testimony of the early church is that the Mark of this gospel is John Mark of the New Testament. The first mention of him is in connection with his mother, who had a house in Jerusalem that served as a meeting place for believers (see Acts 12:12). This house was also thought to be the upper room (see Mark 14:12–15). When Paul and Barnabas returned to Antioch from Jerusalem after the famine visit, Mark accompanied them (see Acts 12:25). Mark next appears as a helper to Paul and Barnabas on their first missionary journey (see Acts 13:5), but he deserted them at Perga, in Pamphylia, to return to Jerusalem (see Acts 13:13). Paul must have been deeply disappointed with Mark's actions on this occasion, because when Barnabas proposed taking Mark on the second journey, Paul flatly refused—a refusal that broke up their working relationship (see Acts 15:36–39). Barnabas took Mark, who was his cousin, and departed for Cyprus. No further mention is made of either of them in the book of Acts. Mark reappears in Paul's letter to the Colossians, written from Rome. Paul sent a greeting from Mark and added: "touching whom ye received commandments: if he come unto you, receive him" (Col. 4:10; see Philemon 24, written about the same time). At that point, Mark apparently had begun to win his way back into Paul's confidence. By the end of Paul's life, Mark had fully regained his favor; the apostle now considered Mark "profitable to me for the ministry" (2 Tim. 4:11). It is also thought that the one Peter mentioned as "Marcus my son" (1 Peter 5:13) was this same Mark. He was Peter's son in the faith.

The most important evidence regarding John Mark and the authorship of the second gospel comes from Papias (ca. AD 140), who quoted an even earlier source as saying:

(1) John Mark was a close associate of Peter, from whom he received the tradition of the things the Lord said and did; (2) this tradition did not come to Mark as a finished, sequential account of the life of Jesus but rather as the preaching of Peter, which was directed to the needs of the early Christian communities; (3) Mark accurately preserved this material. Thus, the gospel of Mark largely consists of the preaching of Peter, arranged and shaped by John Mark. In composing his gospel, Mark drew from Peter's preaching those reminiscences that especially contributed to his own distinctive theological purposes.

Since the gospel contains eyewitness accounts of the life of Jesus — accounts of the apostle Peter himself — it stands as weighty historical evidence that attests to the life and deeds of Jesus. Those eyewitness accounts in which Peter himself appears represent words and events that must have had special significance for him as a disciple of Jesus. Peter's successes (see 8:29) and failures (see 14:66 – 72) serve as examples for other disciples. John Mark, recognizing the value of these personal disclosures in Peter's preaching, related them to his own audience as he sought to build them up in the ways of discipleship.

Date

Precise dating of the gospel of Mark is virtually impossible. Some have proposed dates in the mid- to late-40s or in the 50s. Others have suggested that Mark wrote in the early to mid-60s before Peter's death, which occurred circa AD 64 – 67. Still others believe that the content of the gospel and statements made about Mark by the early church fathers indicate that the book was written shortly after Peter's death in Rome but before the destruction of Jerusalem in AD 70. The date for Mark in this view is therefore circa AD 67 – 70.

Regardless of the difficulty in precise dating, a good case can be made for a date sometime before AD 70, even before 64. According to the two-source hypothesis, Matthew and Luke both utilized Mark and a hypothetical document called Quelle (German for "source"), or Q, in the composition of their gospels. If this hypothesis is true, Mark must predate Matthew and Luke-Acts (Luke's two-volume work). Paul was under house arrest in Rome at the end of Acts, and since neither the outcome of Paul's trial nor his martyrdom (ca. AD 64 – 67) are mentioned in Acts, Luke-Acts (and Mark's gospel, which was used by Luke) was most likely written sometime before AD 64.

Some recent scholars have suggested that the date of Mark is as late as circa AD 70 – 73. The saying of Jesus about "the abomination of desolation" (13:14) enters the discussion at this point. Mark's editorial comment in 13:14 ("let him that readeth understand") infers that Jesus' words in that verse have relevance for his contemporary audience, not just for readers in the distant future. Luke understood the saying to refer to the siege and conquest of Jerusalem by the Romans in the war of AD 66 – 70 (see Luke 21:20), and one may assume that Mark had the same understanding. Mark recalled for his audience Jesus' prophecies of events that were some forty years distant when the Lord spoke. The fulfillment of Jesus' prophecy regarding Jerusalem's fate was still future for Mark, but that fulfillment could be seen on the horizon as he wrote.

Place of Composition

According to early church tradition, Mark was written "in the regions of Italy" (Anti-Marcionite prologue) or, more specifically, in Rome (as stated by Irenaeus and Clement of Alexandria). These same authors closely associate Mark's writing of the gospel with the apostle Peter. The above evidence is consistent with (1) the historical probability that Peter was in Rome during the last days of his life and was martyred there and (2) the biblical evidence that Mark also was in Rome about the same time and was closely associated with Peter (see 2 Tim. 4:11; 1 Peter 5:13, where the word "Babylon" is possibly a cryptogram for Rome).

Further evidence that points to Rome as the place of composition is an incidental reference in 15:21, which describes the Roman soldiers compelling Simon, a Cyrenian, to carry Jesus' cross. Mark noted that Simon was "the father of Alexander and Rufus," a detail that evidently was unimportant for Matthew and Luke (they omitted it from their versions of Jesus' passion) but was important for Mark. He assumed that his readers knew and appreciated the identity of these sons of Simon. But who were Alexander and Rufus? Since Alexander was, in all likelihood, not the same person as any of the other men of that name in the New Testament, nothing can be known about him. An identification of Rufus is more promising, however. In Romans 16, Paul instructed the believers in Rome to greet various members of the church there, including a person named Rufus ("Salute Rufus chosen in the Lord," Rom. 16:13). Since no other Rufus besides the one whom Mark mentioned appears in the New Testament, the Rufus of Mark 15:21 and of Romans 16:13 are probably the same man. If so, the gospel of Mark is closely linked to Rome by the name Rufus. Mark mentioned Rufus in his gospel as one whom the Roman Christians would know; he was one of them. Although some interpreters have suggested other places of composition (Alexandria, Antioch, Galilee), a Roman provenance is most likely.

Recipients

The evidence indicates that Mark's audience was the church at Rome, or at least to Gentile readers there. Mark explained Jewish customs (7:2–4; 15:42) and translated Aramaic words (3:17; 5:41; 7:11, 34; 15:22, 34). Aramaic was one of the languages of the Holy Land in the first century AD, and probably the language Jesus and His disciples ordinarily spoke (though they probably also spoke Hebrew and Greek). Mark's use of Latin technical terms does not absolutely prove that he wrote in the imperial capital and for the believers there, but it does allow for that possibility. In two instances, Mark explained common Greek words by Latin terms. The first instance is in 12:42. In the temple, a poor widow came to the treasury and "threw in two mites [Greek, *lepta duo*], which make a farthing [Greek, *kodrantēs*; Latin, *quadrans*]." In the second instance, at 15:16, Jesus had been delivered over to be crucified, "And the soldiers led him away into the hall [Greek, *aulē*], called Pretorium [Greek, *praitōrion*; Latin, *praetorium*]." These explanations agree with the view that this gospel was written in Rome for the church there. Furthermore, Mark also seems to have had a special interest in persecution and martyrdom (8:34–38; 13:9–13), subjects perhaps of special concern to Roman believers. A Roman origin and audience would explain the almost immediate acceptance of this gospel and its rapid dissemination. In short, Mark's original readers and hearers were quite likely Christians within the city of Rome.

Theme and Theological Message

Throughout Mark, Jesus is consistently portrayed as a person of stature and honor. He receives popular approval in His exchanges with religious leaders, subdues forces of nature, exorcizes demons, and teaches with authority. Even Jesus' opponents must grudgingly withdraw in their attempts to discredit Him. They are finally able to force a trial and condemnation of Jesus, but even in the legal proceedings and execution, Jesus is seen as a person of honor. The shame of the cross is counteracted throughout the gospel. Mark's intention, therefore, may have been to convince unbelievers, and to encourage believers, that Jesus ultimately has honor despite the shame of crucifixion.

Since Mark's gospel is traditionally associated with Rome, it may have been occasioned by the persecutions of the Roman church in the period circa AD 64–67. The famous fire of Rome in 64, probably set by Nero himself but blamed on Christians, resulted in the severe persecution, even martyrdom, of the Roman believers. Whatever the precise circumstances, the gospel of Mark addresses a community or communities under distress. Mark may have wanted to prepare his readers for this suffering by placing before them the life of the Lord, as his gospel contains many references, both explicit and veiled, to suffering and discipleship (see 1:12–13; 3:22, 30; 8:34–38; 10:30, 33–34, 45; 13:8, 11–13). Mark's audience needed a refresher course reviewing the honorable identity of Jesus, the one who inaugurated the kingdom of God in His life and ministry. The confusion of the disciples in the gospel narrative parallels that of Mark's audience. The narrative reminded them that Jesus has glory and honor as the Christ, the Son of God. The anguished disciples in Mark's audience could therefore count it an honor to follow Him.

Mark particularly emphasized several themes in his gospel. (1) *The cross.* Both the human cause (12:12; 14:1–2; 15:10) and the divine necessity (8:31; 9:31; 10:33) of the cross are emphasized. (2) *Discipleship.* Special attention should be paid to the passages on discipleship that arose from Jesus' prophesy of His passion (8:34–9:1; 9:35–10:31; 10:42–45). (3) *The teachings of Jesus.* Although Mark recorded far fewer actual teachings of Jesus than did the other gospel writers, he placed a remarkable emphasis on Jesus as teacher. The words "teacher," "teach" or "teaching," and "Master" are applied to Jesus nearly forty times in Mark. (4) *The messianic secret.* On several occasions, Jesus warned His disciples or the person for whom He had worked a miracle to keep silent about His true identity as the Messiah or what He had done (1:34, 44; 3:12; 5:43; 7:36–37; 8:26, 30; 9:9). Some scholars theorize that Mark invented the messianic secret to remove an embarrassing failure of Jesus to proclaim Himself as Messiah. Words are put into Jesus' mouth that prohibit demons and people from talking about Him and His mighty deeds. According to this theory, Jesus' privately teaching some that He is the Messiah is a fiction. There is no reason to assume, however, that Jesus did not indeed instruct people against revealing His messianic characteristics. He did not want to encourage the masses to follow Him merely as a political liberator who would lead them in revolt against the Roman occupation. The early Christian belief in Jesus as the Messiah and Son of God could have originated only as a result of Jesus' own statement about this. (5) *The Son of God.* Although Mark emphasized the humanity of Jesus (see 3:5; 6:6, 31, 34; 7:34; 8:12, 33; 10:14; 11:12), he did not neglect His deity (see 1:1, 11; 3:11; 5:7; 9:7; 12:1–11; 13:32; 15:39).

Literary Features

Mark's gospel is a simple, succinct, unadorned, yet vivid account of Jesus' ministry, emphasizing more what Jesus did than what He said. Mark moves quickly from one episode in Jesus' life and ministry to another, with frequent use of the adverb translated "immediately." The book as a whole is characterized as "The beginning of the gospel" (1:1). The life, death, and resurrection of Christ comprise the "beginning," of which the apostolic preaching in Acts is the continuation. In recent scholarly study of the second gospel, its literary features (narration, setting, plot, and character) have been a focus. The craftsmanship of Mark as a skilled storyteller has justly been recognized.

Outline

I. The Beginnings of Jesus' Ministry (1:1–13)
    A. His Forerunner (1:1–8)
    B. His Baptism (1:9–11)
    C. His Temptation (1:12–13)
II. Jesus' Ministry in Galilee (1:14–6:29)
    A. Early Galilean Ministry (1:14–3:12)
        1. Call of the First Disciples (1:14–20)
        2. Miracles in Capernaum (1:21–34)
        3. A Tour of Galilee (1:35–45)
        4. Ministry in Capernaum (2:1–22)
        5. Sabbath Controversy (2:23–3:12)
    B. Later Galilean Ministry (3:13–6:29)
        1. Selection of the Twelve Apostles (3:13–19)
        2. Teachings in Capernaum (3:20–35)
        3. Parables of the Kingdom (4:1–34)
            a. The Parable of the Sower (4:1–20)
            b. The Parable of the Candle under a Bushel (4:21–23)
            c. The Saying about Measure (4:24–25)
            d. The Parable of the Growing Seed (4:26–29)
            e. The Parable of the Mustard Seed (4:30–34)
        4. Trip across the Sea of Galilee (4:35–5:20)
        5. More Galilean Miracles (5:21–43)
        6. Unbelief in Jesus' Hometown (6:1–6)
        7. Six Apostolic Teams Tour Galilee (6:7–13)
        8. King Herod's Reaction to Jesus' Ministry (6:14–29)
III. Withdrawals from Galilee (6:30–9:32)
    A. To the Eastern Shore of the Sea of Galilee (6:30–52)
    B. To the Western Shore of the Sea of Galilee (6:53–7:23)
    C. To Phoenicia (7:24–30)
    D. To the Region of the Decapolis: More Miracles (7:31–8:10)
    E. To the Vicinity of Caesarea Philippi (8:11–9:32)
        1. The Pharisees' Demand for a Sign and the Danger of Yeast (8:11–21)
        2. The Healing of a Blind Man at Bethsaida (8:22–26)
        3. Peter's Confession and Jesus' Prophesy of His Death and Resurrection (8:27–9:1)
        4. The Transfiguration (9:2–13)

8. The Soldiers Mock Jesus (15:16–20)
9. The Crucifixion and Death of Jesus (15:21–39)
10. The Burial of Jesus (15:40–47)
VII. The Resurrection of Jesus (chap. 16)
A. The Empty Tomb (16:1–8)
B. The Longer Ending of Mark (16:9–20)

Select Bibliography

Cole, R. Alan. *The Gospel according to Mark: An Introduction and Commentary*. 2nd ed. Tyndale New Testament Commentaries 2. Grand Rapids, MI: Eerdmans, 1989.

Edwards, James R. *The Gospel according to Mark*. Pillar New Testament Commentary. Grand Rapids, MI: Eerdmans, 2001.

France, R. T. *The Gospel of Mark: A Commentary on the Greek Text*. New International Greek Testament Commentary. Grand Rapids, MI: Eerdmans, 2002.

Guelich, Robert A. *Mark 1–8:26*. Word Biblical Commentary 34A. Dallas, TX: Word, 1989.

Gundry, Robert H. *Mark: A Commentary on His Apology for the Cross*. Grand Rapids, MI: Eerdmans, 1993.

Hurtado, Larry W. *Mark*. A Good News Commentary. San Francisco, CA: Harper & Row, 1983.

Lane, William L. *The Gospel according to Mark*. The New International Commentary on the New Testament. Grand Rapids, MI: Eerdmans, 1974.

Taylor, Vincent. *The Gospel according to St. Mark*. New York: St. Martin's Press, 1963.

Witherington, Ben. *The Gospel of Mark: A Socio-Rhetorical Commentary*. Grand Rapids, MI: Eerdmans, 2001.

EXPOSITION

I. The Beginnings of Jesus' Ministry (1:1–13)

A. His Forerunner (1:1–8)

1:1–8. In the opening section, Jesus' activity is linked with God's activity and Old Testament prophecy.

1:1. The beginning (Greek, *archē*) suggests the opening verse of Genesis (see John 1:1). The word **gospel** is from the Old English *godspel*, "good story" or "good news"; the latter term accurately translates the Greek. The good news is that God has provided salvation through the life, death, and resurrection of **Jesus Christ, the Son of God**. "Gospel" could refer to Mark's gospel or to the good news whose story and unfolding begins in 1:2. The significance of **Christ**

and **Son of God** for Mark become clear in the unfolding of his gospel. In brief, however, "Christ" designates the divinely anointed and commissioned Messiah, the deliverer of God's people. For Mark, the title "Son of God" complements "Son of man" (see discussion on 2:10) and refers to the One who has power over the natural and supernatural realms, the authority to bring salvation and judgment, the right to declare the meaning of the Scriptures, and a unique relationship with God the Father. The reader knows from the outset who Jesus is and takes His side against His antagonists.

1:2–3. The prophets (v. 2) should read "Isaiah the prophet" (NIV), the most accurate reading of the manuscripts. Since the quotation of these verses is a combination of texts (v. 2 is from Mal. 3:1; v. 3 is from Isa. 40:3), Mark simply attributed the entire formula to the more prominent prophet, Isaiah. The passages cited speak of the **messenger** (v. 2), **the wilderness** (v. 3), and **the Lord**, each of which is stressed in 1:4–8.

1:4. Mark, like John, has no nativity narrative but begins with the ministry of **John** the Baptist. The name John means "the Lord is gracious." John's practice of baptizing those who came to him in repentance was so characteristic of his ministry that he became known as "the Baptist" or "the Baptizer." **The wilderness** refers to the unpopulated region near the Jordan River. The wilderness setting reminds the reader of the exodus; the One whom John announced would duplicate God's salvation of His people in the wilderness. John's travels may have taken him into the arid region west of the Dead Sea, whose inhabitants included those who wrote and preserved the Dead Sea Scrolls. No evidence exists to connect John conclusively with the settlement of Qumran, near the caves where the scrolls were found. **The baptism** that he preached, however, is similar to the washings practiced at Qumran. John was preaching repentance-baptism, baptism that was preceded or accompanied by **repentance**. The word "repentance" (Greek, *metanoia*) involves turning one's entire person to God, not just feeling sorrow for sin. As did the community at Qumran, John taught that forgiveness (**the remission of sins**) is based on repentance, not baptism. God always grants forgiveness when one has truly repented. John's emphasis on repentance recalls the preaching of the prophets (e.g., Hos. 3:4–5); his stress on forgiveness pointed to the salvation bestowed by the coming One.

1:5. All the land of Judaea and **were all baptized** are obvious hyperboles, indicating the high interest John's preaching created. For centuries, Israel had had no prophet. John created intense excitement throughout Judea: at last God was at work to fulfill His promises and reveal the kingdom of God! Even though **the river of Jordan** is the principal river in the Holy Land, it is located in the rift valley, away from the population centers. It begins from the snows of Mount Hermon and ends at the Dead Sea. Its closest point to Jerusalem is about twenty miles.

1:6. John was a man of simple means: he **was clothed with camel's hair, and with a girdle of a skin** (clothing worn by Elijah and other prophets, see 2 Kings 1:8; Zech. 13:4), and his diet was **locusts and wild honey**. "Locusts" could refer to the insects (allowed as food in Lev. 11:22–23) or to the carob bean or nut.

1:7. Mark's account of John's message is brief (see Matt. 3:7–12; Luke 3:7–17). He **preached** with a focus on the coming of the mighty One. The reader's interest is aroused by this message. Who is **mightier than** the honored prophet John? Whoever he is, he must be a person of great honor since even John was **not worthy to stoop down and unloose** the thongs of His sandals. As great as John's ministry was, the ministry of the coming One would be greater.

1:8. John **baptized … with water: but [Christ] shall baptize you with the Holy Ghost**. An eschatological outpouring of the Holy Spirit, the coming of the Holy Spirit upon God's people in the last days, is an Old Testament expectation (see Isa. 32:15; Ezek. 36:27; Joel 2:28–32). The baptism carries two aspects: salvation conveyed by the Holy Spirit and the fire of judgment (see Matt. 3:11; Luke 3:16).

B. His Baptism (1:9–11)

1:9–11. In those days (v. 9), when Jesus began His public ministry, He was approximately thirty years old (see Luke 3:23), probably circa AD 27. As far as can be known, He had spent most of His earlier years in **Nazareth**. When Jesus **was baptized of John in Jordan**, all three persons of the Trinity were involved (vv. 10–11): (1) the Father spoke, (2) the Son was baptized, and (3) the Holy Spirit descended on the Son. All three persons are characters in Mark's drama. Although distinct, they act in complete and divine harmony with one another. Jesus is shown, at the beginning of His ministry, to be a person with the highest honor and approval. Throughout the gospel, the opponents' slanders and schemes are therefore unjustified and fail to cast Jesus in a negative light for the alert reader. **The Spirit like a dove descending upon him** (v. 10) is Mark's way of describing Jesus' anointing for ministry. The simile of a dove represents the gentleness, purity, and guilelessness of the Holy Spirit (see Matt. 10:16). In certain Jewish literature, the dove symbolizes the Holy Spirit as well as Israel itself. The picture in Mark may convey the idea that the One on whom the Spirit rested would recreate Israel. **Thou art my beloved Son** (v. 11) alludes to Psalm 2:7, and **in whom I am well pleased** alludes to Isaiah 42:1. The allusions bring together the tradition of David's royal descendant and the suffering Servant of the Lord, respectively. The degrading treatment of Jesus in the gospel does not determine Jesus' true status of honor.

C. His Temptation (1:12–13)

1:12–13. A distinctive characteristic of Mark's style is his use (some forty-seven times) of the Greek word *euthys*, "immediately," also translated as "just then," "straightway," "forthwith," and "anon." Rapidity of movement in Mark's narrative lends urgency to the drama. The reader senses the urgency of the mission and message (see 1:14–15) of Jesus, the protagonist in the drama.

Upon Jesus' baptism and anointing for ministry, **immediately the Spirit driveth him into the wilderness** (v. 12). A preferable translation is, "Immediately the Holy Spirit compelled Jesus to go into the wilderness" (NLT). One might think that the next event in the narrative would involve some miraculous deed or victory, but not so. The Father's will was that Jesus be **tempted of Satan** (v. 13) for a time. Nevertheless, divine resources were adequate for the divine plan: **the angels ministered unto him** as they had attended Israel in the wilderness (see Exod. 23:20, 23; 32:34). Jesus' followers today can also face temptations with confidence that God will supply what is necessary for those temptations to be endured (see 1 Cor. 10:13).

The setting (**in the wilderness**; v. 13) and the duration (**forty days**) of Jesus' time there recall the theophany that Moses experienced (Exod. 24:18) and the forty-year wandering of God's people when He led and protected them (see Deut. 8:1–5). A new

exodus was beginning, with Jesus as the new Moses. The severity of Jesus' testing is emphasized by the reference to **the wild beasts**. In Jesus' day, there were many more wild animals, including lions, in Israel than there are today. Only Mark reported their presence in this connection, emphasizing that God kept Jesus safe in the wilderness.

II. Jesus' Ministry in Galilee (1:14–6:29)

A. Early Galilean Ministry (1:14–3:12)

1. Call of the First Disciples (1:14–20)

1:14. Mark did not explain why **John was put in prison**, arousing the reader's curiosity. The details of John's imprisonment are not given until chapter 6. The message of Jesus' preaching at this time was **the gospel of the kingdom of God** (some manuscripts have "the gospel of God"). The kingdom of God is God's rule in which His perfect will for righteousness, justice, and peace is revealed and experienced. In Jesus' life and ministry, the reign of God had come into earthly history and, unexpectedly, overlapped for a time with the present age. In the future, the rule of God will be fully revealed in the final judgment of the wicked and the salvation of the righteous. Now the kingdom is God's saving activity; in the future, the kingdom will be an actual place or realm. In the New Testament, the kingdom of God has both an "already" and a "not yet" aspect.

1:15. Jesus' proclamation that **The time is fulfilled** relates to the hope of the Old Testament and Judaism for God's redemptive purpose to be accomplished. That hope was realized with Jesus' coming, which is why the good news (the gospel) announces that **the kingdom of God is at hand**. Scholars debate the proper translation of the Greek verb *ēngiken*; varying translations are "at hand," "is near" (NIV), "has come near" (NRSV), and "has come." One may conclude that, at least, the powers of the age to come were at work in Jesus and His ministry even if the kingdom was not yet present.

Jesus' announcement of the kingdom demanded a response: **repent ye** (see discussion on 1:4)**, and believe the gospel**. In light of the drawing near of God's dominion, one must make a total commitment of oneself to God, trusting God to work out His gracious purposes of that reign. The verbs "repent" and "believe" are plural; Jesus called for a corporate response from the Jewish people, but an individual response was necessary as well.

1:16 – 20. These verses illustrate what repentance and belief are all about. Mark included the story of the calling of the first disciples to inform his audience what true discipleship entails. Discipleship is a major concern of Mark's gospel, and this is a crucial passage on that topic. The call-and-response pattern and the fishing imagery are powerful literary devices in Mark's theology of discipleship.

1:16 – 18. The sea of Galilee (v. 16) is a beautiful lake, almost 700 feet below sea level, 14 miles long and 6 miles wide, fed by the waters of the upper Jordan River. It was also called "the lake of Gennesaret" (Luke 5:1) and "the sea of Tiberias" (John 6:1; 21:1). In Old Testament times, it was known as "the sea of Chinnereth" (Num. 34:11, e.g.). The metaphor of fishing for people is striking, seizing the attention of **Simon and Andrew his brother** as they were **casting a net into the sea.** The name Simon is probably a contraction of the Old Testament name Simeon. Jesus later gave Simon the name Peter (see 3:16; Matt. 16:18; John 1:42).

Jesus called Simon and Andrew in the midst of their daily lives, speaking to the fishermen in their own language. He called them to a task for which they had preparation and capability; He would supply all that was yet needed (**I will make you to become fishers of men,** v. 17). This was not Jesus' first encounter with Simon and Andrew (see John 1:35 – 42). John 2 – 3 states that they were with Jesus at the wedding at Cana and at the Passover in Jerusalem, where they encountered Nicodemus. They had been with Jesus on a part-time basis; now Jesus called them to follow Him full-time. **Come ye after me** demanded a response of total comittment.

By Jesus' own words, He is an honorable person of unusual authority: He calls individuals of His own choosing to be His disciples (unlike the rabbis, who were chosen by their followers), and He promises to transform the lives of those who follow Him. The immediacy of the brothers' response conveys to the reader that there is urgency in the call of discipleship: **and straightway they forsook their nets, and followed him** (v. 18).

1:19 – 20. The call and response of another pair of brothers, James and John, was also urgent: **he called them: and they left** (v. 20), not only their fishing business (which was evidently thriving, since **hired servants** are mentioned) but also their family (**their father Zebedee**). Discipleship is costly, but those whom Jesus calls are called according to their capabilities and are given even greater resources — the transforming power of Christ Himself.

2. Miracles in Capernaum (1:21 – 34)

1:21 – 34. This section serves as an introduction to Jesus' ministry. He is a person of great honor in that He has authority in His teaching, over supernatural forces of evil, and over oppressive powers of nature. Once again Mark created urgency in the narrative by using the word *euthys* four times in this section ("straightway," v. 21; "Just then," v. 23 [NASB; omitted in KJV]; "forthwith," 1:29; "anon," 1:30). The action is fast-paced and intense.

1:21. The village **Capernaum,** on the northwest shore of the Sea of Galilee, was the nearest Galilean settlement to the Jordan River. A fishing village of not more than one thousand people in the first century, it served as Jesus' ministry headquarters (see Matt. 4:13; Mark 2:1). Recent archaeological discoveries have identified the traditional house of Peter as part of a church that incorporated it. A splendid fourth-century **synagogue** has been excavated, perhaps on the site of the synagogue where Jesus ministered. The synagogue was a very important religious institution among the Jews of that day. Originating during the exile, it provided a place where Jews could study the Scriptures and worship God. A synagogue could be established in any town that had at least ten married Jewish men. Jesus, like Paul (see Acts 13:15; 14:1; 17:2; 18:4), took advantage of the custom that allowed visiting teachers to participate in the worship service by invitation of the synagogue leaders.

1:22. Mark frequently reported the amazement that Jesus' teaching and actions produced (see 2:12; 5:20, 42; 6:2, 51; 7:37; 10:26; 11:18; see also 15:5). In these instances, it was Christ's inherent authority that amazed the people. **They were astonished at his doctrine** since He did not quote human authorities, as did **the scribes** ("the teachers of the law," NIV). His authority was directly from God. The scribes had a threefold function: (1) the preservation of the law (i.e., oral legal applications of the Mosaic law); (2) the instruction of pupils who would pass on their teaching without alteration; and (3) to serve as judges in the Sanhedrin (the national Jewish legal council). The scribes' work often tended toward legalism.

1:23–24. A man with an unclean spirit (v. 23) was present in the synagogue, **and he cried out**. It was actually the demon who cried out. Demonic possession intends to torment and destroy those who are created in God's image, but the demon recognized that Jesus is a powerful adversary, capable of destroying the forces of Satan. The title **the Holy One of God** (v. 24) is used elsewhere in the New Testament only in the parallel passage in Luke 4:34 and points to Christ's divine origin rather than to His Messiahship (see Luke 1:35). The demon's use of this name was perhaps in accordance with the occult belief that the precise use of a person's name gave certain control over him. One of the ironies of Mark's gospel is that religious leaders, who should have been in the know, failed to recognize Jesus' identity, but the demons recognized it.

1:25–28. With the commands, **Hold thy peace** (lit., "Be muzzled!"), **and come out of him** (v. 25), Jesus' superior power silenced the shrieks of the demon-possessed man. In the synagogue episode, Jesus is shown to be a person of the highest honor and authority—authority demonstrated in His teaching and in His confrontation with demonic forces. Jesus' **fame** ("news about him," NIV; v. 28) thus spread throughout Galilee.

1:29–31. The intensity extended beyond the synagogue and **into the house of Simon and Andrew** (v. 29). Jesus and the disciples probably went there for a meal, since the main Sabbath meal was served im-

mediately following the synagogue service. **Simon's wife's mother lay sick of a fever** (v. 30), but she was cured by the power of Jesus. Simon's mother-in-law demonstrated a lesson of discipleship: life in the kingdom of God demands a response of thanksgiving and obedience. Upon being raised up, **she ministered unto them** (i.e., Jesus and His disciples; v. 31).

1:32–34. The news of the day's events prompted others to seek Jesus' help for neighbors and loved ones. They waited until the Sabbath was over (after sunset) before carrying the sick to Him (see Jer. 17:21–22). Those who were brought to Jesus were healed of **divers diseases** ("various diseases," NKJV; v. 34), and Jesus **cast out many devils**. Jesus' authority over the demons is seen in the prohibition He gave them: they were not to speak about Him. Jesus probably wanted first to show by word and deed the kind of Messiah He was (in contrast to popular notions) before He clearly declared Himself, and He would not let the demons frustrate this intent. Mark showed that Jesus is able and willing to heal people. His ability and willingness are still available today for those who need His healing touch.

3. A Tour of Galilee (1:35–45)

1:35. A great while before day, he went ... into a solitary place, and ... prayed. Jesus' prayer life was effective because it was planned, private, and prolonged. He got up early enough, went far away enough, and stayed long enough to commune with the Father. The Greek word for "solitary place" is *erēmos*, meaning "wilderness" (see 1:3–4, 12–13), and reminds the reader of the wilderness wanderings where God gave His people guidance and rest through the Spirit (Isa. 63:11, 14). Jesus initiated a new exodus, a new age of deliverance, and His source of power is His relationship with the Father. Guidance (see 1:38), preaching (see 1:39), power over the forces of evil (see 1:39), and miraculous healing (see 1:40–41) all emerge from the center that is His communion with God.

"How can God pray to God?" is a question that arises for some here and at the other passages in Mark that describe Jesus praying (e.g., 6:46; 14:32–39).

Mark apparently did not see a problem with Jesus' act of praying; he offered no explanation or rationale. For Mark, Jesus is the Son of God, who exercises the very prerogatives of God the Father. Jesus shares the divine power and authority of God the Father, with whom He, the Son, is in the most intimate communion. No doctrine of the Trinity is present in Mark, but the basis of its later development is present.

1:36–39. Simon and others **followed after him** (lit., "hunted him down"; v. 36). Despite the prayerful interlude, urgency surrounded Jesus. He decided to leave the area of Capernaum and **go into the next towns** (v. 38). Neither Jesus nor His followers could meet all the requests made of them. The same is true for believers today, but prayerfully seeking God's guidance helps one distinguish between what is good and what is better. Jesus now embarked upon the first of what seem to be three tours of Galilee (second tour, Luke 8:1; third tour, Mark 6:6 and Matt. 11:1).

1:40–45. The story of the leper's cleansing is a masterful piece of storytelling. The action is vivid and fast-paced. In this section, Mark used the "historical present" tense of certain verbs; the dramatic nature of past action is described as if it were happening right now. The KJV preserves this tense with **saith** in verses 41 and 44. Mark's details in verse 41 create suspense as the reader awaits Jesus' answer to the leper's request: **I will; be thou clean**. The conclusion is full of irony: instead of obeying Jesus' fourfold command (v. 44), the cured leper **began to publish it much, and to blaze abroad the matter** (v. 45). One would expect this person of faith to be as obedient as the demons (see 1:25, 34), but he was not.

The characters in the story are well developed. The **leper** suffered from some sort of skin disease; "leper" or "leprosy" refer not only to leprosy proper but also to other maladies. Leprosy rendered one ceremonially unclean (see Lev. 13–14), and lepers were quarantined to prevent the spread of disease. They were thus completely cut off from religious and social life, and those who had the more severe forms of the illness experienced a living death. Often the leper was thought to be a person under divine judgment. In this story, the leper is a person of exemplary

faith. His faith is shown in his coming to Jesus, **beseeching him, and kneeling down to him** (an act of submission and worship; v. 40), and in his words: **If thou wilt, thou canst make me clean**. He did not doubt Jesus' power but left room in his request for Jesus' will to be done (see Mark 14:36).

Jesus' actions reveal not only that He indeed has power over destructive forces of nature (leprosy) but also that He loves. The Lord, **moved with compassion** (some manuscripts, e.g., NRSV marginal note, have "moved with anger"—probably toward the devastation of disease), **put forth his hand, and touched him** (v. 41). According to Mosaic law, touching a leper was an act that brought defilement (see Leviticus 13, especially vv. 45–46; see also Lev. 5:2). Jesus' compassion for the man superseded ceremonial considerations. A similar act today would be touching an AIDS sufferer. Jesus' followers become His hands of compassion and healing as they reach out to suffering outcasts.

The sacrifices **which Moses commanded** (v. 44) were to be evidence to the priests and the people that the cure was real and that Jesus respected the law. The healing was also a **testimony** to Jesus' divine power, since Jews believed that only God could cure leprosy (see 2 Kings 5:1–14). Although Jesus had allowed Himself to become ritually unclean, He commanded the leper to observe legal regulations. For Jesus, the requirement of the law to love one's neighbor (see Lev. 19:18) sometimes superseded a ritual ordinance. Only by following Jesus' instructions could the healed man be fully integrated back into Jewish society. The kingdom of God involves the total restoration of persons, including spiritual, physical, and social restoration.

Jesus' growing popularity with the people finally made it necessary for Him to withdraw into **desert places** (v. 45). The people were still determined to find Him, however, and they did.

4. Ministry in Capernaum (2:1–22)

2:1–12. The "pronouncement story" in these verses, the healing of the paralytic, introduces a set of five pericopes (2:1–12, 15–17, 18–22, 23–28;

3:1–6) in which Mark further established Jesus' honor as the Son of God. Each of the five brief narratives describes a contest for honor between Jesus and His opponents. In ancient Mediterranean society (and in many cultures today), virtually every social exchange outside one's family was such a contest. Honor was the highest cultural value. By contrast, money, possessions, and rank tend to be the prime cultural values in North American society. In honor cultures, the honor contest follows the challenge-riposte pattern, in which one person issues a *challenge* to the honor of another person, who answers with a counterchallenge, or *riposte*. The exchange may take several turns. Finally, honor is publicly ascribed (the *verdict*) to the party that most effectively responds to challenge or counterchallenge. Positive expressions (e.g., gifts) and negative challenges (e.g., insults) must both be answered appropriately; otherwise, one loses face.

2:1–5. When Jesus returned to **Capernaum** (v. 1), news quickly spread that He was in a certain **house**. So many people gathered to see Him that there was **no room** (v. 2) for all of them. **One sick of the palsy** (v. 3). Nothing definite can be said about the nature of the man's affliction beyond the fact that he could not walk. The determination of the **four** men to reach Jesus suggests that his condition was desperate. **They uncovered the roof** (v. 4). A typical Palestinian house had a flat roof accessible by means of an outside staircase. The roof was often made of a thick layer of clay (packed with a stone roller), supported by mats of branches across wood beams. **Jesus saw their faith** (v. 5). The bold action of the paralyzed man and his friends was evidence of their faith. Jesus' pronouncement, **Son, thy sins be forgiven thee**, signifies that He first met the man's deepest need: forgiveness.

2:6–12. With His pronouncement, "Son, thy sins be forgiven thee" (2:5), Jesus had issued a challenge (for challenge and riposte, see discussion on 2:1–12) to the religious perceptions and security of **certain of the scribes sitting there** (v. 6), in the house. According to their understanding, Jesus spoke **blasphemies** (v. 7). After all, **who can forgive sins but God only?**

Jesus knew that they **so reasoned within themselves** (v. 8), that they were silently issuing a riposte to Him. Jesus had extraordinary perception, in fact omniscience, and before the scribes could even speak their riposte, He began to issue His second challenge: **Why reason ye these things in your hearts?** Jesus' challenge continued in verses 9–10 with a rhetorical question. Of course, the answer is that it is **easier to say … Thy sins be forgiven thee** (v. 9), since the effectiveness of that statement cannot be verified, whereas a pronouncement of healing can be. The effective command for the sick man to **Arise, and take up thy bed, and go thy way into thine house** (v. 11) continued the challenge and demonstrated that Jesus indeed has power to forgive sins. Mark recorded the verdict of the observers: **they were all amazed, and glorified God, saying, We never saw it on this fashion** (v. 12). Jesus won the contest in that the scribes could not effectively answer his second challenge. His honor was upheld despite the opposition from certain religious leaders.

Who can forgive sins …? (v. 7). In Jewish theology, even the Messiah could not forgive sins, and Jesus' forgiveness of sin was a claim to deity, a claim that certain scribes considered to be blasphemous. Here Mark used irony. The scribes uttered something the importance and truth of which escaped them. Yes, only God can forgive sins. Since Jesus forgives sins, He is God incarnate who brings the kingdom of God. The scribes, however, did not recognize Jesus' true identity. The reader, however, knows who Jesus is and thus is in tension with these opponents. The reader begins to ask, "Will the antagonists ever see the truth?" and "What will happen to Jesus if the opponents continue in their ignorance?"

The Son of man (v. 10). This is Jesus' most common title for Himself, used eighty-four times in the Gospels and never used by anyone but Jesus. Whereas in the Old Testament, the term may be used in the sense of "human being" or "mortal" (see, e.g., Ps. 8:4; Ezek. 2:1), Jesus' usage of it requires a different sense. In Daniel 7:13–14, the Son of Man is pictured as a heavenly figure who in the end times is entrusted by God with absolute authority, divine glory, and sovereign power. That Jesus used "Son of man" as a messianic title is evident by His use of it (see 8:31) in juxtaposition to Peter's use of "Christ" (8:29). When Jesus referred to Himself as "the Son of man" before the Sanhedrin, they called it blasphemy, understanding it to be a claim of deity (see Mark 14:62-64). In Mark, the association of "Son of man" with the authority to forgive sins (v. 7) and with the power of judgment and salvation (see 8:38; 13:26-27) requires the term to be understood in light of Daniel 7.

2:13-17. The dramatic calling of Levi is another pronouncement story. Jesus was once again **by the sea** of Galilee (v. 13), where He had first called disciples (see 1:14-20). In scene 1 of the story, **he saw Levi the son of Alphaeus** (v. 14), also known as Matthew (see Matt. 9:9; 10:3), and He called to him, **Follow me.** Levi was probably his given name, and Matthew ("gift of the Lord") his apostolic name. **The receipt of custom** ("the tax collector's booth," NIV) was probably a tollbooth on the major international road that went from Damascus through Capernaum to the Mediterranean coast and on to Egypt. Levi was a tax collector under Herod Antipas, tetrarch of Galilee. The immediacy of Levi's positive response (**he arose and followed him**) demonstrates Mark's view that the call to discipleship is urgent and to be answered without hesitation.

In scene 2 of the short drama, **as Jesus sat at meat in his [Levi's] house** (v. 15), a large number of people who were considered disreputable joined those gathered for the meal. Jewish tax collectors (**publicans**; v. 15; see discussion on Matt. 5:46) were regarded as outcasts. They could not serve as witnesses or judges and were expelled from the synagogue. In the eyes of the Jewish community, their disgrace extended to their families. Popular disdain of them may have been more for the widespread dishonesty in their profession than for anything else. The term **sinners** (v. 15) refers to notoriously evil people as well as to those who refused to follow the Mosaic law as interpreted by the scribes. The term was commonly used of tax collectors, adulterers, robbers, and the like. To eat with a person was a sign

of friendship, and Jesus extended that honor to those considered to be sinful people. Levi opened his home so that such people could meet Jesus—still a good evangelistic method.

Jesus' response to the challenge of **the scribes and Pharisees** (v. 16) was effective and maintained His honor. Not all scribes were Pharisees—successors of the Hasidim, pious Jews who had joined forces with the Maccabees during the struggle for freedom from Syrian oppression (166-142 BC). They first appeared under the name Pharisees during the reign of John Hyrcanus (135-105). Although some Pharisees, no doubt, were godly, most of those who came into conflict with Jesus were hypocritical, envious, rigid, and formalistic. According to Pharisaism, God's grace extended only to those who kept His law.

The pronouncement saying ends the story: **They that are whole have no need of the physician, but they that are sick: I came not to call the righteous, but sinners to repentance** (v. 17). The statement does not mean that some people do not need salvation, whereas others do. Jesus' point was that self-righteous people do not realize their need for salvation; as long as they think that they are okay, a Savior cannot help them. Those who admit that they are sinners, however, find that Jesus offers them healing. Jesus brings salvation for all who recognize their need.

2:18-20. In the following text (another pronouncement story), the question of fasting and Jesus' view on the topic arose. **The disciples of John** (v. 18) were those of John the Baptist, who may have been fasting because he was in prison (see 1:14), or fasting may have been a practice among them as an expression of repentance, intended to hasten the coming of the redemption announced by John. The **disciples ... of the Pharisees** may refer to people influenced by the Pharisees and thus may be a nontechnical expression. In Jesus' time, the Pharisees fasted twice a week (see Luke 18:12). These two groups came to Jesus and asked, **Why do [we] fast, but thy disciples fast not?** In the Mosaic law, only the fast of the Day of Atonement was required (see Lev. 16:29, 31; 23:27-32; Num. 29:7). After the Babylonian exile, the Jews observed four other yearly fasts (see Zech. 7:5; 8:19).

In His question, **Can the children of the bride-chamber fast, while the bridegroom is with them?** (v. 19), Jesus compared His disciples with the guests of a bridegroom. A Jewish wedding was a particularly joyous occasion, and the celebration associated with it often lasted a week. It was unthinkable to fast during such festivities, because fasting was associated with sorrow. Jesus is the "bridegroom"; when He would be **taken away from them** (v. 20) by death, fasting would then be in order. In the life of the kingdom, joy is the controlling element. Those religious observances that gave expression to sorrow and penitence could now give way to celebration of the kingdom's presence in Jesus' life and ministry.

Jesus upheld His honor in effectively answering the objectors of verse 18. He also prophesied His death, although in a cryptic manner. Jesus' predictions of His death in the gospel (see, e.g., 8:31) minimize the shamefulness of it: His execution was something for which He had come and which He accepted.

The value of this story for the early church was that it gave Jesus' view on what evidently was a controversial subject: fasting. The practice is valuable as a spiritual discipline in which one can seek and find God's strength and guidance. While the church awaits the fullness of the kingdom of God to come, this exercise of self-denial has value. One's voluntary abstinence for a period of time from certain foods (or from food altogether), from a particular practice, or from a daily comfort can sharpen one's focus on God. Certain Christian traditions advocate abstention in such areas during Lent as a spiritual preparation for Holy Week. The New Testament has little to say about fasting; Jesus assumed that His followers would follow the practice (see v. 20; Matt. 6:16-18), but He did not clearly command it.

2:21-22. Two parables supplement the discussion of fasting. Their common element, the relationship of the new and the old, continues an idea introduced in 2:18-20. Both parables contain folk wisdom. The parable of **new cloth on an old gar-** ment (v. 21) teaches that the new way of life in the kingdom of God is incompatible with the old legalistic observances of the scribes and Pharisees regarding ritual purity and fasting. Such practices were overly restrictive applications of ceremonial laws of the Old Testament, and the result was arrogance and the exclusion of those who had need. The life of the kingdom cannot simply be superimposed on old legalism (whose lack is signified by the tear that must be covered). Without an abandonment of the old scribal interpretations of the law, the tension of the new and the old cannot be eased (**the rent is made worse**; "making the tear worse," NIV; v. 21).

A completely new expression of the new life of the kingdom is necessary—that of joy and a joyous welcome of those in need—otherwise that new life will not be preserved. That is the point of the parable of **new wine** (v. 22) in old **bottles**, or "wineskins" (NIV). Old wineskins have already reached their limits of expansion, which occurs when the wine that they hold ferments. If new wine is poured into them, therefore, they will burst. New wineskins, which provide greater elasticity, are necessary for new wine that has not yet completed its fermentation process. **No man putteth new wine into old bottles**, Jesus said.

5. Sabbath Controversy (2:23-3:12)

2:23-28. The incident recorded in these verses is the fourth of five controversies of Jesus with scribes and/or Pharisees. Following the pattern of a pronouncement story, the account reveals Jesus' attitude to the Sabbath (and the law generally), which was a controlling principle for His actions throughout the gospel. There was nothing wrong in the action itself **to pluck the ears of corn** (v. 23), which comes under the provision of Deuteronomy 23:25.

According to Jewish tradition (in the Mishnah), however, harvesting (which is what Jesus' disciples technically were doing) was doing **on the sabbath day that which is not lawful** (v. 24; see Exod. 34:21). **What David did** (v. 25) in regard to the **shewbread** ("the consecrated bread," NIV; v. 26; see Exod. 25:30; Lev. 24:5-9) is related in 1 Samuel 21:1-6. Although

Ahimelech, Abiathar's father, was then high priest, the general time frame is the tenure of **Abiathar the high priest**, son of Ahimelech. The relationship between the Old Testament incident and the apparent infringement of the Sabbath by the disciples lies in the fact that on both occasions godly men did something forbidden. Since, however, it is always "lawful" to do good and to save life (even on the Sabbath), both David and the disciples were within the spirit of the law (see Isa. 58:6–7; Luke 6:6–11; 13:10–17; 14:1–6).

The pronouncement saying that concludes the story completely frees a person from the chains of legalism: **The sabbath was made for man, and not man for the sabbath** (v. 27). Jewish tradition had so multiplied the requirements and restrictions for keeping the Sabbath that the burden had become intolerable. Jesus cut across these traditions and emphasized the God-given purpose of the Sabbath, a day intended for man (for spiritual, mental, and physical restoration; see Exod. 20:8–11). Whatever contributes to that restoration on the Christian's day of worship and rest ought to be undertaken with joy and thanksgiving. Sports, games, movies, television, computers, and other so-called secular pursuits may contribute significantly to the refreshment of the Christian soul on the Lord's Day. The individual must decide in her or his own conscience the suitability of these things. In any case, worship and devotion ought not to be replaced by such things but rather augmented by them.

Jesus claimed that, as **the Son of man** (v. 28), He had the authority to define, regulate, and overrule the Sabbath and its restrictions because it is His by right. The astounding assertion that He is **Lord also of the sabbath** was put to the test by His opponents in the following story.

3:1–6. In the account of Jesus' healing of the man with the **withered hand** (v. 1), the challenge-riposte pattern is again evident (see discussion on 2:1–12). Jesus issued the challenge regarding the appropriate actions on the Sabbath: is that which effects wholesomeness or destruction to be permitted? Since the riposte was not forthcoming (**they held their peace**; v. 4), Jesus' honor was upheld. The healing of the man was a further challenge that could not be answered. The verdict is not explicit but may be inferred (see 2:12). **The Pharisees** (v. 6) then consulted with **the Herodians** on **how they might destroy** Jesus. "The Herodians" evidently were influential Jews who favored the Herodian dynasty, meaning they were supporters of Rome, from which the Herods received their authority. They joined the Pharisees in opposing Jesus because they feared He might have an unsettling political influence on the people. The plotting of the Pharisees and the Herodians is seen again on Tuesday of Passion Week (see 12:13). Their antagonism toward Jesus from 3:6 on is seen by the reader in light of the honor contest: Jesus had bested His opponents, and their malice resulted from their refusal to ascribe to Him the honor that He deserves.

Whether he would heal him on the sabbath day (v. 2) is an indication that the Pharisees believed in Jesus' power to perform miracles. The question was not "Could he?" but "Would he?" Jewish tradition prescribed that aid could be given the sick on the Sabbath only when the person's life was threatened, which obviously was not the case here. Jesus' presence demanded a decision about His preaching, His acts, and His person. The hostility of the religious establishment, first seen in 2:6–7, continued to spread.

Jesus asked, **Is it lawful to do good on the sabbath days, or to do evil? to save life, or to kill?** (v. 4). Which is better, to preserve life by healing or to destroy life by refusing to heal? The question is ironic since, whereas Jesus healed a man, the Pharisees were plotting to put Him to death. It is obvious who was guilty of breaking the Sabbath.

Mark's language in the short account of the man with the withered hand is graphic and intense. He employed the historical present to create for the reader a sense of actually hearing Jesus' words as He spoke them (**saith**; vv. 3, 4, 5). In the last instance, Jesus spoke only after **he had looked round about on them with anger** (v. 5), thus creating tension and suspense in the narrative. The narrator reveals the inner Jesus: He was righteously angry, and He was **grieved for the hardness of their hearts**. The Lord has compassion even for those who are hardhearted; He is "grieved to find them so obstinate" (NJB). Once again the Greek *euthys* (**straightway**; v. 6) conveys urgency, this time of the danger beginning to confront Jesus.

3:7–12. In a scene reminiscent of John the Baptist's ministry (see 1:5), Jesus attracted large crowds for His ministry. The reach of Jesus' notoriety was greater than John's, however, thus denoting that Jesus is a figure of even greater honor than John. The geographical list in verses 7–8 indicates that the crowds came not only from areas in the vicinity of Capernaum but also from considerable distances. The regions mentioned included virtually all of Israel and its surrounding neighbors. Mark wrote of Jesus' work in all these regions except **Idumea** (v. 8). "Idumaea" is the Greek form of the Hebrew "Edom" but here refers to an area south of Judea, not to earlier Edomite territory. For Jesus' entry into the other regions, see 1:14 for **Galilee** (v. 7); 10:1 for **Judea**; 5:1 and 10:1 for the region across the **Jordan** (v. 8); 7:24, 31 for **Tyre and Sidon**; 11:11 for **Jerusalem**.

Jesus' honor is evident from his widespread reputation, His extraordinary power to heal (even by **touch**; v. 10), and the submissive recognition of the **unclean spirits** (v. 11) that He is **the Son of God**. The time for revealing Jesus' identity had not yet come (see 1:34), and since demons were hardly the proper channel for such disclosure, He **straitly charged them that they should not make him known** (v. 12).

B. Later Galilean Ministry (3:13–6:29)

1. Selection of the Twelve Apostles (3:13–19)

3:13–15. According to Mark, Jesus' custom was to withdraw for solitude after having encountered the demands of the crowds, after meeting opposition, or before crucial decisions. Quiet seclusion afforded Him time for prayer and for His Father's guidance and strength for what lay ahead (see 1:35; 6:46; 8:10; 9:2; 14:32–42). Although Mark did not mention that Jesus was praying on the **mountain** (v. 13), Luke stated that He was (see Luke 6:12). Jesus'

choice of those whom He wanted to be particularly close to Him was a result of prayer. He **ordained twelve** [some witnesses add "whom he also named apostles" (NRSV)], **that they should be with him, and that he might send them forth to preach, and to have power to heal sicknesses, and to cast out devils** (vv. 14–15).

This appointment, of twelve individuals from a larger number of disciples (see Luke 6:13), was to four responsibilities. Primarily, and often overlooked by students of the subject of discipleship/leadership in the Gospels, was (1) "that they should be with him"(v. 14), or as translated elsewhere, "to be his regular companions" (NLT). The training of the Twelve included not only instruction and practice in various forms of ministry but also continuous association and intimate fellowship with Jesus Himself. Jesus wants fellowship and friendship before He wants service. Some ministers of the gospel are so busy "doing" for Jesus that they neglect "being" with Jesus. Just as Jesus' ministry often grew out of His time with God, so Christ's workers must allow service to arise out of their intimacy with the Lord. After being with Jesus, the Twelve were then sent out with (2) the responsibility "to preach," to announce the kingdom of God and its blessings, (3) "to have the power to heal sicknesses" (v. 15), and (4) to have the authority "to cast out devils." (The words "and to have power to heal sicknesses" are not found in some witnesses.)

3:16–19. The Twelve are known from this list and from the other lists in the New Testament (see Matt. 10:2–4; Luke 6:14–16; Acts 1:13 [eleven at that point]). The name **Boanerges** (v. 17), or **sons of thunder**, was probably descriptive of the dispositions of James and John (see 10:37; Luke 9:54–55). **Thaddaeus** (v. 18) is apparently the same as "Judas the brother of James" (Luke 6:16; Acts 1:13). **Simon the Canaanite** (see Matt. 10:4) is Simon Zelotes in Luke 6:15 and Acts 1:13. The best manuscripts have "Cananaean" rather than "Canaanite." The former is Aramaic for "zealot." A fanatical Jewish nationalistic party named "the Zealots," pledged to oppose the Roman occupation of Israel to the extreme of murder if necessary, may be indicated by the term. Some scholars contend, however, that the Zealots did not emerge as an identifiable movement until the war of AD 66–70. The title may still characterize Simon as a fervent nationalist.

Judas (v. 19) has the additional name **Iscariot**, which probably means "the man from Kerioth," the town Kerioth-hezron (see Josh. 15:25), twelve miles south of Hebron (see Jer. 48:24). For Judas's betrayal of Jesus, see 14:10–11, 43–46. The **house** was probably the home of Peter and Andrew (see 1:29; 2:1).

2. Teachings in Capernaum (3:20–35)

3:20–21. Here the scene is set once again for a controversy narrative that puts Jesus in debate with the scribes. In the passage, even those closest to Jesus do not recognize who He is or understand His mission. **His friends** (v. 21) could refer instead to "His own people" (NKJV) or "his family" (NRSV). Christians commonly share this experience of Jesus: a believer's own family members or close friends fail to comprehend his or her faith. In Jesus' case, the misunderstanding was so severe that His loved ones attempted to seize Him, **for they said, He is beside himself** ("out of His mind," NKJV). No doubt they had come all the way to Capernaum from Nazareth, some thirty miles away (**they went out**; see 3:31). The only course to take in the face of resistance from others is to endure in faith in company with God's people (see 3:34–35).

3:22–27. The controversy concerned **Beelzebub** (v. 22) and the source of Jesus' miraculous power of exorcism. Jesus' opponents did not deny His miracles but rather denied that they were from a divine source. The name "Beelzebub" (alternate spelling "Beelzebul," NRSV) is not found among extrabiblical Jewish writings. The name could refer to an entity who was believed to have prominence in a hierarchy of demons. The charge that Jesus was a sorcerer is attested in early Jewish and Christian texts. Jesus used **parables** (v. 23) to answer the charge of collusion with Satan. (In this context, the word "parables" is used in the general sense of comparisons.) Unity and division can coexist neither within a **kingdom** (v. 24) nor within a **house** (v. 25). Neither is it possible, Jesus said, for Satan to oppose his own purposes. Jesus' exorcisms, therefore, were not the work of Satan. Jesus had bound **the strong man** (Satan; v. 27), entered his house, and plundered **his goods** (released through exorcism his captives).

When did this binding of Satan take place? Was it during the temptation in the wilderness (see 1:12–13)? Mark did not say, but the parable makes it clear that the eschatological defeat of Satan, his final defeat and judgment at the end of history, had already occurred. Jesus' victory was already being experienced in lives that had been freed from the Devil's malignant power.

3:28–30. Jesus then uttered a solemn affirmation, **Verily I say unto you** (v. 28)—an expression that He often used to strengthen His assertions (see 8:12; 9:1, 41; 10:15, 29; 11:23; 12:43; 13:30; 14:9, 18, 25, 30). Anyone who has been in ministry for even a few years has probably been asked by a worried Christian, "Have I committed the unpardonable sin of blasphemy against the Holy Spirit?" The very fact that someone is agitated about this sin is evidence that he or she has not committed it. Just what, then, did Jesus mean when He spoke about a person who **shall blaspheme against the Holy Ghost** (v. 29)? The context furnishes the answer: the teachers of the law attributed Jesus' healing to Satan's power (**an unclean spirit**; v. 30) rather than to the Holy Spirit (see 3:22). When a person refuses obstinately and finally to give reverence and worship to Jesus and instead attributes His power to satanic influence, that person has made a grim and irrevocable choice. Such a one **hath never forgiveness, but is in danger of** ("subject to," NKJV) **eternal damnation** ("but is guilty of an eternal sin," NASB). A person who does not accept the evidence of Jesus' miracles (now attested in the Gospels) has not necessarily come to the point where salvation is impossible. That point may be reached, however, if he or she continues in willful unbelief.

3:31–35. After their special appointment (see 3:14–15), the Twelve viewed nothing but opposition to Jesus. His friends had said that He was "beside himself" (3:21), and His opponents went so far as to say that He was in league with "the prince of the devils" (3:22) and that Jesus had "an unclean spirit" (3:30). Now **his brethren and his mother** (v. 31) summoned Him. Jesus' question (**Who is my mother, or my brethren?** v. 33) and answer (**For whosoever shall do the will of God, the same is my brother, and my sister, and mother**; v. 35) emphasize three facts. (1) His relationship with His followers is precious to Him. They are His family. (2) His followers enjoy intimacy with Him that transcends the closeness that they have with their own family members. Membership in God's spiritual family, evidenced by obedience to Him, is more important than membership in human families. (3) Jesus' disciples have one another as spiritual siblings and are able to find with one another the closeness that they may have missed within their own biological family. The story does not indicate that Jesus excluded His family members from the circle of people around Him; they were simply unable to approach Him because of the crowd.

3. Parables of the Kingdom (4:1 – 34)

a. The Parable of the Sower (4:1 – 20)

4:1 – 2. Mark carefully set the scene for the reader before presenting the first, and lengthiest, of several parables to appear in his gospel. The details in these verses are sharp; readers can imagine themselves actually present. Jesus **entered into a ship, and sat** (v. 1). He is described not just as teaching while sitting (sitting was the usual position for Jewish teachers; see Matt. 5:1; Luke 5:3; John 8:2); He was in the unusual position of sitting in a boat on the lake.

The imperfect tense of the verbs **taught** (v. 2) and **said** demonstrate these actions as actually going on. Jesus "was teaching" **many things by parables.** "Parables" (lit., "something thrown alongside") are stories or illustrations from everyday life or nature that are used to illustrate spiritual or moral truths. Sometimes parables are in the form of brief similes, comparisons, analogies, or proverbial sayings. Ordinarily they have a single main point, and not every detail is necessarily meant to have significance. Jesus' parables are striking and vivid, intended to

startle people and help them think in new ways. If one includes illustrative sayings among "parables," as many as sixty-five parables are found in the Synoptic Gospels. About one third of Jesus' teaching in those gospels is therefore in parables.

4:3 – 9. The parable of the sower serves as a key to the other parables in Mark's gospel (see 4:13). It highlights the various possible responses to the message of the kingdom of God and is one of only two parables (see 7:14 – 23) in Mark for which Jesus gave detailed explanations (for Jesus' interpretation of this parable, see 4:14 – 20). The other parables describe, expand, or bring about the ideas of this parable.

The parable describes common first-century agricultural practices in Israel for the production of barley, wheat, and other grains. Arable land in Galilee was divided into strips separated by narrow footpaths. Each person cultivated his own strip of land, scattering seed as he walked along. In that day, seed was broadcast by hand, and therefore some seed would naturally fall on unproductive ground. Seed that happened to fall on the path, **the way side** (v. 4), would not penetrate the earth and **the fowls of the air** found it ready food. **Stony ground** (v. 5) refers not to earth with rocks in it but rather to a limestone shelf with a veneer of soil. Seed that fell on such ground had no chance of taking firm root and developing. Neither was there hope for the seed to thrive when it **fell among thorns** (v. 7). Only the **good ground** (v. 8), earth that was soft, deep, and clean, gave seed any hope of survival.

4:10 – 12. Before giving His detailed explanation of the parable of the sower, Jesus gave His reason for speaking in parables. In answer to a question from His followers (including **the twelve**; v. 10), Jesus affirmed that they had been given the privilege of understanding **the mystery of the kingdom of God** (v. 11). In the New Testament, "mystery" refers to something God has revealed to His people. The mystery (that which was previously unknown) is proclaimed to all, but only those who have faith understand. In this context, "the mystery" seems to be that the kingdom of God had drawn near in the coming of Jesus Christ. For those who harden themselves to Jesus and His message, the parables have the effect of causing misunderstanding and further hardening. The perplexing phrase **seeing they may see, and not perceive; and hearing they may hear, and not understand** (v. 12; see Isa. 6:9) is helpfully rendered in the NLT as, "They see what I do, but they don't perceive its meaning. They hear my words, but they don't understand." Of course, the possibility of repentance is open to those who harden themselves: **lest at any time they should be converted, and their sins should be forgiven them**. Many do not repent, however, and thus remain outside the circle of faith and the kingdom ("So they will not turn from their sins and be forgiven," NLT). The parables of Jesus are invitations to investigate and pursue the way of the kingdom of God. If one refuses the invitations, however, one cannot expect to understand spiritual realities.

4:13–20. The interpretation that Jesus gave of the parable of the sower reveals that it is an allegory, an extended comparison in which something on one level points to another reality altogether. Each detail in the narrative corresponds to a detail in the alternate reality. Some interpreters argue that this passage constitutes a secondary interpretation that did not originate with Jesus, but there is no reason to believe that Jesus could not have given such an allegorical interpretation of one of His own parables.

The parable balances three negative responses and three positive responses. The conditions upon which the seed falls represent typified responses to the good news of the kingdom. The seed that fell on the path, or **way side** (v. 15), represents those who stubbornly resist the message of the kingdom. "The fowls of the air" (4:4) represent **Satan, who cometh immediately, and taketh away the word that was sown in their hearts**. The seed on **stony ground** (v. 16) represents those who **receive [the Word] with gladness** but, at the first sign of trouble, abandon their promising start in the way of the kingdom, being **immediately ... offended** ("they quickly fall away," NIV; v. 17). Their experience is comparable to that of the newly sprouted plant that lacks sufficient roots to survive in the rocky soil. The seed

that fell **among thorns** (v. 18) represents those who **becometh unfruitful** (v. 19) because of **the cares of this world, and the deceitfulness of riches, and the lusts of other things entering in**. Such things **choke the word**, just as thorny weeds spring up and choke young grain plants. Prosperity tends to give a false sense of self-sufficiency, security, and well-being (see 10:17–25; Deut. 8:17–18; 32:15; Eccl. 2:4–11; James 5:1–6). People under duress, as Mark's readers were, often turn to material pursuits in an attempt to find relief from the pressure. Finally, there appear three degrees of good harvest that come from **good ground ... some thirtyfold, some sixty, and some an hundred** (v. 20). Those who respond to Jesus' message bear fruit; that is, they manifest in their lives the very saving power of God. Jesus' promise of the harvest is striking: in His day, normally only a fivefold increase of grain would have been expected in reaping (today, with the aid of modern fertilizers and technology, it is thirty- or fortyfold). The abundance of the harvest highlights the miraculous nature of the kingdom and its effects.

The conclusion of the parable stresses the continual hearing and receiving of the Word plus the continual bearing of fruit that the proper response produces (the verb "hear/heard" [Greek, *akouō*] is in the aorist tense in vv. 15, 16, 18 and in the present tense in v. 20). The disciples may have already become disillusioned about the fledgling Jesus movement: although Jesus had been popularly acclaimed, He had met resistance from the religious establishment and even from His own family (see chaps. 2–3). This kind of opposition threatened to squelch widespread recognition of Jesus as the bringer of the kingdom. The parable of the sower served to encourage Jesus' disciples that despite opposition or lack of response to the good news of the kingdom, good fruit would nevertheless certainly come forth. Mark's readers, who were also suffering persecution and opposition, could take comfort that their witness would bring results. Jesus' recognition that positive and negative responses to the Word occur neutralizes the shame of the cross that some might attach to the Christian message.

b. The Parable of the Candle under a Bushel (4:21–23)

4:21–23. The parable about the **candle … under a bushel** (v. 21) relates to the fact that the kingdom of God is presently hidden from the understanding of outsiders (see 4:10–12). The purpose of its coming, however, is that it might be manifested to the world. The comparison to a practice from ancient Palestinian life makes that purpose clear. The "candle" (Greek, *lychnos*) is the small clay lamp that, burning olive oil, gave light to the single living area of the home. No one lit the lamp only to hide its light "under a bushel" ("basket," NKJV) or under the couch on which people reclined at mealtime. Rather, it was **to be set on a candlestick** ("the lampstand," NASB).

The ministry of Jesus will one day emerge from the shadows of obscurity and be vindicated as the coming of the very reign of God. That which is now **secret** (v. 22) will **come abroad**. Jesus' followers can expect the same for their ministry in the kingdom as well. God will honor their service to Him even when they are apparently unsuccessful. The Lord emphasized His point with His call to urgent attention: **If any man have ears to hear, let him hear** (v. 23).

c. The Saying about Measure (4:24–25)

4:24–25. This saying underscores the necessity for one who hears Jesus' preaching to continue thoughtfully contemplating its meaning. The one who does so **shall more be given** (v. 24). The one who is inattentive, however, shall begin to be confused and lose his grasp on whatever degree of truth regarding the kingdom of God that he had attained. Paradoxically, Jesus said, **And he that hath not, from him shall be taken even that which he hath** (v. 25). Inattentiveness to Jesus' message means that the hearer has virtually nothing, and even that will soon disappear. The saying, therefore, has this warning, but a promise as well: **For he that hath, to him shall be given**. The teaching on measure serves as an effective introduction to the seed parables of 4:26–32: their instruction on the kingdom must be heeded. An application today is that, the more truth is appropriate now, the more it will be received in the future;

and if one does not respond to what little truth one may know already, one will not profit even from that.

d. The Parable of the Growing Seed (4:26–29)

4:26–29. Only Mark recorded this parable. Whereas the parable of the sower stresses the importance of proper soil for the growth of seed and the success of the harvest, here the mysterious power of the seed itself is emphasized. **The kingdom of God** (v. 26), sown as a mere seed in the ministry of Jesus, contains its own power. One day, a harvest will come. Humans cannot do anything but sow the seed of the kingdom. They cannot bring the reign of God themselves, and the New Testament never speaks of the kingdom being "built" by anyone. This parable takes the pressure off the disciple of Jesus to feel that he or she must "do" anything to establish the kingdom. Its success is God's work; people can only act for the sake of the kingdom (see Matt. 19:12; Luke 18:29–30) and preach about it (see Matt. 10:7; Luke 10:9). Only God, however, can give the kingdom to people (see Luke 12:32). The phrase **immediately he putteth in the sickle, because the harvest is come** (v. 29) is a possible allusion to Joel 3:13, where harvest is a figure for the consummation of God's kingdom.

e. The Parable of the Mustard Seed (4:30–34)

4:30–32. This parable, unlike the parable of the growing seed (4:26–29), is also in Matthew and Luke (see Matt. 13:31–32; Luke 13:18–19). Like that parable, however, the parable of the mustard seed emphasizes the paradoxical nature of the kingdom: its manifestation has insignificant beginnings, but that manifestation will spread and become great. What a comfort to Jesus' disciples, who were discouraged by opposition and lack of response to His message.

The kingdom of God (v. 30), Jesus said, **is like a grain of mustard seed** (v. 31), or more precisely, "like a mustard seed" (NKJV). Jesus was perhaps referring to the black mustard, a plant that was cultivated for its seeds, which were used for oil and for cooking. Proverbially, the mustard seed was the smallest of all things. In the parable, the seed becomes **greater than all herbs** ("larger than all the garden plants," NASB;

v. 32). The mustard plant can grow to a height of more than fifteen feet but is usually much smaller.

Mustard also grew wild, and farmers tried to eradicate it from their fields. Here is a further paradox: mustard is, on the one hand, something to cultivate and nurture; on the other hand, it is a nuisance and must be controlled. The mustard, therefore, is perfectly suited for a comparison to the kingdom of God. Hearers would have asked themselves, "How can the kingdom of God be small and yet large?" "If the kingdom is desirable, why is it also like a big, intrusive weed?" Jesus' parables are designed to provoke just these kinds of thought so that people will be drawn in to His message.

Birds are attracted to the mustard plant; they love the seeds, which they pick out of the pods. In the parable, **the fowls of the air** (v. 32) find refuge in the shade of the mustard bush. One interpretation of the parable identifies the birds as evil influences within a monstrous plant that is Christendom. Birds correspond to Satan in the parable of the sower (see 4:4, 15), but the same correspondence need not occur in another parable. Jesus' hearers would not have imagined "Christendom," in which the presence of the kingdom of God coexists with evil. They would have understood what the reign of God is (the subject of the comparison, see v. 30), however. And they would have understood the Old Testament allusions to Israel (see Ezek. 17:22–24) and Assyria (see Ezek. 31:3–9) as great trees in which the nations (birds) roost. The kingdom of God is not exclusive; all the nations are welcome to its shelter. Jesus concluded this parable with a missionary interest that contradicted the nationalistic dreams prevalent in the Judaism of His day.

The way of the kingdom of God is one of small beginnings that become great. Such is the presence of the kingdom in a Christian's life: anything that one does for God usually has a small beginning that takes time to progress (a ministry, an education, a job, a new habit). A person must be patient with oneself and others during the initial stages of growth.

The kingdom of God is also inclusive. Believers should ask themselves, "Is there a particular person against whom I hold a grudge that keeps me from extending the welcome of the kingdom?" "Do I hold a judgmental attitude against a kind of people so that I reject them as equals in the kingdom?"

4:33–34. These verses indicate that Jesus habitually used parables to teach the disciples. He spoke to their level of understanding while **he expounded all things** (v. 34) to them. When alone with His disciples, Jesus taught more specifically than He did to the crowds, but even the disciples usually needed to have things explained.

4. Trip across the Sea of Galilee (4:35–5:20)

4:35–5:20. The two stories in this section establish Jesus' honor in contests that were not against human foes but against the forces of nature (4:35–41) and against supernatural foes (5:1–20). Previous contests with human foes (see 2:1–3:6) had revealed that Jesus could maintain His honor in the face of opposition. Jesus showed that He is a person of honor in His handling of all three kinds of challengers. His exalted status argues against the shame of the cross in Mark's gospel. Not only was His honor that of a human, but in all these contests, He claimed and exercised the very authority of God.

4:35–41. An apparently serene trip across the Sea of Galilee was threatened with danger when **there arose a great storm of wind** (v. 37) so fierce that **the waves beat into the ship, so that it was now full.** Situated in a basin surrounded by mountains, the Sea of Galilee is particularly susceptible to sudden, violent storms. Cool air from the mountains, including nearby Mount Hermon, the highest point in all the Middle East, descends rapidly and clashes with the hot, humid air lying over the lake, which is 700 feet below sea level. The picture of Jesus, tranquilly **asleep on a pillow** (the cushion customarily kept under the coxswain's seat; v. 38) in the stern of the boat, is in sharp contrast with the panicked disciples. After they had awakened Jesus, they protested to him, **Master, carest thou not that we perish?** They should not have been afraid but rather should have believed in His present power to protect them.

The main point of the story, however, is the almighty power of Jesus over the destructive forces of nature. The sea typified for the Jewish mind the chaos of the primeval ocean, to which God brought order (see Gen. 1:1–10). Jesus **rebuked the wind** (v. 39) and, with a terse command, brought an immediate and absolute calm to the lake: **and there was a great calm**. Because Jesus exercises the very sovereignty of God over wind and sea, His disciples may entrust themselves to His protection.

Jesus' disciples exclaimed, **What manner of man is this …?** (v. 41). In view of what Jesus had just done, the only answer to this rhetorical question was, He is the very Son of God. God's presence, as well as His power, was demonstrated (see Pss. 65:7; 107:25–30; Prov. 30:4). Mark indicated his answer to this question in the opening line of his gospel (1:1). By such miracles, Jesus sought to establish and increase the disciples' faith in His deity. The disciples **feared exceedingly** in the presence of Jesus' power. The motif of fearful awe runs throughout Mark and reveals that, rather than seeing Jesus as a disreputable person, very frequently people regard Him with a reverent, though at times a perplexed, amazement— even terror (see 1:27; 2:12; 4:41; 5:15, 20, 42; 16:8).

5:1–20. The second story of the section is the healing of the demoniac in **the country of the Gadarenes** (v. 1). Some witnesses read "Gerasenes" (see NASB, NRSV); others "Gadarenes" (as in the KJV), probably due to a later harmonization with Matthew 8:28. "Gergesenes" is yet another reading found in some manuscripts. "Gerasenes" is the best reading, although the site of the city of Gerasa (modern Jerash) is thirty-seven miles southeast of the Sea of Galilee. Gadara is five miles in that direction. If Mark associated a wide region around the Sea of Galilee with Gerasa, no geographical inaccuracy is present. The proximity of the sea in Mark's account suggests a location near the Sea of Galilee for the exorcism, and the environs of the town of Gergesa are possible settings. Apparently, in Mark's thinking, the town was within a region that might be associated with Gerasa, one of the Ten Cities (Decapolis) to the east of the Sea of Galilee. The territory was largely

inhabited by Gentiles, as indicated by the presence of the large herd of pigs, animals that Jews considered "unclean" and therefore unfit to eat.

5:1–5. Mark's account of the demon-possessed man is vivid, colorful, and full of suspense. The urgency of the situation confronting Jesus is underscored by Mark's use once again of **immediately** (Greek, *euthys*; v. 2). No sooner had Jesus emerged from the boat than a terrifying figure encountered Him: **a man with an unclean spirit**, of whom, Mark said, **no man could bind him** (v. 3) **… neither could any man tame him** (v. 4). He had been chained hand and foot, but he broke his shackles apart. Though the villagers no doubt chained him partly for their own protection, this harsh treatment added to his humiliation.

The shameful and desperate condition of the demoniac is evident: **and always, night and day, he was in the mountains, and in the tombs, crying, and cutting himself with stones** (v. 5). He was continuously isolated from the society of the living— alone in the mountains and among the tombs of the dead—all the while "howling" (NRSV) in agony and "gashing" (NASB) himself with stones. It was not unusual for the same cave to provide burial for the dead and shelter for the living. Very poor people often lived in such caves.

5:6–9. The superior strength that the demoniac exhibited toward others who attempted to subdue him completely vanished when he saw Jesus. Jesus' presence completely changed a situation that appeared desperate. The tormented man, after having seen Jesus from **afar … ran and worshipped him** (v. 6). Although the second verb is at times translated "worshipped" (Greek, *proskyneō*), as it is here in the KJV (see Matt. 28:9, 17: Luke 24:52), the idea is not that the demons gave devotion and homage to Jesus but that they recognized His absolute authority to command them. A better translation is "bowed down before him" (NASB). **What have I to do with thee …?** (v. 7) is a way of saying, "What do we have in common?" Similar expressions are found in the Old Testament (see, e.g., 2 Sam. 16:10; 19:22), where they mean, "Mind your own business!" The demoniac feared that Jesus would **torment** him (that is, the demons within) when He commanded the demons to **Come out of the man** (v. 8). The man's statement is ironic since he was already immeasurably tormented in his present state. When Jesus demanded that the demons identify themselves, they answered, **My name is Legion: for we are many** (v. 9). A legion of Roman infantry was six thousand men. A common supposition in Jesus' day was that if one named the demon in a ritual of exorcism, one could exercise control over it. Jesus' question and the demons' answer publicly demonstrated the reality of Jesus' power over evil supernatural forces.

5:10 – 13. The complete possession of the man by the "Legion" (5:9) is evident in Mark's language: the reader is unclear whether the man or the demons are speaking: **he besought him much that he would not send them away out of the country** (v. 10). The demons knew that they must go wherever Jesus commanded them and were fearful of being sent into eternal punishment, "into the deep" (Luke 8:31). Evidently, the evil spirits longed for habitable bodies and/or residence in a particular locality. The only bodies readily available were those of the **swine feeding** (v. 11) nearby. Jesus allowed the demons to enter them and, consistent with the destructive intention of the demons, the pigs were drowned in the lake after running over the cliff into the water (v. 13).

5:14 – 20. Mark then profiled two distinct witnesses to Jesus' power and authority over the demons. Their testimony was to the power of the kingdom of God and the salvation that it brings. The first witness was that of the swineherds, who **fled, and told it in the city, and in the country** (v. 14). Their testimony was widespread and initially effective: many came to see for themselves what had happened. When the residents of the area came in response to the swineherds' testimony, they found an astounding sight: the demoniac **sitting, and clothed, and in his right mind** (v. 15), completely transformed from his previous possessed state. The Gerasenes were confronted with a paradox: how could this calm and tranquil person be the same lunatic who had roamed among the dead? Here is good Markan irony: the reader knows that the power of Jesus had everything to do with the transformation that had occurred, but the onlookers did not. Rather, in their misunderstanding, **they were afraid**. Not even the explanation of the herdsmen sufficed to convince them that here was something powerful but good: **And they began to pray him to depart out of their coasts** (v. 17). Faithful and accurate testimony for Jesus does not always bring about a good response. The drowning of the pigs seemed to be a major concern, no doubt because it was so dramatic and brought considerable financial loss to the owners (although the text is unclear whether monetary damages were an issue here). Jesus had effectively answered the challenge to His honor brought by supernatural forces of evil. His honor remained to be established through the witness of the demoniac, however. According to their request, Jesus prepared to take leave of the Gerasenes.

The second witness was that of the former demoniac himself. When Jesus was about to depart from the Gerasene country, the man **prayed him that he might be with him** (v. 18). Jesus did not permit this but rather gave him a command that continues to be a recipe for evangelism for anyone who has encountered the saving power of Jesus: **Go home to thy friends, and tell them how great things the Lord hath done for thee, and hath had compassion on thee** (v. 19). This is in marked contrast to Jesus' exhortation to silence in the case of the man cleansed of leprosy (1:44; see 1:34; 3:12; 8:30), perhaps because the healing of the demoniac occurred in Gentile territory, where there was little danger that erroneous messianic ideas about Jesus might be circulated. The Gerasene man is an example of faithful obedience: going away, he **began to publish** ("proclaim," NKJV; v. 20) all that Jesus had done for him. He is a foil (contrast) to the women in Mark 16:7 – 8, who were silent despite being commanded to announce the resurrection and Jesus' plan to meet with the disciples in Galilee. The former madman complied with Jesus' command and preached widely (in the Ten Cities, or **Decapolis**; v. 20) and effectively. Jesus, although abruptly and rudely rejected at the scene of the miracle, received honor through the faithful testimony about Him: **and all men did marvel**.

5. More Galilean Miracles (5:21–43)

5:21–43. In this section, Mark related two more astounding miracles exhibiting Jesus' power over natural forces of destruction: disease and death. The construction is interesting; the raising of Jairus's daughter is related in two "acts" (vv. 21–24; vv. 35–43) that are "sandwiched" around the healing of the woman who touched Jesus' clothes (vv. 25–34). Other "Markan sandwiches" occur in the gospel (see 11:12–24, the fig tree around the cleansing of the temple; 14:1–11, plots on Jesus' life around His anointing at Bethany; 14:53–72, Peter's denial around Jesus' hearing before the high priest). Such a framing of one story around another provides suspense. When the action shifts to another scene, the reader wonders what will happen next. Sandwiching also provides internal commentary: two stories clarify the meaning of one another by comparison and contrast. Both stories in the Markan sandwich of chapter 5 follow the general pattern of healing stories in the Gospels: the setting, the miracle, and the effect or confirmation of the miracle. In both stories, the hopeless situation of each supplicant is emphasized.

5:21–24. Jesus crossed over the sea westward to Galilee (v. 21). **Jairus** (v. 22), who was **one of the rulers of the synagogue**, approached Jesus and **fell at his feet**. "Rulers of the synagogue" were laymen whose responsibilities were administrative and included such things as looking after the building and supervising the worship. Though there were exceptions (see Acts 13:15), most synagogues had only one ruler. Sometimes the title was honorary, with no administrative responsibilities assigned. Jairus's **daughter** (v. 23) was dying, but he had faith that if Jesus would only **lay ... hands on her ... she shall live**. A crowd followed as Jesus and Jairus began making their way to his house.

5:25–34. It was while Jesus was on his way to Jairus's house that a seeming interruption occurred, which was not an interruption at all but a divine appointment, one which revealed even more clearly the uniqueness of Christ. The woman who **had an issue of blood twelve years** (v. 25) **... was nothing bettered, but rather grew worse** (v. 26) after she **had spent all that she had** on doctors' failed efforts. The Jewish Talmud preserves a record of medicines and treatments prescribed for illnesses of this sort. Her condition, probably continuous vaginal bleeding, rendered her unclean spiritually and socially (see Lev. 12:1–8; 15:19–30). The woman could be restored to ritual cleanliness only when her bleeding stopped and the appropriate sacrifice had been made. Those who came in contact with her or articles she had touched would be unclean as well. If married, her husband would be unclean if he had sexual intercourse with her. The woman had faith that Jesus could heal her: **If I may touch but his clothes, I shall be whole** (v. 28). Although it needed to be bolstered by physical contact, her faith was rewarded. She came to Jesus out of the most extreme desperation and found that, when nothing else had worked, Jesus' power healed her because of her belief. Jesus was aware that **virtue** ("healing power," NLT) **had gone out of him** (v. 30), that God had graciously determined to heal the desperate woman through the power then active in Jesus.

Jesus **looked round about to see her that had done this thing** (v. 32). Jesus would not allow the woman to recede into the crowd without publicly commending her faith and assuring her that she was permanently healed. Her healing, to be complete, involved the restoration of her social relationships by His recognition. He assured her, **thy faith hath made thee whole** (lit., "has saved you"; Greek, *sōzō*; v. 34). The woman could therefore **go in peace, and be whole of thy plague**. Here both physical healing ("be whole of thy plague") and spiritual salvation ("go in peace") are meant. Jesus' healing "saved" her in the sense of complete restoration and wholeness, with God, within herself, and with others. The idea of peace in the Bible is the notion of reconciliation and peace in all one's relationships. Mark's use of the word *sōzō* in this context may have signified for his audience salvation from sin and all its effects. The story is still a lesson for today: Jesus saves from the most desperate crises of life.

5:35–43. Faith was also the basis of the restoration of Jairus's daughter to life. Although his daughter was reported to be already **dead** (v. 35), Jesus did not consider His continued involvement in the father's crisis as troublesome. **Be not afraid, only believe** was the Master's response (v. 36). Then followed the miracle that is the summit of the miracles related in Mark's gospel to this point: a dead girl was raised to life. At Jesus' command, **Damsel (I say unto thee) arise** (v. 41) **… straightway the damsel arose, and walked** (v. 42). Was the girl genuinely dead or just in a coma or a similar state, a kind of deep sleep? According to the text, the bystanders believed that the girl had died; they mocked Jesus' words that she was only sleeping (vv. 39–40). Mark's language also emphasizes that she was "dead" (vv. 35). If those who **wept and wailed greatly** (v. 38) were hired mourners, their presence in the house signifies that the girl's death had been confirmed. In this case, however, it is not certain that enough time had elapsed for professional mourners to have been secured. The people in grief may have been friends and family members. Jesus, knowing that He would raise the girl to life, could say that **the damsel is not dead, but sleepeth** (v. 39). From His perspective, her death, being a temporary state, was but a "sleep." Although the girl's recovery was more of a resuscitation than a resurrection, the event foreshadows Jesus' own resurrection and that of those who are united to Him in faith. The story also stresses the necessity of faith and that Jesus is willing and able to save us from life's most extreme crises.

Mark is the only gospel writer who preserved the original Aramaic Talitha cumi (v. 41; "Damsel [I say unto thee] arise"), a feature that indicates Mark was in touch with eyewitness material in his gospel. Only the few chosen especially by Jesus (the girl's parents, Peter, James, and John) witnessed this extraordinary miracle. Those who were outsiders (v. 40; see 4:11–12) remained in their skeptical unbelief, although they may have been among those who were **astonished with a great astonishment** (v. 42).

6. Unbelief in Jesus' Hometown (6:1–6)

6:1–6. Though Mark did not specifically mention Nazareth, it is obviously implied by the words **his own country** (v. 1). The setting of Jesus' hometown is significantly ironic. One would expect greater recognition of the native son, but not so here. Jesus' proverbial statement underlined the irony: **A prophet is not without honour, but in his own country, and among his own kin, and in his own house** (v. 4). Mark's point is that any dishonor that Jesus experienced from His own people did not negate His honorable status. The fact that **he could there do no mighty work** (v. 5) besides a few healings was not because Jesus did not have power to perform miracles at Nazareth but because He chose not to in such a climate of unbelief. His honor was intact.

Despite their astonishment, Jesus' own townspeople and family **were offended at him** ("They were deeply offended and refused to believe in him," NLT; v. 3). **Is not this the carpenter …?** While Matthew reports that Jesus was called "the carpenter's son" (Matt. 13:55), only in Mark is Jesus Himself referred to as a carpenter. The Greek word can also apply to a mason, wood-worker, or builder in general. The question is derogatory, meaning, "Is He not a common worker with His hands like the rest of us?" They saw no reason to believe that He was different from them, much less that He was specially anointed by God.

7. Six Apostolic Teams Tour Galilee (6:7–13)

6:7–13. Jesus had already chosen the Twelve, "that they should be with him, and that he might send them forth to preach, and to have power to heal sicknesses, and to cast out devils" (3:14–15). Now that they had been with Jesus and had seen His power, the Twelve were sent out **two** (by) **two** (v. 7) to fulfill the other purposes of their calling. Sending them in pairs may have been to bolster credibility by having the testimony of more than one witness (see Deut. 17:6), as well as to provide mutual support during this training period. Jesus instructed the Twelve to take **no scrip** (a scrip was a small bag; we might call it a knapsack), **no bread, no money in their purse** (v. 8). Their clothing was to be extremely simple: **be shod with sandals; and not put on two coats** (v. 9). An extra tunic was helpful as a covering to protect from the cold night air, and the implication here is that the disciples were to trust in God to provide lodging each night. Jesus' instructions regarding meager provisions and clothing may seem strange, but the point was for the disciples to depend on the hospitality of the villages that they entered on their itinerant ministry.

Jesus knew that the honor contest would occur every time that a commissioned pair entered a settlement. The preachers would enter a town, and because of their lack of provisions for travel, whatever household they approached was, in an honor culture, required to extend hospitality. That involved lodging, food, and provisions for further journeying. Those who refused to offer such hospitality dishonored themselves, and in the Mediterranean world, an adequate response to the refusal was necessary to maintain one's honor. To **shake off the dust under your feet for a testimony against them** (v. 11) was a public challenge to the mistreatment that the messengers of the kingdom of God had received. Such an act was a vehement insult and rejection; shaking the dust off one's feet conveyed the idea of being unwilling to touch anything that the villagers had touched since it was common or unclean. In the judgment, the messengers will be vindicated: **Verily I say unto you, It shall be more tolerable for Sodom and Gomorrha in the day of judgment, than for that city**. This mission marks the beginning of the disciples' own ministry in Jesus' name, and their message was precisely the same as His (1:15). Evidently, the Twelve received a welcome in some places that they visited: the tense of the verbs **cast out** (v. 13), **anointed**, and **healed** is imperfect. The disciples were continually doing these things.

8. King Herod's Reaction to Jesus' Ministry (6:14 – 29)

6:14 – 29. Having recorded Jesus' announcement of the kingdom of God (see 1:14 – 15), as well as that of the Twelve whom He had commissioned to preach the same message (see 6:12), Mark addressed the reader's interest in the fate of John the Baptist. What happened to John after his imprisonment (see 1:14)? Mark's flashback in this section satisfies the reader's curiosity.

Here Mark may have used the title **king** (v. 14) with a bit of sarcasm (since Herod was actually a tetrarch), or perhaps he simply used Herod's popular title. At any rate, **king Herod** is Herod Antipas, one of the sons of Herod the Great. The region over which Herod Antipas ruled was Galilee and Perea, but his reign was under the auspices of Roman overlords. Disturbed by an uneasy conscience and disposed to superstition, Herod feared that Jesus was **John … risen from the dead** (vv. 14, 16) and come back to haunt him. Herod, who **feared John** (v. 20) and willingly listened to him, had arrested John only **for Herodias' sake, his brother Philip's wife** (v. 17). Herodias resented John's preaching against her adulterous marriage with Herod, **for John had said unto Herod, It is not lawful for thee to have thy brother's wife** (v. 18). Josephus says that John was imprisoned at Machaerus, the fortress in Perea on the eastern side of the Dead Sea. Herodias's daughter danced at Herod's birthday party, something which prostitutes normally did. Her stepfather was so pleased with her that he made a foolish vow: **Whatsoever thou shalt ask of me, I will give it thee, unto the half of my kingdom** (v. 23), a proverbial reference to generosity, not to be taken literally (see Est. 5:3, 6). Generosity suited the occasion and would win the approval of the guests. The hasty nature of his vow is reminiscent of Jephthah's vow (see Judg. 11:29 – 40); in both cases, the one who vowed later regretted that to which he had committed himself.

John was **beheaded … in the prison** (v. 27). His death was by no means a just sentence, however. Instead, the Baptist's death was brought about by Herodias's hostility toward John in response to his righteous preaching against her adulterous affair with Herod. Herod's shameless arrogance led him to fulfill the heinous request for John's execution. Justice had been trodden into the ground by the dysfunction of the royal house. This dysfunction was so terrible and perverse that a mother and stepfather, after permitting a questionable dancing display by their daughter for their dinner guests, honored her gruesome request for John's beheading (v. 25)—a request encouraged by the girl's mother.

The flashback not only answers the reader's question about John's fate; it also foreshadows Jesus' fate. If John was so abused, what would happen to Jesus, who also announced the kingdom? Moreover, Jesus was greater than John and posed more of a threat. Mark again emphasized that a person who dies ignominiously is not necessarily a person without honor. A travesty of justice may be the reason for a seemingly dishonorable death. Such a travesty had occurred in John's case, as it would in Jesus' case also. All the while, Mark's readers, who faced opposition for their faith in Jesus, had this sober warning: commitment to the righteousness of the kingdom of God entails suffering. The realization of this fact is to be prepared to face the onslaught of hostility when it arrives. Any distress that Mark's audience might have been undergoing, however, was itself for an honorable cause since it was on behalf of the One who has honor despite the shame of the cross.

III. Withdrawals from Galilee (6:30–9:32)

A. To the Eastern Shore of the Sea of Galilee (6:30–52)

6:30–44. The story of the feeding of the five thousand is masterful storytelling. Suspense builds and draws the reader into the tale, from the introduction of the crowds' hunger by the disciples' request (vv. 35–36); through Jesus' command (v. 37a), the disciples' incredulous reply (v. 37b), the period of waiting until the disciples returned with the disheartening disclosure of insufficient resources (v. 38), Jesus' apparently hopeless measure of seating the crowd in groups (vv. 39–40), and the prayer for the utterly impossible supply of food for all (v. 41); to the unbelievable provision underscored by Mark's terse climactic statement, "And they did all eat, and were filled" (v. 42).

6:30. Here Mark picks up his story from 6:13 and focused once again on **the apostles** and their minis-

try. The Twelve were returning from a third preaching tour in Galilee and reported to Jesus **both what they had done, and what they had taught**. In Mark's gospel, the word "apostles" occurs only here and in 3:14 (in some manuscripts). The apostles were Jesus' authorized agents or representatives. In the New Testament, the word is sometimes used quite generally (see John 13:16, where the Greek *apostolos* is translated "he that is sent"). In the technical sense, it is used (1) of the Twelve, in which sense it is also applied to Paul (see Rom. 1:1), and (2) of a larger group including Barnabas (see Acts 14:14), possibly James the Lord's brother (see Gal. 1:19), and less probably Andronicus and Junias (see Rom. 16:7).

6:31–34. So that they could get some rest, Jesus instructed the disciples to **Come ye yourselves apart into a desert place** (v. 31). Being a disciple of Jesus does not mean one must work to exhaustion and deny oneself rest and recreation. It is still true that if the Christian worker does not "come apart," he or she will "come apart." So **they departed** (v. 32). John reports that they went to the other side of the Sea of Galilee (see John 6:1). Luke, more specifically, says that they went to Bethsaida (see Luke 9:10), which locates the feeding of the five thousand on the northeast shore. **The people saw them departing** (v. 33), however, and outran them on foot. Perhaps a strong headwind slowed the boat so that the people had time to go around the lake and arrive before the boat. Jesus **saw much people, and was moved with compassion toward them** (v. 34). Despite His intention and desire to retire with His disciples, Jesus had time for the crowd and their needs. Interestingly, Jesus Himself preached and did not delegate this task to His weary disciples.

6:35–41. Two hundred pennyworth (v. 37). The usual pay for a day's work was one penny or denarius (see Matt. 20:2), meaning that about two hundred denarii would take about eight months to earn. **Green grass** (v. 39). Grass is green around the Sea of Galilee after the late winter or early spring rains. **In ranks, by hundreds, and by fifties** (v. 40) recalls the order of the Mosaic camp in the wilderness (e.g., Exod. 18:21). The word translated "ranks" means "garden plots," a picturesque figure.

6:42-44. And they did all eat, and were filled
(v. 42). Attempts to explain away this miracle (e.g.,
by suggesting that Jesus and His disciples shared
their lunch, and the crowd followed their good example) are inadequate. If Jesus was, as He claimed
to be, God incarnate, the miracle presents no difficulties. God had promised that when the true
Shepherd came, the wilderness would become rich
pasture where the sheep would be gathered and fed
(Ezek. 34:23-31), and here the Messiah feasts with
followers in the desert (see Isa. 25:6-9). Jesus is the
Shepherd who provides for all needs so that there is
no lack (see Ps. 23:1).

**Twelve baskets full of the fragments, and of the
fishes** (v. 43). The Jews regarded bread as a gift of
God, and it was required that scraps that fell on the
ground during a meal be picked up. The fragments
were collected in small wicker baskets that were carried as part of daily attire.

Five thousand men (v. 44). The size of the crowd
is amazing in light of the fact that the neighboring
towns of Capernaum and Bethsaida probably had
populations of only 2,000-3,000 each. "Men" are literally "males," as in all four gospels. Matthew further
emphasized the point by adding "beside women and
children" (Matt. 14:21).

6:45-52. Linking the feeding of the five thousand to the story of Jesus walking on the water, Mark
emphasized the disciples' failure to appreciate Jesus'
power and compassion, which He had just demonstrated so clearly. **For they considered not the
miracle of the loaves: for their heart was hardened**
(v. 52). Here was a lesson of discipleship for Mark's
readers, who could see their own weaknesses in those
of the Twelve. The failure to learn from demonstrations of God's compassion, provision, and power
means that future distress will appear overwhelming. If the Twelve had remembered that their Lord
was sympathetic to their needs and could provide
for their needs just as He had in the immediate past,
they would not have responded with terror when
Jesus was **walking upon the sea** (v. 49). Even though
they supposed it had been a spirit ("ghost," NRSV),
if the disciples had truly believed in Jesus' sufficient

power, fear would not have overtaken them as it did
(note that Jesus said, **Be of good cheer: it is I; be not
afraid**; v. 50).

The sight of Jesus walking on the sea must have
been initially fearsome. It occurred deep in the night,
during **the fourth watch** (i.e., 3:00-6:00 a.m.; v. 48),
and popular Jewish superstition held that the appearance of spirits during the night brought disaster. The disciples' terror was prompted by what they
may have thought was a water spirit. Jesus meant
to reveal His divine glory as He walked in front of
them, however, and the disciples' "heart was hardened" (v. 52). Their failure to recognize the divinity
of Jesus, revealed in the miracle of the loaves and
fish, precluded them from believing that the strange
sight that they saw from the boat could be Jesus
Himself. If they had understood the feeding of the
five thousand, they would not have been amazed at
Jesus' walking on the water or His calming the waves,
which were special displays of the majestic presence
and power of the transcendent Lord, who rules over
the sea. Jesus' closest followers were showing themselves to be similar to Jesus' opponents, who also
exhibited hardness of heart (see 3:5). The disciples'
lack of faith thus prevented them from apprehending yet another theophany of Jesus. Incidentally, this
significant event in Jesus' ministry followed a period
when He devoted Himself to prayer (see v. 46; see
also 1:35; 3:13).

B. To the Western Shore of the Sea of Galilee (6:53-7:23)

6:53-56. This section is a hinge in Mark's gospel. It serves as a climactic summary of Jesus' ministry up to this point, but it also introduces the next
rounds of activity, back on the western side of the
Sea of Galilee (**Genessaret** [v. 53], either the fertile
plain along the northwest shore of the sea or the
town of that name). In language reminiscent of the
healing of the woman in 5:25-34, many **besought
him that they might touch if it were but the border
of his garment: and as many as touched him were
made whole** (v. 56). The Greek word used for "made
whole" is *sōzō* ("to save"). Mark may have chosen

this word rather than the word *therapeuō* ("to heal") so that he might point to Jesus' power to save spiritually, socially, and physically. The verb is in the imperfect tense: His healing ministry was continuous and widespread.

7:1–23. The significance of the controversy between Jesus, **the Pharisees, and ... the scribes** (v. 1) cannot be overestimated. Jesus' teaching in this section established a precedent regarding the Jewish legal tradition, a precedent that was reiterated and developed in the earliest days of the church (see Acts 10:9–16, 28, 34–35; Gal. 2:11–21). The statement in verse 19 about **purging all meats** probably should be considered an editorial comment by Mark (as the NRSV does by enclosing it in parentheses). Thus, the participial construction "purging all meats" ("Thus he declared all foods clean," NRSV; v. 19) modifies Jesus' entire saying in vv. 18–19, not just the phrase **goeth out into the draught** ("goes out into the sewer," NRSV; v. 19). Cole's helpful paraphrase catches the meaning: "by saying this, He was abolishing all distinction between ceremonially clean and unclean foods" (Cole, *The Gospel according to Mark*, p. 186). Mark's editorial addition possibly extends all the way through verse 23. The point of the passage for Gentile Christians at Rome and everywhere in the Mediterranean world would have been of great relevance, assuring them that they had been absolved from the requirement of strict obedience to Jewish purity laws.

In this passage, Jesus convincingly set forth the danger of legalism. By focusing on the minutiae of human standards and traditions, the Pharisees and scribes whom Jesus addressed had missed the actual intention of the Old Testament law. The rabbinic standards involving the washing of hands and utensils were very rigorous; even contact in **the market** (v. 4) with Gentiles, or with Jews who did not observe the ceremonial law, rendered one ceremonially unclean. Jesus denounced such legalism in no uncertain terms: **This people honoureth me with their lips, but their heart is far from me** (v. 6; see Isa. 29:13); **in vain do they worship me, teaching for doctrines the commandments of men** (v. 7); **laying aside the commandment of God** (v. 8); **Full well ye reject the commandment of God, that ye may keep your own tradition** (v. 9); and **making the word of God of none effect through your tradition** (v. 13). This accumulation of condemnations highlights the extreme to which the hypocrisy of the legalists had gone (see v. 6).

Jesus' denunciation targeted a particularly outrageous practice among the Pharisees that illustrates their legalistic hypocrisy: the practice of **Corban, that is to say, a gift** (v. 11). "Corban" is the transliteration of a Hebrew word meaning "offering." That Mark explained this Hebrew word reveals that he was addressing Gentile readers, probably Romans primarily. An irresponsible Jewish son, by using this word in a religious vow, could formally dedicate to God (i.e., to the temple) his earnings that otherwise would have gone for the support of his parents. The money, however, did not necessarily have to go for religious purposes. The Corban formula was simply a means of circumventing the clear responsibility of children toward their parents as prescribed in the law. (**Honour thy father and thy mother; and, Whoso curseth father or mother, let him die the death**; v. 10; see Exod. 20:12; Deut. 5:16; and Exod. 21:17; Lev. 20:9). The teachers of the law held that the Corban oath was binding, even when uttered rashly. The practice was one of many traditions that adhered to the letter of the law while ignoring its spirit.

The teachers of the law appealed to Numbers 30:1–2 in support of the Corban vow, but Jesus categorically rejected the practice of using one biblical teaching to nullify another. They were "making the word of God of none effect through your tradition" (v. 13). The scribal interpretation of Numbers 30:1–2 satisfied the letter of the passage but missed the meaning of the law as a whole. God never intended obedience to one command to nullify another.

The teaching of verses 21–23 replaced the normal Jewish understandings of defilement with the truth that defilement comes from an impure heart, not from the violation of external rules. Fellowship with God is not interrupted by unclean hands or food, but by sin. Perhaps the strangest member of the vice list is **an evil eye** (v. 22). During the first century (and in some cultures today), many people feared that certain persons, gods, demons, or even animals could cast a spell or cause misfortune for humans by looking at them. Although the evil eye is associated with envy or jealousy (the NRSV has "envy" here), demonic power is elsewhere recognized in Mark's gospel, and that power may well be involved in a given practice of the evil eye. The attempt to jealously harm others with occult power compounds the sin of envy (**covetousness**), also condemned in Mark's list.

Two very important principles for the church today emerge from this section. First, Jesus affirmed the commandment to honor one's parents. This command continues to be obligatory for Christians. During their minority, children show their honor by obedience to their parents; during their majority, honor is still to be demonstrated. Grown sons and daughters who regularly and willingly visit or contact their parents fulfill this commandment. Expressions of appreciation and thanks for parental care are never overly repetitive. When aged parents can no longer take care of themselves, children give them honor by opening their home to the parents or by doing what they can to help their parents acquire appropriate residential care.

Second, Jesus focused on a person's inner life instead of on legalistic rules. Christians often set up their own human standards of righteousness and neglect the habits of the heart that replace the sins enumerated in verses 21–22 with the fruit of the Spirit (Gal. 5:22–23). Christian leaders are especially prone to legalism: an increase in church attendance, the size of church buildings, the number of decisions for Christ, a workweek of sixty to eighty hours, all can too easily become false benchmarks for spiritual success. The passage at hand is an effective antidote to legalism.

C. To Phoenicia (7:24–30)

7:24–30. What does this remarkable story of a Greek woman's faith convey? Does it teach that Jesus'

assistance is available only to those who are quick-witted enough to come back at the Master with a snappy and effective retort? Was Jesus outmatched in verbal exchange by this woman? Does it teach that certain people are second-class citizens ("dogs," vv. 27–28)? Is it possible that Luke omitted this story because he found it potentially offensive to Gentile readers?

Mark's placement of this event is also important: it comes immediately after Jesus' definition of what is pure and impure. The woman who came to Jesus was **a Greek** (v. 26), more specifically, **a Syrophenician by nation**. "Greek" here has general reference to a Gentile who has Hellenism as a cultural background. At the time, Phoenicia belonged administratively to Syria. Mark possibly used the term to distinguish this woman from the Libyan-Phoenicians of North Africa. Her home was **the borders** ("region," NKJV) **of Tyre and Sidon** (v. 24). Tyre was a Gentile city located in Phoenicia (modern Lebanon), which bordered Galilee to the northwest. A journey of about thirty miles from Capernaum would have brought Jesus to the vicinity of Tyre. Ever since the feeding of the five thousand (see 6:30–44), Jesus and His disciples had been, for the most part, skirting the region of Galilee. In Tyre, His purpose was to remain secluded for a time, but to no avail. Despite her status as "unclean" regarding Jewish purity laws, the woman was exemplary in her faith, which demonstrates again that old distinctions of clean and unclean are no longer valid in the kingdom of God.

The woman is one of the "little people" of Mark's gospel who are examples of faith, often in contrast to the disciples. Her request was **that he would cast forth the devil** ("the demon," NASB) **out of her daughter** (v. 26). Her belief in Jesus was demonstrated by her immediate and urgent plea ("as soon as she heard about him," NIV; v. 25), her desperate reverence, and her respectful persistence in her entreaty despite an apparent rebuff by Jesus. His initial response has the ring of a proverb: **Let the children first be filled: for it is not meet** ("fair," NRSV) **to take the children's bread, and to cast it unto the dogs** (v. 27). Indeed, for a Jew to call a Gentile a "dog" was an insult (although the Greek word used for "dog," *kynarion*, is diminutive). The idea behind the metaphor of the table is that the Gentiles have second claim on the blessings of God enjoyed by Israel. Jesus may have been testing the woman's faith: did she believe that Jesus' concern and power could transcend ethnic distinctions and boundaries? Her answer proves that she did so believe: **Yes, Lord: yet the dogs under the table eat of the children's crumbs** (v. 28). This is the only time in Mark's gospel that Jesus is addressed as "Lord." In this context, however, it may have the sense only of "Sir," or "Master." Because of the woman's unshakable and persistent faith expressed through her retort, Jesus cast **the devil** ("the demon," NASB; vv. 29–30) out of her daughter.

The challenge-riposte pattern (see discussion on 2:1–12) is once again evident in this story, but with a twist. The woman issued the initial challenge to Jesus when He entered her social space (v. 26). His riposte was that "the dogs" have no equal claim on "the children's bread" (v. 27). The woman continued the contest with yet another challenge: even "the crumbs" may be eaten by "the dogs" (v. 28). She had the last say, and gained the honor in this debate with Jesus. Still, the Master retained His honor through the exorcism of the demon. Faith brings with it its own honor from the Lord.

D. To the Region of the Decapolis: More Miracles (7:31–8:10)

7:31–37. The challenge-riposte pattern (see discussion on 2:1–12) is evident yet again in the healing of the deaf-mute. This time, however, the miracle occurred when Jesus directly and physically contacted the person in need, not by means of His powerful word spoken at a distance (see 7:29–30). The itinerary (**departing from the coasts of Tyre and Sidon, he came unto the sea of Galilee**; v. 31) suggests that Jesus went north from Tyre to Sidon (about twenty-five miles) and then southeast through the territory of Herod Philip to the east side of the Sea of Galilee. The route was circuitous possibly to avoid entering Galilee, where Herod Antipas was in power (see 6:17–29).

In Galilee, many people wanted to take Jesus by force and make Him king (see John 6:14–15). Herod had intimated a hostile interest in Jesus.

The description of the healing sounds somewhat bizarre. Having drawn the deaf-mute away privately, Jesus **put his fingers into his ears, and he spit, and touched his tongue** (v. 33). Then, **he sighed** (as He looked to Heaven in dependence on the power of the Father) and commanded the deaf man's ears to **Be opened** (v. 34). Mark's typical **straightway** (Greek, *eytheōs*; v. 35) emphasizes the overwhelmingly great power of Jesus over physical impediments and disease. The man's **ears were opened, and the string of his tongue was loosed, and he spake plain** (see Isa. 35:5–6). Why did Jesus not merely say the word and permit the healing to take place? Why the rigmarole?

In ancient acts of healing, the very words spoken were thought to have power. Mark preserved the Aramaic form of Jesus' command, Ephphatha ("Be opened"; v. 34), out of this assumption. Healers (not professional physicians) touched their clients, and spittle was believed to ward off evil. Jesus adopted commonly accepted healing gestures as an accommodation to folk understanding and expectation of what genuine healers would do. Of course, His power is from His own divine person and not from magical or occult sources.

8:1–10. Although there are striking similarities between the accounts in 8:1–10 and 6:34–44, they are two distinct incidents, as indicated by the fact that Jesus Himself referred to two feedings (see 8:18–20). The differences in details are as definite as the similarities.

Since the feeding of the four thousand took place in the region of the Decapolis (see 7:31), **the multitude being very great** (v. 1) probably was made up of both Jews and Gentiles. As Jesus had compassion formerly because the people were like sheep without a shepherd (see 6:34), He now had **compassion** (v. 2) because they had been so long without food. The outreach that neglects human need for food, clothing, and shelter is not following the model of Jesus. He was moved with pity at others' physical pain and discomfort and enlisted His disciples to meet that need.

The disciples' question, **From whence can a man satisfy these men with bread here in the wilderness?** (v. 4), displays an astonishing dullness in the face of the need as it was defined by Jesus. How could these same disciples who witnessed the feeding of five thousand not even imagine that their Lord could meet the need of the hour? The lesson of discipleship for any age is embarrassingly clear: the believer's forgetfulness of the Lord's provision in the past dooms that believer to fret over and try to muddle through new challenges. Believers often encounter challenges that are simply tests of their willingness to recall God's blessing in the past. The Twelve would soon be faced with the inadequacy of their recollection of His past blessing. As they and Jesus proceeded to the area of **Dalmanutha** (v. 10), the stage was set. The place was south of the plain of Gennesaret. A cave has been found bearing the name "Talmanutha," perhaps the spot where Jesus landed. Matthew says Jesus went to the vicinity of Magdala (see Matt. 15:39). Dalmanutha and Magdala, located on the western shore of the Sea of Galilee, may be names for the same place or for two places located close to each other.

E. To the Vicinity of Caesarea Philippi (8:11–9:32)

1. The Pharisees' Demand for a Sign and the Danger of Yeast (8:11–21)

8:11–13. The unwillingness to believe the obvious manifestations of the kingdom of God in Jesus' life and ministry had led some of **the Pharisees** (v. 11) to demand yet further proof of the origin of His work. Mark reported that they were **tempting** ("testing," NKJV) **him.** Their motive was not sincere but rather one of putting Jesus into a corner by demanding a **sign** that He could not produce. Of course, Jesus **sighed deeply in his spirit** (v. 12) at this stubbornness. Because the request came from disbelief, He refused their demand, although He was capable of meeting it: **There shall no sign be given unto this generation.** Even today, resistance to the gospel is often rooted in a refusal to accept the clear testimony of the New Testament and its requirements

of faith and obedience. With a satisfactory answer to each objection comes yet another one. Eventually, a decision of faith must be made regarding the overwhelming evidence of the truthfulness of the biblical record. Sometimes what seems like determined resistance is simply ignorance of the witness of the biblical documents. An open and inquiring reading of the texts may very well dispel such a lack of knowledge and lead to faith. All believers need do initially with skeptics is to challenge them to read the New Testament for themselves. Sincere doubts are one thing, hardness of unbelief another.

8:14–21. The disciples' failure to remember bread for the journey across the lake gave Jesus an opportunity to teach the disciples about the dangers of unbelief. **Take heed, beware of the leaven of the Pharisees, and of the leaven of Herod** (v. 15) was a warning for them not to miss the significance of the miraculous deeds that they observed Him do. These deeds, like the miraculous provision of loaves for the five thousand and then the four thousand (19–20), were ample testimony to Jesus' power, compassion, and honor. "Leaven" ("yeast," NIV) often has a negative connotation in the New Testament; it is a symbol of evil or corruption (Matt. 16:6, 11; Luke 12:1; 1 Cor. 5:6–8; Gal. 5:9; but see Matt. 13:33 and Luke 13:20–21, where the kingdom of God is compared to leaven). The idea of the metaphor is that a tiny amount of leaven is able to ferment a large amount of dough. In Mark's context, it refers to the evil disposition of the Pharisees who called for Jesus to produce a sign (i.e., a proof of His divine authority); the leaven represents their stubborn refusal to believe. The disciples were already slipping into this sin, so Jesus questioned them as if they were outsiders, **Having eyes, see ye not? and having ears, hear ye not? and do ye not remember?** (v. 18; see v. 21; 4:12).

2. The Healing of a Blind Man at Bethsaida (8:22–26)

8:22–26. The context of the healing of the blind man is important in appreciating the significance of this story for Mark. The link between the myopia of the disciples in 8:18 and the blindness of the man at **Bethsaida** (on the northeast shore of the

Sea of Galilee; v. 22) is no coincidence. The disciples were like the blind man after Jesus' first touch upon him: they could see, but not clearly. They were not completely blind, like the outsiders in Mark (the scribes, 3:22–23; Pharisees and Herod, 8:10–13; those outside, 4:11–12). The Twelve had been specially taught by Jesus (4:10–13, 33–34), but they had failed to understand Jesus' status (see 8:17–18, 21). They needed a second touch from Jesus, just as the blind man did, to clearly see Jesus' true identity. That perception would not come for them until after the resurrection. At that time, the disciples would clearly see (the verbs in v. 25 denote complete restoration of sight: "Then his eyes were opened, his sight was restored, and he saw everything clearly," NIV). Meanwhile, they were like the unsighted man who, before Jesus' second touch, stated, **I see men as trees, walking** (v. 24).

This second laying on of hands is unique in Jesus' healing ministry, but as in God's original creation over six days, He can choose to do things in stages. Giving sight to the blind was another indication that Jesus was doing what God had promised to do when He came to bring salvation (see Isa. 35:5). Note the similarities of this text with 7:31–37. Once healed, the formerly blind man was to **neither go into the town, nor tell it to any in the town** (v. 26) so as not to broadcast what Jesus had done for him and precipitate a crisis before Jesus had completed His ministry.

3. Peter's Confession and Jesus' Prophecy of His Death and Resurrection (8:27–9:1)

8:27–33. While traveling near or among the villages of **Caesarea Philippi** (v. 27), Jesus asked His disciples, **Whom do men say that I am?** Popular opinions of Jesus were somewhat strange; many people viewed Jesus as some sort of reincarnation of prophetic figures from the past. Then Jesus posed the question that every reader of Mark's gospel since its composition must ask of himself or herself: **But whom say ye that I am?** (v. 29). All objections, arguments, and smokescreens aside, this is the bottom line, and all Christian witness and apologetics must

ultimately arrive at it. Of all the disciples, Peter alone answered as the reader knows is correct. The fisherman appears finally to have begun to believe the evidence about Jesus. His great confession, **Thou art the Christ**, is a high point of Peter's career as a disciple, and the confession to which Mark's gospel is intended to lead the reader. Because popular Jewish ideas associated with the term "Christ" were largely political and national, Jesus seldom used it. Of its seven occurrences in Mark, only three appear in the sayings of Jesus (9:41; 12:35; 13:21), and in none of these did He use the title of Himself (with the possible exception of 9:41). Mark identified Jesus as the Christ in 1:1. Jesus answered affirmatively the high priest's question whether He is the Christ (14:62) but defined His identity as Messiah in terms of the Son of Man.

With Peter's confession, the reader senses that perhaps, finally, the entire group of the Twelve might begin to understand Jesus' power, compassion, and identity. But even Peter's insight broke down immediately after Jesus prophesied His coming death and resurrection. The second touch signified by the healing of the blind man (see 8:22–26) still awaited.

Verse 31 represents the first of three prophecies of Jesus' death in Mark (here; 9:31; 10:33–34). It also indicates a geographical shift from Galilee, where most of Jesus' public ministry reported by Mark took place, to Jerusalem and the closing days of Jesus' life on earth. Jesus would now define the true meaning of "Christ" as the title applies to Him. Some scholars discount Jesus' prophecy regarding His own passion. They maintain that it was impossible for Jesus to foresee that He **must suffer many things, and be rejected ... and be killed, and after three days rise again** (v. 31) and that these words were put into Jesus' mouth by the early church as a way to explain His death as something that He willed and ordained. Since His death and resurrection were foretold in Scripture, however, Jesus, as the Son of God, knew His destiny and acquiesced accordingly in the dire events that occurred around Him. If one accepts Mark's testimony from the outset, that he wrote of "Jesus Christ, the Son of God" (1:1), Jesus' foresight is not problematic. If one's worldview disallows the possibility of God incarnate and of miraculous deeds wrought by Jesus as God-man, then there is no room for Jesus' prophecy. Such a worldview is certainly not that of Mark, however.

Suffering and rejection had no place in Peter's conception of the Messiah, which left no room for God to do the unexpected. Therefore, **Peter took him, and began to rebuke him** (v. 32). Peter's own rebuke was rebuked by Jesus, however: **Get thee behind me, Satan**. Peter insisted that Jesus play a role fitting for the Messiah, one that did not allow suffering. By this insistence, Peter ended up playing the part of the adversary (the basic meaning of "Satan") and even allied himself with the Devil at this point. Peter's refusal to allow his Master's suffering (perhaps because of what it might have meant for himself) led Jesus to say to him, **thou savourest not the things that be of God, but the things that be of men** ("you are setting your mind not on divine things but on human things," NRSV).

8:34–38. Jesus now spelled out for the crowd the call, the cost, and the conditions of discipleship. The Twelve needed to grasp this instruction to be able to receive the second touch that was signified in the healing of the blind man (see 8:22–26). **Whosoever will come after** (Greek, *erchomai opisō*) **me** (v. 34) has, in effect, received the call to follow Jesus. The implication is that a person has a choice in the matter of discipleship (and salvation). God's sovereignty and human freedom intersect. The phrase "come after" is typical Markan language for following Jesus in discipleship. Jesus bluntly stated the cost for the potential disciple: **let him deny himself, and take up his cross, and follow** (Greek, *akoloutheō*) **me**. Self-denial is not rigorous asceticism that believes that any pleasure in life is sinful. Rather, it means saying no to one's inclination to self-preservation, comfort, self-justification, and protection of reputation and status. The readiness to share abuse, and even the same ignominious death, with Jesus is also part of discipleship; in this way, the disciple bears his or her cross. This kind of sacrifice, however, is a daily commitment to walk with Jesus; a one-time decision for

martyrdom can come out of only daily discipleship. Luke therefore wrote, "let him … take up his cross daily" (9:23).

The church must not evade the rigorous conditions of discipleship either in its own corporate life or in its proclamation to the world. Otherwise, the church is guilty of fostering "cheap grace." As Dietrich Bonhoeffer wrote, "Cheap grace is the preaching of forgiveness without requiring repentance, baptism without church discipline, Communion without confession, absolution without personal confession. Cheap grace is grace without discipleship, grace without the cross, grace without Jesus Christ, living and incarnate." Rather, he said, the grace of God is costly: "Such grace is *costly* because it calls us to follow, and it is *grace* because it calls us to follow *Jesus Christ*. It is costly because it costs a man his life, and it is grace because it gives a man the only true life" (*The Cost of Discipleship*, rev. ed., trans. R. H. Fuller and Irmgard Booth [New York: Macmillan, 1959], p. 47). Bonhoeffer, the great German theologian and martyr, echoes the Markan Jesus: **For whosoever will save his life shall lose it; but whosoever shall lose his life for my sake and the gospel's, the same shall save it** (v. 35). The great paradox of life is that one can find life only when one gives it up for Jesus and for His service.

Whosoever … shall be ashamed of me and of my words (v. 38) refers to that person who is concerned more about fitting into and pleasing his own "adulterous and sinful generation" than about following and pleasing Christ. That person will have no part in God's kingdom. To "be ashamed of" someone also means refusing to acknowledge his honor and claims to honor. To preserve one's own status and honor, one dissociates oneself from the claimant. Since Jesus claims, maintains, and deserves honor, to be ashamed of Him places oneself in a dishonorable position. One's refusal to acknowledge Jesus and His honor as Son of God means that Jesus will dissociate Himself from that person **when he cometh in the glory of his Father with the holy angels** (see 2 Thess. 1:6–10). The situation in which Jesus was rejected, humiliated, and put to death will be reversed when

He returns in glory as the Judge of all people. The way to honor for Mark's harassed community was not to compromise with the world around them, nor was it to dissociate itself from Jesus and be "anonymous Christians." The way to honor, for all believers, is to live for Christ and to proclaim Him before an **adulterous and sinful** society.

9:1. Jesus' prophecy that **some … shall not taste of death, till they have seen the kingdom of God come with power** links Jesus' prophecy of His death, resurrection, and second coming in 8:31–38 with the transfiguration (see 9:2–13). The transfiguration not only shows that God's rule and power for salvation are centered and revealed in Jesus; it also demonstrated Jesus' power to prophesy His own future. Since the transfiguration fulfilled Jesus' prophecy in this verse, the fulfillment of His prophecy in 8:31–38 became more certain. Jesus' ability accurately to prophesy His destiny mitigates the shame of the cross.

4. *The Transfiguration (9:2–13)*

9:2–4. In the Bible, a **mountain** (v. 2) is typically the setting for theophanies (see Exod. 19:16–23; 20:18–21; 1 Kings 19:8–13), and the transfiguration (9:2–13) is one of those appearances, here of the Father and the divine Son of God. The imagery in Mark's account is stunning and thus vividly conveys that the transcendent reality of heaven intersected earthly and ordinary reality. Jesus' garments **became shining, exceeding white as snow** ("dazzling white," NRSV)**; so as no fuller** ("launderer," NKJV) **on earth can white them** (v. 3). **Elias** (i.e., Elijah; v. 4) may signify the time of eschatological fulfillment (see Mal. 4:5); **Moses** (v. 4) signifies that Jesus is the Prophet whose coming he prophesied (see Deut. 18:15).

9:5–10. The **cloud that overshadowed** (v. 7) Jesus, Elijah, and Moses sufficed as a shelter, rather than the **three tabernacles** (v. 5) that Peter suggested that the disciples build. He may have been thinking of the booths used at the Feast of Tabernacles (see Lev. 23:42). His plan arose out of confusion and awe at the theophany: **For he wist not what to say; for**

they were sore afraid ("because he did not know what to say, for they were greatly afraid," NKJV; v. 6). **A cloud** (v. 7) is frequently a symbol of God's presence to protect and guide (e.g., Exod. 16:10; 19:9; 24:15–18; 33:9–10). The Father's **voice came out of the cloud, saying, This is my beloved Son: hear him**, an echo of Psalm 2:7.

The Father's command to "hear" (v. 7) the Son was especially relevant in light of Jesus' command that the disciples not say anything about what they had seen on the mountain until **the Son of man were risen from the dead** (v. 9). A report of the glorious event would have detracted from the suffering that was Jesus' purpose. So the "messianic secret" here is explainable as something that really happened in Jesus' life: He was Messiah, and He revealed His messianic glory. At this time, however, that glory had to be downplayed. Nevertheless, the disciples still did not understand the notion of **rising from the dead** (v. 10). As Jews, they were familiar with the doctrine of the resurrection; it was the resurrection of the Son of Man that baffled them, because their theology had no place for a suffering and dying Messiah.

9:11–13. Jesus' destiny of suffering was tied to the coming of **Elias** (i.e., Elijah; vv. 11–13). John the Baptist, as a second Elijah, **cometh first, and restoreth all things** (v. 12). His suffering foreshadowed that of the Son of Man. No prophecy of suffering is associated with Elijah's ministry in the end times. What happened to Elijah under the threats of Jezebel (see 1 Kings 19:1–10), however, foreshadowed what would happen to John the Baptist. The order of events suggested in Mark 9:11–13 is as follows: (1) Elijah ministered in the days of wicked Jezebel; (2) Elijah was a type of John the Baptist, who in turn suffered at the hands of Herodias; (3) **the Son of man** (v. 12) suffered and was rejected a short time after John was beheaded.

5. *The Healing of a Boy with an Unclean Spirit (9:14–29)*

9:14–26. This story of the boy **which hath a dumb spirit** ("possessed with a spirit which makes him mute," NASB; v. 17) is one of the most colorful and dramatic in Mark's narrative. The story displays Jesus' power and honor in challenges from a desperate supplicant and from demons, features dominical instruction on faith with an example of true faith by the boy's father, and teaches a valuable lesson for discipleship through a failure of Jesus' followers. Mark's characteristic **straightway** (Greek, *euthys*) appears three times in this section (vv. 15, 20, 24) and propels the narrative forward. The severity of the boy's affliction is highlighted by Mark's vivid descriptions of the demonic torment, made even more striking by the rare and graphic vocabulary in the following list (some terms are accompanied by the number of times the particular Greek word appears in the New Testament and/or with an alternative translation): **taketh** (v. 18; thirteen times; "seizes," NASB), **teareth** (seven times; "throws him violently to the ground," NLT), **foameth** (two times, both in Mark; "foams at the mouth," NIV), **gnasheth with his teeth** (one time), **pineth away** ("and becomes rigid," NKJV), **the spirit tare him** (v. 20; two times; "it convulsed the boy," ESV), **fell on the ground, and wallowed** (one time; "lay writhing," NJB), **foaming** ("foaming at the mouth," NRSV), **ofttimes it hath cast him into the fire, and into the waters, to destroy him** (v. 22), **the spirit cried** (v. 26; "shrieked aloud," REB), **and rent him sore** (three times; "throwing him into terrible convulsions," NASB).

9:27–29. Although the boy appeared dead after the exorcism, **Jesus took him by the hand, and lifted him up; and he arose** (v. 27). Despite the power of the spirit that had oppressed the boy, Jesus met the challenge and further established His honor as one who cannot be thwarted by demonic opponents.

Jesus' instruction on faith surprisingly came in the form of a rebuke to what appears to be a genuine and believing prayer. The pleading parent begged Jesus, **but if thou canst do any thing, have compassion on us, and help us** (v. 22). Jesus' retort, **If thou canst believe, all things are possible to him that believeth** (v. 23) picked up the supplicant's own language "thou canst" and turned the tables on him. The question was not whether Jesus had the power to heal the boy but whether the father had faith to

believe it. A person who truly believes will set no limits on what God can do. He is able to do whatever one asks. Some New Testament manuscripts read, "Jesus said to him, 'If you are able!—All things can be done for the one who believes'" (NRSV). The lesson is the same whichever reading one adopts.

Jesus demanded not perfect trust but genuine trust. He honored the man's desperate (**with tears**; v. 24), honest, and genuine prayer for his son and for his own faith (**I believe; help thou mine unbelief**). The miracle itself assisted his unbelief. Since faith is never perfect, belief and unbelief are often mixed. **When Jesus saw that the people came running together, he rebuked the foul spirit** (v. 25). Jesus wanted to avoid further publicity, as much as possible, and therefore answered the father's plea without further delay.

Next came the disciples' lesson in the matter of the failed exorcism. The construction **His disciples asked him privately, Why could not we cast him out?** (v. 28) reflects an intensive questioning since the verb "asked" is in the imperfect tense. "His disciples kept on asking him privately" (Wuest) is the sense here. The exact wording of Jesus' reply, **This kind can come forth by nothing, but by prayer and fasting** (v. 29), is uncertain because of differences among the New Testament manuscripts. The words "and fasting" are not in some of the oldest and best manuscripts. As time went on, fasting received increased emphasis in the church. "And fasting" is therefore probably a gloss to the text of Mark that reflects this emphasis.

The expression "This kind" (v. 29) seems to suggest that there are different kinds of demons. The disciples apparently had taken for granted the power given to them or had come to believe that it was inherent in them. Their lack of prayer indicates they had forgotten that their power over the demonic spirits was from Jesus. A prayerless approach to the challenges of spiritual warfare is bound to end in frustration for the church, just as it did for the Twelve. When people are demonically oppressed or possessed, urgent and protracted times of corporate prayer by the church are most critical. Sometimes fasting is also required. It demonstrates to God one's determination and perseverance, one's willingness to sacrifice to see His will accomplished. All things, including release from spiritual bondage, are possible to the believing church (see 3:15; 6:7, 13).

6. Jesus Again Foretells His Death and Resurrection (9:30–32)

9:30–32. Jesus and the disciples **departed thence, and passed through Galilee** (v. 30) quietly and privately. Jesus' public ministry in and around Galilee was completed, and He was now on His way to Jerusalem to suffer and die (see 10:32–34). Once again Jesus discussed His passion and resurrection. As He had been doing for several months, Jesus continued to focus His teaching ministry on the Twelve, **But they understood not** (v. 32; see v. 10; 8:32–33). The significant difference between this prophecy and that in 8:31 is that Jesus now spoke of the process of His suffering as having already begun: **The Son of man is delivered** (present tense) **into the hands of men** (v. 31). The outcome of this deliverance would be that **they shall kill him** and that **he shall rise the third day** (both future tense). Jesus knew His destiny and allowed the gruesome injustices of it to come upon Him. This means that His suffering was voluntary, and He thus maintained His honor in the face of it.

IV. Final Ministry in Galilee (9:33–50)

A. True Greatness (9:33–37)

9:33–37. The disciples' obtuseness regarding Jesus' prophecy that He would suffer at the hand of men is highlighted by His instruction on true greatness. As often happens in Mark's gospel, Jesus instructed His disciples privately (see 4:34; 6:31–32; 9:28; 13:3; see also 9:2), now **in the house** (v. 33; probably the one belonging to Peter and Andrew; see 1:29) at **Capernaum.** That Jesus asked, **What was it that ye disputed among yourselves by the way?** does not imply that Jesus was unaware of the subject of the dispute among the Twelve. He intentionally put them in the awkward position of having to face their ambitiousness and confess it, for the disciples

had argued about **who should be the greatest** ("who was the greatest," NIV; v. 34). Their silence (no doubt due to embarrassment) gave Jesus the perfect opening for teaching about true greatness.

In this passage, Jesus was not forbidding a desire for leadership but rather defining leadership in the kingdom of God as being **last of all, and servant of all** (v. 35), two synonymous descriptions in which the emphasis is on others, not on self (the Greek is literally, "of all last and of all servant"). Jesus' teaching is still relevant for today's Christian leader. Oftentimes a believer thinks that the way to influence others for Christ is to give them orders, that the believer always know what's best, and that to listen to advice or criticism is weakness. Many leaders never admit mistakes, nor extend appreciation to others for their achievements, out of an erroneous belief that the leader must do it all and do it right all the time. Jesus instead demonstrated servant-leadership in the object lesson of the **child** (v. 36) whom he took up **in his arms.** To **receive one of such children in my name** (v. 37) is to receive Jesus and the Father Himself. The emphasis should be on not "who should be the greatest" but rather on humble service to the point of welcoming a child. This passage affirms the necessity of ministry to children as people who are just as worthy of adults' attention as other adults are. Working in the church nursery, teaching preschool and elementary children, and leading teens are just as important in the kingdom as ministry to adult learners.

B. Jesus Forbids an Exclusive Attitude (9:38–41)

9:38–41. Not only does humble service involve service to children; it also has no room for an exclusive attitude that refuses to recognize others outside its own circle of ministry. John (representing the Twelve) is portrayed in this text as zealous for the maintenance of discipleship boundaries. In his opinion, only those immediately around Jesus were legitimately to be identified as His followers. **We forbad** (v. 38), John said, an exorcist outside the circle of the Twelve **because he followeth not us.** "We forbad" may mean either "We tried to forbid him" or "We were forbidding him." In any case, Jesus said, **Forbid him not** (v. 39). Ironically, the Twelve were trying to stop someone who was successfully carrying on the very work (casting out demons) that they themselves had failed in doing (see 9:17–18). Rather than being something noble, John's zealous action may have been jealous action.

Jesus' explanation, **For he that is not against us is on our part** (v. 40), serves as a warning to all His disciples against exclusivity. Just because a person belongs to another church or denomination, or differs on some points of doctrine, or worships differently than another does not invalidate that person's service for Christ. The litmus test is, **For whosoever shall give you a cup of water to drink in my name, because ye belong to Christ, verily I say unto you, he shall not lose his reward** (v. 41). The "outsider" who extends even the smallest service to others within another circle of disciples reveals herself to be identified with and included within Jesus' larger circle of citizens of the kingdom.

C. Teaching on Temptation and Sin (9:42–50)

9:42. Jesus' teaching on welcoming children (9:36–37) led to a prohibition on exclusivity (9:38–41) and here to a further consideration of children. To **offend one of these little ones that believe in me** means to cause "one of these little ones who believe in me to sin" (NIV). This is a heinous injustice. Jesus focused on the adult who, by example, deed, or persuasion, takes advantage of a child who, being weaker, is incapable of resistance to the stronger adult. These words contain a dire warning for those who abuse children physically or emotionally and for leaders who are careless about the role model that they present. The "little ones" may also be adults who are either innocent or relatively immature in faith. Nevertheless, the principle still holds true: a believer's influence on others is to be carefully considered. The hyperbole **it is better for him that a millstone were hanged about his neck, and he were cast into the sea** effectively conveys the seriousness of leading children astray. The "millstone" to which

Jesus referred was a heavy circular stone slab laid on its side and turned by a donkey in grinding grain.

9:43–48. The hyperbole of the "millstone" (9:42) is the first of several hyperbolic warnings. In these verses, the warnings concern the need for one to radically eliminate sin in one's life. The treatment of sin should be so decisive that it is as if one cuts off the very member of the body associated with a particular sin. The phrase **if thy hand offend thee, cut it off** ("If your hand causes you to sin, cut it off," NLT; v. 43) is paralleled in **if thy foot offend thee, cut it off** (v. 45) and in **if thine eye offend thee, pluck it out** (v. 47). In each case, the member of the body is closely associated with the sin it practices and so is used in place of it in Jesus' command to expunge sin from one's life. Jesus therefore employed not only hyperbole (exaggeration) but also metonymy (association) in His shocking instructions. The element of shock conveys the seriousness of dealing radically with sin in one's life. **To enter into life** (v. 43, 45), that is, **the kingdom of God** (v. 47), with loss (being **maimed**, v. 43; **halt** ["lame," NKJV], v. 45; **with one eye**, v. 47) is better than to go into **hell** without loss of those things that ultimately destroy anyway and prevent one from entering the kingdom.

The repetitions in this text emphasize the gravity of the situation: every kind of sin is considered, and the terrible destiny of those who practice sin in these ways comes up again and again in Jesus' speech. **Hell** appears three times (vv. 43, 45, 47); **worm** three times (vv. 44, 46, 48); **dieth not** three times (vv. 44, 46, 48); **fire** six times (vv. 43, 44, 45, 46, 47, 48); and the negated **quenched** five times (vv. 43, 44, 45, 46, 48). The repetition of so many words lends intensity and urgency to Jesus' warnings. (Such an effect does not arise in some more recent translations, such the NIV and the NRSV, which omit verses 44 and 46. Although these two verses are in the majority of manuscripts, major early witnesses to the original reading of Mark 9 do not include these verses. They are included by several early church fathers, however.)

"Hell" (vv. 43, 45, 47) is *geenna*, Gehenna ("the valley of the sons of Hinnom"; see discussion on Matt. 5:22). This valley near Jerusalem was once the site of abhorrent sacrifices of children by fire to Molech (see 2 Kings 23:10; 2 Chron. 28:3; 33:6; Jer. 7:31; 32:35). Later, the area was a smoldering dump, where fires and worms perpetually consumed the garbage and offal of the city. It thus had become an apt image for the place of eternal punishment by the time of Jesus. Isaiah 66:24 speaks of sinners who have perished, whose "worm shall not die, neither shall their fire be quenched"—the punishment for rebellion against God. As the final word of Isaiah's message, the passage became familiar as a picture of endless destruction. The Bible clearly teaches the reality of eternal judgment for those who practice sin and refuse to repent in faith. Jesus' words are a warning, however, not a condemnation. The person who hesitates to follow Christ because of his or her disinclination to forsake a particular sin should hear these words. Likewise for a Christian who refuses to deal with a sinful habit.

9:49–50. The saying about **salt** (vv. 49–50) corresponds to the discussion of judgment in 9:43–48. The saying may mean that everyone who enters hell will suffer its fire, or (if only loosely connected with the preceding passage) it may mean that every Christian in this life can expect to undergo the fire of suffering and purification. **For every one shall be salted with fire** (v. 49) is metaphorical: the fire as judgment (see 1 Cor. 3:13) will thoroughly test every person and their work, as if they were permeated with fire just as food is permeated with salt. In other words, **every sacrifice shall be salted with salt.**

Jesus affirmed the disciples to be salt and the possibility of that salt going bad. Matthew wrote, "Ye are the salt of the earth: but if the salt have lost his savour, wherewith shall it be salted?" (Matt. 5:13). The idea of salt becoming insipid is the same here in Mark. Jesus is warning His disciples against the power of sin to corrupt one's spiritual life, thus infecting the whole community. Such corrupting influences are to be "cut off" (see 9:43–48), drastically removed from the community. Such extreme measures are not unknown in the New Testament (see Matt. 18:15–17; 1 Cor. 5:1–13; 2 Thess. 3:14–15). To **Have salt in yourselves** (v. 50) points to the main-

tenance of the positive influence that Jesus' disciples exerted toward one another and toward the "little ones." Only by guarding against contaminating influences can citizens of the kingdom **have peace one with another.** A disciple of Jesus is marked by his or her diligence to maintain harmonious relationships with others through extending and seeking forgiveness, showing honor and appreciation, praying for others, and developing nondefensive openness to advice and criticism.

V. Jesus' Ministry in Judea and Perea (chap. 10)

A. Teaching concerning Divorce (10:1–12)

10:1–12. In this passage, the discussion involving three parties (Jesus, the Pharisees, and the disciples) may follow an early threefold pattern of Jewish debate: (1) a question from an opponent (v. 2); (2) a public response that answers the opponent only partially (vv. 3–9); and (3) a private elaboration to one's followers (vv. 10–12).

10:1. Jesus' travels now took Him **into the coasts of Judea by the farther side of Jordan** (v. 1). "Judea" is the Greek and Roman equivalent to the Old Testament land of Judah, essentially the southern part of the Holy Land (now exclusive of Idumea), which formerly had been the southern kingdom. Jesus' journey took Him south from Capernaum, over the mountains of Samaria into Judea, and then east across the Jordan into Perea, where He was in the territory of Herod Antipas.

10:2. Stage 1 of the debate (see discussion on 10:1–12) consists of the question posed by Jesus' opponents. **The Pharisees came to him, and asked him** about divorce: **Is it lawful for a man to put away** ("divorce," NKJV) **his wife?** Their intention was hostile, however; they were once again attempting to trap Him. It was for unlawful divorce and remarriage that John the Baptist denounced Herod Antipas and Herodias (see 6:17–18), and this rebuke cost him first imprisonment and then his life. Jesus was now within Herod's jurisdiction, and the Pharisees may have hoped that Jesus' reply would cause the tetrarch to seize Him as he had John. Jews of that day generally agreed that divorce was lawful, the only debated issue was the proper grounds for it.

10:3 – 9. Stage 2 of the debate consists of Jesus' public answer. He immediately turned the tables and put His questioners on the defensive with a question of His own. His honor was upheld in that Jesus effectively parried the challenge and had the last word that could not be successfully countered. The Lord inquired, **What did Moses command you?** (v. 3). The opponents were correct in their answer that Moses permitted a woman to be given **a bill of divorcement** (v. 4). However, the Mosaic legislation (see Deut. 24:1) was not a license for people simply to bail out of a difficult marriage; it was meant to release a woman from an irremediably oppressive situation. The bill was a means of grace that allowed women, socially unequal to men in Israel, to be free to marry again. Divorce was an accommodation to human weakness and was used to bring order in a society that had disregarded God's will. The purpose of Deuteronomy 24:1 was not to make divorce acceptable but to reduce the hardship of its consequences. **For the hardness of your heart** (a husband's callousness) **he wrote you this precept** (v. 5), Jesus said. God's original intention in the creation of **male and female** (v. 6) is that **they twain** ("the two," NKJV) **shall be one flesh** (v. 8). The marital union, especially signified by sexual intercourse, is to be permanent (**let not man put asunder**; v. 9).

10:10 – 12. Stage 3 of the debate consists of Jesus' instruction to the disciples in private. If this is the elaboration stage of traditional Jewish debate, we must understand verses 11 – 12 to be explanatory. **Whosoever shall put away his wife, and marry another, committeth adultery against her** (v. 11) would thus pinpoint the specific circumstances to which Jesus was referring in His public response. If 10:9 is restricted to those marriages formed under the special guidance of the Holy Spirit, who works within citizens of the kingdom, verses 11 – 12 apply only to disciples. If 10:9 refers to the institution of marriage in general, however, then these verses impose universal obligation. Jesus may have been addressing the practice of divorce with the purpose of remarriage

to another. He did not nullify the Mosaic permission to divorce but did disallow subsequent remarriage. Hence, according to the Markan text, one who divorces his or her spouse must remain single. (For Jesus' exception to this rule, see discussions on Matt. 5:32; 19:9. Another exception may be 1 Cor. 7:15.)

In Jewish culture, only the man traditionally was allowed to initiate divorce proceedings. By Jesus' day, however, Jewish women in Israel may have occasionally exercised the right of writing a bill of divorce and pronouncing the standard divorce formula. Jesus' instructions therefore concern a divorce initiated by either spouse: **And if a woman shall put away her husband, and be married to another, she committeth adultery** (v. 12). In this historical and geographical context, Jesus' pronouncements confirmed John the Baptist's bold denunciation of Herod Antipas and Herodias (see 6:17 – 19) and equally condemned them. The society of Mark's Roman audience allowed either husband or wife to file for legal divorce. Jesus forbade either husband or wife from divorcing in order to remarry. In verse 11, the words "against her" could also be translated "with her." In the first case, Jesus indicated adultery *against* the wife who is divorced; in the second, the man commits adultery *with* the new partner.

Pastors and counselors too often overlook the permission of divorce that Jesus recognized in this text and advise a woman to remain in an abusive marriage in which her health or life (and that of her children) are in danger. Divorce, according to Jesus, is clearly not in God's original plan for marriage. In a fallen world, however, it may have to occur as a recognition of human callousness and of the irredeemable nature of the marital breakdown. Only as a last resort should divorce be counseled or contemplated. Although Mark did not envisage a situation in which remarriage is legitimate, the text may leave open that possibility if the remarriage is not the purpose of the divorce in the first place. At any rate, Jesus' other teaching on divorce (see Matt. 5:32; 19:9) must be considered also.

Anglican and Episcopal churches around the world are debating the consequences of the consecration of an openly gay American bishop. Any such debate must consider the words of Jesus on marriage in Mark 10–12. Although the passage does not directly address the issue of homosexual bishops or gay/lesbian unions, marriage as monogamous, heterosexual, and permanent is the paradigm of Jesus, one that affirms the divinely intended order in creation (Gen. 1:27; 2:24; 5:2).

B. Teaching concerning Children (10:13–16)

10:13–16. Mark's narrative proceeds from the sanctity of marriage to the privileged status and example of children in the kingdom of God. The brief story in these verses constitutes an honor contest (see discussion on 2:1–12). When children were brought to Jesus for Him to touch (as a blessing, see v. 16), the disciples perceived some kind of threat to the apostolic company and the Master's ministry. They judged these children to be unworthy of Jesus' attention. The disciples issued a challenge: **his disciples rebuked those that brought them** (v. 13). The antecedent of "them" is not clear in some very early witnesses; later scribes apparently replaced "them" (see NASB, NIV) with "those that brought them." Jesus **was much displeased** (v. 14) with this action and came to the defense of the children. He answered with the riposte **Suffer** ("Permit," NASB) **the little children to come unto me, and forbid them not**. No one could answer His riposte in this story; He upheld the honor of the parents and/or children and shamed the disciples for their harshness. Jesus gave a specific reason for His command: **for of such is the kingdom of God**. The kingdom belongs to people who have the same utter sense of dependence upon God (**receive the kingdom of God as a little child**; v. 15) as children have upon their parents. The kingdom may be entered only by those who know they are helpless, without claim or merit.

This text is a complete endorsement by Jesus of the importance of ministry to children. Many in the church regard "real" ministry as involving adults. Since adults pay the bulk of tithes and offerings to support the church, children are often regarded as having little to contribute. The honored place of children in the kingdom of God means, however, that they have much to teach the church about faith. Children are not just "the church of tomorrow"; they are of inestimable value to Jesus today and deserve every opportunity to be taught the ways of the kingdom. Parenting, teaching of children, and caregiving of youngsters should be valued as ways to "suffer the little children to come" to Jesus.

C. The Rich Young Ruler and Teaching on Wealth (10:17–31)

10:17–22. Discussion of wealth in two separate units comprise this section. First, Jesus engaged in discussion with one who **came … running, and kneeled** (v. 17). Mark does not identify the man, but Luke 18:18 calls him a "ruler," meaning he was probably a member of an official council or court, and Matthew 19:20 says he was "young." The acquisition of eternal life was his concern (**Good Master, what shall I do that I may inherit eternal life?**). With Jesus' objection, **Why callest thou me good? there is none good but one, that is, God** (v. 18), He was not denying His own goodness but was forcing the man to recognize that his only hope was in total reliance on God, who alone can give eternal life. Jesus may also have been encouraging the young man to consider the full identity and nature of the one he was addressing.

In verse 19–21, Jesus did not invalidate the Decalogue (the Ten Commandments). Rather, by forcing the inquirer to choose between treasure on earth and **treasure in heaven** (v. 21), He defined the condition of eternal life to be a matter of the heart and its affections. **Come, take up the cross, and follow me** (elsewhere defined as faith in the New Testament) becomes the condition for eternal life; the fulfillment of the commands is its solid evidence in a person's life. The prohibition of fraud may have represented the tenth commandment (against covetousness). If so, Jesus here mentioned all six commandments that prohibit wrong actions and attitudes against one's fellowman (see Exod. 20:12–16; Deut. 5:16–21). **All these have I observed** (v. 20). The inquirer probably spoke sincerely, because for him keeping the law was a matter of external conformity. That the law also required inner obedience, which no one can fully satisfy, apparently escaped him completely. Paul spoke of having had a similar outlook before his conversion (see Phil. 3:6). The rich man's observance of the commandments **from my youth** (v. 20) is probably a reference to the age of thirteen, when a Jewish boy assumed personal responsibility for obeying the commandments.

Jesus' command to **sell whatsoever thou hast, and give to the poor** (v. 21) originated in His love for the seeker. It was obligatory upon the rich man only (**One thing thou lackest**). The injunction would apply to others only if their riches are the focus of their lives to the point that they would not part with them even if their souls were at stake. The story has a tragic outcome: the rich man was **sad** (v. 22) at Jesus' demands and **went away grieved** since he was unwilling to part with his many **possessions**. "Sad" and "grieved" are both strong terms to describe the man's response. The first term is used in Matthew 16:3 to describe an "overcast" (NIV) sky, and can be used of a gloomy appearance ("the man's face clouded at these words," TCNT Mark 10:22). The Greek word for "grieved" (*lypoumenos*) could be translated to be "in heaviness" (1 Peter 1:6) or to be "with a heavy heart" (NEB). The tragic decision to turn away reflected the man's greater love for his possessions than for eternal life ("treasure in heaven"; v. 21).

Money (and the comfort, possessions, and prestige that it can acquire) keeps many from coming to Christ initially or from continuing in the way of discipleship. A good test of one's attitude toward wealth is the degree to which one is actively sharing it to meet needs. Regular financial support of one's church and of outreach to the poor demonstrates that wealth has not gained mastery over a person, but that he or she has mastery over it.

10:23–25. The necessity and difficulty of coming to terms with riches was Jesus' point in these verse. The urgency of this matter is apparent in Jesus' repetition of the point: **How hardly** ("hard," NKJV) **shall they that have riches enter into the kingdom of God!** (v. 23; with variations in v. 24) and in His hyperbole, **It is easier for a camel to go through the eye of a needle, than for a rich man to enter into the kingdom of God** (v. 25). The camel was the largest animal found in the Holy Land. The vivid contrast between the largest animal and the smallest opening represents what, humanly speaking, is impossible.

10:26–27. Who then can be saved? (v. 26), exclaimed the disciples. Jesus' rejoinder was, **With men it is impossible, but not with God** (v. 27). Salvation is totally the work of God. Every attempt to enter the kingdom on the basis of human achievement or merit is futile. Apart from the grace of God, no one can be saved. Through Jesus' life and ministry, the kingdom of God broke into human history and can now reach even the most unreachable. As demonstrated in the story of the rich ruler (10:17–22), a willingness to be reached must be present, however, for the kingdom to manifest itself in an individual's life.

10:28–31. Peter's claim, **Lo, we have left all, and have followed thee** (v. 28), was not disputed by Jesus. It accurately expressed the sacrifice that the Twelve had made in behalf of their Lord. The claim, since it contains Mark's characteristic term of discipleship ("follow"; Greek *akoloutheō*), contains an indispensable condition for life in the kingdom of God. Jesus' list of sacrifices for His **sake, and the gospel's** (v. 29), whether **house, or brethren, or sisters, or father, or mother, or wife, or children, or lands**, is not exhaustive, nor is it in every case obligatory (Peter maintained his family after deciding to follow Jesus; see Mark 1:29–30). The call of Jesus upon a person might temporarily or permanently involve a separation from family, home, and present livelihood. In such cases, the disciple receives more than enough to make up for any loss incurred: **an hundredfold now in this time** (v. 30). With this provision, however, the disciple must be ready for **persecutions**. The life of discipleship is a combination of promise and persecution, blessing and suffering. God takes nothing from a Christian without making multiplied restoration in a new and glorious form.

The maxim with which Jesus concluded this section on wealth could be a warning against pride in sacrificial accomplishments (an attitude that Peter may have manifested, see v. 28). More likely, the saying speaks of the reversal of honorable status that the kingdom of God effects. Those who presently are honored and enjoy the benefits of this life (**first**; v. 31) will find themselves in a place of disadvantage (**last**). Jesus' followers now appear to have nothing, having forsaken whatever advantages they had in this present world to follow Jesus. They are **last**, but they shall be **first**.

D. Prophecy of Jesus' Death (10:32 – 34)

10:32 – 34. The importance of this brief section is the link it provides between the preceding discussion of discipleship and wealth (10:13 – 31) and the following discussion of discipleship and humble service (10:35 – 45). This last journey **in the way going up to Jerusalem** (v. 32) began in a city called Ephraim (see John 11:54) and took Jesus into Galilee (see Luke 17:11), south through Perea to Jericho (see Luke 18:35), then to Bethany (see Luke 19:29), and finally to Jerusalem (see Luke 19:41). Those who **followed**, probably pilgrims on their way to observe the Passover in Jerusalem, **were amazed** and **afraid**. The note of fearful wonder runs throughout Mark's gospel.

In the hearing of the Twelve, Jesus foretold His suffering, His cross, and His resurrection—a third forecast of His destiny (see 8:31; 9:9 – 13). The threefold prophecy shows that Jesus was in control of His fate and was not robbed of His honor by others. The word "crucify" does not occur in any of the passion prophecies in Mark's gospel, but the statement that Jesus would be handed over to Gentiles to be killed by them suggests crucifixion, since this was the usual means of Roman execution of non-Romans. The absolute control that Jesus had over His destiny is demonstrated by Mark's threefold witness to it: the Old Testament law maintains that "A matter must be established by the testimony of two or three witnesses" (Deut. 19:15 NIV). Jesus' death and resurrection were an incontrovertible element of God's plan for the salvation of humanity.

E. A Request of Two Brothers (10:35 – 45)

10:35 – 45. This passage and 9:33 – 37 both deal with true greatness, and both follow a prophecy of Jesus' suffering and death. Both also show how spiritually undiscerning the disciples were. The irony in this section is stunning: immediately after Jesus foretold His own gruesome fate, James and John (the sons of Zebedee; see 1:19; 3:17) came with a request to be co-rulers with Him in His **glory** (v. 37). Their request was not only audacious (**Master, we would that thou shouldest do for us whatsoever we shall desire**; v. 35); it also showed their complete unwillingness to hear and share Jesus' suffering (see 10:32 – 34). One might have expected the disciples to be more attuned to the necessity of self-denial by this time (see 8:34), but not so. The brothers' petition did not express confidence in Jesus' future triumph after suffering; it revealed their abject greed for positions of prestige and power (to sit at His **right hand** and **left hand**; v. 37) above others. Mark recorded that **when the ten heard it, they began to be much displeased** ("began to feel indignant," NASB) **with James and John** (v. 41), not merely because James and John were so unspiritual, but possibly because they desired the positions of prestige and power for themselves. Apparently, all the disciples sorely lacked even a basic grasp of true leadership in the kingdom.

To **drink of the cup that I drink of** (v. 38) is a Jewish expression that means to share someone's fate. In the Old Testament, the cup of wine was a common metaphor for God's wrath against human sin and rebellion (see Ps. 75:8; Isa. 51:17 – 23; Jer. 25:15 – 28; 49:12; 51:7). Accordingly, the cup Jesus had to drink refers to divine punishment of sins that He bore in place of sinful humankind (see 10:45; 14:36). In the words **be baptized with the baptism that I am baptized with**, the image of baptism is parallel to that of the cup; thus Jesus was referring to His suffering and death as a baptism (see Luke 12:50). The brothers were ambitious (**We can**; v. 39), and Jesus affirmed that they would share a fate similar to His. He could not promise them, however, that their request for positions of honor would be granted (**is not mine to give**; v. 40). Jesus would not usurp His Father's authority.

Here Jesus defined greatness, not in terms of power but in terms of service. His own life was the model for leadership that the disciples were to imitate; they were not to imitate those **accounted to rule over the Gentiles** (v. 42). In relationship to those who are led, such rulers **exercise lordship over them; and … exercise authority upon them** (lit., "lord it down" and "use power down" on their subjects; v. 42). Contrary to such tyranny, Jesus said, **Whosoever will be great** (chiefest) **among you, shall be** (the) **minister** (v. 43) and **servant** ("slave," NIV) **of all** (v. 44). Since Jesus as the **Son of man came not to be ministered unto, but to minister** ("did not come to be served, but to serve," NKJV), **and to give his life a ransom for many** (v. 45), His followers should do likewise. The Christian leader serves others by tolerating others' imperfections, by readily forgiving and seeking forgiveness of others, by desiring and seeking to recognize others before being recognized, by using persuasion and not coercion, and by listening to criticism in a spirit of openness.

"Ransom" (Greek, *lytron*; v. 45) is a word that refers to the purchase of a slave's freedom. In this case, the ransom "for ['instead of,' 'in place of'] many" means freedom for the many from the guilt, penalty, and power of sin. One should not press the metaphor too far so that the Devil is seen as the one to whom the ransom is paid. The idea is that God's justice is fully satisfied by Jesus' willing sacrifice on behalf of sinful humanity. Verse 45 is a key verse in Mark's gospel. Jesus came to this world as a servant—indeed, the Servant—who would suffer and die for humanity's redemption, as Isaiah clearly prophesied (see Isa. 52:13–53:12).

F. Restoration of Bartimeus's Sight (10:46–52)

10:46–52. Jericho (v. 46) is a very ancient city located five miles west of the Jordan River and about fifteen miles northeast of Jerusalem, but down a decline of 3,700 feet to more than 1,000 below sea level. In Jesus' time, Old Testament Jericho was largely abandoned, but a new city, south of the old one, had been built by Herod the Great. In contrast to Mark (**as he went out of Jericho**) and Matthew ("as they departed from Jericho; Matt. 20:29), Luke reported that Jesus "was come nigh unto Jericho" (Luke

18:35). He may have been referring to the new Jericho, while Matthew and Mark may have meant the old city. The presence of a blind beggar just outside the city gates, on a road pilgrims followed on the way to Jerusalem, was a common sight in that day and is not unknown in Israel today.

This section could well be entitled "A Model Disciple" (Edwards, *The Gospel according to Mark*, p. 328) because **Bartimeus** (v. 46; of all those healed in this gospel, his is the only name that Mark recorded) exhibited the qualities of discipleship that none of the Twelve possessed. The story of the healing of this blind beggar is a climax to chapter ten and its numerous references to discipleship (10:10, 13, 23–24, 27–28, 32, 35–36, 46, 52). Three characteristics of Bartimaeus in this story make him an example of discipleship.

(1) The blind beggar had faith. Twice he cried out, **Thou Son of David, have mercy on me** (vv. 47–48). The request expressed the belief that, through Jesus, God shows His covenant love to His people. Bartimaeus was convinced that Jesus could save Him, and the beggar persisted in his urgent cries despite the opposition of the bystanders. **Many charged him that he should hold his peace** ("'Be quiet!' some of the people yelled at him," NLT), **but he cried the more a great deal** (v. 48). The beggar's example would have inspired Mark's Roman audience, who were undergoing opposition and ridicule to their worship and witness.

(2) Bartimaeus also had insight that other disciples have not displayed in this chapter. He confessed Jesus to be "the Son of David." By using this address, the beggar confessed Jesus as Messiah, He who fulfills God's ancient promises to David of the coming One who would sit on David's throne forever (see 2 Sam. 7:11–16; see Isa. 11:1–3; Jer. 23:5–6; Ezek. 34:23–24). Jesus affirmed to the beggar that **thy faith hath made thee whole** (lit., "has saved you"; Greek, *sōzō*). **And immediately he received his sight** (v. 52). The healing demonstrates Jesus' powerful status as God's anointed one. In this passage, the title **Lord** (ascribed to Jesus; v. 51) translates the Hebrew word *Rabboni*, which means literally "(my) teacher."

(3) Once he was "saved" from his blindness, Bartimaeus **followed Jesus in the way** (v. 52). In Mark, the verb "follow" characterizes true discipleship, and so the formerly blind man demonstrated that being a disciple of Jesus means to associate with Jesus continually (the verb is in the imperfect tense, "and was following") and publicly, even on a path that leads to suffering and death. The decision was intentional and final for Bartimaeus. Mark conveyed with vivid details the suspense and seriousness of the moment when Jesus **called** (v. 49): **And he, casting away his garment, rose, and came to Jesus** (v. 50).

VI. The Passion of Jesus (chaps. 11–15)

A. The Triumphal Entry (11:1–11)

11:1–11. The reader now enters Mark's passion narrative, all of which must be seen against the backdrop of this opening scene. In His triumphal entry into Jerusalem, Jesus received the public honor that is His due, despite the outrageously brutal suffering that lay ahead of Him. The theme of discipleship, so prominent in chapter 10, carries over into this new major section of the gospel. In the vicinity of Jericho, Bartimaeus had chosen to "[follow] Jesus in the way" (10:52), and following Jesus continues to be a theme in the environs (Bethphage and Bethany; v. 1) of Jerusalem. Discipleship involves both the fulfillment of Jesus' commands (vv. 1–7) and the worship of the One in whose person the kingdom of God is present (vv. 8–11).

11:1–7. Jesus arrived in **Jerusalem** (v. 1), and the rest of his ministry took place within the confines of the Holy City. The triumphal entry, which inaugurated Passion Week, was a deliberate messianic action, and the clue to its understanding is found in Zechariah 9:9 (quoted in Matt. 21:5; John 12:15). Jesus purposefully offered Himself as the Messiah, knowing that this would provoke Jewish leaders to take action against Him. **The mount of Olives** is directly east of Jerusalem, where it rises to a height of about 2,700 feet (some 200 feet higher than Mount Zion). Its summit commands a magnificent view of the city and especially of the temple. Olive trees still grow on this mount, and the garden of Gethsemane, with its ancient olive trees, is at the base of its western slope.

The task of the two disciples whom Jesus **sendeth forth** (Greek, *apostellō*, related to the word "apostle"; v. 1) was to **find a colt tied, whereon never man sat; loose him, and bring him** (v. 2). The Greek word for "colt" can mean the young of any animal, but here it means the colt of a donkey. If questioned about their task, the disciples were simply to say that **the Lord hath need of** (v. 3) the colt. The task might seem mundane, but since unused animals (**whereon never man sat**) were regarded as especially suitable for religious purposes (see Num. 19:2; Deut. 21:3; 1 Sam. 6:7), the responsibility was sacred. The Lord's purpose of proclaiming the kingdom was served by the finding of the colt. Any commission from the Lord that a disciple undertakes is a sacred duty.

11:8–11. Jesus entered Jerusalem amid much fanfare and jubilation. As in the feast of Sukkoth, the Jewish festival when celebrants dwelt outside in "booths," the **branches off the trees** (v. 8) were used, but now for a new and higher purpose. The triumphal entry was the eschatological celebration of Sukkoth that Zechariah foretold (see Zech. 14:16–19). King Jesus' riding on the colt over branches and **garments** enacted Zechariah's prophecy, which said that the horses in Jerusalem would bear the inscription "HOLINESS UNTO THE LORD" (Zech. 14:20) as the Lord was recognized as King. Among those celebrating were **they that went before, and they that followed** (Greek, *akoloutheō*; v. 9), the latter verb designating disciples in Mark. The cry of **Hosanna** has the sense of "Save now." This word and the following line (**Blessed is he that cometh in the name of the Lord**) echo Psalm 118 (vv. 25–26), one of the Hallel ("Praise") psalms sung at Passover and especially fitting for this occasion. The disciples' worship of Jesus was a recognition that in Jesus is salvation, since He is the one who comes with the authority ("name") of Yahweh. All the promises to **David** (v. 10) for a perpetual **kingdom** are fulfilled in Him as Messiah (see Bartimaeus' confession in 10:47–48). Throughout Mark, faith is that trust which stems from a confession of Jesus' person and character. Faith without accurate knowledge, and belief without proper theology, are not to be found in the gospel. Faith never has exhaustive understanding, but it does have true understanding. The description of Jesus' victory parade ends with a foreshadow of activity in the temple soon to come: **when he had looked round about upon all things … he went out unto Bethany with the twelve** (v. 11).

B. The Fig Tree and the Cleansing of the Temple (11:12 – 26)

11:12 – 26. This segment of the gospel of Mark, comprising two distinct pericopes, must be read as a whole. The entire construction is an example of a "Markan sandwich" (see discussion on 5:21 – 43) in which the story of the fig tree (vv. 12 – 14; 20 – 26) is a commentary on the cleansing of the temple (vv. 15 – 19).

11:12 – 14. The incident involving the fig tree was perhaps a parable of judgment, an acted prophecy in the vein of certain Old Testament prophecies of Isaiah, Jeremiah, Ezekiel, and Hosea. In the Old Testament, the **fig tree** (v. 13) represents Israel's relationship to God (see Jer. 8:13; 29:17; Hos. 9:10, 16; Joel 1:7; Mic. 7:1 – 6; Nah. 3:12). A tree full of leaves normally should have fruit, but this one was cursed because it had none. That the cleansing of the temple (11:15 – 19) is sandwiched between the two parts of the account of the fig tree (here and 11:20 – 26) may underscore the theme of judgment. If this suggestion is correct, Jesus' malediction against the tree (**No man eat fruit of thee hereafter for ever**; v. 14) was not a selfish, uncontrolled outburst because He was denied breakfast. It was a pronouncement against Israel's religious establishment, represented by the temple that He cleansed (see 11:15 – 19). When the disciples later saw "the fig tree dried up from the roots" (11:20), they beheld the corrupted condition of Israel that already existed. That condition would reach its culmination in the destruction of the temple in AD 70.

11:15 – 19. The temple (v. 15) refers to the court of the Gentiles, the only part of the temple in which Gentiles could worship God and gather for prayer

(see v. 17). Pilgrims coming to the Passover feast needed animals that met the ritual requirements for sacrifice, and the vendors set up their animal pens and money tables in the court of the Gentiles. There they **sold and bought** (v. 15). That pilgrims needed their money changed into the local currency because the annual temple tax had to be paid in that currency explains the presence of **the tables of the money-changers**. The Mishnah required Tyrian currency for some offerings. **Doves** were required for the purification of women (see Lev. 12:6; Luke 2:22 – 24), the cleansing of those with certain skin diseases (see Lev. 14:22), and other purposes (see Lev. 15:14, 29). They were also the usual offering of the poor (see Lev. 5:7). Apparently, the temple area was being used as a shortcut between the city and the Mount of Olives. Jesus thus forbade anyone to **carry any vessel through the temple** (v. 16), a detail found only in Mark. Jesus acted against the commercialization of the temple and the careless use of it. It had become **a den of thieves** (v. 17) and was no longer **of all nations the house of prayer**. Isaiah 56:7 assured godly non-Jews that they would be allowed to worship God in the temple. By allowing the court of the Gentiles to become a noisy, smelly marketplace, the Jewish religious leaders were interfering with God's provision. The religious leaders' response to Jesus was hostile, but fearfully so: they **sought how they might destroy him** (v. 18).

11:20 – 26. Jesus had yet another purpose in the incident of the fig tree. The entire occurrence, according to this passage, is a fivefold lesson on believing prayer. (1) Any formidable task or obstacle (**this mountain**; v. 23) can be completely altered (**Be thou removed, and be thou cast into the sea**) through prayer. Jesus' language is metaphorical; although in the comparison, the mountain itself is addressed, the context makes clear that He was referring to prayer to God (vv. 22, 25 – 26). In other words, (2) anything that one desires (**what things soever ye desire**; v. 24) may be requested, but one must (3) **believe that ye receive them** (24) and (4) without **doubt** (v. 23) (5) one must **forgive** (v. 25 – 26) so that he or she may be forgiven by God. This condition is true whether the "mountain" for which one prays is the forgiveness (removal) of sins or not. Since some very early and reliable witnesses omit verse 26, it is relegated to the margin (NIV, NRSV) or is bracketed (NASB) in certain English translations. A later scribe probably added the verse to Mark's text to harmonize the passage with Matthew 6:15.

C. Concluding Controversies with Jewish Leaders (11:27–12:44)

11:27–12:44. Mark's passion narrative includes a series of controversies between Jesus and the religious leaders. These controversies include important teachings of Jesus, but they also show the reader how Jesus had maintained His honor despite numerous challenges to it. Ultimately, the opponents' attempts to trap Jesus in debate failed, and they had to resort to even more desperate measures to fulfill their murderous intent (see 11:18).

1. Jesus' Authority and the Question regarding John's Baptism (11:27–33)

11:27–33. Jesus skillfully turned the tables in His favor when He was questioned about His **authority** (v. 28). The Sanhedrin was asking why Jesus performed what appeared to be an official act if He possessed no official status. His riposte to the challenge (see discussion on 2:1–12) was to ask **the chief priests, and the scribes, and the elders** (v. 27) whether **The baptism of John** (v. 30) had a divine commission or a purely human impulse behind it. Mark provided the reader with insight into the aptness of this question, insight that Jesus Himself had. His opponents were now in jeopardy of falling into their own trap. Because they did not believe John, they could not maintain a divine origin for his prophetic work, but since the people counted John **a prophet** (v. 32), they dared not attribute a purely human inspiration to his prophetic activity. Hence, the opponents were stymied and could not give an answer. Jesus won the debate. Since they could not respond to His counterchallenge, Jesus maintained honor. He did not need to continue the debate: **Neither do I tell you by what authority I do these things** (v. 33).

2. The Parable of the Husbandmen (12:1–12)

12:1–12. The details of the parable of the husbandmen fit the social situation in Jewish Galilee in the first century. Large estates, owned by absentee landlords, were put in the hands of local peasants who cultivated the land as tenant farmers (**husbandmen**; v. 1). The key in interpreting this parable is given by the narrator: **for they knew that he had spoken the parable against them** (v. 12; i.e., the chief priests, scribes and elders of 11:27). The parable exposed the planned attempt on Jesus' life and God's judgment on the planners. The details of the parable correspond to the elements of the dispute between the religious leaders and Jesus. The correspondence is in three notable ways: (1) by this story, Jesus condemned those who maliciously sought His life, (2) He prophesied His own death at their hands (**they took him, and killed him, and cast him out of the vineyard**; v. 8), and (3) He identified Himself as the beloved **son** (v. 6), **the heir** (v. 7). One shows reverence or disregard for the owner by how one treats his agents, especially the son. A citation of Psalm 118:22–23 affirms Jesus' honor despite the infamy of His suffering: He is **The stone** (v. 10) that, although **rejected**, has the honored prominence of the cornerstone. Parallel versions of this parable are found in Matthew 21:33–46 and Luke 20:9–19.

3. The Question regarding Payment of Taxes to Caesar (12:13–17)

12:13–17. In an attempt to trap Jesus, some **Pharisees** (v. 13) and **Herodians** (for their alliance, see 3:6) questioned Jesus about the payment of a poll tax: **Is it lawful to give tribute to Caesar, or not?** (v. 14). Their question was out of **hypocrisy** (v. 15) but was clever. Would Jesus effectively maintain His honor in the face of a challenge that potentially could lead to a charge of either idolatry or rebellion against Rome? Jews in Judea were required to pay tribute money to the emperor. The tax was highly unpopular, and some Jews flatly refused to pay it, believing that payment was an admission of Roman right to rule.

Jesus effectively parried the challenge and took the offensive. The request for the **penny** (v. 15) itself slows the narrative and takes the momentum away from the questioners. The coin, a "denarius" (NASB), was a common coin worth the daily wage of a laborer (see Matt. 20:1–16). Jesus' question, **Whose is this image and superscription?** (v. 16), relates to the image of Tiberius Caesar on the obverse of the coin; the inscription read, "Tiberius Caesar Augustus, Son of the Divine Augustus." The inscription was considered by some to be a blasphemous claim of Caesar to deity. The opponents were now on the defensive, and their answer became the very basis for Jesus' concluding saying in this pronouncement story: **Render to Caesar the things that are Caesar's, and to God the things that are God's** (v. 17).

Jesus' honor was maintained: the opponents could not retort with a counterchallenge; they only **marvelled at him** (v. 17). Jesus recognized the state and its right to govern but affirmed the necessity of humans and human institutions to give God His due. The earthly power may not usurp God's sovereignty since the human ruler is only a created individual who bears His image (see Gen. 1:27). This story would have encouraged Mark's audience to remain loyal to the state insofar as it did not exceed its legitimate demands. (See Acts 4:29 and Dan. 3:16–18, where, for religious reasons, one must be ready to respectfully obey God rather than men, if the occasion clearly warrants it.)

4. The Question regarding the Resurrection (12:18–27)

12:18–27. The next controversy was initiated by **the Sadducees** (v. 18), a Jewish party that represented the wealthy and sophisticated classes. They were located largely in Jerusalem and made the temple and its administration their primary interest. Though they were small in number, in Jesus' time, they exerted powerful political and religious influence. The Sadducees said **there is no resurrection**. They denied the resurrection, accepted only the five books of Moses as authoritative, and flatly rejected the oral tradition. These beliefs set them against the Pharisees and common Jewish piety.

Of course, the question was a trap. For the Sadducees, one of the difficulties of the doctrine of the resurrection arose in the light of levirate marriage. A dead brother who died without an heir could still perpetuate his lineage and inheritance through a living brother. The latter married the widow of the former, and children from their union were legally considered the offspring of the dead brother. The Sadducees correctly cited Genesis 38:8 and Deuteronomy 25:5 for this practice, but they implied that it made resurrection impossible. Seven brothers cannot have one wife, nor can one woman have seven husbands! **Whose wife shall she be of them? for the seven had her to wife** (v. 23), they asked. The questioners anticipated an answer that would be invalidated by their denial of resurrection since any solution would obviously be unjust to six of the brothers (polyandry was not practiced by the Jews).

The Sadducees' denial of the resurrection revealed an ignorance of **the scriptures** (and) **the power of God** (v. 24). Jesus affirmed that resurrection life is of a different order: people **neither marry, nor are given in marriage** (v. 25). Furthermore, the fact of the resurrection is established by the incident at the burning bush. There, God claimed to Moses, **I am the God of Abraham, and the God of Isaac, and the God of Jacob** (v. 26; see Exod. 3:6). Jesus took that to mean that **He is not the God of the dead, but the God of the living** (v. 27). But was that interpretation a misapplication of the original divine utterance in Exodus (**the book of Moses**; v. 26)? Did God mean that the patriarchs were alive in a resurrected state when He spoke with Moses, or did God mean that He was the God whom these Old Testament heroes worshiped as their own God before their deaths? The answer may be both/and: God's faithfulness to His covenant people continues even after their deaths. Once again Jesus' answer could not be contradicted, and His honor was maintained.

5. The Question regarding the Greatest Commandment (12:28–34)

12:28–34. In response to the question **one of the scribes**, Jesus identified, **the first commandment of all** (v. 28), the heart of the Old Testament law: **thou shalt love the Lord thy God** (v. 30). Love for God is a complete response of devotion, trust, and obedience in each dimension of the human person and the entirety (**all thy**) of each dimension. The reason for complete dedication is that **The Lord our God is one Lord** (v. 29). One loves God with the **heart** (v. 30; the seat of one's affections and will; "passion," MSG), with the **soul** (one's entire life activities and pursuits), the **understanding** (the intellect in a pursuit of truth, or mind; v. 33), and **strength** (all one's energies are focused on service to God; v. 30).

Jewish rabbis counted 613 individual statutes in the Law and attempted to differentiate between "heavy" (or "great") and "light" (or "little") commands. **Hear, O Israel** (v. 29), came to be known as "the Shema," named after the first word of Deuteronomy 6:4 in Hebrew, which means "hear." The Shema became the Jewish confession of faith, which was recited by pious Jews every morning and evening. To this day, it begins every synagogue service.

Jesus added, **And the second is like, namely this** ("And the second, like it, is this," NKJV), **Thou shalt love thy neighbour as thyself** (v. 31). Love for God and neighbor summarize all that the Old Testament law intended to accomplish for Israel (Jesus cited Deut. 6:4–5 and Lev. 19:18). The scribe therefore **answered discreetly** ("wisely," NIV; v. 34) in affirming that love for God and neighbor are **more than all whole burnt offerings and sacrifices** (v. 33). With such insight, he was **not far from the kingdom of God** (v. 34). Since a member of the opposition, a scribe (see 11:27), had come to recognize that Jesus spoke **the truth** (v. 32), Jesus' honor in the controversies was upheld. The series of five controversies from 11:27–12:34 begins with scribal opposition to Jesus and ends with scribal affirmation of Jesus. Mark commented, **And no man after that durst ask him any question** ("And after that, no one dared to ask him any more questions," NLT; v. 34). The controversies that occurred from this point on were at Jesus' own instigation.

6. The Question regarding the Son of David (12:35–37)

12:35–37. In recording Jesus' question, Mark did not intend to deny **that Christ is the Son of David** (v. 35). After all, he endorsed both titles in his gospel (e.g., 8:29; 10:47–48). Rather, Jesus' question indicates that His Davidic ancestry does not mean that He is only a human descendant of the great king. Jesus is also Lord; David himself called him such by the inspiration of the Holy Spirit (in Ps. 110:1). Although in Greek, the word *kyrios* is used for both instances of "Lord" (**The LORD said to my Lord**; v. 36), the KJV capitalizes entirely the first instance and only the initial letter of the second. The KJV thus indicates the distinctions in the Hebrew text: "YHWH said to my *'ādōn*" (see Ps. 110:1). Thus, the Messiah was more than a descendant of David; He was David's Lord. Jesus' honor was once again affirmed: **And the common people heard him gladly** (v. 37).

7. The Scribes Are Denounced (12:38–40)

12:38–40. In this denunciation of **the scribes** (v. 38), Jesus redefined the honor code for His hearers. The characteristics of the scribes, which they held to be badges of honor, were actually badges of shame. Rather than being indicative of God's favor, they brought **greater damnation** (v. 40) since the scribes sought them out of wicked motives. The list results in the climactic **devour widows' houses, and for a pretence make long prayers**, two practices that revealed the scribes' self-interest, as did their **love** (v. 38) of going around **in long clothing** and other practices mentioned. The scribes wore long, white linen robes that were fringed and almost reached to the ground. The **chief seats in the synagogues** (v. 39) refer to the bench in front of the "ark" that contained the sacred scrolls. Those who sat there could be seen by all the worshipers in the synagogue. The hyperbolic "devour" (lit., "eat down"; "shamelessly cheat widows out of their property," NLT; v. 40) expresses abusive greed that preys on the powerless. Since the scribes were not paid a regular salary, they were dependent on the generosity of patrons for their livelihood. Such a system was open to abuses, and widows were especially vulnerable to exploitation. A spiritual leader may appear successful, and even win the admiring praise of people, but without love for God and neighbor (see 12:30–31), religious achievements are worthy of condemnation. They are deceptive, destructive, and dishonorable.

8. The Widow's Offering (12:41–44)

12:41–44. In immediate and stark contrast to the greed of the scribes, who exploited widows, is the widow who exhibited a selfless and sacrificial love for God in the giving of her offering. **The treasury** (v. 41) was located in the court of the women. Both men and women were allowed in this court, but women could go no farther into the temple buildings. It contained thirteen trumpet-shaped receptacles for the worshipers' contributions. The **poor widow** (v. 42) was a contrast not only to the scribes but also to the **rich** (v. 41). The rich members of the synagogue **cast in [out] of their abundance, but she ... cast in all that she had** (v. 44). They **cast in much** (v. 41); **she threw in two mites** (i.e., a farthing; "two very small copper coins," NIV v. 42). The *lepton* was the smallest coin then in circulation in the Holy Land, worth less than one hundredth of a denarius (the daily wage of a laborer). Jesus commended the widow for her sacrificial devotion to the work of the temple (she gave up **all her living**). The heart of the giver, not the amount of the gift, is what pleases God. What the world considers as spiritually successful is not necessarily what brings honor from God. This passage does not constitute a condemnation of wealth, but it does serve as a warning about the proper motivation in giving. It should cause twenty-first-century Christians in the West, all of whom are wealthy by the standards of the world, to question whether their giving is merely perfunctory or truly sacrificial.

D. The Olivet Discourse concerning the End of the Age (chap. 13)

13:1–37. The Olivet Discourse, as this chapter of Mark is commonly called, falls into five sections: (1) Jesus' prophecy of the destruction of the temple and the disciples' questions (vv. 1–4); (2) events surrounding the fall of Jerusalem and the destruction of the temple (vv. 5–23); (3) the coming of the Son of Man (vv. 24–27); (4) the lesson of the fig tree (vv. 28–31); and (5) an exhortation to watchfulness (vv. 32–37).

The Olivet Discourse is obviously a prophetic text, but precisely which future events it describes is debated. Three views that surface are the following. (1) Jesus' discourse exclusively forecasts the end of history. This view is unlikely in light of the Markan context: Jesus was responding to the disciples' questions about the destruction of the temple, and certain events in the discourse are definitely localized (vv. 14–18). (2) The entire discourse is a description of events that took place in Israel during the war of AD 66–70. The coming of the Son of Man (vv. 24–27) refers to God's vindication of Jesus and the overthrow of the temple and the sacrificial system. An obstacle to this view is the gathering of the elect from the ends of the earth in verse 27 — a strongly eschatological image. (3) Jesus prophesied both the fall of Jerusalem and the last days. According to this view, Jesus was describing events surrounding the fall of Jerusalem (vv. 5–23) and His second coming (vv. 24–37). Some who hold to this view see some of the events in verses 5–23 as happening in the future as well.

1. Jesus' Prophecy and the Disciples' Questions (13:1–4)

13:1–4. Mark's "Little Apocalypse" is a discourse of Jesus in response to the questions of certain disciples about the destruction of the magnificent edifices of the temple complex, for Jesus had told them, **there shall not be left one stone upon another, that shall not be thrown down** (v. 2). The **manner of stones** (v. 1), according to Josephus (*Antiquities* 15.11.3), was impressive: they were white, and some of them were 37 feet long, 12 feet high, and 18 feet wide. The remains of some of these stones may be seen today in the tunnel of the western wall and in the excavation of the temple stones at the corner of the western and southern walls beneath the temple mount. When Jesus was on **the mount of Olives** (v. 3), a vantage point east of the temple mount across the Kidron Valley, **Peter and James and John and Andrew asked Him privately** about the catastrophe to befall the temple. The four asked Jesus about the time (**when**; v. 4) and the accompanying circumstances (**the sign**) for the event.

2. Events Surrounding the Fall of Jerusalem and the Destruction of the Temple (13:5–23)

a. Hardships (13:5–8)

13:5–8. Jesus foretold the coming of false Christs who shall **deceive many** (v. 6) and issued the appropriate warning: **Take heed** (v. 5). It is clear from such words as "take heed" (both here and in 13:9), "But take ye heed" (13:23), "Take ye heed, watch and pray" (13:33), "Watch ye therefore" (13:35), and "Watch" (13:37) that one of the main purposes of the Olivet Discourse was to alert the disciples to the danger of deception. **Wars and rumours of wars** (v. 7) are not to cause excessive alarm. Such things have already been foreseen by God and do not indicate that the end is at hand. Jesus did not minimize the gravity of warfare, nor the misery it brings. Christians should always strive to be peacemakers. His point here was to fortify the disciples to endure during times of conflict since **the end** was still some distance in the future. **Nation** (v. 8) and **kingdom** shall fight one another, a reference to the ongoing conflict of the nations. **Earthquakes in divers** ("various," NKJV) **places ... famines and troubles** are only **the beginnings of sorrows**. The "earthquakes" (Greek, *seismoi*) may be a metaphor for the violent upheavals that nations experience during combat. The word has a figurative meaning in the Septuagint (see Isa. 29:6; Jer. 10:22; Ezek. 38:19). "Famines," tragic accompaniments to war throughout the ages, were to be expected in the coming war in Jerusalem. The word "troubles" does not appear in some Greek manuscripts; therefore it is absent from English translations such as the NASB, NIV, and NRSV. The woes that Jesus mentions are harbingers of agonies yet to come.

b. Mistreatment of the Disciples (13:9–13)

13:9. The company of Jesus' followers would experience the distress of the general populace but also the sufferings that came with their relationship to Christ. These troubles necessitated Jesus' command of watchfulness: **take heed to yourselves**. The troubles would be threefold: arrests on local charges, beatings, and formal hearings before imperial rulers. **They shall deliver you up to councils** probably refers to arraignments before local Jewish law courts (perhaps connected with synagogues). In Israel, the synagogue had the authority to adjudicate on matters relating to Jewish law and to administer corporal punishment (**ye shall be beaten**). Infraction of Jewish regulations was punishable by flogging, the maximum penalty being thirty-nine strokes with the whip (see 2 Cor. 11:23–24). Roman officials (**rulers**) might hear more serious charges; a Christian's case might even go to the emperor (**kings**), as Paul's case did (see Acts 25:10–11). A formidable legal proceeding has redeeming merit, Jesus said, when it is **for my sake, for a testimony against them** ("as a testimony to them," NRSV).

13:10. This verse has the character of a parenthesis since v. 9 and v. 11 seem to represent unbroken thought. Verse 10, then, could be an editorial comment by Mark or an insertion of a saying of Jesus that Mark imported from another context. In any case, the statement reminds the readers that they too have a responsibility to see that the good news **first be published** ("preached," NIV) **among all nations**. This has been the task of the church through world evangelism since the time of Pentecost. Many believe that its final completion will not come until the preaching of the gospel during the tribulation period.

13:11. Jesus did not forbid the disciples to prepare thoughtfully before legal proceedings when they would give testimony for Jesus. The single Greek word that the KJV translates **take no thought beforehand** is *promerimnaō* and has the sense of "do not worry beforehand" (Phillips). A. T. Robertson suggests "not to be stricken with fright beforehand" as an English equivalent. Since Jesus was referring not to preaching but to legal defenses, Robertson adds, "There is no excuse here for the lazy preacher who fails to prepare his sermon out of the mistaken reliance upon the Holy Spirit" (*Word Pictures in* the New Testament, vol. 1, *The Gospel according to Matthew, The Gospel according to Mark* [Nashville: Broadman, 1930], p. 376). The disciple may rely on the Holy Spirit to give the right word for the right occasion when he or she is called to account.

13:12–13. The opposition that Christ's followers can expect is seriously tragic since it may come even from one's own immediate family. One's **brother** (v. 12), **father**, and even one's **children** may **betray** one **to death**. Jesus stated that His disciples will **be hated of all men for my name's sake** (v. 13). To what does **endure unto the end** refer? It could be the culmination of the catastrophic events to which this section points. The expression **shall be saved** would thus have the sense of "shall be preserved from destruction" (Wuest). If "unto the end" has the sense of "forever" or "for as long as it takes," however, eschatological salvation may be in view here.

Christian discipleship does not mean immunity from the world's suffering. Warfare, political turmoil, and economic hardship affect Christians just as they do all people. Furthermore, God's people are subject to suffering for His name's sake. This section of the Olivet Discourse is a serious warning for believers of any age to "take heed to yourselves" (13:9). In the midst of sorrows and opposition, however, the mandate still stands to preach the gospel "among all nations" (13:10). The Holy Spirit assists God's people in this task (see 13:11).

c. The Abomination of Desolation (13:14–23)

13:14. Perhaps no single image in Mark 13 is as controversial as **the abomination of desolation**. The translation of the phrase poses problems enough. Other renderings of the Greek *to bdelygma tēs erēmōseōs* are "the desolating sacrilege" (NRSV), "the abomination that causes desolation" (NIV), "the sacrilegious object that causes desecration" (NLT). The phrase comes from **Daniel the prophet** (see Dan. 9:27; 11:31; 12:11 Septuagint). The image originally referred to Antiochus Epiphanes who, by installing a statue in the temple and offering swine's flesh on the altar, profaned the temple. In AD 70, the temple was overrun by the Romans, whose standards were

placed over the ruined temple. This abomination reached its ultimate heinousness for the Jew when, after the revolt of AD 135, the Romans placed Zeus's statue in a shrine dedicated to him on the site of the Jewish temple that had been destroyed some sixty-five years earlier. Later, the site was further profaned in the Jewish mind by the erection of the Moslem shrine, the Dome of the Rock, on this site in AD 638.

At this point in the narrative, Mark interjected an editorial comment: **(let him that readeth understand)**. The KJV's parentheses note the editorial nature of the phrase. Mark may have intended for his readers to consider some phenomenon with which they were familiar, to give evidence that the tragic events of this verse were already unfolding. Luke understood the "desolation" to be near whenever Jerusalem was surrounded by Roman armies (see Luke 21:20). Luke's paraphrase of Mark's expression is strong evidence that Jesus was referring to the events of AD 66–70, and Mark wanted his readers not to miss the reference. Though Jesus' prophesied in this verse has a first-century reference, it also provides an eschatological warning of an even greater "desolation" by the Antichrist in the future.

The command **let them that be in Judaea flee to the mountains** indicates that the abomination would be in Jerusalem. The subsequent instructions that Jesus gave are obviously intended for residents of Israel. The immediate referent of the prophecy was a warning to first-century believers to flee Jerusalem before the destruction of the temple, but many believe it also provides a warning for those who will be living there in the end times. Jesus' warnings thus foreshadow a final fulfillment just prior to His second advent.

13:15–18. The housetop (v. 15) refers to the living and sleeping areas atop typical first-century Jewish homes in the area. The flat roof was also used for midday prayer. Escape from the coming disaster could only be made if one left in extreme haste; individuals were not even to go down into the **house** to retrieve anything. Everyday business activity—the one **in the field** (v. 16) represents a typical worker in the agrarian economy of Israel—should be abandoned. One was not to go back even for the outer coat that had been cast aside during working hours. **Them that are with child** (v. 17) represents anyone forced to flee under especially difficult circumstances, which might cause them to perish. **Winter** (v. 18) would be a difficult time for anyone in Israel, particularly pregnant or nursing women. The season would bring discomforting rain and cold. Rivers and fords would be impassable, making escape perilous, if not impossible.

13:19–20. The **affliction** (v. 19) of the Jewish War of AD 66–70 would bring with it unprecedented catastrophe. In fine prophetic fashion, Jesus employed hyperbole to emphasize the severity of the woes ahead: **such as was not from the beginning of the creation**. One could argue that distress of greater intensity and duration has been seen in human history. From the perspective of the hearers, however, Jesus' words proved true. A similar hyperbolic expression is that **no flesh should be saved** (v. 20). For the sake of those **whom he hath chosen**, the Lord cut short the period of suffering. The notions of an **elect** and of a predetermined amount of time for the affliction (**he hath shortened the days**) should be appreciated for their intended function in the discourse. Those who faced the grim prospect of seeing their homeland devastated could take courage from knowing that God was watching out for them as His people and that an end of suffering lay beyond the devastation.

13:21–23. Jesus' prophecy of the catastrophe to come to Judea concluded as it began (see 13:5–6), with a warning about **false Christs and false prophets** (v. 22). The same command **But take ye heed** (v. 23) is reiterated. The intention of the pretenders would be to **seduce** ("to lead astray," NRSV; v. 22) even those who are the **elect**, if that were possible (arguably it is not!). To be forewarned is to be forearmed, and the disciples now had no excuse to be deceived by bogus messiahs or prophets in the days ahead when they longed for deliverance from the distress that Jesus had prophesied.

Although the first part of the discourse relates specifically to the period leading up to the devastation of the temple and the city (ca. AD 66–70), its

warnings also speak in at least four ways to Christians who live in the time after this event. (1) The believer is not immune from the fallout of political and military turbulence in the world. Troubles of this kind should not cause the believer to think that God has failed, or that he or she has sinned and lost God's favor. A certain amount of human suffering is common to all people. For the Christian, God is powerfully present to help and guide during times of distress. (2) Vigilance is needed so that one does not succumb to the seductions of false teachers. Jesus' words throughout Mark's gospel are themselves a solid foundation for Christian stability. (3) The Holy Spirit gives the words to all who are called on to give a testimony for their Lord before unbelievers. Preparation in the way of study, knowing an outline of the facts of the gospel, or the rehearsal of one's personal conversion experience are not forbidden by Jesus. Worry about the outcome of witnessing for Christ is forbidden, however. (4) Every Christian must determine to live a life of endurance. Persecution will come, but Jesus guarantees that the Lord Himself has determined our destiny for the sake of the elect.

3. The Coming of the Son of Man (13:24–27)

13:24–25. In those days (v. 24) must not be taken as a reference to the time under discussion in the immediately preceding section (13:14–23). The prepositional phrase is a common Old Testament expression having to do with the end time (see Jer. 3:16, 18; 31:29; 33:15–16; Joel 3:1; Zech. 8:23). Jesus identified the time more precisely as **after that tribulation** (i.e., "after those horrible days end" [NLT], the days of the battle for Jerusalem). Jesus, in genuine prophetic fashion, now blended the near view with the far view. That is, the events near to the prophet's time blend with events that are distant from his perspective. The upheavals of the siege of Jerusalem are similar, albeit on a smaller scale, to the cosmic upheavals that the coming of the Son of Man will inaugurate. The events at the end of history will come after an unspecified amount of time.

The language that Jesus used to describe His second coming reflects the poetry and symbolism of

Old Testament apocalyptic language. The intensity of the eschatological events is conveyed through two synonymously parallel constructions (typical of Hebrew poetry):

First Parallelism (v. 24)

(a) **the sun shall be darkened,**
(b) **and the moon shall not give her light,**

Second Parallelism (v. 25)

(a) **and the stars of heaven shall fall,**
(b) **and the powers that are in heaven shall be shaken.**

The failure and disintegration of heavenly bodies are common in Old Testament language regarding the Day of the Lord. When God acts in judgment, both historically and eschatologically, life's predictability and routine comes to an end. Sin is requited; righteousness is vindicated (see Isa. 13:10; 24:21 – 23; 34:4; Ezek. 32:7 – 8; Joel 2:10, 31; 3:15; Amos 8:9; see Rev. 6:12 – 14; 8:12). Jesus' words are not to be taken literally, but as a poetic description of the power, scope, and finality of the judgment that He brings at His coming.

"The powers" (v. 25) could designate angelic beings (good and/or evil) since "stars" (with which "powers" is synonymous in this passage) in ancient Jewish literature sometimes signify angels (see Rev. 1:20; 9:1; 12:4). The stars/powers, however, may simply represent planetary or stellar objects that will be transformed or destroyed. These conditions may also refer to severe judgments on the earth that will shake the planet and thus appear to be shaking the heavens.

13:26 – 27. Although the expression **the Son of man** (v. 26) can point to a human being (see Ezek. 2:1), the details surrounding the term in Mark unmistakably recall the description of "one like the Son of man" in Daniel 7:13 – 14: he comes with **the clouds,** attended by **glory.** The Son of Man in Mark is given universal right of judgment in that He dispatches **his angels** (to) **gather together his elect** (v. 27) from every place they inhabit (hyperbolically

from the uttermost part of the earth to the uttermost part of heaven). Daniel's Son of Man likewise has "an everlasting dominion" (Dan. 7:14) and represents His people in exercising sovereignty (see Dan. 7:22). In both cases, "the Son of man" refers to Jesus Christ, who will return in power and great glory to gather His own.

4. The Lesson of the Fig Tree (13:28 – 31)

13:28 – 31. As Jesus often did, here he used a common everyday image (**the fig tree**; v. 28) as an illustration of a spiritual reality. A sure sign that **summer** is close at hand is the profusion of **leaves** from **tender** shoots or branches on the tree. Certain events are also the sign of the nearness of a new season — in this case, a season that will involve upheaval in the present cosmic order for judgment and salvation. Four questions arise upon which the interpretation of this **parable** hinge: (1) What are **these things** (v. 29), and (2) what is **it** that will be **nigh** upon their occurrence? (3) What is **this generation** (v. 30), and (4) what are **all these things** whose accomplishment must precede its passing?

This part of the prophecy points to the distant eschatological future since it involves the triumphal return of Jesus Christ, which did not occur in AD 70. Remember, Jesus was answering questions regarding two things: (1) the destruction of the temple and (2) the sign of His second coming. In 13:24, Jesus used the word "But" (Greek, *alla*) to designate a contrast between the appearance of false messiahs and the coming of the true messiah in "that day" ("those days," NASB; 13:32).

The reference to the "fig tree" is for illustrative purposes. It is not likely a symbolic reference to Israel, as some have claimed. The cross-reference in Luke 21:29 refers to "the fig tree, and all the trees," indicating that Jesus was simply saying that one can determine the seasons by the budding of the trees. So it is that one can determine the prophetic time by the "signs" of the times. **See these things come to pass** (v. 29) refers to the events of the tribulation (see 13:24). **This generation** (v. 30) refers to the generation of the tribulation period, which will live to "see these things come to pass" (v. 29). There is no way this can be limited to the generation of Jesus' time, since He did not (1) come in power and great glory (see 13:26), (2) gather his elect (see 13:27), (3) come at a time when no one expected him (see 13:32).

5. Exhortation to Watchfulness (13:32–37)

13:32. But of that day and that hour knoweth no man, no, not the angels which are in heaven, neither the Son, but the Father is an unusual expression, found only in Mark, because it seems to rob Jesus of the omniscience that one associates with this figure who acts and speaks with the authority of God Himself. The saying ought to be understood as an indication that in the divine economy, Jesus Christ the Son is subordinate to the will and purpose of His Father. This was part of Jesus' voluntary self-emptying. He chose not to use some of His divine attributes at certain times, so that He could function fully as a man. The certainty with which He spoke of His return in Revelation 22:20 indicates that the risen, glorified Christ fully knows the time of His return. The verse emphasizes that the time of Jesus' coming in power and glory (see 13:24–27) is completely unknown to human reckoning. A map of the future would be a hindrance, not a help, to faith. Certain signs have been given, but not for the purpose of making detailed, sequential prophecy. "That day" is an Old Testament expression for the day of the Lord's appearance (see Amos 8:3, 9, 13; 9:11; Mic. 4:6; 5:10; 7:11). Here it refers specifically to the coming of the Son of Man (see 13:26). The "day" and "hour" refer to the coming of the Son of Man in glory (see 13:24–27), the time "when the master of the house cometh" (13:35).

13:33–37. Here Jesus cited a familiar occurrence in Israel: the owner of an estate would leave on business for an undisclosed period of time and delegate responsibilities to his slaves during his absence. Lack of diligence in their assigned tasks would result in the master's displeasure when he suddenly returned, which could be **at even, or at midnight, or at the cockcrowing, or in the morning** (the four watches of the night used by the Romans; v. 35). The obvious meaning is that Jesus could return at any time.

Three distinct commands for Jesus' servants appear in this passage: **Take ye heed** (Greek, *blepete*; "stay alert," NLT), **watch** (*agrypneite*; "keep awake," ESV) **and pray** (v. 33). The final admonition is widely attested in the manuscripts and witnesses. Since it is missing in some witnesses (including some early Latin manuscipts), however, the term is omitted in several recent English translations (e.g., ESV, NASB, NIV, NLT). The emphasis in these commands reinforces the concept of the imminent coming of Christ. Believers are told to watch for the coming of the Lord, who could potentially return at any time (see discussion on Matt. 24:40–42).

All too often Christians become obsessed with fixing the dates for the events surrounding Jesus' second coming. Jesus Himself said that no one knows the time, so we can be sure that any calculation that claims to have figured out the precise time is erroneous. Of far greater importance than date-setting is the necessity of watchfulness. Since His followers cannot know the precise time of His return, the proper conduct in anticipation of the Lord's return is wakeful alertness. Laziness and inattentiveness to responsibilities at hand are how *not* to wait for Jesus' coming!

E. The Anointing of Jesus (14:1–11)

14:1–11. The story of Jesus' anointing is a stunning study in contrasts: the extravagance of devotion for Jesus that the anonymous woman displayed is offset by the revulsion that the bystanders felt for what they believed was a monumental squandering of an invaluable commodity. Between the two parties in this picture of devotion and the lack of it is Jesus. He was honored by the woman in the anointing, and He honored her in His commendation of her. Once again Mark portrayed Jesus as a person of honor. Not only was He given an honorable anointing with ointment of almost incalculable worth, but He associated the anointing with His burial. The prediction of His death reveals that He willingly underwent it for purposes that have already been mentioned.

14:1–2. The chief priests and the scribes (v. 1) determined to seize Jesus before **the feast of the**

passover, and of unleavened bread. The leaders feared **an uproar of the people** (v. 2) if their murderous plot was effected during the holy days. The Jewish festival of Passover commemorates the time when the angel of the Lord passed over the homes of the Hebrews rather than killing their firstborn sons as He did in the Egyptian homes (see Exod. 12:13, 23, 27). The lambs or kids used in the feast were killed on the fourteenth of Nisan (March-April), and the meal was eaten the same evening between sundown and midnight. Since the Jewish day began at sundown, the Passover feast took place on the fifteenth of Nisan. The Feast of Unleavened Bread followed Passover and lasted seven days (see Exod. 12:15–20; 23:15; 34:18; Deut. 16:1–8).

14:3. In Bethany, Jesus **sat at meat**. The usual posture for eating a banquet meal was to recline. **Ointment of spikenard** was an unguent made from an herb that was imported from northern India. It was popular among the Hebrews and Romans in the anointing of the dead. Balms like the one in this story were preserved most effectively in **an alabaster box** ("jar," NRSV) since the container contributed to an aging process that made the ointments of great value after a number of years. Mark thus said that the oil was **very precious** ("very costly perfume, pure oil of nard," NEB).

14:4–5. The violence of the bystanders' reaction was in inverse proportion to the devotion of the woman. Her devotion was exorbitant: the value of the ointment she poured on Jesus was **more than three hundred pence** (v. 5). The monetary unit denoted is the denarius, a day's wage for a common laborer (see Matt. 20:1–15). Almost a year's pay was invested in this expression of love for Jesus! The bystanders' response was **indignation** (v. 4). In other words, **they murmured against her** (v. 5).

14:6–9. The protesters seem to have had a valid criticism: the ointment could have been sold, and the proceeds of the sale could have been given to the poor. Instead, the oil was used up in one action that apparently did no one any good. On the contrary, said Jesus. The pouring was **a good work on me** (v. 6). The expense of the ointment spoke of the

honor Jesus would have even in death. The woman's work was of the utmost importance since the opportunity to anoint Jesus before burial was rare and fleeting. Jesus certainly advocates care of the poor (**whensoever ye will ye may do them good**; v. 7), but never to the extent that His honor is overlooked. Since what the woman had done has become **a memorial of her** (v. 9), she is honored as she honored Jesus.

Costly expressions of devotion to Jesus still draw responses of contempt and derision. Those who labor in ministries or missions in which responses to the gospel are few and far between are sometimes seen as wasting their time and resources. Christian work with the derelict and despondent is viewed by many as poor stewardship. Jesus could be better served in more strategic and important ministries, according to the critics. In this story, however, Jesus affirmed the one who gave extravagantly and "wastefully" for Him. Good stewardship should always be a consideration, but that may involve a costly expression of devotion that others may disapprove.

14:10–11. The treachery of **Judas** (v. 10) is another contrast to the devotion of the woman in Simon's house. **The chief priests** offered him **money** (v. 11), but not nearly as much as the 300 denarii that the spikenard would have brought had it been sold. The lack of specificity by Mark regarding the betrayal price shows that the repudiation of Jesus ultimately brings nothing of value to the one who rejects Him (see 8:36–37).

F. The Arrest, Trial, and Death of Jesus (14:12–15:47)

1. Jesus and the Disciples Celebrate Passover (14:12–17)

14:12–17. This passage sets the scene for the climactic events that occurred at the Passover table. **The first day of unleavened bread** would ordinarily mean the fifteenth of Nisan, the day after Passover. However, the added phrase, **when they killed the passover**, makes it clear that the fourteenth of Nisan is meant because Passover lambs were killed on that day (see Exod. 12:6). The entire eight-day celebration was sometimes referred to as the Feast of Unleavened Bread, and there is evidence that the fourteenth of Nisan may have been loosely referred to as the "first day of unleavened bread."

The preparations for the feast were carried out by two disciples according to Jesus' prearrangement of **a large upper room furnished and prepared** (v. 15). The disciples' encounter with **a man bearing a pitcher of water** (v. 13) is unusual in itself (women fetched the household water from the well or spring) but even more remarkable because Jesus knew that the disciples would encounter the man in a crowded city teeming with pilgrims. Jesus' honor continues to be upheld in this section: He is a person of divine foresight.

The question **Where is the guestchamber …?** (v. 14) infers the Jewish custom that anyone in Jerusalem who had a room available would give it upon request to a pilgrim to celebrate the Passover. It appears that Jesus had made previous arrangements with the owner of the house. To **make ready** (v. 15) would have included preparation of food for the meal: unleavened bread, wine, bitter herbs, sauce, and the lamb. **And in the evening he cometh with the twelve** (v. 17) is full of suspense and tension in light of the plots against Jesus that were being formed.

2. The Last Supper (14:18 – 26)

14:18 – 21. They sat and did eat the Passover meal (v. 18). Originally, the meal was eaten standing (Exod. 12:11), but in Jesus' time, it was customary to eat it while reclining. **Verily I say unto you**. The disciples finally comprehended the grim reality of Jesus' prophecy of His death (unlike earlier prophesies that were met with miscomprehension; see 8:32; 9:10; 10:35 – 45). Jesus stated that **One of you which eateth with me shall betray me**. Although they are **sorrowful** (v. 19), their concern was not so much for the fate awaiting Jesus as it was for their own self-defense: **one by one** the Twelve asked, **Is it I? and another said, Is it I?** Jesus affirmed that the betrayer was indeed of their number, one **that dippeth with me in the dish** (v. 20). The predetermined

plan of God required that **The Son of man indeed goeth** (i.e., to death)**, as it is written of him** (v. 21); the Scripture prophesies such. Jesus no doubt had the suffering Servant passage of Isaiah 53 in mind. Despite the Son's predestined fate, however, the delivery of Him was not something forced upon the individual who would betray Him. Verse 21, reveals the mysterious mixture of God's predestined will that cannot fail to be accomplished and the free choice of individuals. In their freedom, they ultimately serve the purposes of the Lord of history. **Woe to that man by whom the Son of man is betrayed**!

During the first course of the Passover meal, the participants all shared from a common bowl that contained a mixture of bitter herbs and stewed fruit. Jesus did not specifically identify the betrayer but merely affirmed three times (vv. 18, 20, 21) that it was one of the Twelve. His threefold affirmation corresponds to the certainty of a threefold witness in Jewish legal contexts (see Deut. 17:6; 19:15). Jesus affirmed the veracity of His prophecy also by the formula, "Verily I say unto you" (v. 18). The foreknowledge of Jesus contrasts with the ignorance of the disciples regarding the traitor's identity.

14:22 – 26. The New Testament gives four accounts of the Lord's Supper (Matt. 26:26 – 28; Mark 14:22 – 24; Luke 22:19 – 20; 1 Cor. 11:23 – 25). Matthew's account is very much like Mark's, while Luke's and Paul's have similarities. All the accounts include the taking of the bread, the thanksgiving or blessing, the breaking of the bread, the saying "this is my body," the taking of the cup, and the explanation of the relation of blood to the covenant. Only Paul and Luke recorded Jesus' command to continue to celebrate the Supper. The **bread** (v. 22) that Jesus distributed during the meal may represent the *afikoman* of the Passover celebration — the bread that comes after the meal proper and that represents the Passover lamb's flesh. Jesus thus inaugurated a new Passover, a deliverance for the entire world, by His own flesh. **Take, eat: this is my body** constitutes a metaphor: the bread represents Jesus' body.

Similarly, **the cup** (v. 23) represents **my blood of the new testament** (v. 24). In the Jewish Passover

Seder, the cup of Elijah follows the *afikoman*. That may be the cup for which Jesus gave **thanks** (v. 23) and distributed to the Twelve. The word "Eucharist" is derived from the Greek term that is here translated "had given thanks." Some manuscripts do not have the word "new" (*kainos*), but the meaning is clear even without it: Jesus' blood ratified the new covenant and put it into effect (see Heb. 9:15–22). The redemptive value of the blood is evident since it is that **which is shed for many** (v. 24). The word "for" (Greek, *hyper*) has the idea of substitution. Jesus foretold His own death and claimed that it has atoning significance. Any interpretation of Jesus' death must begin here with His own statement regarding its significance (see Mark 10:45).

There is finality in Jesus' assertion that the meal was His last (**I will drink no more of the fruit of the vine**; v. 25), but it is counterbalanced with the affirmation of a future vindication and victory on **that day that I drink it new in the kingdom of God**. The church's own celebration of the Lord's Supper from the earliest time has included this same affirmation of the glorious future that was opened by Jesus' death (see 1 Cor. 11:26). The **hymn** (v. 26) that Jesus and His disciples sang before going out to **the mount of Olives** may have been the second part of the Hallel (Psalms 115–118).

3. Peter's Denial Foretold (14:27–31)

14:27–31. The abandonment of Jesus by His followers now shifted from the one who would betray Him (see 14:18) to the wholesale scattering of the entire flock (**the sheep shall be scattered**; v. 27). Jesus spoke as a prophet in this passage (probably while en route to the Mount of Olives), thus further highlighting that His death was not a deserved result of dishonorable conduct. Rather, it was part of the foreordained will of God and undeserved. The words of prophecy are a quotation of Zechariah 13:7. At the same time, Jesus prophesied, **after that I am risen, I will go before you into Galilee**.

Peter then spoke up, claiming, **Although all shall be offended** (see v. 27)**, yet will not I** (v. 29). The verb "be offended" (Greek, *skandalizō*) is related to

the word for bait in a trap. The verb can have the sense of "to entrap," "to trip up," "to fall away." Jesus' response to this boast was, **in this night, before the cock** ("rooster," NKJV) **crow twice, thou shalt deny me thrice** (v. 30). Protesting, Peter vowed in the strongest terms possible that he would not deny Jesus: the phrase **more vehemently** ("emphatically," NIV; v. 31) is the double-negative *ou mē* paired with the verb: **I will not deny thee in any wise**. Peter's rejection of the possibility of denying Jesus was picked up by all the Twelve at this point (**Likewise also said they all**).

Peter's exhibited brave intentions here, but they outran his capacities for loyalty and faithfulness in the face of danger. Whenever the Christian becomes confident in his or her own strength and refuses to face one's own weakness and inclinations to sin, a catastrophe looms ahead. Perhaps Peter's threefold denial might have been avoided if he had heeded Jesus' prophecy as a warning of his own weakness.

4. In the Garden of Gethsemane (14:32–52)

14:32–34. Jesus and the disciples reached their destination: the lower slopes of the Mount of Olives, specifically, **a place which was named Gethsemane** (v. 32). This was one of Jesus' favorite places (see Luke 22:39; John 18:2). The name is Hebrew and means "oil press," that is, a place for squeezing the oil from olives. East of the old city of Jerusalem, one can still see extremely old olive trees in this place that may be described as "a garden" (John 18:1), "a grove of olive trees" (John 18:1 NLT), or an orchard. Jesus intended to **pray** in the solitude of the place and separated Himself from the larger company of disciples, taking only **Peter and James and John** (v. 33) with Him. These three were to **tarry ye here, and watch** (v. 34), instructions that probably involved serious and concentrated prayer for Jesus in His time of need. The word "watch" has the idea of alert vigilance (see Mark 13:34–35, 37) in the face of impending danger or stress. Mark's descriptions of Jesus signify His extreme anguish before the events that He knew awaited Him. He **began to be sore amazed, and to be very heavy** ("And he began to feel terror and anguish," NJB; v. 33), and Jesus' soul was **exceeding sorrowful** (v. 34). The adverbial **unto death** could indicate either the basis of Jesus' overwhelming dread or the intensity of His distress (see "my heart is ready to break with grief," REB).

14:35. Mark emphasized that private prayer was Jesus' practice during critical points of His life (1:35–39; 6:46), and He continued that habit at this most extreme crisis. Mark further highlighted the duress of the occasion in that Jesus **fell on the ground** (v. 35) and then **prayed that … the hour might pass from him**.

14:36. Mark recorded the very words of Jesus' prayer, indicating their importance as a model for His followers who face crises in their lives of discipleship. Four elements of Jesus' crisis prayer are evident.

(1) He addressed God as **Abba** (v. 36). (Mark provided his Greek readers with the translation, **Father**, of the Aramaic word). This term of familiar endearment is equivalent to "Daddy" or "Dad." Little children as well as grown sons and daughters used it to address their fathers. Jesus' use of it in this anguished situation shows His union with the Father and His willingness to do the will of God. As Christ's disciples, believers also have an intimate relationship with God, by which they can and should cry in prayer, "Abba, Father" (see Rom. 8:15; Gal. 4:6).

(2) Jesus recognized God's omnipotence when He exclaimed, **all things are possible unto thee** (v. 36). Biblical affirmations of God's power to accomplish anything exclude those absurdities that the skeptic often raises, such as, "Can God make a stone so big that He can't lift it?" God's power is consistent with His wisdom and nature. Ludicrous phenomena are excluded by the reality of God and of the universe that He has created. A believer's prayer, like that of Jesus, must be founded on the recognition of God's limitless might in order for it to qualify as a prayer of faith to a loving Father.

(3) An urgent and agonized plea, **take away this cup from me** (v. 36), followed Jesus' recognition of God's power to do anything that might be asked of Him. The word "cup" (Greek, *potērion*) echoes 10:38–39 (where the cup represents Christ's bear-

ing the divine punishment of sins on behalf of others) and 14:23–24 (where the cup represents Christ's blood). The Son prayed to be spared the sufferings that lay ahead. His followers also may pray to be spared trials, temptations, and persecutions. The granting of such a request, however, is not guaranteed. The fourth element of Jesus' crisis prayer makes that clear.

(4) The proviso for Jesus' prayer and for any prayer of His followers must be **nevertheless not what I will, but what thou wilt** (v. 36). One must not presume that one will receive an answer to prayer as it has been prayed. Although God is able to do everything, He may not will to do what one has asked. Our individual wills must thus bend to His. If Jesus prayed with subordination of His will to that of His Father, how much more must one pray in this fashion? God always answers prayers, but not always in the way that one would like.

14:37–42. The perfect example of what prayer should *not* be like is Peter's and the other disciples' sleepy prayerlessness. Rather than **watch** (v. 37) but **one hour**, Peter and the disciples failed three times (see v. 41) to fulfill Jesus' instruction to **Watch ye and pray, lest ye enter into temptation** (v. 38). The threefold failure emphasizes the laxity of the Twelve in the face of danger and foreshadows Peter's imminent threefold denial (see 14:66–72). The present tense of the two verbs lends them special emphasis in this context ("Be constantly watching and praying," Wuest).

Jesus' word "temptation" (v. 38) refers not just to an enticement to evil but also to the testing that any challenge to faith brings. Here the temptation was to be unfaithful in face of the threatening circumstances confronting the disciples. The failure to meet the test is to sin, to fall into temptation (see 1 Tim. 6:9). The testing of the disciples, and especially Peter, in this context becomes a lesson on temptation for the disciple today. The testing may come by way of an attraction to sin, persecution for one's testimony to Christ, illness, depression, fatigue, financial hardship, loss of a loved one, or demands of work and life's responsibilities. Regardless of its source, the time to prepare for challenges is not after they have sprung and are overwhelming, but beforehand. The strength and direction that God grants through vigilant prayer then enable us to withstand the evil onslaught, or allow one to be spared it altogether. The proverbial statement of Jesus, **The spirit truly is ready, but the flesh is weak** (v. 38), provides a basis for the approach to prayer that is presented in the Gethsemane story.

When Jesus found His followers sleeping **the third time** (v. 41), He said, **Sleep on now, and take your rest: it is enough**. This was not a command to keep on in their indolence; the statement rather conceded that the disciples had been asleep and has the notion of, "Are you going to sleep all night? No— you've slept long enough. Time's up" (MSG). Jesus summoned His disciples to alertly witness the events about to unfold around them when **the Son of man is betrayed into the hands of sinners**. The enormity of these events is underscored by the phrase **he that betrayeth me is at hand** (v. 42). The phrase "is at hand" is the second of two instances of this form in the gospel. In Mark 1:15, Jesus announced that "the kingdom of God is at hand." The kingdom of God was now about to be manifested in an ultimate sense. The events of Jesus' passion make it possible for the rule of God to come into the lives of people. Jesus' death is "a ransom for many" (Mark 10:45), the fact of which is demonstrated by His resurrection from the dead. In this sense, the kingdom of God was also "at hand" in Gethsemane.

14:43–52. To this point, the Twelve had not known who the betrayer was. Jesus had known, and His foreknowledge means that the course of events was completely and divinely predetermined. His death occurred not because of dishonorable conduct but because He willed it. **Judas, one of the twelve** (v. 43) led Jesus' foes to Him. These foes were auxiliary police or servants of the court assigned to the task of maintaining public order beyond the precincts of the temple. They carried **swords and staves** ("clubs," NRSV), weapons that the reader knows are completely unnecessary because of Jesus' intention to go to His death (see 10:32–34). By the prearranged

token ("signal," NKJV; v. 44) of a **kiss**, Judas identified the one whom those **from the chief priests and the scribes and the elders** were to seize (v. 43). Jesus was taken into custody after Judas **kissed him** (v. 45). The kiss was a token of respect with which disciples customarily greeted their teacher. A kiss as a greeting in Mediterranean culture, then and now, represents friendship and esteem (without sexual connotations). Jesus' statement that **the scriptures must be fulfilled** (v. 49) is perhaps a reference to Isaiah 53, or more particularly to Zechariah 13:7, which Jesus quoted in 14:27 and which was fulfilled (at least in part) at this time. In fulfillment of 14:27–31, **they all** (i.e., the disciples) **forsook him** (v. 50).

Two questions arise at this point in the narrative. (1) Why did Judas instruct those arresting Jesus to **lead him away safely** (v. 44)? Did Judas not realize what was in store for Jesus if He fell into the hands of the Jewish authorities, or did he have second thoughts and now wanted Jesus to be given protection? (2) If those seeking Him had been with Jesus **daily** (v. 49) while He was **in the Temple teaching**, why would they have needed Judas to distinguish the Master from His disciples? Would those who had come to arrest Jesus not have known who He was? The answer to the first question is that the word translated "safely" (v. 44) should be understood in the sense of "securely" (NAB) or "under guard" (NIV, NRSV). Judas did not want Jesus to escape, nor did he want His followers to stage a rescue. The second difficulty is cleared up when one understands that those seizing Jesus were not the religious authorities themselves but police sent by them to capture Jesus. The opponents who arrived in Gethsemane were "a great multitude" (14:43) sent by Jewish leaders.

Among the minor characters or character groups in Mark's gospel, four of the most intriguing appear in Gethsemane. They are (1) an unnamed **servant of the high priest** (v. 47) whose ear was cut off; (2) an anonymous bystander, presumably one of the Twelve, who **drew a sword, and smote [the] servant … and cut off his ear**; (3) **a certain young man** (v. 51) who **left the linen cloth** (v. 52) with which he had been clothed when (4) **the young men laid**

hold on him (v. 51). The young man **fled from them naked** (v. 52). These characters stand in opposition to one another and reveal the only two positions that could be taken regarding Jesus at this crucial hour. One was either for Jesus (the bystander and the young man) or against Him (the servant and the young men).

In his superb storytelling, Mark even presented the bystander and the young man as foils to one another: the former took his loyalty to an unnecessarily bold and violent extreme, while the latter shows the other extreme in his panicky and timid flight. In their contrasting responses to the situation, both characters were ineffective allies for Jesus at this fatal moment. Mark's treatment of these minor characters clearly presents the only two alternatives between which the reader may choose regarding Jesus. If one chooses the way of discipleship, one must then avoid the two undesirable extremes (fight or flight), and that can be done only by watchful prayer (see 14:38).

The exact identities of these minor characters is left tantalizingly obscure by Mark. John recorded that Simon Peter drew the sword and struck the servant. It was his right ear that was cut off and that the servant's name was Malchus (see John 18:10). Malchus may have ducked his head to avoid having his entire head severed. Perhaps Peter, whose sermons Mark had collected, according to Papias, was ashamed to identify himself as the recklessly bold wielder of the sword. "The young men" (v. 51) may have been the police sent from the religious authorities (see 14:43). The "certain young man" (v. 51) also is not specifically identified, but his anonymity may suggest that this was John Mark, the writer of this gospel. If the upper room were indeed at his mother's house (see Acts 12:12), he may have followed Jesus and the others to the garden after the supper. The young man had **a linen cloth cast about his naked body**. Ordinarily, the outer garment was made of wool. The fine linen garment left behind in the hand of a guard indicates that the youth was from a wealthy family. The absence of an undergarment (he "fled from them naked"; v. 52) suggests that he had dressed hastily to follow Jesus. This was

an embarrassing fact. Who would have known of this incident, since all of Jesus' disciples had fled, and why place this in the gospel unless to indicate that the author was there also? Whoever he was, the young man is evidently a disciple of Jesus who fled in terror and shameful nakedness. In the narrator's mind, the linen cloth may have been an association with the death of Jesus. The Greek word for "linen cloth" (*sindōn*) also appears in 15:46, where Jesus was wrapped in a linen cloth and laid in a tomb. Abandoning Jesus at the hour of His death (represented by the forsaken linen), the young man displayed an imperfect and cowardly discipleship.

5. Jesus before the Sanhedrin (14:53–65)

14:53–59. Here the scene shifts to the residence of **the high priest** (v. 54), but the motif of timid discipleship continues, only now with Peter as one who **followed him afar off**. The word "followed" is Mark's usual word (Greek, *akoloutheō*) for following Jesus in discipleship, but here it is modified with the adverbial "afar off." Peter may not have fled completely (see 14:52), but his coming after Jesus was now more out of fearful curiosity than out of an intention to give testimony on behalf of his Lord. Peter's failure of nerve is especially lamentable in light of the fact that, while he **warmed himself at the fire** (v. 54) ... **many bare false witness against** (v. 56) Jesus. Their contradictory testimonies perhaps could have been silenced by a bold and truthful defense by Peter.

The council (v. 55) refers to the entire Sanhedrin, the high court of the Jews. In New Testament times, it was made up of three kinds of members: chief priests, elders, and scribes. Its total membership numbered seventy-one, including the high priest, who was presiding officer. At this time, he was Caiaphas, son-in-law of Annas, the former high priest. Under Roman jurisdiction, this council was given a great deal of authority, but it could not impose capital punishment. This Sanhedrin **sought for witness against Jesus to put him to death; and found none**. In Jewish judicial procedure, witnesses functioned as the prosecution. According to Deuteronomy 19:15, a person could not be convicted unless two or more witnesses gave testimony, which assumes that their testimonies had to agree. The **false witnesses** (v. 56) given included the erroneous accusation that Jesus said, **I will destroy this temple that is made with hands, and within three days I will build another made without hands** (v. 58). Jesus, according to John, did indeed make a claim like this. His accusers, however, had misconstrued His words (see John 2:19–21). Their stories did not **agree** (vv. 56, 59).

14:60–61. The drama in the high priest's residence now reaches its climax. Jesus, as the suffering Servant who does not open his mouth in his affliction (see Isa. 53:7), **held his peace, and answered nothing** (v. 61) during the inquest. To answer the accusations would have elevated baseless and treacherous lies to the status of legitimate charges. When questioned by the high priest, however, Jesus did respond. **Art thou the Christ, the Son of the Blessed?** The high priest used "the Blessed" as an epithet for "God" out of respect for the very name of God, which was not uttered in Jewish piety. The question concerned not a charge of false identity but Jesus' true identity as "the Christ" (the Anointed One) who is the Son of God. In this context, "the Son of the Blessed" might be understood to refer not to deity but to royal messiahship (since in popular Jewish belief, the Messiah [Christ] was to be a man, not God).

14:62. Jesus' answer is stunning, because in three ways He asserted His divine nature and prerogatives. (1) His affirmation **I am** (Greek, *Egō eimi*) echoes the language of Exodus 3:14. The identical phraseology appears there (in the Septuagint) as well as here. The association that the statement has with the high priest's reaction (14:63–64) makes it an unmistakable claim to Jesus' identification with Yahweh. (2) Jesus' claim to be **the Son of man** recollects Daniel 7:13 where "one like the Son of man came with the clouds of heaven, and came to the Ancient of days." The Son of Man, granted an everlasting dominion, is worshiped by all (see Dan. 7:14). (3) Jesus added to this description an affirmation that He is the Messiah, who shall be seen **sitting on the right hand of power**—a reference to Psalm 110:1 (a passage that Jesus had already identified as messianic,

see Mark 12:35–37). "The right hand of power" is an anthropomorphic epithet that signifies a position of absolute authority in the universe. The threefold claim of Jesus—"I am," the Son of Man, the Christ—is the most significant proclamation that Jesus made of Himself in the gospel. His possession of divine nature and power cannot be any more clearly or forcefully stated.

14:63–64. That Jesus made claims to share in divine authority and power was recognized in the high priest's response to Jesus' words. After he **rent** ("tore," NIV) **his clothes** (v. 63; an impassioned show of protest, outrage, grief, or shock [see Gen. 37:29; 2 Kings 18:37; 19:1]), the high priest addressed the Sanhedrin: **Ye have heard the blasphemy: what think ye?** (v. 64). The answer was a unanimous condemnation: **they all condemned him to be guilty of death,** or "deserving death" (NRSV). The sin of blasphemy not only involved reviling the name of God (see Lev. 24:10–16) but also included any affront to His majesty or authority (see Mark 2:7; 3:28–29; John 5:18; 10:33). Jesus' claim to be the Messiah and, in fact, to have majesty and authority belonging only to God, was therefore regarded by Caiaphas as blasphemy. For blasphemy, the Mosaic law prescribed death by stoning (see Lev. 24:16). "They all condemned him" may refer to a unanimous or nearly unanimous vote. Certainly it did not include the commendable Joseph of Arimathaea, who obtained Jesus' body from Pilate after the crucifixion to give Him a proper burial (see 15:43). Joseph was probably not present when the council met, nor was Nicodemus likely present. He accompanied Joseph in the burial procedures, according to John 19:39. Perhaps any council member who was sympathetic to Jesus was not invited to the sham trial, or perhaps such a member refused to attend out of protest.

14:65. Rather than receiving the honor that is His due as the Son of Man, Jesus underwent treatment that was outrageously brutal. The severity of the abuse is emphasized by the present tense of the verbs in Mark's description: **to spit on him, and to cover his face, and to buffet him.** Furthermore, **the servants did strike him with the palms of their**

hands. The NASB has "the officers received Him with slaps in the face." "Slaps" translates the Greek *rhapisma*, a word that, in a sixth-century AD papyrus, has the sense of a facial scar resulting from a blow. The violence of the word's later usage might have been in Mark's mind as he wrote. The word appears in the Septuagint of Isaiah 50:6 ("I gave my cheeks to slaps of the hand"). The indignity of the entire scene is highlighted in the tormentors' mocking call for Jesus to **Prophesy**, that is, to identify the one who stuck Him while He was unable to see (His face was covered). An old interpretation of Isaiah 11:2 – 4 held that the Messiah could judge by smell without the aid of sight.

6. Peter's Denial of Jesus (14:66 – 72)

14:66 – 72. What little hope, humanly speaking, there might have been for even a faint voice to be raised in Jesus' defense dissolved with Peter's threefold denial of Jesus. The way was now clear for His own prophecies to be fulfilled regarding His death (8:31; 10:33 – 34). Peter denied Jesus exactly as the Lord had foretold—three times before the rooster crowed twice (see 14:30). Some manuscripts omit certain words that are in the Greek text that is the basis for the KJV: **and the cock crew** (v. 72), **the second time**, and **twice**. Nevertheless, the meaning is clear: Peter succumbed to fear and denied association with Jesus the accused.

While Jesus was being beaten in an upstairs room of Caiaphas's house, **Peter was beneath in the palace** (i.e., below in the courtyard; v. 66). The resoluteness with which Peter denied Jesus is evident in that the denial was threefold ("on the evidence of two or three witnesses a matter shall be confirmed," Deut. 19:15 NASB). Ironically, Peter the disciple furnished the testimony-in-agreement that was being sought in Jesus' own trial before the high priest. Mark also emphasized Peter's resolute denial in recording that Peter **began to curse and to swear, saying, I know not this man of whom ye speak** (v. 71). "To curse" is *anathematizō*. Since the object of the cursing is unclear, the meaning may be that Peter was invoking a curse on himself ("He began to call down curses on

himself," NIV) if what he said was untrue. "To swear" is to add gravity to the curse and may have the sense of "May God do such and such to me if I am not telling the truth." The object of the curse may, however, have been Jesus. If so, Peter—the disciple of the great confession that Jesus is the Christ—was guilty of the very sin that true Christians can never commit: cursing Jesus (see 1 Cor. 12:3). Peter would then be the blasphemer, not Jesus (see 14:64)—more Markan irony. Peter had regressed from saying, **I know not, neither understand I what thou sayest** (common in Jewish law for a formal, legal denial; v. 68) to saying, **I know not this man of whom ye speak** (v. 71). This is further irony in that such an absolute denial is not what one would have expected of Peter.

Peter could not easily escape or deny his association with Jesus since he was readily marked as **a Galilean** (v. 70). Galileans were easily identified by their dialect. Peter's speech showed him to be a Galilean, and his presence among the Judeans in the courtyard suggested he was a follower of Jesus. When the apostle realized that he had denied his Lord—at the crowing of the rooster (v. 72; see 14:30)—**he wept** ("and he went out, and wept bitterly," Matt. 26:75; Luke 22:62).

William Barclay's comment on Peter's denial is striking: "Peter's failure was the kind of failure that could have happened only to a brave man. He alone was in a position to fail; the others had fled long ago. Again, it must always be remembered that this tragic story of Peter's denial must go back to none other than Peter himself. If Mark consists of the preaching material of Peter, then one of Peter's favorite sermons must have been on how he had failed and how Christ had forgiven" (*The Master's Men* [Nashville: Abingdon, 1959], pp. 23 – 24).

7. Jesus before Pilate (15:1 – 15)

15:1 – 5. The Jewish authorities **delivered [Jesus] to Pilate** (v. 1) because only the Roman governor had the authority in Judea to issue a capital sentence. Such a sentence had already been determined by the Sanhedrin to be appropriate in Jesus' case (see 14:64). The scene before Pilate occurred **straightway in the morning** ("Early in the morning," NASB). The working day of a Roman official began at daylight. It was now Friday of Passion Week.

Pilate was the Roman governor (prefect) of Judea from AD 26 to 36, whose official residence was in Caesarea on the Mediterranean coast. (In 1961, archaeologists working at Caesarea unearthed a stone contemporary with Pilate and inscribed with his name.) When he came to Jerusalem, he stayed in the magnificent palace built by Herod the Great, located west and a little south of the temple area. Mark used the Latin word "Pretorium" to indicate this palace in 15:16, and it was here that the Roman trial of Jesus took place.

Pilate's question, **Art thou the King of the Jews?** (v. 2) probably reflects the accusation that councilors made against Jesus before Pilate when they came to him with Jesus. The charge of blasphemy (see 14:64) was a Jewish concern, not a Roman one. A charge of treason against the emperor, however, was definitely a Roman concern, and a claim to kingship would be deemed a challenge to the supreme imperial authority in territory occupied by Rome, such as Judea was.

The Greek (*Sy ei*) of Pilate's question contains the emphatic personal pronoun: "Are you, a man like you, the King of the Jews?" Pilate's question was thus one of incredulity. Jesus immediately turned the tables, however. His answer, **Thou sayest it** (v. 2), also contains the emphatic pronoun *sy*; "you yourself are the one who says so" is the idea. The dynamic of reversal in the exchange is captured in Wuest's translation of verse 2: "And Pilate asked Him, 'As for you, are you the King of the Jews?' And answering him He says, 'As for you, you are saying it.'" Once again Jesus responded to questions about His own identity, **but he answered nothing** to false accusations (v. 3; see v. 5; 14:61). Pilate then became quite insistent and **asked him again, saying, Answerest thou nothing? behold how many things they witness against thee**. If Jesus made no defense, then according to Roman law, Pilate would have to pronounce against Him. Pilate was left with his own words to consider as he **marvelled** at Jesus and His refusal to answer the accusers. Did the governor consider Jesus to be the King of the Jews? Pilate was now the one on trial.

What would he do with Jesus? It is the question that every reader of Mark's gospel must also answer.

15:6-8. Beside what little about it is in the New Testament accounts (see Matt. 27:15; Luke 23:17; John 18:39), nothing specific is known about the **prisoner** (v. 6) release that Mark reported was a custom at the time of the Passover feast. Such a practice, however, is hinted at in the Mishnah, the ancient collection of rabbinic teaching. **Barabbas** (v. 7), in custody for the crime of insurrection and murder along with others charged with the same crimes, nevertheless was released by Pilate (see 15:15). Barabbas may have been a member of the Zealots, a revolutionary Jewish group. This group, however, may not have existed as an identifiable group until the period of the Jewish War, AD 66-70. Nothing from other sources is known about this insurrection, or uprising, though Mark wrote of it as if it were well known. Under the Roman prefects, however, such revolts were common.

Barabbas's presence in the narrative has a twofold function in Mark's narrative. (1) Barabbas is an ironic foil for Jesus. Despite the fact that Barabbas was guilty of insurrection and murder (Mark, as the narrator, did not say that he and the others were merely accused), the criminal was released — effectively pronounced innocent of the charges for which he was guilty. Jesus, on the other hand, was condemned on the charge of treason despite being innocent of hostility to Rome (see Mark 12:13-17). Jesus maintained His honor, however, since "the chief priests had delivered him for envy" (15:10) and Pilate was "willing to content the people" ("anxious to please the crowd," NLT; 15:15). All legal proceedings against Jesus were a corruption of justice.

(2) The second function of Barabbas's presence in the narrative is a theological one. Mark's audience could see a dramatization of their own release from sin when Barabbas went free and Jesus took his place. Jesus' death was a substitutionary ransom (see 10:45) for their sins, and the Barabbas story vividly demonstrated the practical benefits of that ransom.

15:9-15. Sadly and tragically, Pilate's shifting of the decision that he had to make about Jesus onto the crowd ended in the death of the Son of God. The feeble **Will ye …?** (v. 9), **What will ye …?** (v. 12), and **Why, what evil …?** (v. 14) all introduce questions of Pilate that sought to shirk his responsibility for deciding what to do with Jesus. Ultimately, not to decide about Jesus is to decide against Him. Pilate's threefold evasion is equivalent to Peter's outright threefold denial since the result was the same. The call of the multitude to **Crucify him** (vv. 13–14) was certainly not a verdict by a reasonable and impartial jury. The crowd had been moved by the envious **chief priests** (vv. 10–11). So, at the behest of the pliable crowd, the jealous priests, and the ingratiating Pilate, Barabbas was **released** (v. 15). Jesus was **delivered** to His executioners to be **scourged** and **crucified**.

The scourging that preceded the crucifixion of Jesus was the Roman practice of flogging. The Romans used a whip made of several strips of leather into which were embedded (near the ends) pieces of bone and lead. Such a whip could flay the victim's flesh so that bones and organs were exposed. The Jews, in their whippings, limited the maximum number of stripes to forty (in practice, to thirty-nine in case of a miscount), but no such limitation was recognized by the Romans, and victims of Roman floggings often did not survive. Mel Gibson's cinematic presentation *The Passion of the Christ* portrays accurately the gruesomeness of the torture of Roman scourging. It was this scourging that Jesus received.

8. The Soldiers Mock Jesus (15:16–20)

15:16. This section is one of the best examples of Markan irony. Jesus, whom the reader knows to be the Christ, the Son of God, and the Son of Man— a figure of supreme honor—was now ridiculed shamefully by Roman soldiers. They were not aware, as is the reader, that their crude and malicious jesting of Jesus as a pretender to kingship was in reality a recognition of that kingship. **The whole band** is "the whole cohort" (NRSV) of Roman soldiers attached to the governor and the palace that was his headquarters, the **Praetorium**. The word "Pretorium" was used originally of a general's tent or of the head-

quarters in a military camp. The soldiers quartered in the Pretorium were recruited from non-Jewish inhabitants of the Holy Land and assigned to the military governor. A cohort was a tenth part of a Roman legion—about six hundred men (but the number could vary). A great number of soldiers took part in the mockery of Jesus.

15:17. The derision was vicious and continual, and Mark presented it graphically. Jesus was given a robe of **purple**, and after the soldiers had **platted** ("twisted," NKJV) **a crown of thorns**, they **put it about his head**. Purple robes signified power; they were often an element of the insignia of field commanders, magistrates, and kings. Although Jesus' crown was undoubtedly painful, it mainly served to mock Him as a clown-king. The acanthus shrub would have been readily available for the crude wreath. Its spikes would have been a parody of ancient images that show monarchs with crowns whose points symbolically radiate their glory.

15:18–20. After mocking Jesus with the salutation, **Hail, King of the Jews!** (v. 18; a mocking salutation that corresponded to "Hail, Caesar!"), the soldiers inflicted continual abuse on Him: **And they smote him on the head with a reed, and did spit upon him, and bowing their knees worshipped him** (v. 19). The NASB captures well the torrential nature of the indignities (the verbs in v. 19 are in the imperfect tense): "They kept beating His head with a reed, and spitting on Him, and kneeling and bowing before Him." The spitting was probably a parody on the kiss of homage that was customary in the Near East when in the presence of royalty. When the mockery had ceased, the soldiers **took off the purple from him, and put his own clothes on him, and led him out to crucify him** (v. 20). A crucifixion detail was normally comprised of four soldiers and a commanding officer for each prisoner.

9. The Crucifixion and Death of Jesus (15:21–39)

15:21. Simon a Cyrenian (Cyrene was an important city of Libya in North Africa that had a large Jewish population) was compelled by the Roman soldiers to carry Jesus' cross. Men condemned to death were usually forced to carry a beam of the cross, often weighing thirty or forty pounds, to the place of crucifixion. Jesus started out by carrying His cross (see John 19:17), but He had been so weakened by flogging that Simon was pressed into service. Simon becomes an example of discipleship in Mark's account. The words **to bear his cross** recall Jesus' words regarding those who would follow Him: "let him … take up his cross" (8:34). The same Greek construction (*airō ton stauron*) appears in both places. To bear one's cross is to publicly identify with Jesus in the shamefulness of His death. Simon proves to be a foil, however unwilling he might have been in carrying the cross, to those who had already forsaken Jesus in the hour of His suffering. Mark's Roman audience would have taken courage in their suffering from Simon's example. Apparently, they were acquainted with his sons since Simon is identified as **the father of Alexander and Rufus**. Only Mark mentioned these men, and he referred to them in a way that suggests they were known by Mark's readers. Rufus may be the same person spoken of in Romans 16:13. Otherwise, who would care to know the names of this man's children? When Simon took up Jesus' cross, he dignified the suffering Jesus (His cross is worth bearing) and dignified himself as an ideal disciple.

15:22. Jesus was brought to **Golgotha, which is, being interpreted, The place of a skull**. The actual location of Golgotha is uncertain. One suggested site, known as Gordon's Calvary, is a rocky knoll pockmarked with caves, atop which has been a Muslim cemetery for centuries. Its perennial association with death, its situation outside the old city walls of Jerusalem (see Heb. 13:12), and its proximity to a tomb like that described in the Gospels has persuaded some that it was the execution site of Jesus. But one cannot be certain. Whatever the location of Jesus' execution, it was outside the city walls, was in a conspicuous place (perhaps near a highway and a city gate), and may have been a place that the Romans habitually used for crucifixions.

15:23 – 25. They crucified him (v. 25) by means of the execution that the Romans reserved for slaves,

people of the provinces, and dangerous criminals. Roman citizens were exempt from it, except in extreme instances like high treason. Its ghastliness made crucifixion generally effective as a deterrent to rebellion against Roman authority in Judea. Death typically came torturously slowly, through shock and asphyxiation, sometimes days after the victim had been bound or nailed to a cross, stake, or tree. The public disgrace of the victim was compounded by the executioners if they left the body on the cross to rot and/or to feed carrion birds. First-century authors vividly describe the agony and disgrace of being crucified. In Mark's account, however, the shame of Jesus' crucifixion is mitigated by several factors. The notation of crucifixion at **the third hour** (i.e., "nine o'clock in the morning," NLT) suggests that Mark wanted his audience to know the time at which Jesus' crucifixion began and ended (see discussion on 15:34). The brevity of Jesus' time on the cross reduces the shame associated with His death; the time that Jesus was exposed to public disgrace was short.

Jesus was fully alert to the pain and shame of His crucifixion. He refused the **wine mingled with myrrh** (v. 23), a concoction whose narcotic effects would have lessened the pain to some degree. The Talmud gives evidence that incense was mixed with wine to deaden pain. Myrrh is a spice derived from plants native to the Arabian deserts and parts of Africa. Jesus died wakeful and strong, not in any kind of undignified stupor.

When the soldiers of the crucifixion detail **parted** ("divided," NKJV) **his garments, casting lots upon them, what every man should take** ("They gambled for his clothes, throwing dice to decide who would get them," NLT; v. 24), they demonstrated that Jesus' garments were desirable. Hence, the wearer of them is dignified in the narrative. Mark's intention may have been to highlight that fact as much as to show that the gambling fulfilled Old Testament prophecy (see Ps. 22:18). It was the accepted right of the executioner's squad to claim the minor possessions of the victim. Jesus' clothing probably consisted of an undergarment, an outer garment, a belt, sandals, and possibly a head covering.

15:26–28. Further Markan irony lies in his identification of **the superscription of his accusation** ("The written notice of the charge against him," NIV; v. 26) affixed to the cross: **THE KING OF THE JEWS.** It was customary to write the charge on a wooden board that was carried before the victim as he walked to the place of execution, after which the board was affixed to the cross above his head. Although Jesus' judges had not ascribed the title "the King of the Jews" to Him, their identification on the basis of His condemnation (a political challenge to imperial sovereignty) unwittingly substantiated Jesus' claims.

Mark's term (Greek, *lēstēs*) to describe the **two thieves** (v. 27) could simply designate them as robbers or bandits. However, Josephus used the term to designate Jewish resistance fighters against Roman domination. Since according to Roman law, robbery was not a capital offense, Mark's term must signify men guilty of insurrection, crucified for high treason. The thieves might have been revolutionaries whose activities against the Romans involved banditry. Perhaps they were accomplices of Barabbas and others who at this time were in custody for sedition (see 15:7). Whatever their identity, the thieves' presence was a fulfillment of prophecy: **And he was numbered with the transgressors** (v. 28). Mark did not include many Old Testament quotations in his gospel, writing as he was for a non-Jewish audience, but these words are from Isaiah 53:12. The contents of verse 28 were almost certainly added to the original wording of Mark. Nevertheless, though the verse does not appear in older witnesses to the text of Mark's gospel, the hand responsible for it rightly appreciated Jesus' position between thieves as a symbol of His death for sinners.

15:29–32. Yet more irony is embedded in the mockery that Jesus' opponents hurled at Him as He hung on the cross. **He saved others; himself he cannot save** (v. 31), exclaimed **the chief priests** together **with the scribes.** Their statement was true; they unwittingly ascribed to Jesus' death an atoning quality (see 10:45; 14:24). For this reason, He could not save Himself. To do so would have meant that the ransom would not be paid. Mark thus portrayed Jesus' death

to be His own willing self-sacrifice—a death of inestimable worth and honor, not of dishonor. Passersby **railed on him** ("were hurling abuse at Him," NASB)**, wagging their heads** ("shaking their heads in mockery," NLT; v. 29). They also rehearsed the accusation that Jesus would destroy **the temple** only to rebuild it **in three days,** a charge that Mark already showed to be false (see 14:57–59). The readers of Mark's crucifixion account know Jesus' honor to be intact despite His apparently ignominious death. Whatever slander Mark's readers might experience because they are Christians is parallel to the suffering of their Lord. Their honor too remains intact.

15:33–34. Mark's careful chronology designates a time of **darkness over the whole land** (v. 33) from **the sixth** up to **the ninth hour** (i.e., from noon until 3:00 p.m.; see NRSV). In the Bible, darkness connotes judgment and death, particularly the eschatological day of the Lord (see 13:24). Darkness at the crucifixion scene symbolizes God's judgment on sin. The judgment on the sin of all men was focused on the Son of Man hanging on the cross since His death was "a ransom for many" (10:45). **At the ninth hour** (v. 34), Jesus therefore cried, **My God, my God, why hast thou forsaken me?** These words were so important to Mark's concept of salvation that he preserved their Aramaic form along with his Greek translation. The words from Psalm 22:1 indicate that Jesus is the ultimate righteous sufferer who cried to God in His distress. For Jesus to quote the initial verse of this psalm was to declare its fulfillment in His own life. Jesus' cry further signifies that He had entered human "godforsakenness." Humans may therefore now have Jesus' Father as their Father too. Through the cross, Jesus is the one present with humanity in its estrangement from God and in its sense of abandonment and loneliness, whatever the cause. In Mark, Jesus is both one's representative in this sense and one's ransom who died as one's substitute (see 10:45; 14:24).

Readers may ask, but how can God forsake God? How can He be separated from Himself? German theologian Jürgen Moltmann says, "To understand what happened between Jesus and his God and Father on the cross, it is necessary to talk in trinitarian terms. The Son suffers dying, the Father suffers the death of the Son. The grief of the Father here is just as important as the death of the Son. The Fatherlessness of the Son is matched by the Sonlessness of the Father, and if God has constituted himself as the Father of Jesus Christ, then he also suffers the death of his Fatherhood in the death of the Son" (*The Crucified God: The Cross of Christ as the Foundation and Criticism of Christian Theology*, trans. R. A. Wilson and John Bowden [New York: Harper & Row, 1974], p. 243).

15:35 – 37. Some of the bystanders misunderstood Jesus' cry and thought that He had called for **Elias** ("Elijah," NASB; v. 35). It was commonly believed that Elijah would come in times of critical need to protect the innocent and rescue the righteous. The mockers sarcastically urged one another to await the great prophet's rescue of Jesus. At the same time, a **spunge full of vinegar** (a type of wine used by laborers and soldiers; v. 36) was offered to Jesus to drink.

It may have quenched Jesus' thirst, but it did not deaden His pain. He may well have refused it altogether (see 15:23). **Jesus cried with a loud voice, and gave up the ghost** ("Jesus breathed his last," NIV; v. 37). The strength of His cry indicates that Jesus did not die the ordinary death of those crucified, who normally suffered long periods of complete agony, exhaustion, and then unconsciousness before dying. The shame of the cross is counteracted by Jesus' sturdiness at this point.

15:38. The effect of Jesus' expiration was that **the vail of the temple was rent in twain** ("torn in two," NJB) **from the top to the bottom**. This is a curious statement and appears somewhat out of place in the narrative, which has focused so precisely on the suffering of Jesus, but the tearing of the veil was important for Mark as another symbol of the meaning of Jesus' death. "The vail" (Greek, *katapetasma*) may refer to the "curtain" (NRSV) that separated the Holy of Holies from the Holy Place in the temple, or it may refer to the curtain that hung at the entrance from the courtyard into the Holy Place, the place where incense was burned. Both curtains were

enormous (perhaps 60 feet by 30 feet and about 5 inches thick). If Mark identified the former curtain, the theological meaning is clear: the way to God's presence (localized in the Holy of Holies and accessible only to the high priest) is now open to all by the death of Jesus (see Heb. 6:19; 9:3; 10:19 – 20). If the latter veil is Mark's reference, however, the tearing was more of a public event and vindicated Jesus in terms of the slanderous mockery that He had endured (v. 29). In Jesus' death, God had begun the destruction and replacement of the temple. In either case, the tearing of the curtain symbolizes a new era that began with Jesus' death. This new era could have been inaugurated only by the work of God ("from the top to the bottom"). Jesus' crucifixion has inestimable importance and great honor attached to it. His was not the execution of a common criminal but a death for the sins of the world.

15:39. The confession of **the centurion** who witnessed the crucifixion and observed Jesus' death is the climax of Mark's gospel. In the Roman army, a centurion was a commander of one hundred men. The centurion at the cross was in a Roman auxiliary unit that was attached to a legion and that had the same number (six thousand) of soldiers. This officer of an infantry cohort was perhaps a Roman citizen. His utterance, **Truly this man was the Son of God**, forms a parallel between the end of the narrative and Mark's opening statement, "The beginning of the gospel of Jesus Christ, the Son of God" (1:1). In His death, Jesus was given the highest ascription of honor that a man can receive. Rather than being inglorious and demeaning, Jesus' death established and revealed His glory in an ultimate way. Although the phrase "the Son of God" could be translated "a son of God" (Goodspeed), the parallel with 1:1 suggests that the reader ought to understand the title in the way Mark has repeatedly portrayed Jesus' sonship in his gospel: Jesus Christ is uniquely *the* divine Son of God.

10. The Burial of Jesus (15:40 – 47)

15:40 – 41. Mark's mention of **women looking on afar off** (v. 40) is important to his narrative for three reasons. (1) Women who observed Jesus' death and burial were the ones who came to the tomb to anoint His body (see 16:1). They could not have mistakenly visited the wrong tomb on Easter morning since two of the three women whom Mark named in 16:1 "beheld where he was laid" (15:47). Any skepticism of the Resurrection that says the women went to the wrong tomb is thus effectively silenced.

(2) Mark specifically named some of the many women who observed Jesus' death: **Mary Magdalene, and Mary the mother of James the less and of Joses, and Salome** (v. 40). Mark 16:9 and Luke 8:2, reveal that Jesus had driven seven demons from Mary Magdalene. Salome was probably the wife of Zebedee and the mother of James and John (see Matt. 27:56). The author thus furnished the names of three eyewitnesses to Jesus' death and of the empty tomb (see also 16:1–8), two of whom witnessed His burial also (see 15:47). Their individual testimonies about the events of Good Friday and Easter morning could have been independently corroborated. The fact that theirs is *female* testimony further validates the historical reliability of the account since a woman's testimony was legally inadmissible in official Judaism. No one concocting the series of events Mark describes would invent witnesses who were women.

(3) Within the wider circle of disciples (beyond the Twelve) were women who **followed him** (Greek, *akoloutheō*; Mark's usual term for designating disciples; v. 41). They also **ministered unto him**, which indicates that they were women of means who shared their wealth with Jesus and His apostolic band. Their commitment was solid, for they "were accustomed to follow with Him and minister to Him the necessities of life" (Wuest). Even while Jesus was alive, a group of women counterpart to the Twelve were disciples and had a distinct and important ministry.

15:42–47. Jesus' burial was handled by **Joseph of Arimathaea** (v. 43). Mark described him as **an honourable counsellor** ("a prominent member of the council," NASB) whose sympathies lay with the Jesus movement since he awaited **the kingdom of God**. He **went in boldly unto Pilate, and craved the body of Jesus** ("asked for the body of Jesus,"

NRSV). Since victims of crucifixion normally suffered much longer, sometimes for days, before dying, **Pilate marvelled if he were already dead** ("Pilate couldn't believe that Jesus was already dead," NLT; v. 44). The Roman centurion officially verified the death of Jesus, a fact that should not be missed lest one is inclined to think that Jesus did not really die but merely swooned only to revive later. It was the "corpse" (ASV; v. 45) that Pilate gave to Joseph. Joseph then took Jesus' body and **wrapped him in the linen** (v. 46) that he had bought for the occasion. The release of the body of one condemned for high treason, and especially to one who was not an immediate relative, was quite unusual.

Joseph placed Jesus' body **in a sepulchre which was hewn out of a rock**. There is archaeological evidence that the traditional site of the burial of Jesus (the Church of the Holy Sepulchre in Jerusalem) was a cemetery during the first century AD. There is also good evidence, however, that the site known as the "Garden Tomb" was also used in the first century and that an early church was once constructed over that site as well. Before the **door** was **rolled a stone**, a large, disc-shaped boulder that rolled in a sloped channel. The placement of the stone was Joseph's responsibility but almost certainly occurred with assistance. Jesus' burial was completed **before the Sabbath** (v. 42), on **the preparation** (Friday). Since it was now late in the afternoon, there was an urgency to get Jesus' body down from the cross before sundown, when the Sabbath began.

In Mark's account of Jesus' burial, the shame of the cross is counteracted in several ways: (1) Jesus was buried after hanging on the cross but a short time; (2) a pious and noble person attended to Jesus' burial; (3) Jesus did not suffer the indignity of hanging on a cross overnight and into the Sabbath day, as the burial was complete before the Sabbath (when these procedures were prohibited); (4) Pilate allowed the burial to proceed although the Romans forbade such a burial to those who were put to death under the charge of high treason, as Jesus was; (5) Jesus received the dignity of a new burial shroud of fine linen; (6) He was placed in a tomb that allowed a dignified and careful placement of the corpse within it; and (7) the blocking of the tomb with a stone shielded Jesus' remains from predatory animals and public exposure. Mark, as he did throughout the gospel, established Jesus as a figure who received honor in life and death. The shame of His cross and the travesty of justice that led Him to it are effectively counteracted. When Mark's readers were abused for their association with Jesus the crucified, they would have been encouraged that their Lord is honorable and to be honored as the Son of God.

VII. The Resurrection of Jesus (chap. 16)

A. The Empty Tomb (16:1–8)

16:1–2. Now that **the sabbath was past** (v. 1), the women could attend to the body of Jesus in such a way that the haste of Friday's burial had not allowed. The same three women mentioned in 15:40 **had bought sweet spices**, which they now brought to the tomb of Jesus that they might **anoint him**. The women probably bought the spices during the brief interval after sundown on Saturday (about 6:00 p.m. Saturday evening) when the shops opened for business at the conclusion of the Sabbath. There would have been no time, however, to visit the tomb then. Therefore, **very early in the morning** (v. 2) on Sunday they came to pay Jesus one last act of devotion and honor. "Anoint" is probably used here in the sense of "to apply to the body," not specifically "to pour over the head." The stench of decomposition was lessened by the application of spices. In light of Jesus' prophcies of His resurrection (8:31; 9:9–10; 10:34), suspense builds for the reader: what will the women find when they arrive at the tomb? How will they react to what they find? In captivating irony, the reader knows that Jesus will rise, but the actors in the story do not expect that event. The women certainly did not since they came expecting to find a corpse to anoint.

16:3–4. The stone (v. 3) now becomes the focus of the narrative. Setting the large stone in place was a relatively easy task, but once it had slipped into the groove cut in bedrock in front of the entrance, it was very difficult to remove. Boulders that covered entrances of tombs like the tomb of Jesus were from five to six feet in diameter, and although of varying thicknesses, their average weight was hundreds of pounds. Mark's description of the stone as **very great** (v. 4) might have been his way of saying that its removal was a supernatural event.

16:5. Inside the large opening of the facade of the tomb was a forechamber, at the back of which a low rectangular opening led to the burial chamber. **Entering** (v. 5) the forechamber, the women encountered **a young man**. He is not identified, and he is described only as **clothed in a long white garment**. Could this be the young man who fled from Gethsemane, leaving his garment behind (14:51–52)? Had he now been reinstated by the Lord, had his nakedness covered, and had been entrusted by the Lord Himself with a message for the band of Jesus' followers whom he had previously forsaken? The word "young man" (Greek, *neaniskos*) is the same word in both accounts, as is the word "clothed" (Greek, *periballō*). Almost certainly, however, here the "young man" is an angelic figure and is to be distinguished from the mere youth in 14:51–52. The same term could describe both. The word for garment here (Greek, *stolē*) is different from that in 14:51–52 (Greek, *sindōn*) and is described as "white," suggesting a supernatural origin. The women would not have been **affrighted** ("alarmed," NRSV), so distressed, at the sight of a mere youth in the tomb, although they would have undoubtedly been surprised. Matthew understood him to be an angel (see Matt. 28:2–4; see also Luke 24:4–5).

16:6. The announcement of this alarming figure was that **Jesus of Nazareth, which was crucified**, whom the women seek, **is risen**. The proof of His resurrection was the absence of a corpse on the shelf within the tomb where the body would have been laid. The use of the passive verb here (lit., "was raised") indicates that the resurrection was accomplished by the power of God. Jesus was not merely resuscitated; He, though dead, was raised up to a totally new plane of existence: **he is not here**. The stranger's announcement is the early Christian preaching in a nutshell: Jesus, who was crucified, had risen from the dead by the power of God.

16:7. The women were to carry the astounding message of Jesus' resurrection to **his disciples**. In **Galilee**, they would see Him once again, just as His promise (unrecorded by Mark) had guaranteed. The two words **and Peter**, found in no other gospel, powerfully express the forgiveness of any sin. "How that message must have cheered Peter's heart when he received it! He must have been tortured with the memory of his disloyalty, and suddenly there came a special message for him. It was characteristic of Jesus that he was concerned not so much because of him, but due to the remorse he was undergoing. Jesus was far more eager to comfort the penitent sinner than to punish the sin" (William Barclay, *The Gospel of Mark*, rev. ed. [Philadelphia: Westminster, 1975], p. 369).

16:8. The women did not heed the young man's command not to be afraid (see 16:6). Rather, they **fled from the sepulchre; for they trembled and were amazed** ("because they were frightened out of their wits," JB; they were "beside themselves with terror," NEB). The women said nothing to anyone, **for they were afraid**. The reader would expect these faithful disciples (see discussion on 15:41) to deliver the message that they had been enjoined to deliver by the angelic stranger in the tomb. That message had Christ's own authority behind it. Here is more Markan irony: the women at the tomb, who were commanded to speak, did not. The leper, who had been commanded to silence, nevertheless spoke out (see 1:44–45). Only the formerly demon-possessed man (see 5:19–20) and the evil spirits themselves were obedient in this matter (see 1:27; 3:12; see also 9:10, where the disciples' silence stemmed from confusion, not obedience).

B. The Longer Ending of Mark (16:9–20)

16:9–20. Some textual critics, even some conservative scholars, have serious doubts as to whether these verses belong to the gospel of Mark. They point out that Mark 16:9–20 is absent from important early manuscripts and displays certain peculiarities of vocabulary, style, and theological content that are unlike the rest of Mark, noting that his gospel probably ended at 16:8 or that its original ending has been lost.

In modern translations of the New Testament (e.g., NASB, NIV, NRSV), this passage is distinguished from the rest of Mark 16 by brackets and/or marginal notes. Since the seventeenth century, when the KJV was translated, older and more reliable manuscripts have become available. The textual tradition of these manuscripts does not have verse 9–20, whereas the textual tradition of more recent manuscripts includes them. One witness (an Old Latin manuscript) concludes Mark with an unnumbered "shorter ending." Furthermore, some manuscripts not only have the so-called longer ending of Mark but also have the shorter ending as well. One manuscript contains verses 9–20 with an expansion of verse 14.

Various positions have been taken regarding the ending of Mark in light of the different readings among the witnesses (Greek New Testament manuscripts, early versions of the New Testament in other languages, lectionaries, and citations among the early church fathers). Among the views regarding Mark 16:9–20 are the following: (1) Mark's gospel originally included the longer ending of Mark. Verses 9–20 should therefore be considered genuine. (2) The ending of the gospel was lost. The various readings that follow verse 8, including the longer ending of verses 9–20, represent attempts to complete the gospel. (3) Mark intended his gospel to end with verse 8. The ending, therefore, is not lost.

An argument in favor of the first view is that the majority of witnesses to the text of the gospel of Mark include verses 9–20 and, therefore, the longer ending should be accepted as the original closing to the book. Only a small handful of manuscripts omit these verses, and the arguments for seeing them as original are equally compelling to some. The number of witnesses, however, does not in itself constitute a conclusive argument.

For the second view to be a viable theory, one must establish that Mark was virtually unnoticed after the practically immediate publication of two other, more popular gospels, Matthew and Luke. Mark, however, undoubtedly enjoyed a substantial circulation before Matthew and Luke drew from it for their gospels, and no reason exists to doubt widespread recognition of Mark after these gospels were composed. There never was a time when a lost ending could not have been retrieved.

Finally, in favor of the third view is that the tone of fearful amazement by the women at the tomb is consistent with responses to Jesus elsewhere in Mark. According to this view, the author intended to leave the reader in a state of awe. One must decide for oneself what to do in response to the empty tomb. Will one take the challenge and proclaim the risen Jesus or fall into fearful silence? Nevertheless, the third view may be challenged by the fact that, in Mark, Jesus' prophecies always come true. One would expect the prophecy of a Galilean appearance (see 16:7) to be followed with a record of its fulfillment.

If Mark intended his gospel to end with verse 8, the reader is thus left with the decision whether to be a bold witness of the resurrected Lord or not. The element of alarm and terror with which the gospel ends is an effective literary device and reinforces the motif of awe that has already emerged in the narrative (see 4:41; 5:15, 33; 6:20, 50; 9:15, 32; 10:32; 11:18, 32; 12:12). The fulfillment of Jesus' prophecy in 14:28 of meeting them in Galilee, which is mentioned and reinforced by the angel in 16:7, is unrecorded because Mark wanted to leave the reader in a place where he or she must decide whether to go on with Jesus in obedient discipleship or not.

How is one to regard verses 9–20? Whether integral to the gospel or not, they represent old tradition — historically reliable — and ought to be considered carefully in any study of Mark. The material offers insight into early understandings of Jesus and the apostolic mission. It ought to be used with reserve, however, in teaching and preaching. No doctrine or practice should be based exclusively on Mark 16:9–20.

16:9–11. Jesus **appeared first to Mary Magdalene, out of whom he had cast seven devils** ("demons," NASB; v. 9). This information is also given in Luke 8:2 and represents a motif in the gospel of Mark: Jesus is sovereign over the powers of darkness (see 1:21–28, 34; 3:22–28; 5:1–20; 7:24–30; 9:14–29), and He delegates His sovereignty to His followers so that they may be victorious in their encounters with demonic foes (see 3:15; 9:29; 16:17). Mary **went and told** (v. 10) the disciples as they **mourned and wept** that Jesus had risen from the tomb. But they **believed not** (v. 11).

16:12–13. The disciples persisted in their unbelief even when Jesus **appeared in another form unto two of them** (v. 12) as they were in the countryside. The NLT expands the translation to include the effect of the metamorphosis: "but they didn't recognize him at first because he had changed his appearance." The phenomenon is recorded in Luke 24:13–35 but in a much expanded form. When these two disciples reported to the others that they had seen Jesus, **neither believed they them** (v. 13). Throughout the narrative, the disciples display fear and unbelief. The reader does not condemn them, for they are not outright enemies, but the reader criticizes their obtuseness and disbelief. By evoking such responses, the narrator enables the reader to judge the quality of his or her own discipleship. "Would I have been willing to believe in the miraculous and have acted on it, or would I have let only what I could have seen for myself determine my faith?'

16:14–15. Later, **as they sat at meat** ("as they sat at the table," NKJV; v. 14), Jesus **appeared unto the eleven** (the original group now missing Judas Iscariot). He **upbraided** ("reproached," NASB) **them with** ("for," NASB) **their unbelief and hardness of heart**. The testimony of those **which had seen him after he was risen** is sufficient as a basis for faith, according to Jesus. That testimony is preserved in the New Testament. The seeker should investigate the evidence firsthand in the gospels in order to decide whether belief in a risen Jesus is reasonable. In Mark's gospel, it most certainly is!

Faith in Jesus is lived out in a commitment to **preach the gospel to every creature** (v. 15; the word "go" is grammatically subordinate to "preach": "having gone into the whole world, preach!"). The one who believes what is preached — the good news of Christ's death as a ransom and His resurrection from the dead — will be saved. The Great Commission is found here, in the other three gospels (see Matt.

28:19–20; Luke 24:47–48; John 20:21), and in Acts 1:8. Jesus' final words are our "marching orders."

16:16. According to Mark, **he that believeth and is baptized shall be saved**. One cannot teach that baptism is necessary for salvation from this doubtful text. In the New Testament, as important as baptism is (see Matt. 28:19), it is the public demonstration of salvation, which takes place inwardly through faith in Christ. Faith in the New Testament has a public dimension to it (see Mark 8:34–38), and baptism is an integral feature of that public quality. Baptism does not save, nor is it required for salvation. Notice that to **be damned** one has only not to believe. Nothing is said about not being baptized.

16:17–18. Accompanying **signs** (v. 17) should probably be understood as miraculous phenomena that serve to confirm the truthfulness of the gospel and the reality of the faith that believers have placed in Christ (see 16:16). Jesus mentioned five such phenomena. Those who believe shall (1) **cast out devils**; (2) **speak with new tongues** (not necessarily in the sense of languages that were previously unspoken, but perhaps "new" in the sense of unknown to the speaker; see Acts 2:1–12); (3) **take up serpents** (v. 18; see Acts 28:3–6); (4) not be **hurt** if they happen to **drink** something poisonous (an accidental ingestion of poison, not an intentional act of proving one's faith by doing something foolish); and (5) **lay hands on the sick**, effectively being God's agents of healing (see James 5:14–15).

A word of caution is in order here. One is ill-advised to base a practice on this text. Any doctrine or practice derived from this section of Scripture ought to have a basis in passages of the New Testament whose genuineness is certain. Furthermore, simply because a practice is mentioned in Scripture does not mean that it is normative for every believer. Because a biblical passage is *descriptive* does not mean that it is *prescriptive*. Hence, unless the author clearly indicated that he intended to establish a phenomenon as a precedent, the reader must not conclude that its presence is equivalent to a command for him or her. This text does not require the reader to consider anything in it as prescriptive rather than simply descriptive.

16:19–20. Jesus' authority was confirmed in His ascension to **heaven** (v. 19), where He sits at **the right hand of God** (both ideas, that of Jesus sitting in one place and that of God having a physical hand, are examples of anthropomorphism). Jesus is seen in this concluding passage as the Lord who accompanied the obedient disciples in their ministry wherever they might go: He was **working with them** (v. 20) and **confirming the word with [the] signs** that He promised in 16:17–18. Whatever the specific task in Christian service, the disciple has the very power of Jesus working with him or her. One's ministry is Jesus' ministry, and He will energize His servants and bring through them the results that He wills, and when He wills. **Amen.**

THE GOSPEL ACCORDING TO ST. LUKE

INTRODUCTION

Author

The author's name does not appear in the book, but much unmistakable evidence points to Luke. This gospel is a companion volume to the book of Acts, and the language and structure of these two books indicate that both were written by the same person. They are addressed to the same individual, Theophilus, and the second volume refers to the first (see Acts 1:1). The author was not present in Palestine during the ministry of Christ but relied on testimony gathered later (see Luke 1:2–4). He was present during at least part of Paul's ministry, however, as certain sections in Acts use the pronoun "we" (Acts 16:10–17; 20:5–15; 21:1–18; 27:1–28:16), indicating that the author was with Paul at that time. Paul mentioned Luke in the epistles as one of his companions, further strengthening the association and thus the authorship of this gospel as well as Acts.

By process of elimination, "Luke, the beloved physician" (Col. 4:14) and Paul's "fellowlabourer" (Philemon 24), becomes the best possible candidate for authorship. This is supported by the uniform testimony of early Christian writings (e.g., the Muratorian Canon, AD 170, and the works of Irenaeus, ca. 180). Other early church writers allude to Luke as the author of this gospel as well, including Clement and Justin Martyr (see *Dictionary of Jesus and the Gospels*, s.v. "Luke, Gospel of").

Luke was probably a Gentile by birth, well educated in Greek culture, a physician by profession, a companion of Paul at various times from his second missionary journey to his first imprisonment in Rome, and a loyal friend who remained with the apostle after others had deserted him (see 2 Tim. 4:11). Some, citing Luke's knowledge of the Old Testament, have argued that he was a Hellenistic Jew who had become a Christian, but this has not gained much popularity. Antioch (of Syria) and Philippi are among the places suggested as his hometown, though it is not certain.

Although Luke acknowledged that many others had written of Jesus' life (1:1), he did not indicate that he relied on these reports for his own writing. He used personal investigation and arrangement, based on testimony from "eyewitnesses and ministers of the word" (1:2), including the preaching and oral accounts of the apostles. His language differences from the other Synoptics and his blocks of distinctive material (e.g., 10:1–18:14;

19:1–28) indicate independent work, though he obviously used some of the same sources. While Paul was imprisoned at Caesarea, Luke would have had ample time to research Jesus' life and to talk with many eyewitnesses then living in Israel.

Date and Place of Composition

The two most commonly suggested periods for the composition of the gospel of Luke are: (1) AD 59–63 and (2) the 70s or the 80s (see chart, *Zondervan KJV Study Bible*, p. 1349). Luke's gospel was written before the Acts of the Apostles and is referred to as Luke's "former treatise" (Acts 1:1). Since the book of Acts closes with Paul in Rome awaiting trial, about AD 62, some assume that Luke was written while Paul was imprisoned in Caesarea awaiting the appeal of his trial before the Roman emperor. That would date the gospel's publication at about AD 60.

The place of writing was probably Rome, though Achaia, Ephesus, and Caesarea also have been suggested. The place to which it was sent would, of course, depend on the residence of Theophilus. By its detailed designations of places in the Holy Land, the gospel seems to be intended for readers who were unfamiliar with that land. Antioch, Achaia, and Ephesus are possible destinations.

Recipient

The gospel is specifically directed to Theophilus (1:3), whose name means "one who loves God" and almost certainly refers to a particular person rather than to lovers of God in general. The use of "most excellent" (1:3) with the name further indicates that this was an individual and supports the idea that he was a Roman official or at least someone of high position and wealth. He was possibly Luke's patron, responsible for seeing that the writings were copied and distributed. Such a dedication to the publisher was common at that time. Theophilus, however, was more than a publisher. The message of this gospel was intended for his instruction (1:4) as well as for the instruction of those among whom the book would be circulated.

Theme and Theological Message

The third gospel presents the works and teachings of Jesus that are especially important for understanding the way of salvation. Its scope is complete from the birth of Christ to His ascension, and it appeals to both Jews and Gentiles. That the gospel was initially directed to Theophilus does not narrow or limit its purpose. It was written to inform and undergird the faith of believers and to displace disconnected and ill-founded reports about Jesus. Luke wanted to show that the place of the Gentile Christian in God's kingdom is based on the teaching of Jesus; he wanted to commend the preaching of the gospel to the whole world.

Since the Synoptic Gospels (Matthew, Mark, and Luke) report many of the same episodes in Jesus' life, one would expect much similarity in their accounts. The dissimilarities reveal the distinctive emphases of the separate writers. Luke's characteristic themes include: (1) universality, recognition of Gentiles as well as Jews in God's plan; (2) emphasis on prayer, especially on Jesus' praying before important occasions (see discussion on 3:21); (3) joy over the announcement of the gospel or "good news" (see discussion on

1:14); (4) special concern for the role of women; (5) special interest in the poor (some of the rich were included among Jesus' followers, but He seemed closest to the poor); (6) concern for sinners (Jesus was a friend to those deep in sin); (7) stress on the family circle (Jesus' activity included men, women, and children, with the setting frequently in the home); (8) repeated use of the title "Son of man" (e.g., 19:10); (9) emphasis on the Holy Spirit (see discussion on 4:1). The main theme of this gospel, however, is the nature of Jesus' messiahship and mission, and the key verse is 19:10.

Literary Features

Luke had outstanding command of the Greek language. His vocabulary is extensive and rich, and his style at times approaches that of classical Greek (as in the preface, 1:1–4), while at other times it shows Semitic influences (1:5–2:52), much like the Septuagint Greek translation of the Old Testament. His vocabulary reveals geographical and cultural sensitivity in that it varies with the particular land or people being described. When Luke referred to Peter in a Jewish setting, he used more Semitic language than when he referred to Paul in a Hellenistic setting.

The writing is characterized by literary excellence, historical detail, and warm, sensitive understanding of Jesus and those around Him. The arrangement of Luke's gospel is orderly, and his account of Jesus' ministry can be divided into three major parts: (1) the events that occurred in and around Galilee (4:14–9:50), (2) those that took place in Judea and Perea (9:51–19:27), and (3) those of the final week in Jerusalem (19:28–24:53). Luke's uniqueness is especially seen in the amount of material devoted to Jesus' closing ministry in Judea and Perea. This material is predominantly made up of accounts of Jesus' discourses. Sixteen of the twenty-three parables that occur in Luke are found there (9:51–18:14; 19:1–28). Of the twenty miracles recorded in Luke, only four appear in these sections. Already in the ninth chapter, Jesus is seen anticipating His final appearance in Jerusalem and His crucifixion (see discussions on 9:51; 13:22).

Outline

I. The Preface (1:1–4)
II. The Coming of Jesus (1:5–2:52)
    A. The Annunciations (1:5–56)
    B. The Birth of John the Baptist (1:57–80)
    C. The Birth and Childhood of Jesus (chap. 2)
III. The Preparation of Jesus for His Public Ministry (3:1–4:13)
    A. His Forerunner (3:1–20)
    B. His Baptism (3:21–22)
    C. His Genealogy (3:23–38)
    D. His Temptation (4:1–13)
IV. Jesus' Ministry in Galilee (4:14–9:9)
    A. The Beginning of the Ministry in Galilee (4:14–41)
    B. The First Tour of Galilee (4:42–5:39)
    C. A Sabbath Controversy (6:1–11)
    D. The Choice of the Twelve Disciples (6:12–16)

G. Jesus' Arrest (22:47–65)

H. Jesus on Trial (22:66–23:25)

I. The Crucifixion (23:26–56)

J. The Resurrection (24:1–12)

K. The Post-Resurrection Ministry (24:13–53)

Bibliography

Bock, Darrell L. *Luke 1:1–9:50*. Baker Exegetical Commentary on the New Testament. Grand Rapids, MI: Baker Academic, 1994.

———. *Luke*. The IVP New Testament Commentary. Downers Grove, IL: InterVarsity Press, 1994.

Godet, Frederick Louis. *Commentary on Luke*. Grand Rapids, MI: Kregel, 1982.

Liefeld, Walter L. "Luke." In *The Expositor's Bible Commentary*, edited by Frank E. Gaebelein, vol 8. Grand Rapids, MI: Zondervan, 1995.

Marshall, I. Howard. *The Gospel of Luke*. The New International Greek Testament Commentary. Grand Rapids, MI: Eerdmans, 1978.

Morris, Leon. *Luke: An Introduction and Commentary*. Tyndale New Testament Commentaries 3. Grand Rapids, MI: Eerdmans, 1988.

Robertson, A. T. *A Harmony of the Gospels*. San Francisco: HarperOne, 1932.

Stein, Robert H. *Luke*. The New American Commentary 24. Nashville: Broadman & Holman, 1992.

EXPOSITION

I. The Preface (1:1–4)

1:1–4. Using language similar to classical Greek, Luke began his gospel with a formal preface, common to historical works of that time, in which he stated his purpose for writing and identified the recipient. He acknowledged other reports on the subject, showed the need for this new work, and stated his method of approach and sources of information.

1:1. Things which are most surely believed among us. Things prophesied in the Old Testament and now fully accomplished.

1:2. Delivered them unto us. A technical term for passing on information as authoritative tradition. **Eyewitnesses, and ministers of the word.** Luke, though not an eyewitness himself, received testimony from those who were eyewitnesses and were dedicated to spreading the gospel. Apostolic preaching and interviews with other individuals associated with Jesus' ministry were available to him.

1:3. Having had perfect understanding of all things. Luke's account is exact in historical detail, having been checked in every way. Inspiration by the Holy Spirit does not rule out human effort. The account is complete, extending back to the very beginning of Jesus' earthly life. It has an orderly, meaningful arrangement that is generally chronological. **Most excellent.** Paul used this respectful term for governors Felix (Acts 24:3) and Festus (Acts 26:25). **Theophilus.** See Introduction: "Recipient."

1:4. That thou mightest know the certainty of those things. While John focused on a personal outcome, that his readers might know Christ (see John

20:31), Luke focused on a more informational outcome: that Theophilus might know about the events that happened.

II. The Coming of Jesus (1:5–2:52)

A. The Annunciation (1:5–56)

1:5. Herod, the king of Judea. Herod the Great reigned 37–4 BC, and his kingdom included Samaria, Galilee, much of Perea, and Coele-Syria (see discussion on Matt. 2:1). The time referred to here is probably circa 7–6 BC. **Zacharias ... Elisabeth.** Both were of priestly descent from the line of Aaron. **The course of Abia.** From the time of David, the priests were organized into twenty-four divisions, and Abia (Abijah) was one of the "priests, the chief of the fathers" (Neh. 12:12, 17; see 1 Chron. 24:10).

1:6. Righteous ... blameless. Zacharias and Elisabeth were not sinless but were faithful and sincere in keeping God's commandments. Simeon (see 2:25) and Joseph (see Matt. 1:19) were given similar praise.

1:7. For **no child**, see discussion on 1:25.

1:9. To burn incense. One of the priest's duties was to keep the incense burning on the altar in front of the Most Holy Place. He supplied it with fresh incense before the morning sacrifice and again after the evening sacrifice (see Exod. 30:6–8). **His lot was.** Ordinarily, a priest would have this privilege very infrequently, and sometimes never, since duty assignments were determined by lot (see discussions on Neh. 11:1; Prov. 16:33; Jonah 1:7; Acts 1:26).

1:11. An angel of the Lord (see 1:19). In this story, the angel appears to make an announcement of tremendous importance (the coming birth of John as forerunner to Christ). Whenever angels appear in Scripture, they are always on very important business related to God's overall plan for His people. We should remember that angelic appearances in Scripture are rare, sometimes separated by hundreds of years. We should not expect to see angels appearing before us, nor should we expect to see them on trivial business, such as giving moral advice (we have God's Word for that) or "helping out" in little ways, though Hollywood often treats angels in this way. Jesus' statement in Matthew that little chil-

dren receive the attention of angels is no exception, for Jesus said that "in heaven their angels do always behold the face of my Father" (Matt. 18:1), not that they make appearances on earth. **The right side of the altar.** The south side, since the altar faced east.

1:12. Fear fell upon him. A common reaction to the appearance of an angel, as with Gideon (see Judg. 6:22–23) and Manoah (see Judg. 13:22). Readers are told nothing of the angel's physical appearance or whether that was what evoked fear in Zacharias. The angel may have resembled the living creatures that Ezekiel saw, but more likely, it had a more human appearance. Zacharias's fear may have stemmed simply from the angel's sudden and supernatural appearance.

1:13. Fear not. This word of reassurance is given many times in both the Old Testament and the New Testament (see, e.g., 1:30; 2:10 and discussion; 5:10; 8:50; 12:7, 32; Gen. 15:1; 21:17; 26:24; Deut. 1:21; Josh. 8:1). Often it accompanies a commission for an important task or an assurance of success. Here it simply means that the angel posed no threat to Zacharias. **John.** The name (derived from Hebrew) means "The Lord is gracious."

1:14. Joy. A keynote of the opening chapters (see 1:44, 47, 58; 2:10).

1:15–16. These verses describing John's life begin with a general statement that is then further explained. **He shall be great in the sight of the Lord** (v. 15), not in terms of human greatness but in terms of the spiritual influence that his life would have on others. First, his greatness would be seen in his high level of moral purity; he would take neither **wine nor strong drink.** It appears likely that John was subject to the Nazarite vow of abstinence from alcoholic drinks (see Num. 6:1–4). If so, he was a lifelong Nazarite, as were Samson (see Judg. 13:4–7) and Samuel (see 1 Sam. 1:11). Second, he would be great in that **he shall be filled with the Holy Ghost.** This is often a reference to one's anointing for a speaking ministry. In the book of Acts, someone is said to be "filled with the Holy Ghost" (e.g., Acts 4:8, 31; 13:9) just before preaching, and Paul linked this phrase with singing and worship (see Eph. 5:18–19).

John would have a preaching ministry that the Lord would anoint with power and effectiveness. Third, he would be great in the sight of the Lord because of the influence of his ministry. **Many** (v. 16) would **turn to the Lord** through him.

1:17. Elias. John was not Elijah returning in the flesh (see John 1:21), but he would function like that Old Testament preacher of repentance and would therefore be a contingent fulfillment of Malachi 4:5–6 (see Matt. 11:14; 17:10–13). Three results would flow from the revival that John's preaching would engender. (1) John's ministry would **turn the hearts of the fathers to the children** (see discussion on Mal. 4:6). When revival comes, it should turn people who are absorbed with themselves and their own needs toward the future and the needs of others. It should also emphasize family. A sure sign that revival is more than just emotions is when fathers take responsibility for their families. (2) John's ministry would turn **the disobedient to the wisdom of the just**. Revival always brings about true repentance. Disobedience here is contrasted with wisdom. No matter how much people may know, until they humble themselves before the Lord in obedience, they lack wisdom. (3) John's ministry would create **a people prepared for the Lord**. John would help fulfill Isaiah's prophecy (see Isa. 40:3–5; Luke 3:4–6). He would spiritually prepare the people to receive the message Christ preached and to receive Him as Lord.

1:18. Whereby shall I know this? Like Abraham (see Gen. 15:8), Gideon (see Judg. 6:17), and Hezekiah (see 2 Kings 20:8), Zacharias asked for a sign (see 1 Cor. 1:22).

1:19. Gabriel. The name can mean "God is my hero" or "mighty man of God." Only two angels are identified by name in Scripture: Gabriel (see Dan. 8:16; 9:21) and Michael (see Dan. 10:13, 21; Jude 9; Rev. 12:7).

1:20. Thou shalt be dumb, and not able to speak. The punishment fit the crime. The angel sentenced Zacharias to months of silence, unable to form words, **because thou believest not my words**, that is, the angel's message regarding John's birth and ministry (see 1:13–17).

1:21. And the people waited for Zacharias. They were waiting for him to come out of the Holy Place and pronounce the Aaronic blessing (see Num. 6:24–26).

1:22. He could not speak. Luke begins with a priest who cannot speak to bless the people and ends with Christ, our High Priest, being lifted up into heaven as He dispenses a final blessing. The people **perceived that he had seen a vision**, probably because he indicated with gestures something of what had happened.

1:23. The days of his ministration. Each priest was responsible for a week's service at the temple once every six months. For **his own house**, see 1:39.

1:24. Elisabeth … hid herself. Perhaps in joy, devotion, and gratitude that the Lord had taken away her childlessness.

1:25. The Lord … looked on me, to take away my reproach. Not only did lack of children deprive the parents of personal happiness, but it was generally considered an indication of divine disfavor and often brought social reproach (see Gen. 16:2, Sarai; 25:21, Rebekah; 30:23, Rachel; 1 Sam. 1:1–18, Hannah; see also Lev. 20:20–21; Ps. 128:3; Jer. 22:30).

1:26–35. This section speaks clearly of the virginal conception of Jesus (vv. 27, 34–35; see Matt. 1:18–25). The conception was the work of the Holy Spirit; in this act, the eternal second person of the Trinity, while remaining God, was also "made flesh" (John 1:14). From conception, Jesus was fully God and fully man.

1:26. In the sixth month. That is, from the time of John's conception. For **Nazareth**, see discussion on Matthew 2:23.

1:27. For **espoused**, see discussion on Matthew 1:18.

1:28–30. Hail. "Ave" in the Latin Vulgate (from which comes "Ave Maria"). **Thou that art highly favoured, the Lord is with thee.** The Lord found in Mary a special quality of servanthood. She was willing to serve God in whatever way He wanted. God resists the proud but gives grace to the humble (see James 4:6). It is interesting that the angel had to say to Mary, "Fear not" (v. 30), just as Zecharias was told the same. Angelic appearances must have been quite frightening.

1:31. JESUS. The name Jesus is the Greek form of Joshua, which means "the Lord saves."

1:32–33. He shall be great (v. 32), but His greatness would differ from that of John the Baptist. Jesus would change not just Israel for a time but the world for all time. **The Son of the Highest.** This title has two senses: (1) the divine Son of God and (2) the Messiah born in time. The context makes it clear that Jesus' messiahship is referred to in these verses. "The Highest" is a title frequently used of God in both the Old Testament and the New Testament (see 1:35, 76; 6:35; 8:28; Gen. 14:19 and discussion; 2 Sam. 22:14). After His resurrection, Jesus would be given **the throne** that was promised in the Old Testament to the Messiah descended from David (see 2 Sam. 7:13, 16; Pss. 2:6–7; 89:26–27; Isa. 9:6–7). Jesus promised His disciples that they would sit upon twelve thrones, ruling over the twelve tribes of Israel, in conjunction with His own reign (see Matt. 19:28). **His father David.** Mary was a descendant of David, as was Joseph (see Matt. 1:16), so Jesus could rightly be called a "son" of David.

He shall reign ... for ever (see Ps. 45:6; Rev. 11:15)**; and of his kingdom there shall be no end** (v. 33). Although Christ's role as mediator will one day be finished (see 1 Cor. 15:24–28), the kingdom of the Father and Son, as one, will never end. David's lineage, of which, humanly speaking, Jesus is a part, will thus never cease to rule over Israel.

1:34. How shall this be ...? Mary did not ask in disbelief, as Zacharias had (see 1:20, 45). She sought information rather than expressing doubt. Rather than centering on how it could be that her Son would be so great, her question centered on her virginity: how could she be with child, **seeing I know not a man.**

1:35. Holy thing. Jesus never sinned (see 2 Cor. 5:21; Heb. 4:15; 7:26; 1 Peter 2:22; 1 John 3:5). He was born sinless because the supernatural overshadowing of the Holy Spirit prevented sin from being passed to Him from His mother. The virgin birth (conception) was necessary for three prominent

reasons: (1) to fulfill prophecy (see Isa. 7:14); (2) to be a sign; (3) to avoid the curse on Coniah (see Jer. 22:30).

1:36. Thy cousin Elisabeth. It is not known whether Elisabeth was Mary's cousin, aunt, or other relation. The Greek word has a breadth of meaning, suggesting simply a "relative." Given the likely age difference between the two women, it is not wrong to suppose that another relationship is in view here.

1:37. With God nothing shall be unpossible. This verse is often quoted out of context. All things are indeed possible to Him who has all power and all knowledge. Believers must not presume, however, that God will always smooth the way for them or give them success in whatever schemes they cook up. The reality is that since all things are possible to Him, believers can be confident that His plans will be worked out. No barrier is too great for God to overcome in the fulfillment of His plan for the ages. The believer's task is not to invoke His aid for one's personal plans but rather to submit to Him and be a part of His plan.

1:38. Be it unto me. Mary submitted to God's will for her life. The context reveals that sometimes God's plan may not always be the easiest for us. A pregnancy would certainly cause problems for Mary, who was not yet married. She would also be taking on the responsibilities of motherhood right on the heels of marriage and would have no time to adjust to her new circumstances before starting a family. Truly, God's plan may not be the easiest or most comfortable path. God loves us and wants to bless our lives, but living according to His will sometimes means moving out of one's comfort zone and change one's plans in response to His. Mary could react to the announcement in this way because of how well she knew God, through knowing His Word. This becomes clearer in light of her words in 1:46–55. Knowing God as she did, Mary fortunately had no false illusions about God wanting to always make her happy. She instead saw herself as His servant and humbly accepted His will.

1:39–40. Saluted Elisabeth (v. 40). This simply means that Mary greeted Elisabeth in the usual respectful manner of a younger person toward her elders in that day and setting.

1:41–43. Elisabeth, **filled with the Holy Ghost** (v. 41), spoke under divine inspiration. Being filled with the Spirit is here again associated with speaking (see discussion on 1:15). Elisabeth recognized that Mary was **the mother of my Lord** (v. 43). It is unclear whether she had already heard of the angel Gabriel's announcement to Mary or whether she received a revelation from the Lord at that moment. In either case, she recognized the lordship of Jesus Christ as a reality that touched her life personally, even before He was born.

1:44. Leaped … for joy. In some mysterious way, the Holy Spirit produced this remarkable response in the unborn baby.

1:45. Elisabeth recognized that Mary had been singled out for the work of bearing Jesus because she was submitted to the Lord. It is noteworthy that Luke cast Mary's role in all of this as humble rather than exalted. Mary was the humble servant of God and was willing to be an instrument of His plan. She saw herself not as exalted in any sense but merely as a humble servant of God (see 1:46–55).

1:46–55. This is the first of four hymns preserved in Luke 1–2 (see 1:68–79; 2:14; 2:29–32 and discussions). This hymn of praise is known as the "Magnificat" (meaning, "exalts"), from its opening word in the Latin Vulgate Bible. This song is like a psalm and should also be compared with the song of Hannah (see 1 Sam. 2:1–10 and discussions). It was not at all unusual for young girls of that day to write poetry; thus, it is not surprising that Mary handled the astounding news that she would be the virgin mother of the Christ child by writing poetry about it, nor that she shared her poem with an older relative whom she respected. Mary had something unique to write poetry about, and her poem reveals a deep understanding of who God is and what He does.

1:46–47. The poem opens with Mary's heart reaction to what God had said. **My soul doth magnify the Lord** (v. 46). This means she sought to make Him great in the world as well as to give Him a bigger

place in her life. She wished to give Him the glory for what was happening to her.

1:48–49. Mary then wrote what God had done for her: **He hath regarded the lowly estate of his handmaiden** (v. 48). He had noticed her even though her place in the world was small. Note that she again called herself "handmaiden" (see 1:38), which in this context means a very humble and lowly servant (*Holman Bible Dictionary*, s.v. "Maid"). **All generations shall call me blessed**. God had done something great for her, and she recognized this. It had not changed her estimation of herself, however, which is rather surprising. When God uses one in a great way, the temptation to become proud is very real. Mary is an example and encouragement to remain humble even when great things happen through one's life and ministry. Believers must remember that when God does great things for a person, it reveals not so much how wonderful that person is as how wonderful He is.

1:50–55. This section reveals how Mary found it in her heart to accept from God's hand such a blessing as this, to be His instrument for bringing God's Messiah into the world. She could accept God's surprising will for her life because she knew something of His character. The Old Testament had given her clues as to how God works in the world. She revealed her understanding of these things in this part of her poem.

1:50. His mercy is on them that fear him. God is merciful. Mary recognized that people need mercy; they deserve wrath, but God is a God of grace. If people fear Him, that is, revere Him and live in harmony with His will, He will show them mercy.

1:51–53. He hath shewed strength with his arm (v. 51). God is powerful. He is able to accomplish what He intends. Mary knew that God had acted powerfully in the past. These verses explain how God is powerful. **He hath scattered the proud**. Mary knew her Bible well. God had done this for Israel many times, and she had heard in the synagogue how God had overthrown the mighty Assyrian Empire and how He had swept away the Egyptian army in the Red Sea. Mary knew how God treated the proud, and she would have expected Him to do the same again. God never changes.

Put down the mighty ... exalted them of low degree (v. 52). One cannot help but think of Saul and David here, and perhaps Mary did too. Mighty Saul was removed from the throne of Israel, and lowly David, the little shepherd boy and the youngest of his family, was raised by the appointment of God to be king.

He hath filled the hungry with good things (v. 53). Elijah was fed by ravens in the wilderness. The Israelites received the manna. Mary knew these things and knew that God would take care of those in need. He has regard for "them of low degree" (v. 52), that is, the poor.

1:54–55. In remembrance of his mercy (v. 54). The song ends with an assurance that God will be true to His promises to His people. Mary's faith was in a God who puts down the proud, exalts the humble, shows mercy to those who fear Him, and fulfills His promises to His people. Mary knew the Old Testament stories of what God had done in the past. She knew that a Messiah was promised to Israel, and she expected God to fulfill that promise. It did not surprise her one bit that God would choose someone like her, someone of a lowly background, to bear Christ. A God who puts down the proud and exalts the humble would do that. Mary could humbly accept what God intended for her because she knew God so well.

B. The Birth of John the Baptist (1:57–80)

1:56–63. Three months (v. 56). Mary evidently remained with Elisabeth until John's birth and then returned to her home in Nazareth. **Called him ... after the name of his father** (v. 59). An accepted practice in that day, as seen in Josephus (*Life* 1). **They made signs to his father** (v. 62). Apparently assuming that since he was mute, he was also deaf. **A writing table** (v. 63). Probably a small wooden board covered with wax.

1:64–67. Filled with the Holy Ghost, and prophesied (v. 67). Prophecy not only but also proclaims God's word. Both Zacharias and Elisabeth

(see 1:41–45) were enabled by the Holy Spirit to express what they otherwise could not have formulated.

1:68–79. This is the second of four hymns preserved in Luke 1–2 (see 1:46–55; 2:14; 2:29–32 and discussions). This hymn is called the "Benedictus" (meaning, "Blessed be"; v. 68), from its opening word in the Latin Vulgate. Whereas the Magnificat (see discussion on 1:46–55) is similar to a psalm, the Benedictus is more like a prophecy. Here we have the content of Zacharias's words of praise to God mentioned in 1:64.

1:68. He hath visited and redeemed his people. Not limited to national security (see 1:71) but including moral and spiritual salvation (see 1:75, 77). "Visited" may simply mean that God had made His power known among them in the way that John was born, and "redeemed" here means that He would bring people to repentance through John's ministry. This prophetic hymn needs to be seen in light of what the angel had told Zacharias months before. Zacharias, certainly being aware of the circumstances of his wife's relative, Mary, may have had Jesus Christ in mind as well (see 1:69).

1:69. Horn. Here symbolizes strength, as in the horn of an animal (see Deut. 33:17; Ps. 22:21; Mic. 4:13). Jesus, the Messiah from **the house of ... David**, has the power to save.

1:70–73. Zacharias saw what was happening in his family and in his community as evidence that God was about to fulfill the promises made to Abraham and to his descendants. Jesus embodied that fulfillment in His earthly life and ministry and will complete it when He returns.

1:74. We being delivered. No doubt including liberation from all kinds of oppression and bondage as well as deliverance from sin. **Might serve him without fear.** Perfect love casts out all fear, and Zacharias foresaw a time when, according to the promises of God, serving Him would be a response of love to a loving God rather than a response of fear of God's judgment. That judgment was surely accomplished at the cross, that all who are in Christ may serve without fear, knowing God's mercy.

1:75. In holiness and righteousness. This carries forward the theme of service after Christ's had accomplished redemption for all sinners. Servants of Christ are set apart by Christ and justified by the Father. Believers therefore not only are free of fear but are secure in their position in Christ.

1:76. John would be **called the prophet of the Highest**, whereas Jesus would be called "the Son of the Highest" (see 1:32 and discussion). **To prepare his ways** (see discussion on 3:4). The angel had told Zacharias that his son would go before the Lord to ready the people for His coming (see 1:16–17). Well might he have remembered those words in this moment, for it was right after hearing them that he had expressed the doubts that had caused his voice to cease.

1:77. John's ministry would be characterized by evangelism, something else Zacharias had learned from the angel (see 1:16–17).

1:78. The dayspring. A reference to the coming of the Messiah (see also similar figures in Num. 24:17; Isa. 9:2; 60:1; Mal. 4:2). Zacharias not only praised his own son, "the prophet of the Highest" (1:76), but also gave honor to the coming Messiah (see 1:79).

1:79. This verse describes the ministry of Jesus. Under divine inspiration, Zacharias said, He will **give light to them that sit in darkness**, that is, to the lost, those who are separated from God (see Isa. 9:1–2; Matt. 4:16). "Light" here means truth, and "darkness" means error. This imagery is common in Scripture and is one of the keys to John's gospel. **To guide our feet into the way of peace** (see discussion on 2:14). Here is the idea of the reversal of the fall, which will be fully accomplished when Christ returns. The fall put man at enmity with God, with others, and with himself. Jesus reconciles us to God so that "we have peace with God through our Lord Jesus Christ" (Rom. 5:1), just as He reconciles each to one another so that all might "live peaceably with all men," and to oneself so that one might have His peace, "which passeth all understanding" (Phil. 4:7).

1:80. Was in the deserts. John's parents, old at his birth, probably died while he was young, and

he apparently grew up in the desert of Judea, which lies between Jerusalem and the Dead Sea. **Till … his shewing unto Israel**. John's preaching and announcing the coming of the Messiah marked his public appearance. He was about thirty years old when he began his ministry (see discussion on 3:23).

C. The Birth and Childhood of Jesus (chap. 2)

2:1. Luke is the only gospel writer who related his narrative to dates of world history. **Cesar Augustus**. The first and, according to many, greatest Roman emperor (31 BC–AD 14). Having replaced the republic with an imperial form of government, Augustus expanded the empire to include the entire Mediterranean world, established the famed *Pax Romana* ("Roman Peace"), and ushered in the golden age of Roman literature and architecture. Augustus (which means "exalted") was a title voted to him by the Roman senate in 27 BC. **The world**. That is, the Roman Empire. **Taxed**. This was a type of census or enrollment used for military service and taxation. Jews, however, were exempt from Roman military service. God used the decree of a pagan emperor to fulfill the prophecy of Micah 5:2.

2:2. Cyrenius. This official was possibly in office for two terms, first in 6–4 BC and then in AD 6–9. A census is associated with each term. This verse refers to the first term; Acts 5:37 refers to the second.

2:3. Every one into his own city. Probably the city of their ancestral origin.

2:4. God not only used the decree of a pagan emperor; He also provided Joseph and Mary with an opportunity to demonstrate submission to earthly authority, for **Joseph also went up** in obedience to the command. Joseph may not have been aware of the prophecy of the Messiah coming from Bethlehem, and how obedience to a Roman decree would bring about the will of God. One must be wary of assuming that God cannot work His will through those who do not acknowledge Him. The Romans, due to their tendency for meticulous record-keeping, ensured that this prophesy would be fulfilled. **Nazareth … Bethlehem**. Bethlehem, the town where David was born (see 1 Sam 17:12; 20:6), was at least a three-day trip from Nazareth. **Judea**. The Greco-Roman designation for the southern part of the Holy Land. Judea had earlier been included in the kingdom of Judah.

2:5. With Mary. Mary too was of the house of David and probably was required to enroll. In Syria, the Roman province in which the Holy Land was located, women twelve years of age and older were required to pay a poll tax and therefore to register. For **espoused**, see discussion on Matthew 1:18.

2:6–7. How long Joseph and Mary stayed in Bethlehem is not known. Mary may have been near to term when they arrived, or perhaps they could not leave because of her condition once they had registered. **Swaddling clothes** (v. 7). Strips of cloth were regularly used to wrap a newborn infant. **Manger**. The feeding trough of animals. This is the only indication in the Bible that Christ was born in a stable. Very early tradition suggests that Christ was born in a cave, perhaps used as a stable.

2:8. Shepherds abiding in the field. This does not necessarily mean that it was summer, the dry season. The flocks reserved for temple sacrifice were kept in the fields near Bethlehem throughout the year. **Keeping watch**. Against thieves and predatory animals.

2:9. The angel of the Lord. A designation used throughout the birth narratives (see 1:11; Matt. 1:20, 24; 2:13, 19). The angel of 1:11 is identified as Gabriel (1:19; see 1:26). **The glory of the Lord shone**. This was the Shekinah glory, which had once rested upon the temple (see 1 Kings 8:11).

2:10. Fear not. Fear was the common reaction to angelic appearances (see discussion on 1:13), and encouragement was needed. The angel's message was one of good news, over which the shepherds should rejoice. In addition, the universal implication of the gospel is emphasized: **which shall be to all people**. Luke was writing to a Gentile audience and emphasized early that the coming of Christ was an event with worldwide consequences, not just local ones.

2:11. City of David. Bethlehem. **Saviour**. Many Jews were looking for a political leader to deliver them from Roman rule, while others were hoping for a savior to deliver them from sickness and physical hardship, but this announcement concerns the Savior who would deliver from sin and death (see Matt. 1:21; John 4:42). **Christ**. Or "Messiah." "The Christ" (Greek) and "the Messiah" (Hebrew) both mean "the Anointed One." **The Lord**. A designation originally reserved for God but later applied to the Messiah as well (see Acts 2:36; Phil. 2:11).

2:14. This is the third hymn preserved in Luke 1–2 (see 1:46–55; 1:68–79; 2:29–32 and discussions). This brief hymn is called the "Gloria in Excelsis Deo," from its opening words in the Latin Vulgate Bible (meaning, **Glory to God in the Highest**). The angels recognized the glory and majesty of God by praising Him. "In the highest" is a reference to heaven, where God dwells (see Matt. 6:9). **Peace, Good will**. Peace is assured not to all but only to those who are pleasing to God, the objects of His good pleasure (see Luke's use of the words "well pleased," 3:22; "good," 10:21; and "good pleasure," 12:32). The Roman world was experiencing the *Pax Romana* ("Roman Peace"), which was marked by external tranquillity, but the angels proclaimed a deeper, more lasting peace than that, a peace of mind and soul made possible by the Savior (see 2:11). Peace with God is received by faith in Christ (see Rom. 5:1), and it is believers who, through faith, are pleasing to God (Heb. 11:6). The Davidic Messiah was called "The Prince of Peace" (Isa. 9:6), and Christ promised peace to His disciples (see John 14:27). Christ also brought conflict (the "sword," Matt. 10:34–36; see also Luke 12:49), however, for peace with God involves opposition to Satan and his work (see James 4:4).

2:15–18. The shepherds had heard the word of God, and now they sought to see for themselves what God was doing. These shepherds dropped every other priority to be involved personally with what God was doing. **With haste** (v. 16) can literally mean, "jumping fences."

2:19. Mary's life at this time was a whirlwind of new experiences, many of which were overwhelming. Being a new mother is a major turning point in itself, but when the shepherds showed up with their story, confirming what she had heard from the angel, from Joseph no doubt, and from Elisabeth, her store of **all these things** grew. Certainly she had much to ponder **in her heart**. It may be that Mary was still alive when Luke wrote his gospel, and if so, she certainly would have been among the people that he talked with during his preparation and research (see Luke 1:2–3).

2:20. Glorifying and praising God. Terms of praise and giving glory to God often used by Luke (see 1:64; 2:13, 28; 5:25–26; 7:16; 13:13; 17:15, 18; 18:43; 19:37; 23:47; 24:53).

2:21–28. Her purification (v. 22). Following the birth of a son, the mother had to wait forty days before going to the temple to offer sacrifices for her purification. If she could not afford a lamb and a pigeon (or dove), then two pigeons (or doves) were acceptable (see Lev. 12:2–8; 5:11). **To Jerusalem**. The distance from Bethlehem to Jerusalem was only about six miles. **To present him to the Lord**. The firstborn of both man and animal were to be dedicated to the Lord (see 2:23; Exod. 13:12–13). The animals were sacrificed, but the human beings were to serve God throughout their lives. The Levites served in the place of all the firstborn males in Israel (see Num 3:11–13; 8:17–18).

The consolation of Israel (v. 25). Refers to the comfort the Messiah would bring to His people at His coming (see 2:26, 38; 23:51; 24:21; Isa. 40:1–2; Matt. 5:4). **The Holy Ghost was upon him**. Not in the way common to all believers after Pentecost. Simeon was given special insight by the Spirit so that he would recognize the Christ.

2:29–32. This is the fourth hymn preserved in Luke 1–2 (see 1:46–55; 1:68–79; 2:14 and discussions). This hymn of Simeon has been called the "Nunc Dimittis" (meaning, "Now … You are releasing"), from its opening words in the Latin Vulgate Bible.

2:29–30. Simeon had seen the means by which God would bring salvation to the world. He could die in peace knowing that the promises of God were being fulfilled. It is not that he had doubted but rather that he wanted to see the Savior, so great was his devotion to God and to his people.

2:31–32. All people (v. 31). Simeon recognized, as had some of the Old Testament prophets (see, e.g., Isa. 11:1; 42:6; Mal. 1:11), that God's plan would include the Gentiles. As a Gentile himself, Luke was careful to emphasize the truth that salvation would now be offered to **the Gentiles** (v. 32) as well as to Jews. This may be why he recorded Simeon's hymn. It does not advance the narrative significantly, although it does point out that spiritually sensitive people recognized Jesus for who He is.

2:33. Joseph. Luke, aware of the virgin birth of Jesus (see 1:26–35), never referred to Joseph as Jesus' human father. He was, however, Jesus' legal father. Mary and Joseph **marvelled at those things which were spoken of him**. This seems strange at first, as both Mary and Joseph had been given supernatural revelation regarding this child (see 1:26–38; Matt. 1:20). They were wise to expose themselves to people who were spiritually sensitive. Often when God does something significant in one's life, He will confirm it among those who are spiritually sensitive.

2:34. Fall and rising again of many in Israel. Christ raises up those who believe in Him but is a stumbling block for those who disbelieve (see 20:17–18; 1 Cor. 1:23; 1 Peter 2:6–8). **A sign which shall be spoken against**. In the years ahead, Jesus would be spoken against by the Pharisees, later on by the Romans, and afterward by yet others. The church has suffered persecution through the centuries, no less in current time than in earlier ones.

2:35. A sword shall pierce through thy own soul also. The word "also" indicates that Mary, as well as Jesus, would suffer deep anguish. This is the first reference in this gospel to Christ's suffering and death.

2:36. Anna. The same name as the Old Testament's Hannah (see 1 Sam. 1:2), which means "gracious." Anna praised God for the child Jesus, as Hannah had praised God for the child Samuel (see 1 Sam. 2:1–10). **Prophetess**. Other prophetesses were Miriam (see Exod. 15:20), Deborah (see Judg. 4:4), Huldah (see 2 Kings 22:14), and the daughters of Philip (see Acts 21:9).

2:37. Departed not from the temple. Herod's temple was quite large and included rooms for various uses, and Anna may have been allowed to live in one of them. This statement, however, probably means that she spent her waking hours worshiping in the temple. Both Anna and Simeon are presented as quite elderly.

2:38. Jerusalem. This is the holy city of God's chosen people (see Isa. 40:2; 52:9). Naturally, people would have looked there, the center of Jewish worship, for Israel's **redemption**.

2:39. They returned into Galilee. Luke did not record the coming of the wise men, the danger from Herod, or the flight to and return from Egypt (see Matt. 2:1–23). Harmonizations of the Gospels, however, often place those events between verses 38 and 39 (see Robertson, *Harmony*, 12–13). Luke's omission of these events is no error. His audience would hardly have cared about these details in the way that Matthew's certainly did. Luke's birth narrative was already long, and he included material that was relevant for his Gentile audience (such as the hymn of Simeon) and left out other matters that would not be as relevant.

2:40. Jesus laid aside certain attributes of His deity when He took on flesh. It is no denial of His deity to recognize that He **grew** and changed in the days of His flesh. He was not, as medieval painters often depicted Him, a child-sized adult.

2:41. The feast of the passover. The law commanded that all adult males (normally accompanied by their families) annually attend three feasts: Passover, Pentecost, and Tabernacles (see discussions on Exod. 23:14–17; Deut. 16:16). Distance prevented many from attending all three, but most Jews tried to be at Passover.

2:42–46. Twelve years old (v. 42). At age twelve, Jewish boys began preparing to take their places in the religious community the following year. **Three days** (v. 46). One day traveling away from Jerusalem, a second traveling back, and a third looking for Him. **The doctors**. The rabbis, experts in Judaism.

2:47–52. I must be about my Father's business (v. 49). Jesus pointed to His personal duty to His Father in heaven. He contrasted His "my Father" with Mary's **thy father** (v. 48). At twelve years of age, He

was aware of His unique relationship to God, but He was also obedient to His earthly parents (v. 51).

And Jesus increased … in favour with God and man (v. 52). Here Luke appears to have borrowed the words of 1 Samuel 2:26. Although Jesus was God, there is no indication that He had all knowledge and wisdom from birth. He seems to have matured like any other boy as to the regular elements of His human nature.

III. The Preparation of Jesus for His Public Ministry (3:1–4:13)

3:1–4:13. This section describes the events that led to Jesus beginning His public ministry. Luke described the ministry of John the Baptist (3:1–20) in terms that echo statements made in chapters 1–2, showing that he fulfilled the ministry that had been ordained for him as Christ's forerunner. After recording John's baptism of Jesus (3:21–22), Luke offered his genealogy of Christ (3:23–38), followed by his account of the temptation of Jesus (4:1–13).

A. His Forerunner (3:1–20)

3:1. The fifteenth year of the reign of Tiberius Cesar. Historians frequently dated an event by giving the year of the ruler's reign in which the event happened. Several possible dates could be indicated by this description, but the date AD 25–26 (Tiberius had authority in the provinces beginning in AD 11) best fits the chronology of the life of Christ. The other rulers named do not help pinpoint the beginning of John's ministry but only serve to indicate the general historical period. **Pontius Pilate**. The Roman prefect who then ruled in Judea, Samaria, and Idumea. **Herod being tetrarch of Galilee**. At the death of Herod the Great (4 BC), his sons—Archelaus, Herod Antipas, and Herod Philip—were given jurisdiction over his divided kingdom. Herod Antipas became the tetrarch of Galilee and Perea (see discussion on Matt. 14:1). **Lysanias the tetrarch of Abilene**. Nothing more is known of this Lysanias than that his name has been found in certain inscriptions.

3:2. Annas and Caiaphas being the high priests. Annas was high priest from AD 6 until the Roman official Gratus deposed him in AD 15. He was followed by his son Eleazar, his son-in-law Caiaphas, and then four more sons. Even though Rome had replaced Annas, the Jews continued to recognize his authority (see John 18:13; Acts 4:6), so Luke included his name as well as that of the Roman appointee, Caiaphas. **The word of God**. The source of John's preaching and authority for his baptizing. God's message came to John as it came to the Old Testament prophets (see Jer. 1:2; Ezek. 1:3; Hos. 1:1; Joel 1:1). **Wilderness**. Refers to a desolate, uninhabited area.

3:3. Baptism of repentance (see discussion on Matt. 3:11). John's baptism represented a change of heart, which includes sorrow for sin and a determination to lead a holy life. **Remission of sins**. Christ would deliver the repentant person from sin's penalty by dying on the cross.

3:4. Prepare ye the way. Before a king made a journey to a distant country, the roads he would travel were improved. Similarly, preparation for the Messiah was made in a moral and spiritual way through John's ministry, which focused on repentance, forgiveness of sin, and the need for a Savior. The words in 3:4–6 are a quotation of Isaiah 40:3–5.

3:5. While it is tempting to find allegorical meaning in **every valley … every mountain and hill … and the crooked** ways, this verse is a literal description of the way a road might be prepared. At most, the verse simply means that as the preparation for the king should be thorough, so also should be the spiritual preparation for the Messiah. It does, however, point to the need for full rather than partial repentance.

3:6. All flesh. God's salvation was to be made known to both Jews and Gentiles—a major theme of Luke's gospel (see discussion on 2:31–32).

3:7. The wrath to come. A reference to both the destruction of Jerusalem (see 21:20–23), which occurred in AD 70, and the final judgment (see John 3:36; but see also discussions on 1 Thess 1:10; 5:9). John was not forbidding the people to repent; he was attempting to shock them into recognizing that his ministry was more than just an entertainment, more than just a wonder. He had come to do serious busi-

ness with God's people and was questioning whether they had come to do serious business with God.

3:8. Bring forth … fruits worthy of repentance. John exhorted the people to show a lifestyle of repentance. Works do not save, but salvation is shown by works. Fruit, that is, good works, is the inevitable result of a genuine change of heart. **Children unto Abraham**. John reminded the people that their background, heritage, and ancestry did not matter. God looks upon the heart. Only by faith and a genuine repentance toward God, which show forth in one's actions, can one claim that they are truly made new in Christ.

3:9. The axe is laid unto the root. A symbolic way of saying that judgment is near for those who give no evidence of repentance. **Fire**. A symbol of judgment (see Matt. 7:19; 13:40–42).

3:10. What shall we do then? Luke presented this general question, followed by specific examples of what genuine repentance looks like.

3:11. Two coats. The coat, or tunic, was something like a long undershirt. Since two such garments were not needed, the second should be given to a person in need of one (see 9:3).

3:12–13. Publicans (v. 12). Taxes were collected for the Roman government by Jewish agents, who were especially detested for helping the pagan conqueror and for frequently defrauding their own people. John said the best way they could show that they had repented was to treat people fairly in matters of taxation.

3:14. Soldiers. Limited military forces were allowed for certain Jewish leaders and institutions (such as those of Herod Antipas, the police guard of the temple, and escorts for tax collectors). The professions of tax collector and soldier were not condemned, but the common unethical practices associated with them were. **Do violence to no man**. Obviously, as soldiers, they might find themselves in conflict. To mistreat the people and take by force what one wanted, however, was a violation of the power given to a military force. **Neither accuse any falsely**. Those who have been given a little power may be tempted to abuse it, either to get back at someone or simply to show that they have power over others. John said people should be treated fairly, even if one has the power to mistreat them. **Be content with your wages**. Again, the soldiers had the power to take things from people but not the right to do so. Officials expected corruption among soldiers and did little about it. John's applications are good advice for anyone in any age. If one seeks to live peaceably, to tell the truth, and to live simply on what God supplies, one shows forth the fruits of repentance, whatever one's occupation or circumstances.

3:15. Luke apparently included this statement simply as a way of demonstrating how influential John's ministry was. Many thought he might be the Christ, something John squelched as soon as he heard it (see 3:16).

3:16. One mightier than I cometh. John knew that his ministry was not about himself but pointed to another. This is something all believers would do well to remember. Christians serve not themsevles but one who is mightier and who has the real power. **He shall baptize you with the Holy Ghost**. Fulfilled at Pentecost (see Acts 1:5; 2:4, 38). **And with fire**. Here fire is associated with judgment (see 3:17; compare the fire of Pentecost in Acts 2:3 and the fire of testing in 1 Cor. 3:13).

3:17. Whose fan. Or "winnowing fork" (see discussion on Ruth 1:22). **The chaff** represents the unrepentant, and **the wheat** represents the righteous. Many Jews thought that only pagans would be judged and punished when the Messiah came, but John declared that judgment would come to all who did not repent, including Jews.

3:18. And many other things. This is a summary statement indicating that Luke did not record all that John preached but rather gave a representative sampling of the kinds of things he preached.

3:19–20. These verses carry the story forward before returning in 3:21 to the baptism of Jesus. That is, they summarize what happened some months later before returning to the most important event in John's ministry. **Herod … being reproved … for Herodias** (v. 19). Herod Antipas had married the daughter of Aretas IV of Arabia but divorced her to marry his own niece, Herodias, who was already his brother's (Herod Philip's) wife (see Matt. 14:3; Mark 6:17). Aretas is mentioned in 2 Corinthians 11:32.

He shut up John in prison (v. 20; see Matt. 4:12; Mark 1:14). According to Josephus (*Antiquities* 18.5.2), John was imprisoned in Machaerus, east of the Dead Sea. This did not occur until sometime after the beginning of Jesus' ministry (see John 3:22–24), but Luke mentioned it here to conclude his section on John's ministry before beginning his account of the beginning of Jesus' ministry (4:14–41). He later briefly alluded to John's death (see 9:7–9).

B. His Baptism (3:21–22)

3:21. For **being baptized**, see discussion on Matthew 3:15. **And praying**. Only Luke noted Jesus' praying at the time of His baptism. Jesus in prayer is one of the special themes of Luke's gospel (see 5:16; 6:12; 9:18, 28–29; 11:1; 22:32, 41; 23:34, 46).

3:22. The Holy Ghost descended. Luke specified that the Holy Spirit descended **in a bodily shape**. To John, the Spirit's descent was a sign (see John 1:32–34; see also discussion on Mark 1:10). **Thou art my beloved Son** (see Ps. 2:7; Isa. 42:1; Heb. 1:5). The gospel writers recorded the declarations of a voice from heaven addressing Jesus on two other occasions: (1) on the Mount of Transfiguration (see 9:35) and (2) in the temple area during Jesus' final week (see John 12:28).

C. His Genealogy (3:23–38)

3:23–38. There are several differences between Luke's genealogy and Matthew's (see Matt. 1:2–16). Matthew began with Abraham (the father of the Jewish people), while Luke traced the line in the reverse order, going all the way back to Adam and showing Jesus' relationship to the whole human race (see discussion on 2:31). From Abraham to David, the genealogies of Matthew and Luke are almost the same, but from David on, they are different. Some scholars suggest this is because Matthew traced the legal descent of the house of David, using only heirs to the throne, while Luke traced the complete line of Joseph to David. A more likely explanation, however, is that Matthew followed the line of Joseph (Jesus' legal father), while Luke emphasized that of Mary (Jesus' blood relative). Although tracing a genealogy through the mother's side was unusual, so was the virgin birth. Luke's explanation here that Jesus was the son of Joseph, "as was supposed" (v. 23), brings to mind his explicit virgin birth statement (see 1:34–35) and suggests the importance of Mary's role in the genealogy of Jesus.

3:23. About thirty years of age. Luke, a historian, related the beginning of Jesus' public ministry both to world history (see 3:1–2) and to the rest of Jesus' life. Thirty was the age when a Levite undertook his service (see Num. 4:47) and when a man was considered mature. **As was supposed**. Luke had already affirmed the virgin birth (see 1:34–35) and here again made it clear that Joseph was not Jesus' physical father.

3:24–38. Cainan (v. 36). The mention of Cainan here, and not in Genesis 10:24, demonstrates that the earlier genealogy was not meant to be complete. Thus, not too much should be made of adding up all the years given in the earlier genealogies, although extremely long gaps in them are probably not to be found either. **Adam, which was the son of God** (v. 38). Luke was not saying that Adam was a biological son of God, nor that he held sonship in the same sense as Jesus Christ. In the original, "the son" does not appear. The idea is that while the others owed their origins and family identities to their fathers, Adam owed his to God, being a direct creation of God.

D. His Temptation (4:1–13)

4:1. Full of the Holy Ghost. Luke emphasized the Holy Spirit not only in his gospel (see 1:35, 41, 67; 2:25–27; 3:16, 22; 4:14, 18; 10:21; 11:13; 12:10, 12) but also in Acts, where the Holy Spirit is mentioned fifty-five times. **Returned from Jordan** puts the reader back into the time frame that Luke had been describing before the genealogy. This is a necessary help to the reader, a matter of which Luke, a master at literary craftsmanship, was well aware. **Into the wilderness**. The desert of Judea (see discussion on 1:80; Matt. 3:1).

4:2. Being forty days tempted (see discussions on Matt. 4:1–11; Heb. 2:18; 4:15). Luke stated that Jesus was tempted for the forty days He was fasting, and the three specific temptations recounted in Matthew and Luke seem to have occurred at the close of this period, when Jesus' hunger was greatest and His resistance lowest. The sequence of the second and third temptations differs in Matthew and Luke. Matthew probably followed the chronological order, since at the end of the mountain temptation (Matthew's third), Jesus told Satan to leave (see Matt. 4:10). To emphasize a certain point, the gospel writers often brought various events together, not intending to give chronological sequence. Perhaps Luke's focus here was geographical, as he concluded with Jesus in Jerusalem (see 4:9).

4:3. For If thou be the Son of God, see discussion on Matthew 4:3. **Command this stone that it be made bread**. The Devil always makes his temptations seem attractive. In fact, error will often look good to us. It rarely comes in an unpleasing package.

4:4. It is written. Three times Jesus met Satan's temptations with Scripture. Only God's Word can provide the strength needed to overcome Satan's wiles. All of Jesus' quotes were from Deuteronomy. Note that Jesus did not challenge Satan's assertion that He *could* turn the stone to bread if He wished. His reply pointed to a higher value than the one to which Satan was appealing. Satan sought to induce Him to satisfy His physical need. Jesus pointed out that something more important than the physical would guide Him, and should guide believers as well.

4:5–6. The Devil's control of this world is asserted here, and Jesus did not contest the fact. Satan rules in this world, a fact believers would do well to remember when they are tempted to put this world's pleasures and this world's offer of power and prestige ahead of their calling to love God and to serve Him.

4:7. Worship me. The Devil was tempting Jesus to avoid the sufferings of the cross, which He came specifically to endure (see Mark 10:45). The temptation offered an easy shortcut to world dominion.

4:8. Jesus' answer, from Deuteronomy 6:13, again pointed to a higher value. There is no power, no glory, no prestige, and no dominion in this world that is worth more than just being God's servant. No pursuit in this world is more glorious than that of worshiping the Lord. Let Christians be diligent to put the Lord first in all things and let nothing stand in the way of loving Him and serving Him with all that they have and are.

4:9. A pinnacle of the temple. Either the southeast corner of the temple colonnade, from which there was a drop of some 100 feet to the Kidron Valley below, or the pinnacle of the temple proper. For **If thou be the Son of God**, see discussion on Matthew 4:3. **Cast thyself down**. Satan was tempting Jesus to test God's faithfulness and to attract public attention dramatically.

4:10–11. For it is written (v. 10). This time Satan also quoted Scripture, though he misused Psalm 91:11–12.

4:12. Jesus answered with Scripture from Deuteronomy (Deut. 6:16), as He did in the first (Deut. 8:3) and second (Deut. 6:13) temptations.

4:13. The devil ... departed from him for a season. Satan continued his testing of Jesus throughout His ministry (see Mark 8:33), culminating in the supreme test at Gethsemane.

IV. Jesus' Ministry in Galilee (4:14–9:9)

A. The Beginning of the Ministry in Galilee (4:14–41)

4:14. For **in the power of the Spirit**, see discussion on 4:1. **There went out a fame of him**. Jesus' ministry was accompanied by early success in Galilee.

4:15. For **He taught in their synagogues**, see discussion on Mark 1:21. **Being glorified of all**. This means that everyone spoke well of him.

4:16. He came to Nazareth. Not at the start of His ministry but perhaps almost a year later (4:23 presupposes that Jesus had already been ministering). All the events described in John 1:19–4:42 probably occurred between Luke 4:13 and 4:14. **As his custom was**. Jesus' custom of regular worship sets an example for all His followers. **To read**. Jesus probably read from Isaiah in Hebrew, and then He or someone else paraphrased it in Aramaic, one of the other common languages of the day.

4:17. The book of the prophet Esaias. The books of the Old Testament were written on scrolls, which were kept in a special place in the synagogue and handed to the reader by a special attendant. The passage Jesus read about the Messiah (Isa. 61:1–2) may have been one He chose to read, or it may have been the assigned passage for the day.

4:18. This verse tells of the Messiah's ministry of preaching and healing, to meet every human need. **He hath anointed me**. Not with literal oil (see Exod. 30:22–31) but with the Holy Spirit. **To preach the gospel to the poor**. Both the financially poor and the spiritually poor. The financially poor know they need to depend on God, for so much in this life is clearly uncertain. The spiritually poor have no less need but may have a harder time accepting the message. **To heal the broken-hearted**. The fall changed the world so that life is full of disappointments, but in His mercy, Jesus Christ will heal the broken-hearted, whatever the cause. **To preach deliverance to the captives**. Those caught in sin as well as victims of injustice. **And recovering of sight to the blind**. Spiritual as well as physical blindness. Christ healed many physically blind people, but His greater work was to remove spiritual blindness that people might see their sin and God's gracious offer of salvation. **To set at liberty them that are bruised**. Again, this includes a spiritual dimension. Everyone has been bruised by this world; sin has left its mark, but in Christ, one can find healing for the heart.

4:19. The acceptable year of the Lord. Not a calendar year but the period when salvation would be proclaimed — the messianic age. This quotation from Isaiah 61:1–2 alludes to the Year of Jubilee (see Lev. 25:8–55), which occurred every fifty years and during which slaves were freed, debts were canceled, and ancestral property was returned to the original family. Isaiah prophesied primarily the liberation of Israel from the Babylonian captivity, but Jesus proclaimed liberation from sin and all its consequences.

4:20. Sat down. It was customary to stand while reading Scripture (see 4:16) but to sit while teaching (see Matt. 5:1; 26:55; John 8:2; Acts 16:13).

4:21. Today is this scripture fulfilled. Jesus, by His presence and His teaching, fulfilled the prophecy before them, for He was proclaiming these things and had been doing them in His ministry.

4:22. The people were surprised. They had all known Jesus from childhood. Too often people fail to see the extraordinary in the familiar.

4:23. For **Capernaum**, see discussion on Matthew 4:13. **Thy country.** Nazareth. Although Jesus was born in Bethlehem, He was brought up in Nazareth, in Galilee (see 1:26; 2:39, 51; Matt. 2:23).

4:24. No prophet is accepted in his own country This has become a proverb in the English language, and there is some truth to it. Jesus went on, however, to point out that it is not wise to reject the message simply because the messenger is familiar.

4:25–27. Jesus here began to show examples from Scripture in which a prophet went outside Israel to minister to needs. The idea seems to be that if Israel, or here specifically Nazareth, rejected His message, God would open it to the Gentiles. Mention of Jesus' reference to God's helping two non-Israelites (see 1 Kings 17:1–15; 2 Kings 5:1–14) also reflects Luke's special concern for the Gentiles. Jesus' point was that when Israel rejected God's messenger of redemption, God sent him to the Gentiles, and so it would be again if Israel refused to accept Jesus (see 10:13–15; Rom. 9–11). **Sidon** (v. 26). One of the oldest Phoenician cities, twenty miles north of Tyre. Jesus later healed a Gentile woman's daughter in this region (see Matt. 15:21–28). **Naaman** (v. 27) was not an Israelite but found healing though the ministry of Elisha.

4:28–29. Filled with wrath (v. 28). Because of Jesus' inclusion of Gentiles as recipients of God's blessings, the people took Him up a **hill** (v. 29), intending to kill Him. This may seem extreme, but apparently the crowd was quite upset.

4:30. Passing through the midst of them. Luke did not explain whether the escape was miraculous or simply the result of Jesus' commanding presence. In any case, His time to die had not yet come (see John 7:30).

4:31–32. Jesus did what anyone who encounters resistance to the gospel should do. He went to another place and began to teach the Word of God there. God always has a place where people are prepared to hear the Word. Here, rather than being indifferent or angry, the people **were astonished at his doctrine: for his word was with power** (v. 32; see discussion on Mark 1:22).

4:33. A spirit of an unclean devil. This was an evil spirit. Such a demon could cause mental disorder (see John 10:20), violent action (see Luke 8:26–29), bodily disease (see 13:11, 16), and rebellion against God (see Rev. 16:14).

4:34. The Holy One of God (see discussion on Mark 1:24). This title is used in the Gospels only here and in Mark 1:24 and John 6:69. It emphasizes that Jesus was set apart for a special mission (see Morris, *Luke*, p. 109). As such, it was a confession of the truth about Jesus, but was offered in a spirit that indicates the demon was not expressing faith but rather seeking to blunt the effect of Jesus' ministry simply by describing it. Perhaps he wanted to see if he could catch Jesus off guard.

4:35. Jesus was not ruffled in the slightest by the words of the demon but spoke authoritatively to it and made it **come out of** the man.

4:36–37. The people **were all amazed** (v. 36) that Jesus could do this. That **he commandeth the unclean spirits, and they come out** demonstrated His power over the forces of darkness in the world. **The fame of him went out into every place** (v. 37). Jesus used this type of ministry as a way to meet spiritual needs and to demonstrate who He is, but He may not have wanted to gain a reputation as a sorcerer.

4:38. Simon's wife's mother. Peter was married (see 1 Cor. 9:5). **A great fever.** All three Synoptics tell of this miracle (see Matt. 8:14–15; Mark 1:29–31), but only Luke, the doctor, used the more specific phrase "a great [i.e., 'high'] fever."

4:39. Immediately she arose and ministered unto them. A genuine supernatural healing is a complete healing. Simon's mother-in-law was restored fully and immediately. She did not need rest in the aftermath of her fever breaking.

4:40. When the sun was setting. The Sabbath (see 4:31) was over at sundown (about 6:00 p.m.).

Until then, according to the tradition of the elders, Jews could not travel more than about two-thirds of a mile or carry a burden. Only after sundown could they carry the sick to Jesus, and their eagerness is seen in that they set out while the sun was still setting.

4:41. Jesus rebuked the demons and ordered them **not to speak**, perhaps due to His experience with the unclean spirit who had proclaimed His true identity (see 4:33–37), **for they knew that he was Christ** (see discussion on Mark 1:34). Jesus certainly wanted time to teach and to demonstrate who He is before He gained too much publicity. He would not let events prevent Him from going to the cross or from doing so at the right time.

B. The First Tour of Galilee (4:42–5:39)

4:42. Jesus **went into a desert place.** Mark included the words "and there prayed" (Mark 1:35).

4:43. The kingdom of God (see discussion on Matt. 3:2). This is Luke's first use of this phrase; it occurs over thirty times in his gospel. Some of its different meanings in the Bible are (1) the eternal kingship of God, (2) the presence of the kingdom in the person of Jesus, the King, (3) the approaching spiritual form of the kingdom, (4) the future kingdom.

4:44. This summary statement includes not only the beginning of Jesus' ministry (4:14–43) but also what lay ahead in His ministry. No express mention is made in the Synoptics of the early Judean ministry recorded in John 2:13–4:3, though it may be reflected in Matthew 23:37 and Luke 13:34.

5:1. The lake of Gennesaret. Luke is the only gospel writer who called it a lake. Josephus always used this term. The other gospel writers called it the Sea of Galilee, and John twice called it "the sea of Tiberias" (John 6:1; 21:1). It is the largest fresh water lake in Israel. Capernaum, which was a major center for Jesus' Galilean ministry, was a major fishing center.

5:2. Washing their nets. After each period of fishing, the nets were washed, stretched, and prepared for use again.

5:3. He sat down. The usual position for teaching (see discussion on 4:20). The boat provided an ideal arrangement, removed from the press of the crowd but near enough to be seen and heard. Sound carries well over water, and Jesus was better able to be heard by the crowd spread out on the shore than He would have been on land.

5:4–6. Jesus was not only interested in helping **Simon** (Peter; vv. 4–5) catch fish. He wanted to demonstrate His power to him and to make a point (see 5:10). **Their net brake** (v. 6). Work prospers as God wills. Not only did they catch fish; they caught way too many fish.

5:7. For **their partners,** see 5:10.

5:8–9. Depart from me (v. 8). Simon Peter got the message that this was no ordinary man and that He had supernatural power. The nearer one comes to God, the more he feels his own sinfulness and unworthiness, as did Abraham (Gen. 18:27), Job (42:6), and Isaiah (6:5). Sometimes when one encounters God, one's own unworthiness comes to the forefront, as happened here.

5:10. Jesus issued the call to **James, John,** and **Simon** to leave fishing and **catch men** instead. At least part of what Jesus was trying to communicate to them was that their success in life was in His hands. He could make them successful and prosperous fishermen if He chose, or He could call them to another occupation. If God could care for them by blessing their fishing efforts, so also could He care for them if they left their profession. All honorable work is service to God if it is done at His call and for His glory, but no work is more important than spiritual service to Him.

5:11. They forsook all, and followed him. This was not the first time these men had been with Jesus (see John 1:40–42; 2:1–2). Their periodic and loose association now became a closely knit fellowship as they followed the Master. The scene is the same as Matthew 4:18–22 and Mark 1:16–20, but the accounts relate events from different hours of the morning.

5:12–16. The healing of the man with leprosy is described in all three of the Synoptic Gospels (see Matt. 8:1–4; Mark 1:40–45), but the setting is different in each. In Matthew, it is part of a collection of miracles; in Mark and Luke, it is probably one incident that occurred on the first tour of Galilee.

5:12. A man full of leprosy. Luke alone noted the extent of this man's disease. The Greek term for "leprosy" could refer to other skin diseases as well as leprosy and was not used for leprosy in medical literature (see *KJV Study Bible* note on Lev. 13:2). The man expressed faith. His **if thou wilt** was not doubt but rather allowance for God's sovereignty in the matter.

5:13. Jesus replied, **I will**, and healed the man.

5:14. For **tell no man**, see discussions on Matthew 8:4; 16:20. **But go, and shew thyself to the priest**. By this command, Jesus urged the man to keep the law, to provide further proof for the actual healing, to testify to the authorities concerning His ministry, and to supply ritual certification of cleansing so the man could be reinstated into society. For **a testimony unto them**, see discussion on Mark 1:44.

5:15–16. The more went there a fame abroad of him (v. 15). The man could not keep the matter quiet. Jesus may well have known that this would be the case and that, at least among the man's family and friends, the matter would cause quite a stir. It may be that the man himself could not help but tell the miracle to all who would listen. In any case, Jesus' increased reknown forced Him to withdraw **into the wilderness** (v. 16), where He **prayed**. The press of responsibility must not take precedence over prayer and dependence on God.

5:17–26. In Luke's gospel, this incident, the healing of a paralyzed man, begins the active confrontation between Jesus and the religious leaders. They recognized that Jesus' claim to be able to forgive sins was tantamount to a claim to deity. Jesus proved His ability to do the higher work of forgiving sins by doing the lower work of healing. While healing is not as difficult as forgiving sins, at least not for God, anyone can *say* that sins are forgiven. To say "Arise" (v. 24) to a paralyzed man and have the power to make it happen requires more than mere words. It demonstrates divine power, the power that can also forgive sins.

5:17. Pharisees and doctors of the law (see discussions on Matt. 2:4; 3:7; Mark 2:16). Opposition was rising in Galilee from these religious leaders. "Pharisees," meaning "separated ones," are mentioned here for the first time in Luke. They numbered about six thousand and were spread over the whole of the Holy Land. They were teachers in the synagogues, religious examples in the eyes of the people, and self-appointed guardians of the law and its proper observance. They considered the interpretations and regulations handed down by tradition to be virtually as authoritative as Scripture (see Mark 7:8–13). "Doctors of the law" refers to scribes, who studied, interpreted, and taught the law (both written and oral). The majority of these teachers belonged to the party of the Pharisees. Already Jesus had run counter to the Jewish leaders in Jerusalem (see John 5:16–18). Now they came to a home in Capernaum (see Mark 2:1–6) to hear and watch Him.

5:18–19. These men brought their friend who could not come on his own. Their great desire to see him healed was evident in their zealously lowering him through the roof. For **housetop** (v. 19), see discussion on Mark 2:4. **Tiling**. Probably ceiling tiles. How long the man had been in this condition or whether it was due to disease or accident is not known. He had probably not been born this way, however. That he had a network of friends willing to do so much for him indicates that he had probably once been vigorous.

5:20. Man, thy sins are forgiven thee. Jesus met the man's spiritual need first. He did not always do this. Here He wanted to make a point to the Pharisees and scribes in the crowd. By forgiving the man's sins, which cannot be demonstrated and which only God could do, Jesus implicitly claimed to be deity.

5:21. Who is this which speaketh blasphemies? (see discussion on Mark 2:7). The Pharisees considered blasphemy to be the most serious sin a man could commit (see discussion on Mark 14:64). If Jesus were saying that the man's sins were forgiven when they were not, not only was He claiming to be God but He was promising what only God could do. If He were not God, He was making a false promise in God's name. All of this was included in the Pharisees' charge of blasphemy.

5:22-23. Jesus perceived their thoughts (v. 22), but then He had created the situation under which they would raise questions in their minds as to His motive and identity. **Whether is easier, to say …?** (v. 23; see *KJV Study Bible* note on Mark 2:9-10). In asking this question, Jesus showed that it is easier to promise what cannot be proven than to promise what can be proven.

5:24. That ye may know. Jesus had every intention of doing what could be seen by all, however. His power to heal was a visible affirmation of His power to forgive sins. Both are things only God can do.

5:25-26. The man was healed **immediately** (v. 25) and was able to leave on his own. It is ironic that his friends could not get him in due to the crowd, but he was able to get out. The people must have backed away from him in wonder.

5:27. For **A publican**, see discussion on 3:12-13. **The receipt of custom** (see discussion on Mark 2:14). The place where customs were collected. **Levi.** This was Matthew.

5:28. He left all, rose up, and followed him. Since Jesus had been ministering in Capernaum for some time, Levi probably had known Him previously (see discussion on 5:11).

5:29. A great feast. When Levi began to follow Jesus, he did not do it secretly. He sponsored a public dinner to introduce people to Jesus personally.

5:30. Their scribes and Pharisees murmured. They may have stood outside and registered their complaints from a distance, or perhaps some of them had been invited to the party. **Why do ye eat with and drink with publicans and sinners?** (see discussion on Mark 2:15). They assumed guilt by association, but it was instead ministry opportunity by association. Christians can never reach the lost if they never get involved with them. As a new believer, Levi knew many lost people and wanted to help them meet the Lord.

5:31-32. They that are whole need not a physician; but they that are sick (v. 31). Implies not that the Pharisees were "They that are whole" but that a person must recognize himself as a sinner before he can be spiritually healed (see discussion on Mark

2:17). The people Levi had invited to his dinner had no illusions about their righteousness. The Pharisees had only illusions about theirs.

5:33. The disciples of John fast often, and make prayers. John the Baptist had grown up in the wilderness and learned to subsist on a meager, austere diet of locusts and wild honey. His ministry was characterized by a sober message and a strenuous schedule. (For a contrast between Jesus' ministry and John the Baptist's, see 7:24-28; Matthew 11:1-19.) The Pharisees also had rigorous lifestyles (see discussion on 18:12). Jesus, however, went to banquets, and His disciples enjoyed a freedom not known by the Pharisees. **Fast** (see discussion on Mark 2:18). While Jesus rejected fasting legalistically for display (see Isa. 58:3-11), He Himself fasted privately and permitted its voluntary use for spiritual benefit (see Matt. 4:2; 6:16-18).

5:34-35. This is more of an analogy than a parable, though the function is the same. Jesus here is the bridegroom. **The days will come** (v. 35), after His resurrection and ascension, **when the bridegroom shall be taken away from them, and then shall they fast** (see discussions on Mark 2:19-20). This was a time of celebration, for Jesus was with them. The time for fasting would come later.

5:36. This again is more like an analogy but is specifically called **a parable** (see discussions on Matt. 13:3; Mark 4:2). The point is that God was doing something new and different, something that would not fit the old mold. The **new garment** was the offer of grace to the Gentiles, something Luke was eager to emphasize for his audience.

5:37-39. For **old bottles** (v. 37), see discussion on Matthew 9:17. **The old is better** (v. 39). Jesus was indicating the reluctance of some people to change from their traditional religious ways and try the gospel.

C. A Sabbath Controversy (6:1-11)

6:1-11. This passage presents two incidents in which Jesus (or His disciples) seemingly violated Sabbath laws. In both cases, Jesus defended the action as consistent with what God has revealed. In the first case (6:1-5), the disciples were plucking grain to eat on the Sabbath. Jesus' point was that Sabbath-keeping is not a ritual that should violate meeting needs. As David and his men had eaten what was technically not lawful, because taking care of hunger is more important than following a rule, so Jesus' disciples were doing nothing wrong by taking care of their hunger on the Sabbath. In the second case (6:6–11), Jesus healed a man on the Sabbath. The need in this case was that of another, not that of Jesus or the disciples.

6:1. He went through the corn fields; and his disciples plucked the ears of corn, and did eat (see discussion on Mark 2:23). "Corn" refers not to the yellow grain that grows on stalks but more likely to wheat. Corn as commonly known was found only in the Western Hemisphere at that time. When the King James Bible was translated, "corn" referred to any kind of grain. In much of the world today, what Americans refer to as "corn" is called "maize."

6:2. The Pharisees had sought to keep the Sabbath very strictly because of the cultural changes brought about by Alexander the Great's conquest of the area three centuries earlier. One clear way to distinguish between those Jews who were "pure" and those who had been "tainted" by Greek culture was their strict observance of the Sabbath. The Pharisees' contention with Jesus over Sabbath-keeping was motivated, in part, by a fear that He was being a traitor to pure Judaism.

6:3. What David did (see discussion on Mark 2:25). Jesus invoked the Old Testament here, demonstrating by the Jewish Scriptures that what His disciples were doing was not out of line with God's Word.

6:4. For **shewbread**, see discussion on Matthew 12:4.

6:5. For **the Son of man**, see discussion on Mark 2:10. **Lord also of the sabbath**. Jesus has the authority to overrule laws concerning the Sabbath, particularly as interpreted by the Pharisees (see Matt. 12:8; Mark 2:27). Jesus never broke the Mosaic law, and since meeting one's genuine needs is more important than a ritual observance, this was not a genuine case of breaking the law.

6:6–7. By now, **the scribes and Pharisees** (v. 7) were watching Jesus and His disciples for occasions of Sabbath-breaking, looking for an opportunity to make **an accusation against him**.

6:8. Stand forth. So there would be no question about the healing.

6:9. Is it lawful … to do good …? (see discussion on Mark 3:4). Jesus had been enduring questions and attacks from the Pharisees and now took the initiative by putting the questions to everyone in the synagogue. Here He was invoking not a specific Old Testament law or incident but rather a general principle. His question was rhetorical; the answer is obvious.

6:10. Looking round about upon them all. Jesus wanted to see whether anyone objected to His question or to the implied answer, but no one was bold enough to do so. By their silence, the people agreed with Him.

6:11. They were filled with madness because they could not withstand Jesus' reasoning. Instead of humbly admitting they were wrong, they became enraged. Already the Pharisees were plotting to take His life (see John 5:18; see *KJV Study Bible* note on Mark 3:6). Their reaction is typical of human nature. When people are proven wrong, they often become angrier rather than repenting of their error.

D. The Choice of the Twelve Disciples (6:12–16)

6:12. Characteristically, Jesus spent the **night in prayer** before the important work of selecting His twelve apostles. Perhaps he had names in mind and spent time laying each name before His Father, meditating on their strengths and potential. Luke does not indicate how many people He considered before settling on the twelve He would call when day came.

6:13. He called unto him his disciples. Among those who came to hear Jesus was a group that regularly followed Him and who were committed to His teachings. At least seventy men were included, since this many disciples were sent out on an evangelistic campaign (see 10:1, 17). Later, 120 believers waited and worshiped in Jerusalem following His ascension (see Acts 1:15). From such disciples, Jesus at this time chose **twelve** to be His **apostles**, meaning "ones sent with a special commission" (see discussions on Mark 6:30; 1 Cor. 1:1; Heb. 3:1).

6:14–16. Lists of the apostles appear also in Matthew 10:2–4; Mark 3:16–19; Acts 1:13. Although the order of the names varies, Peter is always first and Judas Iscariot last. The same disciples are always listed in each of the same three groupings of four each.

6:14. Bartholomew. Seems to be (in the Synoptics) the same as Nathanael (in John). Nathanael is associated with Philip in John 1:45.

6:15. Matthew. Another name for Levi. **James the son of Alpheus.** Probably the same as James the Less (see Mark 15:40).

6:16. Judas the brother of James. Another name for Thaddeus (see Matt. 10:3; Mark 3:18). **Judas Iscariot** (see discussion on Mark 3:19). Probably the only one from Judea; the rest likely came from Galilee.

E. The Sermon on the Plain (6:17–49)

6:17. Stood in the plain. Perhaps a plateau, which would satisfy both this context and that in Matthew 5:1. The crowd that gathered here **came to hear him, and to be healed of their diseases.**

6:18–19. Jesus met the people's need for healing before preaching to them. Often, when one meets a person's felt needs, he or she is then ready to hear the Word of God.

6:20–49. Luke's Sermon on the Plain is apparently parallel to Matthew's Sermon on the Mount (Matt. 5–7). Although this sermon is much shorter than the one in Matthew, they both begin with the Beatitudes and end with the lesson of the builders. Some of Matthew's sermon is found in other portions of Luke (e.g., 11:2–4; 12:22–31, 33–34), suggesting that Jesus may have presented the material on various occasions. It is not unusual for itinerant preachers to have one basic sermon that they give on different occasions and that they vary according to circumstances and time constraints.

6:20–23. The Beatitudes (see Matt. 5:3–12) go deeper than material poverty (v. 20) and physical **hunger** (v. 21). Matthew's account indicates that Jesus spoke of poverty "in spirit" (Matt. 5:3) and hunger "[for] righteousness" (Matt. 5:6).

6:24–26. This section is a point-by-point negative counterpart of 6:20–22.

6:24. Woe unto you that are rich contrasts with "Blessed be ye poor" (6:20). **Ye have received your consolation** means that the rich have their reward in this life. This is not a blanket condemnation of all rich people. Jesus' point seems to be that those who look for rewards only in this life will find them only in this life. Those who set their hearts on things above will find their reward there.

6:25. Woe unto you that are full contrasts with "Blessed are ye that hunger" (6:21). Jesus pointed out how transitory the goods of this world are. Hunger and plenty are both temporary. One should look beyond the temporary to what is permanent. The same is true of laughter and weeping. Those who **laugh … shall mourn and weep**, as those who "weep … shall laugh" (6:21). When life is good, one should remember that temporal goods will pass. When life is bitter, one should take comfort in knowing that even that is temporary.

6:26. Woe unto you, when all men shall speak well of you contrasts with "Blessed are ye, when men shall hate you" (6:22). Another parallel is that the prophets were hated in olden times (6:23), while **the false prophets** were well spoken of in those days. The contrast warns one that others speaking well of them is not an indication that one is blessed of God.

6:27–28. Love your enemies (v. 27). The heart of Jesus' teaching is love. While the Golden Rule (6:31) is sometimes expressed in negative form outside the Bible, Jesus not only forbade treating others spitefully but also commanded that believers love everyone, even one's enemies. This can be done only when one has faith that God is in control and that He will work justice in the end. Hatred for an enemy arises when he has frustrated one's goals, when one fears he will do so, or when he has taken what is rightfully another's. That is how one's enemies **curse** (v. 28) or **despitefully use** one. In such cases, people can love the person more easily if they are seeking something higher than this world's goods, as Jesus encouraged in 6:22–23, or if one believes that God will bring about justice in the end. Loving one's enemies, then, is an act of faith in God.

6:29. Offer also the other. Believers are not to have a retaliatory attitude but rather are to trust that God will right all wrongs and that one need not do so oneself (see Rom. 12:9).

6:30. Give to every man that asketh of thee again requires faith that God is in control. This can be done only by those who believe that God will take care of their needs. Jesus was not saying that one is obligated to honor every request. In certain circumstances, honoring another's request may do more harm than good. His point was that one should not regard one's possessions as sacrosanct when another has a genuine need.

6:31. This general principle is often called the "Golden Rule." People should treat others as they wish to be treated. Fundamental to this is a belief in basic human equality: I will treat others' needs as being as important as my own, because others are as important as I am. In the hierarchical society of the Greco-Roman world of that day, this was a radical idea, and it still is today in many non-Christian societies.

6:32 – 34. Here Jesus elaborated on the reasoning behind the Golden Rule as well as His other instructions in 6:27 – 30. He was not saying that we should do good to others in hope of recognition. **What thank have ye?** (vv. 32, 33, 34) simply means "what have you really accomplished?" Loving those who love us is easy. Loving those who are difficult or demanding is the hard part.

6:35 – 36. These two verses summarize what Jesus said in 6:27 – 34. If everyone followed these three commands, **love ye your enemies, and do good, and lend, hoping for nothing again** (v. 35), the world would certainly be better for it. Not only would one's **reward … be great** in heaven but blessings on earth would abound to all. Finally, Jesus summed up the matter in terms of mercy: **Be ye therefore merciful, as your Father also is merciful** (v. 36). God's perfection should be the example and goal (see Matt. 5:48). Mercy is important because it is goodness given to the undeserving. Enemies, difficult people, and those who borrow have no claim. They do not "deserve" kindness and have not earned it, but as God gives kindness to those who do not deserve it, including Christians, so believers should give kindness to those around them who do not deserve it.

6:37. Judge not. Jesus did not relieve His followers of the need for discerning right and wrong (see 6:43 – 45), but He condemned unjust and hypocritical judging of others. In addition, He recognized that human nature is such that the person who criticizes will draw criticism. In the same way, the one who forgives **shall be forgiven**. It is easy to forgive a good-hearted person who has made a mistake. One recognizes such people by the way they treat others. It is hard to believe that the man who forgives others easily really means to do wrong, and thus one can more easily forgive and understand him.

6:38. Jesus extended the principle of 6:37 to the area of giving. As the one who forgives will be forgiven, someone who is generous will receive generosity. This is also the case in ministry. This passage clearly teaches that one cannot outgive God. **Give into your bosom.** Probably refers to the way the outer garment was worn, with a fold over the belt that could be used as a large pocket to hold a measure of wheat.

6:39 – 40. Can the blind lead the blind? (v. 39). This has become a proverb in the English language. In light of verse 40, Jesus was enjoining His disciples to heed His words. Until the light of God's truth shines, people are blind. One should therefore look to the source of light for truth and turn to God, not worldly sources, for the true meaning of life. This passage serves as a reminder that one should look to godly teachers, who know the truth, rather than to those who are not spiritually qualified to give advice. Likewise, one should examine one's own qualifications before presuming to teach others (see 6:41 – 42).

6:41 – 42. Mote … beam (v. 41). Jesus used hyperbole (a figure of speech that uses exaggeration for emphasis) to emphasize how foolish and hypocritical it is to criticize someone for a fault while remaining blind to one's own considerable faults. Jesus did not say that one cannot advise others. One should in fact do so, but one must **cast out first the beam** (v. 42) that hinders one's vision. This relates to Jesus' question, "Can the blind lead the blind?" (6:39). Jesus' point was not about whether one has the right to advise another, though that is how this passage is often taken. His point was that one must be qualified, one must **see clearly**, if one presumes to do so. The warning is against attempting to counsel others if one is unqualified to do so because of one's own spiritual inadequacy.

6:43–44. For **every tree is known by his own fruit**, see discussion on Matthew 7:16–20.

6:45. Jesus emphasized the importance of the **heart**. Believers should guard their heart's condition, that is, pay attention to their spiritual life. Those who are given over to evil desires can speak only evil. Those who seek what is good and are oriented toward the things of the Lord will show this in what they say.

6:46. Jesus here raised the central question that every Christian must ask: **Why call ye me, Lord, Lord, and do not the things which I say?** All who profess that Jesus is Lord must check their obedience in light of that profession and try to bring the two into line. If one calls Him Lord and does not act like He is Lord, one becomes hypocritical.

6:47–49. Jesus drew an analogy between responses to His words and building a house. The one who obeys what Jesus says builds a house **on a rock** (v. 48), while the one who does not heed His words builds **upon the earth** (v. 49). The house on the rock stands, and the other falls. Everyone builds their life on some foundation. No other foundation will stand the tests of life as well as Jesus Christ.

F. Miracles in Capernaum and Nain (7:1–18)

7:1. Jesus returned to **Capernaum**, where His ministry was headquartered. There He performed two healings.

7:2. The first healing was due to the faith of a Gentile. Luke's concern was always to show that Gentiles were a part of God's plan. The person healed was a **centurion's servant**. The centurion was probably a member of Herod Antipas's forces, which were organized in Roman fashion, ordinarily in companies of one hundred men. Many Roman

centurions referred to in the New Testament showed characteristics to be admired (see, e.g., Acts 10:2; 23:17–18; 27:43). This centurion showed genuine concern for his slave, **who was dear unto him**, and he was admired by the Jews, who spoke favorably of him even though he was a Gentile (see 7:5, 9).

7:3. The elders of the Jews. These were highly respected Jews of the community, though not necessarily rulers of the synagogue (see discussion on 8:41). They were willing to come and plead for the centurion. In Matthew's account, the centurion spoke with Jesus Himself (see Matt. 8:5–13), while in Luke's account, he spoke with Jesus through his friends. Either way, the centurion was the originator and cause of the communication. There is no contradiction between the two accounts (see discussion on Matt. 8:5).

7:4–5. The elders of the Jews approached Jesus on the basis of the man's worthiness, though he had sent them because he believed himself to be unworthy (see 7:7). **He loveth our nation, and he hath built us a synagogue** (v. 5). He certainly had impressive credentials, but one must not suspect that Jesus went to him because he had done these things. There was no sense of obligation that Jesus should perform this healing in return for what the man had done for the people. In all likelihood, the elders mentioned the centurion's good deeds at their own behest, not at his. Had he approached Jesus on his own behalf with these words, he might have been dismissed. God will not make deals.

7:6. As Jesus neared, the man again spoke through intermediaries, sending a humble message: **I am not worthy that thou shouldest enter under my roof** (see discussion on Matt. 8:8).

7:7–8. But say in a word, and my servant shall be healed (v. 7). The centurion showed genuine faith in Jesus' ability to heal. In verse 8, he used an analogy to show that he believed that Jesus has authority over diseases. As a leader, the centurion was used to giving orders and seeing them obeyed. As evidenced by his sending others on his behalf to Jesus, he was used to his word being carried out even when he was not present. Likewise, he believed that Jesus could "say in a word" and it would be done.

7:9. Jesus ... marvelled. The Greek word (*ethaumasen*) for "marvel" is used of Jesus only twice. Here He "marvelled" at faith, while in Mark 6:6, He "marvelled" at a lack of faith. Jesus marveled not that the centurion had built a synagogue but that he had faith. Christians do well to remember this when they are inclined to view their works as a sign of spiritual life. God looks at one's faith. While one may admire those who do mighty works, God admires the one who has a mighty faith.

7:10. Found the servant whole that had been sick. Jesus' word, without His physical presence, was enough to heal the man.

7:11. The second work of healing that Jesus did upon returning to Capernaum was done at **Nain**, not Capernaum itself. The two towns were probably in close proximity, however, since **many of his disciples ... and much people** accompanied Him there.

7:12. There was a dead man carried out who was the sole support of his mother, for **she was a widow**. Death is normal in the course of life in this fallen world. Jesus rarely raised the dead, though He did so at times (see discussion on 7:14–15). This miracle was on a different order than most of the healings He did.

7:13. He had compassion on her. Jesus was motivated by the widow's need as well as by the desire to show His glory.

7:14–15. Bier (v. 14). The man was probably carried in an open coffin, suggested by Jewish custom and by the fact that he **sat up** (v. 15) in response to Jesus' command. This is the first of three instances of Jesus' raising someone from the dead, the others being Jairus's daughter (see 8:40–56) and Lazarus (see John 11:38–44).

7:16–18. Besides compassion for the widow, Jesus may have had two additional purposes in performing this exceptional miracle. The people who accompanied Jesus said **That God hath visited his people** (v. 16). Jesus' miracles were designed to show that He was God.

The second reason for performing this miracle may have been to attract the attention of **the disciples of John** (v. 18). They went to John and **shewed him of all these things**. Despite John the Baptist's

imprisonment, his disciples kept in contact with him and continued his ministry. Jesus may have wanted word of this miracle to reach John for purposes of encouraging him in his imprisonment or so that he would face some of his own doubts.

G. The Inquiry of John the Baptist (7:19–29)

7:19–21. Look we for another? (v. 19). John had announced the coming of the Christ, but now John had been languishing in prison for months, and the work of Jesus had not brought the results that John apparently expected. His disappointment was natural. He wanted reassurance, and perhaps he also wanted to urge Jesus to further action. John's disciples came to Jesus on a day when He performed many miracles of healing (v. 21). This gave shape to Jesus' answer (see 7:22–23).

7:22. Tell John what things ye have seen and heard. Jesus pointed to the healing and life-restoring miracles that He performed, such as those that John's disciples had just witnessed. He gave not promises but clearly observable evidence—evidence that reflected the prophesied ministry of the Messiah. **To the poor the gospel is preached**. In Jesus' review of His works, He used an ascending scale of impressive deeds, ending with the dead being raised and the gospel being preached to the poor. Jesus thus reminded John that these were the things prophesied of the Messiah in the Scriptures (see Isa. 29:18–21; 35:5–6; 61:1; see also Luke 4:18).

7:23. Whosoever shall not be offended in me. Jesus did not want discouragement and doubt to ensnare John. John's doubts may well have been engendered by his imprisonment. Often believers expect God to bless their ministry by smoothing the path and bringing them success. This had not happened in John's situation. His early high-profile ministry had been replaced by a time of waiting in prison day after day, not knowing his fate, possibly having only limited contact with his disciples and others. Jesus' answer showed that God's work was being done, and that without John's active involvement at this point. It is believers who need God, not the other way around, as John should have known.

7:24–29. Jesus always recognized a teachable moment. The people certainly knew who John's disciples were and that they had been consulting with Jesus. What better moment than this to preach on John and his message?

7:24–27. Jesus structured the first part of the message around the phrase **What went ye out ... to see?** (vv. 24, 25, 26). Jesus proposed answers to His question each time He asked it.

A reed shaken with the wind? (v. 24). A reed shaken by the wind is a small thing, not something that would draw a crowd. It might make a little noise, as John certainly made noise, but that alone would not draw a crowd either. John was not a weak messenger, swayed by the pressures of human opinion. On the contrary, he was a true prophet. Jesus' point was that the people went out to hear John because he had something worthwhile to say.

A man clothed in soft raiment? (v. 25). The answer to this one is obvious. Such people are not found in the wilderness where John preached but rather **in kings' courts**. John's raiment was much rougher than this. The people certainly were not attracted to John's ministry by the clothing he wore.

A prophet?... and much more than a prophet (v. 26). John was the unique prophet sent to prepare the way for the Messiah. Jesus' answers to the question moved from the lesser to the greater: a reed, a man in nice clothing, and a prophet. Jesus implied that the last answer was the only worthy reason to have gone out into the wilderness: to hear the words of a prophet.

7:28. For **he that is least in the kingdom of God**, see discussion on Matthew 11:11.

7:29. Justified God. Jesus meant that their response to John's ministry demonstrated that God had anointed him and was using him greatly. It showed that God was truly at work in John's ministry. The people saw the righteousness of God because of the preaching of John and responded by being baptized.

H. Jesus and the Pharisees (7:30–50)

7:30. Lawyers. A designation used by Luke (see 10:25; 11:45–46, 52; 14:3; see also Matt. 22:35) for the scribes (the teachers of the law), most of whom were **Pharisees** (see discussion on 5:17). **Rejected the counsel of God**. Tax collectors had shown their willingness to repent by accepting John's baptism, whereas the Pharisees had shown their rejection of God's message by refusing to be baptized. The contrast is between the ones who knew they were sinners and those who thought they were righteous (see Luke 5:31–32).

7:31–34. Jesus said that the people of His day were **like unto children sitting in the marketplace** (v. 32). They had rejected both John and Jesus, but for different reasons — like children who refuse to play either a joyful game or a mournful one. They would not associate with John when he followed the strictest of rules, nor with Jesus when He freely associated with all kinds of people.

7:34. A friend of publicans and sinners. Jesus ate and talked with people who were religious and social outcasts. He even called a publican to be an apostle (see 5:27–32).

7:35. Wisdom is justified of all her children (see discussion on Matt. 11:19). In contrast to the foolish critics who rejected the ministries of John and Jesus, spiritually wise persons could see that both ministries were godly, despite their differences.

7:36. One of the Pharisees (see discussion on 5:17). Jesus, who was "a friend of publicans and sinners" (7:34), would also give time to a Pharisee who wanted it. Jesus did not reject the self-righteous in favor of the lowly but rather opened Himself to all and accepted those who came to Him. The motive of this Pharisee may have been to entrap Jesus rather than to learn from Him, but Jesus used the situation as a teaching opportunity anyway.

7:37. A woman ... which was a sinner. A prostitute. She must have heard Jesus preach, and in repentance, she determined to lead a new life. She came to Jesus out of love and gratitude, in the understanding that she could be forgiven. **An alabaster box**. A long-necked, globular bottle. **Ointment**. A perfumed ointment.

7:38. Stood at his feet behind him. Jesus reclined on a couch with His feet extended away from the table, which made it possible for the woman to wipe **his feet** with her hair and still not disturb His eating. **Anointed them with the ointment**. The anointing, perhaps originally intended for Jesus' head, was instead applied to His feet. A similar act was performed by Mary of Bethany the week before the crucifixion (see John 12:3).

7:39–40. What manner of woman this is … for she is a sinner (v. 39). It is odd that the Pharisee apparently invited the woman into his home but believed that Jesus should have rejected her attention. The Pharisee, **Simon** (v. 40), may have been looking for an opportunity to discredit Jesus and may have thought he had found it here. If so, Jesus proceeded to prove him wrong.

7:41–42. Five hundred pence (v. 41). Pence is the plural of penny, the denarius, a coin worth about a day's wages. This amount was thus over a year's wages. **The other fifty**. This was about six weeks' wages. The contrast was to make the point that the one forgiven the most would love the most.

7:43. When Simon answered that the creditor would be most loved by the one **whom he forgave most**, Jesus replied, **Thou hast rightly judged**. The more sin one has in one's life, ironically, the less willing one is to approach the Lord. This is why younger people are more easily reached for Christ than older people. Once one who has a major burden of sin finds forgiveness, however, the love is greater. This is not to say that believers should go out and sin more so that they may be forgiven more and thus be more grateful (see Rom. 6:1–16).

7:44–46. The Pharisee had gotten the point, and thus Jesus moved on to apply it to his situation by contrasting his treatment of Him with that of the woman. Simon had given **no water for my feet** (v. 44), which was the minimal gesture of hospitality. She, however, **hath washed my feet with tears**. He had given Jesus **no kiss** (v. 45), again a Middle Eastern custom that the Pharisee had ignored. He had not provided oil for anointing Jesus' head, but she **hath anointed my feet** (v. 46). Jesus, then, had been shown much more honor by her than by His host.

7:47–50. For she loved much (v. 47). The woman's love was evidence of her forgiveness but not the basis for it (see Eph. 1:7). **Thy faith hath saved thee** (v. 50) clearly states that she was saved by faith. She had done no wrong in anointing Him, and Jesus had already made it clear that He would associate with sinners, not to participate in sin but to open the gates of God's mercy to those who would repent. Her sins were forgiven and she could experience God's **peace** (see 1:79; discussion on 2:14).

I. The Second Tour of Galilee (8:1–3)

8:1. He went throughout every city and village. Jesus' ministry had been centered in Capernaum, and much of His preaching was in synagogues, but now He traveled again from town to town on a second tour of the Galilean countryside (for the first tour, see 4:43–44; Matt. 4:23–25; Mark 1:38–39; for the third tour, see discussion on 9:1–6.) For **the kingdom of God**, see discussion on 4:43.

8:2. Mary called Magdalene. Her hometown was Magdala. She is not to be confused with the sinful woman of chapter 7 or Mary of Bethany (see John 11:1).

8:3. Susanna. Nothing more is known of her. **Ministered unto him of their substance**. Jesus and His disciples did not provide for themselves by miracles but were supported by the service and means of grateful people, such as these women. Miracles were the exception rather than the norm. Jesus could have fed Himself and His disciples as He did the five thousand. God, however, most often uses people to accomplish His work by normal means. These women were blessed through their giving, as they were a blessing through their gifts. Jesus depended on the donations of faithful disciples, and so His work does today.

J. Parables of the Kingdom (8:4–21)

8:4. Parable. From this point on, Jesus used parables (see discussions on Matt. 13:3; Mark 4:2) more extensively as a means of teaching. They were particularly effective and easy to remember because He used familiar scenes. Although parables clarified

Jesus' teaching, they also included hidden meanings that needed further explanation. These hidden meanings challenged those who were sincerely interested to inquire further and taught truths that Jesus wanted to conceal from unbelievers (see 8:10). From His parables, Jesus' enemies could find no direct statements to use against Him. The parable of the sower is one of three parables recorded in each of the Synoptic Gospels (8:5–8; Matt. 13:1–23; Mark 4:1–20). The others are those of the mustard seed (13:19; Matt. 13:31–32; Mark 4:30–32) and of the vineyard (20:9–19; Matt. 21:33–46; Mark 12:1–12).

8:5–8. In the parable of the sower, almost every element has an allegorical meaning. This is not always true of parables, and a wise interpreter ensures that the point of the parable governs the interpretation of its various elements. The point of the parable of the sower is that people respond differently to the Word of God (for Jesus' interpretation of the parable, see 8:11–15).

8:5. To sow his seed. In Eastern practice, the seed was sometimes sown first and the field plowed afterward. **Some fell by the way side**. Roads and pathways went directly through many fields, and the traffic made much of the surface too hard for seed to take root in.

8:6. Some fell upon a rock. On a thin layer of soil that covered solid rock. In such conditions, moisture quickly evaporates, and germinating seeds soon wither and die (see Matt. 13:5–6).

8:7. Some fell among thorns. Or plants that grow thorns, that is, weeds and useless plants.

8:8. And other fell on good ground ... and bare fruit an hundredfold. Luke's description of the harvest is more abbreviated than Matthew's and Mark's (see Matt. 13:8; Mark 4:8), but the point is the same: the quantity of increase depends on the quality of soil. **He that hath ears to hear, let him hear**. A challenge for listeners to understand the message and appropriate it for themselves.

8:9. His disciples. This included "they that were about Him with the twelve" (Mark 4:10).

8:10. The mysteries of the kingdom of God (see discussion on Mark 4:11). These are truths that can

be known only by revelation from God (see Eph. 3:2–5; 1 Peter 1:10–12). **That seeing they might not see** (see discussion on Mark 4:12). This quotation of Isaiah 6:9 does not express a desire that some would not understand but simply states the sad truth that those who are not willing to receive Jesus' message will find the truth hidden from them. Their ultimate fate is implied in the fuller quotation in Matthew 13:14–15.

8:11–15. In this passage, Luke recorded Jesus' interpretation of the parable.

8:11. The word of God. The message that comes from God. Jesus had in mind the specific messages He had been preaching, but it may be extended to include all of the Bible, for truly, people respond differently to the whole of God's Word.

8:12. Lest they should believe and be saved. The Devil's purpose is that people will not hear with understanding and therefore will not appropriate the message and be saved. Often the Devil uses various distractions to ensure that God's Word will not take root within a person.

8:13. For a while believe. This kind of belief is superficial and does not save. It is similar to what James calls "dead" faith (James 2:17, 20, 26). Faith is more than emotions. It is a decision made with one's will to trust God and what He has said.

8:14. These people hear and believe the word but are distracted by three things: **cares**, the sheer busyness of life, making a living, caring for family and self, contributing to the community, and so on; **riches**, either the pursuit of them or the enjoyment and contemplation of them; and **pleasures**, entertainment and fun. None of these things are bad in themselves, but any of them can distract Christians from letting God's Word bear fruit in their lives.

8:15. Here, in one verse, is a manual for making the most of God's Word. The first requirement is **an honest and good heart**. This means one must come to God's Word ready to receive it, not predetermining what it says, nor seeking to misuse it. **Having heard the word**. This means exposure to it. Too often Christians hear or read the Bible only on Sundays and wonder why they never grow. Believers should seek regular exposure to God's Word. **Keep it**. This means doing what God's Word says, applying it to life and shaping one's beliefs according to what it says. **And bring forth fruit**. Hearing the Word of God with a receptive heart brings about results in life, for the glory of God. **With patience**. Christians must persevere. If they are to bring forth fruit consistently, hearing and keeping the Word for a few weeks is not enough. Rather, one must be dedicated to a lifestyle of regularly hearing the Word of God with a receptive heart and applying it to life.

8:16. Lighted a candle (see discussion on 11:33). Although Jesus couched much of His message in parables, He intended for the disciples to make the truths known as widely as possible. For **setteth it on a candlestick**, see discussion on Matthew 5:15.

8:17. This verse explains 8:16. The destiny of the truth is that it will be made known (see 12:2). The disciples were to begin a proclamation that would become universal.

8:18. Take heed therefore how ye hear (see Mark 4:24; James 1:19–22). The disciples heard not only for themselves but also for those to whom they would minister. Truth that is not understood and appropriated will be lost (see 19:26), but truth that is used will be multiplied.

8:19–20. Then came to him his mother and his brethren (v. 19; see discussion on Mark 3:21). More is known about their motive from Mark 3:21, 31–32. The family, thinking "He is beside himself" (Mark 3:21), probably wanted to get Him away from His heavy schedule. Jesus' brethren did not believe in Him at this time (see John 7:5). Various interpretations concerning their relationship to Jesus arose in the early church: they were sons of Joseph by a previous marriage (according to Epiphanius) or were cousins (said Jerome). The most natural conclusion (suggested by Helvidius) is that they were the sons of Joseph and Mary, younger half brothers of Jesus. Four of these brothers are named in Mark 6:3, where it also says that Jesus had sisters. Since Joseph is not mentioned here, it is possible that he had died, or perhaps he was home taking care of the carpenter's shop.

8:21. Jesus' reply was not meant to reject His natural family but to emphasize the higher priority of His spiritual relationship to those who believed in Him. The Bible presents reality as interconnected. Jesus shares a connection with those who **hear the word of God, and do it**.

K. The Trip across the Sea of Galilee (8:22–39)

8:22–23. Jesus said to the disciples, **Let us go over unto the other side of the lake** (v. 22), and then **he fell asleep** (v. 23). For **a storm of wind**, see discussion on Mark 4:37. **They … were in jeopardy** only apparently as the boat was swamped, but Jesus had said they would go to the other side. When God says you will go to the other side, circumstances cannot prevent that from happening. The discples were being tested, and they did not pass the test (see 8:25).

8:24. We perish. The disciples had their own ideas about how this would turn out. In the midst of the storm, however, the disciples did turn to Jesus, which was the right thing to do. The parallel to how one should behave in the storms of life is apt, but one should not push the analogy too far. Believers may apply these verses to the storms of life, but they must remember that this is not the meaning of the passage. The passage is not an allegory. It is an account of what really happened.

8:25. Where is your faith? The disciples certainly did not have faith that they would make it to the other side of the lake, as Jesus had said (see 8:22).

8:26. The country of the Gadarenes. The Gospels describe the location of this event in two ways: (1) the region of the Gergesenes (see discussion on Matt. 8:28) and (2) the region of the Gadarenes (see discussion on Mark 5:1–20). Some manuscripts of Mark and Luke read "Gergesenes," but this spelling may have been introduced in an attempt to resolve the differences with Matthew. The significance of this region was that is was Gentile territory and was thus considered unclean by Orthodox Jews.

8:27. A certain man, which had devils (see discussion on 4:33). Matthew recorded that there were two demon-possessed men, but Mark and Luke mentioned only one, probably the one who was prominent because he did the talking (see Matt. 8:28; Mark 5:2). **Tombs**. An isolated burial ground avoided by most people (but see discussion on Mark 5:5). Graveyards were considered unclean by many Jews.

8:28. Son of God most high (see 1:32; 4:34). The title "God most high" was commonly used by Gentiles (see Gen. 14:19 and discussion; Acts 16:17); its use here perhaps indicates that this man was not a Jew (but see discussion on Mark 1:24).

8:30. What is thy name? Jesus asked the man his name, but it was the demons who replied, thus showing they were in control. For **Legion**, see discussion on Mark 5:9.

8:31. The deep. Or "the Abyss," a place of confinement for evil spirits and for Satan (see *KJV Study Bible* note on Rev. 9:1).

8:32. Swine. Pigs were unclean to Jews, and eating them was forbidden (see Lev. 11:7–8), but this was the Decapolis, a predominantly Gentile territory. For **he suffered them**, see discussion on Matthew 8:31–32. The point of this passage, from a Jewish perspective, is that Jesus went to an unclean place to minister to an unclean man.

8:33. The Scriptures always present demon possession as a real, supernatural happening, not just a form of mental illness. **The herd ran violently down a steep place into the lake**. It will not do to explain this away on the basis that the man's screams scared the pigs. The biblical account emphasizes the demonic influence throughout the entire incident.

8:34–37. Such an incident caused a stir in the town. **They were afraid** (v. 35). A major supernatural event had happened, and the people were afraid due to the unfamiliar nature of it and due to the power that Jesus had demonstrated in this event. They thus **besought him to depart from them** (v. 37). Jesus did so.

8:38. Jesus sent him away. Jesus had another call on this man's life. When God does a work in a life, often one wants to sit and contemplate His goodness. That is not usually God's plan, however.

8:39. Return to thine own house, and shew how great things God hath done unto thee. Jesus directed the man to make the miracle known in his native territory. The testimonies of those to whom Jesus ministered were incredible evidences of His divine power.

L. The Third Tour of Galilee (8:40 – 9:9)

8:40. Even though Jesus' ministry in the Gadarenes was rejected, **when Jesus was returned** to Galilee, **the people gladly received him**. There will always be a place where God's Word is accepted with joy, just as there will always be places where it is rejected. Believers should never be discouraged if the Word is rejected but rather should move on until they find people who are prepared to receive it.

8:41–56. In this section, Jesus performed two healings. Here is proof that "the people gladly received him" (8:40). Two people made their way through the crowd to come to Jesus with their needs, knowing that He could heal them. These were people with faith, people who knew the value of Jesus' ministry. What a contrast to those across the lake, in the Gadarenes, who had just rejected Him (see 8:26–39).

8:41. A ruler of the synagogue (see discussion on Mark 5:22). The "ruler of the synagogue" was responsible for conducting services, selecting participants, and maintaining order. **He fell down at Jesus' feet**. This man humbled himself before the Lord. No one can demand anything of God, but if one asks, He is eager to bless His children.

8:42. The people thronged Him. Jesus was at the height of His popularity in His Galilean ministry.

8:43. An issue of blood. This woman's hemorrhage had made her ceremonially unclean for **twelve years** (see Lev. 15:19–30). **Neither could be healed of any**. Comparison with Mark 5:26 shows the restraint of Luke, the physician, in describing the failure of doctors to help her.

8:44. Immediately. The woman was healed instantly by the power of God. When all human efforts fail, one must turn to God in faith. No one should wait twelve years, as this woman did, but here there is no condemnation. This may have been her first opportunity.

8:45. Who touched me? Jesus was not asking for information but rather, for the woman's good and for a testimony to the crowd, He was insisting that the miracle be made known.

8:46. Virtue is gone out of me (see discussion on Mark 5:30). To the Greeks, "virtue" had the idea of fulfilling something's purpose, involving the power to do what it was intended to do. Jesus' purpose was to meet needs by His power. Healing power, the power to meet the woman's need, had gone out of Him. As God, Jesus' power was unlimited and this was no weakening thereof but was a matter of His power being used effectually.

8:47. The woman **came trembling** and **declared unto him before all the people**. Believers should never let fear keep them from giving testimony to what God has done in their lives. This woman's faith was honored even though her voice may have quavered and her words may have been hesitant and unsure.

8:48. Daughter. This woman is the only individual Jesus addressed with this tender term (see 23:28). **Thy faith hath made thee whole.** The woman was healed not by the touch of His garment but by faith. This was not magic; the garment was not a talisman or charm. Instead, her faith in Christ was the key. For **go in peace**, see 7:50.

8:49. Thy daughter is dead. Seemingly, the delay had led to disaster. The man's daughter had died before Jesus could heal her. God is not limited by circumstances, however, as the crowd would soon see.

8:50. She shall be made whole (see discussion on Mark 5:34). Jesus offered a word of comfort. This is another situation in which Jesus, while not directly claiming to be God, said something that makes sense only on the assumption that He is God.

8:51. Jesus wanted only His closest disciples and the girl's parents with Him.

8:52. For **all wept, and bewailed her**, see discussion on Mark 5:38. **She is not dead, but sleepeth.** Jesus meant that she was not permanently dead (for a similar statement about Lazarus, see John 11:11–14).

8:53. They laughed him to scorn. Their lack of faith is in sharp contrast to the faith of the woman who had just been healed by touching Jesus' garment (see 8:43–48).

8:54–55. Jesus raised the girl with no fanfare. Jesus was not a "miracle worker"; rather, He did miracles. He was not a magician or charmer; rather, He showed the power of God while meeting genuine human needs. Jesus never engaged in stunts or used dramatic effects for the sake of showmanship or publicity. His simple words to the child here are just the opposite of what one would expect of a charlatan. His quiet confidence and the fact that the girl returned to life were further evidence of the truth of His claim to deity.

8:56. He charged them that they should tell no man (see discussion on Matt. 8:4; *KJV Study Bible* note on Mark 5:43). Further publicity at this time concerning someone being raised from the dead would have been counterproductive to Jesus' ministry.

9:1–6. A new phase of Jesus' ministry began when He sent out the apostles to do the type of preaching, teaching, and healing that they had observed Him doing (see Matt. 9:35). This was the third tour of Galilee by Jesus and His disciples (see discussion on 8:1). On the first tour, Jesus traveled with the four fishermen; on the second tour, all twelve were with Him; on the third tour, Jesus traveled alone after sending out the Twelve two by two.

9:1–2. His twelve disciples (v. 1). The apostles (see 6:13). **Power and authority.** Special power to heal (see 5:17; 8:46), authority in teaching, and control over evil spirits. **Devils.** Evil spirits (see discussion on 4:33). Jesus sent His disciples out **to preach the kingdom ... and to heal the sick**.

9:3. Take nothing. The disciples were to take no excess baggage that would encumber travel, not even the usual provisions. They were to be entirely dependent on God's provision through the people with whom they were staying (see discussions on Mark 6:8–9). Such dependence led them to exercise faith every day and demonstrated God's faithfulness. This leant further authenticity to the message they were bringing.

9:4. There abide. They were not to move from house to house, seeking better lodging, but rather were to use only one home as their headquarters while preaching in a particular community. This kept them from being distracted from their ministry by thinking about themselves and their needs and wants. It also made it easy for people to find them, as everyone would quickly learn where they were staying.

9:5. Shake off the very dust from your feet. A sign of repudiation for a community's rejection of God's message and a gesture showing separation from everything associated with the place (see 10:11; see also discussions on Matt. 10:14; Acts 13:51).

9:6. The disciples were obedient. Christians today would do well to cultivate a habit of obedience to the promptings of the Lord.

9:7. For **Herod the tetrarch**, see discussion on Matthew 14:1. **John was risen from the dead** (see discussion on Mark 6:14, 16). Luke did not record details about John's death (see Matt. 14:1–12; Mark 6:17–29), which occurred about this time, but simply noted that it had taken place (see 9:9).

9:8. For **Elias had appeared**, see discussions on 1:17; Mark 9:11–13.

9:9. He desired to see him. Herod's desire to see Jesus was not fulfilled until Jesus' trial (see 23:8–12).

V. Jesus' Withdrawal to Regions around Galilee (9:10–50)

A. To the Eastern Shore of the Sea of Galilee (9:10–17)

9:10–17. The feeding of the five thousand is the only miracle besides Jesus' resurrection that is reported in all four gospels (see discussions on Mark 6:30–44; John 6:1–14).

9:10. The disciples reported to Jesus the results of their ministry. In doing so, they also reported to one another. The stories of the others encouraged the disciples and motivated them to further ministry. Surely a time of rejoicing followed. **Bethsaida** (see discussion on Matt. 11:21). Jesus and the disciples must have retired to a remote area near the town (see 9:12).

9:11. Although He sought time alone, Jesus welcomed the crowds. People who interrupt may not always be aware that they are doing so, and a minister should at times make allowances for such inter-ruptions, seeing them as opportunities rather than distractions.

9:12. The day began to wear away. After the preaching and healing, the question of food and lodging was raised because they were in an isolated place. Jesus may have introduced the question (see John 6:5), but the Synoptics indicate that the disciples were also concerned.

9:13. Jesus challenged the disciples, knowing that their resources were not adequate but knowing also what He was about to do. When God calls Christians to a ministry, often they do not see the provision until they have begun the work. God is faithful, however, and will provide the resources when believers are committed to doing His will for His glory.

9:14. For **Make them sit down by fifties in a company**, see discussion on Mark 6:40.

9:15–16. And they did so. The disciples obeyed the Lord, even though they did not know where the food would come from. Christians today also should simply be obedient, trusting Him to provide. The disciples distributed the food at His direction. Apparently, the food was multiplied as they distributed it, and not before.

9:17. There was taken up of fragments … twelve baskets. This act served as an example of avoiding wastefulness and as a demonstration that everyone had been adequately fed (see discussion on Mark 6:43).

B. To Caesarea Philippi (9:18–50)

9:18–19. Whom say the people that I am? (v. 18). The disciples' report was the same as the one that had reached Herod (see 9:7–8). This event occurred to the north, outside Herod's territory, in the vicinity of Caesarea Philippi (see Matt. 16:13 and discussion; see also discussion on Mark 7:24).

9:20. Peter answering said. He was the spokesman for the disciples. **The Christ of God** (see discussion on 2:11). This predicted Deliverer (the Messiah) had been awaited for centuries (see John 4:25; see also discussions on Matt. 16:16; Mark 8:29).

9:21. He straitly charged them … to tell no man. The people had false notions about the Messiah and needed to be taught further before Jesus identified Himself explicitly to the public. He had a crucial schedule to keep and could not be interrupted by premature reactions (see discussions on Matt. 8:4; 16:20; Mark 1:34).

9:22. For **The Son of man**, see discussion on Mark 2:10. **Must suffer.** This was Jesus' first explicit prophecy of His death (for later references, see 9:44; 12:50; 17:25; 18:31–33; see also 24:7, 25–27). The disciples did not really understand what He said. Perhaps they thought He was using figurative language or speaking a mystery. This passage should remind one that God means what He says, and unless the context demands otherwise, one should take God's Word literally.

9:23. Take up his cross daily. To follow Jesus requires self-denial, complete dedication, and willing obedience. Luke emphasized continued action; "daily" is not explicitly mentioned in the parallel accounts (Matt. 16:24–26; Mark 8:34). Disciples from Galilee knew what the cross meant, for hundreds of men had been executed by this means in their region.

9:24. Whosoever will lose his life for my sake. This saying of Jesus is found in all four gospels and in two gospels more than once (Matt. 10:38–39; 16:24–25; Mark 8:34–35; Luke 14:26–27; 17:33; and, in slightly different form, John 12:25). No other saying of Jesus is given such emphasis. Jesus, in this context, is emphasizing self-sacrifice. Most people want to "save" their lives; that is, they want to live for themselves and make themselves happy. The one who loses his life, that is, gives up personal aggrandizement to live for Christ, giving his life to Him, will find his life. In other words, true happiness and satisfaction will be the result of a life lived not for true happiness and satisfaction but for the sake of Jesus Christ and the gospel.

9:25. This verse is an example of hyperbole. If to **gain the whole world** is worth less than the soul, then certainly any lesser material goal one might set is worth far less than the soul. People should be far more concerned with their spiritual condition than with the things they own. Jesus' words should be a corrective when one begins to measure their quality of life by what one owns rather than by identifying with Christ.

9:26. Whosoever shall be ashamed of me (see 12:9; see also discussion on Mark 8:38). In this context, there are three kinds of errors people make. Some focus on themselves and their own happiness, others seek material goods, and some trust Christ but keep that fact hidden because they fear what people will think. None of these paths lead to real satisfaction in life. Only open, committed discipleship will lead to true happiness.

9:27. See discussion on Matthew 16:28. For **the kingdom of God**, see discussion on Matthew 3:2.

9:28–36. The transfiguration. This is a turning point in Jesus' ministry. He soon after sends out the seventy (10:1–24), and the level of conflict with His opponents increases (11:14–28; 37–54).

9:28. An eight days. Frequently used to indicate a week (see John 20:26; discussion on Matt. 17:1). **Peter and John and James.** These three were also with Jesus when He healed Jairus's daughter (see 8:51) and during His last visit to Gethsemane (see Mark 14:33). **Into a mountain.** Although Mount Tabor is the traditional site of the Mount of Transfiguration, its distance from Caesarea Philippi (the vicinity of the last scene), its height (about 1,800 feet), and its occupation by a fortress make it an unlikely location. Mount Hermon fits the context much better by being both closer and higher (over 9,000 feet; see Mark 9:2). **To pray.** Luke again pointed out the importance of prayer to Jesus, especially before special occasions.

9:29. The fashion of his countenance was altered. The change in Jesus' appearance is not specified, but the brightness of His clothing is described as "white and glistening." It may have been due to the brightness of the light that shone on Him or due to a physical change.

9:30. Moses and Elias. Moses was the great Old Testament deliverer and lawgiver, and Elijah was the representative of the prophets. Moses' work was finished by Joshua, Elijah's by Elisha (another form of the name Joshua). Moses and Elijah now spoke with Jesus (whose Hebrew name was Joshua) about the new exodus He was about to accomplish, by which He would deliver His people from the bondage of sin and bring to fulfillment the work of both Moses and Elijah (see discussion on 1 Kings 19:16).

9:31. Decease. Greek *exodos*, a euphemism for Jesus' approaching death. It may also link Jesus' saving death and resurrection with God's saving of His people out of Egypt.

9:32. Heavy with sleep. Perhaps the event was at night. For **they saw his glory**, see *KJV Study Bible* note on Exodus 33:18.

9:33. Three tabernacles. Temporary structures to prolong the visit of the three important persons: lawgiver, prophet, and Messiah. The idea was not appropriate, however, because Moses and Elijah were outshone by Jesus' glory.

9:34–35. My beloved Son (v. 35). Or "my Chosen One," related to a Jewish title found in Dead Sea Scrolls literature and possibly echoing Isaiah 42:1 (see Luke 23:35). God the Father spoke in such a manner to emphasize the priority of Jesus over the two greatest figures of the Old Testament.

9:36. The event ended with **the voice**. The disciples well knew that any attempt to describe this event would be met with disbelief, until after Jesus' resurrection. Then it became one more sign of His messiahship.

9:37–38. Much people met him (v. 37). As so often happened, a crowd was waiting to hear Jesus, and someone had a desperate need to call His attention to.

9:39–40. A spirit taketh him (v. 39). This evil spirit was causing seizures (see Matt. 17:15) and a speechless condition (see Mark 9:17). Evil spirits were responsible for many kinds of affliction (see discussion on 4:33). The disciples were unable to drive out this spirit (v. 40).

9:41. Jesus' concern was not with the man who wanted his son to be delivered. This man had come to His disciples, and to Him, in faith. Perhaps Jesus was frustrated with His disciples, who lacked the faith needed for the situation and had failed miserably. Also, He may have been frustrated with the crowd, who may have been more interested in wit-

nessing a spectacle than in seeing the boy healed. Jesus' ministry was designed to point to Himself as Messiah and as God. The people did not perceive this (see Morris, *Luke*, p. 174).

9:42–43. Jesus easily **rebuked the unclean spirit** (v. 42), even as it was tormenting the boy.

9:44. Another prophecy of Jesus' coming death (see discussion on 9:22), with an indication of how it would be brought about (see 22:21).

9:45. Once again, the disciples **understood not** what He meant. **It was hid from them**. Here it is made clear that God was keeping the true import of Jesus' words from them. This may have been because they would have sought to engineer events to prevent His death. Some will wonder why Jesus foretold His death, knowing that the disciples would not understand. It may have been that He knew they would remember after the events took place, thus confirming and strengthening their faith in Him.

9:46. Which of them should be greatest. This subject arose on a number of occasions (see 22:24; see also Mark 10:35–45). The question revealed, as in 9:45, their lack of full understanding of what Jesus' mission and message were all about. Their lack of understanding may have been due to the pride revealed in this incident (see Morris, *Luke*, p. 175).

9:47–48. Jesus ... took a child (v. 47). Children had no status at that time and were certainly not treated with the type of consideration they receive in modern times. A child thus served as a perfect example of what Jesus wanted to teach about humility. **Receive this child in my name**. Here Jesus was teaching that service given in Christ's name to those who are not important, those who cannot help themselves, is accepted as service to Him. People who exalt themselves will not want to take note of the least important members of society. No one who believes they have attained a place in society will want much to do with those who have not earned their place. Children have not earned anything. Everything they receive is by grace. Jesus' point was that as His grace is given to those who have not earned it and cannot help themselves, so His followers should willingly give grace to those in like condition. **He that is least ... shall**

be great. A person will become great as he or she sincerely and unpretentiously looks away from self to revere God. One who serves the lowest in society (as modeled by the child) must esteem oneself even lower. The key to greatness in God's sight is humility.

9:49. This did not immediately follow from what Jesus said in 9:46–48. Luke apparently moved on to another topic. For **he followeth not with us**, see *KJV Study Bible* note on Mark 9:38.

9:50. He that is not against us is for us. Spoken in the context of opposition to the disciples' work (see 11:23, set in a different context). Jesus wanted the disciples to see that service rendered in His name is acceptable to God. Nothing in the context would lead to religious pluralism, nor does it mean that any ministry that uses the name of Jesus Christ is automatically above question on matters of doctrine and practice.

VI. Jesus' Ministry in Judea (9:51–13:21)

A. Journey through Samaria to Judea (9:51–62)

9:51. He stedfastly set his face to go to Jerusalem. Luke emphasized Jesus' determination to complete His mission (see discussion on 13:22; Isa. 50:7). This journey to Jerusalem, however, was not the one that led to His crucifixion but marked the beginning of a period of ministry in Judea, of which Jerusalem was the central city. Mark 10:1 notes this departure for Judea, which John more specifically describes as a journey to Jerusalem during the Feast of Tabernacles (see John 7:1–10). The Judean ministry is recounted in 9:51–13:21 and John 7:10–10:39.

9:52. A village of the Samaritans. Samaritans were particularly hostile to Jews who were on their way to observe religious festivals in Jerusalem. It was at least a three-day journey from Galilee to Jerusalem through Samaria, and Samaritans refused overnight shelter for the pilgrims. Because of this antipathy, Jews traveling between Galilee and Jerusalem frequently traveled on the east side of the Jordan River.

9:53. His face was as though. The words "his face" appear three times in 9:51–53 and once again in 10:1. In each case, it simply means that Jesus had

set His intention to go in that direction. Since it involved movement in a certain direction, He naturally would be looking in the direction He was going, and so He "set his face" (9:51). With this passage, Luke emphasized the turning point in Jesus' ministry. From this point on, His teaching and activities would be determined by the need to prepare His disciples for the rising opposition from the leadership and for the time after His ascension.

9:54. Command fire to come down from heaven. As Elijah had (see 2 Kings 1:9–16). James and John were known as "The sons of thunder" (Mark 3:17). The Samaritans had rejected Jesus and His disciples. While their anger was understandable, they needed to recognize the purposes of God.

9:55–56. Jesus **rebuked them** (v. 55; see discussion on 2 Kings 1:10). Jesus' purpose was to save lives, not to bring judgment. This should not be treated as applying to all times and places. Scripture makes it clear that, in His own time, God will come in judgment.

9:57–62. In this passage, three people indicated their desire to follow Christ. Each of them had conditions under which he would fulfill that commitment. Jesus made it clear, however, that this commitment must be absolute. One cannot place conditions on God. He must come first, and all other considerations in life must be placed in the background.

9:57–58. As they went in the way (v. 57). Continuing their journey through Samaria to Jerusalem. **I will follow thee whithersoever thou goest**. This man indicated that he would make any sacrifice in order to be Christ's disciple, but Jesus' reply revealed the shallowness of his commitment. **The Son of Man hath not where to lay his head** (v. 58). The man was unwilling to suffer personal discomfort for the glory of the Lord. Jesus spoke of the lack of sleeping accommodations, and that was enough to cool his ardor. When a specific sacrifice was called for, his commitment withered away.

9:59. The second man made his condition clear at the outset. He wished **first to go and bury my father**. If his father had already died, the man would have been occupied with the burial then, so evidently, he wanted to wait until after his father's death, which might have been years away. Jesus told him that the spiritually dead could bury the physically dead and that the spiritually alive should be busy proclaiming the kingdom of God. Jesus did not believe that family is unimportant, only that one's priorities must be right.

9:61–62. The third man laid down another condition: **let me first go bid them farewell, which are at home** (v. 61). This seems to be a proper request. Jesus would never have counseled rudeness. His reply to this man indicates that He discerned a deeper problem than a mere desire to say goodbye. **Having put his hand to the plough and looking back** (v. 62). This man was too attached to home and to familiar surroundings. His ministry would have been hindered by constantly looking back to an earlier day. A plowman who constantly looks over his shoulder does not have his eyes on the goal and tends to plow crooked rows.

Jesus' reply does not mean that anyone who lapses in their service to the Lord has thus lost their salvation. Nor does it mean that there is no second chance for a Christian who is active in church work and then backslides. If "all have sinned, and come short of the glory of God" (Rom. 3:23), then none **is fit for the kingdom of God.** Jesus here was speaking in terms of service, not salvation. His words mean that as long as someone is looking back to a previous time of bliss, his service is hindered. Such a person should repent and turn to the task at hand and to his commitments. Once the focus is on the present demands of the ministry, the problem will cease to exist.

B. The Mission of the Seventy (10:1–24)

10:1. The Lord appointed other seventy also. Recorded only in Luke, though similar instructions were given to the Twelve (see 9:3–5; Matt. 9:37–38; 10:7–16; Mark 6:7–11). Jesus covered Judea with His message (see discussion on 9:51) as thoroughly as He had Galilee. **Sent them two and two.** During His ministry in Galilee, Jesus had also sent out the Twelve in pairs (see 9:1–6; Mark 6:7 and discus-

sions), a practice continued in the early church (see Acts 13:2; 15:27, 39–40; 17:14; 19:22).

10:2. The harvest. Souls as "fruit" is the idea here. Jesus was encouraging His disciples with the promise of results in their ministry. Evangelism and missions are surely in view here. We should pray for workers and should be willing to go ourselves. Jesus urged believers to pray for those who are going as **labourers into his harvest.**

10:3. As lambs among wolves. As with so many metaphors, this one has layers of meaning. (1) It points out the physical danger they might face. Fallen humanity does not like to hear the message of repentance. (2) It implies that their message might be "devoured" by those who would twist it into something else. In like manner, Christians today should expect to meet opposition to the message of the gospel. Increasingly, such opposition is not a matter of friendly disagreement. (3) It indicates the manner in which opposition to the message will come. (4) It indicates the manner in which the gospel is to be shared. Lambs are a symbol of meekness and gentleness. (5) It indicates the nature of the message as well. The call to repentance, that is, to give up one's pride for humility, selfishness for servanthood, bitterness for forgiveness, and anger for gentleness, is a call that must be demonstrated in the life of the witness. A witness who goes forth as a wolf rather than as a lamb will hinder the message rather than help it.

10:4. Carry neither purse, nor scrip, nor shoes. The seventy disciples were to travel light, without a money bag, luggage, or extra sandals. **Salute no man by the way.** They were not to stop along the way to visit and exchange customary lengthy greetings. The mission was urgent.

10:5–7. Jesus here simply meant that the disciples should not stay where they were not welcome. They were not to go **from house to house** (v. 7) but were to find permanent lodging in a place fairly quickly (see discussion on 9:4).

10:8. Here Jesus gave a final word about accepting hospitality: **Eat such things as are set before you.** This is proper for several reasons. For one thing, it is polite. No one likes a picky eater, and no one appreciates having to make special accommodations for one person. Graciously accepting what is offered creates an atmosphere of friendliness that can hasten the acceptance of the message. When people eat together in harmony and fellowship, it creates a sense of common participation and bonding. In addition, pickiness can expose selfishness and a demanding spirit that is antithetical to the Lord's message of repentance and humility. Finally, food choices and standards vary from place to place, and even from family to family. Believers should not treat certain foods or presentations as being beneath them. Again, that is a kind of pride that is counterproductive to preaching and teaching about humility before the Lord. Humble acceptance of whatever food is offered is more in line with a life of faith in the sovereignty of God and His care for His people.

10:9. The kingdom of God is come nigh (see discussions on 4:43; Matt. 3:2). This was the heart of Jesus' message.

10:11. For **the very dust … we do wipe off**, see discussion on 9:5.

10:12. More tolerable in that day for Sodom. Although Sodom was so sinful that God destroyed it (see Gen. 19:24–28; Jude 7), the people who heard the message of Jesus and His disciples were even more accountable, because they had the gospel of the kingdom preached to them. This passage clearly teaches degrees of punishment. Some sins are worse than others and bring more judgment. "That day" is a reference to the judgment day.

10:13. Chorazin … Bethsaida (see discussion on Matt. 11:21). Jesus here turned on the fulcrum of judgment to discuss various cities where He had already preached the gospel. These cities faced judgment.

10:14. Tyre and Sidon were Gentile cities in Phoenicia, north of Galilee, which had not had opportunity to witness Jesus' miracles and hear His preaching as the people had in most of Galilee (see discussion on 10:12).

10:15. Capernaum. Jesus' headquarters on the north shore of the Sea of Galilee (see Matt. 4:13 and discussion), whose inhabitants had many opportu-

nities to see and hear Jesus. The condemnation for their rejection was therefore greater.

10:16. Jesus here offered His disciples some encouragement. They were to preach in His name and to consider opposition to their message as opposition to Jesus, not to them. As "lambs among wolves" (10:3), they would face opposition, but it was opposition to Christ. A believer's responsibility is simply to bear witness to the message of the truth.

10:17–18. The seventy disciples returned and reported the results of their ministry, with great joy. Jesus replied, confirming their experience, **I beheld Satan as lightning fall from heaven** (v. 18). Even the demons were driven out by the disciples (v. 17), which meant that Satan was suffering defeat. This could also refer to Satan's original fall from glory (see 2 Peter 2:4; Jude 6; Rev. 12:9). In any case, Jesus was offering affirmation, confirmation of what they had seen, and encouragement to continue preaching the truth, for God's power was with them.

10:19. Serpents and scorpions … the power of the enemy. In this context, the snakes and scorpions most likely represent evil spirits (see 10:20); the enemy is Satan himself. Jesus was not saying that Christians do not need to be careful of natural evils in the world. People should avoid things that are dangerous. Someone has said that Christians, the same as everyone else, should look both ways before crossing the street. Not to do so is a presumptuous test of the sovereignty of God.

10:20. Man's salvation is more important than power to overcome the Evil One or escape his harm. **Your names are written in heaven.** Salvation is recorded in heaven (see Ps. 69:28; Dan. 12:1; Phil. 4:3; Heb. 12:23; Rev. 3:5). The focus of believers' lives and preaching should be "God is merciful and will save," not "We have power; look at us." Christians should focus their ministries on the gospel of salvation, on God's great work on the cross, and not get sidetracked with other matters, especially those that would draw attention to themselves and how God may be using them.

10:21–22. This is one of Jesus' prayers of thanksgiving. **Thou hast hid these things from the wise**

and prudent, and hast revealed them unto babes (v. 21). This should be seen in context of Jesus' statement elsewhere that one should become "as a little child" (18:17) to enter the kingdom. God reveals truth to those who come in childlike faith, not to those who are wise in their own eyes. This is not to say that education is useless; it certainly has an important place in God's plan. Rather, it is to say that attitude is important. Jesus commends simplicity, trust, and humility. He never commends ignorance.

10:23–24. Jesus followed up His prayer with a word of commendation and encouragement for His disciples. They had seen things that the **prophets and kings** (v. 24) of old would have wanted to see, that is, the power of God at work in their ministries, and numbers coming to faith. How many of the Old Testament prophets never saw the kinds of numbers that Jesus and His disciples saw coming in repentance and faith.

C. The Lawyer and the Parable of the Good Samaritan (10:25–37)

10:25. Lawyer (see discussions on 5:17; 7:30). A scholar well versed in Scripture asked a common question (see 18:18; Matt. 22:36), either to take issue with Jesus or simply to see what kind of teacher He was. **What shall I do to inherit eternal life?** There was nothing wrong with this question. In context of what Jesus had just told the disciples in 10:24, it was quite proper. People were coming with spiritual needs wanting them met, which the prophets and kings had longed to see.

10:26. Jesus answered the question with a question. He was not trying to put the man off but was pushing him to work through the answer. Sometimes people will learn more if they are led to discover the truth rather than merely told the truth. Jesus, the master teacher, knew this and sought to offer the man a lesson he would not forget.

10:27–28. Love … God … and thy neighbour (v. 27). Elsewhere Jesus used these words in reply to another question (see Matt. 22:35–40; Mark 12:28–32), putting the same two Scriptures together (Deut. 6:5; Lev. 19:18). Whether a fourfold love (heart, soul, strength, and mind, as here and in Mark 12:30) or a threefold love (as in Deut. 6:5; Matt. 22:37; Mark 12:33), the significance is that total devotion is demanded. **This do, and thou shalt live** (v. 28). Jesus was not teaching salvation by works. He was leading the man to see how high the demands of the law are. Believers must help people understand the nature of righteousness before they can see the depth of sin. The high demands of the law will lead people to despair and to seeking reconciliation with a God who is holy. People repent lightly, and serve God poorly because they have not been challenged to look beyond the surface. God's requirements are high, and the sin that separates people from Him creates a vast chasm.

10:29. Willing to justify himself. The answer to the lawyer's first question was obviously one he knew, so to gain credibility, he asked for an interpretation. In effect he said, "But the real question is, Who is my neighbor?" This was the right question to ask. Obviously, the easy answer would be, whoever you see around you. Sometimes, though, one fails to see certain people. Those who are significant, those with whom one identifies, can be easy to love. Jesus, wanting to challenge this man with an even higher demand, offered a parable (see 10:30–37), specifically to challenge him to a higher requirement for love than he had known in the past.

10:30–37. The parable of the good Samaritan. As with so many of Jesus' parables, this one should be carefully interpreted with its context in view. There is so much temptation to allegorize the parables. The context offers no warrant to see this as an allegory of sin (the thieves), Jesus (the Samaritan), and the church (the inn). In fact, such an approach would take away from the meaning that Jesus intended. The parable contains a message of grace (see note on v. 37), which should not be ignored, but Jesus mainly wanted the lawyer to see that genuine love demands much more than he had been willing to do in the past. The parable was designed to convict him of not loving God or his neighbor with all his heart.

10:30. Jerusalem to Jericho. A distance of seventeen miles and a descent from about 2,500 feet above sea level to about 800 feet below sea level. The road ran through rocky, desolate country, which provided the perfect setting for robbers to waylay defenseless travelers.

10:31–34. Priest (v. 31) ... **Levite** (v. 32) ... **Samaritan** (v. 33). It is significant, and a completely shocking reversal, that the person Jesus commended was neither the religious leader nor the lay associate but rather a hated foreigner. Jews viewed Samaritans as half-breeds, both physically (see discussion on Matt. 10:5) and spiritually (see discussions on John 4:20, 22). Samaritans and Jews practiced open hostility (see discussion on 9:52), but Jesus asserted that love knows no national boundaries. He wanted the lawyer to see that loving your neighbor includes loving the one who is unlovely, the one whom society rejects. Christians do not have the luxury of choosing their neighbors, only the responsibility to meet their needs. Nor does one have the luxury of choosing the time and occasion for practicing love. Their need creates the time and occasion. Finally, one does not have the luxury of determining what resources will be used. The Samaritan used resources that he had planned for other uses, and he left the matter of the final bill open-ended.

10:35. Two pence. Two days' wages. This was a demonstration of grace. Jesus may have intended, as a subtheme, to demonstrate that God's love is given to those who have not earned it and who do not deserve it, that grace is given to sinful people who have no resources within themselves and who need grace and mercy. If so, it is not the main theme of the parable, which should be kept in mind. It does, however, fit in with the lawyer's question (see 10:25). Eternal life is impossible with one's own resources. All need the help of Christ, who comes in genuine love and mercy and meets the need.

10:36. Which ... was neighbour unto him ...? (v. 36). The question now became, who proved he was the good neighbor by his actions? Notice, the self-righteous theologian could not bring himself to say "the Samaritan." He begrudgingly said, **He that shewed mercy** (v. 36), or kindness. Jesus replied, **Go, and do thou likewise** (v. 37). The call to live out the gospel of grace, to humbly demonstrate to others that grace and mercy are realities, is the essence of love.

D. Jesus at Bethany with Mary and Martha (10:38–42)

10:38–40. A certain village (v. 38). Bethany, about two miles from Jerusalem, was the home of Mary and Martha (see John 12:1–3). These two women demonstrated two different approaches to the Christian life. While it is not a deliberate allegory, the comparison is too apt to miss and may have been intended by Luke. Martha may be likened to busy Christians who are always serving. Many saintly women through the years have served on church committees and done over and above in their work for God's glory. Mary may be likened to the contemplative Christian who adores her Lord. Martha complained to Jesus that Mary was not helping enough, which demonstrates that wherever He went, He was "in charge." His authority was recognized even above the normal authority structure of the household, so much so that Martha appealed to Him rather than directly to her sister or to their brother Lazarus.

10:41–42. Jesus' answer reveals that too much service may be a distraction. **Thou art careful and troubled about many things** (v. 41). Martha may have become busy for busyness' sake. Jesus did not question the quality of Martha's faith or her heart. An important person had come into the household, and Martha wanted to mark the occasion properly. In her preparations, however, she forgot the one for whom they were being done. **One thing is needful** (v. 42). Jesus did not need a lavish feast or everything laid out perfectly; He needed only the devotion of those who loved Him. Devotion should lead to service, not be a replacement for it, and vice versa. Jesus said that **Mary hath chosen that good part**, not that Martha had chosen something bad.

E. Teachings in Judea (11:1–13:21)

11:1. He was praying. Jesus prayed not only on special occasions (e.g., His baptism, 3:21; choosing the Twelve, 6:12; at Gethsemane, 22:41) but also as a regular practice (see 5:16; Matt. 14:23; Mark 1:35).

Teach us to pray. The disciples' request was met with a model prayer and some teaching on prayer. At this point, Jesus was headed toward Jerusalem, and His teaching was increasingly aimed at preparing the disciples for the time when He would no longer be with them. The Lord's model prayer given here is similar to Matthew 6:9–13, where it is a part of the Sermon on the Mount. Matthew included six petitions in the prayer in the Sermon on the Mount (combining the last two petitions into one), whereas Luke included five petitions.

11:2. Our Father. Jesus was addressing a group of disciples here, not a lone individual. He was teaching them about praying together. Much of the Bible is directed at groups. The address to "our Father" rather than to "my Father" should be a reminder that the church is to pray together, express its needs and dependence on God together, and find strength for prayer in lifting up concerns together.

Thy kingdom come. Thy will be done. The first part of the prayer concerns the will of God. The church should be concerned first and foremost that God's will be done. This concern cannot honestly be expressed if church members are not seeking the will of God in all that they do. During prayer, it is wise to always do some soul-searching to be certain that one can honestly pray, "Thy will be done."

11:3. Our daily bread. It is interesting that physical needs are mentioned ahead of forgiveness. It is a measure of God's love and of one's confidence in His love that believers pray for their physical needs.

11:4. Forgive us our sins. Matthew 6:12 has "debts," but the meaning is the same as "sins." Jesus taught this truth on other occasions as well (see Matt. 18:35; Mark 11:25). The prayer is a pattern for believers, who have already been forgiven for their sins. Jesus spoke here of daily forgiveness, which is necessary to restore broken communion with God.

11:5–13. Jesus next urged persistence in prayer (vv. 5–8) and gave assurance that God answers prayer (vv. 9–13). The argument is from the lesser to the greater (see v. 13). If some humans will grant one's petitions, "how much more" (v. 13) will God help His dear children.

11:5–8. The parable of a friend in need. This parable encourages persistence in prayer. Having just given the model prayer, Jesus wanted the disciples to understand that merely praying it as a rote prayer and then forgetting it would not do. One must be persistent in prayer. As with so many parables, the analogy should not be pushed too far. The man got out of bed and gave to his friend because he was annoyed and wanted his rest. God answers prayers not out of annoyance but out of love. The analogy is to the good result of persistence, not to the attitude with which the petition is granted. Believers should pray persistently, in confidence that God loves them and wants to answer their prayers.

11:9–10. Ask … seek … knock (v. 9). These verses are a commentary on the parable in 11:5–8. As the man persisted with his friend, so should one persist with God. Again, interpreters should not push the analogies here too far. The asking, seeking, and knocking are different ways of saying the same thing: be persistent. Jesus used this formula as a mnemonic device to make His oral teaching more memorable.

11:11–12. Having discussed the need for persistence, Jesus turned to the need for faith and confidence in God's goodness. The analogy is to the father-son relationship. The rhetorical questions assume the answer will be, "No, of course not!"

11:13. To make sure the analogy was not missed, Jesus made it explicit here. If even **evil** men (here Jesus assumed that His listeners knew that "all have sinned" Rom. 3:23) give good gifts to their children, God, who is good, will not give evil things to His children who pray. Instead, He will **give the Holy Spirit**. Matthew 7:11 has "give good gifts," probably referring to spiritual gifts. Luke emphasized the work of the Spirit, however, the greatest of God's gifts. Jesus was not saying that believers should pray only for the Holy Spirit. Nor was He saying that believers do not have the Spirit and must pray for Him to come into their lives. Rather, He was saying that Christians should pray for things that are in accord with the working of the Spirit, in their lives and churches.

11:14. A devil, and it was dumb (see discussion on 4:33). This evil spirit caused muteness. The probable parallel passage in Matthew 12:22–30 (see also Mark 3:20–27) indicates that the man was also blind.

11:15. Beelzebub the chief of the devils (see discussion on Matt. 10:25). Satan (see 11:18).

11:16. A sign from heaven. Jesus had just healed a mute (see 11:14). That was the sign, but the Pharisees would not recognize it.

11:17–18. Kingdom divided against itself (v. 17). If Satan gave power to Jesus, who opposed Him in every way, Satan would be supporting an attack on himself.

11:19. By whom do your sons cast them out? Jesus did not say whether the followers of the Pharisees (see Matt. 12:24) actually drove out demons (see discussion on 11:24), but they claimed to drive them out by the power of God, and Jesus claimed the same. To accuse Jesus of using Satanic power was implicitly to condemn their own followers as well. **Your judges**. The Pharisees would be condemned by those whom they had taught, because their accusation against Jesus would apply also to their followers (sons).

11:20. The kingdom of God is come. In the sense that the King was present in the person of Jesus (see discussion on 4:43) and that the powers of evil were being overthrown.

11:21. Here Jesus introduced an analogy to what He was doing. The devil is the **strong man**. **His goods are in peace**. This means not that those in Satan's dominion have peace but that the Devil is not worried about them, until one stronger comes along.

11:22. A stronger than he shall overcome him. Jesus was stronger than Beelzebub, and by His exorcism of demons, He demonstrated that He had overpowered Satan and disarmed him. It was therefore foolish to suggest that Jesus cast out demons by Satan's power.

11:23. The one who does not intentionally support Jesus opposes Him, making neutrality impossible. Even the worker of whom the disciples said "he followeth not with us" (9:49) was apparently a believer, acting in Jesus' name (see *KJV Study Bible* on Mark 9:38), and Jesus did not condemn him.

11:24–28. The unclean spirit is gone out (v. 24; see Matt. 12:43–45, where Jesus makes a similar comment about the Jewish nation of that day). Jesus was perhaps referring to the work of Jewish exorcists, who claimed to cast out demons (see 11:19) but who rejected the kingdom of God and whose exorcisms were therefore ineffective. **He findeth it swept** (v. 25). The place had been cleaned up but left unoccupied. A life reformed but lacking God's presence is open to reoccupancy by evil.

11:29. They seek a sign (v. 29). On several occasions, Jews asked Jesus for miraculous signs (see 11:16; Matt. 12:38; Mark 8:11), but He rejected their requests because they had wrong motives.

11:30. As Jonas was a sign. Jonah spent three days "buried" in the huge fish, just as Jesus would be buried for three days before His resurrection (see discussion on Matt. 12:40).

11:31–32. A greater than Solomon (v. 31) **… a greater than Jonas** (v. 32). Jesus argued from the lesser to the greater. If the **queen of the south** (the queen of Sheba; v. 31) responded positively to the wisdom of Solomon (see 1 Kings 10:1–13 and discussions), and the men of Nineveh to the preaching of Jonas, how much more should the people of Jesus' day have responded positively to the ministry of Jesus, who is infinitely greater than Solomon or Jonas!

11:33. A bushel. A container holding about one peck. **May see the light**. A lamp is meant to give light to those who are near it (see 11:36). Jesus had publicly exhibited the light of the gospel for all to see, but "an evil generation" (11:29) requested more spectacular signs. The problem was not with any failure on Jesus' part in giving light; it was with the faulty vision of His audience.

11:34. Thine eye is single. Those asking for a sign do not need more light; they need clear eyes to allow the light to enter.

11:35. This warning flows from 11:34. Obviously, **light** cannot be literal **darkness**. Figuratively speaking, however, darkness can look like light to fallen minds. Jesus was warning His detractors that they might not recognize truth when they saw it. Evil can keep one from knowing what is good. Christians today should indeed **Take heed** of this warning. They often reject the truth simply because it is uncomfortable. This could be a result of sin in the heart that resists or rejects God's truth.

11:36. Here is a word of encouragement. If Jesus' detractors repented of all sin, then they would see the truth more clearly. One sure sign that sin is present in one's life is an inability to take in spiritual truth and apply it. Sometimes a stagnant spiritual life is nothing more than a result of unconfessed sin.

11:37 – 38. He had not first washed before dinner (v. 38). Not commanded in the law but added in the tradition of the Pharisees (see Mark 7:3; see also Matt. 15:9).

11:39. Clean the outside. Engage in ceremonial washings of the body. **Ravening and wickedness**. These Pharisees were more concerned about keeping ceremonies than about being moral (see Mark 7:20 – 23). God is concerned with the heart. Here Jesus used another analogy. **The cup and the platter** represent outward deeds.

11:40. Did not he … make that which is within also? The inside of man (the "heart" and inner righteousness) is more important than the outside (ceremonial cleansing). God made them both, and to give attention to one without the other is an error.

11:41 – 42. Jesus continued His warning and exhortation here but changed His focus. The statement **rather give alms** (v. 41) does not fit the previous context. It becomes clear in verse 42 where Jesus was going with this. He was using almsgiving as an example of an outward act. Jesus was not saying that inward attitudes are all that matter. The outward deed is important, but the heart must be right as well. **All things are clean** (v. 41). Jesus may have been referring to the dietary regulations of the law. The Pharisees needed not only to do the outward action of giving but also to observe the law outwardly too. Jesus issued a **woe unto you, Pharisees!** (v. 42) because they were doing the outward things, even being fastidious to **tithe mint and rue**, but were ignoring the inward matters of **judgment and the love of God**. Jesus said they should continue to do the one and not fail to do the other.

Too many Christians today are lax about obedience and justify it on the basis that the heart attitude is all that matters. Jesus here made it clear that obedience is both inward and outward. He was rebuking the Pharisees not for tithing but for tithing without a heart for the things of God. Believers should ensure that their hearts are right and then live daily for God's glory in everything they do.

11:43. Ye love the uppermost seat … and greetings. The Pharisees loved the outward trappings of respectability but not the substance of it. There is nothing wrong with being well known or locally prominent, but they should not pursue these things; nor should Christians deceive themselves that they are spiritual merely because the religious community thinks they are. God looks upon the heart.

11:44. Graves which appear not. The Jews whitewashed their tombs so that no one would accidentally touch them and be defiled (see Num 19:16; Matt. 23:27). Just as touching a grave resulted in ceremonial uncleanness, being influenced by these corrupt religious leaders could lead to moral uncleanness. They were "graves which appear not," in that they looked respectable and thus spiritual, but in truth, they were corrupt. People should be on the inside what they appear to be to others.

11:45. One of the lawyers (see discussions on 5:17; 7:30). This man recognized that Jesus' words had a broader application than just to the Pharisees: **thus saying thou reproachest us also**.

11:46. Ye lade men with burdens. By adding rules and regulations to the authentic law of Moses (see discussion on Matt. 15:2) and doing nothing to help others keep them (see Matt. 23:4), while inventing ways for themselves to evade them, these lawyers had been guilty of the same sin as the Pharisees. That is, they had made themselves look respectable or spiritual, while their hearts remained unchanged.

11:47. Ye build the sepulchers of the prophets. Outwardly, these "lawyers" (11:46) appeared to honor the prophets by building or rebuilding memorials, but inwardly, they rejected the Christ the prophets announced. They lived in opposition to the teachings of the prophets, just as their forefathers had done.

11:48. Ye allow the deeds of your fathers. This means that the lawyers approved of their fathers' deeds. They honored the prophets by building their tombs but not by doing what the prophets said. They did outward deeds that looked good to the public but missed what is most important. By not following the teachings of the prophets, they wound up approving their fathers' deeds in killing the prophets. The connection between their deeds and their fathers' deeds is that neither did what God wants, and both had some connection to the prophets' deaths.

11:49 – 50. Said the wisdom of God (v. 49). The saying in these verses is not a quotation from the Old Testament or any other known book. It may refer to God speaking through Jesus, or it may refer in quotation form to God's decision to send prophets and apostles even though He knew they would be rejected. Jesus was saying that those who hear His teaching and have the teaching of all the prophets found in the Old Testament as well have an even greater burden of sin and will be judged more harshly, for their sin comes with greater knowledge.

11:51. The blood of Abel unto … Zacharias (see discussion on Matt. 23:35). Jesus was reenforcing what He said in 11:49 – 50 by emphasizing the specific prophets.

11:52. The key of knowledge. The lawyers, the very ones who should have opened the people's minds concerning the law, instead obscured their understanding with faulty interpretation and an erroneous system of theology. They kept themselves and the people in ignorance of the way of salvation, or as Matthew's account puts it, they "shut up the kingdom of heaven against men" (Matt. 23:13).

11:53. The Pharisees began to urge him vehemently simply means that the Pharisees began to question Him intently. Their motive, as the next verse reveals, was not a thirst for knowledge or a desire for righteousness, however.

11:54. Laying wait … to catch something. The determination of the religious leaders to trap Jesus is evident throughout Luke (see 6:11; 19:47 – 48; 20:19 – 20; 22:2).

12:1 – 12. Jesus here offered words of exhortation and encouragement to His disciples. After issuing a warning against hypocrisy (vv. 1 – 3), He gave them advice on dealing with persecution (vv. 4 – 12), telling them (1) not to fear, (2) not to deny Christ, and (3) to trust God in the hour of persecution.

12:1. Jesus wanted the disciples to **Beware … of the leaven of the Pharisees** (see discussion on Mark 8:15). By this, he meant **hypocrisy**. In the previous chapter, Jesus condemned the Pharisees and the lawyers for doing outward deeds while ignoring matters of the heart and for teaching laws that they themselves did not follow. Now He warned His disciples against doing the same things.

12:2. There is nothing covered, that shall not be revealed. In this context, the meaning is that nothing hidden through hypocrisy will fail to be made known. It is not clear whether Jesus meant that one's hypocrisy will be exposed and proclaimed at the judgment seat of Christ or that it will become evident in the natural course of life. Most likely, He meant the latter.

12:3. In closets. Storerooms were surrounded by other rooms so that no one could dig in from outside. Even things that were said that deeply in the house would become known. One's hidden motives are usually clearer to others than one might think. Jesus' words should challenge believers to examine their lives and the extent to which they live consistently with their testimony. Believers' lives should be transparent, especially to one another within the church; indeed, one's life is more transparent than one might think.

12:4 – 7. Jesus moved on to exhort and encourage His disciples regarding persecution. This passage has no direct relationship to the previous context. Again, however, Jesus was headed toward Jerusalem and was preparing His disciples in a variety of ways for the ministry they would perform after He was gone.

12:4. Them that kill the body, and after that have no more that they can do. Encouragement in the face of persecution (see Matt. 10:28). Persecution can bring about death, but the soul cannot be killed by any man. In the hour of trial, disciples of Jesus Christ should remember this and face whatever comes with a confidence that will be a testimony of the reality of their eternal relationship with God.

12:5. Hath power to cast into hell. God alone has this power. The Greek word for "hell" is *geenna* ("gehenna"; see discussion on Matt. 5:22), not to be confused with Hades, the general name for the place of the dead. In the New Testament, *geenna* is used only in Matthew, Mark, James 3:6, and here. **Fear him**. Respect His authority, stand in awe of His majesty, and trust in Him. When the disciples faced persecution, they would be standing between the men who would kill them and the God who has ultimate power over all men. As believers, they themselves did not face hell but were to be aware that their persecutors would have to deal with the one who would one day judge them. That knowledge would give the disciples a measure of courage and trust.

12:6–7. Five sparrows sold for two farthings (v. 6). God cares even for little birds, which were sold cheaply for food. God cares even more for His children, and even when the situation is bad, God is aware of them and will preserve their souls. Three Greek words used for Roman coins are *dēnarion* (denarius; Matt. 18:28), *assariōn* (Matt. 10:29), and *kodrantēs* (Matt. 5:26), very loosely related to each other as are a fifty-cent piece, a nickel, and a penny. The word for "farthings" is *assariōn*, so the transaction would be something like five birds for two nickels.

12:8–12. These verses deal with the matter of confessing or denying Jesus. Jesus was encouraging the disciples in the face of future persecution.

12:8. Confess me. When a person acknowledges that Jesus is the Messiah, the Son of God (see Matt. 16:16; 1 John 2:22), Jesus acknowledges that individual as His loyal follower (see Matt. 7:21). When the disciples faced persecution, they would be tempted not to confess their faith. Jesus wanted them to recognize their responsibility.

12:9. Shall be denied (see 9:26; 2 Tim. 2:12; Matt. 7:21; 25:41–46). The same word is used for Peter's denial (see 22:34, 61). This is not to say that such

people will lose their salvation. Rather, they will be embarrassed before heaven.

12:10. In this context, Jesus may have had in mind those who persecute believers. If someone who has spoken against Jesus Christ repents, forgiveness is available. Luke may have had in mind Paul's conversion as he recorded Jesus' words here, and Jesus Himself may have looked ahead to that important event and to other occasions when the church would need to admit to their number those who had persecuted them in the past. **Blasphemeth against the Holy Ghost** (see discussion on Matt. 12:31; Mark 3:28–29). Jesus here contrasted those who spoke against the Son of Man with those who go beyond that to blasphemy against the Spirit Himself. Such people have hardened their hearts to the point that they will never repent.

12:11–12. These verses are often misused. They are not teaching that it is wrong to prepare before going into the pulpit. Jesus was not endorsing laziness in sermon preparation. Rather, the context is the persecution of believers. Jesus was telling the disciples that **in the same hour** (v. 12) that they were brought before the authorities, the Holy Spirit would inform them what to say. They were not to worry that their faith would fail in the last moment and that they would deny Christ. Nor were they to plan ahead as to what they might say if they were to face persecution. If the disciples were active in ministering to God's people, building churches, and evangelizing, they would do well. If persecution arose, the Spirit would be with them to help them at that time.

12:13–21. The parable of the rich fool. This well-known parable arose from a question raised by "one of the company" (v. 13). Presumably, this was one of Jesus' disciples.

12:13. Divide the inheritance. Deuteronomy 21:17 gave the general rule that an elder son was to receive double a younger one's portion. Rabbis normally settled disputes over such matters. This man's request of Jesus was selfish and materialistic. There is no indication that the man had been listening seriously to what Jesus had been saying (see 12:1–11).

Jesus replied with a parable about the consequences of greed.

12:14. Jesus is indeed **judge** over all men. In this specific situation, however, He was asserting that He would not get involved in such a minor matter. His ministry was to point people to spiritual realities. Any rabbi could have helped this man if he had a legitimate claim.

12:15. In speaking to the assembled group about the evil of covetousness and materialism, Jesus mildly rebuked the man. It is possible that the group did not overhear the private conversation between Him and the man. In any case, Jesus saw a teachable moment and a lesson that the disciples needed to remember, as do believers today.

12:16. For **parable**, see discussion on 8:4. **The ground ... brought forth plentifully**. The man likely prospered due to rich soil, good farming methods, and careful management. None of these things are sins in themselves, nor is prospering from them. The man's sin was not that he prospered but that he believed prosperity counted for more than spiritual matters (see 12:21).

12:17-19. The man, looking only to this life, planned to store up his wealth and retire early and live for himself.

12:20-21. Fool (v. 20). A strong word (see 11:40; Eph. 5:17). The man would die that very night. None of his wealth would do him any good. This parable is not teaching that it is wrong to be wealthy, nor that it is wrong to plan for the future. Life is more than the wealth one can accumulate, however. One's heart should be focused on eternal matters, even if one prospers in temporal ones. Even early retirement is not a sin, as long as one sees it as an opportunity for service to the Lord and for focusing on more than making oneself happy. This was the man's sin. He thought only of his own happiness in this life and gave no thought to eternity. Eternity came for him quickly, and he was unprepared.

12:22-30. In these verses, Jesus explained the application of the parable for His disciples. If they focused on spiritual riches rather than material riches, it would have important implications for

their behavior and for their faith. These verses need to be examined closely to avoid misunderstanding them.

12:22. Jesus instructed the disciples to **Take no thought** for two things: **your life** and **the body**. In other words, they should not worry about whether they would eat or whether they would have anything to wear. These are concerns for all people at different levels. The poor worry about whether they will have *anything* to eat or to wear. Wealthier people are too often concerned about having the *best* food and the *most stylish* clothes. Jesus was saying that these things, at either end of the spectrum, are of no consequence. He did not mean that there is any virtue in dressing poorly or eating meager fare. The disciple who endeavors to have the poorest and the worst of these things, thinking that this is the path to a truly spiritual life, is just as guilty of "taking thought" for these things as is the one who is obsessed with having the best. Similarly, these verses cannot be used to say that there is any virtue in not looking one's best. Jesus' point was that His disciples should accept what God provides, trust Him to provide it, and then focus on more important things.

12:23. This verse explains why food and clothing are of little importance and echoes the point of the parable Jesus had just told (see 12:16-21). One's life and body have uses far more important than mere feeding and adornment. These are means to an end, not an end in themselves.

12:24-28. Here Jesus began a series of examples. The example of the ravens (v. 24) relates to God's provision of food, and the example of the lilies (vv. 27-28) relates to God's provision of clothing. Between these is the matter of stature (vv. 25-26), which relates to trusting God.

12:24. In the first example, Jesus focused on **the ravens**. They do not toil for their food. Rather, **God feedeth them**. People are more important than birds, and God, who feeds the birds, will feed His people as well.

12:25-26. In the second example, Jesus spoke of one's **stature** (v. 25), pointing out that no one can change height. People can do nothing about it since it is determined apart from a willing of it. Jesus' point was that since one cannot change **that thing which is least** (v. 26), why should one worry about **the rest**? All should accept God's provision of food and clothing in the same way that one accepts His will for one's height.

12:27–28. Finally, in the third example, Jesus considered **the lilies** (v. 27). They are more beautiful than even **Solomon in all his glory**, yet they do not worry about their raiment. God takes care of plants, and He will take care of His children.

12:29–31. These verses sum up Jesus' teaching in 12:16–28. Disciples should not seek food and clothing; that is, they should not worry about these matters but rather should accept them as God gives them, trusting and not doubting that He will provide. **Rather seek ye the kingdom** (v. 31) is a word of exhortation. Since 12:32 suggests that Jesus was speaking to believers, who already possess the kingdom, this command probably means that Christians should seek the spiritual benefits of the kingdom rather than the material goods of the world (see Matt. 6:33).

12:32. Jesus ended this teaching with a word of comfort: **Fear not.** That is, do not be afraid about food or clothes. **Give you the kingdom.** God had given them the kingdom; providing for their physical needs was a small thing. It would be inconsistent for the disciples to say that God had given them the kingdom and yet worry over whether they would eat the next day. It would betray the kind of hypocrisy that Jesus had just warned them against (see 12:1–3).

12:33–34. Give alms (v. 33). The danger of riches and the need for giving are characteristic themes in Luke (see 3:11; 6:30; 11:41; 14:13–14; 16:9; 18:22; 19:8). Jesus, having exhorted His disciples not to worry, now told them to sell their goods and give to the poor. He tied this to the idea that caring for the poor will result in **treasure in the heavens**. He was not saying that this is like an economic transaction. That is, one cannot "buy shares" in heaven by giving to the poor here. It is not the outward action but rather the heart that is important. Those who care nothing for this world's goods but who are

concerned, in the Lord, to meet the needs of others care more about the things of heaven than the things of this world. They exhibit grace, by giving to those who have not earned it, and thus show forth the grace that is a living reality in their hearts. Being focused on God's riches, they are free to share what they have of this world's riches with those in need. They thus have treasure in heaven, not because of an "investment" in this world but because that is where their hearts are (v. 34).

12:35–40. The parable of the watchful servants. This parable points to the need to be busy about serving the Lord at all times, for He may return at any time.

12:35. This is an exhortation to busy oneself with the work of the Lord.

12:36. His disciples were to be like servants awaiting their master's return so that **they may open unto him immediately**, that is, servants who are ready to serve. By analogy, Jesus was going to leave, but when He returns, He wants to find His people busy doing His work.

12:37. He shall gird himself. In this parable, the master reversed the normal roles and served the slaves (see 22:27; Mark 10:45; John 13:4–5, 12–16). So also, when Christ returns, He will bring blessings and joy to His people, not a heavier burden.

12:38. If he shall come in the second watch, or come in the third (see discussion on Matt. 14:25). Night was divided into four watches by the Romans (see Mark 13:35) and three by the Jews (see Judg. 7:19). These were probably the last two of the Jewish watches. The feast would have begun in the first watch.

12:39. Jesus, still thinking of His second coming, changed to another analogy here, that of His coming "as a thief in the night" (1 Thess. 5:2; 2 Peter 3:10).

12:40. Christ's return is certain, but the time is not known (see Matt. 24:36).

12:41. Jesus taught the people in parables but usually used a more direct approach with the disciples. Peter's question, then, was proper. In context, it appears that Jesus was aiming this teaching directly at the disciples. Jesus, still keeping to the analogy of earthly servants and their master, emphasized the duty to fulfill one's responsibilities (see 12:42–28).

12:42–44. Wise steward (v. 42). An outstanding slave was sometimes left in charge of an estate (see 16:1). This had happened to Joseph, whom the Pharaoh put in charge of all of Egypt (see Gen. 41:37–46). By analogy, Jesus was saying that those who serve Him faithfully will be rewarded.

12:45. By contrast, Jesus warned of a disciple who takes advantage of any delay in the Lord's coming, using God's gifts to him for his own pleasure rather than in God's service. If God has given certain gifts and responsibilities, then one must see them as tools to be used in His service. Those who do not will not be rewarded.

12:46–48. Will cut him in sunder (v. 46) ... **shall be beaten with many stripes** (v. 47) ... **shall be beaten with few stripes** (v. 48). Three grades of punishment meted out, in proportion to both the privileges each person enjoyed and his response to those privileges (see Rom. 2:12–16). Those who have much to offer in service to the Lord will be called to do more, and those who have less will not be burdened with ministries for which they are unsuited. Jesus was not threatening His disciples with literal punishment, for He would take care of that at the cross. His point was that there is no room for laziness or self-serving in God's ministry.

12:49–59. Jesus wanted His disciples to understand the seriousness of the ministry and mission to which He was calling them. It was not a ministry of "being nice." It would involve conflict, and they needed to be prepared.

12:49. Fire. Applied figuratively in different ways in the New Testament (see discussion on 3:16). Here it is associated with judgment and division (see 12:51). Judgment falls on the wicked, who are separated from the righteous.

12:50. Baptism. The suffering that Jesus was to endure on the cross (see discussion on Mark 10:38). **Till it be accomplished.** Christ's words on the cross would pronounce the completion of redemption and the end of His suffering on humanity's behalf (see John 19:28, 30). Jesus wished that His hour of suffering were already past.

12:51. Division (see discussion on Matt. 10:34). Jesus brought division, for He would not compromise on the truth. His followers should not compromise on matters of truth for the sake of unity. Division is inevitable as long as people insist on believing things contrary to what God has revealed in His word. Jesus wants His disciples to stand squarely on the truth regardless of the consequences.

12:52–53. Division will happen even within households, but disciples of Jesus Christ should stand firm, even if their families oppose their faith.

12:54–56. Wind from **the west** (v. 54) was from the Mediterranean Sea; wind from **the south** (v. 55) was from the desert. Although people could use such indicators to forecast the weather, they could not recognize the signs of spiritual crisis, the coming of the Messiah, the threat of His death, the coming confrontation with Rome, and the eternal consequences these events would have for their own lives.

12:57. Of yourselves judge. Despite the insistence of the Pharisees, despite the Roman system, and even despite the pressure of one's family, the people needed to accept God on His terms. The signs of the times called for immediate decision, before judgment came on the Jewish nation.

12:58–59. Here Jesus began a new subject related to His teaching in 12:49–53. As an earthly judge will judge a case strictly according to the law, God will do no less. **Give diligence that thou mayest be delivered from him** (v. 58). Settle accounts before it is too late. This is only sensible if one wants to avoid judgment. In the same way, Jesus' disciples were to preach repentance and not waver on this. People should settle with God now rather than later. The disciples were to stand firm on the reality of judgment and the need for repentance before that day comes. **Last mite** (v. 59). If a *kodrantēs* corresponds to a penny (see discussion on 12:6–7), a mite (Greek, *lepton*) corresponds to half a penny.

13:1. There were present at that season is a clue that what follows happened at about the same time as the events of chapter 12. The teaching in chapter 13 did not necessarily happen the same day. In the Bible, the setting often changes with only the barest of clues. The events of 11:1–13:35 all could have taken place on the same day (13:31), though not necessarily so. The events of 13:20–30 and of 13:31–35 certainly did happen on the same day (13:31). (It is possible that 12:1 indicates a break, but the context does not demand it, as Jesus continued to teach on the same theme.) **The Galileans**. This incident is otherwise unknown, but having people killed while offering sacrifices in the temple fits Pilate's reputation. These Galileans may have broken an important Roman regulation, which led to their bloody punishment.

13:2–3. Sinners above all … because they suffered such things? (v. 2). In ancient times, it was often assumed that a calamity would befall only those who were extremely sinful (see John 9:1–2; see also Job 4:7; 22:5, where Eliphaz falsely accused Job). Jesus, however, pointed out that all are sinners who must repent or face a fearful end. This should stand as a warning for believers today. It is easy for those who know Jesus Christ and who live for Him to begin to think of themselves as morally superior to others. Nothing in the Bible gives warrant for this. Christians are sinners who have admitted it and who have cast themselves on the mercy of God through faith in Jesus Christ. Believers seek to live lives that are pure before the Lord and before the world, with the help of the Spirit. They are not "less bad sinners" in any sense, only sinners who have found, in Christ, the remedy.

13:4–5. Those eighteen (v. 4). Another unknown incident. **The tower in Siloam**. Built inside the southeast section of Jerusalem's wall. Jesus Himself mentioned this incident, perhaps anticipating what the people would ask next or perhaps taking advantage of the teachable moment. He was nearing Jerusalem, and some in the crowd may have seen the fallen tower and perhaps knew some of those who had been killed. His point was the same as in verses 1–3: accidents happen. They are not necessarily the result of divine judgment. All have sinned, and all must repent. An unfortunate demise is not a sign of greater sinfulness. The misfortune of others should not lead to spiritual complacency. Misfortunes happen in this world, and one must therefore be ready to meet God at any moment.

13:6–9. The parable of the fig tree. As with other parables, one should not look for an allegorical meaning for every element of this parable. Many of the elements simply reflect how fig trees were cultivated. Jesus' point was simply that God could judge all men quickly, but He is merciful and gives further time to repent.

13:6. A fig tree. Possibly refers to the Jewish nation (see discussion on Mark 11:12–14) but most likely applies to the individual soul.

13:7. These three years. A period of ample opportunity. The three-year delay relates to the fig tree. This is not an opportunity to look for hidden meanings as to when God's judgment will occur, nor for some sign as to how much sin God will tolerate before He judges.

13:8–9. The implication is that the man allowed the fig tree more time to produce, though the account does not say so. Likewise, God is patient and gives people ample opportunity to repent.

13:10. This is a transition sentence. As Jesus traveled to Jerusalem, apparently at a leisurely pace, He often stopped to teach in the towns and synagogues.

13:11. A spirit of infirmity. Evil spirits caused various disorders (see discussion on 4:33). The description of this woman's infirmity suggests that the bones of her spine were rigidly fused together.

13:12–13. Woman, thou art loosed (v. 12). The spirit had been cast out, and the woman was freed from the bond of Satan and from her physical handicap.

13:14. For **the ruler of the synagogue**, see discussion on 8:41. **Jesus had healed on the sabbath**. A focal point of the Jewish leaders' attacks against Jesus was His conduct on the Sabbath (see 6:6–11; 14:1–6; Matt. 12:1–8, 11–12; John 5:1–18; see also Exod. 20:9–10). For Jews who felt threatened by the inroads of Greco-Roman culture, observing the Sabbath was an important way of maintaining the distinction between Jews and Gentiles. This is why it was elevated to such a position of importance in the first century. Jesus' healings on the Sabbath was disturbing to these leaders, who saw it as a challenge to the very heart of Jewish life and culture. Still, it is surprising that the ruler of the synagogue reacted as he did. His words indicate that he was aware that a miracle had taken place; he exhorted the people to come on other days of the week for healing miracles.

13:15 – 16. Loose his ox (v. 15). The Jewish leaders had more regard for the needs of an animal than for the far greater need of a person. Jesus exposed what must have been a common exception among many people who were otherwise strict observers of the Sabbath. In healing the woman, Jesus also made an exception, but with much greater warrant. **Thou hypocrite.** Jesus called His critics hypocrites because they pretended zeal for the law, but their motive was to attack Him and His ministry of healing. Believers should take warning from this. It is easy to speak in terms of spiritual ideals and yet make exceptions personally.

13:17. It was altogether right that **his adversaries were ashamed**. He had left them with no credibility. The Lord did this not as a matter of playing intellectual games. He knew that the issue was deadly serious. He sought to goad them into repentance, not just to win points. **And all the people rejoiced**, not that their leaders' pretensions had been punctured but that good things had happened.

13:18 – 21. Jesus offered two short parables, that of the mustard seed (vv. 18 – 19) and the leaven (v. 20 – 21), to describe the kingdom of God.

13:18. With an introductory statement, Jesus alerted His hearers that He was about to make an analogy (also in 13:20).

13:19. Mustard seed (see discussions on Matthew 13:31 – 32; Mark 4:31). Its growth symbolizes that the kingdom will grow not through military conquest but as people repent and come into it. **A great tree.** In Scripture, trees are sometimes symbols of nations (see Ezek. 17:23; 31:6; Dan. 4:12, 21). **The fowls of the air** nesting in the tree symbolize that the kingdom of God brings blessings and benefits to those who are within it.

13:20. Jesus varied the introductory statement, using one question here, where He had used two in verse 18. Nothing should be made of this, as it was most likely simply an oratorical device to prevent too much repetition. Jesus was a master teacher who knew when to repeat Himself for emphasis and when to vary His words to add interest.

13:21. Jesus emphasized the permeating quality of **leaven** (see discussion on Matt. 13:33); it works from the inside to affect all the dough. This parable could speak of the powerful influence of God's kingdom to change things, or it could represent how evil can pervade and grow even in God's institutions. **Three measures.** About one-half bushel, or twenty quarts (twenty-two liters); Sarah used the same amount in Genesis 18:6.

VII. Jesus' Ministry in and around Perea (13:22 – 19:27)

A. The Narrow Gate (13:22 – 30)

13:22 – 19:27. Somewhere between the events of 11:1 and 13:21, Jesus left Judea and began His work in and around Perea, which is recorded here and in Matthew 19:1 – 20:28; Mark 10; John 10:40 – 42. During the last part of the Perean ministry, it appears that Jesus went north to Galilee and then traveled south again through Perea to Jericho and to Jerusalem. Some of Jesus' sayings that Luke attributes to the period of ministry in Perea are found in different settings in Matthew (see Matt. 7:13 – 14, 22 – 23). Perhaps He repeated various sayings on different occasions.

13:22. He went through the cities and villages. Jesus was **journeying towards Jerusalem**, where He would die. Although Jesus was ministering throughout Perea, His eyes were constantly set on the Holy City and His ultimate destiny.

13:23. Are there few that be saved? Perhaps the questioner had observed that in spite of the very large crowds that came to hear Jesus' preaching and to be healed, only a few followers were loyal. Jesus did not answer directly but warned that many would try to enter the kingdom after it was too late.

13:24. Some have seen this verse as teaching works salvation, but it instead teaches exclusivity. Jesus' use of the term **the strait gate** is a reference not to morals but to the exclusive means of salvation. There is no salvation apart from Jesus Christ. **Many … will seek to enter in**, that is, by means other than by repentance and faith in Christ, **and shall not be able**. This passage should be seen in light of Jesus' words "except ye repent" (13:3, 5). In this context, Jesus may have been warning the people not to depend on mere exposure to the gospel. Merely having heard the message of Jesus, and even rejoicing in it, will not be enough.

13:25. Jesus told a parable to illustrate the problem. **The master of the house** is Jesus. Those who **knock** are the ones who did not repent when they had the chance.

13:26. Those outside will protest that they **have eaten and drunk in thy presence, and thou hast taught in our streets**. They were exposed to the message of repentance and faith.

13:27. I know you not whence you are (see Matt. 7:23; 25:12). Jesus called these people **workers of iniquity**, demonstrating that the problem was that they had not repented. People should take warning from these words today as well. Merely being a church member does not guarantee salvation. Jesus indicated that such protests will fall on deaf ears.

13:28. Weeping and gnashing of teeth is often used to describe those who are in hell or those who are excluded from heaven, as here. It indicates that those who are not allowed to enter heaven will be conscious of their exclusion, and they will sorrow and suffer because of it.

13:29. They shall come from the east, and from the west, and from the north, and from the south. From the four corners of the world (see Ps. 107:3) and from among all people, including Gentiles.

13:30. A theme in Jesus' teaching has been that God values humility (see Luke 14:11; 18:14). This is rooted in the Old Testament (2 Chron. 7:14; Prov. 16:19; Isa. 57:15). Jesus gives it creative expression here. **Last which shall be first, and ... first which shall be last**. Earthly greatness has little to do with greatness in God's sight. In this context, Jesus was telling His hearers not to look to their standing in the community as an indicator of standing with God. Today many who are "pillars" of the church will be less than others who are unknown but who serve faithfully wherever God has put them.

B. Warning concerning Herod (13:31–35)

13:31. Herod will kill thee (see discussion on Matt. 14:1). Jesus was probably in Perea, which was under Herod's jurisdiction (see discussion on 3:1). The Pharisees may have wanted to frighten Jesus into leaving this area and going to Judea. On the other hand, these Pharisees may have viewed His ministry positively and wanted to protect Him. Some Pharisees had such a view, as evidenced by Nicodemus (see John 3).

13:32. Jesus called Herod a **fox**, a crafty animal. The reference is to Herod's tendency to trickery and slyness. **To day and to morrow**. In Semitic usage, this phrase could refer to an indefinite but limited period of time. Jesus, then, was not being literal. He meant that His ministry would continue for a while longer. **I shall be perfected**. Jesus' life had a predetermined plan that would be carried out, and no harm could come to Him until His purpose was accomplished (see 4:43; 9:22). He did not mean that He would move from a state of imperfection to a state of perfection. Jesus never sinned. The Greek word for "perfected" carries the idea of completion. Jesus would complete His ministry, no matter what others might attempt to do.

13:33. Out of Jerusalem. Jesus' hour had not yet come (John 7:30; 8:20; see also John 8:59; 10:39; 11:54). He would die in Jerusalem, as had numerous prophets before Him. This, then, is yet another prophecy of His death. It led Him to lament over the city that had killed so many of the prophets (see 13:34–35).

13:34–35. How often ...? (v. 34). This lament over Jerusalem may suggest that Jesus was in Jerusalem more often than the Synoptics indicate (see John 2:13; 4:45; 5:1; 7:10; 10:22). The statement in these verses may have been uttered some distance from Jerusalem, however, possibly in Perea. According to Matthew 23:37–38, the same utterance was spoken on Tuesday of Passion Week. Jesus repeated many of His teachings and sayings. Perhaps He had said this on many occasions when the subject of Jerusalem came up.

Your house is left unto you desolate (v. 35). God would abandon His temple and His city (see

21:20, 24; Jer. 12:7; 22:5). For **Ye shall not see me, until the time come,** see Zechariah 12:10; Revelation 1:7 (see also Isa. 45:23; Rom. 14:11; Phil. 2:10–11). **Blessed is he that cometh in the name of the Lord.** The crowds spoke like this upon his triumphal entry (see Luke 19:38), but here Jesus was referring to His second coming.

C. At a Pharisee's House (14:1–24)

14:1. On the sabbath. Of the seven recorded miracles that Jesus performed on the Sabbath, Luke recorded five (4:31, 38; 6:6; 13:14; 14:1); the other two are John 5:10; 9:14. For the importance of the Sabbath to the Pharisees, see discussion on 13:14. Sabbath meals were prepared the day before. The Pharisees were seeking an opportunity to trap Jesus. He sought an opportunity to challenge them. They both found it in the same incident. Jesus did not avoid the controversy but rather met it head-on (see 14:3–4).

14:2. Dropsy. An accumulation of fluid that would indicate illness affecting other parts of the body. The Greek for this word is a medical term, *hydrōpikos,* found only here in the New Testament (see Introduction: "Author").

14:3–4. Lawyers (see discussions on 5:17; 7:30). By questioning them before the miracle, Jesus made it difficult for them to protest afterward.

14:5. Have an ass or an ox fallen into a pit. In Deuteronomy 5:14, the law says that even animals were not to work on the Sabbath, but it was never wrong to help an animal that was in need. Jesus' action was unlawful only according to rabbinic interpretations, not according to the Mosaic law itself.

14:6. By meeting the controversy head-on, Jesus had left these Jewish leaders unable to raise any objections: **they could not answer him.** Jesus had appealed to them before healing the man (see 14:3) and instructed them afterward, pointing out how their own behavior was consistent with Jesus' practice (see 14:5). Sometimes more trouble brews by avoiding controversy until it boils over. If one is in the right, then it is appropriate to meet one's opponents and challenge them, not in a way that antagonizes them but merely to show the rightness of one's position.

14:7. This incident took place at the same dinner party (see 14:1). **The chief rooms.** Maneuvering for better seats may have caused trouble at the Last Supper also (see 22:24). Jesus seized the opportunity for a teachable moment as a result of this incident.

14:8–10. Jesus' words here are a bit of practical advice, but they illustrate a spiritual truth.

14:8. Sit not down in the highest room. Jesus was telling the lawyers and Pharisees to do something contrary to normal expectations. God's Word will often startle the reader and challenge one's assumptions. Many times the right thing to do is not what human nature would indicate. Everyone wants to have a place of honor. Jesus said not to seek it, however, contrary to normal human desires.

14:9. Thou begin with shame to take the lowest room. Following Jesus' advice will prevent embarrassment. In Roman times, honored guests at a meal often were given better treatment than the normal guests, for example, a better seat and better food. No one thought this was unusual. It would be embarrassing, however, if one assumed he was honored when he was not.

14:10. Here is a further reason for taking the **lowest** place. One may find oneself called up to the head table, in a sense, and thus honored before the whole assembly.

14:11. Jesus applied the lesson of 14:7–10 in spiritual terms: **he that humbleth himself shall be exalted.** This is a basic principle repeated often in the Bible (see 11:43; 18:14; 20:46; 2 Chron. 7:14–15; Prov. 3:34; 25:6–7; Matt. 18:4; 23:12; James 4:10; 1 Peter 5:6). This principle played out in Jesus' own experience as well. He humbled Himself when He became a man in order to die for humanity's sins, and God highly exalted Him (see Phil. 2:5–11). He is the ultimate example of what He was teaching here.

14:12–13. Jesus, speaking to His host, taught another lesson: **when thou makest a feast, call the poor** (v. 13). By inviting those who cannot return the favor, disciples become an example of grace in action. Again, what one can do on a small scale, God did on a large scale in the work of the cross. God gives grace to sinners who have nothing to offer.

There is no way we can ever pay Him back for what He has done. Those who have been given grace can demonstrate grace, and that is what Jesus was encouraging here.

14:14. The resurrection of the just. All will be resurrected (see Dan. 12:2; John 5:28–29; Acts 24:15). The resurrection of the righteous (see 1 Cor. 15:23; 1 Thess. 4:16; Rev. 20:4–6) is distinct from the resurrection of the unrighteous. There is no "general resurrection" (see 1 Cor. 15:12, 21; Heb. 6:2; Rev. 20:11–15). "The just" are those whom God has pronounced so on the basis of Christ's atonement and whose actions have evidenced their faith (see Matt. 25:34–40).

14:15. Eat bread in the kingdom. The great messianic banquet to come. The association of the future kingdom with a feast was common (see 13:29; Isa. 25:6; Matt. 8:11; 25:1–10; 26:29; Rev. 19:9).

14:16–24. The parable of the great supper, which warns that not everyone will enter the kingdom.

14:16. Then said he unto him. Jesus used the man's remark as the occasion for the parable. In this parable, the **certain man** represents God. The **great supper** is the kingdom of God.

14:17–20. I have bought a piece of ground (v. 18). The initial invitation must have been accepted, but when the final invitation came (by Jewish custom, the announcement that came when the dinner was ready), other interests took priority. None of the reasons given was genuine. For example, one did not buy a field without first seeing it, nor oxen without first trying them out (v. 19).

14:21–23. The master sent the servant out to bring in those who had not originally been invited and who would not normally have been invited to a rich man's feast. These guests most likely represent the Gentiles, to whom the gospel would be taken after Israel rejected it.

14:24. Those men which were bidden. Without explicitly mentioning them, Jesus warned "the lawyers and Pharisees" (14:3) that those who refused the invitation to his messianic banquet would not get one taste of it, but others would (see 20:9–19). Luke wrote to a Gentile audience, who would have found assurance of their position in Christ in this parable, which emphasizes the calling of those who were not part of the original guest list (see discussion on Matt. 21:41).

D. The Cost of Discipleship (14:25–35)

14:25–35. In this section, Jesus challenged those who were following Him whether they really had the commitment to be His disciples. Things would get rough once He was in Jerusalem, and tougher times lay ahead for them all. Those whose discipleship was nothing more than a lark would not be prepared for persecution, opposition, and hardships.

14:25. This is a transition statement, moving the reader from the context of the dinner party to that of Jesus teaching in a town or on the roadside.

14:26. If any man … hate not his father. Vivid hyperbole. Jesus' point was that one must love Him even more than one's immediate family (see Matt. 10:37). The word "hate" in the Bible does not always carry the emotional connotation that it does today. (Remember that God "loved Jacob" but "hated Esau" [Mal. 1:2–3; Rom. 9:13], meaning simply that Jacob received favor from God, whereas Esau, and his descendants, did not. This had nothing to do with God's emotional feelings about them but rather indicated His choice of one over the other.) Jesus was saying that those who follow Him must choose Him over family if a conflict arises from their commitment to Christ.

14:27. Bear his cross (see 9:23; Matt. 10:38 and discussions). One must be willing to follow Jesus before one knows where the journey will lead.

14:28–32. Jesus used two analogies to make His point clear. The cost of discipleship is like that of building a tower (vv. 28–30) or going to war (vv. 31–32). In both cases, one must consider what the commitment will cost before starting out.

14:28–30. Counteth the cost (v. 28). Jesus did not want a blind, naive commitment that expected only blessings. **Build a tower**. As a builder estimates costs, so a person must consider what Jesus expects of His followers. Being a disciple is like building a building; it is a long-term project that demands one's full attention, not something done quickly or in one's spare time. Jesus was looking for long-term commitment.

14:31–32. Going to make war (v. 31). This is like being a disciple in that it requires the expenditure of one's resources. When someone trusts Christ, their money is no longer their own, nor are their time and talent. It is all given over to the cause of Christ, much like when a nation goes to war and wartime realities determine its policies and the use of its resources and time.

14:33. Whosoever … forsaketh not all that he hath. The cost of being a disciple, Jesus warned, is complete surrender to Him.

14:34–35. Salt is good (see *KJV Study Bible* note on Mark 9:50). This ties into Jesus' analogies in 14:28–32. Salt that has lost its flavor is like someone who starts to build a tower and cannot finish or like someone who goes to war without adequate resources. Such salt does not complete its purpose, and it lacks the resource, the saltiness, to do the job it was intended for. A disciple who does not maintain his commitment is like such salt. Believers must determine never to be "useless Christians," like salt that has **lost his savour**.

E. The Parables of the Lost Sheep, the Lost Piece of Silver, and the Lost Son (chap. 15)

15:1. This is a transition sentence. Jesus was still teaching either in a town or along the roadside (see 14:25). He had a new audience, however: **publicans and sinners** (see discussions on 3:12; Mark 2:15).

15:2. The Pharisees and scribes murmured. They complained among themselves but not openly. **Eateth with them**. More than simple association, eating with a person indicated acceptance and recognition (see Acts 11:3; 1 Cor. 5:11; Gal. 2:12). Jesus came to save sinners, and that required identifying with them. This is in line with His teaching that His followers must humble themselves (see 14:1). He cared not about being "respectable" but rather about being identified with the spiritually needy, whatever the cost. Because He humbled Himself, the Father has exalted Him.

15:3–32. In this section, Jesus told three parables intended to explain the importance of His mission to bring sinful people to repentance. "That which is lost" (v. 4) sets the tone for these three parables, each an illustration of being spiritually lost: the lost sheep (vv. 4–7), the lost piece of silver (vv. 8–10), and the lost son (vv. 11–32). The theme throughout is that when something that was lost is found, one rejoices. The lesson is that God seeks lost sinners to reclaim them, and there is great rejoicing in heaven when one of them repents.

15:3. This parable. Of the three parables in chapter 15, the word "parable" appears only here. Some see these parables as one parable with three parts. The subject matter of each is different, though the point is the same, and thus it is best to see these as three parables that teach the same lesson.

15:4–7. The parable of the lost sheep. This parable contrasts the love of God with the exclusiveness of the Pharisees.

15:4. Sheep. The shepherd theme was familiar (see Psalm 23; Isa. 40:11; Ezek. 34:11–16) to Jesus' audience. As Israelites, it was easy to identify themselves as God's sheep.

15:5. The image here points to the idea that God loves His people and treats them with gentleness and kindness.

15:6. The shepherd rejoices more over one lost sheep that was found than over the ones that were never lost.

15:7. To ensure that the people did not miss the lesson of the parable, Jesus spelled it out for them. **Joy shall be in heaven**. God's concern and joy over the sinner's repentance are set in stark contrast to the attitude of the Pharisees and the scribes (see 15:2). **Just persons which need no repentance** is probably irony. Jesus was referring to those who think they are righteous (such as the Pharisees and the scribes) and feel no need to repent. The parable reveals the value God places on each individual. Like the shepherd who valued a single sheep, so God loves each individual person. It also explains why Jesus spent time with sinners (see 15:2). As the shepherd in the parable sought the lost sheep, so also Jesus pursued sinners, seeking to bring them to repentance and faith.

15:8–10. The parable of the lost coin. The coin lost represents the sinner whom God seeks and values.

15:8. Ten pieces of silver. Ten drachmas. A drachma was a Greek coin approximately equivalent to the Roman denarius and worth about an average day's wages (see Matt. 20:2). **Seek diligently.** Near Eastern houses frequently had earthen floors and no windows, making the search for a single coin difficult. Sweeping would move the coin in the midst of the dust.

15:9–10. Rejoice with me. Again there is celebration and rejoicing, and again Jesus explained the lesson.

15:11–32. This parable is popularly known as "the prodigal son," though modern translations have begun calling it "the lost son" to parallel "the lost sheep" and "the lost coin."

15:11–12. The portion of goods (v. 12). The father might divide the inheritance (the older son received a double portion; see discussion on 12:13; Deut. 21:17) but retain the income from it until his death. To give a younger son his portion of the inheritance upon request was highly unusual, however. **He divided unto them.** The son's request is strange enough, but that the father met his request is even more startling. The story is implausible, but not so completely as to be beyond the bounds of believability. Jesus, like any storyteller, took certain liberties and assumed a certain suspension of belief for the sake of the story. This is not intended to deceive the listener but to spark his interest and curiosity.

15:13. The younger son gathered all together. The son's motive became apparent when he departed, taking with him all his possessions and leaving nothing behind. He wanted to be free of parental restraint and to spend his share of the family wealth as he pleased. **Wasted his substance with riotous living.** More details are provided in 15:30, though the older brother may have exaggerated because of his bitter attitude.

15:14. The younger son failed to plan for the future and instead lived only for the moment. When problems arose, he was unprepared. While this is not the main point of the parable, one can certainly see

here a lesson on the wisdom of restraint and foresight. Fulfilling every sensual desire just because one wants to and has the means to is never wise. Living just for the moment, not worrying about tomorrow, is never wise. This young man had done both and was thus doubly foolish. Worse, he had squandered his father's hard-earned money.

15:15. To feed swine. The ultimate indignity for a Jew. Not only was the work distasteful, but pigs were considered unclean animals (see Lev. 11:7).

15:16. Husks. Or "pods," seeds of the carob tree.

15:17. He came to himself. He came to his senses and realized how much worse his condition was than even that of his father's servants. The flow of the story indicates that he truly repented.

15:18. The young man made plans for his return, even as to what he would say. When one has wronged someone, as this young man had done to his father, it is only proper to seek reconciliation. This should be done with all the seriousness the situation requires. **I have sinned against heaven, and before thee.** The young man recognized that his sin was against God as well as against his father.

15:19. He had left home as an arrogant, self-willed young man. He returned as a willing servant. He left wanting to serve himself. He returned ready to serve his father. He left as one unwilling to be a son to his father. He returned as one knowing he was unworthy to be a son to his father. There is much to be learned about the nature of repentance here. No one can come to God as one who has a "right" to salvation.

15:20. In his eagerness, the father **ran** to meet his returning son. So also, God eagerly accepts the repentant sinner. God is eager to save, certainly, but that gives people no warrant to demand it of Him.

15:21. The young man's speech appears to have been cut short by the father's warm welcome. Jesus may have assumed that people would know that he would have given the entire speech he had planned and so did not repeat it, or He may have wanted to emphasize the father's eagerness to forgive.

15:22–23. Bring forth the best robe (v. 22) … **ring … shoes … fatted calf** (v. 23). Each was a sign of position and acceptance (see Gen. 41:42; Zech. 3:4): a long robe of distinction, a signet ring of authority, sandals as a son wore (slaves went barefoot), and the fattened calf for a special occasion.

15:24. Again, the picture is one of rejoicing: **they began to be merry.** In each of these parables, rejoicing is the result of recovering what was lost. Jesus wanted to emphasize that God is eager for sinners to repent, which is why Jesus spent so much time with them.

15:25–27. The **elder son** (v. 25) discovered what had happened.

15:28. The older brother's resentment represents the attitude of the Pharisees and teachers of the law who opposed Jesus, whereas the forgiving love of the father symbolizes the divine mercy of God. The older son resented that much was made of his brother's return. His sense of justice required that his brother be punished or rejected. So also was the Pharisees' attitude toward those to whom Jesus ministered.

15:29. A kid. Cheaper food than a fattened calf. The older brother was not really worried about having a party for himself, only that his younger brother got one. Given his father's demonstrated generosity, he certainly could have thrown a party whenever he wanted. He brought this up as a ploy, to shame his father, as people will often do. Children often use such tactics to try to manipulate their parents. Jesus' stories are very much in touch with human nature, which is why they have such appeal.

15:30. This thy son. The older brother would not even recognize him as his brother, so bitter was his hatred. Like the Pharisees and others that Jesus dealt with, this son did not understand grace at all.

15:31. All that I have is thine. He did not allow the son to manipulate him into guilt. The father's love included both brothers. The parable might better be called the parable of "the father's love" rather than "the prodigal son." It shows a contrast between the self-centered exclusiveness of the Pharisees, who failed to understand God's love, and the concern and joy of God over the repentance of sinners.

15:32. Thy brother was dead, and is alive again. A beautiful picture of the return of the younger son,

which also pictures Christian conversion (see Rom. 6:13; Eph. 2:1, 5). The words **lost, and is found** are often used to mean "perished, but is saved" (see 19:10; Matt. 10:6; 18:10–14). Jesus did not reiterate the lesson at the end of this parable. He had done so twice already (see 15:7, 10), and this parable is so clear that He may have believed it was not necessary.

F. The Parable of the Unrighteous Steward (16:1–18)

16:1. After addressing the Pharisees who had criticized His association with sinful people, Jesus turned to **his disciples.** Perhaps this was more than just the Twelve (see 6:13; 10:1). The Pharisees were still nearby and heard His words, however (see 16:14). **A steward** was one who handled all the business affairs of his master. **Wasted.** The steward had squandered his master's possessions, just as the prodigal (or "wasteful") son had squandered his inheritance (see 15:13).

16:2. The steward was put into a difficult situation. He now had to give **an account** of his management of his boss's financial affairs. Apparently, the master did not ask for an immediate accounting. His holdings must have been vast enough that the steward was given time to get the books into order.

16:3. What shall I do? The steward was unable to do physical work and was ashamed to become a beggar. Under the circumstances, merely finding another household to manage would have been impossible, as his current boss would give him a poor reference.

16:4. I am resolved is analogous to "Aha!" or "I've got it!" as in getting a sudden inspiration (see Morris, *Luke,* p. 247).

16:5–7. The unjust steward had no scruples about using his position for his own benefit, even if it meant cheating his master. Knowing he would lose his job, the steward planned for his future by discounting the debts owed to his master to obligate the **debtors** (v. 5) to himself. Interpreters disagree as to whether his procedure of discounting was in itself dishonest. Was he giving away what really belonged to his master, or was he forgoing interest payments his master did not have a right to charge? The steward may have originally overcharged the debtors, a common way of circumventing the Mosaic law that prohibited taking interest from fellow Jews (see Deut. 23:19). To reduce the debts, he may have therefore returned the figures to their initial amounts, which would both satisfy the steward and gain the good favor of the debtors. In any event, the point remains the same: the steward was shrewd enough to use the means at his disposal to plan for his future well-being. A sinner also must take extraordinary measures if he would plan for the future time when God will cast him out. He must obtain salvation.

16:6. An hundred measures of oil. The yield of about 450 olive trees.

16:7. An hundred measures of wheat. The approximate yield of about 100 acres.

16:8. The man was **commended** by his boss, not for being unjust — he was being fired for that — but for acting wisely under the circumstances. Here Jesus began to make the point of the parable: lost people are often wiser with material things than God's people, **the children of light** (see John 12:36; Eph. 5:8; 1 Thess. 5:5), are with spiritual things.

16:9. This continues the spiritual lesson of the parable by pointing out an application: **Make to yourselves friends**. By helping those in need, who in the future will show their gratitude when they welcome their benefactors into heaven (**everlasting habitations**). In this way, worldly wealth may be wisely used to gain eternal benefit. **The mammon of unrighteousness**. Or "worldly wealth." God's people should make use of what God has given them.

16:10. Faithful also in much (see 19:17; Matt. 25:21). Faithfulness is determined not by the amount entrusted but by the character of the person who uses it. He who is faithful in little things will also be faithful in big things. When choosing leaders in the church, we should seek those who are faithful in minor details and unimportant matters. The person who handles this world's goods poorly because they are not worthy of bother will not handle eternal matters well either. Faithfulness is learned by practicing it every day. People naturally spend more time on lit-

tle things than on things of eternal value. That is the way life is. These little things are given as exercises so that one might learn to handle them well and thus develop the habit of faithfulness. One should learn to manage the small details of life well so that when eternal matters come into one's area of concern, one will be well practiced in good management.

16:11–12. True riches (v. 11). The things of highest value, ultimately matters of the spirit, the eternal. If one is not faithful in the little things, one cannot expect to be trusted with these important matters.

16:13. No one **can serve two masters** (see Matt. 6:24; James 4:4). Jesus was stating something that is obvious when one thinks about it, yet so many people try to do just this. Christians should determine that they will serve God only and that all other relationships and obligations will be subsumed under that. Doing so will resolve much of the conflict so many face in their lives as they try to serve their own desires and God at the same time.

16:14. Jesus was telling the truth. He was stating things that were self-evident, that should have been obvious, but which needed stating due to spiritual blindness and foolishness. It is a measure of the spiritual blindness and foolishness of these Pharisees that **they derided him**. Could they not see that He was telling the plain truth in plain language? Did they believe that faithfulness in little things had nothing to do with faithfulness in the things that really mattered and that one could indeed serve God and mammon? Surely not. They were so set on opposing Him that even when He stated the obvious, truths that were self-evident, they still found fault with Him. Believers should remember this when they encounter opposition to the gospel. People who oppose the gospel and Christianity will do so even when confronted with clear evidence of the goodness and truth of the gospel and of the gentleness and humility of Christian people. This is not to say that one should not be gentle and humble, thinking that it does not matter. Disciples should practice these virtues because they are right, not because they will make the gospel attractive. One should not be surprised, however, when one's good life does not convert those who oppose the truth.

16:15. Jesus confronted the Pharisees directly in His reply to their derision. The Pharisees justified themselves before men. One is reminded of Jesus' condemnation of those who pray in the public squares and who love greetings in the marketplace. **God knoweth your hearts.** This refers back to Jesus' teaching that denounced the Pharisees for doing outward deeds but having no inward spiritual life to go with it (see 11:27–44).

16:16. Until John. The ministry of John the Baptist, which prepared the way for Jesus the Messiah, was the dividing line between the Old Testament (**the law and the prophets**) and the New Testament (see *KJV Study Bible* note on Jer. 31:31–34; discussions on Heb. 8:6–12). **Every man presseth into it.** The meaning of this is disputed, but it probably speaks of the fierce earnestness with which people were responding to the gospel of the kingdom. Multitudes were coming to hear Jesus and to receive His message.

16:17. The ministry of Jesus (introducing the new covenant era) was a fulfillment of the law (defining the old covenant era) in the most minute detail (see 21:33; discussion Matt. 5:17). For **one tittle,** see discussions on Matthew 5:18.

16:18. Putteth away his wife (see Matt. 5:31–32; 19:9; Mark 10:11–12; 1 Cor. 7:10–11). Jesus affirmed the continuing authority of the law. For example, adultery was still adultery, still unlawful and still sinful. Matthew's treatment is fuller in that (1) it shows that the law was given because of man's hardened heart in regard to divorce, and (2) it includes one exception as permissible grounds for divorce: marital unfaithfulness (see Matt. 19:9).

G. The Parable of the Rich Man and Lazarus (16:19–31)

16:19–31. Longer than most of Jesus' parables, the parable of the rich man and Lazarus condemned the Pharisees for their attitude toward society's outcasts and for their focus on this world's goods at the expense of spiritual matters. The parable begins as does that of the unrighteous steward (see 16:1–8).

It appears to be the real history of two individuals, yet like a parable, it has one basic lesson: once death comes, one cannot change his eternal destiny.

16:19. A certain rich man. Sometimes given the name Dives (from the Latin for "rich man"). **Purple and fine linen.** Characteristic of costly garments.

16:20. Lazarus. Not the Lazarus whom Jesus raised from the dead (see John 11:43–44). **Full of sores.** The Greek for this phrase is a common medical term found only here in the New Testament.

16:21. Lazarus did not ask for much. He humbly accepted his position and sought only **the crumbs which fell from the rich man's table.** Jesus, on many occasions, taught that God honors humility.

16:22. Abraham's bosom. Both Abraham's bosom and paradise (see 23:43) are mentioned in the Talmud as the home of the righteous. "Abraham's bosom" refers to the place of blessedness to which the righteous dead go to await future vindication. Its bliss is the quality of blessedness reserved for people like Abraham. Simply put, it is being with Abraham.

16:23. Hell. The place to which the wicked dead go to await the final judgment. That torment begins in Hades is evident from the plight of the rich man. The location of Abraham's bosom is not specified, but it is separated from Hades by an impassable chasm. It could be the distance that separates heaven from hell. Hades includes the torment that characterizes hell (fire, Rev. 20:10; agony, Rev. 14:11; separation, Matt. 8:12). Some understand Jesus' description of Abraham's side and Hades in a less literal way, but the passage gives no direct warrant for this.

16:24. Here the positions of the rich man and Lazarus are reversed. On earth, Lazarus had desired "crumbs ... from the rich man's table" (16:21); now the rich man desired that Lazarus be sent to give him just a few drops of **water.** This is in line with Jesus' statement that the first shall be last and vice versa (see 13:30). This is a spiritual principle that those who are not honored in this world will be honored in the kingdom and those who "had it made" in this life will have no place in the kingdom.

16:25–26. The rich man's request was refused on two grounds: (1) justice: he had already received his

good things (v. 25) in life and now received his just punishment; (2) opportunity: even if helping him were just, it was impossible. The lesson, then, is that people should take care of spiritual matters in this life, for it will be too late in the next.

16:27–28. I have five brethren (v. 28). For the first time, the rich man showed concern for others. He wanted them to be warned.

16:29. Moses and the prophets. A way of designating the whole Old Testament. The rich man had failed to pay attention to Scripture and its teaching and feared his brothers would do the same. People are responsible for what spiritual truth they have received. In the next world, they will have no warrant to plead ignorance.

16:30–31. If one went unto them from the dead (v. 30). The parable may suggest that Lazarus was intended here, but Luke's account seems to imply that Jesus was speaking also of His own resurrection (see v. 31; 9:22). If a person's mind is closed and Scripture is rejected, no evidence, not even a resurrection, will change his mind. It is human nature, however, to believe that somehow a miracle or a spectacle of some kind will change people's hearts, and one often wishes that this would happen. Congregations sometimes use special events of various kinds in their churches, thinking that they will lead people to the gospel. These events may draw a crowd and thus may be useful, but the preaching of God's Word is what will bring about true repentance and faith. **If they hear not Moses and the prophets** (v. 31), they will not be impressed by anything else.

H. Miscellaneous Teachings (17:1–10)

17:1. Jesus again turned His attention to the disciples but began a new subject. He laid down a general truth: people will hinder the spread of the gospel. Their lives and words will be **offences** in that they will turn people away from the truth. Jesus recognized that this is inevitable. Those who do so, however, will still bear responsibility.

17:2. A millstone. A heavy stone for grinding grain. **One of these little ones.** Either young in the faith or young in age (see 10:21; Matt. 18:6; Mark 10:24).

17:3. Since it is inevitable that offenses will occur, believers must learn to forgive **thy brother** (see Matt. 18:15–17; see also Matt. 12:50).

17:4. Seven times. That is, forgiveness is to be unlimited (see Ps. 119:164; Matt. 18:21–22). Here seven is not a limitation; it is the number of perfection. Jesus meant that as many times as one is offended, one must forgive. If not, the problem is compounded.

17:5. Increase our faith. The disciples felt incapable of measuring up to the standards set forth in 17:1–4. They wanted greater faith so that they might have the power to live up to Jesus' standards.

17:6. Faith as a grain of mustard seed (see Matt. 17:20; Mark 11:23; see also discussions on Matt. 13:31–32; Mark 4:31). Jesus was in no way commending miracles done as a stunt or for amusement. He was simply saying that great things may be accomplished with very little faith if that faith is applied in a godly direction.

17:7–8. A servant (v. 7). A slave is used to illustrate performance of duty (see 12:37). Naturally, the servant serves the master first, not the other way around.

17:9. Does he thank that servant …? Jesus was not commending ingratitude. Naturally, when one does what is expected and routine, one does not expect thanks.

17:10. This is the application of verses 7–9. Believers should never expect special commendation from God for being obedient to His will. They should never be proud of their record of service in the church or of their spiritual activities. Were believers perfect in every way, which is impossible, they still would have done only what the Lord commanded.

I. Ten Healed of Leprosy (17:11–19)

17:11. He passed through the midst of Samaria and Galilee. From this point, Jesus seems to have journeyed to Perea, where He ministered on His way south to Jerusalem (see discussions on 9:51; 13:22).

17:12–13. The **ten … lepers** recognized Jesus as Lord, for they addressed Him as **Master** (v. 13). They also knew that they did not deserve to be cured. They had no "right" to be healthy, for they said to Him,

have mercy on us. Mercy is always undeserved favor. These men were asking for grace, something God is eager to give. Perhaps they knew they were sinners and saw their illness as a part of God's judgment on their sin. In any case, they were not demanding a right but rather were asking for something above and beyond that.

17:14. Shew yourselves unto the priests. This was normal procedure after a cure (see Lev. 13:2 – 3; 14:2 – 32). In this case, it was an act of faith. The only way the men could carry out this command was to do so in faith that they were healed, and **as they went, they were cleansed**. The best way to demonstrate repentance and faith is to be obedient to Jesus Christ. These men did what Jesus said, thus showing their willingness to submit to Him as Lord and their faith that He would heal them. God moved in response to their faith.

17:15 – 16. One of them (v. 15). Only one of the men returned to thank Jesus for healing him. **Samaritan** (v. 16; see discussion on 10:31 – 33). Jews did not normally associate with Samaritans (see John 4:9), but it appears that leprosy broke down some social barriers while erecting others.

17:17 – 18. Jesus was not ungrateful to this man who showed such dedication. Rather, He was making an observation about human nature. People often turn to God in a crisis, see Him move in response to their faith, and then forget Him when their situation improves. This passage should be a reminder that God notices this and is not pleased. One's gratitude and faith should be constant, not something given only in time of need.

17:19. Thy faith hath made thee whole (see Matt. 9:22). The phrase may also be rendered "thy faith hath saved thee" (7:50). That the Samaritan returned to thank Jesus may indicate that he had received salvation in addition to the physical healing all ten had received (see 7:50; 8:48, 50).

J. The Coming of the Kingdom (17:20 – 37)

17:20. Jesus was now questioned by **the Pharisees**. They wanted to know when the kingdom of God will come. Either they were looking for a way to trick Him or they misunderstood completely the nature of the kingdom. Jesus assumed the latter and offered them a theologically rich and truthful answer. He began, **The kingdom of God cometh not with observation**. They were to look not for an earthly kingdom at that time with all of its trappings but rather for a spiritual reality.

17:21. Again, the kingdom cannot be pointed out, as one would point out the temple or a city. **The kingdom of God is within you** (see discussion on 4:43). Probably indicating that the kingdom is present in the person of its King, Jesus (see 19:11; 21:7; Acts 1:6). "Within you" could mean that the kingdom is spiritual and internal (see Matt. 23:26), rather than physical and external (see John 18:36). If this is the correct view, the pronoun "you" in the phrase "within you" is to be taken in a general sense rather than as referring to the unbelieving Pharisees personally. The kingdom certainly was not within them. If "you" is specific rather than general, it argues for an interpretation of "in your midst." Thus, the reality of the kingdom was present in the person of the King.

17:22. Jesus turned to His disciples, and His teaching moved to a deeper level than that given to the Pharisees. **Ye shall desire to see**. In time of trouble, believers will desire to experience the day when Jesus returns in His glory and delivers His people from their distress. One should be aware that in prosperous and peaceful times, it is easy to forget the Lord's second coming. Those who suffer persecution and distress understand far more the need for His return.

17:23. Go not after them, nor follow them. Do not leave your work to pursue predictions of Christ's second advent. Many in history, and even these days, would have been spared a lot of trouble by heeding this admonition.

17:24. As the lightning. His coming will be sudden, unexpected, and public (see 12:40).

17:25. First must he suffer. Jesus repeatedly foretold His coming death (see 5:35; 9:22, 43 – 45; 12:50; 13:32 – 33; 18:32; 24:7; see also Matt. 16:21), which had to occur before His glorious return.

17:26–27. As it was in the days of Noe, so shall it be also in the days of the Son of man (v. 26). Much misunderstanding often accompanies this passage. Many see it as a statement that the sin in this world during the end times will be like that in Noah's day. Certainly, Scripture teaches that sin will abound before Christ's coming, but that is not the meaning here. Jesus was reinforcing the idea that His coming will be sudden and unexpected. The activities Jesus mentioned are the normal activities of life, **they did eat, they drank** (v. 27), and normal plans for the future, **they married wives, they were given in marriage**. These people were not shutting down their lives in anticipation of the flood. When Christ returns, people will likewise be engaging in normal daily life and planning for the future. His coming will cut across all of that.

17:28–29. Also as it was in the days of Lot (v. 28; see Gen. 18:16–19:28). Again, in Lot's day, the people were engaging in the normal activities of life until Sodom was suddenly destroyed. Neither here nor in 17:26–27 was Jesus saying that these activities are wrong. Both situations saw God's judgment because of sin, not because of normal life. In both cases, however, the judgment came without warning. So also, when Christ returns, there will be no warning, no time to arrange one's affairs, no diminution in the hum of daily activity, until His coming breaks into history and changes everything.

17:30. When the Son of man is revealed. At Jesus' second coming, He will be plainly visible to all (see 1 Cor. 1:7; 2 Thess. 1:7; 1 Peter 1:7, 13; 4:13). His coming will be sudden and unexpected.

17:31. Upon the housetop. In Jesus' day, it was customary to relax on the flat rooftop. When the final hour comes, however, the individual there should not even think of going into the house to retrieve some material objects. Matthew and Mark referred similarly to flight at the fall of Jerusalem, and indirectly to the end time (see Matt. 24:17–18; Mark 13:15), but here the reference is explicitly to Jesus' return (see 17:30; see also 21:21).

17:32. This short verse recalls when **Lot's wife** looked back (see Gen. 19:26) and was turned into a pillar of salt. Whoever looks back on this world's goods, on what God will judge, shows that their heart is not perfect toward God. When Christ returns, nothing else will matter.

17:33. Whosoever shall seek to save his life shall lose it (see discussion on 9:24; Matt. 10:39). Seeking to save one's life, in this context, refers to seeking to hold on to the material goods of this life, to make one's life as comfortable and pleasurable as possible. A person seeking to "save his life" in this way will find himself uncomfortable and miserable. The pleasures of this world do not last, nor, in the end, do they really satisfy. **Whosoever shall lose his life shall preserve it**. That is, the one who lets go of what this world offers will find real satisfaction in the things of the Lord. He may seem to have less of a "good life" in this world's terms but will, in reality, find true happiness and satisfaction. He will thus "preserve" his life. In the context of the second coming of Christ, believers hearts should be so filled with the riches of heaven that they are ready to leave this world behind. If one is attached to any material pleasures in this world, one is not truly ready for His coming. This teaching harks back to the parable of the rich fool (see 12:13–21) who sought to "save his life" by building bigger barns but lost it all when his soul was required.

17:34–35. Taken (v. 34). Could refer to being "taken to/from destruction" or "taken into the kingdom." What is clear is that no matter how close two people may be in life, they have no guarantee of the same eternal destiny. One may go to judgment and condemnation, the other to salvation, reward, and blessing. The reference here seems to be about judgment, however. The context talks about the people in the days of Noah (see 17:26–27) and of Lot (see 17:28–29) being swept away to destruction. At Christ's return, a similar separation will occur.

17:36. The one shall be taken, and the other left. This probably refers not to being taken in the rapture but rather being taken away to judgment, as the next verse seems to indicate.

17:37. Wheresoever the body is, thither will the eagles be gathered together (see discussion on

Matt. 24:28). A proverb. Those taken away will become a feast for eagles and other birds of prey (see Rev. 19:17 – 18).

K. The Parable of the Persistent Widow (18:1 – 8)

18:1. Luke introduced the parable of the persistent widow with an explanation of its purpose: to teach the disciples that **men ought always to pray, and not to faint**. Jesus had just been describing things related to judgment and the end times (see 26 – 37). He may have believed that the disciples needed some encouragement. As was often the case, Jesus chose to offer it with a parable so that the point would be more memorable.

18:2. The story concerns **a judge, which feared not God, neither regarded man**. He did not recognize the law of God and was unconcerned about the needs of others or about their opinion of him. As a judge, he was in a position to judge legal matters, but his moral and spiritual character made him unable to do so well. Jesus emphasized this point, because He wanted the disciples to see that even the unjust can be made to behave justly. How much more could they, then, expect good things from God, who is just? Persistence is the key.

18:3. A widow. This woman was particularly helpless and vulnerable because she had no family to uphold her cause. Only justice and her own persistence were in her favor, and the judge cared little for justice.

18:4 – 5. The judge granted her justice, not because he cared but because he wanted to be left alone.

18:6 – 7. What the unjust judge saith (v. 6). Jesus was referring not so much to the judge's literal words but rather to what the story about him says about the value of persistence. **Shall not God avenge his own elect …?** (v. 7). If an unworthy judge who feels no constraint of right or wrong can be compelled by persistence to deal justly with a helpless individual, how much more will God answer persistent prayer? **Though he bear long with them**. Although God may delay coming to the aid of His chosen ones, His intention to do so is certain because He is just. He

is not like the unjust judge, who had to be badgered until he wearied and gave in.

18:8. He will avenge them speedily. This does not contradict the previous verse. Jesus simply meant that when God's judgment happens, it will be swift and certain. Those who have suffered wrong should exercise faith, then, and not waver, for to do so would be to doubt God. In fact, Jesus asked whether when He returns, **shall he find faith on the earth?** Particularly, will He find faith that perseveres in prayer and loyalty (see Matt. 24:12 – 13)? Here Christ made a second application that looks forward to the time of His second coming. A period of spiritual decline and persecution is assumed, a time that will require perseverance such as the widow demonstrated.

L. The Parable of the Pharisee and the Publican (18:9 – 14)

18:9. Jesus offered another parable, **unto certain which trusted in themselves that they were righteous**. Apparently not the Twelve but perhaps other disciples who had not completely understood repentance, faith, and grace. **And despised others**. One of the worst things about self-righteousness is that it leads to contempt for those who seem to be less righteous than oneself. Christians should remember that "all have sinned" (Rom. 3:23) and none of us has a corner on righteousness. Many Christians, unfortunately, see themselves as people who have grown beyond major sins. It is well not to commit such sins, but one should all remember that, in the end, none are really superior to the worst of sinners.

18:10. A Pharisee, and … a publican. These two men represent the "best" and "worst" of Jewish society of that day. One was a pillar of the community, and the other an outcast. Jesus chose these two figures to ensure that the contrast was not missed. **To pray**. Periods for prayer were scheduled daily in connection with the morning and evening sacrifices. People could also go to the temple at any time for private prayer.

18:11. The Pharisee … prayed thus with himself. Standing for prayer was normal in that day, but the fact that he prayed "with himself" says that his prayer was uttered in a spirit of self-praise and was more for his own edification than to make contact with God. When engaging in public prayer, Christians today should be careful that they are seeking God rather than merely hoping to sound spiritual. **Extortioners, unjust, adulterers.** The man offered a list of sins he had not committed. Would that he had considered the sin of pride. It would have stopped his prayer in its tracks. **Even as this publican.** The Pharisee's insensitivity is astonishing. He used the presence of the publican as an occasion for self-praise, and that in a prayer to God.

18:12. In his prayer, the Pharisee mentioned two things he did that were spiritual. **I fast twice in the week.** Fasting was not commanded in the Mosaic law except for the fast on the Day of Atonement, but the Pharisees fasted also on Mondays and Thursdays (see 5:33; Matt. 6:16; 9:14; Mark 2:18; Acts 27:9). **I give tithes of all that I possess.** As a typical first-century Pharisee, he tithed all that he acquired, not merely what he earned. Again, as in some of His earlier parables and sayings, Jesus condemned spiritual life that is merely a matter of outward actions. Luke emphasized these teachings more than the other gospel writers did. Being influenced by Greek thought and culture, his Gentile audience may have been receptive to these teachings. The Greeks emphasized the mind over the body, and Luke's readers would have readily agreed that what is in the heart is more essential than outward actions. By the second century, however, this led to Gnosticism, which saw the body as evil and as a trap for the mind. This heresy is never in view in Luke, nor anywhere in Jesus' teachings. The emphasis is not that the mind (or heart) is more important than the body but rather that both the inner heart and the outward actions are essential to a healthy spiritual life. Luke made this point clear in 11:42, where Jesus said, "these ought ye to have done, and not to leave the other [outward actions] undone." Here He said nothing to indicate that the Pharisee's outward actions were wrong. He had done good, even commendable, things. His heart was wrong, however, for he trusted in his own righteousness, unlike the publican whose prayer is presented in 18:13–14.

18:13. Be merciful to me. The verb used here means "to be propitiated" (see discussion on 1 John 2:2). The tax collector did not plead his good works but rather the mercy of God in forgiving his sin. He had nothing to offer God, but then, neither did the Pharisee. The difference was that he knew it and the Pharisee did not.

18:14. Justified. God reckoned him to be righteous; that is, his sins were forgiven and he was credited with righteousness, not his own (see 18:9) but that which comes from God. This passage is one of the clearest presentations of righteousness through faith and not by works that is to be found anywhere in the Gospels.

M. Jesus and the Children (18:15–17)

18:15–16. The disciples here were diligently ensuring that their Master's time was well spent. Their sense of priorities, however, was quite different from that of Jesus. He made this clear in His gentle rebuke.

18:17. As with so much in Jesus' ministry, His receiving the children illustrated a spiritual truth: people should **receive the kingdom of God as a little child**, that is, with total dependence, full trust, frank openness, and complete sincerity (see Matt. 18:3; 19:14; Mark 10:15 and discussion; 1 Peter 2:2). For Jesus, the visual imagery of little children coming to Him and being received and welcomed would impact people's minds as they considered their own approach to God.

N. The Rich Young Ruler (18:18–30)

18:18–27. For this event, see also discussions on Mark 10:17–27. Jesus' point to the man was that he needed grace and should live so as to demonstrate grace as well.

18:18. Eternal life (see discussion on Matt. 19:16). This man asked a legitimate question.

18:19. Why callest thou me good? This may seem like a diversion at first, but Jesus wanted the man to acknowledge that he himself needed grace to have eternal life, pointing out that God alone is good. He used the man's address to Him ("Good Master," 18:18) as a touchstone to gently suggest the truth.

18:20–21. Jesus cited some of the Ten Commandments, and the young ruler asserted, **these have I kept** (v. 21). He had not grasped the import of Jesus' words in 18:19. He still, like the Pharisee in the parable Jesus had just related (see 18:9–14), believed that he was righteous.

18:22. Yet lackest thou one thing. Jesus knew that the one thing this man needed was to recognize that grace was what he needed. He told the man to do three things. (1) **Sell all that thou hast**, that is, rid himself of every encumbrance that tied him to this world. Like the rich fool in the parable related in 12:16–21, this man had "much goods" (12:19) and may have been in danger of relying too much on them. (2) **Distribute unto the poor**. Here was the crux of the matter. The poor had not earned any wealth. Jesus wanted him to go and be an example of grace, giving people what they had not earned and did not deserve. He would have thus learned something about grace and prepared his heart to receive it. In Luke 14:13 Jesus taught about being an example of grace (see 14:13) and perhaps saw this as a key to living the Christian life before the world. Disciples could all stand to learn ways to be an example of God's grace in their dealings with the lost world. (3) **Come, follow me**; that is, He invited the man into the open-ended adventure of faith. Unencumbered by worldly goods, living a life of grace, he would be ready to hear the message of repentance and faith and thus would find eternal life. This kind of commitment cannot be made halfway or with reservations. Jesus had already sent away others who had placed conditions on their discipleship (see 9:57–62). Following Jesus will lead one to places they know not and into situations they cannot have predicted. It was true then and still is true today. Such a commitment requires faith in the goodness and sovereignty of God and a willingness to suffer any hardship. It is to abandon oneself to the belief that God is good and that His will is better than anything one could accomplish without Him.

18:23. The man was not equal to the challenge. It is interesting, and certainly an insight into the darkness of human nature after the fall, that this man left.

He had asked about eternal life but then refused to do what Jesus said, knowing that it meant he would not inherit eternal life. He loved the riches of this world so much more that he was willing to give up eternity, knowing he was doing so, to enjoy the pleasures of this life for a short time.

18:24–25. Jesus, sorrowing, offered a commentary on the situation. He did not say that no rich people will ever be saved. He only said that people in such circumstances see little need to depend on God. Those who have made a financial fortune may have trouble understanding grace. In any case, they see little need to depend on God or anyone else, having the means to live physically with little expenditure of effort. They experience this world as a pleasant place to live and thus have trouble longing for a better world to come.

18:26. Who then can be saved? Those who heard Jesus' commentary asked the right question, considering the culture of the day. Wealth was often seen as a sign of God's favor. If even the rich, the favored of God, would have trouble being saved, then who had any hope of it at all?

18:27. Jesus' reply brought the discussion right back to grace. It is possible for the rich, as well as the poor, to be saved. Neither can depend on themselves, for salvation is **unpossible with men**. But salvation does not depend on men, on their striving and effort. It depends on God and His grace and power; thus, salvation is **possible with God** for anyone who repents, rich or poor.

18:28–29. Peter's words were not a matter of pride. He was stating the fact that they had done what Jesus counseled the rich young ruler to do: they had **left all, and followed thee** (v. 28). Jesus' reply was a word of assurance for those who had made sacrifices. His words are as true today as they were then, and Christians should not be afraid to leave behind **house, or parents, or brethren, or wife, or children** (v. 29), for Jesus promised that it will be worth it (see 18:30).

18:30. Who shall not receive manifold more. Jesus was not saying those who leave something behind to follow Him will receive the same things, houses and family, but that what they receive will be of greater value. Among them is the joy of knowing they have lived a life of service to God, that they have made the very best of what God has given them, and that their life and work will count for eternity. Notice that Jesus did not say that anyone who follows Him must leave their families, only that if one must do so, the reward will be worth it. Nor did He say that one may not care about family. He did not teach that Christians should not love those dearest to them. In fact, His words recognize that family and possessions have a legitimate value, which is why it is hard to leave them and why God rewards those who do so for His sake; He understood the sacrifice involved. No one should use this verse as a basis for saying that they should not care about their families. The verse says only that the call to follow Jesus may involve leaving behind things and people one legitimately cares about. It will always be worth it to do His will, however, both **in this present time, and in the world to come**. In that future day, eternal rewards will be given out at the judgment seat of Christ.

O. Christ Foretells His Death (18:31–34)

18:31–33. All things that are written by the prophets (v. 31). Sometimes referred to as the third prophecy of Jesus' death, though the total number is more than three (see discussion on 17:25). The first distinct prophecy is in 9:22, and the second is in 9:43–45. The Messiah's death had been prophesied and/or prefigured centuries before (see, e.g., Psalm 22; Isaiah 53; Zech. 13:7; see also Luke 24:27; Matt. 26:24, 31, 54). For **the Son of man**, see discussion on Mark 2:10.

18:34. The disciples **understood none of these things** that Jesus said regarding His death. Perhaps Jesus' use of the third person made it difficult for them, or perhaps it was the natural inclination to take something obscure and out of one's experience and try to spiritualize it. This passage is an example that God's Word is best taken literally unless the context demands that it be seen in an allegorical or figurative sense. Also, God may have worked supernaturally, for the import of these words **was hid from them**.

P. A Blind Beggar Given His Sight (18:35–43)

18:35. For **as he was come nigh unto Jericho**, see discussion on Mark 10:46. **A certain blind man**. Bartimeus (see Mark 10:46). Matthew recorded that two blind men were healed (see Matt. 20:30). Probably since one was the spokesman and thus more outstanding, Mark and Luke did not record the presence of the other.

18:36–37. The man was probably well known to the crowd.

18:38–39. Son of David (v. 38). A Messianic title (see Matt. 22:41–45; Mark 12:35; John 7:42; see also 2 Sam. 7:12–13; Ps. 89:3–4; Amos 9:11; Matt. 12:23; 21:15–16).

18:40. Jesus apparently stopped to deal with the man. This brought the entire procession to a halt. It is testimony to the Lord's commitment to meet people's needs. He could have sent one of the disciples to tell the man where He would be stopping to rest and to meet Him there. Instead, He halted everything to meet the man's need.

18:41–42. Thy faith (v. 42; see discussion on 17:19). Jesus healed the man when he told Him what he wanted. Surely Jesus could see that the man was blind but wanted him to confess his need and thus express his faith. That faith was what made it possible for him to be healed. God knows human needs before they are expressed but often waits until one comes to Him, expressing a need and faith in His ability and willingness to act, before He meets the need. God loves to hear the prayers of His people, and faith opens doors for His mercy to be shown in one's life.

18:43. Having **received his sight**, the man followed Jesus, **glorifying God**, as did **all the people**. When God answers prayer, it is an opportunity for us to give Him glory, and we should be sure to do so.

Q. Jesus and Zaccheus (19:1–10)

19:1. Earlier Jesus had "come nigh unto Jericho" (18:35). Here He **entered and passed through Jericho** (see discussion on Mark 10:46). This is a transition sentence. It establishes that the events of 19:1–10 happened just shortly after the healing of the blind man (see 18:35 – 43). It also serves to quicken the pace of Jesus' journey toward Jerusalem. Luke wanted to increase the tension as he drew close to Jesus' trial and passion. Earlier in the narrative, events that took place on the same day might not have these kinds of markers.

19:2. The chief among the publicans. A position referred to only here in the Bible, probably designating one in charge of a district, with other tax collectors under him (see discussions on 3:12; Mark 2:14 – 15). The region was prosperous at this time, so it is no wonder that **Zaccheus … was rich.**

19:3. For the press means the press of the crowd. Zaccheus could not see Jesus because the people would not let him through. It is ironic that their interest in Jesus, the teacher of humility and servanthood (in this gospel especially), led them to be inconsiderate of others.

19:4. A sycamore tree (see discussion on Amos 7:14). A sturdy tree from thirty to forty feet high, with a short trunk and spreading branches, capable of holding a grown man.

19:5. I must abide at thy house implies a divine necessity.

19:6. Zaccheus **made haste** and obeyed what Jesus said. He was already interested in being a disciple of Jesus, for he sought Him and he obeyed Him. However, Luke did not intend to provide a paradigm for discipleship here; he was simply telling the story as it happened. One can take this lesson from it, however, as long as we keep Luke's intention in mind.

19:7. When they saw it. Just who "they" are is not made clear here. Was it the crowd? They were usually supportive of Jesus. Was it the Pharisees? This is the most likely possibility, for they had raised this very issue before.

19:8. If I have taken any thing. Zaccheus was not holding back in the sense of saying, "I don't think I have done so, but *if* I have …" Instead, he meant, "Wherever I have …" **Fourfold.** Almost the extreme repayment required under the law in case of theft (see Exod. 22:1; 2 Sam. 12:6; see also Prov. 6:31).

19:9. A son of Abraham. A true Jew, one not only of the lineage of Abraham but who also walked "in the steps of [Abraham's] faith" (Rom. 4:12). Jesus recognized the tax collector as such, though Jewish society excluded him. His faith was demonstrated by his repentance. He genuinely repented of what he had stolen, because he was willing to make restoration.

19:10. This is the key verse in Luke's gospel (see Introduction: "Theme and Theological Message"). In his gospel, Luke showed over and over that Jesus spent time with sinners, and he recorded Jesus' parables (the lost sheep, the lost coin, and the lost son) that reveal His heart for seeking the lost. **The Son of man** (see discussion on Mark 2:10). This Messianic title (see Dan. 7:13) was used only by Jesus in the four gospels, by Stephen (see Acts 7:56), and in John's vision (see Rev. 1:13). **To seek and to save** (see discussion on 15:32). This was an important summary of Jesus' purpose: to bring salvation, meaning eternal life (see 18:18), and the kingdom of God (see 18:25).

R. The Parable of the Pounds (19:11 – 27)

19:11. He was nigh to Jerusalem. Here again is a geographical reminder, serving to build tension because of what would soon happen there. Jesus chose to tell the parable of the pounds (see 19:12 – 27) because of the proximity of Jerusalem, the location of His coming trial and death. The reader presumably knows this, something Jesus' hearers did not. Also, Jesus told this parable because His disciples **thought that the kingdom of God should immediately appear.** They expected the Messiah to appear in power and glory and to set up His earthly kingdom, defeating all their political and military enemies. Events would soon dash that hope, something that must have been in Jesus' mind at this time.

19:12 – 27. The parable of the pounds. This parable is again one in which some elements do not parallel to the real situation, and it is best not to push the analogies too far. For example, the ruler in the parable is hardly a picture of the loving, gracious, and just Savior that Jesus is. Many elements of the parable do illustrate spiritual truths, however, specifically the ones Jesus wanted to emphasize at this point. The ruler left to receive a kingdom and returned much later to give rewards to those who had served him well and to bring judgment on the people. This is what Jesus Himself would do.

19:12. To receive for himself a kingdom. A rather unusual procedure, but the Herods did just that when they went to Rome to be appointed rulers over the Jews. Similarly, Jesus would soon depart and in the future will return as King. During His absence, His servants are entrusted with their Master's affairs (for a similar parable, see Matt. 25:14–30).

19:13. Ten pounds. Each pound, or mina, was about three months' wages. One talent equaled sixty minas (see Matt. 25:15), and a mina equaled one hundred drachmas, each drachma being worth about a day's wages (see discussion on 15:8). The total amount thus equaled between two and three years' average wages, and a tenth would be about three months' wages. This was small, however, compared with the amounts mentioned in Matthew's version of the parable (see Matt. 25:14–30). Here all **ten servants** were given the same amount and had equal responsibility to use what they were given.

19:14. Sent a message. Such an incident had occurred over thirty years earlier in the case of Archelaus (Josephus *Wars* 2.6.1; *Antiquities* 17.9.3), when the Jews complained to Rome of his cruelty, as well as in a number of other instances. This aspect of the story may have been included to warn the Jews against rejecting Jesus as King.

19:15. He commanded these servants to be called unto him. It may be pressing the point to see this as an allusion to the rapture of the church, prior to the Lord's return to judge the world, but it certainly seems to fit.

19:16–17. The first servant was rewarded in accordance with what he had done.

19:18–19. The second servant, who had produced less, was nevertheless commended but given less reward. There will be degrees of reward in heaven.

19:20–21. The third servant had done nothing with what he was given. This illustrates primarily a lack of faith on his part. He assumed the worst of his master and yet did not do even the minimum to attempt to please him. His action stemmed from fear, and fear is the opposite of faith.

19:22–23. Thou knewest that I was an austere man …? (v. 22). The master did not admit to the statement of the servant but repeated it in a question. If this was the servant's opinion, he should have acted accordingly. The master pointed out to the servant the safest and easiest kind of investment he could have made (v. 23). God will accept even the most meager service from one who, for whatever reason, can do no more. Again, however, that is not central to Jesus' point but may be inferred from it. Of course, one should not use this inference as an excuse to do little for the Lord but should instead make the most of every opportunity for service that He provides.

19:24–25. What the servant had was taken from him and was given to the one who had the most, in spite of the surprised reaction of those who wondered why one who had so much would be given more.

19:26. Jesus explained the actions of the ruler and drew a spiritual parallel. To the one who has much, more **shall be given**, and to the one who has little, **even that he hath shall be taken away** (see 8:18; 17:33; Matt. 13:12). Those who seek spiritual gain in the gospel, for themselves and others, will become richer, and those who neglect or squander what is given them will become impoverished, losing even what they have.

19:27. Those mine enemies … slay them. Perhaps a reference to Jerusalem's destruction in AD 70. The punishment for those who rebelled and actively opposed the king (see 19:14) was much more severe than that of the negligent servant.

VIII. Jesus' Last Days: Sacrifice and Triumph (19:28–24:53)

A. The Triumphal Entry (19:28–44)

19:28–44. The triumphal entry occurred on Sunday of Passion Week.

19:28. He went before, ascending up to Jerusalem. Here Luke finished the chronology of the journey to Jerusalem. Having built up to this moment, he summed it up in a single sentence. Beginning with the next verse, he went back and filled in the details of Jesus' entry into the city. It is well to remember that Jerusalem sat on a hill. Going to Jerusalem meant to "ascend," for the journey was uphill.

19:29. Bethphage. A village near the road going from Jericho to Jerusalem. **Bethany**. A village about two miles southeast of Jerusalem (see John 11:18) and the home of Mary, Martha, and Lazarus. **The mount called the mount of Olives**. A ridge a little more than a mile long, separated from Jerusalem by the Kidron Valley, east of the city (see *KJV Study Bible* note on Zech. 14:4; discussion on Mark 11:1). **Two of his disciples**. Not named here or in the parallel passages (Matt. 21:1; Mark 11:1; see also John 12:14).

19:30. The village. Probably Bethphage. **A colt**. Other accounts specify a donkey colt (see John 12:15) and that the disciples were to take the mother of the colt also (see Matt. 21:2, 7). Luke used a Greek word that the Septuagint frequently employed to translate the Hebrew word for "donkey." Jesus chose to enter Jerusalem mounted on a donkey to claim publicly that He was the son of David chosen to sit on David's throne (see 1 Kings 1:33, 44), the one of whom the prophets had spoken (see Zech. 9:9). **Whereon yet never man sat**. One that had not been put to secular use (see Num. 19:2; 1 Sam. 6:7). Perhaps He wanted to demonstrate His lordship over nature by riding a donkey that would normally balk at being ridden.

19:31. The Lord. Either God or, more likely, Jesus Himself, here claiming His unique status as Israel's Lord.

19:32–34. The two disciples whom Jesus sent to get the colt found the situation as He had described. He thus showed His disciples that He knew the future and could make accurate predictions even of details. This was important because they would soon lose Him; they needed reminders and assurances of His deity.

19:35. They cast their garments upon the colt. They made a more comfortable seat for Jesus than the colt's spine would have been. In verses 30–35,

Luke combines inferences of His deity and His humanity. This is because Jesus could describe a situation he could not see, humanly speaking, yet He would have been uncomfortable, like any man, riding bareback. The Bible moves easily between His divine and human attributes. We should note these inferences, however, so that we may never forget that He was fully human and fully divine, not half of one and half of the other.

19:36. They spread their clothes in the way. This prevented dust from being kicked up by the colt or by those surrounding Him in the procession. It would not do for the Lord to arrive in Jerusalem covered with dust. It was a practical way to honor Him.

19:37. All the mighty works. The raising of Lazarus (John 11) and the healing of blind Bartimeus (Mark 10:46; Luke 18:39–43) were recent examples but included also were the works that John recorded of various occasions in Jerusalem, as well as the whole of His ministry in Galilee (see Matt. 21:14; John 12:17).

19:38. The disciples quoted from Psalm 118:26 and used words similar to ones used at His birth (Luke 2:14). One wonders if they had heard the story of the shepherds and the angels and were alluding to that event. It is impossible to know for sure.

19:39–40. The Pharisees told Jesus, **rebuke thy disciples** (v. 39). They may have wanted to see whether He would claim the kingship, which would give them a basis for accusing Him, or refuse it. He did neither specifically. His reply indicated that what the disciples were saying about Him was true, but He did not give them much basis for a serious charge that He was set to challenge Rome.

19:41–42. Jesus **wept** (v. 41) when He saw the city. Once again we see the compassion and tenderness of God and yet the very human emotions of the Lord.

19:43. Thine enemies shall cast a trench (see 21:20). Fulfilled when the Romans took Jerusalem in AD 70, using an embankment to besiege the city. The description is reminiscent of Old Testament prophecies (see Isa. 29:3; 37:33; Ezek. 4:1–3). Having just accurately foretold small details about the disciples finding and taking the colt, His prophecy here must have made quite an impression on their minds. Surely they knew by now that His prophecies were not to be taken lightly. Little wonder that this one was remembered in detail and reported to Luke.

19:44. The time of thy visitation. God came to the Jews in the person of Jesus the Messiah, but they failed to recognize Him and rejected Him (see John 1:10–11; see also Luke 20:13–16).

B. The Cleansing of the Temple (19:45–48)

19:45. Mark 11:11–17 makes it clear that this cleansing occurred the day after the triumphal entry, that is, on Monday of Passion Week. **The temple**. The outer court (the court of the Gentiles), was where animals for sacrifice were sold at unfair prices. John recorded a cleansing of the temple at the beginning of Jesus' ministry (see John 2:13–25), but the Synoptics (see Matt. 21:12–13; Mark 11:15–17) speak only of a cleansing at the close of His ministry (see discussions on Matt. 21:12–17; John 2:14–17).

19:46. Jesus quoted from Isaiah 56:7 and Jeremiah 7:11. The entire incident must have been dramatic, but it demonstrated to His disciples that holiness in worship was important to Him and that He is Lord over matters related to worship. By His actions, He claimed the authority over the temple to determine what was proper behavior and to enforce it. This must have made an impression on them, as had His prophecy concerning Jerusalem (see 19:43–44).

19:47. Having cleansed the temple, Jesus **taught daily** there, again demonstrating His lordship and authority in that place. It is interesting that Jesus taught there openly, considering the controversy caused by His cleansing the temple on Monday. His authority and presence must have been obvious and overwhelming. **The chief priests** (see 3:2; 22:52; 23:4; 24:20). They were part of the Sanhedrin, the ruling Jewish council (see discussion on Mark 14:55). For **sought to destroy him**, see 20:19–20; John 7:1; 11:53–57.

19:48. The people supported Jesus and heard Him eagerly. This prevented the chief priests from

being able to act. The people had no authority over them, but they were attentive to public opinion. It would not do for them to act in ways that would discredit them before the people. In their challenge of Jesus' authority (see 20:1–8), however, the leadership demonstrated that they both recognized His authority and yet were spiritually blind as to its source.

C. The Last Controversies with the Jewish Leaders (chap. 20)

20:1. The events of this chapter and the next all occurred on Tuesday of Passion Week, a long day of controversy. **One of those days**. The day is not specified, but Mark's parallel accounts (Mark 11:19–20, 27–33) indicate that this day (Tuesday) followed the cleansing of the temple (Monday), which followed the triumphal entry (Sunday). For **chief priests**, see 19:47 and discussion on Matthew 2:4; **scribes**, see 5:30; discussions on 5:17; 7:30; Matthew 2:4; **elders**, see discussion on Matthew 15:2. Each of these groups was represented in the Jewish council, the Sanhedrin (see 22:66).

20:2. Who … gave thee this authority? The religious leaders had asked this of John the Baptist (see John 1:19–25) and of Jesus early in His ministry (see John 2:18–22). Here the reference is to the cleansing of the temple, which not only defied the authority of the Jewish leaders but also hurt their monetary profits. The leaders may also have been looking for a way to discredit Jesus in the eyes of the people or raise suspicion of Him as a threat to the authority of Rome. In asking this question, they implicitly recognized that Jesus' actions and the confidence and presence with which He did them betrayed a certain level of authority. It also showed that they were clueless as to His deity and messiahship.

20:3. As He often did, Jesus answered a question with a question. There is no hint that He hesitated or that He was not prepared to challenge the leaders.

20:4–6. The baptism of John, was it from heaven, or of men? (v. 4). For **From heaven** (v. 5), see *KJV Study Bible* note on Mark 11:30. By replying with a question, Jesus put the burden on His opponents, indicating only two alternatives: the work of John was either God-inspired or man-devised. **They reasoned with themselves**. The leaders recognized that they were in a spot. They saw that either answer would be trouble for them. It is interesting that they could not harm Jesus during these days, for fear of the people (see 19:48), and here they could not honestly answer this question, in part due to **all the people**. By refusing to answer, they placed themselves in an awkward position anyway.

20:7 – 8. Jesus was not required to answer since they would not. The obvious answer was that His authority, as that of John, had come from God. Their refusal to answer in this way was because they had not recognized God's authority in the preaching of John. If they had not recognized God's authority in John (which would have been shown by being baptized), they would not recognize God's authority in Jesus. He therefore had no reason to tell them where His authority came from, as they would have rejected it anyway.

20:9 – 18. The parable of the husbandmen. This parable was aimed directly at the Jewish nation. As they had rejected the prophets, so now they rejected God's own Son. The parable foretells what, in fact, did happen a few years later. The nation was destroyed, and the gospel went to the Gentiles. The parable does not say this, but nothing here gives warrant to assume that God will not fulfill His promises to Israel. Jesus' parables teach what they have to teach and one should not try to impose more on them than is legitimately there.

20:9. Planted a vineyard. This parable is best seen in light of Isaiah 5:1 – 7. There, the Lord describes Israel as His vineyard, which has disappointed Him. The idea of comparing Israel to a vineyard would have been familiar to Jesus' audience. In Jesus' parable, those who are in charge of the vineyard are the ones who disappoint. The **certain man** represents God, and the **husbandmen** may be seen as the chief priests and Pharisees.

20:10 – 12. He sent a servant (v. 10). Those who were sent to the husbandmen represent the prophets God sent in former times who were rejected (see Neh. 9:26; Jer. 7:25 – 26; 25:4 – 7; Matt. 23:34; Acts 7:52; Heb. 11:36 – 38). **Give him of the fruit**. In accordance with a kind of sharecropping agreement, a fixed amount was due the landowner. At the proper time, he would expect to receive his share.

20:13. My beloved son. The specific reference to the "beloved son" clarifies that the intended application of the son in this parable is to the Son, Jesus Christ (see 3:22; Matt. 17:5).

20:14. That the inheritance may be ours (see *KJV Study Bible* note on Mark 12:7). It is chilling to know that, in just a few days, these leaders would have Jesus arrested and tried, for fear that the Romans would "take away both our place and our nation" (John 11:48). They wanted to maintain their role and not give spiritual leadership over to another (Jesus), just as the husbandmen wanted to keep the vineyard for themselves.

20:15 – 16. Give the vineyard to others (v. 16; see discussion on Matt. 21:41). This means that God would cease to work through Israel (for a time), and the center stage of His activity in the world would move to the Gentiles. **When they heard it, they said, God forbid**. The crowd's reaction indicates either that they were very caught up in the story or that they at some level understood the meaning.

20:17. Jesus felt the need to make the point even more clearly, however well the people may have understood it. He made an analogy: **The stone which the builders rejected, the same is become the head of the corner** (see *KJV Study Bible* note on Psalm 118:22). "The stone" is Jesus; "the builders" are the Pharisees and chief priests.

20:18. It will grind him to powder. As a pot dashed against a stone is broken, and as one lying beneath a falling stone is crushed, so those who reject Jesus the Messiah will be doomed (see Isa. 8:14; see also Dan. 2:34 – 35, 44; Luke 2:34).

20:19 – 44. In this passage, two different groups challenged Jesus. He answered their questions in ways that affirmed the authority of Scripture and the teachings they already accepted as true. They thus had no basis for their opposition to Him. Then He offered a challenge of His own, designed to help them see that the Messiah must be the Son of God.

20:19. The chief priests and the scribes. For their opposition to Jesus, see 5:30; 9:22; 19:47; 22:2; 23:10. For the third time, Luke reported that **they feared the people** (see also Luke 22:2). These leaders were "men pleasers." It delayed, in this case, their doing evil, but it still indicates a character flaw. No one who regards the opinions of others is free, whether they seek to do right or wrong, and they may even be unable to distinguish between them.

20:20. They ... sent forth spies. They apparently sent people whom Jesus had not spoken with before, hoping to trap Him. These people pretended to be righteous so that they could catch Him in His words, which shows just how dark the human heart can be. These men pretended to be good in order to do evil, by trapping one who really was good, pretending that He was evil. **Authority of the governor.** Fearing to take action themselves, the Jewish religious leaders hoped to draw from Jesus some statement that would bring action from the Roman officials and remove Him from His contact with the people.

20:21. The spies' words reek with insincerity. What they said was technically true, but the reader knows that the spies themselves did not believe it. It makes the wickedness and hypocrisy of these men all the more apparent.

20:22. To give tribute unto Cesar. The questioners hoped to trap Jesus with this dilemma. If He agreed to the taxes demanded by Caesar, it would disappoint the people; if He advised no payment, it would disturb the Roman officials.

20:23. Jesus **perceived their craftiness.** He was not fooled for a moment. Those who seek to flatter often overstate their case and make themselves obvious.

20:24. A penny (see discussion on Matt. 22:19). The denarius, a Roman coin, was worth about a day's wages. **Whose image ... hath it?** In answering Jesus' question, the spies answered their own.

20:25 – 26. Render ... unto God the things which be God's (v. 25; see discussion on Matt. 22:21). Jesus avoided the dilemma of seeming either to support or to oppose an invading power, but at the same time, He put the question back into their laps. In doing so,

He turned the situation into a teachable moment. Human government is a legitimate institution, set up by God (see Rom. 13:1 – 7). At the same time, one owes God one's ultimate allegiance. One is to render to each whatever is proper. **They marvelled at his answer** (v. 26). None of Jesus' listeners, whatever their motive, could disagree with His statement. It did not commit Him to the legitimacy or the illegitimacy of the Roman government. That question was left to the listener to decide. As long as that government coined the money, however, they had some legitimate claim to it.

20:27. The second group seeking to trap Jesus now approached. The challenges in this chapter may have happened in immediate succession or at different times during the day. This group was **the Sadducees** (see discussions on Matt. 2:4; 3:7; Mark 12:18; Acts 4:1), an aristocratic, politically minded group willing to compromise with secular and pagan leaders. They controlled the high priesthood at this time and held the majority of the seats in the Sanhedrin. They did not believe in the resurrection or an afterlife, and they rejected the oral tradition taught by the Pharisees (Josephus *Antiquities* 13.10.6).

20:28. His brother should take his wife. The levirate law (see Gen. 38:8; discussion on Matt. 22:24 – 28).

20:29 – 32. This passage sets up the dilemma. The woman's husband had brothers, and each married her in turn as the one before him died.

20:33. Now the Sadducees attempted to spring the trap. Not believing in **the resurrection**, they saw their question as the kind of argument that would reduce belief in a bodily resurrection to absurdity. They thus sought to prove the Pharisees wrong and, at the same time, to trap Jesus in a contradiction. Either, they believed, He must deny the resurrection or He must assert that a woman would have seven husbands.

20:34 – 36. This world (v. 34) **... that world** (v. 35; see discussion on 18:30). Jesus did not fall into the trap. He pointed out that the world to come will be different in quality from this one. Marriage is an institution of the present creation. It will not be of the next. An indicator of that change in quality is the lack of death in that world; rather than having a mortal life span, people will be **equal unto the angels** (v. 36). The resurrection order cannot be assumed to follow present earthly lines. In the new age, there will be no marriage, no procreation, and no death. **The children of the resurrection**. Those who are to take part in the resurrection of the righteous (see Matt. 22:23–33; Mark 12:18–27; Acts 4:1–2; 23:6–10).

20:37–38. Jesus turned to the Old Testament Scriptures to demonstrate a point. The Saducees accepted only the first five books of the Old Testament. Jesus thus referred them to the book of Exodus: **Moses shewed at the bush** (v. 37). Since Scripture chapters and verses were not used at the time of Christ, the passage was identified in this way, referring to Moses' experience with the burning bush (see Exod. 3:2). There, God had called Himself **the God of Abraham, and the God of Isaac, and the God of Jacob**. The use of the present tense here indicates that these men lived on after the grave. The Saducees' insistence that this life is all there is was thus discredited by the Scriptures they themselves accepted as true.

20:39–40. Master, thou hast well said (v. 39). Even though they had great animosity against Jesus, **the scribes** (who were Pharisees) sided with Jesus against the Sadducees on the matter of resurrection. **And after that they durst not ask him any question at all** (v. 40). Again, Jesus left His opponents speechless.

20:41–43. Jesus threw out a challenge of His own. The dilemma He presented was that the Messiah is the son of David and yet David called Him **Lord** (v. 42; Ps. 110:1).

20:44. David therefore calleth him Lord (see *KJV Study Bible* note on Psalm 110:1). If the Messiah was a descendant of David, how could this honored king refer to his offspring as Lord? Unless Jesus' opponents were ready to admit that the Messiah was also the divine Son of God, they could not answer His question.

20:45–46. Jesus turned to **his disciples** (v. 45) but addressed them **in the audience of all the people**.

He wanted His words to be heard by the people and by **the scribes** (v. 46), whom He was chastising. Luke recorded this teaching because it once again sounds a theme that is important in this gospel: the need for inner righteousness, not just the outward appearance of it. **Long robes ... chief rooms** (see discussions on Mark 12:38–39). The scribes liked to be recognized, honored, and treated as leading members of the community.

20:47. These scribes had only the outward show of respectability, however. They did not hesitate to **devour widows' houses**. They took advantage of this defenseless group by fraud and schemes for selfish gain. **And for a shew, make long prayers**. Their religious practices were only to show off to the people. **Receive greater damnation** (see 12:47–48). The higher the esteem of men, the more severe the demands of true justice, and the more hypocrisy (see Matt. 23:1–36), the greater the condemnation. Jesus wanted the people to see that the external appearance is not as important as the heart. If these scribes were worthy of the honor they received, they would have lived lives that were morally different: they would have used their power to do good rather than to take advantage of the people, and they would have prayed to communicate with God rather than for show.

D. The Olivet Discourse (chap. 21)

21:1. And he looked up. This incident happened right after the teaching given just previously (Luke 20:45–47) and served as an illustration of the principle that making a show of religion has no value in the sight of God. **Rich men** were **casting their gifts into the treasury**. In the court of women, thirteen boxes, shaped like inverted megaphones, were positioned to receive the donations of the worshipers.

21:2. A certain poor widow casting in thither two mites. Mites were Jewish coins worth very little.

21:3–4. Naturally, people would have thought well of the generous gifts of the rich. They saw the outer reality of the large amounts of money they placed into the treasury. The poor widow's money seemed insignificant. From God's perspective, however, she was worthy of more honor than the rich were. She could well have justified giving nothing at all. Such was her heart for God, however, that she gave **all … that she had** (v. 4; see *KJV Study Bible* note on 2 Cor. 8:12; discussion on Mark 12:41 – 44) counting His glory as worth more than her comfort. The rich had given what had cost them little in terms of comfort but had gained them much in terms of public recognition. She had given what had cost her much but gained her little in the sight of men. The connection to what Jesus had just taught in Luke 20:45 – 47 is that He had just warned His hearers not to look at the outward appearance. Public recognition and esteem count for less than what is in the heart. The widow valued the things of God highly, from her heart, and this was worth much to God.

21:5 – 36. This passage is known as the Olivet Discourse (see discussion on Mark 13:1 – 37.)

21:5. Some of Jesus' disciples were impressed with the outward appearance of **the temple**, remarking on **how it was adorned**. One stone at the southwest corner was some thirty-six feet long. "Whatever was not overlaid with gold was purest white" (Josephus *Jewish Wars* 5.5.6). Herod had given a golden vine for one of the temple's decorations. Its grape clusters were as tall as a man. The full magnificence of the temple as elaborated and adorned by Herod has only recently come to light through archaeological investigations on the temple hill. It was indeed a magnificent building.

21:6. Jesus took advantage of the teachable moment that the disciples' comments offered. Outward adornment is not impressive to God. This temple would in fact be destroyed, Jesus said, so thoroughly that **there shall not be left one stone upon another** (see discussion on Matt. 24:2). This was fulfilled in AD 70 when the Romans took Jerusalem and burned the temple.

21:7. When shall these things be? Jesus' statement must have startled the disciples, even in light of the teaching they had just heard (Luke 21:34). This, certainly, was the effect Jesus intended. Like any good teacher, He wanted to reinforce the lessons He taught, and He used opportunities to evoke

questions from His disciples. He knew that people would pay attention to the answers to questions that the disciples asked. Had Jesus merely launched into a lecture on the destruction of Jerusalem and on the end times, they might have been bored. Mark reported that this question was asked by four disciples: Peter, James, John, and Andrew (see Mark 13:3). Matthew gave the question in a fuller form, including an inquiry for the sign of Jesus' coming and the end of the age (see Matt. 24:3). **What sign will there be …?** What signs would announce the imminence of these events?

21:8. I am Christ, or I am Jesus the Messiah (having come a second time). **The time** refers to the end time. False messiahs would come, and the disciples were not to be deceived by them.

21:9 – 10. The end is not by and by (v. 9). Refers to the end of the age (see Matt. 24:3, 6). All the events listed in 21:8 – 18 are characteristic not only of the end of the age but also of the entire present age.

21:11. Great signs shall there be from heaven (see 21:25). For prophetic descriptions of celestial signs accompanying the day of the Lord, see discussion on Mark 13:24 – 25.

21:12. Delivering you up to the synagogues. Synagogues were used not only for worship and school but also for community administration and confinement of those awaiting trial. **Brought before kings and rulers.** The disciples would face official governmental persecution.

21:13 – 15. The disciples were to see times of persecution as opportunities **for a testimony** (v. 13), but they were not to make a prepared speech. The context rules the proper understanding of this passage. Jesus was not saying that preachers should not prepare a sermon. He was saying that before people in authority or in a trial setting, a prepared, "canned" testimony would not be the best thing. The disciples were instead to depend on God for a testimony at the time. This would, Jesus said, be effective so that **your adversaries shall not be able to gainsay nor resist** (v. 15; see Acts 6:9 – 10).

21:16 – 17. The disciples would face opposition from unofficial sources as well, including family.

21:18–19. Although the disciples would face persecution and possibly even death, God was in control, and the ultimate outcome would be eternal victory. **There shall not a hair of your head perish** (v. 18). In view of 21:16, this cannot refer to physical safety. The figure indicates that there will be no real, that is, spiritual, loss. For **In your patience possess ye your souls** (v. 19), see *KJV Study Bible* note on Mark 13:13.

21:20–24. This section deals with the destruction of Jerusalem in AD 70.

21:20. Jerusalem compassed with armies (see 19:43). The sign that the end was near (see 21:7) would be the surrounding of Jerusalem with armies. Associated with this event would be "the abomination of desolation" (Matt. 24:15). This has three stages of fulfillment. The first was when Antiochus Epiphanes desecrated the temple. The second was when Rome destroyed the temple in AD 70. The third will be during the Great Tribulation.

21:21. Flee to the mountains (see discussion on Matt. 24:16). When an army surrounds a city, one's natural inclination would be to seek protection inside the city walls, but Jesus directed His followers to seek the safety of the mountains because the city was doomed to destruction.

21:22. The days of vengeance. God's retributive justice was the consequence of faithlessness (see Isa. 63:4; Jer. 5:29; Hos. 9:7).

21:23. Bearing children and nursing children is difficult during times of siege and while traveling, when food is hard to get.

21:24. Jerusalem shall be trodden down of the Gentiles. Except for brief revolts in AD 66–70 and AD 132, Jerusalem remained under Gentile rule until June 1967. Since that time, the Jews have retaken their city, signaling that God's time clock for the Jews perhaps is now set in motion once again. **The times of the Gentiles.** The Gentiles would have both spiritual opportunities (see 20:16; Mark 13:10; Rom. 11:25) and domination of Jerusalem.

21:25–28. Jesus returned to the theme of His second coming. These **signs** (v. 25) are associated with the time of the great tribulation. **Then shall they see the Son of man coming** (v. 27). The time of

Christ's second coming (see Dan. 7:13). **Lift up your heads** (v. 28). Do not be downcast at the appearance of these signs, but look up in joy, hope, and trust. **Redemption.** Final, completed redemption.

21:29–31. The parable of the fig tree. Jesus offered this parable as part of His response to the disciples' question regarding signs (see 21:7). **Behold the fig tree** (v. 29; see Matt. 24:32–35; Mark 13:28–31). The coming of summer is announced by the greening of the trees. Likewise, one can anticipate the coming of the kingdom when certain signs are seen.

21:32. This generation. If the reference is to the destruction of Jerusalem, which occurred about forty years after Jesus spoke these words, "generation" is used in its ordinary sense of a normal life span. All these things were fulfilled in a preliminary sense in the AD 70 destruction of Jerusalem. If the reference is to the second coming of Christ, "generation" might indicate the Jewish people as a nation, who were promised existence to the very end, or it might refer to the future generation who will be alive at the beginning of these things. It does not mean that Jesus had a mistaken notion that He would return immediately. The context indicates that He was referring to a future generation that would experience "all these things" (21:36), that is, the signs of the end of time.

21:33. This verse seems to be something of an aside to Jesus' main point. **My words shall not pass away.** He used the words "pass away" as an opportunity to reiterate the permanence of His word, in contrast with the physical universe, **Heaven and earth**, which is not permanent (see Morris, *Luke*, p. 301).

21:34. That day come upon you unawares. This does not mean that Christ's second coming will be completely unannounced, since there will be introductory signs (see 21:28, 31). Those caught up in the affairs of this life will miss the signs, however. As the rich fool was unprepared for his death because he was caught up in the affairs of this life (see 12:13–21), so Christians may be unprepared when Christ returns.

21:35. The whole earth. The second coming of Christ will involve the whole of mankind, whereas the fall of Jerusalem did not.

21:36. Jesus ended with an exhortation to **Watch ... and pray**. In telling His disciples to pray that they **may be accounted worthy to escape all these things that shall come to pass**, He was not telling them to pray that they might be worthy of salvation. Remember that part of this chapter has dealt with the events surrounding the siege of Jerusalem as well. Other portions have dealt with things that will happen around the time when Christ returns ("wars and commotions ... but the end is not by and by," 21:9). It would be well to escape any kind of hardship at any time, but the Lord was warning that the siege of Jerusalem and the tribulation in the distant future would be especially dire.

21:37–38. Luke ended his account of the Olivet Discourse with a summary statement: **in the day time he was teaching** (v. 37). Each day during the final week of His life, from His triumphal entry to the time of the Passover (Sunday to Thursday), Jesus was teaching the kinds of things Luke recorded here. Nights He spent at **the mount that is called the mount of Olives** (see discussions on 19:29; Matt. 21:17). He may have been camping there with His disciples, or He may have gone there to be alone. **All the people** (v. 38). Right up to the end, Jesus drew large crowds.

E. The Last Supper (22:1–38)

22:1. The feast of unleavened bread ... Passover. The word "Passover" denotes two things: (1) a specific meal that began at twilight on the fourteenth of Nisan (see Lev. 23:4–5) and (2) the week following the Passover meal (see Ezek. 45:21), otherwise known as the Feast of Unleavened Bread, a week in which no leaven was allowed (see Exod. 12:15–20; 13:3–7). By New Testament times, the two names for the weeklong festival were virtually interchangeable.

22:2. The chief priests and scribes (see 20:1 and discussion). They **sought how they might kill him; for they feared the people.** The Jewish leaders were in a quandary. They needed some way to accomplish their aim either without public knowledge or with public approval.

22:3. Then entered Satan into Judas. In the Gospels, this expression is used on two occasions: (1) before Judas went to the chief priests and offered to betray Jesus (here) and (2) during the Last Supper (see John 13:27). The gospel writers thus depicted Satan's control over Judas, who had never displayed a high motive of service or commitment to Jesus.

22:4. Captains. These men were Jews selected mostly from the Levites. Judas' motive is not known, though many have speculated on it.

22:5–6. Judas offered the leaders the one thing they wanted: an opportunity to capture Jesus without the multitude, whom, as Luke repeatedly pointed out, "they feared" (20:19; 22:2).

22:7. When the passover must be killed. The Passover lamb had to be sacrificed on the fourteenth of Nisan according to the Jewish calendar, between 2:30 and 5:30 p.m. in the court of the priests—Thursday of Passion Week.

22:8–9. Jesus delegated this matter to **Peter and John**, who asked for instructions on carrying out His command.

22:10. A man ... bearing a pitcher of water. It was extraordinary to see a man carrying a pitcher of water, since this was normally women's work. Perhaps Jesus had somehow arranged this earlier as a way for the two to identify him.

22:11. The Master saith. This form of address may have been chosen because the owner was a follower already known to Jesus.

22:12. A large upper room furnished. Jesus basically had them rent a banquet hall. They continued to use this place for at least several weeks after the events of this week (see Acts 1–6).

22:13. As he had said unto them. It may be that Jesus had made previous arrangements with the man to ensure that the Passover meal would not be interrupted. Since Jesus did not identify ahead of time just where He would observe Passover, Judas was unable to inform the enemy, who might have interrupted this important occasion.

22:14–30. Apparently, Luke did not attempt to be strictly chronological in his account of the Last Supper. He recorded the most important part of the occasion first, the sharing of the bread and the cup. Then he recorded Jesus' comments about His betrayer and about the argument over who would be greatest, though both of these subjects seem to have been introduced earlier. John's gospel, for example, indicates that Judas had already left the room before the bread and cup of the Lord's Supper were shared (see John 13:26–30), but Luke did not say when Judas left.

22:14. He sat down. The usual posture for eating a banquet meal was to recline. It is significant that **the twelve apostles** are mentioned specifically here. It is likely that they alone observed the Passover meal with Jesus. The other disciples in and near Jerusalem were most likely at their own homes (the apostles had come with Him from Galilee, remember), and the room most likely would not have accommodated more people anyway. The identification of the Twelve as the specific group is important in that it identifies "the disciple whom Jesus loved" (John 21:7, 20) as one of the apostles. This has helped scholars to defend the apostle John as the author of the gospel that bears his name since the identity of this disciple is limited to the Twelve.

22:15–16. Until it be fulfilled (v. 16). Jesus yearned to keep this Passover with His disciples because it was the last occasion before He would be slain as the perfect Passover lamb (see 1 Cor 5:7) and thus fulfill this sacrifice for all time. Jesus said He would eat no more Passover meals until the coming of the future kingdom. After this, He will renew fellowship with those who through the ages have commemorated the Lord's Supper. Finally, the fellowship will be consummated in the great messianic "marriage supper" (Rev. 19:9) to come.

22:17. He took the cup. Either the first or the third of the four cups shared during regular observance of the Passover meal.

22:18. Until the kingdom of God shall come (see discussions on 22:16; 4:43). A reference to Jesus' second coming.

22:19–20. These two verses comprise Luke's account of the institution of the Lord's Supper. Perhaps Luke made little of it because his readers, being Christians, were already very familiar with what happened since they were regular celebrants of the Supper.

22:19. This is my body. Jesus meant it represents or signifies His body. **Given for you**. He was anticipating His substitutionary sacrifice on the cross, where His body would be given as a sacrifice. **This do in remembrance of me**. The purpose of the Lord's Supper is to remember what Jesus Christ did on the cross. Just as the Passover was a constant reminder and proclamation of God's redemption of Israel from bondage in Egypt, so the keeping of Christ's command would be a remembrance and a proclamation of the deliverance of believers from the bondage of sin through Christ's atoning work on the cross.

22:20. For **also the cup**, see *KJV Study Bible* note on Mark 14:24. **After supper**. This fact is mentioned only here and in 1 Corinthians 11:25 (see *KJV Study Bible* note on 1 Cor. 11:23–26). **This cup is the new testament in my blood** (see *KJV Study Bible* note on 1 Cor. 11:25). This refers to the new covenant promised through the prophet Jeremiah (see Jer. 31:31–34); it is the fuller administration of God's saving grace, founded on and sealed by the death of Jesus ("in my blood"). **Which is shed for you**. Here again is the truth that the blood of Jesus was shed for the salvation of others. He did not die for His own sins, for He had no sin. He died for our sins.

22:21–22. Jesus foretold His betrayal. He also indicated that the one who would betray Him was present. One wonders what Judas must have thought at that point.

22:23. The disciples had no clue as to which of them it would be. At Jesus' words, the disciples did not all immediately turn and look at Judas. Sometimes, in paintings, Judas is portrayed as a somewhat sinister-looking figure. Such could not have been the case. Anyone who has been betrayed by someone they trusted will understand that. When one is betrayed, one should take comfort in knowing that the disciples were similarly deceived about the character of one among them. At this point, Judas must have done a first-rate acting job, as he drew no suspicion to himself.

22:24. Strife among them, which of them should be accounted the greatest. This was not the first time this issue came up (see 9:46).

22:25. Benefactors. A title assumed by or voted for rulers in Egypt, Syria, and Rome as a display of honor. Frequently, however, it did not represent actual service rendered.

22:26. As he that doth serve. Jesus urged and exemplified servant leadership, a trait that was as uncommon then as it is now.

22:27. I am among you as he that serveth. Jesus used Himself as an example. He recognized that the disciples had some idea of His greatness. If He was in the position of a servant, they could aspire no higher.

22:28. In my temptations. Including temptations (see 4:13), hardships (see 9:58), and rejection (see John 1:11).

22:29. I appoint unto you a kingdom. The following context (see 22:30) indicates that this refers to the future form of the kingdom (see discussions on 4:43; Matt. 3:2).

22:30. Sit on thrones. As the disciples shared in Jesus' trials, so they will share in His rule (see 2 Tim. 2:12). **Judging** here is meant in the Hebrew sense of leading or ruling **the twelve tribes of Israel** (see Matt. 19:28).

22:31. Sift you. The Greek for "you" is plural. Satan wanted to test the disciples, hoping to bring them to spiritual ruin.

22:32. Jesus' comments here apparently were directed at Peter, who would have a ministry of encouragement and exhortation after his failure. Jesus, even before Peter sinned, already had his reconciliation and recommissioning for ministry in mind.

22:33. Peter, with his usual impetuosity, made a rash statement of the extent of his commitment to Christ. When one looks at how Peter failed, in light of his desire to be the best servant of Christ he could be, one should never be too surprised at one's own failures. However sincere the heart, sin is always waiting to catch people unaware. God, in His grace, gives people a second chance, and more.

22:34. Jesus specifically foretold of Peter's denial. **This day**. The Jewish day began at sundown. When the cock crowed in the early morning hours, it would still be the same day by Jewish reckoning.

22:35. Jesus reminded the Twelve of how He had sent them out to preach, trusting for their every physical need (see Matt. 10:9).

22:36. Purse ... scrip. Compare Jesus' previous instructions in 9:3; 10:4. Until now, the disciples had been dependent on generous hospitality, but future opposition would require them to be prepared to pay their own way. This is a warning and reminder not to absolutize any one form of missions support. Jesus gave different instructions to the disciples, and thus different circumstances may demand different means of support. **He that hath no sword, let him ... buy one**. Jesus did not mean that they would stop on the way to the garden to buy weapons right then. Rather, Jesus used this extreme figure of speech to warn them of the perilous times that would soon come. They would need defense and protection, as Paul did when he appealed to Caesar (see Acts 25:11) as the one who "beareth not the sword in vain" (Rom. 13:4).

22:37. He was reckoned among the transgressors. Jesus would soon be arrested as a criminal, in fulfillment of prophetic Scripture, and His disciples also would be in danger for being His followers.

22:38. Here are two swords ... It is enough. Sensing that the disciples had taken Him too literally, Jesus ironically closed the discussion with a curt "That's plenty!" Not long after this, He rebuked Peter for using a sword (see 22:50).

F. Jesus Praying in Gethsemane (22:39–46)

22:39. The mount of Olives (see 21:37; John 18:2). Matthew specified Gethsemane (see Matt. 26:36), and John specified an olive grove (see John 18:1). The place apparently was located on the lower slopes of the Mount of Olives.

22:40. Temptation. This refers to severe trial of the kind referred to in 22:28–38, which might lead to a faltering of the disciples' faith.

22:41. A stone's cast. Jesus would have been about forty or fifty feet away from the disciples. He wanted to pray alone but was not far away from them.

22:42. Remove this cup (see *KJV Bible Study* note on Mark 14:36). The cup of suffering (see Matt. 20:22–23; see also Isa. 51:17; Ezek. 23:33). One should recognize that sometimes God's answer to prayer will be no and that this is just as legitimate and real an answer as yes. Christians are no greater than their Master and Lord. If His Father could refuse His request, how much more might He refuse them. Jesus qualified His prayer with **nevertheless, not my will, but thine, be done.** Disciples too should find, through prayer, the grace to accept their Father's will, even if it is not the same as their own.

22:43. An angel. Matthew and Mark reported that angels ministered to Jesus at the close of His fasting and temptations (see Matt. 4:11; Mark 1:13), but Luke did not. Here, however, Luke reported the strengthening presence of an angel, but the other gospel writers did not.

22:44. Drops of blood. Probably hematidrosis, the actual mingling of blood and sweat, as occurs in cases of extreme anguish, strain, or sensitivity.

22:45–46. Jesus offered comfort and encouragement to His disciples. He exhorted them to pray, knowing better than they the trials and stress they would soon face.

G. Jesus' Arrest (22:47–65)

22:47. A multitude. These people were sent by the chief priests, elders (see Matt. 26:47), and teachers of the law (see Mark 14:43), and they carried swords and clubs. Included was a detachment of soldiers with officials of the Jews (see 22:52; John 18:3). **To kiss him.** This signal had been prearranged to identify Jesus to the authorities (see Matt. 26:48). It was unnecessary because Jesus identified Himself (see John 18:5), but Judas acted out his plan anyway.

22:48. Jesus was aware of the irony of betrayal carried out with a sign of friendship and affection.

22:49–50. The disciples were ready to fight. True to their commitment, they, at this point, feared no foe in the service of their Lord. Peter was especially eager, something to remember when reading of the following hours, when he denied Jesus. **The servant**

of the high priest. Malchus by name; Simon Peter struck the blow to his ear (see John 18:10).

22:51. Healed him. Jesus rectified the wrong done by His follower. No faith on the part of Malchus was involved, but to allow such action would have been contrary to Jesus' teaching.

22:52–53. This is your hour (v. 53). It was the time appointed for Jesus' enemies to apprehend Him, the time when the forces of darkness (the powers of evil) would do their worst in their attempt to defeat God's plan. Jesus was an example of submission to authority here, in contrast with His disciples.

22:54. The high priest's house. Caiaphas, the son-in-law of Annas, the former high priest (see discussion on 3:2).

22:55. Peter sat down among them. Peter was certainly concerned but did not want to be identified, yet he could not stay away.

22:56. A certain maid. She may have seen Peter with Jesus as He taught in the temple or along the roadsides. She too may have been seeking to hide her association with Him by deflecting attention onto Peter. This is uncertain; but certainly she had seen Peter with Jesus at some point and recognized him.

22:57. Woman, I know him not. Peter's first denial of Jesus.

22:58. Another saw him. If deflection had been the maid's motive, it worked. **I am not.** Peter's second denial of Jesus.

22:59. He is a Galilean. Peter was recognized by his speech (see Matt. 26:73) and identified by a relative of Malchus, the high priest's slave (see John 18:26).

22:60. I know not what thou sayest. Peter's third denial of Jesus. **And immediately, while he yet spake, the cock crew.** Lest anyone think that Jesus merely made a guess based on the probability that Peter would deny Him before dawn and on His knowledge of Peter's character, one should look at the specifics of the matter. Jesus had foretold that Peter would deny Him, that it would happen three times, and that it would happen before the cock crowed. Consider that, to have made a "best guess," Jesus would have had to guess the maid's tendency to ask questions and to remember faces, Peter's tendency to buckle when things got uncomfortable, the tendency of the rest of the crowd to ask follow-up questions, not to mention the tendency of the high priest's cook to decide not to make chicken soup on cold nights when the high priest had been up late. It truly is one of the more remarkable prophecies found anywhere in Scripture.

22:61. The Lord … looked upon Peter. Peter was outside in the enclosed courtyard, and perhaps Jesus was being taken from the trial before Caiaphas to the Sanhedrin when Jesus caught Peter's eye. **Peter remembered the word** Jesus had spoken (see 22:34).

22:62. Peter … wept bitterly. He had acted contrary to his own profession of loyalty, had been shamed before the one who meant most to him, and had failed to live up to his own ideal of zeal for the Lord. It is difficult to imagine the depth of despair he felt in that hour. He may have drawn little comfort from Jesus' promise that he would be "converted" and His call for Peter to "strengthen thy brethren" (22:32).

22:63 – 65. Jesus was treated with contempt and suffered great pain even before being brought before the Sanhedrin. One can only wonder at the motivation of these men.

H. Jesus on Trial (22:66 – 23:25)

22:66. As soon as it was day. Only after daylight could a legal trial take place for the whole council (the Sanhedrin) to pass the death sentence. Considering that the trial was based on trumped-up charges, their zeal for minor points of legality seems odd, except that human nature often is to "major on the minors" when someone wants to avoid the real issue.

22:67 – 68. Art thou the Christ? tell us (v. 67). This demand is related to a question asked later: "Art thou then the Son of God?" (v. 70). Jesus' answer was not direct but rather was designed to point to their spiritual blindness.

22:69. Jesus foretold His ascension in these words. The assembly could not have understood what He meant at the time.

22:70. They asked Him again directly, **Art thou then the Son of God?** This time Jesus' reply was

more direct. He apparently was saying that although He would not have put it in those words, He would not deny what the leaders were asserting by them (see Morris, *Luke*, pp. 318 – 19).

22:71. We ourselves have heard. The reaction to Jesus' reply shows that the leaders understood it as a strong affirmative. Mark has simply, "I am" (Mark 14:62). It was blasphemy to claim to be the Messiah and the Son of God (see discussion on Mark 14:64) — unless, of course, the claim was true.

23:1. The whole multitude of them. The multitude of the Sanhedrin (see Matt. 26:59; 27:1), who had met at the earliest hint of dawn (see 22:66). **Led him unto Pilate** (see discussions on Matt. 27:2; Mark 15:1). The Roman governor had his main headquarters in Caesarea, but he was in Jerusalem during Passover to prevent trouble from the large number of Jews assembled for the occasion.

23:2. Perverting the nation. Large crowds followed Jesus, but He was not misleading them or turning them against Rome. **Forbidding to give tribute to Cesar.** Another untrue charge (see 20:25). **Saying that he himself is Christ a King.** Jesus claimed to be the Messiah but not a political or military king, the kind Rome would have been anxious to eliminate.

23:3. Thou sayest it. Jesus affirmed that He is a king but then explained that His kingdom is not the kind that characterizes this world (see John 18:33 – 38).

23:4. Pilate could find no basis in Roman law to convict Jesus. The Romans, at their best, believed in the rule of law over the rule of men and especially of mobs. Pilate could not be easily moved to execute an innocent man.

23:5. Throughout all Jewry. This phrase may here refer to the whole of the land of the Jews (including Galilee) or to the southern section only, where the region of Judea proper was governed by Pilate.

23:6 – 7. Herod's jurisdiction (v. 7; see discussion on 3:1). Although Pilate and Herod were rivals, Pilate did not want to handle this case, so **he sent him to Herod** (see 23:12). Pilate could have freed Him but knew that doing so would be politically risky and may have believed that the issues could be better sorted out in a Jewish court. **At Jerusalem.** Herod's main headquarters was in Tiberias on the Sea of Galilee, but like Pilate, he had come to Jerusalem because of the crowds at Passover.

23:8. He was desirous to see him. Herod was worried about Jesus' identity (see 9:7–9) and had desired to kill Him (see 13:31), though the two had never met. There is no record that Jesus ever preached in Tiberias, where Herod's residence was located.

23:9. Jesus did not answer either Herod or His accusers, but this was not due to defiance on His part. Perhaps He knew that no answer would satisfy them, and certainly He knew that the events must take their course according to His Father's will.

23:10. Jesus' accusers were fervent. Often, the less merit to one's words, the more fervently one asserts them; the less grounds one has, the more vehemently one defends the matter. Luke was very much aware, here as elsewhere, of human nature.

23:11–12. A gorgeous robe (v. 11; see *KJV Study Bible* note on Mark 15:17). Herod found no basis in the charges brought against Jesus **and sent him again to Pilate.** This incident forged a new friendship between the two men (v. 12). Again, human nature is such that sin loves company, something Luke did not fail to note.

23:13–15. Pilate's speech reveals that he honestly believed in Jesus' innocence.

23:16. I will therefore chastise him. Although Pilate found Jesus "not guilty" as charged, he was willing to have Him illegally beaten to satisfy the chief priests and the people and to warn against any possible trouble in the future. Scourging, though not intended to kill, was sometimes fatal (see discussion on Mark 15:15). Pilate was attempting a compromise. Rather than release Jesus, as the law would require, or crucify Him, as the chief priests wanted, Pilate offered a halfway measure. The problem is that, in doing so, he revealed a willingness to punish Jesus even though he knew He was innocent. Once you have given ground on your opponent's main point, it is difficult not to go the whole way. It is like

pulling an unraveling thread from a sweater. Soon the sweater is gone. Once Pilate gave in on the main point, there was no going back.

23:17–18. Pilate wanted to release Jesus, but now he could not. Another, any other, would be accepted in this charged atmosphere. **Barabbas** (v. 18). Means "son of Abba." Pilate offered a choice between Jesus and an obviously evil, dangerous criminal (see Matt. 27:15–20; Mark 15:6–11; John 18:39–40), in an effort to manipulate the situation. It only made matters worse, for it solidified their desire to see Jesus crucified. Once the chief priests and rulers had begun on that path, any movement Pilate made toward them only strengthened their resolve.

23:19. Sedition … murder. This particular uprising is otherwise unknown but, coupled with murder, it shows the gravity of Barabbas's deeds (see John 18:40).

23:20. Pilate was by now desperate. Having agreed to punish Jesus at all, and having offered them a choice as to whom to release, he found himself maneuvered into a corner from which there was no way out. All of this reveals Pilate was a weak-willed man and a poor politician.

23:21. But they cried … Crucify him. Reading Luke's short sentences describing these events, one can sense the intensity of the situation increasing and the rising fervor of the people who called for Jesus' death.

23:22–23. The third time (v. 22; see 23:4, 14). Pilate made one last futile attempt to release Jesus. Had Pilate been a better student of human nature, he would have known that his position was by now impossible. **And the voices of them and of the chief priests prevailed,** as they inevitably would under such circumstances.

23:24. Pilate gave sentence … as they required. What else could he do? This is not to absolve Pilate of any guilt in this matter; he condemned someone he knew to be innocent. His choice of strategy in the matter, however, made the outcome inevitable.

23:25. He delivered Jesus to their will. Luke's account is abbreviated. Pilate had already handed Jesus over to the soldiers for scourging before He was convicted (see John 19:1–5). He now handed Him over for crucifixion.

I. The Crucifixion (23:26–56)

23:26. Simon. His sons, Rufus and Alexander (see Mark 15:21), must have been known in Christian circles at a later time and perhaps were associated with the church at Rome (see Rom. 16:13). **Cyrenian**. Cyrene was a leading city of Libya, west of Egypt. For **on him they laid the cross**, see discussion on Mark 15:21.

23:27–28. Weep for yourselves, and for your children (v. 28). Because of the terrible suffering to befall Jerusalem some forty years later, when the Romans would besiege the city and utterly destroy the temple. Jesus chose this time to bring these matters up because this devastation would come as punishment for Jerusalem's rejection of the Messiah. He was on His way to crucifixion, and many people **bewailed and lamented** because He had been rejected. It is a measure of His love that He expressed concern for the welfare of His followers even in the midst of His own pain and anguish.

23:29. Blessed are the barren (see Jer. 16:1–4; 1 Cor. 7:25–35). It would be better not to have children than to have them experience such suffering.

23:30. Fall on us. People would seek escape through death rather than endure continuing suffering and judgment (see Hos. 10:8; Rev. 6:16).

23:31. In a green tree … in the dry. If the people of Jerusalem treated the Messiah this way when the "tree" was well-watered and green, what would their plight be when He withdrew from them and they suffered, in the dry period, for their rejection of Him?

23:32. Malefactors (see discussion on 23:18). Luke mentioned them here, because he intended to deal with them in some detail a few verses later (23:39–43), and as a master literary craftsman, he wanted his readers to have them in mind as the crucifixion scene is described. It is better to set the scene or its essential elements early than to introduce a new factor later on that will surprise the reader.

23:33. Calvary (see *KJV Study Bible* note on Mark 15:22). The Latin word for skull is *calvaria*,

hence the name "Calvary." For **they crucified him**, see *KJV Study Bible* note on Mark 15:24.

23:34. They parted his raiment. Any possessions an executed person had with him were taken by the executioners. The soldiers (see John 19:23–24) were unwittingly fulfilling the words of Psalm 22:18 (but see introduction to Psalm 22; *KJV Study Bible* notes on Ps. 22:17, 20–21).

23:35. The chosen of God (see discussion on 9:35). The words of the Jewish leaders and people made clear their rejection of Jesus as Messiah.

23:36–37. Vinegar (v. 36). Or wine vinegar, a sour drink the soldiers carried. Jesus refused a sedative drink (see Matt. 27:34; Mark 15:23) but later was given the vinegar drink when He cried out in thirst (see John 19:28–30). These verses show that it was offered in mockery.

23:38. A superscription. Indicated the crime for which a person was dying. This was Pilate's way of mocking the Jewish leaders as well as announcing the crime for which Jesus had been accused. For **THIS IS THE KING OF THE JEWS**, see discussion on Mark 15:26.

23:39–40. One of the malefactors (v. 39; see Mark 15:32). Ungodly men, even in the hour of death, will sometimes hurl abuse at God. This man died bitter. **But the other** (v. 40). These two men are a study in contrasts. Both were evil, and both deserved the sentence they received, most likely. Luke never indicated that they were other than "malefactors." One had faith, however, while the other did not. One of the thieves wanted proof, **If thou be the Christ** (v. 39), while the other believed without proof.

23:41. The first thief was unrepentant. He wanted to avoid the punishment for his crime but would not admit the evil he had done. The second thief recognized himself as a sinner: **we receive the due reward of our deeds**. In addition, the first thief taunted Jesus for His claim to be the Christ. The second believed in Him and in His innocence: **this man hath done nothing amiss**.

23:42–43. Finally, the second thief acknowledged Jesus as Lord: **Lord, remember me when thou comest into thy kingdom** (v. 42). It is true that the

Greek word here rendered "Lord" can mean nothing more than "sir," but in this context, more than that is demanded. This man knew that Jesus was innocent of any wrongdoing. He also knew, as this verse reveals, that Jesus would live after the crucifixion, that He will return, and that He will usher in a new kingdom. Notice that he made this request of Jesus while He was dying on a cross; this man must have believed that Jesus had a future beyond the cross and that He would have a kingdom, otherwise the request makes no sense. The man also believed in his own immortality. Otherwise, he would not have asked anything for himself; he too was dying at that moment. He also must have had faith that God is merciful to sinners. If he had believed that there was no hope for him because of his sins, his request would have made no sense.

When a sinful person approaches Jesus, acknowledges his or her sinfulness, expresses faith in Him as Lord, and believes that He is merciful and will pardon a sinner, this is the kind of answer such a person will receive: **To day shalt thou be with me in paradise** (v. 43). In the Septuagint (the Greek translation of the Old Testament), the word "paradise" designated a garden (as in Gen. 2:8–10) or a forest (as in Neh. 2:8), but in the New Testament (used only here and in 2 Cor. 12:4; Rev. 2:7), it refers to the place of bliss and rest between death and resurrection (see Luke 16:22; 2 Cor. 12:2), which is apparently in the very presence of God. The salvation of the repentant thief proves the reality of deathbed conversions. Luke recorded as the heart of his gospel Jesus' statement that He had "come to seek and to save that which was lost" (Luke 19:10). Little wonder that he alone recorded this remarkable incident.

23:44. About the sixth hour ... until the ninth hour. From noon to three in the afternoon, by the Jewish method of designating time. Jesus had been put on the cross at the third hour (9:00 a.m.; see Mark 15:25). "The sixth hour" of John 19:14 (see discussion there) may be Roman time (6:00 a.m.), when Pilate gave his decision.

23:45. The vail of the temple. The curtain between the Holy Place and the Most Holy Place. Its

tearing symbolized Christ's opening the way directly to God (see Heb. 9:3, 8; 10:19–22).

23:46. Jesus died, having given up His life. His life was not taken but was given up willingly, for the sins of the world. At the end, He commended His spirit into the hands of His Father, having completed the work of redemption on the cross.

23:47. The centurion ... glorified God. Either for having seen God publicly vindicate Jesus by mighty signs from heaven or, out of fear (see Matt. 27:54), to appease the heavenly Judge and thus ward off a divine penalty for having carried out an unjust judgment. **Certainly this was a righteous man.** The centurion realized that Jesus was completely innocent. Matthew and Mark report the centurion's words as "Truly this was the Son [or son] of God" (Matt. 27:54; Mark 15:39). "The Righteous One" and "the Son of God" would have been essentially equivalent terms. Similarly, "the son of God" and "a righteous man" would have been virtual equivalents. Which one the centurion intended is difficult to determine (see discussion on Matt. 27:54). It is likely that the centurion spoke in Latin and that his words had a wide enough range that Greek translations could encompass both possibilities. It seems clear, however, that the gospel writers saw in his declaration a vindication of Jesus, and since the centurion was the Roman official in charge of the crucifixion, his testimony was viewed as significant (see also the declarations of Pilate, 23:4, 14–15, 22; Matt. 27:23–24).

23:48. Smote their breasts. A sign of anguish, grief, or contrition (see 18:13).

23:49. All his acquaintance, and the women ... from Galilee (see 24:10; Matt. 27:55–56; Mark 15:40–41; John 19:25). One often assumes Jesus was abandoned by the disciples after His arrest. This apparently was not the case. They were watching from a distance, but given their emotional ties to Him, that may be understandable. In addition, their emotional anguish may have caused the Roman officials to bar them from the site for fear of what they might do.

23:50. Joseph, a counseller. Either Joseph was not present at the meeting of the Sanhedrin (see 22:66), or he did not support the vote to have Jesus killed (see 23:51). Mark's account suggests Joseph was not present, for the decision was supported by "all" (Mark 14:64).

23:51. Arimathea. A village in the hill country of Ephraim, about twenty miles northwest of Jerusalem. For **waited for the kingdom of God**, see 2:25.

23:52. The remains of an executed criminal often were left unburied or, at best, were put in a dishonored place in a pauper's field. A near relative, such as a mother, might ask for the body, but it was a courageous gesture for Joseph, a member of the Sanhedrin, to ask for **the body of Jesus**.

23:53. Wherein never man before was laid (see discussion on 19:30; *KJV Study Bible* note on Mark 15:46). Rock-hewn tombs were usually made to accommodate several bodies. This one, though finished, had not yet been used.

23:54. That day was the preparation. Friday, the day before the Sabbath, was when preparation was made for keeping the Sabbath. This phrase could be used for Passover preparation, but since in this instance it is followed by the Sabbath, it indicates Friday.

23:55. The women (see 23:49; 24:10; see also 8:2–3). They **beheld the sepulchre** where Jesus was buried and would not have mistaken the location when they returned (see 24:1–8).

23:56. Spices and ointments. Yards of cloth and large quantities of spices were used in preparing a body for burial. About a hundred pounds of myrrh and aloes (see John 19:39) were used on that first evening. More was purchased for the women's return to the tomb after the Sabbath. **According to the commandment.** This phrase makes it clear that the Sabbath in question was Saturday, the day the fourth commandment enjoins to be kept holy. That Christ died on Friday seems beyond question.

J. The Resurrection (24:1–12)

24:1. The first day of the week. According to Jewish time, Sunday began at sundown on Saturday. Spices could then be bought (see Mark 16:1), and the women were ready to set out early the next day. When they started out, it was dark (see John 20:1),

and by the time they arrived at the tomb, it was still early dawn (see Matt. 28:1; Mark 16:2).

24:2. They found the stone rolled away. A tomb's entrance was ordinarily sealed to keep vandals and animals from disturbing the bodies. This stone, however, had been sealed by Roman authority for a different reason (see Matt. 27:62–66).

24:3–4. They ... found not the body of the Lord Jesus (v. 3). The women were **much perplexed** when they found the tomb empty. **Two men** (v. 4). They looked like men, but their clothes were remarkable (see 9:29; Acts 1:10; 10:30). Other reports call them angels (see 24:23; John 20:12). Although Matthew speaks of one angel (not two, see Matt. 28:2) and Mark of a young man in white (see Mark 16:5), this is not strange because frequently only the spokesman was noted and an accompanying figure was not. Another difference in the accounts is the posture of these two figures (standing, here; seated, John 20:12), but since one's posture often changes during the course of a conversation, these variations are not necessarily contradictory but are merely evidence of independent accounts. Angels are connected with Christ's birth and temptation, as well as His agony, resurrection, and ascension.

24:5. Why seek ye the living among the dead? The angels' question contains irony. They were waiting there because they knew that the women would come looking for Jesus. This was a way of announcing to them that Jesus was alive.

24:6–7. When he was yet in Galilee (v. 6). Jesus had His death and resurrection on a number of occasions (see 9:22), but the disciples failed to comprehend or accept what He was saying.

24:8–9. Unto the eleven, and to all the rest (v. 9). "The eleven" is sometimes used to refer to the group of apostles after the betrayal by Judas (see Acts 1:26; 2:14). Judas was dead when the apostles first met the risen Christ, but the group was still called the Twelve (see John 20:24). "The rest" included disciples who, for the most part, came from Galilee.

24:10. Mary Magdalene (see discussion on 8:2). She is named first in most of the lists of the women (see Matt. 27:56; Mark 15:40; but see John 19:25) and was the first to see the risen Christ (see John 20:13–18). **Joanna** (see 8:3). Only Luke listed Joanna as present at this time (and only Mark listed Salome as being present, see Mark 16:1). **Mary the mother of James** (see Mark 16:1). She is "the other Mary" of Matthew 28:1. The absence of the mother of Jesus is significant. She was probably with John (see John 19:27).

24:11. It is surprising that the apostles **believed them not**, considering that Jesus had prophesied that He would rise on the third day. That they did not believe the women helps establish that the resurrection appearances were not a matter of mass hallucinations, which happen only if there is a clear expectation of seeing something. The disciples, however, had no expectation of seeing Jesus alive again.

24:12. Peter … ran unto the sepulchre. John 20:3–9 says that Peter went to the tomb with another disciple: John himself.

K. The Post-Resurrection Ministry (24:13–53)

24:13–14. Two of them (v. 13). One was named Cleopas (see 24:18). Many have surmised that the other was Cleopas's wife. Obviously, the events of that morning would have been a major topic of conversation between them.

24:15–16. Jesus himself drew near (v. 15). He appeared to them, without revealing His identity. **But their eyes were holden** (v. 16). By special divine intervention, they could not recognize Jesus.

24:17. Jesus knew what they were discussing. He wanted to begin a conversation with them and to help them put together in their minds the order of events. He wanted to help them understand what was happening.

24:18. Cleopas's words indicate that the trial and crucifixion of Christ had attracted quite a bit of attention. This would be expected, considering His triumphal entry a week earlier and the crowds He had drawn while teaching in the temple. Details like this give Luke's account a ring of authenticity. Cleopas's response to the Lord is just what someone would say, given the events Luke recorded earlier, yet the reader does not get the feeling that Luke was justify-

ing his account by making up the words. They seem quite natural, a part of the total event. Verses like this one are helpful in establishing the authenticity of the gospel accounts.

24:19–20. A prophet (v. 19). They had respect for Jesus as a man of God, but after His death, they apparently were reluctant to call Him the Messiah.

24:21. We trusted. The verb tense indicates that they used to be trusting. Their hopes had been dashed, however. **He which should have redeemed Israel.** To set the Jewish nation free from bondage to Rome and usher in the kingdom of God (see 1:68; 2:38; 21:28, 31; Titus 2:14; 1 Peter 1:18–19). It is ironic that Cleopas used these words since it was this very death that brought about true redemption to all who will believe. **The third day.** A reference either to the Jewish belief that after the third day, the soul left the body or to Jesus' remark that He would be resurrected on the third day (see 9:22). In any event, this time reference indicates that Jesus was crucified on a Friday, since Jews counted the day on which the event occurred as day one. They would have said it was the fifth day, for example, if Christ had been crucified on Wednesday.

24:22–23. Certain women (v. 22) **… had also seen a vision of angels, which said that he was alive** (v. 23; see discussion on 24:4). Cleopas's account shows that he did not believe the women.

24:24. For **Certain of them … with us,** see 24:12 and discussion. **But him they saw not.** Cleopas had not made the connection between these events and Jesus' words in Galilee.

24:25–27. Jesus gently chastised them for their lack of understanding. **All that the prophets have spoken** (v. 25). Here Jesus provided a hermeneutical key to the Old Testament. It all points to Him and to the redemption He wrought. **Moses and all the prophets** (v. 27). A way of designating the whole of the Old Testament Scriptures. **The things concerning himself.** Everything in the Old Testament ultimately refers back to Jesus. While one should be careful not to force an interpretation onto a passage, one should read the entire Old Testament with an eye to how it points ahead to Jesus Christ.

24:28. As though he would have gone further. He knew that they would invite Him in. He could not politely assume He was invited but had to act as if He would continue His journey until He was asked. This was not deception in any sense. He was only doing what a normal traveler would do, until invited to join the couple for dinner.

24:29. Abide with us. Cleopas and his fellow traveler did invite Jesus to stay with them.

24:30–31. Their eyes were opened (v. 31; see 24:16). This indicates that they had been supernaturally prevented from seeing who He was. Perhaps also, as they took the bread from His hands, they saw the nail marks, but this is not indicated. **He vanished out of their sight**. Apparently, He just disappeared.

24:32. Did not our heart burn within us …? They realized that their engagement with Him in conversation and the emotions they had felt were a result of His "teaching as one having authority" (Matt. 7:29), as had happened during His pre-resurrection ministry. They realized that they should have recognized who was teaching them.

24:33. For **the eleven gathered together, and them that were with them**, see discussion on 24:9.

24:34–35. The two disciples related the account of what had happened. It is possible that Luke spoke with these two in the preparation of his gospel. At the beginning of his gospel, he indicated that he had spoken with "eyewitnesses" (1:2).

24:36. As they thus spake, Jesus himself stood in the midst of them. Behind locked doors (see John 20:19), indicating that His body was of a different order. It was the glorified body of the resurrection (see Mark 16:12).

24:37–38. Jesus' appearance frightened the disciples. This is understandable. People do not normally suddenly materialize in a room. Nothing Jesus could have said would have prevented the panic that ensued. It is safe to infer that the two disciples who had seen Him on the road to Emmaus were there and may have been somewhat less frightened than the others.

24:39. Behold my hands and my feet (see John 20:20, 27). Indicating that Jesus' feet as well as His hands were nailed to the cross (see *KJV Study Bible*

note on Mark 15:24). **A spirit hath not flesh and bones, as ye see me have**. Jesus retained His physical body, yet it had other powers as well. All ideas such as that Jesus was raised "spiritually" or that the disciples used "resurrection language" to account for their sense of God's presence with them after the death of Christ must be utterly rejected in light of Jesus' words here.

24:40–41. The disciples were still reluctant to believe. This fact contradicts those who attempt to show that the disciples were credulous, eager to believe in a miracle, and looking for the risen Christ.

24:42–43. A piece of a broiled fish (v. 42). Jesus ate, thus demonstrating that He had a physical body that could consume food.

24:44. In the law of Moses, and in the prophets, and in the psalms. The three parts of the Hebrew Old Testament (Psalms was the first book of the third section, called "the Writings"), indicating that Christ (the Messiah) was foretold in the whole Old Testament.

24:45. Opened he their understanding. Jesus again taught regarding the Old Testament Scriptures that teach about Him (24:27).

24:46. To suffer, and to rise from the dead the third day. The Old Testament depicts the Messiah as one who would suffer (see Psalm 22; Isaiah 53) and rise from the dead on the third day (see Ps. 16:9–11; Isa. 53:10–11; compare Jonah 1:17 with Matt. 12:40).

24:47. Repentance and remission of sins (see Acts 5:31; 10:43; 13:38; 26:18). The prophecy of His death and resurrection (see 24:46) is joined with the essence of man's response (repentance) and the resulting benefit (forgiveness; see Isa. 49:6; Acts 13:47; 26:22–23). **Beginning at Jerusalem** (see Acts 1:8). This is very much like the Great Commission (see Matt. 28:18–20). The difference in wording is easily understood. The setting is different (the upper room rather than outdoors), and the timing is different (the evening of the same day He rose, not several weeks later). Surely, Jesus gave them this all-important commission to go and preach the gospel to all the world on more than one occasion.

24:48. Ye are witnesses of these things. They were witnesses of the "repentance and remission of sins" (24:47) through Jesus Christ, that would be preached in all the world.

24:49. The promise of my Father (see Joel 2:28–29). The reference is to the coming power of the Spirit, fulfilled in Acts 2:4.

24:50. Bethany (see discussions on 19:29; Matt. 21:17). A village on the Mount of Olives. This is a transition sentence, moving the action to a time forty days later.

24:51. While he blessed them. Luke's gospel begins with a priest who had no blessing to impart (Zacharias) and ends with the great High Priest giving a blessing as He was departing from His disciples. **Carried up into heaven**. Different from His previous disappearances (see 4:30; 24:3; John 8:59). They saw Him ascend into a cloud (see Acts 1:9).

24:52. They worshipped Him. By this time, the disciples understood Christ's deity. Worship is a proper response to deity.

24:53. Continually in the temple. During the period immediately following Christ's ascension, the believers met continually in the temple (see Acts 2:46; 3:1; 5:21, 42), where many rooms were available for meetings (see discussion on 2:37). Luke ended his account with the disciples meeting there. The context is Jewish, and the gospel ends with a small group of disciples, in Jerusalem, worshiping Jesus within that context. In the book of Acts, which is a sequel to this gospel, Luke recorded how the gospel spread far beyond Jerusalem to encounter the Gentile world, bringing in many converts as churches began in Asia and eastern Europe and as far away as Rome.

THE GOSPEL ACCORDING TO ST. JOHN

INTRODUCTION

Author

The author is the apostle John, the disciple "whom Jesus loved" (13:23; 19:26; 20:2; 21:7, 20, 24). John was prominent in the early church but is not mentioned by name in this gospel, which would be natural if he wrote it but is hard to explain otherwise. The author knew Jewish life well, as seen from references to popular messianic speculations (e.g., 1:20–21; 7:40–42), to the hostility between Jews and Samaritans (4:9), and to Jewish customs, such as the duty of circumcision on the eighth day taking precedence over the prohibition of working on the Sabbath (see discussion on 7:22). He knew the geography of the Holy Land, locating Bethany about fifteen furlongs (about two miles) from Jerusalem (11:18) and mentioning Cana (2:1; 21:2), a village not referred to in any earlier writing known to us. The gospel of John has many touches that were obviously based on the recollections of an eyewitness, such as the house at Bethany being filled with the fragrance of the broken perfume jar (12:3; see Matt. 14:3). Early writers such as Irenaeus and Tertullian say that John wrote this gospel, and all other evidence agrees (see 1 John, Introduction: "Author"). The earliest manuscripts have as their title, "The Gospel According to John."

The internal evidence makes it clear that the author was Jewish. He had a thorough knowledge of Jewish feasts and customs, including weddings (2:1–12), ceremonial purification (3:25), religious feasts (2:13; 6:4; 13:1; 18:28), and burial customs (11:38; 19:40). It also indicates he was (or had been) a resident of Israel. He knew the exact distance from Bethany to Jerusalem (11:18) and that Jacob's well is deep (4:11). He also provided several details that indicate he was one of the twelve disciple and an eyewitness of Jesus' earthly ministry. He knew the number and size of the waterpots used in Cana (2:6), the distance from the shore to the apostles' boat (21:8), the number of fish they caught (21:11), and the details of the private conversations that occurred at the Last Supper (chaps. 13–17). The accumulative weight of all these factors favors John the apostle as the author.

Date

The traditional view dates this gospel toward the end of the first century, circa AD 85 or later (see 1 John, Introduction: "Date"). John has always been known as "the fourth gospel." The early church fathers believed it was written toward the end of John's life, between AD 85–95. Those who hold this view maintain that John 21:18, 23 requires a later date, with Peter becoming old and John outliving him. This view may be supported by the statement of Clement of Alexandria that John wrote to supplement the accounts found in the other gospels (Eusebius *Ecclesiastical History* 6.14.7), and thus his gospel is later than the first three. It has also been argued that the seemingly more developed theology of the fourth gospel indicates that it originated later.

An earlier date has been suggested, between AD 50–70, because it has been thought more recently that John wrote independently of the other gospels. This does not contradict the statement of Clement referred to above. Also, those who hold this view point out that developed theology does not necessarily argue for a late origin. The theology of Romans (written ca. AD 57) is every bit as developed as that in John. Further, the statement in 5:2 that there "is" (rather than "was") a pool "by the sheep market" may suggest a time before AD 70, when Jerusalem was destroyed. Others, however, observe that elsewhere John sometimes used the present tense when speaking of the past.

Most liberal scholars advocate a late date, sometime in the second century (ca. AD 150). They agree that this gospel's developed Christology, with an emphasis on the deity of Christ, must have come later than the first century. However, archaeological discoveries of fragments of John's gospel (namely, p52, which contains parts of John 18) predate the supposed late date. This fragment is conservatively dated no later than AD 125, and accounting for circulation pushes its origin no later than AD 100.

Theme and Theological Message

Some interpreters believe that John's aim was to set forth a version of the Christian message that would appeal to Greek thinkers, but his gospel is so thoroughly steeped in Jewish and Old Testament thought that this could hardly have been his main goal. Others have seen a desire to supplement (or correct) the Synoptic Gospels, to combat some form of heresy, to oppose the continuing followers of John the Baptist, or to achieve a similar goal. The writer himself, however, stated his main purpose clearly: "But these are written, that ye might believe that Jesus is the Christ, the Son of God; and that believing ye might have life through his name" (20:31). John may have had in mind mainly Jews and proselytes to Judaism, especially those of the Diaspora (see Carson, *The Gospel According to John*, pp. 91–92), but his primary intention was evangelistic. It is possible to understand "might believe" in the sense of "may continue to believe," in which case, John's intention was to build up believers as well as to win new converts.

John was the only gospel writer to mention more than one Passover. In fact, he listed three (2:13; 6:4; 13:1) and hinted at a fourth (5:1). This enumeration allows one to reconstruct a full three-year ministry for Christ on earth. It also helps to demonstrate that John was familiar with the other three gospels and consciously supplemented as necessary. Fully 92 percent of John's gospel is unique, that is, not contained in any of the other accounts. For the main themes of this gospel, see discussions on 1:4, 7, 9, 14, 19, 49; 2:4, 11; 3:27; 4:34; 6:35; 13:1–17:26; 13:31; 17:1–2, 5; 20:31. A convenient picture of some of the important themes in the gospel of John can be created by comparing vocabulary:

	Matthew	Mark	Luke	John
Love (*agapē*)	9	5	14	44
Truth (*alētheia*)	2	4	4	46
Know (*ginoskō*)	20	4	4	56
Scripture (*graphē*)	0	1	1	11
I am (*eimi*)	14	4	16	54
Work (*ergō*, ergon)	9	3	18	35
Life (*zoē*)	7	4	5	36
World (*kosmos*)	8	2	3	78
Judge (*krinō*)	6	0	6	19
Witness (*martyreō*)	4	6	5	47
Remain (*menō*)	3	2	7	39
Father (*patēr*, used of God)	44	4	16	118
Send (*pempō*)	4	1	10	32
Send (*apostellō*)	22	20	26	28
Send (Jesus, object of)	2	1	4	42
Manifest (*phaneroō*)	0	1	0	9
Light (*phōs*)	7	1	6	23

Adapted from C. K. Barrett, *The Gospel according to St. John*, 5–6.

Perhaps the most prominent theme in John's gospel, however, is that the Father sent the Son to earth as His representative. Not only is it said that "God sent … his Son into the world" (3:17), but Jesus routinely identified God as "the Father which hath sent me" (e.g., 5:30, 37; 6:44; 8:18; 12:49) or "him that sent me" (e.g., 4:34; 5:24; 6:38, 40). Opposed to other backgrounds to explain this emphasis, Jewish ideas of sending a representative in one's place are conventional in John (13:16; 1:19–24) and best explain the character of Jesus' representation of the Father. The cardinal tenet in Jewish agency, that the one sent is equivalent to the one who sends him, presumes the fidelity of the representative to the will and purpose of the sender, whose authority is resident in the representative. The human institution is the starting point for apprehending the Father's supernatural sending of Jesus and accounts for the otherwise perplexing tension between Jesus' humble subordination to the Father and Jesus' exalted authority.

Gauged by just the verbs used for "to send," the gospel of John contains no less than forty direct references to the fact that Jesus was sent by the Father. A cursory survey of these references leads to a distinct picture of Jesus as *the* representative of the Father. The coming of Jesus is conveyed as a representation commissioned by the Father: "I proceeded forth and came from God; neither came I of myself, but he sent me" (8:42; see 7:28–29; 10:36). To the one whom the Father sent to represent Him, He "hath given all things into his hand" (3:35; 13:3), authorizing Jesus to act on behalf of "the Father which hath sent him" (5:24; see 5:22–24, 27). Accordingly, Jesus stated, "I am come in my Father's name" (5:43) and that the works that He did, He did "in my Father's name" (10:25). The Father gave these works, which Jesus called "the works of him that sent me" (9:4), to Jesus to accomplish during His earthly ministry (5:36; 4:34; 17:4).

Jesus' will, therefore, was to do the will and command of the one who sent Him (3:34; 5:30; 6:38–39; 10:18, 12:49–50; 14:31); He sought not His own glory but the glory of the one who sent Him (7:18; 8:50; 17:4; see also 5:41; 8:54): "he that sent me is with me … I do always those things that please him" (8:29). Jesus did "nothing of himself" (5:19; see 5:30; 7:16–18; 28–29; 8:26–28, 42; 12:49). His "doctrine" (7:16), His "word" (14:24), what He "[spoke] to the world" (8:26), was not His own but what He had "heard" from (8:26) or been "taught" by (8:28) the Father to speak: "the Father which sent me … gave me a commandment, what I should say, and what I should speak … whatsoever I speak therefore, even as the Father said unto me, so I speak" (12:49–50). Consequently, "the word which you hear is not mine, but the Father's which sent me" (14:24), and "he whom God hath sent speaketh the words of God" (3:34; see 17:8).

In the gospel of John, Jesus' representation of the Father, who commissioned and authorized Him, serves as the basis for His legally validated authority (5:36, 38; 6:29, 57; 10:36; 11:42; 17:3, 8, 18). Accordingly, to "honour the Son" is to "honour the Father … which hath sent him" (5:23; see 8:49), to receive Jesus is to "receiveth him that sent me" (13:20), to believe in Jesus is to "believeth … on him that sent me" (12:44; see 14:1), to behold Jesus is to "seeth him that sent me" (12:45).

After completing His commission, Jesus was to return to the one who sent Him (7:33; 13:1, 3; 14:28; 16:5, 17, 27–28). In anticipation of His return, Jesus reported to the Father what He had accomplished (chap. 17). That Jesus had faithfully represented the Father in all that He was sent to do is summed up most clearly in the refrain that punctuated His report to the Father: "that the world may believe [or 'know'] that thou hast sent me" (17:21, 23; also 17:3, 8, 25; see 6:29; 11:42).

Outline

Bibliography

Barrett, C. K. *The Gospel According to St. John: An Introduction with Commentary and Notes on the Greek Text*. 2nd ed. Philadelphia: Westminster John Knox, 1978.

Beasley-Murray, George R. *John*. Word Biblical Commentary 36. Waco, TX: Word, 1987.

Borchert, Gerald L. *John 1–11*. The New American Commentary 25A. Nashville: Broadman & Holman, 1996.

Brown, Raymond, E. *The Gospel According to John*. 2 vols. The Anchor Bible 29–29A. Garden City, New York: Doubleday, 1966–70.

Bruce, F. F. *The Gospel of John: Introduction, Exposition, and Notes*. Grand Rapids, MI: Eerdmans, 1983.

Carson, D. A. *The Gospel According to John*. Pillar New Testament Commentary. Grand Rapids, MI: Eerdmans, 1991.

Danby, Herbert. *The Mishnah*. Oxford: Oxford University Press, 1933.

Dodd, C. H. *Studies in the Fourth Gospel*. Ed. F. L. Cross. London: A. R. Mowbray, 1957.

Hendriksen, William. *A Commentary on the Gospel of John*. Grand Rapids, MI: Eerdmans, 1953.

Morris, Leon. *The Gospel According to John*. The New International Commentary on the New Testament. Grand Rapids, MI: Eerdmans, 1971.

Smalley, Stephen S. *John: Evangelist and Interpreter*. Exeter, UK: Paternoster, 1978.

Talbert, Charles H. *Reading John: A Literary and Theological Commentary on the Fourth Gospel and the Johannine Epistles*. New York: Crossroad Publishing, 1992.

Westcott, B. F. *The Gospel According to St. John*. 1881. Reprint, Grand Rapids, MI: Eerdmans, 1975.

EXPOSITION

I. Prologue (1:1–18)

1:1–18. The gospel of John opens with the most towering vista of Jesus as the Word (Greek, *logos*) found in all of the New Testament. Perched on the horizon between heaven and earth, the reader is granted an omniscient perspective of Jesus that holds within its scope the creation of the cosmos and the redemptive history of the world. Colossians 1:15–20, Philippians 2:5–11, and Hebrews 1:1–13 offer this vista, but none matches the scope of Jesus' celestial and terrestrial significance, nor the glory, majesty, and intimacy of Jesus' sonship, as presented in John's prologue. As one reads John's gospel, the omniscient knowledge of the prologue will return again and again to inform the reader of the true identity of Jesus.

1:1–2. John's gospel and Genesis begin alike. The connection is strong. John's opening words are the Greek translation of the very first word of Genesis 1:1 in Hebrew: *bereshith*. If one were to open the old Greek Bible, the Septuagint, one would find that the opening words of Genesis are the same as John's opening. As those familiar with the Genesis account of creation will recognize, John featured the agency of the Creator and revealed the preeminent role of the Word, or Logos (Jesus), in the action of creation.

In the beginning (v. 1) is not only the Greek translation of the very first word of the Bible in Hebrew but is also the Hebrew title of the book of Genesis (Hebrew, *bereshith*). The English title "Genesis" (Greek, *genesis*; "source," "origin") comes from the Septuagint, the old Greek translation of the Hebrew Bible.

In the beginning was the Word (v. 1) was a powerful and pregnant expression for both Greeks and Jews. Greeks used the term "Word" (Greek, *logos*) not only of the spoken word but also of the unspoken word, the word still in the mind, the reason. When they applied it to the universe, they meant the rational principle that governs all things. Jews, on the other hand, were acquainted with its near equivalent in Hebrew (*davar*). "The word of the LORD" was a common expression linked to God's action in both

revelation and creation. These associations with "the Word" were already in place when a Greek or Jewish listener heard the opening words of John's gospel. Using this one term, meaningful to both Jews and Gentiles, John joined two hemispheres to communicate a new and unique fact (see Dodd, *Studies*, p. 12).

The words **was with God** (v. 1) make it clear that the Logos is distinct from God. In John 1:14 (also 1:18), the relationship of the Logos to God is clarified as the relationship of the Son and Father. **The Word was God** clearly identifies the Logos (Jesus) as God in the fullest sense (see discussion on Rom. 9:5). Perhaps the best alternative translation to capture the full sense is that of the New English Bible: "what God was, the Word was." The opening and closing of John's prologue (1:1, 18) present a ringing affirmation of Jesus' deity (see discussion on 1:18).

The verb "was" functions uniformly in each of the four clauses of this passage, to predicate or assert something about the Logos. Different nuances of meaning are suggested by the complete predicate and not by the verb "was" alone: (1) "In the beginning was," preexistence; (2) "was with God," relationship; (3) "was God," identity. The combination of these clauses climaxes into one indissoluble burst of thought: **The same** (lit., 'this one') **was in the beginning with God** (v. 2). This is the crown of the clauses in that it is the sum of its parts. John opened his gospel with a concise and concentrated command of the language to communicate that the Logos, Jesus, is uniquely qualified to reveal God.

1:3. All things were made by him (see Col. 1:16–18). Jesus was the agent of creation. John's pattern of speech is exclusive; "all or nothing" becomes "all and nothing," with the final addendum **that was made** sealing the circle: (1) all through Him came, and (2) without Him came nothing. The parallel (positive and negative) statements are an antiphonal chorus of one truth: everything, without exception, is the work of the Logos.

1:4. Life is always eternal life in this gospel and 1 John (see 1:1–2). One of the great concepts of this gospel, "life" (Greek, *zōē*) is found thirty-six times in John, while no other New Testament book uses it more than seventeen times. Life is Christ's gift (see 10:28), and He, in fact, is "the life" (14:6). **The life was the light of men** specifies the relation of the Life to men as light. As eternal Life (see 1 John 5:11), the Logos (Jesus) is the source of natural life (see 1:3), but only as eternal Life is the Logos "the light" (1:5) and "the light of men." In John's gospel, eternal life is more than endless natural life. It is a quality of life defined by the life of God. The revelation of the Logos (see discussion on 1:14) thus gives eternal life to "men" (or "the world"). "Light" features the spiritual illumination that the Logos presents to the world. Jesus is "the "light of the world" (8:12), who holds out wonderful hope for the world. For an Old Testament link between "life" and "light," see Psalm 36:9.

1:5. The stark contrast between **light** and **darkness** is a striking theme in this gospel (see, e.g., 12:35). "Darkness" connotes not only the absence of light and the spiritual ignorance of the heart but also the evil that breeds in its retreat from the light (see 3:19–21). As "light" cannot be disassociated from the scope of the Life, so "darkness" cannot be disassociated from the specter of death. In this gospel, judgment belongs to sphere of the revelatory nature of light (see 3:18–19; 12:44–47).

1:6–7. In this gospel, the name **John** (v. 6) always refers to John the Baptist, and he is never called "the Baptist." His role as witness is emphasized in this gospel. If there is a model witness, it is John (see 1:19–37). His singular ministry was to testify to Jesus (see 10:41), and the first disciples were introduced to Jesus through the testimony of John.

That all men through him might believe (v. 7) identifies the Baptist's important role as a witness to Jesus. People were to believe not "in" John the Baptist but "through" him. Similarly, the author's purpose was to draw them to belief in Christ (20:31); he used the verb "believe" (Greek, *pisteuō*) ninety-eight times. **Witness** is an important concept in this gospel. The Greek noun for "witness" or "testimony" is used fourteen times (in Matthew not at all, in Mark

three times, in Luke once), and the verb ("testify") thirty-three times (found once each in Matthew and Luke, not at all in Mark)—in both cases, more often than anywhere else in the New Testament. John (the author) thereby emphasized that the facts about Jesus are amply attested.

1:9–10. As the light coming into the world, Jesus **lighteth every man** (v. 9). Although the punctuation of the KJV suggests that "every man" is the subject of **cometh into the world**, the Greek grammar and the clear allusion to the technical epithet for Jesus as the "Coming One" make clear that it is the Light coming into the world that illumines every man. John was referring to the incarnation of Christ, not to a prenatal illumination. Jesus is He who "cometh into the world," and He is "the light of the world" (8:12; 9:5; see 3:19; 6:14; 11:27; 16:28; 12:46). Here John introduced the grand truth that Jesus is the Light of the World (see 8:12; 9:5). Jesus is the **true Light** (v. 9). The adjective "true" (Greek, *alēthinos*) denotes that which is genuine, real, and authentic. **World** (Greek, *kosmos*; vv. 9, 10) is a common word in John's writings, found seventy-eight times in this gospel and twenty-four times in his letters (only forty-seven times in all of Paul's writings). It can mean the universe, the earth, the people on earth, most people, people opposed to God, or the human system opposed to God's purposes. John emphasized the word by repetition and moved without explanation from one meaning to another (see, e.g., 17:5, 14–15 and discussions). Here "the world" clearly denotes "humankind," for the reader is told that **the world knew him not**; that is, it did not recognize or acknowledge its Creator.

1:11. Here the meaning of "the world" (1:9–10) is narrowed by the words **his own** (Greek, *idios*; see 19:27). The notion of Israel as "a peculiar treasure unto me above all people" (Exod. 19:5) may be in view here: the "framework of life to which as Messiah he belonged" (Barrett, *The Gospel According to St. John*, p. 163). The second occurrence of **his own** (a different gender from the first) refers to those who belong to "his own" (perhaps meaning Israel). They **received** (or "accepted") **him not**.

1:12–13. By birth, people are not **the sons** (Greek, *tekna*; "children") **of God** (v. 12). Unlike the Stoic or the Hermetic systems that taught one's divine origin needs only to be realized or exercised, the revelation of God in Jesus Christ is redemptive and calls one to receive Jesus through a trust relationship of faith. Membership in God's family is by grace alone; it is a gift of God (see Eph. 2:8–9). It is never a human achievement (**gave he**; v. 12), yet the imparting of the gift is dependent on man's reception of it, as the words **received** and **believe** make clear. **Power** (Greek, *exousia*) denotes an "authority" or "status" granted through Jesus (see 14:6). The status of the children of God is thus associated with **his name**, the name of Jesus.

1:14. The Word, the Logos (Jesus), existed before He became man, as indicated by the words **was made**. To state that God (the Logos) had become frail and transitory flesh (see Isa. 40:6) was poignant, if not scandalous. **Flesh** is a strong, almost crude, word that stresses the reality of Christ's manhood. The Greek for **dwelt** is connected with the word for "tent" or "tabernacle." The verse would have reminded John's Jewish readers of the tabernacle, which was filled by the glory of God (see Exod. 40:34–35). This is an important clue to the background of John's thought regarding the glory of the Son. **His glory** points to the unique character qualities of God revealed to Moses in answer to his request to see God's glory (see Exod. 33:18): "I will make all my goodness pass before thee" (Exod. 33:19); "While my glory passeth by ... I will put thee in a clift of the rock" (Exod. 33:22); "And the LORD passed by before him, and proclaimed, The LORD, The LORD God, merciful and gracious, longsuffering, and abundant in goodness and truth" (Exod. 34:6).

Significantly, God's character qualities are synonymously associated with, if not synonymous with, the revelation of His glory. The crowning qualities, "abundant in goodness and truth" (Exod. 34:6), are the Hebrew equivalent to John's Greek wording, **full of grace and truth** (see 1:17; *Zondervan KJV Study Bible* note on Ps. 26:3; discussion on Prov. 16:6). These qualities are the glory of **the only begotten of the Father**. One expects the Son to bear the unique stamp of the Father, but the resemblance is the glory of grace and truth. Now too the relationship of the Logos with God (see 1:1) is viewed through a new lens of intimacy, that of Father and Son.

1:15. John again placed the testimony of the Baptist (the chief historical witness in the prologue) strategically. Here the Greek is in the present tense, even though when John wrote it, the action was in the past. The present tense suggests that John the Baptist's message still sounded in people's ears beyond his death. John characteristically used present-tense verbs in his writing. The Baptist's testimony corroborates 1:14 and the eternal existence of the Logos. This is supported by the closing words of his witness: **He that cometh after me is preferred before me: for he was before me**. In ancient times, the older person was given respect and regarded as greater than the younger. People would normally have ranked Jesus lower in respect than John, who was older. John the Baptist explained that this was only apparent, since Jesus, as Logos, existed before He was born on earth. Westcott (*The Gospel According to St. John*, p. 13) maintains it was a reference not merely to relative priority but to absolute priority: the Logos was not just "former" (prior to the Baptist) but was "first" in an absolute sense. It may be understood as, "He who comes after me has precedence over me, because he was (existed) prior to me (and all else)."

1:16–17. Of his fulness (v. 16; see 1:14) points to the full complement of grace and truth in Jesus Christ. The scope of grace experienced (**have all we received**) is defined by the words **grace for grace**, or "grace upon grace," which suggests the continuous disbursement of grace from His fullness. In view of John the Baptist's testimony ("he was before me," 1:15) and the preexistent Logos "made flesh" (1:14), John's clarification that **grace and truth came by Jesus Christ** (v. 17), makes it clear that there is only one mediator of God's grace, just as there was only one agent of creation (see 1:3), and both are none other than Jesus Christ. Sinai and Moses give a telltale historical vantage point to the range of His mediation. The highly esteemed role of Moses as mediator of God's Law and his exclusive witness to God's glory on Sinai (see Exod. 34:29–35; 2 Cor. 8:7–18) offer a historical comparison by which to measure the superior mediation of Jesus Christ, who mediates grace and truth, the very glory of God (see discussion of 1:14). John will go on to express the unparalleled and exclusive role of Jesus as mediator and revealer of God in v. 18.

1:18. The only begotten Son is an explicit declaration of Jesus' uniqueness (see 1:1, 14 and discussions; 3:16). The "Son" (other Greek manuscripts read "God") is clearly implied by the repetition of "the only begotten" (see 1:14), and the word **bosom** indicates the intimacy of the relationship of the Father and Son. The manuscript support for either reading ("Son" or "God") is strong and cannot be decided on the manuscript support alone. Both readings make sense based on the teaching of John's prologue (1:1–18). "Son" fits well the immediate sense by complementing "Father" and echoes " the only begotten of the Father" of 1:14. "God" strikes one as awkward but would round out the prologue by echoing the opening (1:1) at the end and tying the prologue together with a literary inclusion. In either case, this verse forms a climax to the prologue and clarifies the peerless status of Jesus as the one uniquely qualified to reveal the Father: **he hath declared him**. Indeed, **No man hath seen God at any time**. In the Old Testament, people are sometimes said to have seen God (see, e.g., Exod. 24:9–11), but they are also told that no one can see God and live (see Exod. 33:20). Therefore, since no human being can see God as He really is, those who saw God saw Him in a form He took on Himself temporarily for the occasion. Those events are termed "Christophanies," Old Testament appearances of Christ in human form. It seems John was saying that they saw none other than Jesus preincarnate (see discussion on 12:41). Now, however, Christ "hath declared him," or "has made him known."

II. Beginnings of Jesus' Ministry (1:19–51)

A. The Ministry of His Forerunner (1:19–34)

1:19. And this is the record of John points to the Baptist's role as witness (see 1:6–7). "Record"

(Greek, *martyria*) is literally "testimony." Here the testimony of John was given a formal venue with the inquest of the delegation that **the Jews sent ... from Jerusalem**. The phrase "the Jews" occurs about seventy times in this gospel. It is used in a favorable sense (see, e.g., 4:22) and in a neutral sense (see, e.g., 2:6), but generally John used it of the Jewish leaders who were hostile to Jesus (see, e.g., 8:48). Here it refers to the delegation sent by the Sanhedrin to look into the activities of an unauthorized teacher. **Levites** are descendants of the tribe of Levi, who were assigned to specific duties in connection with the tabernacle and temple (see Num. 3:17–37). They also had teaching responsibilities (see 2 Chron. 35:3; Neh. 8:7–9), and it was probably in this role that they were sent with the **priests** to John the Baptist.

1:20. The Baptist used the emphatic "I" to establish a stark contrast. His disavowal, **I am not the Christ** implies the question "Are you the Christ?" according to the pattern of the questions and answers that follow. It may be, however, that the unique introduction of **And he confessed, and denied not; but confessed** suggests the leading question was more benign, such as, "Who are you?" to which the Baptist assumed a proactive posture ("I am not the Christ"). If so, that triggered the follow-up questions (all associated with messianic expectations). The Baptist's emphatic use of "I" implies the avowal that another was the Christ. Throughout the following verses, this emphatic "I" occurs frequently, and almost invariably implies a contrast with Jesus, who is always given the higher place.

1:21. Art thou Elias? ... I am not. The Jews remembered that Elijah had not died (see 2 Kings 2:11) and believed that the same prophet would come back to earth to announce the end time. In this sense, John properly denied that he was Elijah. When Jesus later said the Baptist was Elijah (see Matt. 11:14; 17:10–13), He meant it in the sense that John was a fulfillment of the prophecy of Malachi 4:5 (see Luke 1:17). **That prophet** refers to the prophet of Deuteronomy 18:15, 18. The Jewish people expected a variety of persons to be associated with the coming of the Messiah. The Baptist emphatically denied being "that prophet." He had come to testify about Jesus, yet they kept asking him about himself. His answers became progressively more terse.

1:22–23. The voice of one crying in the wilderness (v. 23). The Baptist applied the prophecy of Isaiah 40:3 to his ministry of calling people to repent in preparation for the coming of the Messiah. The men of Qumran (the community that produced the Dead Sea Scrolls) applied the same words to themselves, but they prepared for the Lord's coming by isolating themselves from the world to secure their own salvation. John concentrated on helping people come to the Messiah (the Christ). In 1:31, the Baptist expressly stated that the objective of his baptism was to reveal to Israel the Coming One.

1:24. Within Judaism, **the Pharisees** (see discussions on Matt. 3:7; Mark 2:16; Luke 5:17) were the conservative religious party and most influential among the people. Here they probed deeper than the rest of the delegation (see 1:19).

1:25. Christ (Greek) and "Messiah" (Hebrew) both mean "Anointed One." In Old Testament times, anointing signified being set apart for service, particularly as king (see 1 Sam. 16:1, 13; 26:11) or priest (see Exod. 40:13–15; Lev. 4:3). People were looking for not just an anointed one, however, but the Anointed One, the Messiah. The Pharisees appear to have associated baptism with initiation, an activity appropriate to one with a title. The Baptist, who refused all titles, saw his baptism as an anticipation of and preparation for the Messiah.

1:26–27. The Baptist responded to the question "Why baptizeth thou …?" (1:25) with a twofold answer that compared what he did and who he was with the one whom his ministry anticipated. First, the Baptist defined what he did: **I baptize with water** (v. 26). The Baptist was not just stating the obvious; he was inviting a comparison of his water ministry with a ministry greater than water (see Mark 1:7–8; Luke 3:16; Matt. 3:11). This impending ministry, which would supercede the Baptist's, belonged to none other than the Messiah. The Baptist alluded to this with the words **there standeth one among you, whom ye know not**, echoing a popular belief that

the Messiah would remain hidden until He was suddenly revealed (see 1:33). Second, the Baptist defined who he was with the description of a slave. How much greater was the Unknown One if the Baptist, who commanded the attention of the religious authorities, was no more important that His slave? Disciples would perform all sorts of service for their rabbis (teachers), but loosing their **shoe's latchet** (sandal thongs; v. 27) was expressly excluded. This was a menial and lowly task. Unloosing another's shoe's latchet was a prelude to footwashing (compare Peter's reaction to his Master, 13:4–8). The Baptist describes the greatness of Jesus by defining his worthiness as beneath that of a slave.

1:28. The site of **Bethabara** ("house of the ford," or crossing point) is not known, except that it was located on the east side of the Jordan.

1:29–30. The next day (v. 29). For the sequence of days enumerated by John, see discussion on 2:1. It would seem that the baptism of Jesus had already taken place. In 1:32–35, the Baptist recounted the event and the Spirit's revelation, which now allowed him to identify Jesus as **the Lamb of God**. Was the occasion of the Baptist's questioning also the occasion of Jesus' baptism (see 1:26)? In verse 30, John linked the events of the previous day with the Baptist's testimony ("bare record," 1:32, 34) to Jesus, who now approached. "Lamb of God" (v. 29) is an expression found in the Bible only here and in 1:36. Many suggestions have been made as to its precise meaning (e.g., the lamb offered at Passover, or the lamb of Isa. 53:7, of Jer. 11:19, or of Gen. 22:8). The expression seems to be a general reference to sacrifice, however, not the name for a particular offering. The Baptist was saying that Jesus would be the sacrifice that would atone for **the sin of the world**. A sacrifice was offered first for the individual (see Genesis 4), then for a family at Passover (see Exodus 12), and then for the nation on the Day of Atonement (see Leviticus 16). With Jesus' death, it would be broadened: He would be a sacrifice for the entire world.

1:31. I knew him not suggests that the Baptist was unable to identify the Messiah by appearance alone. John the Baptist, who lived "in the deserts till the day of his shewing unto Israel" (Luke 1:80), may not have known Jesus in a familiar sense. The words probably mean only that he did not know that Jesus was the Messiah until he saw the sign mentioned in 1:32–33.

1:32–33. The baptism of Jesus is not recorded in John, only recounted (for Jesus' baptism, see discussions on Matt. 3:15–17). The descent of the Spirit upon Jesus (v. 32) took place at His baptism according to all four gospels (see Matt. 3:16; Mark 1:10; Luke 3:22). The perfect tense "I have seen" is not apparent in the KJV's **I saw**, but it underscores the Baptist's testimony to the dwelling of the Spirit upon Jesus (**it abode upon him**), which John witnessed and which characterized Jesus' ministry. John baptized **with water** (v. 33), but Jesus would baptize **with the Holy Ghost**. If a specific event is intended by these words, the fulfillment was the sending of the Holy Spirit on the day of Pentecost (see Acts 2).

1:34. This is the Son of God (see 1:14, 18; 3:16; 20:31). Here the Baptist definitively bore witness to Jesus as the Son of God with a capstone statement that additionally pointed to the very purpose of this gospel (see 20:31).

B. Jesus' Introduction to Some Future Disciples (1:35–51)

1:35–37. Again the next day (v. 35) reveals an unfolding sequence of days (see 1:29, 35, 43; 2:1; for the possible importance of the pattern, see discussion on 2:1). The Baptist was **Again** there (**stood**) with **two of his disciples**. One was Andrew (see 1:40). The other is not named, but from early times, it has been thought that he was John, the author of this gospel. The two were his disciples in the sense that they had been baptized by John the Baptist and looked to him as their religious teacher. The Baptist again identified Jesus as **the Lamb of God** (v. 36; see discussion on 1:29) with the call to **Behold**, an interjection intended to draw the listeners' attention to what the speaker was about to say. From the disciples' response, the Baptist's intent seems to have been understood as a call to heed and not just ob-

serve, for the two **followed Jesus** (v. 37). Because "to follow" means to move behind someone in the same direction, it is also used figuratively of discipleship (see 1:43; 8:12; 10:4–5, 27; 12:26; 21:19–21). Here not only did the two disciples walk after Jesus, but their steps led to a shift in allegiance from the Baptist to Jesus.

1:38–40. Jesus asked the two, **What seek ye?** (v. 38), or "What are you searching for?" The question appears innocent enough, but more was at work here. The two deferentially called Him **Rabbi** (lit., "my lord" or "my master"), which John translated as **Master** (or "Teacher"), bringing together two important qualities of discipleship: devotion and instruction. One may infer that the two understood that Jesus was expressing more than a benign curiosity in the reason they were walking after Him. The invitation to **Come and see … where he dwelt** (v. 39; Greek, *menō*; also used for **dwellest** [v. 38] and **abode** [v. 39]) would gain deeper significance in Jesus' teaching on discipleship (see 12:26; chap. 15) and is anticipated here. Their stay with Jesus gave the two deeper insight into Him and caused **Andrew** (v. 40) to bring his brother Peter to Jesus (see 1:41–42). For **that day** (v. 39), see discussion on 2:1.

1:41–42. Andrew (see 6:8; 12:22) brought his brother Peter to Jesus based on insight he had gained from his stay with Jesus (see 1:39). Jesus' question, "What seek ye?" (1:38) is here answered: **We have found the Messias** (see discussion on 1:25). Both **Cephas** (Aramaic; v. 42) and Peter (Greek, *Petros*) mean "rock." In the Gospels, Peter was anything but a rock; he was impulsive and unstable. In Acts, he was a pillar of the early church. Jesus named him not for what he was but for what, by God's grace, he would become.

1:43–44. Jesus made His way **into Galilee** (v. 43) and called to **Philip … Follow me. Bethsaida** (v. 44; see discussion on Matt. 11:21) was **the city of Andrew and Peter** and Philip. Had Andrew, now joined by his brother Peter, influenced Jesus to travel to their hometown? The Greek does not specify the subject of what literally reads, "he decided to leave for Galilee." Carson (*The Gospel According to John,* pp. 157–58) argues that it was Andrew who made the decision. If so, this would reinforce a chain of witness and belief, showing that everyone who came to Jesus in 1:35–42 did so because of someone else's witness. On the other hand, the chain of witness (Baptist, Andrew, Peter, Philip, Nathanael), if broken by Jesus' intention to find Philip, does show Jesus to always be the common denominator of the faith that resulted. Each person in the chain had an encounter with Jesus.

1:45–46. Philip findeth Nathanael (v. 45) and said, **We have found him, of whom Moses in the law, and the prophets, did write** points notably to Deuteronomy 18:15–19 and a store of other references in what the prophets wrote. "The law, and the prophets" at that time denoted the Torah, the Jewish Bible. **Nazareth, son of Joseph** is a stock reference to a man in first-century Palestine by his village and lineage (see Carson, *The Gospel According to John*, p. 159) and is not a denial of the virgin birth of Christ (see Matt. 1:18, 20, 23, 25; Luke 1:35). Joseph was Jesus' legal, though not His natural, father. **Can ... any good thing come out of Nazareth?** (for "Nazareth," see 7:52; discussion on Matt. 2:23). Since Nathanael was from Cana (see 21:2), it has been suggested (see Brown, *The Gospel According to John*, p. 83; Carson, *The Gospel According to John*, p. 160) that the fault-finding question reflected a local rivalry between the nearby towns. Certainly Philip's testimony had created an expectation of Jesus that did not match His village and lineage.

1:47–49. Nathanael asked, **Whence knowest thou me?** (v. 48), and Jesus answered with a knowledge that showed His greater-than-human ability and fulfilled Philip's advanced billing of Jesus. A **fig tree** (v. 48) was known for its shade and was a favorite place for study and prayer in hot weather. In view of Nathanael's confession, Jesus' identification of Nathanael as **an Israelite indeed** (v. 47), or "truly an Israelite," becomes important. Athough "indeed" or "truly" is explained by the words **in whom is no guile** (or deceit), there appears to be an added significance. As the "true Israelite," Nathanael confesseed, **Rabbi, thou art the Son of God; thou art the King of Israel** (v. 49). The confession not only formed a faith acknowledgment of Jesus but harkened back (a literary inclusion) to the Baptist, whose testimony revealed to Israel that this was the Son of God (see 1:31, 34). Nathanael's confession thus provided John's readers a dependable confirming testimony that Jesus is the Son of God, the King of Israel, and served as a climax to the chain of witness starting with the Baptist. The title "the Son of God" (see 1:14, 18, 34; 3:16; 20:31) was later used in mockery (see 19:7; Matt. 27:40). "The King of Israel" (see 12:13) and "Christ" are equated in Mark 15:32.

1:50–51. Only the gospel of John records Jesus' use of the double **Verily, verily** (v. 51), which appears exactly twenty-five times in the book. This phrase signifies important sayings and carries the sense of firm or solemn conviction. Jesus addressed not only Nathanael (**saith unto him**) but also the other disciples present (**ye** is plural). **Ye shall see ... the angels ... ascending and descending upon the Son of man** alludes to a definitive moment in Israel's history when it was similarly revealed that Jacob was God's elect one and would be the progenitor of God's people (see Gen. 28:12 and discussion). Here the symbolism of angelic traffic between heaven and earth marked Jesus, the Son of Man, as God's elect one through whom redemption would come to the world, perhaps identifying Jesus as the true Israelite (see 1:47). Carson (*The Gospel According to John*, p. 164) puts it well: "Every Jew honoured Jacob/Israel, the father of the twelve tribes; now everyone must recognize that this same God has appointed Jesus as his Messiah." In Jesus' ministry, the disciples would see heaven's (God's) testimony to Jesus as plainly as audibly hearing an announcement from heaven concerning Him. "The Son of man" was Jesus' favorite self-designation (see discussions on Mark 2:10; Luke 19:10).

III. Jesus' Public Ministry: Signs and Discourses (chaps. 2–11)

A. Changing Water into Wine (2:1–11)

2:1–2. And the third day (v. 1) probably should be understood as the third day after the last event,

Jesus' meeting with Nathanael, placing the wedding and Jesus' first miracle on the seventh day. This accounting, based on the pattern of days numbered from the opening day at 1:19, is widely acknowledged, although opinions as to its significance vary. At minimum, the days of testimony to Jesus now culminated in a most important event: "This beginning of miracles did Jesus in Cana of Galilee, and manifested forth his glory; and his disciples believed on him" (2:11).

Cana (v. 1) is mentioned only in John's gospel (see 2:11; 4:46; 21:2). It was west of the Sea of Galilee, but the exact location is unknown. John expressly paired this first miracle, the wedding at Cana, with the second miracle (or "sign"; see discussion on 2:11) of Jesus in his gospel (compare 2:1, 11 with 4:46, 54).

Little is known of how a wedding was performed in the Holy Land in the first century, but clearly the feast was very important and might go on for a week. To fail in proper hospitality was a serious offense. Whether the invitation to **Jesus ... and his disciples** (v. 2; meaning the disciples of chap. 1) came from Jesus' mother or Nathanael, who lived in Cana (see 21:2), is not plain. It is more likely that it came from Mary, given her initiative in 2:3, and with it the sense of responsibility for the shortage of wine when Jesus and His disciples arrived. Whether the wedding was that of a relative is no more than a hunch, albeit not an inconceivable one.

2:3. When they wanted wine is more exactly translated, "when the wine was gone," indicating a shortage of what was required. The shortage was more than a minor social embarrassment, since the family had an obligation to provide a feast of the socially required standard. There was no great variety in beverages in that day, and people normally drank water or wine.

2:4 – 5. To address your mother as **Woman** (v. 4) sounds impersonal and rude to the modern ear. In that day, however, it was a polite form of address, and Jesus used it to address his mother (19:26), the Samaritan (4:21), the adulteress (8:10), and Mary Magdalene (20:13, 15). Even so, the address does not match what one would expect of a son to his mother. In a mother-child relationship, the distance

"woman" implies matches Jesus' question to Mary: **what have I to do with thee?** or literally, "what to me and to you?" This expression was not uncommon (see Mark 1:24; 5:7; Luke 8:28; Judg. 11:12; 1 Kings 17:18; 2 Kings 3:13; 2 Chron. 35:21) and could serve either to rebuke or to contest an obligation. Here Jesus introduced a higher obligation, that of His **hour**, which in this gospel pictures Jesus moving inevitably toward the destiny for which He had come: the time of His sacrificial death on the cross (see 7:6, 8, 30; 8:20). In this gospel, Jesus' use of the word "hour" (Greek, *hōra*; v. 4; also in 4:21, 23; 5:25, 28, 29; 7:30; 8:20; 12:23, 27; 13:1; 16:25, 32; 17:1) refers to more than a division of time as an hour of the day. Its meaning is shaped by the critical events of Jesus' death and resurrection, an incumbent period of Jesus' life when He was to leave this world and return to the Father (see 13:1), the hour when the Son of Man would be glorified (see 17:1).

In His reply to Mary, Jesus altered and redefined the normal expectations of a mother-child obligation. Mary's instruction to the servants reflect her acceptance: **Whatsoever he saith unto you, do it** (v. 5). Mary left the matter to Jesus. Did she expect a miracle? It is unlikely in view of 2:11. This was Jesus' first miracle.

2:6 – 7. Jews became ceremonially defiled during the normal circumstances of daily life and were cleansed by pouring water over the hands. For a lengthy feast with many guests, a large amount of water was required for this purpose. The word **containing** (v. 6) refers to capacity, not to actual content. These **waterpots of stone** could contain **two or three firkins apiece**, about twenty to thirty gallons each. The presence of these emblems of religious practice even in Galilee (**after the manner of the purifying of the Jews**) attests to the prominence of outward purification far and wide. Here the emblems were literally empty, and they would be transformed in value by Jesus, who appropriated them to provide an abundance of wine for the joyous occasion of a wedding.

2:8 – 10. Following Jesus' instructions, the waterpots were filled with water, and out of them a sampling was drawn for the approval of **the governor of the feast** (v. 8), or **the ruler of the feast** (v. 9; the same Greek word), identifying the one in charge of the banquet. His qualified evaluation was not only discriminating but impartial; he **knew not whence it was**. Had he known he was drinking from purification jars, he would never have tasted it. The sampling produced a call to the bridegroom, the one presumed responsible for the wine.

When men have well drunk (v. 10) is an indication not of drunkenness but simply of having consumed a lot of the particular beverage that was served. His remark attests to the clever custom of serving the superior wine before the inferior. Moreover, and without knowing it, he attested that the superior wine had been served last. Indeed, a new standard had been established, with implications for the transcending work of God in Jesus (see 2:11).

2:11. This beginning of miracles. Unlike the other gospel writers (Matthew, Mark, and Luke), John always used the Greek word for "signs" (Greek, *sēmeion*) to refer to Jesus' miracles, emphasizing the significance of the action rather than the marvel (see, e.g., 4:54; 6:14; 9:16; 11:47). Elsewhere (e.g., 2:18; 6:14, 30; 10:41), people emphasized the miraculous feature of a *sēmeion* when it signified and revealed insight to Jesus. These signs revealed Jesus' glory (see 1:14). The first sign, changing water into wine, thus had the same purpose that all the following signs would have: revelation about the true stature and person of Jesus.

Seven "signs" are listed in John's gospel: (1) changing water into wine (2:1–11), (2) healing an official's son (4:46–54), (3) healing the invalid at Bethesda (5:1–18), (4) feeding the five thousand (6:5–14), (5) walking on the water (6:16–21), (6) healing a blind man (9:1–7), and (7) raising Lazarus from the dead (11:1–45). A final miracle, though not specified as a "sign," involved the miraculous catch of fish (21:6–11).

B. Cleansing the Temple (2:12–25)

2:12. The city of **Capernaum** was on the shore of the Sea of Galilee (below sea level) and geographi-

cally at a lower level than Cana, which was in the hill country to the west. This cameo of Jesus with His mother, brothers, and disciples features an interval of **not many days** in which Jesus and His disciples enjoyed the company of His family. This historical detail brings before the reader the very human and very divine features of Jesus. This interlude links the events at the marriage in Cana and at the temple in Jerusalem and places side by side, almost at once, Jesus the son of His earthly mother and Jesus the Son of His heavenly Father. Jesus' **brethren** most likely were the children of Joseph and Mary, His half brothers (see discussion on Luke 8:19).

2:13. Passover (see *KJV Study Bible* notes on Exod. 12:11–23; discussions on Matt. 26:17, 18–30; Mark 14:1–2, 12; Luke 22:1; chart, *KJV Study Bible*, p. 92) was one of the annual feasts that all Jewish men were required to celebrate in Jerusalem (see Deut. 16:16). This is the first of at least three (and possibly four) Passovers noted in John's gospel (see 5:1 and discussion; 6:4; 11:55; 12:1; 13:1; 18:28, 39; 19:14). The chronology of Jesus' three-year ministry is based on the gospel of John and its attention to the Passovers. The other gospels only narrate one Passover in the life of Jesus.

2:14–17. Matthew, Mark, and Luke recorded a cleansing of the temple toward the end of Jesus' ministry (see discussion on Matt. 21:12–17). Jesus also began His ministry with such a cleansing.

Oxen and sheep and doves (v. 14) were required for sacrifices. Jews who came great distances had to be able to buy sacrificial animals near the temple. The merchants, however, were selling them in the outer court of the temple itself, the one place where Gentiles could come to pray. **Changers of money** were necessary (see discussion on Mark 11:15) because many coins had to be changed into currency acceptable to the temple authorities. They should not have been working in the temple itself, however.

From strands of rope lying about, Jesus fashioned a whip and drove out the merchants and livestock. He could not very well drive out the **doves** (v. 16), so He reproached the vendors. **House of merchandise** (Greek, *emporion*; "market," "emporium") identifies a marketplace and the moneymaking (buying and selling of goods) that had eclipsed the purpose of sacrificial offering and the sanctity of the temple. The disciples connected the authority of Jesus' action with Zechariah 69:9: **The zeal of thine house hath eaten me up** (v. 17).

2:18. The Jews (see discussion on 1:19), probably temple authorities of the Sanhedrin, **answered** Jesus' action with a request for a **sign** (Greek, *sēmeion*) to authorize His action in the temple. Jesus resisted such demands (see 6:30; Matt. 16:1). The authorities were looking for miraculous credentials to match the authority one presumed with such an act in the temple. There is probably a note of irony here, for John's use of the word *sēmeion* ("sign"), in contrast with the request, emphasizes the significance of a sign over the miracle itself, which is what Jesus gave them in His response (see 2:19). Jesus' answer alluded to a future miracle, His resurrection (see 2:19, 22), and to His ultimate authority over life and death (see 5:24–29).

2:19. The Jews thought Jesus was referring to the literal temple, but John made it clear that He was not (see 2:21). Just a few years later, Jesus was accused of saying that He would **Destroy** (the) **temple, and ... raise it up** again (see Matt. 26:60–61; Mark 14:57–59). Mockers repeated the charge as He hung on the cross (see Matt. 27:40; Mark 15:29). The same misunderstanding may have been behind the charge against Stephen (see Acts 6:14).

2:20–22. When therefore he was risen ... his disciples remembered (v. 22; see 14:26). Like the temple authorities, Jesus' disciples were thinking only in material terms at this point. The temple was not finally completed until AD 64. Work had been going on for **Forty ... six years** (v. 20). Since it had begun in 20 BC, the event recorded here occurred in AD 26 or 27.

2:23–25. This summary of Jesus' actions and the people's response during **the passover** (v. 23) feast (see discussion on 2:13), is closely connected with what follows. Jesus performed **miracles** ("signs," Greek, *sēmeion*), and people **believed in his name** (see 1:12; 3:18). In ancient times, an individual's "name" summed up his whole person, and here John used the characteristic expression "believed in" (or "on"), which is elsewhere used in the most positive sense of moving into a believing relationship with Jesus. Only with verses 23–24 does one become aware of some inadequacy in the people's belief and seek an explanation for Jesus' reservation to **commit himself**, or "entrust himself," to them. The reason is found in what Jesus knew. **He knew all men** (lit., "all" in the masculine gender), signifying His knowledge of the human heart. Initial "belief in" Jesus at this stage in His ministry may have been uninformed fascination, as the story of Nicodemus, who sincerely sought Jesus, illustrates (see 3:1–21). One should thus probably understand Jesus' response as "a general reference to having no confidence in their enthusiasm" (Brown, *The Gospel According to John*, p. 127) and read the conversation of Jesus with Nicodemus as an illustration (see 3:1–21). Nevertheless, just as the disciples had grown in their belief, Nicodemus appears to have grown in his (see 7:50; 19:39).

C. Interview with Nicodemus (3:1–21)

3:1–2. A man of the Pharisees (see discussions on Matt. 3:7; Mark 2:16; Luke 5:17), **named Nicodemus** (v. 1), probably witnessed the signs of Jesus during Passover (see 3:23), for he said, **for no man can do ... that thou doest, except God be with him** (v. 2). Nicodemus may have connected the miraculous actions of Jesus with the expected kingdom of God (see 3:3, 5; discussion on Matt. 3:2). He visited Jesus **by night** because he was afraid to come by day, or perhaps because he wanted a long talk, which would have been difficult in the daytime with the crowds around Jesus. Each time John introduced Nicodemus, he is identified by his night visit (see 7:50; 19:39).

3:3–4. Born again (v. 3) also means "born from above." The Greek word *anōthen* (here and in 3:7), with its double meaning of "again" and "from above," is important to the conversation between Jesus and Nicodemus. English translations must choose one or the other, but both meanings are in play. Nicodemus obviously understood Jesus in the first sense and quite literally, but he is presented as misunderstanding Jesus and failing to comprehend the second sense, the origin of this birth "from above." No one can **see** (or "enter"; see 3:5) **the kingdom of God** without this birth from above. The question of Nicodemus implies not only his incomprehension but also his sense of disqualification and disappointment: **How can a man be born when he is old?** (v. 4).

3:5–6. The phrase **born of water** (v. 5) has been understood in various ways: (1) It means much the same as "born of the Spirit" (3:8; see Titus 3:5). (2) "Water" here refers to purification (see 2:6). (3) "Water" refers to baptism, that of John (see 1:31) or that of Jesus and His disciples (see 3:22; 4:1–2). (4) "Water" refers to natural birth. Even as one is born of water, he must experience a second birth, a spiritual birth. Option 1 has much to commend it. "Born of water" must not be separated from **and of the Spirit**. On the strength of Jesus' parallel wording in 3:3 and the grammatical bond of the words "water" and "Spirit" (the Greek preposition "of" binds them together), "born from above" is the counterpart of "born of water and … Spirit" here. Only one birth is in view, not two. Moreover, the water-spirit bond has an Old Testament connection. If Jesus expected Nicodemus, a religious teacher (see 3:10), to understand His amplification and explanation in verse 5, one may look to the Old Testament, where water and spirit come together most forcefully in Ezkeiel 36:25–27 to denote the work from above that God does in people's hearts (see Carson, *The Gospel According to John*, pp. 191–96). Jesus went on to confirm this with His distinction between **flesh** (v. 6) and **Spirit**, a contrast of origin (human and superhuman).

3:7. Ye must be born again. This assertion applies to everyone, not just to Nicodemus (the Greek for "Ye" is plural here). "Must" makes it clear there are no exceptions. For **born again**, see discussion on 3:3.

3:8–10. The work of the Holy Spirit, superhuman and sovereign, is as real and as mysterious as **The wind** (v. 8) in the renewal of the human heart. Again there is a play on words or dual meaning at work. The word "wind" (Greek, *pneuma*; like English "pneuma-tic") is also the word for "Spirit" (*pneuma*).

As with the wind, one cannot fathom or control the Spirit, yet the effects are undeniable. The incomprehension of Nicodemus (**How can these things be?** v. 9) points to the very truth of Jesus: **so is every one that is born of the Spirit** (v. 8). Nicodemus had to be born from above to understand, for these truths are spiritually appraised. In chiding Nicodemus, Jesus made a case in point out of the **master** ("teacher") **of Israel** (v. 10).

3:11–13. The plural **We** (v. 11), on the face of it, associated others, perhaps the disciples, with Jesus. It may also be the case, and likely is, that Jesus was employing "we" as Nicodemus used it in 3:2, representatively. In saying, **ye receive not our witness** (for "witness," see discussion on 1:7), Jesus further strengthened the contrast between the earthly (elementary), which the teacher of Israel could not comprehend, and the heavenly, which he longed to understand. **No man hath ascended … but he that came down from heaven** (v. 13) points to Jesus' unique and unparalleled qualification to speak of heavenly things. In other words, no one has been up but He who came down: Jesus. Jesus is the heavenly man, **even the Son of man which is** ("dwells") **in heaven**, whom the Jews associated with residence in heaven. "The Son of man" was Jesus' favorite self-designation (see discussions on Mark 2:10; Luke 19:10), and in the gospel of John, it emphasizes Jesus as the heavenly one who descended and revealed the Father (see 1:18).

3:14–15. As Jesus had just identified Himself with the heavenly Son of Man, He now revealed that He must **be lifted up** (v. 14; see discussions on 12:31–32), even **as Moses lifted up the serpent** (see Num. 21:4–9). Jesus was alluding to His crucifixion and being lifted up on the cross. The primary connection to the action of Moses and the bronze serpent on a pole is that of being lifted up for the sake of salvation. Just as the people looked in faith to that serpent, so must they look to Jesus or perish. **Eternal life** (v. 15) is an infinitely high quality of life in living fellowship with God, both now and forever. By contrast, **perish** suggests eternal death and the specter of being forever cut off from God.

It may be that verse 15 concludes the conversation between Jesus and Nicodemus and the words of John begin again.

3:16–17. God so loved the world (v. 16) is the great truth that motivated God's plan of salvation (see 1 John 4:9–10). In English, "so" can suggest quality ("in this way") and quantity ("so much"). Although the Greek word emphasizes "in this way," the way in which God loved suggests "so much." "World" identifies all people on earth, or perhaps all creation (see discussion on 1:9–10). For **only begotten Son**, see 1:14, 18 (see also Gen. 22:2, 16; Rom. 8:32). Although believers are also called "sons of God" (see 1:12; 2 Cor. 6:18; Rev. 21:7), Jesus is God's Son in a unique sense; sons by adoption do not become members of the Godhead. The divine purpose of God's love in sending His Son (**that whosoever believeth … have everlasting life**) is restated (**that the world through him might be saved**; v. 17). A comparison of the wording brings to the forefront the importance of belief in Jesus and His agency.

3:18–21. Here John was not speaking of momentary beliefs and doubts but of continuing, settled attitudes. The person who refuses to believe in Jesus stands **condemned already** (v. 18) by virtue of his or her refusal. **Darkness** (v. 19) is John's expression for the condition of a perishing world in which evil is compounded by self-rule and rejection of God. The **light** of God, Jesus Christ, **is come into the world** to intervene and offer deliverance. People who cling to the darkness and to that which is condemned (see 3:17) reject the light and will perish (see 3:16). Conversely, what is **wrought in God** (v. 21) shows its origin in the truth that operates in the light and demonstrates its difference from the darkness by gravitating to the light.

D. Parallel Ministry with John the Baptist (3:22–4:3)

3:22. And baptized. According to 4:2, only the disciples baptized; Jesus did not.

3:23. The location of **Aenon** is unclear. Possibly, it was about eight miles south of Scythopolis (Bethshan), west of the Jordan.

3:24. John offered a brief explanation of the presence of John the Baptist. For the reason the Baptist was imprisoned, see Luke 3:19–20.

3:25. Purifying. Many viewed baptism as a ceremonial purification, and proper purification was a matter of great concern to some Jews (see, e.g., Mark 7:1–5). The religious authorities had questioned John about his baptism (see 1:25), and such differences of opinion may have led to that interrogation.

3:26. The Baptist's disciples knew that he had testified about Jesus, but they loved their master and were envious of Jesus' success. For **barest witness**, see discussion on 1:7.

3:27. Except it be given. These words were true of both Jesus and John (and of everyone). Both had what God had given them, so there was no place for envy. The Greek for "to give" is used frequently in this gospel (seventy-five times), especially of the things the Father has granted or entrusted to the Son. **Heaven** is frequently a respectful substitute for "God."

3:28–30. The bridegroom (v. 29) is the most important man at a wedding. It refers here to Jesus, **the Christ** (v. 28), and alludes to the Baptist's testimony that he was not the bridegroom but rather the best man. It is the function of **the friend** (the best man; v. 29) to handle the marriage arrangements and to help the bridegroom, which describes the role of John the Baptist. Customary was the joyous delight of the best man, enough so that the Baptist could compare his disposition toward Jesus to the wedding experiences of his disciples. The best man was known to **rejoiceth greatly** at the arrival of the groom and would then turn **the bride** over to the him. At that point, the friend would **decrease** and the groom would **increase**. Similarly, John the Baptist had been sent to prepare the way for the Messiah, and here he reaffirmed his subordinate position and joy in the role that God had granted him.

3:31–36. Here John (the author) apparently reflected on Jesus' distinguishing characteristics, with comparisons to John the Baptist and themes from the entire chapter as background.

3:31. Jesus **cometh from above** (Greek, *anōthen*; see discussion on 3:3) and is of heavenly origin, which puts Him above people and things of earth. **Earth** (Greek, *gē*) and **earthly** emphasize finite limitation; unlike *kosmos* ("the world"; see discussion on 1:10), these words lack John's insinuation of sinfulness. They could apply to anyone, but here they particularly refer to John the Baptist.

3:32–33. Jesus spoke from divine experience **what he hath seen and heard** (v. 32; see 3:11–13). **No man** means not that no person accepted what Jesus said (see v. 33) but rather that people in general refused His teaching (see 3:11). Those who **received** (accepted) **his testimony hath set to his seal** (v. 33), or "certified," the truth that Jesus came from heaven and that God was acting in Him for the world's salvation. That reception thereby certified not only that Jesus is truthful but also that God is truthful. John repeatedly stated that to believe in Jesus is to believe in God because Jesus reveals the Father, and nothing but what the Father has shown Him and told Him (see 5:19–30; 6:37–40; 8:29).

3:34–36. He whom God hath sent speaketh the words of God (v. 34). Communication in the ancient Mediterranean world depended on reliable messengers. Jesus was more than a messenger, however; He was an authorized agent, able to transact business as well as to deliver messages. In the Jewish institution of agency, the authority of the agent is defined this way: the one sent is as the one who sends. Moreover, Jesus is a unique agent in that He is the Son of the one who sent Him (similar to the householder's son in Matt. 21:33–39). John set out the credentials of Jesus' agency: (1) He has been given the Spirit without **measure**. (2) He is the beloved **Son** (v. 35). (3) **The Father … hath given all things into his hand**, which in Jewish law indicated right of ownership to legally transact business (see also 13:3). In view of these credentials, the offer of eternal life is guaranteed. Jesus is fully authorized to speak for God and act for God. **Everlasting life** (v. 36) is a present possession, not something the believer will obtain only later (see discussion on 3:15). Conversely, **the wrath of God** also is guaranteed. This is a strong expression meaning that God is actively opposed to everything evil. The word "wrath" occurs only here in John's gospel (see discussion on Rom. 1:18). The offer of life is held out in Jesus, and for one who rejects it, the wrath of God **abideth on him**. One may put God out of mind, but John made it clear that God's wrath does not eventually fade away. His opposition to evil is both total and permanent.

4:1–3. The gospel record of partisan Jewish views about ceremonial purity and baptism (see 1:25; 3:22–23, 24–26) offers a hint as to why the baptisms conducted by Jesus' disciples attracted the interest of **the Pharisees** (v. 1). The religious leaders took a close interest in John the Baptist (see discussion on 1:24) and then also in Jesus. The disciples did not baptize without Jesus' approval (see 3:22) and quite possibly baptized in Jesus' name (under His authority). Success in baptizing many disciples (which aroused opposition; see 7:1), as well as God's timetable (see 4:4), was why Jesus **left Judea** (v. 3) and went **again into Galilee**. It was in Galilee that most of Jesus' work was done.

E. Journey through Samaria: The Woman at the Well (4:4–42)

4:4. Must needs go through Samaria expresses a necessity that lay in Jesus' mission, not in the geography. Jews often avoided Samaria by crossing the Jordan and traveling on its east side (see discussions on Matt. 10:5; Luke 9:52). To proceed through Samaria was the direct route to Galilee, but Jesus' necessity to travel through this region apparently was due to spiritual opportunities that demanded His presence. According to Josephus (*Life* 52§269), it took three days to travel from Jerusalem (in Judea) to Galilee by way of Samaria.

4:5. Sychar was a small village near Shechem (see Map 11, p. 2149). Jacob bought some land in the vicinity of Shechem (see Gen. 33:18–19), not far from Mount Gerizim, and it was apparently this land that he gave to Joseph (see Gen. 48:21–22).

4:6. At **about the sixth hour** (reckoned from sunup), or about 12:00 noon, Jesus, fatigued from the journey and the midday heat, **sat thus on the**

well, a detail suggesting that the shaft of the well was protected by stone blocks. For all of Jesus' divinity, John was equally at ease with recording His humanity. **Jacob's well** is mentioned nowhere else in Scripture, but modern identification of the well agrees with John's detail. Its depth of approximately one hundred feet corresponds to the words of the Samaritan woman in 4:11.

4:7–9. A woman of Samaria (the region and not the city, which was further north; v. 7) came to **draw water** at noon (see 4:6). People normally drew water earlier or later in the day to avoid the midday heat (see Gen. 24:11 and discussion), but the practice of drawing water at midday is attested by Josephus, who says that the young ladies whom Moses helped (see Exod. 2:15–17) came to draw water at noon. Even so, the Samaritan woman came alone rather than with other women, as was common. Her solitary presence may reflect a loss of social acceptance owing to her many alliances with men; even her current one was not her husband (see 4:16–18).

Give me to drink (v. 7). A weary traveler asking for a drink was not unusual. What surprised the woman was that Jesus, being a Jew (see v. 9), was not deterred by the social and religious liabilities, so obvious to her, of His association with "a woman of Samaria" (v. 7). Issues of hereditary pedigree and theological purity divided the two peoples and resulted in deep-seated historical prejudice. Jesus broke the mold, and His uncharacteristic request intrigued her. The woman knew well that the Jews viewed all Samaritans as unclean. The Greek words translated **have no dealings with** imply "do not use dishes Samaritans have used." A Jew would become ceremonially unclean if he used a drinking vessel handled by a Samaritan. This meaning squares with verse 8 and the "dealings" of the disciples with the Samaritans to purchase food.

4:10. Jesus implied that the woman lacked knowledge of **the gift of God** and the identity of **who it is that saith to thee, Give me to drink**. Otherwise, she would have been the one asking for water, **living water**. "The gift of God" (only here in the gospel of John) has been variously understood. Two strong possibilities

are (1) Jesus Himself (see 3:16) and (2) the Torah (the Pentateuch, revered by both Jews and Samaritans). Knowing the identity of Jesus functions a little differently in each case, however. If, on the one hand, Jesus is the gift, then knowing His identity functions as a repetition tying His very presence to the wonderment of God's gift and an expectancy of things divine. If, on the other, Torah is "the gift of God" (a description used in Judaism), then knowing the identity of Jesus (Messiah) would be an additional piece of knowledge. In other words, if she had the combined knowledge of the Torah and the identity of Jesus as Messiah, she would have asked Him for a drink of living water, for together, Torah and the presence of Messiah points to the fulfillment of Deuteronomy 18:18. Both have much to commend them, but the latter has the advantage of addressing the Samaritan expectation of a prophet like Moses (see Deut. 18:15–18), and that expectation of prophet and Messiah surfaced later in the conversation (see 4:19, 24–25).

The "living water" (or "flowing water," a dual meaning) that springs from a fountain is preferable to the standing water of a cistern. Jesus would make it clear that He is the fountain, the source of water far superior to that of a cistern like Jacob's well (see 4:12–14). In 7:38–39, "living water" is explained as meaning the Holy Spirit, but here it refers to eternal life (see 4:14).

How dramatic is the contrast between the status of this woman, whom Jesus met at midday, and that of Nicodemus (see 3:1–21), whom Jesus met at night. The two are polar opposites, and almost back-to-back in John's account, they together show the inner reality of human need and the truth that Jesus knows the inner person (see 2:25).

4:11. In the arid setting, the woman could only entertain one source of water, **the well**, in the midst of her conversation with Jesus. Christian pilgrim sources as early as the fourth century mention a well in this area that was about 100 feet deep. When the well was cleaned out in 1935, it was found to be 138 feet deep.

4:12–13. Art thou greater than our father Jacob? (v. 12) is a question that in Greek expects a negative answer. Respect for the past and the prized provision of the patriarch prevented the woman from seeing the great opportunity of the present. For her to conceive of Jesus as greater than their founding father, He would have to produce a water unlike that upon which they had depended since the time of Jacob himself. Her response led Jesus to underscore her point: she had to depend on that water, because as often as she came to the well, she would always **thirst again** (v. 13; see 4:15).

4:14–15. Jesus offered the Samaritan woman a water that perpetually satisfies one's thirst. This variety of water quenches the imbiber because it produces an internal and eternal fountain **springing up** (v. 14) that never runs dry. The expression is a vigorous one, with a meaning like "leaping up." Jesus was speaking of vigorous, abundant life (see 10:10). Compare her misunderstanding with that of Nicodemus (see 3:4). In both cases, the way was opened for further instruction.

4:16–18. Jesus had already bridged gaping social and religious divisions to offer this woman "living water" (4:10). Now He needed to cross the personal barriers she had erected to guard her heart and conceal her shame. The woman could not, however, protect her past from Jesus, who knows what is in a person (see 2:25), and His knowledge of her would lead to her recognition of Him (see 4:29). When Jesus touched on the subject of her marital status with His invitation **Go, call thy husband** (v. 16), her response was preemptory: **I have no husband** (v. 17). Her truth was not the whole truth. What she concealed, Jesus revealed: **For thou hast had five husbands** (v. 18). The Jews held that a woman might be divorced twice or at the most three times. If the Samaritans had the same standard, at best the woman's past had certainly been marked by unquestionable troubles and questionable morality.

4:19–20. In calling Jesus **a prophet** (v. 19), the woman acknowledged His special insight. The reason she diverted the focus from her personal life to a long-standing and divisive religious debate over the proper place **to worship** (v. 20) was mixed. She may have wished only to change the subject, but she may

have also wanted to test His prophetic power and status (see 4:25). Samaritans held that **this mountain** (Mount Gerizim; see Map 11) was especially sacred. Abraham and Jacob had built altars in the general vicinity (see Gen. 12:7; 33:20), and the people had been blessed from this mountain (see Deut. 11:29; 27:12). In the Samaritan Scriptures, Mount Gerizim (rather than Mount Ebal) was the mountain on which Moses had commanded an altar to be built (see Deut. 27:4–6). The Samaritans had built a temple on Mount Gerizim circa 400 BC, which the Jews destroyed circa 128 BC. Both actions, of course, increased hostility between the two groups.

4:21. Woman (see discussion on 2:4) was a polite form of address and was in no way disrespectful. Jesus asserted that her question, although not irrelevant, was shortsighted. Jesus pointed her beyond the present to a time when worship would not be enhanced nor thought proper by virtue of its location. For the Samaritan woman, the word **hour** would have conveyed little more than an indication of a time in the future. The reader of John's gospel, however, knows that it bore a special meaning for Jesus and signified the world-altering events of His death, resurrection, and exaltation (see discussion on 2:4), which would inaugurate that time. Jesus characteristically called God **Father**, and strikingly so in the gospel of John. Whereas the Old Testament identifies God as Father only rarely (15 times), in the gospel of John, God is called Father 119 times, and 96 of them in the words of Jesus Himself.

4:22. The Samaritan Bible contained only the Pentateuch. Although Samaritans worshiped the true God, their failure to accept much of His revelation meant that they knew little of Him. They were therefore ignorant not only of the rich fund of prophetic revelation heralding God's promised salvation but also that the Messiah would be a Jew. Accordingly, **salvation is of the Jews**, for "unto them were committed the oracles of God" (Rom. 3:2).

4:23–24. The hour cometh (v. 23) recalls Jesus' earlier declaration that "ye shall neither in this mountain, nor yet at Jerusalem, worship the Father" (4:21). Standing logically on this declaration, Jesus now emphasized the reality that would come into effect when that hour arrived and its present impetus (**and now is**): the Father desires **worship ... in spirit and in truth** from **true worshippers**. True worship must be in keeping with God's nature, which is spirit. The KJV mars the Greek emphasis on God's nature or essence as spirit. The grammatical construction is qualitative and should be translated "God is spirit" rather than **God is a spirit** (v. 24). The KJV's "in spirit and in truth" (vv. 23, 24) suggests two elements to true worship, but the Greek has one preposition ("in") governing the two nouns (as in 3:5) and is equivalent to "the Spirit of truth" (14:17, 15:26; 16:13). This serves as a clue to the nature of true worship; it corresponds not only to the nature of God, who is spirit, but also to the coming of the Spirit, the endowment of God whose coming belonged to the hour of Jesus' death, resurrection, and exaltation (see 7:37–39; 14:26; 15:26, see also 3:6, 34).

4:25. The Samaritan woman's last attempt to evade the issue came with an appeal to the **Messias** (see discussion on 1:25) **... he will tell us all things**. The matter was too important, she reasoned, for people like Jesus and herself to work out. Understanding would have to await the coming of the Messiah. The Samaritans expected a Messiah, but their rejection of all the inspired writings after the Pentateuch meant that they knew little about Him. They thought of Him mainly as a teacher.

4:26. With the words **I ... am he**, Jesus told the Samaritan woman that the Messiah to whom she would defer the issue was none other than the one to whom she was talking. Now she knew the identity of Jesus and "who it is that saith to thee, Give me to drink" (4:10), the very one who could supply her with "living water" (4:10). This was the only occasion before His trial on which Jesus specifically said that He was the Messiah (but see Mark 9:41). The term "Messiah" did not have the political overtones in Samaria that it had in Judea, which may be part of the reason Jesus used the designation here, although He was also speaking to the woman privately.

4:27. His disciples ... marvelled that he talked with the woman. Jewish religious teachers rarely spoke with women in public, and with the continuous tense (Greek imperfect), John reported the sustained surprise of the disciples. The questions the disciples swallowed and never voiced illustrate the need-centered love of Jesus that looks beyond custom, culture, race, and gender.

4:28–30. Upon hearing Jesus say that He was the Messiah, **the woman left her waterpot, and went ... into the city** (v. 28) to tell others. Why did John report this small detail? Brown (*The Gospel According to John*, p. 173) suggests it was John's way of emphasizing the waterpot's uselessness for the living water that interested her. Also, leaving her waterpot is reminiscent of the disciples leaving their nets to follow Jesus (see Matt. 4:20; Mark 1:18). What had preoccupied them lost its commanding interest upon their recognition of Jesus. Her haste corresponds to her eager interest in broadcasting her discovery. The woman's testimony (**all things that ever I did**) was an exaggeration, but it shows the impression Jesus made on her. **Is not this the Christ?** Her question seems full of longing, as though she did not expect the people to say yes, but she could not say no.

4:31–33. This misunderstanding is similar to that of the woman (see 4:15). The disciples, presumably sent by Jesus to buy food (see 4:8), now returned to the once weary and thirsty Jesus (see 4:6–7). Jesus had been energized by provisions they could only assume were like those that they went to purchase. Once again, the theme of heavenly versus earthly determined the disciples' mindset and confusion.

4:34. My meat (Greek, *brōma*; "food," "that which is eaten") **is to do the will of him that sent me** (see Matt. 4:4). John often mentioned that Jesus depended on the Father and did the work that the Father sent Him to do (see, e.g., 5:30; 6:38; 8:26; 9:4; 10:37–38; 12:49–50; 14:31; 15:10; 17:4).

4:35. There are yet four months, and then cometh harvest apparently was a proverb that meant something like, "Harvest cannot be rushed." Crops take time to ripen, but in **the fields** to which Jesus referred, the harvest was already ripe (see Matt. 9:38).

4:36. Receiveth wages implies that the work, or at least part of it, had been done, and others were working hard. The disciples were not to think that the harvest was far off. Jesus was speaking not of grain but of **fruit unto life eternal**. There was urgency, for the crop would not wait. Joint effort brings joint rejoicing. There is no competition among Christ's faithful servants, and sower and reaper share in the joy of the crop.

4:37. For **One soweth, and another reapeth**, see 1 Corinthians 3:6–9.

4:38. Other men may refer to John the Baptist and his supporters, on whose work the apostles would build. Perhaps Jesus was looking further back, to the prophets and other godly men of old. Either way, He expected the apostles to be reapers as well as sowers.

4:39–42. The Samaritan woman's testimony brought many to belief in Jesus, and **his own word** (v. 41) brought **many mo[r]e**. Although this contrast records the unequal strength of their respective "words" and the superiority of a direct encounter with Jesus, it would be a mistake to overlook the confirmation of the woman's testimony to Jesus: **this is indeed the Christ** (v. 42). What the people found in Jesus was a confirmation of her testimony to Jesus. In the New Testament, the expression **the Saviour of the world** occurs only here and in 1 John 4:14. It points to the facts (1) that Jesus not only teaches but also saves and (2) that His salvation extends to the world (see discussion on 3:16).

F. Healing of the Nobleman's Son (4:43–54)

4:43–45. After two days (v. 43) in Samaria, Jesus resumed His journey north to Galilee (see 4:1–3). John clarified that Jesus did not go to Galilee for honor. Indeed, Jesus testified that **a prophet hath no honour in his own country** (v. 44). Nonetheless, Jesus went to Galilee, because He came to die for our salvation (see 1:29).

4:45–47. The welcome of **the Galileans** (v. 45) actually was a kind of rejection, for they were interested only in his miracles (see 4:48). They were welcoming not the Messiah who could save them but only a miracle worker who could amaze them. Nevertheless, news of the arrival of this miracle worker, known to those from Galilee who had seen what Jesus **did at Jerusalem** over Passover, piqued the

interest of **a certain nobleman** (v. 46) whose little boy (Greek, *paidion*) was very sick. The "nobleman," or royal official (Greek, *basilikos*; "of the king"), was evidently an officer or advisor in Herod's service.

4:48. Except ye see signs and wonders, ye will not believe reveals the general attitude of the Galileans who had flocked to Jesus, not that of the official. "Signs [Greek, *sēmeion*] and wonders [Greek, *teras*]" connoted authenticating miracles associated with God's great deliverance of the Jews out of Egypt (see, e.g., Deut. 6:22; Neh. 9:10; Jer. 32:20) and were expected to be met with belief. Jesus looked for belief that was not conditioned on a steady diet of the miraculous.

4:49–50. The nobleman **believed the word** (v. 50) of Jesus in advance of seeing its miraculous fulfillment. **Thy son liveth** was not simply a prophecy but a powerful pronouncement. Jesus was healing the little boy with these words, not forecasting a happy ending (see 4:51, 53). The man believed; he took Jesus at His word, believed what Jesus said about his little boy, and turned to go home.

4:51–53. It was no happy coincidence that the boy's **fever left him** (v. 52). The effect and the cause corresponded to the time of Jesus' pronouncement: **the seventh hour**, or 1:00 p.m. Not only did the nobleman rightly attribute the break in the little boy's fever to Jesus, but his household did too. That he **believed** (v. 53) implies that he believed Jesus was more than a miracle worker (see the aim of this gospel in 20:31).

4:54. The second miracle was hardly the second of only two. There had, of course, already been many such miracles (see 2:23; 3:2), but this was the second time Jesus performed a miracle after coming from **Judea into Galilee**. The numbering of this miracle as a "sign" (see discussion on 2:11) also shows John's focus on the purpose of such miracles: to bring about belief in the person of Jesus.

G. Trip to Jerusalem for an Annual Feast (chap. 5)

5:1. After this (lit., "after these things") is an indefinite expression (see 6:1; 7:1), and given the context, it suggests "some time later." In 4:46, Jesus was in Cana of Galilee. Now **a feast of the Jews** had brought Jesus to Jerusalem. One can only surmise the passage of some time. "A feast of the Jews" probably refers to one of the three pilgrimage feasts to which all Jewish males were expected to go: Passover, Pentecost, and Tabernacles. The identity of this feast is significant for the attempt to ascertain the number of Passovers included in Jesus' ministry and thus the number of years His ministry lasted. John explicitly mentioned at least three different Passovers: the first in 2:13, 23 (see discussion on 2:13), the second in 6:4, and the third several times (e.g., in 11:55; 12:1). If three Passovers are accepted, the length of Jesus' ministry was between two and three years. If, however, the feast of 5:1 was a fourth Passover or assumes that a fourth Passover had come and gone, Jesus' ministry would have lasted between three and four years.

5:2. Note the wording **there is** rather than "there was." This may mean that the **pool** was still in existence at the time this was written, that is, that John wrote before the destruction of Jerusalem (AD 66–70). This falls short of proving the time of writing, however (see Introduction: "Date"). More likely, John used the present tense as a literary expression to vividly recount past events. The manuscripts have a variety of names for **Bethesda** (e.g., Bethzatha and Bethsaida), but one of the Dead Sea Scrolls seems to show that Bethesda is the right name. **By the Sheep Gate** (rather than **sheep market**) likely indicates the narrow entrance where sheep were brought to the temple for sacrifice. The site is generally identified with the twin pools excavated near the present-day Saint Anne's Church, where colonnades correspond to the five porches (v. 2).

5:3–4. Waiting for the moving of the water (v. 3). Some manuscripts do not have this phrase or verse 4, but these verses explain why people waited by the pool in large numbers: **For an angel went down ... into the pool** (v. 4). This picture of desperate hope underscores the dire condition of those who waited, many without success (see 5:7). While others were preoccupied with the feast, Jesus was preoccupied with people not far from the festivities but forgotten and lying in a pathetic state.

5:5–7. John did not record what the man's **infirmity** (v. 5) was, but judging from Jesus' command, "Rise ... and walk" (5:8), it was a form of paralysis or at least lameness. That **Jesus saw ... and knew** (v. 6; see 2:23) matched His extraordinary offer: **Wilt thou be made whole?** He who has the power to heal also has the power to see and know what others do not. The question was important. The man had no means of getting to the water, and his answer to Jesus may have harbored the hope that, if He truly cared as His question implied, Jesus Himself would help him to the water. Clearly, the man did not see Jesus as his healer, and the question led his mind only to the water and the supposed place of God's power to cure. In healing the man, Jesus demonstrated where the power of God is truly located.

5:8–9. Rise, take up thy bed, and walk (v. 8; see Mark 2:11) is the evidence of the man's healing (**immediately the man was made whole**; v. 9). Without uttering a word in reply, a man debilitated thirty-eight years (see 5:5) by physical malady and discouraged hope was made whole; he needed only to "stand up ... and walk around" (as the Greek conveys). Ordinarily, faith in Jesus was essential to the cure (see, e.g., Mark 5:34), but this man did not even know who Jesus was (see 5:13). One can see the man's faith, however, in his obedience to Jesus' command. For at the word of Jesus, he attempted to do what on so many occasions he had surely tried and failed to do at the moving of the water: "Rise." The man "was made whole," not only sound but also robust. No physical therapy was necessary for his muscles and limbs withered by atrophy. The healing was complete. John, however, added a retrospective and repercussive note: **and on the same day was the sabbath** (v. 9).

5:10–11. Jesus had run afoul of the Sabbath law and up against **The Jews** (the religious authorities; v. 10; see discussion on 1:19) in performing this act of healing on **the sabbath** (see 5:9, 16, 18). They declared to the healed man, **it is not lawful for thee to carry thy bed**, and Jesus had commanded the man to do just that (see 5:8). The gravity of the violation was clear to the man, and he shifted responsibility to the one who had cured him. The Jews had very strict regulations on keeping the Sabbath. To "carry thy bed" belonged to the last of the thirty-nine classes of work prohibited on the Sabbath ("taking out aught from one domain to another," Mishnah, Shabbat 7:2). The Jews contested such a violation, however, not specifically by the law of Moses (see Exod. 20:8–11) but by application of the law that prohibited carrying loads of any kind on the Sabbath (see Jer. 17:21).

5:12–13. Then asked they him, What man is that …? (v. 12). The Jews were contrasting the authority of the law of God, which in their view prohibited the action, and that of a mere man (as they considered Jesus to be) who promoted it. Sadly, the marvelous and glorious healing of the disabled man was completely ignored. The violation and "What man" had endorsed it were all that occupied the attention of the religious authorities. Jesus was unknown to the man by name, and as suddenly as Jesus had come to the man, He **conveyed himself away** (v. 13) as the man walked around among the crowd that had assembled in the precincts of the temple for the feast of the Jews (see 5:1).

5:14–15. Later, in the temple area, **Jesus findeth** (present tense; v. 14) the man. The tense implies that Jesus was deliberately looking for him. More important than the man's physical need was his spiritual need. The sequence of what Jesus told him, **thou art made whole: sin no more, lest a worse thing come unto thee**, makes it clear that the spiritual well-being of the man was more important than the physical. A number of interpreters connect the man's infirmity to sin because of Jesus' command. There is not enough in the text to assure this conclusion, however. Certainly, Jesus did not accept this conclusion in the case of the blind man (see 9:2–3 and discussions; see also Luke 13:1–5). Although suffering (physical or emotional) ultimately may be traced to sin and the broken condition of a fallen world, here Jesus' command is in the present imperative, "stop sinning," pointing to a continuous issue of

the man's life and outlook toward God that had not been arrested or exhausted by either his infirmity or his healing. What Jesus was addressing in the man's life is not known. "A worse thing" points to the judgment of God rather than men (e.g., the Pharisees), and just as the man obeyed Jesus when he was told to "Rise" (5:8), there is no reason to believe he did not obey Jesus' additional command. Just as the man promptly obeyed Jesus at His command to rise (v. 8), the man now directly professed Jesus; he went away and **told** (Greek, *anangellō*; "proclaimed"; always positive in John; see 4:25; 16:13–15) the Pharisees **that it was Jesus, which had made him whole** (v. 15). One may infer that because of Jesus' command, God's authority over his life was given its rightful place, an authority mediated by "He that made me whole" (5:11), whom the man now proclaimed by name.

5:16. The authority of Jesus had been displayed to the man in his miraculous healing, in Jesus' command that trumped the Sabbath prohibition, and in His admonition to sin no more. In identifying Jesus to the religious authorities, this was the very authority the man claimed for carrying his bed on the Sabbath (see Talbert, *Reading John*, p. 123). Apart from any motive one may discern in the man, however, the religious authorities were now armed with the information they needed to prosecute Jesus. It should be noted that the word **persecute** (Greek, *diōkō*) may in this context mean "prosecute." John did not report what form the action took, but the continuous action of the Greek verb, **he had done**, points to more than one incident, and the Jews apparently discerned a pattern.

5:17. Without a shift in setting, John conveyed a verbal exchange between the authorities and Jesus over the Sabbath violation in which Jesus defended Himself. Not evident in English translation, the word **answered** (Greek, *apokrinomai*; middle voice; only here and 5:19), indicates a formal reply with legal overtones. Such a reply matches the implication of "prosecution" in 5:16. With this reply, Jesus offered a formal defense against the charge of questionable Sabbath activity by identifying His actions with the actions of His Father: **My Father worketh hitherto**. The Jews did not refer to God as "My Father," regarding the term as too intimate, though they might have used "Our Father" or, in prayer, "My Father in heaven." Jesus also exemplified the way the Sabbath should be observed. God does not stop His deeds of compassion on that day, and neither did Jesus.

5:18. The authorities understood well the implications of Jesus' defense: **he not only had broken the sabbath, but said also that God was his Father, making himself equal with God**. The Jews did not object to the idea that God is the Father of all, but they strongly objected to Jesus' claim that He stood in a special relationship to the Father, a relationship so close as to "mak[e] Himself equal with God." This indictment is ominous and was later formally called "blasphemy" (10:33) when Jesus was condemned to stoning, and it eventually fueled the punishment of crucifixion sought from Pilate (see 19:7).

5:19. Jesus again formally replied (see 5:17) and began an extended and uninterrupted defense against the leaders' charges, which now included blasphemy. **The Son can do nothing of himself**. Because of who and what He was, it was not possible for Jesus to act except in dependence on the Father who sent Him. Such dependence (see 5:30) and Jesus' emphasis that the Father had sent Him (5:23, 24, 30, 33, 36, 37, 38) pointed to His role not only as the Son but also as the agent of the Father's will. As Jesus' defense in this chapter reveals, because He is the beloved Son, He is the familial choice to act as the Father's agent, a legal form of representation. In the Jewish institution of agency, the one sent is as the one who sends, and the validity of Jesus' authority to act and transact business on behalf of the sender (the Father) rests on the fidelity of the agent (Jesus) to the will of the one who sent Him (see Introduction: "Theme and Theological Message"). The Jews charged Jesus with "making himself equal with God" (5:18). In Jesus' extended defense, again and again He emphasized that the "making" came from the Father and that the equality was not the maverick action of a man who would be equal with God, but was that of a beloved and fully authorized Son who

dutifully and dependently represented the will of the Father who sent Him.

5:20. Because **the Father loveth the Son**, He revealed to the Son His plans and purposes, and the Son obediently carried them out. Even **greater works** belong to the Father's purposes than have been attested to in the Sabbath healing of the lame man that brought the charges of the religious authorities to which Jesus now defends His actions (see vv. 14–18). As Brown (*John*, p. 2114) aptly puts it, "Physical healing ('life') is merely a sign of the power to give eternal life" (see, e.g., the Son's activities in raising the dead and judging in 5:21–29). The word "loveth" is the Greek word *phileō* (only here in the gospel of John), capturing the affection of any father for his son but here used of the divine relationship between God and Jesus.

5:21. That **the Father raiseth up the dead** was a firm belief among the Jews. They also held that He did not give this privilege to anyone else. Jesus claimed a prerogative that, according to His opponents, belonged only to God. **The Son quickeneth** probably refers to Christ's gift of abundant life here and now, though possibly also to the future resurrection (see 11:25–26).

5:22. Not only has the Father given Jesus the right of giving life (see 5:21); He **hath committed all judgment unto the Son**. The Jews believed that the Father is Judge of the world, so this teaching seemed heretical to them.

5:23. In legal terms, Jesus had claimed the right to act as the Father acts (5:17), not only because of His relationship as Son (see 5:19–20) but also because the Father has "given" (5:26–27; 3:35; 13:3) to Him God's quintessential rights as Life-giver and Judge (see 5:22–23, 26–27). As a defense, this not only explained but also justified Jesus' unity of action with the Father and Jesus' right to intervene between God and His creation. It brought to the forefront the importance of Jesus' obedience to the Father who sent Him, for He acted not alone but in concert with the Father's will. The honor that God deserves is therefore the honor that His Son deserves; the Son is His duly authorized representative.

5:24–25. Because Jesus possesses God's divine prerogatives (power and rights), not least of which are the rights of Life-giver and Judge (see 5:21–23), to hear His word and believe the one who sent Him is to pass from under judgment into eternal life. **Heareth** (v. 24) and **believeth** are not separate but rather twin actions because the word of Jesus is the word of the Father who sent Him (see 5:38). **Everlasting life** is a present possession (see discussion on 3:15). The decisive action (**is passed**) has taken place, and the believer no longer belongs to **death**. The words **is coming, and now is** (v. 25) clearly underscore that Christ gives life now. The spiritually dead who hear Him receive life from Him and do not come into judgment. There is no undoing of this action, and Jesus solemnized this promise with the words **Verily, verily.**

5:26–27. These two verses reiterate the authority of the Son in terms of the special prerogatives of God (Life-giver and Judge) He has been given (see 5:21–23). **Hath life in himself** (v. 26) must be understood against the background of the Old Testament, where life is spoken of as belonging to God and as being His gift (see, e.g., Deut. 30:20; Job 10:12; 33:4; Pss. 16:11; 27:1; 36:9). The Son has been given the same kind of life that the Father possesses (for the benefit to man, see 1 John 5:11). Here the Son is identified as **the Son of man** (v. 27; see discussion on 1:51).

5:28–29. Do not marvel at this (v. 28) refers to Jesus' claims of authority as life-giver and judge. The present exercise of His rights will have a corresponding and irreversible impact on the future raising of the dead. Existing Jewish notions of the final judgment and resurrection of the dead are subject to the **voice** of Him whom they now heard (see 5:24–25). As always in Scripture, judgment is on the basis of works, though salvation, of course, is a gift from God in response to faith (see 5:24).

5:30. In saying, **I can of mine own self do nothing,** Jesus again stressed His dependence on the Father (see discussions on 5:19, 23). He judges only as He hears from the Father, which makes His judgment not only fair but also a proof that His representation

as the Father's agent is valid and intact. Jesus had in no way violated the trust of His responsibility to act on the behalf of His Father. Again, in legal terms, He had not "[made] himself equal to God" (5:18) but rather had acted on the behalf of and in accordance with the representation of the Father's making. Jesus' representation was an equality of agency established by the will of the Father.

The correspondence of this verse and 5:19, the opening and closing of the first part of Jesus' defense, has been noted by numerous scholars. This is called an *inclusio* and serves to highlight the main line of Jesus' defense against the indictment of 5:18.

5:31–47. If Jesus' representation of the Father was disputed on the grounds that He had overreached the authority of His commission, the testimony of the Father, the one who sent Him, became vital to His defense. His testimony could not stand alone. This section stresses the testimonies (see discussion on 1:7) of John the Baptist (v. 33), of the works of Jesus (v. 36), of God the Father (v. 37), of the Scriptures (v. 39), and of Moses (v. 46). A close reading reveals that the testimony of the Father who sent Jesus was most important; He above all could verify that Jesus had been duly authorized to act on His behalf.

5:31–32. Another (v. 32) points to a greater testimony than that of Jesus (see 5:36), the testimony of the Father who sent Him. The Jews might not have accepted this testimony, but it was the testimony that mattered most.

5:33–34. Ye sent unto John (v. 33) refers to the delegation of representatives that the Jewish leaders sent to John the Baptist (see 1:19). The leaders therefore understood the tenets of representation. The representatives had acted under strict orders to question John and return with his testimony, and the leaders had received that testimony (see 1:19–23). The testimony of John was important, though not, of course, equal to the testimony of the Father. Had the Jews believed John, however, they would have believed Jesus and recognized His authority and the offer of salvation.

5:35. The past tense **he was** may indicate that John the Baptist was dead or at least imprisoned. In any case, his work was done. John himself was sent from the Father (see 1:6) and **was a burning and a shining** that the Jews themselves enjoyed **for a season**. John's giving light was costly to him. The Jewish leaders never came to grips with John's message, and their responses to him were always at best tentative and superficial.

5:36. The works refers to the authorized actions of Jesus, which testified to His true identity and to His divine mission (see 10:25). Since the actual testimony of the Father has been ambiguous to interpreters, proposals have pointed to (1) the Scriptures, (2) direct internal testimony, (3) the Torah, and (4) the word of the Father which He has given to Jesus and which Jesus gives to the world. In view of the agency of Jesus, the testimony of God can be nothing other than "the works" that Jesus performed, which testified that He had been commissioned and authorized as God's representative agent and Son (see 10:25, 36–38). Jesus' works, His words and deeds, realized what God the Father had commissioned Him to do. Because Jesus did not deviate from the will of His Father, nor act on His own, His works testified to their origin and source in the commission of God. Since the legal validity of Jesus' agency stood open to challenge, and the very fact of agency presumed that the Father was not accessible to offer direct testimony to the commission in question, the only way to demonstrate its validity was to argue on the presumptions of agency: because Jesus was faithfully executing His commission, the commission of the Father in fact remained valid. In this sense, the works themselves offered the direct testimony of the Father.

5:37–40. The Jews had never heard the very voice of God, but it found concrete expression in Jesus' works, which **hath borne witness of me** (v. 37; see 5:36) that **the Father ... hath sent me**. That they had **neither heard his voice at any time, nor seen his shape** underscored the history of God's representation upon which the Jews had depended for knowing God. Even that had failed. If they had **His word** (v. 38) in them, the correspondence between the Father's word from earlier representatives in Scrip-

ture and the word of Jesus would have led to belief. **Search[ing] the Scriptures** (v. 39) is not an end in itself. The Jewish leaders studied Scripture in minute detail. Despite their reverence for the very letter of Scripture (see discussions on Matt. 5:18–21), they did not recognize the one to whom Scripture bears supreme testimony.

5:41–44. In these verses, the ongoing issue of Jesus' valid representation of the Father is picked up in the opening disavowal, **I receive not honour from men** (v. 41). The word "honour" (Greek, *doxa*; "glory") points to the question of motive. The implication is that Jesus' enemies may have imagined He sought His own advantage or benefit, but Jesus' disavowal again pointed to His faithful pursuit of someone else's honor (advantage or benefit): that of the Father who sent Him (see 7:18). They did not have love for God in them because they dishonored (see 5:23) the one God had sent, the one who came **in [the] Father's name** (v. 43). To come in the name of someone is to function under the authority of the one named. A person's name is the quintessential token of his personal identity, his status, and his character. Jesus not only executed His commission in the Father's name but also shares the identity, status, and character of the name because He is not only the agent of God but also the Son of God ("I am," 8:58). When Jesus said, **if another shall come in his own name, him ye will receive**, He was stating that His opponents would accept anyone who came in his own authority because that one would function as their peer and not as their superior. In Jesus, God had a claim on them that they rejected. The question Jesus asked is rhetorical. The answer was clear already. They did not want to submit to God. They therefore rejected the one who came in His name. Their self-seeking honor (advantage and benefit) showed that they did not accept the one who came from God, and therefore they missed the advantage and benefit that comes from God.

5:45–47. Jesus' opponents prided themselves on their attachment to **Moses** (v. 45), their great lawgiver. It was thus an unexpected thrust for Jesus to say that Moses himself **accuseth** them before

God. Jesus came back to the testimony of Scripture (5:39): it is Moses, who wrote of Jesus, who will be the accuser of the Jews who reject Him. All the New Testament writers stressed or assumed that the Old Testament, rightly read, points to Christ (see Luke 24:25–27, 44). Jesus applied this truth specifically to the writings of Moses (see, e.g., discussion on Gen. 49:10; *KJV Study Bible* notes on Exod. 12:21; Lev. 16:5; Num. 24:17; Deut. 18:15).

What began with the accusation of Jesus, an indictment of blasphemy in 5:18, closes with the indictment of His accusers. Those who would prosecute Jesus on the basis of the law of Moses and the witness of the Scriptures found their star witnesses condemning them.

H. The Feeding of the Five Thousand and the Sermon on the Bread of Life (chap. 6)

6:1–14. The feeding of the five thousand is the one miracle, apart from the resurrection, found in all four gospels. It shows Jesus as the supplier of human need and sets the stage for His testimony that He is the bread of life (see 6:35). This was perhaps Jesus' greatest miracle, and it was witnessed by the largest number of people.

6:1. After these things (see 5:1 and discussion) is John's general notation indicating the elapse of time and events between what precedes and what follows. John drew a geographical connection between **the sea of Tiberias**, probably the official Roman name, and **the sea of Galilee**, the popular name. The name came from the town of Tiberias (named after the emperor), the capital city of Galilee founded circa AD 20.

6:2. The crowd **followed him** (vividly depicted in the present tense in the Greek)**, because they saw** more than once (imperfect active tense) **his miracles**. Here John again used *sēmeion*, "signs," to refer to Jesus' miracles (see discussion on 2:11). Indeed, the picture is one of a crowd eager to see more of the miraculous, but John's use of the word "signs" alerts readers to a deeper significance that the crowd was missing.

6:3. The **mountain** cannot be located with certainty, and its identity is of no importance in and of itself. The parallels that Jesus drew between Moses and Himself (see 6:31–32) and the reference to Passover (see 6:4) have prompted a symbolic allusion to Sinai as a constituent piece of the overall motif.

6:4. This is the second **Passover** expressly identified by John (for the chronological significance of this Passover, see discussion on 2:13). Here significance is attached to its nearness and Jesus' comparisons with Moses; the people's yearning for a new Moses and a new exodus was seasonally high.

6:5–7. Since **Philip** (v. 5) came from nearby Bethsaida (see 1:44), it was appropriate for Jesus to ask him, **Whence shall we buy bread …?** Brown (*The Gospel According to John*, p. 233) points out that the **great company** hardly could have been made up of pilgrims to the Passover feast since the Sea of Galilee was en route to Jerusalem and pilgrims would have carried their own provisions. There are subtle comparisons and contrasts between Numbers 11 and the actions of Jesus in this chapter, not least of which is the question Jesus posed here (compare Num. 11:13). Practically, the question begged for a supernatural solution to a human impossibility (clarified in 6:7–9). Jesus **knew what he would do** (v. 6) and used the question to draw out the impossibility of human ingenuity to meet the need. Philip quickly sized up the challenge. Not even **Two hundred pennyworth** (v. 7; the equivalent of as many days' wages), or denarii, could meet the demand, assuming that much bread was available. John reported that Jesus was testing (**prove**; v. 6; Greek, *peirazō*; "test" in a good sense, "tempt" in a negative sense) Philip to expose what he thought or how he would behave. Perhaps Jesus was not only looking for Philip to prove the impossibility of feeding the crowd but was also providing an opportunity for Philip to look to Him in faith.

6:8–9. Andrew (v. 8) explored the crowd for resources and located the equivalent of one lunch. The lunch of one person, and that of a child, was hilariously insufficient, **What are they among so many?** (v. 9), for Philip had just established the minimum bid of eight months' wages to provide food for the crowd (see 6:7). **Barley loaves** refers to cheap bread, the food of the poor. The **two small fishes** were probably dried and pickled for eating with bread.

6:10. The note that **there was much grass** indicates it was springtime. **About five thousand** does not include the women and children. Only the men were numbered, as Matthew made clear (Matt. 14:21). Consequently, one may easily imagine a number twice that.

6:11–13. Jesus gave **thanks** (Greek, *eucharisteō*; "praise," "thanks," "bless"; v. 11), acknowledging God; His focus was on praising the Father rather than on blessing the food. Jesus Himself **distributed to the disciples**, who then distributed the food to the people. **As much as they would** indicates there was more than enough bread and fish to satisfy their desire; **they were filled** (v. 12). **Gather up the fragments that remain** (see discussion on Mark 6:43) and the **twelve baskets** (v. 13) indicate not only that the surplus was ample but that more remained than was available at the start.

6:14. Once again, **the miracle** (Greek, *sēmeion*) was for John a "sign" (see discussion on 2:11). It pointed people to the Son of Man and the food for eternal life that He gives (see 6:27), but those who witnessed it thought of Him only as **that prophet** (see 1:21 and discussion), that is, the prophet of Deuteronomy 18:15 who would be like Moses. Through Moses, God had provided food and water for the people in the wilderness. They saw in Jesus a similar leader and provider.

6:15. Emboldened by Jesus' display of power, the crowd saw in Jesus the attributes necessary to displace the rule of Rome and its client king Herod. Convinced of this opportunity, the people had a mind to **take him by force, to make him a king**. Jesus wanted no part of such rebellion or such kingship. He rejected the world's version of kingship (see discussion on 18:36) as a temptation of the Devil (see Matt. 4:8–10). Jesus was sent by the Father to achieve not a political and temporal victory but a spiritual and eternal one. Jesus therefore went in another direction, going up **a mountain … alone**.

6:16–19. As the sun was setting, the disciples made their way **down unto the sea** (v. 16). Mark 6:46

reports that Jesus left the disciples to pray. Perhaps as Brown (*The Gospel According to John*, p. 251) suggests, the disciples were initially making their way to Capernaum, not far off the shore, hoping to spot Jesus. As darkness fell and the weather changed, however, they pushed on. The distance of **five and twenty or thirty furlongs** (v. 19) would have been about three or four miles. Mark reported that they were "in the midst of the sea" (Mark 6:47). Fighting the winds and making little progress, they saw a figure coming toward them, **walking on the sea**. John summed up the situation with the words **they were afraid**. All together, it was a very ominous state: the storm, the foreboding darkness, and an approaching figure that Matthew said the disciples thought was a ghost (see Matt. 14:26).

6:20–21. What sweet relief to hear the words of Jesus, **It is I; be not afraid** (v. 20). To know that Jesus was there was enough, but this natural form of self-identification has added meaning: "I am" (see 8:58; Exod. 3:14). When the disciples **received him into the ship** (v. 21), it was **immediately … at the land**, pointing to the presence of the Lord who commands the sea and all creation.

6:22–24. Here John narrated details bridging the events of the previous day and the setting of a significant discourse by Jesus on the Bread of Life. John made it clear that a number of people, enough to occupy a small flotilla, had remained the night in the vicinity of the feeding of the five thousand in the hope that Jesus would return. In the morning, unable to locate Him or figure out what had happened to Him, they boarded their small boats, crossed the lake, and looked for Him in the most likely place, **Capernaum** (v. 24). They found Him in the synagogue (see 6:59).

6:25–27. When camest thou hither? (v. 25). The question the people posed expressed more than curiosity about when and how Jesus had arrived. It implied that they thought Jesus was beholden to them. Indeed, His answer pointed to their demanding spirit. If the "signs" (**miracles**; v. 26; see discussion on 2:11), which revealed who it was that performed them, had motivated the people, they would have sought Jesus for who He was and not for what He could do for them. Rather, they wanted Jesus to satisfy their hunger over and over again. He is more than that. He is the giver of **everlasting life** (v. 27), **the Son of man** (see Mark 8:31), approved (**sealed**; see 3:33) by none other than **the Father**.

Labour (v. 27) implies the toil and unending endeavor that goes into acquiring daily bread, something the people believed Jesus could ease, if not eliminate. Like the contrast between well water and living water (see 4:10–15), Jesus was contrasting bread that must be earned and eaten over and over with the bread that He offers and that satisfies (**endureth**; Greek, *menō*; "stay," "remain") once and for all (compare 4:14). Therefore, eternal life is something not to be achieved but to be received by faith in Christ (see 6:28–29; discussion on 3:15).

6:28–29. What shall we do …? (v. 28). The people missed the point that eternal life is Christ's gift and instead thought in terms of achieving it by pious works. They asked for a listing of specific **works** to perform (**work**), but Jesus said the **work of God** (v. 29) is singular in focus: to **believe on him whom he hath sent**. Believing in Jesus Christ is the indispensable "work" God calls for, the one that leads to eternal life. John's use of "believe" is dynamic and emphasizes an ongoing trust and dependence on the one whom the Father sent. John used the verb ("believe") ninety-eight times and never the noun ("faith") in his gospel. Notable is the verb "believe" used with the preposition "in" or "on" to emphasize this dynamic trust in Jesus (thirty-four times in John, three times in 1 John; all other New Testament uses of this expression total five uses, once each in Matthew, Mark, and Acts and twice in Romans).

6:30–31. What sign shewest thou …? (v. 30). The people sought from Jesus a sign greater than the gift of **manna** (v. 31) that had accompanied Moses' ministry. A popular Jewish expectation was that when the Messiah came, He would renew the sending of manna. The crowd probably reasoned that Jesus had done little compared to Moses. He had fed five thousand people; Moses had fed a nation. He did it once; Moses did it for forty years. He gave ordinary bread; Moses gave **bread from heaven**.

6:32–33. Jesus corrected them, pointing out that the manna in the wilderness came not from Moses but from God and that the Father still **giveth** (the present tense is important) **… the true bread from heaven** (life through the Son; v. 32). **The bread of God** (v. 33), Jesus alluded, is the one the Father sent (see 6:29), **he which cometh down from heaven, and giveth life unto the world**. Jesus moved the discussion to something (and someone) much more important than manna.

6:34–35. Lord (v. 34) is closer to "sir" here. The people had not made the connection between Jesus and the "bread from heaven" (6:32). Their misunderstanding, like that of the woman at the well (see 4:15; see also Nicodemus, 3:4), ran along materialistic lines, as seen in their request: **give us this bread**. Jesus replied, **I am the bread of life** (v. 35). What Jesus offers can never be separated from who He is; they are inextricably united in a way that is unique and unparalleled in the history of world religion and philosophy. "The bread of life" may mean "the bread that is living" and/or "the bread that gives life." What Jesus implied in 6:33 He now made explicit and repeated with minor variations in 6:41, 48, 51.

This "I am" saying is the first of seven self-descriptions: (1) "I am the bread of life" (here), (2) "I am the light of the world" (8:12), (3) "I am the door" (10:7), (4) "I am the good shepherd" (10:11), (5) "I am the resurrection, and the life" (11:25), (6) "I am the way, the truth, and the life" (14:6), (7) "I am the true vine" (15:1). In the Greek, the words are solemnly emphatic and echo Exodus 3:14, where God identified Himself as the "I AM."

6:36. Earlier the people had asked, "What sign shewest thou then, that we may see, and believe thee?" (6:30). As the "bread from heaven" (6:32), Jesus was the sign, the manna from God greater than that given through Moses. Everything Jesus had said pointed out that He was what the people ostensibly sought, yet they did not believe (compare 20:29).

6:37–40. Jesus put His declaration of the people's unbelief into perspective. Here Jesus made it plain that He was the authorized agent and representative of God. The people had not believed Him or responded to Him as such, and their unbelief was a rejection of God's own purposes expressed in sending Jesus (see 6:27; 3:33; 5:23–24). Jesus now outlined the implications of such unbelief. In Jewish thought, "to give" means to put into one's control and responsibility. "Giving" falls into two parts: transfer and custody. From 3:35 and 13:3, we know of the transfer: the Father has put all things into Jesus' hands. Here Jesus emphasized the second part, the custody of all that comes under His control. He will not cast out those who come to Him (believe) but rather will safeguard all whom His mission brings under His control. Jesus was saying that the people's unbelief had grave implications. Despite the good will of God expressed in Jesus' mission to gain custody of those who believe in Jesus (vv. 39–40), their unbelief did not dismiss His sovereign authority. In fact, they were rejecting it and the protection of His custody that brings eternal life.

6:38. I came down from heaven occurs six times in this context (6:33, 38, 41, 50, 51, 58) and emphasizes the divine origin of Jesus and His mission: **the will of him that sent me** (see 4:34).

6:39. I should lose nothing points to the believer who perseveres because of Christ's firm hold on him (see Phil. 1:6). **The last day** is an expression found only in John in the New Testament (see 6:40, 44, 54).

6:40. For **everlasting life**, see discussion on 3:15. The one who puts his or her trust in Jesus will be **raise[d] … up at the last day**. The life that Christ gives cannot be destroyed.

6:41–42. The Jews (v. 41; see discussion on 1:19) were murmuring because they did not acknowledge the origin or the heavenly credentials of Jesus and therefore did not acknowledge the invitation of the Father expressed in Jesus' mission. Rather, they dismissed Him as the "bread from heaven" (6:32); they could not see past His earthly rearing. How often is it that one fails to see the extraordinary work of God in what is for all appearances ordinary and familiar? Yet the words of Jesus as to who He is and what He came to do were far from ordinary.

6:43–45. Jesus admonished the Jews to **murmur not** (v. 43). Such murmuring characterized the Isra-

elites during the exodus (see Exod. 16:2, 7–8). Shared faultfinding, such as was expressed in their murmuring to one another, is harmful. It reinforces resistance to what God is doing in the heart of the individual. People do not come to Christ strictly on their own initiative; the Father draws them. Murmuring reinforces human negativity and rehearses human answers to divine queries. Group negativity can create a democratic din that makes it harder to hear the voice of God and easier to resist it. One must beware of inhibiting the tutoring of God. Only those who learn from God come to salvation, and all who learn from Him are saved. The quotation from the Old Testament drawn from that division known as **the prophets** (v. 45) corresponds to a free quotation of Isaiah 54:13.

6:46. Jesus asserted in yet another way His credentials as the one uniquely qualified to represent and reveal God the Father. No one has **seen the Father** (v. 46; see 1:18; 5:37; 14:7; 1 John 4:12). No one has such privileged knowledge of the Father, **save he which is of God, he hath seen the Father**. The word "of" is the Greek preposition *para*, denoting "from the side of" or "originating from" God. If the people took this to heart and responded to the one who stood before them, they would know eternal life (see 5:24, 26).

6:47–51. As is profoundly expressed in 1 John 5:11–12, **everlasting life** (v. 47), eternal life, is not a possession but a person. Life eternal cannot be separated from the Life-giver. The metaphor of bread to denote Jesus Himself illustrates this truth: **I am that bread of life** (v. 48). The image of ingesting the Bread of Life is powerful and graphic. The comparison of eating the **manna in the wilderness** (v. 49) brings a certain literalness to eating the Bread of Life and creates a strong impression that the appetite for life must be satisfied by the true **bread … from heaven** (v. 50), not the manna, but Jesus. In contrast to that which could neither give nor sustain spiritual life, Jesus is the bread that brings eternal life. To **eat of this bread** (v. 51) is to appropriate Jesus as the sustenance of one's life. **My flesh** looks to the cross. Providing eternal life was won at great cost by the one who conquered death.

6:52. The literal character of Jesus' language led to a literalness on the part of His listeners. Language that emphasized the necessity of Jesus Himself over temporal and earthly substitutes had led the materially minded to a gory misconception rather than spiritual insight.

6:53–58. Jesus' absolute statement that **Except ye eat … ye have no life in you** (v. 53) precludes a direct reference to the Lord's Supper. He clearly did not teach that receiving that sacrament is the one requirement for eternal life or that it is the only ordinance through which Christ and His saving benefits are received. In this very discourse, Jesus emphasized the commitment of faith in response to His testimony (see vv. 35, 40, 47, 51). Now, Jesus mandates faith acceptance in the alarming language of wholly ingesting Him as a sacrifice, eating and drinking Jesus' **Flesh** and **blood** (cf. "life," v. 53, resurrection, v. 54), a foreshadowing of His sacrificial death on the cross. Furthermore, the deepest mutual bond between Jesus and the partaker is expressed by the words **dwelleth in me, and I in him** (v. 56 "dwelleth" is Greek *meno*, "bide," "remain"). It should be noted that "flesh and blood" carries Old Testament relevance as an idiom for the whole person (Brown, *The Gospel According to John*, p. 282). Here it points to the totality of Jesus and His cross as the object of faith.

In these verses, Jesus ostensibly responded to the query of His listeners (see 6:52), but what He elaborated did nothing to ease or civilize their literal comprehension. Nevertheless, the graphic wording of verse 54 conceptually corresponds to the wording of 6:40, where looking to Jesus and believing in Him brings eternal life and the assurance of being raised on the last day. Carson (*The Gospel According to John*, p. 297) cites Augustine of Hippo (In Tract. Ev. Jo. xxvi.1): "Believe, and you have eaten." As graphic as it is ("eateth" in Greek is *trōgō*; "chew"), Jesus was talking about a graphic belief that comes to grips with the exclusiveness of the life He offers by virtue of His flesh-and-blood death.

As in 6:49, the value of the **manna** (v. 58) is limited and is contrasted with the heavenly food that Christ gives. **Came down from heaven.** This is the tenth reference in this chapter to Jesus' coming down from heaven or to the bread from heaven.

6:59. John made it clear that the entire exchange between Jesus and the people took place **in the synagogue … in Capernaum** (see 6:24).

6:60. The thought of eating the "flesh" of the Son of Man and drinking His "blood" (see 6:53–58) was doubtless shocking to most of Jesus' Jewish hearers (taboos and purity laws notwithstanding). Even some who considered themselves **disciples** (clearly not the Twelve but a wider circle of followers; see 6:22–24; discussion on 6:67) found these words harsh. **Hard** (Greek, *sklēros*) is an adjective derived from a Greek verb meaning to be dry or parched. These words were very unpleasant. After **they had heard this** saying, they said, **who can hear it?** The same Greek word is used for both instances of "hear." It is similar to the saying, "I can't swallow what you're saying."

6:61. Jesus knew in himself implies supernatural discernment. **Offend you** is quite literally "cause you to stumble."

6:62. In the Greek, this is an "if-then" sentence that lacks a "then" statement. To resolve this, translators supply the word **What** to stand in the place of the "then" statement. One may presume that Jesus expected His listeners to supply the "then" themselves. Earlier Jesus said He "came down from heaven" (6:38). Now He asked what they would conclude **if they saw the Son of man ascend up where he was before**. Judging from 6:61, the offense they experienced at Jesus' words would be either heightened or lessened by this sight. Such a sight would vindicate Jesus' claim of heavenly origin. For "the Son of man," see discussions on 1:51; 3:13.

6:63. Jesus now put the literal misunderstanding of His hearers into perspective. His words were of the **spirit** that generates **life**; the **flesh**, or the human, does not profit. What He had been telling them had a dimension that transcended the natural, and if they would hear it as such, it would be transforming, indeed life-giving, because it was of the Spirit (see 3:5–6, 8).

6:64. This verse is another evidence of Jesus' supernatural knowledge and is reminiscent of 2:25.

From the beginning refers to the beginning of Jesus' ministry (see 16:4).

6:65. Coming to Christ for salvation is never a merely human achievement (see 6:37, 39, 44–45).

6:66. Jesus had already made it clear what discipleship meant, and many were not ready to receive life in the way He taught. His words brought His hearers to a threshold that their lack of faith prevented them from crossing, and they turned away.

6:67–68. The twelve (v. 67) were now singled out and distinguished from the broader category of disciples identified in 6:60. This is the first use of "the twelve" in the gospel of John. **Will ye also go away?** The wording of the question in Greek (interrogative *mē*) implies the expectation of a negative answer: "You do not wish to go away also, do you?" This rhetorical element in the question may have had Judas in view (see 6:64, 70–71). As in the Synoptic Gospels, Peter acted as spokesman. The expression **words of eternal life** (v. 68) is general. Peter perceived the truth of 6:63 and was speaking not of a formula but of the thrust of Jesus' teaching.

6:69. We believe and are sure. The Greek verbs are in the perfect tense and convey the meaning, "We have entered a state of belief and knowledge that has continued until the present time." **Thou art that Christ, the Son of the living God** (as in Matt. 16:16). A well-attested alternative reading is, "You are the Holy One of God." If the former reading entered the stream of manuscript copies through a scribe's inadvertent harmonization of Peter's answer to his well-known confession in Matthew, the harder reading of "Holy One of God" is preferred. It too has messianic implications and squares with the disciples' incomplete but firm grasp of Jesus' mission and consecration to the Father. In Peter's later speeches, recorded in Acts 3:14; 4:27, 30, he called Jesus "holy" (see Brown, *The Gospel According to John*, p. 298).

6:70–71. A devil (v. 70) alludes to **Judas** (v. 71), who would oppose Christ with the very desires of the Devil (see 8:44). **Iscariot** means "a man from Kerioth" (in Judea; see Josh. 15:25) and would apply equally to the father and the son (see 12:4). Judas seems to have been the only non-Galilean among the

Twelve. Judas was **one of the twelve** and therefore one of the last persons likely to betray Jesus. Carson (*The Gospel According to John*, p. 304) puts it well: "The supreme adversary ... of God so operates behind failing human beings that his malice becomes theirs. Jesus can discern the source, and labels it appropriately."

I. Jesus at the Feast of Tabernacles (chaps. 7–8)

7:1–8:59. In chapters 7–8, John recorded strong opposition to Jesus, including repeated references to threats on His life (see 7:1, 13, 19, 25, 30, 32, 44; 8:37, 40, 59). The apostle seems to have gathered the major arguments against the messiahship of Jesus and here answered them.

7:1. After these things. As in 5:1 and 6:1, the time is indefinite. Since, however, 6:4 refers to the Passover feast and 7:2 to the Feast of Tabernacles, the interval was about six months.

7:2. Feast of tabernacles. The great feast in the Jewish year, celebrating the completion of the harvest and commemorating God's goodness to the people during the wilderness wanderings (see Lev. 23:33–43; Deut. 16:13–15; Zech. 14:16–19). The name came from the leafy shelters in which people lived throughout the seven days of the feast.

7:3–5. His brethren (vv. 3, 5), the sons of Mary and Joseph, His half brothers (see discussion on Luke 8:19). **Disciples** may refer here to a broad number of followers (see 6:60) who now were in Judea for the feast. It is not clear whether the brothers claimed some knowledge of Jesus' miracles (lit., **works**) that other people did not have or were suggesting that any claim to messiahship must be decided in Jerusalem. Their advice was not given sincerely, for they did not yet **believe in him** (v. 5).

7:6. My time (Greek, *kairos*; "right time," "proper time") **is not yet come.** Unlike His brothers, whose time was **alway ready** ("right"), Jesus moved in accordance with the will of God (see discussion on 2:4).

7:7. The world is either (1) people opposed to God or (2) the human system opposed to God's purposes (see discussion on 1:9–10). Jesus' brothers belonged to the world and therefore could not be the objects of its hatred. Jesus, however, rebuked the world and was hated accordingly.

7:8–9. I go not up yet (v. 8). Jesus was not refusing to go to the feast but rather refusing to go in the way the brothers suggested, as a pilgrim. When He went, it would be to deliver a prophetic message from God, for which He awaited His "time" (7:6).

7:10. Not openly, but as it were in secret (see 7:4) suggests that Jesus went privately and not among the crowds or pilgrims. In this way, He rejected His brothers' suggestion to show Himself (see 7:4).

7:11–13. The Jews (v. 11; see discussion on 1:19), or religious authorities of Jerusalem, are contrasted with **the people** (v. 12; lit., "the crowds," plural only in John). **Where is he?** (v. 11) is literally, "Where is that man?" and typifies the misunderstanding of Jesus echoed among the people. **Murmuring** (v. 12), the same Greek expression used in 6:41, 46, characterizes the significant disagreement about who Jesus was. **A good man** is obviously an inadequate appraisal of Jesus, but it clearly conveys a perception of His pure intentions, a view contested by others who argued His intentions were impure and aimed at deception (**deceiveth**; Greek, *planaō*; "cause to go astray," see English "planet"). **Openly** (v. 13; Greek, *parrēsia*; "frankly," "boldly"; see 7:4, 25) contrasted with **fear** suggests a "gag order" discouraging any mention of Jesus.

7:14. The midst of the feast, or the middle of the weeklong feast, connotes a time when the crowds would be at their maximum. Teaching in the temple courts at such a time would reach many.

7:15. The Jews (see discussion on 1:19), distinct from "the people" (7:12), who were also Jews, were especially observant of Jesus as He taught in the temple precincts. **Having never learned,** Jesus' knowledge of **letters** (Greek, *grammata*; lit., "letters"; fig., "knowledge") points not to literacy but to recognized schooling. Jesus had never been schooled under a rabbi or recognized Jewish teacher.

7:16. If Jesus' knowledge was not the studied knowledge of a recognized rabbi, where had He acquired such learning? Jesus answered the query directly. **My doctrine** (lit., "teaching") **is not mine, but his that sent me** (see discussion on 4:34). "The Father which hath sent me" (5:30, 37; 6:44) had been His "rabbi."

7:17. Will do his will reflects a disposition or attitude of open and receptive willingness to hear and obey God. A person sincerely set on doing God's will welcomes Jesus' teaching and believes in Him (see 6:29). Commenting on the words **he shall know,** Augustine said, "Understanding is the reward of faith … What is 'If any man be willing to do his will'? It is the same thing as to believe."

7:18. Jesus truly represented and revealed the will of the Father because, as He argued, He sought not **his own glory** (or "benefit"; see 5:41–44): **but … his glory that sent him.** As so often in the gospel of John, the credibility of Jesus' representation of the Father is cast in the language of Jewish agency: the one sent is as the one who sends. His righteousness verified His faithfulness (**true**). In this gospel, no one is spoken of as being "true" except God the Father (3:33; 8:26) and Jesus (here). Once again, John ranked Jesus with God.

7:19. The Jews congratulated themselves on being the chosen recipients of **the law** (see Rom. 2:17), but Jesus told them that they all broke the law of which they were so proud. **Keepeth the law** is literally "doing the law," and Jesus charged each of them (**none of you**) with the failure (see 3:10–11).

7:20. The people probably refers to the pilgrims who had come up to Jerusalem for the feast, different from "the Jews" who were trying to kill Jesus (see 7:1) and the Jerusalem mob that knew of the plot (see 7:25). **Thou hast a devil** is an accusation of demon possession made elsewhere in John (see, e.g., 8:48–52; 10:20–21; see also Matt. 12:24–32; Mark 3:22–30). This was an unfortunate but typical human response to discredit the person (ad hominem) when one cannot discredit the word of the person. Such a response is atypical of a person with a "will [to] do his will" (7:17).

7:21. One work apparently refers to the healing of the lame man (see 5:1–9), as the discussion about the Sabbath shows (see 7:22–23).

7:22–23. The requirement of **circumcision** (v. 22) was included in the law Moses gave (see Exod. 12:44, 48; Lev. 12:3), yet it originated not with Moses but rather with Abraham (see Gen. 17:9–14). The Jews took such regulations as that in Leviticus 12:3 to mean that circumcision must be performed on the eighth day even if it was **the sabbath day**, a day on which no work should be done. This exception is of critical importance in understanding the controversy. Jesus was not saying that the Sabbath should not be observed or that the Jewish regulations were too harsh. He was saying that His opponents did not understand what the Sabbath meant. The command to circumcise showed that sometimes work not only might be done on the Sabbath but must be done then. Deeds of mercy were in this category. **Whole** (v. 23) is a direct reference to the healing of chapter 5; the word is found only here and there (in 5:6, 9, 11, 14–15) in John.

7:24. Judge not is a command to "stop judging" superficially. On the contrary, Jesus admonished them to **judge [the] righteous judgment**, which is equivalent to the whole truth or "the one true and complete decision of which the case admits" (Westcott, *The Gospel According to St. John*, p. 120). The Old Testament (see Deut. 16:18; Isa. 11:3; Zech. 7:9) is an ally to Jesus' admonition.

7:25. Them of Jerusalem is an expression found only here and in Mark 1:5 in the New Testament, probably referring to the Jerusalem mob (see discussion on 7:20). They did not originate the plot against Jesus, but they knew of it.

7:26. That Jesus could **speaketh boldly** in a climate where fear (see 7:13) and plots (7:24) abounded was matched by an equally peculiar silence on the part of the rulers. This strange juxtaposition led to an uneasy suspicion: **Do the rulers know indeed …?** In Greek, the question is in a form that expects a negative answer. The people thought it unlikely, but what else could such silence mean but that Jesus **is the very Christ?** (see discussion on 1:25).

7:27. Howbeit we know proved to be another instance of superficial judgment (see 7:24). What first presented itself caused them to stumble over the whole truth. At face value, He was Jesus of Nazareth. **No man knoweth whence he is.** Some Jews held that the Old Testament gave the origin of the Messiah (see 7:42; Matt. 2:4–6), but others believed that it did not.

7:28–29. Ye … know me (v. 28). Irony, because in a sense they knew Jesus and that He came from Nazareth, but in a deeper sense, they did not know Jesus or the Father (see 8:19) who sent Him. Jesus mentioned again His dependence on the Father (see 4:34) and went on to declare that He had real knowledge of God and that they did not. Both His origin and mission were from God. **He hath sent me** (v. 29) is the confirmation of Jesus' knowledge of the Father and another bold declaration that the people were dealing with the authorized representative of God.

7:30. They sought to take him. Jesus' enemies were powerless against Him until His "time" (7:8) or "hour" (2:4) came (see discussion on 2:4).

7:31. Many of the people, the pilgrims (see discussion on 7:20), **believed on him** and accepted His miraculous signs (**miracles**; see discussion on 2:11) as a peerless credential that the Christ (the Messiah) was before them (compare 6:26).

7:32. The Pharisees (see discussions on Matt. 3:7; Mark 2:16; Luke 5:17) confirmed earlier expressed fears (see 7:12–13), and the **murmured** acclamation of Jesus prompted them to seek a warrant from **the chief priests**. There was only one ruling chief priest, but the Romans had deposed a number of chief priests, and these retained the title by courtesy.

7:33–34. Yet a little while … then I go (v. 33). Jesus changed the topic from His miracles to His death, to which He referred enigmatically (v. 34). Even as the warrant for His arrest directed the temple guards to apprehend Jesus and take Him away, Jesus spoke of leaving. He would return to **him that sent me.** His departure was not in the hands of human authority but was dictated by the commission of the Father who sent Him. In agency, every sending is completed with the fulfillment of the commission and the return and report of the one who was sent. As Passover and the cross loomed, Jesus saw at hand the completion of His commission and return to the Father. Since His commission was of divine origin, His return was also divine and beyond human parallel.

7:35–36. The dispersed among the Gentiles (or "Greeks"; v. 35) points to what is commonly referred to as "the dispersion." From the time of the exile, many Jews lived outside the Holy Land, and Jews were found in most cities throughout the Roman Empire. Without a grasp of Jesus' heavenly origin, human explanations of Jesus' enigmatic talk of departure led to distant locations and realms outside of Judea.

7:37–38. The last day … of the feast (v. 37). The Feast of Tabernacles lasted seven days (see Lev. 23:34; Deut. 16:13, 15) but had a "holy convocation" on the eighth day (see Lev. 23:36). Each morning of the feast, the Jews attended a ceremony in which a priest drew water from the Pool of Siloam as the words of Isaiah 12:3 were recited. Upon drawing the water, the joyful procession set out for the temple, singing from the Hallel Psalms (Psalms 113–118). With the priest carrying the water in a golden pitcher and each participant carrying a *lulab* (myrtle and twigs tied with a palm, symbolizing the construction of a tabernacle hut) and an *ethrog* (a lemon, symbolizing harvest), the procession approached the temple. Upon reaching the Water Gate, the procession was greeted with three blasts of the ram's horn (*shofar*) as the procession made its way to the altar of sacrifice, where it circled the altar, singing the Hallel (Psalm 118:25) and waving its *lulabs*. On the seventh day, the procession would circle the altar seven times before the priest would commence with the pouring of the water, which the rabbis associated with the blessing of rain. It was on this final day of the festivities that Jesus stood up in the temple court and proclaimed that He was the source of **living water** (v. 38). John recorded that Jesus **stood and cried, saying** (v. 37). Teachers usually sat, so Jesus drew special attention to His message. **Thirst** refers to a basic human need that was a feature of the water ceremony associated with the feast. Here Jesus pointed beyond physical demands to spiritual necessities, even as He did with

the woman at the well (see discussion on 4:10). Jesus is the true source of abundant water, and it is obtained by placing one's trust and belief in Him.

7:39. Explaining the "living water" (7:38), John commented that Jesus was referring to **the Spirit**. He further clarified that the Spirit **was not yet given** in the manner in which He would be given at Pentecost (see Acts 2). **Glorified** refers to Jesus' crucifixion, resurrection, and exaltation (see discussion on 13:31). The fullness of the Spirit's work depends on Jesus' work of salvation. Associations of the Spirit with water or liquid imagery are found in the Old Testament (see, e.g., Isa. 44:3; Joel 2:28–32). Luke spoke of the Spirit poured out (see Acts 2:17, 18, 2:33; 10:45), and Paul spoke of being filled with the Spirit (see Eph. 5:18).

7:40–42. The people (v. 40; see discussion on 7:20) identified Jesus as **the Prophet**, probably the one who would be like Moses (see Deut. 18:18). Even as Jesus' miraculous feeding of the five thousand (see 6:1–14) linked Jesus to Moses and the manna (see 6:14), Jesus' water pronouncement may have evoked images of the water Moses provided the people at the rock of Horeb (see Exod. 17:6). **Others** deemed Jesus **the Christ** (v. 41), or Messiah, but this was met with skepticism because Jesus hailed from **Galilee** (Nazareth) and not from **Bethlehem** (v. 42). There is irony here. Just as the people did not know His heavenly origin (see 3:8; 8:14, 23), they did not know His nativity. Nonetheless, there were different ideas about the Messiah's place of origin (see 7:27).

7:43–46. The officers (v. 45) knew they would be in trouble for failing to arrest Jesus but did not mention the hostility of part of the crowd, which would have given them something of an excuse before the Pharisees. **Never man spake like this man** (v. 46). The officers were favorably impressed by the teaching of Jesus and were not inclined to cause Him trouble.

7:47–48. Then answered them the Pharisees (v. 47). The Pharisees must have been greatly irritated. Ordinarily, the chief priests would have rebuked the temple guards. For the position that Jesus **deceived** the people, see 7:12. The wording of both questions expects a negative answer. The first question (v. 47) appears genuinely inquiring, if not hopeful. The second question (v. 48) appears rhetorically bolstering and reassuring; it led to a comparison of opinions. When it came to assessing Jesus, the opinion of the religious authorities, the elite, mattered most, not the religious inferiors or common people.

7:49. This people refers to commoners, the Am HaAretz, or people of the land. The elitist view of the pilgrim crowd (see discussion on 7:20) was that they were ignorant, or **knoweth not**. The Pharisees exaggerated the people's ignorance of Scripture (see 7:42), but the average Jew paid little attention to the minutiae that mattered so much to the Pharisees. The traditions of the elders were too great a burden for people who earned their living by hard physical work, and consequently, these regulations were widely disregarded.

7:50–51. There is irony here. The Pharisees implied that no leader believed in Jesus, yet **Nicodemus** (v. 50), "a ruler of the Jews" (3:1), spoke up. They called for people to observe the law, but Nicodemus pointed to their own disregard of the law in this instance.

7:52. Out of Galilee ariseth no prophet (see 1:46). The Pharisees were angry, and wrong. Jonah came from Galilee, and perhaps other prophets as well. Moreover, the Pharisees overlooked the right of God to raise up prophets from wherever He chooses.

7:53–8:11. This story is absent from some early manuscripts, and of those that have it, some place it elsewhere (e.g., after Luke 21:38). This passage is contained in more than 1,700 New Testament Greek manuscripts, however. Although the location of the story is debated, it is largely regarded as authentic.

7:53–8:2. Jesus went to the **mount of Olives** (v. 1; see discussion on Mark 11:1). This is the only time that the Mount of Olives is mentioned in John. Luke recorded, however, that Jesus spent the day teaching in the temple and the night on the Mount of Olives, as He did during His final days in Jerusalem (see Luke 21:37).

8:3. Scribes (see discussions on Matt. 2:4; Luke 5:17) **and Pharisees** are a frequent couplet found in the other gospels, but only here in John. The expression **a woman taken in adultery** points to sin that cannot be committed alone. Consequently, the question arises as to why only one offender was brought before Jesus. The incident was staged to trap Jesus (see 8:6), and provision had been made for the man to escape. The woman's accusers must have been especially eager to humiliate her, since they could have kept her in private custody while they spoke to Jesus. Her position **in the midst**, or in front of everyone, is indicative of a formal and legal inquiry.

8:4. Taken … in the very act reflects the fact that compromising circumstances were not sufficient evidence, as Jewish law required witnesses who had seen the act.

8:5. Such should be stoned. Death was prescribed (in Lev. 20:10 and Deut. 22:22) for an unfaithful wife and the male counterpart, but the method was not. Stoning was not prescribed unless the woman was a betrothed virgin (see Deut. 22:23–24). This distinct prescription has lead some to suppose the woman was betrothed and not married. Ezekiel 16:38–40, however, shows that stoning was the typical method of execution for all types of adultery (see Brown, *The Gospel According to John*, p. 333). At any rate, that the paramour was not standing beside the woman indicates an uneven application of the law.

8:6. This they said, tempting him. The Romans did not allow the Jews to carry out death sentences (see 18:31), so if Jesus had said to stone her, He would have been in conflict with the Romans. If He had said not to stone her, He could have been accused of being unsupportive of the law. What was it that Jesus **wrote on the ground**? Educated guesses have ranged from a portion of Jeremiah 17:13, to successive portions of Exodus 23:1 (here) and 23:7 (in 8:8). Others have suggested that any content was incidental and that the act of writing was parabolic or a tactic of delay and suspense. Whatever the case, no one knows.

8:7. The phrase **without sin** is quite general and means "without any sin," not "without this sin." Jesus' answer disarmed them. Since He spoke of throwing a stone, He could not be accused of failure to uphold the law. The qualification for throwing it, however, prevented anyone from acting.

8:8 – 9. After His pronouncement, Jesus **again … wrote on the ground** (see discussion on 8:6). The people **went out one by one** (v. 9) because they were not "without sin" (8:7). **The eldest** were the first to realize what was involved, but all the people were either conscience-stricken or afraid, and in the end, only Jesus and the woman remained.

8:10. Woman is not a harsh form of address (see discussion on 2:4; 19:26).

8:11. Go, and sin no more. Jesus did not condone what the woman had done. The ostensible purpose of the law is to sin no more. Even as her accusers had failed, so had she. The grace of God now compelled her to go and live out the law. Her accusers left because they lacked the moral validation to impose the penalty of the law. She was compelled to go for a different reason: the compelling power of grace.

8:12. I am the light of the world (see discussion on 6:35). It is also true that "God is light" (1 John 1:5). As Jesus' followers reflect the light that comes from Him, they too are "the light of the world" (Matt. 5:14; see Phil. 2:15). **Darkness** connotes both the darkness of this world and that of Satan. **The light of life** points not only to Jesus as "the light of men" (see 1:4 and discussion; 9:5; 12:46) but also to the grand truth that "God is light" (1 John 1:5). Jesus is also the light from God that lights the way for life, as the pillar of fire lighted the way for the Israelites (see Exod. 13:21; Neh. 9:12).

The pronouncement of Jesus was magnified by its timing against the background of the Feast of Tabernacles. The Feast of Tabernacles, which lasted seven days (see 7:37), was inaugurated with a grand opening ceremony that featured the lighting of specially prepared beacons of light. Pillars of light, branched candlesticks or candelabras 50 cubits (about 75 feet) high according to the Jewish Talmud, were set up in the temple courtyard. Each pillar was affixed with four basins holding fifteen gallons of oil, with wicks fashioned from the garments of the priests. When these were lit, the Mishnah (Mishnah, Sukkah 5:3) records, "there was not a courtyard in Jerusalem that

did not reflect the light." As a highpoint of the opening festivities, these words were repeated: "We are the Lord's and our eyes are turned to the Lord." With the rich symbolism of the Feast of Tabernacles in view, Jesus declared, "I am the light of the world."

8:13. The Pharisees (see discussions on Matt. 3:7; Mark 2:16; Luke 5:17) opposed Jesus on the basis that He offered unsupported attestation. Jesus was well aware of the legal objection (see 5:31) and the position was later codified in the Mishnah: "No man can give witness for himself" (Mishnah, Ketuboth 2:9). Jesus had already answered such an objection with additional witnesses, citing the testimony of the Baptist, His works, the Father, the Scriptures, and Moses (see 5:32 – 47). Jesus, however, never conceded that He alone testified to Himself. His testimony was not His alone but also that of the Father who sent Him (see 5:32; 8:16, 18).

8:14. Jesus made two points in reply to His opponents' objection that He bore witness to Himself (see 8:13). The first is here, and the second is in 8:16 – 18. He based both points on the fact that He was the commissioned representative of the Father. Just as a human agent representing a potentate from a foreign land might arrive to transact official business, so now He stood before them. They were challenging the authority of Jesus without knowing **whence I come, and whither I go.** Even if He were to bear witness (**record**) to Himself, but He was not, His testimony **is true** (verifiable). **I know whence I came, and whither I go** is a direct reference to the fact that Jesus operated under the authority of a commission that remained intact; He was not a rogue operating on His own, as the reference to His return makes clear. In short, the argument of the Pharisees showed their ignorance of His official representation.

8:15. The judgment of the Pharisees was limited and worldly. **After the flesh** is literally "according to the flesh," or human standards. As Jesus would make clear, His judgments are not His own but those of the one who sent Him (see 8:16).

8:16 – 18. Jesus' second point in replying to His opponents' objection that He bore witness to Himself (see 8:13) was that His testimony was not unsupported. The Father was behind Jesus' testimony (see 5:31–39). In legal terms, He and the Father were the two witnesses required by the law (see Deut. 17:6; 19:15). Jesus was always aware of His mission (see discussion on 4:34). **The Father that sent me** (v. 16) drew the argument against Jesus' testimony into the larger question of the authority of the one Jesus represented.

8:19. If ye had known me. John made it clear that "the Word [Jesus] was with God, and ... was God" (1:1) and revealed God (see 1:18). Jesus here stressed that the Father is known through the Son and that to know the one is to know the other. Of course, Jesus' opponents were thinking in terms of a human father. **Where is thy Father?** Their question may express some rhetorical sarcasm, as if to bring Him down to earth. They were confident they knew who they were dealing with and where He was from (see 6:42; 7:27). Jesus' answer contested that hidden supposition.

8:20. The treasury identifies the precinct within the temple where Jesus was teaching and where this verbal exchange took place. The location appears to correspond to the setting of Mark 12:41–43. Significant is the point that hostility toward Jesus remained high, and one would expect His presence in the temple to result in His arrest, but **no man laid hands on him**, because the Father who sent Him determined **his hour** (see discussion on 2:4).

8:21–24. I go my way (v. 21) was Jesus' manner of speaking about His death and return to the Father (see 7:33–34). Despite His indirect language, **the Jews** (v. 22; see discussion on 1:19) suspected that Jesus spoke of His death. Ostensibly, the death of Jesus would please His opponents, but Jesus exposed them to the grave jeopardy attached to such a hostile disposition: **ye ... shall die in your sins** (vv. 21, 24). **And ye shall seek me** (v. 21) pointed to their ongoing quest for the Messiah (see Carson, *The Gospel According to John*, p. 341), a search that would continue in vain unless they came to believe **that I am he** (v. 24), the Messiah and more (see 8:58; discussion on 6:35; *KJV Study Bible* note on Exod. 3:14). Two realms, one characterized by that which is be-neath ... of this world (v. 23) and sin, is contrasted with its opposite, that which is **above ... not of this world** and, by inference, salvation. In rejecting Jesus, the Jews were turning from the very one they sought.

8:25. The question **Who art thou?** confirms the ambiguity of "I am he" (8:24), for its sense is subject to more than one interpretation. The Jewish leaders were disinclined to automatically attach a higher meaning to it. Its range of meaning is reflected in the distance between the two realms that characterized the difference between Jesus and His opponents ("not of this world" and "of this world," 8:23). Here the leaders' question itself implies that they suspected Jesus meant something higher than any of the denotations to be found in a conversational dictionary. **Even the same that I said unto you from the beginning**. Jesus' answer is a notoriously difficult sentence in the Greek. It may read as a question or an affirmation. Presuming it is an affirmation, Jesus was saying one of two related things: either (1) "You have the answer in what I have just told you" or (2) "You have the answer in what I have been telling you from the beginning of my ministry."

8:26–27. Jesus refused to give the Jewish authorities any explanation beyond what He had already told them (see 8:25). Here He put His refusal into perspective. Notice how Jesus turned their original question ("Who art thou?"; 8:25) into an appraisal of His opinion of them (**I have many things to say and to judge of you: but ...**; v. 26). In saying this, Jesus implied that the answer they sought would have hinged on His opinion of them rather than on the testimony He brought from the one who sent Him. That testimony was as true as its source, and it was the same for the whole **world**. Once again, Jesus' reply focused on the fact that He was the representative of the one who sent Him, and **he that sent me is true**. Two implications, therefore, may apply: (1) the message the Father deemed clear enough for the whole world must suffice for them; and (2) their lack of spiritual discernment had to do more with them than with the message, whose source was true. As if to confirm this, John added, **They understood not that he spake to them of the Father** (v. 27).

8:28–29. Jesus' mission and message would be vindicated and verified in the death that He had spoken about (see 8:21–24). **Lift up** (v. 28) is normally used in the New Testament in the sense of "exalt," and in Acts 2:33, the word is used of the ascension of Jesus, but John used it of the crucifixion (see 3:14; 12:32–33). The certainty of Jesus' claim ("then shall ye know") is based on the fidelity (**I do nothing of myself**) of Jesus to the mission and message of His commission. All that He said and did was prescribed by the will of the Father who sent Him. His ability to carry out what the Father had set before Him was fortified by the faithfulness of God. For **I am he**, see discussions on 8:24, 58.

8:30–31. John left **many** (v. 30) unqualified, and one may presume that it included a considerable number of those who had observed the exchange between Jesus and His more hardened opponents (see 8:22, 25, 27). What is clear is that they had responded to the Jesus' compelling prescriptions to believe in Him or die in their sin (see 8:21–24). **Believed on him** is the same positive expression John used elsewhere to characterize authentic belief (2:11; 4:39; 7:31; 10:42; 11:45; 12:42; see 20:31).

It is notoriously difficult to reconcile the characterization of those who believed on Jesus in these verses with those characterized in 8:33, 37. John's description of their belief in 8:30 is used elsewhere of authentic faith. It may be that John's narrative does not adequately partition two different groups within one crowd, or perhaps he intended the description of their belief to point up the issue at hand: they made some discernible expression of faith ("many believed in him," v. 30) but did not **continue** (Greek, *menō*; "abide"; v. 31) as Jesus prescribed. In that case, they were professors. If we are to take "the many that believed" as possessors, John's description of their belief in verse 30 stands as a bold anomaly in his otherwise consistent pattern of language used to describe authentic faith.

8:32. The truth is closely connected with Jesus (see 8:36; 14:6). The truth that belongs to the disciple who abides in Christ's word (see 8:31) is not philosophical truth but the truth that leads to salvation, the revelation of the Father that comes in Jesus Himself (see 8:36). **Free** thus means freedom from the slavery of sin, not from ignorance (see 8:34–36). Given the following context, one may understand "an implicit contrast between the power of Jesus' revelation and that of the Law" (Brown, *The Gospel According to John*, p. 355).

8:33. Abraham's seed. The word "seed" is singular and refers collectively to the descendants of Abraham. For Paul, the singular "seed" was a significant pointer to Jesus, the true descendant of Abraham (see Gal. 3:16). If John chose the singular for the same reason, there is irony in this protest. On a physical plane, **We … were never in bondage to any man** presented an amazing disregard of their Roman overlords. The words, however, are probably to be taken on a spiritual plane, as suggested by the topics of "truth" (8:32) and "sin" (8:34).

8:34–36. Jesus spoke of **the servant of sin** (v. 34) because the sinner cannot break free by his own strength. The consequences of sin are grave, as underscored by Jesus' use of **Verily, verily**. Jesus illustrated the consequences with a metaphor drawn from the household of a landowner. In the master's household are servants and heirs. A servant's affiliation with the household is conditional and temporary, whereas an heir is a son who belongs to the household without limit or condition. The way Jesus developed the metaphor, the Jewish leaders, who thought they belonged to the household were, as are all sinners, no more than servants, temporarily and conditionally affiliated, unless the Son intervened and set them free. Paul used this metaphor of the household to argue that in Christ believers are no longer servants but are sons and heirs through adoption (see Gal. 4:4–7).

8:37. Ye seek to kill me (see discussion on 7:1–8:59). Biological paternity is not the same as spiritual paternity. Harboring murderous intentions was an evidence that His opponents were servants to sin and had not been freed by the word of Jesus, which liberates true disciples (see 8:31–32).

8:38. Note the contrasts: **I … my Father** and **ye … your father**. Not until later (8:44) did Jesus say who their father was, but it was clear even at this point that it was neither God nor Abraham, as they claimed (see 8:39).

8:39–41. The **deeds** (v. 41) of Jesus' opponents revealed their parentage. Today, paternity may be confirmed by blood or DNA tests. Yet even today, parents rear their children to share their values and cherish what they cherish. To hear that your child is a "chip off the old block" points to signs of parenting more highly prized than the genetics of paternity. For Jesus, the test of paternity was the desire of one's father detectable in the behavior of the child (see 8:38–39; 44; Luke 6:35–36; Mark 3:33–35). **Born of fornication** may have been a slander aimed at the circumstances surrounding Jesus' birth.

8:42. I proceeded forth and came from God specified Jesus' commission and mission (**He sent me**) and was itself an evidence of Jesus' desire to fulfill the will the Father. **Neither came I of myself** shows Jesus' subordination to the will of the Father. Animosity rather than love for Jesus was evidence that His opponents' desires were not from God.

8:43. Jesus said His opponents could not **understand** (lit., "know") **my speech**, His vocalized words, because they were not able to **hear** (accept and therefore obey) **my word**. These descendants of Abraham (see 8:33) were so convinced of their own preconceptions that they did not really hear what Jesus was saying (see 8:47).

8:44–45. Your father the devil (v. 44) specifies explicitly the Jewish leaders' relationship to Satan by virtue of common desires and the common influence of falsehood. Jesus performed a spiritual autopsy to expose inner motives that were inconsistent with outward appearances and their professions of allegiance to Abraham. Mimicking the "right" things may fool others, but not Jesus. **Ye will do** points to the determination of the will. Their problem was basically spiritual, not intellectual. Being oriented toward Satan, they were bent on seeing Jesus put to death (see 8:37) and eventually would (see 8:28). **Truth** is foreign to Satan, and those who are his (see 14:6) do not believe Jesus because He speaks **the truth** (v. 45).

8:46. Which of you convinceth me of sin? That Jesus asked this question was more significant than the Jews' failure to answer in that it showed He had a perfectly clear conscience. Jesus knew no one could prove Him guilty of sin.

8:47. Heareth God's words (compare 8:43; see 10:3–4; 1 John 4:6). Jesus represented the Father as His agent and messenger. Therefore, Jesus' opponents could not **hear** His word (see 8:43), nor could they "hear" God's word because the word of Jesus is the word of God. Those who oppose Jesus are **not of God.**

8:48. The Jews, Jesus' opponents (see discussion on 1:19), took up personal slurs in an attempt to disqualify what they could not refute on the strength of theological argument. *Ad hominem* aspersions were calculated to dismiss any accountability or responsibility for what Jesus had said. Such aspersions attacked Jesus' character rather than answered His contentions. They could not "hear" His word (see 8:43, 47), so they characterized the word of Jesus, and thus of God, as the ravings of an unqualified and demonically controlled unworthy. Since Samaritans did not recognize the exclusive claim of the Jews to Abraham, calling Jesus **a Samaritan** demeaned Him as an adherent of false and unorthodox beliefs, "no better than a Samaritan." **Thou ... hast a devil** (see 10:20; discussion on 7:20), or literally, "a demon." Their accusation was that Jesus was not in control of Himself and was the tool of an ungodly force. The opponents of Jesus thought that they could dismiss the message by "killing" the messenger.

8:49–50. I have not a devil; but I honour my Father (v. 49) points to the mistreatment of God Himself in the dishonoring treatment of His representative (see 5:23). In Jewish agency, the one sent is as the one who sends, and the dishonor shown to Jesus was dishonor shown to the Father who sent Him. If Jesus had glorified Himself or sought His own benefit, He would have been representing Himself and not the Father who sent Him. If Jesus had acted on His own ("If I honour myself" 8:54), slurs such as His opponents had thrown at Him in 8:48 would have been against Him alone (see v. 54). Jesus did not glorify Himself, however. In saying that He honored the Father, Jesus confirmed that He represented the Father faithfully. Jesus certified this fact by deferring to **one that seeketh and judgeth** (v. 50). In other words, Jesus sought the Father's glory (implied in **I seek not my own glory**), and it was the Father who would judge the Jesus' faithfulness and therefore His opponents' dishonor and rejection of Him.

8:51. My saying refers to the whole of Jesus' message, which when accepted, brings deliverance from death.

8:52–53. Never taste of death (v. 52) expresses the experience of physical death, as even **Abraham ... and the prophets** experienced. Jesus, however, was speaking of spiritual death. **Art thou greater ...?** (v. 53). The question was framed to expect the answer no. This is ironic, since Jesus was indeed far greater than Abraham, even as He was greater than Moses (see 6:30–35 and discussions).

8:54–55. Jesus answered the Jewish leaders' question, "whom makest thou thyself?" (8:53), in terms of His agency as the representative of the Father who had sent Him. His opponents claimed as their own the God that sent Him, yet they accused Jesus of seeking His own **honour** (lit., "glory"; v. 54) and failed to recognize that God's honor was at stake in the way they treated Jesus, because God honored Him. Knowing God is confirmed by **keep[ing] his saying** (v. 55), or word; they could not "hear" (8:43, 47) God's word because they did not know Him. Jesus was so faithful to God's word that to say He did not know God would have been as much a lie as them saying they knew God. All in all, Jesus was answering their question by declaring that it was not so much what He made of Himself (see 8:53) as what God made of Him by virtue of His faithful representation of the Father. The honor of God was vested in Jesus in that the Father conferred on Jesus His quintessential rights of life and judgment (see 5:21–27) and put "all things into his hand" (3:35; 13:3). Jesus stood before His opponents as the supreme plenipotentiary of God.

8:56. Abraham rejoiced to see my day. "My day" probably refers to all that was involved in the incar-

nation. It is unlikely that Jesus was referring to any one occasion but rather to Abraham's general joy in the fulfilling of the purposes of God in Christ, by which all nations on earth would receive blessing (see Gen. 18:18). **He saw it** in faith, from afar (see Heb. 11:1, 9–13).

8:57. Not yet fifty years old was a generous allowance for Jesus' maximum possible age. Jesus was "about thirty" (Luke 3:23) when He began His ministry.

8:58. I am. A solemnly emphatic declaration echoing God's great affirmation in Exodus 3:14 (see 8:24, 28; see also discussion on 6:35). Jesus said not "I was" but "I am," expressing the eternity of His being and His oneness with the Father (see 1:1). With this climactic statement, Jesus concluded His speech that had begun with the related claim, "I am the light of the world" (8:12).

8:59. Stones to cast at him. The Jews could not interpret Jesus' claim as other than blasphemy, for which stoning was the proper penalty (see Lev. 24:16).

J. Healing of the Man Born Blind (chap. 9)

9:1–12. Jesus performed more miracles of restoring sight than of any other. Giving sight to the blind was prophesied as a messianic activity (see Isa. 29:18; 35:5; 42:7). These miracles were thus additional evidence that Jesus was the Messiah (see 20:31).

9:1–2. The question of the disciples, **who did sin ...?** (v. 2), presupposed the wide influence of a common theological and cultural view of suffering (see 9:34). The rabbis had developed the principle that there is no death without sin, and there is no suffering without iniquity. They were even capable of thinking that a child could sin in the womb or that its soul might have sinned in a preexistent state. They also held that terrible punishments came on certain people because of the sin of their parents. Jesus plainly contradicted these beliefs.

9:3–5. The disciples also looked at the man's blindness in the way that most Jews and the Pharisees did; they sought to know whose sin had caused the man's blindness, who was responsible (see 9:2).

Jesus wanted them to look at the man the way He did, as an opportunity for doing the work of God as expressed in Jesus' mission (see 9:4–5). He objected to the presupposition of responsibility and turned the question of cause into one of opportunity. He addressed no ostensible cause, only the purpose **that the works of God should be made manifest in him** (v. 3). The KJV properly renders this phrase as the Greek reads. In English, one must supply a main sentence, as do other translations by adding the words, "this happened" (NIV) or "it was" (NASB). It is not necessary to suppose the wording of the main sentence, however, since it is supplied in verse 4. The passage should read, "but, that the works of God should be made manifest in him, I [we] must work the works of him that sent me, while it is day" (vv. 3b–4a). Although this grammatical construction is hard to see in English as opposed to Greek, it is found elsewhere in John (1:31; 13:18; 14:31; 15:25).

Jesus connected the opportunity that this man's blindness provided and His mission as the Father's representative. There is good manuscript evidence that **I must** (v. 4) should read "we must." If so, the disciples were included in this work. **Day** and **night** signify the open-and-closed cycle of a regular workday and the occasion and cessation of work. That daytime alone provides an opportunity suitable for work is proverbial. Jesus' higher meaning was that the works of His mission and its opportunity belonged to the day, the period before the cross and Jesus' return to the Father. Just as there are natural time constraints in a normal workday, Jesus was under the constraints of His impending death. Accordingly, the word "night" (see 13:30) has an ominous quality. Both the proverbial and the higher significance of "day" and "night" are evident in 11:9–10. Nonetheless, there is no reason to think this an allegory. It is unlikely that Jesus was saying work could not be conducted after He died, only that there was urgency for Him to do the work of God, an urgency He called His disciples to share.

The healing of the blind man and the following irony and interplay of physical and spiritual vision and blindness must not be separated from Jesus' self-declaration, **I am the light of the world** (v. 5; see discussion on 8:12). Surely the man heard this pronouncement as Jesus and the disciples stood over him. Its meaning for the man, as for the reader, gains dimension as the chapter unfolds. Initially, it meant physical sight. What more it meant emerged as the man opened his physical eyes to discover he was not among the seeing but rather among the blind.

9:6–7. He spat ... and made clay (v. 6). Jesus used variety in His cures. Such mediums were not necessary, as the healing of 5:8–9 attests. Later, the procedure Jesus chose was directly linked to the violation of sabbath law (see 9:14). **Siloam** (v. 7), already an ancient name (see discussions on 2 Kings 20:20; Neh. 2:14; Isa. 8:6; *KJV Study Bible* note on Job 28:10), was a rock pool on the southern end of the main ridge on which Jerusalem was built. It served as part of the major water system developed by King Hezekiah. For its significance during the Feast of Tabernacles, see 7:37. John drew out the meaning of Siloam (**Sent**), alluding to the true source of the healing, Jesus, the one whom the Father sent as His representative.

9:8–12. John now revealed that **neighbours** (v. 8) and acquaintances had known the man as a beggar. Begging was about the only way a blind person of that day could support himself. His transformation was dramatic, and the questions about his identity are a reminder that people seldom look intently at beggars. His new mobility and manner of bearing caused people to question not only whether it was truly the same man they had known as a beggar but also how such a transformation had taken place. The man identified his healer, whom he knew by name although not by sight, and detailed step by step what Jesus had done and what He had instructed him to do. This would prove significant. The neighbors who wished to know the whereabouts of Jesus and who took the man to the Pharisees proved to be the only source of the detail that Jesus made clay and instructed him to wash in the Pool of Siloam. The man himself never disclosed these details to his official interrogators (see discussion on 9:13–16).

9:13–16. John disclosed that **it was the Sabbath day when Jesus made the clay, and opened his eyes** (v. 14). Both of these activities were violations of the Sabbath. "Kneading," involved in making clay, is one of the thirty-nine works prohibited on the Sabbath by Jewish law, according to Mishnah, Shabbat 7:2. "Opening eyes" was not necessary on the Sabbath, because there are six other days on which to heal a person whose life is not in jeopardy (see Luke 13:14). Notably, the man omitted these details in his testimony to the Pharisees: **He put clay upon mine eyes, and I washed, and do see** (v. 15). Although he apparently was protecting Jesus, the Pharisees nonetheless concluded that **This man** (Jesus) **is not of God** (v. 16) and that the Sabbath had been violated. Beside the man himself, only the neighbors who brought him to the Pharisees were in a position to convey such detail. The Pharisees were divided. Three questions occupied the investigation. (1) Had a miracle happened? This question would not be resolved until the man's parents testified (see 9:18–23). (2) How had it happened? This question focused on the specifics of whether or not Sabbath prohibitions had been violated. (3) Who had performed this miracle? This question focused not only on the identity of the healer but also on His culpability. Until the first question was confirmed, the Pharisees debated the second and third questions as theological lawyers. **There was a division among them**. The first group (v. 16a) started from the position that Jesus had violated the Sabbath and ruled out the possibility of His being from God. The second group (v. 16b) started from the fact of the miraculous sign and ruled out the possibility of His being a sinner (see 9:31–33).

9:17. What sayest thou of him …? It is curious that the Pharisees would pose this question to a man of inferior learning; it indicates their perplexity. At this point, the man identified Jesus as **a prophet**, probably the highest rank appropriate. There is, however, a notable progression to be seen in the man's understanding. His conception of Jesus grew and gained dimension, moving from "A man" (9:11), to "a prophet" (here) who might be followed by "disciples" (9:27), to one who was "of God" (9:33), to one

who was properly to be worshiped (9:38). Ironically, the interrogators' questions, and even their misrepresentations of Jesus, pushed the man to see more and more clearly the unique character of Jesus.

9:18–23. The man's parents confirmed that he was their son and that **he was born blind** (v. 20). This dual confirmation corresponds to the dual question of identity, **Is this your son, who ye say was born blind?** (v. 19). The parents were only as specific as the questions. They stuck to what they knew (**We know**; v. 20). When they came to what they did not know (**we know not**; v. 21), they actually went beyond the Pharisees' question of **how … doth he now see?** (v. 19; **by what means**; v. 21) to the unexpressed question of **who hath opened his eyes**. It may be that the question was asked and John omitted it. From the sequence of questions and answers, however, it appears their additional answer was intended to circumscribe all they knew and did not know to end the interrogation as quickly as possible. There was much to which the parents could not testify, but their emphasis on the son's responsibility, **he is of age** (vv. 21, 23), showed their fear of getting involved. It dramatically illustrates a climate of fear and the high stakes of being associated with Jesus. Excommunication is reported as early as the time of Ezra (see 10:8), but there is practically no information about the way it was practiced in New Testament times. The synagogue was the center of Jewish community life, so excommunication cut a person off from many social relationships (although in some of its forms, at least in later times, not from worship).

9:24. This begins the second interrogation of the man whose sight Jesus had restored. **Give God the praise**, or "glory," was a solemn admonition charging the man to tell the truth (see Josh. 7:19) under oath. There is irony here. The man's testimony would give glory to God, but it would not be the truth that his interrogators want to hear. **We** is emphatic in the Greek, showing the consensus that had emerged among the authorities.

9:25–27. The man refused to alter his previous testimony even when his interrogators prompted him as to what they wanted to hear. How eloquent and powerful is the truth of what he knew, all the more so against the background of what John recorded had frightened his parents (see 9:22).

What the authorities had professed to know ("we know that this man is a sinner"; 9:24) proved to be more an opinion than substantiated fact. They had yet to acquire any incriminating evidence from the man himself, apart from the evidence of a healing, which he himself represented. They lacked firsthand testimony as to how this miracle substantiated a violation of the Sabbath. They therefore resumed an earlier line of questioning (see 9:15), but the man refused to review it all again, saying only, **I have told you already, and ye did not hear: wherefore would ye hear it again?** (v. 27). In effect, the man said, "My testimony will not change, and hearing it again will not produce what you want to hear." His rhetorical question, **Will ye also be his disciples?** shows that he already counted himself a disciple.

9:28–29. The authorities **reviled** (v. 28) the man. In all likelihood, they had contempt for him from the outset. They would have viewed him as an inferior not only because he was a beggar but because they believed his blindness from birth was evidence of sin (see 9:2); this underlying prejudice is expressed openly in 9:34. That such a man as this should insult their dignity by suggesting they would give their allegiance to his healer (Jesus), a man they had declared a sinner (see 9:24), was more than they could tolerate. With a condescending attitude, evidenced by their expressed allegiance to Moses, they belittled the man. In declaring that **God spake unto Moses** (v. 29), they elevated Moses above the healer they knew nothing about, implying that Moses was not a sinner (see 9:31).

9:30–33. In these verses, the exceptional reasoning of a man, presumably unschooled, is revealed, especially when compared to the training of his interrogators. With a dash of sarcasm, the man chided the learned ones for missing the obvious: **Why herein is a marvellous thing, that ye know not from whence he is, and yet he hath opened mine eyes** (v. 30). In other words, how could anyone who

had performed such a miraculous work as opening his eyes go unrecognized as coming from God? The man then proceeded to adduce proof of his healer's higher origin. The first part of his proof he based on the premise that God answers only the prayers of the godly man who **doeth his will** (v. 31). This starting point built on what his interrogators had already expressed with their description of Moses (see 9:29). The second part of his proof he based on the extraordinary character of his healing (v. 32). The implication was clear. Only God could effect such a healing. The third and final part of his proof brought the deduction: **If this man were not of God, he could do nothing** (v. 33), yet his prayers had been answered in a way no other man's prayers had ever been answered. The conclusion is clear: Jesus must be from God. It may be remembered that earlier some of the Pharisees had followed this same line of reasoning (see 9:16b).

9:34. They cast him out may mean they expelled him physically from their assembly, but judging from 9:22, it is more likely that they excommunicated him.

9:35. John's wording sets the scene for the question Jesus posed to the man. The specifics of this man's life portray what is characteristic of John's gospel: no outcast is beyond the love of Jesus. Hearing how the man had been treated, Jesus sought him and **found him**. The question Jesus posed to the man, **Dost thou believe on the Son of God?** is a question more of trust than of whether the man acknowledged the existence of the Son of God. Strong manuscript evidence and the widest scholarly support suggest that "the Son of God" should read "the Son of man." It is certainly easier to explain why copyists might have inadvertently introduced the more common "Son of God" than the rarer "Son of Man." Where "Son of man" occurs in John, it is rich in meaning (1:51; 3:13, 14; 6:27, 53, 62; 8:28; 12:23, 34; 13:31). Jesus invited the man to put his trust in the one who is the revelation of God to man (see Carson, *The Gospel According to John*, p. 376).

9:36. The man was ready to follow any suggestion from his benefactor. Certainly he had become disenchanted, if not exasperated, with the traditional religion that had rejected him and with the authorities that had no place in their theology for the one who had restored his sight. He asked only that Jesus identify the one in whom he had been asked to put his trust: **that I might believe on him**. At this point, **Lord** is probably closer to "sir," but it is appropriately rendered "Lord" in 9:38.

9:37. With the words **Thou hast both seen him, and it is he that talketh with thee**, Jesus revealed His identity to the man, as He had to the Samaritan woman (see 4:26). What the man's heart was eager to embrace, he now realized stood before him. He had already come to see Jesus as more than a man, even before he set eyes on Him; now his physical eyes behold much more: the Son of Man.

9:38. Lord, I believe (see discussions on 1:7; 20:31). **And he worshipped him**. The man expressed his belief and worshiped Jesus, giving Him the reverence due to the very revelation of God.

9:39. Although 9:39–41 may have occurred a little later, it is possible the conversation of 9:35–38 occurred in a public place, where the intimate words of a personal conversation could have been overheard by the Pharisees. Jesus turned the occasion of restoring the man's sight into an opportunity to speak of spiritual realities. **For judgment I am come into this world** points to a function of Jesus' commission. Jesus defined specifically the nature of what He meant by "judgment" (Greek, *krima*): **that they which see not might see; and that they which see might be made blind**. The mission and ministry of Jesus is a catalyst. The foundational condition of humankind is that all people are in darkness, and Jesus is the light. John 3:17–19 states that Jesus came not to "condemn" (or "judge"; Greek, *krinō*) but to save (see 12:47), yet belief (coming to the light) and unbelief (retreating to the darkness) is defined by Jesus' mission in terms of being condemned (or "judged"; Greek, *krinō*): "He that believeth on him is not condemned: but he that believeth not is condemned already" (3:18; see 12:47). Here the same reality applies (see "your sin remaineth," 9:41), and Jesus emphasized the outcome of His ministry and not the intent (see 3:17; 12:47).

9:40–41. The Pharisees found it incredible that anyone would consider them spiritually blind. Their claim to sight showed their complete unawareness of their spiritual blindness and need. **If ye were blind, ye should have no sin** (v. 41). These words of Jesus are striking in view of 9:2–3. As at the beginning of chapter 9 with physical blindness, so here at the end of chapter 9 with spiritual blindness: blindness is an opportunity to manifest the work of God. **But now ye say, We see; therefore your sin** (your blindness) **remaineth**.

K. Parable of the Good Shepherd (10:1–21)

10:1–30. The parable of the good shepherd should be understood in light of the Old Testament (and ancient Near Eastern) concept of a "shepherd," symbolizing a royal caretaker of God's people. God Himself was called the "Shepherd of Israel" (Ps. 80:1; see Ps. 23:1; Isa. 40:10–11; Ezek. 34:11–16), and He had given great responsibility to the leaders ("shepherds") of Israel, which they failed to respect. God denounced these false shepherds (see Isa. 56:9–12; Ezekiel 34) and promised to provide the true Shepherd, the Messiah, to care for the sheep (see Ezek. 34:23).

10:1–3. The sheepfold (v. 1) was a court surrounded by stone walls but open to the sky and with only one entrance. The walls kept the sheep from wandering and no doubt protected them from certain wild animals. The twofold description **a thief and a robber** conveys not only theft but also a note of violent force with the addition of Greek *lēstēs* ("robber," "bandit," "insurrectionist"). Access had to be gained by stealth and force unless one was **the shepherd** (v. 2), whom **the porter** (lit., "doorkeeper"; v. 3) recognized as authorized to enter. The porter functioned as a watchman, especially at night, when the flocks were in the fold. Apparently, a large fold might house several flocks belonging to different shepherds yet be monitored by a joint porter. The porter recognized a shepherd, but the sheep responded to **his voice**. Sheep recognized the voice of their own shepherd and responded only to him. The shepherd did not call sheep randomly but only those that belonged to him (**his own sheep**). Commentators cite the shepherding practice of giving names to individual sheep.

10:4–5. He goeth before them (v. 4). The Palestinian shepherd led his sheep (he did not drive them), and the sheep followed because they knew **his voice**. Recognition of their shepherd's voice was how the sheep distinguished their shepherd from a stranger ("a thief and a robber"; 10:1). The well-being and safety of the sheep depended on this bond.

10:6. A **parable** (Greek, *paroimia*; "proverb," "figure of speech," John's equivalent to the Greek *parabolē* found in Matthew, Mark, and Luke) is a similitude with a primary and generally single point of emphasis. Jesus' hearers were familiar with the practices described in the parable **but they understood not** its meaning.

10:7–10. To make the moral of the parable plain, Jesus gave a fuller explanation. In the parable, Jesus is not only the shepherd (see 10:11), the authorized and recognized caregiver of the sheep, who enters and leads His sheep through the door; He is **the door** (or "entrance"; vv. 7, 9) itself. There is no legitimate access to the blessings of the fold's protection (v. 9a) or the pasture's forage (v. 9b) without Jesus. It appears, however, that Jesus was attributing to His role as the true Shepherd the exclusive attributes of "the door" to metaphorically magnify the exclusive rights of the true Shepherd (see 10:11–18). Consequently, **All ... before me** (v. 8) were "false shepherds," or **thieves and robbers**, like the Pharisees and the chief priests (but not the true Old Testament prophets; see discussion on 10:1–30). As "the door," Jesus is the one way to salvation. Inside the fold is safety, and one is able to **go ... out, and find pasture** (v. 9), the supply of all needs. Conversely, **the thief** (v. 10) has only one interest, himself. Christ's interest is in His sheep, which He enables to **have life** to the full (see discussion on 1:4). For Jesus' use of **I am** (vv. 7, 9), see discussion on 6:35.

10:11. Jesus declared, **I am** (see discussion on 6:35) **the good** (Greek, *kalos*; "beautiful," "praiseworthy") **shepherd**, probably in the sense of the ideal shepherd who puts his sheep ahead of himself.

Jesus **giveth his life for the sheep**. A shepherd might risk danger for his sheep (see Gen. 31:39; 1 Sam. 17:34–37), but he expected to come through alive. Jesus, however, said that the Good Shepherd would die for His sheep.

10:12–13. A **hireling** (v. 12) is interested in wages, not sheep. In time of danger, he runs away because of what he is (v. 13) and abandons the flock to predators.

10:14–15. I ... **know my sheep, and am known of mine** (v. 14) expresses a deep mutual knowledge, like that of the Father and the Son. **I lay down my life** (v. 15; see 10:11) reiterates a fact of central importance. Jesus is unlike any other shepherd because He is willing to set His sheep above Himself. His knowledge of the Father makes this possible.

10:16. Other sheep already belonged to Christ, though they had not yet been brought to Him. **Not of this fold** refers to those outside Judaism. Here Jesus gave a glimpse of the future worldwide scope of the church. There is **one fold** because all God's people have the same Shepherd (see 17:20–23).

10:17–18. That Christ would die for His people runs through 10:11–18. Both the love and the plan of the Father were involved, as well as the authority He gave to the Son. Christ obediently chose to die; otherwise, no one would have had the power to kill Him. **I have power to take it again** (v. 18). Jesus effected His own resurrection, though the Father and the Holy Spirit were also involved (see Rom. 8:11 and 1 Peter 3:18).

10:19–21. Division (v. 19; see 7:43; 9:16), or divided opinions, about Jesus was voiced **again among the Jews**. Some attributed His words to **a devil** (lit., "a demon"; v. 20; see 7:20) or to madness, as of one who is out of control and not in his right mind. **Others** (v. 21), however, protested these opinions. How could one who was under the control of a demon or not in control of himself **open the eyes of the blind?** (see 9:16). The assumption was that even if Jesus was not under His own control, it was a benevolent and good power His opponents were ignoring. Psalm 146:8 reminds us that "the LORD openeth the eyes of the blind."

L. Debating at the Feast of Dedication (10:22–39)

10:22. The feast of the dedication. The commemoration of the dedication of the temple by Judas Maccabeus in December, 165 BC, after it had been profaned by Antiochus Epiphanes (see discussions on Ezra 6:16; Dan. 8:9–12). This was the last great deliverance the Jews had experienced. This is what modern Jews celebrate at Hanukkah. Its origination antedates Christmas. **It was winter**. A description for those unfamiliar with the Jewish calendar.

10:23. Solomon's porch (see Acts 3:11; 5:12) was a roofed structure, somewhat similar to a Greek stoa, commonly but erroneously thought to date back to Solomon's time.

10:24. If thou be the Christ (see discussion on 1:25; 20:31). This was the critical question, but it was not easy to answer because of the different ideas of messiahship then in vogue. **Plainly** (see 7:13, 26 and discussions), or "openly," as His brothers had requested in 7:4.

10:25. I told you. Jesus had not specifically affirmed His messiahship except to the Samaritan woman (see 4:26). **The works that I do in my Father's name, they bear witness of me** points again to Jesus' authorization as the Father's agent and representative (see 5:36). Jesus' messiahship was contained within His faithful representation of the Father and the works He performed as a part of that commission. He may have meant here that the general thrust of His teaching made His claim clear or that such statements as that in 8:58 were sufficient. Or He may have been referring to the evidence of His whole manner of life (including the miracles), all He had done in the Father's name (for "name," see discussion on 2:23).

10:26–27. Jesus said that His opponents' failure to **believe** (v. 26) confirmed that they were **not of my sheep**. This not only was the topic of His parable but may have indeed classified them as wolves (see 10:12). If they were sheep, they would have known His **voice** (v. 27; see 10:3–5), Jesus would **know them** (see 10:14), and they would **follow** Him (see 10:4–5).

10:28. The sheep of the ideal shepherd (see 10:11) are safe in His care. Jesus now turned the metaphor into spiritual certainties. **Eternal life** (see discussion on 3:15) is the positive assurance, and **never perish** is a restatement in opposite terminology. The Greek construction here is a strong denial that the sheep will ever perish. The sheep's security is in the power of the Shepherd, who will let no one take them from Him.

10:29. My Father (see discussion on 5:17) **is able**. The Father's power (**hand**) is greater than that of any enemy, making the sheep completely secure.

10:30. I and my Father are one. The Greek for "one" is neuter: "one thing," not "one person." Jesus and the Father are one in essence or nature (see 17:21–22), but they are not identical persons. This great truth is what warranted Jesus' "I am" declarations (see discussion on 6:35; see also 8:24, 28, 58).

10:31. The Jews (see discussion on 1:19) **took up stones again to stone him**. They took Jesus' words as blasphemy and therefore prepared to carry out the law (see Lev. 24:16), though without due process. This reaction to Jesus' statement of "oneness" with His Father (see 10:30) was evidence that they perceived Jesus to be claiming equal authority with God (see 5:18).

10:32. Good works, as in 10:25, are the works that the Father had authorized Jesus and entrusted Him to carry out in the Father's authority ("name"; 10:25). The underlying Greek words refer in general to works that are fine and noble in character. Here Jesus defined their character as being **from my Father** (see 5:36, 43; 10:38 and discussions). Jesus turned His opponents' raised stones into an appraisal of the Father since He acted on the Father's behalf. Obviously, they vehemently disliked the claims of Jesus, but no work that He had performed had been carried out on His own (see 5:19, 30; 7:16–18, 19–20).

10:33. The clarification that the Jewish leaders would stone Jesus **for blasphemy** shows that they correctly understood the thrust of Jesus' words, but their preconceptions and unbelief prevented them from accepting His claim as true. **Makest thyself God**. To the Jews, Jesus was guilty of "making"

Himself God; they clearly understood Jesus to be claiming that He was God.

10:34 – 36. In its strictest sense, the term **law** (v. 34) meant the Pentateuch, but it was often used, as here, of the whole Old Testament, as evidenced by Jesus' reference to the Psalms. **Ye are gods** echoes Psalm 82:6 and refers to the judges (or other leaders or rulers), whose tasks were divinely appointed (see Exod. 7:1; 22:28 and *KJV Study Bible* note; Deut. 1:17; 16:18; 2 Chron. 19:6). The judges of Psalm 82 were unfaithful to their office, and God, who had **called them gods** (v. 35; see Ps. 82:6) because they were His representatives, judged them for their failure to faithfully represent Him (see Ps. 82:7). This figured prominently in Jesus' defense against the religious leaders who had challenged His claims as God's representative.

Since the religious leaders were taking the law into their own hands (10:31), Jesus challenged them on legal grounds. Unlike the judges, whom God called "gods," Jesus had been faithful to represent the Father who sent Him. The evidence Jesus presented was His faithful execution of the works the Father sent Him to do on His behalf (see 10:32; 5:36 and discussion). Since the religious leaders admitted that they had no grounds to stone Him for His "good work[s]" (10:33), Jesus took up their charge of blasphemy ("thou … maketh thyself God," 10:33).

As the crux of His defense, Jesus used their own judicial standard to legally demonstrate the contradiction of their indictment. If **in your law** (v. 34), He said, other representatives were called "gods," albeit unfaithful ones, how much more legitimate was it for a faithful representative to be so identified? Jesus argued, however, that He was more than a peer. Whereas the **word of God came** (v. 35) to them and they were legally (**the scripture cannot be broken**) called "gods," how much more did "God" befit the one **whom the Father hath sanctified, and sent into the world** (v. 36).

10:37 – 38. Here Jesus turned from a defendant into a plaintiff, from defense to prosecution. His accusers now had to defend themselves against the claims of His authoritative representation of the Fa-

ther. **The works of my Father** (v. 37; see discussion on 10:32) demonstrated the claims and validated the obligations imposed by Jesus' representation: **that the Father is in me, and I in him** (v. 38).

10:39. They sought again to take him. It is not clear if this was to arrest Him for trial or to take Him out for stoning. **But he escaped** (see Luke 4:30). John did not record why they failed, but he often made it clear that Jesus could not be killed before the appointed time (see discussion on 2:4).

M. Ministry in Perea (10:40 – 42)

10:40 – 42. Jesus left Jerusalem and crossed the Jordan to the east and the vicinity where John the Baptist had begun his ministry. The narrative's focus here on the ministry of the Baptist, who had prepared the way for Jesus' public ministry, is thematically the fitting echo to the closing of Jesus' public ministry. The raising of Lazarus (see 11:1 – 44) would initiate a sequence of events that thematically climb toward the cross and resurrection. Using the words of the people, John (the author) confirmed the Baptist's success in what Carson (*The Gospel According to John*, p. 400) calls a fitting epitaph: **all things that John spake of this man were true** (v. 41). The Baptist's testimony is highlighted once again (see 1:6, 15, 19 – 34; 3:27 – 30; 5:33 – 34). Here it is favored by two garlands. First, the Baptist **did no miracle** (v. 41), a point which magnified the praise of his testimony. Second, the Baptist's testimony bore fruit in the people's response to Jesus: **many believed on him there** (v. 42).

N. The Raising of Lazarus (chap. 11)

11:1 – 3. Lazarus (v. 1) is mentioned only in chapters 11 – 12 of John's gospel (the name is found also in the parable of Luke 16:19 – 31, but it is not the same Lazarus). **His sisters** (v. 3) are mentioned in Luke 10:38 – 42. **Bethany** (v. 1) was near Jerusalem, not quite two miles to the east (see 11:18 and discussion). John introduced Lazarus (**a certain man**) by linking him to his sisters, **Mary and … Martha**, with a tone of implied familiarity that prepares even the uninformed reader to recognize that an exceptionally close relationship existed between Jesus, these two sisters, and Lazarus, **he whom thou lovest** (v. 3). Yet despite such mutual affection (see 11:5), Jesus would wholly conduct Himself, not according to the constraints of human pressure (see 2:3–4; 7:8–9), but according to the will and leading of God (see Talbert, *Reading John*, p. 172). For **Mary ... anointed the Lord**, see 12:1–8.

11:4. This sickness is not unto death anticipates the raising of Lazarus (see 11:44), since Jesus already knew his death would occur (see 11:14). In fact, Lazarus must have died shortly after the messengers left Bethany, accounting for the "four days" of 11:17, 39: one day for the journey of the messengers, the two days when Jesus remained where He was (see 11:6; 10:40), and a day for Jesus' journey to Bethany (but see discussion on 11:17). **The glory of God** (see 9:3) and the glorification of Jesus (see discussions on 7:39; 12:41; 13:31–32) are linked by Jesus' agency and representation of the Father (see discussion on 5:41–44). **The Son of God [would] be glorified** through what happened to Lazarus, partly because the miracle would display the glory of God (who alone can raise the dead; see 5:21) in Jesus (see 11:40) and partly because it would help initiate events leading to the cross (see 11:46–53).

11:5–6. Jesus loved (v. 5) this family (see discussion on 11:1–3). As John thus underscored, it was not indifference that led Jesus when **he abode ... where he was** (v. 6). Jesus moved as the Father directed, not as people (here Mary and Martha) wished (see 2:3–4).

11:7–8. Then (v. 7) clarifies the divine will and timetable (see 11:4) according to which Jesus acted, despite His personal relationships (see 11:5) or safety. To **go into Judea again** clearly presented danger, for **the Jews** (see discussion on 1:19) **... sought to stone thee** (v. 8; see discussion on 10:31).

11:9–10. Twelve hours in the day (v. 9) specifies daylight hours allotted each person to accomplish what is obligated. Jesus was under obligation to the Father, which transcended the danger of returning to Judea (see 11:8). There was enough time for what needed to be done, but no time for waste. To help the disciples to grasp this, Jesus placed Himself in the metaphor: He was their daylight, and they must trust Him (see 8:12; 9:5; 12:35–36, 46).

11:11–13. Sleepeth (Greek, *koimaomai*; v. 11) is a euphemism for death, used by the unbelieving world as well as by Christians (see 1 Thess. 4:14–15). The disciples took Jesus literally, thereby assuming that Lazarus would recover, which would obviate any need to go to Judea.

11:14–16. Jesus dispelled the disciples' confusion and their hope of staying out of Judea with a blunt clarification of Lazarus's condition: **Lazarus is dead** (v. 14). Jesus' obligation had become their obligation (see 11:9–10 and discussion), and they could learn to trust Him (**believe;** v. 15) through this trip into Judea with its attendant danger (see 11:7–8). The Hebrew word from which **Thomas** is derived (v. 16) and the Greek word **Didymus** both mean "twin." Thomas is usually remembered for his doubting, but he was also capable of devotion and courage. Knowing the danger Jesus faced in Judea, Thomas said, **Let us also go, that we may die with him**.

11:17. Four days (see discussion on 11:4) confirmed what Jesus had already revealed, that Lazarus was unquestionably dead (see 11:14). Many Jews believed that the soul remained near the body for three days after death in the hope of returning to it. If this idea was in the minds of these people, they obviously thought all hope was gone; Lazarus was irrevocably dead.

11:18–19. It was usual for friends to visit the family **to comfort them** (v. 19). John's details of the distance of Bethany from Jerusalem implies that many who came to comfort the family traveled from Jerusalem. **Fifteen furlongs** (v. 18) was just less than two miles. A "furlong" identifies the Greek *stadiōn* (compare English "stadium"), which measures 606 feet 9 inches, or an eighth of a Roman mile. Jewish custom provided for three days of very heavy mourning, then four days of heavy mourning, followed by lighter mourning for the remainder of thirty days.

11:20. Martha ... went and met him, perhaps because as the elder, she was hostess and was alerted to Jesus' near arrival (see 11:30). **Mary sat ... in the house**, mourning (see 11:31) with those who had gathered (for Martha and Mary, see Luke 10:38–42). It is possible that Mary was unaware of Jesus' arrival (see 11:28–30; note "secretly," 11:28).

11:21. When Martha saw Jesus, she said, **If thou hadst been here, my brother had not died**. Mary repeated this statement in 11:32. Perhaps the sisters had said this to one another often as they awaited Jesus' arrival. Clearly, they had every confidence in Jesus' power to heal their brother, and with the window of opportunity closed by Lazarus's death, their grief spilled forth in a contrary-to-fact wish: "If you had been here, but you were not; my brother would not have died, but he did."

11:22. Whatsoever thou wilt ask. This comment seems to indicate that Martha hoped for an immediate resurrection in spite of the fact that Lazarus's body had already begun to decay. Nothing is too difficult for God to do.

11:23–24. On the surface, it appears that Jesus assented to fulfill Martha's request: **Thy brother shall rise again** (v. 23). Martha's answer, however, makes it clear that she received this apparent assent as holding no more promise than a pious consolation to the grieving, expressing confidence in the final **resurrection** (v. 24). Martha heard **at the last day** (v. 24) and not "today." Strictly worded, Jesus expressed nothing more than the Pharisaic belief in the resurrection (see Acts 23:8; Josephus *War* 2.8.14; Mishnah, Sanhedrin 10:1), which was the more widely held view of life after death than that of the Sadducees (see Mark 12:18–27).

11:25–26. Martha wanted Jesus to petition God (see 11:22). Jesus wanted Martha to understand that the Father had "given all things into his hands" (3:35; 13:3) and that the resurrection and the life she sought were not only His to bestow (5:21, 24–29) but were resident in Him and realized through personal faith in Him. What she abstractly attributed to God is to be identified with the person of Jesus: **I am the resurrection, and the life** (v. 25; see discussion on 6:35). Jesus is life (see 1:4; 14:6; Acts 3:15; Heb. 7:16; 1 John 5:11–12). **He that believeth ... shall**

he live is the confirming confidence that death will never triumph over the one who finds the resurrection and the life in Jesus (see 1 Cor. 15:54–57).

11:27. Yea, Lord; I believe. Martha is often remembered for her shortcoming recorded in Luke 10:40–41, but she was a woman of faith, as this magnificent declaration shows. It succinctly embodies the highest tenets of personal belief in the person and work of Jesus in John's gospel (see 20:31). Indeed, it closes Martha's concern with an assent of trust marked by her departure (see 11:28).

11:28–30. The Master (v. 28), or literally, "the Teacher," a significant description to be given by a woman. The rabbis would not teach women (see 4:27), but Jesus taught them frequently. **Secretly**, or without others being aware, either privately or with whispers, Martha alerted Mary to the arrival and whereabouts of Jesus. Carson (*The Gospel According to John*, p. 414) has suggested that Jesus remained outside the village for the purpose of separate private time with the sisters, an impossibility in a house full of mourners and a better explanation in light of 11:11 than that of protection or anonymity.

11:31. Wailing at a tomb was common, and **the Jews** (see discussion on 1:19) immediately thought Mary had in mind **to weep there**. Jesus may have requested a private meeting with Mary, but her hasty departure caught the attention of the mourners. Because they followed her, Jesus got maximum publicity.

11:32–34. Lord, if thou hadst been here (v. 32). Mary repeated Martha's statement (see 11:21). The two occurrences of the word **weeping** (v. 33) both denote a loud expression of grief, that is, "wailing." Jesus was deeply and internally moved: **he groaned in the spirit** is matched by "groaning in himself" in 11:38. In both places, the word "groaned" (Greek, *embrimaomai*) is closer to an "an articulate expression of anger" (Brown, *The Gospel According to John*, p. 425) and implies a sense of indignation or emotional vexation within Jesus (see Matt. 9:30; Mark 1:43). It was more than empathy or grief and closer to ire welling up within Him. For **troubled** (Greek, *tarassō*; "agitated") see 12:27; 13:21; discussion on

14:1. Jesus' strong inner reaction is probably best understood as His reaction to the despoiling effects of sin and its most potent outcome: death, with its wake of anguish and grief. Before this triumph of death, with its victory trumpeted in wailing, stood Jesus, "the resurrection, and the life" (11:25), and the scene brought forth not only His guttural indignation but also His intervention: **Where have ye laid him?** (v. 34.)

11:35 – 37. Jesus wept (v. 35). The Greek word used here for "wept" is not the one for loud grief, as in 11:33, but one that denotes quiet weeping, that is, "shed tears." Observing the tears of Jesus, perhaps more authentic than some of the mourning at that point, others noted Jesus' love for Lazarus (v. 36, see 11:5). Their position, **Could not this man …?** (v. 37), echoes that of Martha (see 11:21) and Mary (see 11:32): there could have been a different outcome if Jesus had arrived prior to Lazarus's death. Although Jesus **opened the eyes of the blind** (see chap. 9), the reality of the power of death prevailed in the beliefs of those who had yet to realize that Jesus is "the resurrection, and the life" (11:25).

11:38 – 39. Again groaning in himself (v. 38; see 11:33). John clarified that **the grave**, or tomb, **was a cave** with an horizontal approach rather than a vertical shaft. The **stone** prevented the approach of animals. Martha's objection proves how startling was the command of Jesus to remove the stone. It also confirms that she did not expect Jesus to raise her brother that very day and that she had more to fathom from her earlier conversation with Jesus (see 11:23 – 27 and discussions). For **four days**, see discussions on 11:4, 17.

11:40. Jesus had used the expression **the glory of God** with the disciples (see discussion on 11:4) but not expressly with Martha. Carson (*The Gospel According to John*, p. 418) deems His use of this expression a summary of what was promised in 11:23 – 26.

11:41 – 42. The prayerful acknowledgment of the Father accorded with Jesus' purpose here, as elsewhere: to glorify God (see 11:4, 40). As in 11:4, the glory of God was inextricably linked with the glorification and acknowledgment of His representative,

the one whom God had sent, who acted on God's behalf and for His benefit.

11:43 – 44. He cried with a loud voice (v. 43) is proleptic of that day when the dead shall hear the voice of the Son of God (see 5:25, 28 – 29). No one present could mistake that it was the voice of Jesus to whom Lazarus **came forth** (v. 44). **Graveclothes** were narrow strips of cloth, like bandages. Sometimes a shroud was used (see discussion on 19:40). **A napkin** was a separate item (see 20:7). **Loose him, and let him go** signaled that Lazarus was alive.

11:45 – 46. Many of the Jews (see discussion on 1:19) **… believed on him** (v. 45; see 20:31) implies that perhaps some who had been opposed to Jesus now came to believe in Him. On the other hand, **some** (v. 46) could only defer what they had seen with their own eyes to the opinion of **the Pharisees**. The actions of these people may not have been hostile. The Pharisees believed in the resurrection (see discussion on 11:23 – 24), and those who **told them what … Jesus had done** may have had an agreeable intent. The consequent action of the Pharisees (see 11:47), however, underscored their opposition to Jesus.

11:47. The chief priests and the Pharisees. In all four gospels, the Pharisees appear as Jesus' principal opponents throughout His public ministry. They lacked political power, however, and it was the chief priests who were prominent in the events that led to Jesus' crucifixion. Here both groups associated in a meeting of the Sanhedrin (see discussion on Mark 14:55). They did not deny that Jesus did **many miracles** ("signs"; see discussion on 2:11), but they did not understand their meaning, for they failed to believe.

11:48. Our place most likely refers to the temple (see Acts 6:13 – 14; 21:28), though sometimes the Jews used the expression to denote Jerusalem.

11:49. Caiaphas, the high priest circa AD 18 – 36, was the son-in-law of Annas (see 18:13), who had been deposed from the high priesthood by the Romans in AD 15. **The high priest that same year** means "the high priest at that time." The high priesthood was not an annual office but one supposed to be held for life. **Ye know nothing at all** is a remark typical of Sadducean rudeness (Caiaphas, as high priest, was a Sadducee). Josephus (*Jewish War* 2.17.14) says that the Sadducees "in their intercourse with their peers are as rude as to aliens." (For the Sadducees, see discussions on Matt. 2:4; 3:7; Mark 12:18; Luke 20:27; Acts 4:1.)

11:50. It is expedient for us. Caiaphas was concerned with political expediency, not with guilt and innocence. He believed that **one man**, no matter how innocent, should perish rather than that **the whole nation** be put in jeopardy. Ironically, the Jews went ahead with their execution of Jesus, and in AD 70, the nation perished nonetheless.

11:51. Being high priest, Caiaphas was not a private citizen but God's high priest, and God ruled over what he said. For **that year,** see discussion on 11:49. Caiaphas **prophesied** in that his words were true in a way he could not imagine. Prophecy in Scripture is the impartation of divinely revealed truth. In reality, Caiaphas's words meant that Jesus' death would be **for [the] nation**, not by removing political trouble but by taking away the sins of those who believed in Him.

11:52. The children of God ... scattered abroad makes it clear that Jesus' death would have effects far beyond the nation (see, e.g., 1:29; 3:16; 4:42; 10:16).

11:53 – 54. Jesus' opponents now sought to **put him to death** (v. 53), but **went thence** (v. 54) again shows that Jesus was not to die before His "hour" (see discussion on 2:4). He did not act imprudently, however. Knowing the attitude of His opponents, He withdrew. He would die for others, but in His own time, not that of His enemies. If **Ephraim** was the city known as Ophrah, it was about fifteen miles north of Jerusalem.

11:55. For **passover,** see discussions on 2:13; 5:1. It was especially important for the Jews **to purify themselves** at a time like Passover, because otherwise they could not keep the feast (see 18:28; see discussion on 2:6 – 7).

IV. The Passion Week (chaps. 12 – 19)

A. The Anointing of Jesus' Feet (12:1 – 11)

12:1 – 11. All four gospels present an account of a woman anointing Jesus. John's account seems to tell

of the same incident recorded in Matthew 26:6 – 13 and Mark 14:3 – 9, while that in Luke 7:36 – 50 is different.

12:1 – 2. Key words such as **Bethany** (see discussion on Matt. 21:17) and **Lazarus** easily set the scene, connecting Jesus' demonstration of His identity as "the resurrection, and the life" (11:25) in the events of chapter 11 with Mary's anointing of Him, which presaged His own death (see 12:7) at Passover, six days away. For **Martha served,** see Luke 10:38 – 42. The note that **Lazarus ... sat at the table with him** shows the normal life to which Lazarus had been restored with being raised from the dead by Jesus.

12:3. Spikenard denotes both a plant and the fragrant oil it yielded. Since it was **very costly** (Greek, *polytimos*; "very precious," "very valuable"), Mary's act of devotion was costly. It was also an unusual act, both because she poured the oil on Jesus' **feet** (normally it was poured on the head) and because she used **her hair** to wipe them (a respectable woman did not unbind her hair in public). Further, it showed her humility, for it was a servant's work to attend to the feet (see discussions on 1:27; 13:5).

12:4 – 5. What Jesus saw as a costly and humble act of devotion worthy of His death (see 12:7), **Judas Iscariot** (v. 4; see discussion on 6:71) saw as an extravagant and prodigal waste. Judas estimated the value of the costly ointment at **three hundred pence** (v. 5), or denarii. One denarius was a day's wage (see Matt. 20:2), and thus Mary's anointing equaled the annual wage of a laborer and could have fed many who were without food (see 6:7).

12:6. Perhaps a gauge of Mary's extravagance is to be discerned in what John's readers might have thought, for John was quick to clarify and separate the motives of Judas from those of the observer, with the revelation that **he was a thief.** This is the one passage from which we learn that Judas was dishonest. He must have been thought to be a man of some reliability, however, for he was the keeper of the money bag.

12:7 – 8. Jesus defended Mary's action by exposing an intention entirely foreign to the mindset of Judas. The meaning of **kept** (v. 7) is probably "saved for this purpose." Perfume was normally associated with festivity, but it was also used in burials (see 19:39–40), and Jesus linked it with His burial, which Mary's anointing unwittingly anticipated. It is not that **the poor** (v. 8) are unimportant, but unlike the priority of Jesus, the precedence of the poor is limitless (see Deut. 15:11; see Matt. 26:11; Mark 14:7).

12:9–11. The crowd that came to see not only Jesus but **Lazarus also, whom he had raised from the dead** (v. 9), heightened the resolve of the Jewish leaders to eliminate the threat (see v. 11). The Jewish leaders previously had spoken of the death of Jesus (see 11:50–53), but now they conspired to **put Lazarus also to death** (v. 10). Sin grows.

B. The Triumphal Entry (12:12–19)

12:12. Much people identifies the pilgrims who had come up from the country for the Passover feast. Many of the pilgrims had doubtless seen and heard Jesus in Galilee, and they welcomed the opportunity to proclaim Him as Messiah.

12:13. Branches of palm trees were used in celebration of victory. Later in his life, John saw a multitude with palm branches in heaven (see Rev. 7:9). **Hosanna** was a Hebrew expression meaning "Save!" that became an exclamation of praise (see *KJV Study Bible* note on Jer. 31:7). The people added an acclamation, **the King of Israel**, to the words of the psalm (see Ps. 118:25–26), which John alone recorded. It reflects his special interest in Jesus' royalty, which he brought out throughout the passion narrative. **In the name of the Lord** carries a notable significance in John, for Jesus was the unique one sent in the Father's divine name (see 5:43; 10:25; 17:11–12).

12:14–15. A young ass (v. 14; see Matt. 21:2, 7; Mark 11:2; Luke 19:30) has messianic overtones in light of Zechariah 9:9. The political and nationalistic aspirations of the crowd implied in the acclamation "King of Israel" (12:13) were different from those of the humble King who fulfilled Zechariah 9:9.

12:16. Only after the crucifixion and the coming of the Holy Spirit did the disciples appreciate the meaning of the prophecy of Zechariah 9:9 and its fulfillment. The later illumination of the disciples is

an example of the meaning of 16:13. For **glorified**, see discussions on 12:41; 11:4; 13:31.

12:17–19. Two crowds are described in John's account of the triumphal entry. The crowd that had witnessed the raising of **Lazarus** (v. 17) came with Jesus and was met by the crowd of 12:12–13, which had come out of Jerusalem to see Him. The one bore witness to what they had seen as it met the second, which had heard the news and had come from Jerusalem. This general enthusiasm was loaded with political implications, and the ramifications were not lost on the frustrated **Pharisees** (v. 19; see 11:46–50).

C. The Coming of the Greeks (12:20–36)

12:20–22. The **Greeks** (or Gentiles; v. 20) who sought an audience with Jesus represent "the whole world" (Carson, *The Gospel According to John*, p. 435). They belonged to the ranks of "God-fearers," people attracted to Judaism by its monotheism and morality but repelled by its nationalism and requirements such as circumcision. They worshiped in the synagogues but did not become proselytes. As Brown (*The Gospel According to John*, p. 466) insists, "only the understanding that the first Gentiles have come to Jesus explains his exclamation that the hour has come" (see 12:23).

Philip (v. 21) is a Greek name, which may be why the Greeks came to this disciple (though he was not the only one of the Twelve to have a Greek name). **See** means "to have an interview with." The roundabout approach to Jesus is left unexplained but may underscore the novelty and therefore the uncertainty of how Jesus would receive Gentiles (see Carson, *The Gospel According to John*, p. 427). After verse 22, John recorded no more about these Greeks (but see discussion on 12:32). He regarded their coming as important but not their conversation with Jesus. Jesus came to die for the world, and the coming of these Gentiles indicated the scope of the effectiveness of His approaching crucifixion.

12:23–24. The hour is come (v. 23). The hour to which Jesus' whole ministry had led (see discussions on 2:4; 12:20). **Glorified**. Jesus was speaking about

His death on the cross and His subsequent resurrection and exaltation (see discussions on 11:4; 12:41; 13:31). Jesus used the metaphor of **a corn of wheat** (v. 24) to convey the necessity of His death: **if it die, it bringeth forth**. The principle of life through death is seen in the plant world. The kernel must perish as a kernel if there is to be a plant.

12:25 – 26. He that hateth his life … shall keep it (v. 25; see Matt. 16:24 – 25; Mark 8:34 – 35; Luke 9:23 – 24). To love one's life here and now — to concentrate on one's own success — is to lose what matters. Supremely, of course, the principle is seen in the cross of Jesus and the implications of His hour, with its glorification for those that follow and serve Jesus. "Hateth" is a Semitic expression that implies "loves less." One's love for God must be such that all other loves are, by comparison, hatred. For **life eternal**, see discussion on 3:15.

12:27. Now is my soul troubled (Greek, *tarassō*) is John's equivalent to the agony in Gethsemane described in the other gospels. **This hour** (see 12:23 – 24) held for Jesus the prospect of becoming sin (or a sin offering) for sinful people (see 2 Cor. 5:21). He considered praying for God to save Him from this death but refused to pray it because the very reason He had come was to die.

12:28. Father, glorify thy name. Jesus' prayer was not for deliverance but for the Father to be glorified. **A voice from heaven** gave the answer. For "name," see discussions on 2:23; 5:43; see also 10:25; 17:11 – 12.

12:29 – 30. Jesus heard distinctly what the crowd mistook for thunder or the voice of an **angel** (v. 29). Although our knowledge of what **This voice** (v. 30) said must have been mediated by Jesus, who presumably revealed it to the disciples, in the language of exaggerated contrast, Jesus explained it was more for their sake than for His. This point is confirmed by the existing record.

12:31. Of this world. The cross was God's judgment on the world. **The prince of this world** identifies Satan (see 16:11). The cross would seem to be his triumph, but in fact, it was his defeat. Out of it would flow the greatest good ever to come to the world.

12:32 – 33. Lifted up (v. 32; see discussion on 3:14) alludes to the cross, the supreme exaltation of Jesus (see discussions on 12:41; 13:31). It is significant that Greek Gentiles were present on this occasion (see 12:20). Through His death and resurrection, Christ would **draw all** people to Himself, without regard for nationality, ethnic affiliation, or status. "Draw" renders a form of legal Jewish acquisition. Through the cross, Jesus acquired, or took legal possession of, "all" by drawing to Himself that which rightfully belongs to God and thereby divested (evicted) the ruler of this world from his hold on God's possession. **Signifying what death** (v. 33) refers to the manner of His death ("lifted up") and its purpose (to "draw all").

12:34. The law here seems to mean Old Testament Scripture in general (see discussion on 10:34), the reference being to passages such as Psalms 89:36; 110:4; Isaiah 9:7; Daniel 7:14. No particular Scripture says the **Christ abideth for ever**, but Psalm 89:36 is a close possibility (see Brown, *The Gospel According to John*, p. 469). For "Christ" (or "Messiah"), see discussion on 1:25. In Aramaic, **the Son of man** is the equivalent of "I" (12:32), but in context, it could have messianic overtones. The people sensed the "more" in what Jesus was saying and inquired how what He was saying related to their understanding of the Messiah. Here is the only place in the Gospels where anyone other than Jesus used the expression "the Son of man," and even here Jesus was being quoted (see discussion on Mark 2:10).

12:35 – 36. The light (v. 35) is closely identified with Jesus, as seen from the call to **believe in the light** (v. 36; see discussions on 1:4; 8:12). **Lest darkness come upon you** (v. 35) is literally, "lest darkness overcome you," as in "the darkness comprehended it not" (1:5), or "the darkness did not overtake it (the light)." Jesus did not debate but, as "the light of men" (1:4; see 8:12), challenged them to acknowledge the light (Jesus), that is, to believe and walk in it. **Children** (or "sons") **of** is a Semitic idiom. The hereditary meaning led to the figurative "characterized by" (see, e.g., "Barnabas … The son of consolation," Acts 4:36).

D. Continued Jewish Unbelief (12:37–50)

12:37–40. They believed not on him (v. 37). God's ancient people should have responded when He sent His Messiah. They should have seen the significance of the signs Jesus did. John related this hardened unbelief to the fulfillment of Isaiah 53:1 (see Rom. 10:16). The idea of seeing and not believing is also prominent in God's judgment in verses 39–40 (compare 9:39–41 and the sign of healing the blind man). The words **could not believe** (v. 39) mean not that the people in question had no choice. They purposely rejected God and chose evil, therefore **He hath blinded their eyes, and hardened their heart** (v. 40). These words from Isaiah 6:10 were quoted by Jesus (see Matt. 13:14–15; Mark 4:12; Luke 8:10) and by Paul (see Acts 28:26–27). Many Jewish leaders did believe in Jesus as the Messiah, however (see 12:42).

12:41. Saw his glory. Isaiah spoke primarily of the glory of God (see Isa. 6:3). John spoke of the glory of Jesus and made no basic distinction between the two, attesting Jesus' oneness with God. Thus, if "his" refers to Jesus (preincarnate), the judicial hardening (see 12:40) belongs to Him as well (see Carson, *The Gospel According to John*, p. 450). The thought of "glory" here is complex and includes majesty and the idea (which meant so much to John) that Jesus' death on the cross and His subsequent resurrection and exaltation showed His real glory. Isaiah foresaw the rejection of Christ, as the passages (Isa. 53:1; 6:10) quoted in 12:38–40 show. He spoke of the Messiah in the words both about blind eyes and hard hearts, on the one hand, and about healing, on the other. This is the cross and this is glory, for the cross and resurrection and exaltation portrayed both suffering and healing, rejection and triumph, humiliation and glory.

12:42–43. Among the chief rulers ... believed (v. 42; see discussion on 1:7). John did not give a picture of unrelieved gloom. Many Jewish leaders believed, though they remained secret believers for fear of excommunication (see discussion on 9:18–23). **They loved the praise** (lit., "glory") **of men more than the praise of God** (v. 43; see 5:44).

12:44–45. Words that are said to have been **cried** (v. 44) or spoken in a loud voice give what was uttered a special emphasis. **Believeth on me**. John ended his story of Jesus' public ministry with an appeal for belief. He did not say when Jesus spoke these words (they may have been uttered earlier), but they are a fitting close to this part of his account. Belief in Jesus is ultimately belief in **him that sent me** (see 1:18). Jesus' mission and representation of the Father, as well as the inseparability of the Father and the Son, are stressed throughout this gospel and given summary emphasis here.

12:46. The words **I am come ... into the world** point to both Jesus' preexistence and His mission. For **light**, summarized here, see discussions on 1:4; 8:12.

12:47–49. To judge (v. 47) was not the purpose of Jesus' coming. Judgment, however, is the other side of salvation. It is not the purpose of the sun's shining to cast shadows, but when the sun shines, shadows are inevitable. The theme of judgment is tied to Jesus' mission and representation of the Father's will (see 5:30; 7:42; 8:15–16, 26; see also 9:39–41). **The Father ... gave me a commandment, what I should say** (v. 49). Because Jesus is the authorized representative of the Father, Jesus' hearers have a great responsibility. His **word** (v. 48) is that which the Father commanded Him to say. To reject it, therefore, is to reject God.

12:50. Life everlasting (see discussion on 3:15) is the content of the Father's command and the purpose of His sending Jesus to the world. Jesus **therefore** said what He did to fulfill the will of the Father, a wonderful note on which to end the account of Jesus' public ministry.

E. Farewell Discourses (chaps. 13–17)

1. Discourse at the Last Supper (chaps. 13–14)

13:1–17:26. John has by far the longest account of the upper room, though curiously, he recorded nothing about the institution of the Lord's Supper. Nonetheless, John records the most detail about what the Lord said to His disciples on that night. One feature of the discourse is Jesus' emphasis on love. The Greek noun (*agapē*) and verb (*agapaō*) for "love" occur only eight times in chapters 1–12 but thirty-one times in chapters 13–17.

13:1. Before the feast of the Passover (see discussions on 2:13; 5:1) suggests to some that this feast was a fellowship meal or "supper" (13:2) eaten sometime before the Passover feast. This would mean that the Last Supper could not have been the Passover meal as the Synoptic Gospels clearly indicate. However, this was probably intended to be a Passover-like meal and celebrated as a substitute in significance. In the gospel of John, Jesus is crucified at the time the Passover lambs were being slaughtered for the Passover feast (see 19:14; compare Dabny, *Mishnah*, Pesa 5.1, 3). **His hour** (see discussion on 2:4) would demonstrate the extent of Jesus' love. **He loved them unto the end** (Greek, *eis telos*) may express adverbially the extent of His love as "fully" or "utterly."

13:2. The desires of **the devil** (Greek, *diabolos*; "slanderer"; see 6:70; 8:44; see 13:27) had already influenced a plan in **the heart of Judas Iscariot** (see discussion on 6:71). John emphasized this influence with a play on words. In accordance with his name, the Devil had "cast deception" and **put** (lit., "cast"; Greek, *ballō*) into Judas's heart the plan **to betray** Jesus. And Judas received it.

13:3. The Father had given all things into his hands (see 3:35). The Father vested the Son with all authority and control in carrying out His will. His death was by no means outside of the Father's purpose for sending His Son. John again emphasized the fulfillment of God's plan and Jesus' control of the situation.

13:4–5. Began to wash the disciples' feet (v. 5). Sandaled feet become grimy with travel. It was customary hospitality to provide water for a guest to wash his own feet (see Luke 7:44). To wash another's feet was viewed as such a menial task (see discussion on 1:27; see 1 Sam. 24:41) that even Jewish slaves should not be required to perform it (Midrash, Mekilta 82a on Exodus 21:2). On this occasion, Jesus deliberately washed His disciples' feet during the meal (v. 4) rather than upon their arrival to emphasize a point. It was a lesson in humility, but it also set forth

the principle of selfless service that would so soon be exemplified in the cross. John alone recorded this incident, but Luke reported that in rebuking the disciples over a quarrel concerning who would be the greatest, Jesus said, "I am among you as he that serveth" (Luke 22:27). Jesus' life of service would culminate on the cross (see Phil. 2:5–8 and discussions).

13:6–9. Never (v. 8). Characteristically, Peter objected, though apparently no one else did. Jesus' reply, **If I wash thee not, thou hast no part with me**, shows that a crucial lesson was being taught and Peter had to learn it if he was to have anything to do with Jesus. Peter then realized what was at stake and thus asked Jesus to wash every part of him that might need to be cleaned (because of exposure), including **my hands and my head** (v. 9). What was the crucial lesson? Peter, like all disciples, had to accept the reversal of roles that the Master and Lord willingly accepts in order to love. What was menial service for any person, none other than the Lord and Master Himself assumed to exemplify what the cross would epitomize. As Jesus later taught (see 13:12–15), and as every disciple must learn, no title is too majestic and no service is too menial for such sacrificial love. It is a most profound lesson that every disciple must learn to be identified with Jesus; such is the thrust of much of this chapter.

13:9–11. Peter first refused Jesus' humble service, then, still not understanding, connected the washing to cleanliness. Wanting to "have a part with Jesus" (see 13:8), Peter asked for more washing, dramatically reversing his initial refusal. He did not need more, however, **save to wash his feet** (v. 10). A man would bathe himself before going to a feast. When he arrived, he needed to wash only his feet to be entirely clean again. Although Jesus corrected Peter's request for an extended washing, He then pivoted from the physical to the spiritual, by exempting one (Judas) from the declaration **ye are clean**. John immediately explained Jesus' shift. **He knew** (v. 11), as the others did not, that Judas, whose feet Jesus had washed, would **betray Him**.

13:12–13. After washing the feet of each disciple, Jesus fully interpreted His actions and explained the lesson shown to be so crucial at Peter's initial refusal (see 13:8). He who is **Master and Lord** (v. 13) became lower than a servant to wash their feet (see discussion on 13:4–5). Such a reversal of roles by none other than the Master and Lord demonstrated the obligation of love for those who call Him Master and Lord. An instructor would normally be called "master," or "teacher," but "Lord" referred to one occupying the supreme place. Jesus accepted both titles. Some Christians believe that Christ intended to institute a footwashing ordinance to be practiced regularly. More than an ordinance, however, Jesus was exemplifying a lowly and humble attitude that comes from sacrificial love, is epitomized in the cross, and is identified with His own character.

13:14–15. To wash one another's feet (v. 14) is symbolic (**an example**; v. 15), as was Jesus' action, and not limited by its literal wording. Disciples must be willing to perform the most menial services for one another. **Do as I have done to you** is tantamount to saying, "Let not your status or a menial task get in the way of serving one another with the love I have shown you."

13:16. Jesus used easily recognizable social institutions to illustrate clearly demarcated roles of obligation: the **servant** ("slave") and the **lord**; the representative (**he that is sent**) and the sender. A little later, Jesus would personalize the connections made here between His disciples and both the "servant" (see 15:15, 20) and the representative (see 13:20; 20:21). For now, the implication was clear: no servant has any right to judge a task menial which his master has already performed, and no representative is excluded from undertaking what his sender has deemed worthy of doing. With minor variations, this saying, which Jesus used often, is found in 15:20; Matthew 10:24; Luke 6:40 (see also Luke 22:27).

13:17. Happy points to a spiritual reality that defied the social judgments of Jesus' day, as it does still today. It can be affirmed only by doing; obedience is the path to knowing and understanding.

13:18. I speak not of you all. Jesus was leading up to His impending betrayal (see 13:21). **Eateth bread with me.** To eat bread together was a mark of close fellowship (see *KJV Study Bible* note on Ps.

41:9). **Hath lifted up his heel against me** is perhaps derived from a horse's preparing to kick or from shaking off the dust from one's feet (see Luke 9:5; 10:11); both are signs of contempt.

13:19. That, when it come to pass, ye may believe (see 20:31) shows Jesus' concern for the disciples, not Himself. **I am he** is an emphatic form of speech, such as that in 8:58 (see discussion there).

13:20. Whomsoever I send receiveth me; and … him that sent me. Jesus' mission as the representative of the Father is a major theme of this gospel (see Introduction: "Theme and Theological Message"). Jesus now linked the mission of His followers with His own mission (see 20:21).

13:21. For **troubled**, see 11:33 and discussion on 14:1. Though Jesus knew long before it happened that a friend would betray Him, He was nonetheless grieved.

13:22. Doubting of whom he spake. The disciples' astonishment shows that Judas had concealed his collaboration with Jewish authorities to betray Jesus. No one suspected him (see 13:28), but all seem to have thought that the betrayal would be involuntary (see Mark 14:19).

13:23. At a dinner, guests reclined on couches, **leaning** on the left elbow with the head toward the table. **One of his disciples, whom Jesus loved** is usually thought to be John, the author of this gospel (see 19:26; 20:2; 21:7, 20). The expression does not, of course, mean that Jesus did not love the others but rather that there was a special bond with this man.

13:24–26. He it is, to whom I shall give a sop, when I have dipped it (v. 26). Evidently Judas was near Jesus, possibly in the seat of honor. In the Mediterranean with its code of honor and shame, it was a gesture of intimacy to allow a guest to dip his "sop," or "piece of bread," in one's bowl. The intimacy of Jesus' act starkly contrasted the act of betrayal it identified. Reciprocity to such intimacy was expected. Ironically, in the other gospels, Judas met it with the kiss of betrayal (see Matt. 26:48; Mark 14:44; Luke 22:47), but John did not report it or what happened to Judas following the betrayal, which Matthew reported in his gospel (Matt. 27:3–10).

John used Judas's full name (see discussion on 6:71) in recording this solemn moment.

13:27 – 29. After the sop (v. 27) identifies the critical moment. If giving bread to Judas was a mark of honor, it also seems to have been a final appeal, which Judas did not accept. Rather than reciprocity, the hardness of Judas's resistance is seen in the expression **Satan entered into him** (compare the language of possession in Mark 5:12; Luke 8:30). The name Satan (Hebrew, *ûâṭân;* "adversary") is used only here in John (see 13:2). Jesus' words, **Do quickly**, once more indicate His control. He would die as He directed, not as His opponents determined.

For what intent (v. 28) Jesus said this to Judas was not clear to the disciples. John, who was reporting, excluded himself (see 13:25 – 26) and reported only what the others surmised. Some thought Jesus intended Judas to purchase food for **the feast** (v. 29; see discussion on 13:1), perhaps the Feast of Unleavened Bread, which follows Passover; others thought He intended Judas to care for **the poor** (see 12:5).

13:30. In light of John's emphasis on the conflict between light and darkness, **night** may here be more than a time note, picturing also the darkness of Judas's soul.

13:31 – 32. The Son of man (v. 31; see discussion on Mark 2:10) and **glorified** (see discussion on 7:39) are connected here with the inevitability of the cross (see 3:13 – 14; 6:62; 8:28; 12:34 see 13:23), which was now impending. As inglorious as crucifixion was meant to be, Jesus' sacrificial death on the cross was far from inglorious. It manifested the glorious salvation that the Father sent His Son to achieve. Therefore, **God is glorified in him** (v. 32). The glory of the Father is closely bound to the attainment of what the Father sent the Son to do.

13:33 – 34. In a sense, **a new commandment** (v. 34) was an old one (see Lev. 19:18), but for Jesus' disciples it was new because it was the mark of their brotherhood, created by His great love for them (see Matt. 22:37 – 39; Mark 12:30 – 31; Luke 10:27). The standard is Christ's love for us: **as I have loved you**.

13:35. Love is the distinguishing mark of Jesus' followers (see 1 John 3:23; 4:7 – 8, 11 – 12, 19 – 21).

13:36. Whither goest thou? Peter seems to have ignored Jesus' words about love and was more concerned about his Master's departure. In Jesus' reply, **thou** is singular and thus personal to Peter, whereas in 13:33, "ye" is plural.

13:37. The words **I will lay down my life** are similar to those of the good shepherd in 10:11. Peter was characteristically sure of himself, when in fact he would not at this time lay down his life for Jesus. Exactly the opposite would be true.

13:38. Denied me thrice. Peter's denial of Jesus is prophesied in all four gospels (see Matt. 26:33 – 35; Mark 14:29 – 31; Luke 22:31 – 34).

14:1. Jesus' talk of death and departure distressed the disciples, and He offered them words of confident encouragement: **Let not your heart be troubled**. "Troubled" (Greek, *tarassō*) is a vivid word that can mean "agitated" or "disturbed." John used it of the water that was "troubled" in 5:7. Jesus Himself knew what it was to be troubled (see 11:33; 12:27; 13:21). "Your" is plural. All the disciples needed comfort. The "heart" is the seat of the emotional, intellectual, and volitional life. In this sense, all of life is lived out of the heart. In speaking of the heart, Jesus was speaking not only to their feelings but also to their faith: **ye believe in God, believe also in me**. This is Jesus' antidote for a troubled heart. The KJV translates this as a statement (indicative mood) followed by a command (imperative mood). The grammar permits this, but it also permits other combinations. The strongest option is two imperatives: "Believe in God; believe also in me." This corresponds not only to "Let not your heart be troubled" (imperative) but also to the underlying need of a troubled heart: faith in God. The heart of God is known through Jesus. The certainty of His word, the basis of the peace He offers the troubled heart, is that His word is as God's word; His heart is as God's heart.

14:2 – 3. My Father's house (v. 2) refers to heaven, the abode of **many mansions**. "Mansions" is literally "dwellings," or places to abide (Greek, *monē*, from the verb *menō;* "remain," "abide"). In the Father's house, there is ample room for permanent living. There is no rival in all Scripture to the tender picture that these verses present of God the Father's household filled with rooms and, by extension, alive with His children. They need not fear the future. **I go to prepare a place for you**. The Father's house already exists. Jesus was saying not that He must go to build it but rather that He must go because His departure and return to the Father (the cross and resurrection) was the means of enabling believers to inhabit the house of the Father. In addition to preparing the way, however, He is also preparing a dwelling place for them in the Father's house. The terminology is reminiscent of the Jewish wedding custom in which the betrothed groom (Christ) prepares a place for his bride (the church) in his father's house (heaven). **I will come again** (v. 3) refers to the rapture, when Jesus will return to take the believers home to the Father's house (see 1 Thess. 4:13–17).

14:4. The emphasis here is on **the way**, which anticipates Jesus' statement, "I am the way" (14:6). Peter's question of 13:36 had been answered (see 14:2–3), and the disciples now knew not only "whither goest thou?" (13:36) but "the way" (Jesus), even though they continued to think geographically.

14:5. Thomas was candid and plainly told the Lord that he and the others (**we**) did not understand the answer to Peter's original question (see 13:36). If **whither thou goest** remained unclear, **the way** was all the more unclear. In the gospel of John, Thomas is portrayed as a loyal disciple with a penchant for the concrete and tangible (see discussion on 11:16; 20:24–25): what he could not see, he could not accept. One may discern here a desire on the part of Thomas to become familiar with the topography of getting from one place to another, as if the disciples should be able to visualize the turns and the milestones that would incrementally mark a successful journey. Jesus had already confirmed that He would return to get them (see 14:3). It appears characteristic of Thomas's loyalty and bent for the observable to push for a backup plan to follow Jesus (see 13:37). Note that although Thomas spoke for the other disciples, Jesus directed His answer to Thomas ("him," 14:6).

14:6. I am the way (see discussion on 6:35) expressly answered the question of Thomas. The coor-dinate and additional words, **truth** and **life**, expand and confirm the virtue of why Jesus is "the way." In other words, "I am the way (to the Father) in that I am the truth and the life." **No man cometh unto the Father, but by me** is an exclusive truth that is general in scope, and it certainly envelops any thought on the part of the disciples that they could go on their own to where Jesus was going. He was going to God the Father (see 13:1), the "Father's house" (14:2), and His death and resurrection was the only way. Jesus is not one way among many, but the only way (see Acts 4:12; Heb. 10:19–20). In the early church, Christianity was sometimes called the "way" (see, e.g., Acts 9:2; 19:9, 23). Jesus is **the truth** because He is the genuine revelation of God: "he hath declared him" (1:18; see 1:1, 14). Jesus is **the life** because He is the source of life (see 1:3–4; 5:26), the resurrection and life eternal (see 11:25; 1 John 5:20).

14:7. Me … my Father. Jesus once again stressed the intimate connection between the Father and Himself. Jesus brought a full revelation of the Father (see 1:18), so the apostles had real knowledge of Him.

14:8–10. Philip (v. 8) discerned that the Father could indeed be seen in Jesus. It was not the Father's physicality, however, but rather His nature and character that was present in Jesus. Jesus therefore oriented Philip's thinking toward "knowing" Him (v. 9). As the Son of the Father, Jesus was the fitting representative and revealed the Father not only in His person but also in His faithful expression of the Father's will through His words and works.

14:11. Believe … that I am in the Father, and the Father in me. Saving faith is trust in a person, Jesus, but it must also have factual content. Faith includes believing that Jesus is the expression of the Father as apprehended in Jesus' words and works.

14:12–14. Works … greater works (v. 12) point to the actions, even the miraculous ones, that Jesus performed on behalf of the Father in representing the Father's will (see 4:34; 5:20, 36; 9:4; 17:4). Just as Jesus did these works not of His own accord but in the name of the Father (see 5:43; 10:25; 12:28; 17:6, 12, 26), the greater works of the disciples would represent Jesus and be carried out in His name (see 20:21). The glory of the Father is the mutual end of such works. **In my name** (vv. 13, 14) is a reference not to prayer that merely utters Jesus' name but to prayer in accordance with all that the person who bears the name is (see discussion on 2:23). It is prayer aimed at carrying forward the work that Jesus did, prayer that He Himself will answer. The works that the disciples would do depended on Jesus' going to the Father, because they would be done in the strength of the Holy Spirit, whom Jesus would send from the Father (15:26; 16:7; see 14:16–17).

14:15. Love ... keep. Love, like faith (see James 2:14–26), cannot be separated from obedience (see 14:21, 23–24).

14:16. The Father ... shall give you. The first of a series of important passages about the Holy Spirit (14:26; 15:26; 16:7–15), the gift of the Father. After Jesus' departure, the Father would send **another**, besides Jesus, whom Jesus identified as the **Comforter**, or "Counselor" (Greek, *paraklētos*; one who acts on another's behalf, "advocate," "intercessor," "helper"). This was a legal term but had a broader meaning than "counsel for the defense" (see 1 John 2:1). It referred to any person who helped someone in trouble with the law. The Spirit will always stand by believers; **he [will] abide with you for ever** (see 14:18).

14:17. The Spirit of truth. In essence and in action, the Spirit is characterized by truth. He brings people to the truth of God. All three persons of the Trinity are linked with truth (for the Father, see 4:23–24; Ps. 31:5; Isa. 65:16; for the Son, see 14:6). The Spirit of God, **whom the world cannot receive**, or apprehend (see 1 Cor. 2:14), would be **with** Jesus' disciples and **in** them. Some believe the latter relationship (indwelling) specifically anticipated the coming of the Holy Spirit on the day of Pentecost (see Acts 2; Rom. 8:9).

14:18. I will come to you relates to the coming of the Spirit, but Jesus was also speaking of His own appearances after the resurrection and at His second coming (see 14:3, 19, 28; 16:22). **Comfortless**, or "as orphans" (Greek, *orphanos*), suggests helplessness, those who must fend for themselves.

14:19. The world ... but ye. The cross separated the world (who would not see Jesus thereafter) from the disciples (who would see Him). **Because I live, ye shall live also.** The life of the Christian always depends on the life of Christ (see 1:4; 3:15).

14:20. At that day ye shall know. The resurrection would radically change the disciples' thinking.

14:21. Keepeth ... loveth. Love for Christ and keeping His commands cannot be separated (see discussion on 14:15). "Keepeth" means to observe and fulfill the will of Jesus as expressed in His commands. **Shall be loved of my Father, and I will love him** points once again to the oneness of the Father and the Son. Love that is genuine enough to obey Jesus is not only love for Jesus but love for the Father. In turn, not only Jesus but also the Father loves the believer who obeys Jesus' will. The love of the Father cannot be separated from that of the Son.

14:22. How is it ...? Judas (and for that matter, the others) probably looked for Jesus to fulfill popular messianic expectations. It was not easy therefore to understand how that would mean showing Himself to the disciples but not to the world.

14:23–24. Love ... keep ... love (v. 23) forms an unbroken chain. The links of love and obedience are of one piece in an authentic relationship with Jesus and the Father (see 14:15, 21). In answering the question of Judas, Jesus made it clear that no one is excluded, but there is a condition: love must issue in **keep[ing] my words** (v. 24; see 14:21; 1 John 2:3–5). Once more the close relationship between Jesus' words and the Father's is stressed (see 14:10; 7:16).

14:26. The Comforter (see discussion on 14:16) **... is the Holy Ghost**, which is His normal title in the New Testament (though only here and in 1:33; 20:22 in this gospel), emphasizing His holiness rather than His power or greatness. **Whom the Father will send.** Both the Father and the Son would be involved in the sending (see 15:26). **In my name** (see discussions on 2:23; 14:13) points to the Spirit's operation on Jesus' behalf (see 15:26; 16:13–15) in the lives of His disciples. One of the Spirit's functions is to **bring all things to your remembrance, whatsoever I have said unto you.** The sending of the Spirit thus was crucial for the life of the church, as it was for the writing of the New Testament.

14:27. Peace ... my peace is a common Hebrew greeting (see 20:19, 21, 26), which Jesus used here in an unusual way. The Old Testament word for peace (Hebrew, *shalom*) speaks of wholeness, as in altogether well, particularly in relation to God. The way Jesus used the word "peace" incorporated the salvation that His redemptive work would achieve for His disciples: total well-being and inner rest of spirit, in fellowship with God. All true peace is His gift, which the repetition emphasizes. His peace is given **not as the world giveth**. In its greetings of peace, the world can only express a longing or wish, but Jesus' peace is real and present. For **troubled**, see discussion on 14:1.

14:28–29. Heard how I said (v. 28) echoes the explanation of 14:3. **Ye would rejoice** defines the outlook of the disciple that loves Jesus and appreciates His mission, which necessarily involved returning to the one who sent Him. **My Father is greater than I** attests once again to the subordinate role Jesus accepted as a necessary part not only of the incarnation but also of His fidelity to fulfilling the Father's will as His representative (see Introduction: "Theme and Theological Message"). The statement must be understood in the light of the unity between the Father and the Son (see 10:30).

14:30. For **prince of this world**, see discussion on 12:31. **Hath nothing in me.** Satan has a hold on people because of their fallen state. Since Christ was sinless, Satan could have no hold on Him.

14:31. As the Father gave me commandment, even so I do. Jesus had stressed the importance of His followers being obedient (see 14:15, 21, 23), and He set the example. With these words, He went to fulfill His mission (see chaps. 18–19).

2. Discourse on the Way to Gethsemane *(chaps. 15–16)*

15:1. I am the true vine (see discussion on 6:35). The vine is frequently used in the Old Testament as a symbol of Israel (see, e.g., Ps. 80:8–16; Isa. 5:1–7; Jer. 2:21). When this imagery is used, Israel is often shown as lacking in some way. Jesus, however, is "the true vine." For this sense of "true," see discussion on 1:9.

15:2. Taketh away speaks of removal of deadwood and implies judgment (see discussion on 15:6). God, "the husbandman" (15:1), **purgeth** (i.e., prunes) the fruitful branch to increase fruitfulness. In the New Testament, good fruit symbolizes the product of a godly life (see Matt. 3:8; 7:16–20) or virtues of character (see Gal. 5:22–23; Eph. 5:9; Phil. 1:11).

15:3. The word, or message, of Jesus is the pruning instrument that corresponds to the work of the husbandman (see 15:2). It may also be that because of Jesus' word, these branches emerge **clean** and fruitful. The Greek for "clean," however, is the same root word as "purgeth" (15:2). Christ wants to use the Word to cleanse us, but He may use other more severe measures if believers will not allow the Word to do its work in them.

15:4. Abide in me emphasizes the vitality of the vine as the source of fruitfulness. The believer has no fruitfulness apart from his or her union and fellowship with Christ. A branch out of contact with the vine is lifeless.

15:5. For **I am the vine**, see discussion on 15:1. The repetition gives emphasis. **Abideth in me, and I in him** speaks of a living union with Christ, the vine, that is as necessary for the believer as it is for the branch; without that vital connection, there is **nothing**.

15:6. The branches that are not connected to the vine do not bear fruit and are **cast ... into the fire, and they are burned** (see Ezek. 15:1–8). Apart from Christ, there is no life, and the outcome is destruction, a picture of judgment (see discussion on 15:2). In light of such passages as 6:39 and 10:27–28, these branches probably do not represent true believers. Genuine salvation is evidenced by a life of fruitfulness (see discussions on 15:2, 4; see also 15:10; Matt. 7:19–23; Heb. 6:9, "things that accompany salvation").

15:7. The evidence of this vital union, Jesus said, is whether **My words abide in you**. The words of Jesus are like the sap of the vine that brings life to every branch. It is impossible to pray correctly apart from knowing and believing the teachings of Christ. For **ask what ye will**, see 14:13 – 14 and discussion.

15:8 – 9. **My Father [is] glorified** (v. 8) in the work of the Son (see 13:31 – 32), and He is also glorified in the fruit-bearing of His disciples (see Matt. 7:20; Luke 6:43 – 45). A failure to bear fruit results not from any deficiency in the vine; Jesus loves with the same love that the Father has given Him. The admonition **continue** (or "abide") **ye in my love** points to the sufficiency of Jesus' (and the Father's) love for all manner of fruitfulness.

15:10. **Keep … as I have kept** stresses once again the importance of obedience (see 14:15, 21, 23) to the character of love and the example of Christ (see 14:31). **My love … his love** (see 15:12, 14) shows not only that obedience and love go together (see 1 John 2:5; 5:2 – 3) but also that love, as Jesus defined it, is more than a sentiment or emotion (see 15:12, 13).

15:11. **Joy** is mentioned previously only in 3:29 but is one of the characteristic notes of the Upper Room Discourse (see 16:20 – 22, 24; 17:13). The Christian way is never dreary, for Jesus desires His disciples' joy to be complete (see 1 John 1:3 – 4).

15:12 – 13. Christ's love was revealed not only in words but also in His sacrificial death. How selfless is such love? The extent of its depth is immolation of the self for another.

15:14 – 15. **I call you not servants … but I have called you friends** (v. 15). With the emphasis that Jesus put on obedience, one might think He described the servile obedience of a servant or slave, but voluntary obedience inspired by shared purpose points to a different status: friends. Jesus takes His friends into His confidence: **all things … I have made known unto you.** From 16:12, one learns that though Jesus had let His disciples know as much as they were able to absorb of the Father's plan, the revelation was not yet complete. The Spirit would make other things known in due course.

15:16. **I have chosen you … bring forth fruit … ask.** Disciples normally chose the particular rabbi to whom they wanted to be attached, but it was not so with Jesus' disciples. He chose them, and for a purpose: the bearing of fruit. Believers usually desire a strong prayer life so that they may be fruitful, but in this passage, it is the other way around. Jesus enables believers to bear fruit, and then the Father will hear their prayers. Normally, prayer is addressed to **the Father in [Christ's] name** (see discussions on 2:23; 14:13 – 14), meaning on the basis of His access to the Father, and with the help of the Holy Spirit.

15:17. Now that Jesus has detailed their status and privileges, He commences to speak of their obligations. **These things** refers to what follows, notably the obligation to **love one another**.

15:18 – 19. **The world** (vv. 18) refers to the human system that opposes God's purpose (see discussion on 1:9 – 10). **Ye are not of the world** (v. 19), because the believer's essential being, his new life, comes specially from God, and therefore he is not the same as those who oppose God.

15:20 – 21. Disciples, even with their status of friends of the Master (see 15:14 – 15), are not exempt from the world's hatred that association with Jesus will attract. **The servant is not greater than his lord** (v. 20). Here Jesus underscored the point with the pithy, almost proverbial saying He used in 13:16. **All these things will they do unto you** (v. 21). Persecution from the world is inevitable because those who identify with Jesus (for **for my name's sake**, see discussion on 2:23) give their allegiance to Him and not to the world. Jesus explained that the basic reason for such persecution is the world's ignorance and rejection of the Father (see 16:3) who sent Him.

15:22 – 24. Jesus came to the world as the Father's representative, and one's response to Jesus is likewise one's response to God (see 5:23). Because Jesus **had … come and spoken unto them** (v. 22), those who rejected Him had **no cloke**, or "excuse" (see KJV marginal note). The Jews had the great privilege of having the Son of God among them, in addition to having received God's special revelation in the Old Testament. Privilege and responsibility go together. Their rejection of Jesus left them totally guilty and without excuse. Had He not come to them, they would still have been sinners, but they would not have been guilty of rejecting Him directly (v. 24).

15:25. That the word might be fulfilled that is written. In the end, God's purpose is always accomplished, despite the belief of sinful men that they have successfully opposed it. The **law** (see discussions on 10:34; 12:34), the very revelation of God that the Jews jealously guarded as their own, condemned them.

15:26. Testimony to Jesus and His coming would continue after He returned to the Father. **The Comforter** (see discussions on 14:16, 26), whom Jesus said He **will send unto you from the Father** (see discussion on 14:26), would bear witness to Jesus. Thus, **the Spirit of truth** (see discussion on 14:17) would equip the disciples of Jesus. **Proceedeth from the Father** parallels or equivocates what Jesus said about sending the Spirit but emphasizes that the Spirit is the Father's special endowment.

15:27. Ye also shall bear witness is emphatic and accentuates that believers bear their testimony to Christ in the power of the Spirit. It is their testimony, however, and they are responsible for bearing it. **From the beginning** qualifies the witness of the apostles as the definitive testimony, for they were uniquely chosen and taught by Christ and were eyewitnesses of His glory (see Luke 24:48; Acts 10:39, 41).

16:1–2. They shall put you out of the synagogues (v. 2) echoes 9:22 and the jeopardy of identifying with Jesus. **Think that he doeth God service** alerts one to the mindset of religious people who persecute others in the strong conviction that they are honoring God (see Acts 26:9–11; Gal. 1:13–14).

16:3. The service supposedly rendered to God in 16:2 is here shown to be defined by one's relationship to Jesus. Abstract notions of God are supplanted by Jesus' revelation of God as **the Father** (see discussion on 5:17). With the words **nor me**, Jesus again linked the Father and the Son. Not to know Christ is to be ignorant of the Father.

16:4–5. None of you asketh me, Whither goest thou? (v. 5). Peter had asked such a question (see 13:36) but quickly turned his attention to another subject. His concern had been what would happen to himself and the others and not where Jesus was going.

16:6. Jesus again perceived the condition of His disciples' hearts because of His announced departure. Earlier their hearts had been "troubled" (14:1; see discussion there); now that agitation was followed or compounded by sadness (Greek, *lypē*; "pain," often of mind or spirit): **sorrow hath filled your heart.**

16:7. If I go not away. Jesus did not say why the Spirit would not come until He went away, but He clearly taught that His saving work on the cross was necessary before the sending of the Spirit. The Spirit is again identified as **the Comforter** (see discussions on 14:16, 26), and His title was appropriate to the disciples' "sorrow" (16:6). **I will send him** (see discussion on 14:26) assured the disciples that Jesus' departure, or return to the Father (see 13:1), was **expedient** (Greek, *sympherō*), to their "advantage" or "benefit."

16:8–11. In this passage, Jesus amplified the benefit of the Comforter. The New Testament normally speaks of the Spirit's work in believers, but here a wider arena of activity is in view. The dimensions of the Spirit's convicting work are elaborated in verses 9–11.

16:8. One of the Spirit's operations is the threefold work of spiritual prosecution: **He will reprove the world of sin … righteousness … judgment.** To "reprove" means to "expose the guilt of."

16:9. Through the Spirit's convicting work, people are brought to a recognition of their sin. **Of sin, because they believe not** may mean either that their sin is their failure to believe or that their unbelief is a classic example of sin. Typically, John may have had both of these in mind. In either case, it is willful unbelief and not ignorance.

16:10. Unbelief involves a rejection of who Jesus is and that He was sent from God. Jesus' return to the Father would ratify that God sent Him and would show God's approval of Him through the glorifying work of His death and resurrection. This is seen in the words **because I go to my Father**, commonly referred to as the ascension. As part of Christ's exaltation, the ascension placed God's seal of approval on Christ's redemptive act. **Of righteousness** points to the Spirit's work of confirming Jesus' righteousness and, with it, the righteousness brought about by His sacrificial death (see Rom. 1:17; 3:21–22). No one but the Holy Spirit can reveal to a person that a righteous status before God does not depend on good works but on Christ's death on the cross.

16:11. In referring to the Comforter's work **Of judgment,** Jesus was speaking of the defeat of Satan, which was a form of judgment, not simply a victory. More than power is in question. God acts with justice. Satan is referred to as **the prince of this world** (see discussion on 12:31), conveying the power that Satan exercises over this domain.

16:12. Ye cannot bear them now. This may mean "more than you can understand now" or "more than you can perform without the Spirit's help" (to live out Christ's teaching requires the enabling presence of the Spirit).

16:13. For **the Spirit of truth,** see discussion on 14:17. Jesus said the Spirit would speak **whatsoever he shall hear,** but it is unclear whether He hears from the Father or the Son. It obviously does not matter, however, for the verse stresses the close relationship among the three. **Things to come** probably means the whole Christian way or revelation (presented and preserved in the apostolic writings), still future at the time Jesus spoke.

16:14–15. The Spirit draws no attention to Himself but promotes the glory of Christ. For **glorify me** (v. 14), see discussion on 1:14. The Spirit exalts and gives expression to the character, reputation, and presence of Christ, for **All things that the Father hath are mine** (v. 15; see 3:35; 13:3; see 17:10). The three persons are closely related.

16:16. A little while … a little while. Few doubt that the first phrase refers to the interval before the crucifixion, but interpretations differ as to whether the second refers to the interval preceding the resurrection, or the coming of the Spirit, or the second coming of Christ. It seems that the language best fits the resurrection.

16:17–19. Jesus had not linked the words **I go to the Father** (v. 17; see 16:10) with **a little while** (see 16:16), but the apostles saw them as connected.

Apart from their confusion, Jesus had addressed His death and the resurrection, which correspond to **ye shall not see me** and **ye shall see me**. The disciples were speaking to one another, but Jesus clarified the pattern in His question of verse 19.

16:20–21. Weep (v. 20) is the same verb for loud wailing used in 11:33, which carries the idea of deep sorrow and its outward expression. Weeping and **joy** correspond to the sequence of death and resurrection, "ye shall not see me" and "ye shall see me" (16:16). Jesus related this to **A woman when she is in travail** (v. 21). Giving birth usually causes both pain and joy (see Isa. 26:17–19; 66:7–14; Hos. 13:13–14).

16:22. As in 16:16, **I will see you again** is probably a reference to Jesus' appearances after His resurrection. **Your joy no man taketh from you** speaks of the resurrection, which would change things permanently, bringing a joy that the world's assaults cannot remove.

16:23. Ye shall ask me nothing seems to mean asking for information (rather than asking in prayer), which would not be necessary after the resurrection. Jesus then moved on to the subject of prayer. He may have been saying that His disciples previously had been praying to Christ, but after His death and resurrection they were to go directly to the Father and pray in Christ's **name** (see 16:24, 26–27; see also 2:23; 14:13–14 and discussions).

16:24. Hitherto (previously) the disciples had asked the Father or Christ, but they had not asked the Father in Christ's name. **Ask** implies "keep on asking," involving the disciples in persistence when petitioning. For **your joy,** see discussion on 15:11.

16:25. Have I spoken unto you in proverbs points to figures of speech Jesus used throughout the discourse (chaps. 15–16), not just in the immediately preceding words. **The time cometh,** after the resurrection, when Jesus would speak **plainly** (Greek, *parrēsia*; "frankly," "boldly"; see 7:4, 25)

16:26. I say not unto you, that I will pray the Father for you. This is not a contradiction of Romans 8:34; Hebrews 7:25; 1 John 2:1. Those passages mean that Christ's presence in heaven as the crucified and risen Lord is itself an intercession. Here the teaching is that there will be no need for Him to make petitions on believers' behalf.

16:27–29. The Father himself loveth you (v. 27). Christ explained why the disciples could come directly to the Father in prayer. Because they had loved and trusted in Jesus, God would hear their requests in Jesus' name. Jesus' mission, His being sent by the Father and His return to the Father, is crucial to properly apprehending His unique authority to reveal the Father and achieve salvation. The disciples needed to grasp this, and they did (see 16:30).

16:29. For **no proverb**, see 16:25 and discussion.

16:30–31. We believe that thou camest forth from God (v. 30). This statement reflects two recurring themes of this gospel: believing (see discussion on 1:7) and Jesus' coming from God (see 16:27–28; discussion on 4:34).

16:32. Ye shall be scattered. The disciples had faith but not enough to stand firm in the face of disaster. Jesus knew they would fail; however, His church is built not on people's strength but on God's ability to use people even after they have failed.

16:33. Notice the contrasts: between **in me** and **In the world** (see discussion on 1:9–10) and between **peace** and **tribulation**. Just before His death, Jesus encouraged His disciples with an affirmation of His final victory: **I have overcome**.

3. Jesus' Prayer of Intercession (chap. 17)

17:1–26. Jesus' longest recorded prayer is found here in the gospel of John. It is truly deserving of the title "the Lord's Prayer." Jesus devoted this prayer to the primary concerns and issues of His mission (His sending), which was all but completed. The pattern of Jewish agency, which illumines one's understanding of the sending of Jesus (see Introduction: "Theme and Theological Message"), is evident here too, with one significant change. Every human agent returned and reported to his sender. Here Jesus, the divine agent and representative of the Father, took up the concerns and accomplishments of His mission in anticipation of His return. As the Son who was sent (see Mark 12:5; Matt. 21:37), endowed with

the Father's supreme authority, Jesus entailed in His prayer both the intimacy of such an extraordinary relationship as well as the deference of one who had officially and faithfully acted on the Father's behalf.

17:1. Lifted up his eyes to heaven was the customary attitude in prayer (see 11:41; Ps. 123:1; Mark 7:34), though sometimes the person prostrated himself (see Matt. 26:39). **Father** is used of God in John's gospel 119 times, and 96 of them are in the words of Jesus (see discussion on 4:21). **The hour** (see discussion on 2:4) upon which Jesus had focused throughout His ministry was at hand (see 13:1). Glory (**glorify … glorify**) was mutual because the character and will of both the Father and the Son were bound together in what had to be accomplished in this hour (see discussions on 1:14; 7:39; 13:31–32). Glorification involves a benefit that belongs also to believers: the death by which Jesus would glorify God would lead to eternal life for all who believe (see 17:2).

17:2. Thou hast given him all power (see 3:35; 13:1) is elaborated throughout the prayer in references to what the Father had given, or entrusted, to Jesus (see 17:4, 6–9, 11–12, 14, 22, 24; discussion on 3:27). **That he should give eternal life** expresses the purpose the Father had in granting Jesus such vast authority (see discussions on 3:15; 5:21–27). **As many as thou hast given him**, or entrusted to Jesus, shows again God's initiative in salvation.

17:3. Eternal life is the believer's endowment, but as the word **sent** indicates, it is the achievement of Jesus' mission and brings before believers the role of Jesus' agency in the divine plan, mission, and salvation that He achieved.

17:4. I have glorified thee. Christ's mission was not self-centered but on behalf of the Father. **The work which thou gavest me to do** expresses the supreme aegis of the Father in Jesus' mission.

17:5. Glorify thou me … with the glory which I had with thee. Jesus asked the Father to reinstate Him to His previous position of glory, to exchange humiliation for glorification. This occurred at Christ's resurrection and exaltation to God's right hand. The Greek for **world** occurs eighteen times in this prayer. Here it identifies the universe (see discussions on 1:9–10; 17:14).

17:6. I have manifested thy name (see 1:18) is another way of saying "I have glorified you" (17:4), for the "name" stands for the person (see discussions on 2:23; 14:13). **The men which thou gavest me** again points to the divine initiative (see 6:44).

17:7. All things … are of thee expresses the aegis of the Father in His sending Jesus to the world and the fulfillment of Jesus' revelation of the Father: "he hath declared him" (1:18). Throughout John's gospel, Jesus never varied from His faithful dependence on and devotion to the Father's will, expressed in Jesus' words and works. Only as people see the Father at work in Jesus do they have a proper concept of God. The disciples had at last reached this understanding.

17:8. Three things about the disciples are mentioned: (1) They accepted Jesus' teaching (unlike the Pharisees and others who heard it but did not receive it). (2) They knew with certainty Jesus' divine origin. Acceptance of the revelation led them further into truth. (3) They believed (see discussion on 1:7; see 1:12; 20:31).

17:9–10. I pray not for the world (v. 9). The only prayer Jesus could pray for the world was that it cease to be worldly (i.e., opposed to God), and this He did pray (see 17:21, 23).

17:11. Holy Father is a form of address found only here in the New Testament (but see 1 Peter 1:15–16; Rev. 4:8; 6:10). The title suggests both remoteness and nearness; God is both awe-inspiring and loving. To **keep through thine own name** suggests the aegis of the Father, which earmarked Jesus' mission and on which He was totally dependent (see 17:6–7, 12). It was instrumental to the unity of the Father and the Son and was now featured in Jesus' prayer for those entrusted to Him and to whom He had manifested the Father (see 17:6). **That they may be one** summarizes the focus of the latter part of the prayer, which strongly emphasizes unity. The unity was already given, not something to be achieved. The meaning is "that they continually be one" rather than "that they become one." The unity of believers is to be like that of the Father and the

Son. While it is much more than unity of organization, the church's present divisions are the result of the failures of Christians.

17:12. I kept … I have kept makes it clear that Christ's power is adequate for every need. Jesus Himself had kept the disciples safe ("I kept"; Greek, *tēreō*) and guardedly watched over ("I have kept"; Greek, *phylassō*) them. **The son of perdition** means "the son of destruction," that is, one belonging to the sphere of damnation and destined for destruction (but predestination is not here in view). The reference is to Judas Iscariot.

17:13. From the features of Jesus' prayer to this point, it may be inferred that **My joy** (see discussion on 15:11) refers to Jesus' enjoyment of the Father's all-sufficient provision, protection, direction, and authority (aegis) for His mission. His delight was in the Father. Now Jesus prayed that this joy might be replicated in His disciples.

17:14. The world is the domain that is hostile to God and God's people (see discussions on 1:9; 17:5). The disciples were **not of the world**, or having the mindset of the world (i.e., hostility to God), for they had been "born of the Spirit" (3:8) and were "sons of God" (1:12).

17:15–16. Jesus prayed not that God would **take them out of the world** (v. 15) but rather that they would be "in the world but not of the world" (see 1 Cor. 5:9–10; 2 Cor. 10:3). He prayed that the disciples would be resistant to the world's influence. The world is where Jesus' disciples were to do their work; He did not wish them to be taken from it until that work was done (see 17:18). **The evil**, or the Evil One (see 1 John 2.13–14; 3:12; 5:18–19), Satan, who is especially active in the world, makes God's protection indispensable.

17:17. Sanctify means "to set apart for sacred use" or "to make holy" (also in 17:19). **Thy truth: thy word** indicates that sanctification and revelation (as recorded in God's Word) go together. For the connection of Christ's teaching with truth, see 8:31–32.

17:18. Jesus' mission is one of the dominant themes of this gospel, and **As thou hast sent me … even so have I also sent them** shows that the Father's sending of Jesus is the pattern for His followers. **Into the world** (see 17:14–15) is the arena where the disciples would carry on Jesus' commission. One may long for heaven, but it is on earth that one's work is done.

17:19. I sanctify myself is a statement that appears to be unparalleled. In the Septuagint (the Greek translation of the Old Testament), the verb is used of consecrating priests (Exod. 28:41) and sacrifices (Exod. 28:38; Num. 18:9). Jesus solemnly "set himself apart to do God's will," which at this point meant His death. **That they also might be sanctified** (see discussion on 17:17). Jesus died on the cross not only to save all humanity but also to consecrate them to God's service.

17:20. Them also which shall believe on me points beyond those that "have believed" (17:8) to future disciples. Jesus had just spoken of the mission and the sanctification of His followers (see 17:18–19). He was confident that they would spread the gospel, and He prayed for those who would believe as a result. All future believers are included in this prayer.

17:21. For **that they also may be one**, see discussion on 17:11. For **Father**, see discussion on 17:1. **That the world may believe**. The unity of believers should have an effect on outsiders, to convince them of the mission of Christ. Jesus' prayer is a rebuke of the groundless and often bitter divisions among believers.

17:22. The glory (see discussion on 17:1). Believers are to be characterized by humility and service, just as Christ was, and it is on them that God's glory rests. Jesus' repeated emphasis on unity, **that they may be one, even as we are one**, shows the importance of unity among His followers, and again the standard is the unity of the Father and the Son.

17:23. I in them, and thou in me. This refers to two indwellings: that of the Son in believers and that of the Father in the Son. It is because the latter is a reality that the former can take place. **Made perfect in one.** The emphasis on unity again has an evangelistic aim. This time it is connected not only with the mission of Jesus but also with God's love for people and for Christ.

17:24. Father (see discussion on 17:1), as so often and so appropriate to prayer, is in direct address here, as throughout this prayer. Jesus said, **I will**, His last will and testament for His followers. "I will" (Greek, *thelō*) expresses His "desire." Where He Himself was concerned, He prayed, "not that I will, but what thou wilt" (Mark 14:36). **Be with me** (see 14:3) is the Christian's greatest blessing. **My glory** is perhaps used here to refer to Jesus' eternal splendor (see 1 John 3:2). Or Jesus' prayer may have been that in the life to come they might fully appreciate the glory of His lowly service (see Eph. 2:7).

17:25. Righteous Father is a form of address found only here in the New Testament (see "Holy Father," 17:11). The disciples did not know God directly and personally, but **these have known** that God had sent Christ. To recognize God in Christ's mission is a great advance over anything **the world** can know.

F. Jesus' Betrayal and Arrest (18:1–12)

18:1. The brook Cedron lies east of Jerusalem and remains dry except during the rainy season. "Brook" translates a Greek word that compounds "winter" and "flowing" and literally reads as "winter-flowing Cedron." The disciples may have expected to spend the night in the **garden** since the city was crowded with pilgrims for Passover. Judas knew the place (see 18:2).

18:2–3. Judas (v. 2; see discussion on 6:71) led **a band** (v. 3), or "cohort" (the Greek translates the Latin *cohors*), **and officers from the chief priests and Pharisees**. A "cohort" (Greek, *speira*; also in 18:12) always refers to Roman soldiers in the New Testament and need not denote a full detachment of 600 men, nor even a full maniple of 200, which *speira* usually connotes. "Officers" is equivalent to the temple guard sent by the Sanhedrin. **Lanterns** were terra-cotta holders into which household lamps could be inserted, and **torches** were resinous pieces of wood fastened together.

18:4–9. Jesus was not taken by surprise, **knowing all things that should come upon him** (v. 4). Taking the initiative, Jesus controlled the encounter and went out of the garden to meet the advancing company. **Whom seek ye?** One may infer from Jesus' question that Judas, who had guided them, receded behind the officials vested with the responsibility of arresting Jesus. As John parenthetically explained, however, the one **which betrayed him, stood with them** (v. 5). In John, the kiss of Judas is overshadowed (and perhaps for that reason omitted) by the formal exchange: the warrant for **Jesus of Nazareth** answered with the consequential **I am he** (see discussions on 6:35; 8:58). At that, **they went backward, and fell to the ground**. They came to arrest a meek peasant and instead were met in the dim light by a majestic person.

The formal question and answer occurred twice, but John's threefold repetition of **I am he** (vv. 5, 6, 8) emphasizes these solemn words. Twice Jesus made the arresting party say plainly that He was the one they wanted (18:4–5, 7). His petition, **let these go their way** (v. 8), verbalized His concern for the disciples even as He was going to His death. **That the saying might be fulfilled** conveys the authority of Jesus and His words. Carson (*The Gospel According to John*, p. 579) puts it well: "Just as events fulfill the authoritative and prophetic words of Scripture, so this event fulfills Jesus' own words, which cannot be less authoritative (cf. Mark 13:31)." John also bears witness to the certification of Jesus' prayer in 17:12; see also 6:39 and 10:28.

18:10. It is John to whom is owed the information that the man with the **sword** (the Greek for this word refers to a short sword) was **Simon Peter** and that the man he wounded was named **Malchus.**

18:11. The cup often points to suffering (see Ps. 75:8; Ezek. 23:31–34) and the wrath of God (see Isa. 51:17, 22; Jer. 25:15; Rev. 14:10; 16:19). **My Father hath given me** reveals once again that God was in control, but Peter needed to be reminded. The Synoptic Gospels also speak of "the cup" at the time of Jesus' prayer at Gethsemane (see Matt. 26:39; Mark 14:36; Luke 22:42), and John said it came from the Father.

18:12. For **band**, see 18:3 and discussion. The **captain** (Greek, *chiliarchos*) is literally a "leader of a thousand soldiers" but is used of a military tribune

or commander of a cohort. It may be that "band" (or "cohort") here designates the Roman soldiers under this tribune and not a full detachment. The reason they **bound him** is not clear. Perhaps it was standard procedure, much like the modern use of handcuffs.

G. The Trials of Jesus (18:13–19:15)

18:13. Annas had been deposed from the high priesthood by the Romans in AD 15 but was probably still regarded by many as the true high priest. In Jewish law, a man could not be sentenced on the day his trial was held. The two examinations, this one (mentioned only by John) and that before Caiaphas, may have been conducted to give some form of legitimacy to what was done. For **the high priest that same year**, see discussion on 11:49.

18:14. Caiaphas … gave counsel to the Jews is a reference to 11:49–50. For John, it was this unconscious prophecy, **that one man should die for the people**, that mattered most about Caiaphas. John may also have been hinting that a fair trial could not be expected from a man who had already said that putting Jesus to death was **expedient** (see 11:50).

18:15–16. Another disciple (v. 15) perhaps refers to John himself. **Known unto the high priest** refers to more than casual acquaintance; this disciple had entrée to the high priest's house and **brought in Peter** (v. 16) as well.

18:17. The damsel that kept the door, a maidservant, is mentioned in all the accounts of Peter's denial (see Matt. 26:69–75; Mark 14:77–72; Luke 22:54–62). Peter's first challenge came from a slave girl, the most unimportant person imaginable. The form of the girl's question implied a negative answer, and Peter capitalized on her expectation by saying, **I am not**. The other gospels seem to indicate that the other denials followed immediately, but it is likely that they were separated by intervals during which other things happened (see Luke 22:58–59).

18:18. Peter stood with them, for on a cold night, he would have been conspicuous if he had stayed away from the fire.

18:19. Asked Jesus refers not to legal questioning, since witnesses were supposed to be brought in first to establish guilt. The accused was not required to prove his innocence. Perhaps Annas (see 18:13) regarded this as a preliminary inquiry, not a trial, since Caiaphas apparently was not present at this inquiry (see 18:24).

18:20–21. I spake openly (v. 20). It should not have been difficult to find witnesses; **them which heard me … know what I said** (v. 21). When Jesus asserted, **In secret have I said nothing** (v. 20), He was denying not that He taught the disciples privately but that He had secretly taught them subversive teaching different from His public message.

18:22. The **stroke**, or "blow," was one of many indignities and another illegality that Jesus suffered. The word apparently means a blow with the open hand, a slap.

18:23–24. Bear witness (v. 23) is a legal term, indicating an invitation to act according to proper legal form. John stressed the importance of testimony throughout his gospel (see discussion on 1:7). The audience proved to be unproductive, and Annas failed to solicit any information from Jesus that might be used to incriminate Him. This and Jesus' request for witnesses (see 18:21) called for a more formal hearing, and Jesus was sent to **Caiaphas** (v. 24), the presiding **high priest**.

18:25. Some find a difficulty in that Matthew 26:71 says another girl asked this question, whereas Mark 14:69 says it was the same girl, and Luke 22:58 that it was a man. With a group of servants talking around a fire, however, several doubtless would have taken up and repeated such a question, which could be the meaning of John's **They said therefore unto him**. As on the first occasion (see 18:17), the question anticipated the answer no. The servants probably did not really expect to find a follower of Jesus in the high priest's courtyard, but the question seemed worth asking. Again Peter answered, **I am not**, his second denial of Christ.

18:26. Being his kinsman whose ear Peter cut off is another piece of information readers owe to John. A relative would have a deeper interest in the swordsman than other people had. The light **in the garden** would have been dim, however, as it was in the courtyard ("a fire of coals" [18:18] glows but does not have flames). In Greek, the question **Did not I see thee …?** expects the answer yes.

18:27. Peter then denied again, his third denial of Christ. **Immediately the cock crew**, and Jesus' prophecy in 13:38 found fulfillment.

18:28. The hall of judgment (Greek, *praitōrion*; a Latin loanword for *praetorium*) was the palace of the Roman governor, Pilate (see Mark 15:16). John recorded little about the Jewish phase of Jesus' trial but much about the Roman trial. It is possible that John was in the Praetorium, the governor's official residence, for this trial. **It was early**. Evidently, the chief priests held a second session of the Sanhedrin after daybreak to give some appearance of legality to what they did (see Mark 15:1). This occasion would have been immediately after that, perhaps between 6:00 a.m. and 7:00 a.m. Ironically, in order to eat the Passover and avoid being **defiled**, a result of entering a Gentile residence, the Jewish authorities remained outside, yet their hands were sullied with manipulated justice to secure the death of Jesus, the true Passover (Carson, *The Gospel According to John*, p. 589). **Eat the passover** does not mean that the time of the Passover meal had not yet come, for this would contradict the Synoptic Gospels, which have Jesus eating the Passover meal the night before. The term "passover" was used to refer to the whole festival of Passover and Unleavened Bread, which lasted seven days and included a number of meals.

18:29–30. Pilate (v. 29; see discussion on Mark 15:1), the Roman governor, showed himself tolerant of Jewish ways. **What accusation …?** was a normal question at the opening of a formal trial, but it was difficult to answer because the Jews had no charge that would stand up in a Roman court of law. Since Roman soldiers were party to the arrest of Jesus, Pilate likely had been briefed of the apprehension of **a malefactor** (v. 30), or one who had violated the law. Now specific violation of Roman law was required.

18:31–32. Without an opening accusation, Pilate remanded Jesus to **the Jews** (v. 31; see discussion on 1:19) with the words, **Take ye him**. In other words, no Roman charge, no Roman trial.

The retort, **It is not lawful for us to put any man to death**, shows they were looking for an execution, not a fair trial. The restriction was important, for otherwise Rome's supporters could be quietly removed by local legal executions. The Romans seem to have sometimes condoned local executions (e.g., of Stephen; see Acts 7), but normally they retained the right to inflict the death penalty. With **what death he should die**, John recalled the words of Jesus and the necessity of crucifixion (see 12:32–33 and "must" in 12:34). Jewish execution was by stoning, but Jesus' death was to be by crucifixion, whereby He would bear the curse (see Deut. 21:22–23). The Romans, not the Jews, had to put Jesus to death. God was ruling over the whole process.

18:33. Pilate's first words to Jesus, identical in all four gospels, were, **Art thou the King of the Jews?** Since a capital sentence was required for capital punishment (crucifixion), a political charge had to be found, and thus the question. "Thou," or "you," is emphatic and Brown (*The Gospel According to John*, p. 851) suggests that Pilate's question bears a tone of incredulity. If so, Jesus did not meet Pilate's expectation (see 18:34).

18:34–35. Jesus answered Pilate with a question: **Sayest thou this thing of thyself …?** (v. 34). If so, Pilate's question (see 18:33) had meant, "Are you a rebel?" If the question had originated with the Jews, it meant, "Are you the messianic King?" Pilate's retort makes it clear that (1) he was unacquainted with Jesus apart from what he had been told, and (2) he harbored reservations about the Sanhedrin's charges.

18:36. My kingdom. Jesus agreed that He has a kingdom but asserted that it is not the kind of kingdom that has soldiers to **fight** for it. It was not built, nor is it maintained, by military might.

18:37. Jesus admitted to being a king and having a kingdom, but he defined its rule and domain as truth and its subjects as those who hear the truth. It is therefore a kingdom of truth, and Jesus came to **bear witness unto the truth**, two of this gospel's important themes (see 1:7; 1:14; 14:6 and discussions).

18:38. What is truth? Pilate may have been jesting and meant, "What does truth matter?" Or he may have been serious and meant, "It is not easy to find truth. What is it?" Because John specified the immediacy with which Pilate departed, the former is the more likely. Either way, it was clear to him that Jesus was no rebel: **I find in him no fault**, or "cause" ("crime") for which He was worthy of punishment. Teaching the truth was not a criminal offense.

18:39. Ye have a custom. In antiquity, prisoners are known to have been released on special occasions in other places. Pilate's direct appeal to the people may indicate an effort on his part to circumvent the Sanhedrin. Although Pilate had pronounced Jesus innocent of any political crime, his use of the title **King of the Jews** may have been meant to influence the people toward the way he wanted them to decide. At any rate, the note of royalty is a prominent emphasis in John's account.

18:40. Barabbas was a **robber**, a rebel, and a murderer (see Luke 23:19). The name is Aramaic and means "son of Abba," that is, "son of the father." In place of this man, the Son of the Father died.

19:1. Pilate hoped a flogging would satisfy the Jews and enable him to release Jesus (see discussion on Mark 15:15). Brown (*The Gospel According to John*, p. 874) suggests that here and in 19:3, John's selection of vocabulary to describe the treatment of Jesus may have been drawn from Isaiah 50:6.

19:2–3. Thorns (v. 2) is a general term relating to any thorny plant, but fashioned into a wreath, those thorns became a mockery of Jesus and the opposite of the laurel wreath that adorned the emperor. **Purple** was associated with royalty because purple dye was hard to obtain and expensive. John's record of the soldier's mistreatment of Jesus is graphic and brutal. Again and again, one after another, the soldiers humiliated Jesus emotionally and physically with their mocking words and blows. The earthly symbols of power mocked the King whose reign is not of this world.

19:4–5. A second time, Pilate pronounced the innocence of Jesus and, as if to draw attention to it, called out, **Behold the man** (v. 5). This time Pilate did not use the title "King of the Jews" (18:39). Pilate's words were meant not to pour scorn on Jesus but to demonstrate to the Jews the ridiculous nature of their charge that He was a royal claimant. Thus, he said, "Look at this man!" Before them stood a pitiable figure; should they not grant amnesty to such a beaten and broken, bruised and bleeding man?

19:6. Any spark the crowd may have had to grant Jesus amnesty was quickly quenched by the ready and repeated chant of the Jewish officials: **Crucify him**. The exasperated Pilate petulantly replied, **Take ye him, and crucify him**. It was a sarcastic suggestion, not only because Jewish authorities could not carry out this form of execution but because Pilate did not concur with their indictment. **I find no fault**. For the third time, Pilate proclaimed Jesus' innocence (see 18:38; 19:4). Luke also recorded this threefold proclamation (see Luke 23:4, 14, 22).

19:7–8. We have a law … he ought to die (v. 7) refers to the penalty for blasphemy (see Lev. 24:16). **The Jews** (see discussion on 1:19) countered Pilate with their own law, which Pilate would not have known, and the content of the allegation, **he made himself the Son of God**, raising the stakes and a new level of fear for Pilate. That **he was the more afraid** (v. 8) may have had a dual source: (1) Pilate was likely superstitious, and this charge, akin to a claim of divinity, frightened him (see 19:9 and 8:36–37). (2) As a Roman governor, Pilate was responsible for upholding local laws, and the depth of the Jews' resolve and motivation suggested a new level of political jeopardy.

19:9. Whence art thou? Pilate's question belongs to a theme of puzzlement throughout John's gospel (see, e.g., 7:27–28; 8:14; 9:29–30). The answer, of course, is "from above" (19:11), with all that it entails (see 1:1–18), but **Jesus gave him no answer**. The reason is not clear since Jesus had answered other questions readily. Perhaps Pilate would not have understood the answer or would not have believed it.

19:10. I have power. Pilate was incredulous and very conscious of his authority. Ironically, he touted his authority to none other than the one given supreme authority, Jesus (see 3:35; 13:3; 5:24–27). Pilate's second question indicates his personal responsibility for crucifying Jesus.

19:11. These were Jesus' last words to Pilate. The answer to Pilate's earlier question (see 19:9) is embedded in the words **from above**. Jesus, sent to earth as the Father's representative, had come from the realm of all authority, a kingdom not of this world (see 18:36–37). All earthly authority comes ultimately from God. **The greater sin** belonged to Caiaphas (not Judas, who was only a means), but "greater" implies that there was a lesser sin, so Pilate's sin was also real.

19:12. Not Caesar's friend. Some people had official status as "Friends of Caesar," but the term seems to be used here in the general sense. There was an implied threat that if Pilate released Jesus, he would be accused before Caesar. His record was such that he could not face such a prospect without concern. Ties of patronage between Pilate and the Praetorian prefect Lucius Aelius Sejanus, who had recently been executed (AD 31) by Tiberius Caesar on suspicion of plotting against the emperor, magnified the dangers of such a charge: **whosoever maketh himself a king speaketh against Caesar.**

19:13. The judgment seat, or "bench" (Greek, *bēma*), was a platform outside the palace (see 18:28; see also Acts 18:12, 16, 17; 25:6, 10, 17). **The Pavement** is not a translation of **Gabbatha**, which seems to mean "the hill of the house," but a different name for the same place.

19:14. The preparation. Normally, Friday was the day people prepared for the Sabbath. Here the meaning is Friday of Passover week. **About the sixth hour**, or about noon. Mark 15:25 says that Jesus was crucified at "the third hour." It is possible that Mark's gospel contains a copyist's error, for the Greek numerals for three and six could be easily confused. Or it may be that John was using Roman time, in which case the appearance before Pilate would have been at 6:00 a.m. and the crucifixion at 9:00 a.m. (the third hour according to Jewish reckoning; see Mark 15:33; for other time references, see Matt. 27:45–46; Mark 15: 33–34; Luke 23:44). **Behold your King**. John does not let his readers forget the sovereignty of Jesus. Pilate did not mean the expression seriously, but John did.

19:15. The chief priests answered, We have no king but Caesar. More irony. They rejected any suggestion that they were rebels against Rome but expressed the truth of their spiritual condition.

H. The Crucifixion and Burial (19:16–42)

19:16–17. Bearing his cross (v. 17). A cross might be shaped like a T, an X, a Y, or an I, as well as the traditional form. A condemned man would normally carry the crossbeam (Latin, *patibulum*) to the place of execution. Somewhere along the way, Simon of Cyrene took Jesus' cross (see Mark 15:21), probably because Jesus was weakened by the flogging. **Golgotha** is Aramaic for "the skull" (see discussion on Mark 15:22). The name of the site is given in both Greek and Aramaic ("Calvary" is from the Latin, with the same meaning).

19:18. They crucified him (see discussion on Mark 15:25). As with the scourging, John described this horror with one Greek word. None of the gospel writers dwelt on the physical sufferings of Jesus. The positioning of **two others … on either side** of Jesus may have been meant as a final insult, but it brings out the important truth that in His death, Jesus was identified with sinners.

19:19–20. A title (v. 19), or placard, stating the crime for which a man was executed was often fastened to his cross. The full title, **JESUS OF NAZARETH THE KING OF THE JEWS**, and John's detail that Pilate caused it to be written corresponds to the formal criminal charge of sedition. Only John mentioned the languages in which the title was written. **Hebrew** (v. 20) was one of the languages of the Jewish people at that time (along with Aramaic). **Greek** was the common language of communication throughout the empire. **Latin** was the legal and official language of Rome. The threefold inscription may account for the slight differences in wording in the four gospels.

19:21–22. The chief priests of the Jews (v. 21) protested the implications of the charge itself. Pilate needed sufficient reason for the execution, and he was not above mocking the Jews, but for John, Pilate's insistence on the wording may also have served

to underscore that Jesus' kingship is final and unalterable. As Carson (*The Gospel According to John*, p. 611) puts it, "Pilate's malice serves God's ends."

19:23–24. Jesus' **coat** (Greek, *chitōn*; "tunic"; v. 23), a type of shirt that reached from the neck to the knees or ankles, **was without seam** and therefore too valuable to be cut up. Rather than mar the coat, the soldiers **cast lots** (v. 24) for the final division of Jesus' clothing and thus fulfilled **the Scripture** (see introduction to Psalm 22 and discussions on Ps. 22:17–18, 20–21).

19:25. Although the number of women that **stood by the cross** is unclear (two, three, or four), it remains simplest to understand four women, two unnamed and two named. **Cleophas** is mentioned only here in the New Testament. **Mary Magdalene** appears in the crucifixion and resurrection story in all four gospels, but apart from that, one reads of her only in Luke 8:2–3.

19:26–27. The disciple standing by, whom he loved (v. 26) most likely was John (see discussion on 13:23). According to Barrett (*The Gospel According to St. John*, p. 552), the words of Jesus, **behold thy son** (v. 26) **… Behold thy mother** (v. 27), recall the wording of legal adoption formulas. Jesus demonstrated a dying concern for His mother and made provision for her care. **Woman** (see discussion on 2:4), as His concern showed, was not a term of disrespect. The **disciple took her unto his own home** and so took responsibility for her. It may be that Jesus' brothers still did not believe in Him (see 7:5).

19:28–29. I thirst (v. 28; see Ps. 22:15) is a detail of Jesus' agony; dehydration was a cruelty of crucifixion. This detail, however, belonged to the completion of a larger plan now nearing perfection, His sacrificial death, and probably refers to Psalm 69:21. **Vinegar** (v. 29), equivalent to cheap wine, was the drink of ordinary people. **A sponge** was a useful way of giving a drink to one on a cross and may indicate forethought and compassion on someone's part. Affixed to a **hyssop** branch (the name given to a number of plants), the sponge was lifted up to Jesus.

19:30. Jesus … said, It is finished, apparently with the loud cry of Matthew 27:50; Mark 15:37.

Gave up the ghost, or "handed over" His Spirit, is an unusual way of describing death and suggests an act of will (see 19:29). Jesus died as a victor and had completed what He came to do.

19:31–33. The Jews (v. 31; see discussion on 1:19) did not want the Romans to follow the practice of leaving the bodies hanging on the cross since the following day was **a high day**, the Sabbath that fell at Passover time. The Passover meal had been eaten on Thursday evening, the day of preparation was Friday, and the Sabbath came on Saturday, commencing at sunset on Friday. These arrangements may have been discussed earlier (see 19:21) and now came into play. To hasten death, **legs might be broken** (v. 31) so that the victim could not put any weight on his legs and breathing would be difficult. At the time this was implemented, Jesus **was dead already** (v. 33). John elaborated the significance of this in 19:36.

19:34. To be sure Jesus was dead, a soldier **pierced his side** (see 19:37; Isa. 53:5; Zech. 12:10; see also Ps. 22:16). This action was more than a prodding; it was a brutal thrust issuing in **blood and water**, the result of the spear piercing the pericardium (the sac that surrounds the heart) and the heart itself.

19:35. He that saw it points to the significant eyewitness testimony of the Beloved Apostle, who was present at the cross (see 19:25–27; 21:24). The incident proved important because it underscored not only the incarnation but also the additional fulfillment of Scripture (see 19:36–37).

19:36–37. Scripture (v. 36). John again observed God's overruling in the fulfillment of Scripture. It was extraordinary that Jesus was the only one of the three whose legs were not broken and that He suffered an unusual spear thrust that did not break a bone (see Zech. 12:10). The law dictated that no bone of the Passover lamb be broken (see Exod. 12:46; Num. 9:12). Jesus, as "the Lamb of God" (1:29) and "our passover" (1 Cor. 5:7; see 1 Peter 1:18–19), thus fulfilled the Scripture that **A bone of him shall not be broken** (see Ps. 34:20).

19:38. Joseph was a wealthy disciple (see Matt. 27:57) and a member of the Sanhedrin who had not agreed to Jesus' condemnation (see Luke 23:51).

The place-name **Arimathea** (see discussion on Matt. 27:57) points to Joseph's hometown or place of birth. It is likely that he resided in Jerusalem. His allegiance to Jesus had been expressed only **secretly**. It would have been hard for a member of the Sanhedrin to support Jesus' cause openly (see 12:42–43; 3:1). Joseph now expressed courage (see Mark 15:43) when Jesus' closest followers had all run away (see Mark 14:50); it was left to Joseph and Nicodemus to provide for His burial. Permission was required to take the body, **and Pilate gave him leave**. Otherwise, people could take away their crucified friends before they died and revive them.

19:39. John alone reported that **Nicodemus** (see 3:1) joined Joseph in the burial. John characteristically identified Nicodemus as he that **came to Jesus by night** (see 7:50). John's emphasis **at the first** may indicate his perception of a man whose faith had grown. **An hundred pound weight** was a very large amount, such as was used in royal burials (see 2 Chron. 16:14). A "pound" (Greek, *litra*) was about twelve ounces, and thus a "hundred pound weight" was about seventy-five pounds by current standards.

19:40. Linen clothes denotes thin strips like bandages. A shroud, a large sheet, was also used (see Matt. 27:59; Mark 15:46; Luke 23:53).

19:41–42. Jesus' body was placed in **a new sepulchre** (v. 41), a tomb that had never been occupied, hewn out of the rock (see Mark 15:46; Matt. 27:60; Luke 23:53) and situated in **a garden** near Golgotha (see 19:17). It was Joseph's own tomb (Matt. 27:60), and its proximity — **nigh at hand** — was important since labor must cease at sunset, the beginning of the Sabbath. That it was "new" would also readily prove that it was empty upon the resurrection of Jesus. For **preparation**, see discussion on v. 14.

V. The Resurrection (20:1–29)

20:1. Mary Magdalene (see discussion on 19:25; Mark 16:9) went to the garden early, **when it was yet dark**. Mark says it was "at the rising of the sun" (Mark 16:2). Perhaps the women came in groups, with Mary Magdalene coming very early. Or John may have referred to the time of leaving home, and

Mark to that of arriving at the tomb. John's account of the open tomb and Mary's discovery presumes the details of Mark 15:46–47: Joseph "rolled a stone unto the door of the sepulchre. And Mary Magdalene and Mary the mother of Joses beheld where he was laid."

20:2. Despite his denials of Jesus (see 18:15–27), **Simon Peter** was still the leading figure among the disciples. Peter and **the ... disciple, whom Jesus loved** (John; see discussion on 13:23) were the prominent disciples and likely had remained in the vicinity. Unlike the disciples who had fled (see Mark 14:50; Matt. 26:56), Peter and John were around during the interrogations (18:15). The word **we** indicates that others were with Mary (see Matt. 28:1; Mark 16:1; Luke 24:10), though John did not identify them. **They have taken away the Lord ... we know not where they have laid him**. Mary had no thought of resurrection. It was not uncommon for graves to be robbed, as Mary's immediate suspicion confirms.

20:3–7. To describe the exigent concern over the empty tomb, John recorded the running of Mary (see 20:2), then of **Peter** (v. 4) and **the other disciple**. Speculation over John's report that one **did outrun** the other, such as allusions to age, should not lose sight of the individual haste and concern that this detail portrays. Mary's words were troubling and suggested tomb robbery, but John's report emphasizes the short time and the chain of evidence between Mary's finding and the finding of what the disciples closely inspected. The detailed description of the location of the **linen clothes** in vv. 5–7 and the **napkin that was about his head** (v. 7) portrays an evacuation of the bindings, as though passing through them rather than evidence of being humanly removed (compare Lazarus wrapped in grave clothes and his face bound with a napkin, 11:44); see discussion of Carson, *The Gospel According to John*, p. 637.

20:8. He saw, and believed (see 20:29). John did not say what he believed, but it must have been that Jesus was resurrected.

20:9. Peter and John first came to know of the resurrection through what they saw in the tomb;

only later did they see it in **scripture**. It is obvious they did not make up a story of resurrection to fit a preconceived understanding of scriptural prophecy. **Must rise** conveys that Scripture and the will of God coincided. John's placement of this note may explain why "that other disciple ... [who] saw, and believed" (20:8) did not relate what was in his heart as a certainty. As Luke 24:12 tells us, "Peter ... departed, wondering in himself at that which was come to pass."

20:10–11. Nothing in John's account confirms that **Mary** (v. 11) and the two disciples met at the tomb. The word **But** contrasts not only that **the disciples went away** (v. 10) and **Mary stood** (v. 11) but also two perspectives: hers (see 20:2; 20:13), leading to tears, and theirs (see 20:6–8), leading to home. Mary's **weeping** means "wailing" (as in 11:33), a loud expression of grief. Perhaps Jesus appeared first to Mary (see 20:14) because she needed Him most at that time.

20:12–13. When Mary ventured to peer into the tomb, the findings of the disciples were eclipsed by the presence of **two angels** (v. 12; see discussion on Luke 24:4). Matthew has one angel (see Matt. 28:2), Mark a young man (see Mark 16:5), and Luke two men who were angels (see Luke 24:4, 23). The presence of these angels, garmented **in white**, "make clear that the empty tomb cannot be explained by appealing to grave robbers; this is nothing other than the invasion of God's power" (Carson, *The Gospel According to John*, p. 640).

20:14–15. Presumably alerted by the approach of a stranger, Mary turned to see who was there but **knew not that it was Jesus** (v. 14). A number of times the risen Jesus was not recognized (see 21:4; Matt. 28:17; Luke 24:16, 37). He may have looked different, or He may have intentionally prevented recognition. If the disciples who had heard Jesus speak of His resurrection had trouble absorbing the hope of it, how difficult would it have been for Mary to think of any reason for the empty tomb but a robbery? She thus asked **the gardner** (v. 15) if he was responsible.

20:16. Perhaps the familiar tone and that He addressed her by name caused Mary to recognize that the one speaking to her was none other than

Jesus (see 10:3–4). **Rabboni** is a strengthened form of "Rabbi" and in the New Testament is found elsewhere only in Mark 10:51 (in the Greek). Although the word means "(my) teacher," there are few if any examples of its use in ancient Judaism as a form of address other than in calling on God in prayer. However, John's own interpretation of the expression as "teacher" (Greek *didaskalos*, JKV: "Master") casts doubt on any thought that Mary intended to address Jesus as God here.

20:17. The grammar of **Touch me not** suggests that it is to be understood as "Stop clinging to me." The picture of Mary immediately embracing Jesus is altogether in keeping with this unexpected answer to her grief: the appearance of Jesus. Taken with the words **for I am not yet ascended**, Jesus was assuring Mary that she would have opportunity to see Him again, so she need not cling to Him. Conversely, Mary was to go and alert the **brethren** with an important message. Here "brethren" refers to the disciples (see 20:18; Matt. 12:50), and its use coincides with the message Mary was to deliver: **I ascend unto my Father, and your Father**. By virtue of what Jesus accomplished in His death and resurrection, His disciples are able to enjoy the full-fledged status of being a child of God. Jesus succinctly expressed its realization in the message Mary was given.

20:18–19. The disciples (v. 18) probably includes others besides the apostles, "the twelve" (20:24). On the heels of her exciting news **that she had seen the Lord**, Mary delivered His message. The danger remained real, however, and the doors were locked **for fear of the Jews** (v. 19; see discussion on 1:19). That the doors were locked also accentuates the miraculous appearance of the resurrected Jesus **in the midst** of the disciples (see Luke 24:36). **Peace be unto you** (see discussion on 14:27) was the normal Hebrew greeting (see Dan. 10:19). Because of their behavior the previous Friday, they may have expected rebuke and censure, but Jesus calmed their fears.

20:20. In keeping with His greeting of peace, Jesus showed the disciples **his hands and his side**, where the wounds were (John did not refer to the wounds in the feet). According to Luke 24:37, the disciples thought they were seeing a ghost. Jesus was clearly identifying Himself.

20:21. It is unlikely that this second **Peace be unto you** (see discussion on 20:19) indicates a need for added assurance, given John's description of the disciples' joy in 20:20. Rather, the repetition prepares for Jesus' solemn commissioning of the disciples: **as my Father hath sent me, even so send I you** (see discussion on 17:18). Different Greek verbs are used for "sent" and "send," but the order is consistent with John's use throughout his gospel. The first verb (Greek, *apostellō*) is used of the commissioning of Jesus, and the second verb (Greek, *pempō*) is used to identify the Father as the sender. Here Jesus mediated the continuation of His commission to His disciples. Jesus' commission stemmed not from His own authority but from that of the Father, and Jesus now transferred this commission to His disciples in anticipation of His departure.

20:22. John clarified that in the continuation of Jesus' commission and authority (17:8, 22), only the Resurrected One was able to pass on the Spirit to those who would carry on His commission. **Receive ye the Holy Ghost** anticipates what happened fifty days later on the day of Pentecost (see Acts 2). The disciples needed God's help to carry out the commission they had just been given.

20:23. This verse reads literally, "Those whose sins you forgive have already been forgiven; those whose sins you do not forgive have not been forgiven." God does not forgive people's sins because believers do so, nor does He withhold forgiveness because Christians do. Rather, those who proclaim the gospel are in effect forgiving or not forgiving sins, depending on whether the hearers accept or reject Jesus Christ.

20:24–25. Thomas (v. 24; see discussion on 11:16) was not present when Jesus first appeared to the disciples (see 20:19–23), so he met the excited announcement of the disciples with skepticism: **Except I shall see … and put … I will not believe**. Hardheaded skepticism can scarcely go further than this.

20:26–28. A week had passed. Jesus appeared again to the disciples, and this time **Thomas** (v. 26) was present. For **Peace**, see discussions on 14:27; 20:19. Jesus addressed Thomas's unbelief with specific attention to the points of his skepticism. For believers today, Thomas may serve as a model of doubts that can be avoided. **Be not faithless, but believing** (v. 27) is a poignant flip of the Greek adjective *pistos* (here rendered "believing"): "Be not an 'unbeliever' [*a-pistos*, or dis-believer], but [be] a 'believer' [*pistos*]." Although the verb "to believe" occurs frequently in John (100 times), the adjective occurs only here. It appears that "seeing was believing" for Thomas, and rather than resort to touching the Lord, he answered Him with a confession of belief: **My Lord and my God** (v. 28). To acknowledge Jesus as one's Lord and God is the high point of faith (see discussion on 1:1).

20:29. They that have not seen, and yet have believed would have applied to very few at this time. All whom John mentioned had "seen" in some sense. The words, of course, apply to future believers as well. **Blessed** (Greek, *makarios*; "happy," "fortunate"; see Matt. 5:3–11) tells one not only something about those who have not seen yet believe as Thomas did (see 20:28); it tells one something about the regard of the Lord Jesus. In short, Jesus assured future generations of believers that they are in no way at a disadvantage in His eyes because they were not present to touch or see Him.

VI. The Statement of Purpose (20:30–31)

20:30. Signs (Greek, *sēmeion*; see discussion on 2:11) refers to the miraculous actions of Jesus that revealed His significance. John had selected from among many the signs that he recorded in his gospel. **In the presence of his disciples** points to those who could testify to what He had done and who He revealed Himself to be. John again stressed testimony (see discussion on 1:7).

20:31. These signs were chosen for a purpose: **that ye might believe** (see discussion on 1:7). John's purpose in writing his gospel was evangelistic. Faith has content. The signs revealed that **Jesus is the Christ** (see discussion on 1:25), **the Son of God**. This whole gospel was written to show the truth of Jesus' mes-

siahship and to present Him as the Son of God, so that the readers may believe in Him. **That believing ye might have life** expresses another purpose: to bring about faith that leads to life (see discussions on 1:4; 3:15). **Through his name** represents all that Jesus is and stands for (see discussion on 2:23) and points to the authority or credentials of the one who gives life.

VII. Epilogue (chap. 21)

21:1. After these things merely puts the following episode later in the sequence of John's record. **Jesus shewed himself** (lit., "revealed himself") **again**, this time **at the sea of Tiberias** (the Sea of Galilee; see discussion on 6:1). The Greek for **on this wise** means "as follows."

21:2. John identified the disciples that were present, those known to the readers and two not known. For **Simon Peter**, see discussion on Mark 1:16–18. For **Thomas**, see discussion on 11:16. For **the sons of Zebedee**, not mentioned by name in this gospel, see Matthew 4:21, which names them as James and John.

21:3. The outline of an unsuccessful night of fishing provides a prequel to the appearance of Jesus. Nighttime was favored by fishermen in ancient times (as Aristotle, e.g., informs us). One must be cautious about assuming that the disciples had abandoned their charge because they engaged in a night of fishing. Peter's eager reaction to the recognition that it was the Lord who addressed them (see 21:7) is not the response of a man that has knowingly displeased his Master.

21:4–6. The disciples **knew not that it was Jesus** (v. 4; as with Mary Magdalene; see discussion on 20:14). Dim light and distance may have been factors in their not recognizing the Lord. Jesus' question, **have ye any meat?** (v. 5), expected an answer of no even before the disciples confirmed it. "Meat," or "fish," translates a word found only here in the New Testament. Literally, the word refers to "a relish" of whatever sort to go with bread (see 21:9). When the Lord's instruction to **Cast the net on the right side** (v. 6) was met with a great catch (see Luke 5:6), it awakened the recognition that the stranger was none other than Jesus (see 21:7).

21:7. The disciple whom Jesus loved, John (see discussion on 13:23; 21:20), characteristically exhibited quick insight, and Peter quick action (see Carson, *The Gospel According to John*, p. 671). It is curious that Peter put on **his fisher's coat**, or "outer garment" (the word appears only here in the New Testament), before jumping into the water, but Jews regarded a greeting as a religious act that could be done only when one was clothed. Peter may have been preparing himself to greet the Lord.

21:8. Peter recklessly abandoned the others and swam to shore, leaving the rest to labor with the huge catch of fish. **Two hundred cubits** is a distance of about one hundred yards.

21:9 – 10. Jesus had already prepared a breakfast for them of **fish … and bread** (v. 9), to which they could add from their catch. Both supplies were provided by the Lord.

21:11. Peter … drew the net to land apparently means that Peter headed up the effort, for the whole group had not been able previously to haul the net into the boat (see 21:6). One would expect that the size of the catch would cause the net to tear, **yet was not the net broken** (compare Luke 5:6). The number of fish, 153, has triggered not a little speculation over its symbolic importance, but John's emphasis on the net being intact suggests that the number was intended to stress the size of the catch.

21:12 – 13. Come and dine (v. 12), or literally "eat breakfast." The disciples did not ask for confirmation, for they knew **it was the Lord**. In view of 20:28, "master" is an inadequate lexical option here.

21:14. The third time. This was Jesus' third appearance to a group of disciples (see 20:19 – 23, 24 – 29), though He had appeared to individuals (e.g., Mary Magdalene; see 20:14 – 18). John's repetition of **shewed himself** (see 21:1) forms a literary inclusion. An inclusion is an author's device to begin and end a discussion with the same or closely related words (see 1:18). This verse closes the account of Jesus' appearing to the disciples and transitions to His intimate discussion with Peter, which followed breakfast (see 21:15). The setting remains the same, and one can imagine Jesus and Peter strolling beside the Sea of Tiberias (see 21:1), with the Beloved Disciple (and the others) just behind them (see 21:20).

21:15 – 17. The Greek word for "lovest" in Jesus' first two questions (Greek, *agapaō*; vv. 15, 16) is different from the word for "lovest" in His third question (Greek, *phileō*; v. 17), which is the same word Peter used for "love" in all three verses. It is uncertain whether a distinction in meaning is intended since John often made slight word variations, apparently for stylistic reasons. No distinction is made between these two words elsewhere in this gospel. In this passage, however, they occur together, and the variations seem too deliberate to be explained on stylistic grounds. *Agapaō* refers to a love in which the entire personality, including the will, is involved, whereas *phileō* refers to spontaneous natural affection or fondness in which emotion plays a more prominent role than will. Whatever interpretation is adopted, the important thing is that in so serious a matter as the reinstatement of Peter, the great question was whether he loved Jesus. Peter had been restored privately and personally (see Luke 24:34; 1 Cor. 15:5), but now it was to be a public matter. Peter had disowned Christ in public three times. Now he needed to own Christ three times in front of the other disciples.

Intriguing variations are also seen in Jesus' repeated command to Peter.

Verse 15	Feed (*boskō*) my lambs (*arnion*)	
Verse 16	Feed (*poimainō*) my sheep (*probaton*)	
Verse 17	Feed (*boskō*) my sheep (*probaton*)	

Boskō means to "feed as a herdsman," "graze." *Poimainō* means to "tend" or "shepherd" and involves the shepherd's responsibilities of caring, feeding, and protecting (see 1 Peter 5:2). In the end, the distinctions are slight, and the overall emphasis appears to fall on Jesus' thrice-repeated call to fulfill the responsibilities of a shepherd who fully cares for a flock that belongs not to him but to Jesus (see 10:12 – 13).

21:15. Son of Jonas. The name of Peter's father is mentioned only in John's gospel (see 1:42). That Jesus addressed Peter as He had when they first met (see 1:42) may indicate that He was treating Peter less familiarly and questioning his friendship (see Brown, *The Gospel According to John*, p. 1102). **More than these** may mean "more than you love these men," "more than these men love me," or "more than you love these things" (i.e., the fishing gear). Perhaps the second is best, for Peter had claimed a devotion above that of the others (see 13:37; Matt. 26:33; Mark 14:29). Peter did not take up the comparison, and Jesus did not explain it.

21:16–17. The third time (v. 17) matches Peter's threefold denial (see 13:38; 18:17, 25, 27), and Peter's "grief" (see Mark 14:72) expresses a sad remorse that corresponds to the cumulative toll of Jesus' probing questions. The combined effect of Jesus' command amounted to a call for Peter to be more than "a hireling" (see 10:12–13). He was to be a true shepherd of Jesus' flock. **Thou knowest all things**. Peter's replies stressed Christ's knowledge, not his own grasp of the situation.

21:18–19. Stretch forth thy hands (v. 18). The early church understood this as a prophecy of crucifixion. **By what death** (v. 19). Peter would be a martyr. Tradition indicates that he was crucified upside down.

21:20. The disciple whom Jesus loved (see discussion on 13:23) is pictured as **following** Jesus and Peter. He was doing what Peter was twice told to do (see 21:19, 22). For **leaned on his breast at supper**, see 13:23–25.

21:21–23. The Lord censured Peter for entertaining comparisons. What mattered was Peter's faithfulness in what the Lord had called him to do: **follow thou me** (v. 22; see 21:19). **Till I come** (vv. 22, 23) is a clear declaration of the second coming. John repeated Jesus' statement to dispel the rumor of verse 23.

21:24. The disciple which testifieth. Testimony is important throughout this gospel (see discussion on 1:7). The Beloved Disciple was the witness behind this account. **These things** must refer to the whole book. **And wrote these things** makes it clear that the Beloved Disciple was not only the witness but also the author of this gospel. **We know** evidently includes some of John's contemporaries in a position to know the truth.

21:25. Many other things. As in 20:30, one is assured that the author has been selective. **Even the world itself could not contain** is probably a case of hyperbole, exaggeration to stress a point, but our historical knowledge of Jesus is at best partial. Nevertheless, readers have been given all they need to know.

THE ACTS OF THE APOSTLES

INTRODUCTION

Author

Although the author does not name himself, evidence outside the Scriptures and inferences from the book itself lead to the conclusion that the author was Luke.

The earliest of the external testimonies appears in the Muratorian Canon (ca. AD 170), which explicitly states that Luke was the author of both the third gospel and the "Acts of All the Apostles." Eusebius (ca. 325) lists information from numerous sources to identify Luke as the author of these two books (*Ecclesiastical History* 3.4).

The book itself presents some clues as to who the author was:

(1) *Luke, the companion of Paul.* In the description of events in Acts, certain passages use the pronoun "we." At these points, the author includes himself as one of Paul's companions in his travels (16:10–17; 20:5–21:18; 27:1–28:16). A historian as careful with details as this author proves to be would have had good reason for choosing to use "we" in some places and "they" elsewhere. The author was therefore probably present with Paul during events described in the "we" sections.

These "we" passages include the period of Paul's two-year imprisonment at Rome (chap. 28). During this time, Paul wrote several letters, including Colossians and Philemon. In these letters, he sent greetings from his companions, and Luke was included among them (see Col. 4:14; Philem. 24). In fact, after eliminating those who, for one reason or another, would not fit the requirements for the author of Acts, Luke is left as the most likely candidate.

(2) *Luke, the physician.* Although it cannot be proved that the author of Acts was a physician simply from his vocabulary, the words he used and the traits and education reflected in his writings fit well his role as a physician (see, e.g., discussion on 28:6). It is true that doctors of the first century did not have as specialized a vocabulary as that of doctors today, but some terms in Luke and Acts suggest that a physician was the author of these books. Paul himself used the term "physician" in describing Luke (Col. 4:14).

Date

Two dates are possible for the writing of this book: (1) circa AD 63, soon after the last event recorded in the book, and (2) circa AD 70 or even later.

Two arguments support the earlier date. (1) Silence about later events. While arguments from silence are not conclusive, it is perhaps significant that the book contains no allusion to events that happened after the close of Paul's two-year imprisonment in Rome: for example, the burning of Rome and the persecution of the Christians there (AD 64), the martyrdom of Peter and Paul (possibly AD 67), and the destruction of Jerusalem (AD 70). (2) No outcome of Paul's trial. If Luke knew the outcome of the trial Paul was waiting for (28:30), why did he not record it at the close of Acts? Apparently, at the time that Luke wrote, the outcome was still in the future.

Those who prefer the later date hold that 1:8 reveals one of Luke's purposes for writing his historical account and that this purpose influenced the way he ended the book. Luke wanted to show how the church penetrated the world of his day in ever-widening circles (Jerusalem, Judea, Samaria, the ends of the earth; see 1:8) until it reached Rome, the world's political and cultural center. Based on this understanding, mention of the martyrdom of Paul (ca. AD 67) and of the destruction of Jerusalem (AD 70) was not pertinent. This would allow for the writing of Acts circa AD 70 or even later. The evidence for this is so thin, however, that the earlier date is much to be preferred.

Recipient

The recipient of the book, Theophilus, is the same person addressed in the first volume, the gospel of Luke (see Luke, Introduction: "Recipient").

Theme and Theological Message

The book of Acts, as a second volume to Luke's gospel, joins what "Jesus began both to do and teach" (1:1), as told in the Gospels, with what He continued to do and teach through the apostles' preaching and the establishment of the church. It unites the writings of the New Testament by providing a bridge between the Gospels and the Epistles. Without Acts, there would be a gap between Jesus' giving the Great Commission, and a series of letters to already established churches, and no context through which to understand them. In addition, Acts supplies an account of the life of Paul, the author of so many of these letters. Geographically, its story spans the lands between Jerusalem, where the church began, and Rome, the political center of the empire. Historically, it recounts the first thirty years of the church. It also ties the church in its beginning to each succeeding age. This book may be studied to gain an understanding of the principles that ought to govern the church of any age.

The major theme of Acts is best summarized in 1:8. It was ordinary procedure for a historian at this time to begin a second volume by summarizing the first volume and indicating the contents anticipated in his second volume. Luke summarized his first volume in 1:1–3; the theme of his second volume is presented in the words of Jesus: "ye shall be witnesses unto me both in Jerusalem, and in all Judea, and in Samaria, and unto the uttermost part of the earth" (1:8). This is, in effect, an outline of the book of Acts (see "Outline," below).

Luke seems to have written Acts with several themes in mind. His theological and exhortation-encouragement themes are especially prominent, however.

(1) *Historical.* The significance of Acts as a historical account of Christian origins cannot be overestimated. It tells of the founding of the church, the spread of the gospel, the beginnings of congregations, and evangelistic efforts in the apostolic pattern. One of the unique aspects of Christianity is its firm historical foundation. The life and teachings of Jesus Christ are established in the four Gospel narratives, and the book of Acts provides a coordinated account of the beginnings of the church and its geographical spread over the first three decades of its existence (see Ger, *The Book of Acts*, p. 8).

(2) *Apologetic.* One finds embedded in Acts a record of Christian defenses made to both Jews (e.g., 4:8–12) and Gentiles (e.g., 25:8–11), with the underlying purpose of conversion. It shows how the early church coped with pagan and Jewish thought, the Roman government, and Hellenistic society.

(3) *Legal.* Luke probably wrote Acts while Paul awaited trial in Rome. It has been suggested that he wrote with the purpose of helping in Paul's defense before the emperor. If Paul's case came to court, what better court brief could he have had than Luke's account of the life of Jesus, history of the beginnings of the church (including the activity of Paul), and early collection of Paul's letters? Advocates of this view point out that Roman officials always vindicate Paul in Acts.

(4) *Prescriptive.* Luke had no way of knowing how long the church would continue on this earth, but he may have wanted to provide guidance to congregations facing common problems. Indeed, as long as the church pursues its course, the book of Acts will be one of its major guides. In Acts, basic principles are applied to specific situations in the context of problems and persecutions. These same principles will continue to be applicable until Christ returns.

(5) *Theological.* Since Acts is the second volume of the work that Luke began in his gospel, these two books are best viewed together. A major theme in the gospel of Luke is that the grace of God is available to Gentiles as well as to Jews (see Ger, *The Book of Acts*, p. 8). Acts highlights the spread of the gospel to the Gentile world in a manner consistent with the theological theme so prominent in Luke's earlier work: the universality of the gospel. This explains Luke's emphasis on Paul's missionary work, as well as why so much attention is given to the conversion of Cornelius and why the Jersualem church receives comparatively little attention after the early chapters of the book (see Marshall, *Acts of the Apostles*, pp. 18–20).

(6) *Exhortation and encouragement.* Churches in the second half of the first century faced increased persecution in various places. Isolated groups of Christians might easily become discouraged. Despair often results from persecution as the vision wanes and as success continually eludes those seeking to evangelize. The success of the church in carrying the gospel from Jerusalem to Rome and in planting local churches across the Roman Empire demonstrated that Christianity was not a mere work of man; God was in it (5:35–39). Churches could read Luke's account and be strengthened to endure the trials they faced while being emboldened to tell the good news of Jesus Christ to their communities.

Literary Features

The book of Acts is a delight to read. Luke was a master of good style and knew how to tell a story well. Several features are evident to the reader who pays attention to matters of style.

(1) *Accurate historical detail*. Every page of Acts abounds with sharp, precise details, to the delight of the historian. The account covers a period of about thirty years and reaches across the lands from Jerusalem to Rome. Luke's description of these times and places is filled with all kinds of people and cultures, a variety of governmental administrations, court scenes in Caesarea, and dramatic events involving such centers as Antioch, Ephesus, Athens, Corinth, and Rome. Barbarian country districts and Jewish centers are included as well. Yet in each instance, archaeological findings reveal that Luke used the proper terms for the time and place being described. Hostile criticism has not succeeded in disproving the detailed accuracy of Luke's political and geographical designations.

(2) *Literary excellence*. Luke not only had a large vocabulary compared with other New Testament writers, but he also used these words in literary styles that fit the cultural settings of the events he was recording. At times, he employed good, classical Greek; at other times, the Palestinian Aramaic of the first century shows through his expressions. This is an indication of Luke's careful practice of using language appropriate to the time and place being described. Aramaisms are found in Luke's descriptions of events in the Holy Land (chaps. 1–12). These cease, however, in his descriptions of events in the Hellenistic lands beyond the territories where Aramaic-speaking people lived.

(3) *Dramatic description*. Luke's skillful use of speeches contributes to the drama of his narrative. Not only are they carefully spaced and well balanced between Peter and Paul, but the speeches of a number of other individuals add variety and vividness to the account. Luke's use of details brings the action to life. Nowhere in ancient literature is there an account of a shipwreck superior to Luke's with its nautical details (chap. 27). The book is vivid and fast-moving throughout.

(4) *Objective account*. Luke's careful arrangement of material need not detract from the accuracy of his record. He demonstrated the objectivity of his account by recording the failures as well as the successes, the bad as well as the good, in the early church. Luke recorded not only the discontent between the Grecian Jews and the Hebraic Jews (6:1) but also the discord between Paul and Barnabas (15:39). He recognized the divisions and differences within the early church (15:2; 21:20–21).

Outline

Luke wove together different interests and emphases as he related the beginnings and the expansion of the church. The design of his book revolves around (1) key persons: Peter and Paul; (2) important topics and events: the role of the Holy Spirit, pioneer missionary outreach to new fields, conversions, the growth of the church, and life in the Christian community; (3) significant problems: conflict between Jews and Gentiles, persecution of the church by some Jewish elements, trials before Jews and Romans, confrontations with Gentiles, and other hardships in the ministry; (4) geographical advances: five significant expansions of the gospel (see the quotations in the outline; see also map, *Zondervan KJV Study Bible*, p. 1582).

Bibliography

Bruce, F. F. *The Book of Acts*. Rev. edition. The New International Commentary on the New Testament. Grand Rapids, MI: Eerdmans, 1988.

Ger, Steven. *The Book of Acts: Witnesses to the World*. Twenty-first Century Biblical Commentary. Chattanooga, TN: AMG, 2005.

Larkin, William J. *Acts*. The IVP New Testament Commentary. Downers Grove, IL: InterVarsity, 1995.

Longenecker, Richard N. "Acts." In *The Expositor's Bible Commentary*, edited by Frank E. Gaebelein, vol 9. Grand Rapids, MI: Zondervan, 2002.

Macaulay, Joseph C. *Expository Commentary on Acts*. Chicago: Moody Press, 1978.

Marshall, I. Howard. *The Acts of the Apostles: An Introduction and Commentary*. Tyndale New Testament Commentaries 5. Grand Rapids, MI: Eerdmans, 1980.

Polhill, John B. *Acts*. The New American Commentary 26. Nashville: Broadman & Holman, 1992.

Talbert, Charles H. *Reading Acts: A Literary and Theological Commentary on the Acts of the Apostles*. New York: Crossroad, 1997.

EXPOSITION

I. Peter and the Beginnings of the Church in Palestine (chaps. 1–12)

A. First Geographical Expansion of the Church: "Throughout all Judea and Galilee and Samaria" (1:1–9:31; see 9:31)

1. Introduction (1:1–2)

1:1. The former treatise. The gospel of Luke. Luke and Acts are addressed to the same patron, **Theophilus** (see Luke, Introduction: "Recipient"). **All that Jesus began both to do and teach.** An apt summation of Luke's gospel, implying that Jesus' work continued in Acts through His own personal interventions and the ministry of the Holy Spirit.

1:2. Taken up. The last scene of Luke's gospel (see Luke 24:50–52) and the opening scene of this second volume (see 1:6–11). The ascension occurred forty days after the resurrection (see 1:3). **Through the Holy Ghost.** Jesus' postresurrection instruction of His apostles was carried on through the Holy Spirit, and succeeding statements make it clear that what the apostles were to accomplish was likewise to be done through the Spirit (see 1:4–5, 8; Luke 24:49;

John 20:22; see also Judges, Introduction: "Theme and Theological Message"). Luke characteristically stressed the Holy Spirit's work and enabling power (see, e.g., 1:8; 2:4, 17; 4:8, 31; 5:3; 6:3, 5; 7:55; 8:16; 9:17, 31; 10:44; 13:2, 4; 15:28; 16:6; 19:2, 6; see discussion on Luke 4:1).

2. Christ's Postresurrection Ministry (1:3–11)

1:3. For many infallible proofs, see the resurrection appearances in Matthew 28:1–20; Mark 16:1–20; Luke 24:1–53; John 20:1–29; 1 Corinthians 15:3–8. **The kingdom of God.** The heart of Jesus' preaching (see discussions on Matt. 3:2; Luke 4:43).

1:4. The promise of the Father. The Holy Spirit (see John 14:26; 15:26–27; 16:12–13).

1:5. For **John truly baptized with water,** see Luke 3:16. **Not many days hence.** The day of Pentecost came ten days later, when the baptism with the Holy Spirit occurred (see 2:1–4).

1:6. Restore again the kingdom to Israel. Like their fellow countrymen, the apostles were looking for the deliverance of the people of Israel from foreign domination and for the establishment of an earthly kingdom. The reference to the coming of the Spirit (see 1:4–5) had caused them to wonder if the new age was about to dawn.

1:7. The times or the seasons. The elapsing time or the character of coming events (see 1 Thess. 5:1).

1:8. Ye shall be witnesses unto me. An important theme throughout Acts (see 2:32; 3:15; 5:32; 10:39; 13:31; 22:15). This verse is a virtual outline of Acts: the apostles were to be witnesses **in Jerusalem** (see chaps. 1–7)**, and in all Judea, and in Samaria** (see chaps. 8–9)**, and unto the uttermost part of the earth**, including Caesarea, Antioch, Asia Minor, Greece, and Rome (see chaps. 10–28). They were not to begin this staggering task, however, until they had been equipped with the **power [of] the Holy Ghost** (see 1:4–5). Judea was the region in which Jerusalem was located. Samaria was the adjoining region to the north.

1:9. He was taken up. This is the fullest description of the ascension of Jesus Christ is recorded in Scripture. Jesus was not continually with the disciples during the forty days leading up to this incident, and one may suppose that He was already in the heavenly places with His Father. The uniqueness of this disappearance of the Lord lies in the fact that He ascended from the ground, was received into a cloud, and did not appear on earth again to the disciples. (The Lord's appearance to Stephen in chap. 7 was an altogether different matter.) His reception into **a cloud** brings to mind His words to the disciples that He would return again some day in the clouds (see Mark 13:26; 14:62 and Bruce, *The Book of Acts*, p. 38). The cloud here thus marked the fact that this time they would not see Him again until His return.

1:10. Two men … in white apparel. A common description of angels.

1:11. Men of Galilee. The Twelve were all from Galilee except Judas, and he was no longer present. **In like manner**. In the same resurrection body and "in the clouds … with power and great glory" (Matt. 24:30). This also was an indication to the disciples that they should expect no more appearances of the risen Christ but should begin waiting for the promise of the Spirit (see 1:8).

3. The Period of Waiting for the Holy Spirit (1:12–26)

1:12. The mount called Olivet (see Luke 19:28–29, 37; discussions on Zech. 14:4; Mark 11:1; Luke 19:29). The ascension occurred on the eastern slope of the mount between Jerusalem and Bethany. **A sabbath day's journey**. About three-quarters of a mile (1,100 meters). This distance was drawn from rabbinical reasoning based on several Old Testament passages (Exod. 16:29; Num. 35:5; Josh. 3:4). A faithful Jew was to travel no farther on the Sabbath. This is not an indication that the ascension took place on a Sabbath; in fact, it would not have since it occurred forty days after the resurrection. The resurrection happened on a Sunday. The ascension happened on a Friday. The Sabbath would not have begun until sundown.

1:13. An upper room. Probably a room on the upper floor of a large house, such as the one where the Last Supper was held (see Mark 14:15) or that of Mary, mother of Mark (see discussion on 12:12). **Bartholomew**. Apparently, John called him Nathanael (see John 1:45–49; 21:2). **James the son of Alpheus**. The same as James the younger (see Mark 15:40). For **Simon Zelotes**, the same as Simon the Canaanite, see discussion on Matthew 10:4. **Judas the brother of James**. Not Judas Iscariot, but the same as Thaddeus (see Matt. 10:3; Mark 3:18).

1:14. With the women. Possibly wives of the apostles (see 1 Cor. 9:5) and those listed as ministering to Jesus (see Matt. 27:55; Luke 8:2–3; 24:22). **Mary the mother of Jesus**. Last mentioned here in Scripture. **Brethren** (see discussion on Luke 8:19). These brothers would have included James, who later became important in the church (see 12:17; 15:13; Gal. 2:9).

1:15–16. About an hundred and twenty (v. 15). The first of a series of progress reports given periodically throughout the book of Acts (here; 2:41; 4:4; 5:14; 6:7; 9:31; 12:24; 16:5; 19:20; 28:31). Luke often used these reports, which frequently point to a period of growth in numbers for the church, to indicate that he was concluding one topic and moving on to another. **This scripture must needs have been fulfilled** (v. 16; see 1:20). Peter was referring to Psalms 69:25; 109:8. Both before and after Christ came, numerous psalms were viewed as messianic. The psalmist's experiences were typical of the Messiah's experiences. No doubt Jesus' teaching in Luke 24:27, 45–47 included these Scriptures.

1:17–18. This man purchased a field (v. 18). Judas bought the field indirectly: the money he returned to the priests (see Matt. 27:3) was used to purchase the potter's field (see Matt. 27:7). **Falling headlong.** Matthew 27:5 reports that Judas "hanged himself." It appears that when the body finally fell, either because of decay or because someone cut it down, it was in a decomposed condition and so broke open in the middle. Another possibility is that "hanged" in Matthew 27:5 means "impaled" (the Hebrew of Est. 2:23 can be translated "impaled"; see discussion there) and that the gruesome results of Judas's suicide are described here.

1:19. Aceldama … The field of blood. An Aramaic term, no doubt adopted by people who knew the circumstances, for the field was purchased with Judas's blood money (see Matt. 27:3–8).

1:20. It is written (see 1:16). Two passages of Scripture (Pss. 69:25; 109:8) were put together to suggest that Judas had left a vacancy that had to be filled. **His bishoprick** would not have designated a church office. The word means literally "superintendence" or more literally "overseership."

1:21. All the time that the Lord Jesus went in and out among us. The first requirement for the person selected to replace Judas was that he be someone who had been with Jesus during the entire time He ministered publicly.

1:22. A witness with us of his resurrection. The second requirement was that he be someone who had seen the risen Christ. Apparently, several met this requirement. On this occasion, however, the believers were selecting someone to become an official witness to the resurrection, a twelfth apostle (see 1:25). The number twelve here has no mystical significance; it is the number of the tribes of Israel, which Jesus had promised the apostles would judge, sitting on twelve thrones (see Matt. 19:28). It would not do if one of the thrones was vacant.

1:23. Barsabas. Means "son of [the] Sabbath." This patronymic was used for two early Jewish Christians, possibly brothers. One was Joseph (here); the other was Judas, a prophet in Jerusalem who was sent to Antioch with Silas (see 15:22, 32). **Justus.** Joseph's Hellenistic name. Nothing more is known of him.

1:24. Once two qualified men were chosen, the disciples prayed. Their prayer was directed to God but included a relevant fact about God. Since God **knowest the hearts of all men**, He would know who was best suited to the office of apostle.

1:25. Judas by transgression fell. That is, Judas fell from a position of authority and inclusion among the apostles. Some want to determine from this or from **that he might go to his own place** that Judas was unsaved and went to hell. This is reading more into this verse than is warranted. The euphemism "go to his own place" in those days meant one's final destiny and could be either heaven or hell (see Marshall, *Acts of the Apostles*, p. 66). It may be that Luke himself was unsure and deliberately left the matter ambiguous. All that Scripture clearly reveals here is that Judas lost his apostleship. Anything else is a matter of inference, whether from here or from other passages that mention Judas.

1:26. They gave forth their lots. By casting lots, the disciples were able to allow God the right of choice. The use of rocks or sticks to designate the choice was common (see 1 Chron. 26:13–16; see also discussions on Neh. 11:1; Prov. 16:33; Jonah 1:7). This is the Bible's last mention of casting lots. This, at least by implication, indicates that after the coming of the Holy Spirit, such a device was no longer necessary. Again, that is inference as well as argument from silence, but there is no indication that the early church continued the practice, nor was it a part of later practice. **And the lot fell upon Matthias.** One should not make too much of the fact that Matthias plays no major role in the book of Acts. Most of the other apostles do not either. Luke's purpose was not to trace the ministry of each apostle but to focus on Peter and later Paul and the spread of the gospel to the Gentiles.

4. The Filling with the Spirit (chap. 2)

2:1. The day of Pentecost. The fiftieth day after the Sabbath of Passover week (see Lev. 23:15–16), thus the first day of the week. Pentecost is also called "the feast of weeks" (Deut. 16:10), "the feast of harvest" (Exod. 23:16), and "the day of the firstfruits" (Num. 28:26). **They were all with one accord.** The nearest antecedent of "they" is "the eleven apostles" (plus Matthias; 1:26), but the reference is probably to all those mentioned in 1:13–15. **In one place.** Evidently not the upstairs room where they were staying (see 1:13) but perhaps somewhere in the temple precincts, for the apostles "were continually in the temple" (Luke 24:53; see discussion there) when it was open.

2:2. A rushing mighty wind. "Wind" (Greek, *pnoē*), or "breath," is a symbol of the Spirit of God (see Ezek. 37:9, 14; John 3:8). The coming of the Spirit was marked by audible (wind) and visible (fire) signs. **The house.** Some say this may refer to the temple (see 7:47), but that is hardly possible. It would not be referred to as a "house" in this context, and **they were sitting**, which may indicate that they were together in a smaller room, not in the much larger space of the temple.

2:3. Tongues. A descriptive metaphor appropriate to the context, in which several languages were soon to be spoken. In the Old Testament, when the Spirit came upon someone, they would prophesy (declare the message of God; see 2:11; 1 Sam. 19:20–23). This seems to be what happened here. **Fire.** A symbol of the divine presence (see *KJV Study Bible* note on Exod. 3:2), it is also associated with judgment (see Matt. 3:12).

2:4. All could refer either to the Twelve or to the 120 disciples mentioned in 1:15. Those holding that the 120 are meant point to the fulfillment of Joel's prophecy (see 2:16–18) as involving more than the twelve apostles. The nearest reference, however, is to the apostles (see discussion on 2:1), and the narrative continues with "Peter, standing up with the eleven" (2:14) to address the crowd. In addition, the tongues speakers are referred to as Galileans in 2:7, which points to the apostles (see Ger, *The Book of Acts*, p. 38). **Filled with the Holy Ghost.** A fulfillment of 1:5, 8; see also Jesus' promise in Luke 24:49. Their spirits were completely under the control of the Spirit; their words were His words. **With other tongues.** The Spirit enabled them to speak in languages they had not previously learned (the Greek can mean "tongues" or "languages"; also in 2:11). Two other examples of speaking in tongues are found in Acts (10:46; 19:6). One extended New Testament passage deals with this spiritual gift (1 Cor. 12–14). Not all agree, however, that these other passages refer to speaking in known languages. The gift had particular relevance here since people of different nationalities and languages were gathered.

2:5. Jews, devout men. Devout Jews from different parts of the world were assembled in Jerusalem either as visitors or as current residents (see Luke 2:25).

2:6. Every man heard them speak in his own language. Jews from different parts of the world would have understood the Aramaic of their homeland as well as the Greek language, which was common to all parts of the world. More than this was occurring, however; they heard the apostles speak in languages native to the different places represented.

2:7. Are not all these which speak Galileans? This must refer to the apostles (see 2:4), for surely some among the 120 disciples (see 1:15) were Judeans.

2:8. How hear we every man in our own tongue …? This was, however, a miracle not of hearing but of speaking, since the apostles are referred to as speaking in "other tongues" (2:4).

2:9. Parthians. Inhabitants of the territory from the Tigris to India. **Medes.** Media lay east of Mesopotamia, northwest of Persia, and south-southwest of the Caspian Sea. **Elamites.** Elam was north of the Persian Gulf, bounded on the west by the Tigris. **Mesopotamia.** Between the Euphrates and Tigris rivers. **Judea.** The homeland of the Jews, perhaps used here in the Old Testament sense of "from the river of Egypt unto the … Euphrates" (Gen. 15:18), including Galilee. **Cappadocia, in Pontus, and Asia.** Districts in Asia Minor.

2:10. Phrygia, and Pamphylia. Districts in Asia Minor. **Egypt.** Contained a great number of Jews. Two out of the five districts of Alexandria were Jewish. **Libya.** A region west of Egypt. **Cyrene.** The capital of a district of Libya called Cyrenaica. **Rome.** Thousands of Jews lived in Rome. **Proselytes.** Gentiles who undertook the full observance of the Mosaic law were received into full fellowship with the Jews.

2:11. Cretes. Represented an island lying south-southeast of Greece. **Arabians.** From a region to the east. The kingdom of the Nabatean Arabs lay between the Red Sea and the Euphrates, with Petra as its capital. **We do hear them speak in our tongues.** A miracle not of hearing but of speaking. The believers were declaring God's wonders (prophesying) in the native languages of the various visiting Jews.

2:12–13. They were all amazed (v. 12). Everyone was surprised at what they heard. Apparently, it was unusual for fishermen and workmen such as these to be fluent in foreign languages. **Others mocking** (v. 13). Some people will scorn even the most evident work of God. **Full of new wine.** They accused the disciples of being undisciplined and sensual, the opposite of what they were.

2:14–40. The pattern and themes of Peter's Pentecostal sermon became common in the early church: (1) an explanation of events (vv. 14–21); (2) the gospel of Jesus Christ—His death, resurrection, and exaltation (vv. 22–36); (3) an exhortation to repentance and baptism (vv. 37–40). The outline of this sermon is similar to those in 3:12–26; 10:34–43; 13:16–41.

2:14. With the eleven. The apostles had been baptized with the Holy Spirit and had spoken in other languages to various groups. Now they stood with **Peter**, who served as their spokesman.

2:15. The third hour of the day. On a festival day such as Pentecost, a Jew would not break his fast until at least 10:00 a.m. It was therefore extremely unlikely that this group of Jewish men would have been drunk at such an early hour.

2:16–18. Upon all flesh: your sons and your daughters … your young men … and your old men (v. 17) **… on my servants and on my handmaidens** (v. 18). The Spirit is bestowed on all, irrespective of sex, age, and rank (see Gal. 3:26–4:7).

2:16. The prophet Joel. Peter quoted from Joel 2:28–32, an apocalyptic passage. **This is that which was spoken.** Peter meant not that this event was the final fulfillment of Joel's prophecy, for obviously there had been no changes in the sun and moon (see 2:19–20), but rather that this was the kind of event Joel had in mind, and it inaugurated a new dispensation in God's dealings with His people, just as will happen at the end.

2:17. In the last days (see Isa. 2:2; Hos. 3:5; Mic. 4:1; Heb. 1:2; discussions on 1 Tim. 4:1; 2 Tim. 3:1; 1 Peter 1:20; 1 John 2:18). In Joel 2:28, the Hebrew has "after this," and the Septuagint has "after these things." Peter interpreted the passage as referring specifically to the latter days of the new covenant (see Jer. 31:33–34; Ezek. 36:26–27; 39:29) in contrast to the former days of the old covenant. The age of messianic fulfillment had arrived. For **my Spirit**, see discussion on 1:2.

2:19–20. Certain apocalyptic signs are described here, quoted from Joel 2:30–31. Peter was not asserting that these things were happening. He was giving the fuller context of the prophecy and linking the event that had just happened to God's overall plan for His people, which includes the **day of the Lord** (v. 20).

2:21. Whosoever shall call (see 2:39) means faith and response rather than merely using words (see Matt. 7:21). Luke would not have meant that one could merely say the words. In his gospel, he highlighted Jesus' emphasis on the need for genuine faith, faith from the heart, not just outward actions.

2:22. This begins the second theme of Peter's sermon: the presentation of the gospel. He first commended Jesus to his audience in terms of what they had already seen and heard: **as ye yourselves also know.** Even those who were in town just for the feast would likely have heard of the events surrounding the ministry of Jesus. He thus had been **approved … by miracles and wonders and signs.** The mighty works that Jesus did were signs that the Messiah had come.

2:23. Having attested to who Jesus is, Peter next focused on His work on the cross. Peter pointed out that Jesus' crucifixion was not an accident but was done **by the determinate counsel and foreknowledge of God**. The cross was not a tragic end or even a tragic interlude; it was the plan of God to accomplish the work of redemption. **Wicked hands**. The Greek has "those not having the law," that is, Gentiles. The reference is to the Romans involved in the trial and crucifixion of Christ. These Gentiles had acted in an evil ("wicked") way. The counsel of God and His eternal purposes may thus take into account the wickedness of men, without excusing their responsibility for their deeds.

2:24. Peter turned to the resurrection. **Whom God hath raised up**. Once again, this was a work of God. **It was not possible he should be holden of it**. That is, it was not possible for Jesus to be kept in the grave.

2:25–28. In explaining why it was impossible for Jesus to remain in the grave, Peter quoted Psalm 16:8–11. David was prophesying, but even though he used the first person, his words refer not to himself but, Peter asserted, to Jesus. These verses, then, say that Jesus could not be kept in the grave because God had promised not to leave Him there. Peter began with the prophecy's assertion that God is always before Him and God is on His **right hand** (v. 25). Again, as Peter went on to point out (see 2:29–31, 34), David was not speaking of himself here, though it would appear that way on the surface.

My flesh shall rest in hope (v. 26). Jesus went to His death knowing that He would not remain there (see Luke 23:43, where Jesus made a promise to one of the thieves that assumed that they both would live beyond their physical deaths: "To day shalt thou be with me in paradise"). **Thou wilt not leave my soul in hell** (v. 27). David referred ultimately to the Messiah (see 2:31). God would not allow His physical body to decompose in the grave (Hades).

Since God had made known to David **the ways of life** (v. 28), he could face the future with **joy**, and by extension, so could the Messiah, the real first-person narrator here.

2:29. To emphasize that David did not have himself in view in this psalm, Peter pointed to a fact his hearers knew well: **his sepulchre is with us**. The sepulchre of David could be seen in Jerusalem. It still contained the remains of David's body. The words of Psalm 16:8–11 thus did not fully apply to him.

2:30–31. Peter made the point of 2:29 explicit as he began to turn toward a consideration of the exalted Christ in heaven.

2:32. Jesus hath God raised up. Peter again pointed out that the resurrection was a work of God (see 2:23–24).

2:33. The promise of the Holy Ghost refers to "the promise of the Father" in 1:4. **He hath shed forth this** (see 2:17; Joel 2:28). Peter tied his words regarding the work of Christ to the events of that morning, the coming of the Holy Spirit.

2:34–35. The Lord said unto my Lord (v. 34; see discussion on Ps. 110:1). Meaning, "The Lord [God] said unto my Lord [the Son of David, the Messiah]." According to Peter, David addressed his descendant with uncommon respect because he, through the inspiration of the Spirit, recognized how great and divine He would be (see Matt. 22:41–45). Not only was He to be resurrected (see 2:31–32); He was to be exalted to God's **right hand**. His presence there was now being demonstrated by the sending of the Holy Spirit (see 2:33; John 16:7).

2:36. Peter began the final part of his sermon: the call for a response. **Let all the house of Israel know**. Peter called for a response based on knowledge. Faith is always tied to what we know of the truth that is in Christ. **God hath made**. Peter again emphasized that this was the work of God. God allowed the death of Christ, God raised Him up, and God exalted Him to heaven. Peter's audience would have found this a persuasive argument for repentance and faith. Throughout the Old Testament, the Jewish people were blessed when they responded in faith to the mighty acts of God. Peter was letting his Jewish audience know that they were now being confronted with a new mighty act of God, for which they were accountable to respond in faith.

2:37. They were pricked in their heart. Reflects both belief in Jesus and regret over their former rejection of Him.

2:38. Repent, and be baptized. Repentance was important in the message of the forerunner, John the Baptist (see Mark 1:4; Luke 3:3), in the preaching of Jesus (see Mark 1:15; Luke 13:3), and in the directions Jesus gave His disciples just before His ascension (see Luke 24:47). Baptism also was important in the work of John the Baptist (see Mark 1:4), in Jesus' instructions to His disciples (see Matt. 28:18 – 19), and in the preaching recorded in Acts. In Acts, baptism is associated with belief (see 8:12; 18:8), acceptance of the Word (see 2:41), and repentance (here). **In the name of Jesus Christ**. Not a contradiction to the fuller formula given in Matthew 28:19. The abbreviated form emphasizes the distinctive quality of this baptism, for Jesus was now included in a way that He was not in John's baptism (see 19:4 – 5). **For the remission of sins**. Not that baptism effects remission (forgiveness); rather, forgiveness comes through that which is symbolized by baptism (see Rom. 6:3 – 4 and discussion). **The Holy Ghost**. Two gifts had now been given: the forgiveness of sins (see also 22:16) and the Holy Spirit. The promise of the indwelling gift of the Holy Spirit is given to all Christians (see Rom. 8:9 – 11; 1 Cor. 12:13).

2:39. The promise is unto you, and to your children, and to all that … God shall call. Peter here acknowledged that this new work of God, the gift of the Holy Spirit, was not temporary. Those who had witnessed the coming of the Spirit could not pass it off as something merely temporary or local. This was therefore a call to respond in faith, in that moment, to the call of God.

2:40. This verse indicates that Luke did not record all of Peter's message here. The systematic treatment given here, however, shows that readers have the gist and outline of it. This verse may also indicate that Peter (and presumably the disciples with him) followed up the message with personal evangelism.

2:41. They that gladly received his word. Many, but apparently not all, believed. **There were added unto them**. Added to the number of believers. **About three thousand souls** (see discussion on 1:15). It is possible that all three thousand might have heard Peter's sermon. Equally likely, however, is that the entire day was spent in witnessing to the truth of Christ and making converts. The commotion surely attracted latecomers, who then heard the Word expounded or heard the testimonies of new believers. One mark of genuine faith is an eagerness to testify to the Lord's grace. The initial band of hearers thus became a force for evangelism that same day.

2:42. The apostles' doctrine. Included all that Jesus Himself taught (see Matt. 28:20), especially the gospel, which centers on His death, burial, and resurrection (see 2:23 – 24; 3:15; 4:10; 1 Cor. 15:1 – 4). Luke used the term here to emphasize that what "Jesus began both to do and teach" (1:1) He was now doing through His Spirit-anointed apostles. Their doctrine was a unique teaching in that it came from God and was clothed with the authority conferred on the apostles (see 2 Cor. 13:10; 1 Thess. 4:2). Today, this same teaching is available in the books of the New Testament. **Fellowship**. The corporate fellowship of believers in worship. **Breaking of bread**. Although this phrase is used of an ordinary meal in 2:46 (see Luke 24:30, 35), the Lord's Supper seems to be indicated here (see discussion on 20:7; see 1 Cor. 10:16; 11:20). **Prayers**. Acts emphasizes the importance of prayer, private as well as public, in the Christian life (see 1:14; 3:1; 6:4; 10:4, 31; 12:5; 16:13, 16).

2:43. Fear came upon every soul. This was not the fear that comes from a lack of faith or assurance. Everyone took the things of God seriously and were in awe of what God had done and was doing. **Many wonders and signs were done by the apostles**. It is well to note here that these "wonders and signs were done by the apostles," not by believers generally. Later, Stephen would perform "wonders and miracles" (6:8) and then Phillip (see 8:6), but nowhere do these things happen generally by all believers, nor even by all leaders in the church.

2:44. All that believed were together. This expresses the unity of the early church. They were together in their sense of purpose and common life. Obviously, all three thousand (see 2:41) could not have lived in one household. **Had all things common** (see 4:34 – 35). This was a voluntary sharing to provide for those who did not have enough for the essentials of living (for examples of good and bad sharing, see 4:36–5:10).

2:45. Parted them to all men. The disciples sold off surplus goods and gave to the needy. That Luke mentioned this here indicates that a communal lifestyle was not common in the churches of the first century. If it had been, he would not have felt the need to mention this as an unusual thing.

2:46. Breaking bread from house to house. Here the daily life of Christians is described, distinguishing their activity **in the temple** from that in their homes, where they ate their meals—not the Lord's Supper (see discussion on 2:42)—with gladness and generosity. **With gladness and singleness of heart**. The fellowship, oneness, and sharing enjoyed in the early church are fruits of the Spirit. Joy is to be the mood of the believer (see discussions on 8:39; 16:34).

5. Conflict between the New Church and Jewish Authorities (3:1–4:31)

3:1–4:31. These chapters deal with conflict between the new church and the Jewish authorities. Luke's report of it sets up Paul's later conflict with them in Jerusalem, which led to his arrest (see 21:27–36). Luke seems eager to point out that the authorities did not understand the gospel and opposed it on wrong grounds. Since the Jews had hardened their hearts to the gospel, it was to be taken to the Gentiles, and Luke was demonstrating that fact here.

3:1. Peter and John. Among the foremost apostles (see Gal. 2:9). Along with John's brother, James, they had been especially close to Jesus (see Mark 9:2; 13:3; 14:33; Luke 22:8). They may have been going to the temple together because of the pattern that Jesus had established of traveling in twos for ministry (see Marshall, *Acts of the Apostles*, p. 86). They appear together in Acts on several occasions; they were arrested together (see 4:3), and they were together in Samaria (see 8:14). **The hour of prayer**. The three stated times of prayer for later Judaism are midmorning (the third hour, 9:00 a.m.), the time of the evening sacrifice (**the ninth hour**, 3:00 p.m.), and sunset. Most likely, they were at the temple in late afternoon.

3:2. A certain man lame. It is likely that this man had been at the gate daily. Perhaps Peter and John had given him alms in the past. **The gate … called Beautiful**. The favorite entrance to the temple court, it was probably the bronze-sheathed gate that led from the court of the Gentiles to the court of women, on the east wall of the temple proper, though other possibilities have been suggested (see Marshall, *Acts of the Apostles*, p. 87).

3:3. Asked an alms. The man sought financial support from them but may have done so mechanically, without paying much attention to who was walking by (see Marshall, *Acts of the Apostles*, p. 88). That Peter had to ask for his attention (see 3:4–5) indicates this was the case.

3:4–5. Fastening his eyes upon him (v. 4) … **and he gave heed unto them** (v. 5). The encounter moved from an impersonal request of strangers to a personal encounter between one who had great need and the representatives of the One who gives life abundantly (see Marshall, *Acts of the Apostles*, p. 88).

3:6. In the name of Jesus Christ. Not by the apostles' own power, but by the authority of the Messiah. This reinforces that Luke's account records the continuing acts of Jesus through His church.

3:7. And lift him up. Here Peter did a miracle through the power of Jesus Christ, but that is not the whole story. To be healed, the man had to have faith (see 3:16). Perhaps he had heard of Jesus but had not been present to hear Him teach. Perhaps he knew of others who had found healing, and he despaired, knowing that Jesus had been crucified. When Peter evoked His name, however, the man realized that the power of God through Christ was still available, and in that moment, the faith he had not had opportunity to exercise during Christ's earthly ministry was again aroused, and he found the Lord still faithful.

3:8. Entered … the temple. Assuming that this was the bronze-sheathed gate mentioned in 3:2, the man entered from the outer court (for Gentiles also) into the court of women, which contained the treasury (see Mark 12:41–44), and then into the court of Israel. From the outer court, nine gates led into the inner courts.

3:9–10. Many people were present in the temple at this time. **And they were filled with wonder and amazement** (v. 10). This harks back to 2:43, where everyone was amazed as the apostles performed "wonders and signs." The context there seems to require that "every soul" means "everyone in the church," though it is not impossible that Luke had in mind something like "everyone in town." Here it is clear that the witnesses of the miracle were the general population.

3:11. The porch that is called Solomon's (see discussion on John 10:23). A porch along the inner side of the wall enclosing the outer court, with rows of 27-foot-high stone columns and a roof of cedar.

3:12–26. For the pattern and themes common in the sermons of the early church, see discussion on 2:14–40. Once again, as on the day of Pentecost, Peter explained a miracle to the resultant crowd, which provided him an opportunity to preach the gospel. He combined the explanation of the miracle with the fact that Jesus was killed by their action and decision but was raised by God (vv. 13–15). Verse 16 is the hinge of the message, as Peter pointed out that it was faith in Jesus Christ that had made the man well. Verses 17–26 constitute Peter's appeal to the crowd to repent and trust in Jesus, whose coming Moses had promised.

3:12–13. Peter's explanation of the miracle moved quickly to Jesus Christ. God the Father, whom Peter here tied to the people's religious understanding, **hath glorified his Son Jesus** (v. 13; see Matt. 12:18; Acts 4:27, 30), or "his servant," a reminder of the suffering Servant prophesied in Isaiah 52:13–53:12. **Whom ye … denied.** They had voted against Jesus, spurned Him, denied Him, and refused to acknowledge Him as the true Messiah. For **Pilate … was determined to let him go**, see John 19:12.

3:14. The Holy One and the Just. Blameless in relation to God and man. Peter provided a bit of theology here. Jesus was blameless, just as He was the Son of God. Later in this sermon, Peter stated that He is "the Prince of life" (3:15) and the Christ (see 3:20). All of this pointed to His deity, His special mission, and thus to the people's responsibility to own Him as their Lord.

3:15. Killed … God hath raised … we are witnesses. A recurring theme in the speeches of Acts (see 2:23–24; 4:10; 5:30–32; 10:39–41; 13:28–29; see also 1 Cor. 15:1–4).

3:16. Through faith in his name. Here Peter came to the point. Faith in Jesus brings blessing and life. Conversely, by implication, rejection of Jesus brings misfortune. Peter's words up to this point demonstrated that his hearers had been rejecting Jesus, the source of true life.

3:17. I wot (know) **that through ignorance ye did it.** Here Peter turned pastoral. He wanted his audience to repent. Having shown them that they were sinners and had rejected God's grace, he now wanted to make it clear that God still had a door of pardon open for them.

3:18. God before had shewed by … all his prophets. This echoes what Jesus said (see Luke 24:25–27). **That Christ should suffer** was prophesied (compare Isa. 53:7–8 with Acts 8:32–33; Ps. 2:1–2 with Acts 4:25–26; Ps. 22:1 with Matt. 27:46; see also 1 Peter 1:11). In saying these things, Peter was also showing the crowd that their rejection of Jesus had played a part in God's overall plan.

3:19–21. Peter issued his invitation. **Repent** (v. 19). Repentance is a change of mind and will that arises from sorrow for sin and leads to a transformation of one's life (see discussion on 2:38). **Be converted.** Subsequent to repentance and not completely identical with it (see 11:21, "believed, and turned"; 26:20, "repent and turn"; see also 9:35; 14:15; 15:19; 26:18; 28:27). In the strictest sense, repentance is turning from sin, and faith is turning to God. The word "turn," however, is not always used with such precision. **Your sins … blotted out.** One's sins are forgiven as a result of repentance. If the people would repent and trust in Jesus Christ, their former rejection of Him would no longer count against them. God's grace is freely offered to any sinner who repents and turns to Jesus Christ, no matter what one has done in the past. **When.** The Greek for this word normally means "so that." **Until the times of restitution** (v. 21). This refers to the time after the return of Jesus Christ from heaven.

3:22–26. Peter offered his listeners further proof that they should repent. The Old Testament points to Jesus Christ and offers a warning to those who do not accept Him. Christ is the fulfillment of prophecies made relative to Moses, David, and Abraham. He was the prophet like unto Moses (vv. 22–23), He was foretold in Samuel's declarations concerning David (v. 24), and He was to bring blessing to all people, as promised to Abraham (vv. 25–26).

3:22. Him shall ye hear in all things whatsoever he shall say unto you. Moses wrote about Jesus and warned the people that they should believe Him. Peter was appealing to them to do so, and thus this continues the invitation to repentance and faith offered in 3:19–21.

3:23. Peter followed the appeal with a warning for those who refuse to heed Jesus Christ.

3:24. All the prophets from Samuel and those that follow after. Samuel anointed David to be king and spoke of the establishment of David's kingdom (see 1 Sam. 16:13; 13:14; 15:28; 28:17). Nathan's prophecy (see 2 Sam. 7:12–16) was ultimately messianic (see Acts 13:22–23, 34; Heb. 1:5). Peter here provided a hermeneutical principle. All of the prophets point forward to Jesus, and they should be read and understood in that light. Peter's main concern, however, was to link the people's faith in the prophets with the need to believe in Jesus.

3:25. Peter made the invitation personal: **Ye are the children of the prophets.** His hearers owed the prophets their allegiance. If the prophets pointed toward Jesus, they as their "children" should believe in Him. The Bible often presents past and present as intimately interconnected. The Jews recognized genuine obligations to the past, especially to their ancestors. These days, alas, Westerners no longer honor their ancestors by practicing the values and upholding the beliefs they did, and they are the worse off for it. These Jews, however, took the matter seriously. Knowing this, Peter used terminology that would drive home to them their obligation to uphold the values and beliefs passed down to them, which, Peter said, pointed directly to exercising faith in Jesus Christ. **Seed.** The word is singular, ultimately signifying Christ (see Gal. 3:16).

3:26. Peter continued the personal note: **Unto you first God … sent him to bless you.** Peter was appealing to the people to trust Christ because God had opened a door of blessing through Him. This sermon, then, made it clear that repentance and faith in Jesus were what the people needed, that they were in line with the Old Testament teaching they had believed, and that the doors of God's mercy were open to them. In his invitation, Peter thus issued four different appeals to the people (3:19, 23, 25, and 26). We don't know what else Peter might have said. Either Luke did not record it, or as 4:1 seems to indicate, the message was interrupted.

4:1. And as they spake unto the people. The sermon was interrupted by officials who intervened and arrested Peter and John. **The priests.** Those who were serving that week in the temple precincts (see discussion on Luke 1:23). **The captain of the temple.** A member of one of the leading priestly families, next in rank to the high priest (see 5:24, 26; Luke 22:4, 52). He was head of the temple police and responsible for maintaining order (see Bruce, *The Book of Acts*, p. 89). His concern here perhaps lay in the fact that a crowd had gathered for an "unauthorized" meeting. **The Sadducees** (see discussions on Matt. 3:7; Mark 12:18; Luke 20:27). A Jewish sect whose members came from the priestly line and controlled the temple. They did not believe in the resurrection or a personal Messiah but held that the messianic age, an ideal time, was then present and needed to be preserved. They were thus concerned about the content of the disciples' preaching. The high priest, one of their number, presided over the Sanhedrin (see 5:17; 23:6–8; Matt. 22:23–33).

4:2. Being grieved that they … preached through Jesus the resurrection from the dead. In the Greek, this immediately follows the word "Sadducees," and this doctrine of the resurrection is one they did not like. Luke thus may have meant that they were the ones with the specific grievance and that the ones "grieved" did not include the whole company.

4:3. Eventide. The evening sacrifices ended about 4:00 p.m., and the temple gates were closed at that time. Any judgments involving life and death were required to begin and end during daylight hours.

4:4. Many … believed. Peter's sermon must have been effective, though it must be remembered that the Lord was adding "daily" (2:47) to their number. Perhaps only a few hundred more were converted here. **Men**. Literally, "males." **Five thousand** (see discussion on 1:15). A growth from the three thousand converted at Pentecost (see 2:41; for later growth, see 5:14; 6:7). In all likelihood, the entire company of believers did not worship at the temple, at least not at the same time.

4:5. The trial was held off until the next day. Then there came together the **rulers, and elders, and scribes**. These three groups made up the Sanhedrin, Israel's supreme court (see Luke 22:66; see also discussions on Matt. 2:4; 15:2; Mark 14:55; Luke 5:17).

4:6. Annas the high priest. Annas was high priest in AD 6–15 but was deposed by the Romans and succeeded by his son Eleazar (AD 16–17), then by his son-in-law, **Caiaphas** (AD 18–36), who was also called Joseph. The Jews, however, still recognized Annas as high priest (see Luke 3:2; John 18:13, 24). **John**. This may refer to Annas's son Jonathan, who was appointed high priest in AD 36. Others suggest it refers to Johanan ben Zaccai, who became the president of the Great Synagogue after the fall of Jerusalem. **Alexander** is named here but is not further identified. Luke may have been using material gained while in Jerusalem. He could not expect Theophilus or his other readers to know who this Alexander was, yet it had become so much a part of the story that Luke did not see fit to omit it.

4:7. By what power, or by what name, have ye done this? The question holds a note of scorn. In the Greek, "ye" is emphatic, which may offer a clue regarding the word "this." The problem may have been that laypeople, those who were not officially rabbis, had presumed to teach. The question "By what power, or by what name …?" implies that the Sanhedrin wanted to know what authority the apostles had to teach. At this point, the interrogators had not yet identified Peter and John as disciples of Jesus, though they were about to do so (see 4:13).

4:8. Peter, filled with the Holy Ghost (see discussion on 2:4). Here there seems to be a causal link between being filled with the Spirit and the message Peter gave. One might render the idea as "Peter, because he was filled with the Holy Ghost." When Luke wrote of someone, often Peter, being filled with the Spirit, it usually was in the context of public speaking (see 4:31; 13:9). Paul linked being "filled with the Spirit" to "speaking to [one another] in psalms and hymns" (Eph. 5:18–19). Being filled with the Spirit, then, is closely linked to giving a bold witness for Christ and glorifying Him.

4:9. If we this day be examined for the good deed done to the impotent man. Peter, for whatever reason, took the "this" in the question (see 4:7) as a reference to the healing of the lame man. He may have known that there was nothing inherently wrong with healing a man. By focusing on that, he perhaps sought to prevent further trouble for himself and John and effect a quick release.

4:10. By the name of Jesus Christ. Peter went quickly to his main purpose in speaking: to glorify Christ. Their teaching and healing were both done in the name of Jesus, so he gave a correct answer to the question.

4:11. The stone … set at nought. Jesus also used this quotation from Psalm 118:22 (see Matt. 21:42; see also 1 Peter 2:7; Rom. 9:33; Isa. 28:16). Fulfillment of prophecy was an important element in early Christian sermons and defenses. Peter wanted again to point out that the rulers were culpable for their lack of belief. It is as if he picked up the thread of the previous day's message (see 3:19–26) and once again began to preach. His text was a messianic one, which he here applied to the Jewish rulers. They had "set at nought" Jesus, who **is become the head of the corner**. Thus far Peter's sermon followed the format of his sermons in 2:14–40 and 3:12–26, though this one was briefer. He explained what had happened, then pointed to Jesus as the Messiah, whom Peter's listeners had rejected.

4:12. Peter next proclaimed the exalted Christ as the answer to their spiritual needs. **None other name** (see 10:43; John 14:6; 1 Tim. 2:5; see also discussion on Matt. 1:21). This passage is used by those who seek to defend the exclusivity of Christ. This was not Peter's concern here; he did not fear that his hearers might believe that all religions bring salvation. He wanted only to exhort the rulers to faith in Christ as opposed to expecting a future Messiah. In the context of his previous day's preaching (see 3:12–26), Peter was aware that rejecting Jesus meant missing God's blessing and favor.

4:13. Boldness. The apostles' boldness was characterized by assurance, authority, and forthrightness (see 2:29; 4:29; 28:31) and was shared by the believers (see 4:31). **They were unlearned and ignorant men.** Meaning only that Peter and John had not been trained in the rabbinic schools, nor did they hold official positions in recognized religious circles. This may have been the precipitating cause of their arrest. Peter's words left them no doubt that he and John were disciples of Jesus Christ. This did not help their case, but Peter was more concerned to bear witness to Christ than he was to avoid prison.

4:14. The man which was healed. The evidence that the apostles had some kind of spiritual authority could not be denied.

4:15–16. In private conference, the Sanhedrin admitted that the **miracle** (v. 16) was so **notable** and so public that they could not **deny it** or its significance.

4:17. But that it spread no further. Apparently, the council's concern had shifted to the fact that the apostles' healing and teaching were done in the name of Jesus. The Sanhedrin had recently dealt with Jesus as a problem for them politically and morally, or so they had thought. The problem now confronted them again. It is interesting that they did not deny the miracle but were still, as during Jesus' earthly ministry, more concerned with their power and position than they were with doctrinal truth. Truly, the church was continuing the work "that Jesus began both to do and teach" (1:1), often with the same results in people's hearts.

4:18. They called them, and commanded them not to speak at all … in the name of Jesus. Clearly, Jesus was the problem for the Sanhedrin now, though it had not been at the time of the Peter and John's arrest.

4:19. To hearken unto you more than unto God. The apostles did not retreat an inch on the matter of truth. The Sanhedrin was on the wrong side of truth, and the apostles boldly proclaimed themselves to be on God's side in the matter. There is no hint in their response that they were willing to accept a compromise or that they were willing to agree that truth may be seen from different perspectives. To oppose the message of the gospel is to oppose God, and that is the end of the matter.

4:20. We cannot but speak (see 5:29; Jer. 20:9). Peter and John were accountable for telling the truth about what God had done in Jesus Christ. This involved much more than just relating their own experiences. The apostles were not merely telling of their personal experiences; they were reporting what God had done. **The things which we have seen and heard,** not their inner experiences, were the focus of their preaching.

4:21. The Sanhedrin could not punish Peter and John, partly because, as during the ministry of Jesus, the Jewish leaders feared the people. It seems strange that men who were so concerned to hold on to power were so powerless before the public will.

4:22. One reason the miracle caused so much public comment was the man's age, **above forty years old** (v. 22), which means he was known to many in the city, since he had been lame from birth and sat daily at the gate of the temple (see 3:2, 10). Though this information, picked up in Luke's investigation, would have held little interest for his hearers, it points to the truthfulness of the account. Made-up stories rarely have such extraneous details in them.

4:23. Being let go, they went to their own company. Probably where the apostles had met before (see 1:13) and where they may have continued to meet (see 12:12). This would not have been the place where all the believers gathered. They had been three thousand in number (see 2:41) and growing and were now up to five thousand or more (see 4:4). They either met in smaller groups or met in the temple at different times. **And reported all that the chief priests and elders had said**. The other disciples may not have known the cause of Peter and John's disappearance. They had been held overnight and may not have been able to get a message out to the others. Some certainly must have heard of the healing of the lame man by now, but they may not have known that Peter and John were involved.

4:24. In response to Peter and John's report, the believers offered a prayer to God. Luke emphasized that the prayer was offered **with one accord**. More than once he emphasized the unity of the early church in Jerusalem (see, e.g., 2:44–47; 4:32–35). The believers began their prayer with a confession of God's greatness: **Thou art God, which hast made heaven, and earth, and the sea**. Such a confession was appropriate since human authorities were opposing them, yet the one who is greater than man upheld them in their testimony.

4:25–26. Following their initial confession, the believers quoted Scripture applying to the situation they faced. They cited Psalm 2:1–2 as evidence that those in power often oppose the work of God. The message was that this had gone on for centuries and was to be expected; it in fact confirmed their calling as witnesses to the work of God.

4:27. Here the believers made a specific application: **Herod** (Herod Antipas, tetrarch of Galilee and Perea; see Luke 23:7–15), **Pontius Pilate** (Roman procurator of Judea; see Luke 23:1–24), **the Gentiles, and the people of Israel** had all opposed Jesus.

4:28. Though these parties had acted in their own perceived interest, they brought about that which God had **determined**. Not that God had compelled them to act as they did, but He willed to use them and their freely chosen acts to accomplish His saving purpose. Thus, even their opposition to Christ was part of God's overall plan. By extension, the opposition to the work that Christ was continuing to do through the apostles was a part of God's plan too and confirmed that they were in the will of God.

4:29. Only after confessing their faith in God and appling His truth to their specific situation, did the believers offer a petition. They prayed that **with all boldness they may speak thy word**. That they prayed for boldness shows that they were faced with the temptation to fear. Being afraid to witness is not a reason to avoid it but is rather a reason to pray.

4:30. Holy child. Or "holy servant" (see discussion on 3:13). The believers would be emboldened as they saw God continue **to heal** and to work **signs and wonders**, thus vindicating their testimony.

4:31. The place was shaken. An immediate sign that the believers' prayer had been heard (see 16:26). **They spake the word of God**. They continued preaching the gospel despite the warnings of the council (see discussion on 4:18). Again, being **filled with the Holy Ghost** (see discussion on 2:4) is linked to speaking the word of God (see discussion on 4:8). Luke did not mean that they immediately quoted additional Scripture to one another. Instead, in the weeks that followed, they had renewed **boldness** to proclaim the gospel.

6. The Community of Goods (4:32–5:11)

4:32–37. Luke, as a literary master, knew how to bring facts to the table almost casually or incidentally so that they become part of the reader's mindset before they become important. In this passage, Luke related information intricately linked with later events. He again emphasized the extraordinary unity of the disciples and reported that they collected funds to feed the poor among them (vv. 32–35; see 2:44–45). This sets the scene for the situation in 6:1–7, when the apostles had to deal with the issue of the daily distribution of food, an issue that threatened their unity. Here Luke also introduced Barnabas (vv. 36–37), whose example of giving contrasts that of Ananias and Sapphira (see 5:1–11). Barnabas went on to become a companion of Paul (see chap. 13). The alert reader thus will not be completely unfamiliar with these characters and situations when they again take the stage.

4:32. Of one heart and of one soul. In complete accord, extending to their attitude toward personal possessions: **they had all things common** (see 2:44).

4:33. Witness of the resurrection. As significant as the death of Christ was, the most compelling event was the resurrection, an event about which the disciples could not keep silent. No one in Jerusalem at that time sought to refute their testimony on this point. Apparently everyone, at least those in authority, knew of the empty tomb and that a body could not be produced to discredit the apostles.

4:34–35. As many as were possessors of lands or houses sold them (v. 34; see discussion on 2:44). That this was not a forced selling and that everyone was free to do as they were led is made clear by Peter's question "was it not in thine own power?" (5:4).

4:36. Barnabas. Presented as a good example of giving. In this way, Luke introduced the one who would become an important companion of Paul (see 13:1–4; for other significant contributions of this great-hearted leader to the life and ministry of the early church, see 9:27; 11:22, 25; 15:37–39). **The son of consolation.** The name Barnabas means "son of encouragement." "Son" in Jewish thought could mean something like "essential nature" (Ger, *The Book of Acts*, p. 82). **A Levite, and of the country of Cyprus.** Although Levites did not own inherited land in the Holy Land, these regulations may not have applied to the Levites in other countries. Jews had settled in Cyprus, an island in the eastern part of the Mediterranean Sea, since Maccabean times. Perhaps Barnabas sold land he owned in Cyprus and brought the proceeds to the apostles (see 4:37), or perhaps he was married, and the land was his wife's property. It is also possible that the prohibition against Levite ownership of land in the Holy Land was no longer observed.

4:37. Brought the money, and laid it at the apostles' feet. Barnabas's money was given to the apostles for charity.

5:1–11. Having presented Barnabas as a good example of giving (see discussions on 4:36–37), Luke recorded the story of Ananias and Sapphira as a bad example of giving. These two have not been previously introduced to the reader. Luke may have intended to bring them onstage suddenly and without introduction for their one scene. The reader thus has no previous experience of them and no sympathy for them. The sudden deaths of these two strangers to

the reader stand out all the more as a result. **Again,** Luke was very much aware of the literary qualities needed for effective narrative. In the case of these two, love of praise for (pretended) generosity and love of money led to the first recorded sin in the life of the church. It is a warning to the reader that "God is not mocked" (Gal. 6:7). Compare this divine judgment at the beginning of the church era with God's judgments on Nadab and Abihu (Lev. 10:2), on Achan (Josh. 7:25), and on Uzzah (2 Sam. 6:7).

5:1–2. Ananias, with Sapphira … sold a possession, and kept back part. They had a right to keep whatever they chose. The sin was to make it appear that they had given all when they actually had not. Peter made it clear in 5:3–4 that giving was not compulsory. Ananias could well have said, "Here is part of the money; the rest we will use to meet our needs." No one would have thought the worse of them for it, and no sin would have been committed.

5:3. Satan filled thine heart. The continuing activity of Satan is noted (see Luke 22:3; John 13:2, 27; 1 Peter 5:8). **To lie to the Holy Ghost.** A comparison with 5:4 shows that the Holy Spirit is regarded as God Himself present with His people.

5:4. Was it not thine own … in thine own power? Ananias sinned only in that he lied … unto God.

5:5. Ananias died immediately. And great fear came on all. That apparently was God's purpose in Ananias's sudden death: that the new church should take sin and obedience seriously.

5:6. It appears that no funeral service was held for Ananias. They simply **wound him up, carried him out, and buried him.** They wrapped him in the manner that a body would be wrapped at that time, with strips of linen, and placed him in a tomb.

5:7. It is peculiar that no one was sent to inform Ananias's widow. Perhaps the apostles forbade it, knowing that she might have had a part in the sin. Peter apparently wanted to give her the opportunity to repent or to fill up the measure of sin, as she chose. She chose wrongly.

5:8. Peter asked Sapphira a leading question. Still, she had the option of saying, "No, it was for more than that, but that is the amount of our gift."

Had she done so, things would have been different for her. Peter did not tell her of her husband's death until after she answered. Her decision to repent or to participate in the deceit was thus free of outside influence.

5:9. To tempt the Spirit of the Lord. If no dire consequences had followed this act of sin, the results among the believers would have been serious when the deceit became known. Not only would dishonesty have appeared profitable, but the conclusion that the Spirit could be deceived would have followed. It was important to set the course properly at the outset to leave no doubt that God will not tolerate such hypocrisy and deceit.

5:11. Great fear came upon all. Bruce (*The Book of Acts*, p. 107) suggests that one reason for this fear is that many of the members "had reason to tremble and think." He thereby suggests that many others were guilty of similar sins. This may be true, but it is not the most likely interpretation. Fear will grip anyone confronted with the stark realities of God's judgment on sin. **The church**. This is the first use of the term in Acts. It can denote either the local congregation (see 8:1; 11:22; 13:1) or the universal church (see 20:28). The Greek word for "church" (*ekklēsia*) was already being used for political and other assemblies (see 19:32, 40) and, in the Septuagint (the Greek translation of the Old Testament), for Israel when gathered in religious assembly.

7. The Arrest of the Twelve Apostles (5:12–42)

5:12. For the third time, Luke mentioned that **by the hands of the apostles were many signs and wonders wrought** (see 2:43; 5:12; 6:8). This was in answer to the prayer of the church (see 4:30). For **Solomon's porch**, see discussion on 3:11.

5:13. Of the rest durst no man join himself to them. Because of the fate of Ananias and his wife, no pretenders or halfhearted followers risked identification with the believers. Luke could not have meant that no one joined the Christian community, since 5:14 indicates that many were coming to Christ. **But the people magnified them**. This does not mean that people made more of the apostles' significance than

was warranted, only that people had a high level of awareness of the church. Today, one would say that the church had a "high profile."

5:14. Added … multitudes both of men and women (see discussion on 1:15). This is the first specific mention of women believing (compare 4:4; see 8:3, 12; 9:2; 13:50; 16:1, 13–14; 17:4, 12, 34; 18:2; 21:5; but see also 1:14).

5:15–16. Luke often made a general statement and then gave examples of it. Here, having said that the apostles performed "many signs and wonders" (5:12) and having described the results, he went back and offered examples.

5:15. The shadow of Peter. This parallels such items as Paul's handkerchiefs (see 19:12) and the edge of Jesus' cloak (see Matt. 9:20). Not that any of these material objects had magical qualities, but the least article or shadow represented a direct means of contact with Jesus or His apostles. Luke thus again linked the works done by the apostles to those of Jesus, in line with his desire to present in Acts the continuation of all that "Jesus began both to do and to teach" (1:1) during His earthly ministry.

5:16. Out of the cities round about unto Jerusalem. This is testimony not only to the "signs and wonders" (5:12) that the apostles performed but also to the fact that "the people magnified" (5:13) the disciples.

5:17. Then indicates that the reaction of the leadership was in response to the healings the apostles performed and to their teaching. The incident involving Peter and John was most likely still fresh in the minds of the leaders. Possibly, the crowds the apostles were drawing raised fears among the temple authorities that the Romans would crack down on them. More likely, they feared that their credibility and standing with the people would be affected. The crowds being drawn by the miracles were hearing daily that the Jewish leaders had delivered up Jesus to be crucified. It could not have helped their standing (see discussion on 5:28). **High priest**. The official high priest recognized by Rome was Caiaphas, but the Jews considered Annas, Caiaphas's father-in-law, to be the actual high priest since the high priesthood was to be held for life (see discussion on 4:6). **All they that were with him**. His family members. For **the sect of the Sadducees**, see discussion on 4:1.

5:18. Put them in the common prison. To await trial the next day. Apparently, all of the apostles were arrested this time, not just two.

5:19–20. The angel of the Lord (v. 19; see Matt. 1:20–24; 2:13, 19; 28:2; Luke 1:11–38; 2:9; discussions on Gen. 16:7; 2 Kings 1:3; Zech. 1:11). This phrase is used four other times in Acts: (1) Stephen spoke of him (7:30–38); (2) he guided Philip (8:26); (3) he liberated Peter (12:7–10); and (4) he struck down Herod (12:23). **Go, stand and speak** (v. 20). The angel commanded the apostles to preach **all the words of this life**. This may have served as an affirmation to the apostles that they were indeed obeying God rather than men in the matter of preaching. The angel commanded them to preach rather than to perform signs. Perhaps too much attention had been focused on the healing miracles. Crowds were drawn by these, but it is likely that the Lord wanted to keep the focus on the gospel itself.

5:21. The apostles began to teach in the temple in response to the angel's command. Meanwhile, **the high priest … called the council** (see discussion on Mark 14:55) **together** for a meeting. This was the Sanhedrin, the supreme Jewish court, consisting of seventy to one hundred men (seventy-one being the proper number). They sat in a semicircle, backed by three rows of disciples of the "learned men," with the clerks of the court standing in front. The council, unaware that the apostles had been freed, **sent to the prison to have them brought**.

5:22–23. The officers (v. 22) found the prison still **shut** (v. 23) and the guards outside, but the apostles were gone. It seems the officers saw this as a miracle.

5:24. For **the captain of the temple**, see discussion on 4:1. **They doubted of them whereunto this would grow**. The leaders were unsure how all of this would turn out.

5:25. Then came one and told them. The apostles made no effort to hide their activities. It is testimony to the size of the temple complex that the council was able to convene for a meeting without noting the apostles' presence in the temple precincts.

5:26. Brought them without violence: for they feared the people. Luke again pointed out the extent to which the people and the leadership were at odds. Their fear of the people constrained the leaders' actions. In his gospel, Luke mentioned this twice in relation to their desire to take Jesus (Luke 20:19; 22:2). In Acts, Luke again mentioned twice that the leaders could not act aggressively against the apostles because of their popularity with the people (here and 4:21).

5:27–28. Did we not straightly command you that ye should not teach in this name? (v. 28) The leaders had issued a clear command "not to speak at all nor teach in the name of Jesus" (4:18). Their problem was the apostles' teaching in the name of Jesus. **Bring this man's blood upon us**. Probably a reference to the apostles' repeated declaration that some of the Jews and some of their leaders had killed Jesus (see 2:23; 3:13–15; 4:10–11; Matt. 27:25). The leaders feared the people, and the apostles' teaching was casting doubt on their spiritual knowledge, morals, and credibility in the people's eyes.

5:29. We ought to obey God rather than men. Having been encouraged by the angel of the Lord in the rightness of their calling, the apostles boldly asserted their intention.

5:30–32. Peter's message here is similar to his preaching in Acts 2:14–40 (see discussion there) and elsewhere, though much shortened.

5:30. Peter went right to the heart of the authorities' problem. **Jesus … ye slew and hanged on a tree**. "Tree" here is used to describe the cross (see 1 Peter 2:24; Deut. 21:22–23). Like its Hebrew counterpart, the Greek for this word could refer to a tree, a pole, a wooden beam, or some similar object. **God … raised up** the one whom the Jewish leaders had slain.

5:31. Jesus is **exalted** and is now in a position to **give repentance … and forgiveness**. Peter could assume that they had heard this message, and thus he shortened it. This was not a change from the gospel he had preached but rather a summary. The council could not have failed to hear the implicit call for them to repent and turn to Christ.

5:32. Peter finished with a statement about the apostles' calling as Jesus' **witnesses**. They were not alone in this, however, for **so is also the Holy Ghost, whom God hath given to them that obey him** (see John 15:26–27). The disciples' testimony was directed and confirmed by the Holy Spirit, who convicts the world through the Word (see John 16:8–11) and is given to those who respond to God with "obedience to the faith" (Rom. 1:5; see discussion on 6:7).

5:33. They were cut to the heart. Apparently, Peter's words stung sharply. At this point, the council considered killing the apostles. Bruce (*The Book of Acts*, p. 114) indicates that the Sadducean party might have done this, except that the Pharisees, a minority on the council, would not have gone along. Because the Pharisees were more popular with the people, who were supportive of the apostles, the Sadducees' hands were tied in the matter.

5:34. A Pharisee, named Gamaliel. The most famous Jewish teacher of his time and traditionally listed among the heads of the schools of Jewish thought. Possibly he was the grandson of Hillel. Like Hillel (see discussion on Matt. 19:3), he was moderate in his views, a characteristic that is apparent in his cautious recommendation on this occasion. Saul (Paul) was one of his students (see 22:3).

5:35. Take heed. Gamaliel's counsel was to adopt a wait-and-see attitude. He did not want the council to act in haste and went on to provide several reasons for waiting (see 3:36–39).

5:36. Theudas. We know of him from no other historical source. Gamaliel asserted that after Theudas's death, his followers **were scattered**, and his movement came to nothing. The analogy that Gamaliel drew, however, is false. Theudas was **boasting himself to be somebody**; Jesus, who really was somebody, had carried on His ministry humbly. Theudas **was slain** and apparently was still in his grave; Jesus had risen, and the apostles, who were on trial here, were witnesses to that resurrection. Movements often end when their founders die. The "movement" begun by the living Christ has never died, nor ever will, for He lives and reigns in His church. Seen from an unbeliever's perspective, Ga-

maliel's analogy makes sense, but as history has shown, it fails.

5:37. Gamaliel offered a second and similar analogy: **Judas of Galilee**, whom the Jewish historian Josephus refers to as a man from Gamala in Gaulanitis who refused to give tribute to Caesar. His revolt was crushed, but a movement started in his time may have lived on in the party of the Zealots. **The days of the taxing.** Refers to a census for the purpose of taxing, not the first census of Cyrenius (see discussion on Luke 2:2) but the second one, in AD 6. **As many as obeyed him, were dispersed.** The analogy fails here as well. The "movement" that Jesus founded was not dispersed; it was growing and spreading. This was a work of God, energized by the Spirit, not a movement that was running out of steam.

5:38–39. And now I say unto you, Refrain from these men (v. 38). Gamaliel drew this application from his analogies (see 5:36–37). That Gamaliel was wrong about what would happen is a fortunate thing for the church. He ended, however, with a final reason for not persecuting the apostles: **if this counsel or this work be of men, it will come to nought**, as had happened with the two incidents he cited, **But if it be of God, ye cannot overthrow it** (v. 39). Here Gamaliel was absolutely right. The works "of men" that he cited have disappeared, but the church, which is "of God," has never been overthrown.

5:40. To him they agreed, sort of. The council agreed that it would come to nothing if it were not of God, but they did not agree to "Refrain from these men, and let them alone" (5:38). Still apparently insecure about their credibility before the people, they had the apostles **beaten**, that is, flogged with the Jewish penalty of thirty-nine lashes (see 2 Cor. 11:24). Then **they commanded that they should not speak in the name of Jesus, and let them go.** That they could issue this command while agreeing that this work could not be stopped if it was of God is testimony to the ability of fallen and lost men to think and act contrary to even their own counsel in their opposition to God.

5:41. The apostles left **rejoicing that they were counted worthy to suffer shame for his name.** They are an example of the advice given in James 1:2. They rejoiced in the midst of trials. Their rejoicing did not come from suffering in itself. The Bible never teaches that there is any virtue in pain for its own sake; rather, the virtue comes because of some other benefit. Pain and suffering become valuable when these things are a test of faith, or they come because of faith. The cause of the apostles' suffering, the name of Jesus, made it worthwhile. It assured them that they were faithfully following their Lord, who had Himself suffered shame at the hands of these same leaders.

5:42. This verse stands as testimony that the apostles did not obey the council's command. **Daily in the temple**, the disciples were able **to teach and preach Jesus Christ** despite the command they had been given to cease. Perhaps the punishment inflicted was a result of the council's frustration, but their ongoing policy became to adopt Gamaliel's advice to leave them alone (see 5:38–39).

8. The Choice of the Seven (6:1–7)

6:1. The number of the disciples was multiplied. A considerable length of time may have transpired since the end of chapter 5. The church continued to grow (see 5:14), but this gave rise to inevitable problems, both from within (see 6:1–7) and from without (see 6:8–7:60). At this stage of its development, the church was entirely Jewish in its composition, but two groups of Jews existed within the fellowship: (1) **Grecians**. Hellenists, those born in lands other than the Holy Land who spoke the Greek language and were more Grecian than Hebraic in their attitudes and outlook. (2) **Hebrews**. Native Hebrews who spoke the Aramaic and/or Hebrew language(s) of the Holy Land and preserved Jewish culture and customs. **The daily ministration**. Daily funds were given to widows who had no one to care for them and so became the church's responsibility (see 4:35; 11:28–29; see also 1 Tim. 5:3–16).

6:2. The twelve. At this early stage, the apostles were responsible for church life in general, including the ministry of **the word of God** and the care of the needy. The early church was concerned about a spiritual ministry ("prayer, and ... the ministry of the word," 6:4) and a material ministry (**serve tables**).

6:3. Look ye out ... seven men. The number most likely was determined by the size of the task and has no other significance. The men were to have certain qualifications. **Of honest report**. Since they would be handling money and perhaps material goods in the name of the church, it was important not only that they be honest but also that they be known to be honest. **Full of the Holy Ghost** (see discussion on 2:4) **and wisdom**. This presents two sides of good decision making, an ability the men would need since they would be handling funds and making financial decisions. "Full of the Holy Ghost" means that they would need God's wisdom and direction in these matters. "Wisdom" means that they should also possess good sense. Christians should never ignore the importance of having plain wisdom simply because they are led by the Spirit. The early church recognized that human wisdom is not enough by itself, for it is limited. They did not, however, toss it aside on the grounds that being filled with the Spirit was enough. Certainly, the church should not be served by those who have quenched the Spirit in their lives, but these early Christians recognized that it is not a matter of choosing one over the other; both are required for effective ministry. The church elected seven men for the task (see 6:5), and the apostles ordained them (see 6:6). In this way, they were appointed to their work.

6:4. We will give ourselves continually to prayer and the ministry of the word. The apostles were making the point that some things had priority. Meeting physical needs was important, but other believers could do this ministry well, and the apostles had a specific calling as official witnesses of the resurrection. The church had grown to the point that the apostles could no longer do all of the work themselves. That the complaints about the distribution were directed at the apostles was another reason that others needed to be involved in the ministry, so that a misunderstanding on administrative matters might not reflect on them.

6:5. They chose Stephen ... Nicolas. The seven men chosen all had Greek names. The murmuring had come from the Greek-speaking segment of the church (see 6:1), so those elected to oversee the work came from their number to ensure that their interests were represented fairly. Of the seven, only Stephen and Philip receive further notice (for Stephen, see 6:8–7:60; for Philip, see 8:5–40; 21:8–9). **A proselyte of Antioch**. It is significant that a proselyte was chosen and that Luke pointed out his place of origin as Antioch, the city to which the gospel would soon be taken and which would become the headquarters for the forthcoming Gentile missionary effort. That the grace of God was available to the Gentiles is a major theme in both the gospel of Luke and Acts. Here Luke again introduced the names of people and places that become important later on (see discussion on 4:32–37).

6:6. They laid their hands on them. In the Old Testament period, laying on of hands was used to confer blessing (see Gen. 48:13–20), to transfer guilt from sinner to sacrifice (see Lev. 1:4), and to commission a person for a new responsibility (see Num. 27:23). In the New Testament period, laying on of hands was used in healing (see 28:8; Mark 1:41), blessing (see Mark 10:16), ordaining or commissioning (see 6:6; 13:3; 1 Tim. 5:22), and imparting of spiritual gifts (see 8:17; 19:6; 1 Tim. 4:14; 2 Tim. 1:6). These seven men were appointed to responsibilities turned over to them by the twelve apostles. The Greek verb used to describe their responsibility (*diakoneō*; "serve," 6:2) is the root of the noun "deacon" (see Phil. 1:1; 1 Tim. 3:8–13), which can also be translated "minister" or "servant." The men appointed on this occasion were simply called "the seven" (21:8), just as the apostles were called "the twelve" (6:2). It is disputed whether these seven were the first deacons or were later replaced by deacons (see discussion on 1 Tim. 3:8). In actual function, they apparently formed a benevolence committee.

6:7. The number of the disciples multiplied (see discussion on 1:15). Luke apparently saw the division of labor and the settlement of the dispute as the cause of the growth that followed. Freed from administrative duties, the apostles were able to fully devote themselves to preaching. **A great company**

of the priests. Though involved by lineage and life service in the priestly observances of the old covenant, they accepted the preaching of the apostles, which proclaimed a sacrifice that made the old sacrifices unnecessary (see Heb. 8:13; 10:1–4, 11–14). **Were obedient to the faith**. That is, they responded to the gospel. "Faith" here carries the same sense as in Jude 3, where it refers to the body of doctrinal truths revealed concerning the gospel. The priests were obedient to the truth that Christ died for their sins and to the call to repentance inherent in that truth. Exercising faith in Christ is obedience, but faith also produces obedience (see Rom. 1:5; Eph. 2:8–10; James 2:14–26).

9. Stephen's Arrest and Martyrdom (6:8–7:60)

6:8. Stephen ... did great wonders and miracles. Up to this point, Luke reported only the apostles working miracles (see 2:43; 3:4–8; 5:12). Now Stephen worked miraculous signs, and Philip would soon do the same (see 8:6).

6:9. There arose certain of the synagogue ... Libertines. Persons who had been freed from slavery. They came from different Hellenistic areas. **Cyrenians**. Halfway between Alexandria and Carthage, Cyrene was the chief city in Libya and north Africa (see discussion on 2:10). One of its population groups was Jewish (see 11:19–21). **Alexandrians**. Alexandria was the capital of Egypt and second only to Rome in the empire. Two out of five districts in Alexandria were Jewish. **Cilicia**. A Roman province in southeastern Asia Minor, adjoining Syria. Tarsus, the birthplace of Paul, was one of its principal towns. **Asia**. A Roman province in western Asia Minor. Ephesus, where Paul later ministered for a few years, was its major city. **Disputing with Stephen**. Since Saul was from Tarsus, this may have been the synagogue he attended, and he may have been among those who argued with Stephen. He was present when Stephen was stoned (see 7:58).

6:10. They were not able to resist. This means not that they believed what Stephen said but that they were unable to come up with counterarguments to the truths he was defending.

6:11. Since they could not refute Stephen, their reaction was to discredit him falsely. Again, this shows how far fallen men may go in their rejection of the truth. They found men who would accuse him of speaking **blasphemous words against Moses, and against God.** Since Stephen declared that the worship of God was no longer to be restricted to the temple (see 7:48–49), his opponents twisted these words to trump up an accusation that Stephen was attacking the temple, the law, Moses, and ultimately, God.

6:12. With their misrepresentation of what Stephen had said, **they stirred up the people, and the elders, and the scribes** (see discussions on Matt. 2:4; 15:2; Luke 5:17) against Stephen. Nowhere, however, did Luke report that Stephen's preaching itself caused opposition from the people. They opposed Stephen due to what was reported to them, not due to what Stephen had actually said. For **the council,** see discussion on 5:21.

6:13–14. Against this holy place, and the law (v. 13). This is similar to the charges brought against Christ (see Matt. 26:61). The next charge is similar but refers directly to Jesus: **this Jesus of Nazareth shall destroy this place, and shall change the customs which Moses delivered us** (v. 14). Stephen may have referred to Jesus' statement in John 2:19, and his words may have been misunderstood or purposely misinterpreted, as at the trial of Jesus.

6:15. His face as it had been the face of an angel. The meaning of this is unclear. It may simply mean that Stephen faced this tense situation with a supernatural peace that showed on his countenance. Many Christians have reported experiencing supernatural peace in a moment of trial. Or it may mean that Stephen's face glowed supernaturally, as Moses' had, but this is unlikely.

7:1. The high priest. Probably Caiaphas (see Matt. 26:57–66; but see discussion on 4:6; John 18:13, 24). **Are these things so?** "These things" refers to the charges that Stephen had spoken against the law and sought to harm the temple (see discussions on 6:11, 13).

7:2–53. Stephen, in his defense, sought to turn the charges back on the Jewish leaders. It was they,

not he, who had spoken against the law, not directly but by missing its true meaning and intent. In an attempt to show them that they were in a long line of people in Israel's history who had resisted the plan and people of God, Stephen reviewed the history of the patriarchs (vv. 2–16) and the story of Moses and the exodus (vv. 17–43). Then, because he had been accused of speaking against the "holy place" (6:13), he spoke briefly about the sanctuary (vv. 44–50) before issuing his counteraccusations (vv. 51–53).

7:2–16. Stephen began with Abraham and related Israel's patriarchal history up to the time of Jacob's death.

7:2. Abraham … in Mesopotamia, before he dwelt in Charran. "Charran" is the Greek spelling for "Haran." Abraham's call came in Ur, not Haran (see Gen. 15:7; Neh. 9:7). Or perhaps his call came first in Ur and was later renewed in Haran (see discussion on Jer. 15:19–21).

7:3–4. The land of the Chaldeans (v. 4). A district in southern Babylonia, the name was later applied to a region that included all Babylonia. **When his father was dead.** Genesis 11:26 does not mean that all three sons—Abraham, Nahor, and Haran— were born to Terah in the same year when he was 70 years old (see Gen. 11:26–12:1). It may be that Haran was Terah's firstborn and that Abraham was born 60 years later. The death of Terah at 205 years of age thus could have occurred just before Abraham, at 75, left Haran.

7:5. Here Stephen's point was that Abraham believed the promise of God, though he never owned the land that was promised. Stephen's accusers were, by contrast, guilty of a lack of faith in the promises of God fulfilled in Jesus Christ.

7:6. Four hundred years. A round number for the length of Israel's stay in Egypt (Exod. 12:40–41 has 430 years). That four generations would represent considerably less than four hundred years is not a necessary conclusion (see discussion on Gen. 15:16). Exodus 6:16–20 lists Moses as the great-grandson of Levi (son of Jacob and brother of Joseph). This would make four generations from Levi to Moses. In 1 Chron. 7:22–27, however, a list of ten names represents the generations between Ephraim (son of Joseph) and Joshua. The ten generations at forty years each would equal four hundred years, the same period of time noted as four generations in Exodus. The list in Chronicles gives a full genealogy, however, while that in Exodus is abbreviated.

7:7. The nation to whom they shall be in bondage will I judge. Those who oppose the work of God will face judgment. Stephen later accused the Jewish leaders of spurning the work of God in Christ (see 7:51–53).

7:8. The covenant of circumcision (see discussions on Gen. 17:10–11). The essential conditions for the religion of Israel were already fulfilled long before the temple was built and their present religious customs began. For **the twelve patriarchs**, see Genesis 35:23–26.

7:9. The patriarchs … sold Joseph. Israel consistently rejected God's favored individuals. Stephen built his case about Jesus' rejection by noting Joseph's rejection by his brothers (see Gen. 37:12–36).

7:10–12. These verses describe Joseph's rise to power and the famine in Canaan. Stephen's point was that Joseph's situation was part of God's plan to rescue His people and preserve them.

7:13. The second time (see Genesis 43). God used the circumstances and Pharaoh's esteem for Joseph to effect His plan.

7:14. Jacob … and all his kindred, threescore and fifteen souls. Seventy-five people. Although the Hebrew Bible uses the number seventy (see Gen. 46:27; Exod. 1:5; Deut. 10:22), the Greek translation of the Old Testament (the Septuagint) adds at Genesis 46:20 the names of one son of Manasseh, two sons of Ephraim, and one grandson of each. This makes the number seventy-five and was the number that Stephen used.

7:15–16. Jacob went down into Egypt, and died (v. 15), but he was buried in the land God had promised. **He, and our fathers** (v. 16). Stephen greatly compressed Old Testament accounts of two land purchases (by Abraham and Jacob) and two burial places (at Hebron and Shechem). According to the Old Testament, Abraham purchased land at Hebron

(see Gen. 23:17–18), where he (see Gen. 25:9–11), Isaac (see Gen. 35:29), and Jacob (see Gen. 50:13) were buried. Jacob bought land at Shechem (see Gen. 33:19), where Joseph was later buried (see Josh. 24:32). Josephus preserves a tradition that Joseph's brothers were buried at Hebron. Stephen's rhetorical device (by which he recalled that Jacob and the twelve patriarchs were buried not in Egypt but in Canaan) is strange to modern ears but would have been well understood by his hearers. His point was that they were buried in Canaan because God had promised that land to Israel. Canaan, not Egypt, was the homeland of their fathers, and to it they would surely return.

7:17–43. Here Stephen turned to the story of Moses and the exodus, including his time in Egypt (vv. 17–29), his experience at the burning bush (vv. 30–34), the exodus (vv. 35–36), his prophecy that God would send "A prophet … like unto me" (v. 37), and the apostasy of the people in the wilderness (vv. 38–43).

7:17–19. The time of the promise drew nigh. In his review of Israel's patriarchal history (7:2–16), Stephen had been leading up to this point. For **another king arose, which knew not Joseph** (v. 18), see discussion on Exodus 1:8.

7:20–21. Stephen introduced Moses, saying he **was exceeding fair** (v. 20). This, to Stephen's hearers, would have denoted God's favor upon Moses. Stephen was aware that his hearers knew this story well. Their familiarity with the Old Testament accounts allowed him to greatly compress the narrative. His purpose was to show them that God had been at work in all of this, through people who had faith.

7:22. Moses was learned in all the wisdom of the Egyptians. Not explicitly stated in the Old Testament but to be expected if he grew up in the household of Pharaoh's daughter. Both Philo and Josephus speak of Moses' great learning.

7:23. When he was … forty. Moses was 80 years old when he was sent to speak before Pharaoh (see Exod. 7:7) and 120 years old when he died (see Deut. 34:7). Stephen's words agree with a tradition that Moses was 40 years old when he first departed from Egypt.

7:24–25. Moses had avenged a wronged Israelite. Stephen commented that Moses **supposed his bretheren would have understood how that God by his hand would deliver them** (v. 25). Moses had reason to believe that the people would see God at work and trust Him, **but they understood not**. Stephen here introduced the idea that the Jewish people, by their hardness of heart, had failed to discern the work of God. He was leading up to his indictment of his hearers.

7:26–28. Who made thee a ruler and a judge over us? (v. 27). Stephen offered this incident as an example of the Israelites' lack of understanding. It was key to how the Israelites, up to Stephen's own day, responded to God's plan. This is why he devoted so much attention to the incident, though he had just narrated several hundred years in a few verses.

7:29. Madian. Commonly known as Midian. Rejected by his own people, Moses feared that they would inform the Egyptians, and this led to his flight to Midian (see Exod. 2:15), the land flanking both sides of the Gulf of Aqaba. **He begat two sons.** Gershom and Eliezer (see Exod. 2:22; 18:3–4; 1 Chron. 23:15).

7:30–34. When forty years were expired (v. 30). Plus the forty years of 7:23 totals the eighty years of Exodus 7:7. **Mount Sina.** That is, Mount Sinai, which is called Mount Horeb in Exodus 3:1 (see discussion there). In relating Moses' experience at the burning bush, Stephen was contrasting the Israelites' initial rejection of Moses' leadership (see 7:24–29) with God's plan **to deliver them** (v. 34). God had plans for His people, but they lacked faith, which was exactly the situation that Stephen and the church faced with respect to his opponents in the court.

7:35–36. This Moses whom they refused … did God send to be a ruler and a deliverer (v. 35). Israel had rejected Moses, their deliverer, just as the Jews of Stephen's day were rejecting Jesus, their deliverer. Yet both had been sent by God. God did great things for and through Moses. With **wonders and signs**, Moses **brought them out** of Egypt and led them **in the wilderness forty years** (v. 36).

7:37. Here Stephen's narrative took a turn. For the first time, he brought in a reference to Jesus, in a prophecy delivered by Moses: **A prophet … like unto me** (see 3:22–23; discussion on Deut. 18:15). **Him shall ye hear.** This prophet had arisen, His name was Jesus, and the Jewish leaders were not willing to hear His teaching and thus were disobeying God.

7:38. The church in the wilderness. Though the Greek word *ekklēsia* ("church") takes on a technical, theological sense in the New Testament, its more common sense of "assembly" is used here (see discussion on 5:11). **The angel which spake to him.** According to Jewish interpretation at that time, the law was given to Moses through the mediation of an angel, after the manner of Moses' original call (see Exod. 3:2; see also 7:53; Gal. 3:19; Heb. 2:2). **Who received the lively oracles to give unto us.** Moses was the mediator between God and man on Mount Sinai.

7:39. Whom our fathers would not obey. The Israelites again rejected God's representative and His commands. As Stephen neared the conclusion of his speech, he began to heighten the tension in his narrative. The reader can almost sense the air crackling in the court.

7:40–43. Make us gods (v. 40). While Moses was on Sinai receiving the law, the people **made a [golden] calf** (v. 41), rejecting God and His representative (see Exod. 32:1). The people had not traveled far from the idolatry of Egypt. **God … gave them up** (v. 42; see discussion on Rom. 1:24). Stephen compressed the idolatry of the Israelites in the wilderness and their later idolatry, which were essentially different parts of one long act of betrayal on the part of the people. His point was that the Israelites had a history of turning their backs on God and what He had done for them. In these verses, Stephen quoted from Amos 5:25–27 as translated in the Septuagint, except that he replaced "Damascus" with **Babylon** (v. 43) since the Babylonians had carried out Israel's final exile from the Promised Land (Amos was speaking first of the Assyrian exile of the northern kingdom).

7:44–50. Because he had been accused of speaking against the "holy place" (6:13), Stephen concluded his recital with a word about the sanctuary. Presumably, he had been preaching that the risen

Christ had now replaced the temple as the mediation of God's saving presence among His people and as the one ("the place," v. 49) through whom they (and "all nations," Mark 11:17) could come to God in prayer (see discussion on 6:13–14).

7:44. **The tabernacle of Witness**, or "the tabernacle of the Testimony." Stephen used this term because the primary contents of the wilderness tabernacle were the ark of the covenant and the two covenant tablets it contained, which were called "the Testimony" (see *KJV Study Bible* notes on Exod. 25:16, 22).

7:45–46. Stephen speeded up the narrative, carrying the story up to the time of David. His point was that God had continued to work His purpose even though the people may have turned away from Him.

7:47. **Solomon built him a house**. Solomon built the first temple.

7:48. Here Stephen addressed the matter that may have been the touchstone of the accusations against him: **the most High dwelleth not in temples made with hands.**

7:49–50. Stephen quickly cited Scripture to prove his point, quoting from Isaiah 66:1–2, where Isaiah reminded Israel that all creation is the temple that God Himself made. Stephen thus reminded his hearers that ultimately God builds His own temple.

7:51–53. Having traced the history of Israel and her faithlessness, even in the face of God's mighty deeds on her behalf, Stephen made the application to his hearers and issued counteraccusations to their charges against him. **Ye stiffnecked and uncircumcised in heart and ears** (v. 51). Though physically circumcised, these Jews were acting like the uncircumcised pagan nations around them. They were not truly consecrated to the Lord. Their faith was not in God and what He was doing through Jesus Christ. Stephen drew an analogy. As their fathers had persecuted the prophets, who foretold the coming of Jesus Christ, so also his hearers were **now betrayers and murderers** (v. 52) of this same Jesus. For **the law by the disposition of angels** (v. 53), see discussion on 7:38. **And have not kept it**. In that they had not

believed God and had spurned the grace offered in Jesus Christ.

7:54. Stephen's speech affected his hearers: **they were cut to the heart**. Rather than repent, however, they became angry.

7:55. For **full of the Holy Ghost**, see discussion on 2:4; see also 6:5. **And saw the glory of God, and Jesus standing on the right hand of God**. Luke wanted his readers to know that Stephen received affirmation that he had borne true testimony to his Lord.

7:56. Stephen described what he saw as he looked to heaven. **The Son of man** (see discussion on Mark 2:10). Jesus used this title of Himself (see Mark 2:10) to emphasize His relationship to messianic prophecy (see Matt. 25:31; Dan. 7:13–14). It is unusual for someone other than Jesus to apply this term to Him (see also Rev. 1:13).

7:57. **They cried out ... stopped their ears, and ran upon him**. They refused to listen further. The picture is of an irrational mob.

7:58. **Cast him out of the city, and stoned him**. Luke made a general statement here of what happened and gave details in 7:59–60. **Laid down their clothes at a young man's feet ... Saul**. Some have thought that this marked Saul as being in charge of the execution. In any case, it was Luke's way of introducing the main character of the second part of the book (see discussion on 4:32–37).

7:59. **They stoned Stephen, calling upon God**. At first glance, it is hard to tell who was calling upon God. The rest of the verse makes it clear this was Stephen. The idea is that they stoned Stephen, "who was calling upon God," or, "while he was calling upon God."

7:60. **Lord, lay not this sin to their charge**. This is similar to Jesus' words seeking forgiveness for His executioners (see Luke 23:34).

10. The Scattering of the Jerusalem Believers (8:1–4)

8:1. **Saul was consenting unto [Stephen's] death** (see 22:20). Luke recorded this to present Saul as a zealous persecutor of the church. This marks the beginning of persecution in Jerusalem. As a result, the disciples **were all scattered abroad throughout**

... Judea and Samaria. This was the beginning of the fulfillment of the commission in 1:8, not by the church's plan but by events beyond the believers' control. **Except the apostles.** The apostles' presence in Jerusalem would encourage those in prison and provide a center point of communication for those scattered. The church now went underground.

8:2. Luke returned to Stephen one more time, to briefly describe **his burial.** This verse indicates that Stephen was well loved in the church, in contrast to the official condemnation that led to his execution (see Bruce, *The Book of Acts*, p. 162). By first reporting the scattering of the church through persecution and then returning to Stephen, Luke slowed the pace of the narrative and made the transition easier. Rather than finishing with Stephen and then dealing with persecution, he introduced persecution and then finished the account of Stephen on a tender note, thus making both the death of Stephen and the persecution of the church a little easier on the reader's psyche.

8:3. Saul ... made havock of the church (see 22:4). The Greek underlying this phrase sometimes describes the ravages of wild animals. Saul was, "concerning zeal, persecuting the church" (Phil. 3:6), and this in no uncertain terms.

8:4. Preaching the word. Many witnesses to the gospel **went every where,** proclaiming the good news. The number of witnesses multiplied, and the territory covered was expanded greatly (see 11:19–20). Persecution often causes the church to grow, further confounding the wishes of those who would crush it.

11. Philip's Ministry (8:5–40)

a. In Samaria (8:5–25)

8:5. Philip. One of the seven men elected in the Jerusalem church to oversee the care of the needy (see 6:3, 5; discussion on 6:6), Philip now became an evangelist, proclaiming Christ (see 21:8). Philip is an example of one of those who had been scattered (see 8:1). **The city of Samaria.** A reference to the old capital Samaria, renamed Sebaste or Neapolis (modern Nablus).

8:6–8. Luke recounted the success of Philip's preaching in the city of Samaria to show that the gospel was to spread to all the world. Early success in Samaria confirmed Jesus' will in this matter (see 1:8) and must have encouraged the scattered disciples that their activities were not outside the blessing of God even though their circumstances had changed.

8:9. Simon. In early Christian literature, Simon the sorcerer (Simon Magus) is described as the archheretic of the church and the father of Gnostic teaching (see 1 John, Introduction: "Gnosticism").

8:10. This man is the great power of God. The people were saying either that Simon was God Himself or, more likely, that he was His chief representative.

8:11. Simon had deceived many for a **long time.**

8:12. Here Luke provided a hint of the content of Philip's preaching. **The things concerning the kingdom of God.** Philip taught much like what Jesus had taught on these matters. **And the name of Jesus Christ.** This was the specific teaching that there is life in His name for all who repent and believe.

8:13. Simon himself believed ... was baptized. It is difficult to know whether Simon's faith was genuine. Though this verse says Simon believed, Peter's statement that Simon had no part in the apostles' ministry because his heart was "not right in the sight of God" (8:21) casts some doubt on the depth of his belief.

8:14. Samaria had received the word of God. The people were obedient to the gospel proclaimed by Philip. **The apostles ... sent unto them Peter and John.** The Jerusalem church assumed the responsibility of inspecting new evangelistic efforts and the communities of believers they produced (see 11:22). The apostles had responsibility for proper doctrine. In the absence of the New Testament, they were the guarantors of this. Today, the Bible performs that function.

8:15. Prayed for them, that they might receive the Holy Ghost. The apostles may have laid hands on believers individually or at a joint service much like a large ordination service today.

8:16. Was fallen upon none of them. Since the day of Pentecost, those who belong to Christ (see

Rom. 8:9) also have the Holy Spirit. In Samaria, however, the Spirit had not yet been made manifest to the Christians by the usual signs. This deficiency was now graciously supplied (see 8:17).

8:17. For **laid ... their hands on them**, see discussion on 6:6; see also 8:18; 19:1–7; 2 Tim. 1:6.

8:18–19. He offered them money (v. 18). Simon had boasted of having great powers (see 8:9, discussion on 8:10), and now he tried to buy the magical power he believed that the apostles possessed.

8:20–21. Luke recorded in detail Peter's rebuke of Simon. These verses show Peter's integrity; he was unwilling to profit from the gospel. They also show that the apostles' ability could not, and would not, be sold and that Simon's desire to purchase it was itself sinful.

8:22. Peter exhorted Simon to **Repent therefore of this thy wickedness and pray God**. He called Simon to prayer, but **if perhaps** left some doubt **whether** God would answer. The doubt most likely stemmed from the question of whether Simon would actually exercise the faith necessary to trust God to forgive him.

8:23. In the gall of bitterness (see Deut. 29:18). At this point, the state of Simon's heart was such that he could neither receive God's forgiveness nor offer a prayer in faith. If he set his heart in that direction, however, it could result in faith being generated. When one is far from God and has no heart for prayer, one ought the more to pray, that God may soften one's heart and bring one back to Him.

8:24. Pray ye to the Lord for me. It is unclear whether Simon genuinely repented. He asked only for prayer that he not suffer the consequences of his actions.

8:25. Luke used this summary statement to indicate he was finishing one topic and moving on to another. Apparently, **they ... preached the gospel in many villages of the Samaritans** on their way back to Jerusalem. "They" here seems to mean Peter and John since they were the ones who had come from Jerusalem to see what was happening (see 8:14). It is possible, however, that at least Philip returned with them (see 8:26).

b. To the Ethiopian Eunuch (8:26–40)

8:26. For **the angel of the Lord**, see 8:29; discussion on 5:19. **From Jerusalem unto Gaza.** A distance of about fifty miles. Philip most likely was in Jerusalem at this time. Perhaps the persecution that had sent all but the apostles out of the city had eased somewhat (but see 9:1–2). **The way ... unto Gaza, which is desert.** A road through the wilderness, a largely uninhabited area.

8:27–28. A man of Ethopia, an eunuch (v. 27). In this period, Ethiopia corresponded to Nubia, from the upper Nile region at the first cataract (Aswan) to Khartoum. **Candace.** The traditional title of the queen mother, who was responsible for performing the secular duties of the reigning king. The king was thought to be too sacred for such activities. **Had come to Jerusalem for to worship.** If not a full-fledged proselyte (see Deut. 23:1), the Ethiopian was a Gentile God-fearer. **Read Isaiah the prophet** (v. 28). Perhaps he had purchased the scroll while in Jerusalem.

8:29. The Spirit said unto Phillip. This is the first time Luke indicated that certain leaders were led of the Spirit toward a ministry direction. It was not the last time, however (see 10:19, 11:12, 16:7, 21:4). Most likely, the Spirit spoke to Philip's heart rather than in an audible voice.

8:30. Heard him read. It was customary to read aloud. **Understandest thou what thou readest?** Philip's question was the obvious opening and began a conversation that would inevitably lead the eunuch to Christ.

8:31. The Ethiopian's reply, followed with an invitation to **sit with him** in the chariot, was an implicit request for Philip to interpret for him.

8:32–33. The Ethiopian was reading Isaiah 53:7–8, which is a poetic passage. Thus, **as a sheep** (v. 32) and **like a lamb** are parallelisms. **Opened he not his mouth.** The reference to Jesus is clear to readers today, and certainly was to Philip, but it would not have been clear to someone unfamiliar with the details of the trial and crucifixion of Christ.

8:34. Of whom speaketh the prophet this? of himself ...? It was more common in biblical times for writers to refer to themselves in the third person. Paul may have done this in 2 Corinthians 12:2.

8:35. Philip … preached unto him Jesus. Philip proclaimed the way of salvation through Jesus Christ. Beginning with Isaiah 53, Philip may have identified the suffering Servant with the Davidic Messiah of Isaiah 11 or other suffering Servant passages. Depending on the Ethiopian's familiarity with Scripture, Philip may have referred to many other passages as well.

8:36. They came unto a certain water. This could be (1) a brook in the valley of Elah (which David crossed to meet Goliath, see 1 Sam. 17:40), (2) the Wadi el-Hasi just north of Gaza, or (3) water from a spring or one of the many pools in the area. **What doth hinder me to be baptized?** indicates that Philip had explained to him doctrinal matters besides the person of Jesus Christ.

8:37. Philip's reply, **If thou believest with all thine heart, thou mayest**, indicates that the only condition was faith. **I believe that Jesus Christ is the Son of God** indicates the proper content of faith. The Ethiopian had by this time come to more than a general faith in God and a desire to be "a better person."

8:39. Rejoicing (see discussion on 16:34). Joy is associated with salvation in Acts. New believers often radiate joy, with the realization of sins forgiven and burdens lifted.

8:40. Azotus. Old Testament Ashdod (see 1 Sam. 5:1), one of the five Philistine cities. It was about nineteen miles from Gaza and sixty miles from Caesarea. **Cesarea**. Rebuilt by Herod, the city had an excellent harbor and served as the headquarters of the Roman procurators. The account leaves Philip in Caesarea at this time; his next appearance is twenty years later, and he is still located in the same place (see 21:8).

12. Saul's Conversion (9:1–31)

9:1. Saul. Introduced at the stoning of Stephen (see 7:58), Saul was born in Tarsus and trained under Gamaliel (see 22:3; see discussions on Phil. 3:4–14). **Yet breathing out threatenings and slaughter**. It is not known whether Saul was directly involved in the death of anyone other than Stephen (see 8:1), but there appear to have been similar cases (see 22:4; 26:10). **The high priest**. Probably Caiaphas (see discussion on 4:6) and the members of the Sanhedrin, who had authority over Jews both in Judea and elsewhere.

9:2. Desired of him letters. These would have been writs of authority granting him power of arrest. **To Damascus**. Located in the Roman province of Syria, Damascus was the nearest important city outside the Holy Land. It also had a large Jewish population. The distance from Jerusalem to Damascus was about 150 miles, four to six days' travel. **Any of this way** (see discussion on 19:23). "The way" was an early name for Christianity and occurs a number of times in Acts (16:17; 18:25–26; 19:9, 23; 22:4; 24:14, 22; see 2 Peter 2:2). Jesus called Himself "the way" (John 14:6). **He might bring them bound unto Jerusalem**. Where the full authority of the council could be exercised in trial for either acquittal or death. This was in reaction to the fact that persecution at Jerusalem had led to the spread of the gospel elsewhere.

9:3. There shined round about him a light from heaven. This occurred "at midday" and was "above the brightness of the sun" (26:13). The bright (literal) light not only got Saul's attention but also indicated to him that he was in contact with a heavenly reality. Jesus called Himself "the light of the world" (John 8:12).

9:4. Saul, Saul, why persecutest thou me? To persecute the church is to persecute Christ, for the church is His body (see 1 Cor. 12:27; Eph. 1:22–23).

9:5. Who art thou, Lord? In rabbinic tradition, such a voice from heaven would have been understood as the voice of God Himself. The solemn repetition of Saul's name and the bright light suggested to him that he was in the presence of deity. He asked the question because he believed he was serving the God of Israel with his actions; now he was no longer certain. The answer came directly: **I am Jesus whom thou persecutest**. The next statement, **it is hard for thee to kick against the pricks**, has led some to speculate that Saul might have been experiencing guilt over the death of Stephen, and his rabid zeal for persecution was a cover for an uneasy conscience. This is not impossible, but it is more likely that Saul was at this point resisting the grace offered to him. In that case, the phrase expresses Jesus' compassionate understanding of Saul's situation along with an appeal to repent.

9:6. Lord, what wilt thou have me to do? Here is an expression of submission to Christ. Most people assume that Saul's conversion took place here, though some insist that it did not come until Ananias spoke with him (see 9:17–18). The Lord told Saul to **go into the city** and await instructions.

9:7. Hearing a voice. "Heard not" in 22:9 perhaps means that those with Saul did not understand what the voice was saying (see Dan. 10:7). The voice of God from heaven is sometimes described as sounding like thunder (see John 12:29). That may have been the case here.

9:8–9. Saul was blind when he opened his eyes. Perhaps God wanted to symbolize for him the spiritual darkness in which he had been living, but the text neither supports nor denies this. He was **led … by the hand** to Damascus, where he apparently had living quarters already arranged. **Neither did eat nor drink** (v. 9). Saul's fasting was most likely for spiritual enlightenment, not a result of trauma. Bruce (*The Book of Acts*, p. 185) points out that there is nothing to warrant the idea that Saul was engaging in the practice of fasting prior to baptism. That practice came later in the life of the church.

9:10. Ananias. This Ananias is mentioned elsewhere only in 22:12. His was a common name (see 5:1; 23:2). The Greek form is derived from the Hebrew name Hananiah, meaning "The Lord shows grace" (see Dan. 1:6).

9:11. The street which is called Straight. This street probably followed the same route as the long, straight street that today runs through Damascus from east to west. It is a decided contrast to the numerous crooked streets of the city. For **Tarsus**, see discussion on 22:3. **Prayeth.** Prayer is often associated with visions in Luke and Acts (see 10:9–11; Luke 1:10; 3:21; 9:28).

9:12. And hath seen in a vision. This must have reassured Ananias. A believer who ministers as God leads often finds that God has prepared the way for him or her.

9:13. Saints (see discussions on Rom. 1:7; Phil. 1:1). This is the first use of "saints" to describe believers in the book of Acts.

9:14. Apparently, word of Saul's intentions had reached Damascus ahead of him.

9:15. The Lord cut short Ananias's protest. His implied, "I can't go down there!" remained unexpressed. **He is a chosen vessel unto me.** God had called Saul to be a missionary. The image of a person as a "vessel," or container (in this case, a container of the gospel), is common in Scripture. Paul himself made a similar comparison in 2 Corinthians 4:6–7, where he wrote that believers have the treasure of "the light of the knowledge of the glory of God … in earthen vessels." Isaiah said that God is the potter and we are the clay (see Isa. 64:8). **To bear my name before the Gentiles** (see Rom. 1:13–14). The spread of the gospel to the Gentiles is the major theme of Acts. That fact, as much as any other, most likely determined Luke's decision to devote much of the book to Paul's ministry. **Kings.** Agrippa (see 26:1) and Caesar at Rome (see 25:11–12; 28:19). **And the children of Israel.** Paul's ministry was not confined to the Gentiles, though that was his primary focus.

9:16. Great things he must suffer. The things Paul suffered for Christ's name were the product of the times and situations in which he ministered. They happened in the sovereignty of God and for His purposes. In no way, however, is Paul's suffering to be seen as any kind of payback for his persecution of the church. When Saul trusted Christ, all his sins were paid for on the cross. God's grace is sufficient and complete. No Christian pays for his or her sins by increased suffering after salvation (Bruce [*The Book of Acts*, p. 187] is wrong on this point).

9:17. Brother Saul. This form of address indicates just how much Ananias's feelings toward Saul had changed as a result of the Lord's word to him. **Jesus, that appeared unto thee.** Saul's experience on the Damascus road was not merely a vision. The resurrected Christ actually appeared to him, and on this fact Saul based his qualification to be an apostle (see 1 Cor. 9:1; 15:8).

9:18–19. There fell from his eyes as it had been scales (v. 18). This is unique in Scripture. In every case in which Jesus healed a blind man, sight was restored, but no physical barrier to sight fell away. The incident most similar to this is when He put clay on a blind man's eyes (see John 9:6), but that is not really a true analogy. **Was baptized**. Saul's baptism most likely was performed by Ananias.

9:20. Straightway. Following his baptism. **He preached Christ in the synagogues**. It became Saul's regular practice to preach at every opportunity in the synagogues (see 13:5; 14:1; 17:1–2, 10; 18:4, 19; 19:8). For Saul, it really was, "to the Jew first, and also to the Greek" (Rom. 1:16). **He is the Son of God**. Saul's message was a declaration of what he had become convinced of on the Damascus road: Christ's deity and messiahship (see 9:22; discussion on Luke 2:11). Notice that Saul "preached Christ" and gave content to that message ("He is the Son of God"). He apparently did not focus on his own conversion experience, though he was not averse to relating it; rather, he focused on Christ Himself and who He is.

9:21. All that heard him were amazed. This may perhaps be seen as the first "celebrity conversion" in the history of the church. Many came to hear Saul simply because of who he was and what he had done in the past.

9:22. Proving that this is very Christ. Saul, due to his already vast store of Old Testament knowledge, was quickly able to offer proofs of Jesus' messiahship. Luke thus offered here an early example of apologetics in service to the church's evangelistic efforts.

9:23. After that many days were fulfilled. Three years (see Gal. 1:18). It is probable that Saul spent the major part of this period in Arabia (see Gal. 1:17), away from Damascus, though the borders of Arabia extended to the environs of Damascus. That Luke did not discuss Saul's Arabian visit should not trouble readers. It simply played no part in the story he was telling (see Bruce, *The Book of Acts*, p. 191).

The Jews took counsel to kill him. Upon Saul's return to Damascus, the governor under Aretas gave orders for his arrest (see 2 Cor. 11:32). The absence of Roman coins struck in Damascus between AD 34 and 62 may indicate that Aretas was in control during that period.

9:24. Saul was aware that the Jewish leaders were **laying await** for him and likely was careful to stay out of public view. He was now fully identified with the Christians he had sought to persecute, hiding with them from those who would persecute him. **They watched the gates day and night**. This most likely happened in shifts.

9:25. Let him down by the wall in a basket (see 2 Cor. 11:33; Josh. 2:15; 1 Sam. 19:12). Those watching by night did so at the gates of the city. The disciples chose a place on the wall far from any gate. It must be remembered that there were no streetlights in that day. On a moonless night, it would have been extremely dark.

9:26. When Saul was come to Jerusalem. Galatians 1:18–19 relates that the only apostles in Jerusalem at that time were Peter and James, the Lord's brother. James was not one of the Twelve, but he held a position in Jerusalem comparable to that of an apostle. **They were all afraid of him**. The disciples in Jerusalem either had not heard of his conversion, a thing not impossible in those days, or they did not believe the reports they had heard.

9:27. Barnabas (see discussion on 4:36). Barnabas apparently knew details of Saul's conversion, or perhaps he took the opportunity to visit Saul and heard the story from him. In either case, he came to believe in Saul's sincerity and became his advocate.

9:28. He was with them. After Barnabas vouched for Saul, he was admitted to the company of the disciples at Jerusalem and was able to be seen in public with them. Apparently, by this time, persecution in Jerusalem had died down. Perhaps the Sanhedrin felt more secure, since years had passed and there had been no public uprising against them. By this time, there was certainly new leadership in the Sanhedrin as well. In any case, the church must have seemed less of a threat.

9:29. He spake boldly. Formerly Saul had argued against Christ; now he forcefully presented Jesus as the Messiah.

9:30. For **Cesarea,** see discussion on 8:40. **Tarsus** (see discussion on 22:3). Saul's birthplace.

9:31. The churches … throughout all Judea and Galilee and Samaria. The whole Christian body, including Christians in these three districts. **Walking … in the comfort of the Holy Ghost.** The work of the Spirit is particularly noted in the book of Acts (see 13:2; discussion on 1:2), which is why it is sometimes called "The Acts of the Holy Spirit." This verse constitutes one of Luke's progress reports (see discussion on 1:15).

B. Second Geographical Expansion of the Gospel: "As far as Phenice, and Cyprus, and Antioch" (9:32–12:25; see 11:19)

1. Peter's Ministry on the Mediterranean Coast (9:32–11:18)

  a. To Aeneas and Dorcas (9:32–43)

9:32–43. Without Luke's summary statement in 9:31, his shift back to Peter might be jarring. In this section, Luke's account of Peter's activity explains how he came to be in Joppa, where he was called on to take the gospel to Cornelius, a Gentile (see chap. 10). Peter performed miracles of healing at least twice while traveling. Luke wanted to show that the church had spread beyond Jerusalem in preparation for portraying its reception by the Gentiles.

Peter probably did much else besides travel and heal people during the time of Saul's conversion and early ministry. Luke chose these incidents because they reestablish in the reader's mind that the apostles were performing "many wonders and signs" (2:43) and that Peter was a significant leader in the church. An alert reader would not have forgotten these matters entirely, but a good writer knows it is helpful to reestablish things after a significant diversion.

9:32. Lydda. A town two or three miles north of the road connecting Joppa and Jerusalem. Lydda was about twelve miles from Joppa.

9:33. Aeneas. Since Peter was in Lydda to visit the believers, Aeneas was probably one of the Christians.

9:34. Peter put his statement in the present tense: **Jesus Christ maketh thee whole.** This indicates that faith operates when Christians trust as a present reality what God wants to do; "faith is the substance of things hoped for" (Heb. 11:1). Aeneas was called on to believe not that Jesus *could* heal him or *should* heal him but that his healing was present reality. One may wonder, since Aeneas was a Christian, why he had not trusted Christ for healing sooner. Miracles are not common, however, and at no time have Christians been able simply to "claim" healing and have it become reality. God's intention here was to affirm Peter's apostleship before the people and to establish his credibility in preaching the gospel. Aeneas was called on to trust Christ for healing in that very moment, but that moment did not happen until Peter was present and God's purpose could be worked out.

9:35. Saron. The Greek spelling of "Sharon." The fertile plain of Sharon runs about fifty miles along the Mediterranean coast, roughly from Joppa to Caesarea. The reference here, however, may be to a village in the neighborhood of Lydda instead of to a district (an Egyptian papyrus refers to a town by that name in the Holy Land).

9:36. Joppa. About thirty-eight miles from Jerusalem, the main seaport of Judea. Today it is known as Jaffa and is a suburb of Tel Aviv.

9:37. Washed. In preparation for burial, a custom common to both Jews (purification of the dead) and Greeks. **An upper chamber.** If burial was delayed, it was customary to lay the body in an upper room. In Jerusalem, the body had to be buried the day the person died, but outside Jerusalem, up to three days might be allowed for burial.

9:38. For **nigh to Joppa,** see discussion on 9:32. **Would not delay to come.** Whether for consolation or for a miracle, Peter was urged to hurry in order to arrive before the burial.

9:39. Shewing the coats and garment which Dorcas made. Dorcas apparently was a talented and giving woman who was much loved in the community. When loved ones pass on, it is natural to focus on the things they loved and handled and worked on, as these are indicators of why they were loved so much.

9:40. Put them all forth (see 1 Kings 17:23; 2 Kings 4:33). Peter had been present on all three occasions recorded in Scripture when Jesus raised individuals from the dead (see Matt. 9:25; Luke 7:11–17; John 11:1–44). Like Jesus when he raised Jairus's daughter, Peter told the crowd in the room to leave. Unlike Jesus, however, Peter **kneeled down, and prayed**.

9:41. Presented her alive. Peter's prayer was answered, much to the wonder of the assembled people.

9:42. Many believed (see John 12:11). Peter's miracle was an act of compassion, but it also led more people to the church. While works of compassion should never be done with evangelism as the sole motive, nothing is wrong with using the occasion afforded to bear witness to Christ. In fact, it would be wrong not to do so.

9:43. Simon a tanner. Occupations were frequently used with personal names to identify individuals further (see 16:14; 18:3; 19:24; 2 Tim. 4:14), but in this case, it is especially significant. Tanners treated the skins of dead animals, thus contacting the unclean according to Jewish law, so many people would have despised Simon. Peter's decision to stay with him shows his willingness to reject Jewish prejudice and prepares the way for his coming vision and the mission to the Gentiles.

b. To Cornelius (10:1–11:18)

10:1. Cesarea. Located thirty miles north of Joppa and named in honor of Augustus Caesar, it was the headquarters for the Roman forces of occupation (see discussion on 8:40). **Cornelius**. A Latin name made popular when Cornelius Sulla liberated some ten thousand slaves over one hundred years earlier. The freed slaves had all taken his family name, Cornelius. **A centurion**. The commander of a military unit that normally numbered at least one hundred men (see discussion on Luke 7:2). A Roman legion (about six thousand men) was divided into ten regiments, each of which had a designation. This was **the Italian band** (another was the "Augustan," or "Imperial," band; see 27:1). A centurion commanded about a sixth of a regiment. Centurions were carefully selected; all of the centurions mentioned in the New Testament appear to have had noble qualities (see, e.g., Luke 7:5). The Roman centurions provided necessary stability to the entire Roman system.

10:2. A devout man. In spite of all his good deeds, Cornelius needed to hear the way of salvation from a human messenger. The role of the angel (see 10:3) was to bring Cornelius and Peter together (see 8:26; 9:10). **One that feared God**. The term used of one who was not a full Jewish proselyte but who believed in one God and respected the moral and ethical teachings of the Jews.

10:3. A vision. This was not a dream or trance but rather a revelation, through an angel, given to Cornelius while at prayer (see 10:30; discussion on 9:11). **About the ninth hour**. About 3:00 p.m. This is another indication that Cornelius followed Jewish religious practices; three in the afternoon was a Jewish hour of prayer (see 3:1), the hour of the evening incense.

10:4. A memorial. A portion of the grain offering burned on the altar was called a "memorial" (Lev. 2:2). Cornelius's salvation, however, must not in any sense be seen as a reward for his prayers and generosity. The angel was simply saying that Cornelius's **prayers … and alms** had not gone unnoticed. Had these in any way paid for his salvation, there would have been no need to send for Peter, or anyone else.

10:5–6. Joppa (v. 5; see discussion on 9:36) … **Simon a tanner** (v. 6; see discussion on 9:43). The angel told Cornelius exactly where to find Peter.

10:7–8. The three men Cornelius sent to Joppa included a **soldier** (v. 7), possibly for their protection in traveling.

10:9. Upon the house. Eastern houses customarily had flat roofs with outside stairways. The roof was often used for relaxation and privacy. Peter used it as a place for prayer, perhaps regularly.

10:10. He fell into a trance. God produced this state of mind in Peter to communicate with him. It was not merely his imagination or a dream. Peter's consciousness was heightened to receive the vision from God.

10:11–12. All manner of fourfooted beasts (v. 12). Including animals both clean and unclean according to Leviticus 11.

10:13. Rise, Peter; kill, and eat. The command was not literal, as the rest of the story demonstrates, for the "great sheet" (10:11) was taken back up into heaven before Peter could actually kill and eat one of the animals. Peter was meant to learn an important spiritual point from this: God was not restricting the gospel to the Jewish people. It was not necessary for him to actually kill one of the animals; in a sense, God was leading Peter in a role-playing scenario. Killing and eating an unclean animal is something a Gentile would do. Peter, as a Christian, had always seen himself as a "Jewish Christian" and could not imagine any other kind. Even the Samaritans who were saved were at least partially Jewish. Now God was asking him to do something a Jewish person would not do. As a Christian, Peter wanted to obey God; as a Jew, he wanted to avoid unclean foods. He was being asked to obey God in doing something only a Gentile, and therefore a Gentile Christian, could do. God thus put Peter in the role of imagining himself as a Christian and a Gentile, a startling new idea for Peter.

10:14. Not so, Lord. So deeply ingrained was the observance of the laws of clean and unclean that Peter refused to obey immediately. **Common or unclean.** Eating anything common (impure) was forbidden by the law.

10:15. What God hath cleansed. Jesus had already laid the groundwork for setting aside the laws of clean and unclean food (see Matt. 15:11; 1 Tim. 4:3–5). Here the central point was the spiritual truth that Gentiles were now to be accepted in Christ.

10:16. Thrice. To make a due impression on Peter.

10:17. While Peter doubted in himself what this vision which he had seen should mean. Apparently, Peter did not immediately understand the full meaning of the vision. Sometimes one comes to understand God's truth more fully in the midst of service for Him. Peter would soon be called on to preach the gospel to Cornelius, a Gentile, and the vision would then become clear. Even now, the men that Cornelius had sent **stood before the gate**.

10:18. The three men that Cornelius had sent (see 10:5–8) asked either Simon the tanner or a servant whether Peter was staying there.

10:19–20. The Spirit gave Peter direction concerning those who had come. Since Peter had not yet come to an understanding of the vision, he would have had trouble going to Cornelius's home without assurance that this was God's will.

10:21. I am he whom ye seek. Peter spoke thus based on what the Spirit had said to him upstairs.

10:22. Three phrases describe Cornelius. He was **a just man**, meaning that he lived a morally upright life, both personally and in his dealings with others; he was **one that feareth God**, a Gentile who recognized one God and respected the Jewish law; and he was **of good report among all the nation of the Jews**. Preaching to a Gentile was outside of Peter's comfort zone. That Cornelius was an honorable man who feared God made it less of a stretch for Peter. It would have been more difficult for him if he had been called to preach to a sensual and evil Gentile who mocked God.

10:23. Called he them in. By providing lodging for them, Peter was already taking the first step toward accepting Gentiles. Such intimate relationship with Gentiles was contrary to prescribed Jewish practice. Having heard their story, Peter must have realized what God was doing. **On the morrow**. It was too late in the day to start out on the long journey to Caesarea (see discussion on 10:1). **Certain brethren**. Six in number (see 11:12), these men were Jewish in background (see 10:45).

10:24. Had called together his kinsmen and near friends. Cornelius well knew that the message Peter would deliver was important. He eagerly invited all those close to him to be present to hear the word of God.

10:25. Fell down at his feet, and worshipped him. Perhaps Cornelius intended only to honor Peter as one having a rank superior to his own, since he was God's messenger. Even so, this went beyond what would normally be expected in a greeting.

10:26. I myself also am a man. Peter allowed no chance for misunderstanding: he was not to be worshiped because he was not God.

10:27. He went in. Apparently, Cornelius had met Peter outside the house.

10:28. God hath shewed me. Peter recognized that his vision had deeper significance than declaring invalid the distinction between clean and unclean meat; he saw that the barrier between Jew and Gentile had been removed (see Eph. 2:11–22).

10:29. Gainsaying simply means "denying." Peter did not deny the truth that God had shown him, and based on that truth, he had accepted Cornelius's invitation. **I ask therefore for what intent ye have sent for me?** Peter surely knew by now that he had been sent to preach the gospel to Cornelius, but he wanted Cornelius to give testimony to the fact. This would also provide Peter with an opening to broach the subject. He did not want to walk into the house and immediately begin preaching. After all, he was a guest. Cornelius telling his story not only constituted an invitation for Peter to begin preaching; it also allowed Cornelius's assembled family and friends to hear once again what had happened and to establish in their hearts an expectation of hearing the truth of God.

10:30. Four days ago. The Jews counted a part of a day as a day: (1) the day the angel appeared to Cornelius, (2) the day the messengers came to Joppa and Peter received a vision, (3) the day the group set out from Joppa, and (4) the day they arrived at Cornelius's house. **Until this hour**. Exactly what Cornelius meant here is unclear. Had he been praying ever since the incident? Did he simply mean that he normally prayed at this time every day? The latter is the best understanding of the text and is inferred in the KJV's translation (see Marshall, *Acts of the Apostles*, p. 188). **A man … in bright clothing**. Common language to describe an angel when appearing in the form of a man.

10:31–32. Luke summarized these details of the story since the reader already knows them. That he repeated them rather than simply saying, "And Cornelius described all that had happened," was probably due to his great concern that his readers understand that the admission of the Gentiles into the grace of God was a genuine and supernatural act of God.

10:33. We are all here present before God. When people come together to hear the preaching of God's word, God is present with them. This is the only place in the New Testament where this phrase is used in this way, however (see Marshall, *Acts of the Apostles*, p. 189).

Once again, Peter is called upon to speak a word for Christ in light of a miraculous event (see discussion at 2:14–40 and 3:12–26). In this case the event was the appearance of an angel to Cornelius, seen in light of Peter's vision in Acts 10:9–16. Peter recognizes that the gospel sent to Israel (Acts 10:26) is meant for the Gentiles as well. Peter's message emphasizes the universal aspect of the gospel that everyone who believes is forgiven (Acts 10:43).

10:34–35. God is no respecter of persons (v. 34; see discussion on James 2:1). God does not favor an individual because of his station in life, his nationality, or his material possessions. He does, however, respect his character and judge his work. This is evident because **in every nation he that feareth him, and worketh righteousness, is accepted with him** (v. 35). Cornelius already worshiped the true God, but this was not enough; he lacked faith in Christ (see 10:36). Peter was not saying here that God accepts people apart from faith in Jesus Christ. All who come to Him in a true spirit of repentance and faith, however, are accepted. That may be implied in the phrase "feareth him [repentance], and worketh righteousness [faith]." Righteous deeds are an act of faith when they are done not to earn salvation but because, in faith, one believes that they are what God wants done. This happens in the context of Christian discipleship, and thus Peter may be seen as meaning that God accepts all, people from every nation, who repent and have faith in Jesus Christ. He did not explain all of this to Cornelius and his guests, probably because he had not yet preached Christ to them, so it would have been confusing since they did not know yet *how* God accepts people to Himself. Cornelius was about to learn, however.

10:36. Peace. Between God and man (reconciliation). **Lord of all**. Lord of both Jew and Gentile (see 10:34–35).

10:37. After the baptism which John preached. Similar to the outline of Mark's gospel, Peter's presentation of the gospel begins with John's baptism and continues to the resurrection of Jesus (for Peter's preaching, see 2:14–40; 3:12–26; 4:8–12; 5:29–32; discussion on 2:14–40). This is significant since the early church fathers viewed Mark as the "interpreter" of Peter (see Mark, Introduction: "Author"). Peter assumed that Cornelius was aware of John the Baptist. John's ministry, which had ended some years earlier, certainly had made a wide impact (see Acts 18:25; 19:3).

10:38. How God anointed Jesus (see Isa. 61:1–3; Luke 4:18–21). Peter assumed that Cornelius also knew the basic story of the ministry of Jesus. His ministry had attracted much attention, especially after His trial and crucifixion at the hands of Pilate, which would have been known among Roman officials throughout the region.

10:39. Both in the land of the Jews, and in Jerusalem. It may seem that Peter was making a false distinction between the two, but he was not. One might say today, "throughout all the land of the Jews, as well as in Jerusalem itself, the major city there." For **hanged on a tree**, see discussion on 5:30.

10:40. Him God raised up the third day. Peter presented the resurrection as an act of God and therefore something to be reckoned with. It was not something that just happened, nor just another event. When God acts, people must respond, either with faith or with rejection. No one can be neutral in the presence of God's mighty deeds.

10:41. Who did eat and drink with him. Those who ate with Jesus after He rose from the dead received unmistakable evidence of His bodily resurrection (see Luke 24:42–43; John 21:12–15).

10:42. For he commanded us to preach, see 1:8; Matthew 28:18–20.

10:43. To him give all the prophets witness. Luke took every occasion to point out that the Old Testament testifies to Jesus (see Luke 18:31; 24:27, 44; Acts 3:18; 10:43;13:27). It is thus to be read christologically, that is, with reference to its testimony to Jesus Christ. This was not uppermost in Luke's mind; he was relating what happened historically, but he certainly may have been aware of the hermeneutical and spiritual import of what he was recording.

10:44. For **the Holy Ghost fell on all them**, see 8:16 and discussion.

10:45. Astonished … because that on the Gentiles also was poured … the Holy Ghost. Apparently, Peter's associates failed to understand that the gospel was for the Gentiles as well as for the Jews and that they would share alike in the benefits of redemption. Gentile proselytes to Judaism, however, were accepted (see 6:5). Peter himself was still just coming to understand it fully, and his companions may have been skeptical despite his testimony concerning what had happened on the roof in Joppa.

10:46. They heard them speak with tongues. This was, to the Jewish believers, a sign that these Gentiles had received the Holy Spirit. Tongues speaking is rare in the book of Acts and normally happened when a new ethnic group was admitted into the church: the inauguration of the church among the Jews (see 2:3–13); the inauguration of the church among the Samaritans, with no mention of tongues, but it is implied that they had received the Holy Spirit (see 8:14–17); the inauguration of the church among the Gentiles (here); the inauguration of the church among the Ephesians (see 19:6). No other accounts of tongues speaking are found in Acts, though there are many conversions to Christ.

10:47–48. Can any man forbid water, that these should not be baptized …? (v. 47). The Gentiles had received the same gift as the Jewish believers (see 11:17); they spoke in tongues as the Jewish Christians had on the day of Pentecost. This was unavoidable evidence that the invitation to the kingdom was open to Gentiles as well as to Jews. **He commanded them to be baptized in the name of the Lord** (v. 48), in obedience to Matthew 28:19–20.

11:1. The apostles and brethren. "Brethren" sometimes refers to those of common Jewish lineage (see 2:29; 7:2), but in Christian contexts, it denotes those united in Christ (see 6:3; 10:23). In matters of deep concern, the apostles did not act alone. The divine will gave guidance, and the apostles interpreted and exhorted, but the consent of the whole church was sought ("the whole multitude," 6:5; "apostles and brethren," here; "the church," 11:22; "the church, and ... the apostles and elders," 15:4; "the apostles and elders, with the whole church," 15:22).

11:2. They ... of the circumcision. Jewish Christians.

11:3. Men uncircumcised. Gentiles, who did not observe the laws of clean and unclean food and violated Jewish regulations concerning food preparation. The church in Jerusalem was rather startled that their leaders **wentest in ... and didst eat with them**.

11:4 – 17. This section repeats, in summary form, the material from 10:1 – 46 (see discussions there), including Peter's vision (vv. 4 – 6), his conversation with God concerning the vision (vv. 7 – 10), his agreeing to journey to Caesarea (vv. 11 – 12), his encounter with Cornelius (vv. 13 – 14), the results of his preaching (vv. 15 – 17). That Luke repeated these details further indicates the importance of this event to the whole book. Readers have now read of Cornelius's encounter with the angel three times, of his encounter with Peter twice, and of Peter's vision on the rooftop three times. Much of the rest of Acts focuses on the reception of the gospel among the Gentiles.

Thou and all thy house (v. 14; see discussion on Gen. 6:18). Not only Cornelius's family but also the slaves and employees under his authority. **Withstand God** (v. 17). Peter could not deny the Gentiles the invitation to be baptized (see 10:47) and to enjoy full fellowship in Christ with all believers. The Jewish believers were compelled to recognize that God was going to save Gentiles on equal terms with Jews. By divine action rather than by human choice, the door was being opened to Gentiles.

11:18. Then hath God also to the Gentiles granted repentance unto life. God had opened the door for the Gentiles to experience repentance, the change of one's attitude toward sin, which leads to a turning from sin to God and results in eternal life

(see discussion on 2:38). What had been happening among the Jews and the Samaritans was undeniably happening among the Gentiles also. A result of the gospel coming to the Gentiles was that Gentile churches began to appear.

2. The New Gentile Church in Antioch (11:19 – 30)

11:19 – 30. Here Luke returned to the scattering of the disciples after the martyrdom of Stephen (see 8:1). The intervening material has been something of a parenthesis. It has, however, explained how and why the gospel spread beyond Jerusalem and demonstrated clearly that God intended for Gentile churches to be planted. Luke began with a catalogue of several places where new churches were started (v. 19). Barnabas, who comes into this section, was sent to Antioch to provide leadership to a new church plant that was growing there (vv. 22 – 23).

11:19. Phenice. Commonly called Phoenicia, a country about 15 miles wide and 120 miles long, stretching along the northeastern Mediterranean coast (modern Lebanon). Its important cities were Tyre and Sidon. **Cyprus.** An island in the northeastern Mediterranean; the home of Barnabas (see 4:36). **Antioch.** The third city of the Roman Empire (after Rome and Alexandria). It was 15 miles inland from the northeast corner of the Mediterranean. The first largely Gentile church was located in Antioch, and it was from this church that Paul's three missionary journeys were launched (see 13:1 – 4; 15:40; 18:23). **Preaching the word to none but unto the Jews only.** Remember that these disciples had scattered abroad before Peter met Cornelius and would not have heard of the incident until their return to Jerusalem.

11:20. Some of them. Perhaps these disciples had gone out to preach later and knew of Cornelius's conversion, but this is not explicitly stated. For **Cyrene**, see discussion on 2:10. **Grecians.** Not Greek-speaking Jews, but Gentiles. This is the first instance of disciples besides Peter preaching to truly non-Jewish people.

11:21. The hand of the Lord (see 4:30; 13:11; Luke 1:66). Indicates divine approval and blessing, sometimes evidenced by signs and wonders (see

Exod. 8:19). The disciples saw results among the Gentiles perhaps to a greater degree than they had expected.

11:22. They sent forth Barnabas (see discussions on 4:36; 9:27) **... as far as Antioch** (see discussion on 11:19). This apparently was in keeping with the Jerusalem church's policy of sending leaders to check on new ministries that came to their attention (see 8:14). Barnabas would later depart from Antioch to accompany Paul on his first missionary journey (see 13:2–3).

11:23. Was glad. Barnabas was pleased with what he saw. He was originally from Cyprus and may have been more comfortable in a non-Jewish setting than other church leaders at Jerusalem were. He was thus the logical choice to go and investigate and to bring words of exhortation to them.

11:24. He was a good man, and full of the Holy Ghost and of faith. Luke's description of Barnabas resembles his description of Stephen (6:5). That Luke commended Barnabas is important in light of his role in the church at Antioch and especially in light of the division that later arose between him and Paul (see 15:36–39).

11:25. For **Tarsus**, see 9:11, 30; discussion on 22:3.

11:26. Barnabas brought Saul back from Tarsus, an event that would affect the whole future of Christianity, for it was at Antioch that the major missions thrust of the church began. **A whole year.** Luke noted definite periods of time (see 18:11; 19:8, 10; 24:27; 8:30). **Christians.** Whether adopted by believers or invented by enemies as a term of reproach, this is an apt title for those "belonging to Christ" (the meaning of the term).

11:27. Prophets. The first mention of the gift of prophecy in Acts. Prophets preach, exhort, explain, or as in this case, foretell (see 13:1; 15:32; 19:6; 21:9–10; Rom. 12:6; 1 Cor. 12:10; 13:2, 8; 14:3, 6, 29–37; see also *KJV Study Bible* notes on Jonah 3:2; Zech. 1:1; discussion on Eph. 4:11).

11:28. Agabus. Agabus later foretold Paul's imprisonment (see 21:10). In Acts, prophets engaged in foretelling (see 11:27; 21:9–10) at least as often as in "exhortation" (see 15:32).

11:29. Every man according to his ability. Apparently, some gave more and others less, but no one was forced to give a set amount. **To send relief.** This is the first instance in Acts of one congregation reaching out to help another in a time of physical need. This incident must have made a deep impression on Paul, since he later led the churches of Asia and Greece in a larger offering for the church in Jerusalem (see 1 Cor 16:1–4). No word is given regarding any motive here, other than the need itself. Paul's later offering, however, may have been an act of gratitude to the Jerusalem church as the place from which the blessing of the gospel had come to the other congregations (see Rom. 15:27).

11:30. To the elders. This is the first reference to "elders" in Acts (see discussions on 1 Tim. 3:1; 5:17, 19). That the offering was not presented "to the apostles" is at first surprising. Since the Jerusalem church had elected seven men to oversee the ministry of physical needs (see 6:1–7), it may be that they were the ones who officially received the offering. Perhaps they were now referred to as "elders" by virtue of their long service, Christian example, and leadership abilities (see Marshall, *Acts of the Apostles*, p. 205).

3. Herod's Persecution of the Church and His Subsequent Death (chap. 12)

12:1. About that time. There are two views regarding the time frame of chapter 12. (1) Some hold that it groups together matters concerning Herod, and the events may not be in strict chronological order. For example, the arrival of Barnabas and Saul in Jerusalem (see 11:30) may have followed Herod's persecution of Christians and Peter's release from prison. Since Herod died in AD 44, these events probably occurred in 43. According to this view, the famine of 11:28 occurred circa 46, following Herod's death (see 12:23). The famine visit of 11:30; 12:25 was the Jerusalem visit recorded in Galatians 2:1–10. (2) Others hold that such juggling of events is not necessary. According to this view, the relief gift of 11:30 was delivered before Herod's death in 44, and Barnabas and Saul returned from Jerusalem (see 12:25) after Herod's death. The Jerusalem council visit of 15:1–29 was the Jerusalem visit recorded in Galatians 2:1–10. **Herod the king**. Agrippa I, grandson of Herod the Great (see discussions on Matt. 2:1; 14:1) and son of Aristobulus. He was a nephew of Herod Antipas, who had beheaded John the Baptist (see Matt. 14:3–12) and had tried Jesus (see Luke 23:8–12). When Antipas was exiled, Agrippa received his tetrarchy as well as those of Philip and Lysanias (see Luke 3:1). In AD 41, Judea and Samaria were added to his realm.

12:2. Killed … with the sword. Beheaded, like John the Baptist. **James**. Brother of John the apostle and son of Zebedee (see Matt. 4:21). This event took place about ten years after Jesus' death and resurrection. Jesus had warned the disciples of coming suffering (see Matt. 20:23).

12:3–5. The days of unleavened bread (v. 3; see discussion on Luke 22:1). Because of this feast, Peter was imprisoned rather than killed immediately (see Marshall, *Acts of the Apostles*, p. 208). **Four quaternions** (v. 4). One company of four soldiers for each of the four watches of the night. **Easter**. The New Testament word is "Passover," which was often used to refer to the whole week of the festival (see discussion on Luke 22:1). **Prayer … without ceasing of the church unto God for him** (v. 5). Perhaps the church held regular prayer sessions or, more likely, around-the-clock home prayer meetings to which people would come and go. Under the circumstances, it probably was best not to have the disciples gather in large groups.

12:6. The same night. For Jews, the day began at sunset. Peter thus was freed the night before he would have been brought before Herod.

12:7. A light shined. The glory of the Lord (see Luke 2:9). The angel awakened Peter, **And his chains fell off from his hands**, apparently miraculously.

12:8–9. The angel allowed Peter time to get dressed. Apparently, those who might have prevented Peter's escape (see 12:6) were asleep, which perhaps had been supernaturally enduced. **He went out** (v. 9). Out of the prison, probably the tower of Antonia, located at the northwest corner of the temple—the "castle" where Paul was later held (see

21:34). **Thought he saw a vision**. The circumstances were so unusual that Peter assumed it was a dream of some kind. James had recently been killed, and Peter had no reason to expect supernatural intervention.

12:10. The iron gate … which opened to them of his own accord. Again, this occurred supernaturally. Normally, Peter never would have gotten out of the tower without being spotted and without having to open barred doors and gates.

12:11. Peter spoke to himself of his assurance of the reality of what had happened. Why Luke recorded this in such detail is unclear. Perhaps he wanted to set the scene for the disciples' disbelief when Rhoda claimed that Peter was free and at the door (see 12:13–14).

12:12. Mary. The aunt of Barnabas (see Col. 4:10). Apparently, her home was a gathering place for Christians. It may have been the location of the upper room where the Last Supper was held (see Mark 14:13–15; see also Acts 1:13) and the place of prayer in 4:31. For **John … Mark**, see discussion on 12:25.

12:13. Rhoda. A hired servant who sympathized with the family and the church.

12:14. Told how Peter stood before the gate. In her excitement, Rhoda forgot to let Peter in but instead **ran in** to tell the others.

12:15. It is his angel. Perhaps this reflects the belief that everyone has a personal angel who ministers to him or her (see Matt. 18:10; Heb. 1:14), but this is unlikely. The word "angel" in the Greek means only "messenger," not necessarily a supernatural being (which may explain why so often in the Bible the term is qualified with "of the Lord" to make it clear that no human messenger is meant). The disciples likely assumed that Peter had sent the church some word of encouragement on the eve of his trial and that Rhoda had heard through the gate the words "a message from Peter" but had latched on to just the word "Peter." Their assumption was reasonable, given that James had recently been killed (see 12:2). They probably had been praying that Herod would relent, not for a supernatural release for Peter. Even in those days, miraculous events were rare, and no one in the church presumed that they would happen.

12:16. They were astonished. Though "prayer was made without ceasing of the church unto God for him" (12:5). God often answers prayers in ways that go beyond what one imagines or thinks.

12:17. James. The Lord's brother, a leader in the Jerusalem church (see Gal. 1:19). James the brother of John had been killed (see 12:2).

12:18. No small stir among the soldiers. The soldiers had been responsible for keeping Peter and feared that they would be held accountable for his escape.

12:19. Cesarea (see discussions on 8:40; 10:1). Not only the headquarters for Roman procurators but also Agrippa's capital when no procurators were assigned to Judea.

12:20. Herod was highly displeased with them of Tyre and Sidon, the leading cities of Phoenicia (Lebanon today). **They came with one accord to him**. Apparently, they sought reconciliation and goodwill. They were dependent on the grain fields of Galilee for their food. **Blastus the king's chamberlain**. The treasurer. Blastus is otherwise unknown.

12:21–22. Upon a set day (v. 21). The historian Josephus (*Antiquities* 19.8.2) provides additional details about this event, a festival that Herod was celebrating in honor of Claudius Caesar. **Royal apparel**. Josephus describes that Herod wore a dazzling silver robe that day. When the people acclaimed him **a god** (v. 22), he did not deny it. This was an error on the part of the people but a much worse error on his part to accept such worship.

12:23. Immediately the angel of the Lord (see discussion on 12:15) **smote him**. Josephus (*Antiquities* 19.8.2) reports that Herod was seized with violent pains, was carried out, and died five days later. **Eaten of worms**. A miserable death associated with Herod's acceptance of acclaim to be divine, but it may also be seen as divine retribution for his persecution of the church. The phrase is often used to describe the deaths of evil men (see Marshall, *Acts of the Apostles*, p. 212). It emphasizes that the one who has died no longer exists in this world and is analogous to today's "and good riddance!"

12:24. The word of God grew and multiplied. One of Luke's progress reports (see discussion on 6:7).

12:25. Here Luke returned to the story of **Barnabas and Saul** in preparation for the account of their mission activity, which begins in chapter 13. **John ... Mark** (see 12:12). The author of the second gospel (see Mark, Introduction: "Author") and a companion of Barnabas and Saul on the first part of their missionary journey (see 13:5, 13; discussions on 15:37–39). He was perhaps the young man who fled on the night of Jesus' arrest (see Mark 14:51–52).

II. Paul and the Expansion of the Church from Antioch to Rome (chaps. 13–28)

A. Third Geographical Expansion of the Gospel: "Throughout Phrygia and the region of Galatia" (13:1–15:35; see 16:6)

1. Paul's First Missionary Journey (chaps. 13–14)

13:1. There were in the church that was at Antioch certain prophets (see discussion on 11:27). These believers had the special gift of inspiration experienced by Old Testament prophets (see Deut. 18:18–20; 2 Peter 1:21) but known also in the New Testament (see 2:17–18; 1 Cor. 14:29–32; Eph. 3:5). Prophets are second to apostles in Paul's lists (see 1 Cor. 12:28–29; Eph. 2:20; 4:11; but see Luke 11:49; Rom. 12:6; 1 Cor. 12:10). For **teachers**, see 11:26; 15:35; 18:11; 20:20; 28:31; 1 Cor. 12:28–29; Eph. 4:11. **Barnabas** (see discussion on 4:36) **... Saul**. These are the church leaders at Antioch, perhaps listed in the order of their importance. Barnabas was originally sent to Antioch by the church in Jerusalem (see 11:22), had recently returned from taking alms to Jerusalem (see 12:25), and was a recognized leader in the church at Antioch. **Simeon that was called Niger**. "Simeon" suggests a Jewish background, and "Niger" is Latin for "dark-complexioned" (see Marshall, *Acts of the Apostles*, p. 214). **Lucius of Cyrene**. Lucius is a Latin name. In the second group of preachers coming to Antioch, some were from Cyrene (see 11:20), the capital of Libya (see discussion on 6:9). **Manaen**. In Hebrew, Menahem. Since he was the foster brother of Herod Antipas, he would have been able to tell of Herod's thoughts and actions (see Luke 9:7–9).

13:2. They refers to the prophets and teachers listed in 13:1. **Ministered to the Lord, and fasted.** Paul's first missionary journey did not result from a planning session but from the Spirit's initiative as the leaders worshiped (see 13:4). **Separate me Barnabas and Saul for the work whereunto I have called them.** The communication from the Holy Spirit may have come through the prophets. "Separate" here means "to set aside" and "to give them exclusive responsibility for." This may have included the idea that the church would support them financially so that they could devote themselves to the work.

13:3. Laid their hands on them. This was a means of appointing Barnabas and Saul and of recognizing the church's participation in their mission. Fasting and prayer accompanied this appointment (see 14:23; Luke 2:37).

13:4. Seleucia. The seaport of Antioch (sixteen miles to the west and five miles upstream from the mouth of the Orontes River). **Cyprus** (see discussion on 11:19). Many Jews lived there, and the gospel had already been preached there (see 11:19–20).

13:5. Salamis. A town on the east coast of the central plain of Cyprus, near modern Famagusta. **John.** John Mark, a cousin of Barnabas (see Col. 4:10; discussion on 12:25).

13:6. Paphos. At the western end of Cyprus, nearly one hundred miles from Salamis, Paphos was the headquarters for Roman rule. **Bar-jesus.** "Bar" is Aramaic for "son of"; "Jesus" is derived from the Greek for "Joshua" (see discussion on Matt. 1:21).

13:7. Deputy. Since Cyprus was a Roman senatorial province, a proconsul was assigned to it.

13:8. Elymas. A Semitic name meaning "sorcerer," "magician," or "wise man" (probably a self-assumed designation).

13:9. Saul, (who also is called Paul,). The names mean "asked [of God]" and "little" respectively. It was customary to have a given name, in this case Saul (Hebrew, Jewish background), and a later name, in this case Paul (Roman, Hellenistic background). From this point on, Saul is called Paul in Acts. This may be because he was now entering the Gentile phase of his ministry. The order in which the names

are mentioned now changes from "Barnabas and Saul" (13:2, 7) to "Paul and Barnabas" (13:43, 46). Upon their return to the Jerusalem church, however, the order reverts to "Barnabas and Paul" (15:12). **Filled with the Holy Ghost** (see discussions on 2:4; 4:8). Here again is an instance in which a disciple's being filled with the Spirit accompanied a speaking ministry.

13:10. Paul's address to Elymas begins with three descriptive names: **O full of all subtilty and all mischief** ("one who is" is understood here to preface this), **thou child of the devil,** and **thou enemy of all righteousness.** By calling him these names, Paul made explicit Elymas's character. Exactly what this man was in his heart was not at all hidden from Paul. Each of these names points to some aspect, and each is more explicit in describing Elymas's motives. A sinful man does not want to have his sin exposed. The one who exposes it will certainly get that man's attention. **Wilt thou not cease to pervert the right ways of the Lord?** In one sense, Paul's question was a plea for Elymas to repent. In another, it gave moral justification for the judgment that came upon him with Paul's next words.

13:11. Thou shalt be blind. Elymas's spiritual blindness is signified by his physical blindness. Sorcery is about having power and being independent, even of the normal laws of nature. Elymas's judgment caused him to depend on **some to lead him by the hand.** What he had treasured most, his power and independence, was thus removed by the One who humbles the proud and exalts the humble.

13:12. The deputy (see discussion on 13:7) ... **believed.** He was convinced by the miracle and the message.

13:13. Perga in Pamphylia. Perga was the capital of Pamphylia, a coastal province of Asia Minor between the provinces of Lycia and Cilicia, and was five miles inland and twelve miles east of the important seaport Attalia. **John departing from them.** Homesickness to get back to Jerusalem, an illness of Paul necessitating a change in plans and a trip to Galatia, and a change in leadership from Barnabas to Paul have all been suggested as reasons for John Mark's return. Paul's dissatisfaction with his departure is noted later (see 15:37–39).

13:14. Antioch in Pisidia (see discussion on 14:24). This is a different Antioch, not the one from which Paul and his companions had departed. Named after Antiochus, king of Syria after the death of Alexander the Great. It was 110 miles from Perga and was at the hub of good roads and trade. The city had a large Jewish population. It was a Roman colony, which meant that a contingent of retired military men was settled there. They were given free land and were made citizens of the city of Rome, with all the accompanying privileges. **Synagogue**. Paul's regular practice was to begin his preaching in the synagogue. He would preach there regularly for as long as the Jews would allow it (see 13:5; 14:1; 17:1, 10, 17; 18:4, 19; 19:8). His reason for doing so was grounded in his understanding of God's redemptive plan: to the Jew first (see 13:46; Rom. 1:16; 2:9–10; see also Romans 9–11). Paul was not neglecting his Gentile mission, for the God-fearers (Gentiles committed to worshiping the one true God) were part of the audience. Moreover, the synagogue provided a ready-made preaching situation with a building, regularly scheduled meetings, and a people who knew the Old Testament Scriptures. It was customary to invite visitors, and especially visiting rabbis (such as Paul), to address the gathering.

13:15. The law and the prophets. Sections from the Old Testament were read, followed by exposition and exhortation. **The rulers of the synagogue**. Those who were responsible for calling readers and preachers, arranging the service, and maintaining order.

13:16–41. This is Paul's first extended speech in Acts. His presentation of the gospel is fairly similar to that of Stephen (see 7:2–53) but with a milder tone. Stephen's speech must have made quite an impression on him. Like Stephen, he rehearsed the history of Israel (vv. 16–22), announced Jesus as the promised Messiah (vv. 23–26), accused the Jews of having Him killed (vv. 27–28), and proclaimed that God had raised Him from the dead (vv. 29–31). In conclusion, he presented Jesus as the fulfillment of the promises of God to the patriarchs (vv. 32–35) and issued an appeal to faith (vv. 36–41).

13:16–22. Paul recounted the history of Israel from the patriarchs through David. This is a quicker recitation than Stephen's, but Luke may have been summarizing Paul's words. Paul presented the history as something God did, not as something that "happened." He wanted to link God's activity in establishing the nation with His activity in sending Jesus Christ and raising Him from the dead.

13:16. For **ye that fear God**, see discussion on 10:2.

13:17–18. The God of this people of Israel chose our fathers (v. 17). The establishment of the nation was a mighty act of God, which the people held to by faith. Paul was laying the groundwork for calling them to faith in another mighty act of God: raising Jesus from the dead.

13:19–20. He divided their land to them (v. 19). Paul's audience knew that God gave them the land; he would go on to tell them that God gave them Jesus Christ also. **About the space of four hundred and fifty years** (v. 20). The Greek manuscripts create some uncertainty whether this phrase identifies the time of the events in verse 19 or 20. If verse 19, then it refers to the four hundred years of the stay "in the land of Egypt" (13:17; see discussion on 7:6) plus the forty years in the wilderness and the time between the crossing of the Jordan and the distribution of the land (see Josh. 14–19).

13:21–22. God gave unto them Saul (v. 21) … **[and] raised up unto them David** (v. 22). Jesus, as Paul would point out, was of the lineage of David (see 13:23) and thus was also one whom God had anointed and chosen.

13:23–25. Paul next moved to contemporary events, connecting them with Israel's past and God's mighty actions on her behalf, and proclaimed that Jesus was the promised Messiah.

13:23. Of this man's (David's) **seed hath God according to his promise** (see, e.g., Isa. 11:1–16) **raised unto Israel a Saviour, Jesus**. This was Paul's main point. God, who had done mighty acts in creating, establishing, and leading the nation, was now doing another mighty act. Just as the Israelites had faith that God was in the previous deeds, so also they were responsible for believing God in this latest deed.

13:24 – 25. Paul then turned to a recent matter that his hearers all knew of, the ministry of John the Baptist. That a prophet had arisen in Israel after centuries of silence from heaven had certainly been the occasion of much discussion among Jews around the Mediterranean world. The impact of this event is difficult to fathom today. Christians today recognize John as the forerunner of Christ and focus on Christ. Jewish people of that time recognized John as a true prophet and focused on his ministry itself. Paul could legitimately use this fact to turn their focus toward Christ. His audience recognized John as one who had announced the will of God, and he had testified of Christ, as One greater than he, **whose shoes of his feet I am not worthy to loose** (v. 25). Paul now had a reasonable expectation that his audience was ready to hear of what God had done in Jesus Christ, whom even John had testified was greater than he, and this at a time when God was again actively dealing with His people, evidenced by the fact that He had sent John at all.

13:26 – 31. Here Paul told of the death and resurrection of Jesus Christ.

13:26. Paul desired that his hearers would come to faith in Jesus Christ. He thus prefaced the story of Jesus' death and resurrection with an appeal: **to you is the word of this salvation sent**. They were the recipients of the word of God, who had created their nation and led them and had now sent Jesus Christ. Paul understood that it was not enough just to tell people to believe in Jesus; they needed to know why they should believe in Him and what He had done that made faith in Him necessary.

13:27 – 28. Paul made it clear that the rulers in Jerusalem were culpable in Jesus' death. He apparently did this more mildly than Stephen had done. The point held, however. **Because they knew him not, nor yet the voices of the prophets** (v. 27), they became accomplices in accomplishing the will of God. Paul assumed that his hearers would not categorize themselves as ones who did not know the prophets. If the prophets foretold Jesus' coming and His death, then surely they would believe it rather than reject it.

13:29. The death of Christ **fulfilled all that was written of him**. It therefore fulfilled the purposes of God, and Paul's hearers should believe this.

13:30. But God raised him from the dead. Just as God "chose our fathers" (13:17), "divided their land to them" (13:19), "gave unto them judges" (13:20), "gave unto them Saul" (13:21), and "raised up unto them David" (13:22). Paul presented each of these as an act of God, and equally to be accepted on faith by Israel. The parallel between "raised him from the dead" and "raised up unto them David" may not have been accidental on Paul's part, as Jesus' right to reign was humanly established by His being in the lineage of David.

13:31. Eyewitnesses, Paul said, had seen the risen Christ and even now bore testimony to Him. **Many days.** Forty days (see 1:3).

13:32 – 35. Paul presented Jesus as the fulfillment of God's promises to the patriarchs.

13:32 – 33. We declare unto you glad tidings (v. 32). Paul had good news to bring: God had fulfilled His promises to Israel in the ministry of Jesus Christ, whom they should trust. To demonstrate the truth of what he preached, Paul quoted from the Old Testament: **Thou art my Son, this day have I begotten thee** (v. 33; Ps. 2:7). Jesus is the Son of God.

13:34. I will give you the sure mercies of David. This, Paul said, was God's promise to Jesus. In Him, the promise to David that his line would rule Israel forever is fulfilled.

13:35. Not suffer thine Holy One to see corruption. This passage from Psalm 16:10, quoted also in Peter's sermon at Pentecost (see discussion on 2:27), testifies to the permanent nature of the resurrection. Jesus lives forever to save His people.

13:36 – 41. Paul concluded his sermon with an appeal to his audience to exercise faith in Jesus Christ.

13:36 – 37. David himself did not see the fulfillment of the promise; he died **and saw corruption**

(v. 36). Jesus, as the fulfillment of the promise, was the one they should trust, for he **saw no corruption** (v. 37).

13:38. That through this man is preached unto you the forgiveness of sins. Since Jesus' resurrection was an act of God, just as the establishment of Israel was, and since God had given Jesus the throne of David, then Israel should trust in Him for whatever they needed; and their greatest need was for forgiveness of sins.

13:39. All that believe are justified from all things. Justification combines two aspects: (1) the forgiveness of sins (here) and (2) the gift of righteousness (see Rom. 3:21–22).

13:40–41. Paul's appeal included a warning not to be like those who disbelieved in the mighty acts of God, including and especially His most recent act in sending Jesus Christ and raising Him from the dead.

13:42. After the worship time, the Jews left the synagogue, but **the Gentiles**, those "that fear[ed] God" (13:16), remained and invited Paul to speak to them again **the next Sabbath**.

13:43. That **many of the Jews** also wanted to hear Paul does not contradict 13:42, which speaks of the time right after the service. **When the congregation was broken up** could well imply later that same day, or even during the week. **Continue in the grace of God**. Apparently, Paul and Barnabas saw from that first meeting some converts of both Jews and **proselytes**, God-fearing Gentiles.

13:44. Those who had heard Paul must have spread the word, including the fact that grace was offered to non-Jews as well, for **the next Sabbath day came almost the whole city together to hear the word of God**.

13:45. The Jews ... were filled with envy. The idea that Gentiles also might be shown grace did not set well with many of the Jews. It had been difficult even for Peter and the Jerusalem church to accept this idea.

13:46. It was necessary that the word [be] first ... spoken to you (see discussion on 13:14). This was necessary because the gospel came from and was for the Jews first and because Paul was himself a

Jew with great compassion for his people (see Rom. 9:1–5; 10:1–3).

13:47. The Lord commanded us ... to be a light of the Gentiles ... for salvation unto the ends of the earth. Luke again emphasized that the grace of God was available to the Gentiles. This is a major theme in both the gospel of Luke and Acts.

13:48. As many as were ordained to eternal life believed. Possession of eternal life involves both human faith and divine appointment.

13:49. Though this appears to be one of Luke's summary statements, it is not, for the verses that follow continue the same story. Luke simply wanted to show that Paul and Barnabas had a successful ministry in the district.

13:50. The Jews ... expelled them. Paul and Barnabas were exiled from the city. While most of the people in the city had heard the gospel and many had believed, still more had not. Rarely does the gospel penetrate to the point that the majority of people in an area are saved.

13:51. They shook off the dust of their feet (see discussion on Luke 9:5). To show the severance of responsibility and the repudiation of those who had rejected their message and had brought suffering to the servants of the Lord. **Iconium**. Modern Konya. It was an important crossroads and agricultural center in the central plain of the province of Galatia.

13:52. Filled ... with the Holy Ghost (see discussion on 2:4). Luke wanted to emphasize that rejection did not daunt the disciples in their mission. This is one of the rare times that Luke mentioned disciples being filled with the Spirit without a direct reference to speaking.

14:1. Their mixed results at Antioch of Pisidia did not discourage Paul and Barnabas. It was time to move on, as a growing body of disciples had been established there. They went on to **Iconium** (see discussion on 13:51), where they preached to many and **a great multitude ... believed**. Paul continued his practice of going to **the synagogue** first.

14:2. Following their initial success, Paul and Barnabas faced bitter opposition from **the unbelieving Jews**. They evidently failed in this attempt to cause trouble, for Paul and Barnabas remained in Iconium a considerable time (see 14:3). A second wave of persecution was planned, however, involving violence (see 14:5).

14:3. Gave testimony ... and granted signs and wonders. A major purpose of miracles in Acts was to confirm the truth of the words and the approval of God.

14:4. The apostles. Paul and Barnabas are both called "apostles" (see 14:14; see also discussion on Mark 6:30). The term is used here not of the Twelve but in its broader sense of persons sent on a mission, that is, missionaries (see 13:2–3).

14:5. Stone them. Stoning was a Jewish mode of execution for blasphemy. Mob action probably was planned.

14:6. Lystra. A Roman colony (see discussion on 13:14) and probable home of Timothy (though he was known in Iconium as well), Lystra was about 20 miles from Iconium and 130 miles from Antioch. **Derbe** (see discussion on 14:20). About 60 miles from Lystra, Derbe was the home of Gaius (see 20:4). **Cities of Lycaonia.** Lycaonia was a district east of Pisidia, north of the Taurus Mountains. It was part of the Roman province of Galatia.

14:7. And there they preached the gospel. Most likely, Paul and Barnabas preached in all of the cities in this region as well as the surrounding areas. Wherever they found success, they stayed a while and taught. Otherwise, they moved on more quickly.

14:8–10. In Paul's time, **Lystra** (v. 8) was a minor place, a "small country town" (Polhill, *Acts*, p. 312). There, Paul saw a man crippled and healed him supernaturally. There is no mention of Paul having gone to a synagogue there, and it is possible that this was a wholly Greek city. In Judea and Samaria, the "signs and wonders" (2:43; 5:12) the apostles performed had validated their message. In Lystra, however, Paul's miracle was completely misunderstood (see 14:11–13).

14:11. In the speech of Lycaonia (see discussion on 14:6). The main language of these people apparently was not Greek, though certainly they knew it. Since Lystra had no Jewish population of any size,

the people had no knowledge of a religion in which miracles validated the message of God rather than indicating that the miracle worker was himself a god.

14:12. Jupiter ... Mercurius. The Latin names for the Greek gods Zeus and Hermes, respectively. Zeus was the patron god of the city, and his temple was there. People who had come to bring sacrifices to Zeus apparently decided to make an offering to Paul and Barnabas instead. That Barnabas was identified as the god Zeus may indicate that his appearance was more imposing, and Paul was identified as the god Hermes **because he was the chief speaker** (see 28:6). This incident may have occurred because of an ancient legend that told of a visit of Zeus and Hermes to the same general area. The gods, however, were not recognized by anyone except an old couple. The people of Lystra thus were determined not to allow such an oversight to happen again.

14:13. Gates. The Greek can refer to the temple gates, the city gates, or house gates.

14:14. They rent their clothes. A Jewish way of expressing great anguish (see Gen. 37:29, 34).

14:15. Vanities. Used in the Old Testament to denote false gods (see 1 Sam. 12:21).

14:16–17. In bearing testimony to the living God, Paul did not cite Scripture because these people would not have recognized it. He turned instead to natural revelation.

14:18. Scarce restrained they the people, that they had not done sacrifice unto them. Paul and Barnabas barely prevented the people from offering a sacrifice to them.

14:19. Apparently, some of Paul's opponents now began to follow him. **Stoned Paul.** This was done inside the city rather than at the usual place of execution outside the city walls. This incident may have happened several days or several weeks after the people's initial encounter with Paul and Barnabas. Enough time had passed for a body of disciples to have been established (see 14:20).

14:20. The disciples stood round about him. Young Timothy may have been present (see 2 Tim. 3:10–11). **Derbe.** A border town in the southeastern part of the Lycaonian region of Galatia (see discussion on 14:6). An inscription naming the city has been discovered about thirty miles east of what was previously thought to be the city site.

14:21–22. Paul and Barnabas returned to the cities they had preached in, **confirming the souls of the disciples** (v. 22), that is, helping them grow in the faith and in assurance and knowledge. **We must through much tribulation enter into the kingdom of God**. This has always been the case, though among Western Christians of the past two centuries, there has been little real tribulation. These circumstances, however, are an aberration for which believers should be thankful. Even today, tribulation is not the usual experience of the church in other parts of the world.

14:23. Ordained. The Greek for this word (used also in 2 Cor. 8:19) can mean (1) to stretch out the hand, (2) to appoint by show of hands, or (3) to appoint or elect without regard to the method. In 6:6, the appointment of the seven included selection by the church and presentation to the apostles, who prayed and laid their hands on them. **Elders in every church**. Because these were new churches, at least partly pagan in background, Paul and Barnabas may have both selected and appointed the elders.

14:24. Pisidia. A district about 120 miles long and 50 miles wide, north of Pamphylia (13:13–14). Bandits frequented the region (see perhaps 2 Cor. 11:26). **Pamphylia**. A district 80 miles long and 20 miles wide, on the southern coast of Asia Minor. After AD 74, Pisidia was included in the Roman province of Pamphylia (see 13:13).

14:25. For **Perga**, see discussion on 13:13. **Attalia**. The best harbor on the coast of Pamphylia (see 13:13).

14:26. For **Antioch**, see 11:20; discussion on 11:19.

14:27. Opened the door of faith. God had brought Gentiles to faith. He had, as it were, opened the door for them to believe (see 11:18).

14:28. Long time. Possibly more than a year.

2. The Jerusalem Council (15:1–35)

15:1. Certain men … came down from Judea. To Antioch. These men, probably from "the sect of the Pharisees which believed" (15:5), were believers who insisted that to become a true Christian, one must first keep the law of Moses, and the test of such compliance was circumcision. They in no way correctly represented the apostles and elders of Jerusalem (see 15:24). The content of their preaching was that circumcision was necessary for salvation. This added a work to simple faith. Circumcision was the rite of initiation into the covenant God had made with Abraham, which was renewed in the law of Moses. In other words, these Judaizers maintained that the Gentile Christians had to become Jewish to be true Christians. This violated the doctrine of salvation by faith alone.

15:2. Paul and Barnabas had no small dissension and disputation with them. The argument went on apparently for weeks and was rancorous. Perhaps these Judaizers argued that Christ had come to the Jews and that while all are admitted to God's grace, so were all admitted into Judaism if they would be circumcised. Gentiles wishing to become Christians therefore needed first to become Jews, the people to whom Christ came. Cast this way, the argument is not completely unplausible. These men were not arguing mere nonsense. They were, however, arguing contrary to the truth of the gospel, which is that God saves by grace through faith, and no works of any kind are required. **Go up to Jerusalem** (see discussions on 12:1; Gal. 2:1). It was decided that these Judaizers (or legalists) would be given a hearing by the church in Jerusalem. Those who hold that Galatians 2:1–10 refers to the famine visit of 11:27–30; 12:25 argue that since Galatians 2:2 says that the visit mentioned there was occasioned by a revelation, it must refer to Agabus's prediction of the coming famine (see 11:27–28). Those who believe that Galatians 2:1–10 refers to the Jerusalem council visit of 15:1–22 assert that the famine visit occurred at the time of Herod Agrippa's death in AD 44 (see 11:27–30; 12:25).

15:3. Being brought on their way by the church. The Antioch church paid their travel expenses. **Declaring the conversion of the Gentiles**. In those days, when news traveled slowly, many of the churches had not heard about the missionary journey of Paul and Barnabas, nor about the conversion of Cornelius. This was completely new information for them, and it understandably **caused great joy unto all the brethren**. Hearing reports from missionaries encourages local churches in their own outreach and brings joy in knowing that God's word is going forth with power.

15:4–22. The sequence of meetings described in this section is: (1) a general meeting of welcome and report (vv. 4–5); (2) a meeting of the apostles and elders (perhaps to one side) while the church was still assembled (vv. 6–11); (3) a meeting of the apostles, the elders, and the whole assembly (vv. 12–22).

15:4. The first meeting was a report, cordially received, about the work done among the Gentiles.

15:5. Certain of the sect of the Pharisees which believed. Some Pharisees became Christians and brought their Judaic beliefs with them. They believed that Gentiles must first become converts to Judaism and be circumcised (see 15:1), and then they would be eligible to be saved by faith. Perhaps some of them had gone to Antioch and now returned to present their case.

15:6. The apostles and elders came together for to consider of this matter. The idea is that this was an official meeting. Since all the believers in the Jerusalem church were Jewish, the issue had not arisen, other than theoretically. If Cornelius had moved to Jerusalem and sought admission to the church there, the matter might have come up much sooner.

15:7. Peter rose up. After the apostles and elders had discussed the matter for a considerable period, Peter addressed them. **Gentiles by my mouth should hear**. Peter's argument was his own experience: God had sent him to preach to the Gentiles (see 10:28–29).

15:8. Giving them the Holy Ghost. This for Peter was the irrefutable proof of God's acceptance (see 10:44, 47; 11:17–18). Since Cornelius had received the Spirit without circumcision, then circumcision was not necessary.

15:9. Purifying their hearts by faith. This was Peter's way of saying what Paul affirmed (see Rom.

5:1; Gal. 2:15–16). Peter recognized that, as Jesus had taught, faith is a matter of the heart, not of outward acts. Genuine faith results in moral behavior, but mere outward behavior of any kind cannot be substituted for faith.

15:10. A yoke. The law (see Gal. 5:1; Matt. 11:28–29). No one had been able to keep the law, and in fact, it served mainly to demonstrate how far short of perfection one fell. It was assumed that when anyone was circumcised, they thereby agreed to abide by the law of Moses.

15:11. Through the grace of the Lord. Circumcision was not required. **We shall be saved, even as they** (see Rom. 3:9). Peter could have said, "They shall be saved, even as we." He said it this way to emphasize that Gentiles were saved by faith but that circumcision offered no barrier to the Jews' salvation, which was also by faith.

15:12. The multitude kept silence (see discussion on 15:4–22). Apparently, the people had remained in place while the apostles and elders met. The assembly had not remained quiet during that time but now became silent to listen to the leaders. **Barnabas and Paul**. Here Barnabas is mentioned first, perhaps reflecting his importance in Jerusalem, whereas in the account of the missionary journey the order was "Paul and Barnabas" after the events on the island of Cyprus (see 13:7, 9, 13, 42, 46). **Miracles and wonders** (see 8:19–20; 14:3). Barnabas and Paul had ministered more extensively among the Gentiles than had Peter or any of the others. They therefore had the greatest store of anecdotal evidence of God's grace at work among them.

15:13. James. The brother of the Lord. His argument added proof from Scripture (see 15:15–18).

15:14. Simeon. Peter (see 15:7). James used Peter's Hebrew name in its Hebrew form (Simeon is a variant of Simon). **A people for his name**. A new community largely made up of Gentiles but including Jews as well (see John 10:16; 1 Peter 2:9–10).

15:15. James invoked Scripture. The prophets. Specifically, Amos 9:11–12. Anecdotal evidence is good and must not be totally dismissed, but the controlling factor in determining truth is what God's

Word says. It provides the authoritative interpretation of human experience and thus was used to validate what Barnabas and Paul reported.

15:16–18. After this I will return (v. 16). This quotation from Amos 9:11–12 may set forth a sequence of the end times, including (1) the church age ("God ... did visit the Gentiles, to take out of them a people for his name," 15:14), (2) the restoration of Israel as a nation (**build again the tabernacle of David**), and (3) the inclusion of the Gentiles (**all the Gentiles, upon whom my name is called**; v. 17).

15:19–20. Trouble not them (v. 19). Circumcision was not required, but four stipulations were laid down (see discussion on 15:20) regarding areas where the Gentiles had specific weaknesses and where the Jews were especially repulsed by Gentile violations. **Abstain from pollutions of idols** (v. 20; see 15:29; 1 Cor. 8:7–13; Rev. 2:14, 20); **from fornication**, a sin taken too lightly by the Greeks and also associated with certain pagan religious festivals; **from things strangled**, which thus retained the blood that was forbidden to be eaten (see Gen. 9:4); **from blood**, expressly forbidden in Jewish law (see Lev. 17:10–12). Reference here may be to consuming blood apart from meat. If these stipulations were observed, it would help both the individual Gentile and the relationship between Gentile and Jew. These were things that the foreigner residing in Israel would be expected to do according to Leviticus 17 and 18 (see Talbert, *Reading Acts*, p. 142).

15:21. Moses of old time hath in every city them that preach him. These four stipulations were not put upon the Gentiles as conditions for salvation. Instead, the concern most likely was that the Gentiles in the churches should behave in ways that would not offend Jewish believers or potential converts. The church at Antioch and in most of the places Paul had preached had mixed memberships of Jewish and Gentile believers, and the law was **read in the synagogues every Sabbath day**. The stipulations were intended to promote unity and to prevent barriers to outreach, not to secure salvation, which as James had made clear, was evidently by grace through faith alone.

15:22. The apostles and elders, with the whole church. Apparently, there was unanimous agreement on the choice of messengers and the content of the letter (see 15:23–29). **Judas surnamed Barsabas.** The same surname as that of Joseph Barsabas (see discussion on 1:23). The two may have been brothers. **Silas.** A leader in the Jerusalem church, a prophet (see 15:32), and a Roman citizen (see 16:37).

15:23. Here begins the content of the letter. Most likely, many copies were made, to be kept by the churches the delegation visited (see 16:4). Luke surely would have had access to these copies in his research for this book. **In Antioch and Syria and Cilicia.** Antioch was the leading city of the combined provinces of Syria and Cilicia.

15:24. To whom we gave no such commandment. The early church was already facing the problem of maintaining doctrinal purity and of separating themselves from those who preached falsely in the church's name. This problem has plagued the church throughout its history. Separating from false teachers has sometimes caused sharp division and hurt feelings, but the protection of the truth must always be uppermost (see John 17:17).

15:25. Being assembled with one accord emphasized that the church was unified in this matter, **to send chosen men unto you.** The delegation members had been chosen for the task; they were not acting on their own authority. This may have set a precedent. Official declarations on doctrinal matters coming from the Jerusalem church would have certification, while preachers claiming such authority but unable to produce written credentials might be suspect.

15:26. Men that have hazarded their lives. This refers to the hardships Paul and Barnabas had endured on their first missionary journey (see chaps. 13–14). Their testimony was the more credible because they had suffered for it.

15:27. Shall also tell you the same things. Perhaps the letter was read to the congregations and then explained in more detail by the delegation.

15:28. It seemed good to the Holy Ghost, and to us. Prior authority was given to the Spirit (whose working in the assembly was thus claimed), but "the apostles and elders and brethren" (15:23) also agreed on the matter.

15:29. For **abstain from ... fornication**, see discussion on 15:20.

15:30. Luke skipped over details of other congregations the delegation might have visited along the way. Antioch was the main church in the region that was being disturbed and the home church of Barnabas and Paul.

15:32. Prophets. One of the primary functions of prophets in the early church was to encourage and strengthen the believers.

15:33. In peace. Apparently, the letter and the testimony of Judas and Silas ended the dispute. The church had wisely chosen the right people to carry the letter and to add their verbal testimony to its authority (see Talbert, *Reading Acts*, p. 143).

15:34. Silas decided to stay in Antioch. He became an associate of Paul in his later missionary work.

15:35. The church at Antioch was blessed with a multitude of knowledgeable and talented teachers and preachers.

B. Fourth Geographical Expansion of the Gospel: "Over into Macedonia" (15:36 – 21:16; see 16:9)

1. Paul's Second Missionary Journey (15:36 – 18:22)

15:36. In every city where we have preached the word. In the towns of Paul's first missionary journey (see 13:4 – 14:26).

15:37. Barnabas determined to take with them John, whose surname was Mark (see discussion on 12:25). Barnabas was perhaps more willing than Paul to offer a second chance to Mark, who now had another year or more of maturity.

15:38. Who departed from them (see discussion on 13:13). Mark had turned back at Perga and did not go to Antioch, Iconium, Lystra, and Derbe.

15:39. They departed asunder. That Paul and Barnabas would come to such a division is startling. It demonstrates that unity among believers has always been difficult, no matter how desirable it may be. Barnabas and Mark do not appear again in Acts. In 1 Corinthians 9:6, however, Paul named Barnabas as setting a noble example in working to support himself. Galatians 2:11 – 13 describes another scene in Antioch that includes Barnabas. Mark evidently returned from his missionary work with Barnabas and became associated with Peter (see 1 Peter 5:13). During Paul's first imprisonment, Mark was included in Paul's group (see Col. 4:10; Philem. 24). By the end of his life, Paul came to admire Mark so much that he requested Mark to come to be with him during his final days (see 2 Tim. 4:11; Mark, Introduction: "Author"). **Cyprus.** The birthplace of Barnabas (see discussion on 4:36).

15:40. And Paul chose Silas. Apparently, Paul and Silas had become friends, beginning with the journey from Jerusalem to Antioch (see 15:22, 30 – 35). Luke's statement that Paul and Silas were **recommended by the bretheren unto the grace of God** is in no way meant to take away from whatever ministry Barnabas and Mark might have had. Luke's purpose now was to trace Paul's journeys.

15:41. Confirming the churches. Paul and Silas may have used the opportunity not only to deliver news of the Jerusalem council's letter but also to check up on doctrinal matters and to encourage the churches in their outreach and service to the Lord.

16:1. Derbe (see discussions on 14:6, 20). Paul had approached Derbe on the first trip from the opposite direction, so the order of towns is reversed here. For **Lystra,** see discussion on 14:6. **Timotheus.** Since Paul addressed him as a young man some fifteen years later (see 1 Tim. 4:12), Timothy must have been in his teens at this time. **His father was a Greek.** Statements concerning his mother's faith (here and in 2 Tim. 1:5) and silence concerning any faith on his father's part suggest that his father was neither a convert to Judaism nor a believer in Christ.

16:2. Which was well reported of by the bretheren. "Which" refers back to "Timotheus" not to "his father" (16:1), which might appear to be the immediate antecedent.

16:3. Circumcised him. Timothy's circumcision was a matter of expediency so that his work among the Jews might be more effective. This was different from Titus's case (see Gal. 2:3), in which circumcision was refused because some were demanding it as necessary for salvation. Timothy's standing among the Jews could have been problematic given his mixed Jewish-Gentile parentage.

16:4. They delivered them the decrees. Paul, Silas, and Timothy circulated among the churches copies of the letter written at Jerusalem. These may have been some of the copies produced there, or perhaps additional copies were made at Antioch. Silas, having been part of the Jerusalem church, would have been able to authenticate their contents.

16:5. The churches ... increased in number daily. Luke used this progress report (see discussion on 1:15) to set the scene for the gospel's spread into Europe.

16:6. They. Paul, Silas, and Timothy. **Phrygia.** The district was formerly the Hellenistic territory of Phrygia, but it had more recently been divided between the Roman provinces of Asia and Galatia. Iconium and Antioch were in Galatian Phrygia. **The region of Galatia.** The name had been used to denote the Hellenistic kingdom, but in 25 BC, it had been expanded considerably to become the Roman province of that name. **Asia.** This also had been a smaller region but now was a Roman province including the Hellenistic districts of Mysia, Lydia, Caria, and parts of Phrygia.

16:7. Mysia. In the northwest part of the province of Asia. Luke used these old Hellenistic names, but Paul preferred the provincial (Roman) names. **Bithynia.** A senatorial province formed after 74 BC, Bithynia was east of Mysia. **The Spirit suffered them not.** The Spirit may have led Paul and Timothy in any of a number of ways: vision, circumstances, good sense, or the gift of prophecy.

16:8. Troas. Located ten miles from ancient Troy, Alexandria Troas (its full name) was a Roman colony and an important seaport for connections between Macedonia and Greece on the one hand and Asia Minor on the other. Paul returned to Troas following his work in Ephesus on his third journey (see 2 Cor. 2:12). On Paul's second or third journey, a church was started in Troas. Later, Paul ministered to believers there, following his work in Ephesus and again when he returned from his third journey on his way to Jerusalem (see 20:5–12).

16:9. A vision. One of the ways God gave direction (see 10:3). **A man of Macedonia.** Macedonia had become a Roman province in 148 BC. There is no indication that the man of the vision was Luke, as some have suggested, but he did join the group at this point.

16:10. We endeavoured to go. This is where the "we" passages of Acts begin (see Introduction: "Author"), indicating that Luke had joined the party at Troas.

16:11. Samothracia. An island in the northeastern Aegean Sea. It was a convenient place for boats to anchor rather than risk sailing at night. **Neapolis.** Known today as Kavalla, Neapolis was the seaport for Philippi, which was ten miles away.

16:12. Philippi. A city in eastern Macedonia named after Philip II, father of Alexander the Great. Since it was a Roman colony, it was independent of provincial administration and had a governmental organization modeled after that of Rome (see discussion on 13:14). Many retired legionnaires from the Roman army settled there but few Jews (see Philippians, Introduction: "The City of Philippi"). **The chief city.** Thessalonica was the capital of Macedonia. Macedonia had four districts, however, and Philippi was in the first of these.

16:13. By a river side, where prayer was wont to be made. So few Jews lived in Philippi that it had no synagogue, so the Jews who were there met for prayer along the banks of the Gangites River (see Bruce, *The Book of Acts*, p. 311). It was customary for such places of prayer to be located outdoors near running water. Paul chose this place because it was as near to being a synagogue as he could find. Wanting to proclaim religious truth, he naturally went to a location where religious concerns, especially connected to the one true God, were expressed.

16:14. Lydia. A businesswoman. Her name may be associated with her place of origin, the Hellenistic district of Lydia. **Thyatira** (see Rev. 1:11; *KJV Study*

Bible note on Rev. 2:18). In the Roman province of Asia, twenty miles southeast of Pergamum (in the Hellenistic kingdom of Lydia). It was famous for its dyeing works, especially royal **purple** (crimson). **Worshipped God**. Lydia was a Gentile who, like Cornelius (see 10:2), believed in the true God and followed the moral teachings of Scripture. She had not, however, become a full convert to Judaism. **Whose heart the Lord opened**. After the resurrection, the minds of the disciples were opened to understand the Scriptures (see Luke 24:45); similarly, Lydia's heart was opened to respond to Paul's gospel message.

16:15. If ye have judged me to be faithful to the Lord. In other words, if the disciples believed that her conversion was genuine. She had not been saved long enough, nor had they known her long enough, for "faithful to the Lord" to mean what it usually does for people today. She offered them the hospitality of her home, which may have been large, as she was active in a prosperous business.

16:16. A spirit of divination. A "python" spirit, a demonic spirit. The python was a mythical snake worshiped at Delphi and associated with the Delphic oracle. The term "python" came to be used of the persons through whom the python spirit supposedly spoke. Since such persons spoke involuntarily, the term "ventriloquist" was used to describe them. To what extent the woman actually predicted the future is not known.

16:17. Us. The "we" section (see discussion on 16:10) ends here and begins again in 20:5. Perhaps Luke was not traveling with Paul on that day, as he was not arrested with Paul and Silas (see 16:19–24). Apparently, Timothy also was not with them on this day. It is pure speculation, but it is possible that Luke stayed at Philippi after Paul and Silas left, to help establish the new church there, or even that he returned to Troas. He may have intended to go with them only as far as Philippi. **The most high God**. The man possessed by an evil spirit in Mark 5:7 also used this title. It was a common title among both Jews (see Num. 24:16; Isa. 14:14; Dan. 3:26) and Greeks (found in inscriptions), but in the New Testament, the title is not used of God by Christians or Jews (see 7:48).

16:18. And this she did many days. It is surprising that Paul did not act sooner to deal with this problem. He either was very patient or believed that his preaching alone might deliver the woman or drive her off.

16:19. The motivation of **her masters** was simply financial. When **their gains** were taken away, they found reason to arrest Paul and Silas.

16:20. Magistrates. The Greek term *stratēgos* (Latin, *praetor*) is not the usual word for magistrates but rather a term of courtesy used in some Roman colonies, such as Philippi. **These men, being Jews, do exceedingly trouble our city**. The woman's masters knew that magistrates want, above all else, to maintain order. Such a charge would be hard to disprove and would motivate them to act.

16:21. Customs ... not lawful. If a religion failed to receive Roman approval, it was considered *religio illicita*. Judaism had legal recognition, but Christianity did not. Since Paul and Silas were not preaching "normal" Judaism, they could be seen as troublemakers by the magistrates.

16:22–23. Beat them (v. 22). With rods. **Cast them into prison** (v. 23). Apparently, all of this was done in haste, without checking the facts.

16:24. Inner prison ... stocks. Used not only for extra security but also for torture.

16:25. Paul and Silas prayed, and sang praises unto God. They knew joy in the midst of hardship. **And the prisoners heard them**. The disciples used the opportunity to give testimony to God's goodness, in spite of less than good circumstances, and their testimony seems to have made an impact on those near them.

16:26. All the doors were opened, and every one's bands were loosed. Apparently, not just Paul and Silas but all the prisoners were freed, a fitting picture of the spiritual freedom found in Christ (see Gal. 5:1). This incident recalls Isaiah 61:1 (which Jesus quoted in Luke 4:18), which states that the Messiah would "proclaim liberty to the captives, and the opening of the prison to them that are bound."

16:27. The keeper … would have killed himself. If a prisoner escaped, the life of the guard was demanded in his place (see 12:19). The guard would have taken his own life to shorten his shame and distress.

16:28–29. We are all here (v. 28). No one had actually escaped, though their chains were off. The other prisoners may have found the situation so startling that they did not take advantage of the opportunity to escape.

16:30. What must I do to be saved? The jailer had heard that Paul and Silas were preachers of a way of salvation (see 16:17). He had heard them singing and praying, and it had certainly worked on his heart.

16:31. Believe on the Lord Jesus Christ. A concise statement of the way of salvation (see 10:43). The word "believe" here means more than mental assent; it means to actively trust in or rely on Jesus.

16:32–33. The word of the Lord (v. 32; see 10:36). Paul and Silas explained the gospel more thoroughly to the jailer and the members of his household, and they all believed in Christ and were saved (see 16:34).

16:34. They enjoyed a meal together, in fellowship. **Rejoiced.** The consistent consequence of conversion, regardless of circumstances (see discussion on 8:39).

16:35. For **magistrates**, see discussion on 16:20. **Let those men go.** Cooler heads prevailed after the initial excitement. The magistrates knew they had no grounds to hold Paul and Silas under Roman law.

16:36. The jailer probably saw this as good news for Paul and Silas. Paul did not see it this way; there was a legal matter still to settle.

16:37. Beaten us … uncondemned, being Romans. Public beating as punishment for Roman citizens would have been illegal (see 16:38), let alone beating them without a trial. **Let them come themselves.** There is no sin in asserting one's legal rights, if it is done in the right spirit. In this case, the gospel and its credibility were at stake. Paul and Silas were not asking for an escort to salve their injured pride as much as they were establishing their innocence for

the sake of the church in Philippi and its future. They wanted a public declaration of their innocence and, by extension, the legitimacy of the new church there.

16:38–39. The magistrates … feared (v. 38), but they need not have. As Christians, Paul and Silas had no intention of pressing the legal point out of spite.

16:40. Rather than leave the city, they went back to Lydia's house. **Comforted them.** Paul and Silas, having been beaten and imprisoned, were more concerned for the comfort of the new believers than for their own circumstances.

17:1. Amphipolis … Thessalonica. The Egnatian Way crossed the whole of present-day northern Greece east to west and included Philippi, Amphipolis, Apollonia, and Thessalonica on its route. At several locations, such as Kavalla (Neapolis), Philippi, and Apollonia, the road is still visible today. If a person traveled about thirty miles a day, each city could be reached after one day's journey. Located about a hundred miles from Philippi, Thessalonica was the capital of the province of Macedonia and had a population of more than 200,000, including a colony of Jews (and **a synagogue**). These factors contributed to Paul's decision to preach there (see 1 Thessalonians, Introduction: "Thessalonica: The City and the Church").

17:2. Paul … went in unto them. To the synagogue (see 17:1; discussion on 13:14). **Three sabbath days.** These two weeks represent the time spent in the synagogue reasoning with the Jews, not Paul's total time in Thessalonica. An analysis of the Thessalonian letters reveals that Paul had taught them much more doctrine than would have been possible in two or three weeks.

17:3. Paul's message was that it was necessary for the Messiah to suffer and be resurrected and that Jesus, who suffered, died, and rose again, is the Messiah. This was a message tailored for a Jewish audience.

17:4. For **the devout Greeks**, see discussions on 10:2; 16:14. **The chief women.** These women were perhaps the wives of the leading men of the city but also deserved notice and position in their own right (see 17:12).

17:5. Moved with envy. Because of the large number of people (including some Jews, many God-fearing Gentiles, and many prominent women) who responded to Paul's ministry (see 13:45). **The house of Jason**. Paul had probably been staying there.

17:6. The rulers of the city. The Greek term *politarchēs* (lit., "city ruler"), used here and in 17:8, is found nowhere else in Greek literature, but it was discovered in 1835 in a Greek inscription on an arch that had spanned the Egnatian Way on the west side of Thessalonica. (The arch was destroyed in 1867, but the block with the inscription was rescued and is now in the British Museum in London.) The term has since been found in sixteen other inscriptions in surrounding towns of Macedonia and elsewhere.

17:7–8. Do contrary to the decrees of Caesar (v. 7). Blasphemy was the gravest accusation for a Jew, but treason—to support a rival king above Caesar—was the worst accusation for a Roman. **And they troubled the people and the rulers of the city** (v. 8). Once again, the local leaders were motivated as much by a desire to prevent civil disorder as they were to enforce specific laws.

17:9. Taken security of. Jason was forced to guarantee a peaceful, quiet community, or he would face the confiscation of his properties and perhaps even death.

17:10. Paul and Silas. It has been suggested that Timothy was left at Philippi and rejoined Paul and Silas at Berea (see 17:14). **By night unto Berea**. Modern Verria, located fifty miles from Thessalonica in another district of Macedonia. For **synagogue**, see discussion on 13:14.

17:11. These were more noble. It may be that Luke was not so much complaining about the Thessalonians as merely reporting that the Bereans received the word more openly. **Searched the scriptures daily**. This is the best reaction one can make to any new religious ideas one encounters, to see what the Scriptures say on the matter (see Bruce, *The Book of Acts*, p. 327).

17:12. Therefore, because they had searched the Scriptures, **many of them believed**. There is a direct connection between exposure to the Word of God and the moving of faith in the heart ("Faith cometh by hearing, and hearing by the word of God," Rom. 10:17).

17:13. The Jews of Thessalonica. Sometimes when people are emotionally engaged, they cannot leave a matter alone, and that seems to have been the case here. The Thessalonians had no rational reason to go to Berea, but uncontrolled emotions can cause people to do many things. Apparently, they came to Berea and told stories which upset the populace against Paul. We have no idea what they said, but it may have been charges similar to ones found elsewhere in Acts (13:45, 50; 16:19–21).

17:14. To go as it were to the sea. One might conclude that Paul went by boat to Athens. The road to Athens was a coastal road, however, and Paul may have walked the distance after having been escorted to the coast (some twenty miles). In any event, Christian companions stayed with him until they reached Athens.

17:15. Athens. Five centuries before Paul, Athens had been at the height of its glory in art, philosophy, and literature. She had retained her reputation in philosophy through the years and still maintained a leading university in Paul's day. **Silas and Timotheus** were called to join Paul there. They may have been in different locations. Paul could have expected a wait of more than just a few days.

17:16. His spirit was stirred in him. Paul was unable to see the level of idolatry in Athens without being disturbed. Much of the prophetic writings, not to mention the law of Moses, forbids idolatry. As a Christian, Paul knew even better that such activity diminished God and misrepresented Him.

17:17. For **disputed he in the synagogue**, see discussion on 13:14. **Devout persons**. God-fearing Gentiles (see discussions on 10:2; 16:14). Paul was not simply being combative; he was using Scripture and reason to point the Athenians to Christ. His method probably was much like the one he used in Antioch of Pisidia (see 13:14–44), perhaps with a more pointed defense of the truth since the synagogue was located in an idolatrous city. **In the market daily**. Paul engaged in what today would be called "street witnessing." The circumstances in Athens encouraged this approach; people gathered in the marketplace for conversation as well as to buy and sell, and there may have been something of a festival atmosphere on certain days.

17:18. Philosophers of the Epicureans. Originally, these philosophers taught that the supreme good is happiness, but not mere momentary pleasure or temporary gratification. By Paul's time, however, this philosophy had degenerated into a more sensual system of thought. **Stoicks**. The Stoics taught that people should live in accord with nature, recognize their own self-sufficiency and independence, and suppress their desires. At its best, Stoicism had some admirable qualities, but like Epicureanism, by Paul's time, it had degenerated into a system of pride. The two systems were at opposite poles, with the Epicureans emphasizing physical pleasures as the chief end in life, and the Stoics emphasizing moral duty as the chief end. **Babbler**. The Greek word originally meant "seed picker," a bird picking up seeds here and there. Then it came to refer to the loafer in the marketplace who picked up whatever scraps of learning he could find and paraded them without digesting them. **A setter forth of strange gods**. Some of the philosophers at least dimly understood the religious nature of Paul's message, though unclearly.

17:19. Areopagus means "hill of Ares." Ares was the Greek god of thunder and war (the Roman equivalent was Mars). The Areopagus was located just west of the acropolis and south of the agora and had once been the site of the meeting of the court or council of the Areopagus. Earlier the council had governed a Greek city-state, but by New Testament times, it retained authority only in the areas of religion and morals and met in the Royal Portico at the northwest corner of the agora. The council members considered themselves the custodians of teachings that introduced new religions and foreign gods. Paul thus had an opportunity to present the gospel to the people who had some authority in religious matters in Athens. If he could win this group to Christ, or even gain their sympathetic approval, the way would be cleared for many in Athens to believe.

17:20. Certain strange things. To the Greeks, the ideas that there is only one God and that people are morally responsible to Him would have been odd indeed. It was certainly encouraging to Paul that the group wanted to know more.

17:21. Luke seems to have dismissed as mere curiosity the Athenians' motive for wanting to hear more. Even if that were so, Paul did not waste the opportunity to tell them the truth about God. Luke here presented a picture of Paul as knowledgeable on matters of Greek thought, something he did nowhere else in Acts (see Ger, *The Book of Acts*, p. 237).

17:22. Too superstitious. The Greek for "superstitious" could be used to congratulate a person or to criticize him, depending on whether the person using it included himself in the circle of individuals he was describing. The Athenians would not know which meaning to take until Paul continued. In this context, it is clear that Paul wanted to be complimentary in order to gain a hearing. Paul, because he was not speaking to a Jewish-oriented audience, did not begin with a recounting of God's mighty acts in history, as that would have meant nothing to these people. He tailored his presentation to the awareness level of the audience. Here he had to begin with theology, not with history, as he did with Jewish audiences. Jews would have already known the theology Paul presented here.

17:23. TO THE UNKNOWN GOD. The Greeks were fearful of offending any god by failing to give him attention, so they felt they could cover any omissions with the label "the unknown god." Other Greek writers confirm that such altars could be seen in Athens. This was a striking point of contact for Paul. **Him declare I**. Paul could claim that the God he preached was this "unknown god," because God really is unknown apart from His self-revelation in Scripture and especially in Jesus Christ. He may be known partially from the evidences in nature and the human heart that He has put there, but men have rejected this revelation and turned away from the truth.

17:24. God that made the world. A personal Creator, in contrast with the views of pantheistic

Stoicism. **Lord of heaven and earth**. God is in authority and must be believed. With the Jews, Paul had pointed out that God was to be believed because of His mighty acts in history. With the Athenians, Paul took a more philosophical approach. **Dwelleth not in temples made with hands**. Paul thus invalidated all of the temples of Athens. He saw no need to accommodate the truth to their understanding but instead challenged their beliefs. He accommodated their lack of understanding by beginning with theology rather than history, but he never accommodated their beliefs by compromising the truth.

17:25. Neither is worshipped with men's hands. That is, sacrifices do no good, in the sense of appeasing God or buying His favor, for He needs nothing. In fact, it is the other way around: **he giveth to all life, and breath, and all things**.

17:26. Hath made of one blood all nations. All people are of one family (whether Athenians or Romans, Greeks or barbarians, Jews or Gentiles). All are descended from Adam (had Paul been able to finish this address, he might have discussed universal sin). **Determined the times before appointed**. God planned the exact times when nations should emerge and decline. **The bounds of their habitation**. He also planned the specific area to be occupied by each nation. He is God, the Designer (things are not left to chance, as the Epicureans thought).

17:27. God set the nations in place to **seek the Lord**, which they had not done.

17:28. Certain also of your own poets. Paul alluded to two Greek poems here: (1) "In him we live and move and have our being," from the Cretan poet Epimenides (ca. 600 BC) in his *Cretica*, and (2) "For we are also his offspring," from the Cilician poet Aratus (ca. 315–240 BC) in his *Phaenomena*, as well as from Cleanthes (331–233 BC) in his *Hymn to Zeus*. Paul quoted Greek poets elsewhere as well (see *KJV Study Bible* note on 1 Cor. 15:33; discussion on Titus 1:12). Here he used truth familiar to the Athenians as a bridge to introduce them to truth they had not yet heard.

17:29. Paul here used logic: **we are the offspring of God**, and therefore God cannot be **like unto gold, or silver, or stone**. No effect can be greater than its cause. God is not an idol, because God created humans, and humans are greater than man-made idols.

17:30. The times of this ignorance God winked at. God had not judged them for worshiping false gods in their ignorance (see 17:31). **But now commandeth all men every where to repent**. Paul was calling the Athenians to repudiate false gods and to acknowledge the one true living God who had created them.

17:31. That man whom he hath ordained. Jesus, the Son of Man (see 10:42; Matt. 25:31–46; Dan. 7:13). **He hath raised him from the dead**. Here is the point of contact with Paul's preaching to the Jews. Paul moved from the philosophical theology of the previous verses to historical reality. God will judge (something the Jews knew), and He will do it through Jesus Christ, whom He raised from the dead. It was at this point that Paul hit a roadblock.

17:32–34. The resurrection of the dead (v. 32). The Greeks accepted immortality of the soul but not resurrection of a dead body. Paul's speech produced three reactions: (1) **Some mocked**. They were unwilling to engage in an idea so new to them. (2) **Others said, We will hear thee again of this matter**. They delayed making a decision but were at least open to the possibility. (3) **Certain men clave unto him, and believed** (v. 34). These men had faith. "Clave" here means "attached themselves," with the idea of separating themselves from their prior beliefs. **Dionysius**. Later tradition states that he became the bishop of Athens, though it cannot be proved. **Damaris**. Some have suggested that she must have been a foreign, educated woman to have been present at a public meeting such as the Areopagus. It is also possible that she was a God-fearing Gentile who had heard Paul at the synagogue (see 17:17).

18:1. Came to Corinth. Either by land along the isthmus (a distance of about fifty miles) or by sea from Piraeus, the port of Athens, to Cenchrea, on the eastern shore of the Isthmus of Corinth (see 1 Corinthians, Introduction: "The City of Corinth").

18:2. Pontus. In the northeastern region of Asia Minor, a province lying along the Black Sea between

Bithynia and Armenia (see 2:9). **Aquila … Priscilla** (the diminutive form of Prisca). Since no mention is made of a conversion and since a work partnership was established (see 18:3), it may be that they were already Christians. They may have been converted in Rome by those returning from Pentecost or by others at a later time. **Claudius.** Emperor of Rome (AD 41–54). **Commanded all Jews to depart from Rome.** Recorded by the Roman historian Suetonius (*Claudius* 25). The expulsion order was given, Suetonius writes, because of "their [the Jews'] continual tumults instigated by Chrestus" (a common misspelling of "Christ"). If "Chrestus" refers to Christ, the riots obviously were "about" Him rather than led "by" Him.

18:3. Tentmakers. Paul would have been taught this trade as a youth. It was the Jewish custom to provide manual training for sons, whether rich or poor. Tents were provided to the Roman army and to people who wanted shade for outdoor events or other reasons.

18:4. He reasoned in the synagogue (see discussion on 13:14). Here again Paul used reason to defend the truth of Christ. One may infer from Paul's earlier speeches that he used Scripture as a basis and then reasoned from that to the truth that Jesus is the Messiah. **And persuaded the Jews and the Greeks.** Among the Greeks, Paul may have used tactics similar to those he used in Athens (see 17:19–31). Luke did not say, but it would seem logical. In any case, Paul found ways to present the truth concerning Christ logically to whomever he encountered.

18:5. When Silas and Timotheus were come from Macedonia. Paul had instructed these two to come to him at Athens (see 17:15). Evidently they did (see 1 Thess. 3:1), but they may have been sent back to Macedonia almost immediately to check on the churches, perhaps Silas to Philippi and Timothy to Thessalonica. **Paul was pressed in spirit.** This means that Paul sensed the Lord leading him strongly to devote himself to preaching the gospel. He may have given up tentmaking to preach full time. **And testified to the Jews that Jesus was Christ.** Apparently, Paul pressed the claim with more emotional fervor than he had previously.

18:6. When they opposed themselves. That is, to Paul. **And blasphemed.** The Jews spoke evilly against Christ. **I am clean.** Paul had done his part in sharing the gospel with them. He bore no responsibility for their reaction. A faithful witness for Christ has only to tell the truth and call people to repentance and faith. The results are in God's hands. **From henceforth I will go unto the Gentiles.** Paul indeed did this during his long stay in Corinth (but see 18:19, where Paul went straight to the synagogue in Ephesus). Truly, Paul's fervent "desire and prayer to God for Israel is, that they might be saved" (Rom. 10:1).

18:7. Paul's desire to see his Jewish brethren saved may be why he moved into a house next door to **the synagogue.** It may have been coincidence, but one cannot be sure.

18:8. Crispus. Paul baptized him (see 1 Cor. 1:14). For **ruler of the synagogue**, see discussion on 13:15. **Believed, and were baptized.** The tense of the Greek verbs indicates that this response to this gospel was an ongoing, daily process.

18:9–10. By a vision (v. 9). Paul had seen the Lord in His resurrection body at his conversion (see 9:4–6; 1 Cor. 15:8) and in the temple at Jerusalem while in a trance (see 22:17–18). Now he saw Him in a vision (see 23:11). **Be not afraid, but speak.** Apparently, Paul felt some fear. It should comfort Christians today to know that even the apostles experienced fear about witnessing. Jesus' words of encouragement to him should speak to every Christian in every time; the Great Commission is not suspended due to local opposition. **For I am with thee** (v. 10). There is no fear in the presence of Christ for those who know Him and serve Him. "With thee" may also mean that Jesus was in favor of what Paul sought to do in Corinth. When Christians are doing His will, He is "on our side" or "with us," and one has no reason to fear.

18:11. A year and six months. During this time, Paul may have taken the gospel also to the neighboring districts of Achaia (see 2 Cor. 1:1).

18:12. Gallio. The brother of Seneca, the philosopher, who was the tutor of Nero. Gallio was admired as a man of exceptional fairness and calmness.

From an inscription found at Delphi, it is known that Gallio was proconsul of Achaia in AD 51–52. This information helps to date Paul's visit to Corinth on his second journey as well as his writing of the Thessalonian letters.

18:13. Contrary to the law. The Jews were claiming that Paul was advocating a religion not recognized by Roman law, as Judaism was. If he had been given the opportunity to speak, he could have argued that the gospel he was preaching was the faith of his fathers (see 24:14–15; 26:6–7) and thus was authorized by Roman law.

18:14. If it were a matter of wrong. According to Roman law, or local ordinance. Since Paul had committed no such crime, Gallio had no reason to punish him.

8:15. If it be a question of words and names, and of your law. Gallio saw the problem as an internal one among Jewish people about religious beliefs and the roles and identities of various persons and beings. Gallio was very fair, having only a passing familiarity with either Judaism or Christianity, and recognized at least that his government had nothing to say in a dispute involving the matter.

18:16. He drave them. That is, Gallio dismissed the case and moved on to other matters. To modern imaginations, the image of "drave them" is probably stronger than what actually happened.

18:17. The Greeks took Sosthenes … and beat him. It is not clear whether the Greeks beat Sosthenes to vent their feelings against the Jews or beat him, their own synagogue ruler, because he was unsuccessful in presenting their case, but probably the former. A Sosthenes is included with Paul in the writing of 1 Corinthians (see 1 Cor.1:1). Perhaps he was the second ruler of the synagogue at Corinth to become a Christian in response to Paul's preaching (see 18:8).

18:18. Priscilla and Aquila. The order of the names used here (but see 18:2) may indicate Priscilla's prominent role or her higher social position (see Rom. 16:3; 2 Tim. 4:19). **He had a vow**. Grammatically, this could refer to Aquila, but the emphasis on Paul and his activity makes Paul more probable.

It was probably a temporary Nazarite vow (see Num. 6:1–21). Different vows were frequently taken to express thanks for deliverance from grave dangers. Shaving one's head marked the end of a vow.

18:19. Ephesus (see Ephesians, Introduction: "The City of Ephesus"; see also map, *KJV Study Bible*, p. 1694). The leading commercial city of Asia Minor, the capital of provincial Asia, and the warden of the temple of Artemis (Diana). **Left them there**. Priscilla and Aquila would give valuable aid upon Paul's return, providing advice about where and how the work in Ephesus could be started. For **synagogue**, see discussion on 13:14.

18:20–21. He consented not (v. 20) to tarry with Priscilla and Aquila in Ephesus, wanting to continue his church-planting activities. Paul always was focused more on planting new churches than on staying with one church for a time. This was a matter of his calling and ministry.

18:22. Saluted the church. This could refer to a congregation in Caesarea, but the explanation that Paul went **up** makes it more likely that it was the church in Jerusalem, some 2,500 feet above sea level. **Down to Antioch**, his home church. He did not stay long there either (see 18:23).

2. Paul's Third Missionary Journey (18:23–21:16)

18:23. The country of Galatia and Phrygia. The same route Paul had taken when starting on his second missionary journey but in the reverse order (see 16:6). The use of the phrase may indicate the southern part of Galatia in the Phrygian area (see discussion on 16:6).

18:24. Alexandria. Alexandria, in Egypt, was the second most important city in the Roman Empire and had a large Jewish population. **Apollos … an eloquent man**. This means that Apollos knew much and perhaps had a large vocabulary. **Mighty in the scriptures**. Education is no barrier to faith, especially if one is well educated in matters related to Scripture. Apollos knew the Scriptures well and knew how to present scriptural truths persuasively.

18:25. The baptism of John. It was not in the name of Jesus (see also 19:2–4). Apollos knew something about Jesus, but basically he, like John, was still looking forward to the coming of the Messiah. John's baptism was based on repentance rather than on faith in the finished work of Christ.

18:26. Expounded unto him the way of God more perfectly. Apollos's heart was prepared due to his knowledge of Scripture. He was ready to receive Jesus Christ as soon as he heard the truth concerning Him.

18:27. Achaia. The Roman province of which Corinth was the capital. **The bretheren wrote, exhorting the disciples to receive him**. It may be that the letter from the Jerusalem church (see chap. 15) established a precedent that traveling speakers carried letters of commendation to certify their credentials. Apollos's ministry in Achaia was effective, for he **helped them much which had believed through grace**. The word "grace" is used ten times in Acts. The nearest parallel to this occurrence is 15:11, "But we believe that through the grace of the Lord Jesus Christ we shall be saved, even as they."

18:28. He mightily convinced the Jews ... that Jesus was Christ. Because Apollos was "mighty in the scriptures" (18:24), he was able to show the Jews that Jesus was the Messiah promised in the Old Testament.

19:1. Apollos was at Corinth. Apollos was introduced at Ephesus (see 18:24) in the absence of Paul and moved to Corinth before Paul returned to Ephesus. Apollos later came back to Ephesus during Paul's ministry there (see 1 Cor. 16:12). **Through the upper coasts**. Not the lower direct route down the Lycus and Meander valleys but the upper Phrygian route approaching Ephesus from a more northerly direction. If Paul got to northern Galatia, which is unlikely, it must have been on one of these trips through the interior (see 16:6; 18:23). For **Ephesus**, see discussion on 18:19. **Certain disciples**. These twelve men (see 19:7) seem to have been followers of Jesus, but indirectly, through John the Baptist or some of his followers. Or perhaps they had received their teaching from Apollos himself in his earlier state of partial understanding (see 18:26). Like Apollos, they had a limited understanding of the gospel (see discussion on 18:25).

19:2. Have ye received the Holy Ghost ...? The men's response to Paul's question was that they had **not so much as heard** of the Holy Spirit. Since they knew the Old Testament and John's preaching, they probably did know of the Holy Spirit. What they apparently did not know was the fulfillment of John's preaching that occurred on the day of Pentecost with the coming of the Holy Spirit. That they were rebaptized (see 19:5) clearly indicates the uniqueness of Christian baptism.

19:3. Unto what then were ye baptized? ... Unto John's baptism. Apparently, these disciples preached about baptism, for Paul knew that they had received some kind of baptism, and hence his question.

19:4. John verily baptized with the baptism of repentance (see discussions on Matt. 3:11, 15; Mark 1:4). A summation of John's teaching. It was preparatory and provisional, stressing man's sinfulness and thus creating a sense of need for the gospel. John's baptism looked forward to Jesus, who by His death would make possible the forgiveness of sins.

19:5. The mark of true discipleship is willing obedience to the truth. These disciples did not argue that their previous baptism was "good enough," nor that baptism was unimportant. They had not had Christian baptism, and they needed to do things properly. Their willingness to do so is a mark of God's grace at work within them.

19:6. For **laid his hands upon them**, see discussion on 6:6. **The Holy Ghost came on them; and they spake with tongues, and prophesied**. The same experience that the disciples had at Pentecost (see 2:4, 11) and the Gentiles had in Caesarea (see 10:46).

19:7. One should not make too much of the fact that there were **about twelve** of these disciples. It is not a parallel to the apostles but only a passing fact that Luke recorded because he had it in his records.

19:8. Three months. Much longer than the "three sabbath days" (17:2) that Paul spent in Thessalonica, but he used the same approach: Jews first, then Greeks (see discussion on 13:14).

19:9. For **that way**, see discussions on 9:2; 19:23. **The school of one Tyrannus**. Probably a school used regularly by Tyrannus, a philosopher or rhetorician.

Instruction at the school was probably given in the cooler, morning hours. One Greek manuscript adds that Paul did his instructing from 11:00 a.m. to 4:00 p.m. This would have been the hot time of the day, but the hall was available then and the people were not at their regular work.

19:10. Two years. Paul's stay in Ephesus, totaling two years and three months (see 19:8), was the longest stay in one missionary location that Luke recorded. By Jewish reckoning, any part of a year is considered a year, so this period can be spoken of as "three years" (20:31). **All they which dwelt in Asia heard the word**. One of the elements of Paul's missionary strategy is seen here. Many of the cities where Paul planted churches were strategic centers that, when evangelized, served as focal points from which the gospel radiated out to the surrounding areas. Other examples are Antioch in Pisidia (see 13:14), Thessalonica (see 17:1), Athens (see 17:15), and Corinth (see 18:1).

19:11. God wrought special miracles by the hand of Paul. Luke mentioned this also in 14:3. It may be that such miracles were intermittent. One certainly does not get the impression from reading Acts that Paul constantly did miracles everywhere he went, though they did happen at times.

19:12. Handkerchiefs or aprons. Probably used by Paul in his trade of tentmaking (see discussion on 18:3): one for tying around his head, the other around his waist. Luke recorded this as something unusual; it was not an everyday occurrence in Paul's ministry. A similar phenomenon occurred in Peter's ministry (see 5:15).

19:13. By Jesus whom Paul preacheth. The name of Jesus cannot be used as a talisman or incantation. That these Jews referred to Jesus in this way also indicates that they had no personal knowledge of Him. It was thirdhand knowledge, and their efforts came to nothing. One cannot rely on the faith of another.

19:14. Sceva, a Jew, and chief of the priests. Sceva may have been related to the high-priestly family of Jerusalem, but more likely, he took this title himself to make a greater impression with his magical wiles. Drawn by Paul's ability to drive out

evil spirits, Jewish exorcists wanted to copy his work (see 13:6; 19:13), but the genuine power of God cannot be successfully copied.

19:15. The evil spirit asked, **but who are ye?** The men had no spiritual standing of their own.

19:16. Overcame them. The power of the evil spirit was such that the man was able to defeat seven others and send them fleeing (for another example of supernatural strength coming from an evil spirit, see Mark 5:3–4).

19:17. And the name of the Lord Jesus was magnified. This incident impressed upon people that the name of Jesus was not to be taken lightly or misused. That Jesus was the Messiah became well known to many people as a result of Paul's ministry, the outreach of the church, and the incident with the sons of Sceva.

19:18. Confessed, and shewed their deeds. One mark of a genuine revival or awakening is that people will openly confess their sins.

19:19. Books. Such documents bearing alleged magical formulas and secret information have been unearthed. Ephesus was a center for magical incantations. **And burned them before all men**. By publicly repudiating magical arts, they glorified the Lord and gave public testimony to the lordship of Jesus Christ over all matters of spiritual life and truth. **Fifty thousand pieces of silver**. The high price was not due to the quality of the books but to the supposed power gained by their secret rigmarole of words and names.

19:20. Mightily grew the word of God. This progress report (see discussion on 1:15) concludes Luke's account of the significant events at Ephesus.

19:21. Paul purposed in the spirit. Paul made the determination to go through Greece, then to Jerusalem, and on to Rome from there. Luke did not say so, but part of Paul's purpose in this itinerary was to collect an offering for the church in Jerusalem to be distributed to the poor (see 1 Cor. 16:1).

19:22. Erastus (see discussion on Rom. 16:23). An important figure at Corinth, the city treasurer at one time (see Rom. 16:23). Here Erastus returned to Corinth by way of Macedonia with Timothy. He is also located later at Corinth (see 2 Tim. 4:20).

19:23 – 41. The success of the preaching of the gospel caused a major upheaval in Ephesus. This indicates that as widespread as the gospel was, a sizable majority in the area had not believed in Jesus Christ. The Christian minority had, however, made an impact on at least one segment of the local economy (see 19:24 – 27), and it was economic hardship more than religion that drove the opposition.

19:23. No small stir. One wonders if this is a bit of understatement on Luke's part. What happened was a near riot. **That way.** Luke first used this phrase in 9:2 to describe Christianity. It recalls Jesus' statement "I am the way" (John 14:6). It also implies that faith in Christ is more than a onetime event; it is a way of life radically different from the way most people live. Paul had once opposed people who followed "this way" (9:2); here local merchants opposed "that way." In both cases, the emphasis is on how different living for Christ is from living like other people. If the Christians had been indistinguishable by their lifestyles from the respectable people around them, there would have been no opposition. Christians in all ages are called to follow a different "way."

19:24. Demetrius, a silversmith. Each trade had its guild, and Demetrius was probably a responsible leader of the guild for the manufacture of **silver shrines** and images. **Diana.** The Greek name for the Roman goddess Diana is Artemis, which is found in the Greek New Testament. The Ephesian Artemis, however, was very different from the Greco-Roman goddess. She had taken on the characteristics of Cybele, the mother goddess of fertility worshiped in Asia Minor and served by many prostitute-priestesses. A meteorite may be the basis of the many-breasted image of heavenly workmanship claimed for Artemis (see 19:35; some have identified the objects that cover the torso of the image as ostrich eggs). Reproductions of the original image from the time of the emperor Domitian (AD 81 – 96) have been found in Ephesus.

19:25. Wealth. Since the temple of Diana (Artemis) was one of the seven wonders of the ancient world, people came from far and wide to view it. Their purchase of silver shrines and images produced a lucrative business for the craftsmen.

19:26. Saying that they be no gods, which are made with hands. Paul was right on this point, but it is interesting that Demetrius mentioned this second. His main concern was financial, but religion was useful in inspiring others to action.

19:27. The temple of the great goddess. This temple was the glory of Ephesus. It was 425 feet long and 220 feet wide, having 127 white marble columns 62 feet high and less than 4 feet apart. In the inner sanctuary was the many-breasted image that supposedly dropped from heaven. **Her magnificence should be destroyed.** Demetrius used inflammatory language here. There was no evidence that anyone in Ephesus wanted to destroy the building itself. He implied, however, that should the craftsmen's trade be hindered, destruction of the building would soon follow. **Whom all Asia and the world worshippeth.** This was exaggeration on his part. Many people worshiped at the temple of Diana certainly, but not everyone. This is an example of the "bandwagon" fallacy. Worshiping Artemis was something, Demetrius said, that everyone did. Therefore, it was right, and such worship should not be interfered with. He implied that this interference came from a small minority who opposed what "everyone" believed and did. Demetrius shaped the argument in ways that were inaccurate and that isolated the Christian minority, making them appear more of a threat to society than a help. Unbelievers in every age do this, and no less so today, in which those who have the public "megaphone" often use inflammatory language and inaccuracies to shape people's perceptions of Christians as people whose existence threatens the fabric of society.

19:28. They were full of wrath. The inflammatory speech Demetrius had given had the intended effect. **Great is Diana of the Ephesians.** The angry crowd reacted with fervor in upholding the religious concept that both shaped their worldview and filled their pocketbooks.

19:29. Aristarchus. He later traveled with Paul from Corinth to Jerusalem (see 20:3 – 4) and also accompanied Paul on the voyage from Jerusalem to Rome (see 27:1 – 2; Col. 4:10).

19:30. Paul would have entered in. Paul's motivation was to speak to the people, not to run away. Under the circumstances, he might not have wanted to present the gospel, but he certainly would have wanted to correct misperceptions about Christians and to defend their right to live in Ephesus. Had the crowd calmed down at this, surely Paul would then have seized the opportunity to present Christ as the true God, in contrast to idols made with human hands (at least that part of Demetrius's speech was accurate).

19:31. The chief of Asia (Greek, *Asiarchēs*). Members of a council of men of wealth and influence elected to promote the worship of the emperor. Paul had **friends** in this high circle. Their primary concern here may have been maintaining order and preventing a murder from taking place.

19:32. The assembly was confused. Demetrius's words were not accurate, and the efforts of some to correct them led to further confusion. **Knew not wherefore they were come together.** Many in the assembly had gathered simply because a crowd was gathering and had no idea what the issue was but did not want to miss it. "Wherefore" simply means "why."

19:33. Alexander. Why he was pushed forward by the Jews is unclear. It may have been to make clear the disassociation of the Jews from the Christians or perhaps to accuse the Christians further of an offense against the Greeks. **Would have made his defense** indicates that Alexander may have sought to defend the Christians, since the Jews agreed with the Christians that idolatry is wrong. It may be that he was a better choice for this than Paul, who was new in town and was the center of controversy. In any case, the crowd did not even give him the chance to speak (see 19:34).

19:34. When they knew that he was a Jew. The crowd recognized that the Jews were not worshipers of Diana any more than the Christians were. Alexander's presence only fanned the flames further.

19:35–40. "The townclerk" (v. 35) was the secretary of the city who published the decisions of the civic assembly. He was the most important local official and the chief executive officer of the assembly, acting as go-between for Ephesus and the Roman authorities. In contrast to Demetrius's rhetoric, the clerk made a speech offering common sense and truth.

19:35–36. When the townclerk had appeased the people (v. 35), he made his first point: everyone knew **that the city of the Ephesians is a worshiper of … Diana.** The city's position as the center for that kind of worship had not been threatened, and thus the people had overreacted. **These things cannot be spoken against** (v. 36). In other words, no one could bring any evidence that the city's position was threatened. Demetrius had claimed that Paul had "persuaded and turned away much people" (19:26), and while this was true, there were still many who practiced pagan ways. In that first century, the church had not completely demolished the pagan worldview. It was not until the fifth century, after the fall of Rome, that paganism ceased to be the majority worldview in that part of the world. At that time, Augustine devoted a major portion of his *City of God* to refuting paganism as a false and illogical understanding of reality.

19:37. The clerk's second point focused on the Christians themselves. They had not done anything wrong before the law. **Robbers of churches.** Literally, he meant that the Christians had not broken into any pagan temples and stolen anything. They were not guilty of sacrilege (see Bruce, *The Book of Acts*, p. 377). **Nor yet blasphemers of your goddess.** The Christians had said that idolatry is wrong and that a god made with human hands is not real. They had not, however, launched a deliberate attack against a specific deity, or so the clerk claimed. He may or may not have been correct in this. His goal was to prevent a riot and to restore order.

19:38–39. The town clerk next offered a legal remedy for Demetrius and the craftsmen. **The law is open, and there are deputies.** Any real problem could be brought before the courts. Apparently, the clerk understood that the only real complaint they had was that their business had been hurt. The government could not do anything about the law of supply and demand. Since the Christians had not prevented anyone from worshiping wherever they chose, any harm to the craftsmen's trade was a result of the wholly legal success of the Christians' preaching, not due to a violation of the law.

19:40. We are in danger to be called in question. This was the clerk's main concern. Rome wanted order and peace, and a riot over a point of conflict between religious perspectives would only make the leadership at Ephesus look bad in the eyes of Rome. By implication, the town clerk had upheld some principles that are recognizable today: (1) people have the right to preach their religious views without hindrance by government or society; (2) people have the right to believe as they choose, without hindrance; (3) that some people do not like the religious views of others is not sufficient reason for the government to step in; (4) genuine complaints about actual behavior should be brought before the proper authorities, in the courts, not made fodder for public approbation. Would that certain people and organizations today recognized these principles when Christians assert their right to meet and preach the gospel in the public square.

19:41. He dismissed the assembly. By the time the town clerk finished speaking, the crowd had quieted. Truth won out over inflammatory rhetoric in the end, and a riot was averted.

20:1. Departed ... into Macedonia. Paul wanted to (1) leave Ephesus, (2) preach in Troas on his way to Macedonia, (3) meet Titus at Troas with a report from Corinth (see 2 Cor. 2:12–13), and (4) continue collecting the offering for Judea (see 1 Cor. 16:1–4; 2 Cor. 8:1–9:15; Rom. 15:25–28).

20:2. He had gone over those parts. This may cover a considerable period of time. Paul may have gone as far as Illyricum (see Rom. 15:19) at this time.

20:3. There abode three months. Probably a reference to the stay in Corinth, the capital of Achaia. These would have been the winter months, when ships did not sail regularly. Paul probably wrote Romans at this time (see Romans, Introduction: "Background"). **The Jews laid wait for him.** The Jews were determined to take Paul's life. Since he was carrying the offering for the Christians in Judea, there would have been a temptation for theft as well. The port at Cenchrea would have provided a convenient place for Paul's enemies to detect him as he entered a ship **to sail into Syria.**

20:4. The men listed in this verse seem to be the delegates appointed to accompany Paul and the money given for the needy in Judea (see *KJV Study Bible* note on 2 Cor. 8:23). Three were from Macedonia, two from Galatia, and two from Asia. Luke may have joined them at Philippi ("we sailed," 20:6; see discussion on 16:10). **Sopater.** May be the same as Sosipater (see Rom. 16:21). For **Aristarchus**, see discussion on 19:29. **Secundus.** Not mentioned elsewhere. His name means "second," as Tertius (see Rom. 16:22) means "third" and Quartus (see Rom. 16:23) means "fourth." **Gaius of Derbe.** A Gaius from Macedonia was associated with Aristarchus (see 19:29), but the grouping of the names in pairs (after the reference to Sopater) indicates that this Gaius was associated with Roman Galatia and is different from the Macedonian Gaius. **Timotheus.** May have represented more than one congregation. He was from Lystra but had been responsible for working in other churches (see 1 Cor. 16:10–11; Phil. 2:19–23). He had been sent to Macedonia before Paul left Ephesus (see 19:22). **Tychicus.** A constant help to Paul, especially in association with the churches of Asia (see Eph. 6:21–22; Col. 4:7–9; 2 Tim. 4:12; Titus 3:12). **Trophimus** (see 2 Tim. 4:20). Appears again in 21:29. He was an Ephesian, and it is implied that he was a Gentile.

20:5. Troas. Was to be the rendezvous for Paul and those who went on ahead by sea from Neapolis, the seaport of Philippi (see 16:11). Paul and his immediate companions stayed in Philippi before sailing a week later. This is the beginning of the "we" passages in Acts (20:5–15; 27:1–29; 28:2–16), passages written in first-person plural, indicating that the author was a participant in the events recorded.

20:6. From Philippi. From the seaport, Neapolis, about ten miles away. **The days of unleavened bread.** Began with Passover and lasted a week. Paul spent the period in Philippi. He had initially hoped to reach Jerusalem sooner (see 19:21), but now he hoped to arrive there for Pentecost (see 20:16). The voyage from Neapolis to Troas took **five days**. It had taken about two days going the other direction (see 16:11). Although Paul was in a hurry to arrive at Jerusalem by Pentecost, he remained **seven days** at Troas. This might have been because of a ship schedule, but more likely, Paul wanted to meet with the believers on the first day of the week to break bread.

20:7. The first day of the week. Sunday. Although some maintain that they met on Saturday evening since the Jewish day began at six o'clock the previous evening, there is little indication that Luke was using the Jewish method of reporting time to tell of happenings in this Hellenistic city (but see 20:8, 11). **To break bread**. Here refers to the Lord's Supper, since breaking bread was the expressed purpose for this formal gathering. The Lord's Supper had been commanded (see Luke 22:19), and it was observed regularly (see 2:42).

20:8. Many lights. The disciples were meeting at night (see 20:11). It may have been Saturday night, by modern reckoning, or Sunday night. It is interesting that Luke recorded this small detail. He may have been an eyewitness.

20:9. Eutychus. A name common among the freedman class (see discussion on 6:9). **Paul was long preaching**. This tendency has not died out in the life of the church.

20:10. His life is in him. As Peter had raised Tabitha (9:40), so Paul raised Eutychus. It may be that life returned when Paul embraced him (see Bruce, *The Book of Acts*, p. 385).

20:11–12. Were not a little comforted (v. 12). Everyone rejoiced that Eutychus was alive. Verse 12 did not happen chronologically later than verse 11. Luke was summing up Paul's ministry that night before finishing his account of Eutychus.

20:13. Assos. On the opposite side of the peninsula from Troas, about twenty miles away by land. The coastline, however, was about forty miles. Paul thus was not far behind the ship that sailed around the peninsula.

20:14. Mitylene. After the first day of sailing, the ship put into this harbor on the southeast shore of the island of Lesbos.

20:15. Chios. Paul and his companions spent the second night off the shore of this larger island, which lay along the west coast of Asia Minor. **Samos**. Crossing the mouth of the bay that leads to Ephesus, they came on the third day to Samos, one of the most important islands in the Aegean. **Miletus**. Thirty miles south of Ephesus, Miletus was the destination of the ship Paul was on. He would have had to change ships to go to Ephesus, which would have cost him time (see 20:16). If he had gone to Ephesus, he would have had to visit a number of families, which would have taken more time. If trouble arose, such as the riot of a year ago (see 19:23–41), even more time would be lost. A delay could not be risked.

20:16. The day of Pentecost. Fifty days after Passover. Five days plus seven days (see 20:6) plus four days (see 20:13–15) had already gone by, leaving only about two-thirds of the time for the remainder of the trip.

20:17. The elders of the church. The importance of the leadership of elders was evident throughout Paul's ministry. He delivered the famine gift from the church at Antioch to the elders of the Jerusalem church (see 11:30). He appointed elders on his first missionary journey (see 14:23) and addressed elders later in Philippi (see Phil. 1:1, where they are called "bishops"). He requested the Ephesian elders to meet with him on this solemn occasion (see 20:28). Some years later, he wrote instructions regarding the qualifications for elders (see 1 Tim. 3:1–7; Titus 1:5–9).

20:18–35. Paul's speech has more in common with his letters than with any of his addresses in Acts (see Polhill, *Acts*, p. 422). This may be because Paul would soon be absent from the Ephesians and because of his concern for their doctrinal purity, a matter he addressed often in his letters.

20:18–21. Paul began his speech by laying out his philosophy of ministry, describing his manner of conducting his ministry (vv. 18–19), the scope of his ministry (v. 20), and the content of his ministry (v. 21).

20:18–19. What manner I have been with you at all seasons (v. 18). Paul could point to a life of consistency, both in terms of ethics and in terms of performing his ministry. This involved two factors: **humility of mind, and with many tears** (v. 19; see 20:31). There is no inconsistency between standing up for truth and being humble. Paul had proclaimed the gospel without compromise and yet with humility. "Humility" indicates Paul's attitude as a servant of God, and "tears" indicate his burden that people would come to know Christ. Both are necessary if one is to fulfill the call to ministry. Paul's ministry at Ephesus was conducted with emotional fervency and a sense of urgency.

20:20. Paul turned to the scope of his ministry: **I kept back nothing that was profitable**. Paul preached the whole truth of God. **Shewed you, and ... taught you**. Paul's ministry included living out the truths of the gospel as well as teaching them. Both are essential for a fully effective ministry. Paul's ministry among the Ephesians, then, was characterized by humility and genuine caring, and it included both living out and teaching the truth.

20:21. Paul concluded this section with the content of his ministry: **repentance toward God, and faith toward our Lord Jesus Christ**. This is the gospel in a sentence. "Repentance" is turning from evil and sin and toward God and His will. "Faith" is directed toward the Lord Jesus Christ, that is, toward His work on the cross. Anyone who comes to God in genuine repentance of sin and who trusts in the finished work of Christ will be saved. Thus, repentance and faith, properly understood, constitute the essence of the gospel.

20:22. Paul then moved on to matters related to his travel plans. **I go bound in the spirit unto Jerusalem**. Paul did not go to Jerusalem against the guidance of the Spirit, as some have suggested, but because of the guidance of the Spirit. People pleaded with him not to go (see 21:4, 12), not because the Spirit prohibited his going but because the Spirit revealed the capture that awaited him there (see 21:11–12).

20:23. Witnesseth in every city. Perhaps Paul was hearing in all of the churches warnings that he should not go to Jerusalem, similar to what Luke recorded in 21:12. **Bonds and afflictions abide me**.

Paul was aware of what awaited him but was also convinced that God wanted him to go. Sometimes God's will is the path of joy, peace, and comfort. Other times, it is a path of hardship and opposition. One must not let such matters be a hindrance us from doing the will of God.

20:24. None of these things move me, neither count I my life dear unto myself. Paul would rather die because he had done God's will than live for many more years outside of His will.

20:25. Shall see my face no more. This was not a message from God but rather what Paul anticipated. He had been mistaken before in his plans: he had intended to stay in Ephesus until Pentecost, but he had to leave earlier (see 20:1; 1 Cor. 16:8–9). His prophetic power was not used to foresee his own future, just as his healing power was not used to heal his own disease (see 2 Cor. 12:7–9). As it turned out, it seems Paul did revisit Ephesus (see 1 Tim. 1:3).

25:26–27. I am pure from the blood of all men (v. 26). Paul meant not that he had not committed murder during his ministry (his supporters were certainly well aware of that) but that he had faithfully preached the gospel. Perhaps Paul had in mind the passage in Ezekiel 3:18–19, which says that one must warn the wicked man or be guilty of his blood. Paul had preached "repentance toward God" (25:21) and had done it "both publickly, and from house to house" (25:20) and thus was not guilty before God of failing to warn the wicked.

20:28. Overseers. "Elders" (20:17) were called "overseers" and were told to pastor ("shepherd") the flock, demonstrating that they could be called "elders," "overseers," or "pastors." **His own blood**. Literally, "the blood of his own one," a term of endearment (such as "his own dear one," referring to His own Son).

20:29. Shall grievous wolves enter in among you. Paul had seen what had happened in the churches in Galatia and Corinth when certain men posing as apostles or their representatives came and preached a "works" salvation. They had avoided Ephesus, probably because of the presence of Paul and his associates. Paul did not need a prophet's vision to see that his absence would mean these false teachers would attempt to influence this large and important church.

20:30. Of your own selves. That is, men who would preach false doctrine would arise among the Ephesians, not just come in from the outside. Paul well knew the reality of fallen human nature. Humans need little help to be led astray into heresy. Christians need much help from God if they are to stay true to His Word.

20:31. Three years (see discussion on 19:10). Paul's ministry in and around Ephesus had been long and influential. Even though he had traveled from Ephesus to other places, his ministry had been headquartered there for some time, and his associates—Timothy, Titus, and perhaps Luke himself—had carried on his work even when he was away.

20:32. I commend you to God. That is, Paul left the Ephesians in God's care **and to the word of his grace**. Paul left them under the authority of God's Word. They would face doctrinal heresy from outside and from within (see 20:29–30), but their protection would be from God and from His Word. Paul was especially concerned that they would depart from the truth of salvation by grace through faith, as this had so often been the point of departure for other churches, to salvation by works. That Paul was primarily concerned about the church's doctrinal purity is a reminder of its importance in the life of the church today. Paul was not worried about their relevance to the culture, nor about their external unity or number of programs, so long as they remained true to the gospel and to God's Word. **Are sanctified**. Positional sanctification (see 26:18; see *KJV Study Bible* note on 1 Cor. 1:2).

20:33. Paul then turned to the matter of financing his ministry. **I have coveted no man's silver, or gold, or apparel**. Paul had not charged a fee for preaching the gospel. He may have been contrasting his behavior with that of those who had disturbed the Corinthian church (see 1 Corinthians 9). Paul had asserted to the Corinthians that he had the right to charge for the gospel but had not done so (1 Cor. 9:14, 18). He hinted that others, perhaps the false

teachers at Corinth, had charged a fee for their ministries (1 Cor. 9:11–12). None of these Scriptures are to be used to justify not paying ministers today. Paul even asserted that it is right to pay the minister (see 1 Cor. 9:3–11). A minister should be paid so that he can devote himself to the work of the ministry, not having to be concerned for physical needs. Paul, believing God had called him to ministry in a special way, believed that he should not charge for ministry, perhaps to contrast himself with the false teachers of his time.

20:34. Ministered unto my necessities. Paul had worked in Thessalonica (see 1 Thess. 2:9) and Corinth (see Acts 18:3).

20:35. Remember the words of the Lord Jesus. A formula regularly used in the early church to introduce a quotation from Jesus (see 1 Clement 46:7). This is a rare instance of a saying of Jesus that is not found in the canonical Gospels.

20:36–38. Paul ended the meeting with prayer and goodbyes. Many tears were shed, especially over the possibility that the Ephesians would not see him again. Nothing is wrong with Christians bidding tearful goodbyes to one another. Believers will see each other in heaven, but especially among close family and friends, leave-taking in this world is always tearful, yet sometimes necessary, in answer to God's call.

21:1. A straight course unto Cos. Favorable winds took Paul and his fellow travelers to a stopping place at this island. **Rhodes**. The leading city on the island of Rhodes, once noted for its harbor colossus, one of the seven wonders of the ancient world (but demolished over two centuries before Paul arrived there). It took them a day to get to Rhodes. **Patara**. On the southern coast of Lycia.

21:2. Paul changed ships from a vessel that hugged the shore of Asia Minor to one going directly to Tyre and Phoenicia.

21:3. For **Cyprus**, see 13:4. **Tyre**. Paul had passed through this Phoenician area at least once before (see 15:3; Mark 7:24).

21:4. Seven days. These, added to the twenty-nine days since the Passover in Philippi, would leave only two weeks until Pentecost. **Finding disciples**. Apparently, Paul and his associates did not know of these Christians, at least not directly. **Who said to Paul through the Spirit, that he should not go up to Jerusalem**. The Spirit warned of the coming trials in store for Paul at Jerusalem. Because of these warnings, Paul's brothers urged him not to go on, knowing that trials lay ahead, but Paul felt "bound in the spirit" (20:22) to go.

21:5–6. We kneeled down on the shore, and prayed (v. 5). This was much like Paul had done with the Ephesian elders (see 20:36). Luke did not record what Paul said to the disciples, but most likely, it was a less personal and tearful goodbye due to the different circumstances. Praying together on the occasion of a departure may have already become a common practice among Christians. **And they returned home again** (v. 6). This again is a detail Luke did not need to supply but indicates he was with Paul during this "we" section.

21:7. Ptolemais. The modern city of Acco, north of and across the bay from Mount Carmel. It was one day's journey from Tyre on the north and another thirty-five miles to Caesarea on the south.

21:8. Cesarea. A Gentile city, the capital of Roman Judea (see discussions on 8:40; 10:1). **Philip the evangelist**. Philip's evangelistic work may have focused on Caesarea for almost twenty-five years (see discussion on 8:40). "Evangelist" is a title used only here and in Ephesians 4:11; 2 Timothy 4:5.

21:9. Four daughters, virgins. They may have been dedicated in a special way to serving the Lord. For **which did prophesy**, see 1 Cor. 11:5; 12:8–10; see Luke 2:36. For Old Testament prophetesses, see Exodus 15:20; Judges 4:4; 2 Kings 22:14; Nehemiah 6:14.

21:10. A certain prophet, named Agabus. Evidently he held the office of prophet, as Philip held the office of "evangelist" (21:8). This is the same prophet who, some fifteen years earlier, had been in Antioch prophesying the coming famine in Jerusalem (see 11:27–29).

21:11. He took Paul's girdle. That is, Paul's belt. Agabus acted out the prophecy, as Jeremiah had done centuries earlier when he shattered a clay pot

and said, "Thus saith the LORD of hosts; Even so will I break this people and this city, as one breaketh a potter's vessel" (Jer. 19:11). Ezekiel also had acted out his prophecy of the siege of Jerusalem by laying siege to a model of the city (see Ezek. 4:1–4). The use of visual aids or object lessons was thus an old tradition among prophets. Agabus was not just being dramatic; he was prophesying in a manner that Jewish people would recognize as valid. The content of his prophecy was that Paul would be bound and that his captors would **deliver him into the hands of Gentiles**. Indeed, this is exactly what happened.

21:12. We, and they of that place. Luke, in the company of travelers with Paul, joined in urging him not to go to Jerusalem. Agabus did not say that Paul should not go, only that these things would happen if he did. Naturally, Paul's friends did not want him to endanger himself.

21:13. Paul, however, was willing **not to be bound only, but also to die at Jerusalem for the name of the Lord Jesus**. This was not mere bravado on his part. If Paul had any doubt whether going to Jerusalem was God's will, he would not have gone.

21:14. The will of the Lord be done. This may mean that Paul's companions finally recognized that it was the Lord's will for him to go to Jerusalem. Or it could mean that they simply cast the situation into God's hands and prayed for Paul's protection.

21:15. We took up our carriages. The idea is that they prepared for the trip. The expression could imply that they were provided with horses (see Bruce, *The Book of Acts*, p. 402, who translates this rather freely as "got ready for the road"). **Went up to Jerusalem**. Jerusalem was one of the highest elevations in the region.

21:16. Mnason. He must have been a disciple of some means to be able to accommodate Paul and a group of about nine men traveling with him.

C. Paul in Jerusalem and Caesarea (21:17–26:32)

1. Paul Arrested in Jerusalem (21:17–23:35)

21:17. We were come to Jerusalem. No more than a day or two before Pentecost. **The brethren**

received us gladly. May indicate the grateful reception of the offering as well.

21:18. James. The brother of the Lord, author of the letter of James, and leader of the church in Jerusalem (see Gal. 1:19; 2:9). He is called an apostle but was not one of the Twelve.

21:19. He declared particularly what things God had wrought among the Gentiles by his ministry. When Paul had last departed from Jerusalem, he had taken the letter to the Gentile churches with him (see chap. 15). Since then, churches had been planted in many places in Asia and had spread to Europe through Macedonia and Achaia. Paul had much to tell the Jerusalem church.

21:20. They glorified the Lord. The believers gave credit to God for the things that had happened in Paul's ministry. **Thousands of Jews there are that believe**. These were disciples in and around Jerusalem. Apparently, this was a time of relative peace and freedom from the persecution experienced earlier (see chaps. 3–4, 6–7). **And they are all zealous of the law**. James and the elders apparently meant that many of the Christians among the Jews still believed that circumcision was necessary for salvation (see Bruce, *The Book of Acts*, p. 405).

21:21. Thou teachest all the Jews … to forsake Moses. The leadership of the church did not believe this, but they were quite aware that many of the laity did. How tragic it is that once an ugly rumor gets started in a church, it is often impossible to squelch it. The very people who most need to believe the truth often refuse to accept it and cause much heartbreak for God's noblest servants, often damaging their ministries for years to come.

21:22. The multitude. That is, the entire body of believers in and around Jerusalem would come together once they knew that Paul was there.

21:23. The leadership proposed a plan that would demonstrate publicly that Paul had not repudiated Moses. **Four men which have a vow on them**. They were evidently under the temporary Nazarite vow (see Num. 6:2–12) and became unclean before the completion time of the vow (perhaps from contact with a dead body). Apparently, the Jewish practice

of this vow continued among those who believed in Christ.

21:24. Purify thyself. In some instances, the purification rites included the offering of sacrifices. Some Jewish Christians observed such rites by choice, but they were not required of Christians, whether Jew or Gentile. **Be at charges with them**. Paul's part in sponsoring these men would include (1) paying part or all of the expenses of the sacrifices (in this case, eight pigeons and four lambs; see Num. 6:9–12) and (2) going to the temple to notify the priest when their days of purification would be fulfilled so that the priests would be prepared to sacrifice their offerings (see 21:26). **Keepest the law**. Paul had earlier taken a vow himself (see 18:18), he had been a Jew to the Jews (see 1 Cor. 9:20–21), and Timothy had been circumcised (see 16:3). Paul was very careful, however, not to sacrifice Christian principle in any act of obedience to the law (he would not compel Titus to be circumcised; see Gal. 2:3).

21:25. The leadership assured Paul that they still abided by the Jerusalem council's decree that the Gentiles were not under the law of Moses in any way, only that they should observe the four restrictions set forth in the letter to the Gentile churches, for the sake of unity and peace (see chap. 15).

21:26. Paul complied with the church's request that he sponsor the men who were taking vows. It involved nothing that would compromise his own convictions regarding Christ, and the public testimony it would provide would only further the spread of the gospel and the credibility of his own ministry.

21:27. Seven days (see Num. 6:9). These were the days required for the men's purification, shaving their heads at the altar, the sacrifice of a sin offering and a burnt offering for each, and announcing the completion to the priests. **Jews which were of Asia**. Paul had already suffered at the hands of Asian Jews (see 20:19).

21:28. Brought Greeks also into the temple. Explicitly forbidden according to inscribed stone markers (still in existence). Any Gentiles found within the bounds of the court of Israel would be killed. There was no evidence, however, that Paul had brought anyone other than Jews into the area. Paul's willingness to comply with the request of the church leaders in the matter of the vow indicates that he was sensitive to the situation and would not, in any case, have violated the custom and beliefs of the Jews.

21:29. Trophimus. Paul probably would not have taken him into the forbidden area. If he had, they should have attacked Trophimus rather than Paul.

21:30. The doors were shut. By order of the temple officer to prevent further trouble inside the sacred precincts.

21:31. The chief captain (Greek, *chiliarchos*). A commander of one thousand men (a regiment). This captain was named Claudius Lysias (see 23:26) and was stationed at the Fortress of Antonia (see discussion on 21:37).

21:32. Centurions. Since the plural is used, it is likely that at least two centurions and two hundred **soldiers** were involved.

21:33. Two chains. Paul's hands probably were chained to a soldier on either side. At this point, Agabus's prophecy (see 21:11) was fulfilled.

21:34–36. Since there was confusion as to exactly what Paul had done, the chief captain had him taken away until he could sort out the problem. **The multitude** (v. 36) may have included Jewish believers as well as members of the general populace, as there was a serious misunderstanding among the believers about Paul's preaching and activities (see 21:21–22).

21:37. Castle. The Fortress of Antonia, which was connected to the northern end of the temple area by two flights of steps. The towers overlooked the temple area.

21:38. That Egyptian, which … madest an uproar. Josephus tells of an Egyptian false prophet who some years earlier had led four thousand Jews (Josephus, through a misreading of a Greek capital letter, says thirty thousand) out to the Mount of Olives. These Jews were Zealots, members of a party that sought to overthrow Rome and achieve independence for Israel. Roman soldiers killed hundreds, but the leader escaped. **Men that were murderers**. The Greek here is a loanword from Latin *sicarii*, mean-

ing "dagger-men," who were violent assassins. One might almost think that the chief captain was disappointed that he had not captured so notorious and wanted a criminal.

21:39. No mean city. The Greek means that Tarsus was not an obscure or insignificant city (see discussion on 22:3). Paul asked to be allowed to speak to the multitude still gathered outside. He certainly had confidence in his persuasive powers. It may have been warranted, given the amount of speaking he had done in his travels. He had earlier sought to speak to the Ephesians when they were on the verge of a riot (see 19:30), and those with him had dissuaded him. Here he was allowed the opportunity to speak.

21:40. The Hebrew tongue. More likely Aramaic than Hebrew, since Aramaic was the most commonly used language among Palestinian Jews.

22:1–21. Paul's defense before the Jews. Here Paul once again recounts his conversion on the Damascus Road, emphasizing how he had once opposed Christians. He also tells of God's call to him to preach to the Gentiles since the Jews were rejecting his message. His purpose was to convince the crowd to repent of their opposition to what was clearly the will of God.

22:1. Paul began his speech with the following address: **Men, brethren** (see discussion on 11:1)**, and fathers**. He thus identified with the people. The accusation was that he had betrayed Jewish law and tradition. He wanted to begin in a way that said he was one of them. The word "fathers" especially acknowledged that he saw them as people to be respected and treated as authorities. Someone who wanted to challenge rather than affirm would not have addressed them in this way.

22:2. The Hebrew tongue (see discussion on 21:40). Luke meant the tongue used by the Hebrews (Aramaic), not the Hebrew language.

22:3. Verily. Means "truly," "certainly." **Born in Tarsus**. Paul was a citizen of Tarsus (see 21:39) as well as of Rome. "No mean city" (21:39) was used by Plato to describe Ephesus (in the dialogue *Ion*), and the term may have been in common use up until Paul's day. Tarsus was ten miles inland on the Cydnus River and thirty miles from the mountains, which were cut by a deep, narrow gorge called the Cilician Gates. It was an important commercial center, university city, and crossroads of travel. **Brought up in this city at the feet of Gamaliel**. Paul must have come to Jerusalem at an early age. Another translation ("brought up in this city, being educated under Gamaliel, strictly according to the law of our fathers" NASB) suggests that Paul came to Jerusalem when he was old enough to begin training under Gamaliel. Gamaliel was the most honored rabbi of the first century. Possibly he was the grandson of Hillel (see 5:34–40). By pointing out his association with Gamaliel, Paul again emphasized his knowledge of and respect for Jewish law and traditions. **Was zealous towards God, as ye all are**. Paul meant that his training was effective, and he was not an enemy of God and His revelation.

22:4. I persecuted this way (see 9:1–4). Remember that Paul was speaking to an audience of both Christians and unbelievers who were all zealous for the law, with many from both groups convinced that he opposed the law of Moses and sought to commit sacrilege in the temple. With this statement, he said to the unbelievers that he had stood with them in opposition to Christianity before his conversion; to the believers, he emphasized how much his life had changed after he trusted Christ. To both groups, he wanted to emphasize that he was not an impious or unholy man who would speak or behave in ways that would denigrate Moses and the law.

22:5. The high priest. Caiaphas, the high priest over twenty years earlier, was now dead, and Ananias was high priest (see 23:2). The records of the high priest, however, would show Paul's testimony to be true.

22:6–21. Paul related his encounter with Christ on the road to Damascus. To unbelievers, he wanted to emphasize that what had happened to him was from God. To believers, he wanted to emphasize that his conversion was genuine. One may wonder why Paul spoke of this incident now, so many years later, and how it related to the specific problem the crowd

had with him. Because it had happened so long ago, many in the crowd, both believers and unbelievers, would not have heard the story or would have heard it only secondhand. In addition, his personal testimony of his encounter with Christ established his credentials as a man who was called of God and thus was not an enemy of God and His truth. The basic charge against him here was that he was living and teaching in opposition to God.

22:6. About noon. A detail not included in the earlier account (see 9:1–22).

22:7–8. Why persecutest thou me? (v. 7; see discussions on 9:4–5). By persecuting the church, Paul was persecuting Jesus. For **Who art thou, Lord?** (v. 8), see discussion on 9:5.

22:9. They heard not the voice. They heard the sound (see 9:7) but did not understand what was said.

22:10. Paul was told to **go into Damascus** and there receive instructions. **Appointed for thee to do**. God had a specific call and plan for Paul.

22:11. I could not see for the glory of that light. Paul's attributed his blindness to the light itself, which left him temporarily unable to see.

22:12–13. Ananias, a devout man according to the law (v. 12; see discussion on Luke 1:6). This fact would have been important to Paul's audience. The crowd was upset that he was overturning the law. Affirmation of him from one who followed the law would make this charge more difficult to sustain.

22:14. See that Just One (see 3:14). Seeing the resurrected Jesus was all-important to Paul (see 26:16; 1 Cor. 9:1; 15:8). It was that experience that had convinced him of the truth of the gospel and became the foundation of his theology.

22:15. Thou shalt be his witness unto all men. Paul made no distinction between Jew and Greek here, nor mentioned his desire to carry to gospel to the Gentiles. He would mention this later in the speech (see 22:21).

22:16. Be baptized, and wash away thy sins (see discussion on Rom. 6:3–4). Baptism is the outward sign of an inward work of grace. The reality and the symbol are closely associated in the New Testament (see 2:38; Titus 3:5; 1 Peter 3:21). The outward rite, however, does not produce the inward grace (see Rom. 2:28–29; Eph. 2:8–9; Phil. 3:4–9).

22:17. When I was come again to Jerusalem. Refers to the visit described in 9:26 (see also Gal. 1:17–18). **While I prayed in the temple, I was in a trance** (see 10:10; 11:5; see also 2 Cor. 12:3). Paul was not a blasphemer of the temple but continued to hold it in high honor. Paul saw the temple as a proper place for prayer, which would ameliorate the charge that he wished to defile it.

22:18. They will not receive thy testimony concerning me. Paul's audience knew that the preaching of Christ was controversial. He had no need to hide it.

22:19–20. Paul's reply indicates that he believed he would gain a hearing as a former persecutor of the church. God, however, had other plans for him (see 22:21). **Standing by, and consenting** (v.20). This does not necessarily mean that Paul had been a member of the Sanhedrin, though some believe he was (see discussion on 26:10). He could have shown his approval by allowing them to put their cloaks at his feet.

22:21. Jesus told Paul, **I will send thee far hence unto the Gentiles**. Paul was coming to the point of contention between him and the crowd. He presented this as a call from God that was given to him while he was praying in the temple (see 22:17). In other words, his ministry to the Gentiles was something God had given him, not something by which he sought to oppose the things of God.

22:22–23. Paul's effort to clarify these matters did not work. At this point, the crowd became upset. Paul had sought to present himself as a loyal Jew who had a call from God to present Christ to the Gentiles, but the people's assumptions about his ministry activities got in the way of what he was actually saying.

22:24. For **The chief captain**, see discussion on 21:31. For **castle**, see discussion on 21:37. **Scourging**. Not with the rod, as at Philippi (see 16:22–24), but with the scourge, a merciless instrument of torture. It was legal to use it to force a confession from a slave or alien but never from a Roman citizen. The scourge consisted of a whip of leather thongs with pieces of bone or metal attached to the ends.

22:25. They bound him with thongs. The Greek implies tying a person to a post for whipping. For **centurion**, see discussion on 10:1. **A Roman, and uncondemned**. Roman citizenship did not mean that one lived within the city of Rome, nor even that one lived in the empire. Citizenship was a special privilege not extended to all and gave certain rights not shared by all who lived under Roman rule. According to Roman law, all Roman citizens were assured exclusion from all degrading forms of punishment, including beating with rods, scourging, and crucifixion. See 16:37.

22:26–27. This man is a Roman (v. 26). Luke did not record whether or how the officers verified Paul's claim. Perhaps falsifying the claim would have brought worse punishment, or perhaps Paul carried documents authenticating his Roman citizenship.

22:28. With a great sum obtained. There were three ways to obtain Roman citizenship: (1) receive it as a reward for some outstanding service to Rome; (2) buy it at a considerable price; (3) be born into a family of Roman citizens. How Paul's father or an earlier ancestor had gained citizenship, no one knows. By 171 BC, a large number of Jews were citizens of Tarsus, and in the time of Pompey (106–48 BC), some of these could have received Roman citizenship as well.

22:29. They departed from him which should have examined him. Paul's Roman citizenship made a great difference. "Should have examined him" does not mean that they were supposed to do so and changed their minds but rather that they "would have examined him" had he not been a Roman citizen. As it was, they had no authority to do so. **The chief captain also was afraid … because he had bound him**. This could have gotten him into trouble if Paul had sought to pursue the matter out of spite. The captain should have ascertained Paul's status before acting. Paul did not take action against the captain, however. It is no part of a Christian's calling to act out of spite or revenge or to be petty toward others, even if he or she has a legal right to do so.

22:30. He loosed him. Paul was no longer bound, and presumably he would have been free completely if the council had not wished to detain him. **The chief priests**. Those of the high-priestly line of descent (mainly Sadducees), but the council now included a considerable number of Pharisees. These men constituted the ruling body of the Jews. The Jewish court was respected by the Roman governor, whose approval had to be obtained before sentencing someone to capital punishment.

23:1. For **the council**, see discussion on 5:21. **Brethren**. Fellow Jews (see discussions on 11:1; 22:1). **Good conscience**. A consistent claim of Paul (see 24:16).

23:2. Ananias. High priest AD 47–59, son of Nebedaeus. He is not to be confused with the high priest Annas (AD 6–15; see discussion on Luke 3:2). Ananias was noted for cruelty and violence. When the revolt against Rome broke out, he was assassinated by his own people. **Them that stood by him**. Apparently a guard detachment, whether of Romans or Jews is not clear. Most likely, they were Jews, since they were under Ananias's authority. That Paul's defense was interrupted and in such a manner indicates that the chances of his getting a fair hearing before this group were impossible.

23:3. Thou whited wall. Whitewashed, having an attractive exterior but filled with unclean contents, such as tombs holding dead bodies (see Matt. 23:27), or walls that look substantial but fall before the winds (see Ezek. 13:10–12). It is a metaphor for a hypocrite. Paul certainly showed courage here. He pointed out that he was being judged under Jewish law but that the command to hit him was contrary to that law. He pointed out both the injustice of the proceeding and the inconsistency between their profession and practice. He also demonstrated his knowledge of and commitment to the law, the very matter under contention.

23:4–5. I wist not (did not realize)**, brethren, that he was the high priest** (v. 5). Paul's failure to recognize the high priest is explained in different ways: (1) He had poor eyesight (suggested by such passages as Gal. 4:15; 6:11) and failed to see that the

one who presided was the high priest. (2) He failed to discern that the one who presided was the high priest because on some occasions others had sat in his place. (3) He was using pure irony: a true high priest would not have given such an order. (4) Having been away from Jerusalem for many years, Paul did not recognize him on sight. Pictures of people were rare in those days, even of public officials other than the emperor.

23:6. Sadducees (v. 6; see discussions on 4:1; Matt. 3:7; Mark 12:18; Luke 20:27). The Sadducees denied the resurrection and angels and spirits (see 23:8). For **Pharisees**, see discussions on Matt. 3:7; Mark 2:16; Luke 5:17. **Of the hope and resurrection of the dead I am called in question**. Since these two groups disagreed on the resurrection, Paul was able to shape the proceedings to his advantage by creating division and confusion among them, getting one group to sympathize with him. That several stories had been told about the specific charge against Paul (see 21:34) only added to the confusion. Paul was not being untruthful in this matter for the sake of his own legal advantage. The resurrection is a central doctrine of Christianity, and the basis on which Christians have this hope is faith in Jesus Christ, not works of the law. To the extent that Paul was on trial because he preached a gospel of grace rather than law, he was there because of the hope of the resurrection from the dead. Paul's strategy worked: the assembly **was divided** (v. 7).

23:8. Luke felt the need to explain to his readers the nature of the disagreement between the Pharisees and the Sadducees. He was writing to a Gentile audience, who would not have been familiar with the distinctions between the Jewish groups.

23:9. Paul was also successful in getting the Pharisees on his side.

23:10. The chief captain (see discussion on 21:31) once again rescued Paul from what threatened to become a mob. Luke often presented the Roman officials as enlightened, sympathetic, and just. To the extent that Luke wanted to commend the gospel to a Gentile audience, the circumstances Paul found himself in were often helpful, as the Gentiles were usually more open to the message and the messenger than the Jews. For **castle**, see discussion on 21:37.

23:11. The Lord stood by him. In times of crisis and need for strength, Paul was given help (see 18:9; 22:18; 27:23). **Jerusalem ... Rome**. One was the spiritual capital of Judaism; the other was the political capital of the Mediterranean world. That the Lord would call Paul to bear testimony in both places affirmed the universality of the gospel. It was for all the world, not just for the Jews. It also points out how God's concerns span both the sacred and the secular. Both realms are under his reign, both realms need to be brought to an awareness of the truth, and both realms evidence the same spiritual needs.

23:12–13. Bound themselves under a curse (v. 12). Under an oath. Probably these Jews were Zealots (see discussion on 21:38), who were later responsible for a revolt against Rome. This was a large group, **more than forty** (v. 13), and was a force to be reckoned with.

23:14–15. The Jews who had vowed to kill Paul did not hide their plot from **the chief priests and elders** (v. 14), who would have been sympathetic to this plan. Their goal was to get rid of Paul, and Roman authority must have seemed an impediment. Bureaucratic procedure can be slow and ponderous, but it protects innocent people from the whims of those who would use power in corrupt ways.

23:16. Paul's sister's son. This is the first time Luke mentioned that Paul had relatives in Jerusalem, but until now, it was not important to his story. How Paul's nephew heard of the plot and how he gained access to Paul is unknown. Perhaps family members were allowed to visit prisoners.

23:17. For **centurions**, see discussion on 10:1. For **the chief captain**, see discussion on 21:31.

23:18–19. By now, **the chief captain** (vv. 18–19) apparently was sympathetic to Paul and more than willing to hear **privately** (v. 19) a message from him. The commander had seen the proceedings before the high priest and could not have been impressed from a legal standpoint.

23:20–21. Paul's nephew provided a succinct account of what was to happen. Once again, this

Roman official is shown to be committed to truth and justice and determined to prevent an injustice from happening under his watch.

23:22. Tell no man. For the boy's own safety and because of the commander's plans to transfer Paul under cover of night (see 23:23).

23:23–24. Soldiers ... horsemen ... spearmen. Heavily armed infantry, cavalry, and lightly armed soldiers. The commander assigned 470 men to protect Paul, the Roman citizen (see 22:25–29). The Greek for "spearmen," however, is an obscure word and could perhaps be translated "additional mounts and pack animals." The numbers indicate that the commander took the threat seriously. The assassination of a Roman citizen in his custody would have been a blot on his record (see Bruce, *The Book of Acts*, p. 433), something that must have been on his mind as well as his desire to see justice done.

23:25. He wrote a letter after this manner. Luke apparently did not quote the letter verbatim but gave the substance of it.

23:26. Cladius Lysias unto. This is the way first-century letters normally began. Whereas today the sender's name is at the bottom of the letter, at that time, the letter began with it.

23:27. Having understood that he was a Roman. The commander inserted this to gain favor with Rome. It was not a true statement, however, because the commander did not learn of Paul's citizenship until he was about to scourge him to gain information.

23:28–29. This is a true statement of what happened. **Accused of questions of their law** (v. 29). This had been the Roman perception of charges against Paul earlier in his ministry (see 18:14–15). **Nothing ... worthy of death or of bonds**. The chief captain pronounced Paul innocent of any charge under Roman law.

23:30. If Paul was not guilty, the captain had to explain why he was holding him and, further, why he was sending him to Caesarea. He apparently believed that the exact accusations against Paul could be better set forth outside the emotionally charged atmosphere of Jerusalem. Many of his less credibile accusers would not want to make the trip, and a fairer hearing would result.

23:31. Antipatris. Rebuilt by Herod the Great and named for his father. It was a military post between Samaria and Judea, thirty miles from Jerusalem.

23:32 – 33. The soldiers did not complete the journey, returning from Antipatris and letting **the horsemen** (v. 32) take him the rest of the way. The main danger was past; they were away from Jerusalem, and Paul's enemies had not yet learned of his departure. Also, the chief captain may have wanted to emphasize that Paul was not at this point charged with any specific crime under Roman law and thus was not a prisoner but rather one under protection. **Cesarea** (v. 33; see discussions on 8:40; 10:1). Twenty-eight miles from Antipatris, Caesarea was the headquarters of Roman rule for Samaria and Judea.

23:34. The governor. Antonius Felix (see 23:26). The emperor Claudius had appointed him governor of Judea circa AD 52, when Felix's brother was the emperor's favorite minister. The brothers had formerly been slaves, then freedmen, then high officials in government. The historian Tacitus said of Felix, "He held the power of a tyrant with the disposition of a slave." Felix married three queens in succession, one of whom was Drusilla (see discussion on 24:24). **Of Cilicia.** If Paul had come from a nearby province, Felix might have turned him over for trial under another's jurisdiction.

23:35. Herod's judgment hall. Erected as a royal residence by Herod the Great but now used as a Roman government center (a praetorium), where official business of the emperor was conducted and/ or personnel directly responsible to the emperor was housed. Praetoria were located in Rome (see Phil. 1:13), Ephesus, Jerusalem (see John 18:28), Caesarea, and other parts of the empire.

2. Paul's Defense in Caesarea (chaps. 24 – 26)

a. Paul before Felix (chap. 24)

24:1. After five days. After the departure from Jerusalem. This would have allowed just enough time for a messenger to go from Caesarea to Jerusalem, the council to appoint their representatives,

and the appointees to journey to Caesarea. **Ananias** (see discussion on 23:2). The high priest made the sixty-mile journey to supervise the case personally. **The elders.** The council was made up of seventy-one elders. The designation was used of both the religious and the political councils (see discussions on Exod. 3:16; 2 Sam. 3:17; Matt. 15:2; *KJV Study Bible* note on Joel 1:2). **Orator.** In a court trial, one trained in forensic rhetoric would serve as an attorney-at-law. **Tertullus.** A common variant of the name Tertius. He possibly was a Roman but more likely was a Hellenistic Jew familiar with the procedures of the Roman court.

24:2 – 3. Great quietness (v. 2) **… with all thankfulness** (v. 3). The expected eulogy with which to introduce a speech before a judge. In his six years in office, Felix had eliminated bands of robbers, thwarted organized assassins, and crushed a movement led by an Egyptian (see discussion on 21:38). In general, however, his record was not good. He was recalled by Rome two years later because of misrule. His reforms and improvements are hard to identify historically.

24:4 – 5. A pestilent fellow … a ringleader of the sect of the Nazarenes (v. 5). In other words, a troublemaker. To excite dissension in the empire was treason against Caesar. To be a leader of a religious sect that did not have Roman approval was contrary to law. "The sect of the Nazarenes" was a term for Christianity.

24:6. Hath gone about to profane the temple. The charge against Paul was now qualified by "an attempt" rather than the former claim (see discussion on 21:28).

24:7. Lysias … with great violence took him away out of our hands. Note the contrast between this account and the one Lysias sent in his letter (see 23:27). Tertullus presented the Jews as having been ready to judge Paul fairly "according to our law" (24:6) and Lysias presented them as having been violent and too swift to act. Felix had Lysias's letter before him, which Tertullus would not have known. The reader has seen both accounts, plus Luke's own account in 21:27 – 36. The significant and perhaps self-serving differences in these accounts could not have been lost on Luke. He intended for his readers to note them as well, surely.

24:8. Commanding his accusers to come unto thee. Tertullus treated it as if Lysias's intent was from the first to send this case to Felix for trial. In fact, the case was sent to Felix only because the Jews were plotting to assassinate Paul, a fact that Tertullus neglected to mention but that Felix knew (see 23:30).

24:9. The Jews also assented. The group, in all likelihood, had gotten their story straight with Tertullus before the proceedings began. When everyone in a group agrees to all the details of a story, one may be certain that it is just that: a story.

24:10. Paul's reserved introduction lacks the flattery that Tertullus employed (see 24:2 – 4).

24:11. Yet but twelve days. Paul answered each accusation. He was not a troublemaker, and he had not been involved in disturbances. He had but recently arrived in Jerusalem. He had spent five days in Caesarea and nearly seven in Jerusalem.

24:14 – 15. After the way … so worship I … God (v. 14). Paul admitted to his part in "the way," (see discussion on 19:23) but he still believed **the law and the prophets**. He shared the same hope as the Jews: resurrection and judgment.

24:16. For **a conscience void of offence**, see discussion on 23:1.

24:17. To bring alms to my nation. This is the only explicit reference in Acts to the collection that was so important to Paul (see discussion on 20:4). **Offerings**. May refer to Paul's help in sponsoring those who were fulfilling their vows (see 21:24). He also may have intended to present offerings for himself. In any case, this was the kind of thing a devout Jew would do and thus helped refute the case made by Paul's accusers (see Talbert, *Reading Acts*, p. 207).

24:18 – 19. Jews from Asia (see 21:27 – 29). Paul is careful to point out that the absence of these Asian Jews suggests that they could not substantiate their accusations. The trial was stacked against him. Paul was not accusing Felix, who would not have known this fact. It did provide a basis for Felix delaying a decision, however (see 24:22).

24:20. Paul was so certain that no solid evidence could be brought against him that he was willing to forgo having his associates brought to testify. He believed that even his accusers could prove nothing that would stand up in court.

24:21. Touching the resurrection. Paul again introduced the point of contention between the Pharisees and Sadducees. His accusers knew that Paul had said this, and he did not dispute it. This issue was of no concern under Roman law.

24:22. Having more perfect knowledge of that way (see discussion on 19:23). Felix could not have governed Judea and Samaria for six years without becoming somewhat familiar with the beliefs and activities of the Christians. Felix intended to question Lysias. Apparently, he considered Lysias's letter a more accurate account of events than Tertullus's but wanted Lysias's testimony officially entered before he rendered a decision.

24:23. Let him have liberty. Perhaps Paul was under house arrest (as he later was while awaiting trial in Rome, see 28:30 – 31), in recognition of the fact that he was a Roman citizen who had not been found guilty of any crime.

24:24. Drusilla. Felix's third wife, daughter of Herod Agrippa I. At age fifteen, she married Azizus, king of Emesa, but deserted him for Felix a year later. Her son, also named Agrippa, died in the eruption of Vesuvius (AD 79). **Heard him concerning the faith in Christ**. Felix had knowledge about Christianity but probably had not heard firsthand about the faith. Having Paul at hand, Felix did not pass up the opportunity to learn more about Christianity.

24:25. He reasoned of righteousness, temperance, and judgment. Paul is again shown as an apologist for the truth. He did not merely quote Scripture, nor did he merely tell of his own and others' experiences. He sought to show why the doctrines of the faith were true and reasonable. **Felix trembled**. Hearing Paul speak of righteousness, self-control, and the judgment, Felix looked at his past life and was filled with fear. He had a spark of sincerity and concern. Paul was persuasive. He did not merely give dry lectures on doctrine. He sought, even as a prisoner, to lead this man to make a personal commitment to Christ. Paul's example should encourage believers today. No one, no matter how high their position, is above the need for the gospel. Nor is anyone so far from God that the word of the truth, persuasively presented, cannot have some effect. **When I have a convenient season**. Lust, pride, greed, and selfish ambition made it continually inconvenient to change.

24:26. Money should have been given him. Felix supposed that Paul had access to considerable funds. He had heard of his bringing an offering to the Jewish Christians in Jerusalem (see 24:17). He wanted Paul to give him money to secure his release. Paul no longer had that money, nor would he have offered a bribe if he did have it.

24:27. Festus came into Felix' room. Festus succeeded Felix. Readers who forget which of these men is first and which is second should remember that they served in this office in alphabetical order. Felix comes before Festus. Felix was recalled to Rome in AD 59/60 to answer for disturbances and irregularities in his rule, such as his handling of riots between Jewish and Syrian inhabitants. Festus is not mentioned in existing historical records before his arrival in Judea. He died in office after two years, but his record for that time shows wisdom and honesty superior to both his predecessor, Felix, and his successor, Albinus. **Willing to shew the Jews a pleasure**. To do them a favor. Felix did not want to incite more anger among the Jews, whom he shortly would be facing in Roman court. To release Paul from prison would have done just that.

b. Paul before Festus (25:1–12)

25:1. From Cesarea to Jerusalem. Sixty miles, a two-day trip. Festus was anxious to go immediately to the center of Jewish rule and worship.

25:2. The high priest and the chief of the Jews. The council (see discussions on 5:21; Mark 14:55). This group was aware that Festus would not have had time for much, if any, briefing on Paul's case. They took advantage of the opportunity to shape his perceptions before he had seen a legal document on the case.

25:3. Laying wait. To ambush Paul. Probably the same group that had earlier made a vow to take Paul's life (see discussion on 23:12).

25:4. Festus wisely discerned that these men had more interest in the case than merely wanting justice done. He decided to do nothing until he had further knowledge of the matter. Once again, Luke took the opportunity to show a Roman official being fair-minded in judging between Christians and their accusers.

25:5. Festus was willing to hear the council's accusations against Paul, but only in a proper setting.

25:6. Sitting in the judgment seat. To make his decision binding as a formal ruling.

25:7. Which they could not prove. Again, as in the first hearing, Paul's adversaries produced no witnesses or evidence of any kind.

25:8. Neither against the law of the Jews ... have I offended. Paul had respect for the law (see Rom. 7:12; 8:3–4; 1 Cor. 9:20). **Against the temple** (see discussions on 21:28–29). Paul had not defied temple customs by taking Trophimus into forbidden areas (see 21:29). Jesus had prophesied the temple's destruction, but He was not responsible for its plight (see Luke 21:5–6). **Against Caesar**. Paul proclaimed the kingdom of God, but not as a political rival of Rome (see 17:6–7). He advocated respect for law and order (see Rom. 13:1–7) and prayer for civil rulers (see 1 Tim. 2:2).

25:9–10. Wilt thou go up to Jerusalem ...? (v. 9). Obviously not. Festus had said that the trial would be before him, so Paul insisted that he was standing in the Roman civil court, where his case should be tried. He wanted to keep his trial there rather than suffer at the hands of a Jewish religious court. As a Roman citizen, he could refuse to go to a local provincial court.

25:11. I refuse not to die. Paul was willing to accept the penalty for any crime he had committed, but he had committed no crime. **I appeal unto Caesar**. Nero had become the emperor by this time. It was the right of every Roman citizen to have his case heard before Caesar himself (or his representative) in Rome. This was the highest court of appeal, and winning such a case could have led to more than just Paul's acquittal; it could have resulted in official recognition of Christianity as distinct from Judaism.

25:12. The council. The officials and legal experts who made up the advisory council for the Roman governor. Since Paul's appeal to Caesar was valid and legal, it was granted.

c. Paul before Agrippa (25:13 – 26:32)

25:13. King Agrippa. Herod Agrippa II. He was seventeen years old at the death of his father in AD 44 (see 12:23). Being too young to succeed his father, he was replaced by Roman procurators. Eight years later, however, a gradual extension of territorial authority began. Ultimately, he ruled over territory north and northeast of the Sea of Galilee, over several cities in Galilee, and over some cities in Perea. During the Jewish revolt, when Jerusalem fell, he was on the side of the Romans. He died circa AD 100, the last of the Herods. **Bernice**. The oldest daughter of Agrippa I, she was sixteen years old at his death. When only thirteen, she married her uncle, Herod of Chalcis, and had two sons. When Herod died, she lived with her brother, Agrippa II. To silence rumors that she was living in incest with her brother, she married Polemon, king of Cilicia, but soon left him to return to Agrippa. She became the mistress of the emperor Vespasian's son Titus but was later ignored by him. **To salute Festus**. To pay their respects. It was customary for rulers to pay a complimentary visit to a new ruler at the time of his assignment. It was advantageous to each that they get along (see Luke 23:6 – 12, which led to a friendship between Herod Antipas and Pilate).

25:14. Many days. Apparently, Agrippa and Festus spent several days celebrating and consulting on matters of mutual concern, perhaps cutting some deals for their mutual benefit. Once the major business had been conducted, Festus wanted to present Paul, perhaps as a kind of entertainment. He was not seeking advice except in the matter of how to word his statement to Nero (see discussion on 25:26). That Paul would be sent to Caesar had already been decided (see 25:12).

25:15 – 18. Festus gave an accurate account of what had happened, pointing out that Paul was guilty of no crime against Rome.

25:19. The only problem Festus could find, like Felix and Gallio (see 18:12 – 16) before him, lay in the matter of religious claims, not Roman law. **Superstition**. Or "religion," the same word used by Paul in 17:22 (see discussion there).

25:20 – 21. Paul would have been foolish to go back to Jerusalem. His appeal to Caesar not only was strategically sound, but it also ended a stalemate situation.

25:22. I would also hear. Agrippa had been wishing to hear Paul (as Antipas had wanted to see Jesus; see Luke 9:9; 23:8).

25:23. The place of hearing. Not the judgment hall, for this was not a court trial. The hearing took place in an auditorium appropriate for the **great pomp** of the occasion, with the king, his sister, the Roman governor, and the outstanding leaders of both the Jews and the Roman government present. **The chief captains** (see discussion on 21:31). Five regiments were stationed at Caesarea, so their five commanders would have been in attendance.

25:24 – 25. Festus made the opening remarks, perhaps introducing Paul to the group. **Nothing worthy of death** (v. 25). Festus mentioned this again, possibly because Jewish officials were present, and he wanted to keep matters crystal clear with them.

25:26. I have no certain thing to write. Festus was required to send Caesar an explicit report on a case when an appeal was made. He hoped for some help from Agrippa in this matter. This was not an official trial but a special hearing to satisfy the curiosity of Agrippa and to provide an assessment for Festus. **Specially before thee, O king Agrippa**. Agrippa would have been sensitive to differences between Pharisees and Sadducees, expectations of the Messiah, differences between Jews and Christians, and Jewish customs pertinent to these problems.

25:27. Unreasonable to send a prisoner, and not … to signify the crimes. Festus wanted to protect his own credibility before Roman officialdom.

26:1. Thou art permitted to speak. Agrippa gave permission for Paul to speak because Festus allowed the king to have charge of the hearing.

26:2. Paul began with the usual courtesies required of one who is speaking to a superior in an official setting.

26:3. Expert in all customs and questions ... among the Jews. As king, Agrippa controlled the temple treasury and the investments of the high priest and could appoint the high priest. The Romans consulted him on religious matters. This was one of the reasons Festus wanted him to assess Paul.

26:4. All the Jews. Paul's assertion here, that all of them knew of his life and religious commitments, seems designed to imply that his accusers had knowingly fabricated the charges against him.

26:5. I lived a Pharisee (see Gal. 1:14). Paul again emphasized this fact, as he had on a previous occasion when it helped his case (see 23:6). Pharisees were zealous in keeping the law, and since Paul was identified with them, it made no sense that he would teach Jewish people to scorn and disobey the law.

26:6. The hope of the promise made of God. Including God's kingdom, the Messiah, and the resurrection (see 26:8). Paul wanted to show that the religious beliefs he now preached were in line with traditional Old Testament teaching. He also may have been harking back to his statement in 23:6, for that had divided the Pharisee and Sadducee camps and gained the support of the Pharisees at that time.

26:7. Paul said that he was **accused of the Jews** for the hope of the promise given to Israel. Once again, Paul presented himself as being on trial for opposing the Jewish faith, yet his teachings were the fulfillment of that faith's promises and teachings.

26:8. Paul had been speaking to Agrippa but at this point must have addressed others as well, such as Festus and the chief captains (see discussions on 21:31; 25:23), who did not believe in the resurrection. Agrippa was allied with the Sadducees, whom he appointed high priests, and was likely to reject both the resurrection of Christ and resurrection in general.

26:9. Paul presented himself as someone who had sincerely believed that opposing Jesus was the right way to uphold Jewish beliefs, just as his accusers believed now. Since Paul had been wrong on this point, so must they be wrong and should see that Paul was the true defender of the hope and promises God gave to Israel, which were fulfilled in Jesus Christ.

26:10. I gave my voice against them. Meaning "I cast my vote against them," since the Greek word translated "voice" literally means "pebble," which was used to vote. This does not necessarily mean that Paul was a member of the Sanhedrin (see discussion on 22:20). He may have been appointed to a special commission to carry out the prosecution of the Jerusalem Christians (see 26:12), where his vote was given.

26:11. Compelled them to blaspheme. Paul tried to force them either to curse Jesus or to confess publicly that Jesus is the Son of God, in which case they could be condemned for blasphemy, a sufficient cause for death (see Matt. 26:63–66).

26:12. As I went to Damascus. Once again, Paul gave an account of his conversion (see 9:1–19; 22:4–21 and discussions).

26:13. At midday. Once again, Paul said his conversion happened around noon (see 22:6).

26:14. For **I heard a voice,** see discussions on 9:7; 22:9. **To kick against the pricks.** A Greek proverb for useless resistance: in kicking the pricks on the goad, the ox succeeds only in hurting itself.

26:15–16. Paul reported that Jesus had called him to be **a minister and a witness** (v. 16) of what he had seen that day on the Damascus road and of things which he would soon learn. In giving this testimony, Paul was fulfilling that calling.

26:17. Unto whom now I send thee. Not only to the Jews but also to the Gentiles (see 22:21; Gal. 1:15–16). Paul's mission was from God (see Gal. 1:1).

26:18. From darkness to light. A figure especially characteristic of Paul (see Rom. 13:12; 2 Cor. 4:6; Eph. 5:8–14; Col. 1:13; 1 Thess. 5:5). **Are sanctified.** Positional sanctification (see *KJV Study Bible* note on 1 Cor. 1:2). This is the most extensive account of what Jesus said to Paul. It differs from previous accounts in Acts. Most likely, Luke, as a master of literary style, knew that this book would include several accounts of this incident. With each retelling, he intentionally provided certain details not given previously, both to maintain the reader's interest and to emphasize different facts that were important at that point in his narrative. Here, because Paul was speaking before a mostly Gentile audience, the details of his call to preach to them were of major importance for his evangelistic purpose, as well as for his defense of his ministry. Bruce (*The Book of Acts*, p. 491) proposes that Paul may have brought together some things the Lord said to him on the road, through Ananias, and later in Jerusalem at the temple. This is not likely, however. Paul heard from Ananias things in line with this passage, but the text indicates that Paul heard this directly from Jesus. Luke was not so much of a literary stylist that he would have changed facts to fit his literary needs.

26:19 – 20. Here Paul's account of his ministry, except for beginning in **Damascus** (v. 20), echo Jesus' words in Acts 1:8: Paul had indeed taken the gospel to **Jerusalem ... the coasts of Judaea, and then to the Gentiles**. His ministry had involved taking the gospel outward from Jerusalem to the Gentiles. His goal was to go "unto the ends of the earth" (13:47), that is, to Spain (see Rom. 15:24, 28, which he had written before coming to Jerusalem). In his overall ministry, Paul had gone "to the Jew first, and also to the Greek" (Rom. 1:16), just as he did in each town he visited. **Repent and turn to God.** Paul knew that his accusers believed, in theory at least, that God's people should obey Him. Paul was pointing out that his preaching was in line with that belief, not contrary to it.

26:21. It was Paul's preaching of Christ that caused the Jews to want to kill him, he said, not desecration of the temple or teaching Jewish believers to denigrate the law. Paul was not trying to confuse matters here. He was looking beyond the false charges against him, to the motivation behind them. Those who had spread false rumors about his preaching opposed Christ, as he once did. His accusers included some believers, but surely they had been led astray by the false accusations of those who opposed Christ. Paul had seen a spiritual truth that is important to remember today. People may and often do oppose Christianity for a multitude of reasons that hold no water. The real problem is spiritual; they oppose the preaching of Christ as the answer to sin. Truly, "men loved darkness rather than light" (John 3:19), and still do to this day.

26:22. The prophets and Moses. The Old Testament Scriptures (see Luke 24:27, 44). Paul reiterated his main defense: he preached only what God Himself had promised Israel, and he pointed people toward these truths rather than away from them.

26:23. The Gentiles (see Isa. 49:6). The prophets and Moses pointed directly to Christ, whom Paul preached, and for which he was on trial. Luke used every opportunity to emphasize that the gospel was intended, even from the days of the prophets, to be preached to the Gentiles as well as the Jews. Luke's purpose, at least in part, was to present Jesus and the gospel as the answer to the spiritual needs not just of the Jews but of the whole world. This guided his selection of material in both his gospel and Acts.

26:24. Thou art beside thyself ... mad (see John 10:20; 1 Cor. 14:23). In other words, "You are out of your mind!" The governor felt that Paul's education and reading of the sacred Scriptures had led him to a mania about prophecy and resurrection.

26:25. Truth and soberness. Paul's assertion, made so clearly, in itself testified that he was not insane or manic.

26:26. Was not done in a corner. The gospel that Paul proclaimed was based on actual events, lived out in historical times and places. The king himself had to attest to the truth of what Paul had affirmed.

26:27. Believest thou the prophets? Paul's question presented King Agrippa with a dilemma. If he said yes, Paul would press him to recognize that their words were fulfilled in Jesus; if he said no, he would be in trouble with the devout Jews, who accepted the message of the prophets as the very word of God. It is altogether proper to press people to make a decision about Christ. Paul was defending himself, but he could not resist such a great opportunity to present Christ as the answer to Agrippa's need as well.

26:28. Almost thou persuadest me to be a Christian. The Greek phrase has the sense of, "You will persuade me to become a Christian by few words" or "in a short time." Agrippa's answer was an evasion of Paul's question and an answer to what he anticipated Paul's next question to be. His point was that he would not be persuaded by such a brief statement. Aggrippa was no different from many today, for whom no amount of proof is enough. Their problem is not intellectual, but spiritual.

26:29. These bonds. Paul was still bound as a prisoner. Paul revealed his heart's desire here. Preaching Christ was more important than his own defense, and he spoke in hope of bringing his audience to faith.

D. Fifth Geographical Expansion of the Gospel: "Into Italy" (chaps. 27–28; see 27:1)

1. Sea Voyage and Shipwreck (chap. 27)

27:1. We should sail. The "we" narrative (see discussion on 16:10) begins again (the last such reference appeared in 21:18). Luke probably had spent the two years of Paul's Caesarean imprisonment nearby, perhaps researching material for his gospel, and now he joined those ready to sail. **Julius, a centurion**. Otherwise unknown. Perhaps he was given the specific duties of an imperial courier, which included delivering prisoners for trial. **Augustus' band**. A Roman band, or cohort, was a military unit composed of 300–600 men. The Roman legions were designated by number, and each of the regiments also had designations (see discussion on 10:1). The identification "Augustan," or "Imperial" (belonging to the empire), was common.

27:2. Adramyttium. A harbor on the west coast of the province of Asia, Adramyttium was southeast of Troas and east of Assos. **By the coasts**. At one of these stops, Julius would have planned to transfer to a ship going to Rome. **Aristarchus** (see 19:29; 20:4). Other New Testament passages (Col. 4:10; Philem. 24) indicate that he was in Rome with Paul later.

27:3. Sidon. About seventy miles north of Caesarea.

27:4. We sailed under Cyprus. They sought the protecting shelter of the island by sailing north on the eastern side of the island, then west along the northern side. **The winds were contrary**. The prevailing winds in summer were westerly.

27:5. Cilicia and Pamphylia. Adjoining provinces on the southern shore of Asia Minor. From Sidon to Myra along this coast would normally be a voyage of ten to fifteen days. **Myra ... of Lycia**. The growing importance of the city of Myra was associated with the development of navigation. Instead of hugging the coast from point to point, more ships were daring to run directly from Alexandria in Egypt to harbors like Myra on the southern coast of Asia Minor. Myra was considerably out of the way on the trip to Rome from Egypt, but the prevailing westerly wind would not allow a direct voyage toward the west. Myra became an important grain-storage city as well.

27:6. A ship of Alexandria. A ship from Egypt (with grain cargo; see 27:38) bound for Rome. Paul and the others could have remained on the first ship and continued up the coast to Macedonia, then taken the land route over the Egnatian Way across Greece and on to Rome, entering Italy at the port of Brundisium. Julius instead chose to change ships, accepting the opportunity of a voyage direct to Rome. Some suggest that Aristarchus from Macedonia stayed with the first ship and went to his home area to tell of Paul's coming imprisonment in Rome. If so, he later joined Paul in Rome (see discussion on 27:2).

27:7. Cnidus. From Myra to Cnidus, at the southwest point of Asia Minor, was about 170 miles. The trip probably took another ten to fifteen days. **Crete**. An island 160 miles long. Rather than cross the open sea to Greece, the ship was forced to bear south, seeking to sail west with the protection of the island of Crete on the north ("under the shelter of Crete"). **Salmone**. A promontory on the northeast point of Crete.

27:8. The fair havens. A port about midway on the southern coast of Crete. **Lasea**. A city about five miles away.

27:9. The fast. The Jewish Day of Atonement fell in the latter part of September or in October. The usual sailing season by Jewish calculation lasted from Pentecost (May – June) to the Feast of Tabernacles, which was five days after the fast. The Romans considered sailing after September 15 doubtful and after November 11 suicidal.

27:10 – 11. Sirs, I perceive (v. 10). Paul was not engaging in predictive prophecy here (in fact, he suggested that their lives were in danger, though all survived the shipwreck that came; see 27:44). He was making an educated guess as an experienced traveler. Those who stood to profit from the voyage rejected his counsel, and the centurion chose to believe them. One who has no personal or financial incentive often can see the truth more clearly than those who are biased due to the possibility of some benefit to themselves.

27:12. Phenice. Also known as Phoenix, a major city of Crete that served as a wintering place, having a harbor with protection against the storms.

27:13. Supposing that they had obtained their purpose. The wind seemed to be good for sailing. Their decision may not have been foolish based on the evidence of the moment.

27:14. Euroclydon. A typhoon-like, east-northeast wind (a "northeaster"), which drove the ship away from their destination.

27:15. We let her drive. Sometimes the safest thing to do, especially in open water, is to allow the ship to go where it will. Fighting a strong wind puts a strain on the rigging and perhaps even on the ship's structure.

27:16. Clauda. An island about twenty-three miles from Crete. This island provided enough shelter to make preparations for the storm. **To come by the boat.** A small boat was being towed behind the ship, and it was interfering with the progress of the ship and with the steering. It may also have been in danger of being crushed against the ship in the wind and the waves. It had to be taken aboard (see 27:17).

27:17. They used helps, undergirding the ship. They used cables, probably placed crosswise, to keep the ship from being broken apart by the storm. **Fall into the quicksands.** A long stretch of desolate banks of quicksand (called Syrtis) along northern Africa off the coast of Tunis and Tripoli. It was still far away, but in such a storm, the ship could be driven a great distance.

27:18. They lightened the ship. By dumping the cargo. They kept some bags of grain, however (see 27:38).

27:19. The tackling of the ship. Spars, planks, and perhaps the yardarm with the mainsail attached. At times, these were dragged behind the ship, serving as a brake.

27:20. All hope that we should be saved was then taken away. Luke meant that they had given up hope. Of course, they were saved in short order (see 27:44), but that was contrary to hope.

27:21. Ye should have hearkened unto me. The crew had lost the cargo from which they had hoped to profit. Paul was not engaging in triumphalism here. The situation hardly warranted such an attitude. He wanted to establish his credibility before making the next statement. They should have listened to Paul's warning (see 27:10). Although they had not done so, Paul had good news for everyone, to which they now should certainly give ear (see 27:22 – 26).

27:22. There shall be no loss of any man's life. Paul's first statement was one of reassurance.

27:23. The angel of God. Paul had received a supernatural visitor from God. **Whose I am, and whom I serve.** The antecedent is "God." Paul belonged to God, and therefore his life was in His hands. If God had a plan for Paul, it would not be derailed by a storm.

27:24. Thou must be brought before Caesar. God had called Paul to go to Rome. Paul was not making this journey because of the legal system or happenstance. God had used the legal system and circumstances, but these served His will. **God hath given thee all them that sail with thee.** God had granted Paul that all those on board would survive also.

27:25. I believe God, that it shall be even as it was told me. Paul most likely was giving testimony to a mixed group of believers and unbelievers. In these circumstances, he was testifying to his faith that God would keep His word. The pagans on board, having given up hope, were ready to believe anyone who could give a confident word from any deity who might help them. Paul, by giving credit to God for their rescue from these circumstances, was engaging in preevangelism here, showing that God rules in all the affairs of life and is to be believed. Those who came through this experience would certainly be more open to hearing the gospel message later on.

27:26. Paul predicted that they would wash ashore **upon a certain island**. It is likely that the angel had told him this as well.

27:27. The fourteenth night. After leaving "The fair havens" (27:8). **In Adria**. That is, in the Adriatic Sea, which lies between Italy, Malta, Crete, and Greece. In ancient times, the Adriatic Sea extended as far south as Sicily and Crete (some think that it included all the area between Greece, Italy, and Africa and that it was known as the Adrian, not the Adriatic, Sea.) Today its extent is considerably reduced. **Deemed that they drew near**. By now, the men were looking for land, as Paul had gained much credibility with them by what he had said. They may have seen birds or noticed a change in the water color, indicating that land was near.

27:28. Sounded. Measured the depth of the sea by letting down a weighted line. The water, they discovered, was getting shallower.

27:29. Fallen upon rocks. With land close, rocks could wreck the ship and drown all of them, only a few feet from land. They could not take that risk.

27:30. The shipmen were about to flee out of the ship. Without a port for the ship, the sailors felt their chance for survival was better in the single lifeboat, unencumbered by the many passengers.

27:31. Except these abide in the ship. If the sailors had been allowed to desert the ship in seeking to save themselves, the passengers would have been unable to beach the ship the following day.

27:32. The soldiers cut off the ropes. Paul's word was heeded, and the soldiers took charge. Most likely, these were the soldiers guarding Paul.

27:33 – 34. Having taken nothing (v. 33). No provisions had been distributed, nor regular meals eaten, since the storm began. It may have been difficult to hold food down in the midst of the storm.

Now they could think about food, and they would need the strength for swimming ashore soon.

27:35. He took bread, and gave thanks to God. Paul gave two good examples: he ate food for physical nourishment and gave thanks to God. To give thanks before a meal was common practice among God's people (see Luke 9:16; 24:30; 1 Tim. 4:4 – 5). Paul did this in the presence of unbelievers as a testimony of God's provision and protection.

27:36. Then were they all of good cheer. Eating lifted everyone's spirits.

27:37. Two hundred threescore and sixteen souls. Noting the number on board may have been necessary in preparation for the distribution of food or perhaps for the coming attempt to get ashore. The number is not extraordinary for the time. Josephus (*Life* 3[15]) refers to a ship that had six hundred aboard. Luke may have noted the number in preparation for the account of all being saved (see 27:44).

27:38. They lightened the ship. They threw overboard the remaining bags of wheat (see 27:18), which had probably been kept for food supply. The lighter the ship, the farther it could sail in to shore.

27:39. Creek … shore. These details are further evidence that Luke was an eyewitness. The experience must have made quite an impression on him.

27:40. Loosed the rudder bands. They loosed the ropes of the rudder to lower the stern rudders into place so the ship could be steered toward the sandy shore. Ancient ships had a steering oar on either side of the stern.

27:41. A place where two seas met. That is, two currents came together, perhaps near the mouth of the creek. A sandbar normally forms at such locations, as each current deposits whatever it is carrying. **They ran the ship aground; and the forepart stuck fast**. Again, all of these details indicate that Luke was an eyewitness.

27:42. The soldiers' counsel was to kill the prisoners. If a prisoner escaped, the life of his guard was taken in his place. The soldiers did not want to risk having a prisoner escape.

27:43. The centurion. Once more, the centurion is to be admired for stopping this plan and trusting the prisoners. Perhaps Paul's testimony had made an impression on him. Also, he may have been aware that no charge under Roman law could be sustained against Paul and that Paul was thus trustworthy.

27:44. They escaped all safe to land. Since the ship was breaking up, remaining on it was not an option. They made their way to shore as best they could. The ship most likely was quite close to land, not more than a hundred feet or so.

2. Ministry in Malta (28:1–10)

28:1. Melita. Also known as Malta. It was included in the province of Sicily and is located fifty-eight miles south of that large island.

28:2. Barbarous people. The Greeks called all non-Greek-speaking people "barbarians." Far from being uncivilized tribesmen, the islanders were Phoenician in ancestry and used a Phoenician dialect but were thoroughly Romanized. **Rain, and ... cold**. It was the end of October or the beginning of November.

28:3. A viper. This snake must have been known to the islanders to be poisonous. That no poisonous snakes live on the island today is not an objection. In two thousand years, the native animals living in a place that is populated but isolated can easily change (see Bruce, *The Book of Acts*, pp. 521–22).

28:4. Vengeance suffereth not to live. The islanders assumed that Paul was getting the justice due him that had not come by way of the sea. The Greeks had a strong understanding of fate.

28:5. Paul, knowing that God had called him to appear before Caesar, was not concerned. This account, however, in no way supports the idea that any Christian can be bitten by a poisonous snake and survive. God would not allow happenstance to short-circuit his special calling for Paul.

28:6. He should have swollen. The usual medical term for inflammation; in the New Testament, it is used only by Luke (see Acts, Introduction: "Author"). **Said that he was a god**. Parallel to the Lystrans' attempt to worship Paul and Barnabas (see 14:11–18).

28:7. The chief man. The "first man" of Melita, a technical term for the top authority. Luke's designa-

tion is accurate here, as elsewhere, even though the Greek term used is not a common one. Other terms Luke used for authorities include "the deputy of the country," or proconsul (Greek, *anthypatos*; 13:7); "magistrates" (Greek, *stratēgos*; 16:20); "the rulers of the city" (Greek, *politarchēs*; 17:6); "the chief of Asia," or Asiarchs (Greek, *Asiarchēs*; 19:31). **Publius**. A Roman name, but his first name rather than his family name. It must have been what the islanders called him.

28:8–9. Publius's father most likely had gastric fever and dysentery (see Bruce, *The Book of Acts*, p. 499). Paul healed him, which opened the door for further healing ministry. Surely this opened the door for preaching the gospel, though Luke did not say so here. It is likely that no church had been planted on the island and that this was the islanders' first exposure to the gospel. This is conjecture, as Luke is silent on these points, but it seems reasonable. The healings authenticated Paul's preaching.

28:10. Many honours. The islanders honored Paul and his companions greatly, out of gratitude for the healings and perhaps for Paul's preaching.

3. Voyage to Rome and Ministry There (28:11–31)

28:11. After three months. Paul and his fellow travelers had to remain on the island until the sailing season opened in late February or early March. Another ship had wisely wintered there and was able to take them on to Rome. **Castor and Pollux**. The two "sons of Zeus" (Greek, *Dioskouroi*), the guardian deities of sailors. Considering the size of the entire party, it may be that only the soldiers and Paul's party made this portion of the journey, their business in Rome being official, and that the rest waited or took other ships.

28:12. Syracuse. The leading city on the island of Sicily, situated on the east coast.

28:13. Rhegium. A town on the coast of Italy, near the southwestern tip and close to the narrowest point of the strait separating that country from Sicily, opposite Messina. Around the promontory north of the town was the whirlpool of Charybdis and the rock of Scylla. Coming from his triumph in Judea, the general Titus landed here on his way to Rome. **Puteoli**. Modern Pozzuoli, almost two hundred miles from Rhegium. It was situated in the northern part of the Bay of Naples and was the chief port of Rome, though seventy-five miles away. The population included Jews as well as Christians.

28:14. To tarry with them seven days. As at Troas (see 20:6) and Tyre (see 21:4), Paul stayed with the believers for one or perhaps two Sundays to observe the keeping of the Lord's Supper and to teach and preach. Either the centurion had business to care for or he was free to delay the journey at Paul's request (see 27:42–43; see also 27:3).

28:15. Appii forum. The market of Appius, which was a small town forty-three miles from Rome and noted for its wickedness. Some Roman Christians came this far to meet Paul. Beyond this point, they could not be certain of the way he would come. **The three taverns**. Or "The Three Inns," a town thirty-three miles from Rome. Other Roman believers met Paul there. The term "inn" was used to designate any kind of shop.

28:16. To dwell by himself. "In his own hired house" (28:30). Paul had committed no flagrant crime and was not a politically dangerous rival, so he was allowed to have his own living quarters. A guard was with him at all times, however, perhaps chained to him (see Eph. 6:20; Phil. 1:13–14, 17; Col. 4:3, 18; Philem. 10, 13).

28:17–19. The chief of the Jews (v. 17). This refers not to one person but rather to all the leading Jews of Rome. The decree of the emperor Claudius (see 18:2) had been allowed to lapse, and Jews had returned to Rome with their leaders. **Brethren**. An epithet that recognized the common Jewish blood Paul shared with them (but see discussion on 11:1). Paul offered a defense of himself and his presence in Rome on two fronts. First, he had not violated Jewish law: **I have committed nothing against the people, or customs of our fathers**. Paul wisely wanted to make this clear to them, in case they had heard otherwise, which as it turned out, they had not (see 28:21). Second, Paul had committed no crime against Rome (v. 18). The unreasonableness of the

Jewish authorities had led to his being **constrained to appeal unto Caesar** (v. 19), which explained his presence in Rome.

28:20. The hope of Israel (see discussion on 26:6). For Paul, the hope of Israel was Jesus Christ, something he would make clear to the Jews in Rome at the appropriate time (see 28:23).

28:21. We neither received letters out of Judea … neither any of the brethren that came shewed or spake any harm of thee. Perhaps Paul's opponents had not traveled to Rome, or they had not considered the matter worth mentioning since it was now a governmental affair. His opponents had been irrationally enraged, and as is human nature, they may have forgotten their rage since the cause was no longer present. Paul had been away from Jerusalem for some time and had not been actively preaching around the Mediterranean world for over two years. Passions had cooled, and no one thought to mention the matter.

28:22. We desire to hear … what thou thinkest. The Jews in Rome were well aware of the dispute over whether Jesus was the Messiah. There were certainly Jewish Christians in Rome at this time, and these leaders had heard them. The opportunity to hear expert testimony from an apostle was not to be passed up, however. They wanted to hear Paul's presentation of the gospel, and he was eager to present it before the arrival of adverse opinions from the Jewish leaders of Jerusalem.

28:23. Persuading them concerning Jesus, both out of the law of Moses, and … the prophets. The Old Testament Scriptures (see Luke 24:27, 44). Here Paul was once again engaged in apologetics. As he had done previously, he reasoned from the Scriptures, showing them what the Old Testament said about the Messiah and that these things point to Christ.

28:24. As so often happens, **some believed … and some believed not**. No evangelist is ever 100 percent effective.

28:25–26. Paul quoted Isaiah 6:9–10 to show that the Jews did not hear the truth concerning Christ, even as it was presented to them.

28:28. The salvation of God is sent unto the Gentiles. The major theme of the book of Acts. The gospel is meant for all. Paul was a chosen vessel to carry the message to Gentiles as well as to Jews. He had such a heart for his Jewish brethren that he often had to remind himself of his call.

28:29. Paul's words created some controversy among the Jews, as well they might. Paul at least had done his duty before God, to bring the gospel to them.

28:30. Two whole years. Paul served the Lord (see 28:31) during the full period of waiting for his accusers to press the trial in Rome.

28:31. Preaching the kingdom of God, and teaching those things which concern the Lord Jesus Christ. This may be related to what Paul told the Ephesian elders. "Preaching the kingdom of God" may be related to "repentance toward God" (20:21). God rules, and sinful men must acknowledge this and repent, submitting themselves to the truth of God. "Teaching those things which concern the Lord Jesus Christ" may be related to "faith toward the Lord Jesus Christ" (20:21). Paul's ministry was consistent. He preached and taught as he always had, that humankind should repent and put their faith in Jesus Christ as their only hope.

Acts ends here, with no word of Paul's fate. There are a number of indications, however, that Paul was released from this imprisonment: (1) Acts abruptly stops here. (2) Paul wrote to churches of his plans to visit them soon, so he must have anticipated a release (see Phil. 2:24; Philem. 22). (3) A number of the details in the Pastoral Epistles do not fit into the historical setting given in the book of Acts. These details indicate that Paul later returned to Asia Minor, Crete, and Greece. (4) Tradition indicates that Paul went to Spain. Even if he did not go, the very fact that a tradition arose suggests a time when he could have taken that journey.

The ending of Acts is not so abrupt as it might seem, however. Luke closed with a summary of Paul's activities during his two years in Rome, and if the trial had not yet taken place, Luke may have thought this was the best stopping point. He had achieved his objective. He had shown, both in doctrine and in history, that salvation by grace alone, through faith alone, is for everyone. The apostles certified this fact in Jerusalem (see chap. 15), and Paul's ministry demonstrated the truth of it as he established churches among the Gentiles. Luke, like any good writer, knew when to stop. The book of Acts, lying between the Gospels and the Epistles, forms a bridge between the historical and doctrinal aspects of this great truth.

THE EPISTLE OF PAUL THE APOSTLE TO THE ROMANS

INTRODUCTION

Author

The writer of this letter was the apostle Paul (see 1:1). No voice from the early church was ever raised against his authorship. The letter contains a number of historical references that agree with known facts of Paul's life. The doctrinal content of the book is typical of Paul, which is evident from a comparison with other letters he wrote.

Date and Place of Composition

The book was probably written in the early spring of AD 57. Very likely, Paul was on his third missionary journey, ready to return to Jerusalem with the offering from the mission churches for poverty-stricken believers in Jerusalem (see 15:25–27). In 15:26, it is suggested that Paul had already received contributions from the churches of Macedonia and Achaia, so he either was at Corinth or had already been there. Since he had not yet been at Corinth (on his third missionary journey) when he wrote 1 Corinthians (see 1 Cor. 16:1–4) and the collection issue had still not been resolved when he wrote 2 Corinthians (2 Cor. 8–9), the writing of Romans must have followed that of 1–2 Corinthians (dated ca. AD 55).

The most likely place of composition is either Corinth or Cenchrea (about six miles away) because of references to Phebe of Cenchrea (16:1) and to Gaius, Paul's host (16:23), who was probably a Corinthian (see 1 Cor. 1:14). Erastus (16:23) may also have been a Corinthian (see 2 Tim. 4:20).

Recipients

The original recipients of the letter were the people of the church at Rome (1:7), who were predominantly Gentile. Jews, however, must have constituted a substantial minority of the congregation (see 4:1; chaps. 9–11; see also discussion on 1:13). Perhaps Paul originally sent the entire letter to the Roman church, after which he or someone else used a shorter form (chaps. 1–14 or 1–15) for more general distribution (see discussion on 2 Peter 3:15).

Background

When Paul wrote this letter, he was probably at Corinth (see Acts 20:2–3) on his third missionary journey. His work in the eastern Mediterranean was almost finished (see 15:18–23), and he greatly desired to visit the Roman church (see 1:11–12; 15:23–24). At this time, however, he could not go to Rome because he felt he must personally deliver the collection taken among the Gentile churches for the poverty-stricken Christians of Jerusalem (see 15:25–28). So instead of going to Rome, he sent a letter to prepare the Christians there for his intended visit in connection with a mission to Spain (see 15:23–24). For many years, Paul had wanted to visit Rome to minister there (see 1:13–15), and this letter served as a careful and systematic theological introduction to that hoped-for personal ministry. Since he was not acquainted directly with the Roman church, he said little about its problems (but see 14:1–15:13; see also 13:1–7; 16:17–18).

Paul's purposes for writing this letter were varied. (1) He wrote to prepare the way for his coming visit to Rome and his proposed mission to Spain (see 1:10–15; 15:22–29). (2) He wrote to present the basic system of salvation to a church that had not received the teaching of an apostle before. (3) He sought to explain the relationship between Jew and Gentile in God's overall plan of redemption. The Jewish Christians were being rejected by the larger Gentile group in the church (see 14:1) because the Jewish believers still felt constrained to observe dietary laws and sacred days (see 14:2–6).

Theme and Theological Message

Paul's primary theme in Romans is the basic gospel, God's plan of salvation and righteousness for all mankind, Jew and Gentile alike (see 1:16–17). Although some have suggested justification by faith as the theme, it would seem that a broader theme states the message of the book more adequately. "The Righteousness of God" (1:17) includes justification by faith but also embraces such related ideas as guilt, sanctification, and security.

Paul began the letter by surveying the spiritual condition of all mankind. He found Jews and Gentiles alike to be sinners and in need of salvation. That salvation has been provided by God through Jesus Christ and His redemptive work on the cross. It is a provision, however, that must be received by faith—a principle by which God has always dealt with mankind, as the example of Abraham shows. Since salvation is only the beginning of Christian experience, Paul moved on to show how the believer is freed from sin, the law, and death—a provision made possible by his union with Christ in both death and resurrection and by the indwelling presence and power of the Holy Spirit. Paul then showed that Israel too, though presently in a state of unbelief, has a place in God's sovereign redemptive plan. Now she consists of only a remnant, allowing for the conversion of the Gentiles, but the time will come when "all Israel shall be saved" (11:26). The letter concludes with an appeal to the readers to work out their Christian faith in practical ways, both in the church and in the world. None of Paul's other letters states so profoundly the content of the gospel and its implications for both the present and the future.

Literary Features

The letter displays several notable literary features. (1) It is the most systematic of Paul's letters, reading more like an elaborate theological essay than a letter. (2) The emphasis is on Christian doctrine. The number and importance of the theological themes Paul touched on are impressive: sin, salvation, grace, faith, righteousness, justification, sanctification, redemption, death, resurrection, and glorification. (3) Paul used a large number of Old Testament quotations. Although he regularly quoted from the Old Testament in his letters, in Romans, the argument is sometimes carried along by the quotations (see especially chaps. 9–11). (4) The letter displays Paul's deep concern for Israel. He wrote about her present status, her relationship to the Gentiles, and her final salvation.

Outline

Bibliography

Barrett, C. K. *A Commentary on the Epistle to the Romans.* New York: Harper & Row, 1957.

Black, Matthew. *Romans.* New Century Bible. Grand Rapids, MI: Eerdmans, 1981.

Bruce, F. F. *The Epistle of Paul to the Romans.* Tyndale New Testament Commentaries 6. Grand Rapids, MI: Eerdmans, 1963.

Cranfield, C. E. B. *A Critical and Exegetical Commentary on the Epistle to the Romans.* 2 vols. Edinburgh: T&T Clark, 1979.

Luther, Martin. *Luther: Lectures on Romans.* Edited and translated by Wilhelm Pauck. Philadelphia: Westminster, 1961.

Moo, Douglas J. *Romans.* The NIV Application Commentary. Grand Rapids, MI: Zondervan, 2000.

Morris, Leon. *The Epistle to the Romans.* Pillar New Testament Commentary. Grand Rapids, MI: Eerdmans, 1988.

Mounce, Robert H. *Romans.* The New American Commentary 27. Nashville: Broadman & Holman, 1995.

Murray, John. *The Epistle to the Romans.* The New International Commentary on the New Testament. Grand Rapids, MI: Eerdmans, 1965.

Stott, John. *Romans.* Downers Grove, IL: InterVarsity Press, 1994.

EXPOSITION

I. Introduction (1:1–15)

1:1. Paul. In ancient times, writers put their names at the beginning of letters. For more information on Paul, see discussions on Acts 9:1; Philippians 3:4–14. The Greek for **servant** means (1) a "slave," who completely belongs to his owner and has no freedom to leave, and (2) a "servant," who willingly chooses to serve his master (see discussions on Psalm 18 superscription; Isa. 41:8–9; 42:1; *Zondervan KJV Study Bible* note on Exod. 14:31). **An apostle** is one specially commissioned by Christ (see discussions on Mark 6:30; 1 Cor. 1:1; Heb. 3:1). **Gospel** (Greek, *euangelion*), in general, refers to "good news" as proclamation. Here its content concerns God's Son (see 1:3, 9; see also 15:16, 19). "Gospel" occurs sixty times in Paul's writings (see discussion on Mark 1:1).

1:2. His prophets are not just the writers of the prophetic books, for the whole Old Testament prophesied about Jesus (see Luke 24:27, 44). **Holy scriptures** refers to the Old Testament.

1:3–4. God's promised gospel (see 1:1–2) proclaims **his Son** (v. 3). Christ's supernatural status as God's Son is given historical dimension with the addition of two balanced clauses that correspond to and amplify His title, **Jesus Christ our Lord**. As "Christ" (Messiah), He was descended from David (**the seed of David**). As "Lord," He was **declared to be the Son of God with power** (v. 4). The one is **according to the flesh** (v. 3), which reveals His title "Christ" through His messianic birth. The other is **according to the Spirit of holiness** (v. 4), which ratifies His title to "Lord" through His **resurrection from the dead**. Both belong to history and both redound to His proclamation in the gospel of God. The continuum of these two verses and these two historical touchstones not only spans the birth, ministry, death, and resurrection of Jesus but, through His sonship, reaches back into eternity past and ahead into the eternal present and the glorious reign of Christ our Lord.

1:5–6. By whom (v. 5) refers to the Son, who now, in view of 1:2–3 and especially His resurrection, mediates **grace and apostleship**. These two words summarize Paul's mission and authority. As an apostle (see 1:1), Paul belonged to the grand scope of the gospel of God (see 1:1–4) and its objective, **obedience to the faith**, which is both global (**all nations**) and local (**ye also**; v. 6).

1:7. According to the conventional salutation of a first-century letter, Paul, after a digression on the gospel of God (1:2–4) and its relation to him and the recipients (1:5–6), completed the normal X-to-Y salutation, begun in 1:1, by naming the recipients with a greeting. **All that be in Rome,** (who are) **beloved of God** specifies the Christians of the imperial city. The basic idea of the Greek word for **saints** is "holiness." All Christians are saints in that they are positionally "set apart" to God and are experientially being made increasingly "holy" by the Holy Spirit (see *KJV Study Bible* note on 1 Cor. 1:2). For **Grace,** see discussions on Jonah 4:2; Galatians 1:3; Ephesians 1:2. For **peace,** see discussions on John 14:27; 20:19; Galatians 1:3; Ephesians 1:2.

1:8. I thank my God characteristically opens the "thanksgiving" with which Paul regularly began his letters (see 1 Cor. 1:4; Eph. 1:16; Phil. 1:3; Col. 1:3; 1 Thess. 1:2; 2 Thess. 1:3; 2 Tim. 1:3; Philemon 4), following his salutation and greeting. **Through Jesus Christ** points to the New Testament theology of prayer. Christians must go through Christ not only for requests to God (see John 15:16) but also to give thanks. **Throughout the whole world** refers to every place where the gospel had been preached.

1:9–10. The word for **serve** (Greek, *latreuō*; v. 9) has a rich background in sacred and priestly service (see Heb. 9:9; 10:2). For Paul, such dutiful service was spiritual (**with my spirit**); that is, he carried out his service not in a physical temple but in his heart, wherever he went. **The gospel of his Son** is the same as "the gospel of God" (1:1; see 15:16, 19). Paul alluded to God's watchful eye and His ability to bear witness to Paul's service on behalf of the Christians in Rome, for whom he interceded through prayer, just as a priest serves before God on behalf of His people. The extension of Paul's prayerful service was to serve the Roman Christians in person (**to come unto you**; v. 10).

1:11–12. Paul stated that he wished to visit the church in Rome, **that I may impart ... some spiritual gift** (v. 11); that is, he wished "to share" some of his gifts of the Spirit. Paul was an apostle, but more important, he saw himself as an instrument of the Holy Spirit. "Spiritual gift" occurs only here in Paul's letters and was probably used here because he had not yet visited the Romans in person and did not want them to misunderstand the "gift" that he intended to bring them. In chapter 12, Paul taught about "spiritual gifts." Here he states what is fundamental to all of his teaching on the gifts of the Spirit: their purpose is that **you may be established**, to "strengthen" the church. **Together** (v. 12) points out that the work of the Spirit and the mutual exercise of the Spirit's gifts can be anticipated among God's people even when the gifts have yet to be labeled and taught as such. Paul's genuine humility is seen in his desire to be ministered to by the believers at Rome as well as to minister to them.

1:13. Fruit refers to new converts as well as the spiritual growth of those already converted. **Among you ... among other Gentiles** suggests that the church at Rome was predominantly Gentile.

1:14. The Greeks identifies those Gentiles who spoke Greek or followed the Greek way of life, even though they may have been Latin-speaking citizens of the Roman Empire. A further specification of the Gentiles to whom Paul ministered is found in the word **barbarians.** The word is onomatopoetic; it sounds out the bar-bar-bar of non-Greek languages that was unintelligible to Greek ears.

II. Theme: The Righteousness of God (1:16–17)

1:16–17. The theme of the entire book of Romans is found in these two verses.

1:16. Paul was **not ashamed of the gospel** anywhere or at anytime, not even in the capital city of the Roman Empire (see 1:15; for "gospel," see 1:1 and discussion on Mark 1:1). Paul knew of a power to deliver that eclipsed that of Rome. **The power** (Greek, *dynamis*) **of God** (see 1 Cor. 1:18 for the same expression) effects **salvation** for those who believe and reveals "the righteousness of God" (1:17). The Jews come **first** not only in time but also in privilege. "Salvation is of the Jews" (John 4:22), and the Messiah was a Jew. "The oracles of God" (3:2), the covenants, law, temple worship, revelation of the divine glory, and messianic prophecies came to them (see 9:3–5). These privileges, however, were not extended to the Jews because of their superior merit or because of God's partiality toward them. It was necessary that the invasion of this world by the gospel begin at a particular point with a particular people, who in turn were responsible for carrying that gospel to the other nations.

1:17. The righteousness of God points to "a righteousness from God," the state of being "in the right" in relation to God (see discussions on 2:13; 3:21, 24) as well as to "the righteousness of God" (see 3:5, 25–26; 10:3), which is foundational in Romans. The gift must not be separated from the Giver of the gift. Paul's understanding of God's righteousness is informed by the Old Testament, in which God's righteousness is related to His covenant faithfulness and demonstrated in His acts to deliver and save. The words **from faith to faith** and the citation of Habakkuk 2:4 (**The just shall live by faith**; see discussion on Gal. 3:11) point to the two dimensions—righteousness of God and righteousness from God—revealed in the gospel.

III. The Unrighteousness of All Mankind (1:18–3:20)

1:18–3:20. In developing the theme of righteousness from God (see 1:17; 3:21–5:21), Paul set the stage by showing that all have sinned and therefore need the righteousness that only God can provide. He discussed the sin of the Gentiles (1:18–32) and the sin of the Jews (2:1–3:8) and then summarized the sin of all, Gentile and Jew alike (3:9–20).

A. Gentiles (1:18–32)

1:18–20. No one, not even one who has not heard of the Bible or of Christ, has an excuse for not honoring God, because the whole created world reveals Him.

1:18. The wrath of God is not a petulant, irrational burst of anger, such as humans often exhibit, but a holy, just revulsion of what opposes and is contrary to His holy nature and will. God's wrath is not limited to the end-time judgment of the wicked (see 1 Thess. 1:10; Rev. 19:15; 20:11–15), as the words **is revealed** make clear. Here the wrath of God is His abandonment of the wicked to their sins (see 1:24–32). **The truth** is the truth about God that is revealed in the creation order.

1:19–21. God can be acknowledged and known through general revelation, that is, from seeing His revelation in creation (vv. 19–20), as Paul attested with the words **they knew God** (v. 21). Since general revelation is not redemptive, as is God's special revelation distinguished in Scripture, what people know of God through creation is **his eternal power and Godhead** ("deity"; v. 20). **Understood** implies not only the perception but its inference or conclusion. Thus, all people **are without excuse** before the witness of creation if they have not **glorified him** (v. 21) as God. In other words, they had not suitably and properly honored and extolled the divine benefactor for what was understood through creation as divine benefaction. That these people were idolaters (see 1:23) and knew God only through the creation order indicates that they were Gentiles. **Thankful** expresses recognition and gratitude for earthly blessings, such as sun, rain, and crops (see Matt. 5:45; Acts 14:17).

1:22–23. Professing themselves to be wise (v. 22), those who fail to acknowledge God assert their own superiority. When God is the rival, the folly is most calamitous. **Glory** (v. 23) refers to God's unique majesty (see Isa. 48:11), which fallen mankind lost sight of and for which the idolators had substituted deities of their own devising, patterned after various creatures.

1:24. Wherefore, or "For this reason," connects God's reaction to the base behavior described in 1:22–23. Like a bell toll, the refrain **God ... gave them up** (see 1:26), or "God gave them over" (1:28), declares that God allowed sin to run its course as an act of judgment. Here God gave them over **to uncleanness,** with the consequence that **through**

the lusts of their own hearts ... they dishonoured **their own bodies between themselves**. Inasmuch as God was not glorified (see 1:21) but dishonored (see 1:23), Paul portrayed their consequential and commensurate dishonoring of one another. This perversion is spelled out in 1:25–27.

1:25. The idolaters' "exchange" of 1:23 is here fathomed succinctly. **Who** has the sense of "They actually" (Cranfield, *Epistle to the Romans*, p. 123). **The truth of God** refers not only to the truth about God and His self-revelation but to the truth about all things. The **lie**, the worship of creation, is a perversion of the truth, an absurdity of idolatry. **Amen** can mean either "Yes indeed, it is so" or "So be it" (see 9:5; 11:36; 15:33; 16:27; see also *KJV Study Bible* note on Deut. 27:15; 1 Kings 1:36).

1:26–27. For the refrain **God ... gave them up** (v. 26), see discussion on 1:24. **Their women** is a gender reference that refers to females generally, not necessarily their wives, even as **men** (v. 27) refers to males. Interpreters have suggested that the order of Paul's treatment, females before males, was for emphasis on the male perversion. **Likewise** makes it clear that the unnatural sexual relations of the males applied also to the females. Homosexual practice is sinful in God's eyes. The Old Testament condemns the practice (see Lev. 18:22). **Receiving in themselves that recompence of their error** explains that the punishment matched the offense.

1:28–31. Not ... retain God in their knowledge (v. 28; see 1:19, 21) is tantamount to a restatement of 1:22–23, 25, and here summarizes human rejection of God and refusal to acknowledge God. **God gave them over** is the third time (see 1:24, 26, 28) God's response is described as the judgment of abandonment. Paul made the correlation clear through a wordplay. They did not "retain God," or "find Him fit" (Greek, *dokimazō*), so God "gave them over" to **a reprobate** ("an unfit"; Greek, *adokimos*) **mind**. The intent preceded the act (see 1:21; Mark 7:20–23).

The "reprobate mind" that has rejected the knowledge of God has engaged in an exchange (see 1:23, 25). Empty of the knowledge of God, the reprobate mind is filled with **things which are not con-**

venient (v. 28), or "unfitting," meaning "not proper" or "morally wrong." The word has a rich history as a technical ethical term among the Stoics. For people with such a mind, Paul grammatically divides the list of their vices into three categories: (1) they are **filled with all unrighteousness, fornication, wickedness, covetousness, maliciousness** (v. 29); (2) they are **full of envy, murder, debate, deceit, malignity, whisperers**; (3) they are **backbiters, haters of God, despiteful, proud, boasters, inventors of evil things, disobedient to parents** (v. 30), **without understanding, covenantbreakers, without natural affection, implacable, unmerciful** (v. 31). This is the fullest and most detailed list of vices of all of Paul's "sin lists" (see Rom. 13:13; 1 Cor. 5:10–11; 6:9–10; 2 Cor. 12:20–21; Gal. 5:19–21; Eph. 4:31; 5:3–5; Col. 3:5–8; 1 Tim. 1:9–10; 2 Tim. 3:2–6; Titus 3:3).

1:32. Although they rejected the knowledge of God, the people described in 1:28–31 were not void of **knowing**. Their outrageous conduct was not due to total ignorance of what God required but rather due to self-will and rebellion. **Have pleasure in them that do them** points to a culture and pattern of attitude and action that glories not in God but in what is shameful. The extreme of sin is applauding, rather than regretting, the sins of others.

B. Jews (2:1–3:8)

2:1–16. In this section, Paul set forth principles that govern God's judgment. God judges (1) "according to truth" (v. 2), (2) "according to ... deeds" (v. 6–11), and (3) according to the light a person has (vv. 12–15). These principles laid the groundwork for Paul's discussion of the guilt of the Jews (2:17–29).

2:1. Inexcusable. Paul's teaching about judging agrees with that of Jesus (see discussion on Matt. 7:1), who did not condemn judging as such, but hypocritical judging. **Whosoever ... that judgest** posed a warning that had relevance for any moralist but special relevance for Jews. They were inclined to look down on Gentiles because of their ignorance of God's revelation in the Old Testament and because of their immoral lives.

2:2. Paul frequently used the expression **We are sure** (lit., "We know"), which assumed the persons addressed agreed with the statement that followed (see 3:19; 7:14; 8:22, 28; 1 Cor. 8:1, 4; 2 Cor. 5:1; 1 Tim. 1:8). **According to truth** means that justice is impartial and that God is no respecter of persons (see 2:11), either outward appearance or national origin. This theme is spelled out in 2:3 – 11.

2:3. Jesus also condemned this attitude (see Matt. 7:3; see Luke 18:9). It is the height of perverted miscalculation to presume on the judgment of God.

2:4. The purpose of God's kindness is to give opportunity for **repentance** (see 2 Peter 3:9). The Jews had misconstrued His patience to be a lack of intent to judge. **Despisest** conveys the sense of looking down with contempt, but the Greek word can also convey disregard and presumption. In this context, **not knowing** comes closer to the sense of "ignoring" rather than "ignorant."

2:5. The day of wrath, or judgment, at the end of time stands in contrast to the judgment discussed in 1:18 – 32.

2:6 – 8. God is impartial in His judgment (see 2:2, 11) and **will render to every man according to his deeds** (v. 6; see Ps. 62:12; Prov. 24:1). Paul was not contradicting his continual emphasis in all his writings, including Romans, that a person is saved not by what he does but by faith in what Christ does for him. Rather, he was discussing the principle of judgment "according to … deeds" (see discussion on 2:1 – 16). If anyone persists in doing good deeds (i.e., lives a perfect life), he will receive eternal life. No one can do this (see 3:10 – 12), but if anyone could, God would give him life, because God judges according to what a person does.

2:9. Every soul … that doeth evil makes it clear that there is no exemption (see 3:9 – 10), although there is an order: **the Jew first**. With spiritual privilege comes spiritual responsibility (see Amos 3:2; Luke 12:48).

2:11. There is no respect of persons with God is a basic teaching of both the Old Testament and the New Testament (see Deut. 1:17; 10:17; 16:19; 2 Chron. 19:7; Prov. 24:23; 28:21; Eph. 6:9; Col. 3:25;

James 2:1; Acts 10:34). "Respect of persons," or partiality (Greek, *prosōpolēmpsia*; "accept face"), is defined quite literally in Galatians 2:6: "God accepteth no man's person [face]." The Lord does not evaluate any person on the basis of "face" (one's pedigree or credentials).

2:12. For as many as have sinned without law refers to Gentiles ("law" refers to the Mosaic law). God judges according to the light available to people. Gentiles will not be condemned for not obeying a law they did not possess. Their judgment will be on other grounds (see 1:18 – 20; 2:15; Amos 1:3 – 2:3).

2:13. In a courtroom, the word **justified**, or "declared righteous," represents the verdict of a judge over the accused. **The doers of the law** are vindicated. Knowledge alone (**the hearers of the law**) is not enough. Paul was setting forth a general principle that Roman hearers, with their sense of justice, could readily appreciate. This principle is the basis of God's pronouncement of acquittal on judgment day (see discussion on 3:24).

2:14 – 15. By nature (v. 14) suggests an inner moral code, **written in their hearts** (v. 15), ratified by **their conscience**, and reflected in **their thoughts**, apart from the external constraint of the law written on tablets, the Mosaic law revealed specifically to Israel. It must be kept in view, however, that **things contained in the law** (v. 14) does not mean that pagans fulfilled the requirements of the Mosaic law. Rather, it refers to practices in pagan society that agreed with the law, such as caring for the sick and elderly, honoring parents, and condemning adultery. **A law unto themselves** also speaks of the moral nature of pagans, enlightened by "their conscience" (v. 15), which functioned for them as the Mosaic law did for the Jews.

2:16. God shall judge all people by the standard of **Jesus Christ**. This verse picks up Paul's thought from 2:12; the material in 2:13 – 15 is parenthetical in Paul's argument.

2:17 – 24. Here the presentation takes the form of a dialogue. Paul knew how a self-righteous Jew thought, for he had been one himself. He cited one advantage after another that Jews considered to be unqualified assets. Those assets became liabilities, however, when profession and practice did not correspond. Paul applied to the Jew the principles of judgment set forth in 2:1–16 (see discussion there).

2:19–20. The blind (v. 19) and **babes** (v. 20) are descriptives of a superior to an inferior. Although Paul sought to chagrin the elitist, not shame the insulted, one may see the Jewish outlook on the Gentiles, to whom Jews regarded themselves as vastly superior because they (the Jews) possessed the Mosaic law.

2:21–24. These verses present several pictures of hypocrisy, double standards, and partiality. **Dost thou commit sacrilege?** (v. 22) is literally, "Dost thou rob temples?" (see Acts 19:37). Large amounts of wealth were often stored in pagan temples. **Makest thy boast** (v. 23) is a case of bragging about the law and at the same time bringing the Giver of the law into disrepute by breaking the law. As Paul's quotation in verse 24 (from Ezek. 36:20, 22; Isa. 52:5) suggests, it would not be the first time that the Jews had given the Gentiles cause to blaspheme God.

2:25. Circumcision was a sign of the covenant that God made with Israel (see Lev. 12:3) and a pledge of the covenant blessing (see Genesis 17 and discussions on Gen. 17:10–11). The Jews had come to regard circumcision as a guarantee of God's favor.

2:26–27. If a Gentile's deeds excelled those of a Jew in righteousness, that very fact condemned the Jew, who had an immeasurably better set of standards in the law of Moses.

2:28–29. That which is **inwardly … in the spirit … of God** (v. 29), in contrast to that which is **outwardly** (v. 28), points to the authenticity of what is subject to God alone as opposed to the partiality of human standards. The true sign of belonging to God is not an outward mark on the physical body but the regenerating power of the Holy Spirit within, which is what Paul meant by **circumcision … of the heart** (v. 29; see Deut. 30:6).

3:1–2. Paul raised two rhetorical questions. He knew the answers and wanted to explain the advantage of the Jew (see 1:16; 2:9–10) more fully in view of what he had just written about them (see

2:17–29). **Chiefly** (v. 2). Paul did not discuss the other advantages of being a Jew until 9:4–5. He used the word **committed** because the advantage of having the very words of God involves a duty. Indeed, the Jews were guilty of infidelity to their greatest treasure, **the oracles of God**, that is, the Word of God, with particular emphasis on His promises. Overall, Paul was arguing that God had been faithful to the oracles, whereas the Jews had not.

3:3. Here **the faith of God** means "faithfulness." The Greek word means either "faith" or "faithfulness." God is faithful to His promises and would punish Israel for its unbelief (see 3:5; 2 Tim. 2:13). Also, although not at this point, Paul will argue in 3:31 that God's faithfulness is preeminently demonstrated in the gospel, in the deliverance of His Son, Jesus Christ.

3:4. God's punishment of sin exhibits His faithfulness to His righteous character.

3:5. By contrast, human **unrighteousness [can] commend the righteousness of God**, in showing it up against the dark background of man's sin. **I speak as a man** was Paul's way of saying, "I am using a human argument," implying its weakness and absurdity.

3:6. God will **judge the world** on judgment day. Here "the world" identifies all moral creatures (also in 3:19) and is a more limited reference than in 1:20.

C. Summary: All People (3:9–20)

3:7–8. Again, although not expressly labeled as a "human argument" (3:5), Paul posed a monstrous proposition in the form of a question to further address God's just condemnation of sin.

3:9. Are we better than they? Are Jews better than Gentiles in the sight of God? Paul's answer was inclusive: **all [are] under sin**, its power and condemnation. Nine times in four verses (3:9–12), Paul declared the universality of sin ("all," twice; "none," four times; "not even one," twice; "together," once).

3:10–18. Paul used this collection of Old Testament quotations to underscore his charge that both Jews and Gentiles are under the power of sin. Several factors explain why the citations are not always verbatim: (1) New Testament quotations sometimes gave the general sense and were not meant to be word for word. (2) Quotation marks were not used in Greek. (3) The quotations were often taken from the Greek translation (the Septuagint) of the Hebrew Old Testament, because Greek readers were not familiar with the Hebrew Bible. (4) Sometimes the New Testament writer, under the inspiration of the Holy Spirit, would purposely adapt an Old Testament passage or combine two or more passages to drive home a point.

3:10–12. In these three verses, Paul set forth the universal indictment of humanity. In logic, the statements are comprehensive, with a universal affirmative, **all** (the totality; v. 12), punctuating a series of universal negatives, "none." **None that understandeth** (v. 11) refers to the failed equation of the perception and that which is perceived, here of God and what is right. **They are all gone out of the way** (v. 12) speaks of "turning away" from seeking God's interests (v. 11) and, as a result, becoming depraved or morally **unprofitable** ("corrupted" or "broken"; v. 12).

3:13–18. In these verses, the depth of human depravity is described in terms of human anatomy: **throat** (v. 13), **tongues, lips, mouth** (v. 14), **feet** (v. 15), and **eyes** (v. 18). **Their throat is an open sepulcher** (v. 13) expresses the corruption of the heart. **Before their eyes** is a cipher for mental and spiritual understanding in which **There is no fear of God** (v. 18). This important Old Testament expression refers to an awesome reverence for God, who is the source of all godliness (see discussion on Gen. 20:11). Fundamentally, what people fear, aside from the emotional associations that predominate contemporary understanding, is that which people give priority. What one fears is what commands one's attention and respect. In the Old Testament, the "fear of God" denotes the positive preeminence that His lordship should receive.

3:19–20. The issue of the advantage of the Jew, which Paul raised at the outset of this chapter, here comes back into focus. In short, **the law** (and circumcision, which binds one to the law; v. 19) does not deliver the Jew from sin. The law ratifies the existence of sin by identifying it and condemning its presence. Here "the law" refers to the Old Testament (as in John 10:34; 15:25; 1 Cor. 14:21). For **we know**, see discussion on 2:2. **Them who are under the law** are the Jews. **Every mouth ... and all the world** is profound, because if the Jews are not vindicated by the law but are in fact indicted by it, Jews as well as Gentiles are guilty. For **justified**, see discussions on 3:24; 2:13. To conclude his argument, Paul drew on Psalm 143:2: "For in thy sight shall no man living be justified." Interestingly, in the preceding verse, the psalmist prayed for and anticipated deliverance, by appealing to God's "faithfulness" and "righteousness" (Ps. 143:1). That is, although the psalmist did not deserve it, he appealed to God's covenant virtues, believing that God would do what he did not warrant. Although not expressly stated by Paul, the twin virtues of God's character and subjects of dispute in 3:3, 7, come forward in 3:21–22 as Paul addresses "the righteousness of God" and "faith ['faithfulness,' as in 3:3] of Jesus Christ" (3:22) expressing apart from the law a deliverance through Christ that is unwarranted by human unrighteousness.

IV. Righteousness Imputed: Justification (3:21–5:21)

A. Through Christ (3:21–26)

3:21–5:21. Having shown that all (both Gentiles and Jews) are unrighteous (1:18–3:20), Paul went on to show that God has provided a righteousness for mankind.

3:21. The words **But now** offer two possible meanings: (1) temporal—all of time is divided into two periods, and in the "now" period, **the righteousness of God** has been made known; (2) logical—the contrast is between the righteousness gained by observing the law (which is impossible; see 3:20) and the righteousness provided by God. For **witnessed by the law and the prophets**, see Genesis 15:6; Psalm 32:1–2; Habbakuk 2:4.

3:22–23. For there is no difference (v. 22) **... all have sinned, and come short of the glory of God** (v. 23) is a parenthetical thought. Thus, **all them that believe** (v. 22) are "justified freely" (3:24), not "all have sinned" (v. 23) are "justified freely" (3:24); "justified" goes with "believe," not with "sinned." "No difference" (v. 22) targets the equal standing of Jews and Gentiles (see 10:12). "All have sinned" (v. 23) is literally defined in the words "come short of." The Greek word that Paul used for "sinned" (a form of the verb *hamartanō*) is the same word that the Greek historian Xenophon (*Anabasis* 1.v.12) used in a scene in which an axe was hurled and missed its target. In other words, it fell short. "The glory of God" includes what God intended man to be. The glory that man had before the fall (see Gen. 1:26–28; Ps. 8:5–6; Eph. 4:24; Col. 3:10) the believer will again have through Christ (see Heb. 2:5–9).

3:24. Justified was a significant term for Paul. He used the Greek verb for "justified" twenty-seven times in his letters, mostly in Romans and Galatians. The term describes what happens when someone believes in Christ as his Savior: from the negative viewpoint, God declares the person to be not guilty; from the positive viewpoint, He declares him to be righteous. He cancels the guilt of the person's sin and credits righteousness to him. Paul emphasized two points in this regard: (1) No one lives a perfectly good, holy, righteous life. On the contrary, "There is none righteous" (3:10), and "all have sinned, and come short of the glory of God" (3:23). "By the deeds of the law there shall no flesh be justified in his sight" (3:20). (2) Even though all are sinners and not sons, God will declare everyone who puts his trust in Jesus righteous rather than guilty. This legal declaration is valid because Christ died to pay the penalty for sin and lived a life of perfect righteousness, which can in turn be imputed to all humans. This is the central theme of Romans and is stated in the theme verse, 1:17 ("the righteousness of God"). Christ's righteousness (His obedience to God's law and His sacrificial death) will be credited to believers as their own. Paul used one Greek word meaning "reckoned," "imputed," or "counted" eleven times in chapter 4 alone. **Freely by his grace** is God's unmerited provision that finds expression in justification. The central thought in justification is that, although man clearly and totally deserves to be declared guilty (3:9–19),

God declares him righteous because of his trust in Christ. This is stated in several ways here: (1) "freely" (for nothing), (2) "by his grace," (3) **through the redemption that is in Christ Jesus**, and (4) "through faith" (3:25). "Redemption" is a word taken from the slave market; the basic idea is that of obtaining release by payment of a ransom. Paul used this word to refer to release from guilt, with its liability for judgment, and to deliverance from slavery to sin, because through His death, Christ paid the ransom for all humanity.

3:25a. To be a propitiation points to an atoning sacrifice and defines Jesus' sacrificial death "as the One who would turn aside God's wrath, taking away sin." The Greek for this phrase speaks of a sacrifice that satisfies the righteous wrath of God; without this appeasement, all people are justly destined for eternal punishment (see discussion on 1 John 2:2). **Through faith in his blood** makes it clear that saving faith looks to Jesus Christ in His sacrificial death for us.

3:25b–26. The sins of God's people, punished symbolically in the animal sacrifices of the Old Testament period, were totally punished in the once-for-all sacrifice of Christ on the cross.

B. Received by Faith (3:27–4:25)

1. The Principle Established (3:27–31)

3:27–28. There can be no **boasting** (v. 27) whatsoever; the grounds for boasting have been **excluded**, or literally "shut out." In short, **works** or merits of any kind are eliminated as a ground for justification. Only what God has done through the sacrificial death of Christ offers justification, which can be claimed only **by the law of faith**. When Luther translated this passage, he added the word "alone," which, though not in the Greek, accurately reflects the meaning (see discussion on James 2:14–26). Verse 28 states in positive terms what 3:20 stated in negative terms.

3:29. If justification were by the "works of the Law" (3:28), then God would indeed be **the God of the Jews only**. But such is not the case. Thankfully, God is the **God of the Gentiles also**.

3:30. Seeing it is one God refers to the first article of Jewish faith ("the LORD our God is one," Deut. 6:4). With this appeal, Paul argued that there is only one way of salvation for both Jew and Gentile, namely, faith in Christ.

3:31. Do we then make void the law through faith? Paul anticipated being charged with antinomianism ("against law"): If justification comes by faith alone, then is not the law rejected? He gave a more complete answer in chaps. 6–7 and reasserted the validity of the law in 13:8–10 (see also 1 Tim. 1:8–10).

2. The Principle Illustrated (chap. 4)

4:1. The great patriarch of the Jewish nation and the true example of a justified person (see James 2:21–23) is **Abraham our father**. The Jews of Jesus' time used Abraham as an example of justification by works, but Paul held him up as a shining example of righteousness by faith (see Gal. 3:6–9).

4:2. Paul raised the question of whether Abraham was **justified by works** but stopped short of saying that Abraham had no works worthy of **glory** (human respect). Indeed, he was a great man, but Paul made it clear that he had no grounds for glory **before God**.

4:3. What saith the scripture? The reference is to Genesis 15:6, where nothing is mentioned about works. Abraham's faith, not his works, was **counted unto him** (or "credited") **for righteousness**. Abraham had kept no law, rendered no service, and performed no ritual that earned credit to his account before God. His belief in God, who had made promises to him, was credited to him as righteousness.

4:4–5. Paul explained in general workday terms the difference between works and grace. **Him that justifieth the ungodly** (v. 5) is truly a remarkable description of God and His grace. In a court of law, such as a Roman one, a reputable human judge vindicates or justifies only the innocent person, one who has been proven righteous and innocent of the charge that landed him before the court. Here, then, is the grace of God and the heart of the gospel, for God justifies the ungodly, the unrighteous, those who are guilty and not innocent.

4:6–8. God does not continue to impute unrighteousness to the sinner who repents but forgives him when he confesses (see Ps. 32:3–5; Ezek. 18:23, 27–28, 32; 33:14–16).

4:9–10. For the Jews, **circumcision** (v. 9) represented the fulfillment of the covenant between God and Abraham (see Gen. 17:10–14), the first divine command of the Pentateuch, that every male child shall be circumcised. By contrast, **uncircumcision** identified the Gentiles. Paul was developing his argument (see 4:1–2) that the covenant between God and Abraham was based on faith, not works. **Not in circumcision, but in uncircumcision** (v. 10) points to the fact that Abraham was declared righteous (see Genesis 15) some fourteen years before he was circumcised (see Genesis 17; for a similar statement, see Gal. 3:17).

4:11–12. Circumcision was, among other things, the outward **sign ... of the righteousness** (v. 11) that God had credited to Abraham for his faith. For this reason, Paul showed that Abraham became **the father of all ... not circumcised** (v. 11) **... and the father of circumcision** (v. 12). Abraham is the father of believing Gentiles (the uncircumcised), because he believed and was justified before the rite of circumcision (the mark of Jews) was instituted. Abraham is also the father of believing Jews. His story thus shows that, for Jew and Gentile alike, there is only one way of justification: the way of faith. All believers (Jews and Gentiles), therefore, are called his spiritual children (v. 12) and referred to as the "seed" or "descendants" of Abraham (see, e.g., Gal. 3:16; Heb. 2:16).

4:13. Paul drew a significant inference here in his argument that the towering figure of Abraham is a model of righteousness by faith, or justification by faith. In 4:9–12, Paul established that the righteousness imputed to Abraham was based on faith apart from and before circumcision. Here Paul made it clear that what was before circumcision was also before and apart from the law, namely, the blessing or divine promise that Abraham would become the father of all, **the heir of the world**. "World" here refers to the creation, as in 1:20. No express mention of this heirship is made in the Genesis account of Abraham. He was promised "seed as the dust of the earth" (Gen. 13:16), possession of the land of Canaan (see Gen. 12:7; 13:14–15; 15:7, 18–21; 17:8), and that all peoples of the earth will be blessed through him (Gen. 12:3; 18:18) or his offspring (Gen. 22:18). Genesis makes it clear, however, that God purposed to work out the destiny of the whole world through Abraham and his offspring; it was therefore implicit in God's promises to Abraham that he and his offspring would "inherit the earth" (see Ps. 37:9, 11, 22, 29, 34; Matt. 5:5). The full realization of this awaits the consummation of the messianic kingdom at Christ's return. **Not … through the law** means that the promise to Abraham was not conditioned on its being merited by works of the law. **His seed** refers to all those of whom Abraham is said to be father (see 4:11–12).

4:14. They which are of the law specifies those whose claim to the inheritance is based on the fulfillment of the law. For **the promise**, see discussion on 4:13.

4:15. Paul could say **the law worketh wrath** because the law reveals sin and even stimulates it (see 7:7–11); it produces wrath, not promise. **Transgression** (Greek, *parabasis*) is an act of crossing, deviating from, or overstepping a clearly defined line. **Where no law is**, there is still sin, but it does not have the character of transgression or violation.

4:16. Here Paul summarized the thought of 4:11–12. For the close correlation between **faith** and **grace**, see 3:24–25; Ephesians 2:8. **Which is of the law** identifies Jewish Christians. **Which is of the faith of Abraham** identifies Gentile Christians, who share Abraham's faith but who, like Abraham, do not possess the law.

4:17. Before him refers to God and here accentuates the importance of God's verdict over that of human opinion or tradition. God considers Abraham to be the **father** of Jews and believing Gentiles alike, no matter how others (especially the Jews) may see him. The specific honorific, **God, who quickeneth the dead**, is primarily a reference to the birth of Isaac through Abraham and Sarah, both of whom were far past the age of childbearing (see 4:19; Gen. 18:11). Secondarily, Paul was alluding also to the resurrection of Christ (see 4:24–25). **Calleth … as though they were** is an expanded description of God, who has the ability to create out of nothing, as He demonstrated in the birth of Isaac. Together, these characterizations of God give focus to the exercise of His divine power in the fulfillment of His promise to Abraham.

4:18. Abraham **against hope believed in hope**. When all hope, as a human possibility, failed, Abraham placed his hope in God. It was not the ambition or gumption of Abraham that generated such hopeful belief, but rather the One who promised (see Heb. 11:11).

4:19–21. Being not weak in faith (v. 19) is a statement that points to the triumph of Abraham's conviction that God would be true to His promise. Abraham had some anxious moments (see Gen. 17:17–18), but God did not count those against him. The words **considered not** illustrate the wisdom of a proper focus. Faith does not refuse to face reality but looks beyond all difficulties to God and His promises. The twin descriptions **his own body now dead** and **the deadness of Sara's womb** underscore the impossibility of human potency as a ground of hope (see 4:18). Sarah was ten years younger than Abraham (see Gen. 17:17) but well past the age of childbearing. Only the power of God (see 4:17), devoted with a promise, can explain such faith and sustain such hope. Because Abraham had faith to believe that God would do **what he had promised** (v. 21), he is characterized as **giving glory to God** (v. 20). Whereas works are man's attempt to establish a claim on God, faith brings glory to Him.

4:22. Therefore means "as a consequence" or "for this reason" and here introduces Paul's quotation of Genesis 15:6. Abraham's faith **was imputed to him for righteousness** because it was true faith, that is, complete confidence in God's promise.

4:23–24. Abraham's experience was not private or individual, **not written for his sake alone** (v. 23), but had broad implications. If justification by faith was true for him, it is universally true, as confirmed in the words **for us also** (v. 24). As Abraham was justified because he believed in a God who brought life from the dead (see 4:19), so Christians will be justified by believing **on him that raised up Jesus our Lord from the dead**.

C. The Fruits of Righteousness (5:1–11)

5:1. Peace with God means more than a subjective feeling (peace of mind); it primarily refers to an objective status, a new relationship with God: once humans were His enemies, but now they are His friends (see 5:10; Eph. 2:16; Col. 1:21–22).

5:2. We have access describes the believer's introduction or entrance to grace. Paul said the believer now stands on the inside, as in an estate that one can admire and enjoy as a resident. Jesus ushers believers into the presence of God. The heavy curtain (of the temple) that separated man from God and God from man has been removed (see discussion on Matt. 27:51). For the Christian, **hope of the glory of God** carries the confidence that the purpose for which God created him will be ultimately realized (see discussion on 3:23).

5:3. The believer can **glory in tribulations** — not "because of" them but "in the midst of" them — because of God's unveiled grace and glorious purpose for the Christian. Paul was advocating, not a morbid view of life, but a joyous and triumphant one.

5:4. A Christian can rejoice in suffering because he knows that it is not meaningless. Part of God's purpose is to produce character in His children.

5:5. Hope maketh not ashamed because hope placed in God is not disappointed. The believer's hope is not to be equated with unfounded optimism. On the contrary, it is the blessed assurance of believers' future destiny and is based on God's love, which is revealed to them by the Holy Spirit and objectively demonstrated to them in the death of Christ. Paul moved from faith (5:1) to hope (5:2, 4–5) to **love** (see 1 Cor. 13:13; see also discussion on 1 Thess. 1:3). **Is shed abroad** is literally, "has been poured out." From this, it may be inferred that God has not held some back but has poured out all there is to pour. The verb indicates a present status resulting from a past action. When we first believed in Christ, the Holy Spirit poured out His love **in our hearts**, and His love for us continues to dwell in us.

5:6. In due time denotes the appointed moment in God's redemptive plan (see Mark 1:15; Gal. 4:4). Compare the words **Christ died for the ungodly** with "justifieth the ungodly" in 4:5 (see discussion there). Christ's love is grounded in God's free grace and is not the result of any inherent worthiness found in its objects (mankind). In fact, it is lavished on believers in spite of their our undesirable character.

5:7–8. The difference of **a righteous man** (v. 7) and **a good man** is one of relationship to the reader. Whereas the former may be thought worthy because of his justness, the latter evokes sympathy because of his benefaction. Paul's point is clear. In the realm of human affairs, what men may aspire to do for the most worthy, God has done for all, even the most unworthy. Christ made the ultimate sacrifice: giving one's life to redeem another. Moreover, we were neither righteous nor good, but **sinners** (v. 8), when **Christ died for us** (see 3:10–12). How profound is the sacrificial love of Christ, a love that acts on our behalf before any "I'm sorry," before any repentance, before any amends — in short, not because of us, but for us. Christ indeed loved His enemies (see 5:10; see Luke 6:27, 34–35).

5:9. By his blood is a reference to Christ's death for humanity's sins (see 3:25), by laying down His life as a sacrifice. **Wrath** refers to the final judgment, as the verb **shall be saved** makes clear (see 1 Thess. 1:9–10).

5:10. Enemies is a word that sums up the status of all for whom Christ died (see 5:7–10). Man is the enemy of God, not the reverse. Thus, the hostility must be removed from man if reconciliation is to be accomplished. God took the initiative in bringing this about through **the death of his Son** (see 5:11; Col. 1:21–22). **Reconciled** points back to 5:1. To "reconcile" is to "put an end to hostility" and is closely related to the term "justify," as the parallelism in 5:9–10 indicates:

5:9	5:10
justified	reconciled
by his blood	by the death of his Son
we shall be saved	we shall be saved

We shall be saved by his life is a reference to the unending life and ministry of the resurrected Christ for His people (see Heb. 7:25). Since believers were reconciled when they were God's enemies, they will be saved because Christ lives to keep them.

5:11. Atonement is the noun form of the verb used twice in 5:10, "reconciled." The noun is translated with the sense of "reconciliation" elsewhere in the New Testament (see 2 Cor. 5:18–19). Reconciliation, like justification (see 5:1), is a present reality for Christians and is something to rejoice about.

D. Summary: Man's Unrighteousness Contrasted with God's Gift of Righteousness (5:12–21)

5:12–21. This passage presents a contrast between Adam and Christ. Adam introduced sin and death into the world; Christ brought righteousness and life. The comparison begun in verse 12 is completed in verse 18. These two verses summarize the whole passage, and these two men, Adam and Christ, sum up the message of the book up to this point. Adam stands for man's condemnation (see 1:18–3:20); Christ stands for the believer's justification (see 3:21–5:11).

5:12. Death, referring to physical death, is the penalty for **sin**. It is also the symbol of spiritual death, man's ultimate separation from God. Although the wording may suggest it, **for that all have sinned** is not a repetition of 3:23. The context shows that Adam's sin involved the rest of mankind in condemnation (see 5:18–19) and death (see 5:15). Humans do not start life with even the possibility of living it sinlessly; humans begin it with a sinful nature (see Gen. 8:21; Pss. 51:5; 58:3; Eph. 2:3).

5:13. Sin is not imputed means that sin is not credited to a person. In other words, God did not lay responsibility or blame. In the period **when there [was] no [Mosaic] law**, sin was not charged against man (see 4:15). Death, however, continued to occur (see 5:14). Since death is the penalty for sin, people between Adam and Moses were involved in the sin of someone else, namely, Adam (see discussion on 5:12).

5:14. A **figure** is an image or type (Greek, *typos*), and **similitude** is a likeness or analogy. The analogy here is one of contrast. Through his sin, Adam brought universal ruin on the human race. In this act, he is the prototype of Christ, who, through one righteous act (see 5:18), brought universal blessing.

5:15. Many is the same as "all men" in 5:12 (see Isa. 53:11; Mark 10:45). **Much more** describes a degree of difference and is a theme that runs through this section. **The grace of God** is infinitely greater for good than is Adam's sin for evil.

5:16. The gift equals salvation. **Many offences** encompasses the sins of the succeeding generations.

5:17. Shall reign in life points to the future reign of believers with Jesus Christ (see 2 Tim. 2:12; Rev. 22:5).

5:18. The free gift came upon all men does not mean that everyone eventually will be saved. Rather, Paul was saying that salvation is available to all. To be effective, God's gracious gift must be received (see 5:17).

5:19. Made righteous refers to a standing (status) before God (see 2 Cor. 5:21), not to a change in character. The latter (the doctrine of sanctification) is developed in chapters 6–8.

5:20–21. The law entered (v. 20) not to bring about redemption but to point up the need for it. The law made sin even more sinful by revealing what sin is in stark contrast to God's holiness.

V. Righteousness Imparted: Sanctification (chaps. 6–8)

A. Freedom from Sin's Tyranny (chap. 6)

6:1–8:39. After explaining how God has provided for redemption and justification (3:21–5:21), Paul proceeded to explain the doctrine of sanctification, the process by which believers grow to maturity in Christ. He treated this subject in three parts: (1) freedom from sin's tyranny (chap. 6), (2) freedom from the law's condemnation (chap. 7), and (3) life in the power of the Holy Spirit (chap. 8).

6:1. Shall we continue in sin, that grace may abound? This question arose out of what Paul said in 5:20: "where sin abounded, grace did much more abound." Such a question expresses an antinomian ("against law") viewpoint. Apparently, some objected to Paul's teaching of justification by faith alone because they thought it would lead to moral irresponsibility.

6:2. Dead to sin refers to a past event and is explained in 6:3.

6:3–4. Here Paul explained the when and how of the Christian's death to sin. In New Testament times, baptism so closely followed conversion that the two were considered part of one event (see Acts 2:38 and discussion). So although baptism is not a means by which one enters into a vital faith relationship with Jesus Christ, it is closely associated with faith. Baptism depicts graphically what happens as a result of the Christian's union with Christ, which comes with faith. Believers are united with Christ through faith, just as they are united with Adam through their natural birth. As they fell into sin and became subject to death in father Adam, so they now have died and been raised again with Christ, which baptism symbolizes. It is noteworthy that although Paul had yet to visit the Christians in Rome, he expected that they shared the church's understanding of baptism and that its enactment corresponded with burial and resurrection.

Buried with him by baptism into death (v. 4) is amplified in 6:5–7. **By the glory of the Father** means "by the power of God." God's glory is His divine excellence, His perfection. Any one of His attributes is a manifestation of His excellence. Thus, His power is a manifestation of His glory, as is His righteousness (see 3:23). Glory and power are often closely related in the Bible (see Ps. 145:11; Col. 1:11; 1 Peter 4:11; Rev. 1:6; 4:11; 5:12–13; 7:12; 19:1). **Walk in newness of life** is amplified in 6:8–10.

6:5–6. Our old man (v. 6) refers to the unregenerate self, what believers once were. **The body of sin** connotes the self in its pre-Christian state, dominated by sin. This is a figurative expression in which the old self is personified. It is a "body" that can be put to death. For the believer, this old self has been rendered powerless so that it can no longer enslave him to sin, whatever lingering vitality it may yet exert in its death throes.

6:7. Is dead describes the believer's death with Christ to sin's ruling power. **Freed from sin** visualizes the believer's emancipation and release from sin's confines; the believer is set free from its shackles and power.

6:8–9. As resurrection followed death in the experience of Christ, so the believer who dies with Christ is raised to a new quality of moral life here and now. Resurrection in the sense of a new birth is already a fact, and it increasingly exerts itself in the believer's life. Assurance of this comes from Jesus Christ and His total victory over death and sin (see 6:10).

6:10. He died unto sin once shows the efficacy (power) of Christ's death; once was thoroughly effective. In His death, Christ, for the sake of sinners, submitted to the reign of sin (see 5:21), but His death broke the judicial link between sin and death, and He passed forever from the sphere of sin's reign. Having been raised from the dead, He now lives forever to glorify God. **Unto God** means "for the glory of God."

6:11. In contemporary language, **reckon … yourselves** is like saying, "Do the math." When one adds up what Christ has done for the believer, the sum is a new way of seeing oneself. Such reevaluation is the first step toward victory over sin (for the succeeding steps, see discussion on 6:12–13). Believers are **dead indeed unto to sin** and **alive unto God**, and by faith, they are to live in the light of this truth.

6:12–13. These verses are a call for the Christian to become in experience what he already is in position: dead to sin (see 6:5–7, 11) and alive to God (see 6:8–11). The second step toward the Christian's victory over sin is a determination to **Let not sin … reign** (v. 12) in his life. The third step is to **yield … unto God** (v. 13). "Yield" denotes putting oneself in the service of another. It may also echo the language of sacrifice, in which supplicants "present" or "bring" a sacrifice. In either case, sin is an unworthy overlord (see 6:14, 16). **Your members** refers to all the separate capacities of one's being (also in 6:19).

6:14. Sin shall not have dominion over you. Paul conceived of sin as a power that enslaves and therefore personified it. It would be a misunderstanding to take **ye are not under the law** to mean that the

Christian has been freed from all moral authority. Rather, the Christian has been freed from the law in the manner in which God's people were under the law in the Old Testament era. The law does not enable one to resist the power of sin; it only condemns the sinner. Conversely, the believer is **under grace**, and grace enables rather than condemns. For the disciplinary aspect of grace, see Titus 2:11–12.

6:15–23. The question raised in verse 15 seems to have come from those who were afraid that the doctrine of justification by faith alone would remove all moral restraint. Paul rejected such a suggestion and showed that a Christian does not throw morality to the wind. To the contrary, he exchanges sin for righteousness as his master.

6:16–17. The contrast between **sin** (v. 16) and **obedience** suggests that sin is by nature disobedience to God. Conversely, faith entails obedience, a willing submission to God that welcomes His loving will and truth (see 1:5, "obedience of faith"). Accordingly, Paul could speak of believers that **have obeyed from the heart** (v. 17). Christian obedience is not forced or legalistic, but willing. **That form of doctrine** probably refers to a summary of the moral and ethical teachings of Christ that was given to new converts in the early church.

6:18. A Christian has changed masters and is numbered among **the servants of righteousness**. Whereas he was formerly a slave to sin, he has become a slave (a willing servant) to righteousness.

6:19–22. I speak after the manner of men (v. 19) was Paul's way of apologizing for using an imperfect analogy. The word **servants** (v. 19–20), when applied to Christians, who are free in Christ, naturally presents problems. As implied in 6:16–17, "obedience unto righteousness" involves a willing heart, not enslavement. Paul argued that serving righteousness is better than any freedom enjoyed under sin (**free from righteousness**; v. 20). He secured this point by asking his readers to survey the **fruit** (v. 21) of their former service to unrighteousness. Indeed, **the end** (or "harvest") **... is death**.

The contrast of fruit in verses 21–22 juxtaposes death and eternal life, the opposing trajectories of unrighteousness and righteousness (see 6:18–21). For **made free from sin** (v. 22), see discussion on 6:6. **Holiness** refers to sanctification (for other uses of various forms of the word "sanctification," see 6:19; 1 Cor. 1:30; 1 Thess. 4:3–4, 7; 2 Thess. 2:13; 1 Tim. 2:15; Heb. 12:14; 1 Peter 1:2) and corresponds to the **fruit** of righteousness. Slavery to God produces holiness (or sanctification), and **the end** of the process is **everlasting life** (viewed not in its present sense but in its final, future sense). Without holiness, one cannot receive eternal life (see Heb. 12:14). Anyone who has been justified will surely give evidence of that fact by the presence of holiness in his life.

6:23. Two kinds of servitude are contrasted here. One brings **death** as its **wages**; the other results in **eternal life**, not as wages earned or merited, but as a **gift of God** (for the contrast between wages and gift, see 4:4).

B. Freedom from the Law's Condemnation (chap. 7)

7:1. The law. Although Paul may have had in mind the Mosaic law, his concern here was with the fundamental character of law as such.

7:2–3. These verses illustrate the principle set down in 7:1. Death decisively changes a person's relationship to the law.

7:4. Wherefore ("For this reason") signifies a direct logical relationship between the principle Paul stated in 7:1 and illustrated in 7:2–3 and the conclusion he drew here. By virtue of the bodily death of Jesus Christ, Christians have been made **dead to the law**. The law's power to condemn no longer threatens the Christian, whose "death" here is to be understood in terms of 6:2–7. There, however, he is "dead to sin" (6:2); here he is "dead to the law." The result is that the law has no more hold on him. **By the body of Christ** underscores the personal and physical death He died, the body (self) crucified. The words **married to another** pick up the theme of freedom from the law, illustrated in 7:3, which now finds expression in new life through the resurrected Christ (see 6:5). The purpose of this union is to produce in the believer the **fruit** of holiness.

7:5. In the flesh identifies the control of the sinful nature, a condition, so far as Christians are concerned, that belongs to the past — the unregenerate state. **The motions of sin, which were by the law** shows the law's instrumental power; it not only reveals sin but also stimulates sin. The natural tendency in man is to desire the forbidden thing. **Death** means physical death and, beyond that, spiritual death — final separation from God — which were the **fruit** of our "union" with the law.

7:6. Christians **are delivered from the law** in the sense of its condemnation (see discussion on 7:4). **Wherein we were held** pictures the law as a captor restraining or checking the captives' freedom (see 7:4, 6). **Newness of spirit** relates to the believer's new condition, also signified by the word **now** at the beginning of this verse (see discussion on 8:4). **The oldness of the letter** points to life under the Old Testament law (see 2 Cor. 3:6).

7:7. Is the law sin? This question was occasioned by the remarks about the law in 7:4–6. Paul's use of the first-person pronoun **I** in 7:7–25 is a topic of considerable interest. He seems to have used the first-person pronoun of himself but also as representative of mankind in general (7:7–12) and of Christians in particular (7:13–25). **I had not known sin** points to the important function that the law fulfilled, that of revealing the presence and reality of sin.

7:8. To better appreciate the words **sin, taking occasion by the commandment**, see discussion on 7:5. **Sin was dead** does not mean that it was nonexistent but that it was not fully perceived.

7:9. I was alive without the law once. Here Paul was reviewing his own experience from the vantage point of his present understanding. He was alive before he realized that the law condemned him to death, meaning either before his bar mitzvah or before his conversion, when the true rigor of the law became clear to him (see Luke 18:20–21; Phil. 3:6). **When the commandment came,** or when Paul came to the realization that he stood guilty before the law, again is a reference either to his bar mitzvah, when he (at age thirteen) assumed full responsibility for the law, or to his conversion, when he became aware

of the full force of the law. With the realization that he was condemned to death, Paul could say **I died**, because law reveals sin, and "the wages of sin is death" (6:23).

7:10. For **ordained to life**, see Leviticus 18:5. As it worked out, the law became the avenue through which sin entered, both in Paul's experience and in that of mankind. Instead of giving life, the law brought condemnation; instead of producing holiness, it stimulated sin.

7:12. The law comes from God and reflects His character. **The law is holy.** Despite the despicable use that sin made of the law, the law was not to blame. The law is God's, and as such, it is **holy, and just, and good** (see 7:13–14).

7:13–25. Whether Paul was describing a Christian or non-Christian experience here has been hotly debated through the centuries. That he was speaking of the non-Christian life is suggested by (1) the use of phrases such as "sold under sin" (v. 14), "I know that in me … dwelleth no good thing" (v. 18), and "wretched man that I am!" (v. 24) — which do not seem to describe Christian experience; (2) the contrast between chapters 7 and 8, which makes it difficult for the other view to be credible; (3) the problem of the value of conversion if one ends up in spiritual misery. In favor of the view that Paul was describing Christian experience are (1) the use of the present tense throughout the passage; (2) Paul's humble opinion of himself (v. 18); (3) his high regard for God's law (vv. 14, 16); (4) the location of this passage in a section dealing with sanctification, the Christian's growth in holiness.

7:13. Sin used a holy thing (the law) for an unholy end (death), which reveals the contemptible nature of sin.

7:14. The law can be called **spiritual** because it had its origin in God. Paul's use of **I am**, the personal pronoun and the verb taken together, suggests that he was describing his present (Christian) experience. **Carnal** ("fleshly") stands in contrast to "spiritual" and describes humanness that cannot rise above a disappointing level of conduct and character. Even a believer has the seeds of rebellion in his heart. Paul's description **sold under sin** is a phrase so strong that many refuse to accept it as descriptive of a Christian. It may graphically point out, however, the failure of even Christians to meet the radical ethical and moral demands of the gospel. It also points up the persistent nature of sin, which in 7:13–25, Paul nearly personified as a tyrannical and irresistible power (see, e.g., 7:17). It must be remembered, however, that sin is resident within all people, part of human nature (see 7:17, 20).

7:15. I allow not renders the Greek for "I do not understand [or 'recognize']." What a person wants to do and what a person does often fail to match. The struggle within creates tension, ambivalence, and confusion.

7:16. I consent unto the law that it is good. Even when Paul was rebellious and disobedient, the Holy Spirit revealed to him the essential goodness of the law.

7:17. It is no more I that do it, but sin is a clear concession to the power of sin; this is in no way an attempt on Paul's part to escape moral responsibility but is a statement of the insidious influence that sin can have over a Christian's life.

7:18–21. In these verses, one can perceive the depth of sin. Humanly, sin is uncontrollable. **In me … dwelleth no good thing** (v. 18) is a reference to man's fallen nature, as the last phrase of the sentence indicates. Paul was not saying that no goodness at all exists in Christians, but certainly aspirations and coordinate actions are flawed by sin. For **sin … in me** (v. 20), see discussion on 7:17.

7:22–23. I delight in the law of God (v. 22) refers to the Mosaic law or to God's law generally. It is difficult to see how a non-Christian could say this (see discussion on 7:13–25). Paul's "delight in" (lit., "experience joy in connection with") the law is assigned to **the inward** (inner) **man**, the "I" of Paul as concerns the aspirations of his **mind** (v. 23). This is contrasted with **another law**, a principle or force at work in Paul preventing him from giving obedience to God's law. **The law of my mind,** Paul's desire to obey God's law, was confounded by **the law … in my members.** By this, Paul meant a power, an au-

thority, or a control exercised in his members, which he revealed is **the law of sin.** Essentially the same as "another law," it opposes and usurps the prerogative of God's law (see Cranfield, *Epistle to the Romans,* p. 364).

7:24. Paul's description **the body of this death** is figurative for "the body of sin" (6:6), which hung on him like a corpse and from which he could not gain freedom.

7:25. The first half of this verse is the answer to the question stated in 7:24: deliverance comes, not through legalistic effort, but through Christ. The second half is a summary of 7:13–24. **I myself** connotes the real self, the inner being that delights in God's law (see 7:22).

C. Life in the Power of the Holy Spirit (chap. 8)

8:1. Therefore now connects the victory sounded in 7:25 to the Spirit-enabled life presented in chapter 8. The law brings **condemnation** because it points out, stimulates, and condemns sin. The Christian, however, is no longer "under the law" (6:14) because the Christian is **in Christ Jesus,** that is, united with Him (see 6:1–10; discussion on 6:11).

8:2. In Christ, there is a different law, **the law of the Spirit of life.** Here "the law" speaks of "the controlling power" (as in 7:22–23) of the Holy Spirit, who is life-giving. Accordingly, **the law of sin and death** refers to the controlling power of sin, which ultimately produces death. Paul used the word "law" in several different ways in Romans, for example, to mean a controlling power (here), God's law (2:17–20; 9:31; 10:3–5), the Pentateuch (3:21b), the Old Testament as a whole (3:19), and a principle (3:27).

8:3. For all of the law's authority, it suffered a power shortage. **What the law could not do** (lit., "the impossibility of the law") is possible, Paul went on to explain, through the power of the Spirit. **The flesh,** which weakened the law, is countered by the Spirit, who comes to believers through **God sending his own Son in the likeness of sinful flesh.** Christ in His incarnation became truly a man but, unlike all other men, was sinless. The final expression **in the flesh** may refer either to man's flesh or to Christ's. If the latter, it states where God condemned sin, namely, in Christ's human (but not sinful) nature. This interpretation seems more consistent with Paul's teaching.

8:4. **The righteousness of the law** cannot be thought of here without an echo of chapter 7. The law still plays a role in the life of a believer—not, however, as a means of salvation but as a moral and ethical guide, obeyed out of love for God and by the power that the Spirit provides. This is the fulfillment of Jeremiah 31:33–34 (a prophecy of the new covenant). **Fulfilled in us** recognizes that God's aim in sending His Son was that believers might be enabled to embody the true and full intentions of the law. **Walk ... after the Spirit** is equivalent to living according to the influence and power of the Spirit, which is how the law's righteous requirements can be fully met—by no longer letting the sinful nature hold sway but instead yielding to the directing and empowering ministry of the Holy Spirit.

8:5–8. Two mindsets are described here, that of the sinful nature and that of the Spirit. The former leads to **death** (v. 6), and the latter to **life and peace**. The sinful nature is bound up with death (v. 6), hostility to God (v. 7), insubordination (v. 7), and unacceptability to God (v. 8).

8:9. To every Christian belongs the indwelling presence and power of the Holy Spirit. **If any man have not the Spirit of Christ, he is none of his.** If a person does not possess the indwelling Holy Spirit, he does not possess Christ either. The Spirit indwells the Christian as a result of his justification. There is a practical identification of the Spirit of God and the Spirit of Christ in Paul's letters. Paul identified the indwelling of the Spirit as "the Spirit of God" (here, 1 Cor. 3:16), "the Spirit of Christ" (here), "the Spirit of his Son" (Gal. 4:6), "the Holy Ghost" (1 Cor. 6:19; 2 Tim. 1:14), as well as writing of Christ's indwelling the believer (Gal. 2:20; Eph. 3:17; Col. 1:27, 29).

8:10–11. The body is dead because of sin (v. 10), even as a Christian's body is subject to physical death, the consequence of sin, **but the** (Holy)

Spirit is life because of righteousness. This is a compact way of saying that the indwelling and life-giving Spirit is an evidence of the believer's justification through Christ, and, Paul continued, it is an evidence, even a guarantee of, the resurrection: **he ... shall also quicken your mortal bodies** (v 11). The life of the Spirit is evidenced by a Spirit-controlled life (see 8:4–9), which in turn provides assurance that one's resurrection is certain even now (for the close connection between the resurrection of Christ and that of believers, see 1 Cor. 6:14; 15:20, 23; 2 Cor. 4:14; Phil. 3:21; 1 Thess. 4:14).

8:12–14. In these verses, Paul very plainly and practically illustrated that the indwelling Spirit can be deduced from the manifestation of the Spirit's life. There are no **debtors ... to the flesh** (v. 12) among those possessing the Spirit. Character and conduct correspond to the rule of the Spirit. **The sons of God** (v. 14) points in the same direction. The "biological" features that distinguish God's children are not physical, but spiritual, as evidenced by a growing likeness in character and conduct. It must be remembered, however, that although God is the Father of all in the sense that He created all and His love and providential care are extended to all (see Matt. 5:45), not all are His children. Jesus said to the unbelieving Jews of His day, "Ye are of your father the devil" (John 8:44). People become children of God through faith in God's unique Son (see John 1:12–13), and the hallmark of this relationship is one's being led by God's Spirit.

8:15. Paul drew on his readers' familiarity with the practices of **adoption** to communicate a spiritual truth greater than its analogy. The underlying Greek term for "adoption" occurs four other times in the New Testament and only in Paul's letters (8:23; 9:4; Gal. 4:5; Eph. 1:5; see discussion on Gal. 4:5). Common among the Greeks and Romans, adoption granted the adopted son all the privileges of a natural-born son, including inheritance rights. Paul, however, went further. In the Mediterranean world, such legal rights were no guarantee of familial affection, whereas the Spirit of God's family assures it. Paul therefore complemented the legal privileges of the child adopted into God's family with a picture of familial affection: God's children greet their Father with the cry, **Abba, Father**. "Abba" (Aramaic for "Father") is expressive of an especially close relationship to God. It is akin in intimacy to "Papa." Through adoption, God's love for His own Son now welcomes His adopted children. Christians are adopted sons by grace; Christ, however, is God's Son by nature.

8:16. Beareth witness with our spirit expresses the inner testimony of the Holy Spirit to believers' relationship to Christ. **The children of God** and "the sons of God" (7:14) are synonymous terms in Paul's letters.

8:17–18. Heirs (v. 17) are those who have already entered, at least partially, into the possession of their inheritance. Adopted sons are **joint-heirs with Christ**. Everything really belongs to Christ, but by grace, Christians share in what is His. The Greek construction of **if so be that we suffer with him** does not set forth a condition but states a fact. The meaning, then, is not that there is some doubt about sharing Christ's glory; rather, despite the fact that Christians presently suffer, they are assured a future entrance into their inheritance. **The glory which shall be revealed in us** (v. 18) most certainly includes a personal glorification, "the recovery of the divine image or glory originally lost at the Fall, but restored in Christ" (Black, *Romans*, p. 120; see discussion on 3:23).

8:19. The creature here means "that which is created," "the creation," and refers to God's creation both animate and inanimate exclusive of human beings (see 8:22–23, where "the whole creation" and "ourselves" are contrasted). **The manifestation of the sons of God** points to the full manifestation of all that this means (see 1 John 3:1–2). Christians are already sons of God, but the full manifestation will not come until Christ returns (see 1 John 3:1–2).

8:20. Was made subject to vanity is a reference to Genesis 3:17–19. In the Bible, "vanity," or that which is "futile," means "without use" or "without result." **In hope** is possibly an allusion to the promise of Genesis 3:15.

8:21. Shall be delivered from the bondage of corruption. The physical universe is destined, not for destruction (annihilation), but for renewal (see 2 Peter 3:13; Rev. 21:1). Living things will no longer be subject to death and decay, as they are today.

8:22. The Greek words for **groaneth and travaileth** occur in the New Testament only here. Futility (see 8:20) compounds the hardships of existence and endurance (see 8:19). Some interpreters surmise that here creation is personified as a woman in labor waiting for the birth of her child. If so, the **now** painfully endures the "not yet" in full expectancy, unable to produce what God alone can deliver.

8:23. The firstfruits of the Spirit is an expression drawn from the imagery of harvest. In general, the firstfruits forecast the quality and delivery of the whole harvest. Similarly, the Christian's possession of the Holy Spirit is not only evidence of his present salvation (8:14, 16) but also a pledge of his future inheritance, and not only a pledge but also the down payment on that inheritance (see 2 Cor. 1:22; 5:5; Eph. 1:14). Christians are already God's children; **the adoption** (see discussion on 8:15) is a reference to the full realization of our inheritance in Christ. **The redemption of our body** points to the resurrection as the final stage of one's adoption (for the Spirit's vital role in this stage, see 8:11; 2 Cor. 1:22; 5:4–5; Eph. 1:13–14; 4:30). The first stage was God's predestination of one's adoption (see Eph. 1:5); the second is one's present inclusion as children of God (see 8:14; Gal. 3:26).

8:24–25. We are saved (v. 24) by faith (see Eph. 2:8), not **by hope**, but hope accompanies salvation. Hope, as Paul alluded, is a close ally of faith, for it appreciates what it cannot see, just as faith does. Real hope brings patient endurance.

8:26. Likewise means "similarly" or "in the same way." As hope sustains the believer in suffering, so the Holy Spirit helps him in prayer. **With groanings which cannot be uttered** suggests "groanings" that are inaudible yet deeply felt. In 8:23, it is the believer who groans; here it is the Holy Spirit. Whether Paul meant words that are unspoken or words that cannot be expressed in human language is not clear—probably the former, though 8:27 seems to suggest the latter. As Barrett (*Epistle to the Romans*, p. 168) put it, "communion between Spirit[-filled worshipper] and God is immediate and needs no spoken word."

8:27. The relationship between the Holy Spirit and God the Father is so close that the Holy Spirit's prayers need not be audible. God knows His every thought.

8:28. Good can best be understood as that which conforms one "to the image of His Son" (8:29). **Called** connotes an effectual calling, the call of God to which there is invariably a positive response.

8:29. Some insist that the knowledge referred to in **did foreknow** is not abstract but is couched in love and mixed with purpose. They hold that God not only knew believers before they had any knowledge of Him but that He also knew them, in the sense of choosing them by His grace, before the foundation of the world (see Eph. 1:4; 2 Tim. 1:9 and discussions). Others believe that Paul was referring to the fact that in eternity past God knew those who by faith would become His people. As it is used here, **predestinate** connotes moral conformity to the likeness of His Son. **That he might be the firstborn amongst many brethren.** God foreknew, predestined, and conformed believers to Christ's likeness so that the Son might hold the position of highest honor in the great family of God.

8:30. Predestinate ... glorified outlines the sequence by which God carries out predestination. The word **glorified** should not be separated from, but rather magnified by, Paul's other references to glory in this chapter (8:17–18, 21). Since this final stage is firmly grounded in God's set purpose, it is as certain as if it had already happened.

8:31. In Greek, **If God be for us** expresses no question mark in Paul's mind. The form of the condition makes it clear that there is no doubt about it.

8:32. The argument (from the greater to the lesser) here is similar to that in 5:9–10. If God gave the supreme gift of **his own Son** to save humanity, He will certainly also give whatever is necessary to bring to fulfillment the work begun at the cross (see discussion on Gen. 22:16).

8:33–34. A court of law is in view here. No charge can be brought against the Christian because God has already pronounced a verdict of not guilty.

8:34. Paul gave three reasons why no one can condemn God's elect: (1) Christ died for them; (2) He is alive and seated **at the right hand of God**, the position of power; and (3) He is interceding for them.

8:35–39. Paul wanted to show his readers that suffering does not separate believers from Christ but actually carries them along toward their ultimate goal.

8:36. Paul quoted Psalm 44:22 to show that suffering has always been part of the experience of God's people.

8:37. Through him that loved us refers especially to Christ's death on the cross.

8:38–39. Nor height, nor depth (v. 38) shows that it is impossible to get beyond God's loving reach. **Nor any other creature** includes all created things. Only God is not included, and He is the one who has justified believers (see 8:33).

VI. God's Righteousness Vindicated: The Problem of the Apparent Rejection of Israel (chaps. 9–11)

A. The Justice of the Rejection (9:1–29)

9:1–2. Paul offered solemn testimony to **the truth** (v. 1) with a triple confirmation: (1) **in Christ**; (2) **I lie not**; (3) **my conscience ... in the Holy Ghost**. The conscience is a reliable guide only when enlightened by the Holy Spirit. Paul wanted his readers to know, and know without reservation, the heartache that accompanied his knowledge of the truth about his own people, the Jews of his own heritage who had rejected Jesus Christ. Their fate without Christ was not something Paul spoke about with indifference or superiority, only with great pain.

9:3. The Greek word for **accursed** is *anathema* and means "delivered over to the wrath of God for eternal destruction" (see 1 Cor. 12:3; 16:22; Gal. 1:8–9). Such was Paul's great love for his fellow Jews that he would have forfeited his own salvation if such a substitutionary action could have benefited them (for a similar expression of love, see Exod. 32:32). That bespeaks the depth of Paul's heartfelt love and longing to see his people accept God's provision, the substitutionary sacrifice of Jesus Christ. Christ alone, however, could make the necessary sacrifice (see Gal. 3:10, 13).

9:4. Israelites denotes the descendants of Jacob (who was renamed Israel by God; see Gen. 32:28). The name was used of the entire nation (see Judg. 5:7), then of the northern kingdom after the nation was divided (see 1 Kings 12), the southern kingdom being called Judah. During the intertestamental period and in New Testament times, Palestinian Jews used the title to indicate that they were the chosen people of God. Its use here is especially relevant because Paul was about to show that, despite Israel's unbelief and disobedience, God's promises to her are still valid. By **adoption**, Israel had been accepted as God's son (see Exod. 4:22–23; Jer. 31:9; Hos. 11:1). Because of Israel's special relationship with God, **glory**, by association, involves the evidence of the presence of God among His people (see Exod. 16:7, 10; Lev. 9:6, 23; Num. 16:19). Israel's unique relationship with God is marked by its **covenants** with God, for example, the Abrahamic (Gen. 15:17–21; 17:1–8); the Mosaic (Exod. 19:5; 24:1–4), renewed on the plains of Moab (Deut. 29:1–15), at Mounts Ebal and Gerizim (Josh. 8:30–35), and at Shechem (Joshua 24); the Levitical (Num. 25:12–13; Jer. 33:21; Mal. 2:4–5); the Davidic (2 Samuel 7; 23:5; Ps. 89:3–4, 28–29; 132:11–12); and the new (prophesied in Jer. 31:31–40). **The promises** refer especially to those made to Abraham (Gen. 12:7; 13:14–17; 17:4–8; 22:16–18) but also include the many Old Testament messianic promises (e.g., 2 Sam. 7:12, 16; Isa. 9:6–7; Jer. 23:5; 31:31–34; Ezek. 34:23–24; 37:24–28).

9:5. The fathers are the patriarchs Abraham, Isaac, Jacob, and his sons. **Christ ... who is over all, God** sets forth one of the clearest statements of the deity of Jesus Christ found in the entire New Testament, assuming that "God" refers to "Christ" (see 1:4; Matt. 1:23; 28:19; Luke 1:35; 5:20–21; John 1:1, 3, 10, 14, 18; 5:18; 20:28; 2 Cor. 13:14; Phil. 2:6; Col. 1:15–20; 2:9; Titus 2:13; Heb. 1:3, 8; 2 Peter 1:1; Rev. 1:13–18; 22:13).

9:6. The word of God includes His clearly stated purpose, which has not failed, because **they are not all Israel, which are of Israel**. Paul was not denying the election of all Israel (as a nation) but rather stating that there is a separation within Israel, that of unbelieving Israel and believing Israel. Physical descent is no guarantee of a place in God's family.

9:7–8. The seed (v. 7) refers to physical descendants (e.g., Ishmael and his offspring), as Paul made clear in the expression **children of the flesh** (v. 8), those merely biologically descended from Abraham. By contrast, **children of God** refers to the Israel of faith (see 9:4). Not all Israelites were God's children.

9:9–13. Paul makes clear that God's promise was given prior to birth and prior to any good or bad behavior in order to dismiss a challenge to his point on the ground that his distinction belonged not to promise but to a difference between Isaac and Ismael.

9:11. Neither having done any good or evil shows that God's choice of Jacob was based on sovereign freedom, not on the fulfillment of any prior conditions. **The purpose of God according to election** means God's purpose is embodied in His election (see discussion on Eph. 1:4). A further proof is presented in the words **not of works, but of him that calleth** (for "calleth," see 8:28 and discussion). Before Rebekah's children were even born, God made a choice; obviously, that choice was not based on works.

9:13. Jacob have I loved, but Esau have I hated sounds very harsh but is the Semitic equivalent of "Jacob I chose, but Esau I rejected" (see Mal. 1:2–3). In 9:6–13, Paul dealt with national election and portrayed the nation Israel (Jacob) over the nation Edom (Esau). His intention is evident in light of the problem he was addressing: How can God's promise stand when so many who comprise Israel (in the Old Testament collective sense) are unbelieving and therefore cut off?

9:14. Is there unrighteousness with God? God forbid. Is He unjust to elect on the basis of His sovereign freedom, as with Jacob and Esau?

9:15. Quoting Exodus 33:19, Paul denied injustice in God's dealing with Isaac and Ishmael, and Jacob and Esau, by appealing to God's sovereign right to dispense mercy as He chooses.

9:16. It refers to God's choice, which is not controlled in any way by man. Paul made it clear, however, that the basis for Israel's rejection was her unbelief (see 9:30–32).

9:17. Pharaoh is the pharaoh of the exodus. **Raised thee up** means "made you ruler of Egypt." God's **purpose** was exercised through Pharaoh, **that I might shew my power ... and that my name might be declared** ("published"). "My name" represents the character of God (see Exod. 34:6–7), particularly as revealed in the exodus (see Exod. 15:13–18; Josh. 2:10–11; 9:9; 1 Sam. 4:8).

9:18. The first part of this verse again echoes Exodus 33:19 (see Rom. 9:15), and the last part echoes such texts as Exodus 7:3; 9:12; 14:4, 17, in which God is said to have hardened the hearts of Pharaoh and the Egyptians. **Whom he will** cannot mean that God is arbitrary in His **mercy**, because Paul ultimately based God's rejection of Israel on her unbelief (see 9:30–32).

9:19. This objection could be phrased, "If God determines whose heart is hardened and whose is not, how can God blame anyone for hardening his heart?"

9:20. Who art thou that repliest against God? Paul was not silencing all of man's questioning of God but was speaking to those with an impenitent, God-defying attitude who wanted to make God answerable to man for what He does and who defamed God's character with their questions.

9:21. The analogy between God and **the potter** and between man and **the vessel** (the pot) should not be pressed to the extreme. The main point is the sovereign freedom of God in dealing with man.

9:22–24. These verses are an illustration of the principle stated in 9:21. The emphasis is on God's mercy, not His wrath, as verse 24 makes clear. No one can call God to account for what He does, but He does not exercise His freedom of choice arbitrarily, and He shows great patience toward even the objects of His wrath. In light of 2:4, the purpose of such patience is to bring about repentance. Both God's judgment and His saving power are magnified and intensified with His continued restraint. For **glory** (v. 23), see

discussion on 3:23. Because of God's forbearance in the service of His purpose, "the children of the promise" (9:8–9), **the vessels of mercy**, are called **not of the Jews only, but also of the Gentiles** (v. 24) .

9:25–26. In the original context, these passages from Hosea (the two quotes are from Hos. 2:23 and 1:10 respectively) refer to the spiritual restoration of Israel. Paul, however, found in them the principle that God is a saving, forgiving, restoring God who delights to take those **which were not my people** (v. 25) and make them **my people**. Paul then applied this principle to Gentiles, whom God made His people by sovereignly grafting them into a covenant relationship (see chap. 11); they are **children of the living God** (v. 26).

9:27–29. The two passages from Isaiah indicate that only a small **remnant** (v. 27) will survive from the great multitude of Israelites. For Paul, the remnant and the **seed** (v. 29) were reduced to one: Jesus Christ (see Gal. 3:16). God's calling includes both Jews and Gentiles (see 9:24), but the vast majority are Gentiles, as 9:30 suggests.

B. The Cause of the Rejection (9:30–10:21)

9:30–32. Here Paul took a new step in his argument: the reason for Israel's rejection lay in the nature of her disobedience; she failed to obey her own God-given law, which in reality was pointing to Christ. She pursued the law, yet not by faith but by works. Thus, the real cause of Israel's rejection was that she failed to believe.

The law of righteousness (v. 31) should be understood as "the law that prescribed the way to righteousness," as is made very clear in verse 32. Paul did not reject obedience to the law but rather rejected righteousness by works, the attempt to use the law to put God in one's debt.

Israel's pursuit of righteousness was **not by faith** (v. 32). The failure of Israel was not that she pursued the wrong thing (i.e., righteous standing before God) but that she pursued righteousness by works in a futile effort to merit God's favor rather than pursuing it by faith. **That stumblingstone** refers to Jesus, the Messiah. God's rejection of Israel was not arbitrary but was based on Israel's rejection of God's way of gaining righteousness: faith.

9:33. Apparently, early Christians commonly used these two passages from Isaiah (Isa. 8:14; 28:16), which are here combined, in defense of Jesus' messiahship (see 1 Peter 2:4, 6 – 8; see also Ps. 118:22; Luke 20:17 – 18).

10:1. Paul often prayed for the churches (see Eph. 1:15 – 23; Col. 1:3; 1 Thess. 1:2 – 3; 2 Thess. 1:3). Here his **prayer to God for Israel** was for the salvation of his fellow countrymen.

10:2. A zeal of God should be understood as zeal "for" God rather than "from" God. The Jews' zeal for God (see Acts 21:20; 22:3; Gal. 1:14) was commendable in that God was its object, but it was flawed because it was not based on right knowledge about God's way of salvation. Paul, before his conversion, had been an example of such zeal (see Gal. 1:14).

10:3. Their own refers to a righteous standing based on mere human effort. **Being ignorant of God's righteousness** led the Jews to **establish their own righteousness** ("establish" means to "set up" or "put into force") and also caused them to resist and not submit to **the righteousness of God**. Paul probably had in mind their rejection of the Messiah, as 9:33 would suggest. Righteous standing based on faith in Jesus Christ (see 1:17) comes from God as a gift and cannot be earned by man's works.

10:4. Christ is the end of the law. Although the Greek word for "end" (*telos*) can mean either (1) "termination," "cessation," or (2) "goal," "culmination," "fulfillment," it seems best here to understand it in the latter sense. Christ is the fulfillment of the law (see Matt. 5:17) in the sense that He brought it to completion by obeying perfectly its demands and by fulfilling its types and prophecies. The Christian is no longer "under the law" (6:15) since Christ has freed him from its condemnation, but the law still plays a role in his life. He is liberated by the Holy Spirit to fulfill the law's moral demands (see 8:4). **For righteousness,** or "So that there may be righteousness," speaks of the righteous standing before God that Christ makes available **to every one that believeth** (see discussions on 1:17; 3:24).

10:5. The man which doeth those things shall live by them is a quotation of Leviticus 18:5, which speaks of the righteousness to which Israel was called under the Sinai covenant (see *KJV Study Bible* note on Lev. 18:5; see also Deut. 6:25). Some understand Paul's purpose in quoting this text as describing the way of obtaining righteousness ("shall live") by keeping the law (see 2:6 – 10). Others think that the reference is to Christ, who perfectly fulfilled the law's demands and thus makes salvation available to all who believe (see Heb. 5:9).

10:6 – 8. In these verses, **the righteousness which is of faith** (v. 6) is personified (**speaketh**), a vivid way of letting the Old Testament speak for itself. Paul's purpose in this quotation was to explain the nature of the righteousness that is by faith. It does not require heroic feats such as bringing Christ down from heaven or up from the grave. In its original context, Deuteronomy 30:12 – 13 refers to the law, and Paul here applied the basic principle to Christ.

"The righteousness which is of faith speaketh" (v. 6) continues to communicate in verse 8, **But what saith it?** The answer is from Deuteronomy 30:14: **The word is nigh thee.** In the Old Testament passage, "the word" is God's word as found in the law. Paul applied the passage to the gospel, **the word of faith**, the main point being the accessibility of the gospel. Righteousness is gained by faith, not by deeds, and is readily available to anyone who will receive it freely from God through Christ. **Even in thy mouth, and in thy heart** corresponds to "shalt confess … and shalt believe" in 10:9.

10:9 – 11. Confess with thy mouth the Lord Jesus (v. 9) echoes the earliest Christian confession of faith (see 1 Cor. 12:3), probably used at baptisms. Since "Lord" (Greek, *kyrios*) is used over six thousand times in the Septuagint (the Greek translation of the Old Testament) to translate the name of Israel's God (Yahweh), it is clear that Paul, when using this word of Jesus, was ascribing deity to Him. What one is to "confess with thy mouth" is his genuine inner belief, which is **in thine heart**. In biblical terms, the heart is the seat not merely of the emotions and affections but also of the intellect and will. **God hath raised him from the dead** is the bedrock truth of Christian doctrine (see 1 Cor. 15:4, 14, 17) and the central thrust of apostolic preaching (see, e.g., Acts 2:31–32; 3:15; 4:10; 10:40). Christians believe not only that Jesus lived but also that He still lives. The future tense in **shalt be saved** brings into focus the certainty of final salvation—salvation at the last day. Salvation involves inward belief (**with the heart**; v. 10) as well as outward confession (**with the mouth**); the two cannot be separated, although the order no longer follows Deuteronomy 30:14 but instead corresponds to experience. Here righteousness and salvation are not separate stages but one and the same. A confirmation of this is Paul's citation of Isaiah 28:16: **Shall not be ashamed** (v. 11), which is a proof of both righteousness and salvation.

10:12. There is no difference between the Jew and the Greek in the sense that both are on the same footing as far as salvation is concerned (see 10:13).

10:13. Peter cited this same passage (Joel 2:32) on the day of Pentecost (see Acts 2:21).

10:14–16. Since it might be argued that Jews had never had a fair opportunity to hear and respond to the gospel, Paul, through a series of rhetorical questions, stated (in reverse order) the conditions necessary to call on Christ and be saved: (1) a preacher sent from God, (2) proclamation of the message, (3) hearing the message, (4) believing the message.

How beautiful are the feet of them that preach the gospel of peace (v. 15). This is a quotation from Isaiah 52:7, which refers to those who brought the exiles the good news of their imminent release from captivity in Babylon. Paul applied it to gospel preachers, who bring the good news of release from captivity to sin. For **obeyed the gospel** (v. 16), see 1:5. Faith not only apprehends the content of the gospel but responds submissively to the Lord of the gospel. **Not all** presents a contrast to the "Whosoever" of 10:11. The testimony of Isaiah verifies that resistance and rejection is based not on the message but on the absence of faith (see Isa. 53:1). What was true in Isaiah's day was relevant in Paul's day and is still relevant today.

10:17. The word of God refers either to the gospel concerning Christ or to Christ speaking His message through His messengers.

10:18. Their sound belongs to Paul's citation of Psalm 19:4 (from the Septuagint), where it is paralleled with "their words" and refers to the testimony of the heavens to the glory of God. Here Paul applied "their sound" to gospel preachers and used it to show that Israel could not offer the excuse that she had not had the opportunity to hear. "Their sound" (originally used to describe God's revelation in nature) aptly describes the widespread preaching of the gospel, showing that Jews had ample opportunity to hear the message of redemption.

10:19. Did not Israel know? The quotation that follows (from Deut. 32:21) answers this question by suggesting that the Gentiles, whom the Jews considered to be spiritually unenlightened, understood. If the Gentiles understood the message, surely the Jews could have. **Them that are no people** refers to the Gentiles, who were not a nation of God's forming in the sense that Israel was.

10:20–21. Isaiah (Isa. 65:1–2) added a second witness to that of Moses (see 10:19). The opportunity that was open-ended (**All day long**) for Israel had been opened to others. The responsibility for Israel's rejection as a nation rested with Israel herself. She had failed to meet God's requirement, namely, faith. Incidentally, Paul himself followed a similar course in his ministry: first to the Jew and then to the Gentile (see Acts 13:46–47).

C. Facts That Lessen the Difficulty (chap. 11)

1. The Rejection Is Not Total (11:1–10)

11:1. Cast away implies total rejection. The expression comes from 1 Samuel 12:22 and Psalm 94:14, where God promises to never forsake Israel (see also Jer. 31:37). In Greek, the question Paul asked clearly expects a negative answer: "God has not cast away His people, has He?" Paul added to what is already explicit in the Greek: an emphatic **God forbid**. Indeed, Paul himself was proof that God had not totally rejected the Jews.

11:2–4. Paul reiterated the impossibility that God should "cast away" (11:1) His people but added the words **which he foreknew** (v. 2). As in 8:29 (see discussion there), God's foreknowledge is associated with His election. Since they are God's chosen people, a faithful remnant has always existed among the Jewish people (see 11:5). Paul made this point by quoting the exasperated pleading of Elijah against Israel (see 1 Kings 19:10, 14, 18). In the face of Israel's apostasy, Elijah lamented that he alone believed in God and that his life was in danger. **I have reserved** (v. 4) points to God's faithfulness, which 11:5 says is "according to [God's] election of grace."

11:5–6. If God had "cast away" (11:1) His people, no **remnant** (v. 5) would have remained. As it was in Elijah's day, so it was in Paul's day (**Even so**). Despite widespread apostasy, a faithful remnant of Jews remained. **According to the election of grace** means the remnant existed because of God's grace, not because of their good works.

11:7. What then? indicates that Paul was drawing a conclusion from 11:1–6. **Israel … seeketh** refers to a righteous standing before God, which eluded the greater part of Israel. **The election hath obtained it.** In other words, the faithful remnant within Israel obtained righteousness through faith in response to the gracious choice of God. **The rest were blinded** because they refused the way of faith (see 9:31–32). God made them impervious to spiritual truth (see discussion on Isa. 6:8–13)—a judicial hardening of Israel.

11:8. Scripture (Isa. 29:10; see Deut. 29:4) accounts for Israel's condition and remains relevant **unto this day.** The spiritual dullness of the Jews had continued from Isaiah's day to Paul's day.

11:9–10. This passage from Psalm 69:22–23 was probably originally spoken by David concerning his enemies. Paul used it to describe the results of the divine hardening of Israel.

2. The Rejection Is Not Final (11:11–24)

11:11. The form of Paul's question corresponds to the pattern of the question in 11:1; it explicitly expects a negative answer, to which Paul again added an emphatic **God forbid** (see 11:1). **Have they stumbled that they should fall?** "They" corresponds to "the rest" in 11:7, and "should fall" (Greek, *piptō*; "fall down") is distinguished from the word "stumbled" (Greek, *ptaiō*; "trip") in a way that suggests a dire fall resulting in destruction. **Their fall** (here and in 11:12) uses yet a different word in Greek (*paraptōma*), denoting a "trespass" or a "transgression," and refers to the Jews' rejection of the gospel. In accordance with Deuteronomy 32:21, God's purpose for "their fall" is **to provoke them to jealousy** (see 11:14; 10:19). Gentiles enjoying the privileges of God's salvation through faith will prod "the rest [who] were blinded" (11:7) to accept what they have hitherto rejected.

11:12. The riches of the world is equivalent to **the riches of the Gentiles** and refers to the abundant benefits of salvation that believing Gentiles already enjoyed, which had come about because of the Jews' rejection of the gospel. That rejection had caused the apostles to turn to the Gentiles (see Acts 13:46–48; 18:6). **The diminishing of them** is equivalent to "their transgression" (see discussion on 11:11) but focuses on the loss that this transgression entailed. **How much more** indicates a correlation based on a pattern of lesser to greater or light to heavy (for more on this correlation, see discussion on 11:15. **Their fulness** speaks of the salvation of Israel (see 11:26–27; see also "the fulness of the Gentiles," 11:25).

11:13–14. Paul positioned his own ministry and his Gentile hearers within God's purpose to provoke **them which are my flesh** (v. 14) to jealousy (see 11:11) and salvation. As **the apostle of the Gentiles** (v. 13; see 1:5; Acts 9:15; Gal. 1:16; 2:7, 9), Paul's ministry was an end in itself, worthy of his greatest endeavor: **I magnify mine office.** Yet in turning to the Gentiles, he could hardly be accused of turning away from unbelieving Jews, for in God's purpose, the ministry to the one is a ministry to the other. **Provoke to emulation** (v. 14) means "provoke to jealousy" (see 11:11)

11:15. As in 11:12, here Paul's train of thought runs from lesser to greater. **Casting away** is here used of God's temporary and partial exclusion of the Jews. **The reconciling of the world** is similar to "the riches of the world" (11:12; see discussion there). **Life from the dead** is equivalent to "how much more" in 11:12. The sequence of redemptive events, each of which leads to the next, is: (1) the "fall" and "diminishing" (11:12) of Israel; (2) the salvation of the Gentiles; (3) the jealousy of Israel; (4) the "fulness" (11:12) of Israel when the hardening is removed; (5) even more riches for the Gentiles. To what, however, does the "how much more" (11:12) for the Gentiles refer, which Paul described here as "life from the dead"? Three views may be suggested: (1) an unprecedented spiritual awakening in the world; (2) the consummation of redemption at the resurrection of the dead; (3) a figurative expression describing the conversion of the Jews as a joyful and glorious event (like resurrection), which will result in even greater blessing for the world. Of these three views, the first seems least likely, since before Israel's spiritual rebirth, the fullness of the Gentiles will have already come in (see 11:25). Since the Gentile mission will then be complete, a period of unprecedented spiritual awakening seems to have no place. The second view also seems unlikely, since the context suggests nothing of bodily resurrection.

11:16. The first half of this verse is a reference to Numbers 15:17–21. Part of the dough made from the first of the harvested grain (the firstfruit) was offered to the Lord, which consecrated the whole batch. **The firstfruit** and **the root** refer to the patriarchs, and **the lump** and **the branches** refer to the Jewish people. In this analogy of the firstfruit, **holy** means "consecrated to God." Paul was saying, not that all Jews are righteous (i.e., saved), but that God will be true to His promises concerning them (see 3:3–4) because of the patriarchs, which involves God's election of grace. Paul foresaw a future for Israel, even though she is for a time set aside.

11:17. In 11:17–24, Paul used the metaphor of a tree to vividly explain what he had taught so far in chapter 11. As he established in 11:16, "the branches" refers to the Jewish people. Even as Paul drew a distinction between the "remnant" (11:5) and "the rest [who] were blinded" (11:7), **some of the branches**

… broken off is a new word picture corresponding to their "fall" (11:11–12), their "diminishing" (11:12), and "the casting away of them" (11:15). **A wild olive tree** refers to Gentile Christians. What Paul earlier described as "the riches of the Gentiles" (11:12) and "the reconciling of the world" (11:15) belongs to the wild olive that was **graffed in**. The usual grafting procedure is to insert a shoot or slip of a cultivated tree into a common or wild one. In Paul's metaphor, however, the grafting procedure is "contrary to nature" (11:24): a wild olive branch (the Gentiles) is grafted into a cultivated olive tree. Such a procedure is unnatural, which is precisely the point. Normally, such a graft would be unfruitful. **The root and fatness** points to the patriarchs. The whole olive tree, the old olive tree with its graft from a wild start, represents the people of God.

11:18–19. Paul warned the graft (the Gentiles) against an attitude of superiority: **thou bearest not the root, but the root thee** (v. 18). The salvation of Gentile Christians is dependent on the Jews, especially the patriarchs (e.g., the Abrahamic covenant; see John 4:22). For **The branches were broken off** (v. 19), see 11:17.

11:20–21. With the word **Well** (v. 20), Paul granted the correctness of the hypothetical rebuttal in 11:19 (compare the same Greek word in John 4:17: "Thou hast well said"). He went on, however, to warn his readers against the attitude behind the statement. Behind **unbelief** is arrogance. The graft that **standest by faith** must remember that pride comes before a fall (see Prov. 16:8; 3:34; 1 Peter 5:5). Better is humility that brings grace, and **fear** that acknowledges God (on "the fear of God," see discussion on Gen. 20:11; see also Prov. 3:7; Phil. 2:12–13; Heb. 4:1; 1 Peter 1:17).

11:22. Any adequate doctrine of God must include **the goodness and severity of God**. These two elements should not be separated. When one ignores His goodness, God seems a ruthless tyrant; when one ignores His sternness, He seems a doting Father.

11:23. God is able to graff them in again. Paul held out hope for the Jews. God is able to restore them (see Matt. 19:26; Mark 10:27; Luke 18:27).

11:24. Paul cautioned the Gentiles against limiting God with the "impossible." What is possible with God (**how much more**) could be seen in their own salvation experience: **contrary to nature**, God had grafted the Gentiles into the family of God (see Eph. 2:12–13). Paul recognized that such a grafting procedure was not commonly practiced (see discussion on 11:17). Obviously, the reasoning in this verse is more theological than horticultural. It would be difficult horticulturally to graft broken branches back into the parent tree, but the Jews really belong (historically and theologically) to the parent tree. Thus, they will "much more" **be graffed into their own olive tree**.

3. God's Ultimate Purpose Is Mercy (11:25–36)

11:25. Paul's teaching on Israel and the Gentiles belongs to God's **mystery**: a divine truth hidden from God's people in the past but now revealed in the gospel. The so-called mystery religions of Paul's day used the Greek word *mystērion* to refer to something that was to be revealed only to the initiated. Paul, however, used it to refer to truth formerly hidden in God's eternal plans but now revealed by God for all to know and understand (see 16:25; 1 Cor. 2:7; 4:1; 13:2; 14:2; 15:51; Eph. 1:9; 3:3–4, 9; 5:32; 6:19; Col. 1:26–27; 2:2; 4:3; 2 Thess. 2:7; 1 Tim. 3:9, 16). Paul used the word "mystery" to refer to (1) the incarnation (1 Tim. 3:16; see discussion there), (2) the death of Christ (1 Cor. 2:7, "the wisdom of God in a mystery"), (3) God's purpose to sum up all things in Christ (Eph. 1:9) and especially to include both Jews and Gentiles in the New Testament church (Eph. 3:3–6), (4) the change that will take place at the resurrection (1 Cor. 15:51), and (5) God's plan by which both Jew and Gentile, after a period of disobedience by both, will by His mercy be included in His kingdom (here). **Lest ye should be wise in your own conceits**, Gentiles must understand their place in the mystery. God's merciful plan to include the Gentiles in His great salvation plan should humble them, not fill them with arrogance. **In part** means that Israel's hardening is partial, not total. Indeed, Israel's hardening

is not final and permanent but temporary and effective, as the word "until" clearly indicates. **The fulness of the Gentiles** refers to the total number of the elect Gentiles.

11:26. And so introduces an emphatic statement that this is the way all Israel will be saved. What did Paul mean by **all Israel**? Three main interpretations of this phrase are: (1) the total number of elect Jews of every generation, or the "fulness" (11:12) of Israel, which is analogous to "the fulness ['full number'] of the Gentiles" (11:25); (2) the total number of the elect, both Jews and Gentiles, of every generation; (3) the great majority of Jews of the final generation. Given Paul's discussion in this chapter, there is no basis for taking the words **shall be saved** in any sense other than that of 11:14. The salvation of the Jews will, of course, be on the same basis as anyone's salvation: personal faith in Jesus Christ, crucified and risen from the dead. **There shall come out of Sion the Deliverer** is a quotation from Isaiah 59:20, where "the redeemer" ("the Deliverer") seems to refer to God. The Talmud understood the text to be a reference to the Messiah, and Paul appears to have used it in this way. For "Sion," see discussion on Galatians 4:26.

11:27. Covenant refers to the "new covenant" of Jeremiah 31:31–34. **When I shall take away their sins** (see Jer. 31:34; Zech. 13:1). Just as salvation for Gentiles involves God's merciful forgiveness of sins, so it is for the Jews. For Jew and Gentile alike, God's forgiveness is based on only repentance and faith (see 11:23; Zech. 12:10–13:1).

11:28. They (the Jews) **are enemies** only temporarily and **for your sakes**, as explained in 11:11. With respect to God's election, **they are beloved for the fathers' sakes**, not because any merit was passed on from the patriarchs to the Jewish people as a whole but because God, out of love, chose Israel, and that choice is irrevocable.

11:29. The gifts and calling of God are without repentance means that God does not change His mind with reference to His call. Even though Israel is presently in a state of unbelief, God's purpose will be fulfilled in her.

11:30–31. In this carefully balanced sentence, Paul articulated the relationship of God's grace to Gentile Christians and to the Jews.

Gentile Christians (v. 30)	Jews (v. 31)
For as ye	Even so have these
in times past	also now
have not believed	not believed
yet now have obtained mercy	that … they also may obtain mercy
through their unbelief	through your mercy

Through your mercy means "Through the mercy that God has shown to you, the Gentiles."

11:32. So that God may have mercy on **them all**, meaning both groups under discussion, Jews and Gentiles have each undergone a period of disobedience. Paul was in no way teaching universal salvation.

11:33–36. The doxology that ends this section is the natural outpouring of Paul's praise to God, whose **wisdom and knowledge** (v. 33) brought about His great plan for the salvation of both Jews and Gentiles.

VII. Righteousness Practiced (12:1–15:13)

12:1–15:13. Here Paul turned to the practical application of all he had written up to this point. This does not mean that he had not yet said anything about Christian living. Chapters 6–8 touched on this, but now Paul went into detail to show that Jesus Christ is to be Lord of every area of one's life. This section is not a postscript to the great theological discussions in chapters 1–11. In a real sense, Paul directed the entire letter toward the goal of showing that God demands one's action as well as one's believing and thinking. Faith expresses itself in obedience.

A. In the Body, the Church (chap. 12)

12:1. Paul called every believer to total sacrifice. His exhortation was not without leverage: (1) **I beseech you therefore** makes it clear that total sacrifice is an important inference drawn from and compelled by the truth set forth in chapters 1–11. (2) Total sacrifice is warranted **by the mercies of God**; it is the fitting response to His gracious action in Christ. Much of the letter has been concerned with demonstrating this. **Present** is a technical term for offering a sacrifice. **Your bodies** (see 6:13 and discussion) is suited to the imagery of sacrifice and is a concrete expression tantamount to "yourselves," as the words **a living sacrifice** confirm. The altars of daily life are concrete occasions to present oneself to God as "a living sacrifice," in contrast to dead animal sacrifices. The words **reasonable service** also belong to the imagery of sacrifice. "Service" in particular alludes to temple duties and the kind of service a priest renders. Here Paul extolled the presentation of living sacrifices as worship that befits what God has achieved in Christ. Accordingly, "reasonable service" is not merely ritual activity in a place such as the temple; it takes place in the heart, mind, and will (see 1 Cor. 3:16; 6:19).

12:2. This world in Greek is the word "age" (*aiōn*), as in Gal. 1:4 and Eph. 2:2. Christians are to resist the shaping and molding forces and philosophies of this world. Instead of being **conformed**, believers are to be **transformed**. Transformation is not attributed to this world. This world conforms, but God's truth (His will) transforms. **Be ye transformed** denotes a process, not a single event. Interestingly, the same word is used in the transfiguration narratives (Matt. 17:2–8; Mark 9:2–8) and in 2 Corinthians 3:18. The **mind**—thought and will as they relate to morality (see 1:28)—must be renewed by God's revealed truth, His will. God's truth renews and transforms. Through faith, God's truth is rooted in the mind and heart, and its transforming action has an outcome: **that you may prove** (or ascertain) **what is … [the] will of God. Good** is that which leads to the spiritual and moral growth of the Christian. **Acceptable** means what is acceptable to God, not necessarily to humans. God's will is **perfect**; no improvement can be made on His will.

12:3. To think soberly, or in a clearheaded, sensible way, calls for seeing oneself accurately. The touchstone is God's grace, or as Paul put it, **according as God hath dealt**. Since the power comes from

God, there can be no basis for a superior attitude or self-righteousness. All believers are on equal footing because any distinctions belong to God's grace and not to anyone's superiority. Accordingly, **the measure of faith** belongs to the power that God gives to each believer to fulfill various ministries in the church (see 12:4–8).

12:4–8. Here Paul likened Christians to members of a human body. There are **many members** (v. 4), and each has a different function, but all are needed for the health of the body. The emphasis is on unity within diversity (see 1 Cor. 12:12–31).

12:5. The key to Paul's concept of Christian unity is found in the words **in Christ** (see discussions on 6:11; Eph. 1:1). Only in Jesus Christ is any unity in the church possible. True unity is spiritually based.

12:6. The Greek word for **gifts** is *charismata*, which refers to special gifts of grace (Greek, *charis*). God freely gives these gifts to His people to meet the needs of the body (see *KJV Study Bible* notes on 1 Cor. 1:7; 12:4). **Prophecy** (Greek, *prophēteia*) is the ability to interpret and communicate in clear speech God's direct and relevant will or purpose for His people (see *KJV Study Bible* note on 1 Cor. 12:10). From 1 Corinthians 14, it is clear that prophesying delivers a message addressed to the church's understanding and comprehension. Its purpose is "edification, and exhortation, and comfort" (1 Cor. 14:3), instruction so "that all may learn" (1 Cor. 14:31). The exercise of this gift, however, must be **according to the proportion of faith**, meaning "according to the standard." The word "proportion" (Greek, *analogia*) is similar to yet different from "the measure of faith" in 12:3 (see discussion there). The "standard" acts as a safeguard and suggests that the exercise of this gift will conform to faith. On the one hand, it suggests that prophecy will not contradict faith in and knowledge of Jesus Christ. On the other hand, it suggests that the one who prophesies is equally subject to the prophecy.

12:7. Ministry (Greek, *diakonia*) connotes any kind of service needed by the body of Christ or by any of its members. For **teacheth** (Greek, *didaskalia*), see discussion on Ephesians 4:11; *KJV Study Bible* note on 1 Corinthians 12:28.

12:8. Paul used the verb **exhorteth** (Greek, *parakaleō*) and the noun **exhortation** (Greek, *paraklēsis*) frequently in his letters—the verb fifty-four times, and the noun twenty times. Judging from his use of these words and his practice of instilling others with courage or encouragement, the gift of exhortation involves an uplifting, cheerful call to worthwhile accomplishment. The teacher often carried out this function. In teaching, the believer is shown what he must do; in encouraging, he is helped to do it. **Giveth** (Greek, *metadidōmi*) connotes giving what is one's own, contributing material resources to the work of God and the needs of others or possibly distributing what has been given by others. **Simplicity** is to accompany giving, suggesting that the hallmarks of the gift of giving are generosity and sincerity. **Ruleth** (Greek, *proistēmi*) suggests leading, modeling, motivating, and inspiring others to accomplish the work of the ministry. "He that ruleth" is possibly a reference to an elder; it clearly alludes to a qualification for church leaders (see Paul's use of *proistēmi* in 1 Thess. 5:12; 1 Tim. 5:17; 3:4–5, 12). The gift of leadership is to be complemented with **diligence**. In Greco-Roman literature and inscriptions, "diligence" characterized extraordinary commitment to civic and religious responsibilities. In relationships, diligence is expressed as devotion and goodwill toward others—an important quality for leaders if others are to follow. **Sheweth mercy** (Greek, *eleeō*) speaks of tenderly and empathetically caring for people who are suffering, certainly the sick, the poor, and the aged. Mercy is to be exercised **with cheerfulness**, a spirit and countenance that dispels gloom.

12:9–21. With short brushstrokes, Paul painted a truly extraordinary and altogether beautiful figure of the transformed and renewed life (see 12:1–2) of the believer. He connected Christ's transformation of one's inner life to the outer application of that life within the community of believers and the concrete world and was thus addressing, not individual believers, but the community.

12:9. Love, the Christian's love for fellow Christians and perhaps here also for his fellow man, must be **without dissimulation**, that is, genuine, true love, not pretense. In view of 12:6–8, with its emphasis on social concern, the love Paul was speaking of here is not mere emotion but active love. **Abhor ... cleave** speaks of a disposition that finds evil repugnant and good attractive.

12:10. Brotherly love (Greek, *philadelphia*) denotes family affection and devotion, love within the family of God. **In honour preferring one another** was once translated, "compete in honoring one another." Paul pictured a noble competition for the privilege of putting others first. Only one whose mind has been renewed by the Holy Spirit (see 12:2) would participate in such a competition (see Phil. 2:3).

12:11. Not slothful in business is literally "not indolent in diligence" (see "diligence" in 12:8), meaning that believers are to exhibit wholehearted devotion and goodwill toward others. If **fervent in spirit** means "fervent in the Holy Spirit," the reference would be to the fervor the Holy Spirit provides. The same expression is used of Apollos in Acts 18:25. Since the Greek word for "fervent" (*zeō*) means "to boil," effervescence, liveliness, and exhilaration befit the spirit of one serving the Lord.

12:12. Rejoicing in hope shows that the certainty of the Christian's hope is a cause for joy (see 5:5; see also 8:16–25; 1 Peter 1:3–9) and implicitly expresses the importance of a forward focus and expectancy that regularly looks to a future grounded in God's favor. Hope makes one **patient in tribulation** (see Rom. 8:25; 1 Thess. 1:3). Patience maintains its belief and its course of action in the face of opposition and affliction. The patience to endure triumphantly is necessary for a Christian, because affliction is the believer's inevitable experience (see John 16:33). As Paul's sequence of thought (hope, patience) suggests, **continuing instant in prayer** calls one not only to pray in hard times but also to maintain communion with God through prayer at all times (see Luke 18:1; 1 Thess. 5:17).

12:13. The Christian has social responsibility to all people, but **distributing to the ... saints** calls the Christian to the necessary responsibility of caring for other believers (see Gal. 6:10). **Given to hospitality** is literally "pursuing" or "aspiring" to hospitality.

Hospitality (Greek, *philoxenia*) is to strangers what brotherly love (Greek, *philadelphia*) is to family.

12:14. Bless them which persecute you. Here Paul echoed Jesus' teaching in Matthew 5:44 and Luke 6:28.

12:15. Identification with others in their joys and in their sorrows is a Christian's privilege and responsibility.

12:16. Be of the same mind. Paul prayed for this in 15:5 and beseeched it in 1 Corinthians 1:10 and Philippians 4:2. It made his joy complete in Philippians 2:2 (see discussion there). What unifies Christians into one mindset is the mind of Christ: "Let this mind be in you, which was also in Christ Jesus" (Phil. 2:5).

12:17. For **Recompense to no man evil for evil**, see Matthew 5:39–42, 44–45; 1 Thessalonians 5:15; 1 Peter 3:9. **Provide things honest in the sight of all men**. Paul's exhortation is quite possibly a reflection of Proverbs 3:4 in the Septuagint (the Greek translation of the Old Testament). Christian conduct should never betray the high moral standards of the gospel, or it will provoke the disdain of unbelievers and bring the gospel into disrepute (see 2 Cor. 8:21; 1 Tim. 3:7).

12:18. If it be possible ... live peaceably. Jesus pronounced a blessing on peacemakers (see Matt. 5:9), and to the extent that it depends on them, believers are to cultivate peace with everyone.

12:19–21. Heap coals of fire on his head. Doing **good** (v. 21) to one's enemy, instead of trying to take revenge, may bring about his repentance (see discussion on Prov. 25:22).

B. In the World (chap. 13)

13:1–7. The question of responsibility and obligation to the state is an important issue for the Christian, whose allegiance and true citizenship belong to the rule of Christ. The question had an added dimension for believers in Rome, the seat of imperial, even world, power. At the time, currents of political unrest over taxes within Rome and winds of religious resistance to human rule within the empire may have prompted Paul to safeguard a proper outlook and attitude toward government and its authority (see Moo, *Romans*, p. 426). Paul called all believers to recognize that they stand under government in God's instituted order for ruling the world.

13:1. Be subject is a significant phrase in 13:1–7. In scripture, to "be subject" is to be volitionally subordinate, not abject. The Greek word *hypotassō* ("to submit," "be subject") is not fully explained by the word "obey." Within the heart of the word is an attitude of willingness; as Paul made clear here, its virtue is deference to the ultimate authority of God. **Higher powers** refers to civil rulers and governing officials (see Titus 3:1), all of whom were probably pagans when Paul wrote this letter. Christians may have been tempted not to submit to them and to claim allegiance only to Christ. **Ordained of God** means that God puts in place the structures of authority. Even the possibility of a persecuting state did not shake Paul's conviction that civil government is ordained by God.

13:2. The word **damnation** concerns either divine judgment or, more likely, punishment by the governing authorities, since 13:3 ("For") explains this verse (see also 13:4).

13:3. Do that which is good, and thou shalt have praise. Paul was not stating that this will always be true but was describing the proper, ideal function of rulers. When civil rulers overstep their proper function, the Christian is to obey God rather than man (see Acts 4:19; 5:29).

13:4. He is the minister of God. In the order of divine providence, the ruler is God's servant (see Isa. 45:1). **Good** means "advantage," "benefit," "well-being" in a general sense. Rulers exist for the benefit of society, to protect the public by maintaining good order. Cranfield, however, giving full weight to the words "a minister of God to thee [the Christian] for good," suggests that "good" should be taken in the sense of 8:28 (*Epistle to the Romans*, pp. 665–66). **The sword** was the symbol of Roman authority on both the national and the international levels. It represented Rome's power of life and death over its citizens (Tacitus, *History* 3.68). This verse illustrates the biblical principle of using force for the maintenance of good order.

13:5. This statement summarizes 13:1–7. The necessity (**must needs**) to **be subject** is **not only for wrath**, fear of the law and punishment (see 13:3–4), **but also for conscience sake** (see 13:1–2). "For conscience sake" points to the deference the Christian owes to the authority of God. He ordains civil authorities, and to maintain a good conscience, Christians must duly honor them.

13:6–7. Pay you tribute (v. 6) refers to "taxes" (see Luke 20:22 for the same word), and **custom** (v. 7) refers to "revenues" (see Matt. 17:25). The pairing of monetary obligations leads to a pairing of obligations concerning deferential recognition: **fear** and **honour**. Paul made the most of similar sounding words to make his point: in Greek, "tribute," "custom," "fear," and "honour" are, in order, *phoron*, *telos*, *phobon*, *timēn*. The spectrum and variation of these pairings appears to have been an effort on Paul's part to open and close loopholes and to ask and answer questions of exception, as if an exemption might apply to something he did not specifically address. Paul's point was that the Christian with a proper attitude of submission to God's authority will in turn exercise a proper attitude of submission to civil authorities, whom God has ordained, and to the various obligations that entails.

13:8. A connection to 13:1–7 comes in the word **Owe**, which can designate a duty or a debt. All debts may be paid and all duties discharged except for the duty **to love**. To love is the one debt that is never paid off, the one duty that is never done. No matter how much one has loved, he is obligated to keep on loving. **One another** includes not only fellow Christians but all people. **The law**, as becomes clear from 13:9, refers to the Mosaic law, which lays down both moral and social responsibilities.

13:9. Here Paul further explained the last statement of 13:8, namely, that love of neighbor encompasses all one's social responsibilities. **Thy neighbour**, as Jesus taught, is anyone in need (see Luke 10:25–37), which is probably the idea that Paul had in mind here. **As thyself** reflects the Golden Rule (see Matt. 7:12; Luke 6:31). This is not a command to love oneself but a recognition of the fact that one naturally does so and knows how one wants to be treated.

13:10. Whereas love has been defined actively with "thyself" as the standard (13:9), here love is defined passively with one's **neighbour** as the standard: **Love worketh no ill**. The word "ill" connotes "harm" or "wrongdoing" of any kind. This so-called negative definition of love corrects a view of love that rests on sentiment and strong emotion. Love is a quality of action that is courteous of God's best for another.

13:11–14. In this section, as in other New Testament passages, the certain coming of the end of the present age is used to provide motivation for godly living (see, e.g., Matt. 25:31–46; Mark 13:33–37; James 5:7–11; 2 Peter 3:11–14).

13:11. The time refers to the time of salvation, the closing period of the present age, before the consummation of the kingdom. **It is high time to awake** means it is time for action. **Salvation** entails the full realization of salvation at the second coming of Jesus Christ (see 8:23; Heb. 9:28; 1 Peter 1:5). **Nearer than** is even nearer today. Every day brings closer the second advent of Christ.

13:12–13. Darkness (v. 12; see 1 Thess. 5:5) belongs to **The night**, a metaphor for the present evil age; **light** belongs to **the day**. With the words **The night is far spent, the day is at hand**, Paul evoked a picture of the dawning of a new day. His image presents a clear example of the New Testament teaching of the "nearness" of the end times (see Matt. 24:33; 1 Cor. 7:29; Phil. 4:5; James 5:8–9; 1 Peter 4:7; 1 John 2:18). These texts do not mean that the early Christians believed that Jesus would return within a few years (and thus were mistaken); rather, they regarded the death and resurrection of Christ as the crucial events of history that began the last days. Since the next great event in God's redemptive plan is the second coming of Jesus Christ, "the night," no matter how long it may last chronologically, is almost gone. "The day" denotes the appearing of Jesus Christ, which will usher in the consummation of the kingdom. Daytime conduct (**as in the day**; v. 13) is to characterize the believer since he belongs to the coming day and not to the passing night.

13:14. Put ye on the Lord Jesus Christ. "Put on" is an expression that Paul used frequently. Even as one "dresses" for the day, the believer is to "put on," or "clothe himself in," the garment of Christ (see Col. 3:10; Eph. 4:24; see also Gal. 3:27, where the metaphor pertains to baptism). Paul exhorted believers to display outwardly what has already taken place inwardly and to practice all the virtues associated with Christ.

C. Among Weak and Strong Christians (14:1–15:13)

14:1. Him that is weak in the faith probably refers to Jewish Christians in Rome who were unwilling to give up the observance of certain requirements of the law, such as dietary restrictions and observing the Sabbath and other special days. Their concern was not quite the same as that of the Judaizers of Galatia. The Judaizers thought they could put God in their debt by works of righteousness and were trying to force this heretical teaching on the Galatian churches, but the "weak" Roman Christians did neither. They were not yet clear as to the status of Old Testament regulations under the new covenant inaugurated by the coming of Christ. Believers are not to receive or succumb to **doubtful disputations**. Fellowship among Christians is not to be based on everyone's agreement on disputable questions. Christians do not agree on all matters pertaining to the Christian life, nor do they need to do so.

14:2. In contrast to "him that is weak in the faith" (14:1), here Paul described the "strong" Christian. **One believeth** denotes assurance or confidence. The strong Christian's understanding of the gospel allows him to recognize that one's diet has no spiritual significance.

14:3–4. For **despise** and **judge** (v. 3), see 14:10. Scruples of conscience, pro or con, must not be allowed to justify disdain or condemnation, **for God hath received him**. How can a fellow believer reject one whom God has received? Paul pursued this train of thought in his question about **another man's servant** (v. 4), which is a thinly veiled reference to God. A Christian must not reject a fellow Christian, who is also a servant of God. **To his own master he stan-**

deth or falleth, meaning the "weak" Christian is not the master of his "strong" brother, nor is the "strong" the master of the "weak." God is Master, and to Him alone all believers are responsible.

14:5. Questions of preference are not limited to food. Paul expanded the range of possibilities by touching on differing views of calendar observance. Some feel that **one day above another** refers primarily to the Sabbath, but it is probably a reference to all the special days of the Old Testament ceremonial law. One who **esteemeth every day alike** is of the conviction that all days are to be dedicated to God through holy living and godly service. Paul was fully aware that powerful personal convictions were at work, as is clear from his words **fully persuaded in his own mind**. The importance of personal conviction in disputable matters of conduct runs through this passage (see 14:14, 16, 22–23).

14:6. The motivation behind the actions of both the strong Christian and the weak Christian is to be the same: both should want to serve the Lord and give thanks for His provision.

14:7–9. None of us liveth to himself (v. 7). "Us" refers to Christians, who live to please the Lord rather than themselves. **No man dieth to himself.** Even in death, the important thing is one's relationship to the Lord. Paul repeated these truths in verse 8 to emphasize that Christians do not live for themselves or for their own gratification but instead live for Him who is greater to them than even life or death, the **Lord** (v. 9; see discussion on 10:9). Christ's lordship over **both ... the dead and [the] living** arises out of His death and resurrection.

14:10–12. Paul asked the weak Christians, **Why dost thou judge thy brother?** (v. 10). To "judge" is stronger than to "consider" or "have an opinion about." Here, as in 14:3, it carries the sense of "criticize," "find fault with," or "condemn," as the context confirms. Paul then asked the strong Christians, **Why dost thou set at nought thy brother?** "Set at nought" means to treat with disdain or as if lacking merit or worth (the same word as "despise" in 14:3). **We shall all**, each and every Christian, whether weak or strong, give an account at **the judgment seat of Christ**. In

the New Testament, "judgment seat" (Greek, *bēma*) refers to the platform or raised place that designates the official seat of a judge, usually the governor or emperor (see, e.g., Acts 25:10) but also Christ (here and in 2 Cor. 5:10). Paul cited Isaiah 45:23, **every knee ... and every tongue** (v. 11; see Phil. 2:10–11), to certify that no one is exempt from accountability to the Lord. **Every one ... shall give account of himself** (v. 12), a formal account or "reckoning" (Greek, *logos*; see Heb. 13:17; Matt. 12:36), especially of one's actions. The problem for the Roman Christians was just the opposite. The "weak" and "strong" were engaged in giving an account of others. Paul therefore urged them to think of giving an account of themselves, for all will be judged, and the judgment will be based on works (see discussion on 2:6–8; 2 Cor. 5:10; 1 Cor. 3:10–15).

14:13. In light of what Paul wrote in 14:10–12, judging one's brother would smack of taking the very "seat" (Greek, *bēma*) of the Lord Jesus Christ, even as Paul questioned the propriety of displacing the Master by judging His servant (see 14:4). **But judge this rather** pointed Paul's readers to self-examination (see "give account of himself," 14:12) and a better use of judgment. The rest of the verse addressed the strong Christians. **A stumblingblock** is anything that causes one to fall into sin. A comparison of 4:13–14 and 15:1 with 1 Corinthians 8:4–9 shows that Paul's own position belonged to that of the strong Christian, but he made it clear that sympathy for those who have understanding must be matched with sensitivity for those who lack understanding.

14:14. I know, and am persuaded by the Lord Jesus. Now that Paul was a Christian, the old food taboos no longer applied (see Matt. 15:10–11, 16–20; Mark 7:14–23). For Paul's teaching **that there is nothing unclean of itself**, see 1 Timothy 4:4; Titus 1:15. **To him that esteemeth any thing to be unclean, to him it is unclean.** Paul's words must not to be generalized to mean that sin is only a matter of subjective opinion or conscience. He was not discussing conduct that is clearly sinful in the light of Scripture but discussing conduct concerning which Christians may legitimately differ (in this case, food regulations). With regard to such matters, a believer's decisions should be guided by his conscience.

14:15. Walkest thou not charitably means that choices and decisions of conduct are not being governed or guided by love. Love is the key to proper settlement of disputes. **For whom Christ died**, the supreme act of love, is a reminder that Christ so valued the weak brother that He died for him. Surely the strong Christian ought to be willing to make adjustments in his own behavior for the sake of such brothers.

14:16. Your good refers to a legitimate good as gauged by one's own understanding of Christian liberty. If, however, one engages in that "good" apart from the guidance of love (see 14:15), it may **be evil spoken of**. To exercise freedom without responsibility may lead to evil results.

14:17–18. The kingdom of God (v. 17; see discussions on Matt. 3:2; Luke 4:43) invites a change of perspective on matters that concern largely the economy and culture of this world. To be concerned with such trivial matters as **meat and drink** is to miss completely the essence of Christian living. **Righteousness** refers to righteous living. Paul's concern for the moral and ethical dimension of the Christian life stands out in all his letters. For **peace**, see 5:1 and discussion. **Joy in the Holy Ghost** identifies joy given by the Holy Spirit. **In these things serveth Christ** (v. 18) includes the aforementioned qualities belonging to the Spirit.

14:19. Edify another refers to the spiritual building up of individual Christians and of the church (see 1:11–12).

14:20–21. The work of God (v. 20) is here not an abstract program but the weak Christian brother, who as a redeemed person is God's work and in whom God continues to work (see Eph. 2:10). Paul recognized a strong Christian's right to certain freedoms but qualified it with the principle of regard for a weak brother's scruples. **With offence**, like the "stumblingblock" of 14:13, speaks of the inconsiderate exercise of freedom that is detrimental to the spiritual growth of those who are weak in faith. It would be wiser to forgo one's

freedom than to exercise it and thereby hinder the advance of God's work.

14:22–23. Have it to thyself before God (v. 22) means that a believer should be secure within himself that before God his faith is valid (see 14:14). The strong Christian is not required to go against his convictions or change his standards, yet he is not to flaunt his Christian freedom but to keep it a private matter. **Which he alloweth** is probably a reference to the eating of certain foods. For **eateth not of faith** (v. 23) and the issue of certainty and uncertainty, see 14:14. **Whatsoever** pertains to the matters discussed in 14:20–21, namely, conduct about which Christians may have legitimate differences of opinion.

15:1–2. With the words **we then that are strong** (v. 1), Paul identified himself with the strong Christians, those whose personal convictions allow them more freedom than the weak. **To bear** means not merely to tolerate or put up with but to uphold lovingly. **Infirmities** are not sins, since Scripture gives no clear guidance on the matters under discussion. **Not to please ourselves** does not mean that a Christian should never please himself but that he should not insist on doing what he wants without regard to the scruples of other Christians.

15:3. Christ pleased not himself. Christ came to do, not His own will, but the will of His Father, which involved suffering and even death (see Matt. 20:28; Mark 10:45; 1 Cor. 10:33–11:1; 2 Cor. 8:9; Phil. 2:5–8). **The reproaches of them that reproached thee fell on me.** In this quotation from Psalm 69:9, "thee" refers to God, and "me" refers to the righteous sufferer, whom Paul identified with Christ. The quotation serves to show that Christ did not please Himself but voluntarily bore man's hostility toward God.

15:4. Here Paul defended his application of Psalm 69:9 to Christ. In so doing, he stated a great truth concerning the purpose of Scripture: it was written for instruction, so that as one patiently endures, one might be encouraged to hold fast one's **hope** in Christ (see 1 Cor. 10:6, 11).

15:5–6. To be likeminded (v. 5) does not mean that believers should all come to the same conclusions on matters of conscience but rather means that believers should agree to disagree in love. What unifies and harmonizes discordant opinions is the greater and higher agreement found in Jesus Christ (see 15:7), which enables believers to glorify God.

15:7. As Christ also received us (see 14:3–4, 15) introduces grace and thus restores humility to both sides of an opinion.

15:8. Jesus Christ was a minister of the circumcision should be understood as "… to the circumcision," the Jews, as clearly revealed in His earthly ministry. Christ was sent to the Jewish people and largely limited His ministry to them (see Matt. 15:24). God gave a special priority, so far as the gospel is concerned, to the Jews (see 3:1–8). **Promises made unto the fathers** refers to the covenant promises made to Abraham (Gen. 12:1–3; 17:7; 18:19; 22:18), Isaac (Gen. 26:3–4), and Jacob (Gen. 28:13–15; 46:2–4).

15:9–12. The purpose God's redemptive work in and for Israel was **that the Gentiles might glorify God** (v. 9). From the beginning, He had in view the redemption of the Gentiles (see Gen. 12:3). Both the Jews and the Gentiles would see God's mighty and gracious acts for His people and hear their praises as they celebrated what God had done for them (a common theme in the Psalms; see discussion on Ps. 9:1; see also Paul's quotations in these verses, from Deut. 32:43; Ps. 117:1; Isa. 15:12). Thus, they would come to know the true God and glorify Him for His mercy (see discussions on Pss. 46:10; 47:9). God's greatest and climactic act for Israel's salvation was sending the Messiah to fulfill the promises made to the patriarchs and thus to gather in the great harvest of the Gentiles. **A root of Jesse** (v. 12) refers to David, whose father was Jesse (see 1 Sam. 16:5–13; Matt. 1:6); the Messiah was "the Son of David" (Matt. 21:9; see Isa. 11:1; Rev. 5:5). **In him shall the Gentiles trust.** The early church's mission to the Gentiles was a fulfillment of this prophecy, as is the continuing evangelization of the nations.

15:13. God is **the God of hope**. Any hope the Christian has comes from God (see discussion on 5:5). Hope comes **through the power of the Holy Ghost**. Hope cannot be conjured up by man's effort; it is God's gift by His Spirit (see 8:24–25).

VIII. Conclusion (15:14–33)

15:14–15. Paul began the close of his letter with an expression of high praise. In case anyone had taken offense after reading the topics of this letter (**I have written the more boldly**; v. 15), the apostle took steps to assure the Roman Christians of his high regard. **I myself also am persuaded of you** (v. 14) indicates that the following opinion was not that of others only: "I am convinced; yes, indeed, I am" (Black, *Romans*, p. 174). **Full of goodness** is tantamount to saying that the Roman Christians were thoroughly characterized by interest in the welfare of others. **Filled with all knowledge** probably pertains to Christian knowledge, certainly a measure of such sufficiency that Paul could commend their fitness **to admonish one another** (elsewhere the word "admonish" [Greek, *noutheteō*] presumes Christian maturity and is associated with teaching; see 1 Thess. 5:12; Col. 1:28; 3:16). **As putting you in mind** (v. 15) means "as a reminder," inasmuch as the topics of Paul's letter were broadly relevant to all the churches and not at every point directed to specific problems in the church at Rome. Since Paul had never preached or taught in Rome, he referred to generally known Christian doctrines of which the Romans needed to be reminded. **The grace that is given to me of God** alludes to Paul's apostleship (see 1:5, 15:16). Paul validated his ministry (particularly in 15:16–19), a ministry he hoped the Roman Christians would support in its expansion to the west and Spain (see 15:24).

15:16. The minister of Jesus Christ to the Gentiles emphasizes Paul's "administrative" role as "the apostle to the Gentiles" (11:13; see discussion there). The word "minister," used one other time in Romans of civil leaders ordained by God (13:6), is here associated with priestly ministry (see Heb. 8:2), as the words **ministering the gospel** confirm. The Greek word that Paul used for "ministering" (only here in the New Testament) refers to "ministering as a priest." Paul's priestly function was different from that of the Levitical priests. They were involved with the rituals of the temple, whereas he preached the gospel. **That the offering ... might be acceptable, being sanctified by the Holy Ghost**. The offering that Paul brought to God was the Gentile church.

15:17 – 18. With the words **I have therefore whereof I may glory** (v. 17), Paul was boasting, not of his own achievements, but of what Christ had accomplished through him.

15:19. Paul's ministry had been credentialed, so to speak, by the power of the Spirit, one evidence of which was **signs and wonders** (see Acts 14:8 – 10; 16:16 – 18, 25 – 26; 20:9 – 12; 28:8 – 9; 2 Cor. 12:12; Heb. 2:3 – 4). The breadth of Paul's ministry ran **from Jerusalem**, the home of the mother church, where the gospel originated and its dissemination began (see Acts 1:8), to **Illyricum**, a Roman province north of Macedonia (present-day Albania and Yugoslavia). Acts mentions nothing of Paul's ministry there, and perhaps he meant only that he had reached the border. **I have fully preached the gospel** does not mean that everyone in the eastern Mediterranean had heard the gospel. Rather, Paul believed that his work there had been completed and that it was time to move on to other places.

15:20 – 21. Paul elucidated a guiding principle or policy of his ministry: to preach in territories where Christ had yet to be named and where no other preacher had yet laid a **foundation** (v. 20; see 1 Cor. 3:10 – 12). In this effort, Paul was conscious of and inspired by Isaiah 52:15.

15:22 – 23. For which cause (v. 22) refers to Paul's great desire to complete the missionary task in the eastern Mediterranean. Completing that task **much hindered** or prevented him from making a trip to Rome. His **having no more place in these parts** (v. 23) can be attributed to the principle stated in 15:20. Paul's **great desire these many years to come unto you** was also expressed at the outset of the letter (see 1:11 – 15).

15:24. To be brought on my way thitherward by you. Paul wanted to use the Roman church as a base of operations for a mission to Spain. **Be somewhat filled with your company** pictures a visit to Rome of some length; more than a quick stop was contemplated (see 1:11 – 12).

15:25 – 26. Before Paul's desired visit to Rome could take place, he first had to fulfill a responsibility to the church **at Jerusalem** (v. 26; see 15:28) and there **minister unto the saints** (v. 25). "Saints" refers generally to believers in Jesus Christ (see discussion on 1:7). Paul wanted to present a gift, **a certain contribution** (v. 26), personally to the Jerusalem church. The gift needed interpretation. It was not merely money; it represented the love and concern of the Gentile churches in **Macedonia and Achaia** for their Jewish brothers and sisters. Paul called the gift "a certain contribution" (Greek, *koinōnia*; as in 2 Cor. 8:4; 9:13; see 1 Cor. 16:1 – 4; 2 Corinthians 8 – 9) because this was its first mention to the Romans.

15:27. Their spiritual things refers especially to Christ and the gospel.

15:28 – 29. This fruit (v. 28) symbolizes the contribution collected from the Gentile churches. Paul assured the Roman Christians that the delay would not diminish his visit but rather cause it to come **in the fulness of the blessing of the gospel of Christ** (v. 29).

15:30 – 31. Paul invited the Roman church to begin supporting him through prayer, **that I may be delivered from them that do not believe in Judea** (v. 31). Paul wanted to go to Jerusalem. The delivery of the collection was important to him (see 15:25 – 28), but he had received warnings about what might happen to him there (see Acts 20:22 – 23). **May be accepted** is perhaps a reference to the way in which the money was to be distributed — often a delicate and difficult task.

15:32. Paul believed that the prayers he requested in 15:30 would accelerate his visit to Rome. For **be refreshed**, see 1:11 – 12.

15:33. This verse is a provisional close to the letter. For **the God of peace**, see discussions on 5:1; 1 Thessalonians 5:23.

IX. Commendation and Greetings (chap. 16)

16:1 – 2. Phebe (v. 1) was quite possibly one of the carriers of the letter to Rome. She was **our sister** in the sense of being a fellow believer. **A servant** (Greek, *diakonos*) is one who serves or ministers in any way. Regarding women serving in the early church, see discussions on 1 Timothy 3:8 – 11. **Cenchrea** was a port located about six miles east of Corinth on the Saronic Gulf. **Assist her** (v. 2) suggests the same kind of help that she had provided Paul and others at Cenchrea. Judging from the word **succourer** (Greek, *prostatis*), Phebe was a benefactor or patron to many Christians.

16:3 – 5. Greet (v. 3, 5) occurs five times in chapter 16. **Priscilla and Aquila** (v. 3) were close friends of Paul who were tentmakers, as he was (see Acts 18:2 – 3). The two had risked their lives for Paul; they had **laid down their own necks** (v. 4). There is no other record of this in the New Testament or elsewhere, but it must have been widely known, as the last part of the verse indicates. **The church that is in their house** (v. 5) clearly shows that the word "church" denoted an assembly of believers that congregated in a residence or home, the people of God and not a building.

16:6 – 7. Six persons in the New Testament are known by the name **Mary** (v. 6). This one is unknown apart from this reference. **Andronicus and Junia, my kinsmen** (v. 7) probably refers to fellow countrymen (as in 16:11, 21), possibly Jews by birth. They were **apostles** in the sense of being "missionaries" or "messengers" (as in 2 Cor. 8:23; Phil. 2:25).

16:8 – 10. Amplias (v. 8), **Urban … Stachys** (v.9), and **Apelles** (v. 10) were all common slave names found in the imperial household. **Aristobulus** may refer to the grandson of Herod the Great and brother of Herod Agrippa I.

16:11. Herodion my kinsman is perhaps a reference to Herodion's being a Jew (see 16:7). **Narcissus** is sometimes identified with Tiberius Claudius Narcissus, a wealthy freedman of the Roman emperor Tiberius.

16:12. Tryphena and Tryphosa were perhaps sisters, even twins, because it was common for siblings and especially twins to be given names from the same root. **Persis** means "Persian woman."

16:14 – 15. None of these persons can be further identified, except that they were slaves or freedmen in the Roman church.

16:16. Justin Martyr (AD 150) tells us that **a holy kiss** (see 1 Cor. 16:20; 2 Cor. 13:12; 1 Thess. 5:26;

1 Peter 5:14) was a regular part of the worship service in his day. It is still a practice in some churches.

16:17 – 20. These verses present a theological application of the story of man's fall (see Genesis 3). We cannot tell who **them which cause divisions and offences** (v. 17) were, but some of their characteristics are mentioned in verse 18. **Wise unto that which is good** (v. 19) shows that Christians are to be experts in doing good. For **the God of peace** (v. 20), see 15:33. **Shall bruise Satan** is a reference to Satan's final doom (see Gen. 3:15). For **shortly**, see discussion on 13:12.

16:21. Jason is possibly the Jason mentioned in Acts 17:5 – 9. **Sosipater** was probably Sopater son of Pyrrhus from Berea (see Acts 20:4).

16:22. I Tertius, who wrote this epistle. Tertius is not mentioned elsewhere in the New Testament. In writing this letter, he functioned as Paul's secretary (for clues to Paul's use of an amanuensis, or secretary, see 1 Cor. 16:21; 2 Cor. 10:1; Gal. 6:11; 2 Thess. 3:17; Col. 4:18).

16:23. Gaius is usually identified as Titius Justus, a God-fearer, in whose house Paul stayed while in Corinth (see Acts 18:7; 1 Cor. 1:14). His full name was Gaius Titius Justus. **The whole church** refers to the church in Corinth (see Introduction: "Date and Place of Composition"). The name **Erastus** has been identified on an inscription at Corinth. Archaeologists have discovered a reused block of stone in a paved square, with the Latin inscription: "Erastus, commissioner of public works, bore the expense of this pavement." This may refer to the Erastus mentioned here. If it does, it is the earliest reference to a Christian by name outside the New Testament. He may also be the same person referred to in Acts 19:22 and 2 Timothy 4:20, though it is difficult to be certain because the name was fairly common. **Quartus** means "fourth (son)."

16:25 – 27. Paul concluded his letter with a grand doxology. **My gospel** (v. 25) refers not to a gospel different from that preached by others but to a gospel Paul received by direct revelation (see Gal. 1:12). **The preaching of Jesus Christ** is a description of the gospel; it is about Jesus Christ, who is its content. For **mystery**, see 11:25 and discussion.

THE FIRST EPISTLE OF PAUL THE APOSTLE TO THE CORINTHIANS

INTRODUCTION

Author and Date

Paul is acknowledged as the author both by the letter itself (1:1–2; 16:21) and by the early church fathers. His authorship was attested by Clement of Rome as early as AD 96, and today practically all New Testament scholars concur. The letter was written circa 55, toward the close of Paul's three-year residency in Ephesus (see 16:5–9; Acts 20:31). It is clear from his reference to staying at Ephesus until Pentecost (16:8) that he intended to remain there somewhat less than a year when he wrote 1 Corinthians.

The City of Corinth

It has been estimated that in Paul's day Corinth had a population of about 250,000 free persons, plus as many as 400,000 slaves. In a number of ways, it was the chief city of Greece. (See map, *Zondervan KJV Study Bible*, p. 1641.)

Its commerce. Located just off the Corinthian isthmus, Corinth was a crossroads for travelers and traders. It had two harbors: (1) Cenchrea, six miles to the east on the Saronic Gulf, and (2) Lechaion, a mile and a half to the west on the Corinthian Gulf. Goods flowed across the isthmus on the Diolkos, a road by which smaller ships could be hauled fully loaded across the isthmus, and by which cargoes of larger ships could be transported by wagons from one side to the other. Goods flowed through the city from Italy and Spain to the west and from Asia Minor, Phoenicia, and Egypt to the east.

Its culture. Although Corinth was not a university town like Athens, it was characterized nevertheless by typical Greek culture. Its people were interested in Greek philosophy and placed a high premium on wisdom.

Its religion. Corinth contained at least twelve temples. Whether they were all in use during Paul's time is not known. One of the most infamous was the temple dedicated to Aphrodite, the goddess of love, whose worshipers practiced religious prostitution. About a fourth of a mile north of the theater stood the temple of Asclepius, the god of healing, and in the middle of the city the sixth-century BC temple of Apollo was located. In addition, the Jews had established a synagogue; the inscribed lintel of it has been found and placed in the museum at old Corinth.

Its immorality. Like any large commercial city, Corinth was a center for open and unbridled immorality. The worship of Aphrodite fostered prostitution in the name of religion. At one time, one thousand sacred prostitutes served her temple. So widely known did the immorality of Corinth become that the Greek verb "to Corinthianize" came to mean "to practice sexual immorality." In a setting like this, it is no wonder that the Corinthian church was plagued with numerous problems.

Background

Paul had received information from several sources concerning the conditions existing in the church at Corinth. Some members of the household of Chloe had informed him of the factions that had developed in the church (1:11). Three individuals — Stephanas, Fortunatus, and Achaicus — had come to Paul in Ephesus to make some contribution to his ministry (16:17), but whether they were the ones from Chloe's household is not known.

Some of those who had come had brought Paul disturbing information concerning moral irregularities in the church (chaps. 5–6). Immorality had plagued the Corinthian assembly almost from the beginning. From 5:9–10, it is apparent that Paul had written previously concerning moral laxness. He had urged believers "not to company with fornicators" (5:9). Because of misunderstanding, he now found it necessary to clarify his instruction (5:10–11) and to urge immediate and drastic action (5:3–5, 13).

Other Corinthian visitors had brought a letter from the church that requested counsel on several subjects (7:1; see also 8:1; 12:1; 16:1).

It is clear that, although the church was gifted (1:4–7), it was immature and unspiritual (3:1–4). Paul's purposes for writing were: (1) to instruct and restore the church in its areas of weakness, correcting erroneous practices such as divisions (1:10–4:21), immorality (chap. 5; 6:12–20), litigation in pagan courts (6:1–8), and abuse of the Lord's supper (11:17–34); (2) to correct false teaching concerning the resurrection (chap. 15); and (3) to give instruction concerning the offering for poverty-stricken believers in Jerusalem (16:1–4).

Theme and Theological Message

The letter revolves around the theme of problems in Christian conduct in the church. It thus has to do with progressive sanctification, the continuing development of holiness of character. Obviously Paul was personally concerned with the Corinthians' problems, revealing a true pastor's (shepherd's) heart.

This letter is timely for the church today, both to instruct and to inspire. Most of the questions and problems that confronted the church at Corinth are still very much current — problems like immaturity, instability, divisions, jealousy and envy, lawsuits, marital difficulties, sexual immorality, and misuse of spiritual gifts. Yet in spite of this concentration on problems, the book contains some of the most familiar and beloved chapters in the entire Bible — for example, chap. 13 (on love) and chap. 15 (on resurrection).

Outline

    I. Introduction (1:1–9)
       A. Greetings (1:1–3)

Bibliography

Barrett, C. K. *The First Epistle to the Corinthians*. Black's New Testament Commentaries. Peabody, MA: Hendrickson, 1996.

Hodge, Charles. *An Exposition of the First Epistle to the Corinthians*. Grand Rapids, MI: Eerdmans, 1956.

Hunter, Jack. "1 Corinthians." In *What the Bible Teaches*, vol. 4. Ritchie New Testament Commentaries. Edited by Tom Wilson and Keith Stapley. Kilmarnock, Scotland: John Ritchie Ltd., 1986.

Kistemaker, Simon J. *1 Corinthians*. Grand Rapids, MI: Baker, 1993.

Lenski, R. C. H. *The Interpretation of 1 and 2 Corinthians*. Minneapolis: Augsburg, 1963.

Lowery, David, K. "First Corinthians." In *The Bible Knowledge Commentary: New Testament*, edited by John F. Walvoord and Roy B. Zuck. Wheaton, IL: Victor, 1983.

MacArthur, John. *1 Corinthians*. MacArthur New Testament Commentary. Chicago: Moody, 1984.

Mitchell, Dan. *The Book of First Corinthians: Christianity in a Hostile Culture*. Twenty-First Century Biblical Commentary. Chattanooga: AMG, 2004.

Vine, W. E. *The Collected Writings of W. E. Vine*. 5 vols. Nashville: Nelson, 1996.

EXPOSITION

I. Introduction (1:1–9)

The letters of the apostle Paul have common introductory remarks. He generally identified himself, addressed his audience, and then added a courteous greeting to the readers that always brought forth his love for the Lord Jesus and for God the Father. As a chief apostle, Paul was compelled to include a loving greeting from both the Father and the Son.

A. Greetings (1:1–3)

1:1. The apostle wanted to make certain the church understood that his authority was imparted by Christ. Paul was **called to be an apostle** ("one sent with a message"), to carry the good news of the glorious work of Christ on the cross for sinners. From chapter 9, it seems that some believers within the church challenged his apostolic role and ministry. Paul made it clear that he bore witness to the truth **through the will of God**. Many scholars believe **Sosthenes** ("of safe strength") was one of the rulers of the Corinthian synagogue who was beaten when an attempt to prosecute Paul failed (see Acts 18:8).

This beating may have driven him to Christ, and he became a devoted helper of the apostle. God sometimes uses persecution to drive people to the Lord.

1:2. The apostle here addressed the issue of the larger church and the local church. The believers in the church in Corinth positionally were **sanctified in Christ Jesus**, but they belonged to the larger body of Christians, **all that in every place call upon the name of Jesus Christ our Lord**. He is the same Lord, **both theirs and ours**. By faith, every child of God is placed "in Christ." Paul was addressing the setting aside that is the result of union with Christ. Believers are "sanctified," or "made holy," by their relationship to Him. The problem of the Corinthian church was that many were not experiencing daily sanctification and were therefore living carnally (see 3:3). Their walk was out of sorts with their position.

1:3. While "grace and peace" was a common greeting in Paul's day, he did not use it in a perfunctory manner. **Grace** (Greek, *charis*) has the idea of undeserved kindness, while **peace** (Greek, *eirēnē*) is the calmness and inner serenity that comes only from God and the Lord Jesus Christ. The grace and peace that humans give are limited, but true satisfaction and blessing come when these qualities are of a spiritual nature.

B. Thanksgiving to God (1:4–9)

Though Paul took the Corinthian church to task for its sins, he also complimented the church. Here he wanted to make certain these believers understood how blessed they were. While setting out to reform them in their carnality, he reminded them how much God was still at work in their midst. The Lord does not throw away even the most sinful believer. This church had an opportunity to change its ways. It had a wide influence throughout the region for the sake of the gospel and had much work to do.

1:4. Despite the many problems in the Corinthian church, Paul still thanked God for this body of believers. Christ benefited this assembly by **the grace of God**. In Greek, **is given** is an aorist passive particle and may better be translated "was given." Paul may have been thinking of the salvation "grace" that is imparted through Jesus Christ. Perhaps concerned that the Corinthians were puffed up in their self-esteem, Paul reminded them that they were saved by the grace of God, not by their goodness.

1:5. In every way and **in every thing**, the Corinthians were **enriched by** Christ. **Utterance** and **knowledge** could refer to the speaking and knowledge gifts, such as prophecies, tongues, and knowledge (see 13:8). The apostle again reminded them of how blessed they were to have these gifts operating in the assembly. He later chided them for their misuse of these impartations of the Holy Spirit (see chaps. 12–14).

1:6. The spiritual gifts mentioned in 1:5 seem to clearly confirm **the testimony of Christ** in their lives. The Christians in Corinth were not fakes, but they did have tremendous problems with carnality. Though Paul considered himself a feeble speaker (see 2:4), the word of salvation in Christ and the message of the cross was delivered "in the power of God" (2:5).

1:7–8. The apostle pointed out that the Corinthians possessed spiritual gifts and did not **come behind** (v. 7) in the exercise of those gifts. He wanted the believers to have full use of what the Holy Spirit imparted to them (see 12:7–11). **Waiting** (Greek, *apekdechomenous*; see 1 Peter 3:20) is here "waiting patiently," with expectation and longing, **for the coming of our Lord Jesus Christ**. The Greek for "the coming" (*apokalypsin*; "the revelation") is not the term one would expect here. Since Paul and the Corinthians were waiting for this to happen, more than likely he was referring to the revelation of Christ in the rapture of the church. Potentially, this could have happened in Paul's day because no one knows God's timetable for this glorious event.

The Lord would **also confirm** (Greek, *bebaiōsei*; v. 8) the believers, meaning He would make them steadfast and preserve them from falling. **Unto the end** of their lives, the believers would be prevented from falling away, kept steadfast in their belief and in obedience to the truth (see 2 Cor. 1:21). They would be kept **blameless** and would not be charged with apostasy. This does not mean that they would live absolutely perfect lives but that they would be kept from walking away from their faith in Christ (see 1 Thess. 5:23).

1:9. In Greek, **God is faithful** has no verb. It simply says "faithful God." God had **called** the Corinthians into fellowship with his Son, and whom the Lord calls to such a relationship, He also justifies and even glorifies (see Rom. 8:30). Being "called" is the effectual calling of the Holy Spirit, by which the soul is renewed and given an eternal inheritance in glory. **The fellowship** (Greek, *koinōnia*) has to do with the personal communication with which the believer is blessed to enjoy his Savior intimately. Believers are also "conformed to the image of [the] Son" (Rom. 8:29), participate in "the blood of Christ" (1 Cor. 10:16), and participate in "the communion of the Holy Ghost" (2 Cor. 13:14).

II. Schisms and Divisions in the Church (1:10–4:21)

In this lengthy section of the book, Paul spelled out the many problems the Corinthian church faced. The apostle pulled no punches. He was specific about the things that were destroying this body of believers and ruining their testimony before the lost. One of the most compelling objects of this letter was to correct the evils that had come to the surface. Human wisdom had brought about divisions and contentions, and from this came all kinds of sinful practices that were hindering the gospel. The apostle set forth a long list of problems he wanted this assembly to contemplate spiritually.

A. Specific Contentions and Divisions (1:10–17)

1:10. Paul pleaded with these brothers in Christ (**I beseech you**), not in his own name, but **by the name of the Lord Jesus Christ**. The final authority was not the apostle but Christ. Paul wanted them to **all speak the same thing**, stressing their spiritual and biblical unity. Their common moral and spiritual thoughts were to come from God, not simply from their own ideas about the Christian walk. He urged the congregation to stop its **divisions** (*schisma*) and **be perfectly joined together**. "Joined" (Greek, *katartizō*) means "cauterized" (meaning to heal), "restored" (as in healing) or "made fit or complete" (as sometimes used to describe the mending of fishing nets; see Matt. 4:21; Mark 1:19). In Galatians 6:9, Paul used the same Greek word to refer to the restoration of a brother who had been caught in a trespass.

The union Paul had in mind has to do with being of **the same mind** and possessing **the same judgment**. "Mind" has to do with the faculty by which truth is grasped, and "judgment" is the opinion formed in regard to truth, not by insistence upon uniformity (Vine, *Collected Writings*, p.). The believers were to move forward in spiritual unity rooted in truth.

1:11. The house of Chloe had reported to Paul what was going on in the Corinthian church. Chloe (meaning "verdant") is mentioned only here in the New Testament. It is not known whether she was a widow or had a husband who was not a Christian. Her "house" could have been her believing children who informed Paul of the **contentions** (Greek, *er-*

ides; "strifes," "wranglings") **among you**. The following verses seem to indicate that these "wranglings" had to do with the religious teachers among the congregation. Jealousies had sprung up.

1:12. The divisions in the church seem to have been sharp and apparently placed members in different camps: **every one of you saith, I am of Paul; and I of Apollos; and I of Cephas; and I of Christ**. Since Paul was an apostle of the Gentiles, and Peter of the Jews (see Gal. 2:8), more than likely the Gentile converts were in a struggle with the followers of Peter (see Hodge, *First Epistle to the Corinthians*, p. 13). These contentions were driven by false teachers who were Jews (see 2 Cor. 11:13, 22). They worked hard to undermine Paul, possibly not realizing that he also was Jewish.

Apollos was a Jew from Alexandria who was well known for his eloquence, education, and literary culture. The more highly educated Corinthians followed his teachings. The name Apollos comes from the Greek god and means "the destroyer." Early on, Priscilla and Aquila had given him instruction in the faith (see Acts 18:26), and he had grown to become one who greatly strengthened the believers by using the Word of God to show that Jesus was the promised Christ (see Acts 18:28). Apollos was last mentioned in Acts 19:1.

1:13. These three questions are rhetorical and demand a clear no. Christ did not die just for certain people. Paul was certainly not the crucified Savior, nor were the Corinthians **baptized** in Paul's **name**. There is only one redeemer, one Savior, and one expression of baptism. Christians worship Christ alone and are committed and consecrated to Him only. Christianity is not a man-centered religion but one that focuses on the Savior Himself (see Hodge, *First Epistle to the Corinthians*, p. 15).

1:14–15. Paul made it clear that he had gone to Corinth, not to make a huge issue of baptism, but to preach the gospel. He initially recalled that he had baptized no one **but Crispus and Gaius** (v. 14; see 1:16). He mentioned this because he suspected that others would want him to baptize them so they could claim some form of religious fame: "I was baptized by the apostle Paul!" (see v. 15). Crispus ("curly") was a leader in the synagogue (see Acts 18:8) and one of the few whom Paul personally baptized. Tradition says Crispus became the bishop of Aegina. Gaius (Latin, Caius; "I rejoice") was Paul's host in Corinth (see Rom. 16:23). The positions of these two men may indicate why the apostle remembered them.

1:16. As Paul wrote, he then recalled that he had also baptized **the household of Stephanas** ("crown"). "The household" indicates that this man's family and maybe even some of his servants had accepted Christ. Stephanas apparently was one of the first converts Paul made in Achaia and may have been the Stephanas who delivered a letter from the Corinthians when Paul was in Ephesus (see 16:17), though this may not be the same individual.

1:17. Paul made an important point about the relation between baptism and the gospel. While baptism is important as a witness of the believer's cleansing through the work of Christ on the cross, it is not part of the gospel message, nor does it save. Paul separated baptism from the gospel by saying, **Christ sent me not to baptize, but to preach the gospel.** The implication of this is important: baptism is not necessary for salvation (see Mitchell, *First Corinthians*, p. 27), which is not to say baptism is not important. It was commanded by Jesus (see Matt. 28:19) and practiced by the early church (see Acts 2:41), and along with the Lord's Supper, it is a symbol of the sacrifice of Christ and His redemption.

Paul focused on the Corinthian believers' attempt to solve their spiritual problems **with wisdom words of** rather than with spiritual and biblical principles. The apostle was not about to ascribe to the simple gospel its power to save by using poetic oratory (see Mitchell, *First Corinthians*, p. 27). He was repudiating, not godly wisdom, but human reason that attempts to justify one's actions and motives. Such self-effort nullifies **the cross of Christ.** Paul was not talking about a loss of salvation. He was saying that the redemptive work of Christ was having no effect in the Corinthians' daily walk. Whatever obscures the cross deprives the gospel of its power (see Hodge, *First Epistle to the Corinthians*, p. 18).

B. The Various Causes of Divisions (1:18–4:5)

In this section, the apostle went to great lengths to spell out the problems the Corinthian Christians were having. The message to them regarding these problems is certainly applicable to congregations today. Paul cited carnality as a major cause of what was happening in the church and addressed the assembly with strong language. Some have noted that he did not address any elders in his correction and therefore surmise that none in the congregation were qualified for the office. If this was the case, Paul was acting as the elder-apostle, governing the believers and chiding them for having allowed divisions to take hold in the church.

1. A Wrong View of the Christian Message (1:18–3:4)

Without a doubt, the Corinthian church was attempting to live the Christian life by unsanctified ways rather than by focusing on Christ. Such self-serving behavior is ultimately self-destructive (see Luke 9:24–25).

1:18. The preaching of the gospel (see 1:17) and **the preaching of the cross** are virtually the same thing. Actually, Paul said "the word [Greek, *ho logos*] of the cross." Hodge (*First Epistle to the Corinthians*, p. 19) sees this as "the doctrine of the cross." It is the cross that brings salvation; otherwise, there is no redemption. To the world and those who are perishing, the cross is **foolishness** (Greek, *mōria*, from which the word "moronic" comes). What Paul wrote here still stands today. Christ made a similar statement in Matthew 7:13–14: "broad is the way [that leads] to destruction … and narrow is the way [that leads] unto life, and few there be that find it." For the saved, the cross is **the power of God.** For the world, the doctrine of salvation through a crucified Savior is absurd. "The Death of Christ seems, to natural wisdom, unfit to attain its end, and therefore foolishness" (Vine, *Collected Writings*, p. 11).

1:19. Paul quoted Isaiah 29:14: **I will destroy the wisdom of the wise, and will bring to nothing the understanding of the prudent.** "Prudent" (Greek, *synesis*) carries the thought of a quickness of comprehension, a mental alertness that precedes action. It is a human quality admired by the world but useless for salvation. Humanity boasts in such attributes, but God says He will destroy such frail and limited thinking. The context of Isaiah 29:14 has to do with Sennacherib's invasion, when Judah sought the assistance of Egypt. Human political wisdom rendered Judah helpless. The nation of Judah was to depend on God.

1:20–21. Here Paul mocked those who relied on natural wisdom. One would think **the wise** (Greek, *sophos*; v. 20), **the scribe**, and **the disputer** (Greek, *syzētētēs*; "debater") would have the answers to spiritual questions. Instead, **God made foolish the wisdom of this world**. The apostle put this last thought in the form of a question as a challenge to every class of people admired by the world. Neither the esteemed Jewish rabbi and scholar nor the Greek philosopher could ever attain to God's thinking.

The world (Greek, *kosmos*; v. 21) has to do with not simply the "globe" but also the worldly system of humanity. This system is controlled by Lucifer, or Satan, who is the god "of this world" (see also Luke 16:8). This is the realm of spiritual darkness and natural thinking that in no way can please God (see Eph. 2:1–3). Satan is described as "the prince of the power of the air, the spirit that now worketh in the children of disobedience" (Eph. 2:2).

The world could not know God **by wisdom** but only by the **preaching to save them that believe**. This encompasses all that is included in the gospel about who Jesus is, what He did at the cross, and what He accomplished through His resurrection, without which there is no salvation (see 15:17).

1:22–23. Further explaining 1:18–21, Paul pointed out that **the Jews require a sign, and the Greeks seek after wisdom** (v. 22). Both Jew and Gentile found it difficult to rely on God's authoritative word about spiritual and eternal issues, especially in regard to the crucifixion. "Both found it equally difficult to accept a dead man on a cross as an eternal Savior" (Mitchell, *First Corinthians*, p. 31). That Christ was **a stumblingblock** (v. 23) to the Jews is made quite clear in the Gospels. They rejected Him outright as a malefactor and refused to see Him as

their Messiah. Christ became a rock of offense (see Rom. 9:33; 1 Peter 2:8). Whether Jew or Gentile, nothing was more absurd than saying that the blood of the cross could remove sin and secure salvation (see Hodge, *First Epistle to the Corinthians*, p. 23).

1:24–25. Unto them which are called (Greek, *klētos*; v. 24) of God in a sovereign way, whether **Jews and Greeks**, the preaching of Christ crucified (and Christ Himself) is **the power of God, and the wisdom of God**. The Lord calls people by opening their eyes to faith and belief in the gospel. The initiative belongs to God, not man. The doctrine of Christ crucified produces effects on those who are saved, effects that only divine power can accomplish (see Hodge, *First Epistle to the Corinthians*, p. 23).

Paul used hyperbole to explain why human wisdom is not enough: if God acted with **foolishness** (v. 25) and **weakness**, this would still be greater, or **stronger**, than anything man could do. Of course, God is neither foolish nor weak. The Corinthians got the point.

1:26–31. In these verses, the apostle's summary furthered his point about human wisdom and God's divine way of doing things. God uses **the foolish things of the world** (v. 27), things the world would consider foolish, **to confound** those who think they are **wise**. He also uses **the weak things … to confound** those who think they are **mighty**. The wise are operating from the **flesh** (v. 29), from their own wisdom, human nature. The hierarchy of "wise" men includes the **mighty** (Greek, *dynatoi*; "the powerful" who have authority; v. 26) and the **noble**, those who are "well-born." "The things which elevate man in the world, knowledge, influence, rank, are not the things which lead to God and salvation" (Hodge, *First Epistle to the Corinthians*, p. 25). "Paul's readers were not the recipients of the grace of God because of their social status" (Mitchell, *First Corinthians*, p. 31). God is not impressed with what impresses men.

God turns around the things that people think are important. He chooses the **base things** (Greek, *ta agenē*; v. 28), the "ignoble," things that are in contrast to what is "wise." "Base things" refers to those who are not well-bred and who do not come from the nobility. He also chooses the **things which are despised**, the lowly, and **things which are not**, meaning "the things that do not even exist." In other words, the Lord uses things that people do not even think about to accomplish His purposes, that is, **to bring to nought things that are**. This proves that man's thoughts are not God's thoughts and that human beings do not counsel Him (see Isa. 55:8; Rom. 11:34).

God rejects human "things" so **That no flesh should glory in his presence** (v. 29). No one can stand before the Lord Almighty and claim that his conversion or his redemption came about through his own wisdom, birth, station in life, or education. Men may use such means to differentiate themselves, but God does not. The glory belongs to God, not man (see v. 31).

Believers are placed **in Christ Jesus** (v. 30), whom God **made unto us wisdom … righteousness … sanctification, and redemption**. God's "wisdom" initiates salvation through certain doctrinal accomplishments that He renders through Christ. "Righteousness" (Greek, *dikaiosynē*) has to do with the "applied" righteousness, or the justification that comes through the infinite merit of Christ (see Rom. 3:21–22; 2 Cor. 5:21). Believers share in His attribute of perfection, or perfect righteousness, which is imputed to them (see Rom. 4:1–10). "Sanctification" (Greek, *hagiasmos*) here is positional sanctification, which credits Christ's holiness to the believer's account because of the union with Him (see 2 Thess. 2:13; 1 Peter 1:2). "Redemption" (Greek, *lytrōsis*) is here also used in a positional sense (see Titus 2:14; Heb. 9:12; 1 Peter 1:18) and pictures one being redeemed from the slave market of sin and freed by the payment of the Redeemer. Christ paid the price by taking our place at the cross. All believers will experience the final redemption of their bodies, "the redemption of the purchased possession, unto the praise of his glory" (Eph. 1:14).

As a conclusion of 1:18–30, Paul quoted Jeremiah 9:23: **He that glorieth, let him glory in the Lord** (repeated in 2 Cor. 10:17). The citation is an abridged combination of Jeremiah and 1 Samuel 2:10. **In the Lord** is the Septuagint's condensed rendering of "Jehovah." "All that is significant in that title is demonstrated in the New Testament to be true of Christ. To glory in the Father is to glory in the Son (cf. John 14:13)" (Vine, *Collected Writings*, p. 15).

2:1–5. Despite the Corinthians' problems, Paul still called them **brethren** (v. 1). He reminded them that he had not come to them with flattery or **excellency of speech or of wisdom**. These things he repudiated. The word "excellency" (Greek, *hyperochē*) denotes that which "overhangs" with preeminence, that which is superior. It is used in 1 Timothy 2:2 to mean "a high place," a place of "authority." Paul had apostolic authority (see 2 Cor. 11), but he did not like to wield that power unless it was necessary to silence those who rebelled against the Word of the Lord.

Paul had gone to the Corinthians declaring **the testimony of God** (v. 1), or "the witness [Greek, *martyrion*] of God," probably referring either to God's own testimony about the gospel or to Paul's testimony about God, that is, what the Lord revealed and testified to be true. What Paul had testified among the Corinthians was **Jesus Christ, and him crucified** (v. 2). Salvation does not come about by believing that Christ was simply a good teacher, a blessed prophet. The cross of Christ cannot be excluded from who He is and what He came to do. Salvation comes about only by Christ's substitution under the wrath of God and His death for sinners. The apostle already stated that such a message is, from the human standpoint, foolishness to those who are perishing (see 1:18).

Paul had not witnessed to the Corinthians with a pompous demeanor but with **weakness … fear, and … much trembling** (v. 3). Again, he was probably using hyperbole here. He came to them with simplicity, though he may have had some anxiousness of mind because of what he perceived as his insufficiency. He realized how important his task was (see 2 Cor. 7:15; Phil. 2:12; Eph. 6:5). "He had a work to do which he felt to be entirely above his powers" (Hodge, *First Epistle to the Corinthians*, p. 31).

Paul's **speech** (Greek, *logos*) **and … preaching** (Greek, *kērygma*) **was not with enticing words of** man's wisdom (v. 4) but in the work of the Holy Spirit. His ability did not come from his talent and oratory skills. Without the dynamic work and power of God's Spirit in the heart of the hearer, the wisdom and eloquence of the human preacher is not effective. In the New Testament, **demonstration** (Greek, *apodeixis*) means a "showing forth" or "proving by force." This "demonstration" manifests the sovereign work **of the Spirit and of power**, the power He wields in working salvation in the chosen. Contrasting the Holy Spirit with the spiritually impotent human spirit, Paul said that the Corinthians' **faith should not stand in the wisdom of men, but in the power of God** (v. 5). The preposition "in" (Greek, *en*) indicates the sphere in which their faith had its roots. "It has been well said that what depends upon a clever argument is at the mercy of a cleverer argument" (Vine, *Collected Writings*, p. 17). "Those who put their faith in God's power to save them, their faith … 'has found a resting place'" (Mitchell, *First Corinthians*, p. 39).

2:6. The Lord puts a premium on ignorance and rejects human wisdom of all sorts, but there is a place for divine wisdom, the **wisdom** of God that is spoken **among them that are perfect** (Greek, *tois teleiois*). "Perfect" refers to believers who are mature, complete, whole, spiritually competent. God's wisdom does not originate with the **world**, nor from **the princes of this world**. All such human wisdom will **come to nought** (Greek, *katargeō*). Human wisdom will be rendered inactive, and the policies of human potentates are destined to become ineffective (see Vine, *Collected Writings*, p. 18).

2:7. The apostle put forth God's secret wisdom, known only to the Lord and made known to humankind only through His revelation (see Matt. 11:25): **the wisdom of God … a mystery … the hidden wisdom, which God ordained**. "Mystery" refers to God's work or purpose that was once "kept secret" (Rom. 16:25–26) but has now been revealed to His people (see Mitchell, *First Corinthians*, p. 41). Such wisdom was **ordained before the world unto our glory** (Greek, *doxa*). "Glory" refers not to the self-glory of the believer but to God's blessing of those

who are in Christ and the working of His glory for their benefit. "The word *glory* is often used for all the benefits of salvation" (Hodge, *First Epistle to the Corinthians*, p. 35). "Ordained" is *proorizō*, which means "predetermined" in reference to human glory. "The idea that the scheme of redemption, which the apostle here calls the wisdom of God, was from eternity formed in the divine mind" (ibid.).

2:8. As did the apostle John (see John 17:1), Paul linked **glory** with the crucified Savior. This was a total paradox for both the Jews and the Gentiles (see 1 Cor. 1:23), who, though not knowing it, were to a degree witnesses of God's great plan for the redemption of His lost creatures (see Luke 23:24). If they had **known it** (the plan), **they would not have crucified the Lord of glory**. "The Lord of glory" literally means "the Lord whose attribute was glory."

2:9–12. The magnificent blessings of redemption were planned by God the Father, carried out by the Son, and then directed toward those who were chosen (see Eph. 1:3–4), those who love God (see 1 John 4:19). This great truth about redemption cannot be known apart from **his Spirit** (v. 10), who **searcheth … the deep things of God** and gives it to His children. This "searching" demonstrates the personality of the Spirit; intelligent activity is ascribed to Him. His divinity is omniscient; He knows all that God knows and progressively shares this with the believers — an activity referred to as "the doctrine of illumination." That which is beyond human knowledge (see 1 Cor. 2:9) is revealed to those who have received the Spirit, who is **not the spirit of the world, but the Spirit which is of God** (v. 12). Besides the knowledge of salvation, the Holy Spirit conveys to the believer "the deep things of God," or "the depths of God," the inmost recesses of His being, His "perfections and purposes" (Hodge, *First Epistle to the Corinthians*, p. 39).

People can know **the things of a man** (v. 11) only through **the spirit of man** by which they are able to communicate with another human being. Likewise, a Christian can know the things of God only through **the Spirit of God**. The Lord's Spirit is given to us so that we can know God the Father. What believers

have received (v. 12) is not the spirit of the world but **the Spirit which is of God**, who helps us better understand what God has **freely given** to us. **That we might know** (Greek, *oida*) stands in contrast to *ginōskō* (used earlier in v. 11), which suggests an understanding of the relation and meaning of things. *Oida* is knowledge, while *ginōskō* is comprehension.

2:13. Which things also we speak probably refers to the apostles and all who were ministering and setting forth the truth. The source was not **man's wisdom** but what **the Holy Ghost teacheth**. The evangelist or teacher, then, is speaking words "taught by the Spirit," **comparing**, or better "combining" (Greek, *synkrinō*; "together judging, evaluating"), spiritual thoughts with spiritual words. In classical Greek, *synkrinō* is always used in the sense of "to compound" or "to interpret" (cf. Gen. 40:8 Septuagint) (Mitchell, *First Corinthians*, p. 43).

2:14. The natural man cannot receive **the things of the Spirit of God** because such things **are foolishness unto him**. He cannot even **know them** because they have to be **spiritually discerned**, and he, in the natural sense, is incapable of this. This verse stresses the depravity of humanity in that the lost are cut off from God and cannot "reason" up to Him (see Rom. 1:18–32). Also, as Paul explained in 2:11–12, one must have the Holy Spirit to know the things of God, which certainly includes the truth about salvation. "The natural man" (Greek, *psychikos*) operates from the center of himself. He cannot reason spiritually from his inner self. James 3:15 renders *psychikos* "sensual," with the idea of "natural" or "animal-like" (see also Jude 19). Spiritual things are therefore distasteful and unintelligible to the lost.

2:15–16. Here Paul drew a conclusion, stating that the one who **is spiritual judgeth all things** (v. 15). "Spiritual" is *pneumatikos* and is in contrast to *psychikos* (2:14), the "natural" man who has no relationship with God and receives no spiritual enlightenment from the Holy Spirit. The spiritual man is able to comprehend spiritual issues and live the life God desires of him because he "judgeth," or "discerns," all things. Because of this, he receives but limited criticism and condemnation and **is judged of**

no man. "The spiritual man is a riddle to the merely natural. This does not mean that he stands above [all] criticism" (Vine, *Collected Writings*, p. 21). Much of what Paul described here happens progressively. No believer is "born again" with perfect spiritual knowledge.

If the Holy Spirit, who dwells within the believer, gives spiritual discernment, the child of God knows **the mind of the Lord** (v. 16) because he has **the mind of Christ**. When the Spirit of God gives inner spiritual instruction, the Christian knows the mind of God the Father and the mind of His Son, Jesus Christ. "That the phrase 'the mind of Christ' is used as the equivalent of 'the mind of the Lord' (Jehovah, in the Old Testament), is a testimony to the Deity of Christ (cf. Gal. 4:6)" (Vine, *Collected Writings*, p. 21). "We have the mind of Christ because we have the words and thoughts stirred up in our minds through the indwelling Holy Spirit (see Col. 3:16–17; cf. also Eph. 3:17; James 4:5)" (Mitchell, *First Corinthians*, p. 46).

3:1–4. Concluding his discussion of the Corinthians' wrong view of the Christian message, Paul aimed his thoughts even more directly at the problems of the Corinthian church. He again called the believers **brethren** (v. 1; see 1:10; 2:1) but said he could speak to them not **as unto spiritual** but rather **as unto carnal** (Greek, *sarkinos*), or "fleshly," believers. Being "carnal" in spiritual maturity, the Corinthians were **babes** (Greek, *nēpiois*; "non-speakers," or "infants") **in Christ**. The apostle put forward the three types of humanity: (1) "the natural man," who operates only from his own soul and "receiveth not the things of … God" (2:14), (2) the "spiritual" man (2:15; 3:1), who listens to the Spirit of God, and (3) immature, or "carnal" (3:1), believers, who are characterized as "babes in Christ" in contrast to the mature believers mentioned in 2:6.

Paul had to feed this body of Corinthian believers with **milk** (v. 2), which means he could not give them the **meat** of the Word of God to help them grow and mature in the Lord. Previously they **were not able to bear it**, and **neither yet now are ye able**, Paul said. "As newborn babes this condition would be natural and to be expected (1 Pet. 2:2). But, at this state in their development, it is embarrassing. They still are acting like spiritual babes" (Mitchell, *First Corinthians*, p. 49). The proof of their immaturity was their **envying … strife, and divisions** (v. 3), which clearly demonstrated that they were **carnal, and walk[ed] as men**. "'Are you not on a purely human level,' lacking spiritual discernment?" (Vine, *Collected Writings*, p. 23). The division continued as it had begun, over baptism (see 1:12). The church was divided into the camps of Paul and Apollos. Some were claiming, **I am of Paul** (v. 4), and others claimed, **I am of Apollos**. Paul pointed to this as final proof that the Corinthians were still **carnal**. They had focused on men, forgetting that God alone is the true source of blessing (see 3:5 – 9).

2. A Wrong View of the Christian Ministry (3:5 – 4:5)

3:5 – 9. Paul explained that there are no divisions with God. In the pioneering ministry of the gospel, **Paul, and … Apollos** (v. 5) were but human instruments used of the Lord, **ministers by whom ye believed**. These two men were means God used for bringing people to salvation; they were not the first cause. They were only servants who had to give an account to God the Father (see 3:10 – 17). Each man had his own ministry and his own particular place in God's plan. Paul said, **I have planted, Apollos watered; but God gave the increase** (v. 6).

Again, Paul stressed God's sovereignty over His servants, saying, **So then neither is he that planteth** (Paul) **any thing, neither he that watereth** (Apollos)**; but God that giveth the increase** (v. 7). Three principles are seen here. Paul and Apollos were practicing (1) *faithfulness*. Since they differed somewhat in ministry, there was (2) *diversity*. The (3) *ownership*, however, belonged to God (see Mitchell, *First Corinthians*, p. 50). The work is God's, and so is the harvest. "Ministers are nothing. They are the instruments in the hands of God" (Hodge, *First Epistle to the Corinthians*, p. 52). Despite the fact that the servants of the Lord are but carrying out His purposes, He will still reward each one **according to his own labour** (v. 8). "Paul does not develop the thought of the *pay*, or reward (*misthos*), received by God's

gardeners, and it is not clear whether he refers to recompense in heaven, or a return for his labours in the growth of his plants" (Barrett, *First Epistle to the Corinthians*, p. 86). In God's providence, Christians are but **labourers together with God** (v. 9). "Labourers" are but **God's husbandry**, or "farm," producing the yield that He has planned. Believers are also called **God's building**, which is being constructed for His purposes.

3:10 – 17. It is interesting to note the various analogies Paul used to get across his point about the ministry: earlier he spoke of planting and watering; here he spoke of laying a foundation and constructing a building. In this building process, the apostle was not reluctant to share the ministry and the rewards. **The grace of God** (v. 10) was given to Paul to make him **a wise masterbuilder**. He **laid the foundation**, but Apollos **buildeth thereupon**. In the Christian life, no **other foundation** (v. 11) can be laid except that **which is Jesus Christ**. Salvation and the entire spiritual life are held up by Him. Once faith establishes Jesus as the foundation, the believer is constructing his spiritual life, his existence, upon Him. The quality of that construction is important. Will it be of precious materials, such as **gold, silver, precious stones** (v. 12), or flimsy building elements, such as **wood, hay, [and] stubble?** "'Gold, silver, precious stones refer to the apostle's teaching, also that of Apollos and other good men, whereas the 'wood, hay, and stubble' refer to teaching that was divisive, marked by the wisdom of this world" (Hunter, *1 Corinthians*, p. 37).

There will be an answering, or a **day** (v. 13) of reckoning, that **shall declare** what kind of work it is. That work **shall be revealed by fire**, and that **fire shall try every man's work of what sort it is**. These verses and others (see, e.g., 2 Cor. 5:9 – 11) describe what is called the *bēma*, or "the judgment seat of Christ," where "every one [will] receive the things done in his body … whether it be good or bad" (2 Cor. 5:10). This judgment, mentioned in both letters to the Corinthians, is not meant to determine the believer's eternal destiny but rather his ministry reward. If the works done in this life, based on the foundation of Jesus Christ, were for His sake, the believer **shall receive a reward** (v. 14).

Some have mistakenly argued that this passage refers to a judgment in which the believer's life will be tested by fire to determine whether he will be admitted into heaven. The believer's eternal destiny, however, was completely and fully settled at the cross. Salvation is assured because of the faithfulness of Christ, not because of human efforts to stay saved. It is one's works that will be tested as by fire, to determine their durability. **If any man's work shall be burnt, he shall suffer loss: but he himself shall be saved; yet so as** if he had passed through **fire.** "If the person's work remains undamaged by the fire, he or she receives rewards (*misthos*, "wages"; cf. v. 8). Of course, it goes without saying that even the wages mentioned here are entirely a gift of grace (cf. Dan. 12:3; 1 Cor. 9:19; 2 John 1:8; Rev. 4:4; 11:18)" (Mitchell, *First Corinthians*, pp. 54 – 55).

As important as rewards may be, Paul reached for a higher incentive. He reminded the Corinthians that they were collectively **the temple of God** (v. 16) in which **the Spirit of God dwelleth**. If someone comes against the temple, **him shall God destroy** (v. 17). The apostle was describing the church as a group, a body of believers with whom God fellowships and resides. He does not want the church to suffer tampering. "The prospect of such people [harming the church] is a fearful one. They will fall under the condemnation of God" (Mitchell, *First Corinthians*, p. 55). "The verb *phtheirō* signifies to destroy by corrupting; here it is used, firstly, of the marring of an assembly by unprofitable teaching and by producing a party spirit thereby, or by leading it away by any means" (Vine, *Collected Writings*, p. 26). God takes this seriously because despite the imperfections of how believers may walk at any specific moment, they are still seen positionally as **holy** because they belong to Christ.

3:18 – 23. The apostle continued to drive home the issue that human wisdom does not bring one to God. In a twist in his argument, he said one needs to put away what the world calls wisdom and **let him become a fool, that he may be wise** (v. 18). He again

said that **the wisdom of this world is foolishness with God** (v. 19; see 1:18). The apostle then quoted Job 5:13, **it is written, He taketh the wise in their own craftiness**, and Psalm 94:11, **the thoughts of the wise ... are vain** (v. 20). **Therefore,** Paul said, one should not **glory in men** (v. 21). He then made what seems to be a strange statement: **For all things are yours.** The answer appears to be, "Only as we belong to Him do things belong to us. Since we are members of Christ, and all things are under His authority and control (Matt. 28:18; Rom. 14:9; 1 Cor. 15:27), they are *ipso facto* subservient to our real welfare" (Vine, *Collected Writings*, p. 27).

Because "all things" (v. 21) belong to believers, the child of God has access to all, **whether Paul, or Apollos, or Cephas** (Peter), **or the world, or life, or death, or things present, or things to come** (v. 22). Paul concluded this section by saying, **ye are Christ's; and Christ is God's** (v. 23). The church belongs to the Lord Jesus, and He is subject to God the Father. Since the church is the possession of Christ, both the church and Christ are in subordination to the Father. The Son and Father are of the same substance, yet the *economic* submission of the Son to the Father exists within the Godhead. This is beyond human comprehension, yet it stands as a solid doctrine in Scripture (see Phil. 2:6 – 11; Heb. 1:3).

4:1. In view of the previous passage, it is clear that all who serve the Lord Jesus Christ are responsible as **ministers** to Him and are **stewards** (Greek, *oikonomos*; "household managers") **of the mysteries of God.** Because the word "mystery" (Greek, *mystērion*) is in the plural, Paul's meaning is open-ended. "Mystery" means "something not before revealed," and the New Testament speaks about many subjects as a mystery: (1) "the mystery of the kingdom of God" (Mark 4:11); (2) the mystery of the unification of Jews and Gentiles into one body, the church (Ephesians 2 – 3); (3) "the mystery of the gospel" (Eph. 6:19); (4) "the mystery of the faith" (1 Tim. 3:9); and (5) the mystery of the rapture of the church (1 Cor. 15:51), among others.

4:2. Because such great truths are revealed to God's **stewards**, it is imperative that they be **found**

faithful. They must be ready to give their Master an account of their loyalty. The Lord certainly sees one's faithfulness, but others also witness it.

4:3. Paul considered himself a faithful servant of Christ. He made it clear, however, that he was not to **be judged** by the Corinthian church or by any other **man's judgment**, adding even, **I judge not mine own self**. The Lord alone was his judge. One of the problems Paul had to contend with in this body of "carnal" (3:3–4) believers was their criticism of him and his apostleship. In 4:6–21 and in 2 Corinthians 10–11, he forcefully answered their criticisms. Though an apostle, Paul still could not judge his own motives or the quality of his service. How could others decide such issues?

4:4–5. In writing, **I know nothing by myself** (v. 4), Paul was not repudiating his apostolic and prophetic offices, nor the revelations that were given to him exclusively. Likewise, **I [am] not hereby justified** does not refer to salvation and justification by faith. In this passage, Paul was discussing motives and actions. He was responsible to God: **he that judgeth me is the Lord**. "'My judgment of myself is not final… Paul felt himself accountable to Christ" (Hodge, *First Epistle to the Corinthians*, pp. 66–67).

Paul stated that judgment needs to be held off **until the Lord come** (v. 5), who will then **bring to light** what is **hidden** and make clear **the counsels of the hearts**, so that all will **have praise of God**. Apparently, this judgment of believers will occur at the rapture of the church. James seems to have had this in mind when he wrote, "The coming of the Lord draweth nigh. Grudge not one against another, brethren, lest ye be condemned: behold, the judge standeth before the door" (James 5:8–9).

C. Overcoming Divisions (4:6–21)

The apostle came out swinging to rebuke those within the Corinthian church who were attempting to discredit his ministry to the church. Having set forth the guidelines that should govern this assembly, he went on to discuss their divisions. With strong appeals against this state of things (vv. 7–8), he maintained that he ministered to them in full in-tegrity and openness, even foregoing any help from them (v. 12) and abiding their defamation of his work and his character (v. 13).

4:6. To make a point, he wrote **in a figure transferred** what he was writing about to himself and Apollos for the sake of the Corinthian believers. "Transferred" is the Greek word *metaschēmatizō*, which means to "change in appearance or form." It is translated "change" in Philippians 3:21, where it refers to the fashioning anew of the believer's body in the rapture of the church. Paul used himself and Apollos to illustrate the principle underlying his instruction. "Paul avoided singling out guilty persons by name. Instead he applied the problem cases to Apollos and himself (and Peter and Christ; cf. 1:12; 3:4–6, 22:33)" (Lowery, "First Corinthians," p. 512). Paul desired for the Corinthians to **learn** (Greek, *manthanō*; "to learn by practice or doing") so that they would not be **puffed up … one against another** in spiritual competition.

4:7. People **differ from** each other because they **receive** unique talents or characteristics from God. Paul therefore asked the Corinthians, **why doest thou glory, as if thou hadst not received** such differences from the Lord? The word "differ" (Greek, *diakrinō*) means to "make a distinction." With those distinctions, however, many in the church were saying that such abilities were self-generated and not divinely imparted. This was bringing about self-conceit.

4:8. Because of God's gifts given to the Corinthian believers, they were **rich**, or **as kings**, but they were taking these blessings and **reign[ing] as kings** over the apostles and their guidance. They were **full** (Greek, *korennymi*; "satiated") with assumed spiritual fullness. They believed they had reached the goal of perfection very quickly, and that **without us**, the apostle added. "Paul represents the Corinthians as thinking that they had already attained the full blessedness of the Messiah's reign … and were already perfect" (Hodge, *First Epistle to the Corinthians*, pp. 71–72).

4:9–13. Using irony and sarcasm, Paul mocked the Corinthians' sense of superiority in the realm of

Christian service and maturity. He said, **God hath set forth us the apostles last** (v. 9), as if destined for **death**. They had been **made a spectacle unto the world**, and even **to angels, and to men**. The apostles were **fools** (v. 10) for the sake of Jesus, but the Corinthians were **wise**; Paul and others were **weak**, but the Corinthians were **strong**. The apostles were **despised**, but the Corinthians were **honourable**.

The apostles were hungry, thirsty, naked, buffeted about, with **no certain dwellingplace** (v. 11). They worked hard with their **own hands** (v. 12) but were **reviled**. They **bless[ed]** but were **persecuted** and **suffer[ed]** it. The apostles were **defamed** (v. 13) and were seen as **the filth** ("refuse," "scum," "rubbish") of humanity. Even **unto this day**, the apostles continued to be treated as **offscouring** (Greek, *peripsēma*; "filth," "that which is wiped off").

4:14–17. While Paul could have written **these things to shame** (v. 14) his critics, he did not. Instead, he wrote to them **as my beloved sons** to **warn** them. While they could have had **ten thousand instructers in Christ** (v. 15) in place of the apostles, they had **not many fathers** who really cared for their spiritual growth. **In Christ Jesus** and **through the gospel**, Paul had **begotten** them. "Instructors" (Greek, *paidagōgos*) means "child leaders." Such an instructor was often a slave that gave supervision over the pedagogical learning of the master's son. For Paul, "a spiritual relationship had been established between him and the saints through the Gospel which he brought to them" (Vine, *Collected Writings*, p. 33). Because of this, Paul said, **I beseech you, be ye followers of me** (v. 16). "Followers" (Greek, *mimētēs*) refers to those who imitate or attempt to emulate a teacher, or in this case the father, in how he thinks and acts (see Eph. 5:1; Phil. 3:17).

For this cause (v. 17), that the Corinthians might become true "followers," Paul had sent **Timotheus** (Timothy), his **beloved son** who was **faithful in the Lord**, to refresh the Corinthians in his **ways ... in Christ**. Paul said that these "ways" were the same spiritual principles he taught **in every church**. This is an important statement because it shows that in the church dispensation, spiritual principles are the same in every local assembly. While some issues each congregation may face, generally problems are the same, and biblical and spiritual answers are for everyone in the body of Christ. Paul sent Timothy because he could trust him, and he gave Paul much comfort. Elsewhere Paul said, "I have no man likeminded" as Timothy (Phil. 2:19–20).

4:18–21. Some members of the congregation in Corinth disregarded Paul, were **puffed up** (v. 18), and argued that he would not give his time to come and visit their church. Paul, however, said that **if the Lord will** (v. 19) allow it, **I will come to you shortly**. He reminded them that **the kingdom of God** (v. 20) is not simply about speaking a **word**; it is about **power**, the power of God. By speaking of "the kingdom of God," Paul was not referring to the millennial reign of Christ, which is yet to come on earth. The ultimate destiny of all things, even believers in Christ in this present dispensation of grace, is the one-thousand-year rule of Christ in Jerusalem. Paul may have had this in mind, but it is also possible that he had in view "the Kingdom of God is as a general term, the realm of His [present] rule. As, however, the earth [now] is the scene of rebellion against Him" (Vine, *Collected Writings*, p. 34).

Paul asked, How **shall I come unto you[?] with a rod, or in love, and in the spirit of meekness?** (v. 21). The "rod" of discipline is a metaphor for the rebuke administered by a pedagogue or teacher. "Love" emphasizes parental patience and concern. "The spirit of meekness" is in contrast with stern discipline. "The question implies that the choice of the alternatives, in his mode of dealing with them, lay with themselves" (Vine, *Collected Writings*, p. 34).

III. Immorality in the Church (chaps. 5–6)

A. The Fruit of a Lack of Discipline in the Church (chap. 5)

Besides the divisions in the Corinthian church, another evil caught Paul's attention. The church had allowed a man guilty of incest to stay within the fellowship; it was reported that fornication was generally tolerated among them, without any punishment or discipline (v. 1). Incest was not allowed even among the pagan Gentiles. With apostolic anger, Paul reproved the Corinthians for being so insensitive and spiritually inflated. They did not have a sense of humility and penance, nor had they excommunicated the one who was engaging in incest (v. 2).

5:1. The incest apparently had to do with a Corinthian Christian who was carrying on with his stepmother, a relationship that is forbidden in the Old Testament (see Lev. 18:8; Deut. 22:22, 30). Such a relationship was forbidden even in Roman law (see Cicero *Cluentes* 6; Gaius *Instutitis* 1.63; Lowery, "First Corinthians," p. 514). That Paul said nothing about the woman may suggest that she was not a believer in the Lord. The incestuous affair was not hidden from the assembly but was engaged in openly and **reported commonly**. The whole community knew about it.

5:2. Instead of feeling shame that one of their members was involved in incest, the congregation was **puffed up**, apparently gloating over their Christian liberty, which was a distortion of the doctrine of grace. The church had not **mourned** before God or others, that this man might be removed from the fellowship. Evidently, no one was doing anything or saying anything to correct the situation.

5:3–5. These verses make up one long sentence, which shows how disturbed Paul was about the matter; he could not stop writing until he had completed his thoughts (see Hodge, *First Epistle to the Corinthians*, p. 83). Though Paul was **absent in body** (v. 3), he was still **present in spirit** and had **judged already** the matter **concerning him that hath so done this deed**. Paul did not have to come to the Corinthian church to determine whether the relationship was right or wrong. In both the Old Testament and the New Testament, God has spelled out His eternal moral principles.

In the name of our Lord Jesus Christ (v. 4), with the church **gathered together**, and **with the power of ... Christ**, the offending brother was to be delivered **unto Satan for the destruction of the flesh** (v. 5). The reason: so that his **spirit may be saved in the day of the Lord Jesus**. Since "the whole world lieth in wickedness" (1 John 5:19), the idea is

that the man would get a taste of what Satan does in his own realm. He brings on the human race severe retribution and affliction, even physical destruction. Satan the "adversary is ever seeking to tempt the children of God to turn aside from the right ways of the Lord, and is occupied in laying snares for them (1 Tim. 3:7)" (Vine, *Collected Writings*, p. 37). The man might have to suffer physically in a terrible way to cause him to drop his sinful ways and thus not be castigated so intensely "in the day of the Lord Jesus," more than likely referring to the *bēma* judgment. The issue was not the man's eternal destiny but rather the sins he was practicing openly in his Christian walk. "It thus became a painful example of the price of self-centered indifference and a powerful reminder of the demand for holiness in God's temple (1 Cor. 3:17; 6:19)" (Lowery, "First Corinthians," p. 514). The man would still be saved, "yet so as by fire" (3:15).

5:6. Having chided them for being "puffed up" (5:2) over this issue, Paul added that they were **glorying** (Greek, *kauchēma*; "boasting") and that such glorying **is not good**. He reminded them of the principle of the **leaven** and **the whole lump** of dough. As does leaven, sin spreads throughout the entire loaf of dough (see discussion on Mark 8:15). The whole congregation was morally polluted because of this issue. "It is no less true of any community, that any [toleration of] evil deteriorates its whole moral sense" (Hodge, *First Epistle to the Corinthians*, p. 86).

5:7–8. Paul commanded the church to **purge out ... the old leaven** (v. 7) that they might **be a new lump**. His next statement may seem contradictory at first: **ye are unleavened** because Christ **our passover ...** is **sacrificed for us**. Walking and living as "a new lump" has to do with believers' daily experience in Christ. The Corinthians were not to be a polluted lump of dough; they were to be dough without leaven. Christ was "sacrificed for us" and yet was without sin. Because He offered a pure sacrificial body, believers are to live in their bodies in a pure and holy way. Jesus fulfilled the true meaning of the Old Testament sacrifice. He was the Passover Lamb of God (see Isa. 53:7; John 1:29). He was crucified on Passover day, a time of celebration that began the evening before the Passover supper was consumed (see Exod. 12:8).

Paul used the Passover feast as an analogy, encouraging the Corinthians to partake of **the feast** (v. 8), not with sinful **old leaven**, satiated with **malice and wickedness; but with the unleavened bread of sincerity and truth.** The apostle was saying, "Let your entire life be as a sacred festival, that is, as a consecration to the Lord." This was to be done in "sincerity" (Greek, *eilikrineia*; "purity," "transparent clarity") and living subjective "truth" that can be seen by all.

5:9–10. Paul had previously written to the Corinthians about not keeping **company with fornicators** (v. 9), but in the providence of the Lord, that letter was not kept as part of the New Testament canon. The church was not to mix with **the fornicators of this world** (v. 10). Moreover, the church was not to associate or have fellowship **with the covetous, or extortioners, or with idolaters.** The covetous defraud, the extortioners exact what is not justly theirs, and the idolaters worship false gods. These descriptions are but the tip of the iceberg of sin and evil in the world. If the Corinthian believers associated regularly with such people, **then must ye needs go out of the world.** Believers would "have to seek another world to live in" (Hodge, *First Epistle to the Corinthians*, p. 90). The believers' "future role should have radically affected their practice in the present (cf. 1 John 3:3)" (Lowery, "First Corinthians," p. 516).

5:11–13. Paul did not want the believers **to keep company** (v. 11) with such people. Here he added in these lines **a railer, or a drunkard** to the list in 5:9–10. The "railer," or "reviler," is one who uses abusive and violent language against someone else. This could also be a "slanderer." The "extortioner" (Greek, *haparx*) is one who robs or takes as spoil another's goods. The believer is **not to eat** with such people.

The apostle made it clear that believers are not to **judge** (v. 12) the lost, those who **are without.** Instead, those in the church should **judge them that are within.** God will take care of those who **are with-**out (v. 13). The responsibility of the local church is to **put away** from the body **that wicked person.**

B. Strife from a Lack of Discipline in the Church (6:1–11)

In this section, Paul addressed an issue that must have been a persistent problem, that of fellow Christians taking each other before secular judges to solve disputes. He questioned why believers should settle issues this way. Why could they not solve their problems in an amicable way? Even if they couldn't, they were not to go before pagan arbitrators but rather to take their cases before qualified Christians.

6:1. Paul spoke his mind on the matter and even called the secular judges **the unjust.** This may indicate that most Gentile judges in the government courts were prejudiced or could be bribed. When a believer has **a matter against another** brother, why does he not go **before the saints** to settle the problem?

6:2–4. Six times in this chapter, Paul said, **Do ye not know** or **Know ye not** (vv. 2, 3, 9, 15, 16, 19). He appears to have been provoking them to their senses in realizing how foolish they were being over certain problems. Did the Corinthian church not realize that someday (probably in the millennium) **the saints shall judge the world** (v. 2) and even **angels** (v. 3)? If believers are someday going to have such responsibility, why can they not now judge **the smallest matters** (v. 2) and **things that pertain to this life** (v. 3) in a proper manner without rumblings? To Paul, something appeared to be out of order. The problems in this church were petty, and the believers had their noses too close to small issues and minor grievances. In their Christian relationships, they had lost their perspective. The peace in the assembly was broken because these problems were taking place **in the church** (v. 4). Some feel Paul was using irony when he instructed the Corinthians to set the **least esteemed** to judge. He could have meant, "Set your least esteemed members to decide such matters" or "Do you set as judges those least esteemed in the church?" (Hodge, *First Epistle to the Corinthians*, p. 96).

6:5–6. I speak to your shame (v. 5) indicates Paul was disgusted with their practice of taking each other before secular courts. He questioned whether there was **not a wise man**, meaning one with spiritual wisdom, among them, **not one that shall be able to judge between his brethren**. He could not understand why **brother goeth to law with brother, and that before the unbelievers** (v. 6). "Such lawsuits certainly did not glorify God (10:31–33)" (Lowery, "First Corinthians," p. 515). When those who claim to be Christians wrangle before the lost, it casts doubt on the effect of the gospel.

6:7–8. Paul said that their practice of **go[ing] to law one with another** was **utterly a fault**. It was a **wrong**, and they **suffer … to be defrauded**. It appears that the main motive for such actions was personal gratification rather than redressing wrongs. Under the Mosaic law, God appointed judges to administer justice among the people, but He did not do so under the dispensation of the church. Believers are to solve issues among themselves, operating from a sense of grace and not from a heart of carnality. In view of this passage, one might question Paul's appeal to Caesar when he was accused of teaching things against the Jewish law, against the temple, and even against Caesar (see Acts 25:8). Did the apostle not wish to be tried by Caesar Augustus (see Acts 25:25)? Being a citizen of the Roman Empire, Paul had the right to such an appeal. The Jews accused him of civil disturbance and even with insurrection against the name of Caesar. Paul was willing to "stand at Cesar's judgment seat" (Acts 25:10) because he had done no wrong against the Jews. The Jews were Paul's natural brethren in the flesh, but since they had not trusted Christ, they were not his spiritual brethren.

6:9–10. Why have a relationship with **the unrighteousness** (v. 9), who **shall not inherit the kingdom of God**? Here Paul used the term "unrighteousness" to describe those who are "unjust," the spiritual state of the lost, in contrast to those who have trusted Christ as their Savior. While believers can do unrighteous acts, they are categorized as "saints" because of their position in Christ. It is only natural for the lost to freely and without conscience practice unrighteousness. The apostle again added to his list of sins (see 5:9–11) that are common to those

without Christ: **adulterers … effeminate … abusers of themselves with mankind**. "Adulterers" implies those who have relations with another's wife. "Effeminate" means "soft" and refers to the male who plays the female role in a homosexual relationship. "Abusers" (Greek, *arsenokoitēs*; "man-bed") seems to refer to homosexual acts.

6:11. Even the vilest person can be saved by the grace of Christ, for, Paul said, **such were some of you**. Now, however, they were **washed … sanctified**, and **justified in the name of the Lord Jesus, and by the Spirit of our God**. "Washing" refers to the baptism of the Holy Spirit, whereby believers are placed into the spiritual body of Christ (see 12:12). "Sanctified" refers to the spiritual sanctification whereby the believer united to Christ is "set aside," or "made holy" (made a "saint"), by his new relation to the Lord (see 1:2; 2 Thess. 2:13; Titus 3:5). Some in the Corinthian church, in fact all of them before their conversion, had been as Paul described in 6:9–10. Now, however, they had a new position in Christ.

C. Failure to Judge Immorality in the Church (6:12–20)

Paul has already written about all the moral failures of the Corinthian church. "All things are lawful" (v. 12) introduces the idea of liberty in Christ. The context, however, makes it clear that this does not include immoral acts. Believers are not free to practice sin without impunity; freedom in Christ does not remove the need for self-governance. If one has been made holy because of his relationship to Christ, it would be foolish to argue that he now has open season to sin as he wishes. In this section, Paul continued to hammer away at the sins this church apparently was practicing without compunction.

6:12. All things are lawful … but all things are not expedient (Greek, *sympherō*). "Not expedient" means "not to be brought together," "not profitable." "All use of Christian liberty must be beneficial" (Vine, *Collected Writings*, p. 45). No matter that there is some freedom in some things, Paul refused to **be brought under the power of any**. Wisdom and self-discipline are the rule in Christian life.

6:13–14. Meats (food; v. 13) and **the belly** are legitimate connections; the Lord designed them to function together. The time will come, however, when **God shall destroy both**, and men will no longer be sustained by this natural order. The human body is not made **for fornication**. The body is for the Lord's use, and the Lord will use the body for His own purposes. "The body was never designed for promiscuous" use (Hodge, *First Epistle to the Corinthians*, p. 103).

By his own power (v. 14), God will **raise up us** as He **raised up the Lord** Jesus from the grave. The intensive form of "raise up us" is "perhaps suggesting that the future act will be no less sure than the past. The same power which wrought in the resurrection of Christ will be put forth in the resurrection of believers" (Vine, *Collected Writings*, p. 45).

6:15–17. Believers' bodies belong to Christ and not to **a harlot** (v. 15). **God forbid**. The believer's union with the Lord Jesus affects both him and the Savior. One cannot act without affecting the other. To prove his point, Paul quoted Genesis 2:24 (and Matthew 19:5), where the Lord said the **two** (v. 16), man and woman, **shall be one flesh**. One of the key doctrines of the Bible is that the union of the believer with Christ creates a community of life. The Bible clearly teaches that this life pertains to the body as well as the soul (see Rom. 8:6–11; Eph. 2:6–7; 5:30).

He that is joined unto the Lord is one spirit (v. 17). In the Upper Room Discourse (John 13–17), Christ expressed this spiritual union to the disciples (see John 14:20; 15:4–5). He mentioned it again in His prayer to the heavenly Father (John 17:21–23). This vital spiritual union with the Lord is kept in place and maintained by the indwelling Holy Spirit of God. This profound truth is all too often simply forgotten. The Christian does not walk through this life alone; he has a new and unbroken relationship with Christ that gives comfort.

6:18. Paul commanded the Corinthians to **Flee fornication**. This indicates that some in this church were flirting with the worst of sins. Most sins are those that go outward, that is, outside, **without the body**. Fornication, however, is more specific and personal. For the Christian, it is sinning **against his own body**.

6:19–20. Paul asked a rhetorical question, something they should have already known: **know ye not that your body is the temple of the Holy Ghost …?** (v. 19). He had earlier told them, "Ye are the temple of God, and … the Spirit of God dwelleth in you" (3:16). This indwelling is made clear in Scripture (see, e.g., 12:13; 1 John 3:24). Because of His indwelling, the Spirit can be grieved (see Eph. 4:30) and quenched (see 1 Thess. 5:19). The believer has been **bought with a price** (v. 20; see Acts 20:28; Gal. 3:13); **ye are not your own** (v. 19). The purchase was made "with the precious blood of Christ" (1 Peter 1:19). The child of God, then, is to **glorify God in your body, and in your spirit** (v. 20), which belong to the Lord.

IV. Various Problems in the Church (chaps. 7–14)

A. Directives concerning Marriage (chap. 7)

The Corinthians had written to the apostle about some troubling issues in their church. Paul wanted to make sure they understood that marriage was not expedient. He wrote that every man should have his own wife, and every wife should have her own husband. The obligation is mutual for both parties; neither has the right to desert the other. Temporary separation for devotional reasons is permissible. What Paul wrote here seems to be only advice (see v. 6). He could only tell them what was expedient under the circumstances; each one must act according to the grace given him (see vv. 6–9). Ideally, divorce was not an option for any Christian, though if an unbelieving spouse left, they would not be judged for their decision. Paul's discussion of marriage logically follows his words about honoring the body (chap. 6).

1. Concerning Celibacy (7:1–9)

7:1. Now concerning shows that Paul knew there was some inappropriate intimacy in Corinth because the Christians there had written him regarding this matter. Because of the dangers of lust, **it is good for a**

man not to touch a woman. While many take this to mean that it is good for a man to remain unmarried, it may refer to actual touching.

7:2. Paul apparently was concerned about fraternization between single (or married) men and women, which could lead to sexual problems. Thus, **to avoid fornication ... every man** should **have his own wife, and ... every woman** should **have her own husband.**

7:3–4. No one can accuse Paul of being against marriage. He commanded **the husband** (v. 3) and **the wife** to **render ... due benevolence** in the marriage relationship. "Render" means that this is an obligation, not simply the granting of a favor. "The recognition of the conjugal rights of marital intercourse is to be regulated by mutual consideration" (Vine, *Collected Writings*, p. 48). Paul stressed the equality and reciprocity of the husband and wife's sexual relationship by emphasizing the "responsibilities of each to satisfy the other" (Lowery, "First Corinthians," p. 517).

7:5–7. Defraud (v. 5) not each other, Paul said, although it is permissible **with consent** to abstain **for a time, that ye may give yourselves to fasting and prayer.** The couple is then to **come together again** so that **Satan** might not win over **for your incontinency.** He told them that his advice was that of **permission, and not of commandment** (v. 6). In general, the apostle's advice seems to have been that he desired that the married couple work these issues out by mutual agreement and with no hard feelings or resentments.

These verses show that the Christian community, even in the carnal Corinthian church, was very serious about their appeals to God. Fasting was practiced, and devoting oneself to intense prayer during a period of isolation seems to have been common. That there is no hint of any special adherence to seasonal prayers or specific times of the year to carry out these spiritual dedications shows that the early church did not observe set ceremonial feasts and holidays, which came about later in church history.

For the sake of the ministry, Paul wanted the church to be **even as I myself** (v. 7). It seems clear

that Paul was unmarried or possibly widowed. He urged celibacy because of the encumbrance that marriage can be when serving the Lord (see Acts 26:29). Paul saw the act of celibacy as a **proper gift** that not all can carry forward in their lives. He added that the gift is not the same for everyone, but instead, **one after this manner, and another after that.** The gift ultimately for celibacy comes from God.

7:8–9. Widows (v. 8) are particularly mentioned here to avoid any thought that Paul was leaving them out of this discussion. **The unmarried,** however, refers not only to widows but also to women who are young and unmarried. Specific issues regarding virgins are addressed in 7:25–28. "As to the apostle himself, there is no indication that he was a widower" (Vine, *Collected Writings*, p. 49). There has been much speculation on Paul's marital state. If he was previously married, either his wife (more than likely Jewish) left him because of his dedication to Christ or she was deceased. In any case, he was free to crisscross the Roman world, carrying the gospel. "Paul affirmed the suitability of remaining single, if they had the appropriate enablement from God" (Lowery, "First Corinthians," p. 518).

2. Concerning Divorce (7:10–24)

7:10–11. The apostle next tackled the difficult issue of divorce. The mixed marriages of believers in Christ and nonbelievers make this a complicated issue. To **the married** (v. 10), Paul said, **I command, yet not I, but the Lord, Let not the wife depart from her husband.** He was drawing on what Christ said regarding divorce (see Matt. 5:32; 19:3–9; Mark 10:2–12). If the wife leaves the marriage, and the marriage is not broken, she is to **remain unmarried, or be reconciled to her husband** (v. 11). The husband is not to **put away his wife** as in divorce. It seems clear in these two verses that the apostle was working to hold marriages together, even mixed marriages. "If the covenant [of marriage] be annulled, it can only be by the sinful act of one of the parties" (Hodge, *First Epistle to the Corinthians*, p. 113). That Paul addressed divorce in this letter indicates that it was rampant within the church.

7:12–14. Here Paul gave his own opinion about divorce, beginning with the issue of mixed marriages between believers and unbelievers. **To the rest** (v. 12) addressed those in the congregation who were married to nonbelievers. More than likely, the unsaved partner was antagonistic to the saved partner. The tension in such circumstances can certainly be appreciated in modern times. A spiritually divided marriage is torn at every corner: spiritually, emotionally, sexually, and domestically.

If either partner **be pleased to dwell with** (vv. 12–13) the other, the marriage should be held together. Paul gave a powerful spiritual reason for this: **the unbelieving** (v. 14) wife or husband **is sanctified** by the believing partner, and in the intact family, even the **children** are kept from being **unclean** and remain **holy.** The words "sanctified" (Greek, *hagiazō*) and "holy" (*hagios*) both come from the same root word. Here Paul used these words in an unusual way. He was saying that the unbelieving partner and the children are especially "blessed" by the Christian husband or wife. Also, keeping the family together means that the unsaved spouse and the children may come to Christ, though Paul did not say this directly.

Paul's statement that the children would be "unclean" (v. 14) if one parent were not a believer means they would no longer have the sanctifying power or influence of that parent. He was convinced of this influence, which comes through the believing spouse. His statement, however, must not be taken too far, as if some kind of sacramental force is at work. All he was saying is that the believing spouse has a strong witness and influence in the family unit.

7:15–16. **If the unbelieving depart** (v. 15), the Christian **brother or … sister is not under bondage.** This means not only that the believing spouse is not held culpable but also that he or she is not held to the marriage. Though he did not say so here, Paul may have been intimating that such a marriage is in continual strife because one in the union is a believer and the other is not. He added, **but God hath called us to peace.** "There were exceptions to the rule of no divorce" (Lowery, "First Corinthians," p. 518). The Christian was not in "bondage" to stay in a marriage

that was truly broken but was free to marry again (see also 7:39). "The point is that the divine standard cannot be imposed upon the unregenerate" (Mitchell, *First Corinthians*, p. 111).

Paul then presented a counterargument. If, for example, the believing wife remains in the marriage, she may **save thy husband** (v. 16). Likewise, the apostle said to the man that he could not know **whether thou shalt save thy wife.** This is certainly a compelling argument for any man or woman who loves his or her spouse. What a blessing if, through perseverance and prayer, the lost companion comes to saving faith in Christ. "We have here, therefore, an additional reason for avoiding separation" (Hodge, *First Epistle to the Corinthians*, p. 119).

7:17. God gives believers the ability to persevere in tough situations. In this verse, Paul was saying that whatever lot in life God has assigned, so the believer must remain. "Accordingly, the believing partner must not take any step to bring about a separation" (Vine, *Collected Writings*, p. 51). Believers must live contentedly where God has placed them. **As the Lord hath called every one, so let him walk.** Paul placed his apostolic authority behind this command and made his a broad rule applicable to all the churches: **so ordain I in all churches.** "Ordain" (Greek, *diatassō*) has the idea to "thoroughly order," "prescribe," "appoint." He was not laying upon the Corinthians undue commands. This was an order that applied to all the congregations.

7:18–19. To pick up on the idea of social status among Christians, Paul shifted the subject to the issue of circumcision and the believers' handling of this "legal" problem. He wanted to make sure the believers knew that **Circumcision is nothing** (v. 19); the important thing is the **keeping of the commandments of God.** Paul was not placing the Corinthian church under the dispensation of law. There are legitimate moral commandments that are eternal in their application to both the period of the Mosaic covenant and the church age. Jewish circumcision or Gentile uncircumcision has nothing to do with being obedient to the Lord. Paul addressed this issue because many Jews were saying, "Yes, you have accepted Christ as your Savior, but now you must also be circumcised." Paul was putting this issue to rest.

7:20–24. Every believer must **abide in the same calling** (v. 20) in which God has called him. Paul was addressing the social status of new believers, but he had a twist in mind: a new Christian was to remain in the social status he held when he was called, whether **servant** (v. 21) or **freeman** (v. 22). If one's position changed, well and good, but a Christian **called in the Lord, being a servant, is the Lord's freeman: likewise also he that is called, being free, is Christ's servant**. "What matters is that every Christian should realize he is Christ's slave and needs to render obedience to Him" (Lowery, "First Corinthians," p. 519). Since the children of God have been **bought with a price** (v. 23), the sacrifice of Christ (see 1 Peter 1:18–19), they are not **the servants of men**. In this calling, what is most important is to **abide with God** (v. 24), that is, "near him, perpetually mindful of his presence and favour. This would secure their contentment and happiness" (Hodge, *First Epistle to the Corinthians*, p. 125).

3. Concerning Marriage and Ministry (7:25–38)

7:25. Young Christian women faced particular problems in the early church. **Virgins** were unmarried and sexually inexperienced. Here the word is used as an adjective to refer to both sexes (see Hodge, *First Epistle to the Corinthians*, p. 126). The natural desire for companionship made marrying an unbeliever a great temptation. Paul was concerned about this issue, but he was also concerned about the marrying of the young in general because of the persecutions he saw coming against Christians. He stated that what he was writing was not a **commandment of the Lord** but his own **judgment**. "Here, Paul means that he is one whose advice can be trusted … even when he has no direct command of the Lord to quote" (Barrett, *First Epistle to the Corinthians*, p. 174).

7:26–28. Paul was concerned about what he called **the present distress** (v. 26), "the impending crises," "the distress standing near" (Greek, *enestōsan anankēn*), that he saw coming against the communities of the faithful. No one knows for certain what

this "distress" was. Persecution seems to be most likely, but some have surmised that Paul was referring to the social upheaval that was taking place in the mixed marriages of the saved with the unsaved. Paul saw persecutions coming upon the church and apparently believed that someone who was single could better handle its onslaught. For those responsible for a spouse and children, martyrdom (see 13:3) would be terrible. Paul was not saying that marriage is wrong; he was simply saying that it would be more prudent not to be married.

7:29–31. Because **the time is short … they that have wives [should] be as though they had none** (v. 29). Likewise, **they that weep … rejoice … buy** (v. 30) or **use this world** (v. 31), should live above these things, because **the fashion of this world passeth away**. This list consists of normal things that make up life. Normal life, however, will be stopped by what is coming. The apostle "was calling for a commitment to eternal matters and a corresponding detachment from the institutions, values, and substance of this world which was passing away (v. 31)" (Lowery, "First Corinthians," p. 519).

7:32–35. A man who remains **unmarried** (v. 32) can take care of **the things that belong to the Lord** and **how he may please the Lord**. A **married** (v. 33) man must care for **the things … of the world** and provide for and **please his wife**. Here Paul did not use the concept of "the world" in the evil sense as the word *kosmos* is usually used. He simply meant that the married man must look after his wife in the provision of living and existing. He must provide food, shelter, comfort, and companionship.

In the same sense, the **virgin** (v. 34), or **unmarried woman**, can care for **the things of the Lord**. She can be a missionary of sorts and totally give herself to Him. She can **be holy both in body and in spirit**. The woman who is **married** must also care for the worldly needs of her husband and **how she may please** him. "The situation illustrates Paul's point that the single life with its greater simplicity in obligations allows a potentially greater commitment of time" (Lowery, "First Corinthians," p. 520). Paul said these things for the Corinthians' **profit** (v. 35).

He was not trying to **snare** them in some kind of spiritual trap. He was saying these things so that they could **attend** to the things of the Lord **without distraction**. "Everywhere the apostle is careful to show that celibacy was preferred merely on the grounds of expediency, and not on the ground of its being a higher state of virtue" (Hodge, *First Epistle to the Corinthians*, p. 132).

7:36–38. There is some question whether **he [who] behaveth himself uncomely** (v. 36) refers to a father or to a potential bridegroom. The point seems to be whether the father (or bridgegroom) is disgracing himself by not allowing this young woman to marry. What **if she pass the flower of her age** and she wants children? What should happen? Paul instructed the father to **do what he will**. He would not be sinning to **let them marry**. If, however, the father **standeth stedfast in his heart** (v. 37), has **power over his own will**, and is determined **in his heart that he will keep** his daughter a **virgin**, he **doeth well**. He who allows her to marry **doeth well, but he that giveth her not in marriage doeth better** (v. 38). It is better if she not marry. The father needs to act with all human and godly wisdom. Paul's twists and turns in this matter show the seriousness of the events that continued to swirl around such problems in the early church. It "is not a case of what is morally right or wrong but of what is expedient or advantageous" (Vine, *Collected Writings*, p. 55).

4. Concerning Remarriage (7:39–40)

7:39–40. Here Paul again addressed the issue of marriage and divorce. **The wife is bound by the law as long as her husband liveth; but if her husband be dead, she is at liberty** (v. 39) to marry again, but **only in the Lord**. Most commentators take these last words to mean she is to marry only a Christian. Paul repeated the advice given throughout the chapter, returned to the issue of remaining unmarried, and said she will **be happier** (v. 40) if she remains unmarried. The apostle stated that this was **after [his] judgment** but added that he thought he had **the Spirit of God** in such a decision. Remarriage is permitted, though not encouraged.

B. Directives concerning Christian Liberty (chaps. 8–11)

1. Eating Meat Offered to Idols (chap. 8)

Paul hit home in regard to a sore issue, that of eating meat offered to idols. Meat was placed on the altars of all the pagan temples in Corinth. When it began to spoil, the meat was taken from the altars and offered in the bazaars for food. Whether Christians could or should eat meat that had been offered to pagan gods became a huge contention among the believers.

8:1. In writing **we all have knowledge**, Paul may have been saying that all the churches knew that this meat, though offered to idols, meant nothing in a spiritual sense. Such knowledge, however, could bring about insensitivity and cause some to **puffeth up** and be short on the **charity** that **edifieth** the brother. Paul may have mentioned the issue of knowledge because of the growing Gnostic religion, which pandered to secretive, hidden "spiritual" knowledge. Christians were continually exposed to some form of idolatrous homage without knowing it. The apostle wanted the believers to focus on "charity," or love, which builds up the brother. In saying "we all have knowledge," he was also reminding the Corinthians that Christians have been given the open truth of God and Christ, and the basics of faith are well-known.

8:2–3. With a twist of argument, Paul then said that the man who boasts **he knoweth any thing** (v. 2) is presumptuous and a spiritual braggart. When one is blessed with understanding spiritual truth, humility should follow, not pride. "He whose knowledge is superficial often displays a readiness to impart instruction. His very readiness betrays his ignorance (3:18)" (Vine, *Collected Writings*, p. 57).

What counts is that **if any man love God, the same is known of him** (v. 3). Some commentators feel the sense of this is not certain. It could mean, "If any man loves God, he has been brought by Him to the true knowledge," which appears to fit the context. Or it could mean, "If a man is without love, he has not true knowledge; but if he love God, he has the right kind of knowledge" (Hodge, *First Epistle to the*

Corinthians, p. 141). The apostle John wrote something similar: "Beloved, let us love one another: for love is of God; and every one that loveth is born of God, and knoweth God. He that loveth not, knoweth not God; for God is love" (1 John 4:7–8).

8:4. Paul then leapt into one of the burning issues that was dividing the Corinthian assembly—the issue of eating meat offered to idols. Some believers had no problem eating meat **offered in sacrifice unto idols**. Paul said, **an idol is nothing … there is none other God but one**. The idol (Greek, *eidōlon*) is but a wooden or stone image of the false deities of the pagans. There is no Jupiter, Juno, or Mars. In the whole of **the world**, the idols mean nothing.

8:5–6. It is true, however, that the pagan world believes in the pantheon of the many **gods** (v. 5) and **lords**, as they **are called**, which are supposed to dwell **in heaven or in earth. … But to us** (v. 6), to believers, **there is but one God**, and He is **the Father**, to whom belongs **all things, and we [are] in him**. There is also only **one Lord Jesus Christ, by whom are all things, and we** too came into existence **by him**. In these short phrases and clauses, the apostle assigned all deity to the person of God the Father and to His Son Jesus Christ. Both the Father and Jesus Christ created everything and own everything.

"The Father is the source of all (Gen. 1:1) and the One for whom the Corinthians should live (1 Cor. 10:31). The Lord Jesus Christ was the agent of Creation (Col. 1:16) and the One through whom the Corinthians lived (1 Cor. 12:27; Eph. 1:23)" (Lowery, "First Corinthians," p. 521).

8:7–8. Some believers in the congregation still did not have full **knowledge** (v. 7) about the falsehood of the pantheon of the gods. They had a **conscience of the idol unto this hour**, even up to that day. If they ate that which was offered to idols, **their conscience being weak is defiled**. These Christians could not indifferently eat meat offered on the pagan altars. Besides, Paul argued, eating such **meat commendeth us not to God** (v. 8). "Commendeth" carries the idea of "approval." Eating or not eating meat sacrificed to idols had no bearing on whether a believer was **better** or **worse**.

8:9–10. Paul issued a caveat for those who were strong in their faith: they should not exercise their **liberty** (v. 9) to eat such meat if it **become[s] a stumblingblock to them that are weak** in this matter. Apparently, "idol meat" restaurants were located near the temples of the gods and served leftover meat that had been previously sacrificed to the deities. The one who had **knowledge** (v. 10) and freedom concerning the issue was to consider carefully whether to **sit at meat in the idol's temple**. The example of the stronger Christian might strike **the conscience** of the **weak** brother, who would therefore **be emboldened to eat** the same food. Unfortunately, "many repeat the mistake of the Corinthians by assuming that liberality in matters of personal conduct is a sign of spiritual maturity and strength, while scrupulosity is a sign of weakness" (Mitchell, *First Corinthians*, p. 127).

8:11–12. Seeing stronger Christians eat meat sacrificed to the idols might lead a weak Christian to eat the same food even if he believed it was wrong. If this happened, his conscience would be "seared" (1 Tim. 4:2), and his ability to distinguish right from wrong would be lost (Titus 1:15), leading to his spiritual ruin, whereby **the weak brother [would] perish** (v. 11). "Perish" often has to do with physical death (see Matt. 2:13; Acts 5:37), but here it is probable that Paul meant the weak brother's spiritual life would be destroyed. The apostle warned the brother who had proper **knowledge** and spiritual understanding about the meat offered to idols that exercising his freedom to eat such meat might cause him to **sin … against the brethren** (v. 12) by harming the **weak conscience** of the one who had stumbled over this issue. Moreover, Paul said, **ye sin against Christ**, because exercising one's freedom to eat the meat caused spiritual confusion for the weaker brother, who also belongs to the body of Christ. Since Jesus died for this soul, the strong should be able to give up eating the meat offered to idols to keep from destroying his brother's conscience.

8:13. Wherefore indicates Paul's conclusion and summary statement on this subject: if eating such meat might cause a weaker brother **to offend**, Paul would never eat it again **while the world standeth**. Paul did not say that a knowledgeable Christian had to set aside his freedom. It was unlikely that Paul saw this weak brother as permanently shackling the freedom of the knowledgeable Christian (Lowery, "First Corinthians," p. 522). The weak brother needed to be properly taught so that he could enjoy his spiritual freedom (see Gal. 5:1).

2. Paul's Apostleship and Authority (chap. 9)

There were rumblings of doubt about Paul's authority. Here Paul set forth his defense against those who questioned whether he had any right to presribe the moral and spiritual behavior of the Corinthian church. He later defended his calling as an apostle in more detail (see 2 Cor. 11–13). Also at issue "was his steadfast refusal to derive material support from those to whom he was ministering, so no one could say he was motivated by money (cf. 2 Cor. 2:17)" (Barrett, *First Epistle to the Corinthians*, p. 522).

9:1. With a staccato of quick and direct questions, Paul asked the Corinthian believers, **Am I not an apostle? am I not free? have I not seen Jesus Christ our Lord? are not you my work in the Lord?** The apostle pulled no punches. He got to the point and attacked their criticisms, which were seething just below the surface. Paul seems especially direct in the Corinthian letters. Some have suggested this was because no men in this assembly were qualified to act as elders, and carnality in the congregation was rampant. Paul made it clear that his authority came from Christ. In 9:1–13, he hammered his readers with sixteen questions, forcing them to think twice about their objections to his ministry.

9:2–6. Paul said that even if he was **not an apostle unto others, yet doubtless I am to you** (v. 2). **The seal of [his] apostleship** was over the Corinthian church. He had birthed this church and was now correcting their spiritual and moral waywardness. He had an **answer** (Greek, *apologia*; v. 3) for those who wished to **examine** (Greek, *anakrinō*) him. "Answer" and "examine" are forensic terms, showing that his opponents felt they had the right to judicially scrutinize his authority. Paul was answering

in so many words, "I have seen the Lord Jesus, and He has set His seal to my calling by the success with which He has crowned my work." This answer satisfied Peter, James, and John, who gave to Paul "the right hands of fellowship" (Gal. 2:9).

In asking whether he had the **power to eat and to drink** (v. 4), Paul probably had in mind whether he had the "right" to do so. Many believe he meant that he had some authority to be helped along the way by the churches in his ministry. He had the right to be supported by the various congregations, but having said that, Paul went on to show that he had not availed himself of that right. On the other hand, he may have meant that he could live as he wished as an apostolic leader. This argument, however, is doubtful (see v. 6; 9:13–14).

Paul said he had the right **to lead about a sister, a wife** (v. 5). Some believe this should be read as "a sister, [who is my] wife" and that it indicates Paul was married. The New Testament and the writings of the church fathers, however, are silent about Paul's marital status. This right to "lead about … a wife" belonged also to **other apostles**, including Christ's **brethren** (who would have been His half-brothers, the children of Joseph and Mary; see Matt. 12:46; 13:55) and **Cephas**, or Peter.

Further pushing the issue, Paul asked, **Or I only and Barnabas, have not we power to forbear working?** (v. 8), that is, "Do Barnabas and I not have the power, the right, to forbear working?" While Paul at times refused to accept remuneration in order to silence criticism, he argued that those working in a teaching ministry should be compensated by those who are blessed. "Let him that is taught in the word communicate unto him that teacheth in all good things" (Gal. 6:6). Paul seems to have been saying, "Are Barnabas and I the only exceptions to the rule that ministers should be supported by their respective churches?" At the beginning of his ministry in Corinth, the apostle had supported himself. When financial aid did come, it did not come from the Corinthian assembly.

9:7–9. Does a soldier go into **warfare** (v. 7) and pay for it himself? **Who planteth a vineyard, and**

eateth not of the fruit ... or who feedeth a flock, and eateth not of the milk? I can say **these things as a man** (v. 8), but **saith not the law the same also?** Paul spoke from the position of a human being who had to find sustenance while he labored. Reminding them that this is **the law of Moses** (v. 9), Paul cites Deuteronomy 25:4 to support his case: **Thou shalt not muzzle ... the ox that treadeth out the corn.** Since God takes care of the oxen and even feeds the young ravens when they cry (see Job 38:41), He certainly will take care of His gospel ministers.

9:10 – 12. Paul maintained that the words of Moses were written not only for those in the past but also **for our sakes, no doubt** (v. 10). If the farmer **should plow** and thresh his grain **in hope** and also **be partaker of his hope**, how much more so for those who plow, plant, and thresh the Word of God to reap a spiritual harvest? The ministers of the gospel had **sown unto** (v. 11) the Corinthian church **spiritual things**; was it not only right that these same ministers should be able to **reap ... carnal things?** If others had the right to benefit from and **be partakers of** (v. 12) blessing, should Paul and his fellow workers not also have that right? Still, Paul said, **we have not used this power** or authority but instead **suffer all things** so as not to **hinder the gospel of Christ.** Paul was saying that he would do anything that did not violate his allegiance to Christ or forgo anything so that no one could criticize and thus besmirch the gospel of the Lord Jesus Christ.

9:13 – 14. Paul asked the Corinthians, Is it not true that **they which minister ... holy things live of the things of the temple** (v. 13) and **are partakers of** the meat placed on the altar, just as the farmer partakes of that which he sows? **Even so hath the Lord ordained that they which preach the gospel should live of the gospel** (v. 14). Paul likely had in mind the temple service in Jerusalem and portion given to the priests from the food taken for offerings (see Lev. 7:31 – 34), but the Corinthians certainly would have been aware that even the pagan priests lived off of their service at the pagan temples and altars.

9:15 – 17. Paul reminded his readers that he had taken nothing from this church, nor had he **writ-**ten these things, that it should be so done unto me (v. 15). He would have preferred to die rather than be deprived of his ground for glorying in their salvation. Paul was not a braggart, but he was genuinely joyful and proud as a parent of the spiritual birth of this congregation. He was not in it for himself. He then reversed that thought and said, **I have nothing to glory** (v. 16) about, because **necessity is laid upon me** to proclaim the truth of Christ. **Woe is unto me, if I preach not the gospel!** Because he did **this thing willingly** (v. 17), he had **a reward.** The apostle was driven because the **dispensation of the gospel [was] committed** to him. Paul made it clear that he was fully committed to the ministry of the gospel. The English word "economy" comes from the Greek word for "dispensation" (*oikonomia*). The gospel dispensation is what governs the church age, the age of grace. This is in contrast to the older dispensation of the Mosaic law. The word is used four times in the New Testament to refer to the church age (1 Cor. 9:17; Eph. 1:10; 3:2; Col. 1:25). This dispensation was especially "committed" to Paul (see Gal. 2:7; Col. 1:25). The word "dispensation" can be translated "stewardship." Paul was given a "stewardship" to preach. That was enough (see 4:1 – 2; Luke 17:10). A steward received no pay. "Such a one was merely a slave doing an assigned task" (Mitchell, *First Corinthians*, p. 134).

9:18. How, then, was Paul rewarded for his service? He preached **the gospel of Christ without charge** so that he would not **abuse** his **power** (i.e., "right") **in the gospel.** No one could deny this claim (see 2 Cor. 11:9 – 10), and Paul could see the gospel at work in those to whom he ministered (see 7:3 – 4). His reward was to sacrifice himself for others. Any satisfaction gained would be made void if there was self-glorification before the Lord.

9:19 – 23. While Paul was **free from all men** (v. 19) and their authority, he still made himself a **servant unto all, that [he] might gain the more.** The apostle did not have to conform to the opinions of others, especially that of his critics. By serving all, however, he could do them good and bring a greater number to the cross of Christ. To prove his point

Paul made a long list of those to whom he ministered in order to gain their confidence for the gospel's sake.

To **the Jews** (v. 20) and others **under the law**, Paul **became as a Jew** and lived **as under the law, that [he] might gain them that are under the law**. By "gain," he meant to win them to the gospel, though their spiritual orientation was the law. He did the same with those who were **without law** (v. 21), more than likely referring to the Gentiles. He related to the religious or ethnic situation of those he was trying to reach. He wanted to make sure, however, that the Corinthians did not think he was antinomian, a rebel against law and reason, **being not without law to [before] God**. Yet he lived as one governed by Christ, **under the law to Christ**. He did this to **gain them that are without law**. He did the same with **the weak** (v. 22) to **gain the weak**. His main purpose was **that I might by all means save some**.

The apostle worked hard to identify with others in situations different from his own. This he did **for the gospel's sake** (v. 23). He did the same thing with the Corinthians; he became a **partaker** ("joint partaker") with them to win them to the Lord. Paul's focus was on great eternal issues over and above temporal issues. It can be said that he went about reaping the joyful harvest of many won to Christ (see John 4:36).

9:24 – 25. Paul saw himself **in a race** (v. 24) to receive **the prize**. He wanted the same spirit of achieving for the sake of Christ to be in the Corinthian believers. **So run, that ye may obtain**. Being an athlete and running the race means that one must **striveth for the mastery** (v. 25). Discipline is required, and one must be **temperate in all things**. The world expends energy for glory **to obtain a corruptible crown**, but the believer is to serve diligently to receive **an incorruptible** reward. In the Olympic games, the prize was a perishable wreath, a garland of leaves that faded quickly after the contest was over. The Lord will reward the believer in Christ, however, a crown given that is incorruptible and lasting (see 2 Tim. 4:8; James 1:12; 1 Peter 5:4; Rev. 2:10; 3:11; 4:10).

9:26 – 27. Paul had explained himself, his motives, and his actions to the congregation at Corinth. **I ... run, not as uncertainly** (v. 26). He fought as a boxer, not without purpose, as one that simply **beateth the air**. He brought the needs and wants of his **body ... into subjection** (v. 27) so that when he **preached to others**, he **should be a castaway**. "Castaway" (*adokimos*) should better be translated "disqualified," "unapproved." While the word in other contexts is applied to the lost (see Rom. 1:28; Titus 1:16), here the apostle was not addressing salvation but rather faithfulness in the Christian walk. He wanted it to be said of him, "I have fought a good fight, I have finished my course, I have kept the faith: Henceforth there is laid up for me a crown of righteousness, which the Lord, the righteous judge, shall give me at that day: and not to me only, but unto all them also that love his appearing" (2 Tim. 4:7 – 8).

3. Temptations (10:1 – 13)

The apostle Paul next turned to the issue of various temptations: lust, drunkenness, fornication, even complaining and doubt. He used the history of the Israelites in the wilderness because they were "our examples" (v. 6), and they were "overthrown in the wilderness" (v. 5). In all of these experiences, the Jews were a warning to every Christian. Therefore, the one who thinks he is secure from such temptations should "take heed lest he fall" (v. 12).

10:1. Lest the Corinthians **should be ignorant** of how God works, it was appropriate to look back at the story of the Exodus. God gave the children of Israel supernatural guidance (see Exod. 13:21) and protection (see Exod. 14:19 – 20) by leading them **under the cloud** of blessing. All of the Israelites experienced a miraculous deliverance from the Egyptians: God led them **through the sea**, the Red Sea (Exod. 14:21 – 29). This blessing of their liberation, however, was not enough. It is not enough to begin well; one must also finish well.

10:2 – 5. Coming out of Egypt, the Jews **were all baptized unto Moses in the cloud and in the sea** (v. 2). Moses was their spiritual head and God's servant. He was the object of their trust (Exod. 14:31). In a similar manner, the Corinthians had been baptized into the body of Christ (1 Cor. 12:13). Christ is the Head (see Eph. 1:22), in whom believers have faith (see Matt.

12:21; Eph. 1:12). What did Paul mean when he said the Jews "were all baptized unto Moses"? He was not using this expression about baptism in a technical sense, though he will discuss spiritual baptism as a distinct New Testament doctrine in 12:12–18. Paul meant that the children of Israel "were immersed into Moses' authority." Thus, the expression speaks of divine leadership (see Exod. 14:31).

The Jews were also said to have eaten **the same spiritual meat** (v. 3). This could refer to the Passover meal, which consisted of slaying a lamb and eating unleavened bread (see Exod. 12:43–51). Passover, though a meal of physical food, was a prophetic event that pointed to the Lord Jesus, who became the spiritual Passover (see Luke 22:19–21; 1 Cor. 5:7). Many believe, however, that the "spiritual meat" is the *manna* (Hebrew; meaning, "What is it?") that miraculously sustained the Jews in the desert. The manna was spiritual in that it was supernatural in origin (see Ps. 78:25). Christ Himself is the Bread of Life (see John 6:31–32).

In addition to the "spiritual meat," Paul referred to the **spiritual drink** (v. 4) that came forth from the **spiritual Rock that followed them: and that Rock was Christ**. The apostle used real historic events that took place when Israel came out of Egypt as symbolic figures representing the supernatural subsistence the Lord used to preserve the Jewish people in the desert (Exod. 16:2–36; 17:1–7; Num. 20:2–11; 21:16). The manna, the water, and the rock all represent the saving work of Christ for His people. Because of the disobedience and doubt of many of the people, however, **God was not well pleased** (v. 5), and **they were overthrown in the wilderness** (see Num. 14:22–24, 28–35; Josh. 1:1–2). Caleb and Joshua, however, were allowed to enter the Promised Land of Canaan because they trusted God.

10:6. These wilderness events became **examples** so that believers today **should not lust after evil things** as that generation did. Though the church is not under the Old Testament economy, it still receives tremendous spiritual blessings that should act as warnings for the child of God. The Corinthian complacency corresponded to what happened to ancient Israel. Christian liberty should not lead to self-indulgence and spiritual compromise.

10:7–10. In these verses, Paul set forth a list of warnings. Each verse begins with "Neither," indicating that the Christian should not act as the Jews did under the leadership of Moses. **Neither be ye idolaters** (v. 7) as the Jews were when they **sat down to eat and drink**. Moses recorded that the people rose up early and made offerings to a molten calf, which was one of the gods they said had brought them out of bondage (see Exod. 32:4–5). Their "eating and drinking" more than likely was a drunken orgy. When they **rose up to play** is an expression of the sexual carousing that followed.

Neither let us commit fornication (v. 8). This specifies what the Jews were doing, and because of their actions, God slew **in one day** 23,000 people (see 32:6; Ps. 106:29). At first, Paul's figure seems to contradict his account of what happened. Some of the Jews had committed whoredom with the pagan daughters of Moab and had also bowed down to the gods of these people. God instructed Moses' judges to slay all who had participated in this idolatry (see Num. 25:1–5). A plague also came upon the congregation. It was the final judgment that wiped out 24,000 (see Num. 25:9). Paul probably did not include those who were killed by the judges (see Num. 25:5). Though Paul says they **fell in one day**, he could have meant that they were judged in one day, but the carrying out of God's sentence took longer. Another view is that Paul was counting only those who fell in one day, while the others followed in death a short time later. Some surmise that the apostle was only rounding down the number. This entire warning is strong and hints that some in the church at Corinth continually practiced fornication and possibly flirted with idolatry also.

Neither let us tempt Christ as some of them also tempted, and were destroyed of serpents (v. 9). A vivid account of this event is found in Numbers 21:6–9. The children of Israel had forgotten God's liberation of them from Egypt and blamed both God and Moses for bringing them into the wilderness to die. They complained, "our soul loatheth this light bread" (Num. 21:5), the manna. As God had authority over Israel in the wilderness, so Christ has authority over the church. For a Christian to resist Christ is the same as when the Jews resisted God. Christians must not "tempt" Him to overlook their spiritual failures, because He will not do so.

Neither murmur ye (v. 10). The Jews in the desert **were destroyed** (see Num. 14:37) by the same death angel that came to the Egyptians and took their first-born sons (see Exod. 12:13, 23). **The destroyer** was "an angel commissioned by God to use the pestilence as an instrument of destruction" (Hodge, *First Epistle to the Corinthians*, p. 180). "The destroyer here mentioned is not Satan, but the destroying angel" of Exodus (Vine, *Collected Writings*, p. 69).

10:11–13. The historical events recorded in the Old Testament became lessons, or **ensamples** (v. 11), for the church. They **are written for our admonition**, both to encourage and to warn. These lessons have an impact on all those who go to **the ends of the world,** by which Paul meant the successive periods of God's entire dealing with mankind. **Are come** (Greek, *katantaō*) signifies arrival at a certain period, to come upon or reach certain persons. The events recorded in the Old Testament will stand as spiritual lessons until the end. Paul warned his audience to avoid moral pride and thinking they would not be judged for their open sins. **Let him that thinketh he standeth take heed lest he fall** (v. 12). Self-satisfaction leads to arrogance, which in turn leads to a downfall.

No one can escape **temptation** (v. 13) because it is **common to man.** The most spiritual person can trip up, but God **will not suffer** (allow) the believer **to be tempted above that ye are able.** When a believer is tempted, God will **make a way to escape, that ye may be able to bear it.** He is **faithful** in doing this. The Lord is aware of the temptations His children face; He is not detached from the events that come upon His own. Through His Holy Spirit, believers can overcome whatever comes against them.

4. Fleeing from Idolatry (10:14–22)

10:14–15. Wherefore (Greek, *dioper*; v. 14) is a strong word for the summary introduction. To show that he was not simply judging the Corinthians, Paul

addressed them as **my dearly beloved.** After moving from a serious admonition to terms of affection, he summarized the admonition very simply: **flee from idolatry.** Idolatry seems to be the central problem from which the other heinous sins originated. "The only safety is keeping at a distance. This includes two things; first, avoiding what is questionable; that is, every thing which lies upon the border of what is allowable" (Hodge, *First Epistle to the Corinthians*, pp. 184–85). Those who heard and heeded Paul's words were the **wise** (Greek, *phronimos*; v. 15), those who are wise practically and who are prudent. He wanted the Corinthians to judge for themselves: **judge ye what I say.**

10:16–18. Some in the church may have been looking at the Lord's Supper as something similar to the idol feasts. **The cup of blessing** (v. 16) is **the communion** (Greek, *koinōnia*), the "fellowship" that centers around **the blood of Christ.** The high churches that believe there is some efficaciousness in the communion service misread this passage. "The cup" and **the bread** presented to those in the fellowship *are* the communion. Together the church centers itself around the **one bread** (v. 17). They **all** become **partakers of that one bread.** Here the unity of the local assembly is emphasized. Paul probably stressed this because the Corinthians had been so divided. This occasion of mutual partaking symbolizes the unity they should have around the body of Christ. In fact, Paul later went further in his description of the new unity: believers, though "being many, are one body: so also is Christ" (12:12).

Returning to what happened to Israel, Paul asked, Did they not become as one **after the flesh** (v. 18) because of what they had experienced together in the wilderness and also when they came into the Land of Promise? And were not the priests who ate **of the sacrifices partakers of the altar?** After a part of the sacrifice had been burned on the altar, the priests partook together of a portion of the animal offerings (see Lev. 7:15–21; Deut. 12:5–7; 18:18). These happenings are types and pictures of how the church is to unite around the remembrance of the death, burial, and resurrection of Christ.

10:19–22. Verse 19 may show how mixed up this church was. Is **the idol … any thing** (v. 19), or are the **sacrifice[s] to idols … any thing?** But **the Gentiles** (v. 20–21) were making such sacrifices, **sacrifice[s] to devils, and not to God**. Paul added, I do not want you to **have fellowship with devils. Ye cannot drink the cup of the Lord, and the cup of devils** (v. 21); you cannot come to both **the Lord's table, and … the table of devils**. In the pagan Greek world, the words *daimōn* and *daimonion* were both used to describe the gods, the deities and spirits of the underworld. Interestingly, here the word Paul used, *daimoniōn*, is the plural. The pagan feasts were in honor of more than one demonic spirit. In no way could the Christian have fellowship both with Christ and with these evil beings. Paul asked, **Do we provoke the Lord to jealousy** (v. 22) in this matter? Did some in the assembly in Corinth think they could worship devils and God? Concerning the worship of other gods, the Lord said in the Old Testament: "They have moved me to jealousy with that which is not God; they have provoked me to anger with their vanities" (Deut. 32:21). Paul asked, **Are we stronger than** God? The answer to this question brings a warning. The child of God cannot arouse the Lord to anger with impunity. Fear of and respect for God should cause believers to do what is right (see Eccl. 6:10; Isa. 10:15; 45:9; Ezek. 22:14).

5. Lawful Things and Maturity (10:23–11:1)

10:23–24. Paul again asserted, **All things are lawful for me** (v. 23; see 6:12), though not everything is **expedient** (Greek, *sympherei*), meaning "right to do," "useful for others." While believers have a wide range of liberty in their Christian walk, wisdom must play a part in what one does. While all things may be **lawful … all things edify not**. "Edify" has the idea of "strengthen," "build up another." The "principle for us all toward others is that we might be a means of edifying" (Vine, *Collected Writings*, p. 72).

A believer is not to simply **seek his own** (v. 24) but is instead to pursue **another's wealth**, or "welfare," "benefit," "gain." Only in this way can a believer really be helpful to others. Self is not to be the object of the actions of the Christian.

10:25–28. Paul here gave permission to **eat** (v. 25) that which was purchased **in the shambles** (v. 25), meaning the public marketplace. In a large city like Corinth, it was difficult to determine what had been slaughtered for general food and what had been offered in sacrifice to the gods. **No question** (v. 27) needed to be asked **for conscience sake**. "For a Christian who bought meat at a market with the intent of eating it at home, Paul recommended that selections be made without reservation. No one could contaminate what God had made clean" (Lowery, "First Corinthians," p. 528). **The earth is the Lord's** (vv. 26, 28), and all that is in it, **the fulness thereof**.

Paul advised his readers that if an unbeliever asked them to dine with him, and they wished to go, **whatsoever is set before you, eat, asking no question for conscience sake**. By this, Paul meant that the believer did not have to worry about what is unclean everywhere he went. It was alright to partake in what was served. If the host told believers, however, that the meat had been **sacrifice[d] unto idols** (v. 28), they were not to eat the meat. Such a refusal would be a witness to him **that shewed it**. The believer needed to be careful that the unbeliever did not get the idea that he might be willing to partake of idolatrous food. As well, if another Christian was present, the refusal would not cause him to sin in regard to meat offered to idols (Rom. 14:14–23). A weak brother might act against his conscience and thus be harmed (see 8:11).

10:29–33. The believer needed to be concerned about others' **conscience** (v. 29) and aware of how exercising one's personal **liberty** in these matters might affect someone else. If **by grace** (v. 30) one partook of meat offered to idols, he might be **evil spoken of**, even if he gave **thanks** for that food. Therefore, whether eating or drinking, all must be done for **the glory of God** (v. 31). "Paul's message is cohesive from start to finish, and each chapter plays a crucial role in demonstrating why and how to correct misconceptions about the practice of Christian liberty" (Mitchell, *First Corinthians*, p. 149). One's actions could offend **Jews … Gentiles … the church of God** (v. 32). To do all to His glory is to manifest

Him in all respects. In these debatable matters, the Christian must **please all men in all things** (v. 33), not being self-serving but profiting others, the **many, that they may be saved.** If they are to be saved, a stumbling block must not be placed before them. To possibly bring the lost to conversion to Christ, good must be done to them.

11:1. The apostle concluded, **Be ye followers of me, even as I also am of Christ.** Paul was perhaps saying that this church was not yet mature enough to follow Christ in a direct manner, in which case, they were to imitate Paul, as he did Christ, who is the ultimate standard of the Christian life.

6. The Veiling of Women (11:2–16)

This section has cultural overtones, but eternal doctrinal principles are established here. Some things Paul said may not be fully clear because observors today do not fully understand the cultural and historical setting, but the conclusions are doctrinally sure. The apostle addressed issues that must have been great concerns in the Corinthian church. Paul's discussion of whether women should wear veils was possibly unsolicited by the congregation. This discussion has to do with behavior in the worship service and with gender leadership.

11:2–9. Paul began by praising the Corinthians that they had **remember[ed]** (v. 2) what he taught previously and that they had kept **the ordinances** he gave to them. The word "ordinances" (Greek, *paradosis*) could best be translated "traditions." Godly traditions should not be cast off lightly.

Paul then established a gender order based on the order of how God relates people to Christ, in relation to prophesying and other matters. Christ is the **head** (v. 3) of every man, the man is the **head** of the woman, and the head of Christ **is God.** The idea of headship does not mean that women are inferior to men or that they have a lesser status before God. It is about an order, an arrangement, in the spiritual "social" order of how the Lord wants to relate to men and women in a church setting.

Because there should be "an openness" between Christ and a man who is **praying or prophesying**

(v. 4), the man is to have his head uncovered or he **dishonoureth his head.** "Prophesying" here is more than likely a teaching ministry not prophesying into the future, as only a few did apart from the other apostles and Paul (such as Abagus, Acts 11:28). The **woman that prayeth or prophesieth with her head uncovered dishonoureth her head** (v. 5). It is as if her hair is **shaven.** Paul instructed, **Let her be covered** (v. 6). Some think he was referring to a face covering, but a veil is more than likely a head shawl.

Notice here how Paul permitted and even encouraged women to pray and to have their own teaching ministry. Since the apostle forbade women to teach a mixed audience (see 1 Tim. 2:11–15), this means women were to be spiritual instructors for other women.

Since Adam was created first, he was to reflect **the image and glory of God** (v. 7; see Gen. 2:26; Ps. 8:4–6). Adam was created first and then **the woman for the man** (v. 9; see Gen. 2:18, 21–22). The woman is the **glory of the man** (v. 7). She is not, however, in his image (see Vine, *Collected Writings*, p. 77). She is his "help meet" (Gen. 2:18). Paul wanted to maintain this gender order even in the affairs of the church. He challenged men to be leaders in the churches. Again, this does not imply that women are inferior or have less intelligence; it simply reflects a proper order for the congregations. The creation order is to be maintained. "God could, indeed, have created both man and woman, Adam and Eve, in one undivided act" (Lenski, *1 and 2 Corinthians*, p. 443), but He did not. What the apostle instructed "is not merely a perfunctory observance ... It is obligatory upon the woman as *agent* to exercise her will in a free demonstration of godly submission" (Mitchell, *First Corinthians*, p. 162).

11:10–16. Paul's continuation of this discussion indicates that it must have been a very contentious issue in the assembly. A woman's hair is her **glory** (v. 15) and it is her **power** (Greek, *exousia*; "authority"; v. 10). This is so on account of **the angels.** This "implies that God's good angels are present when God's people come together to pray" (Lenski, *1 and 2 Corinthians*, p. 445). On "power," Barrett (*First Epis-*

tle to the Corinthians, p. 255) suggests the covering "represents the new authority given to the woman under the new dispensation to do things which formerly had not been permitted her." Still, the man is not **without the woman, neither the woman without the man, in the Lord** (v. 11). The authority of the man does not make him independent of the woman, and the subordination of the woman does not make her dispensable. They are not independent of each other (Hunter, *1 Corinthians*, p. 127).

Paul again used the example of the order of creation. The man and the woman are interdependent. The woman comes from the man, and the man is given birth by the woman. This shows that **all things (are) of God** (v. 12). "Man and woman, everything that pertains to birth, relationships, and married life — all come from God" (Kistemaker, *1 Corinthians*, p. 378).

Paul provoked his readers, asking, **Judge in yourselves: is it comely** (right) **that a woman pray unto God uncovered?** (v. 13). With all that he had said and with what was clearly traditional, and even logical, the answer was no. **Even nature** (Greek, *physis*; "the natural world") shows that **if a man have long hair, it is a shame unto him** (v. 14). **But if a woman have long hair, it is a glory to her** (v. 15). In fact, it is given to her by God **for a covering**.

Paul completed his long argument on this issue and reminded the Corinthians not **to be contentious** (v. 16), because there was no other **custom, neither [in] the churches of God**. No assembly among the new churches being formed across the Roman Empire had any other view on the subject. Long hair was considered a woman's glory because it gave visible expression to the differentiation of the sexes.

7. Practice of the Lord's Supper (11:17 – 34)

Paul was given a report that factions were also developing over the Lord's Supper, which involved practices that dishonored the remembrance of Christ's death for the believer. Possibly some believers were taking the elements of the Lord's Supper in a fashion that echoed the pagans' bacchanalian and debauched practices in the feasts to their gods. Paul needed to continue his criticisms of this church to set doctrinal and practical things in order.

11:17 – 22. The apostle began by saying, **I praise you not** (v. 17), because the church was coming together at the Lord's table **not for the better, but for the worse**. "Better" (Greek, *kreisson*) refers to that which is advantageous, and "worse" (Greek, *hēsson*) refers to something deteriorating, referring to the spiritual effect and the contentious fallout in the congregation. Paul had heard that the Corinthians still came together with their schisms and spiritual **divisions** (v. 18). This he could **partly believe**. While what was taking place was deplorable, it exposed and **made manifest** (v. 19) the **heresies** among them. This celebration, meant to show unity, instead expressed conflict. "Heresy" (Greek, *hairesis*) means an act or choice, an opinion that is different from that of the whole church or a doctrine that is contrary to Scripture.

Paul knew that their main motive when they came together was **not to eat the Lord's supper** (v. 20). Instead, they came to eat and to get drunk. They were dishonest in their motives, and they dishonored the memory of the Lord's sacrifice on the cross. When they came together, apparently the wealthy brought full meals and became intoxicated, while the poor, **them that have not** (v. 22), could bring nothing. They gave the appearance of having a common meal, but this was not the case. Did they not have homes in which to eat their ordinary meals? Were they not despising the church? Regarding this matter, Paul said, "I praise you not" (v. 17).

11:23 – 25. The apostle does not say how he received the revelation about the Lord's Supper. Generally, he received revelation two ways: by direct revelation and maybe also by the instruction of the disciples. The bread represented the body of Christ given unselfishly for the benefit of the lost. It is a constant reminder of why he died (v. 26).

This cup … my blood (v. 25) points to the sacrifice of Christ for the forgiveness of sins (see Heb. 9:22). This is a **new testament** ("contract," "agreement"), the new covenant, made by God (see Heb. 9:14 – 15). The word "testament" has to do with a relationship and contrasts with the old Mosaic covenant of the law (see Exod. 20; 24:1–8). The new covenant (see Jer. 31:31–32) while first promised to Israel spills over to benefit the church, but it will not be "fulfilled" with the Jews until the kingdom. The new covenant represents Christ the Living Word (see John 1:14–18). Jesus meant for this **cup** representing His **blood** to be taken in **remembrance of** Him (v. 25; Luke 22:19).

11:26–28. The Lord's table is to **shew the Lord's death till he come** (v. 26). "Shew" (Greek, *katangellō*) means "exhibit," "show forth," "proclaim," even "preach" (as in Acts 4:2; 13:5, 38; 15:36). The communion meal expresses believers' confidence in the death and resurrection of Christ as well as their confident expectation of His second coming.

To **drink ... unworthily** (v. 27) means to come with an attitude of irreverence. It is a privilege to represent the Lord's sacrifice and partake in the communion of the saints remembering His work on the cross. To be **guilty** (Greek, *enochos*) means being liable to the penal effect of committing a misdeed. Each one in the church was to **examine himself** (Greek, *dokimazetō*) to test or even judge, his actions and then eat and drink the meal with a good conscience. "This is defined in verse 29 as 'not judg[ing] the body rightly.' In other words, an irreverent and careless attitude is displayed at the Lord's Table" (Mitchell, *First Corinthians*, p. 168).

11:29–32. The one who eats and drinks **unworthily** (v. 29) brings **damnation to himself**. "Damnation" (Greek, *krima*) carries the idea of "judgment" in a special sense. While all believers will stand before the Lord for what is done in this life (see Rom. 14:10; 2 Cor. 5:10), this damnation is a special judgment, though not a loss of salvation. The judgment is temporal and has physical consequences. Because of it, **many are weak and sickly** (v. 30) in the congregation, **and many sleep**; that is, they are taken away to the Lord by death. This is a special penalty the Lord has imposed so that the sacrifice of Christ would not be besmirched among Christians and even among the lost in Corinth. Other sins can be equally evil and carry a temporal penalty for the believer. John the apostle adds, "There is a sin unto death: I do not say

that he shall pray for it. All unrighteousness is sin: and there is a sin not unto death" (1 John 5:16b–17).

Believers can escape such a harsh penalty by coming to their senses and **judg[ing] ourselves** (v. 31), and if this is done, **we should not be judged**. If this is not done, however, when the Lord judges, **we are chastened** (v. 32) so that believers will not be **condemned with the world**. "God disciplines us, so that we may turn to him in full penitence. By repenting of our sinful ways, we experience God's forgiveness, grace, mercy, and love (II Cor. 7:10)" (Kistemaker, *1 Corinthians*, p. 404).

11:33–34. Paul concluded this discussion with warmth and conciliation. **Wherefore, my brethren** (v. 33). By addressing the Corinthians as "brethren," he still spoke to them as part of the family of the children of God. He advised them to be considerate **when ye come together to eat**, even to **tarry** and wait for each other. If one was hungry, **let him eat at home** (v. 34) so that he would not bring upon himself **condemnation**. The Lord's Supper is to be more than food and drink. It has a spiritual purpose of reminding all the Christians of what Christ did at the cross. "Paul's primary interest is not reprobation, but restoration" (Mitchell, *First Corinthians*, p. 169). **And the rest**, other issues he was concerned about, he would **set in order** when he came to them. The apostle was hoping he could come to minister to them (see 4:19; 16:5–9). If he was able to come, he would arrive with the full authority of all of the apostles that the Lord had commissioned.

C. The Use of Spiritual Gifts (chaps. 12–14)

The Corinthian church also had problems regarding, and some cases of abuse of, the special spiritual gifts that the Holy Spirit imparts for the edification of the church. Having a gift did not ensure that it would not be used improperly. Many in the church had an inflated idea of their gifts and ostentatiously displayed their extraordinary abilities. Paul put the gifts into a proper balance in the Christian experience. In the midst of this discussion, he wrote that love, and all of its ramifications, is far more important than exercising spiritual gifts.

1. The Varieties of Spiritual Gifts (12:1–11)

In Paul's day, the issue of spiritual gifts was controversial in churches, as is often the case today. The Corinthian believers had spiritual gifts but were abusing them. Paul wanted to show that the gifts are given by the Holy Spirit, they are to help the churches minister, they do not replace love, they are primarily for ministry and not for show, and — especially regarding the gift of tongues — they have guidelines for their use.

12:1–3. That Paul started out with **concerning spiritual gifts** (v. 1), indicates that he was aware of some confusion or that the Corinthians had inquired about spiritual gifts. He did not want this church to be **ignorant** about the subject. He wanted to address the issue clearly so that none in the congregation would have an opportunity to contradict his message (see 14:37). He reminded them that they had practiced a false mysticism when, as **Gentiles**, they had been misled by **dumb idols** (v. 2). Misusing the miracle of the spiritual gifts could cause the church to fall into strange practices that they had all previously experienced as pagans. Paul was concerned both about their attitude on the subject and about the misconceptions taught by false teachers. The test of a lying apostle was that no one with **the Spirit of God** (v. 3) could **calleth Jesus accursed**, nor could one **say that Jesus is the Lord, but by the Holy Ghost**. The false prophets claimed special visions, revelations, and messages (see 2 Cor. 12:1) as if these has been given to them by the Lord, but apparently they were denying the humanity of Christ, as with the words "Jesus accursed."

12:4–6. Paul wanted the Corinthians to understand that there are **diversities** (Greek, *diaireseis*) **of gifts** (v. 4), though it is **the same Spirit** giving them, **And there are differences of administrations, but the same Lord** (v. 5). Both the Holy Spirit and the Lord Jesus Christ are involved in the working of the spiritual gifts. "Administrations" (Greek, *diakonia*) means "service" or "ministry," for each believer has his particular service to render and each has a gift to exercise for Christ's glory. There are **diversities of operations** (Greek, *energēma*)**, but it is the same**

God at work in every believer: (1) the Spirit grants the gift, (2) the Lord Jesus administers it, and (3) the heavenly Father energizes it, or makes it work, for His purposes. Taken all together, these verses "suggest that for each there is a specific *gift* that correlates with a specific *place* and a specific *work*. As he proceeds, Paul weaves these three ideas in and out of his teaching on the subject" (Mitchell, *First Corinthians*, p. 176).

12:7–10. Every man (v. 7) is given **the manifestation of the Spirit** so that he may **profit withal**. The Holy Spirit imparts a gift to each Christian. The gifts come from the same source but are uniquely expressed (see 14:4; 1 Peter 4:10). "Profit" (Greek, *sympherō*) means "bring together." Most gifts are for the edifying of the believers in the body of Christ. Paul noted individuality in his comment, **For to one … to another** (v. 8). **The same Spirit** is at work here, not simply human energy. Spiritual gifts are not simply talents or skills; they are placements and activities that have a distinct purpose in God's plan.

The gift of **the word of wisdom** (v. 8) means that certain believers have a Spirit-given ability to share common sense and wisdom in specific situations, while others may not have this ability to discern. **The word of knowledge** is given to some to comprehend and process spiritual information that is not fully understood by all. This might have been confined to the early apostles and prophets, because it seems to be identified here as a revelatory gift for the apostles.

The **working of miracles** (v. 10), **prophecy**, and **discerning of spirits** were also important gifts. "It was … of importance to have a class of men with the gift of discernment, who could determine whether a man was really inspired, or spoke only from the impulse of his own mind, or from the dictation of some evil spirit" (Hodge, *First Epistle to the Corinthians*, p. 248). On prophecy, "After the canon of the New Testament was completed, the special needs for this gift was substantially diminished" (Mitchell, *First Corinthians*, p. 176).

Divers kinds of tongues (v. 10) and **the interpretation of tongues** work in tandem. They were probably the most exotic and controversial gifts in the early church. Today there are three views as to what "tongues" are about: (1) an ecstatic utterance or an "unknown" (14:2) language, (2) a language spoken by angels (13:1), (3) a foreign language that communicated the message of the gospel to one who could not understand the language being used. Those who hold that it is an ecstatic language argue that when tongues were spoken in Acts (2:4; 10:46; 19:6), they were certainly foreign languages because the text in Acts 2 clearly says that every man at Pentecost heard the disciples speak in "his own language" (Acts 2:6–8) or dialect. It is argued, however, in 1 Corinthians 12 and 14, that tongues are an ectastic utterance or angelic languages, different from what was recorded in Acts. The Greek expression "other tongues" (Greek, *hetera glōssa*) is used in both Acts 2:4 and 1 Corinthians 14:21, which indicates that what happened in Acts 2 was the same as in 1 Corinthians 12 and 14. It would thus be a foreign language that the speaker would not know except by the Holy Spirit working a miracle in the speaker.

12:11. The Spirit of God is required to make **all these worketh**, giving to each believer **severally** (differently) **as he will**. Gifts are sovereignly initiated and divided for God's purposes in the body of believers. "The Spirit chooses what gift shall be given to each Christian, so that none have occasion for boasting, or for a sense of inferiority" (Barrett, *First Epistle to the Corinthians*, p. 286). It is not for the believer to dictate to the Holy Spirit what gifts they, or anyone else, should have.

2. Spiritual Gifts and the Body of Christ (12:12–31)

12:12–17. Here Paul explained the spiritual body of Christ, how the Spirit places the **many members** (v. 12) into Christ. There is but **one body: so also is Christ**. All believers are **baptized into** (v. 13) this one spiritual body, **whether ... Jews or Gentiles ... bond or free**. All classes who trust Christ are united to Him by spiritual baptism and are **made to drink into one Spirit** (see Rom. 12:4–5; Eph. 4:4–5). Since Paul said there is only "one baptism" (Eph. 4:5), he was not here referring simply to water baptism. It is the baptism of the Holy Spirit that actually brings

about salvation by uniting the believer with Christ. "The baptism of the Spirit is experienced by all who believe, at the moment of salvation (cf. Rom. 8:9). In that baptism, believers,... are identified with Christ ... and are indwelt by the Spirit ..." (Lowery, "First Corinthians," pp. 533–34). Jesus prophesied that believers would "drink into one Spirit" (v. 13) in John 4:14; 7:38–39.

Since each believer is a member of the body, and each is given a specific gift for a distinct task, **the foot ... the hand** (v. 15), **the ear ... the eye** (v. 16), **the hearing ... the smelling** (v. 17) cannot say, **I am not of the body** (v. 16). It would be ridiculous for the foot or hand to claim that they were **the whole body** (v. 17). Each member is different and unique and is carrying out its function as given by the Lord. As the members cooperate together, they increase the effectiveness of the ministry of the local church.

12:18–22. God set the members ... in the body, as it hath pleased him (v. 18). No one can request a specific gift, not even the gift of tongues. Nor can the members laud their gifts over other members as if the others' gifts are not as important. Even **those members ... which seem to be more feeble, are necessary** (v. 22). The physical body has small organs and larger members that appear more essential, but all together, they make up the body. If any member is missing or is sickly, the body does not function properly.

12:23–27. The member of the body that is "ill" needs a compensation, another member to bring him strength. Upon the **less honourable** (v. 23) the **more abundant honour** is **bestow[ed]**, and the **uncomely parts** are given more abundance. **We bestow** (Greek, *peritithemen*) means "we clothe." This is like giving someone a coat that bestows honor upon the one who was previously not so blessed. In like manner God is bestowing gifts to the individual "to secure the result that more abundant honor should be given to those which lacked. By making the uncomely parts essential to the well being of the rest ..." (Hodge, *First Corinthians*, p. 260). In this way, **there should be no schism** (v. 25) or competition. Each should **care one for another**. In a healthy body, when **one member suffer, all the members suffer with it; or one member be honoured, all the members rejoice with it** (v. 26). Paul did not single out the weaker members but laid down a principle that all should heed and abide by. Elsewhere the apostle said, "Let us therefore follow after the things which make for peace, and the things wherewith one may edify another" (Rom. 14:19).

12:28–31. To make sure the Corinthians did not suddenly feel they were high and mighty, Paul emphasized that there is an order to how God works in the church. He has **set some in the church, first apostles, secondarily prophets, thirdly teachers, after that miracles, then gifts of healing, helps, governments, diversities of tongues** (v. 28). Here Paul put forth an order of authority when he wrote of the apostles, prophets, and teachers. These were the teaching and writing disciples and included Paul himself.

Paul then asked a rhetorical question: does everyone in the church have the same gifts? (see vv. 28–29). The answer is no. In fact, his list does not include all of the gifts that he could have listed. He concluded that believers should **covet earnestly the best gifts** (v. 31). He had more to say, however. He would show them **a more excellent way**. When he says "covet earnestly" ("desire earnestly"), he was looking forward to chapter 14, where he said that it is good to want to promote the gifts, but only if one is driven by love (see chap. 13). Paul was not trying to arouse a spirit of competition among the believers. The "more excellent way" (or road) leads right into Paul's discussion of being driven by love in all things, rather than being driven by jealousy, as many of the Corinthians had been. Demonstrating the love of God is more important than seeking gifts.

3. The Primacy of Love over Gifts (chap. 13)

All of Paul's great authority and influence, his high and holy office, were because of God's love. The apostle laid open his whole heart for the Corinthians in this chapter. Paul stopped the flow of his discussion on spiritual gifts to point the church to something higher. He had experienced the love and grace of God when he was mercifully knocked down on the road to Damascus (see Acts 9:1–17). Whatever service the Corinthians had through their gifts needed to be tempered with charity that "never faileth" (1 Cor. 13:8).

13:1–3. Even having the gift of **tongues** (v. 1) of **angels**, if there was no **charity** (love) in what was said it would all sound like gonging **brass** or the gentle sound of a small, bell-like **tinkling cymbal**. Angels do communicate with each other, and in some cases the Lord allows them to speak with humans (see Matt. 28:5), but Paul's point was that it would be a miraculous gift to actually know the vocabulary of the angelic realm. He was not saying he had such a gift. And even if one had **the gift of prophecy** (v. 2), and comprehended **all mysteries, and all knowledge**, and had complete **faith** in order to be able to **remove mountains**, and yet had **no charity**, it would be as if one had **nothing**. Paul here used hyperbole and exaggeration to contrast the extremes of being able to do almost anything and yet be devoid of love—such power would be useless. By referring to prophecy, mysteries, and knowledge, he hit upon spiritual abilities that would be attractive to someone religiously ambitious. But such gifts the Lord would discount. When he mentioned the moving of the mountains by faith, he may have been referring to the words of Christ when He said that the faith of a grain of mustard seed could "remove [it] to yonder place" (Matt. 17:20). Some of the Corinthians may have hoped for such authority, but if it was without charity, it would be a spiritually useless gesture.

What if one gave away **all [his] goods to feed the poor** (v. 3), or gave his body as a sacrifice to **be burned**? Without **charity, it profiteth … nothing**. Great acts of charity or the giving of oneself in martyrdom would be wasted without love. "The exercise of the gifts accomplishes something in each case, but without love he who exercises them is himself of no value" (Vine, *Collected Writings*, p. 93).

13:4–7. In poetic fashion, the apostle made a long list of the blessedness of **Charity** (love; v. 4). The list is nearly exhaustive because he wanted the

Corinthians to become a model church. Charity **suffereth long** (v. 4), does not retaliate; **is kind**, outgoing with goodness; **envieth not**, will not show jealousy; **vaunteth not itself**, refuses to exalt oneself; **is not puffed up**, is not conceited; **doth not behave itself unseemly** (v. 5), does not act improperly; **seeketh not her own**, is never selfish; **is not easily provoked**, is not short-tempered; **thinketh no evil**, does not plot to do wrong; **rejoiceth not in iniquity** (v. 6), does not rejoice over wrong; **rejoiceth in the truth**, embraces what is right; **beareth all things** (v. 7), endures quietly even when suffering; **believeth all things**, anticipates what is good; **hopeth all things**, knows no pessimism; **endureth all things**, bears up under trials.

The Christian who exercises such godly love is showing forth the nature of Christ. Love always expects that grace will conquer and win its way in the struggles of the human drama. Exercising love raises the believer into the heights of the spiritual life. Paul would not allow the Corinthians to fall below this standard, which they had not been living and practicing among themselves.

13:8–10. Charity never faileth (v. 8). Some of the more miraculous gifts may cease, but love will not. The grammatical construction of "never faileth" means "does not fall." **Prophecies** will in the future be made inoperative, and the gifts of **tongues** and of **knowledge** will one day **cease**. These three gifts can be called "the communication gifts"; that is, they were used to transmit spiritual truth in the churches where the people spoke different languages. Also, a special source for revealed truth was needed because the New Testament books had not been finally written under the inspiration of the Holy Spirit. There had to be those who could "move the message" and explain doctrine, though revelation had not been finalized. "Perhaps what is most significant is that these gifts *will* stop. Some have agued that tongues are the language of heaven. If that were true, Paul could hardly have said that they will stop" (Mitchell, *First Corinthians*, p. 190).

The gifts of knowledge and prophecy are useful only in an imperfect state of existence. They have a purpose for the present but are limited in vision and scope; they do not tell the believer all there is to know. **In part** (v. 9) means that **we know** partially, or with limitation, but a change will come **when [the] perfect is come** (v. 10). The "perfect" (Greek, *teleion*; "complete," "mature," "finished") apparently does not refer to the coming of Christ because the word is in the neuter gender, not masculine. There are three views on what it means: (1) the completion of the New Testament canon (as suggested in the preceding paragraph), (2) the state of perfection of the new heavens and new earth, and (3) the state of the church when God's program for it is consummated at the coming of Christ.

13:11–12. Paul used two illustrations to get his point across. The first is that of the immaturity of **a child** (v. 11), who has limited speech, understanding, and thinking skills. In saying **I thought** (Greek, *elogizomēn*) **as a child**, the apostle may have been speaking of the church and "hinting that it was childishness that led the Corinthians to overvalue tongues and to undervalue love" (Barrett, *First Epistle to the Corinthians*, p. 306). When Paul **became a man, [he] put away childish things**.

Paul's second illustration argues that Christians can see only as **through a glass, darkly** (v. 12), or dimly. His reference is to a polished bronze mirror, which distorts a reflection and shows it with imperfection. The Christian now only **know[s] in part**, or partially, but someday will know as if seeing the Lord **face to face**. Only when the believer sees God face-to-face will partial knowledge (see 8:1–3) be displaced by the perfect knowledge of God. Elsewhere Paul added, "While we look not at the things which are seen, but at the things which are not seen: for the things which are seen are temporal; but the things which are not seen are eternal" (2 Cor. 4:18).

4. The Primacy of Prophecy over Tongues (14:1–25)

Tongues must have been extremely divisive issue in the Corinthian church. Apparently, when the Spirit imparted such a gift, the receiver could use this miraculous phenomenon on a continual basis. This became a contentious issue because pride set in.

The Corinthians must have had a fascination with this gift and quickly perverted its use. In this chapter, Paul spelled out the guidelines for its manifestation in the assembly.

14:1. Both this verse and 13:13 seem to set the stage for Paul's answer about tongues. The Corinthians were to **Follow after charity** but also **desire spiritual gifts**; the better gift, however, was **that ye may prophesy**. Paul was not saying that everyone should prophesy, for he had already said that not everyone has the same gifts (12:28–30). His point was that prophecy, or teaching, is preferable over the gift of tongues.

14:2–4. Verse 2 may seem confusing. In the Greek, Paul used what is known as "a dative of reference." The verse best reads: "He that speaketh in an unknown tongue speaketh not *in reference to the things* of men, but *in reference to the things* of God." In other words, he speaks of spiritual matters, not simply human matters. The word **unknown** (v. 2, 4) was added to the text for clarification. This **tongue** (v. 2, 4) would not have been understood by most in the company, yet **in the spirit he speaketh mysteries** (v. 2). The "mysteries" were "truths requiring a supernatural disclosure which God had not provided the Corinthians" (Barrett, *First Epistle to the Corinthians*, p. 538). As a result, for the church as a whole, tongues were a futile exercise that few could benefit from, except the speaker, who **edifieth himself** (v. 4) in his own spirit. Because all of the gifts were to edify **the church**, what the "Corinthians are experiencing fails this litmus test and should be laid aside in preference to those gifts" that benefit the church (Mitchell, *First Corinthians*, p. 197). **He that prophesieth speaketh [for] edification, and exhortation, and comfort** (v. 3). Preaching in a known tongue brings greater edification than preaching in an unknown tongue.

14:5–6. When Paul wrote that he wished **all spake with tongues** (v. 5), he was using hyperbole, because he already said that not everyone has the same gifts. He was contrasting this wish with **but rather that ye prophesied** and explained that **except he interpret** (tongues), prophesying was the greater

gift because it edifies **the church**. To understand Paul's statements here, one must consider the context. His point was that if the gift of tongues is used, it must be interpreted by one who has this gift (see 12:30). He probably was not saying that the one who speaks in tongues must then interpret what he has just said.

Paul was not deprecating the gift of tongues, which is a gift the Holy Spirit imparts. He was trying to ensure that the gift was used properly and that the extremes that the Corinthians fell into were avoided. What would **tongues … profit** (v. 6) them unless it came with some deep spiritual substance, such as with special **revelation … knowledge … prophesying, or … doctrine**? While the apostle mentioned his own gifted abilities here, he was trying to communicate to them that unless tongues were used in a way that had meaning, it was simply for show.

14:7–12. Here Paul presented a long illustration. He needed to use object lessons to communicate to this very immature congregation. He pointed out that different sounds are made by the **pipe … harp** (v. 7), and **trumpet** (v. 8), and these sounds have different purposes, such as the trumpet calling the soldier **to the battle. So likewise** (v. 9), **what is spoken** in the general assembly must be **easy to be understood**. Otherwise, **ye … speak into the air**. In this world, **There are … many voices** (sounds) (v. 10), but they have a purpose; they are not **without signification**. So it is with the gift of tongues if not used properly. It must have a spiritual purpose, or one **speaketh [as] a barbarian** (v. 11). A "barbarian" was one who did not speak Greek or one who was simply a foreigner. To illustrate his point, Paul used what was happening in the metropolis of Corinth. The city was a melting pot of races and languages. It was teeming with sailors and traders from all points in the known world. This may be one of the reasons that the Holy Spirit activated the gift of tongues there, so that those who spoke other languages could miraculously hear the gospel and then take it back to their homeland.

Paul came to his point. Because this church was **zealous [for] spiritual gifts** (v. 12), it was best to

excel to the edifying of the church, which meant that the gift of prophecy (teaching) was the most beneficial. Paul wanted the Corinthians to "seek after gifts that will benefit the church. Note that where Paul gives direction to his argument, it moves toward Acts 2 as the normative experience" (Mitchell, *First Corinthians*, p. 198).

14:13 – 17. This is the second time Paul said that **an unknown tongue** (v. 13) should be interpreted (see 14:5). In fact, Paul exhorted the one who spoke in tongues to **pray** that it may be interpreted. "This is always the case when the ability is lacking" (Lenski, *1 and 2 Corinthians*, p. 591). He urged this because the **tongue** (v. 14) given without interpretation is **unfruitful** and will not benefit those who do not know that language. Interpreted tongues, like prophecy, could edify the congregation (see Acts 19:6). If no one present was able to interpret, the tongues speaker was to keep silent (see 1 Cor. 14:28).

If one miraculously spoke in another tongue or language and did not comprehend what he said, the experience had no value. One could **pray** (v. 15) or even **sing** in tongues, but if it was done without understanding, the process was no better than the babbling of the heathen demon worshipers who put themselves into ecstatic trances. The speaker was to use tongues **with the understanding also**. Otherwise, one coming into the assembly or one who is **unlearned** (v. 16) and does not know what is going on would not know **what thou sayest**. Without a lucid understanding of what the Lord is revealing through these gifts the speaker was giving thanks well enough, but others were not edified. What was said may have been good, but no one spiritually benefited from it. **Thanks** (v. 17) and other spiritual expressions may go forth, **but the other is not edified**. "In short, anyone who gives leadership in worship service [including the tongues speaker] must speak intelligently to enlighten and instruct his fellow man" (Kistemaker, *1 Corinthians*, p. 494).

14:18 – 21. Paul had the gift of tongues and used it often: **I speak with tongues more than ye all** (v. 18). **Yet in the church** (v. 19), he preferred to speak clearly, **with my understanding** (v. 19), that

he **might teach others also**, rather than speak **ten thousand words** in a tongue that most could not comprehend. The apostle was chipping away at the abuse and the arrogance displayed at Corinth. He was rebuking the Corinthians, not for speaking in tongues, which is a gift of the Holy Spirit, but for their irresponsible flaunting of the practice, which brought about more confusion than light.

In the midst of correcting the Corinthians' practice of tongues, Paul called them **Brethren** (v. 20) and told them to no longer be **children** in this matter but rather **men** who acted as spiritual adults. Their infatuation with tongues was another manifestation of their immaturity.

The apostle quoted **the law** (v. 21), a broad reference that included even the Prophets, such as Isaiah. The Lord said through Isaiah that Israel will be reached "with stammering lips and another tongue" (Isa. 28:11). Because of their hardness of heart, God will use Gentiles to speak to His people. With a foreign tongue unintelligible to Israel, this stiff-necked people will hear the truth of God's judgment on them.

14:22 – 25. Wherefore tongues are for a sign (v. 22), not for believers, but for unbelievers. **Prophesying**, or teaching, however, was **for them which believe**. Since the church is mainly for the spiritual nourishment of believers, prophecy is the more appropriate gift. If the skeptic, the doubter, the **unlearned**, and the unbeliever were to come into the assembly and hear what seems but a rambling of tongues, **will they not say that ye are mad?** (v. 23). The word "unlearned" ("idiots") refers to the uninitiated regarding tongues. Upon hearing what to them would be gibberish, they and **the unbelievers** would regard the congregation as a company of lunatics, whereas God's purpose in ministry, whether for the saved or unsaved, is to reach the understanding and appeal to the conscience.

If prophecy or teaching was being practiced, however, the unbeliever or the **unlearned** (v. 24) could be taught and **convinced of all**, and even convicted or **judged [by] all. The secrets of his heart** (v. 25), of the one who is so convicted, would cause him to fall **down on his face** and **worship God**. Then he would testify that in this assembly, **God is in you of a truth**. The unbeliever will only come to faith as a result of clearly hearing and understanding God's Word.

5. Regulating Spiritual Gifts (14:26–40)

Paul continued on the subject about tongues and prophecy, but here he laid down certain principles for regulating the use of these gifts. Prophecy has the highest value because it edifies all of those in the body of Christ and even works to bring unbelievers to repentance. Having established the theological and doctrinal issues regarding the gifts of tongues and prophecy, Paul set biblical parameters to eliminate abusive practices.

14:26–28. In the assembly, how should the services be conducted? **When ye come together** (v. 26), whether one brings **a psalm** to sing, gives **a doctrine**, speaks in **a tongue**, gives **a revelation**, or has **an interpretation … Let all things be done unto edifying**. Paul's point was that it must all be done to edify the congregation. If one spoke **in an unknown tongue** (v. 27), it was to be done **by two, or at the most by three … by course** (in turn)**; and let one interpret**. The phenomenon of tongues was a gift of the Spirit of God, but carnality could set in, and the person speaking could be simply uttering his own thoughts. If this happened, it could lead to heresy. That is why the presence of one who had the gift of interpretation was necessary, to assure that this was a word from God, not man. **If there be no interpreter** (v. 28), the tongues speaker was to **keep silence in the church**. Paul added, **let him speak to himself, and to God**, meaning that he should keep his thoughts to himself and to God rather than speak in tongues without the counterbalance of an interpreter.

14:29–33. Turning to prophecy, the apostle applied the same principle and said that those prophesying may speak by **two or three** (v. 29), with others judging what was said. Again, this proves that while these gifts are from God, the flesh can intervene and spoil the message. Therefore, the message must be judged by the wisdom of others to ensure that it fits within the full scope of previous revelation. "When a person who receives such a revelation makes it known to fellow believers, they in turn must subject this revelation to the authoritative teaching of the Scriptures" (Kistemaker, *1 Corinthians*, p. 509).

Teaching and receiving prophecy must "be done decently and in order" (14:40). If a revelation was given **to another**, Paul instructed, **let the first hold his peace** (v. 30). Prophecy was to be given in an orderly fashion, **one by one [so] that all may learn, and all may be comforted** (v. 31). In human terms, **the spirits of the prophets are subject to the prophets**; that is, a consensus must be reached to confirm a teaching or a doctrine. No one could prophesy independently. Paul said that if there was confusion in the church while prophecy was being given, it was not from God, **For God is not the author of confusion** (v. 33); He is the author **of peace**. The obvious conclusion, then, is that confusion comes from the flesh and from believers' carnality and pride. Paul wanted peace to prevail **in all the churches of the saints**. "Saints" refers to those who are spiritually and positionally sanctified in Christ. The church is to be a unified body of believers, not a forum for self-promotion.

14:34–35. Scholars have differing opinions on these verses. Some say that Paul was referring to women who have the gift of tongues. Others believe Paul was simply continuing his argument about order and peace in the church. He was concerned that the women might disrupt the service. If Paul's context was prophecy, it ties into 11:5, where he permitted women to prophesy. Paul's main concern can be found in 1 Timothy 2:12, where he stated that he wanted the women "to be in silence." "Silence" is the Greek word *hēsychia*, which carries the idea "to not be excitable," or "to remain unemotional." Again, his concern was about the decorum and emotional state during the gathering of the congregation. He wanted the wives **to be under obedience** (v. 34), as is stated in **the law**. In a broad sense, it appears he was referring to the demeanor of Jewish women in the synagogues. Peter mentioned this and wrote that wives should be "in subjection unto their own husbands: even as Sara obeyed Abraham, calling him lord: whose daughters ye are, as long as ye do well, and are not afraid" (1 Peter 3:5b–6).

When Paul wrote, **Let your women keep silence** (v. 34), he used the Greek word verb *sigaō*, which comes from the noun *siagōn*, meaning the "jaw." Some have reasoned that, with a bit of humor, he was saying he did not want the woman "to move the mouth" or "flap the jaw" in a disruptive and emotional display. He instead wanted the women to **ask their husbands at home** (v. 35). "This contrasts with a disturbance caused by their talking to their husbands during the service" (Barrett, *First Epistle to the Corinthians*, p. 541). Paul was saying not that women should not speak at all but that they should not disturb the public services.

14:36–40. The church at Corinth was not an exclusive group of believers, acting independently as interpreters or as those handed down **the word of God** (v. 36). They, like all assemblies (see 14:33), were to obey the Lord's Word and truth by obeying its standards of conduct and even the traditions that come from His Word. If anyone claimed **to be a prophet, or spiritual** (v. 37), he must **acknowledge that the things** Paul wrote **are the commandments of the Lord**. This supports the doctrine of the inspiration of Scripture. What the apostle wrote came from the Lord and was not to be ignored or challenged. Whoever wanted to remain **ignorant** (v. 38) about this matter, however, **let him** do so. Paul may have been saying some will remain unconvinced.

The church should **covet** (in the good sense of "earnestly desire") **to prophesy** (v. 39) but **forbid not to speak with tongues**. Paul here emphasized the teaching ministry and held a neutral position on tongues, only because that gift was abused in the Corinthian church. He summarized the discussion with the desire that **all … be done decently and in order** (v. 40). Harmony and order should characterize public church services.

V. The Importance of the Doctrine of the Resurrection (chap. 15)

This entire chapter focuses on one of the most significant doctrines of Christianity, the resurrection, a doctrine which sets it apart from other religions. Without the resurrection, those who profess faith in Christ have no hope. If He did not come forth from the grave, Christians' belief is in vain, and there is certainly no guarantee of being resurrected. Paul also touched on the fulfillment or summing up of all things in the messianic kingdom. The resurrection was an historical event, was witnessed by a large company of the disciples and others, and was even attested to by many others who saw the Lord for themselves. Paul apparently was answering some skeptics who denied the resurrection of Christ and therefore were also repudiating the resurrection of believers. He seems to have been saying that a strong belief "in it would help solve many of the Corinthians' problems. Certainly if the message of Christ crucified were foolishness to the Greek mind (1:23), the corollary doctrine of the Resurrection was no less so (cf. Acts 17:31–32)" (Lowery, "First Corinthians," p. 542).

A. The Historical Fact of the Resurrection (15:1–11)

15:1–2. The essence of **the gospel** (v. 1) is the doctrine of the resurrection. **I declare** (Greek, *gnōrizō*) actually means "I make plain," "I cause [you] to know." Paul was reminding the Corinthians of what they ought never to have forgotten. He spells this out in verse 3 on. **I preached** the gospel and the resurrection, which **ye have received**, and now **ye stand** in it. By this **ye are saved, if ye keep in memory what I preached unto you, unless ye have believed in vain** (v. 2). In writing "keep in memory," Paul was putting forth the idea that if they did not keep in their memory what he had preached to them, it was possible they did not ever have saving faith. Judas Iscariot, for example, showed by his denial of the Lord Jesus that he was never a true believer.

15:3–7. When Paul said he had delivered **first** (v. 3) what the Corinthians believed, he used the Greek word *prōtois*, meaning "among the first things," or the things of primary importance (see Kistemaker, *1 Corinthians*, p. 535). This he had **received** from the Old Testament (see Ps. 16:8–11; Isa. 53:5–6, 11) and from eyewitnesses, the apostles and others (see Acts 1:21–22). These facts, **that Christ**

died (v. 3) and **was buried, and … rose again** (v. 4) are all confirmed and prophesied in the Old Testament, that is, **according to the scriptures**. The Word of God is the first line of defense for all truth.

After His resurrection, Jesus was first seen by one of the most respected disciples, **Cephas** (Peter; v. 5; see Luke 24:34), then by the other apostles, **the twelve**. "The twelve" became a symbolic description of the inner circle of the disciples as a group. Judas had already killed himself when Christ revealed Himself to Peter and the others. In other places in the Gospels, they are often called "the eleven" (Matt. 28:16; Mark 16:14; Luke 24:9; Acts 1:26).

Even more astounding is that others beside the twelve saw Christ. More than **five hundred brethren** (v. 6), or believers, saw Him at the same time (**at once**), many of whom were still alive when Paul was writing, though some had already died, or **fallen asleep** (an often used expression of the death of believers, see Acts 7:60). Paul then mentioned one of the most respected elder leaders of the disciples, **James** (v. 7), and a wider circle of believers, **all the apostles**, who saw the living Jesus. This James is probably the Lord's brother (see Matt. 13:55), since the apostle James was included in "the twelve" (v. 5). The brother James earlier had been an unbeliever (see John 7:5), though he later joined the assembly of disciples (see Acts 1:14; Mitchell, *First Corinthians*, p. 213). Paul could not have mentioned these facts if they were not true. Any skeptic could have searched for eyewitnesses and asked pertinent questions. This was too large of a crowd of eyewitnesses to refute.

15:8–11. Next the apostle added his own firsthand witness. The resurrected Christ **was seen of me also** (v. 8) but as **one born out of due time**, meaning Paul was not saved when the Lord appeared to him (see Acts 9:3–9) and commissioned him as "a chosen vessel unto me, to bear my name before the Gentiles, and kings, and the children of Israel" (Acts 9:15). Paul considered himself **the least of the apostles** (v. 9) because he tormented the early believers in Jerusalem, placing them in chains, using "threatenings and slaughter against the disciples of the Lord" (Acts 9:1). He considered himself the chief of sinners (see 1 Tim. 1:15) and "the least of all saints" (Eph. 3:8). "This recollection of a sinful past is set as an example to all in whom the grace of God has so wrought" (Vine, *Collected Writings*, p. 107). This grace was not **bestowed … in vain** (v. 10) because it brought on a greater appreciation of the gospel, causing Paul to labor **more abundantly than they all**, possibly meaning the other apostles. The apostle shows how personal his ministry was when said, **the grace of God … was with me**. Regardless of who was preaching and teaching, however, **I or they** (v. 11), the message was going forth, **and so ye believed**.

B. No Salvation without the Resurrection (15:12–19)

15:12–14. Paul asked, **If Christ be preached that he rose from the dead, how say some among you that there is no resurrection of the dead?** (v. 12). If there is no promise of resurrection anywhere in God's Word, **then is Christ not risen** (v. 13). In seed form, Job prophesied, "For I know that my Redeemer liveth, and that he shall stand at the latter day upon the earth: and though after my skin worms destroy this body, yet in my flesh shall I see God" (Job 19:25–26). David also echoed the words of the Messiah, "My flesh also shall rest in hope. For thou wilt not leave my soul in hell [the grave]; neither will thou suffer thine Holy One to see corruption" (Ps. 16:9b–10). Ezekiel spoke of the resurrection (Ezekiel 37), and so did Daniel (Dan. 12:1–3). The doctrine of the resurrection was well established and certain for all believing Jews during the time of Christ. Martha said to Jesus, "I know that he [Lazarus] shall rise again in the resurrection at the last day" (John 11:24). Jesus answered with these famous words: "I am the resurrection, and the life: he that believeth in me, though he were dead, yet shall he live" (John 11:25). Christ is the epitome and the embodiment of this doctrine.

15:15–19. All of the great company, including Paul, were **false witnesses of God** (v. 15) if they **testified** that God **raised up Christ** and it was not so. The principle would have been destroyed; there would never be such a thing as the resurrection. If the dead cannot be raised, neither can Christ (v. 16). Here Paul may have been referring to Lazarus, whose resurrection had to be well known among the believers of the church. If there is no resurrection, then **faith is vain** (v. 17) and the Corinthians and all Christians **are yet in your sins**. "Vain" (Greek, *mataios*) means "lacking in result." "Since the resurrection of Christ is essential to our justification (Rom. 4:25), the denial of it vitiates the forgiveness of our sins" (Mitchell, *First Corinthians*, p. 216). Therefore, all who have died, those **fallen asleep in Christ are perished** (v. 18). If there is no hope in this life for a future resurrection, then Christians are among **all men most miserable** (v. 19).

C. All in Christ Shall Be Made Alive (15:20 – 34)

15:20 – 24. Here Paul focused on the central truth of Christ's resurrection from the dead. By Christ's resurrection, He led the way for others to follow, like the first of the spring crops from the field, **the firstfruits of them that slept** (v. 20). Because He came forth from the grave, believers are certain to follow. Christ was the first to be resurrected, **the firstfruits** (Greek, *aparchē*; v. 23). "Paul (in dependence on the Old Testament) takes the word to mean the first installment of the crop which foreshadows and pledges the ultimate offering of the whole" (Barrett, *First Epistle to the Corinthians*, p. 350). This is similar to Him being also called "the beginning, the firstborn from the dead" (Col. 1:18).

By one **man** (Adam) **came death** (v. 21), and by another **man** (Jesus) **came … the resurrection of the dead** (see Rom. 5:12 – 18). Adam brought upon all judgment, but Christ brought upon all the free gift of "righteousness" (see Rom. 5:18). Some have mistakenly seen this as a form of universalism. In verse 21 – 22 and in 15:45, however, Paul made it clear that **in Adam all die, even so in Christ shall all be made alive** (v. 22), and the only way to be "in Christ" is to trust Him as Savior. "Union with Adam is the cause of death; union with Christ is the cause of life" (Hodge, *First Epistle to the Corinthians*, p. 324). There is an order for every man: (1) **Christ**

the firstfruits (v. 23), then (2) they who belong to Him **at his coming**. Paul's nearest reference would be the rapture, which he described in some detail in 15:51 – 54 and 1 Thessalonians 4:13 – 18.

Paul carried his eschatological thought on to the end of history as described in Scripture. **The end** (v. 24) will arrive when Christ has **delivered up the kingdom to God, even the Father**. At that time, Christ **shall have put down all [human] rule and all authority and power**. This is when "every knee shall bow" (Isa. 45:23; Rom. 11:4; 14:11; Phil. 2:10 but "should") and Christ will be a root of His distant fathers David and Jesse and be "an ensign [flag] of the people; to it shall the Gentiles seek: and his rest shall be glorious" (Isa. 11:10). As for putting down "all rule and all authority," the Messiah, the Son of God, shall have the nations as an inheritance and shall "break them with a rod of iron … shalt dash them in pieces like a potter's vessel" (Ps. 2:9). Then begins His kingdom that will last one thousand years (see Rev. 20:1 – 6).

15:25 – 28. For he must reign (v. 25) was Paul's prevailing conclusive statement. At that time, as a conquering king of days gone by, Christ shall place His foot on the neck of His foes, subduing them **under his feet**. As God's Son, the Lord "madest him to have dominion over the works of thy hands" (Ps. 8:6). Meanwhile, in heaven, seated at the right hand of the Father, He waits until His enemies become His footstool (see Ps. 110:1). He will reign from Zion in Israel (see Ps. 110:2a) but will reign over the world. The Father will say to Him: "Rule thou in the midst of thine enemies" (Ps. 110:2b). When God is **all in all** (v. 28; see Rom. 11:36), the new creation will be consummated, and the church will share in Christ's resurrection. At that time, even the Son of God will be **subject unto him**, the God of the universe. Though equal in essence to the Father, the Son remains submissive in carrying out His will.

15:29 – 34. These cryptic verses have generated over two hundred explanations. "It is clear from the context, however, that Paul distinguishes his own practice and teaching from that described here" (Lowery, "First Corinthians," p. 542). The baptism **for the dead** (v. 29) initially raises problems, but considering what Paul may have meant and what he certainly could not have meant sheds light on the passage. The rules of Bible interpretation dictate that one should not hold a doctrine based on an obscure passage, and an obscure passage must be interpreted in light of the more clear verses that contradict what the obscure passage seems to be saying.

Some have tried to explain this passage by saying that Paul was refuting a pagan practice of ritual and religious washings. Mormons try to explain the passage by saying that one can be a substitute in baptism for those who have died, thus "making" them saved by the waters of baptism. Another view is that the Corinthians had distorted water baptism, as they apparently did in chapter 1, and as they had distorted the Lord's Supper (see 11:17–34). Yet another view is that Paul was talking about those who come along as believers, are baptized, and replace those who have fallen asleep in Christ.

The best explanation, which seems similar to the last suggestion, is put forth by Mitchell (*First Corinthians*, p. 221): "The logic of the passage would thus connect to the import of resurrection. People (now dead) have proclaimed the message and have led others to faith in the same gospel promising life and participation with Christ at His coming. What will we do if we now say that there is no resurrection and that the dead are simply gone?" In asking **why stand we in jeopardy** (v. 30), Paul could have meant, "Why do we continue to risk ourselves, giving our lives for the gospel, if all of this is not true?"

By your rejoicing (v. 31) means "By my boasting concerning you." Paul added, **I die daily**, meaning that he was continually exposed to death for the sake of Christ (see 2 Cor. 4:10). In fact, he had even fought with **beasts at Ephesus** (v. 32), probably referring to how he nearly lost his life when the mob tried to kill him (see Acts 19). Paul asked why he would struggle so and **what advantageth it me, if the dead rise not?** If this were the case, **let us eat and drink; for to morrow we die**, as cited by the Epicurean philosophers. Paul advised his readers to be careful what they listen to: **Be not deceived** (v. 33). Do not be fooled by what others say. Hang on to what is right and good.

Awake to righteousness (v. 34), in this case, what is right, and **sin not** by being led into doing what is wrong. Paul reminded the Corinthians that **some have not the knowledge of God**. They are but pretenders. Because some of the Corinthians had thus been led astray, Paul said, **I speak this to your shame**. "False doctrine never aids true moral conduct but works to corrupt that conduct" (Lenski, *1 and 2 Corinthians*, p. 701).

D. The Promise of the Resurrection (15:35–49)

Having proved the authenticity of the resurrection, Paul next focused on the promise of the resurrection. Here he wanted to illustrate its nature and show what kind of bodies the dead are to be raised in. Apparently, the overwhelming objection that Paul was aware of was, How can the future body be different from the one believers now have? The future body will definitely be material and identical to the present one, though it will be "organized" in a very different way. A seed is planted, yet it does not come out of the ground like a seed but like a flower. So it is with the eternal resurrected body.

15:35–38. Some would question, **How are the dead raised up? and ... what [kind of] body** (v. 35) will they have when **they come** out of the place of the dead? With a tinge of anger, Paul said, **Thou fool** (Greek, *aphrōn*; "without reasoning intelligence"; v. 36), a seed does not come alive, **is not quickened**, unless it dies. This is the great mystery of the ground bearing fruit. So it is with the miracle of the resurrection. The body placed in the ground is **not that body that shall be** (v. 37), yet it will not come forth as some other kind, **some other grain**. Every seed has its own essence, its **own body** (v. 38), and that is given, is created, as God has made it **as it hath pleased him**. God has created us, and we shall come forth from the dead as is pleasing to Him, God's "choice not being determined by man's act of sowing ... God himself appoints and chooses [the seed and the body] for various purposes" (Barrett, *First Epistle to the Corinthians*, pp. 370–71). God is in charge of the resurrection.

15:39–45. Paul's main purpose in these verses has to do with the resurrection, yet they provide an excellent explanation of how God created biological kinds and how He specifically created the bodies in space for distinct purposes. Creation and nature are fully in His design and operate by His power and authority.

When God created **men, beasts, fishes,** and **birds** (v. 39), He gave to each **kind** a distinct makeup, or **flesh.** The discovery and workings of the chromosomes of living cells shows that they do not cross over between kinds. They do not have **the same flesh.** The same is true of the **celestial** (v. 40) and **terrestrial** bodies. "As to the stars, their differences in luster and brilliance are endless, and in this they testify to the infinite wisdom and inexhaustible power of God their Creator" (Vine, *Collected Writings*, p. 113). These bodies each have a distinct glory (Greek, *doxa*) that sets them apart, **for one star differeth from another star in glory** (v. 41).

Paul explained, **So also is the resurrection of the dead** (v. 42). The human body is **sown in corruption** and **raised in incorruption.** "Corruption" (Greek, *phthora*) is the state of creation because of the entrance of sin into the universe (see Rom. 8:21; 2 Peter 2:12); because of the resurrection of Christ, however, the very body of the believer is to be raised and redeemed (see Rom. 8:23), with "the redemption of the purchased possession, unto the praise of his glory" (Eph. 1:14). As well, the body **is sown in dishonour** (v. 43) and **weakness** as **a natural body** (v. 44), but it is **raised in glory [and] power** (v. 43) as **a spiritual body** (v. 44). The reader must not assume that the resurrected saint's receiving "a spiritual body" means he is resurrected simply as a nonmaterial being, a floating wisp without form or corporality. By "a spiritual body," the apostle meant that the resurrection is accomplished through the supernatural operation of God the Spirit. God is going to change everything around. Nothing will be the same, and sin will be forever eradicated. Paul drew this conclusion partly from Genesis 2:7, which states that **Adam was made a living soul** (v. 45) that failed the test and succumbed to the temptation placed

before him by Satan, who was embodied in the serpent (see Genesis 3). Because of his disobedience to God's instructions, Adam would die, and the Lord added, "unto dust shalt thou return" (Gen. 3:19). Christ, **the last Adam,** is **a quickening** (life-giving) **spirit,** however, who has given those of Adam's race eternal life. Apart from the coming of the rapture, when the saints who are alive will be taken from the earth, Christians "still face the effect of death, even though we know that its power has been abrogated" (Kistemaker, *1 Corinthians*, p. 572).

15:46–49. The first Adam and his children were from the **earth, earthy.** The second man, the Lord, is from **heaven.** So those who trust in Him will be of the **heavenly.** Redeemed human beings are not meant to be earthbound but are instead bound for heaven. As believers **have borne the image of the earthy** (v. 49), likewise they will **also bear the image of the heavenly.** "*The heavenly* is Christ; *they that are heavenly* are his risen people. The descendants of Adam derive from him an earthly body like his. Those who are Christ's are to have a body fashioned like unto his glorious body, Phil. 3, 21" (Hodge, *First Epistle to the Corinthians*, p. 352).

E. Christ's Victory over Death (15:50–58)

15:50–54. Paul reminded his readers that simple **flesh and blood** (v. 50), humans residing in the same spiritual and physical mold as Adam, as sinful beings, **cannot inherit the kingdom of God** because this is comparable to **corruption inherit[ing] incorruption.** The thousand-year reign of Christ in the millennial kingdom will be the first stage in the eternal state of the new heavens and the new earth (see Rev. 21:1–7) "wherein dwelleth righteousness" (2 Peter 3:13). It is possible that many believers of this present church age may not die (**We shall not all sleep;** v. 51). If the rapture transformation took place today, **we** (the living) **shall all be changed** (see 1 Thess. 4:15; Phil. 3:21). The rapture **trumpet shall sound** (v. 52), and believers who have died **shall be raised incorruptible,** and those believers who are left **shall be changed.** This trumpet is called **the last trump,** meaning the trumpet that ends the church dispensation. This trumpet should not be confused with the seventh trumpet of Revelation (see Rev. 11:15–18). That trumpet is a war trumpet signaling the wrath to come upon the world before the kingdom of Christ is established (see Rev. 11:15). The rapture trumpet will be sounded to call the workers home from the fields of Christian labor. It is a trumpet of blessing, not a trumpet of terror.

The resurrection of those that are asleep will come just before the change that will take place for the living (see v. 52). The living will receive new and eternal bodies like those of the dead in Christ, who will be "raised incorruptible" (v. 52). This entire rapture process is called **a mystery** (v. 51) because it is not revealed in the Old Testament. Paul had written of this earlier in his first letter to the Thessalonians (1 Thess. 4:13–18). Those who are the dead in Christ shall be resurrected, and then "we which are alive and remain shall be caught up together with them in the clouds, to meet the Lord in the air: and so shall we ever be with the Lord" (1 Thess. 4:17). All of this will happen because **this mortal** (that which is dying) **must put on immortality** (v. 53), the state in which dying is eliminated. This fulfills Isaiah 25:8, which states that **Death is swallowed up in victory** (v. 54).

15:55–56. Death's **sting** (v. 55) is gone, and so is the triumph of the **grave** (see Hos. 13:14). John the apostle summarized this when he wrote, "And God shall wipe away all tears from their eyes; and there shall be no more death, neither sorrow, nor crying, neither shall there be any more pain: for the former things are passed away" (Rev. 21:4).

The sting of death (v. 56) came about as a result of the penalty for **sin.** The power and **strength of sin** is administered by the force of God's righteous demands, as laid down in **the law.** The main purpose of the law was to bring conviction about sin, so that "all the world may become guilty before God" (Rom. 3:19). Therefore "by the deeds of the law there shall no flesh be justified in his sight: for by the law is the knowledge of sin" (Rom. 3:20). Justification comes only through faith in Christ (see Rom. 3:26–28).

15:57–58. Because of these wonderful revelations, the apostle concluded with this triumphant message:

But thanks be to God, which giveth us the victory through our Lord Jesus Christ (v. 57). The only way out of the judgment laid upon humanity is to trust in Christ as one's Savior. These facts should make an impact on the **beloved brethren** (v. 58). They should live out the Christian life in a steady and **unmoveable** manner. They should be **always abounding in the work of the Lord,** knowing that their **labour is not in vain in the Lord.** The Christian life has purpose; it is not an empty existence. For Paul, this purpose was found in the sure conviction that he would one day share in the glory of the resurrection.

VI. Practical and Personal Exhortations (chap. 16)

As was his usual custom, Paul closed his letter with words of encouragement. The flow of the last chapter here concludes with an exhortation about very practical matters, focusing on the needs of the persecuted church in Jerusalem and a collection that would be made for them. In this chapter, Paul also cited the work of many who were laboring, sometimes under terrible circumstances, in various places.

A. The Collection for the Needy Saints (16:1–4)

16:1. God's people, **the saints** (see 1:2), needed help. Paul gave the same order to all **the churches of Galatia** that they too should put together a **collection,** probably meaning monies to relieve the lack of temporal things needed for survival. Paul wanted to go to Jerusalem to help (see Rom. 15:25) and had written to the Roman church, "For it hath pleased them of Macedonia and Achaia to make a certain contribution for the poor saints which are at Jerusalem" (Rom. 15:26). These Gentile churches wished to help their Jewish brothers who were suffering. Paul added, "For if the Gentiles have been made partakers of their spiritual things, their duty is also to minister unto them in carnal things" (Rom. 15:27), or temporal things. The apostle continued this reminder in 2 Corinthians 8:1; 9:1–4. The Galatian churches were contributing, and Paul instructed the Corinthian church, **even so do ye.**

16:2–4. The collection was to be taken **Upon the first day of the week** (v. 2), or compiled on a Sunday, when the churches were meeting for teaching and fellowship. The principle was that during the week they were putting aside, laying up **in store**, their money and even possibly some goods to be transported. They were to do this from a spiritual perspective: **as God has prospered.** Paul was always careful about money matters, avoiding solicitations for himself (see 9:12, 15), "but also when he acted to meet the needs of others he avoided direct involvement in handling the gift" (Lowery, "First Corinthians," p. 546). The believer was to do this not out of compulsion but in relation to what the Lord had done for him. Paul wanted the gift to be steadily collected so that there would **be no gatherings when I come.** The church would **approve by [their] letters** (v. 3) whom they chose to deliver their **liberality** (bounty) **unto Jerusalem.** If possible, **if it be meet** (v. 4), Paul would go with this envoy of believers to make the delivery. He may have had other missionary business to accomplish also.

B. Paul's Desire to Visit Corinth (16:5–9)

16:5–9. Paul had travel plans to **pass through Macedonia** (v. 5) and then possibly to **winter** (v. 6) in Corinth. With prayer support and possibly also with supplies, the church could help him on his way: **ye may bring me on my journey whithersoever I go.** This may mean that he wanted to journey straight to Macedonia, but the plans needed to be fluid as circumstances dictated. Though he could not come to Corinth at that time, he still wanted **to tarry a while with you** (v. 7). It is interesting to observe that after having been so "heavy" regarding the situations in the Corinthian church, Paul could now come along side of them and speak with such kind thoughts of intimate fellowship and concern. Paul knew that nothing would happen unless **the Lord permit.** There is human responsibility in the ministry, yet it is God who directs His work for His own purposes. Along his route of evangelization and teaching, Paul wanted to **tarry at Ephesus until Pentecost** (v. 8). Though the Corinth congregation was

mainly a Gentile church, they knew of the Jewish festivals that had their origins in the Old Testament. Paul said, though **there are many adversaries** (v. 9) in Ephesus, still **a great door and effectual is opened unto me.**

C. Personal Exhortations and Encouragements (16:10–18)

16:10–11. Timothy (**Timotheus**; v. 10) was well-known as Paul's traveling companion and ambassador who carried messages and even ministered on behalf of the great apostle. If Timothy went to Corinth, Paul wanted to make sure he labored with them **without fear.** Timothy and Erastus had gone into Macedonia (see Acts 19:22), but then Timothy was to go on to Corinth (see 1 Cor. 4:17). Paul did not want Timothy intimidated by harsh treatment in Corinth, because Timothy, as Paul, **worketh the work of the Lord.** Some argue that the issue was not "fear" but simply that Timothy appeared to be somewhat timid (see 1 Tim. 4:12; 2 Tim. 1:7). The apostle did not want him to be **despise[d]** (v. 11) but rather to come **in peace** and then be able to go back to Paul. Paul wanted him to be a part of the congregations, **for I look for him with the brethren.** Mitchell (*First Corinthians*, p. 230) suggests that Timothy "appears as a man of character, courage, and resourcefulness under whose leadership many crisis situations in the fledgling New Testament churches were confronted (cf. Acts 16–20; Phil. 2:19–24; 1 Thess. 3:1–6)."

16:12. Paul also **greatly desired** for **Apollos** to visit the assembly in Corinth. Apollos, however, had some legitimate reasons not to go. He desired **not at all to come at this time,** but he would come later, at a more **convenient time.** This may indicate that Apollos was operating independently of Paul, though there was no conflict between them.

16:13–16. Here Paul began a short series of pithy commands and encouragements. He wanted the Corinthian church to examine carefully what they were doing spiritually. He said, **Watch ye, stand fast in the faith** (v. 13). They were to look around, be aware of what was going on, and stand firm in their trust in the Lord. Barrett notes that "Watch ye" (Greek, *grēgorein*) is a present infinitive with the idea "to be continually watching" (*First Epistle to the Corinthians*, p. 393). This expression is often used not of purely general events but of eschatological happenings, or signs that may signal the coming of Christ (see 15:51–54). **Quit you like men** (Greek, *andrizesthe*; "play the man") refers to "manliness," which was a virtue recognized in the ancient world. Paul wanted the Corinthian assembly to shape up spiritually and **be strong** for the Lord's sake, yet all things were to **be done with charity** (v. 14), or love.

Paul issued another command that seems to have come from deep personal conviction. Apparently, **the house of Stephanas** (v. 15), whom Paul had baptized in Corinth (see 1:16), had originally come from **Achaia** (Greece), were some of the first converts there, and were viewed as among **the firstfruits** of that region. **They have addicted themselves** means "they have set themselves" to ministering to the believers, **the saints**. The entire household of Stephanas was serving the Lord. The larger body of believers in Corinth needed to **submit** to this family. They had helped Paul and were now laboring for and with him. "Stephanas and his household are not the only members of the church whose lead must be valued, respected, and followed" (Barrett, *First Epistle to the Corinthians*, p. 394).

16:17–18. Stephanas and Fortunatus and Achaicus (v. 17) were coming to Paul to help him with what the whole church had not **supplied**. This could mean that they made up for the absence of the Corinthians as a whole or that they had done what the Corinthians had failed to do. **For** (v. 18) introduces the reason these men were so important to Paul: **they have refreshed my spirit and yours**. Because of this, they were to be **acknowledge[d]**, "recognized" and "appreciated."

D. Final Greetings and Benedictions (16:19–24)

16:19–20. There must have been a great "telegraphing" of communication between the churches of Greece (Achaia) and all the churches **of Asia** (v. 19). Asia was a Roman province that is today western Turkey, including Ephesus and the surround-

ing cities (see Acts 19:10). The churches of Colosse, Laodicea, and Hierapolis were on the border of the province of Asia (see Col. 4:13–16; Rev. 1:11). These churches **salute[d]** (greeted) the Corinthian believers. Paul specifically mentioned **Aquila and Priscilla**, the couple who had helped found the Corinthian church (see Acts 18:1–4) but who had since gone to Ephesus (see Acts 18:18–19). **Much** (Greek, *polla*) means that their greetings were enthusiastic, carrying much delight and fond memories of the church. They sent their greetings **in the Lord**, with His blessing and for His purposes. The salute was also from the house church of Aquila and Priscilla. In fact, the Corinthians were urged to **Greet … one another with an holy kiss** (v. 20), an expression of the day that indicated camaraderie and friendship. "This was the conventional token of Christian affection. In the East, the kiss was a sign either of friendship among equals, or of reverence and submission on the part of an inferior" (Hodge, *First Epistle to the Corinthians*, p. 372).

16:21–24. Paul wrote the **salutation** (v. 21) **with mine own hand**. He generally used the services of an amanuensis or a secretary when writing his letters but often concluded with his own writing as an authentication of his letters (see Col. 4:18; 2 Thess. 3:17). He mentioned in Galatians 6:11 that he had written the entire epistle with his own hand, as something that was unusual (see Hodge, *First Epistle to the Corinthians*, p. 372).

Paul wanted to weed out those in the Corinthian assembly who did not love **the Lord Jesus Christ** (v. 22). Note that he used the full title of the Lord, wanting to ensure undying love and honor for the entire person and all that He represents to the world. The one who did not so love Christ, **let him be Anathema**, or "cursed." These are strong words, but Paul was concerned that the local assembly might become spiritually polluted through the efforts of those who were pretenders to the faith. In a sudden burst of expression, he added, **Maran-atha**, an Aramaic word meaning "the Lord comes." It is both a solemn warning of judgment for those who are false believers and a statement of blessed hope for genuine believers. It is suggested that "the warning is against those whose lack of love proves their lostness. The gracious affection is expressed to those who, with Paul, *do* love the Lord and each other" (MacArthur, *1 Corinthians*, p. 488). **The grace of our Lord … be with you** was a common greeting of the day, but for Paul, it was not a meaningless pious platitude. He really wanted to see this church increasingly graced and blessed by the Lord.

The last thing Paul wanted the Corinthian congregation to read in this letter was that he loved them all **in Christ Jesus**. Christianity is about Christ from start to finish. By closing with **Amen**, Paul was saying "surely," "absolutely," "verily." The epistle ends on a positive note, but the challenges for this church remained, as is evident in the second letter to the Corinthians.

THE SECOND EPISTLE OF PAUL THE APOSTLE TO THE CORINTHIANS

INTRODUCTION

Author, Date, and Place of Composition

Paul is the author of this letter (see 1:1; 10:1). It is stamped with his style and contains more autobiographical material than any of his other writings. The available evidence indicates that AD 55 is a reasonable estimate for the writing of this letter. From 1 Corinthians 16:5–8, we conclude that 1 Corinthians was written from Ephesus before Pentecost (in the spring) and that 2 Corinthians was written later that same year before the onset of winter. Second Corinthians 2:13; 7:5 indicate that it was written from Macedonia.

Recipients

The opening salutation addresses the letter to the church in Corinth and to the Christians throughout Achaia (the Roman province comprising all the territory of Greece south of Macedonia).

Theme

The Corinthian church had been infiltrated by false teachers who were challenging both Paul's personal integrity and his authority as an apostle. Because he had announced a change in his itinerary, with the result that he would pay the Corinthians one (long) visit instead of two (short) visits, these adversaries were asserting that his word was not to be trusted. They were also saying that he was not a genuine apostle and that he was putting into his own pocket the money they had collected for the poverty-stricken believers in Jerusalem. Paul asked the Corinthians to consider that his personal life in their midst was always honorable and that his life-transforming message of salvation was true. He urged them to prepare for his impending visit by completing the collection they had started a year previously and by dealing with the troublemakers in their midst. He warned them that he meant what he wrote.

Literary Features

The structure of the letter relates primarily to Paul's impending third visit to Corinth. The letter falls naturally into three sections: (1) Paul explained the reason for the change in his itinerary (chaps. 1–7); (2) he encouraged the Corinthians to complete the collection in preparation for his arrival (chaps. 8–9); (3) he stressed the certainty of his coming, his authenticity as an apostle, and his readiness as an apostle to exercise discipline if necessary (chaps. 10–13).

Some have questioned the unity of this letter (see discussion on 2:3–4), but it forms a coherent whole, as the structure shows. Tradition has been unanimous in affirming its unity (the early church fathers, e.g., knew the letter only in its present form). Furthermore, none of the early Greek manuscripts breaks up the book.

Outline

I. Paul's Defense of His Apostolic Ministry and Calling (chaps. 1–7)
   A. Salutation and Introduction (1:1–2)
   B. Thanking God for Comfort in Troubled Times (1:3–11)
   C. Paul's Motives and Plans in the Ministry (1:12–2:4)
   D. Forgiveness for the Offender (2:5–11)
   E. The Lord's Leading in the Ministry (2:12–17)
   F. The Corinthians Are a Letter from Christ (3:1–11)
   G. Unveiled Faces Seeing the Glory of God (3:12–4:6)
   H. Treasures in Earthen Vessels (4:7–16a)
   I. Death and Its Meaning for the Christian (4:16b–5:10)
   J. The Ministry of Reconciliation (5:11–6:10)
      1. Reconciliation Accomplished (5:11–21)
      2. The Cost of Reconciliation (6:1–10)
   K. Appealing to Spiritual Children (6:11–7:4)
   L. Comfort from Titus (7:5–16)
II. The Collection for the Jerusalem Christians (chaps. 8–9)
   A. The Blessing of Generosity (8:1–15)
   B. Titus and Companions Sent to Corinth (8:16–9:5)
   C. The Results of Generosity (9:6–15)
III. Paul's Strong Defense of His Ministry Calling and Apostleship (chaps. 10–12)
   A. Paul's Authority Granted by the Lord (chap. 10)
   B. Paul's Service to Christ (chaps. 11–12)
      1. Warning of False Teachers (11:1–15)
      2. Paul's Rightful Claims (11:16–33)
      3. Paul's Testimony of His Vision (12:1–21)
IV. Closing (chap. 13)
   A. Spiritual Concerns (13:1–10)
   B. Farewell and Benediction (13:11–14)

Bibliography

Barrett, C. K. *The Second Epistle to the Corinthians*. Peabody, MA: Hendrickson, 1997.

Hodge, Charles. *An Exposition of the Second Epistle to the Corinthians*. Grand Rapids, MI: Eerdmans, 1956.

Hughes, Philip E. *Paul's Second Epistle to the Corinthians.* The New International Commentary on the New Testament. Grand Rapids, MI: Eerdmans, 1972.

Kistemaker, Simon J. *2 Corinthians.* New Testament Commentary. Grand Rapids, MI: Baker, 1997.

Lenski, R. C. H. *The Interpretation of 1 and 2 Corinthians.* Minneapolis: Augsburg, 1963.

Lowery, David. "2 Corinthians." In *The Bible Knowledge Commentary*, edited by John R. Walvoord and Roy B. Zuck. Wheaton, IL: Victor, 1983.

Stanley, Arthur P. *The Epistle of St. Paul to the Corinthians.* Minneapolis: Klock & Klock, 1981.

EXPOSITION

I. Paul's Defense of His Apostolic Ministry and Calling (chaps. 1–7)

As he did in 1 Corinthians, Paul dealt with moral and spiritual issues in his second epistle. In his second letter, however, he spent many more pages defending his apostolic authority. His first letter must have stirred debate and resistance from the many members of the Corinthian congregation who challenged Paul's leadership. He made it clear to them that he was not speaking from within himself but had been commissioned by Christ Himself to teach the Word and defend the truth.

A. Salutation and Introduction (1:1–2)

1:1. Paul immediately made it clear that he was **an apostle of Jesus Christ** not by his own will but **by the will of God**. God's "will" (*thelēmatos*) implies His sovereign calling and appointment. It was no accident that Paul was an apostle ("one sent forth"). **Timothy** (meaning, "honoring God") also joined Paul in the Corinthian endeavor; he was Paul's spiritual **brother**. Timothy came from a godly family (see 2 Tim. 1:5; 3:15), was converted by Paul possibly on his first missionary journey (see Acts 14:6–23), was referred to by Paul as "my own son in the faith" (1 Tim. 1:2; see 1 Cor. 4:17; 2 Tim. 1:2), and was well-respected by the believing community (see Acts 16:1–2). His father was Greek and his mother was Jewish. He not only accompanied the apostle on many trips but also was his courier and ambassador to various churches. When Paul saw his end coming,

he challenged Timothy to remain true to his calling (see 1 Tim. 1:18), and he asked this younger leader to be with him until the end (see 2 Tim. 4:9). It is believed that Timothy had been imprisoned but was finally released (see Heb. 13:23).

While this letter focuses on the problems of the Corinthian church, it also had application to **all the saints**, mainly, though not exclusively, Greeks who lived throughout the region of **Achaia**. This area was distinct from the northern territory of Macedonia.

1:2. For Paul, **Grace ... and peace** were not polite but empty words. The Corinthians desperately needed to experience these spiritual and emotional qualities because their source was **from God**. God, however, is not seen in the abstract; He is **our Father**. "God's essence consists in mercy, and also that He is the Father and source of mercies" (Stanley, *Corinthians*, p. 370). Since the Lord Jesus is very God, grace and peace originate from Him also.

B. Thanking God for Comfort in Troubled Times (1:3–11)

With all the problems in the Corinthian church, it is interesting that Paul moved quickly to the issue of comfort in times of tribulation. Believers will suffer for Christ's sake but will also experience abounding consolation. The persecutions in Corinth must have been accelerating because these were the apostle's first thoughts as he penned this second epistle.

1:3–4. Despite any persecution or suffering that believers face, God is still **blessed** (Greek, *eulogētos*;

"good-worded"; v. 3). He is not only our Father but also the **Father of our Lord Jesus Christ**. As a loving Father, He showers His children with **mercies** and **all comfort** (Greek, *paraklēseōs*). God is the Author of comfort. At the root of the word "comfort" is the idea of calling one alongside to help. When people fail and even Christians offer no help, God can always be relied on to soothe and repair the soul that is lonely.

Verse 4 has an interesting twist. Paul wrote that God **comforteth us in all our tribulation** (Greek, *thlipsei*; "pressure," "trouble," "distress"), **[so] that we may be able to comfort them which are in any trouble** (v. 4). Christians are to do this with the same **comfort** God uses to aid them. God's purpose in afflicting and consoling Paul was to qualify him for the office of a consoler of the afflicted. In this design, Paul acquiesced; he was willing to be thus afflicted in order to be the bearer of comfort to others.

1:5–7. The **sufferings** (v. 5) that Christ went through **abound in us**, so that our comfort **also aboundeth by Christ**. As union with Christ Jesus was the cause of the affliction that Paul experienced, so it was the source of the comfort that he enjoyed. That Paul and the other servants of Christ were afflicted turned out to be a benefit of comfort for even the Corinthians. **Our hope of you is stedfast** (v. 7) probably carries the thought, "Whenever we are afflicted, it is for your benefit; whenever we are given consolation, it is for your good. It is passed on to you!" No matter what happened, Paul told them, **it is for your consolation and salvation** (v. 6). Hodge explains: "Whether we be afflicted, (it is) for your consolation and salvation, which is effectual in enduring the same sufferings which we also suffer" (Hodge, *2 Corinthians*, p. 7). As **partakers of the sufferings** (v. 7), they likewise received **the consolation**, or comforting. Affliction and comfort are experienced simultaneously, though this does not exclude the thought of future deliverance. Paul's sufferings were a source of strength for those he led to the Lord. He had no motive for concealing his sufferings.

1:8–11. Paul did not hold back on informing the Corinthians of the persecution he had experienced. He did not want them to be **ignorant** ("unknowing"; v. 8) of the **trouble** (Greek, *thlipseōs*; see discussion on 1:4) he had faced **in Asia**, probably broadly referring to Asia Minor, Mysia, Lydia, Caria, and parts of Phrygia. Some have assumed he also included Ephesus (see Acts 19:23–41), but this may not be so. The "trouble" may have been sufferings inflicted on Paul by his many enemies, like the Jews and many pagans who thirsted for his blood. Another suggestion is what happened in Lycus Valley, where he was possibly beaten by the Jews (see 2 Cor. 11:24). Whatever Paul was talking about must have been terrible because he wrote, **we were pressed out of measure**, beyond our strength, so that **we despaired even of life**.

With **the sentence of death** (v. 9) hanging over his head, Paul could in no way **trust in** himself but had to have faith in **God which raiseth the dead**. The apostle may have meant that if he died, the Lord would someday give him resurrection life, but more than likely he meant that God, who has such power, could deliver him from experiencing death. Paul confirmed this by saying, God **delivered us from so great a death** (v. 10). In fact, He **doth deliver**; that is, He delivers believers from the martyrdom of physical death, and He will continue to deliver us: **he will yet deliver us**. God would deliver Paul from impending or immediate threat of death (see 4:8–14) until his course was finished (see 2 Tim. 4:7), and even at that time, Paul would be certain of the final deliverance from death at the resurrection (see 1 Cor. 15:55; 2 Cor. 4:14).

Paul was being helped by the **prayer** (v. 11) of the Corinthians, along with that of **many persons**, and these prayers were the **thanks** given on Paul's **behalf**. Joint prayers were offered as a cooperation in the work of intercession with other churches, rather than with the apostle himself. The design of God in thus uniting His people in praying for each other when in affliction and danger results in common congratulation and praise. **The gift** could refer to their intercession before God but probably refers to the gift of a deliverance. It does not refer to the past deliverance of Paul and of Timothy; most likely, it refers to a future deliverence, to God's wonderful, gracious help in response to the prayers of the many readers.

C. Paul's Motives and Plans in the Ministry (1:12 – 2:4)

While the apostle reserved confrontational words for those questioning him in Corinth, he was more conciliatory in these verses. Although he was more positive here, a mild polemic pervades even these early chapters. Here he laid out his activities and itinerary of ministry.

1:12. With **the testimony** of a good **conscience**, and **in simplicity and godly sincerity**, yet without human **fleshly wisdom**, Paul and Timothy had served the Lord. Their ministry was blessed **by the grace of God**. The word "simplicity" (Greek, *haplotēti*) speaks for itself. Paul's ministry was not complicated but to the point: to give the gospel to as many people as he could, in as many places as he could. "Paul performs his work as a minister of the gospel for everyone to see. In this setting, he demonstrates his love for God's people [also] in Corinth" (Kistemaker, *2 Corinthians*, p. 54). Paul's **conversation** (Greek, *anestraphēmen*; "to move about") **in the world** (Greek, *kosmos*) shows how he conducted himself, but this expression also "includes all the manifestations of his inward life" (Hodge, *Second Epistle to the Corinthians*, p. 15). This spilled over to the Corinthians also; they knew how Paul operated, and they should have known what motivated him. That is, the evidence of his sincerity was **more abundantly** (more especially) **to you-ward** in regard to his ministry as an apostle.

1:13 – 14. Paul wrote to the Corinthians what he did and what drove him, and they **read or acknowledge[d]** (v. 13) what he wrote. "Acknowledge" (Greek, *epiginōskō*) is in the present tense and "is used with the signification of the present ... [It] combines the sense of 'recognition' with that of 'complete knowledge'" (Stanley, *Corinthians*, p. 379). Paul did not want the Corinthians to deny what he informed them about; he **trust[ed]** they would agree to the same **even to the end**. Here Paul may have

been trapping some who wanted to "rewrite" what he was doing for the sake of Christ. He must have known that a clique in Corinth despised him.

Grudgingly, the Corinthians had **acknowledged ... in part** (v. 14) the truth about Paul's ministry, yet even with this, Paul said, **we are your rejoicing**, and in turn, **ye also are ours in the day of the Lord Jesus**, that is, when He returns. The Corinthians should acknowledge Paul and his coworkers, and in like manner, Paul wished to boast about that congregation. Believers should never boast about themselves.

1:15 – 16. With all of this in mind and **in this confidence** (v. 15), Paul wanted to come to them earlier so that they could have **a second benefit** (Greek, *charis*), or "kindness," "blessing," "gifting," "favor." By "second" blessing, Paul meant the act of helping twice. "'Gift' would be a good rendering if not taken in too concrete a sense; a 'second mark of his esteem'" (Barrett, *Second Epistle to the Corinthians*, p. 74). After staying a while in Corinth, he would travel on to **Macedonia** (v. 16), then return back to Corinth on his way **toward Judaea** and Jerusalem. Paul eventually met up with Titus in Macedonia and picked up the collection from the churches (see 8:1 – 7) for the poor believers in Jerusalem. Perhaps Luke and Titus were the couriers whom the assembly in Corinth had chosen to deliver the monetary gifts to the Jerusalem saints (see 8:16 – 19).

1:17 – 18. While Paul was thinking about his itinerary, he used the word **lightness** (Greek, *elaphria*; v. 17), which may refer to the fact that some had accused him of being thoughtless and inconsiderate. Had he planned all of this **according to the flesh**, or for fleshly and selfish reasons? Or was he wishy-washy, going back and forth with **yea yea, and nay nay**? This may be an Aramaic expression like, "Again and again yes and again and again no" (Kistemaker, *2 Corinthians*, p. 59). With the pledge **as God is true** (v. 18), Paul wrote that he did not go back and forth and **was not yea and nay**. God is faithful, and his proclamation of the truth was not uncertain. The gospel is true and trustworthy. Notice **our word**. Paul, Timothy, and their associates were equally involved in this ministry of the Lord.

1:19–22. For (Greek, *gar*; v. 19) gives the reason for all that Paul had previously preached concerning the Son of God. **The Son of God, Jesus Christ**, had been preached among the Corinthians by Paul, **Silvanus** (Silas) **and Timotheus** (Timothy) in the synagogue at Corinth (see Acts 18:5). There had been no **yea and nay**, back and forth, yes and no. God is firm and sure in the work of His Son. It is first mentioned in Psalm 2 that God has a Son who will someday rule over the nations. All are warned in prophecy that someday they will have to "Kiss [honor] the Son, lest he be angry, and ye perish from the way" (Ps. 2:12). About this matter and about **all the promises of God … are yea, and in him Amen** (v. 20), or "absolutely," "verily," "certainly." The promises of God concerning Christ were **unto the glory of God** by proclamation of the gospel by Paul and his cohorts. Here Paul was hinting at the providence of God as He works in the lives of those who serve Him. There are no accidents in the work of the gospel. Paul stated in his letter to the Philippians, "For it is God which worketh in you both to will and to do of his good pleasure" (Phil. 2:13).

God has both **stablishe[ed]** (v. 21) and **anointed** all believers **in Christ**. He has also **sealed us, and given the earnest of the Spirit in our hearts** (v. 22). "Stablisheth" (Greek, *bebaiōn*) means "to give a guarantee" and "to make firm." "Anointed" (Greek, *chrisas*) means a special marking that is given for the benefit of all in the body of Christ (see 1 John 2:20, 27) so that they have spiritual comprehension. Paul mentioned the "sealing" of ownership in several places in his writings (Eph. 1:13–14; 4:30). All who believe in the gospel are sealed "until the redemption of the purchased possession, unto the praise of his glory" (Eph. 1:14). The work of the Spirit of God at salvation is His conformation that what the Lord has begun, He will certainly finish. Present redemption is only a foretaste of what eternal glory holds for the child of God (see Rom. 8:23).

1:23–24. Apparently, Paul's change of plans had caused problems in Corinth. This is why, in a strong statement, Paul said **I call God for a record** (v. 23), or "as a witness" (see Rom. 1:9; Phil. 1:8; 1 Thess. 2:5, 10). The apostle staked his life, his very **soul** (Greek, *psychēn*), his inner being, **that to spare** the Corinthians, he **came not as yet unto Corinth**. "To spare" (Greek, *pheidomenos*) carries the idea, "that I might not have occasion to exert my power to the full and take vengeance on your sins." Because of the incident of incest in the church (1 Corinthians 5), he had decided to go first to Macedonia, then to Corinth, and then on to Jerusalem (see 1 Cor. 16:5–8). Having been charged by those who hated him (see 2 Cor. 1:17) and accused of being afraid to come to Corinth (see 1 Cor. 4:18), he explained why he had altered his plans.

Not for that we have dominion over your faith (v. 24) means, "We do not lord it over your faith." By "we," Paul included his partners in the ministry. He wanted the Corinthians to realize that what he was doing was not simply his own idea but the consensus of others also. "All are free in the Lord but are obligated to help one another. So Paul writes that he and his partners do not lord it over the faith of the Corinthians but instead minister to the believers" (Kistemaker, *2 Corinthians*, p. 70). They wanted to be **helpers of your joy: for by faith ye stand**. The Corinthians were independent and stood before the Lord by their own trust. Paul truly desired their spiritual good.

2:1–2. Paul did not want to return to this congregation with **heaviness** (Greek, *lypē*; v. 1), being pulled down with "grief." This would be his third visit; nothing is known about his second trip except that he was there (see 12:14; 13:1), but it seems apparent that it did not go as the apostle would have hoped. If he visited Corinth and a moral quarrel occurred, he would be making them **sorry** (v. 2), and if that happened, who then could bless him and make him **glad**? The **I** (Greek, *egō*) is the personal pronoun, indicating that whether they liked it or not, he was personally involved with all of the mess in Corinth. On one of his past visits, some painful event had transpired that grieved the Corinthians and Paul. To spare grief for them both, Paul postponed his visit.

2:3–4. Paul wished to avoid a terrible confrontation again with this church, which is why he decided to write them a letter. He wrote **out of much afflic-**

tion and anguish of heart ... with many tears (v. 4), not so they would **be grieved** but so they **might know the love** he had for them. These verses show the heart of the apostle Paul. While he could at times be tough and straightforward, in cases like this, he poured his heart out. He really cared for this flock. Such grief robbed him of the **joy** (v. 3) that he should have had, joy which should have been theirs also, as well as their great comfort.

D. Forgiveness for the Offender (2:5–11)

Here Paul returned to the issue of the incest offender (see 1 Cor. 5:1). The assembly had brought tremendous shame upon itself because of their casual attitude about the problem. The church had become "puffed up" and had "not rather mourned" (1 Cor. 5:2) over this sin, that a man would have intercourse with "his father's wife" (1 Cor. 5:1). Paul had therefore instructed that the man "be delivered to Satan for the destruction of the flesh" (1 Cor. 5:5). With repentance, however, restoration should follow.

2:5. The apostle certainly may **have caused grief** for the man guilty of incest, but Paul was not offended himself **but in part**. As an apostle, he had a duty to chide the church, and in some sense, he did not apologize. Some have questioned whether this incident is the incident described in 1 Corinthians 5, but all evidence indicates that it is identical. Many commentators seem to repudiate the connection, but compare what Paul wrote here with 1 Corinthians 5:5. While Kistemaker (*2 Corinthians*, pp. 82–83) admits there may not be absolute proof that the two incidences are related to the same offender, he gives five reasons that seem to support such a view: (1) Both accounts mention only one offender. (2) The Corinthians had reason to be ashamed of the affair (see 1 Cor. 5:2, 6; 2 Cor. 2:5). (3) In the first account, Paul insisted that the church punish the wrongdoer, and in the second account, the majority of the church followed through (1 Cor. 5:5, 13; 2 Cor. 2:6). (4) The apostle referred to Jesus Christ in both accounts (1 Cor. 5:4; 2 Cor. 2:10). (5) Finally, Satan can advance his cause either with evil and diabolical force or with deliberate deceit.

2:6–8. The **punishment** (Greek, *epitimia*; v. 6), better translated "censure," that the church had placed upon the offender was enough and had been dished out by **many**. They had done their duty to bring conviction and stop this sin so that it would not destroy the church. Thus, **contrariwise** (v. 7), to bring the pendulum back in place, it was now time **to forgive him, and comfort him**. Paul was not suggesting that they should coddle the offender, but lest he become discouraged and be overwhelmed with **overmuch sorrow**, they needed to **confirm** (Greek, *kyrōsai*; General: *kyroō* v. 8), or "ratify," their **love toward him**. When one is truly repentant, restoration then needs to take place, as the apostle so pointedly urged in Galatians 6:1–2. With this, Paul drew to a conclusion: **Wherefore** (Greek, *dio*; a strong word of summary) **I beseech** (Greek, *parakalō*; "call alongside," "counsel") **you** to restore your brother and **confirm your love toward him**.

2:9–11. The apostle tested their resolve, their sensitivity in such spiritual and moral matters. He wanted to **know the proof** (v. 9) of the Corinthians, whether they were **obedient**. "If you forgive, I forgive, and if I forgive, you should forgive." This was to be done **for your sakes ... in the person of Christ** (v. 10). The Devil hates forgiveness and wants to hold people in bitterness. Paul taught the Corinthians to forgive one another in love just as Christ had forgiven them (see Eph. 4:32).

E. The Lord's Leading in the Ministry (2:12–17)

Paul again turned to some of his travel issues. He not only wrote positively of how God was at work to bring people to salvation but also described the open door for the gospel he had encountered, as well as the diabolical opposition to the Word of God. Many who opposed the truth had set out to corrupt the message of grace.

2:12–13. Paul apparently had journeyed from Ephesus to Troas, a city on the Aegean coast, where he hoped to find Titus and get from him any news he might have about the Corinthian church. No matter where Paul was, he seemed to place this congregation at the forefront of his interest and concern, possibly because of the size of the assembly or its vital influence in the Greek world. The city was a cosmopolitan hub teeming with people of mixed races, languages, and cultures. Traders crisscrossed through the Corinthian canal, going into Asia, Europe, and even into Africa. Paul wanted the truth, moral and spiritual, to go forth from Corinth with integrity.

When Paul arrived in **Troas** (v. 12), he had an open door from the providence **of the Lord**. He was troubled **in [his] spirit** (v. 13), however, because he could not find his **brother** in the Lord, **Titus**. Leaving his other companions, Paul traveled on **into Macedonia**.

2:14 – 16. Though he had "no rest in [his] spirit" (2:13), Paul did not want his readers to think he was losing heart. God causes believers **to triumph in Christ, and maketh manifest the savour** (v. 14), as that of votive incense. Here Paul used the imagery of the Roman victory triumph that honored the victorious general. The general rode ahead of the troops and was showered with laurels by the crowds. Christ is the one who is victorious over death (see 1 Cor. 15:57). This truth of the gospel is going forth **by us**, and it is **his knowledge** of salvation **in every place**. While there is opposition and persecution, the gospel still goes forth and brings to the lost the knowledge of Christ. But not everyone hearing receives the message. The manifestation of the knowledge of God does not mean that everyone is saved by it.

Those who witness are **a sweet savour of Christ** (v. 15) to God. Believers are "a savour" both to **them that are saved** and to **them that perish**. Barrett (*Second Epistle to the Corinthians*, p. 99) introduces the word "sacrifice" because Paul seems to have been portraying himself and those with him as the fragrance emanating from the Lord's personal sacrifice, which ascended to honor God. Here is another parallel to the Roman triumph. The enemies of the conquering general were slain following the triumph. In writing "them that perish," Paul was referring to those who reject the gospel and spurn the salvation being offered, as indicated by, **to the one we are the savour of death … and to the other the savour of**

life (v. 16). Paul was saying, "We are to the latter a smell of death to death and to the former an aroma of life to life" (Kistemaker, *2 Corinthians*, p. 91). "We bring both death and life to our hearers."

With emotion, Paul asked, **Who is sufficient for these things?** (v. 16). In other words, "These facts are too overwhelming to comprehend." Paul's own life, which gave forth the knowledge of God, was a "sweet savour" (v. 15) rising up before Him, as described in the Old Testament (see Lev. 1:9; Stanley, *Corinthians*, p. 394).

2:17. Apparently, scores of false prophets and apostles were spreading lies and distorting the gospel (see 2 Peter 2:1). Paul had addressed this in some of his earlier letters (e.g., 1 Thess. 2:1 – 5). These **many** false teachers set out to **corrupt** (Greek, *kapēleuontes*) **the word of God**, to "hawk" or "peddle," as dishonest merchants, a diluted or poisoned gospel. In contrast, Paul and his fellow workers came **as of God** and with **sincerity**, and **in the sight of God speak we in Christ**, meaning they stood before God in connection with the Lord Jesus Christ. Paul was warning the Corinthians to be careful of false messengers. He himself had been commissioned from the Lord. "Here is the source of the sincerity that fills his soul, the impossibility of his dealing with that Word like a haggling, dickering huckster" (Lenski, *1 and 2 Corinthians*, p. 906).

F. The Corinthians Are a Letter from Christ (3:1 – 11)

The apostle again wrote with frankness, asking the Corinthians whether he had to start all over with them again in proving himself in order to gain their confidence. This section shows that many were attempting to discredit him in the eyes of this church.

3:1 – 2. Well aware of the strategies of his critics, Paul knew that his criticism of the false apostles and defense of his own ministry might be turned against him. He therefore asked the Corinthians, **Do we** (need to) **begin again to commend ourselves? or need we** give or receive **letters of commendation …?** (v. 1). "Commendatory" (*systatikos*) letters were common in biblical days. Letters of recommendation were widely used among the churches to vouch for someone's truthfulness and integrity. **Some others** (v. 1) indicates that travelers with questionable credentials were moving about. **Ye are our epistle written in our hearts, known and read of all men** (v. 2). Everyone could see the effect that Paul's ministry had had on them, and they were placed permanently in the "hearts" (Greek, *kardia*) of Paul and his companions.

3:3–6. The Corinthians were as an **epistle of Christ** (v. 3), penned **not with ink, but with the Spirit of the living God**. Paul added a comparison with the Old Testament law: **not in tables** (tablets) **of stone, but in fleshly** (flesh-and-blood) **tables of the heart**. He was pointing out that the church dispensation benefits from the new covenant ("the new testament," 3:6), though it does not fulfill it. The new covenant will be fulfilled for Israel when the Jews return to the land for the millennial reign of Christ. The new covenant, in contrast with the old covenant, the Mosaic covenant written in stone (see Exod. 24:12), is first mentioned in Jeremiah 31:31–34, where it was prophesied that the new covenant would be penned upon human hearts (see also Ezek. 11:19; 36:26). The characteristics of the new covenant include: (1) God's law principles being written within the heart (Jer. 31:33), (2) an intimate relationship with God (Jer. 31:33), (3) a permanent forgiveness of sin (Jer. 31:34), (4) an inner cleansing and the Spirit placed within the heart (Ezek. 36:25–27), (5) and the new birth ("my spirit in you, and ye shall live") (Ezek. 37:14; see Titus 3:5). Besides these spiritual elements, the nation of Israel will have its land restored ("I shall place you in your own land," Ezek. 37:14). The promise of a territorial land is not given to the church.

Paul's **trust** (v. 4) was his conviction that the truth of the gospel of Christ had been entrusted to him and that his vocation as an apostle was given to him by the Lord. The ministry's **sufficiency** (v. 5) came from God; it was not self-driven. Paul said that he and his fellow workers could not **think any thing as of ourselves**. God **hath made us** (v. 6), he continued, **able ministers** (Greek, *diakonos*) **of the new testament; not of the letter** (as of the Old Tes-

tament law)**, but of the spirit ... [who] giveth life**. Again, the comparison is obvious. Paul was writing virtually the same as the prophet Jeremiah wrote concerning Israel in 31:31–32: God would make a new covenant, not like the covenant He made when He brought the Jews out of the land of Egypt, the Mosaic covenant, which they broke. That the church now benefits from the new covenant does not mean that the church has replaced Israel in God's plans. "The physical and national aspects of the New Covenant which pertain to Israel have not been appropriated to the church. Those are yet to be fulfilled in the Millennium. The church today shares in the soteriological aspects of that covenant, established by Christ's blood for all believers [cf. Heb. 8:7–13]" (Lowery, "2 Corinthians," pp. 560–61).

3:7. **The ministration of death**, the law (see Rom. 3:20; Gal. 3:10), was carved **in stones** (tablets; see Exod. 32:15–18; 34:1; Deut. 10:1), and it **was glorious** because it was the law from God, and it came directly from Him to Moses. When Moses returned from Mount Sinai with the two tablets of the law, his "face shone while he talked with [God]" (Exod. 34:29). "And when Aaron and all the children of Israel saw Moses, behold, the skin of his face shone; and they were afraid to come nigh him" (Exod. 34:30). In time, the glow on Moses' face **was to be done away**.

3:8–11. How much greater is the work of the Spirit, how much more **glorious** (v. 8) than even the "glorious" (3:7) law. This new work of the Spirit in the new covenant brings **righteousness** (v. 9) and even **exceed[s] in glory**. If the law, which was **done away** (v. 11) with, was **glorious** (v. 10), how much more will be **the glory** and blessing of the new covenant? The old covenant condemns (see Rom. 7:11), but **the ministration** (v. 8) of the new covenant, by means of **the spirit**, leads men to faith in Christ and the imputation of His righteousness (see Rom. 3:21–22; 4:24).

G. Unveiled Faces Seeing the Glory of God (3:12–4:6)

To focus on the age of grace and the blessings that believers now have under the gospel, Paul presented an illustration referring to Moses and the giving of the law on Mount Sinai as a contrast to the new dispensation of grace. Some in the Corinthian assembly may have had a wrong view about the dispensation of the Mosaic law.

3:12–15. Paul gloried in the new **hope** (v. 12) of the cross and wanted to speak with **great plainness of speech**. "Plainness" (Greek, *parrēsia*) means "outspokenness," "boldness." Here he made his case. It was his firm conviction of his divine mission and of the truth of the gospel, which he preached without regard to the consequences. With the giving of the law, Moses had to cover his face with **a vail** (v. 13), a cloth covering, because **the children of Israel could not stedfastly look** upon his face (see Exod. 34:33–35) after he returned from the mountain with "the two table[t]s of Testimony" (Exod. 34:29). They were overwhelmed by the shining of his face, and he had to cover it until he again went to speak with God (Exod. 34:35).

Did Moses cover his face because the Jews would be less inclined to obey God if they saw a diminishing of this awesome radiance? Or did he believe they were unworthy to see the display of God's glory and so veiled his face as a commentary on the hardness of their hearts? We may never know.

More than their eyes were blinded, however; **their minds were blinded** (v. 14) as well, and it **remaineth the same** now when **the old testament** is read. The **vail** must now be **done away in Christ**; otherwise, Israel will remain in darkness. **But even unto this day, when Moses** (the law) **is read, the vail is upon their heart** (v. 15). They hear the words of Moses, but they cannot look upon the glory of God. "Paul preaches the new covenant of God's justifying righteousness and of the Spirit. This carries with it the abolition of the law ... The law is done away in Christ" (Barrett, *Second Epistle to the Corinthians*, p. 121). Stanley sees "the vail" as a metaphor in that the Jews in the synagogue prayed and read with "veils upon their heads—the Tallith, or four-cornered white scarf, still seen in the Jewish ... worship" (*Corinthians*, p. 407).

3:16–18. There is still hope for Israel: if the Jews **turn to the Lord, the vail shall be taken away** (v. 16).

This will be the work of **the Lord** (v. 17), and He **is that Spirit: and where the Spirit of the Lord is, there is liberty** from the law. The apostle was describing regeneration that only the Spirit can accomplish (see Titus 3:5). Paul made this clear to the Galatians when he wrote that "no man is justified by the law in the sight of God," because "the law is not of faith: but, the man that doeth them shall live in them. Christ hath redeemed us from the curse of the law, being made a curse for us ... Wherefore the law was our schoolmaster to bring us unto Christ, that we might be justified by faith" (Gal. 3:11–13, 24), and not by the law.

Now with an unveiled face, an **open face** (v. 18), and looking **as in a glass** (a polished bronze mirror), we behold **the glory of the Lord**. Believers **are changed into the same image from glory to glory**, as is accomplished **by the Spirit of the Lord**. The glory in Moses' face finally faded away, but the believer in this age of grace is promised ever-increasing glory, "from glory into glory"; that is, this glory just keeps building and will not diminish. The believer's glory is a mirror reflection of the Lord's glory. The indwelling Holy **Spirit** (v. 17) enhances the believer's glory, which is therefore unlimited. Believers are progressively being transformed (**changed**; see Rom. 12:2) into His **image** (Greek, *eikona*; "likeness"). "Christlikeness is the goal of the Christian walk (Eph. 4:23–24; Col. 3:10)" (Lowery, "First Corinthians," p. 562).

4:1–2. Paul and his associates had **this ministry** (Greek, *diakonia*; "task," "service"; v. 1) because they **received mercy**, and therefore they could not stop serving the Lord: **we faint** (Greek, *enkakeō*; "grow weary," "despondent") **not**. "This ministry" has broad meaning and includes the gospel of salvation in Christ, which contrasts the law and includes the work of the Holy Spirit in the life of the individual. Paul said, **we have renounced** once for all (aorist tense, middle voice) **the hidden things of dishonesty** ("shame"; v. 2), refusing to walk **in craftiness, not handling the word of God deceitfully**, that is, not "adulterating" God's Word. Here Paul may have used words that his opponents had used against him.

Unspiritual conduct is paired with adulterating the Word of God. Paul and his friends, however, practiced the opposite. They **manifest[ed] … the truth** (v. 2), showing themselves **to every man's conscience** (see 1:12), not only before the Corinthian congregation and other believers but also **in the sight of God** (see 2:17). "Manifest" (Greek, *phanerōsis*) means to "shed light on," "publish." "Conscience" carries the thought of collective knowledge. Though the conscience may be seared, branded with an iron (see 1 Tim. 4:2), so that it no longer accepts truth, it may also be "deceived so that it thinks truth is falsehood and falsehood truth" (Lenski, *1 and 2 Corinthians*, p. 957). Many despise truth simply because it is truth (see John 8:45), and they hate the light because their works are evil and they want darkness (see John 3:19–21).

4:3–6. Those who do not accept the **gospel … are lost** (v. 3); they are without God and without Christ in this world (see Eph. 2:12). In fact, Satan, **the god of this world** (v. 4), has **hid** (v. 3) the gospel and **blinded the minds** (v. 4) of the lost, those who refuse to believe. He has done this because he hates the truth of Christ. He wants to bring darkness so that **the light of the glorious gospel of Christ, who is the image of God**, does not **shine unto them**. Here Paul's language is similar to the language he used about the law and the veiling of Moses' face (see 3:7–18), but in reverse. The gospel of Christ is glorious and it is light, though Satan tries to extinguish or hide it. Those who serve Christ do not **preach** themselves **but Christ Jesus the Lord**. To the Corinthians, Paul and his companions were but **servants for Jesus' sake** (v. 5). "Paul proclaims Jesus Christ as Lord (Rom. 10:9; 1 Cor. 12:3; Phil. 2:10–11) and thus indicates he and his associates are Christ's servants … Jesus is Lord and the apostles are servants" (Kistemaker, *2 Corinthians*, p. 142).

God … commanded the light of salvation to give **the knowledge of the glory of God in the face of Jesus Christ** (v. 6). At the beginning of creation, God ordered physical light (see Gen. 1:3). Now He commands light to be **shined in our hearts** for salvation. In the face of Christ, the glory of God is made known. God illumines for salvation but then continues the illumination, through the Holy Spirit, so that the believer "might know the things that are freely given to us of God" (1 Cor. 2:13). With Paul, God caused the light to shine both into his heart and into his eyes (see Acts 9:3–9). "Paul recognized the parallel of creation and re-creation, the material and the spiritual domains" (Kistemaker, *2 Corinthians*, p. 143).

H. Treasures in Earthen Vessels (4:7–16a)

Moving to a metaphor of the treasure of the gospel (see 4:6) and clay vessels, or pots, that have no value, Paul continued his contrast between the old covenant and the new covenant. In many places in Israel, the ground is littered with potsherds, or broken pottery. In ancient days, clay vessels were expendable; if they had the slightest crack, they were thrown out on the ground, where they were trampled into broken pieces and dust. Human beings are sinful and frail, but God has elected to use such objects for His design.

4:7–12. The **treasure** (v. 7) of the gospel has been stored away **in earthen vessels**, but **the power** is not in the earthen vessels; it comes from God. The vessels have little resilience and can break easily. Because of God's power, however, believers can be **troubled … yet not distressed … perplexed, but not in despair; persecuted, but not forsaken; cast down, but not destroyed** (vv. 8–9). With great poetry, the apostle listed all the things that had come upon him, things which can also come against all believers in Christ. Believers are given no guarantees of absolute protection in the Christian life, though through it all, the child of God is able to rise above and have the final victory.

As Christ lived and went to the cross to die, so believers carry about a death sentence, so that His life **might be made manifest in our body** (v. 10). Not every believer in every generation faces such pain and even martyrdom, but in the early church, thousands did. This persecution began with the apostles and then came upon average Christians. Living often means facing **death for Jesus' sake**, showing forth Christ **in our mortal flesh**. The early Christians realized that, to a lesser or greater degree, they would be persecuted, and many would face even death.

By speaking of himself first in these verses, Paul was preparing the church at large for troubled times. The apostle and his coworkers would suffer terribly in the future. Paul often mentioned the sufferings of Christ as related to him (see Rom. 8:17; 1 Cor. 15:31; Gal. 6:17; Col. 1:24). Though our souls "hold the priceless treasure, our bodies are nothing but 'earthern vessels' that are liable to be broken at any time (v. 7)" (Lenski, *1 and 2 Corinthians*, p. 981).

Paul's suffering had a distinct purpose. It was placed upon him and his coworkers, even possibly unto **death** (v. 12), but **in you**, the Corinthians, it was **life**. At any moment, the authorities could seize Paul and his companions and deliver them to the door of death; they had no sureties as they traveled about.

4:13–15. The same spirit of faith (v. 13) that was within Paul kept him going. He trusted his Savior and his God. To make his point, he quoted Psalm 116:10, where David said, "I believed, therefore have I spoken: I was greatly afflicted." Paul latched hold of this verse and added, **we also believe, and therefore speak**. In other words, "What is inside us, by faith, we are compelled to set forth in words. We cannot hold back!" Paul was specific about the gospel: **that he which raised up the Lord Jesus shall raise up us also by Jesus, and shall present us with you** (v. 14). Whether through death or the resurrection, all believers will be together and shall stand before the Lord. No single event in history is better authenticated than that the Lord Jesus Christ rose from the dead. Believers too have the same ground for assurance of the resurrection of those who are Christ's when He returns.

4:16a. For which cause, the cause of seeing the Lord someday, **we faint not**, Paul said. The apostle was driven; he could not stop or grow weary. The truth spurred him on. Because of his faith that God will raise us up with Jesus, he could not neglect his duty.

I. Death and Its Meaning for the Christian (4:16b–5:10)

It seems as if verse 16 should be broken at this point. Paul moved from saying that in ministry "we faint not" (4:16a) to discussing heavenly and eternal matters. Here His words seem to transcend his previous discussions; he now looked heavenward.

4:16b–18. The physical body, **our outward man** (v. 16b), is limited in years. It will someday **perish**, though a change awaits all believers. The spiritual soul, **the inward man[,] is renewed** every day. The spiritual nature receives new life and vigor each day. The anticipation for the believer becomes more real as time and age advances. **Day by day** is a Hebrew expression that comes from Genesis 39:10 and Psalm 68:19. This continual renewal of strength is the opposite of weakness and despair.

Light affliction ... which is but for a moment (v. 17). Life is but a wisp, and we are all but grass, here today and gone tomorrow (see Ps. 90:5–6; 103:15–16; Isa. 40:6–8), and life is "soon cut off, and we fly way" (Ps. 90:10b). Working for the believer also is an **eternal weight** (Greek, *baros*; "load") **of glory**. "Weight," or "load," carries the thought of "abundance," and Paul probably chose this word as a suitable contrast with his earlier description of tribulations suffered for Christ's sake (see 4:7–12). What the apostle said here is applicable only to the believer, because he alone has an inner, spiritual, renewable life and the expectation of glorious eternal life in the presence of God.

The child of God looks at **the things which are seen** (v. 18), but he must look not simply at these visible things but also at **the things which are not seen**, the spiritual issues that are **eternal** and not just **temporal** and tangible. Through the prophetic promises in Scripture, the Christian has hope and a clear sense that life consists of much more than that which is visible. This is not the same for the unbeliever (see 1 Cor. 15:19). Paul touched on this subject in his first letter to the Corinthians (1 Cor. 15:46–49). Christians will bear the heavenly and will not simply remain in the earthly.

5:1–4. Here Paul explained the change that is the great expectation of the believers in Christ. **Our earthly house of this tabernacle** (Greek, *skēnous*; "tent"; v. 1) will be **dissolved** ("taken down," "folded up"); of that, there is no doubt. Believers, however, will one day reside in **a building of God, a house**

not constructed with physical **hand[s]**. This "house" will be **eternal** and **in the heavens**. A tent is flimsy and temporary, but this "house," "a building," will be eternal and heavenly and eternal.

Now believers **groan** (v. 2) because of persecution and because of the diminishing of the physical faculties. "Groaning" has a positive value because it means Christians are longing for something to happen; it creates within them an anticipation for heaven, a longing for the time of fulfillment, when the Lord will bring to an end the course of this age and establish the eternal glory. Believers want **to be clothed upon with our house which is from heaven** so that they might **not be found naked** (v. 3). The "house which is from heaven" is the resurrected body. In eternity, believers will not be floating spirits, as if "naked" without a corporal body. A new, eternal body will be given at the resurrection.

In this tabernacle (v. 4), we **groan** and are **burdened**, but the new body will be like that of Christ's. **Mortality [will] be swallowed up [with] life** that is eternal, immortal, and pure, without sin. This temporary "tentlike" existence, which is something that will fade away, shall soon be taken down and no longer used.

5:5–7. God **hath wrought** (v. 5) this transaction for believers, and as assurance that this will take place, He has given the Spirit as **the earnest** (Greek, *arrabōn*; "surety," "pledge," "guarantee"). In Romans 6:5, 8, Paul wrote: "For if we have been planted together in the likeness of his death, we shall be also in the likeness of his resurrection … we believe that we shall also live with him."

This assurance should make the believer **always confident** (v. 6), knowing that no matter what, he will always be with the Lord. "Always" (Greek, *pantote*) signifies "on all occasions," "under all circumstances," even in the midst of dangers, discouragements, and despair. To be **at home** (Greek, *endēmeo*) means to be "in the house," "among one's people," while to be **absent** (Greek, *ekdēmeo*) means "out of the house." Even now, the Christian's conversation, or citizenship, is not here on earth. "For our conversation is in heaven; from whence also we look for the Saviour, the Lord Jesus Christ: Who shall change our vile body, that it may be fashioned like unto his glorious body, according to the working whereby he is able even to subdue all things unto himself" (Phil. 3:20; see also Heb. 11:13; 13:14).

Looking forward to this day of liberation means that **we walk by faith, not by sight** (v. 7). Believers do not see heaven now, nor do they understand what the new body will be like. The day-by-day experience is waiting for the final redemption, that is, the redemption into the final stated of "the purchased possession, unto the praise of his glory" (Eph. 1:14).

5:8. Believers, then, **are confident** (Greek, *tharroumen*; "of good courage") because they are **willing** to wait and, for a time, **to be absent from the body**. They are ready, however, and long "to be absent from the body" so that they can **be present with the Lord** in the glorious state. This shows that there is no intermediate state. The believer passes from this physical life directly into the presence of Christ. This simple but straightforward verse has comforted thousands, if not millions, through the ages as, trusting in the Lord Jesus, they faced eternity in death.

5:9–10. Whether present or absent (v. 9), the believer continues his **labour, that … we may be accepted of him**. The believer is not working for his salvation but is living out his free servitude of gratitude to Christ for eternal life. Whether in this world or the next, the Christian strives to be pleasing to the Lord.

We must all appear (Greek, *phaneroō*) **before the judgment seat of Christ** (v. 10) carries the idea, "We will all be made manifest before Him" or "the light will shine on us in His presence." **The judgment seat** (Greek, *bēma*) is, according to Hodge, "the step," "raised platform," or "seat," used by the Roman magistrate for judgment but also for handing out civil rewards (*Second Epistle to the Corinthians*, p. 125). Paul discussed this in his first letter to the Corinthians (1 Cor. 3:11–15), but here he added some additional thoughts. This appearance is to evaluate what has been **done in** ("by means of") **[the] body, whether it be good or bad**. To **receive** (Greek, *komizō*) means "to take for one's life," "to receive what is entitled."

One will have to give an account of what he did while in his earthly body. "Bad" (Greek, *phaulon*) can mean "foul," "worthless," "of no account," and in some cases, "wicked." This corresponds to the "wood, hay, stubble" of Paul's previous letter (1 Cor. 3:12).

J. The Ministry of Reconciliation (5:11–6:10)

The apostle wanted the Corinthians to understand how important his ministry was in reaching the world. He had a deep, solemn sense of his great responsibility to the Lord his God. Christ's love constrained him to live not for himself but for Christ, who gave His life for him and came forth from the grave to redeem humankind (5:14–15). God had wrought the great transformation that Paul had experienced; it was not a self-willed act. God is the author of the entire work of redemption. Paul's new task was to present Christ, who reconciles the world to the almighty God. The apostle was God's ambassador, exhorting men to accept His offer of reconciliation so that they "might be made the righteousness of God in him" (5:20–21). For his ministry, Paul's paid a high price of pain and suffering (6:1–10), and yet through it all, he saw himself as "yet possessing all things" (6:10).

1. Reconciliation Accomplished (5:11–21)

5:11. Paul began this section with a grammatical perfect participle: **Knowing therefore**, or "having become aware then." He was saying that he had come to realize that he must **persuade men** of **the terror** (Greek, *phobos*; "fear") **of the Lord**. Spiritual issues are serious matters. Paul persuaded the Jews and endeavored to convince them of the truth and bring them to Christ (see Acts 28:23). He was tireless in this effort and did the same thing with the Corinthians. God saw his efforts, he was **made manifest unto God**, but he wanted to be equally manifest to this church. "Manifest" (Greek, *phaneroō*) means Paul wanted to "appear as with a light," transparent to their **consciences.**

While Paul was misunderstood and rejected by so many, he still wanted the Corinthian Christians, as a circle of believers, to have a deep conviction about his integrity. He had won many over with his arguments, but apparently, many still did not trust his motives.

5:12–15. The apostle reminded his readers that he did not again **commend** (v. 12) himself, as if he had to prove himself all over again, as some said he had done before. (He returned to this issue in 12:11–12). Self-laudation was not his style. He did not intend to **give [them] occasion** that would cause them **to glory** over him. Some in the assembly must have sought self-glorification, as did some traveling ministers. Concerning himself, he wanted the Corinthians to have an **answer** for those who sought **glory in** outward and superficial **appearance, and not in heart**. This seems to show that great religious pride was being promoted in Christian circles. Paul vehemently rejected that he could be accused of this.

Whether Paul and his companions were **besides [them]selves** (Greek, *existēmi*; v. 13), "outside of their minds," or whether they were mentally **sober**, they served **God** and the **cause** of the Corinthians. Whether they were crazy or sane did not matter; their service to both God and the Christian community was what mattered. **The love of Christ constraineth us** (v. 14), Paul wrote, **because we thus judge**, make a ruling, a determination, **that if [Jesus] died for all, then were all dead**. By "constraineth" (Greek, *synechō*), he meant that Christ's love, which sent Him to the cross, pressed on Paul, coercing and impelling him to serve. "If one died for all, then were all dead" has four possibilities meanings: (1) all died to themselves and sin, (2) then all *ought* to die, (3) if one died for all, all were subject to death, (4) if one died for all, they all died (Hodge, *Second Epistle to the Corinthians*, p. 136). The word "died" (Greek, *apethanon*) is in the aorist tense and means that this action is completed. The Word of God seems to show that the relationship Christ now has with those for whom He died is analogous to that of Adam and his offspring (see Rom. 5:12–21; 1 Cor. 15:21–22). The fall of Adam affected all humanity, all who were united with him. Christ's death on the cross was for all of those who would be united with Him by faith. All who were in Adam died; all who are in Christ are made alive.

Because Christ **died for all** (v. 15) who would be related to Him in salvation, the same **should not ... live unto themselves, but unto Him which died for them, and rose again**. Paul could not get away from the truth of the death, burial, and resurrection of the Lord Jesus Christ. Christianity was founded on these great doctrines. They are central to living faith and absolutely essential for guaranteeing the promise of eternal life. Quoting and applying Psalm 68:18 in Ephesians 4:8, Paul said, "When he ascended up on high, he led captivity captive, and gave gifts unto men." Paul applied this passage to the spiritual powers and enemies that Christ defeated at the cross.

5:16–19. Here Paul further explained 5:15. **To wit** (Greek, *hōs hoti*; v. 19) means "seeing that," "because," as a clarification to what he has just said. **God was** working within **Christ, reconciling the world unto himself**. "Reconciling" (Greek, *katallassōn*) carries the thought of bringing two parties together, thus making peace. Through the death of His Son, God made the salvation of the world possible. Because of Christ, God was **not imputing their trespasses unto** believers. Here the doctrine of imputation comes into play. The Greek for "impute" (*logizomai*) means to "put something to one's account." Paul addressed imputation at some length in Romans 4:1–25; 5:12–20, using Abraham as an illustration. Abraham's faith "was imputed to him for righteousness. Now it was not written for his sake alone, that it was imputed to him" (Rom. 4:22–23). Here in verse 19, the verb is a present participle in the Greek, meaning that this imputation is a continuous action. God will no longer continuously impute sin to the sinner who comes to Christ for salvation. The Lord has **committed** to all His servants **the word of reconciliation**, who are to declare that God is ready to grant forgiveness and be reconciled to all and that whoever has faith in Christ will live.

5:20–21. Because Paul and his fellow laborers in Christ had been so blessed, they were now **ambassadors for Christ** (v. 20). As they appealed to the Corinthians and others, it was **as though God did beseech** them through Paul and those with him. Those who share the gospel make the appeal as if

they are the very voice of the Lord. Christians are acting for God, in His name, when they go out as His ambassadors.

In Christ's stead (v. 20), for His name's sake, **be ye reconciled** to God. Was this an appeal to some in the Corinthian assembly who had not trusted Christ as Savior or an appeal to the converted to daily avail themselves of the continual offer of peace with the Lord? Kistemaker believes it was both and says, "The imperative *be reconciled* is directed to both the Corinthians and the world" (*2 Corinthians*, p. 200).

Here God's divine "exchange" program is seen: Christ, who **knew no sin** (v. 21), was **made ... to be sin** in behalf of the believer, and in turn, the child of God was **made the righteousness of God** because of being related to Him. The Lord Jesus was without sin, but in the divine transaction, God saw Him bearing the sins of the world. The sins of the human race were "imputed" (see 5:19) to Him, and His righteousness was imputed to the believer. This is a judicial reckoning in the mind of God in order to accomplish redemption. Jesus became the substitute for sinners by taking the place before God of those under condemnation. He is the Lamb of God who removed the sin of the world by His sacrificial death on the cross (see John 1:29; 3:14–15). The prophet Isaiah prophesied, "All we like sheep have gone astray; we have turned every one to his own way; and the LORD hath laid on him the iniquity of us all" (Isa. 53:6).

2. The Cost of Reconciliation (6:1–10)

Paul demonstrated his patient endurance as a minister of God through all kinds of trials and tribulations. In every adverse circumstance, brought against him by the unbelieving world and often even by other brothers, Paul suffered. His list of sufferings is long but so is his list of positives, through which he even received kindnesses "by the Holy Ghost" (v. 6b).

6:1–3. Paul saw the Corinthians **as workers together with** Christ (v. 1). He pleaded that they would not **receive ... the grace of God in vain**. Some think this refers to: (1) salvation grace, (2) a warning of "falling from grace," (3) or spurning grace to live by.

The key could be in the word "vain" (Greek, *kenon*), which means "empty," "without content," "useless." While they were redeemed through saving faith in Christ, their belief was having little effect on their Christian walk. When the Corinthians responded to the gospel, Paul had **succoured** (v. 2) them, giving them encouragement and support. He quoted Isaiah 49:8, where the Lord said through the prophet, "In a day of salvation have I helped thee." This **day of salvation** had come to Israel in the work of Christ at the cross. There may have been some in the Corinthian congregation who spurned grace and were turning to Jewish legalism (see 3:12–16; Gal. 3:1–6). If so, they may have been living out their salvation in a twisted and legalistic way. Paul therefore warned them to give **no offence** (v. 3) so **that the ministry be not blamed**. In the following verses, he illustrated the price one must pay for being true to truth. Suffering will follow, but so will reward.

6:4–10. In all things (v. 4), Paul and his companions were **approving [them]selves as … ministers of God**, before the Corinthians and before the world. With poetic flare, Paul made a long list of what was happening to him for the sake of the gospel. Much that he listed here can be found in his other writings, as well as in the recorded events of his ministry (see the cross-references). In verses 4b–5, he listed words describing negative events and happenings: **in much patience** (v. 4b; see Rom. 12:12); **afflictions** (see 5:3); **necessities** ("needs"; see 1 Cor. 9:16); **distresses** ("anguishes"; see Rom. 8:35); **stripes** (v. 5; see Acts 16:23); **imprisonments** (see 6:24); **tumults** ("uproar"; see 20:1); **labours** ("deeds"; see 2 Cor. 10:11); **watchings** ("absence of sleep"; see 11:27); **fastings** (see Acts 13:2–3). In verses 6–7, he listed positive spiritual qualities: **pureness** (v. 6; see 1 Tim. 5:22); **knowledge** (see 2 Cor. 8:7); **longsuffering** (see Col. 1:11); **kindness** ("gentleness," "goodness"; see Col. 3:12); **by the Holy Ghost** ("by His work within"; see Gal. 5:16); **love unfeigned** ("unprejudiced love"; see Rom. 12:9); **the word of truth** (v. 7; see Eph. 1:13); **the power of God** (see 2 Cor. 13:4); **the armour of righteousness** ("the instruments of righteousness"; see Rom. 6:13). And in verses 8–10, he compared the negative with the positive: **honour and dishonour** (v. 8; Greek, *doxa*, "honour"; *atimia*, "despise"; see Gal. 1:24; 1 Cor. 4:10); **evil report and good report** (defamed report; good report; see 4:13); **deceivers, and yet** (we speak what is) **true** (see 1 Thess. 2:3); **unknown, and yet well known** (see 1 Cor. 4:9–13); **dying, and behold, we live** (see 2 Cor. 1:9–10), **chastened, and not killed** (see Acts 23:11–24); **sorrowful, yet always rejoicing** (see Phil. 1:18); **poor, yet making many rich** (see 1 Tim. 6:18); **having nothing, and yet possessing all things** (see Rom. 9:23).

Paul's list of descriptives about the Christian walk is unmatched. In comparison to what the world offers, in an eternal perspective, believers have everything that is of permanent and lasting value. Even if the child of God has nothing in this world, he has everlasting life in the presence of the God of the universe. What this physical life offers cannot be compared with eternity with Christ.

K. Appealing to Spiritual Children (6:11–7:4)

Here Paul challenged the Corinthian church regarding other moral issues they were facing. What he wrote makes it clear that many in the congregation were compromising their faith and were flirting with evil company among the unsaved. The Christians were being polluted spiritually. They were practicing immorality with those outside of Christ. They were walking in the world "as men" who were lost (1 Cor. 3:3).

6:11–15. With a strong plea from his heart, Paul cried out, **O ye Corinthians, our mouth is open … our heart is enlarged** (v. 11), meaning, we are large-hearted, generous, and warm in our affections. He added, You Corinthians **are not straitened** (restricted, blocked) **in us, but you are straitened in your own bowels** (v. 12). The Greek word for "bowels" (*splanchnon*) means "intestines." For the ancient peoples, the bowels were the seat of affection, compassion, sympathy, and mercy. Paul was saying that there was plenty of room for the Corinthian believers in his affections because he loves them all. He did not hold back his love. Even if the church had some reservations about the apostle, he was wide-open to them.

Paul continued to write to them as his **children** (v. 13) and wanted them to have an **enlarged** heart, to be open to him and to his instructions. Without giving details, he hit them head-on with that which was bothering him, commanding them, **Be ye not unequally yoked together with unbelievers** (v. 14). Believers are in the world, yet they must live morally and spiritually above the world. Addressing the issue of **fellowship** with unbelievers, the apostle focused on the differences: **righteousness** versus **unrighteousness**, **light** versus **darkness**. He elaborated on this in the following verses.

6:16–17. The believer's body is **the temple of the living God** (v. 16), and in this "temple," the heavenly Father dwells. In a spiritual sense, the church is like ancient Israel when the Lord told the Jews of His special relationship with them: **I will be their God, and they shall be my people** (see Exod. 29:45). In the Exodus passage, God said He would dwell "amongst" the children of Israel, whereas now with the church, He takes up residence **in them** personally. How can believers cohabit in a spiritual sense **with idols**? The problem this congregation had seems so elementary, but it escaped the Corinthians, or they simply lived in denial of the facts of their Christianity.

Paul then commanded the Corinthians to depart from idol worshipers: **Come out from among them, and be ye separate** (v. 17). He added that this was not simply an imperative from him; it was God's command (**saith the Lord**). The apostle loosely quoted Isaiah 52:11–12, where the nation of Israel heard the **word** calling forth salvation but also warning His people to "Depart ye" from sinners, and **touch not the unclean thing.** Believers are not to be monkish, to be isolated from sinners, but they are to be "separate" from sin and sinful things. Believers rub shoulders with the lost, but they are not to succumb to the world's sinful ways. Their testimony of purity becomes a witness to the grace of God to deliver from sin.

6:18. While the child of God has a relationship with the heavenly Father that is based on the work of Christ and that positionally cleanses from sin, daily fellowship is based on confession of sin and is conditional. John wrote, "If we say that we have fellowship with him, and walk in darkness, we lie, and do not the truth … If we confess our sins, he is faithful and just to forgive us our sins, and to cleanse us from all unrighteousness" (1 John 1:6, 9). By walking in a close and transparent fellowship with the **Father**, believers are His **sons and daughters**. This is a promise, **saith the Lord Almighty**. While this is an issue for the believers in the church age, Paul may have drawn the illustration from Isaiah 43:6: "I will … bring my sons from far, and my daughters from the ends of the earth."

7:1. In his summary, Paul spoke with affection for the Corinthian Christians, calling them **dearly beloved**. His comments in 6:18 are **promises**, but in similar words to 1 John 1, he urged that all those in Christ, including even himself, should **cleanse ourselves from all filthiness of the flesh and** even of the **spirit**. Doing so brings about a **perfecting holiness** with respect and **fear** of the Lord. Sinning can be both external and internal, of the body and the inner person, the spirit. The word "perfecting" (Greek, *epiteleō*) means "completely finishing," "carrying out," "discharging," or "completely carrying forth" holiness, living separate from sin.

7:2–4. The apostle continued his rapprochement with the Corinthian assembly. He urged the readers to **Receive us** (v. 2), because in no way had the apostle and his ministry companions **wronged** (Greek, *ēdikēsamen*; "treated unjustly"), **corrupted** (Greek *phtheirō*; "injured," "destroyed"), or **defrauded** (Greek, *pleonekteō*; "took advantage of," "made gain of") anyone. The apostle walked carefully to avoid every possibility of suspicion that he was defrauding with monies, fooling the believers spiritually, or bringing them harm in any other way. Therefore, he was to be accepted and not rejected. He did not, however, want to **condemn** (v. 3) them. He told them, **you are in our hearts to die and live with you.** With an exuberant burst of emotion and accolades, Paul spoke positively, with **boldness** (v. 4), in **glorifying** the Corinthians, saying he was **filled with comfort** and was **exceeding joyful**, even when suffering **tribulation**.

In 2:13, Paul said he "had no rest in [his] spirit," because he had hurried to Troas to meet Titus to find out how the Corinthians were doing. His soul was no longer troubled about them, his mind was at rest, and he was full of warm consolations. The favorable account of what was happening in that church had relieved his anxieties and turmoil.

L. Comfort from Titus (7:5–16)

Titus was able to help Paul understand the changes that were taking place in the Corinthian church, which gave the apostle much comfort. Paul did not apologize, however, for his heavy-handedness when dealing with blatant sin. In this section, Paul focused on explaining himself and getting his relationship with the church back on track.

7:5–7. Picking up the discussion from 2:12–14, Paul gave additional details about his side of the story and how he had received from Titus the positive message he had been longing to hear. When he had reached Macedonia, he was in great consternation over the Corinthian assembly with all of its problems. He knew that the news of their sins could affect the entire family of new churches spread throughout the region. Disappointed that he did not find his helper Titus in Troas but having received his report, Paul pressed on into Macedonia. There, he found Titus and was comforted. Before that, however, he **had no rest** (v. 5), was **troubled**, was having **conflicts** without and within, and was full of **fears**. **Nevertheless** (Greek, *alla*; "in contrast") **God, that comforteth** (Greek, *ho parakalōn*, present participle; v. 6), "the One who is continually comforting, "the **cast down** comforted Paul through Titus.

Titus' arrival in Corinth had brought **consolation** (v. 7) and **comforted** the believers. He reported to Paul the repentance of the Corinthian congregation, who, after being reprimanded, had mourned over their sins and focused their **fervent mind** (Greek *zēlos*), or "zeal," "enthusiasm," **toward** Paul. In other words, the church got on the same page with him both morally and spiritually. Titus reported to Paul (see Acts 14:27; 16:38) all that had happened. Their **mourning** (Greek, *odyrmos*; "wailing," "lam-

entation"; see Matt. 2:18), was certainly because of their sins but also possibly because they had so grieved the apostle Paul. Hearing this good report, Paul **rejoiced the more**, that is, beyond the fact that he was glad to see Titus again. These verses show that Paul was not simply a good, theologically oriented apostle; he felt deeply about the human drama going on with the believers he had led to Christ.

7:8–11. Paul knew that he had made the Corinthians **sorry with a letter** (v. 8), 1 Corinthians, in which he had scolded them. On one hand, he **did repent** for hurting them; on the other hand, he said, **I do not repent**, because the letter had caused them to change their ways. Their sorrow was but for **a season**; they would get over it. He had been heavy-handed in the letter so that they might be **sorrowed to repentance** (v. 9), **after a godly manner**, so that in the future, they might not have to **receive damage** (hurt) again. Paul had known that the church in Corinth would be torn up with his comments but that the sorrow he brought would be only temporary, and in the final analysis, he did not regret his judgments.

In the world, **the sorrow** (v. 10) imposed by stern punishment **worketh death**; that is, it destroys and gives no opportunity for forgiveness or hope. **Godly sorrow**, however, brings forth **repentance to salvation** that does not have to be continually **repented of**. Scholars are divided as to how Paul was using "salvation" in this verse. Some believe he was referring to the repentance that causes one to turn to Christ and receive Him for deliverance. Others believe he was using the idea of salvation in the broader sense of a moral deliverance from evils that "destroy," meaning being rescued from the penalty of the wrongs done as Christians (see 1:6). Either way, a true principle is cited here: godly sorrow brings about a repentance that leads to salvation.

Verse 11 had a powerful rhetorical sense. **For behold** (Greek, *idou*; emphatic; v. 11), "For look!" True sorrow is **after a godly sort**. If repentance and sorrow are carefully initiated, they bring forth a **clearing of yourselves**, a certain feeling of **indignation**, even **fear**, but also a **vehement desire**, a zealousness (**zeal**), and possibly a sense of **revenge**. The Corinthians had **approved** themselves and were **clear[ed]** of allowing the incestuous relationship to fester in the church. Some suggest that the Corinthians had not fully understood the seriousness of the matter of the incest until they had received Paul's letter. They had argued with him about the fact that they had not given him proper respect over the matter. They had even shown a desire for revenge to clear themselves of the charge and had issued a countercharge. The people repented not for the wrong they had committed but for their error in not dealing with it.

7:12–14. The apostle clarified himself by noting that he had written the first epistle not simply for the one who had done wrong, nor for his suffering, but to show his **care** (v. 12) for the congregation, which he wanted them to know about, **in the sight of God**. These words seem somewhat exaggerated or extreme, but they show that Paul had a larger principle in view. He wanted the Corinthian assembly, in the greater sense, to know that there was an overall concern for this body of believers, before the eyes of the Lord.

At this point, all seems to be turning out well. Paul and his friends were **comforted** (v. 13) in the Corinthians' **comfort**. Because Titus was joyful and **his spirit was refreshed** by what was happening in the church, Paul and the others could be **exceedingly the more joyed**. He was pleased and **not ashamed** (v. 14) that he had **boasted** of the church in Corinth. Paul's **boasting** to Titus was discovered to be **truth**. "Boasted" (Greek, *kauchaomai*) as used here does not mean Paul had "bragged" about the Corinthians but rather that he had shared news of them with positive conviction, commendation, and pleasantness.

One of the members of the assembly had committed a sin (see 2:5–11). The entire congregation apparently had repented. The church had shown godly sorrow, which was felt and shared by all. Since the believers are one body in the Lord Jesus, and all belong to each other as members of that body, when one suffers, all suffer. The experience is shared among all the members (see 1:6–7).

7:15–16. Because of what he had observed in the church at Corinth, Titus had greater **inward af**fection (v. 15) toward the assembly. He **remembereth the obedience** the Corinthians had shown, **how with fear and trembling you received him**. This caused Paul to **rejoice** (v. 16) and **have confidence** in the church **in all things**.

With these two verses, the entire issue was concluded. The first seven chapters of this letter are tightly connected and seem to revolve around the great all-pervasive sin of the incident of incest. These same chapters can be said to relate to the spiritual and moral state of the church with which Paul was so concerned. Here the problematic issue was put to rest, with a full restoration of confidence.

II. The Collection for the Jerusalem Christians (chaps. 8–9)

In these two chapters, Paul digressed to an issue that weighed heavy on his heart: the collection of funds to help the distressed believers in the church at Jerusalem. The Corinthians had started a relief fund but had not completed it. He reminded the Corinthian congregation of the generosity of the churches in the Macedonian region. Liberality to the poor was only a part of their devotion to the Lord. The conduct of the Macedonians caused Paul to urge Titus, since he had begun the task, to carry it to completion in Corinth (8:6).

Paul did not want to arrive in Corinth to receive the collected funds and find them unprepared to give their pledge. God had commanded that they give, and He would supply their needs. In these chapters, the apostle was not so much concerned about the temporal needs of the poor (though he certainly was); he was more concerned about the mutual love and care that Christians should have for each other. Gifts to the poor cannot be compared to the gift of Christ, given by the heavenly Father (9:15).

A. The Blessing of Generosity (8:1–15)

Give oneself to the Lord is the first principle of sharing with others. The Macedonian believers stood out as a great example for the Corinthian assembly. The ultimate example for believers, however, is the grace of the Lord Jesus Christ in giving of Himself over to the cross. While rich in glory as the Son of God, He became poor on earth for others. Regarding giving, Paul was looking first for "a willing mind" (v. 12).

8:1–5. The Greek word **Moreover** (Greek, *de*; v. 1) begins the transition to the new subject. Paul started this section by reminding the Corinthians of **the grace of God bestowed on the churches of Macedonia**. **To wit** (Greek, *gnōrizomen*) means "cause you to know." Though the Macedonian churches were under **affliction** (v. 2), they still carried on with a great **abundance of … joy**. They experienced **deep poverty** (Greek, *bathous ptōcheia*), "poverty down to the depths," though this **abounded** forth to **the riches of their liberality**. While facing trials, they still had joy and dug deeper into their purses to exercise generosity ("liberality").

The apostle spoke often of God's "riches" (v. 2), His "fullness" (*ploutos*). He spoke of "the riches of his goodness" (Rom. 2:4), "the riches of his grace" (Eph. 1:7), and "the riches of the glory of his inheritance" (Eph. 1:18). He used this word over and over in the sense of God's great abundance. Because of what God was doing with the Macedonian Christians, they were operating in **power** (v. 3), to which Paul bore **record**, and from this **power**, or ability (Greek, *dynamis*), they became **willing of themselves** to give. Furthermore, the Macedonians were **praying … with much intreaty** (v. 4) that Paul would take their **gift** of funds, and thus share even more in **fellowship**, to **the ministering to the saints**. In essence, "They gave far beyond their ability, without any further urging by me." They were giving of **their own selves to the Lord** (v. 5) but also **unto us by the will of God**.

The enthusiasm of the Macedonians far surpassed Paul's expectations. Their liberality was in their gift of money but also in the gift of themselves. Some commentators think that "unto us" in verse 5 means they had offered themselves to go to Corinth or elsewhere, for Paul, to collect more money for the Jerusalem poor.

8:6–7. Paul urged Titus to continue **as he had begun** (v. 6) and to **finish** in the Corinthian church

with the **same grace** of God's riches as seen with the Macedonian believers. Paul had instructed the Corinthians (1 Cor. 16:1) to take a collection for the poor who were suffering in Jerusalem. Titus probably visited Corinth after that epistle had been written and made a start with this endeavor. When Paul discovered how giving the Macedonian congregations were, he then urged Titus to return to Corinth and finish what he had so successfully started. Paul exhorted Titus to go back for a renewed visit. Titus would **finish**, or bring the work to completion.

As the church at Corinth was **abound[ing] … in faith, and utterance, and knowledge, and in all diligence, and in your love to us** (v. 7), they should likewise **abound in this grace also** that the Macedonian congregations were blessed with. With "faith, and utterance [speech], and knowledge," Paul was reminding the church of the spiritual gifts of 1 Corinthians 12:8–10. "Utterance" and "knowledge," however, are also used in the same combination in 1 Corinthians 1:5. "Utterance" (Greek, *logō*) may refer to the teaching of doctrine (see Hodge, *Second Epistle to the Corinthians*, p. 198). The Greek word *spoudē* ("diligence") is used five times in this letter (7:11, 12; 8:7, 8, 16) and twice in Romans 12:8, 11. It could be translated "to be careful," "to be businesslike."

8:8–10. The apostle was continually concerned with the charge that he had dominated unreasonably the churches he had begun (see 1:24). He trusted, however, that their spiritual motivation was not simply externally driven (see 8:7b) or driven **by [his] commandment** (v. 8). He preferred that their motivation be internal devotion, **the sincerity of your love**, and wanted that love to be focused on the **Lord Jesus Christ** (v. 9), who had lavished upon them His **grace**. By grace, they were now **rich**, though for them and all who are saved, **he became poor**. From the glory of the heavenlies, Christ came to earth to die for the sins of condemned humanity.

Paul gave his **advice**, urging the Corinthians to finish their financial pledge begun **a year ago** (v. 10). This material offering for the church in Jerusalem was really for the Lord (see Matt. 25:34–40). Was this too much to ask? "If we have sown unto you spiritual things, is it a great thing if we shall reap your carnal things?" (1 Cor. 9:11). Therefore, it was only **expedient** for the Corinthians to carry forward their promise and pledge they **have begun before**.

8:11 – 14. Therefore, the church was to carry on to **perform the doing of it** (v. 11), or literally, "complete ye also the doing of what you promised." **There was a readiness to will**, and that needed to be put into **performance**, coming from what they had. **For if there be first** (Greek, *prokeitai*; better translated, "If there be present") **a willing mind** (v. 12). Was this congregation mentally prepared to follow through? That willingness was to be **according to [what] a man hath, and not according to [what] he hath not**. The Lord Jesus taught the same principle (see Mark 12:42). The issue was the "readiness" (Greek, *prothymia*), or "disposition," of the mind. God looks at the disposition ("readiness") of the mind and heart, which will be judged based on the individual's resources, related somewhat to ability. Paul did not intend, however, to bring about a church **burdened** (v. 13) in their giving while other congregations went free, being **eased** in their contribution. He argued for **an equality** (v. 14) among the assemblies **now at this time**. Those who can give to the needs of other Christians should, and if the situation is reversed and they have a need, a **want**, some other church can **supply** what is required so **that there may be equality**.

Some have thought Paul was teaching a form of early church communism. The same claim is leveled at the story of the punishment Peter placed upon Ananias and his wife Sapphira (see Acts 4:32 – 5:1 – 11). In the case of that event, the couple sold possessions to help many who were without, but they lied about how much they had taken in, claiming that they were giving funds from the entire sale. Yet they were not! This is not communism, and neither is what Paul taught here. In communism, every possession belongs to the state. In Christianity, every possession belongs to the individual, though whatever one has really comes from God. The Christian is to share out of the resources he is blessed with. All

of one's material goods do not belong to the group. However, from the heart, the one who "soweth bountifully shall reap also bountifully" (9:6).

8:15. To make his point, the apostle quoted Exodus 16:18, about the children of Israel who had to collect the Lord's supply of manna each morning as they traveled through the wilderness. Whether they collected a lot or a little, everyone had plenty. They "gathered every man according to his eating." But if they gathered too much out of selfishness, and could not even eat it all, the manna spoiled and rotted before their eyes (see Exod.16:19 – 20). Paul used this story to tell the church that they need not hoard their possessions. As with the children of Israel wandering in the wilderness, every blessing of food and even clothing came from the Lord. Too much could be a curse. Trusting God's supply is a blessing.

B. Titus and Companions Sent to Corinth (8:16 – 9:5)

In this section, Paul provided some details for how to collect the funds in a judicial manner, so that no one can complain or accuse a brother of stealing. He wanted fail-safe conditions put into place for integrity's sake. The same should be practiced today where money is concerned. It is wise to have a check-and-balance of several eyes when accounting for finances in the congregation.

8:16 – 19. But thanks be to God (v. 16), He had placed **into the heart of Titus** a distinct consideration for this church. While he had accepted Paul's **exhortation** (v. 17) to serve the Corinthian congregation, he did it not out of the apostle's urging but had responded (**being more forward**) on his own account and went to Corinth. This younger man was genuinely "concerned about the welfare of those he served" (Lowery, "First Corinthians," p. 574).

Along with Titus, Paul sent to the Corinthians another **brother, whose praise** (v. 18) in his work **in the gospel** was well-known **throughout all the churches**. This servant of Christ must have been fervent in his presentation of the cross of Christ for sinners. Commentators are undecided about his identity and cannot be dogmatic. The suggestions are Luke, Mark, Barnabas, or Trophimus. Whoever the brother was, he had a zeal and labored hard to promote the gospel.

Because this unnamed servant was **chosen of the churches to travel** (v. 19) with Paul and his fellow workers, many scholars point to the sending forth of Paul and Barnabas to Antioch, and beyond, which is referred to here (see Acts 15:22–35). They were "chosen," "called out," "selected" (Greek, *cheirotoneō*) by the Jerusalem congregation, the elders, and the other apostles for their journey (see Acts 15:22, 25). Other congregations may have joined in approval of the choice of these two men. Whoever this anonymous servant was, he traveled **with this grace, which is administered** through Paul **to the glory** of God. The gospel is being spread through human means, but the God's providence is active to bring about His glory and His purposes.

8:20–22. The reason several other respected disciples would be in charge of the collected offerings for the Jerusalem church was **avoiding** (v. 20) any **blame** over **this abundance which is administered by us.** Every transaction and handling of money must be kept **honest … not only in the sight of the Lord, but also in the sight of men** (v. 21). Apparently, this unnamed brother was not only to accompany Titus but also to help in the distribution of the alms to the churches in Judea, so that there could be no misrepresentation of what was happening. The accounting of two is better than that of one. Paul did not want his or anyone else's integrity questioned. This brother had **proved diligent** (v. 22) in his service to Christ, and the apostle placed **great confidence** in him, as he did also with the saints in the Corinthian church. Paul did not explain how large these funds were, but that was not his point. Whether the collection was large or small, he wanted it handled in an above-board manner so that no one could complain.

8:23–24. If any held doubts about Titus, they should not, Paul said, because **he is my partner and fellowhelper** (v. 23) for the Corinthian church. The **brethren** with him were **messengers of the churches,** and they served for **the glory of Christ.**

Paul urged the Corinthians to show to this entire retinue of traveling servants **the proof of [their] love.** He desires others to see all that he had said about the kindnesses of the Corinthians, to prove his **boasting** (v. 24) about them. He wanted this church to exhibit the evidence of their love in the presence of other congregations. This entire chapter shows how intimately the early churches were bound together. Their influence, sympathy, and love obviously was shown forth and shared from assembly to assembly.

9:1–4. Paul said it was not necessary (**superfluous**; Greek, *perisson*; v. 1) to write concerning the importance of **ministering**, or better, "concerning the ministering," to the believers. This "ministering" was unto **the saints** (Greek, *hoi hagioi*; "the sacred ones"), believers, who are "sanctified" in a positional sense in Christ (see 1:1). In their daily experience, however, believers may "be carnal, and walk as men" (1 Cor. 3:3). In the good sense, the Corinthians had **forwardness** ("readiness"; v. 2) of mind, as he had boasted to those in **Macedonia**, that is, that this church was ready to do its duty in the alms collection. Paul's mention of **Achaia** has caused some scholars to believe that all the Christians of that region belonged to the assembly in Corinth, but this cannot be proven. Since Achaia was the Roman province of southern Greece, with its capital in Corinth, it may be that this congregation was the mother church for the region. It might be noted that Cenchrea, a seaport six miles east of Corinth, had an established church (see Rom. 16:1). It certainly was influenced by the larger Corinthian assembly.

So that Paul's rightful pride (**boasting**; v. 3) in the Corinthian church should not fall short and **be in vain**, he had already **sent the brethren** and urged the Corinthians to **be ready.** This was important lest any from **Macedonia** (v. 4) came with Paul and found this church not prepared with their offering. He did not want anyone to be **ashamed** after all of the **confident boasting** about how generous this church was.

9:5. Though Paul said he was coming to Corinth, he thought it best to send Titus and the other companions first to prepare, **make up beforehand,** the collection of their **bounty** so that that there would be no **covetousness**. He wanted their gift to be genuine, not something extracted from them by compulsion, deceit, or some kind of moral blackmail. Some commentators think Paul wanted to avoid causing some to react by stinginess, but this may not be what he had in mind. It must be noticed again how delicate this matter was emotionally and spiritually. Issues of money can often separate brothers in Christ.

C. The Results of Generosity (9:6−15)

In this section, Paul turned the discussion of the collection for Jerusalem into a positive spiritual lesson by focusing on inner motives for giving. He set the pattern for charity and giving for all of the churches, for all generations to come. Here he takes believers to the heights, into heaven itself, in understanding how giving bountifully is not simply a material matter but a spiritual issue.

9:6. Here Paul laid out the great principle for Christian giving. Unreserved sharing of one's assets brings a blessing and a return from the Lord. Care must be taken with this verse, however. How much one gave was not Paul's major concern; he cared more about one's motive and openness before God as guiding principles. Many believe this verse was a known proverb. Though it is not found in Scripture, it seems to allude to Proverbs 11:24: "There is that scattereth, and yet increaseth; and there is that withholdeth more than is meet, but it tendeth to poverty." The righteous who sow bountifully will always be taken care of by the Lord. The righteous will not be without. **But this I say** means, "You know this is true" (Barrett, *Second Epistle to the Corinthians*, p. 235).

9:7−9. God looks at the **heart** (v. 7), where every man **purposeth**. One is to **give** from the heart, **not grudgingly, or of necessity: for God loveth a cheerful giver**. No one can be forced to give, and the Lord would not want it that way. "Grudgingly" (Greek, *ek lypēs*) means "out of being pulled down," out of sorrow or from a reluctant state of mind, grieving about what is given as something that is lost. "A cheerful giver" (Greek, *hilaron dotēn*) is one whose sharing is a delight, done with "hilarity."

God will not allow His saints to starve. **God is able to make all grace** (v. 8) overflow, so that the giver has **all sufficiency** in everything and may be able to go beyond in **every good work**. God does not prosper His saints simply so they can enjoy material things; He does it so they can share with others, in a ministry of charity or a ministry of promoting the gospel.

The one who generously **hath dispersed** (v. 9) the seed abroad and **hath given to the poor** in charity, **his righteousness** can be seen by all; it **remaineth for ever**. Here Paul was quoting Psalm 112:9, which is full of words such as "righteousness" and "the righteous." Of the righteous man it is said, "He is gracious, and full of compassion, and righteous" (Ps. 112:4).

9:10−14. God is the one who **ministereth seed to the sower** (v. 10). This then **minister[s] bread for … food**, multiples the seed, and in turn, brings an **increase [in] the fruits of your righteousness**. Every farmer can understand Paul's analogy about the seed. Seed has life in itself; it is meant to grow, flourish, feed, and produce more seed so that the process can continue. Giving must come from a spiritual motive, not simply for an economic purpose. God is the one who, by His providence, multiplies generous giving for His unfolding plan. This brings about "enrichment," to **all bountifulness** (v. 11), which then results in **thanksgiving to God**. This is an **administration** (Greek, *diakonia*; v. 12) of **service** (Greek, *leitourgias*; "liturgy") that blesses the public nature of the body of Christ; that is, it spreads and benefits the whole church of the Lord, which God causes to happen and again brings **many thanksgivings unto God**. That this happens, **the experiment** (v. 13), causes many to **glorify God** because the church shows forth a **professed subjection unto the glory of Christ**.

This process set forth the **liberal distribution** (v. 13) to the Macedonians, as it does for all others who receive such bounty. Many give thanks to the Lord because of the shown by the givers. Through the Corinthians' service to their needy brothers, their obedience and fellowship with all the saints in other places was demonstrated (see Hodge, *Second Epistle to the Corinthians*, p. 225). It may have surprised the Corinthian church to know that the recipients of their generosity offered **prayer** (v. 14) for them, **long[ed]** to be with them, and thanked God for **the exceeding grace of God** that could be seen flourishing in them.

9:15. The apostle concluded with a poetic anthem that has blessed believers throughout the ages. It is simple and to the point and gives God the glory. The word **gift** (Greek, *dōrea*) is only used here in 2 Corinthians and is in the singular. Some have assumed it refers to "the gift" of alms the Corinthians were to collect, but more likely, it refers to the gift of the Savior and His wonderful salvation. **Unspeakable** (Greek, *anekdiēgētō*) carries the thought of "unable to recount," "not able to describe fully." Calvin and others believe the gift bestowed on the Corinthians has to do with their generosity. Others apply it to God's unspeakable gift of salvation in His Son, Christ, who was rich but became poor in order to grant spiritual riches (see 8:9).

III. Paul's Strong Defense of His Ministry Calling and Apostleship (chaps. 10–12)

The apostle now turned back to more serious issues concerning his authority and apostleship. He strongly defended his ministry and his calling by the Lord Jesus Christ. He answered criticism about his "weighty" (10:10) letters and showed that it was the Lord who had commended him for service. Reminding his readers that false teachers were stalking the churches, he said their criticisms are motivated by Satan, who is transformed into an angel of light and has followers who appear to be "apostles of Christ" (11:13). Paul gave them the sign of a true apostle (12:11–12).

A. Paul's Authority Granted by the Lord (chap. 10)

The tone and style of this letter drastically changes here. The contrast and differences between chapters 10–13 and some of the preceding chapters are extreme, to say the least. Some have conjectured that this should be a separate letter or that possibly Paul wrote this part of the letter after he heard additional information from the Corinthian church. Such theories are not necessary, however. It is quite reasonable that Paul's tone would change as he took on the evil false prophets and teachers and their followers, about whom he had written earlier. They were falsifying the gospel, and the apostle stepped forth to defend his position as an apostle. He very naturally wrote with a tone of apostolic authority, with firmness and severity.

10:1. Paul began this verse with a strong authoritative attitude: **I Paul myself**. He used the first-person plural often in this letter, to make his words inclusive of the junior apostles traveling with him, but here, he spoke as an individual so that the Corinthians could sense that he alone was dealing with the problems he addressed here.

Paul pleaded with the Corinthian assembly **by the meekness and gentleness of Christ**. He claimed the meek and gentle virtues of the Lord Jesus yet coupled these attributes with a certain boldness and righteous indignation in what he had to say. When with them, he was **base** (Greek, *tapeinos*), meaning "lowly," "humble," but he was **bold** (Greek, *tharreō*), or "confident," "assertive," in what he had to say when away from the church.

10:2–4. This was the second time Paul said, **I beseech you** (Greek, *deomai*; v. 2; see 10:1), which means to "exhort" or "implore." This shows that he did not wish to use force; he wanted to avoid severity in his expression. He preferred persuasion and reason in what he was about to write. With the majority of those in Corinth, he wanted to work from the position of **confidence** and not compulsion, though he would **be bold against some, which think of us as if we walk according to the flesh**. In other words, they refused to listen to him. They thought he was simply blowing up and giving commands from his own fleshly desires rather than from the order of the Lord. Those he was referring to considered Paul just an ordinary man and not an apostle. They said he was acting under the guidance of his own corrupt nature and was but following his selfish or malicious emotions, relying simply on himself.

Showing how his enemies were mistaken, Paul made a clarification. All the apostles **walk[ed] in the flesh** (v. 3), he said, yet the war they were involved in was not simply a fleshly conflict but was instead a spiritual battle, a battle waged not only against evil men but also against unseen spiritual forces lurking in spiritual darkness. Paul amplified this thought in Ephesians 6:12: "We wrestle not against flesh and blood, but against principalities, against powers, against the rulers of the darkness of this world, against spiritual wickedness in high places."

Believers do not fight with the handmade **weapons** (v. 4) of flesh (**carnal**), but the struggle (**warfare**) is waged **through God**, and by His power, **strong holds** ("secure towers," "walls") are **pull[ed] down**. Some have paraphrased verse 4 as, "Our weapons are mighty, in that we pull down strong holds."

10:5–6. Continuing the analogy of war in this spiritual struggle, Paul wrote that, like pulling down the walls of a fortress, we are to be **casting down imaginations, and every high thing that exalteth itself** (v. 5) against what the Lord has revealed about Himself, that is, **the knowledge of God**. "Imaginations" (Greek, *logismous*) has the idea of "opinions," "convictions," "thoughts," referring to human self-reasoning that is contrary to the truth of God. "Every high thing" again refers to the towers and fortresses, the human pride and reasoning that exalts itself against God's revelation of Himself and against the gospel He has given by grace to lost humanity. Human beings will use human logic, philosophy, and wisdom in attempting to defeat what the Lord has said. "A rationalistic Christian, a philosophizing theologian, therefore, lays aside the divine for the human, the wisdom of God for the wisdom of men, the infinite and infallible for the finite and fallible" (Hodge, *Second Epistle to the Corinthians*, pp. 235–36).

Verse 6 is difficult. The word **revenge** means "punishment" and conveys, "We are ready to punish every disobedience." Using military language, the apostle spoke of bringing defeat upon enemies who must suffer the consequences of their actions. When their **obedience** was complete (**fulfilled**), the Lord

Jesus would act to control the unstable situation in Corinth. When the time arrived, and using Paul as His instrument, Christ would bring about a judgment on the false teachers. Some scholars believe Paul was talking about the collection for the Judean saints, but that issue is not mentioned here. It is better to take his statement as looking forward to 11:4. Paul was referring to "another Jesus" and "another gospel" proclaimed by the false apostles. The congregation had to excise the heretical teachers and false prophets and obey the gospel of Christ. The church is responsible for carrying out such discipline to stabilize the church with purity in ministry to which it is called.

10:7. Paul asked how the Corinthian congregation judged issues, by **the outward appearance** or by something more substantive? If those criticizing the apostle trusted Christ and were sure that they belonged to Him, then in this same way, they should look at Paul and his companions, because **so are we Christ's**. Paul's adversaries continually tried to place a division between him and the Corinthian church. They tried to concoct reasons for not trusting his leadership and apostleship. **Let him … think this again**, let him realize that Christians are all in this together; believers belong to the Lord Jesus. From the general drift, it appears that a whole class of persons stood firmly against Paul's authority.

10:8–11. While Paul could **boast** (v. 8) in his **authority**, which was given by the **Lord … for edification**, this power was not given to him for the **destruction** of the Corinthian church. As in 7:14, **boast[ing]** does not mean bragging, but simply stating what was fact. "Edification" means the building up of the church in holiness, spirituality, and peace. Power in the church does not come from civil authority or from the talents of the people but from the Lord Jesus only.

Paul assured his readers that his purpose was not to **terrify** (v. 9) them with the seemingly harsh words in his **letters**. His opponents argued that **his letters … are weighty and powerful** (v. 10). They also criticized him physically, however, claiming, **his bodily presence is weak.** They criticized his speaking abilities, saying, **his speech [is] contemptible**. That Paul cited what his critics said about him shows his great confidence in his appointment as an apostle by the Lord. Whether the claims are true or not, for an ordinary mortal, such comments bring pain to the soul, but apparently not for Paul. Some scholars have an opposite take on these verses. "Weighty" (Greek, *bareiai*) could have the idea of "impressive" in a positive sense, while "powerful" (Greek, *ischyrai*) carries the thought of "vigor," "authority." This could be a way of saying that he was convincing in his speech, though his detractors still disagreed with his claims. Verse 11 may confirm that theory. As truth was given in his **letters** (v. 11) when he was **absent** from the Corinthian church, so it would be **in deed** when he was in their presence. His letters are full of force and energy, and so it would be when he was present. His deeds would correspond to his written words. Because he said **such a one**, some commentators believe that only one person was opposing Paul. But most believe this is a figure of speech, and more than likely, a larger group opposed his ministry.

10:12. Paul assured his readers that he was not playing the comparison game. He and his companions were not looking at the number of those who opposed them, nor did they **measure themselves by themselves**, as their opponents did. Paul was not in a competitive race, nor was he counting heads. This is what the false teachers were doing, and they were **not wise**. The opponents had a faulty standard by which to test themselves; they used their own human standard rather than God's standard. The divine standard was exemplified by Christ. This is what Paul used.

10:13–15. In proclaiming the truth, and in ascertaining whether one is sent by God or man, the **measure** (v. 13) must be of the **rule of God**. God had **distributed** to Paul and his companions the right **measure** based on truth. This **measure** reached even to the Corinthians and blessed them. Paul did not go beyond his commission from Christ. He and his followers did not **stretch** (v. 14) beyond the authority God meted out. Paul, not the opposition, was designated "the apostle to the Gentiles" (see Gal. 2:8).

The Lord authenticated him by producing a bounty among the Corinthians; he came **in preaching the gospel of Christ** (see 1 Cor. 3:6). The false teachers had gone beyond that limit.

Paul did not ride on the back of others, **of other men's labours** (v. 15). As he preached the gospel to the Corinthians, he had **hope**. And when the fruit came forth, when the **faith** of the Corinthians was **increased**, he and his cohorts were **enlarged by** the **rule** they had followed.

10:16–18. As the Corinthian church matured and grew, the believers could help expand his work of evangelizing other Gentiles in the **regions beyond** them, even as far away as Spain (see Rom. 15:23–24). They could help by praying for Paul and his traveling companions (see Eph. 6:19–20) and by giving monetary support (see 1 Cor. 16:6; Phil. 4:15–17). First, however, this congregation needed to get things straight spiritually (see 2 Cor. 10:6). Paul did not want to take the easy route and follow after someone else's efforts, **in another man's line of things** (v. 16). He did not want to minister where it would be easy, where things were **made ready to our hand**. The apostle was a pioneer; he was not a follower. In this, **he that glorieth** would do so **in the Lord**, and not by man. Self-glory goes nowhere and is invalid by all standards. To **glory in the Lord** (v. 17) is to ascribe all good to Him and to realize that by His grace spiritual battles have been won. Final approval comes from the Lord, not from **he that commendeth himself** (v. 18). Paul never commended himself; his claims were founded not on conceit but on the clear calling and appointing of the Lord Himself. If God gave him favor, being judged by puny human judgment would be a small thing (see 1 Cor. 4:3).

B. Paul's Service to Christ (chaps. 11–12)

To prove his servitude to the Lord Jesus, the apostle was forced to do what appeared to be some kind of self-glorification. While he condemned all such personal boasting, he told the Corinthians it was necessary in order to clarify his role as an apostle. The Corinthians appeared to be in jeopardy of turning away from Christ because their respect of

Paul was being undermined by the false accusations of his opponents. It was thus necessary to present the basis on which he had claimed his authority from Christ. He had to support his miraculous calling from the Lord. This was a repugnant task to his sensibilities. Time after time, when he presented his claims, he quickly turned away to some other issue. These chapters were painful for the apostle Paul, though necessary for the sake of the gospel.

1. Warning of False Teachers (11:1–15)

In these verses, Paul begged the Corinthians to bear with him while he appeared to praise himself, though his motive was pure. He spoke this way because he was seen on the same level as the other apostles, who were highly esteemed.

11:1–3. Paul asked that the Corinthians **bear** (v. 1) with him, in his **folly**, in the words to come. He was **jealous over** (v. 2) this church because he had **espoused** (engaged) them to **one husband**, that is, **as a chaste virgin to Christ**. He was zealous for this congregation of believers because he had acted as a matchmaker in bringing them, as a new bride, to the Lord for salvation. In writing **godly jealousy** (Greek, *theou zēlō*), the apostle communicated that the emotions he had arose from his zealous desire to promote the honor of God the Father. **Fear** (v. 3) came upon the apostle because they were being **beguiled** by Satan, **the serpent**, who was attempting to **corrupt** them **from the simplicity** that is found in **Christ**. Satan did the same to **Eve** in the temptation in the garden (see Gen. 3:4). His work was to corrupt their **minds**. "Beguile" (Greek, *exēpatēsen*) means to "thoroughly deceive," "seduce by means of deception." Their "minds" (Greek, *noēmata*) has to do with their "thoughts" and "understanding" of what is right. Satan attempts to sidetrack the thinking of believers to derail them from what God intends for them. "Simplicity" (Greek, *haplotētos*) has to do with single-mindedness for the things of Christ, the undivided devotion to Him that is like the loyalty of a bride to her spouse (see Hodge, *Second Epistle to the Corinthians*, p. 253).

11:4–6. Verse 4 is one of the strongest verses in this section. Paul hit the church head-on, warning them not to accept the words from one who **preacheth … another gospel** (v. 4), a gospel **not preached** by Paul. If they **receive[d] another spirit**, which they had not previously, that was **not accepted**, they were **bear[ing] with** the messenger, or with his message. In the Greek text, **ye might well bear** (Greek, *kalōs anechesthe*) is in the imperfect tense, and seems to infer that they would be tolerating or accepting this message. At the least, they would be giving it some credence, which would be terribly confusing for the doctrinal stability of the church. The congregation had come close to forsaking their commitment to Christ, choosing a form of doctrinal liberty, and departing from the truth. It is interesting that Paul spoke of this "new" message as receiving "another spirit." Ideas have a "spirit" about them, a driving philosophy that can mislead the spirit of the hearer. To keep out error, vigilance always must be maintained in the assemblies.

Paul then brought himself forward in the right sense, saying that he **was not a whit behind the very chiefest apostles** (v. 5). He was saying something like, "I want you to put up with me, and my bringing forth my position, because I am not in any way less that the chief apostles." He wanted to make certain that they did not think of him as any less in gifts, labors, or success than the other apostolic leaders. He was clearly authenticated as a servant of Christ and was completely entitled to all the deference and authority that was due them.

While he seemed to have to be **rude in speech** (v. 6), he did not fall short **in knowledge** of Christ and the gospel. And he knew what the Lord Jesus Christ had called him to do, and he had **been throughly made manifest** (Greek, *phaneroō*; "to shed light on") before them in everything he did, **in all things**. Paul's motives and his work were carried out not in the dark but in the light, and the Corinthians knew this well. At every point, in every respect, "in all things," he was clearly known; he stood revealed before them in every way as an apostle of Jesus Christ.

11:7–9. No one could claim **an offence** (v. 7) with Paul when he **abas[ed]** himself so that the Corinthians **might be exalted**. He did this when he **preached ... the gospel of God** to them **freely**. He was not under compulsion, nor was he seeking monetary compensation. Paul gave them the gospel to raise them up spiritually; he had no other motive.

With tongue in cheek, with hyperbole, and with a figurative sense, Paul said he had **robbed other churches** (v. 8) by **taking wages** from them so that he could be of **service** to the Corinthians. Though Paul was a traveling evangelist and teacher, the principle still stands in what he wrote to Timothy: "For the scripture saith, Thou shalt not muzzle the ox that treadeth out the corn. And, The labourer is worthy of his reward" (1 Tim. 5:18).

When Paul had been with the Corinthians, probably during his first visit, he had **wanted** (v. 9), that is, had been "reduced to want" since he had run out of the support that came from the Macedonian churches. He was **chargeable** to no one, literally, "I pressed as a dead weight upon no one" or "I was a burden to no one." **The brethren** of the Macedonian churches **supplied** (Greek, *prosaneplērōsan*; "supplied in addition") what he needed so that he was not **burdensome** to anyone. This is reminiscent of what he wrote to the Ephesians: "I have coveted no man's silver, or gold, or apparel. Yea, ye yourselves know, that these hands have ministered unto my necessities, and to them that were with me" (Acts 20:33 – 34). The "hands" that ministered to him probably refers to the generosity of the Thessalonian church to help him along the way.

11:10 – 14. The truth of Christ (Greek, *alētheia*; v. 10), or the "veracity" or "truthfulness" that Christ produces, **is in me**, Paul said, and **this boasting** shall not be stopped. In all the **regions of Achaia**, he was not willing to accept help, though he did from the churches in Macedonia. The attitudes of the Corinthians seem to have had a negative impact on the Achaians. Paul did not love the Corinthians any less than those in other congregations **God knoweth** (v. 11). It seems clear from what he wrote in 1 Corinthians 9:15 – 18 that His "boasting" was that he shared the gospel of Christ gratuitously and not for gain. The number of verses given over to this issue clearly show that the issue of money and compensation was huge in the eyes and minds of the Corinthian church.

Paul's opponents (**false apostles**; v. 13) fueled this issue and infected the entire congregation with suspicion about Paul. They were **deceitful workers, transforming themselves into the apostles of Christ**. The Devil is behind those who oppose the gospel. **Satan himself is transformed** (Greek, *metaschēmatizō*; v. 14) literally means that he is able to "change the schematics" or "alter the configurations." Satan then appears as **an angel of light**, making people think that his lies are the truth. He is "the spirit that now worketh in the children of disobedience" (Eph. 2:2).

11:15. Satan's lackeys, **his ministers**, are capable of doing what he does; they can **be transformed** as workers of **righteousness**. Their **end**, however, will come about because of their self-righteous **works**. Revelation 20:11 – 15 vividly describes the judgment of the lost: books are opened that describe their evil sins, by which they are to be judged, because they have not trusted the only one who gives a way of escape—the Lord Jesus Christ. These who are unsaved are resurrected for this great white throne judgment (Rev. 20:11), before which they will be judged "out of those things which were written in the books, according to their works" (Rev. 20:12). Without trusting in Christ, men will have no recourse, and they must face "the second death" (Rev. 20:14). They then will be "cast into the lake of fire" (Rev. 20:15).

2. Paul's Rightful Claims (11:16 – 33)

In these verses, Paul gave his strongest attestation to his calling and authority as an apostle. This was not his first desire, but it was necessary in order to put down once and for all the criticisms that were continually being hurled at his character, his calling, and his motives. He reaffirmed his calling but also showed that he was no less than the other twelve apostles of Christ. He had the same authority and the same miraculous demonstrations of the power of the Spirit to prove it.

11:16 – 20. Paul repeated some of the thoughts he had previously shared. He was not **a fool** (v. 16). Even if he were, however, he should still be accepted so that he could **boast** about himself **a little**. Here he again used exaggeration to get his point across. He was speaking **not after the Lord, but … foolishly** (v. 17), with a certain **confidence of boasting**. In other words, "If you have to, then accept me as if I was a fool. Give me a little slack, let me boast a little!" His readers would have noticed that he was spoofing them somewhat, but his comments would have caused them to think twice about the opinions of those attacking him. The Corinthians ought to take him as a apostle of Christ, even though he ironically let himself be called a fool. With irony, Paul said that if he was a fool, and others who had gloried in their **flesh**, should allow him **glory also** (v. 18). Since the Corinthians saw themselves as wise and yet they put up with fools (v. 19), the Corinthians in their wisdom should bear with the apostle.

Verse 20 is a hypothetical thought. What if **ye suffer** (v. 20) because you are put in chains, **devour[ed]**, taken captive, **exalt[ed]** over, and smitten **on the face**? What if the Corinthians were so abused? All of this had been done to Paul, yet he said, "I still love you" (see 1 Cor. 4:21). If they had been fooled by false teachers, it was time to admit they were blinded and were wrong. They needed to take action to get rid of the "invaders" who so mistreated and misled them. As with many Christians even today, the Corinthians were slow to realize the truth that what God says is different from what the world says. Paul had tried to put forth the message of the cross and that the wisdom of God is foolishness to the world (see 1:18 – 25). Yet if the Corinthians continued to look at things from the world's vantage point, he would accommodate himself to their thinking.

11:21 – 27. This is a long list of all that Paul had suffered for the sake of Christ. He mentioned this punishment to prove to the Corinthians how he had suffered for truth. Because most of this torment came from the Jews who hounded Paul because of the gospel, this passage may be proof that the false prophets who spiritually poisoned the Corinthians were also Jewish.

Paul mentioned his **reproach** (Greek, *atimian*; "shame"; v. 21) and admitted, with a bit of irony, that he had been ministering somewhat as a weakling (**weak**). Those who hated him marked him in this way (see 10:10; 1 Cor. 2:3). While he had tried to be gentle, his foes used force. So what they had said about him must have been true. Yet Paul came right back and asserted that if they had been **bold** or brash, he would be **bold also**.

Were his enemies Jews (**Hebrews**; v. 22)? Paul answered, **so am I**. Were they **Israelites … the seed of Abraham? so am I**. The word "Hebrew" was one of the first designations for Abraham (see Gen. 14:13). Most scholars believe the word comes from *eber*, meaning "from the other side." This could be a reference to the fact that Abraham had crossed over the Euphrates River to enter the land of Canaan. Israel (which means "He strives [with God]") is the name given to Jacob after he wrestled with the angel of Jehovah (see Gen. 32:28). "The seed [descendants] of Abraham" encompasses the entire nation of the Jewish people. Paul used all of these expressions and names in a synonymous sense. He was proud of his Jewish heritage, but to his grief, the Jews were vehemently against the message of the gospel (see Rom. 9:2 – 5; 10:1 – 3, 16 – 21).

With tongue in cheek, Paul asked, **Are they ministers of Christ? (I speak as a fool)** (v. 23). He hoped this question would cause the Corinthian church to think. If they were ministers of Christ, he was even **more**. Actually, they were opposing the gospel; Paul was proclaiming it. He listed all that he had suffered at the hands of the Jews, or from their influence, for the sake of the truth. He **labour[ed] more abundant[ly]** (see 1 Cor. 15:10), suffered **stripes above measure** (see Acts 9:16), was **in prisons more frequent[ly]** (see Acts 16:23; 23:10; 24:27; 28:16), was left for dead, **in deaths oft** (see Acts 14:19; 1 Cor. 15:30), was beaten **five times** (v. 24) by the Jews with **forty stripes save one**, was **beaten with rods** (v. 25; see Acts 16:22), was **once … stoned** (see Acts 14:19), **suffered shipwreck** three times (see Acts 27:41), spent **a night and a day** in the sea, **in the deep**.

In all of his **journeyings** (v. 26), he had often been **in perils of waters … of robbers … by [his] own countrymen … by the heathen** (Gentiles) **… in** the city ... in the wilderness ... in the sea ... among **false brethren**. He had suffered **in weariness and painfulness, in watchings often** (sleepless nights)**, in hunger and thirst, in fastings often, in cold and nakedness** (v. 27).

While it may seem that Paul was seeking sympathy, this is not the case. He simply wanted the Corinthians to be aware of what he had gone through for the sake of Christ. While the believers in other churches may have known of Paul's ordeals for the gospel, this congregation needed some historical perspective on what he had endured. Everything that he experienced is not recorded in Scripture, but the truthfulness of these experiences was certainly well known by his traveling companions.

11:28. Paul added that **Besides those things that ... cometh upon me daily** (see 11:21 – 27), he still had the **care of all of the churches**. The many letters Paul wrote to the widely scattered congregations throughout the Roman and Greek world certainly verify this and that he had great personal care and interest in the many believers whose names he mentioned in his writings. Most scholars believe that the apostle wrote many more letters, letters that the Holy Spirit deemed not to include in the canon of Scripture (Christians have just the epistles He wanted them to possess). Paul was an amazing apostle. He traveled thousands of miles by land and by sea, wrote probably dozens of letters, counseled and taught night and day—all for the love of his Savior, Jesus Christ.

11:29 – 31. Paul had sympathy for his believing brothers in Christ, who were his children in the faith. Their sorrows were his also. In the best sense, this was the blessed result of the fellowship of the saints. Paul had earlier written, "And whether one member suffer, all the members suffer with it; or one member be honoured, all the members rejoice with it" (1 Cor. 12:26). If one was **weak** (v. 29), so also was Paul. If one was **offended** (Greek, *skandalizō*; "caused to stumble"), so also was Paul **burn[ed]**, that is, left "indignant" or moved with concern. He was never indifferent about what was happening with the believers. He was filled with grief when the weak fell or when someone stumbled.

The apostle never gloated over the weaknesses of other brothers in Christ. Rather, his own weaknesses and deficiencies made him **glory** (v. 30) over only the things that had to do with his own **infirmities**, that is, that God's grace and strength carried him through such experiences. This testimony was confirmed by **The God and Father of our Lord Jesus Christ, which is blessed for evermore** (v. 31). He knew that Paul **lie[d] not**. Because Paul knew that the Corinthians were not trusting him (see 1:12 – 18), he cited this witness that he was not a liar.

11:32 – 33. To illustrate how he began his ministry with his life in jeopardy, Paul briefly related the story of his early witnessing of the Lord Jesus Christ (see Acts 9:20 – 31). When **Aretas** (v. 32) was **the king** of **Damascus**, his **governor** tried to capture Paul because he was boldly endangering his life by proclaiming in the synagogue the message that Jesus was the Son of God (Acts 9:20), and that He was the Christ, the promised Messiah (Acts 9:22). The Jews in Damascus tried to kill him (Acts 9:23) and placed watches at the gates to capture him (Acts 9:24). The disciples had lowered him down the wall in a basket, and he had escaped to Jerusalem (Acts 9:25 – 26). Paul "had preached boldly at Damascus in the name of Jesus" (Acts 9:27). Was this not proof enough that his ministry had been genuine from the very beginning? The genuineness of Paul was witnessed by those who saved his life even though he continued to preach the Lord Jesus before the hostility of the Jews. God confirmed that what he had said was true. What more could this apostle add in regard to his genuineness?

3. Paul's Testimony of His Vision (12:1 – 21)

In this chapter, Paul did give additional testimony to his calling as an apostle. This calling was not simply that he would be a New Testament prophet but that he would be given equal status with the twelve apostles. To show God's revelations to him, Paul spoke of being "caught up to the third heaven" (v. 2) and given visions that no one had seen before. In spite of this great proof of the Lord's divine favor, Paul was still left with painful bodily afflictions that would not be removed. This was to demonstrate further God's grace but also to keep him humble.

12:1–5. Paul did not have to **glory** (v. 1) before the Corinthians about his reputation. "Glorying," or "boasting," was **not expedient** or necessary. It did not become him, was not profitable, and was not the proper thing to do. He had a better way of demonstrating his divine mission and calling. To boast in the fleshly sense would be foolish, derogatory, and painful. The better way was to give testimony to the **visions and revelations** he had received from **the Lord**. The visions were what he saw, and the revelations were the content of those visions.

Paul began by speaking about himself in the third person: **I knew a man in Christ** (v. 2), one who was a believer and part of the body of Christ. This man had been saved **above fourteen years**. He did not know whether this one was physically carried away **in the body** or not when he was **caught up to the third heaven** (the very presence of God). The ancients considered the sky and clouds as the first heaven, the starry heavens as the second heaven, and the presence of the Lord as the third heaven. Only **God knoweth** the true state of this experience and whether the man (Paul) was simply transported in spirit into this vision or was caught up physically. The word translated "caught up" (Greek, *harpazō*) means to "snatch away suddenly" and is used to describe the miracle of the rapture of the church (see 1 Thess. 4:17).

This man had been elevated **into paradise, and heard unspeakable words, which it is not lawful** (right) **for a man to utter** (v. 4). The word "paradise" (Greek, *paradeisos*) is from a Sanskrit word meaning "park" or "garden." To the Jews, it was the designation for heaven, or the abode of those who have died believing in the Lord. Christ told the repentant thief that he would be with Him "in paradise" upon his death (Luke 23:43). The word is used in the same sense of "heaven" in Revelation 2:7. Other verses add to this understanding of what Paul saw and where the Lord now resides. When He ascended, He passed "into the heavens" (Heb. 4:14), to be exalted and "ascended up far above all heavens" (Eph. 4:10), to be

"made higher than the heavens" (Heb. 7:26). Believers who have passed away are now "at home with the Lord" (2 Cor. 5:8; "with Christ" in Phil. 1:23).

Paul could not **glory** (v. 5) in a personal way that this miracle had happened to him, but he could glory because it indeed had taken place. His greatest **glory**, however, was in his **infirmities**. Why did Paul wish to deny self-glory? He probably was saying, "This event is just grounds for giving glory, but not to me personally." He did not want to take on any personal superiority that would cause boasting about his particular qualities, entitling him to religious admiration. One of the proofs that God was using him, however, is seen in his personal infirmities, which he explained in 12:9.

12:6–9. Humanly speaking, Paul wanted **to glory** (v. 6), but this would have been **foolish[ish]**. He said, **now I forbear** ("hold back"), yet he desired to speak only **the truth**. He did not want anyone to think wrongly of him based on what they saw in him or heard about him. He did not want to be judged by what he said about himself or of his experiences. His focus was on Christ. What mattered most were not his achievements for the Lord but how God was working through his ministry of proclaiming the gospel message.

Because he was being so used, and to keep him from being **exalted** (v. 7), because of the many **revelations** he was given, God gave him **a thorn in the flesh**. Paul called this "thorn" **the messenger of Satan**. Its purpose was to **buffet** him, as he said, **Lest I should be exalted above measure.** Paul's use of the present tense of "buffet" means that this is a permanent, ongoing affliction to ensure he kept the proper perspective about his service for the Lord. The role of Satan is uncertain. Did Paul mean that Satan had direct influence on the physical problem, or was he saying that the problem was as painful as if Satan were administering the ailment? Scholars disagree on this.

"Buffet" (v. 7) is a boxing term, again indicating that this "thorn" (Greek, *skolops*) was continually beating up on him. A thorn is an object that pierces the flesh and injures. Most scholars believe that this is to be taken in a physical sense, that it was some kind of malady he had to painfully endure. Many suggestions are given as to what this affliction might have been: neuralgia, hysteria, malaria, epilepsy, leprosy, rheumatism, or eye difficulties. Paul wrote about "my temptation … in my flesh" (Gal. 4:14). He also spoke of having to write with large letters, which might mean he had eye problems (ophthalmia; see 6:11). When the Lord struck him down on the road to Damascus, a bright light "shined round about him … from heaven" (Acts 9:3), which was followed by blindness (Acts 9:7–8). Paul's blindness was removed by God's righteous messenger, Ananias, who put his hands on him, by which the Lord restored his sight (Acts 9:17). "Scales," or scabs, fell from his eyes (Acts 9:18). While he could then see again, his eyesight may have suffered permanent damage.

Paul **besought the Lord thrice** (v. 8) to remove this affliction, but He had answered: **My grace is sufficient for thee: for my strength is made perfect in weakness**. The apostle **Most gladly** accepted the **infirmities** so that he would receive no personal **glory**. He would carry out his calling by **the power of Christ**. God always answers prayer: "yes," "no," or "later!" This was a case of "no" because the Lord had spiritual purposes beyond simply giving Paul physical relief from a painful situation. The Lord's power is sometimes best displayed against the backdrop of human frailties so that He alone receives the praise. Rather than removing the problem, He supplies the believer with grace to allow one to endure with contentment (see Lowery, "First Corinthians," p. 583).

12:10. For Christ's sake, Paul was able to **take pleasure** (joy) in his **infirmities**, and even **in reproaches, in necessities, in persecutions, in distresses**. He added other difficulties to what he may have been experiencing for the name of the Lord. He embraced these problems because of the principle that when he was **weak**, then he was **strong** in the strength of Jesus Christ. It would have been natural for Paul to abhor such experiences in his ministry and in his personal life, but he welcomed them from the supernatural point of view because Christ's power was made evident through these adversities.

When Paul arrived at the end of himself, the Lord Jesus alone could be manifested.

12:11–13. With a twist of irony, Paul added that he had **become a fool** (v. 11) with his **glorying**. He had not wanted to get into all that had happened to him, but the Corinthians' doubts had **compelled** him to do so. The Corinthian church should have **commended** him because they should have recognized who he was. For in no way, **in nothing**, was he less than (**behind**) the **chiefest apostles**, while in another sense he said, **I be nothing**.

To prove that he was no less than the recognized apostles, Paul said, **the signs of an apostle were wrought among you in all patience, in signs, and wonders, and mighty deeds** (v. 12). Paul must have been performed such signs among the Corinthians, but apparently they had refused to acknowledge them. Hodge believes these nouns are different designations for the same thing (*Second Epistle to the Corinthians*, p. 292). They could have been miracles of healings and of speaking in tongues (see 1 Cor. 12:29–30). Paul knew that he was equal with the Twelve (see 11:5), as illustrated by the long list of abilities he had just put forth. It was foolish to argue about this, however, because ultimately his credentials came from God; they were not his own. It is interesting to note that Paul included "patience" (probably with the believing sheep) as a sign that verified apostleship.

The Corinthian congregation may have felt they **were inferior to other churches** (v. 13) because Paul did not want to be **burdensome** to them. He had founded many assemblies that were replete with gifts and graces. This demonstrates that he was equal to the other disciples. At one time in the past, however, he had not wanted to ask for their help because they had not trusted him. What God did through Peter with the Jews was done in like manner through Paul with the Gentiles: "For he [God] that wrought effectually in Peter to the apostleship of the circumcision, the same was mighty in me towards the Gentiles" (Gal. 2:8). The apostolic pillars, James, Cephas (Peter), and John, also "perceived the grace that was given unto me," Paul added, and he and Barnabas had received "the right hands of fellowship," with all the apostles, "that we should go unto the heathen" (Gal. 2:9).

12:14–16. Paul must have made two other visits to Corinth, as indicated in 2:1 and 13:1–2. On this **third** visit, he would act on the same principles as before in that he would take for himself nothing from this church, though their alms for the Judean church would be received by Titus and others. Paul was their spiritual parent and believed he should not receive anything from the children he spiritually birthed. Since he was their spiritual father, he would **gladly spend** ("give out"; v. 15) himself, though **the more abundantly I love you, the less I [am] loved.**

Paul was saying he forfeited their love by doing what love forced him to do. This is the strongest statement of disinterested love. He was willing to give his possessions and himself, his life and strength, not only without pay but at the cost of their love. He repeated that he did not want to place a **burden** (v. 16) on them, though he thought it important to guard against unfounded insinuations from the antagonists who doubted the purity of his motives. He **caught** them **with guile** (Greek, *dolō*), as an animal is fooled by a camouflaged trap.

12:17–18. Paul pointedly asked, **Did I make a gain of you by any of them whom I sent unto you?** (v. 17). The critics and the naysayers, if they were honest, could only answer no. With this, he appealed to facts they could not deny. The mention of **Titus** (v. 18) visiting Corinth is not the visit discussed in chapter 8, which had not yet been accomplished, but rather that discussed in chapter 7. Titus and another **brother** (see 8:18) had been sent earlier. Had Titus sought personal **gain**? Was not everyone walking **in the same spirit** and **in the same steps**? By "same spirit," Paul meant with the same inward thinking or walking in the same Holy Spirit. The believers were to be imbued and led by the same divine agent who controls the conduct of all believers.

12:19–21. Paul did not **excuse** (Greek, *apologeomai*; v. 19) himself and his fellow workers, meaning "apologize," "talk to oneself," "answer for oneself." The problems were with the Corinthians, not with Paul and his companions. **We speak before God in Christ**; God was their witness. **All things** were done for the **dearly beloved** for their **edifying**, for their benefit. Paul's aim was to build them up, **For** (v. 20), he said, he **fear[ed]** their spiritual state of mind was not what he wanted it to be. He was concerned that they would not be acceptable to him and he would not be in favor with them. He was afraid that the evil contentions that had been going on still existed among the Corinthians. These evils were **debates** (Greek, *eris*; "contentions"), **envyings** (*zēlos*; "feelings of jealousy"), **wraths** (*thymoi*; "outbreaks of anger"), **strifes** (*eritheiai*; "partisan factions"), **backbitings** (*katalaliai*; "evil speakings"), **whisperings** (*psithyrismoi*; "gossip"), **swellings** (*physiōseis*; "full of pride and insolence"), **tumults** (*akatastasiai*; "taking a stand with disorder"). The explanation for all of this uproar was that part of the assembly was penitent and humble, while the others were just the opposite. It must be remembered that most at this church were Gentiles who were ignorant of Christian sensibilities and ways of doing things. In Paul's writings, there are abundant examples of such behavior among them. The first part of 1 Corinthians is full of the strongest words of praise, but what follows speaks of contentions that could have ripped the church apart.

When he arrived in Corinth, Paul did not want to be **humble[d]** again in the presence of the church by those who had sinned and not repented (v. 21). He would also **bewail many which have sinned** and continue in that state. They had **not repented of the uncleanness and fornication and lasciviousness which have committed.** "Lasciviousness" (Greek, *aselgeia*) is a common word for "filth." Most of these words hint at sexual sins, open debauchery, and possibly even orgies. With this, Paul reached the bottom of his accusations. They could not escape or deny that this was going on in the church, not that many who had participated had not "repented" (Greek, *metanoeō*), "changed their minds."

To turn around a sinful church in the midst of heathenism was virtually impossible without the sanctifying work of the Holy Spirit. The transformation of these Christians would not be instant, for God's omnipotent power often works gradually. These early believers were but babes in the Lord Jesus.

IV. Closing (chap. 13)

Paul closed with positive words for this church, saying that he desired to speak to them with kind words and not with words that are sharp in nature.

A. Spiritual Concerns (13:1–10)

Having given strong warnings in the previous chapters, Paul intended to exercise his apostolic authority in punishing the heretical offenders (vv. 1–2). They had questioned him about his apostleship; he would now show that although he was weak in his own power, he was invested with the supernatural authority and power of the Lord Jesus. As Christ seemed to be weak in His death yet nonetheless was imbued with divine power, as proved by His resurrection, so the apostle Paul in some ways was weak but in other ways was strong in the Lord (vv. 3–4). By giving the church warning before his impending visit to Corinth, he hoped to avoid judging them as an apostle, as he had been invested by Christ.

13:1–3. Paul's second trip to the Corinthian church (see 2:1) must have been a spiritual disaster and a humiliating experience (see 12:21). Many challenged his person and his right to be an apostle (see 2:5–11), and they were living out their Christian walk in defiance of God's desire and will (see 12:21). The apostle had given ample warning about their sins, and did so again in this epistle. As Christ used Deuteronomy 19:15 against sinners (see Matt. 18:16), so Paul promised harsh discipline aimed at those walking in carnality without repentance. They would be wise to avoid his apostolic authority (see 1 Cor. 5:5).

Paul reminded the Corinthians that when he came **the third time** (v. 1), he would seek out **two or three witnesses** to verify their sinful, errant ways. As he had told them on **the second** visit, for all who **have sinned**, and sinned grievously, that when he

returned, he would **not spare**. The **proof of Christ speaking in me** (v. 3) would not come in weakness, which they had been counting on, but would come **mighty in you**.

13:4–6. As the Lord Jesus **was crucified** (v. 4) because of what seemed **weakness, yet he liveth by the power of God**, likewise Paul and his followers were **weak in him** yet would **live with him by the power of God** through the Corinthians. The apostle was proclaiming that the Lord Jesus is not dead but alive. "Liveth" (Greek, *zaō*) is present tense in the Greek text. "He is right now, presently alive!"

The Corinthians needed to look at themselves carefully. Paul urged them to **examine** (v. 5) and **prove** themselves, whether they were in **the faith**. While it appears he was concerned about their salvation, this may not be the case. Many commentators believe Paul had some doubts about the salvation of some of the Corinthians. "Those therefore in whom Christ does not dwell cannot stand the test, and are proved to be Christians, if at all, only in name" (Hodge, *First Corinthians*, p. 306). He may have been saying, "If you are saved, do you not know that Jesus Christ is in you?" And, "if He is not in you," **ye be reprobates?** Hodge thinks Paul was trying to goad the Corinthians to look at the issue of sanctification in the daily experience (see *Second Epistle to the Corinthians*, p. 306). Paul appealed directly to the consciences of his readers: "Do you not recognize in yourselves, that is, in your consciences, that Christ is in you?" The thought that **Christ is in you** does not mean "Christ is among you as a people" but refers to an indwelling of Christ in the child of God, as the apostle said, "Christ liveth in me" (Gal. 2:20; 4:19; see also Rom. 8:11). Paul **trust[ed]** (v. 6) that the Corinthians were well aware that he and his companions were **not reprobates**. "Reprobates" refers to the lost who are judicially condemned.

13:7–9. Paul did not want the Corinthians to practice **evil** (v. 7). He did not have to stand **approved** (Greek, *dokimos*). "The good state of the Corinthian church was therefore an evidence that he was approved, i.e. could stand the test" (Hodge, *First Corinthians*, p. 308) like someone concerning whom there was not a shadow of a doubt that Christ was dwelling in him. He had many verifications and proofs that he was a believer, a child of God, and that he was an apostle called to a special mission by Christ. Even if Paul and his companions were **reprobates**, the Corinthians needed to do the moral and **honest** thing. Because the spotlight was on him and on his many ministry workers, he could **do nothing against the truth, but [only] for the truth** (v. 8). He was delighted and **glad** (v. 9) to be **weak** (limited and human), for then the Corinthians had to look at what was right, and not simply at Paul. Then they would be **strong**, resulting in their **perfection** (Greek, *katartisis*), their "being put in order," "being made complete." This would liberate them from carnality, confusion, contention, and evil.

13:10. Paul concluded this section (**Therefore**) by reminding the Corinthians that he wrote while **being absent, lest being present** with them, he **should use** (Greek, *chraomai*; "to necessarily act") **sharpness**. This "sharpness" came not from his own carnality and meanness but from **the power** (Greek, *exousian*; "ability," "authority," "right") **the Lord** had given to him for **edification, and not [for] destruction** (see 1 Cor. 4:21).

B. Farewell and Benediction (13:11–14)

13:11–13. This letter is unusual in that Paul did not address anyone personally, as he did in most of his epistles. In writing **farewell** (Greek, *chairete*, present imperative; v. 11), he meant "you be rejoicing" or "may joy be continually coming to you." **Be perfect** (Greek, *katartizō*; present imperative) means "be sound," "be complete," "be put in order," "be mended," as in fixing a torn fishing net. The Corinthians were also to walk in **good comfort**, and with **one mind**. If they were to do these things and **live**

in peace … the God of love and peace shall be with you. If they had claimed the Lord Jesus as Savior, the God of love was already dwelling within them (see John 14:23; 1 John 4:12–13). Paul meant that they would have fellowship established with the Father for their daily Christian walk (see 1:6–7). God's fellowship presence gives perfect peace and inner contentment.

To **greet one another with a holy kiss** (v. 12) was an expression of communion and love within the early church. This practice did not go out of usage in the Western churches until about the thirteenth century, though it is still carried on in the Eastern Orthodox churches. It is not a command or a required ordinance for fellowship. It is a practice that some are comfortable with, and some are not. **All the saints** (v. 13) with Paul, and possibly from other churches as well, **salute[d]** their Corinthian brothers. The "salute" (Greek, *aspazomai*) was a slight gesture, a hand motion, even an embrace and a kiss. Here it is a verbal greeting, used to wish the other brothers in Corinth well.

13:14. This verse is a Trinitarian benediction that has remained as a traditional Christian farewell. All three persons of the Trinity are included and are attributed as passing on to the believers some aspect of love and communion. To **be with you all**, Paul mentioned **the grace of the Lord Jesus Christ, and the love of God [the Father], and the communion** (Greek, *koinōnia*; "sharing") **of the Holy Ghost**. It is obvious that the personality and divinity of each person in the Trinity is addressed here. Each person in the Godhead, with their particular work in salvation, is mentioned separately. This passage is recognition of the doctrine of the Trinity, which is basic to Christianity. Paul could not have written a better ending for this important letter.

THE EPISTLE OF PAUL THE APOSTLE TO THE GALATIANS

INTRODUCTION

Author

The opening verse identifies the author of Galatians as the apostle Paul. Apart from a few nineteenth-century scholars, no one has seriously questioned his authorship. The author calls himself Paul both in the opening verse and in the body of the letter (5:2). Most of the first two chapters are autobiographical and harmonize with the events in Paul's life as recorded in the book of Acts.

Date

The date of Galatians depends to a great extent on the destination of the letter. There are two main views: (1) The older North Galatian theory holds that the letter was addressed to churches located in north-central Asia Minor (Pessinus, Ancyra, and Tavium), where the Gauls had settled when they invaded the area in the third century BC. Paul visited this area on his second missionary journey, though Acts contains no reference to such a visit. This view maintains that Galatians was written between AD 53 and 57 from Ephesus or Macedonia. (2) According to the South Galatian theory, Galatians was written to churches in the southern area of the Roman province of Galatia (Antioch, Iconium, Lystra, and Derbe) that Paul founded on his first missionary journey. Some believe that Galatians was written from Syrian Antioch in AD 48–49 after Paul's first journey and before the Jerusalem council meeting (see Acts 15). Others say that Galatians was written in Syrian Antioch or Corinth between AD 51 and 53.

Background

"Judaizers" were Jewish Christians who believed, among other things, that a number of the ceremonial practices of the Old Testament were still binding on the New Testament church. Their "gospel" proclaimed not only the Messiah, Jesus, as God's fulfillment of His promises to His people the Jews but also the covenant made to their father Abraham and the law given to Moses. In some sense, then, the special status of the Jews was folded into the messianic privileges of believing in Jesus, the Messiah. In short, the Judaizers insisted on Jesus plus Judaism. For Gentiles, that meant Jesus plus becoming a Jew through circumcision (the sign of the covenant with Abraham/Jesus) and the law (which binds the covenant). Consequently, after Paul's successful campaign in Galatia, they insisted that Gentile converts to Christianity become circumcised and abide by observations of the law (see, e.g., 5:2–4; 4:21; 6:12–13). Other motives apparently heightened their opposition to the preaching of Paul. The Judaizers argued that Paul was not an authentic apostle and that, desiring to make the message more appealing to Gentiles, he had removed from the gospel certain legal requirements. The Judaizers may have been motivated also by a desire to avoid the persecution of Zealot Jews, who objected to their fraternizing with Gentiles (see 6:12).

Paul responded by clearly establishing his apostolic authority and thereby substantiating the gospel he preached. By introducing additional requirements for justification (e.g., works of the law), his adversaries had perverted the gospel of grace and, unless prevented, would have brought Paul's converts into the bondage of legalism. It is by grace through faith alone that man is justified, and it is by faith alone that he is to live out his new life in the freedom of the Spirit.

Theme and Theological Message

For Paul, the acknowledgment of the crucified Jesus as God's Messiah logically implied the nullification of the law (see 3:15–26), and with it circumcision. "I do not frustrate [lit., "nullify"] the grace of God: for if righteousness come by the law, then Christ is dead in vain" (2:21). Therefore, Galatians stands as an eloquent and vigorous apologetic for the essential New Testament truth that man is justified by faith in Jesus Christ—by nothing less and nothing more—and that he is sanctified not by legalistic works but by the obedience that comes from faith in God's work for him, in him, and through him by the grace and power of Christ and the Holy Spirit. It was the rediscovery of the basic message of Galatians that brought about the Reformation. Galatians is often referred to as "Luther's book," because Martin Luther relied so strongly on this letter in his writings and arguments against the prevailing theology of his day. A key verse is 2:16 (see discussion there).

Outline

I. Introduction (1:1–9)
   A. Salutation (1:1–5)
   B. Denunciation (1:6–9)
II. Personal: Authentication of the Apostle of Liberty and Faith (1:10–2:21)
   A. Paul's Gospel Was Received by Special Revelation (1:10–12)
   B. Paul's Gospel Was Independent of the Jerusalem Apostles and the Judean Churches (1:13–2:21)
      1. Evidenced by His Early Activities as a Christian (1:13–17)
      2. Evidenced by His First Post-Christian Visit to Jerusalem (1:18–24)
      3. Evidenced by His Second Post-Christian Visit to Jerusalem (2:1–10)
      4. Evidenced by His Rebuke of Peter at Antioch (2:11–21)
III. Doctrinal: Justification of the Doctrine of Liberty and Faith (chaps. 3–4)
   A. The Galatians' Experience of the Gospel (3:1–5)
   B. The Experience of Abraham (3:6–9)

C. The Curse of the Law (3:10–14)
D. The Priority of the Promise (3:15–18)
E. The Purpose of the Law (3:19–25)
F. Sons, Not Slaves (3:26–4:11)
G. Appeal to Enter into Freedom from Law (4:12–20)
H. The Allegory of Hagar and Sarah (4:21–31)
IV. Practical: Practice of the Life of Liberty and Faith (5:1–6:10)
A. Exhortation to Freedom (5:1–12)
B. Life by the Spirit, Not by the Flesh (5:13–26)
C. Call for Mutual Help (6:1–10)
V. Conclusion (6:11–18)

Bibliography

Barclay, William. *The Letters to the Galatians and Ephesians*. Daily Study Bible. Rev. ed. Philadelphia: Westminster, 1976.

Bruce, F. F. *Commentary on Galatians*. Grand Rapids, MI: Zondervan, 1982.

George, Timothy. *Galatians*. The New American Commentary 30. Nashville: Broadman & Holman, 1994.

Guthrie, Donald. *Galatians*. Grand Rapids, MI: Zondervan,1973.

Lightfoot, Joseph Barber. *The Epistle of St. Paul to the Galatians*. 1865. Reprint, Grand Rapids, MI: Zondervan, 1957.

McKnight, Scot. *Galatians*. Grand Rapids, MI: Zondervan, 1995.

Witherington, Ben, III. *Grace in Galatia: A Commentary on Paul's Letters to the Galatians*. Grand Rapids, MI: Eerdmans, 1998.

EXPOSITION

I. Introduction (1:1–9)

A. Salutation (1:1–5)

1:1. Paul, as was customary and conventional in letters of the time, put his name at the beginning of his letters (for more information on Paul, see discussions on Acts 9:1; Phil. 3:4–14). **An apostle**, Paul was sent on a mission with full authority of representation, as an ambassador (see *Zondervan KJV Study Bible* note on 1 Cor. 1:1). Given the Judaizers' opposition to his apostleship (see Introduction: "Background"), Paul opened his letter with the credentials of his apostleship and its character, defined by its origin through Christ. With the words **raised him from the dead**, Paul gave principal emphasis to the resurrection, the central affirmation of the Christian faith (see Acts 17:18; Rom. 1:4; 1 Cor. 15:20; 1 Peter 1:3), for two reasons: (1) because it validated the message of his apostleship, the gospel, and (2) because he had seen the risen Christ, Paul was qualified to be an apostle (see Acts 1:22 and discussion; 2:32; 1 Cor. 15:8).

1:2. Brethren, or fellow Christians (see 3:15; 4:12; 5:11; 6:18), in this case probably coworkers in spreading the gospel and planting churches (see Phil. 4:21). The plural **churches** makes it clear that this letter was a circular letter, intended to be read to several congregations. The term **Galatia** occurs four times in the New Testament. In 2 Timothy 4:10, the reference is uncertain. In 1 Peter 1:1, it refers to the northern area of Asia Minor occupied by the Gauls.

Here and in 1 Corinthians 16:1, Paul probably used the term to refer to the Roman province of Galatia and an additional area to the south, through which he traveled on his first missionary journey (see Introduction: "Date"; see also Acts 13:14–14:23).

1:3. Grace be to you and peace is characteristic of the opening of Paul's epistles (see Rom. 1:7; 1 Cor. 1:3; 2 Cor. 1:2; Gal. 1:3; Eph. 1:2; Phil. 1:2; Col. 1:2; 1 Thess. 1:1; 2 Thess. 1:2; Philem. 1:3). "Grace" is a Christian adaptation of a common Greek form of greeting (see discussions on John 4:1–3; Eph. 1:2). "Peace" is the common Hebrew form of greeting (see discussions on John 14:27; 20:19; Eph. 1:2). The meaning of both is informed by the added words, **from God the Father, and from our Lord Jesus Christ**.

1:4. For our sins. See Matthew 1:21; John 1:29; 1 Corinthians 15:3; 1 Peter 2:24. **This present evil world**, or "age," refers to the present period of the world's history (see *KJV Study Bible* note on 2 Cor. 4:4; discussion on Eph. 1:21), which stands in stark contrast with the "age" to come (the climax of the messianic age). This present age is characterized by wickedness (Eph. 2:2; 6:12), and its influence is to be countered with new thinking, God's revealed truth (Rom. 12:2).

1:5. For other doxologies, see Romans 9:5; 11:36; 16:27; Ephesians 3:21; 1 Timothy 1:17.

B. Denunciation (1:6–9)

1:6–7. So soon (v. 6) likely refers to the shortness of time between the Galatians' conversion (Paul's founding visit) and the coming of the Judaizers. The gospel they brought (see Introduction: "Background") swayed some to defect (**removed**) from the true gospel to **another gospel**. Paul impressed on them not only his surprise but something that may have surprised them. Contrary to claims, "another gospel" did not move them toward God but away **from Him that called you into the grace of Christ**. The call of God comes by virtue of the grace of Christ. Grace is the "good" in the "good news" of the gospel. The grace of Christ is the core of the true, unadulterated gospel and the chief characteristic by

which one appreciates its difference ("another," v. 6) and its uniqueness ("not another," v. 7) from other so-called gospels. **Some that trouble you** (v. 7) specifies the Judaizers (see Introduction: "Background"). Their message, the un-gospel, had done two things among the Galatian churches: (1) unsettled the Galatian believers and (2) perverted the true gospel. As the word **pervert** implies, the Judaizers had contorted the gospel to such a degree that it could no longer be called the gospel; it had been disfigured and no longer resembled "good news."

1:8–9. Paul made it clear that the messenger, whether earthly or heavenly, was not what mattered most. The message, **that which we have preached unto you** (v. 8), was what mattered most. For, as Paul wrote to the church at Rome, the gospel "is the power of God unto salvation" (Rom. 1:16). Since salvation itself was at stake, it was not too strong for Paul to call **accursed** (v. 8–9) the one who preaches **any other gospel**. The Greek word for "accursed" (*anathema*) originally referred to a pagan temple offering in payment for a vow and devoted to sacred destruction. Later it came to represent a curse (see v. 9; 1 Cor. 12:3; 16:22; Rom. 9:3).

II. Personal: Authentication of the Apostle of Liberty and Faith (1:10–2:21)

A. Paul's Gospel Was Received by Special Revelation (1:10–12)

1:10. Paul was in the business of persuading men, not God, and pleasing God, not men. If matters had been the other way around, as evidently some had charged, then Paul would have not been a **servant of Christ**. Paul once wore "the yoke of bondage" (5:1), but having been set free from sin by the redemption that is in Christ, he became a slave of righteousness, a slave of God (see Rom. 6:18, 22).

1:11–12. I certify you, brethren (v. 11). A similar phrase is found in 1 Corinthians 15:1, where Paul sets forth the gospel he received. **The gospel … preached of me**, Paul called "my gospel" in Romans 2:16; 16:25. As F. F. Bruce (*Commentary on Galatians*, p. 88) aptly pointed out, Paul also called his gospel "the gospel of God" (1 Thess. 2:8, 9; 2 Cor. 11:7) because God authored it and "the gospel of Christ" (1 Thess. 3:2; 2 Cor. 2:12; Rom. 15:9) because Christ is its content (see Rom. 1:1 – 3). The words **not after man** make it plain that Paul's gospel, in nature and character, was not of human ingenuity or authority, nor was he indebted to any human for its reception or instruction. The validity of Paul's gospel was ensured by none other than **the revelation of Jesus Christ** (v. 12; see Eph. 3:2 – 6).

B. Paul's Gospel Was Independent of the Jerusalem Apostles and the Judean Churches (1:13 – 2:21)

In defense of his gospel, Paul opened with an autobiography of his changed life, a powerful witness to the genuine gospel over against the Judaizers' gospel (see Introduction, "Background"). Paul's opening point and evolving case is clear: Why would one who was so completely committed to the values of Jewish faith and practice turn to embrace that which he persecuted as wrong? One would not, Paul argued, unless God Himself intervened and revealed to him his error, calling him to what is right and therefore bringing about a conversion so radical it owed nothing to his once beloved life with its law and its circumcision but only to the risen Christ. The very gospel he had once persecuted he now preached, and it was this very gospel that Jerusalem approved when it was later compared with that of the apostles before him. Indeed, even Peter had to accede and submit to this very gospel. In the end, the implicit question to the Galatians became, by what means do the Judaizers leverage your faith with another gospel?

1. Evidenced by His Early Activities as a Christian (1:13 – 17)

1:13 – 14. Paul's **conversation** (v. 13), or "manner of life," **in the Jews' religion** ("Judaism") attested to his piety in the Jewish faith and way of life to the degree that he was a **zealous** (v. 14; see Phil. 3:6) champion of every effort to annihilate the church of God (see 1:23). Further attestation came from none other than the ruling Sanhedrin, which had deemed him fit and granted him formal authoriza-

tion to arrest and imprison Christians (Acts 9:1 – 2; 22:4 – 5; 26:10 – 11). **Ye have heard** (v. 13) may point to Paul's own testimony among the Galatians, but his reputation for piety and persecution was evident to both peers and opponents (see v. 14, 1:23). **The traditions of my fathers** (v. 14) were authoritative ancestral doctrines and customs that regulated religious and social life. These traditions, which may be described as complementary explanation and illustration of the law, were orally transmitted from previous generations and contrasted with the written law of Moses (see the "tradition of the elders," Matt. 15:2 and discussion).

1:15 – 17. When Paul wrote of how God **separated me from my mother's womb** (v. 15), he declared his calling and apostleship (see Rom. 1:1) to be rooted in the foreordained purposes of God, even as God's servant (Isa. 49:1) and prophet (Jer. 1:5). His professed role in the economy of God's salvation plan was not the consequence of Paul's claim to it but God's calling to it.

Paul's point in 1:15 – 2:10, that the apostles of Jerusalem recognize (2:6 – 10) his God-given commission to preach to the Gentiles, begins here with the declaration that God had **called** (v. 15) him and had **reveal[ed] his Son in [him]** (v. 16), which initiated Paul's preaching to the Gentiles and not any conference with human authorities, not even in Jerusalem. **Heathen** (lit., "nations" or "peoples") is the term commonly designated "foreigners," hence pagans, or the non-Jewish world. **Jerusalem** (v. 17) was important because it was not only the religious center of Judaism but the birthplace of Christianity and the recognized capital of apostolic rule. Paul had not been led there but to **Arabia**, the Nabatean kingdom in Transjordan stretching from Damascus southwest to the Suez, and to **Damascus**, the ancient capital of Syria (Aram in the Old Testament). Paul had been converted en route from Jerusalem to Damascus (Acts 9:1 – 9). That Paul received his message from God and did not confer with **flesh and blood** (v. 16) contested any notion that his gospel omitted crucial tenets (e.g., circumcision) of the gospel that the Judaizers (see Introduction, "Background") asserted came from Jerusalem and the apostles. Remember, it was by grace, Paul asserted, that he had been called (v. 15). In the New Testament, "flesh and blood" always carries the implication of human impotence or imperfection (see Matt. 16:17; 1 Cor. 15:50; Eph. 6:12).

2. Evidenced by His First Post-Christian Visit to Jerusalem (1:18–24)

1:18. Then after three years, or from the time of his departure into Arabia (see 1:16–17). The text does not say he spent the three years in Arabia. **I went up to Jerusalem** probably refers to the visit recorded in Acts 9:26–30, though some equate it with the visit recorded in Acts 11:30. **Peter**, from the Greek word for "stone," is the Aramaic equivalent to "Cephas" (see Matt. 16:18 and discussion). The name designates a like quality in the bearer (see discussion on John 1:42). Paul went **to see**, or "to make the acquaintance of" (Greek, *historeō*; to know by inquiry), Peter. This meeting followed Barnabas's endorsement of Paul (see Acts 9:26–27).

1:19. The only other apostle Paul **saw**, that is, set eyes upon, a verb different from the word "see" in 1:18, was **James** (see James, Introduction: "Author") **the Lord's brother** (see discussion on Luke 8:19). Whether Paul viewed James as numbered among the "other apostles" pivots on the question of whether the word **save** introduces an exception to the whole statement or just the verb "see." Like Paul, James was converted by an appearance of Jesus (see 1 Cor. 15:7). Although not among the original twelve, James rose to prominence in the Jerusalem church (see Acts 12:17; 15:13; 21:18–19).

1:20. Here Paul inserted a solemn oath (**before God**) to underscore his central and vital point: his gospel was not derived from any source save the "revelation of Jesus Christ" (1:12). In other words, it did not come from Jerusalem, despite his visit with Peter and his "sighting" of James.

1:21. Afterwards, or "then," introduces the second of three instances (1:18, 21; 2:1) in which Paul used the same adverb to produce an unbroken account of his missionary movements, independent of Jerusalem, as he was led from the reception of his gospel and calling (see 1:12) to the conference and formal presentation of his gospel in Jerusalem (2:1–10). **Syria and Cilicia** were provinces in Asia Minor. Specifically, Paul went to Tarsus (see Acts 9:30), his hometown.

1:22–24. As a further testimony to Paul's independent missionary work, the churches of Judea didn't even know what Paul looked like, although they **had heard** (lit., "kept hearing"; v. 23) of his preaching. Their response was a tacit confirmation of Paul's gospel apart from any recognition out of Jerusalem. That recognition, as Paul recounted in 2:1–10, came next in Paul's argument. For the moment, as it were, the Galatian readers were standing at the doorstep of the Jerusalem meeting and proceeded to it with these words from the Judean churches ringing in their ears: **they glorified God in me** (v. 24).

3. Evidenced by His Second Post-Christian Visit to Jerusalem (2:1–10)

2:1. Then fourteen years after is probably to be reckoned from the date of Paul's conversion, or "call" (see 1:15–16 and "immediately," 1:16). This probability is strengthened by Paul's use of the same Greek adverb, *epeita* ("Then," or "thereupon"; 1:18, 21; 2:1), that he used to show he was omitting nothing from the succession of events stemming from God's call and revelation of His Son. **I went up again to Jerusalem**. According to some, this refers to the visit mentioned in Acts 11:30; according to others, the one in Acts 15:1–4 (see discussions on Acts 12:1; 15:2). "Went up" is consistently used with reference to Jerusalem in the New Testament, not only because of its elevation but because of its prestige. **Barnabas** means "one who encourages." His given name was Joseph, and he was a Levite from the island of Cyprus (see Acts 4:36 and discussion). Barnabas endorsed Paul in Jerusalem (see Acts 9:26–27) and was Paul's companion on the first missionary journey (see Acts 13:1–14:28). **Titus** was a Gentile Christian who served as Paul's delegate to Corinth and later was left in Crete to oversee the church there (see Titus 1:5). It is likely that Titus was a convert of Paul's early ministry ("mine own son after the common faith," Titus 1:4) and accompanied Paul as a prime example of the gospel Paul preached.

2:2. I went up by revelation. Paul disclosed that the impetus for visiting Jerusalem this time came not from a felt need on his part but from the prompting of God. To whom this revelation came, Paul did not specify (as in 2:12, 16); whether it came to Paul himself, to Barnabas, to fellow believers as at Antioch (Acts 11:27–30), or in some other way, Paul did not make clear. What is clear is that it was not Paul's idea but God's. **Them which were of reputation** points to men of acknowledged authority and refers to James, Peter, and John (see 2:6, 9). To them, Paul had communicated **that gospel which I preach**. Why them? Paul had not been summoned by them. Paul had taken pains to establish that the validity of his gospel was subject not to them but only to Christ. In part, an answer has already been supplied: Paul had been compelled by God ("by revelation"), which accounts for Paul's humility on a matter of such importance. The further answer comes in Paul's use of an athletic metaphor picturing a race than cannot be won but is **run** nonetheless (see 1 Cor. 15:58; Phil. 2:16). Paul did not want to run such a race if there was any possibility (**by any means**) its victory can be assured. The prize to be won was a more unified church and the recognition of the one gospel. That is what was won (see 2:2–10). The words "that gospel which I preach" (present tense) made clear to Paul's Galatian readers that the same gospel he had always preached, and had preached to them, was the very gospel that those "of reputation" heard and recognized. It was "that gospel which I preach" that some Galatians were abandoning at the time of his letter.

2:3–5. In different words, Paul stated that the subject of circumcision, so prominent among the Judaizers (see Introduction: "Background"), was not even raised by "them … of reputation" (2:2), let alone any insistence of it being a necessity, and **Titus** (v. 3) had been right there. On the contrary, the matter was introduced by others, by **false brethren** (v. 4), the Judaizers, who imposed on Gentile converts cir-

cumcision and adherence to the law of Moses (see Acts 15:5; 2 Cor. 11:26). This Paul called **bondage**. The **liberty which we have in Christ Jesus** (see 5:1, 13; Rom. 6:18, 20, 22; 8:2) they sought only to detect and **spy out**. The Greek word *kataskopeō* can carry a tone of treachery and is used in the Septuagint (the Greek translation of the Old Testament) in 2 Samuel 10:3 and 1 Chronicles 19:3 to refer to spying out a territory. Paul not only describes the manner of their admission, but his vocabulary decries their motives: they were clandestinely smuggled in **that they might bring us into bondage**. It should not be missed that Paul saw a parallel between their earlier actions in Jerusalem and their present actions in Galatia. Paul fixed the connection between the two situations when he addressed his readers directly (**with you**; v. 5). His Galatian readers may have fairly imagined that as Paul had given the Judaizers and their gospel of bondage no quarter then, nothing now had changed.

2:6. These who seemed to be somewhat (see discussion on 2:2) refers to James, Peter, and John (see 2:9). Paul's use of the present tense here (as well as in 2:2, 9) points to the issue: they were "being reputed" (see 2:2) at the time of his writing by the Judaizers in what had become among the Galatians a contest over the right gospel. Paul stated that it did not matter what he or anyone else thought about them. What mattered was what God thought. **God accepteth no man's person** (see Deut. 10:17; 1 Sam. 16:7; Luke 20:21; James 2:1). Literally, the Greek reads, "God does not accept the face of man" (or a human being), an expression that is common in the New Testament (see Luke 20:21; Acts 10:34; Rom. 2:11; Eph. 6:9; Col. 3:25; 1 Tim. 5:21; James 2:1, 9). In a Mediterranean culture that valued the giving and accepting of honor, Paul asserted quite powerfully that God has a different outlook on outward human evaluations of honor or status: they matter not at all. In short, Paul was saying that those who were esteemed—and it did not matter what they were because it was irrelevant to God—**added nothing to me**. They neither added nor subtracted anything with respect to the gospel that he preached, nor to his honor or status as an apostle. Paul's tone, although not one of disrespect (as 2:2, 9, make clear; see "pillars," 2:9), may well have been agitated by the echo of reported appeals to just such reputation by the Judaizers who had attacked the gospel he had preached among the Galatian churches.

2:7–9. But contrariwise (v. 7), or just the opposite of any recommended alteration, there was only recognition of (**saw**, v. 7; and **perceived**, v. 9) Paul's calling from God to the **gospel of the uncircumcision** (v. 7). Paul's ministry was not exclusively to the Gentiles. In fact, he regularly went first to the synagogue when arriving in a new location (see discussion on Acts 13:14). He did, however, consider himself to be foremost an apostle to the Gentiles (see Rom. 11:13 and discussion). Paul acknowledged **James** (see discussion on 1:19), **Cephas** (see discussion on 1:18)**, and John** (v. 9) as the ascribed church **pillars**, a common metaphor for those who represent and strongly support an institution. **The right hands of fellowship** they had extended, a common practice among both Hebrews and Greeks, indicating a pledge of friendship and cooperation, was a proof of their recognition of Paul. The message to Paul's readers was clear: any claim from the Judaizers that the Jerusalem leadership disapproved of Paul's ministry is patently false and contrary to the divine approval they duly recognized.

2:10. One thing James, Peter, and John asked was that Paul encourage Gentile churches to **remember the poor**. Even that was not novel to Paul's attitude or practice. It may have fallen into line with an impetus for coming to Jerusalem in the first place if, as some have suggested, the revelation of 2:2 was in any way connected to the events of Acts 11:27–30.

4. Evidenced by His Rebuke of Peter at Antioch (2:11–21)

2:11. Antioch was the leading city of Syria and third-leading city of the Roman Empire (after Rome and Alexandria). From there, Paul had been sent out on his missionary journeys (see Acts 13:1–3; 14:26). Peter **was to be blamed** for yielding to the pressure of the circumcision party (the Judaizers; see Introduction: "Background") and thus going against what

he knew to be right. The seriousness of Paul's action was due to the seriousness of Peter's. God stands behind the passive "was to be blamed," which is more accurately rendered "stands condemned" (perfect tense). "God condemns what Peter has done" (Witherington, *Grace in Galatia*, pp. 151–52; see Bruce, *Commentary on Galatians*, p. 159).

2:12–13. Paul set forth the reason for Peter's condemnation and opposition and indirectly painted a picture of the early church at Antioch, that influential church where the disciples were first called Christians (Acts 11:26). Peter was there, as were Barnabas and other Jews. Like Peter, they were comfortable living after the manner of Gentiles (2:14). **He did eat with the Gentiles** (v. 12) summarizes the regular and unrestricted fellowship Peter and others enjoyed. This was as it should be, as Peter well knew from his rooftop vision in Joppa and subsequent fellowship with Cornelius (see Acts 10:9–11:18). Such was the atmosphere before the arrival of certain men of James. After their arrival, Paul described Peter's actions as a contagious reduction of and final withdrawal from fellowship with the Gentile Christians. **Other Jews** (v. 13) and even **Barnabas**, Paul's ally in the evangelism of the Gentiles, followed Peter's lead out of fear of **them which were of the circumcision** (v. 12). These were not them who **came from James**, nor were they Jewish Christians, but Zealot Jews (see Introduction: "Background") who persecuted (see 6:12) Jews and Jewish Christians for fraternizing with Gentiles. It is probable that James and the others thought the mission of bringing the gospel to the Jews, of which Peter was the apostle to the Jews (see 2:7–8), was in jeopardy because of Peter's open fellowship with Gentiles in flagrant violation of Jewish purity and dietary laws.

2:14. Paul publicly and directly challenged Peter, addressing him as one who **livest after the manner of Gentiles**. In other words, Paul told Peter: You do not observe Jewish customs, especially dietary restrictions (see 2:12). For Peter to now resume Jewish practices was to **compellest … the Gentiles to live as do the Jews**. Peter's actions amounted to imposing Jewish purity and dietary laws as a condition for fellowship with Peter and other like-minded Jewish Christians.

Such conditions for acceptance struck at the heart of the gospel. "To live as do the Jews" translates the Greek verb *Ioudaizō*, from which comes the expressions "Judaize" and "Judaizer." It is a significant word that Paul used here only, and it occurs nowhere else in the New Testament. It means to adopt Jewish customs and practices, including Sabbath observance, laws concerning purity and diet, and circumcision. In effect, Peter's actions were not "Christianizing" but "Judaizing" the Gentiles. Paul made clear to Peter that his actions were promoting a unity of believers found, not in Christ, but in Judaism.

2:15–16. Paul made it plain that Jews and Gentiles alike are justified by faith and not by works of the law. Verse 16 is a key verse in Galatians (see Introduction: "Theme and Theological Message"). Three times it tells us that no one is justified by observing the law, and three times it underscores the indispensable requirement of placing one's faith in Christ. **Justified by ... the faith of Jesus Christ** (v. 16) is the essence of the gospel message (see Rom. 3:20, 28; Phil. 3:9; see also discussions on Rom. 3:24, 28). Faith is the means by which justification is received, not its basis. On the other hand, no one is justified **by the works of the law.** Paul was not depreciating the law itself, for he clearly maintained that God's "law is holy ... and just, and good" (Rom. 7:12). He was arguing against an illegitimate use of the Old Testament law that made the observance of that law the grounds for God's acceptance.

2:17–18. We ourselves also (v. 17) underscores the perspective of the Jewish Christians (see 2:15–16) or Jews who sought justification in Christ (2:15–16) and not in the law. As such, they came to justification just as "sinners of the Gentiles" (2:15); seeking justification in Christ and not in the law implies the recognition of sin and the ineffectiveness of the law to justify. Of course, Paul quickly clarified that justification apart from the law did not mean that Jesus promotes or services immorality (v. 17b). It means that Jesus does what the law cannot: justify. Then Paul addressed in principle what Peter, Barnabas, and other Jews had done by resuming Jewish practices: **If** (v. 18) as a Jewish Christian

I build again what I effectively destroyed (i.e., the law) when I accepted justification by faith in Jesus, **I make myself a transgressor** of that which cannot justify. Moreover, such a rebuilding of the law communicates that justification in Christ is ineffective.

2:19–20. Paul had rhetorically identified himself with Jews who sought justification through Christ. Now the "I" became most personal as he distanced himself from any notion of the law's vitality in justification: there could be no transgression of the law because he was **dead to the law** (v. 19; see discussion on Rom. 7:4). Where did Paul die to the law? He died at the cross. Every believer who identifies with the accomplished work of Christ recognizes that he or she has been **crucified with Christ** (v. 20; see 5:24; 6:14; Rom. 6:8–10; 7:6; see also discussion on Rom. 6:7). The only life that has ever followed crucifixion is the resurrected life of Jesus Christ. That was the life Paul now enjoyed. The words **gave himself for me** (see 1:4; 1 Tim. 2:6; Titus 2:14) tenderly and personally summarizes the profound truth that the death of Jesus abolished the law's indictment by sacrificially settling the debt that the law emphatically points out is owed to God's holiness. Now there is no indictment for those in Christ and therefore no law with power to inhibit the life God wants believers to live through Jesus Christ. Such life and its power can only be gained through a lively relationship with God made possible by Jesus Christ.

2:21. However, Paul said, to empower the law by making it the means of righteousness is to **frustrate** (or nullify) **the grace of God.** When that is done, one nullifies the power and effect of Christ's death: **Christ is dead in vain.** In short, to mingle legalism with grace distorts grace and makes a mockery of the cross.

III. Doctrinal: Justification of the Doctrine of Liberty and Faith (chaps. 3–4)

A. The Galatians' Experience of the Gospel (3:1–5)

3:1. Paul's use of the word **foolish** (see Luke 24:25; Rom. 1:14; 1 Tim. 6:9; Titus 3:3) to vocalize the absurdity of the Galatian defection, corresponds to his use of **bewitched**. The Galatians were not mentally deficient, but their powers of perception had been so sorely altered, it was if they had been put under a spell. The question, **who hath …?** (see 5:7), although rhetorical since Paul knew the answer, prodded the Galatians into picturing the legalistic Judaizers (see Introduction, "Background") that had been among them pedaling "another gospel" (1:6). Rhetorical questions, however, prod one into looking beyond the obvious answers in the mind to the deeper issues in the heart. **Evidently set forth, crucified** (see 1 Cor. 1:23; 2:2) translates the Greek verb meaning "to publicly portray or placard as crucified." With this expression, Paul was recalling not only the portrayal but also the purpose of Jesus' death on the cross. In other words, Paul was asking how the importance of Jesus' crucifixion and death could be ignored or overlooked; it is the crux of the gospel. How could they get around something so obvious? Yet some of them were acting as though they had never seen the cross, by embracing the legalism of the Judaizers' gospel.

3:2. Paul knew the answer. Works of the law were not the substance of the gospel he preached or the basis for **the Spirit** they received. Their experience of the Spirit (see 3:5; 4:6) could not be denied, and the admission was a concession they owed not to works of the law but to **the hearing of faith** (see 3:5). It was also an admission to Paul's argument against the Judaizers' **works of the law**. The work of the Spirit could in no way be attributed to "works," and from this point on in Galatians, Paul refers to the Holy Spirit sixteen times.

3:3 – 4. Begun in the Spirit … made perfect (v. 3). The Spirit is the hallmark of life in Christ (Eph. 1:13 – 14; Rom. 8:9). Both salvation and sanctification are the work of the Holy Spirit. To try to perfect **by the flesh** what only God can do through the power of the Spirit is folly (**foolish**). "Flesh" is a reference to human nature in its unregenerate weakness. All attempts to achieve righteousness by works, including circumcision, belong not to faith but to the "flesh." Paul hoped that by leading his Galatian converts through a course of right thinking, those who had been misled would return to the true gospel (v. 4).

3:5. Paul reiterated the contrast between **the works of the law** and **the hearing of faith**, (as in 3:2). Although the Spirit's **miracles**, or "mighty deeds" (Greek, *dynamis*), belonged to the marks of an apostle (2 Cor. 12:12), there is no grammatical or theological reason in Paul's teaching on the Spirit to exclude from his meaning here the whole range of the Spirit's ministry, both **among you** and "in you" (see 4:6; 5:16 – 25). Paul's use of the Greek word *epichorēgeō*, here translated **ministereth**, suggests (as in 2 Cor. 9:10 and Col. 2:19) the provision or supply of a necessity. Accordingly, Paul conveyed that God's provision of the Spirit supplies to faith what is necessary for a relationship with God. The Spirit belongs to God's grace and the reception of faith; its provision is not a payoff for works, performance, or earnings.

B. The Experience of Abraham (3:6 – 9)

3:6 – 7. Abraham provides a crucial example. **Even as** (v. 6) "the hearing of faith" (3:5), not works, was operative in God's supply of the Spirit, Abraham was justified (accounted righteous) by faith, not works. Abraham's example was pivotal to Paul's argument with the Judaizers. If, for all intents and purposes, the Judaizers required Gentiles like the Galatians to become Jews to be justified in Christ, one might ask how Abraham was justified and became the father of the Jews. Was it by works of the law and circumcision, as required by the Judaizers, or by faith alone? Paul's answer came in a declaration: it is through faith that a person belongs to **the children of Abraham** (v. 7). Abraham was the physical and spiritual father of the Jewish race (see John 8:33, 39, 53; Acts 7:2; Rom. 4:12). Here all believers (Jews and Gentiles) are called his spiritual children (see discussions on Rom. 4:11 – 12). They are also referred to as the "seed" (3:16; Heb. 2:16), or "descendants," of Abraham.

3:8. The scripture, foreseeing is a personification of the Scripture that calls attention to its divine origin (see 1 Tim. 5:18). By virtue of the Scripture, the testimony of Abraham's example is unimpeachable. This very same Scripture provided the divine and advance testimony to the gospel preached to the Galatians, not by the Judaizers, but by Paul. At the very inception of all that became Jewish, Abraham, the Gentile who became the father of the Jews, was justified by faith. Thus, the blessing of **all nations** ("Gentiles") in Abraham was conceived with Abraham and consummated with Christ (see 3:14–15).

3:9. The expression **faithful Abraham** again highlights and underscores the role of faith; Paul uses the adjective (*pistos*) of the verb "believed" (*pisteō*) in 3:6. Paul develops this theme at length in Romans 4 (see also Heb. 11:8–19).

C. The Curse of the Law (3:10–14)

3:10. Are of the works of the law is Paul's shorthand to describe those who insist on pursuing righteousness through works. Seeking to fulfill the demands of the law serves only to confirm **the curse** because no one under the law ever perfectly keeps the law. God's blessing has never been earned but has always been freely given. **All things ... do them** (Deut. 27:26) defines the scope of the demand and also the potential for failing to keep the law (see James 2:10).

3:11. That no man is justified by the law ... is evident. Not only is it plain and clear, but Abraham's justification by faith was not an exception or a special case. In his argument, Paul moved from the principle in particular (Abraham, 3:6) to the principle in general, citing Habakkuk 2:4 to show that the law was never God's method for justification. Paul's citation comes from the Septuagint, the Greek translation of the Old Testament. The wording in Greek reads, "The just on the basis of faith shall live." The curse of the law (3:10) is contrasted with life that comes "on the basis of [by] faith." **Just** (or "righteous") is the noun and **justified** its verb; thus, the sense becomes clear: "the one justified on the basis of faith shall live." F. F. Bruce (*Commentary on Galatians*, p. 161) rendered it, "It is the one that is righteous (justified) by faith [not by law] that will live (find life)" and therefore not come under the curse.

3:12. Paul cited Leviticus 18:5 (see Luke 10:28) to demonstrate that the law has to do with only works (**doeth them**; see 3:10), not faith. Anticipating 3:13

and comparing Romans 10:5, one may infer that only one, Jesus Christ, has fulfilled the demands of the law.

3:13. Christ hath redeemed us from the curse of the law (see 4:5; Rom. 8:3). **Tree** is used in classical Greek of stocks and poles on which bodies were impaled. Here it is used of the cross (see Acts 5:30; 10:39; 1 Peter 2:24). The **curse** (see 3:10), or penalty of death, that must be met or suffered because of the law's demand has been met and suffered by Christ. To capture the sense of what Christ has done for us, Paul used the word **redeemed**, a metaphor familiar to his contemporaries from the formal emancipation of a slave. At the price of His own life, Jesus has satisfied the debt demanded (see 1 Cor. 7:23). To the same realm of thought belong Paul's associations of bondage (slavery) under the law (see 4:9; 4:24; 5:1).

3:14. Two promises stated as purposes (Greek, *hina*; "that") are realized through the redeeming death of Jesus Christ. First, **the blessing of Abraham** (see 3:8; Rom. 4:1–5) to the Gentiles is fulfilled through "his seed" (see 3:16), and second, **the promise of the Spirit** is supplied (see 3:5; Ezek. 36:26; 37:14; 39:29; John 14:16; Eph. 1:13).

D. The Priority of the Promise (3:15–18)

3:15. Brethren (see discussion on 1:2) solicited not only the Galatians' attention but also their identification with Paul and the human comparison he was about to draw between earthly and heavenly covenants. **After the manner of men**, or "drawn from our common human experience," established the vantage point of Paul's argument as he moved from the lesser to the greater. The Greek word for **covenant** (*diathēkē*) normally indicates a last will or testament, which is the legal instrument Paul was referring to here. In the Septuagint (the Greek translation of the Old Testament), it had been widely used of God's covenant with His people (see Matt. 26:28; Luke 1:72; Acts 3:25; 7:8; 2 Cor. 3:14; Heb. 8:9), so Paul's choice of analogy was apt for his purpose. Paul's point was that everybody acknowledges and counts on the inviolable and irrevocable character of a man's last will and testament. Paul argued that if a covenant a man sets up is binding, how much more so when God sets up a covenant?

3:16 – 18. The promises (v. 16; see discussions on Rom. 4:13; 9:4) of which Paul wrote were made in a covenant with **Abraham and his seed**, which is Jesus Christ. This covenant, Paul argued, God set up apart from and before the law given much later to Moses. That law cannot change or amend the covenant previously made by God. **Four hundred and thirty years** (v. 17; see Exod. 12:40 – 41) is the period of time the children of Israel dwelt in Egypt. The law was given to Moses after they left. The period in Egypt is designated in round numbers as "four hundred years" in Genesis 15:13; Acts 7:6.

E. The Purpose of the Law (3:19 – 25)

3:19. From the time of Abraham, the promise covenanted to him (Gen. 12:2 – 3, 7; 15:18 – 20; 17:4 – 8) had stood at the center of God's relationship with His people. After the exodus, the law contained in the Sinaitic covenant (Exod. 19 – 24) became an additional element in that relationship — what Jeremiah by implication called the "old covenant" when he brought God's promise of a "new covenant" (Jer. 31:31 – 34). Paul posed and answered an obvious question. If the law does not change or amend the covenant with Abraham, why was it introduced or **added**? Paul expounded a twofold answer: (1) to make evident the **transgressions** (v. 19) being committed (see Rom. 5:13, 20) and (2) to "conclude [or confine] all under sin" (3:22, see Rom. 11:32). Thus, the law was added **till the seed should come**. After God promised to regenerate the nations through Abraham's seed (Jesus Christ), He added the Mosaic law to reveal and restrain sin until Christ should come and provide righteousness to all who believe (Rom. 10:4). The purpose of the law has been fulfilled within those who have obtained righteousness and sonship in Christ (see 3:24 – 25). **By angels** (see Deut. 33:2; Acts 7:38, 53; Heb. 2:2) **in the hand of a mediator** (Moses) serves to describe the mediation involved in God's giving of the law. Paul's argument capitalized on contemporary rabbinic views of the law's mediation to contrast the superiority of the promise given directly by God (see 3:20).

3:20. The Mosaic covenant was a formal arrangement of mutual commitments between God and Israel, with Moses as the mediator. Since the promise God covenanted with Abraham involved commitment only from God's side (and God is one; see *KJV Study Bible* note on Deut. 6:4), no mediator was involved.

3:21. The reason the law is not opposed to God's promise to Abraham is that, although in itself it cannot save, it serves to reveal sin, which alienates God from man, and to show the need for the salvation that the promise offers.

3:22. The Greek word translated **concluded** means "to catch by enclosing," as when a shoal of fish is netted on every side. The same word is translated "shut up" in 3:23. No one can escape the confining and imprisoning effect of the Scripture, which is here equivalent to the written law.

3:23. Faith, or faith in Christ (see 3:22), is the only key that liberates one confined or **kept under the law.** Paul's terminology was consistent with the Roman practice of using prisons primarily for holding prisoners until the disposition of their cases. To be a prisoner of sin (see 3:22) and a prisoner of the law amounts to much the same, because law reveals and stimulates sin (see 4:3; Rom. 7:8; Col. 2:20).

3:24 – 25. Was our schoolmaster (v. 24) translates the Greek *paidagōgos* (from which "pedagogue" is derived). It refers to the personal slave-attendant who supervised a freeborn boy wherever he went and had charge over the child's rearing and behavior. Contrary to the English use of the word pedagogue, the *paidagōgos* was not the teacher but was responsible for getting the child to the teacher for his education. After this analogy from daily life, Paul portrayed the law as the *paidagōgos* that leads one to the teacher, Jesus Christ. Once the child is in the hands of the teacher, the *paidagōgos* steps back and does not interfere with the teacher. In Roman culture, the duties of the *paidagōgos* were concluded when the boy assumed the toga of adulthood.

F. Sons, Not Slaves (3:26 – 4:11)

3:26 – 27. By adoption, the justified believer enters a relationship with God the Father as a full-fledged heir in God's family, with all the attendant rights and privileges (see 4:1 – 7; Rom. 8:14 – 17). Since Paul was writing to Christians, some of whom were struggling with their identity and privileges because of the misinformation of the Judaizers, he stressed that they were the full-fledged children of God through faith. The act of being **baptized into Christ** (v. 27; see Rom. 6:3 – 11; 1 Cor. 12:13) was outward proof of their inward faith and commensurate adoption. To **put on Christ** is to be clothed in His identity and cloaked in the privileges of His sonship.

3:28 – 29. Unity in Christ transcends ethnic, social, and sexual distinctions (see Rom. 10:12; 1 Cor. 12:13; Eph. 2:15 – 16). These earthly distinctions and roles remain, but all who are **in Christ** (v. 28) are positioned as full and equal sons and heirs of God. **Free** (see 5:1, 13; Rom. 6:18, 20, 22; 8:2) and "freedom" are key words in Galatians, occurring ten times (here; 4:22 – 23, 26, 30 – 31; 5:1, 13; see "liberty" in 2:4). All who are "in Christ," or Christians, regardless of ethnic heredity or pedigree, are Abraham's true, spiritual descendants (v. 29).

4:1. In the ancient Mediterranean world, customs connected to a child's status and advance to adulthood were more uniformly observed than are customary today. Once again, these human customs helped to make plain the spiritual truths of the gospel as Paul communicated them to the Galatians. A minor, or **a child** (compare "men" in 1 Cor. 14:20; "perfect" in Phil. 3:15), regardless of pedigree or inheritance, has no decision-making authority; the heir has no more freedom in this regard than a slave does.

4:2. In Roman and Greek law, **tutors and governors**, or guardians and trustees, have distinct legal responsibilities in the charge of a minor. Here, like the *paidagōgos*, they represent the role of the law governing the child until he comes of age, or **until the time appointed of the father**. Paul's wording has a double duty, strategically drawing on the meaning of familiar customs while anticipating new spiritual meanings. In this case, the "time appointed" is echoed in "the fulness of the time" in 4:4.

4:3. Even so we are the words Paul used to draw a spiritual comparison to the human customs surrounding the custody of a minor (4:1 – 2). **In bondage**, as defined by the restricted status of a minor (4:1), goes back also to 3:23 (see discussion there). The Greek term used for **elements** meant essentially "things placed side by side in a row" (as the ABCs) and then came to mean fundamental principles or basic elements of various kinds. The context here suggests that it refers to the elemental forms of religion, whether those of the Jews ("under the law," 4:5) or those of the Gentiles (under their old religious bondage, 4:8).

4:4. The fulness of the time was come. "The time appointed" (4:2) by God for His children to become adult sons and heirs. In Paul's immediate argument, the words **God sent forth his Son** (see John 1:14; 3:16; Rom. 1:1 – 6; 1 John 4:14) are descriptive not only of the divine initiative but also the full authority of an heir (see 4:2) as He undertakes His representation of the Father who sent Him. **Made of a woman** shows that Christ was truly human. **Made under the law** shows that Christ was subject to the Jewish law.

4:5. The adoption of sons not only incorporates a child into the family but invests the child with all the rights of sonship (see Rom. 8:15, where "the Spirit of adoption" is contrasted with "the spirit of bondage"; see also Eph. 1:5). God takes into His family as fully recognized sons and heirs both Jews (those who had been under law) and Gentiles who believe in Christ. Adoption is linked with "redemption" (see 3:13; 1:10), the emancipation from slavery, leading to a startling reversal of status, with the slave becoming a son with full rights and an inheritance.

4:6 – 7. The Spirit of his Son (v. 6), the selfsame "Spirit of God" in Romans 8:9 (see Rom. 8:2; Eph. 1:13 – 14), identifies the believer as belonging to God and being His child, just like His Son, Jesus. "Of His Son" profiles the Christlike character and quality of the believer's experience of the Spirit. Through the Spirit, a Christian's character and relationship with God is patterned on Jesus and shaped by the image of Christ. Thus, the Spirit is a new "tutor" (4:2). The Greek for **crying** is a vivid verb expressing deep emotion, often used of an inarticulate cry. In Matthew 27:50, it is used of Jesus' final cry. **Abba, Father,**

is the instinctive and intimate cry of the Spirit, here given expression first in Aramaic (*abba*) and then in Greek (*patēr*). "Abba" (see Mark 14:36; Luke 11:2), expressive of an especially tender relationship with God as Father, is likened to the affectionate use of "Papa." All in all, the Spirit **sent forth** initiates the kind of spontaneous recognition that accompanies a homecoming, the spiritual reunion with one's father experienced at the core of one's being, the heart. Such a cry belongs not to a slave but to a son, a son who is an heir to all the Father's benevolent love.

4:8. When ye knew not God, that is, before being liberated ("redeem[ed]," 4:5) and adopted to sonship (4:7), the Galatians were slaves or in bondage to masters (see 1 Cor. 12:2; 1 Thess. 4:5) that **are no gods**. When the Galatians were pagans, they thought that the beings they worshiped were gods, but when they became Christians, they learned better.

4:9–10. As with the questions of 3:1–3, Paul appealed to the Galatians' experience when they became Christians (see 4:6–7). In verses 8–10, the question, **how turn ye again …?** (v. 9), drew a comparison between their former allegiance to the feasts and observances of the pagan calendar of public emperor worship and their acceptance of the Jewish calendar of the Mosaic covenant. **The weak and beggarly elements** (see discussion on 4:3), regardless of whether they belonged to pagan or Jewish religion, demanded the observance of sacred dates and rites. Paul declared that they were impotent and impoverished because they had no power to liberate, only to enslave: **ye desire again … bondage**. Legalistic trust in rituals, moral achievement, law, good works, or even cold, dead orthodoxy may invigorate a personal sense of achievement, but these achievements fall under the curse of the law and far short of sonship. **Days** (v. 10), such as the Sabbath and the Day of Atonement (the tenth day of Tishri; see Lev. 16:29–34), **months, and times**, such as new moons (see Num. 28:11–15; Isa. 1:13–14), Passover (Exod. 12:18) and the Feast of Firstfruits (Lev. 23:10), **and years**, such as the Sabbath year (see Lev. 25:4), had never been, and can never be, in themselves means of salvation or sanctification. The

Pharisees meticulously observed all these to gain merit before God.

4:11. In vain characterizes primarily the failed potential of Paul's labor invested in those who returned to the old covenant law but secondarily characterizes the equivocal failure of pagan and Jewish religion. In Paul's argument, changing from one to the other is merely a shift in the duties of a slave and is empty of the emancipating sonship Christ won on the cross and confirmed through His Spirit.

G. Appeal to Enter into Freedom from Law (4:12–20)

4:12. Paul adjured the **brethren** (see discussion on 1:2) with a real, not a rhetorical, request: **be as I am**, which implies "not as I was" (see 1:13–14). Some of the Galatians were moving to that which Paul had been in Judaism, not to what he had become in Christ (2:19–21). When Paul was with them, he was like them; they enjoyed harmonious Christian fellowship apart from any observance of the Mosaic law. With the coming of the Judaizers with their introduction of the Mosaic law and animosity toward Paul had brought discord to the Galatians and their relations with Paul. In favor of returning to better times (see 4:13), Paul easily dismissed any notion of personal injury.

4:13. On the basis of 4:15 and 6:11, a strong suggestion for Paul's **infirmity of the flesh** is recurring or chronic eye trouble. Others have suggested malaria or epilepsy. **I preached … at the first** refers to the occasion when Paul visited Galatia on his first missionary journey (see Acts 13:14–14:23).

4:14. Received me implies that under the influence of Judaizers, the Galatians had changed their attitude toward him. In the Mediterranean world, superstition and corollary social conventions were attached to encounters with illness and disease. For example, the Greek word for **rejected** is literally "spit out." Although a gesture of disrespect, it was a convention of defense in the presence of disease, averting a demon or warding off the "evil eye." The Galatians treated Paul just the opposite; they received him as a messenger (**an angel**) of God, even the representation of Jesus Christ. Paul's argument is clear: if they had at first seen Paul as God's agent, indeed, as the very representation of Christ, they should now have no problem imitating Paul and becoming more Christlike (Witherington, *Grace in Galatia*, p. 312).

4:15. Where is then the blessedness you spake of? Because of the restraints of legalistic Judaism, the Galatians had lost their blessing and joy. **Plucked out your own eyes** may legitimately gain significance if Paul's infirmity was situated in his eyes, but even so, the hyperbole stressed the Galatians' willingness, for his benefit, to part with that which was most precious to them (see Mark 2:4, where the same verb is used of digging through a roof).

4:16 – 18. Your enemy (v. 16) marks the dramatic shift that had come to pass. **They** (v. 17), the Judaizers (see 2:4, 12), **zealously affect you**. The language of zeal, often associated with the law, alludes to the exclusionary not inclusive effect of the law. As the law shut out Gentiles, it made Gentiles zealous for inclusion. The exclusion may have made Paul and some of the Galatians "enemies," for it put them on opposite sides of the law.

4:19 – 20. My little children (v. 19), although more affectionate, is in keeping with Paul's tenderhearted use of "brethren" and his frequent use of "we." Given the distance that had come between him and some of the Galatians, this expression of affection is a remarkable testament to Paul's selfless, pastoral heart. It is akin to a parent's affirming love in the face of a child's hasty "I hate you!" (for Paul's affectionate relationship to his converts, see Acts 20:37 – 38; Phil. 4:1; 1 Thess. 2:7 – 8). The expression occurs only here in Paul's writings but is common in John's (see, e.g., John 13:33; 1 John 2:1; 3:7). Paul expressed the goal of his ministry with **until Christ be formed in you** (see Rom. 8:29; Eph. 4:13, 15; Col. 1:27). That goal was real to Paul's own experience (see 2:19 – 20) and explains the eclipse of his own ego in the way he handled relationships of great personal interest.

H. The Allegory of Hagar and Sarah (4:21 – 31)

4:21 – 23. Here Paul was teaching all the Galatians, but he wanted the special attention of those among them who were near to embracing the law. Abraham had **two sons** (v. 22). Ishmael was born to the slave woman, Hagar (Gen. 16:1 – 16), and Isaac to the free woman, Sarah (Gen. 21:2 – 5). In the allegory to follow, Hagar and Sarah illustrate law and grace, with their sons corresponding to bondage and freedom in as much as they contrast that which is born after the flesh and after the promise (the Spirit; see 4:24 – 26, 28).

4:24. Which things are an allegory, or literally "allegorized" (Greek, *allēgoreō*). This is the only place in Scripture where this word occurs. The Sarah-Hagar account is not an allegory in the sense that it was nonhistorical but in the sense that Paul used the events to illustrate a theological truth. For the word **covenants**, see discussion on 3:15. **Mount Sinai** is where the old covenant was established, with its law governing Israel's life (see Exod. 19:2; 20:1 – 17).

4:25. Answereth to Jerusalem which now is. Jerusalem could be equated with Mount Sinai because it represented the center of Judaism, which was still under bondage to the law issued at Mount Sinai.

4:26. Jerusalem which is above represents the opposite of Jerusalem below. This contrast between heavenly and earthly Jerusalem is not unique to Paul. Rabbinical teaching held that the Jerusalem above was the heavenly archetype that would be let down to earth in the messianic period (see Rev. 21:2). Here it refers to the heavenly city of God in contrast to the "Jerusalem which now is" (4:25). Elsewhere in the New Testament, it symbolizes the place of Christ's reign and the realm of Christian citizenship. Thus, **the mother of us all** identifies Jerusalem as the spiritual complement to Sarah and as the mother of the freeborn citizens of the heavenly Jerusalem; Christians are her children.

4:27. Paul applied Isaiah's (54:1) joyful promise to exiled Jerusalem (in her exile **barren** of children) to the ingathering of believers through the gospel, by which "Jerusalem's" children have become many.

4:28. Even **as Isaac was**, Christians are now **children of promise** by virtue of God's promise (see 3:29; Rom. 9:8).

4:29. Persecuted him that was born after the Spirit is most likely suggested by Genesis 21:9 (see

Ps. 83:5–6). **So it is now** points to the opposition and persecution suffered for the gospel (see Acts 13:50; 14:2–5, 19; 1 Thess. 2:14–16).

4:30. Cast out the bondwoman. Paul used Sarah's words in Genesis 21:10 as the scriptural basis for teaching the Galatians to put the Judaizers out of the church.

4:31. We are not children of the bondwoman. The believer is not enslaved to the law but is a child of promise and lives by faith (see 3:7, 29).

IV. Practical: Practice of the Life of Liberty and Faith (5:1–6:10)

A. Exhortation to Freedom (5:1–12)

5:1. Made us free is emphasized by its position in the Greek sentence. Paul also prominently underscored its thematic importance by opening the sentence with "the freedom believers enjoy in Christ." The freedom spoken of here is freedom from the entangling bonds of the law. In classical Greek, the verb **entangled** means "to be held, caught or entangled in." **The yoke of bondage** points to the burden of the rigorous demands of the law as the means for gaining God's favor—an intolerable burden for sinful man (see Acts 15:10–11).

5:2–4. To be **circumcised** (v. 2) as a condition for God's acceptance represented a grave choice in two ways. First, Paul said, **Christ shall profit you nothing,** for such a condition nullified the work of Christ on the cross, the very grace of God (see 2:21). Second, one who accepted such a condition would become **a debtor to do the whole law** (v. 3; see 3:10; James 2:10); its demand cannot be satisfied through selective submission nor tokens of compliance (circumcision). The Galatians were **fallen from grace** (v. 4) because they no longer relied on it and no longer put their **faith** (believed) in it. Accepting circumcision and the was tantamount to saying that the cross of Jesus Christ was inadequate and grace was insufficient. Gaining God's favor by observing the law and receiving it by grace are mutually exclusive (see 2 Peter 3:17).

5:5. The hope of righteousness refers to God's final verdict of "not guilty," assured presently to the believer by faith and by the sanctifying work of the Holy Spirit. This is one of the few eschatological statements in Galatians (see Rom. 5:1–5; 8:10–21; 2 Cor. 5:5; Eph. 1:13–14).

5:6. Neither circumcision availeth any thing, nor uncircumcision (see 5:2; 2:21; 6:15; 1 Cor. 7:19), for they are external and irrelevant to the expression of faith. Faith works from the inside out. The operation of faith is not invisible; it shows itself at work in love. Therefore, **faith which worketh by love** speaks not of a faith that is mere intellectual assent (see James 2:18–19) but of a living trust in God's grace that expresses itself in acts of love (see 1 Thess. 1:3).

5:7–8. Ye did run well (v. 7), before the Judaizers (see Introduction: "Background") hindered them. Paul was fond of depicting the Christian life as a race (see, e.g., 2:2; Phil. 2:16). The picture of a race preempted by onlookers who obstruct the progress of those running is vividly contrasted with God, **him that calleth you** (v. 8). The metaphor pictures God inspiring them to run and run well. **Persuasion** refers to the Judaizers' coaxing to abandon the race; Paul was coaching them to continue the race.

5:9. Here Paul used a proverb to stress the pervasive effect of Judaism. When the word **leaven** is used as a symbol in the Bible, it indicates evil or false teaching (see discussion on Mark 8:15), except in Matthew 13:33.

5:10. Through the Lord expresses the source of Paul's optimism even as it alludes to the unseen work of God in the Galatians' hearts through the Spirit and the truth (see 5:7). **Whosoever he be** is here probably generic, ruling out any exception. Elsewhere, Paul used the plural to identify the agitators (the Judaizers), as in 1:7; 5:12.

5:11. Brethren (see discussion on 1:2) is here an alert to capture the Galatians' attention as Paul took up an allegation, presumably the false charge that he preached circumcision. If such were the case, Paul asked, why the persecution and why were his opponents offended by the cross? In short, Paul asked, would not **the offence of the cross** (see Rom. 9:32–33; 1 Cor. 1:23) disappear if he preached circumcision?

5:12. The allegation that Paul himself preached circumcision was so outrageous that he could imagine only one form of circumcision that he would preach: **I would they were even cut off**. The Greek word "to cut off" or "to castrate" connotes that the agitators should go even further and make themselves eunuchs. F. F. Bruce (*Commentary on Galatians*, p. 238) points out the term identifies eunuchs in Deuteronomy 23:1 (Septuagint), where they are debarred from the congregation of the Lord. The Galatians would be better off if these Judaizers who were preaching circumcision were themselves "cut off." In Philippians 3:2, Paul used a related word to describe the same sort of people as "the false circumcision." His sarcasm is evident.

B. Life by the Spirit, Not by the Flesh (5:13–26)

5:13. Use not liberty for an occasion to the flesh (see Rom. 6:1; 1 Peter 2:16). Liberty is not license but rather freedom to serve God and each other in love.

5:14. All the law is fulfilled. Doing to others what you would have them do to you expresses the spirit and intention of "the law and the prophets" (Matt. 7:12; see Mark 12:31). The words **as thyself** are not a condition but a standard. The meaning of "as thyself" is explained by the Golden Rule (Luke 6:31): treat others the way you would have them treat you. This is the great doctrine that must not be diminished under the banner of defending either the law or some other doctrine in the service of God. Jesus significantly linked the application of this doctrine to the first great commandment, "Thou shalt love the Lord thy God" (Luke 10:27).

5:15. Paul represented those involved in quarrels and controversy as wild animals that **bite and devour one another**. Here, in contrast to 5:13–14, Paul addressed the potential harm of partisan strife, presumably incited by doctrinal disputes among the Galatians over the teachings of the Judaizers (see Introduction: "Background"). Untempered by love, such acrimony is fueled by the flesh, not by the Spirit (see 5:16, 18). Seeking to attain status with God and man by mere observance of the law breeds a self-righteous, critical spirit.

5:16. Walk is a meaningful Jewish metaphor that Paul frequently used to express the way one conducts oneself or lives. The present tense, "go on living," prescribes a pattern of habitual conduct. Living by the promptings and power of the Spirit is the key to conquering sinful desires (see 5:25; Rom. 8:2–4). Paul used various metaphors to communicate the necessity of submitting to the Spirit's control (see 5:18, "be led"). In addition to "Walk in the Spirit" (see Rom. 8:4), Paul admonished Christians to "mind [set the mind on] ... the things of the Spirit" (Rom. 8:5) and to "be filled with the Spirit" (Eph. 5:18). All these expressions underscore the occupying and controlling influence of the Holy Spirit as the defining reality of the Christian life.

5:17. Are contrary the one to the other. See Romans 7:15–23; 1 Peter 2:11.

5:18. Led of the Spirit expresses the guidance and direction the Spirit gives to those who follow or willingly submit to the Spirit's supervision (see 5:16; Rom. 8:14). Under the supervision of the Spirit, one is **not under the law**, not under the bondage of trying to please God by minute observance of the law for salvation or sanctification (see Rom. 8:4; discussion on Rom. 6:14).

5:19–21. For other lists of vices, see 1 Corinthians 6:9–10; Ephesians 5:5; Revelation 22:15.

5:22–23. For other lists of virtues, see 2 Corinthians 6:6; Ephesians 4:2; 5:9; Colossians 3:12–15. Christian character is produced by the Holy Spirit, not by the mere moral discipline of trying to live by law. Paul made it clear that justification by faith does not result in libertinism. The indwelling Holy Spirit produces Christian virtues in the believer's life.

5:22. Fruit of the Spirit. Compare the singular "fruit" with the plural "works" (5:19).

5:23. No law. See 1 Timothy 1:9.

5:24. Crucified the flesh. See 2:20; 6:14.

5:25. Walk in (Greek, *stoicheō*) is a military term meaning "to keep in step with" or "to walk in line with." A different Greek word for "walk" (*peripateō*) was used in 5:16, meaning "to walk" or "to live" and involving one's conduct. Interestingly, Paul used the noun (*stoicheia*) translated "elements" in 4:3, 9, to refer to elementary principles of religion (pagan and Jewish). Paul purposely used the verb (*stoicheō*) here to suggest that the Galatians did not have to align themselves with any elementary principles when they aligned themselves with the Spirit of God.

C. Call for Mutual Help (6:1–10)

6:1. In addition to expressing the affection of familial brotherly love, **Brethren** (see discussion on 1:2), as often in this letter, marks the opening of a new thought or section. For a contrast that further defines **ye which are spiritual**, see 1 Corinthians 3:1–3. **Restore** (Greek, *katartizō*; see Matt. 4:21) is used elsewhere for setting bones, mending nets, or bringing factions together.

6:2. Bear ye one another's burdens. The translation "burden" here and in 6:5 represents two different Greek nouns. In 6:5, the term requires that each one is to bear their own normal load. Believers are to help others, however, when they have an overload or are overburdened. The emphasis here is on moral burdens (see 6:1; Rom. 15:1–3). **The law of Christ** (see *KJV Study Bible* note on 1 Cor. 9:21) cannot be legislated but is articulated by the Spirit, the Spirit of His Son (4:5–6; Rom. 8:2), that engenders the character of what Christ would do, or the measure of Christlikeness in one's daily walk.

6:4. Let every man prove his own work. The emphasis here is on personal responsibility (see 1 Cor. 11:28; 2 Cor. 13:5). The alternative is to "prove" (Greek "test" or "examine") the work of others, which can lead to comparison, fault-finding, and **rejoicing** by subtraction. Here the word "rejoicing" points to a proper "pride" that is grounded in the substance of one's own work. Paul may also have been implying that one should keep his "rejoicing" to himself and not direct it toward others. In 6:14, Paul featured the sure ground of his pride, or "glory," in the work of Jesus Christ and the cross and nothing other.

6:5. Bear his own burden. The **For** at the beginning of this verse connects it with 6:4. Each of us is responsible before God. The reference may be to the future judgment (the verb is in the future tense), when every person will give an account to God (see Rom. 14:12; 2 Cor. 5:10).

6:6. Communicate unto him that teacheth in all good things elucidates a general principle (see Luke 10:7; Matt. 10:10; 1 Tim. 5:18) calling those that are taught to support the teacher (see Phil. 4:14–19).

6:7–9. Mocked (v. 7) translates a Greek word that visualizes a gesture of contempt: "to thumb the nose at." Paul warned that God will not ignore such disdain. **Whatsoever a man soweth, that shall he also reap** (see 2 Cor. 9:6). As verses 8–9 show, the principle applies not only negatively but also positively (see Rom. 8:13). On the negative side, sowing to the flesh reaps **corruption** (v. 8; see 5:19–21). On the positive side, sowing to the Spirit reaps **life everlasting**. In 5:21, Paul wrote of inheriting "the kingdom of God," here of reaping "life everlasting." The first focuses on the realm (sphere, context) that will be inherited (as Israel inherited the Promised Land); the second focuses on the blessed life that will be enjoyed in that realm. **Weary in well doing** speaks of losing one's motivation when the payoffs ("harvest") for doing what is right are not timely. Keep doing what is good and right, Paul said; do not lose heart when you cannot see the results. A harvest will come in due season.

6:10. Especially unto them who are of the household of faith (see 1 Tim. 5:8). Sow good without discrimination, but make sure to sow within the household of faith, the fellowship of believers.

V. Conclusion (6:11–18)

6:11. The words **how large a letter** may have been used for emphasis or, as some have suggested, because Paul had poor eyesight (see discussion on 4:13). **With mine own hand** indicates that the letter up to this point had probably been dictated to a scribe, after which Paul took the pen in his own hand and finished the letter (see Rom. 16:22; 1 Cor. 1:1; 16:21; 2 Thess. 3:17; Col. 4:18).

6:12–13. Constrain you to be circumcised (v. 12) points to not only the pressure but the conditional necessity that must be met before acceptance and inclusion may be experienced (see 2:3).

Lest they should suffer persecution. By advocating circumcision (see 5:11), the Judaizers (see Introduction: "Background") were less apt to experience opposition from the Jewish opponents of Christianity and were thinking only of themselves.

6:14. Glory, save in the cross. See 1 Corinthians 1:31; 2:2. **The world**. All that is against God. **Crucified unto me, and I unto the world**. See 2:19–20; 5:24; see also discussions on James 4:4; 1 John 2:15.

6:15. In Christ, a person undergoes a transformation and becomes **a new creature**, an entirely new being. Creation again takes place (see 2 Cor. 5:17).

6:16. This rule. See 6:14–15. **Peace … and mercy**. See Psalms 125:5; 128:6. **The Israel of God**, or the Christian Jews. If the conjunction is translated "even" instead of "and," the phrase stands in contrast to "Israel after the flesh" (1 Cor. 10:18; a literal rendering of the Greek for "national Israel"). The New Testament church, made up of believing Jews and Gentiles, is included in the seed of Abraham and is an heir according to the promise (3:29; see Rom. 9:6; Phil. 3:3).

6:17. In ancient times, the Greek word **marks** (*stigma*) was used of the brand marks that identified slaves or animals. Paul's suffering (stoning, Acts 14:19; beatings, Acts 16:22; 2 Cor. 11:25; illness, 2 Cor. 12:7; Gal. 4:13–14) marked him as a "servant of Christ" (1:10; see 2 Cor. 4:10).

6:18. Amen. A word of confirmation often used at the close of a doxology or benediction.

THE EPISTLE OF PAUL THE APOSTLE TO THE EPHESIANS

Introduction

Author, Date, and Place of Composition

The author identifies himself as Paul (1:1; 3:1; see also 3:7, 13; 4:1; 6:19–20). Some have taken the absence of Paul's usual personal greetings and the verbal similarity of many parts to Colossians, among other reasons, as grounds for doubting Paul's authorship. This was probably a circular letter, however, intended for other churches in addition to the one in Ephesus (see discussions on 1:1, 15; 6:21–23). Paul may have written Ephesians about the same time as Colossians, circa AD 60, while he was in prison in Rome (see 3:1; 4:1; 6:20).

The City of Ephesus

Ephesus was the most important city in western Asia Minor (modern-day Turkey). It had a harbor that, at that time, opened into the Cayster River, which in turn emptied into the Aegean Sea (see map, *Zondervan KJV Study Bible*, p. 1694). Because it was also at an intersection of major trade routes, Ephesus became a commercial center. It boasted a pagan temple dedicated to the Roman goddess Diana (Greek Artemis; see Acts 19:23–31). Paul made Ephesus a center for evangelism for two years and three months (see discussion on Acts 19:10), and the church there apparently flourished for some time but later needed the warning of Revelation 2:1–7.

Theme and Theological Message

Unlike several of Paul's other letters, Ephesians does not address any particular error or heresy. Paul wrote to expand the horizons of his readers, so that they might better understand the dimensions of God's eternal purpose and grace and come to appreciate the high goals God has for the church. Indeed, Ephesians may well be called Paul's chief theology of the church. To view the church as God does, one must appreciate the message of this grand epistle.

The letter opens with a sequence of statements about God's blessings, which are interspersed with a remarkable variety of expressions drawing attention to God's wisdom, forethought, and purpose. Paul emphasized that believers have been saved not only for their personal benefit but also to bring praise and glory to God. The climax of God's purpose, in "the fulness of times" (1:10), is to bring all things in the universe together under Christ. It is crucially important that Christians realize this, so in 1:15–23, Paul prayed for their understanding (a second prayer occurs in 3:14–21).

Having explained God's great goals for the church, Paul proceeded to show the steps toward their fulfillment. First, God has reconciled individuals to Himself as an act of grace (see 2:1–10). Second, God has reconciled these saved individuals to each other, Christ having broken down the barriers through His own death (2:11–22). God has done something beyond even that: He has united these reconciled individuals in one body, the church. This is a "mystery" not fully known until it was revealed to Paul (see 3:1–6). Paul was then able to state even more clearly what God has intended for the church, namely, that it be the means by which He displays His "manifold wisdom" (3:10) to "the principalities and powers in heavenly places" (3:10; see 3:7–13). The repetition of "heavenly places" (1:3, 20; 2:6; 3:10; 6:12) makes it clear that Christian existence is not merely on an earthly plane. It receives its meaning and significance from heaven, where Christ is exalted at the right hand of God (see 1:20).

Nevertheless, Christian life is lived out on earth, where the practical daily life of the believer continues to work out the purposes of God. The ascended Lord gave gifts to the members of His church to enable them to minister to one another and so promote unity and maturity (see 4:1–16). The unity of the church under the headship of Christ foreshadows the uniting of "all things ... in heaven, and ... on earth" (1:10) under Christ. The new life of purity and mutual deference stands in contrast to the old way of life without Christ (see 4:17–6:9). Those who are "strong in the Lord" (6:10) have victory over the Evil One in the great spiritual conflict, especially through the power of prayer (see 6:10–20).

Outline

Bibliography

Barclay, William. *The Letters to the Galatians and Ephesians.* Daily Study Bible. Rev. ed. Philadelphia: Westminster, 1976.

Barth, Marcus. *Ephesians.* The Anchor Bible. 2 vols. Garden City, NY: Doubleday, 1974.

Bruce, F. F. *The Epistles to the Colossians, Philemon, and the Ephesians.* The New International Commentary on the New Testament. Grand Rapids, MI: Eerdmans, 1984.

Hendricksen, William. *Galatians, Ephesians, Philippians, Colossians, and Philemon.* New Testament Commentary. Grand Rapids, MI: Baker, 1995.

Martin, Ralph. *Ephesians, Colossians, and Philemon. Interpretation: A Bible Commentary for Teaching and Preaching.* Edited by James L. Mays. Louisville: John Knox, 1991.

Snodgrass, Klyne. *Ephesians.* Grand Rapids, MI: Zondervan, 1996.

Exposition

I. Greetings (1:1–2)

1:1. An apostle is one specially commissioned by Christ (see discussions on Mark 6:30; 1 Cor. 1:1; Heb. 3:1). **By the will of God** stresses not only Paul's authority under God but also anticipates the strong emphasis on God's sovereign plan and purpose that Paul made later in this chapter and the book. The destination, **at Ephesus**, is not found in the oldest available Greek manuscripts, which adds to the opinion that the letter may have been intended as a circular letter to several churches, in particular the chief city in the vicinity, Ephesus (see discussions on 1:15; 6:21–23; Acts 19:10). Interestingly, the oldest Greek manuscripts retain the prescript, "to the Ephesians." This phrase **in Christ Jesus** (or a similar one) occurs eleven times in 1:1–13. It refers to the spiritual union of Christ with believers, which Paul often symbolized with the metaphor "body [of Christ]" (see, e.g., 1:23; 2:16; 4:4, 12, 16; 5:23, 30).

1:2. Grace be to you, and peace are words that were commonly used in the greetings of secular letters. The words that follow show that Paul intended a spiritual dimension. Paul used the word "grace" twelve times and "peace" eight times in Ephesians.

II. The Divine Purpose: The Glory and Headship of Christ (1:3–14)

1:3–14. All one sentence in Greek, this section is often called a "doxology" because it recites what God has done and is an expression of worship to honor Him. Paul spoke first of the blessings through the Father (v. 3), then of those through the Son (vv. 4–13a), and finally of those through the Holy Spirit (1:13b–14). Strikingly, such a long sentence (unparalleled in Paul's letters) is not only typical of doxologies, but its advance, clause by clause, is marked by repeated reference to God's action or decision in, through, or by Christ (or an equivalent).

1:3 in Christ	1:10 in Christ
1:4 in him	1:10 in him
1:5 by Jesus Christ	1:11 In whom
1:6 in the beloved	1:12 in Christ
1:7 In whom	1:13 In whom
1:7 through his blood	1:13 in whom
1:9 in himself (Greek, "in him")	

Clearly, the scope of all of God the Father's (v. 3) redemptive will and work, from beginning to end, in heaven and on earth (compare vv. 3–4 and v. 10) is focused on and featured in the person of Jesus Christ.

1:3. God is worthy of blessing. Moreover, God is hailed as **Blessed** at the opening of the doxology (1:3–14), because He has become expressly recognized and honored as Father: the **Father of our Lord Jesus Christ** (see John 20:17 and discussion) and, therefore, the Father of those who know sonship by virtue of the Son (see 1:5). The sequence of "Blessed" and **blessings … in Christ** fathoms God as Father through the privileged and redemptive (**spiritual**) blessings met in the Son (the Christ). Jewish people used the word "bless" to express both God's kindness to believers and their thanks or praise to Him. Appropriately, the doxology to God's glorious redemptive work in the Son ends with "the praise of his glory" (1:14). **Heavenly places** occurs five times in Ephesians, emphasizing Paul's perception that in the exaltation of Christ (His resurrection and enthronement at God's right hand) and in the Christian's union with the exalted Christ, ultimate issues are involved—issues that pertain to the divine realm and that, in the final analysis, are worked out in and from that realm. At stake are God's eternal eschatological purpose (see 3:11) and the titanic conflict between God and the powerful spiritual forces arrayed against Him—a purpose and a conflict that come to focus in the history of redemption.

Here Paul asserted that through their union with the exalted Christ, Christians have already been made beneficiaries of every spiritual blessing that belongs to and comes from the heavenly places. Paul proclaimed Christ's exaltation to that realm and His elevation over all other powers and titles so that He rules over all for the sake of His church (1:20–22). According to 2:6, those who have been made alive with Christ (2:5) share in Christ's exaltation and enthronement in heaven. Thus, by gathering Gentiles and Jews into one body of Christ (the church), God triumphantly displays His "manifold wisdom" (3:10) to "the principalities and powers in heavenly places" (3:10). As a result, the spiritual struggle of the saints here and now is not so much against "flesh and blood" (6:12) as against the great spiritual forces that war against God in heaven.

1:4. The word **chosen** points to God's elective decision implemented in Christ. Divine election is a constant theme in Paul's letters (see Rom. 8:29–33; 9:6–26; 11:5, 7, 28; 16:13; Col. 3:12; 1 Thess. 1:4; 2 Thess. 2:13; Titus 1:1). In this chapter, it is emphasized in the following ways: (1) **He hath chosen us in him**; (2) "predestined us … by Jesus Christ" (1:5); (3) "In whom also we have obtained an inheritance" (1:11); (4) "being predestined according to [His] purpose" (1:11). God's elective decision was fixed in Christ **before the foundation of the world** (see John 17:24). **Holy and without blame** (see 5:27 for the same pair of words) is used of the church, the bride of Christ. Holiness is the result, not the basis, of God's choosing. It refers both to the holiness imparted to the believer because of Christ and to the believer's personal sanctification (see discussion on 1 Cor. 1:2). Grammatically, the words **in love** (or "by love") may be construed with either what follows (1:5) or with what precedes (in v. 4). Elsewhere (3:17; 4:2, 15–16), "in love" stands at the end of a sentence. Accordingly, here it probably is to qualify both God's elective decision in Christ and the appearance of those whom God has chosen (Barth, *Ephesians*, vol. 1, pp. 79–80).

1:5. Adoption was common among the Greeks and Romans, who granted the adopted son all the privileges of a natural son, including inheritance rights. On God's part, our adoption to such privileged sonship was not an afterthought but a decision predetermined, or **predestined** (Greek, *proorizō*; "to decide upon beforehand"), to become effective for us **by**, or "through," **Jesus Christ**. Christ is the means of God's election ("in him," 1:4) and adoption ("by Jesus Christ"). Christians are adopted sons by grace (**adoption … by Jesus Christ to himself, according to the good pleasure of his will**; compare 1:6); Christ, however, is God's Son by nature. The Greek term for "adoption" occurs four other times in the New Testament (Rom. 8:15, 23; 9:4; Gal. 4:5).

1:6. All the aforementioned benevolence of God is the glory of His grace and is worthy of **praise** (see 1:14; 4:30; Rom. 3:24; Titus 2:14). **Hath made us accepted** translates the verb form of the noun **grace**.

The sense may be rendered, "grace by which he favored [graced] us in the beloved."

1:7–8. Redemption (v. 7) was familiar to the Ephesians. In the Greco-Roman practice of redemption, slaves were freed by the payment of a ransom. Similarly, the ransom necessary to free sinners from the bondage of sin and the resulting curse imposed by the law (see Gal. 3:13) was the death of Christ (**through his blood**; see 2:13; 1 Peter 1:18–19). The word "redemption" is linked and further explained by the words "the forgiveness of sins" (the cancellation of debt) through the vast resources of God's grace. God exercised His lavish and extravagant disbursement of such riches (**abounded toward us**; v. 8) **in all wisdom and prudence**. Far from foolish, the objective and outcome of God's action, as seen in 1:9–12, verifies God's wisdom and prudence.

1:9–11. The mystery (v. 9; see discussions on Rom. 11:25; Col. 1:26) of God's own counsel (**his will**), previously unknown, has been revealed. It accords with His benevolent purpose in Christ: **That in the dispensation of the fulness of times ... in Christ** (lit., "in him"; v. 10). Paul used a significant term (**the fulness of times ... in Christ**) here that not only has the idea of leadership but also was often used of adding up a column of figures. A contemporary way of putting it might be to say that in a world of confusion, where things do not "add up" or make sense, one looks forward to the time when everything will be brought into meaningful relationship under the headship of Christ. With the words **in him** comes the reverberation that Christ is the center of God's plan. This point is amplified in verse 11 (**In whom**). Whether the universe or the individual Christian is in view, it is only in relationship to Christ that there is a meaningful future destiny. Paul went on to speak not of the world as a whole but of those who respond to God's call.

1:12. Who first trusted in Christ is probably a reference to those Jews who, like Paul, had become believers before many Gentiles had. For **to the praise of his glory**, see 1:6.

1:13–14. Ye also probably refers to the majority of the Ephesians, who were Gentiles. **Sealed** in those days was a mark of identification and denoted ownership. **The earnest** (v. 14; Greek, *arrabōn*; "deposit," "down payment," "pledge") is an assurance of what is promised or yet to come (see discussion on Rom. 8:23). The same word is used today in modern Greek of the wedding ring, the symbol of matrimonial pledges. The Holy Spirit is God's "earnest" that identifies and marks ("sealed") the believer as belonging to God.

III. Prayer That Christians May Realize God's Purpose and Power (1:15–23)

1:15–16. Wherefore (v. 15), or "therefore," points back to the doxology and sets Paul's apostolic and pastoral care squarely within the grand scope of God's salvation. What God has accomplished in Christ inspired Paul's intercession (see 1:17–22) and prayers for his readers to grow in their personal understanding of what God has done for them. Coming from one who had spent several years in Ephesus, **after I heard** seems strange. Paul may have been referring either to a greatly enlarged church there, many of whose members he did not know, or, if Ephesians was intended as a circular letter (see discussion on 1:1), to news from the whole area, only a part of which he had visited.

1:17. The God of our Lord Jesus Christ (see discussion on 1:3) **... knowledge of him** is the object of knowledge but not, as Paul made clear, in isolation from "our Lord Jesus Christ." **The spirit** points to a disposition or attitude (see Col. 1:9), not to the "giving" of the Holy Spirit (see 1:13–14). Nonetheless, it is the Spirit of God that generates the new person (4:23) and enables a deeper understanding of God (see 1 Cor. 2:7, 10). With the doxology of 1:3–14 close at hand, **the spirit of wisdom and [of] revelation** points to the believer's acquisition and expression of true understanding and insight into God's mystery made known. The practical side of such a disposition may be implied in Paul's indirect questions that follow: "what is the hope of his calling" (1:18), "what [are] the riches ... of his inheritance" (1:18), and "what is the ... greatness of his power" (1:19).

1:18. The eyes of your understanding is tantamount to "your mind" or "your inner awareness." **Hope** has an objective quality of certainty (see Rom. 8:25). It is the assurance of eternal life guaranteed by the present possession of the Holy Spirit (see 1:14; for **calling**, see Phil. 3:14; 2 Tim. 1:9; Heb. 3:1). **The glory of his inheritance in the saints** refers to either the inheritance the saints have from God (see 1:14; Col. 1:12) or the inheritance God receives, that is, the saints themselves. **Saints** identifies those whom God has called to be His own people, that is, all Christians (see 1:1, 15). The word carried the idea of dedication to a deity.

1:19–20. In verse 19, Paul piled term upon term to emphasize that the extraordinary divine force by which Jesus Christ was **raised** (v. 20) is the same power at work in and through believers (see 3:20). The expression **right hand** is symbolic for the place of highest honor and authority.

1:21. All principality ... every name that is named is inclusive. Paul deliberately calculated his wording here to draw within the scope of Christ's supremacy every conceivable power, natural or supernatural, whatever his contemporaries might imagine. In Paul's day, many people believed not only in the existence of angels and demons but also in that of other beings. Christ is above them all. **This world ... that which is to come**. Like the rabbinic teachers of his day, Paul distinguished between the present age, which is evil, and the future age when the Messiah will consummate His kingdom and there will be a completely righteous society on earth.

1:22. Under his feet further expresses the supremacy of Christ's authority (see Ps. 110:1). Psalm 8:5–6 emphasizes the destiny of man, and Hebrews 2:6–9 shows that ultimately it is the Son of Man who rules over everything (see Heb. 10:13). This is a certainty for the church. Christ, who is **head** of the church, is head over everything (see discussion on 1:10).

1:23. His body (see 2:16; 4:4, 12, 16; 5:23, 30) is Paul's metaphor for the church, all believers incorporated by and under the Head. In addition to the theological implication, an anatomical implication may be connected to 1:22: what is under His feet is

beneath His body. **Fulness ... filleth** explains that the church is the fullness of Christ, probably in the sense that it is filled by Him who fills all things.

IV. Steps toward the Fulfillment of God's Purpose (chaps. 2–3)

A. Salvation of Individuals by Grace (2:1–10)

2:1–10. In chapter 1, Paul wrote of the great purposes and plan of God, culminating in the universal headship of Christ (1:10), all of which is to be for "the praise of his glory" (1:14). He next proceeded to explain the steps by which God will accomplish His purposes, beginning with the salvation of individuals.

2:1–3. These verses describe the Ephesians' past moral and spiritual condition, separated from the life of God. Clearly, this is a condition of being spiritually dead, as they **walked according to the course** (lit., "age") **of this world** (v. 2; see "present evil age," Gal. 1:4) and its ruling **prince**. Satan is "the prince of this world" (see John 14:30). As prince of **the power** (lit., "dominion" or "authority") **of the air**, Satan is no mere earthbound enemy (see 6:12). Satan is a created, but not a human, being (see Job 1:6; Ezek. 28:15; discussion on Isa. 14:12–15). He is **spirit**, in contrast to human, or "flesh and blood" (6:12), and he operates (**worketh**) in ways discernible **in the children of disobedience**. The expression "children of" is a Semitic way of saying "characterized by." Paul used the expression twice, first of disobedience, then of wrath. The first summarizes human culpability in terms of cosmic opposition to God as it is marshaled and organized by the operation of the prince of "the course of this world." The second summarizes human culpability under the penalty of God's wrath. **We all** (v. 3), both Jews and Gentiles, **fulfilling the desires of the flesh and of the mind**, were rebellious and **were by nature the children of wrath** (see Rom. 1:18–20; 2:5; 9:22). In short, Paul wanted to show that the natural bent ("by nature") of the human condition aligns all humanity against God and warrants the penalty of His wrath.

2:4–5. But God (vv. 1–4); our condition that warrants God's anger is, by contrast, met with mercy from His great love, offered not because of any human merit but because of God's divine character. **Quickened us together with Christ** (v. 5) is literally, "made us alive together with Christ," and refers to the joint resurrection of both Jew and Gentile in the resurrection of Christ. This truth is expanded in Romans 6:1–10. **By grace ye are saved** summarizes these two verses. The scope of God's action to deliver children of disobedience and children of wrath is all of God's mercy and love through Jesus Christ, His grace.

2:6. Raised us up ... and made us sit together ... in Christ Jesus gives corroborating meaning to the words "quickened us together with Christ" (2:5). Here is a picture of full participation in the life of Christ through union with Christ. **Heavenly places** (see discussion on 1:3) is best defined by 1:19–21, a position of honor and authority at the right hand of God with Jesus. Paul pictures complete deliverance from "the prince of the power of the air" (2:2) through our union with Christ.

2:7. The word **That** indicates God's purpose. **In the ages to come** (see 1:21), probably referring to the future of eternal blessing with Christ, God will **shew** ("exhibit" or "prove") **the exceeding riches of his grace ... through Christ Jesus**. In view of 1:23 and 3:8–11, the church, "quickened," "raised," and seated "in heavenly places" (2:5–6), is the emblem of God's grace and belongs to God's demonstration to all men and all principalities and powers.

2:8. This verse is a major passage for understanding God's grace, that is, His kindness, unmerited favor, and forgiving love. **Are ye saved**. "Saved" has a wide range of meanings, including salvation from God's wrath, which all had incurred through sinfulness. The tense of the verb (also in 2:5) suggests a completed action, with emphasis on its present effect. **Through faith** (see Rom. 3:21–31 and discussions) establishes the necessity of faith in Christ as the only means of being made right with God. **And that not of yourselves** refers to God's act of saving. No human effort can contribute to salvation; it is the gift of God.

2:9. Not of works. One cannot earn salvation by "the deeds of the law" (Rom. 3:20, 28). Such a le-

galistic approach to salvation (or sanctification) is consistently condemned in Scripture. **Lest any man should boast**. No one can take credit for his or her salvation.

2:10. The Greek for the word **workmanship** (Greek, *poiēma*; "that which is made," see the English word *poem*, which is derived from the Greek word Paul uses here) sometimes has the connotation of a "work of art." **Before ordained** carries forward the theme of God's sovereign purpose and planning, seen in chapter 1.

B. Reconciliation of Jew and Gentile through the Cross (2:11–18)

2:11–22. From the salvation of individuals, Paul moved to another aspect of salvation in which God reconciles Jews and Gentiles, previously hostile peoples, not only to Himself but also to each other through Christ (vv. 11–16). Even more than that, God unites these now reconciled people in one body, a truth introduced in verses 19–22 and explained in chapter 3.

2:11. Wherefore refers to the state of those without Christ, described in 2:1–10. **Ye ... Gentiles in the flesh** addressed most of the Ephesians (see "ye also," 1:13). **Uncircumcision ... Circumcision** demarcates Gentiles and Jews. The rite of circumcision was applied to all Jewish male babies, so this physical act (**in the flesh made by hands**) was a clear distinction between Jew and Gentile. These distinctions "in the flesh"—the Gentile in the flesh ("birth") and the circumcision in the flesh ("body")—have been superceded by a new act of God: Jesus' death "in the flesh" made peace with God for both Jew and Gentile and therefore abolished distinctions between them (see 2:14).

2:12. At that time, or before salvation, stands in stark contrast to "But now" (2:13). **Without Christ ... without God** are expressions emphasizing the distance of unbelieving Gentiles from Israel, as well as from Christ. Paul did not diminish the inherent advantages of the Jews. **The covenants** point to God's blessings promised to and through the Jewish people (see discussion on Rom. 9:4).

2:13. The words **But now** not only pose a contrast with "at that time" (2:12) but also introduce the contrast between "without Christ" (2:12) and **in Christ**. **The blood of Christ** expresses the violent death of Christ as He poured out His lifeblood as a sacrifice (see 1:7).

2:14. He is our peace, who hath made both one means that believing Jews and believing Gentiles enter peace with God through Jesus Christ. If Gentile and Jews have peace with God on the same basis, the blood of Jesus Christ, there are no advantages (for Jews) or disadvantages (for Gentiles) "in the flesh" (2:11). Distinctions have been abolished "in his flesh" (2:15; or "by His death"). **The middle wall of partition** is a vivid description of the total religious isolation that Jews and Gentiles experienced from each other even in the temple.

2:15. Abolished ... the law is an advantage to obtaining peace with God. Since Matthew 5:17 and Romans 3:31 teach that God's moral standard expressed in the Old Testament law was not changed by the coming of Christ, what was abolished here was the effect of the specific **commandments contained in ordinances** in approaching God, on the one hand, and separating Jews from Gentiles, on the other. Observance of the Jewish law (circumcision, ritual cleanness, keeping the festivals) is not the basis of peace with God. The blood of Jesus reconciles (see 2:16; "our peace," 2:14) Gentile and Jew with God. Therefore, all distinctions (advantages or disadvantages) owing to "the flesh" (2:11) are abolished **in himself**, referring to the death of Christ. This makes possible the **one new man**: the united body of believers, the church.

2:16. One body. While this could possibly mean the body of Christ offered on the cross (see "in his flesh," 2:15), it refers to the "one new man" just mentioned, the body of believers.

2:17–18. Afar off ... nigh (v. 17) denotes Gentiles and Jews respectively. Paul made it clear that the Jew has no advantage over the Gentile if nearness or farness is judged "in the flesh" (2:11). Distance from God is bridged not by human effort but by the peace extended through Jesus Christ. The "one new man"

(2:15) has "one body" (2:16) with one Spirit. As the KJV rightly recognizes, the word "spirit" is here not the human spirit or an *esprit de corps*; it is the Holy Spirit (see 2:22; see also "one body, and one Spirit," 4:4).

C. Uniting of Jew and Gentile in One Household (2:19–22)

2:19. With the words **Now therefore**, Paul introduced a comprehensive conclusion to the whole passage. He indicated that the unity described in 2:19–22 is based on what Christ did through His death, described in 2:14–18. **Ye** indicates that Paul had the Gentiles at Ephesus particularly in mind here. **Fellowcitizens ... the household of God** are two powerful metaphors Paul used to communicate the dramatic shift in status and privilege that "outsiders" acquire through Christ. In the first metaphor, the contrast of **strangers and foreigners** with "fellowcitizens" pictures an entire class of disparate people who are not enfranchised with the rights and privileges belonging to the enviable class of equal citizens. "Outsiders" are now "insiders" through Jesus Christ. In the second metaphor, Paul's teaching on "reception" is more intimate. Outsiders are accepted into the family of God. The "household" (Greek, *oikeios*; "belonging to a family or house") in ancient times was what today might be called an extended family. Paul later extended this metaphor of belonging in the direction of a building, turning the inhabitants of God's household into constituent parts of God's house, His temple (see 2:21). It is not by accident that Paul appropriated Greek words formed from the root of "household" (-*oik*-): "built on the foundation" (*epoikodomeō*, 2:20), "building" (*oikodomē*, 2:21), "built together" (*sunoikodomeō*, 2:22), and "habitation" or "dwelling" (*katoikētērion*, 2:22). His readers would not have missed the connections.

2:20–21. The word **foundation** (v. 20) offers further metaphorical language to convey the idea of a solid, integrated structure. **The apostles and prophets** probably refers to the founding work of the early Christian apostles and prophets as they preached and taught God's word (see 1 Cor. 3:10–11). The **corner stone** (see 1 Peter 2:6) as in Isaiah 28:16, which uses the same term in its pre-Christian Greek translation (the Septuagint), refers to a foundation with a "tested" stone at the corner. Such a stone is foundational to the entire structure as the load-bearing stone that forms the plumb of the entire edifice. Christ is the cornerstone, and **In [Him] all the building[is] fitly framed together** (for "fitly framed together," see 4:16). This passage and 4:16 speak of the close relationship between believers. **Groweth** gives a description of a building under construction and conveys the sense of the dynamic growth of the church. Paul used the metaphor of **a holy temple**, thereby indicating the purpose ("to become") for which God has established His church. This is the temple that is a worthy "habitation" (2:22) for God.

2:22. A habitation of God describes the church. The church is to be a people or community in whom the Holy Spirit dwells.

D. Revelation of God's Wisdom through the Church (3:1–13)

3:1–13. Having saved people individually by His grace (2:1–10) and having reconciled them to each other as well as to Himself through the sacrificial death of Christ (2:11–22), God unites them on an equal basis in one body, the church. This step in God's eternal plan was not fully revealed in previous times. Paul calls it a "mystery" (vv. 3–4).

3:1. For this cause reaches back to all that Paul explained in the preceding chapter about what God has done, notably the inclusion of the Gentiles. Indeed, it was for this cause that Paul was called to be an apostle to the Gentiles (see 3:2; Rom. 15:15–16; Gal. 2:7–9; Acts 9:15), a **prisoner … for you Gentiles.** Paul was under house arrest at this time (see Acts 28:16, 30). **Of Jesus Christ** is shorthand for the fact that Paul was imprisoned because of his obedience to Christ's calling (see Acts 9:15–16) to this great cause. This verse was probably meant to begin an intercessory prayer (see 3:14), but Paul paused to further explain his ministry (see 2:7; "dispensation

of grace," 3:2) as it belongs to "the mystery" (3:4). He resumed his initial thought in 3:14.

3:2. The expression **If ye have heard** contains a Greek conjunction used to introduce a justifiable assumption and may be rendered, "Surely you have heard" (Barth, *Ephesians*, vol. 1, p. 328). Most of the Ephesians would have heard of Paul's ministry because of his long stay there earlier. If this was a circular letter (see discussion on 1:1), however, the other churches may not have known much about it from Paul himself. **Dispensation** (Greek, *oikonomia*; "administration," "stewardship," "plan") was used in 1:10 of God's plan consummated and executed in Jesus Christ. With God's administrative plan for the church and for the universe (see especially 1:3–12) as background, Paul now defined his own ministry with the word "dispensation," explaining that he had been given a significant responsibility in the execution of this plan in the dispensation of the church age.

3:3–4. The mystery (v. 3) is a truth known only by divine revelation (see 3:5; Rom. 16:25; discussions on Rom. 11:25; Col. 1:26). Here the word "mystery" refers to the eternal and wise plan of God, once hidden in God but now revealed and proclaimed to the world (see 3:9–10). In Ephesians, "mystery" points to the unification of believing Jews and Gentiles in the new body, the church (see 3:6). **As I wrote afore in few words** (v. 3) may refer to 1:9–10. Paul's **knowledge** (v. 4), or comprehension, of the "mystery" was not a boast but belonged to the special dispensation (see v. 2) of his ministry from God.

3:5. For **not made known unto the sons of men**, see discussion on 3:6. **Holy** means set apart for God's service. **Apostles and prophets** is best defined by Paul's use of the expression in 2:20. Although Paul was the chief recipient of this revelation, others received it also. **By the Spirit** indicates the agency of the Spirit in revealing God's truth (for the role of the Spirit, see 1 Peter 1:10–12).

3:6. The words **fellowheirs** (see discussion on 1:18) **… same body … partakers** indicate the unique aspect of the mystery that was not previously known: the equality and mutuality that Gentiles had with Jews in the church, the one body.

That Gentiles would turn to the God of Israel and be saved was prophesied in the Old Testament (see Rom. 15:9–12); that they would come into an organic unity with believing Jews on an equal footing was unexpected.

3:7–8. Paul understood his strategic role as apostle to the Gentiles as being entirely God's calling through His grace (see 3:2, Rom. 11:32; 15:15–16; Gal. 2:7–9; Acts 9:15) and not of any personal merit. As a result, Paul saw himself as **less than the least** (v. 8; see 1 Tim. 1:15). Paul never ceased to be amazed that one so unworthy as he should have been chosen for so high a task. His modesty was genuine, even though one may disagree with his self-evaluation. **Grace** (v. 7), in this case, was a special endowment that brought responsibility for service (see Rom. 12:6). The **riches of Christ** (v. 8; see 1:3) are **unsearchable,** far beyond what can be known but not beyond appreciation, at least in part (see Rom. 11:33).

3:9–10. Now (v. 10) stands in contrast to the previous "ages." **Fellowship** (v. 9) translates the Greek word *oikonomia* ("administration," "stewardship," "plan"), used also in 3:2. This grand plan of God, the mystery now unfolding, is being executed in Christ (see 1:10), and the incorporation of both the Jews and the Gentiles into the church is manifesting the manifold wisdom of God to all men and no less to **the principalities and powers in heavenly places** (v. 10; see 1:20–21, discussion on 1:3). It is a staggering thought that the church on earth is observed, so to speak, by these spiritual powers and that, to the degree the church is spiritually united, it portrays to them the wisdom of God. This thought may be essential in understanding the meaning of "vocation" in 4:1. What is manifested is demonstrated and known **by the church.** That God has done the seemingly impossible — reconciling and organically uniting Jews and Gentiles in the church — makes the church the perfect means of displaying God's wisdom. **Manifold** means "variegated" or "multifaceted" (in the way that the many facets of a diamond reflect and enhance its beauty).

3:11. In all of Scripture, there is no theology of the church more profound or focused than is given in Ephesians. Human characterizations of "the church" must be elevated and transformed by Paul's majestic illumination of the church according to God's **eternal purpose.** The effective headship of Christ over a united church is in preparation for His ultimate assumption of headship over the universe (see 1:10).

3:12–13. Note well the believer's prerogative in Christ (**In whom;** v. 12). The believer's **boldness and access [to God] with confidence** is a privilege attributed to the manifold wisdom of God made known in the church and observed by the "loftiest" principalities and powers in the heavenly places (see 3:10). By virtue of Jesus Christ and faith in Him, the "lowliest" enjoys prerogatives with God that belong only to the loftiest of the lofty, the exalted status of Jesus Christ (see 1:17–21). "Boldness" (Greek, *parrēsia*; "frank speech," "open expression," "fearlessness"), a word that had a rich history in the Greek *demos*, referring to a citizen's right to speak openly, was also used to "signify the right to stand with uplifted head before a potentate (Luke 21:28)" (Barth, *Ephesians*, vol. 1, p. 348). The latter fits the picture Paul painted here of the believer's comfortable access to and audience with God (see Heb. 4:16). Paul enjoyed this too, even in prison, and therefore assured his readers and encouraged them. His tribulations belonged to the glory of what God is doing in the church according to His eternal purpose in Christ.

E. Prayer for a Deeper Experience of God's Fullness (3:14–21)

3:14–21. Here Paul expressed a prayer that grew out of his awareness of all that God is doing in believers. God's key gifts are "might" (vv. 16, 20) and "love" (vv. 17–19).

3:14–15. For this cause resumes the thought of 3:1. **I bow my knees** expressed Paul's deep emotion and reverence, as people in his day usually stood to pray.

In Greek, **family** (v. 15) is similar to the word for "father," so it can be said that the "family" derives its name (and being) from the father. God's universal preeminence and power as Sovereign Creator is reflected in this absolute use of **Father** (v. 14). Nevertheless, God is our Father, and Christians can commit their prayers to Him in confidence (see 3:12–13).

3:16–19. According to the riches of his glory (v. 16) points to the inexhaustible fund of God's vast resources aligned with the purpose of Paul's prayer for the Ephesians. Three objectives occupy Paul's prayer: (1) inner strength (vv. 16–17), (2) comprehension (v. 18), and (3) fullness (v. 19). The key to inner strength is Christ, who inwardly **dwell[s] in your hearts** (v. 17). When Christ is completely at home in the believer, He is free to exercise power through His effective presence. Christ was already present in the Ephesian believers' lives (see Rom. 8:9). Through faith, however, the believer must rest in the strength of Christ rather than wrest control from Him through independent human effort. "Heart" denotes the whole inner being. **Passeth knowledge** (v. 19) does not mean that the love of Christ is unknowable but that His love is so great that it cannot be completely known (compare God's peace "which passeth all understanding," Phil. 4:7). **Filled with all the fulness of God** conveys the idea of such inconceivable scope and incalculable measure that its conception becomes nearly imponderable. The stature of God's perfection ("fulness"), however, must not obscure the dynamic and qualitative emphasis here on "filling." Believers are to be permeated by God, absorbing His person and His provisions more and more. God, who is infinite in all His attributes, allows one to draw on His resources — in this case, His love.

3:20. Exceeding abundantly above refers specifically to the matters presented in this section of Ephesians but is not limited to these. **Power that worketh in us** (see 1:19–21) refers to the operative presence of the Holy Spirit, the power of **him that is able** to **worketh** in the believer. In Greek, the word "power" (*dynamis*) takes up the verb *dynamai* of "him that is able."

3:21. Unto him be glory expresses the ultimate goal of human existence (see 1:6 and discussion). **In the church by Christ Jesus** poses a remarkable parallel. God has called the church to an extraordinary position and vocation (see 3:10; 4:1).

V. Practical Ways to Fulfill God's Purpose in the Church (4:1–6:20)

4:1–32. The chapter begins (v. 2) and ends (v. 32) with exhortations to love and forgive one another.

4:1–16. Earlier in Ephesians, Paul taught that God brought Jew and Gentile into a new relationship with each other in the church and that He called the church to display His wisdom. Paul now showed how God made provision for those in the church to live and work together in unity and to grow together into maturity.

A. Unity (4:1–6)

4:1. Paul retained the self-designation **prisoner**, introduced in 3:1 (see discussion there). With its repetition, he called not for pity (see 3:13) but carried forward the example of his calling (see 3:1–2, 8–10) on behalf of the Lord as he exhorted the Ephesians to **walk worthy of** (their) **vocation**. Indeed, they now belonged to the same grand vocation (see 3:10, 21 and discussions).

4:2–3. Keep the unity (v. 3) points to the peace that God produced through the reconciling death of Christ (see 2:14–22). **The bond** has already been established by "our peace" (2:14), Jesus Christ, and its unity is maintained in the Spirit. Christians have the heavy responsibility of keeping that unity from being disturbed, a responsibility that is given specific expression in the self-effacing attitude believers are to have toward each other: **lowliness and meekness, with longsuffering, forbearing one another in love.** In Greek, the word **endeavouring** as Paul used it here means to be especially conscientious in discharging an obligation. This responsibility belongs to the very foundation of the church's existence and identity, its oneness (see 4:4–6).

4:4. One body is the church, the union of believers incorporated in Christ (see, e.g., 1:22–23; 2:16; 3:6; 5:30). **One Spirit** is the Holy Spirit (see 1:13; 2:18, 22). **One hope** has different aspects (e.g., 1:5, 10; 2:7), but it is still one hope; its substance is the calling of God in Jesus Christ (1:18) and the glorious future of Christ, in which all believers share.

4:5 – 6. One Lord (v. 5) is Jesus Christ, who is the Head of the church, His body (see 1:2 – 3, 22; 3:11; 4:15). **One baptism** refers not to the baptism of the Spirit (see 1 Cor. 12:13), which is inward and therefore invisible, but to water baptism (see discussion on Rom. 6:3 – 4). Since Paul apparently had in mind that which identifies all believers as belonging together, he would have naturally referred to the church ordinance in which every new convert participated publicly. At that time, it was a more obvious, common identification mark of Christians than it is now, when it is observed differently and is often seen by only those in the church. **One God, and Father of all** (v. 6) is "the God of our Lord Jesus Christ, the Father of glory" (1:17), and the foundation of the church is God's universal rule. His sovereign presence is exemplified by the description of His care for the church in what follows (see Barth, *Ephesians*, vol. 2, p. 429).

B. Maturity (4:7 – 16)

4:7. Grace (see 3:7 – 8) is given **according to the measure of [God's] gift**, the Christ (Messiah). Jesus is the measure (see Rom. 8:32) and, as expressed in what follows, the donor (see 4:11).

4:8. Psalm 68:18 (see *KJV Study Bible* note) speaks of God's triumphant ascension to His throne in the temple at Jerusalem (symbol of His heavenly throne). Paul applied this to Christ's triumphal ascension into heaven. Where Psalm 68:18 states that God "received gifts among men," Paul apparently took his cue from certain rabbinic interpretations current in his day that read the Hebrew preposition "among" in the sense of "unto" (a meaning it often has) and the verb for "received" in the sense of "take and give" (a meaning it sometimes has, but with a different preposition; see Gen. 15:9; 18:5; 27:13; Exod. 25:2; 1 Kings 17:10 – 11). **Captivity** probably refers to the spiritual enemies that Christ defeated at the cross.

4:9 – 10. Ascended ... descended (v. 9) belongs to Paul's elaboration and explanation. Although Paul quoted from the psalm to introduce the idea of the "gifts unto men" (4:8), he took the opportunity to remind his readers of Christ's coming to earth, His incarnation ("descended"), and His subsequent resurrection and ascension ("ascended"). This passage probably does not teach, as some think and as some translations suggest, that Christ descended into hell.

4:11. He gave picks up the leading thought in 4:7, that Jesus is the measure or gold standard of God's grace. His qualifications as donor were established in 4:8 – 10. Consequently, the quotation of Psalm 68:18 has its ultimate meaning when applied to Christ as the ascended Lord, who Himself has given gifts. **Apostles** are mentioned here because of their role in establishing the church (see 2:20; for qualifications of the initial group of apostles, see Acts 1:21 – 22; see also discussions on Mark 6:30; Rom. 1:1; 1 Cor. 1:1; Heb. 3:1). In a broader sense, Paul was also an apostle (see 1:1). **Prophets** are men or women (Acts 21:9; Rev. 2:20; 1 Cor 11:15) who spoke of God's revelation to the particular need or situation of the church (see 1 Cor. 14:3 – 4; see also note on 1 Cor. 12:10). True prophetic utterance for the church adhered to and upheld the apostles' testimony to Jesus. For **evangelists**, see Acts 21:8; 1 Corinthians 1:17. While other gifted people help the church grow through edification, evangelists help the church grow by augmentation. Since the objective mentioned in 4:12 is "for the perfecting of the saints for the work of the ministry," one may assume that evangelists, among their various ministries, help other Christians in their testimony. As Paul's wording indicates, **pastors and teachers** belong closer together than do apostles and prophets or prophets and evangelists; the Greek grammatical construction (also, the word **some** introduces both words together) suggests these gifted people are closely related. Those who have pastoral care for God's people (the image is that of shepherding) will naturally provide "food" from the Scriptures (teaching). They will be especially gifted as teachers (see 1 Tim. 3:2).

4:12. People are given (see 4:11) as gifts for a twofold function: First, they are given **For the perfecting of the saints for the work of the ministry**. Those mentioned in 4:11 were not to do all the work for the people but were to train the people to do the work themselves. "Perfecting" (Greek, *katartismos*) occurs only here. Outside the New Testament the word is used in association with actions taken to make something fit for its intended use. Accordingly, the saints are "trained" or "equipped." All believers are to be enlisted in the work of the ministry. The second function develops and expands the first: **for the edifying of the body of Christ** (see 4:16). Spiritual gifts are for the body, the church, and are not to be exercised individualistically (see 1 Peter 4:10). "Edifying" or "building up" reflects the imagery of 2:19–22. These concepts, body and building, occurring together emphasize the key idea of growth.

4:13. Till (or "until") expresses not merely duration but also purpose. **Unity** carries forward the ideal of 4:1–6. **Of the faith** here refers to the Christians' common conviction about Christ and the doctrines concerning Him, as the following words (e.g., **knowledge**) make clear (see also "the apostles' doctrine" in Acts 2:42). The word **unity** makes it clear that **the knowledge of the Son of God** is not a private or an individual "familiarity." Unity is a matter not just of a loving attitude or religious feeling but of truth and a common understanding about God's Son. The final goal, the **perfect man ... the fulness of Christ**, is conceived not as an individual achievement but as the collective attainment of the church. There is no room in this picture for competition, only for mutual and cooperative fellow ministry that cherishes the words **till we all** (see 4:15–16). More than the maturity of doctrinal conviction referred to by "of the faith" or a personal maturity that includes the ability to relate well to other people (see 4:23), the "perfect man" is the maturity of the perfectly balanced character of Christ.

4:14. For the sense of the word **children**, contrast the maturity described in 4:13. The nautical imagery of **tossed to and fro** and **wind of doctrine** pictures the instability of those who are not strong Christians. Then, as now, there were many distorted teachings and heresies that could easily throw the immature off course. For this reason, the church must be intentional and deliberate about its responsibility (see 4:12–13). Additionally, it must withstand the very

intentional and deliberate nature of its opposition: **sleight ... craftiness ... deceive**. Those who try to draw people away from the Christian faith are not innocently misguided but deliberately deceitful and evil (see 1 Tim. 4:1–2).

4:15. Speaking the truth in love is contrasted with the deceiving practices of those who oppose the truth (4:14). A truthful and loving manner of life is implied. **Grow up into him ... the head** is a slightly different restatement of 4:13, based here on the imagery of Christ as the Head of the body, which is the church. Paul thus was speaking primarily of corporate maturity: "the body of Christ" needs to be edified or built up (4:12); "we all" are to become "a perfect man," or mature (4:13).

4:16. Paul further detailed the body growing under the Head's direction with the anatomical imagery of interconnected parts functioning in a vital and essential design. The parts of the body help each other in the growing process, picturing the mutual ministries of God's people spoken of in 4:11–13. All believers, each and every one, have a vital and essential role and place in the healthy growth of the church. In the physical body, the mechanics are anatomical; in the spiritual body of Christ, the motive is love. **Love** is instrumental, for maturity and unity are impossible without it (see 4:2, 15).

C. Renewal of Personal Life (4:17–5:20)

4:17–5:20. In the preceding section, Paul discussed unity and maturity as twin goals for the church, which God brought into existence through the death of Christ. Here he went on to show that purity is also essential among those who belong to Him.

4:17–19. Christians from a Gentile background were to eschew their former way of life. **The vanity of their mind** (v. 17) points to the empty and futile reasoning of a mind devoid of revealed truth and moral clarity. Accordingly, life without God is intellectually frustrating, useless, and meaningless (see, e.g., Eccl. 1:2; Rom. 1:21). Paul further described the "vanity" of the Gentile mind as **understanding darkened** (clouded judgment; v. 18) and **ignorance** (lacking knowledge, namely, revealed truth), conditions of a heart that is increasingly hardened and calloused (**past feeling**; v. 19). In this kind of internal environment, impurities and immorality thrive. The Ephesians were instructed to **walk not as other Gentiles walk** (v. 17), who **have given themselves over** (v. 19). Just as Pharaoh's heart was hardened reciprocally by himself and by God (see Exod. 7–11), so here the Gentiles had given themselves over to a sinful kind of life, while Romans 1:24, 26, 28 says that God gave them over to that life. The wording of verses 17–19 is comparable to that of Romans 1:21, 24.

4:20–21. Ye (v. 20) is emphatic and complements the strong contrast of the vain ways of "other Gentiles" (4:17) with the way Paul's readers **learned Christ**. This is shorthand for being taught and learning the will of God as it is embodied in Christ. **The truth is in Jesus** (v. 21). The wording and the use of the name Jesus (rather than Christ) suggest that Paul was referring to the embodiment of truth in Jesus' earthly life. The internal benefits of "learning Christ" can be imagined by contrasting the internal degeneration described in 4:17–19, which was associated with "being alienated from the life of God through ... ignorance" (4:18). The contrast is summarized in 4:22–23.

4:22–23. The old man (v. 22) refers to everything humans are naturally, by birth, being part of the fallen human race. It includes the old lifestyle, resulting from natural deceitful desires. **The spirit of your mind** (v. 23) and its renewal is directly contrasted here with "the old man" and the degeneration associated with the vanity of one's mind (see 4:17–18). Romans 12:2 is helpful here. Revealed truth (see 4:20–21) is the medium of transformation and the disposition or spirit of the mind.

4:24. The new man refers to everything believers are in Christ through rebirth (see Rom. 6:6–11; 2 Cor. 5:17; Gal. 2:20; Col. 3:9–10).

4:25. Inner **truth**, such as Christ embodies (see 4:20–21), when it takes root and renews the spirit of the mind, is necessarily matched by truth that graces one's speech (see 4:15). **Neighbour** probably means fellow Christians in this context. **We are members**

one of another, as anatomically illustrated in 4:16, integral to and interconnected in one body, the church.

4:26. Be ye angry. Christians do not lose their emotions at conversion, but their emotions should be purified. Some anger is sinful; some is not. Anger is a God-given emotion that can serve the righteous purposes of God if expressed constructively and not destructively. Anger that does not serve sin must serve the higher demands of God's love. **Let not the sun go down.** No anger is to outlast the day. The sooner it is dealt with, the better.

4:27. Personal sin is usually due to personal evil desires (see James 1:14) rather than to direct tempting by the Devil. However, **the devil** can, as his very name, "Slanderer," indicates, use our sins—especially those, like anger, that are against others—to bring about greater evil, such as divisions among Christians.

4:28. Steal no more ... labour ... give to him that needeth. It is not enough to cease from sin; one must reverse the practice and replace wrongdoing with what is right. The former thief must now help those in need.

4:29. But that ... edifying is an exhortation parallel to the previous one (4:28). The Christian not only stops saying unwholesome things; he also begins to say things that will help build up others.

4:30. Grieve is used of actions that vex, irritate, offend, or insult, actions that cause severe mental or emotional distress. The verb also demonstrates that the Holy Spirit is a person, not just an influence, for only a person can be grieved. "Corrupt communication" (4:29) and the sins mentioned in 4:31 belong to the kinds of sinful actions that "grieve" the heart of God. **Sealed** (see discussion on 1:13) reminds one of the abiding personal presence of God in the person of the Holy Spirit, identifying believers as His **unto the day of redemption** (see 1:14; KJV Study Bible note on 1 Peter 1:5).

4:31. Bitterness ... malice are among the things that grieve the Holy Spirit. **Put away** does not mean to put away for safekeeping but to "remove" and so "renounce" such things (see 22). This continues the instruction concerning one's speech (4:29), which ought to correspond to the truth within (see 4:20–21, 25).

4:32. Kind … tenderhearted are opposites of the negative qualities of 4:31. These are the outward expressions of "the new man" (see 4:21–24), the Christlike person being forged by the presence of the Spirit (see 4:30). **Forgiving** is the basic Christian attitude, which is a result of being forgiven in Christ, and along with being kind and compassionate, it brings to others what Christians have received from God.

5:1. Be … followers of God. One way of imitating God is to have a forgiving spirit (see 4:32). The way one imitates the Lord is to act "even as" (4:32) He did. The sacrificial way Jesus expressed His love is not only the means of salvation (as seen in chap. 2) but is also an example of the way to live, for the sake of others.

5:2. With the imagery of **an offering … a sweet-smelling savour**, Paul's assigned the highest rank to the imitation of Jesus' sacrificial love in attitude and action. In the Old Testament, the offering of a sacrifice pleased the Lord so much that it was described as "a sweet savour" (Gen. 8:21; Exod. 29:18, 25, 41; Lev. 1:9, 13, 17).

5:3. With the sequence of **all uncleanness, or covetousness**, Paul moved from specifically sexual sins to more general sins, such as greed. These sins include sexual lust but refer to other kinds of excessive desire as well. **Not be once named** (see 5:12) adds the perspective of outsiders who observe the relevance of Christ through the lens of His **saints** (lit., "holy ones"). Believers are also "a holy temple" (2:21; see 2 Cor. 6:16; 1 Peter 2:5, 9).

5:4. The context and the word **filthiness** indicate that **foolish talking** and **jesting** refer not to humor as such but to dirty jokes, caustic sarcasm, and the like, which are out of place. Always appropriate and worthy of God's generosity is the **giving of thanks**. By being grateful for all that God has given, one can displace evil thoughts and words.

5:5. The behaviors and attitudes profiled in 5:3–4 belong to the culture of the **whoremonger**

… covetous man and not to the character of those ruled by Christ and God's reign (see 5:3). Paul appealed to what his readers already knew (**For this ye know**), probably alluding to a realization attested by their own conversion as well as his teaching (see 2:1–3; "children of disobedience," 5:6). **An idolater** (see Col. 3:5) is a greedy person who wants things more than he wants God and puts things in place of God, thereby committing idolatry. **Inheritance** literally refers to the property or possessions of a bequest and identifies the spiritual belongings that are bequeathed in salvation to those who belong to God, his heirs (see 1:14, 18; Col. 1:12; 1 Peter 1:4). The person who persists in sexual and other kinds of greed has excluded God, who therefore excludes him from the kingdom (but see discussions on 1 Cor. 6:9, 11).

5:6–7. Paul instructed the Ephesians to withstand any and all efforts to **deceive** (v. 6) them into being drawn aside or led astray from what they knew (see 5:5). Believers will always be confronted with plausible and attractive justifications and rationalizations of worldly ungodliness, but such words are **vain words**. "Vain" may refer to the content of the words (lit., "empty") as being devoid of truth or to the outcome or effect of the words as having no clout or impact. **These things** summarizes not the "vain words" but the ungodly ways represented in the previous verses. **Partakers** (v. 7) refers to taking part in or experiencing something with others. The foundation of this prohibition is laid in 5:8–14. Although Christians live in normal social relationships with others, as did the Lord Jesus (Luke 5:30–32; 15:1–2), they are not to participate in the sinful lifestyle of unbelievers.

5:8. Darkness and **light** are metaphors that convey moral opposites. Behind this polarization lies the contrast of revelation and the illumination of God's truth (see 4:18). The contrast between light and darkness in 4:8–14 shows that those who belong to Him who is "light" (1 John 1:5), that is, pure and true, not only have their lives illumined by Him but also are the means of introducing that light into the dark areas of human conduct (see Matt. 5:14).

5:9–10. Walking in the light (see 5:8; 1 John 1:7) is demonstrable, showing the effects of the light, **the fruit of the Spirit** (v. 9; see Gal. 5:22–23), and what pleases the Lord (see Rom. 12:2).

5:11. Have no fellowship with (see 5:7), or mutual partnership with, **unfruitful works of darkness**. The "fruit" of the light, "goodness and righteousness and truth" (5:9), is contrasted with "unfruitful works": evil and wickedness and falsehood. **Reprove** means "convict, refute, and confute." Light, by nature, exposes what is in darkness, and the contrast shows sin for what it really is.

5:12. Paul wrote with a tone of disdain of the disgraceful things, "the deeds of darkness" done in secret. So disgraceful are they, **it is a shame even to speak of those things**. How unthinkable must it be for the believer to associate with and participate in such darkness as children of the light? Moreover, Christians should not dwell on the evils that their lives expose in others.

5:13–14. All things ... made manifest ... for whatsoever doth make manifest is light (v. 13). The repetition of these words indicates that Paul was stressing the all-pervasive nature of the light of God and its inevitable effect. **He saith** (v. 14) is the opening of what may well be a hymn used by the early Christians (see discussion on Col. 3:16). **Sleepest ... dead** are two images that describe a sinner (see 2:1). **Christ shall give thee light**. As the sun and its dawn arouse and awaken one from physical slumber, Christ and His life-giving light awaken one from spiritual slumber.

5:15–17. Paul challenged his readers to **walk circumspectly** (v. 15), to watch their step, or conduct. With the word **Wherefore** (v. 17), the contrast between light and darkness turns to the contrast between wisdom and foolishness. Walking circumspectly requires wisdom. Paul's method for walking wisely entailed **redeeming the time** (v. 16; see Col. 4:5). The commercial associations of the verb "buy, buy up" makes time the valued commodity to be bought up. "Time" (Greek, *kairos*) connotes opportunity. The present is a precious opportunity to do **the will of the Lord** (v. 17). Perspective on *kairos*

is gained from a different word for time, *chronos*, found elsewhere in the New Testament, which connotes the elapse and measure of time. **Days** (v. 16) are increments of *chronos* that Paul characterized as "evil," not because they are intrinsically so but because people exhaust time with their evil, largely because they are foolish. Christians, on the other hand, are to "buy up" the time, the present, as an opportunity to walk wisely, doing the will of God in an environment of evil, even as light in an environment of darkness reproves the darkness.

5:18. Paul stated that the means of walking wisely as children of the light is the power of the Holy Spirit (see 5:10). Christians are to operate under the influence, or control, of God, His will (4:17), and His power: **be not drunk ... but be filled with the Spirit**. Paul used the Greek present tense to indicate that the filling of the Spirit is not a onetime experience. Repeatedly, as the occasion requires, the Spirit empowers for worship, service, and testimony. The contrast between being filled with wine and being filled with the Spirit is obvious. The two have something in common, which enabled Paul to make the contrast, namely, that one can be under an influence that affects him, whether of wine or of the Spirit. Since Colossians 3:15–4:1 is very similar to Ephesians 5:18–6:9, one may assume that Paul intended to convey a similar thought in the introductory sentences of each passage. When he wrote here of being filled with the Spirit and when he wrote in Colossians of being under the rule of the peace of Christ and indwelt by the "word of Christ" (Col. 3:16), he meant that believers are to be under God's control. The effect of this control is essentially the same in both passages: a happy, mutual encouragement to praise God and a healthy, mutual relationship with people.

5:19–20. Paul encouraged the Ephesians to sing every kind of appropriate song, whether **psalms** like those of the Old Testament, **hymns** directed to God, or other **spiritual songs** Christians were accustomed to singing. Such songs provide a means for **giving thanks** (v. 20) and praise to God. Actually, however, all three terms may refer to different types of psalms (see discussion on Col. 3:16). All in all, music fills the heart when it is filled with God's Spirit.

D. Deference in Personal Relationships (5:21–6:9)

5:21–6:9. In chapters 2–4, Paul showed how God brought believing Jews and Gentiles together into a new relationship in Christ. In 4:1–6, he stressed the importance of unity. In this section, he showed in a practical way how believers, filled with the Spirit, can live together in various human relationships. This list of mutual responsibilities is similar to the pattern found in Colossians 3:18–4:1 and 1 Peter 2:13–3:12 (see also Rom. 13:1–10).

1. The Principle (5:21)

5:21. Submitting yourselves one to another is basic to the following paragraphs. Paul showed how, in each relationship discussed, the partners can have a conciliatory attitude that will help that relationship. The grammar indicates that this submission is associated with the filling of the Spirit in 5:18. The command "be filled" (5:18) is followed by a series of participles in the Greek: speaking, singing, making melody (5:19), giving thanks (5:20), and submitting (v. 21). **In the fear of God** denotes the positive posture of submitting to the rightful priority of God. Honoring God with priority of place over oneself by giving Him rightful power over one's will and wishes makes submitting to one another an easy step (see Col. 3:18). Alternatively, submission owed to another person should never exceed the submission owed to God.

2. Husbands and Wives (5:22–33)

5:22. Wives, submit yourselves is an aspect of the submission taught in 5:21. To be subject to another meant to yield one's own rights. Biblical submission is not to be confused with passivity but rather is a noble act of the will that places another ahead of oneself. If the relationship calls for it, as in the military, the term can connote obedience, but that meaning is not called for here. In fact, the word "obey" does not appear in Scripture with respect to

wives, though it does with respect to children (6:1) and servants (6:5). **As unto the Lord** does not put a woman's husband in the place of the Lord but rather shows that a woman ought to submit to her husband as an act of submission to the Lord (see 1 Peter 3:1–6, especially 3:6).

5:23–33. Throughout this crucial and very practical text, Paul instructed wives and husbands that the husband is to take his cues from Christ and the wife is to take hers from the church. This insight is important both for the marriage partners and for the church (see v. 32).

5:23–24. The husband is the head of the wife (v. 23; see *KJV Study Bible* note on 1 Cor. 11:3) only and in the same way **as Christ is the head of the church**. The words "as Christ" are the control. The analogy between the relationship of Christ to the church and that of the husband to the wife is basic to the entire passage. **He is the saviour of the body** (see 2:16; 4:4, 12, 16) makes it clear that Christ earned, so to speak, the right to His special relationship to the church. As to Christ, the wife is to submit to her husband.

5:25. Paul proceeded to show that this is not a one-sided submission but a reciprocal relationship. The command **Husbands, love your wives** is also a command showing that the husband's headship is under the authority of Christ and subject to His command, even as the wife's submission is. "Love" (Greek, *agapaō*) generally means "the attitude and acts of unselfish giving" (Barth, *Ephesians*, vol. 2, p. 621). Here it is given its supreme example and definition. **Gave himself for it** not only points to the expression of the Lord's love but exemplifies how the husband ought to devote himself to his wife's good. To give oneself up to death for the beloved is a more extreme expression of devotion than the wife is called on to make.

5:26. Many attempts have been made to see marriage customs or liturgical symbolism in the words **the washing of water by the word.** One thing is clear: the Lord Jesus died not only to bring forgiveness but also to effect a new life of holiness in the church, which is His "bride." A study of the concepts of washing, water, and the Word should include John 3:5; 15:3; Titus 3:5; James 1:18; 1 Peter 1:23; 3:21.

5:27. Holy and without blemish (see 1:4) expresses the beauty and splendor of the bride at her presentation. This objective, albeit on a spiritual plane, finds its corollary and application for the husband and his bride in the following verses.

5:28–29. As their own bodies ... loveth himself (v. 28) **... his own flesh** (v. 29). The basis for such expressions and for the teaching of these verses is the quotation from Genesis 2:24 in 5:31. If the husband and wife become "one flesh" (5:31), then for the man to love his wife is to love one who has become part of himself.

5:30. We are members of his body ties the thought of 5:28–29 into the experience of the church and its reception of Christ's love: believers ought to love as they have been loved.

5:31. See Genesis 2:24.

5:32. Mystery. See discussion on Rom. 11:25. The profound truth of the union of Christ and his "bride," the church, is beyond unaided human understanding. It is not that the relationship of husband and wife provides an illustration of the union of **Christ and the church**; rather, the basic reality is the latter, and marriage is a human echo of that relationship.

5:33. Love ... reverence is a rephrasing and summary of the whole passage.

3. Children and Parents (6:1–4)

6:1–2. Children, obey your parents in the Lord (v. 1). The words "in the Lord," or "because of the Lord," are the motivation to obey whether parents are Christians or not. This is borne out by the other pairs of social relationships. In both the preceding example (wives and husbands) and the latter example (slaves and masters), the subordinate is addressed first. In all three cases, the traditional social duty is now configured in relation to Christ. **First commandment** (v. 2) refers here to the "basic" or "primary" command for children. **With a promise** refers to the promise of 6:3, the fifth commandment (Exod. 20:12), and apparently the second commandment with a promise (see Exod. 20:6).

6:3. Note the words **on the earth**. In Deuteronomy 5:16, where this commandment occurs (see also Exod. 20:12), the "promise" (6:2) was expressed in terms of the anticipated occupation of the "land," that is, Canaan. That specific application was, of course, not appropriate for the Ephesians, so Paul made a more general application here.

6:4. Fathers as the governing heads of families are addressed with an obligation to control the spirit of discipline: **provoke not**. Fathers must surrender any right they may feel they have to act unreasonably toward their children.

4. Slaves and Masters (6:5–9)

6:5–7. Servants (v. 5) are to view their responsibilities to their earthly **masters according to the flesh** as they would their service to Christ. Both the Old Testament and the New Testament included regulations for societal situations such as slavery and divorce (see Deut. 24:1–4), which were the results of the hardness of hearts (see Matt. 19:8). Such regulations did not encourage or condone such situations but were divinely given, practical ways of dealing with the realities of the day. **Fear and trembling** was a fairly stock expression for Paul (see 2 Cor. 7:15; Eph. 6:5; Phil. 2:12; 1 Cor. 2:3) and expresses respect. **Singleness of your heart** speaks of "wholeheartedness" or "complete sincerity." The heartfelt service with which one serves Christ is introduced in verse 5 and is amplified in verses 6–7.

6:8. Knowing ... whether he be bond or free points to the general principle and encouragement that properly motivated actions or service to the Lord (see 6:5–7) do not go unrecognized by the Lord (see Rom. 2:6; Ps. 62:12; Prov. 24:12; 1 Peter 1:17).

6:9. Likewise, **masters** are to treat slaves according to the treatment of their **Master ... in heaven**. Once again, Paul stressed reciprocal attitudes (see 5:21–6:4; see discussion on Titus 2:9). **Neither is there respect** (or "partiality"; Greek, *prosōpolēmpsia*; "accept face") **of persons with him** is defined quite literally in Galatians 2:6: "God accepteth no man's person." The Lord does not evaluate any person on the basis of "face" (one's status and credentials). One may be a "master" by earthly standards but not by heavenly ones.

E. Strength in the Spiritual Conflict (6:10–20)

6:10–20. Paul's scope in Ephesians was cosmic. From the very beginning, he drew attention to the unseen world (see discussion on 1:3; see also 1:10, 20–23; 2:6; 6:10); now he described the spiritual battle that takes place against evil "in high places" (v. 12).

6:10–11. Strong ... might (v. 10) implies that human effort is inadequate, but God's power is invincible. Such strength, the Lord's might, is found in **the whole armour of God** (v. 11; repeated in 6:13), and its inventory given in 6:14–17. The ready purpose of the Lord's might and armor is to withstand **the wiles of the devil.** "Wiles," or "methods" (Greek, *methodeia*), are the schemes of Satan, which may be encountered and administered by the forces of darkness identified in 6:12 (see Satan's "devices," 2 Cor. 2:11; Greek, *noēma*; meaning "design" or "intention," as the product of an intellectual process).

6:12. Not against flesh and blood is a caution against lashing out against human opponents as though they were the real enemy and also against assuming that the battle can be fought using merely human resources. Compare **principalities ... spiritual wickedness** with Paul's earlier allusions to powerful beings in the unseen world (see discussions on 1:21; 3:10). The Greek phrase for **high places** is the same as in 1:3 and is better translated "heavenly places" (see discussion on 1:3).

6:13–14. In this context, the imagery of **withstand** (v. 13) and **Stand therefore** (v. 14) is not that of a massive invasion of the domain of evil but of individual soldiers withstanding assault. **Loins girt about with truth** (see the symbolic clothing of the Messiah in Isa. 11:5). Character, not brute force, wins

the battle, just as in the case of the Messiah. **Breastplate of righteousness** is a metaphor Paul used to show that Christians are to put on righteousness to protect their hearts as a soldier puts on a breastplate to protect himself.

6:15. Feet shod with the preparation of the gospel. Whereas the description of the messenger's feet in Isaiah 52:7 reflects the custom of running barefooted, here the message of the gospel is picturesquely connected with the protective and supportive footgear of the Roman soldier.

6:16. Taking the shield of faith ... to quench all the fiery darts is an description pointing to the large Roman shield covered with leather, which could be soaked in water and used to put out flame-tipped arrows.

6:17–18. The sword of the Spirit (v. 17) and **Praying ... in the Spirit** (v. 18) are reminders that the battle is spiritual and must be fought in God's strength, depending on the Word and on God through prayer. Isaiah 59:17 has similar language, along with the breastplate imagery (see discussion on 6:14). As a helmet both protects a soldier and provides a striking symbol of military victory, **the helmet of salvation** (v. 17) caps the spiritual armor and victory of the Lord's might.

VI. Conclusion, Final Greetings, and Benediction (6:21–24)

6:21–23. Paul concluded with greetings that lack personal references, such as are usually found in his letters. This is understandable if Ephesians was a circular letter (see discussion on 1:1). **Tychicus** (v. 21) was an associate of Paul who traveled as his representative (see Col. 4:7; 2 Tim. 4:12; Titus 3:12). Thus, Paul closed with practical advice and personal concern for the believers at Ephesus.

THE EPISTLE OF PAUL THE APOSTLE TO THE PHILIPPIANS

INTRODUCTION

Author, Date, and Place of Composition

The early church was unanimous in its testimony that Philippians was written by the apostle Paul (see 1:1). Internally, the letter reveals the stamp of genuineness. The many personal references of the author fit what is known of Paul from other New Testament books.

It is evident that Paul wrote this letter from prison (see 1:13–14). Some have argued that this imprisonment took place in Ephesus, perhaps circa AD 53–55; others put it in Caesarea, circa AD 57–59. The best evidence, however, favors Rome as the place of composition and the date as circa AD 61. This fits well with the account of Paul's house arrest in Acts 28:14–31. When Paul wrote Philippians, he was not in the Mamertine dungeon as he was when he wrote 2 Timothy. He was in his own rented house, where for two years he was free to impart the gospel to all who came to him. Silva (pp. 5–8) discusses these options in detail, providing a thorough defense of the Roman imprisonment, reconciling the time elements involved.

The City of Philippi

The city of Philippi was named after King Philip II of Macedon, father of Alexander the Great. It was a prosperous Roman colony, which meant that the citizens of Philippi were also citizens of the city of Rome itself. They prided themselves on being Romans (see Acts 16:21), dressed like Romans, and often spoke Latin. No doubt this was the background for Paul's reference to the believer's heavenly citizenship (see 3:20–21). Many of the Philippians were retired military men who had been given land in the vicinity and who in turn served as a military presence in this frontier city. That Philippi was a Roman colony may explain why there were not enough Jews there to permit the establishment of a synagogue and why Paul did not quote the Old Testament in the Philippian letter.

Theme and Theological Message

Paul's primary purpose in writing this letter was to thank the Philippians for the gift they had sent him upon learning of his detention at Rome (1:5; 4:10–19). However, he made use of this occasion to fulfill several other desires: (1) to report on his own circumstances (1:12–26; 4:10–19); (2) to encourage the Philippians to stand firm in the face of persecution and rejoice regardless of circumstances (1:27–30; 4:4); (3) to exhort them to humility and unity (2:1–11; 4:2–5); (4) to commend Timothy and Epaphroditus to the Philippian church (2:19–30); and (5) to warn the Philippians against the Judaizers (legalists) and antinomians (libertines) among them (chap. 3).

Literary Features

Philippians is a missionary thank-you letter in which the missionary reports on the progress of his work and contains no Old Testament quotations (but see discussion on Job 13:16). It manifests a particularly vigorous type of Christian living: (1) a self-humbling attitude (2:1–4); (2) pressing toward the goal (3:13–14); (3) a lack of anxiety (4:6); (4) an ability to do all things (4:13). It is outstanding as the New Testament letter of joy; the word "joy" (Greek, *chara*) in its various forms occurs some fourteen times. Other distinctive terms in Philippians include the word "think" (Greek, *phroneō*), used ten times; "consider" (Greek, *hēgeomai*), used six times; and "bond," used four times. Philippians contains one of the most profound christological passages in the New Testament (2:5–11). Yet, profound as it is, Paul included this passage mainly for illustrative purposes. In general, Philippians has a warm, practical, and personal tone, with an emphasis on rejoicing. Thus, it has often been called the "Epistle of Joy."

Outline

    I. Salutation (1:1–2)
   II. Thanksgiving and Prayer for the Philippians (1:3–11)
  III. Paul's Personal Circumstances (1:12–26)
  IV. Exhortations (1:27–2:18)
      A. Living a Life Worthy of the Gospel (1:27–30)
      B. Following the Servant Attitude of Christ (2:1–18)
   V. Paul's Associates in the Gospel (2:19–30)
      A. Timothy (2:19–24)
      B. Epaphroditus (2:25–30)
  VI. Warnings against Judaizers and Antinomians (3:1–4:1)
      A. Against Judaizers, or Legalists (3:1–16)
      B. Against Antinomians, or Libertines (3:17–4:1)
 VII. Final Exhortations, Thanks, and Conclusion (4:2–23)
      A. Exhortations concerning Various Aspects of the Christian Life (4:2–9)
      B. Concluding Testimony and Repeated Thanks (4:10–20)
      C. Greetings and Benediction (4:21–23)

Bibliography

Fee, Gordon D. *Paul's Letter to the Philippians*. Grand Rapids, MI: Eerdmans, 1995.

Gromacki, Robert. *Philippians and Colossians*. Twenty-First Century Biblical Commentary. Chattanooga, TN: AMG, 2003.

Lightfoot, J. B. *St. Paul's Epistle to the Philippians*. 1913. Reprint, Grand Rapids, MI: Zondervan, 1953.

Martin, Ralph, P. *The Epistle of Paul to the Philippians*. Grand Rapids, MI: Eerdmans, 1959.

O'Brien, Peter T. *The Epistle to the Philippians: A Commentary on the Greek Text*. The New International Greek Testament Commentary. Edited by I. Howard Marshall and W. Ward Gasque. Grand Rapids, MI: Eerdmans, 1991.

Silva, Moises. *Philippians*. Wycliffe Exegetical Commentary. Chicago: Moody Press, 1988.

EXPOSITION

I. Salutation (1:1–2)

1:1–2. As in all his letters, Paul followed the conventional letter format of his day, with its three elements: (1) identification of the sender, (2) identification of the recipients, (3) greeting.

1:1. For **Timotheus**, see 1 Timothy, Introduction: "Recipient." The contents of the letter identify Timothy as Paul's associate but not as coauthor. Here Paul identified himself not as an apostle but as among **the servants of Christ Jesus** (see Rom. 1:1; Titus 1:1; Philemon 1). In Paul's case, this designation brings out an essential aspect of the more usual identification of himself as "an apostle." **Saints** is a common designation that Paul used to address and identify believers. The expression, derived from "holy ones," is descriptive not of individual moral purity but of the believer's status and spiritual union with Christ, as the following **in Christ Jesus** shows (see Rom. 1:7; 1 Cor. 1:2 and discussions). **Philippi.** See Introduction: "The City of Philippi." **Bishops and deacons**. This is the only place in Paul's writings where he singled out church officers as a group as recipients of a letter. "Bishops" (Greek, *episkopos*; "overseer") are equivalent to "elders" (Greek, *presbyteros*) and "pastors" (Greek, *poimēn*), judging from a comparison of Acts 20:17, 28 with 1 Peter 5:1–2 (see discussion on 1 Tim. 3:1). For "deacons," see discussion on 1 Timothy 3:8.

1:2. The opening greeting is not merely a matter of polite custom but has a distinctively Christian tone and content.

II. Thanksgiving and Prayer for the Philippians (1:3–11)

1:3–4. I thank my God (v. 3) **... in every prayer of mine** (v. 4) **... with joy.** Prayers of joyful thanksgiving for his readers' response to the gospel are a hallmark of the opening sentences of Paul's letters (see Rom. 1:8; 1 Cor. 1:4; Col. 1:3; 1 Thess. 1:2; 2 Thess. 1:3; 2 Tim. 1:3; Philemon 4). Here Paul modeled what he later advised the Philippians to practice in their own prayer life (see 4:6–7). Throughout his "thank-you" (1:3–11), the sanctuary doors to Paul's personal prayer life stand wide open, which allowed the Philippians to see not only the vital role that prayer plays in the work of the gospel but also the scope of their partnership in the greater work of God. For God to shape a partnership that is bigger than its partners, it begins with partners mutually dependent on God through prayer.

1:5. Your fellowship in the gospel. The basis of Paul's prayerful thanksgiving was not only their reception of the gospel but also their active support of his ministry (see 4:15). **From the first day.** When Paul first came to Philippi (see Acts 16:12). **Until now.** Toward the close (see 2:24) of Paul's first Roman imprisonment (see Acts 28:16–31).

1:6. The basis of Paul's confidence was God's divine **work in you**. Paul was confident not only of what God had done "for" the readers in forgiving their sins but also of what He had done "in" them (see 1:11). "Work" refers to God's activity in saving them and the dynamic impact of God's presence, "For it is God which worketh in you both to will and to do of his good pleasure" (2:13). **The day of Jesus Christ** specifies the time of His return, when their salvation will be brought to completion (see 1:10; 2:16; 1 Cor. 1:8; 5:5; 2 Cor. 1:14). It is God who initiates salvation, who continues it, and who will one day bring it to its consummation.

1:7. Paul emphasized his partnership with the Philippians by calling them "mutual partners," or **partakers of my grace**, the grace God had extended to Paul in his imprisonment for the gospel. Even in Paul's imprisonment, they willingly identified themselves with Paul by sending Epaphroditus and their financial gifts. They had become one with Paul in his persecution.

1:8. Bowels of Jesus Christ denotes "the affection of Jesus Christ," the deep yearning and intense, compassionate love exhibited by Jesus Himself and now fostered in Paul by his union with Christ. The term "bowels" (Greek, *splagchnon*; pronounced "splanknon") identifies the viscera, where deep emotion is experienced. Although this affection reaches out to all impartially and without exception, here Paul's heart is a human locus of the divine affection. Paul called God as his witness since God alone could verify the emotion of His Son's affection that Paul professed to feel for the Philippians.

1:9. A focal point and petition of Paul's prayer is that the love of the Philippians would **abound yet more and more**. Real love requires growth and maturation (see 1 Thess. 3:12; 4:10; 2 Thess. 1:3). Love grows in two ways: **in knowledge** of God, the source of love, as evidenced by what love approves (see 1:10–11; Col. 1:9), and in **judgment**, or practical discernment and sensitivity. Christian love is not mere sentiment; it is rooted in knowledge and understanding.

1:10. Love operating with the tandem qualities of knowledge and judgment (see 1:9) enables the be-

liever to **approve things that are excellent**. The word "approve" (Greek, *dokimazō*) carries the sense of "put to the test, examine" and then its consequence of "accept as proved, approve." In view of 1:9, the latter sense is prominent here. Christians are to approve (and practice) what is morally and ethically superior. **Sincere and without offence** portrays the outcome and goal of love. A life molded and shaped by love is a life formed without any mixture of evil. Indeed, God's love is the vital and effective power in leading a moral and ethical life. If holiness may be described as the absence of evil, it is the operation of God's love that functionally occupies its space and evacuates it (see 1:11). **Till the day of Christ** points to the occasion when the goal will be perfectly realized (see discussion on 1:6), and then Christians will have to give an account (see 2 Cor. 5:10).

1:11. Filled with the fruits of righteousness may be thought of as the continuous springtime of a flourishing fruit tree, only here it is a flourishing life planted in the heart of God. A life nourished by God's love yields on every limb fruit with the quality of God's character: righteousness. Such character is expected of all Christians (see Matt. 5:20–48; Heb. 12:11; James 3:18; see also Amos 6:12; Gal. 5:22). **By Jesus Christ** means "produced by Christ" (in union with Him) through the work of the Holy Spirit (see John 15:5; Eph. 2:10). **Unto the glory and praise of God** speaks of the ultimate goal of all that God does in believers (see Eph. 1:6, 12, 14).

III. Paul's Personal Circumstances (1:12–26)

1:12. Things which happened unto me, or "my circumstances," pertains to Paul's detainment in prison. **Have fallen out** (lit., "have come moreover" or "have come rather") implies a standard of comparison that has been exceeded. Here the standard, which, as it often is, is unexpressed, was the expectation of the Philippians. Instead of confining the gospel, Paul's imprisonment had served to "advance," or bring about, **the furtherance of the gospel**. Paul's shackles proved strategic to the release of the gospel (see "manifest in all the palace," 1:13).

1:13. The conditions under which Paul had been imprisoned are explained by the words **bonds in Christ**. "Bonds," or "restraints," may refer either to actual chains ("fetters") or broadly to his sufferings and imprisonment (see 1:14). They were **manifest**, or apparent, to all who knew of Paul's situation that he was imprisoned not because he was guilty of some crime but because of his stand for the gospel. **All the palace** (lit., "the whole praetorian"; Greek, *praitōrion*) refers to the imperial guard, a contingent of soldiers numbering several thousand. Many would have had personal contact with Paul or would have been individually assigned to guard him during the course of his imprisonment (see Acts 28:16, 30).

1:14. Not only had the gospel for which Paul was imprisoned circulated in unexpected ways, but timid brethren were **much more bold**. Encouraged by Paul's example, other believers were forcefully proclaiming the gospel. Since **brethren in the Lord** is redundant and occurs nowhere else, the sense and punctuation should read, "many of the brethren, having become more confident in the Lord due to my bonds, dare much more to speak the word without fear."

1:15. Even of envy and strife ... of good will. The preaching of the gospel that Paul's imprisonment had stimulated stemmed from either one of these two sharply opposed motives. These divisions (1:15–17) are grammatically and most naturally categories of the "many" (lit., the "majority") mentioned in 1:14. Paul scrutinized the motive, not the content, of the proclamation.

1:16. The one preach Christ of contention. Those who preached with wrong, insincere motives did so out of a sense of competition with Paul and so thought they were making his imprisonment more difficult to bear. Paul described their motive as insincere (**not sincerely**), or not with "pure" (Greek, *hagnōs*; "purely") intentions. Not all preaching of the gospel is based on proper motives.

1:17. The other of love. Those who preached with a right motive recognized the true reason for Paul's imprisonment (see 1:13) and were encouraged to take the same bold stand that he had taken. The

contrast of motives, "[out] of love" (Greek, *agapē*) and "not sincerely" (Greek, *hagnōs*; "purely"; 1:16), reminds the reader that love is pure.

1:18. Whether in pretence, or in truth, Christ is preached. The insincere preachers were not to be viewed as being heretical. Their message was true, even though their motives were not pure. The gospel has its objectivity and validity apart from those who proclaim it; the message is more than the medium. **I ... rejoice ... and will rejoice** characterizes Paul's hearty and buoyant confidence in Jesus, despite his surrounding circumstances. Although Paul was under arrest and fellow Christians sought, by their preaching, to add to his difficulties, he kept on rejoicing, because his emotional life was ever inspired by an effervescent perspective encouraged by Christ.

1:19. Salvation, or "deliverance," speaks either of Paul's release from prison (see 1:25; 2:24) or, in view of the immediately following verses, of the deliverance brought to the believer by death (see Rom. 8:28). The former interpretation, however, seems to be indicated in 1:25. **Spirit of Jesus Christ** denotes not only the Holy Spirit, the Spirit of God the Father (see Rom. 8:9, 14; 1 Cor. 2:10–11, 14), but also the Spirit of Christ, the second person of the Trinity (see Acts 16:7; Rom. 8:9; Gal. 4:6). He is sent by the Father (see John 14:16–17, 26; Gal. 4:6) and by the Son (see John 15:26; 16:7).

1:20. For the sense of **earnest expectation**, or "eager expectation," see Romans 8:9 for the one other New Testament example of this poignant word of expectancy. The words **hope** and **boldness** aptly attend the expectation expressed by this word (Greek, *apokaradokian*). Rather than **be ashamed**, Paul wanted to magnify **with all boldness** and elevate the reputation of Christ through the actions and attitudes of his life. The circumstances of imprisonment, with all its attendant suffering and oppression, constituted a real temptation for Paul to abandon the gospel and his resolute service for Christ. **My body** is the instrument of human activity and, from this perspective, refers to Paul himself. Accordingly, the body is where the exalted Christ dwells by His Spirit and is at work (see Rom. 8:9–10), and Christ was therefore exalted by what Paul did. **Whether it be by life, or by death**. Whether his service for Christ continued in life or ended in death.

1:21. To live is Christ. Christ was the source and secret of Paul's continual joy (even in prison), for Paul's life found all its meaning in Christ. **Gain** specifies that the gain brought by death is "be[ing] with Christ" (1:23), so that here Paul was saying that his ultimate concern and most precious possession, both now and forever, was Christ and his relationship with Him.

1:22. Fruit of my labour. The spread of the gospel and the upbuilding of the church. **I wot not**, or as some translations word it, "I know not," fails to bring out the sense of this word found elsewhere in the New Testament. Elsewhere (e.g., Luke 2:15; Rom. 9:22; Eph. 6:19) it means "to make known," "to reveal." There is no reason to give it a meaning here other than its usual meaning, which here may be rendered, "What I would choose, I am not going to declare." Why? As 1:23–24 shows, Paul was torn between two positives: his desire to be present with his beloved Christ and his desire to be present with his beloved Philippians.

1:23–24. Depart, and to be with Christ (v. 23) **... abide in the flesh** (v. 24). Either alternative was a good one. While mysteries remain, this passage clearly teaches that when believers die, they are with Christ, apart from the body. The word "depart" has a background of colorful usage, which includes references to weighing anchor (and putting out to sea), breaking camp, and, euphemistically, death.

1:23. Far better, or beyond compare, leaves no room for doubt about the advantages of death for the Christian: to face death is to face Christ. Being with Christ after death must involve some kind of conscious presence and fellowship (see 2 Cor. 5:6, 8).

1:24. More needful for you expresses the pull of Paul's concern and love for the Philippians. Paul put the needs of those he ministered to ahead of his personal preference.

1:25. I shall abide. It is entirely possible that Paul was later released from prison (see map, *Zondervan KJV Study Bible*, pp. 1738–39). Certain unknowns,

however, make a definitive conclusion impossible. **Furtherance and joy of faith** indirectly make it clear that the Christian life is to be one of joyful growth and advance (see discussion on 1:9).

IV. Exhortations (1:27–2:18)

A. Living a Life Worthy of the Gospel (1:27–30)

1:27. Conversation, or "manner of life," translates the Greek word *politeuomai*, "live [behave] as citizens." Given the Philippian pride of Roman citizenship (see Introduction: "The City of Philippi"), Paul was calling them to a healthier pride of conduct, one that **becometh the gospel** and their true citizenship "in heaven" (3:20). Therefore, Paul said the one important thing (**Only**) is to live as citizens "worthy" of the gospel. In other words, live in a way that is appropriate to the privileges, standards, and goals given with the gospel. **In one spirit** speaks of having a common disposition and purpose. Citizens of heaven are to be united **with one mind striving together**. This is particularly necessary when the gospel is under attack. Christians need each other and must stand together.

1:28. The word **token** (Greek, *endeixis*) as a law term denoted "'proof' obtained by appeal to the facts" and connoted a sure sign or clear omen (O'Brien, *The Epistle to the Philippians*, p. 155). In the face of opposition, the Philippians could gain courage from the fact that the demonstration of their heavenly citizenship (1:27–28a) functioned as a proof or "evident token" of their salvation and their opponents' destruction. Persistent opposition to the church and the gospel is a sure sign of eventual destruction since it involves rejection of the only way of salvation. By the same token, when Christians are persecuted for their faith, it is a sign of the genuineness of their salvation (see 2 Thess. 1:5).

1:29. With the words **given** (Greek, *charizomai*) **... to suffer**, Paul expressed suffering **in the behalf of Christ** as a gift or privilege. Through Christ, God had graciously given the Philippians not only the privilege of salvation (**not only to believe on him**) but also the privilege of suffering **for His sake**. Both expressions of God's privilege in Christ (believing and suffering) are balanced by one Greek expression, translated here as "in the behalf of Christ" and "for His sake." Christian suffering, as well as faith, is a blessing (see Matt. 5:11–12; Acts 5:41; James 1:2; 1 Peter 4:14) and is in no way a proof (see 1:28) of anything but salvation and God's privilege in Christ. The Christian life is to be a "not only … but also" proposition: not only believing but also suffering.

1:30. Paul assured the Philippians that the opposition engaging them was not unique; overall, it belonged to the **same conflict**, or "struggle," engaging Paul. They had witnessed it (**Ye saw**) when Paul and Silas first visited Philippi and were imprisoned (see Acts 16:19–40), and now they heard about it (1:12–26). All in all, in 1:27–30, Paul dissuaded the Philippians from any discouragement or any deduction of defeat that they might have drawn from the opposition they faced to their faith in the gospel of Jesus Christ. They needed to stand fast in one Spirit (1:27), strive with one soul for the faith of the gospel (1:27), and do so boldly, in nothing terrified by their adversaries.

B. Following the Servant Attitude of Christ (2:1–18)

2:1. In Paul's teaching, the words **in Christ** refer to the believer's personal union with Christ, the basic reality of salvation. To be in Christ is to be saved. It is to be in intimate personal relationship with Christ the Savior. From this relationship flow all the particular benefits and fruits of salvation, such as encouragement (see, e.g., 3:8–10; Rom. 8:1; 2 Cor. 5:17; Gal. 2:20). **Comfort of love** speaks of the comforting knowledge and assurance that come from God's love in Christ, demonstrated especially in Christ's death for the forgiveness of sins and eternal life (see John 3:16; Rom. 5:8; 8:38–39; 1 John 3:16; 4:9–10, 16). **Fellowship of the Spirit** denotes the fellowship among believers produced by the Spirit, who indwells each of them (see 2 Cor. 13:14). **Bowels and mercies** expresses the experience of intense care and deep sympathy that Christians have for each other (see 1:8; Col. 3:12). Paul viewed all these benefits — encouragement, comfort, fellow-

ship, tenderness, and compassion — as present realities for the Philippians.

Paul's repeated use of **If** with each of these notable Christian benefits served to heighten his readers' awareness of not only their personal experience but also their obligation as beneficiaries. Laced together, these spiritual incentives offered the Philippians a powerful motivation to welcome and fulfill Paul's appeal in 2:2.

2:2. Paul's string of incentives (2:1) is adorned with a cluster of synonymous or matching phrases that reflect one glowing idea: harmonious devotion. The words **likeminded … same love … one accord … one mind** emphasize the unity that should exist among Christians. Rather than uniformity in thought, "one mind" denotes the common disposition to work together and serve one another — the "attitude" of Christ (see 2:5; 4:2; Rom. 12:16; 15:5; 2 Cor. 13:11).

2:3. The mortal enemies of unity and harmony in the church (see 1:17; see also Gal. 5:20, where the Greek for "selfishness" is rendered "disputes" and listed among the "works of the flesh," Gal. 5:19–21) are **strife or vainglory**. Strife, on the one hand, beats one's rival down; vainglory, on the other hand, boosts one's ego up. Both are self-centered and devoted to personal advancement. By contrast, the source of Christian unity is **lowliness of mind**, or humility. Humility is not inferiority. The divine definition given here shows that humility involves a noble and strong act of the will, a decision to put others above oneself, a disposition modeled on Christ (2:5). The key to humility is to put God first (see 2:8). Therefore, Paul's admonition to **esteem other better than themselves** should not be taken to mean that everyone else is superior or more talented but that Christian love sees others as worthy of preferential treatment (see Rom. 12:10; Gal. 5:13; Eph. 5:21; 1 Peter 5:5).

2:4. A person's concern for **his own things** is certainly proper, but only if there is equal concern for the interests of others (see Rom. 15:1).

2:5. Let this mind be in you, which was also in Christ Jesus. In spite of all that is unique and radically different about the person and work of Christ (see 2:6–11), Christians are to have His attitude of self-sacrificing humility and love for others (see 2:2–4; Matt. 11:29; John 13:12–17).

2:6–11. The poetic, even lyric, character of these verses is apparent. Many scholars view them as an early Christian hymn (see discussion on Col. 3:16), taken over and perhaps modified by Paul. If so, they nonetheless express his convictions. The passage treats Christ's humiliation (2:6–8) and exaltation (2:9–11). This kenotic pattern of suffering, followed by glory, became an important one for Paul, who applied it to himself (see 3:7–14) and his readers (see 2:5; 3:15–16; Rom. 8:17–19).

2:6. In the form of God affirms that Jesus is fully God (see discussion on Rom. 9:5). "Form" (only here and in 2:7 in the New Testament) is taken to mean essential form, "the specific character" (Lightfoot, *St. Paul's Epistle to the Philippians*, p. 129) or sum of those qualities that make God specifically God. **Equal with God** points to the status and privileges that inevitably follow from being in very nature God. In Jesus' mind (see "Let this mind be in you," 2:5), this divine equality was not regarded as **robbery**, something to be seized or used for His own advantage. He did not consider that high position to be something He could not give up.

2:7. Made himself of no reputation. He did this not by giving up deity but by laying aside His glory (see John 17:5) and submitting to the humiliation of becoming man (see 2 Cor. 8:9). Jesus is truly God and truly man. Another view is that He emptied Himself, not of deity itself but of its prerogatives — the high position and glory of deity. In either case, the words "made himself of no reputation" should be explained by addition and not subtraction: "He made himself of no reputation by taking the form of a servant and being made in the likeness of men." **The form of a servant** emphasizes the full reality of His servant identity (see Matt. 20:28). As a servant, He was always submissive to the will of the Father.

2:8. Fashion as a man shows not only that Jesus was "like" a human being (2:7) but also that He took on the actual outward characteristics of a man (see

John 1:14; Rom. 8:3; Heb. 2:17). **Humbled** (see 2:7; 2 Cor. 8:9) is the same word Paul used in 2:3, here the verb and there the noun. How Jesus humbled himself and how one can likewise humble oneself is revealed in the word **obedient** (see Heb. 5:7–8). Obedience to God properly enthrones Him above all and puts Him first. A "servant" (2:7) obeys, and Jesus willingly accepted the position of a servant. **Death** stresses both the totality and the climax of Jesus' obedience. **Of the cross** heightens Jesus' humiliation; He died as someone cursed (see Gal. 3:13; Heb. 12:2). Crucifixion was the most degrading kind of execution that could be inflicted on a person.

2:9. With **Wherefore**, the description of Jesus' sacrificial humiliation is matched by a description of His supreme exaltation from on high (2:9–11). Regal imagery abounds, but the servant (2:7) is **exalted** (see Matt. 28:18; Acts 2:33; Isa. 52:13) far above any earthly king. The regal inauguration and reign of Jesus is hailed with the **name … above every name**. Reference doubtless is to the office or rank conferred on Jesus — His glorious position, not His proper name (see Eph. 1:21; Heb. 1:4–5). That name would be God's own name, Yahweh (see "Lord," 2:11; and His attendant worship, 2:10; compare the Septuagint, where "Lord" stands for Yahweh). Thus, "Lord" forms an inclusion with "God" in 2:6, only now all creation is bound to Jesus' glory in an obligatory way because of His redemptive work.

2:10–11. Bow (v. 10) **… confess** (v. 11; see Isa. 45:23) describes the visible posture and vocal profession of every living creature before the supremacy of Jesus. God's design is that all people everywhere should worship and serve Jesus as Lord. Ultimately, all will acknowledge Him as Lord (see Rom. 14:9), whether willingly or not.

2:12. With **Wherefore**, Paul tied two motivations together as he exhorted the Philippians, **work out your own salvation**. One looks back to the incomparable example of Jesus and His obedience (2:5–11); the other looks to the history of obedience on the part of the Philippians. Both were an encouragement to the Philippians. **Obeyed** identifies the commands of God as passed on to the Philippians by Paul (see

Rom. 1:5; 15:18; 2 Cor. 10:5–6). **My presence** refers to the times Paul was with them during the course of his second (see Acts 16:12–40) and third (see Acts 20:1–3, 6) missionary journeys. In saying "work out your own salvation," Paul compelled them to work it out to the finish. He was referring not to an attempt to earn their salvation by works but to the expression of their salvation in spiritual growth and development. Salvation is not merely a gift received once for all; it expresses itself in an ongoing process in which the believer is strenuously involved (see Matt. 24:13; 1 Cor. 9:24–27; Heb. 3:14; 6:9–11; 2 Peter 1:5–8) — the process of perseverance, spiritual growth, and maturation. Rather than expressing doubt or anxiety, **fear and trembling** measures the importance of an active reverence and a singleness of purpose in response to God's grace.

2:13. Imitation depends on incarnation: God is at work **in you**, so work out what He is working within. **To will and to do** speaks of both God's intention and His inner operation to effect **his good pleasure**—what God enables in a believer's life as one obediently works out one's salvation. Faith and obedience cannot be separated (see Gal. 5:6; James 2:18, 20, 22).

2:14–17. These verses list some things involved in working out our salvation.

2:14. Murmurings and disputings, or grumbling and arguing, model not the mind of Jesus Christ (2:5) but the mind of a world preoccupied with its own good pleasure. "Murmurings," or being discontented with God's will, is an expression of unbelief that prevents one from doing what pleases God (see 2:13; 1 Cor. 10:10). "Disputings" are the arguments that erupt and divide people over conflicting points of view. Debatable points that do not need to be settled for the good of the church (see 2 Tim. 2:23; Titus 3:9) are in view. Such will be far from the one who puts the interests of others (see 2:3–4) ahead of his own, because that person's mind is occupied by the mind of Christ (see 2:5).

2:15. Blameless and harmless ... without rebuke speaks not of absolute, sinless perfection but of wholehearted, unmixed devotion to doing God's

will. The objective is to have a character distinctive of God's children, contrasted with the character of **a crooked and perverse nation**, a description of the unbelieving world (see Acts 2:40; Eph. 2:1–3; Matt. 17:17). Children of God should **shine as lights**, standing out like eye-catching stars, all the brighter in darkness; Christians are to shine brighter in the world around them (see Matt. 5:15–16).

2:16. In exhorting the Philippians, Paul added a personal motive to the preceding divine incentives that have dominated the chapter. As if in a race, Paul imagined the finish line drawn by **the day of Christ** (see discussion on 1:6). He pictured a day of joy over a race run well, in part because of what God had done through Paul (see 1 Thess. 2:19), in part because the Philippians had held forth (like a torch) or clutched (like a baton) **the word of life**, as had others in his apostolic work. **In vain** (see 1 Cor. 9:24–27) speaks of running in futility or without effect.

2:17–18. The all too real and near possibility of Paul's martyrdom (see 1:19–26) was surely in Paul's mind as he spoke of his life, a slowly poured drink offering, pictured as being drained in service. Paul assured the Philippians that his service, like the spirit of a drink offering, was offered unreservedly with joy, a joy that is best appreciated with mutual joy: **I** (v. 17) **... rejoice ... also do ye** (v. 18) **... rejoice.** Christian joy ought always to be mutual. **I be offered** (v. 17) portrays Paul's life as a drink offering that accompanies other sacrifices. **Upon the sacrifice** is informed by the Old Testament background of the daily sacrifices described in Exodus 29:38–41. From the first to the last, Paul offered his life with joy.

V. Paul's Associates in the Gospel (2:19–30)

2:19–30. Judging from verses 23–24, Paul had every intention of coming to Philippi, should the Lord grant him his desire. In the meantime, he sent two associates in the gospel. Paul wrote first of his plan to send Timothy (vv. 19–24), "so soon as I shall see how it will go with me" (v. 23), but in advance, it was "necessary to send ... Epaphroditus" (v. 25; vv. 25–30), who carried Paul's letter to the Philippians. Thus, verses 19–30 set forth Paul's travel plans, conveying his apostolic attention and care as outlined in the sending of the letter bearer, Epaphroditus, to be followed by the visit of Timothy, to be followed by the arrival of Paul himself, should he be released from prison as hoped.

A. Timothy (2:19 – 24)

2:19 – 23. Paul planned to send Timothy, who was with him in Rome (see 1:1), to discover and report on conditions in the Philippian church.

2:20 – 21. Likeminded (Greek, *isopsychos*; lit., "of equal soul"; v. 20) is a rare expression, occurring only here in the New Testament. No one could best or equal Timothy's genuine concern (**who will naturally care**) for the best interests of the Philippians. Since all others sought their own interests, Timothy was a good example of the kind of person envisioned in the exhortation of 2:4. There was a wide divide and sharp contrast between Timothy and Paul's other associates — an outstanding commendation for one so young.

2:22. The proof (Greek, *dokimē*; a test with attention to the result, "standing a test," "character") of Timothy's worth had already been demonstrated and so was known to the Philippians. What the Philippians knew of Timothy's character, Paul explained as the outcome of an ongoing devotion to the work of the gospel, which had united Timothy and Paul **as a son with the father**. Paul's own commendation of Timothy could hardly reach higher than this tender description of their ministry partnership. The relationship between Timothy and Paul is developed at length in 1-2 Timothy. The words **served with me** show that Timothy, like Jesus and Paul, had a servant attitude.

2:23 – 24. Given Paul's regard (see 2:20 – 23), sending Timothy to the Philippians was like sending an apostolic letter, the closest substitute for Paul's own presence. Paul anticipated his release and arrival in the near future (see 1:25).

B. Epaphroditus (2:25 – 30)

2:25 – 30. Epaphroditus, too, after a close brush with death (vv. 27, 30), was being sent home to Philippi.

2:25. Paul commended **Epaphroditus**, and thus the Philippians, by describing what their **messenger**, who had **ministered to** Paul, had become to him: **my brother, and companion in labour, and fellow-soldier**. These five phrases characterize the role of Epaphroditus, the first three describing what he became on Paul's behalf, and the last two explaining why he came on the behalf of the Philippians. "Messenger" (Greek, *apostolos*) is a broader use of the Greek word often translated "apostle," applied here to Epaphroditus as a commissioned representative of the Philippian church (see 2 Cor. 8:23). "Ministered" (Greek, *leitourgos*), with its rich connections to the performance of priestly duties, suggests that Epaphroditus as a "priestly minister" had earnestly and fittingly served Paul's need in prison (see "service"; Greek, *leitourgia*; 2:30). Clearly, what Epaphroditus became to Paul fulfilled, if not exceeded, what the Philippians had intended (see 2:30).

2:26 – 28. Having clarified Epaphroditus's value to Paul and the gospel ministry (2:25), Paul further qualified his mutual value, explaining that his return not only brought this letter but safeguarded him who came near to **death** (v. 27; see 1:21 – 26) in their mutual service. **Sorrowful** (v. 28) implies the legitimate cares and concerns that come with the Christian life and the gospel ministry (see discussion on 4:6; see also 2 Cor. 4:8; 11:28).

2:29 – 30. To supply your lack of service toward me (v. 30) refers not to a standard of expectation on Paul's part but to the expectation of what the church wanted to accomplish and fulfill. In other words, a "lack" the Philippians wanted to fulfill, yet unable to do so themselves, they sent Epaphroditus to fulfill it on their behalf. In this pursuit, Epaphroditus nearly gave his life. For that, the Philippians were to have a sense of "mission accomplished" and commensurately honor the man who had acted on their behalf. Paul spoke of this "service" as a priestly service in the most positive terms and imagery (see 2:25; 4:18).

VI. Warnings against Judaizers and Antinomians (3:1 – 4:1)

A. Against Judaizers, or Legalists (3:1 – 16)

3:1. Finally marks a transition to a new section as Paul moved toward his conclusion; this does not mark the close of the letter, however (see 4:8). With the injunction to **rejoice in the Lord** (see 4:4), Paul set the tone both theologically ("in the Lord") and experientially ("rejoice," "express gladness"; Greek, *chairō*) for the reminders that follow on a subject matter that could otherwise be **grievous** or disturbing. Paul stated it was not grievous for him, so the Philippians should not let it be grievous for them. **The same things** refers to matters in the following verses that Paul had previously dealt with either orally when he was in Philippi or perhaps in an earlier letter. For the Philippians, there was a benefit: **it is safe**. Where serious error is present, there is safety in repetition.

3:2. The threefold repetition of **beware** ("watch out"), one with each epithet, underscores how important it was to Paul that his opponents did not overtake the Philippians. **Dogs** is pejorative and a harsh fault-finding word for Paul's opponents. The image portrays not only their aggressive opposition to the gospel but the seriousness of their error and its destructive, "devour[ing]" (Gal. 5:15) results. Their teaching probably was similar to what Paul had to oppose in the Galatian churches (see Galatians, Introduction: "Background"). **Concision**, or "mutilation," is a strong, painfully vivid term; the false teachers had so distorted the meaning of circumcision (see 3:3) that it had become nothing more than a useless cutting of the body.

3:3. The true, inner meaning of **circumcision** is realized only in believers, who worship God with genuine spiritual worship and who glory in Christ as their Savior rather than trusting in their own human effort (see Rom. 2:28–29; Col. 2:12–13; see also Deut. 30:6; Ezek. 36:26). **Rejoice ... no confidence**. Unlike in 3:1, here the word "rejoice" translates the Greek word *kauchaomai*; "boast," "glory," "take pride"). Everyone is a "boaster," either in Christ or in himself. The medium of **the flesh** (weak human nature) is the antithesis of **in** ("by means of") **the spirit**. Although the term "flesh" in Paul's letters often refers to sinful human nature, here it speaks of the frailty of human nature: it is not worthy of our confidence; it cannot save.

3:4–14. Paul's personal testimony, a model for every believer. This is one of the most significant autobiographical sections in his letters (see Gal. 1:13–24; 1 Tim. 1:12–16; Acts 22:1–21; 26:1–23).

3:4–6. Paul's pre-Christian confidence, rooted in his Jewish pedigree, privileges, and attainments, he eschewed in 3:7–8 and thus brought full circle his personal endorsement of "we" in 3:3.

3:5. Circumcised the eighth day (see Gen. 17:12) alludes to the Jewish piety of Paul's family. Paul was born a Jew, **of the stock of Israel**, and was not a proselyte. Paul's family traced its genealogy to **the tribe of Benjamin**, the tribe of Saul—Paul's name. His Jewish roots were deep and unambiguous. Jerusalem, the Holy City, lay on the border of the tribal territory of Benjamin. Narrower than "Israelite" or "descendant of Abraham," **a Hebrew of the Hebrews** draws a distinction located in language, attitudes, and lifestyle (see Acts 22:2–3; Gal. 1:14; 2 Cor. 11:22). **Pharisee** points to the strictness of Paul's allegiance to and observance of the Torah (the Law) and all the authoritative ancestral doctrines and customs that regulated religious and social life (see Acts 22:3; 23:6; 26:5).

3:6. Concerning zeal (see Gal. 1:13–14), Paul's fervor in persecuting the church could be gauged by reference to the zeal of Phinehas (see Num. 25:11; Ps. 106:30–31), who became a prototype and emblem of righteous zeal in Jewish tradition. **Righteousness ... in the law** refers to righteousness produced by using the law as an attempt to merit God's approval and blessing (see 3:9)—a use of the law that Paul strongly opposed as being contrary to the gospel itself (see Rom. 3:27–28; 4:1–5; Gal. 2:16; 3:10–12). Finally, Paul's "confidence" (3:3–4) had come from his legal disposition of being **blameless**. In terms of legalistic standards of scrupulous external conformity to the law, Paul was above reproach.

3:7–14. Paul contrasted his confidence in Christ with his pre-Christian confidence (3:4–6), a confidence he now designated as having belonged to the flesh and its standards (3:3).

3:7. What things, or the things mentioned in 3:5–6, are given an accounting in terms of the bottom line: **gain ... loss**, which refers to the great reversal in Paul, begun on the road to Damascus (see Acts 9:3–16), from being self-centered to being centered in Christ.

3:8. The knowledge of Christ Jesus is not only a knowledge of facts but a knowledge gained through experience that, in its surpassing greatness, transforms the entire person. The following verses spell this out. **Dung** (Greek, *skubalon*) may refer to refuse, such as the excrement of animals, kitchen scraps, or foul-smelling garbage. Although its etymology remains uncertain, its origin has been reasoned from the expression "to fling to the dogs," which if valid, may here have been a knock on Paul's opponents ("dogs," 3:2). What Paul now had as a Christian was not merely preferable or a better alternative; his former way of life was worthless and despicable. **Win** means to gain or acquire by effort or investment.

3:9. Be found in him expresses the premium of Paul's investment (to gain or "win Christ," 3:8) in terms of his union with Christ (see discussion on 2:1; 1 Cor. 1:30)—not simply an experience in the past but a present, continuing relationship. **Righteousness ... of the law** (see discussion on 3:6) is contrasted with its diametrical and polar opposite, righteousness **through the faith**. The latter, a principal benefit of union with Christ (see Rom. 3:21–22; 1 Cor. 1:30; Gal. 2:16), sets forth plainly why Paul radically revised his principles of accounting and how gain became loss on the revised balance sheet.

3:10. Know him, as in 3:8, is not merely factual; it includes the experience of the power of Christ's resurrection (see Eph. 1:17–20), of fellowship in His sufferings (see Acts 9:16), and of being like Him in His death (see 2 Cor. 4:7–12; 12:9–10). Believers already share positionally in Christ's death and resurrection (see Rom. 6:2–13; Gal. 2:20; 5:24; 6:14; Eph. 2:6; Col. 2:12–13; 3:1). Here, however, Paul was speaking of the actual experience of Christ's resurrection power and of suffering with and for Him, even to the point of death. Paul already knew this world and its power; what he wanted to know fully was Christ.

3:11. I might attain does not convey any indication of doubt or uncertainty on Paul's part but

rather his intense yearning to advance his experience of **the resurrection**, the great personal anticipation of every believer (see Dan. 12:2; John 5:29; Acts 24:15; 1 Cor. 15:23; 1 Thess. 4:16). Paul so longed for Christ (see 1:20–23) that if he had his druthers, he would have already been resurrected.

3:12–14. The Christian life is like a race; elsewhere Paul used athletic imagery in a similar way (1 Cor. 9:24–27; 1 Tim. 6:12; 2 Tim. 4:7–8; see also Matt. 24:13; Heb. 12:1). Here Paul describes the athlete's attitude (v. 12), aim (v. 13), and award (v. 14).

3:12. Apprehend ... I am apprehended. Paul's goal was Christ's goal for him, and Christ supplied the resources for him to "press toward the mark" (3:14; see 2:12–13). In light of 3:10–11, the "mark" (3:14, 17), or "goal," may be imagined as the apprehension of Christ Himself (see 1:21).

3:13. Forgetting speaks not of losing all memory of a sinful past (see 3:4–6) but of leaving it behind as something done with and settled.

3:14. The prize denotes an award for exceptional accomplishment. The winner of the Greek races received a wreath of leaves and sometimes a cash award; the Christian receives an award of everlasting glory. The locus of **the high calling of God** is in Christ Jesus (see 3:12), the focus of God's invitation. Paul's ultimate aspirations were found not in this life but in heaven, because Christ is there (see 3:20; Col. 3:1–2).

3:15. Perfect should be set in quotations as follows: "Those of us who are 'perfect' should think this." In view of his own example (**thus minded**; see 3:12–14), Paul recommended an adjustment in the mindset of any among the Philippians who thought of themselves as "perfect." Paul was certainly not dismissing reasonable progress in spiritual growth and stability (see 1 Cor. 2:6; 3:1–3; Heb. 5:14). He was saying that there were heights yet to be scaled; no one should become complacent. **Otherwise minded** was Paul's way of anticipating an opposing view of what he had just written. If the readers accepted the view set forth in 3:12–14 and yet failed to agree in some lesser point, God would clarify the matter for them.

3:16. Let us walk by the same rule, meaning, "Let's agree to conduct ourselves by the same standards," in particular, practicing the truth the Philippians had already comprehended. One is responsible for the truth one currently possesses.

B. Against Antinomians, or Libertines (3:17–4:1)

3:17. Be followers ... of me, or "join with others in following my example" (lit., "be a fellow imitator"), as Paul followed the example of Christ (see 1 Cor. 11.1). **Mark them** (from the Greek verb *skopeō*; "to pay careful attention to") here carries a strong allusion to the related noun in 3:14, "mark" or "goal" (Greek, *skopos*). The lifestyles Christians lead ought to be models worth following. Indeed, believers should run with those who have their eyes on the ultimate goal, Jesus Christ. The writer of Hebrews wrote from the same perspective in Hebrews 12:1–2.

3:18–19. These two verses form an explanation (**For**; v. 18) that served as a supporting incentive to Paul's urging them to join in following him (3:17). **Told you often** (see 3:1) calls to mind Paul's repeated warnings. **Weeping** (see Acts 20:19, 31) reveals the lament that beset Paul's heart; he was not emotionally detached from the pitiable tragedy of those who **are the enemies of the cross**. Such enemies stand in glaring contrast to Paul's conduct (see 3:17) and to the truth of the gospel. The tragedy of their status is described in one poignant word: **destruction** (Greek, *apōleia*; "utter ruin," "annihilation"; v. 19), the opposite of salvation (see 3:20–21). **Whose God is their belly** depicts a deep self-centeredness; their appetites and desires come first. Such people **mind earthly things**, the opposite of heavenly things (see 3:20; Col. 3:1, 3). They set their minds on the things of this life; they are antinomians (libertines), the opposite of the legalists of 3:2.

3:20. The word **conversation** (lit., "citizenship") picks up the theme of 1:27. As a colony of Rome, Philippians were citizens of Rome and governed as if they lived in Italy; their civic life mirrored Rome in every way possible. Now the Philippian believers existed and functioned as a colony of heaven. The Christian has a new citizenship **in heaven**, where Christ is and where believers are, in union with Him

(contrast the "earthly things" of 3:19; see Eph. 2:6; Col. 3:1–4). **From whence ... look** points to the different focus that heavenly citizenship brings (see Rom. 8:19; 1 Cor. 1:7; 1 Thess. 1:9–10; 2 Tim. 4:8). In this world, Christians are aliens, fully involved in it yet not of it (see John 17:14–16; 1 Cor. 7:29–31; 1 Peter 2:11).

3:21. Shall change means to transform, referring to a supernatural and radical alteration by the Holy Spirit at the resurrection (see Rom. 8:11; 1 Cor. 6:14; 15:50–53). **Our vile body** is more literally "lowly" and characterizes the human body's weakness, decay, and death, due to sin (see Rom. 8:10, 20–23; 1 Cor. 15:42–44). **Fashioned like unto his glorious body** (see Rom 8:29; 1 John 3:2). The resurrection body, received already by Christ, who is the "firstfruits," will be received by believers in the future resurrection "harvest" (see 1 Cor. 15:20, 49). It is "spiritual," that is, transformed by the power of the Holy Spirit (see 1 Cor. 15:44, 46). **According to the working ... to subdue** explains the power that is able to effect such a transformation, a power measured by Christ's ability to subject all things to Himself. Christ's present power, earned by His obedience unto death (see 2:8) and received in His resurrection and ascension, is universal and absolute (see Matt. 28:18; 1 Cor. 15:27; Eph. 1:20–22).

4:1. Paul's sincere affection for his "brethren" is expressed in two pairings of four modifiers: **beloved and longed for** (see discussions on 1:8; 2:1), **my joy and crown**. Among Paul's letters, nothing quite equals the tender sentiments expressed in this chain of endearing terms. The word "crown" adds dimension and scope to them all: his outlook on the Philippians was not only true at that time but envisioned the return of Christ (see 1 Thess. 2:19). **So** refers to the closing statements of chapter 3. In the face of libertine practices (3:18–19), the Philippians were to follow Paul's example (3:17), having their minds set on heavenly things (3:20–21), and **stand fast** in the midst of their struggles for the sake of the gospel (see 1:27–30; 1 Cor. 15:58). Paul hallowed the sincerity of his affectionate admonition with a repetition of "beloved."

VII. Final Exhortations, Thanks, and Conclusion (4:2-23)

A. Exhortations concerning Various Aspects of the Christian Life (4:2-9)

4:2-3. The disagreement between **Euodias, and ... Syntyche** (v. 2) was serious enough to be mentioned in a letter to be read publicly, but it seems Paul was confident that **those women** (v. 3) would be reconciled. His handling of the situation is a model of tact; he did not take sides but encouraged others closer to the situation to promote reconciliation (see 2:2). How realistic and true to life that even in this letter of such joy, differences do arise between devoted Christian workers. Paul already prescribed the remedy to differences of the heart in 2:1-5. Here is a reminder that harmony of heart is found "in the Lord" (3:1; 4:4).

Laboured with me ... my fellowlabourers (v. 3) identifies those associated with the apostle in the cause of the gospel (women as well as men) as his equals, not as his subordinates (see 2:25; Rom. 16:3, 9, 21; Philemon 24). **Clement** is not mentioned elsewhere in the New Testament. "My fellowlabourers" refers to coworkers not mentioned but nonetheless known to God, for their names are entered **in the book of life**, the heavenly register of the elect (see *KJV Study Bible* note on Rev. 3:5).

4:4. Rejoice in the Lord (see 3:1) **always**, in all circumstances, including suffering (see Hab. 3:17-18; James 1:2; 1 Peter 4:13). This appeal for uninterrupted rejoicing is repeated for emphasis and the sake of its importance. "In the Lord" is the ground of our rejoicing.

4:5. Moderation refers to Christlike consideration for others (see 2 Cor. 10:1), which is especially essential in church leaders (see 1 Tim. 3:3; "shewing all meekness," Titus 3:2). **At hand** (see Rom. 13:11; James 5:8-9; Rev. 22:7, 12, 20) expresses the imminence of the next great event in God's prophetic schedule, the return of Christ (see 3:20). The whole period from Christ's first coming to the consummation of the kingdom is viewed in the New Testament as "the last time" (1 John 2:18). From God's vantage point, a thousand years are as a day. Thus, there is a sense in which the Lord's coming is near for every generation.

4:6. Be careful (i.e., "anxious") **for nothing** (lit., "not one thing"). Here Paul was speaking of self-centered, counterproductive worry, not legitimate cares and concerns for the spread of the gospel (see 2:28 and discussion; 2 Cor. 11:28; Matt. 6:25-31; 1 Peter 5:7). Note well Paul's alternative: **in every thing by prayer**. Anxiety and prayer are two great opposing forces in Christian experience. **With thanksgiving** is the antidote to worry (along with prayer and petition). To give thanks with prayer and supplication—at the outset, not just at the outcome—honors God's perspective and recognizes that His attentive provision is far above one's ability to care for oneself.

4:7. The peace of God is more than a psychological state of mind; it's an inner tranquility based on peace with God—the peaceful state of those whose sins are forgiven (see John 14:27; Rom. 5:1). The opposite of anxiety, it is the tranquility that comes when the believer commits every care to God in prayer and worries about them no more. Such peace **passeth all understanding**; it achieves "more than our clever forethought and ingenious plans can accomplish" (Martin, *The Epistle of Paul to the Philippians*, p. 170). The full dimensions of God's love and care are beyond human comprehension (see Eph. 3:18-20). **Keep your hearts and minds** draws on a military metaphor to portray God's peace as a sentry guarding or maintaining watch over the heart and mind. God's "protective custody" of those who are in Christ Jesus extends to the core of their beings and to their deepest intentions (see 1 Peter 1:5).

4:8-9. For Paul's use of **finally** (v. 8), see discussion on 3:1. **Whatsoever things** denotes anything of the caliber or quality of what follows: **true ... praise**. Paul understood the influence of one's thoughts on one's life. What a person allows to occupy his mind will sooner or later determine his speech and his action. Paul's exhortation to **think on these things** is followed by a second exhortation: **those things ... do** (v. 9). The combination of virtues listed in verses 8-9 is sure to produce a wholesome thought pattern, which in turn will result in a life of moral and spiritual excellence.

Together the verbs **learned, and received, and heard, and seen** (v. 9) offer a profile of Paul's pastoral care of and personal familiarity with the Philippians. How worthy an example was Paul's own life when he could invite attention to and imitation of both his teaching and the pattern of his conduct (see 3:17). What Paul knew from the pattern of his devotion would be the blessing of their imitation: **the God of peace shall be with you** (see discussion on 1 Thess. 5:23; see also "the peace of God," 4:7).

B. Concluding Testimony and Repeated Thanks (4:10–20)

4:10–20. In this section of the letter, Paul confirmed that it is the thought that counts (v. 10), that happiness is in the heart, not in the circumstances (vv. 11–12), that a "can do" spirit belongs to the inner power of Christ (v. 13), that the Philippians' gift to Paul was first a gift to God (v. 18), who is the true source of ongoing generosity (vv. 15–17).

4:10. Paul targeted the thoughtful concern behind the Philippians' gifts rather than the gifts themselves (see 4:15–18). **At the last … lacked opportunity** expresses his awareness that the thought was there all the time; only the opportunity was lacking. It is likely that the gifts carried by Epaphroditus came with apologies voiced on behalf of the congregation. Paul took pains to let them know that he found no fault in them for the delay, nor did he imagine any lack of concern for him (see 2 Cor. 11:9). Perhaps Paul's uncertain itinerary prior to his arrival at Rome or the lack of an available messenger had prevented the Philippians from showing their concern.

4:11–12. Paul genuinely appreciated the gifts from Philippi (see 3:14, 18), but he was not ultimately dependent on them (see 1 Tim. 6:6–8). **Whatsoever state … to be content** (v. 11) was for Paul a secret (v. 12) to living independently through dependency on Christ. Paul revealed that contentment, or "self-sufficiency" (Greek, *autarkēs*), is actually a sufficiency found not in the self but in Christ

(see 4:13). For all intents and purposes, Paul redefined the meaning of this favorite Stoic expression by converting the highly prized virtue of "self-sufficiency" into "Christ-sufficiency" (Fee, *Paul's Letter to the Philippians*, p. 427). **I know … abased … abound** (v. 12) means in every situation, in all things (see 4:6–7). Paul knew that true contentment is a matter of inner sufficiency that neither poverty can abash nor prosperity can assure. Prosperity too can be a source of discontent.

4:13. All things refers to any and all situations that Paul faced (see 4:11–12). **Through** (lit., "in") **Christ which strengtheneth me** expresses Paul's vital union with the living, exalted Christ—the inner power effecting Paul's strength. The secret of Paul's being content (see 4:11–12) and the source of his abiding strength (see especially 2 Cor. 12:9–10; see also John 15:5; Eph. 3:16–17; Col. 1:11) was a Christ-centered life, powered by the inner presence of Christ.

4:14. The verb **communicate** means to share, participate, or partake in something. Compare the noun "partakers" in 1:7. The Philippians' gifts were a means of involving them in Paul's troubles (see Heb. 10:33).

4:15. Paul appreciated the significant help of his Philippian partners by identifying the strategic importance of their participation (**communicated**) in the travelogue of his second missionary journey (4:15–16). **Beginning** refers to Paul's initial work in the region, when he first preached in Philippi (see Acts 16:12–40). When Paul **departed**, or set out, for the south (Achaia), where Athens and Corinth were located (see Acts 17:14–16; 18:1–4), he left **Macedonia**, the northern part of modern-day Greece, where Berea and Thessalonica, as well as Philippi, were located, and only the church of Philippi helped Paul on his way. **But ye only** expresses the unique and unmatched generosity of the Philippian church (see 2 Cor. 8:1–5). Paul used commercial language to describe **giving and receiving** (credit and debit) between the Philippians and himself (see "abound to your account," 4:17). Yet this commercial imagery clearly was transcended by the mutual concern and self-sacrifice of their relationship.

4:16. Even in Thessalonica, or while Paul ministered there (see Acts 17:1–9), the partnership of the Philippians was evident. The word "even" calls the reader's attention to an unexpressed but implied comparison. Thessalonica was the capital and largest city of Macedonia. Far greater was its influence and prestige than that of Philippi. Even there, in the biggest of the cities, Paul said, it was the church of smaller Philippi that had the bigger partnership in the ministry. **Sent once and again** enumerates two and alludes to three occasions. Clearly, the gifts sent to Rome through Epaphroditus were the latest in a long and consistent pattern of generosity (see 2 Cor. 8:1–5).

4:17. For the commercial character of the words **abound to your account,** see discussion on 4:15. The "investment value" of the Philippians' gift was not primarily what Paul received, but the "spiritual dividends" they received.

4:18. The phrase **a sweet smell, a sacrifice acceptable** is drawn from the language and imagery of Old Testament sacrifice, not of atonement for sin but of thanksgiving and praise (see Lev. 7:12–15; Rom. 12:1; Eph. 5:2; Heb. 13:15–16). Paul had already associated their gifts, involving Epaphroditus, with priestly service (see 2:25, 30); now he spoke of its outcome, the offering **acceptable, well pleasing to God.** For this wording, compare also the language and imagery of Christ's work for believers (see 1 Peter 2:5) and God's work in believers (see Phil. 2:13).

4:19. Paul's use of **my God** added not only a personal touch (see "my God," 1:3) but also a tone of personal testimony to his note of assurance. **Shall supply** is a promise that was given to a church that had sacrificially given to meet Paul's need. **Your need** made it clear that Paul was concerned about not only his own situation but also that of the Philippians. Paul assured them that God has more than enough to cover their need: **his riches in glory by Christ Jesus** sets forth the measure of God's supply (see Eph. 1:18; 3:16–20).

4:20. Paul could not hold back a doxology, especially as he considered the truth of 4:19.

C. Greetings and Benediction (4:21–23)

4:21–22. Final greetings are a typical feature of Paul's letters (see, e.g., Rom. 16:3–16, 21–23; 1 Cor. 16:19–20; 2 Cor. 13:12–13; Col. 4:10–12, 14–15, 18).

4:21. For **every saint,** see discussion on 1:1. **Brethren which are with me** is a reference to Paul's fellow workers at Rome, especially Timothy (see 1:1, 14, 16).

4:22. Cesar's household refers not to blood relatives of the emperor but to those employed (slaves or freemen) in or around the palace area (see "palace," 1:13).

THE EPISTLE OF PAUL THE APOSTLE TO THE COLOSSIANS

INTRODUCTION

Author, Date, and Place of Composition

That Colossians is a genuine letter of Paul is not usually disputed. In the early church, all who spoke on the subject of authorship ascribed it to Paul. In the ninteenth century, however, some thought that the heresy refuted in chapter 2 was second-century Gnosticism. A careful analysis of chapter 2, however, shows that the heresy referred to there is noticeably less developed than the Gnosticism of leading Gnostic teachers of the second and third centuries. Also, the seeds of what later became the full-blown Gnosticism of the second century were present in the first century and already making inroads into the churches. Consequently, it is not necessary to date Colossians in the second century, at a time too late for Paul to have written the letter.

Instead, the letter is to be dated during Paul's first imprisonment in Rome, where he spent at least two years under house arrest (see Acts 28:16–31). Some have argued that Paul wrote Colossians from Ephesus or Caesarea, but most of the evidence favors Rome as the place where Paul penned all the Prison Letters (Ephesians, Colossians, Philippians, and Philemon). Colossians should be dated circa AD 60, the same year Ephesians and Philemon were written.

Colosse: The Town and the Church

Several hundred years before Paul's day, Colosse had been a leading city in Asia Minor (present-day Turkey). It was located on the Lycus River and on the great east-west trade route leading from Ephesus on the Aegean Sea to the Euphrates River. By the first century AD, Colosse was diminished to a second-rate market town, which had long ago been surpassed in power and importance by the neighboring towns of Laodicea and Hierapolis (see 4:13).

What gave Colosse New Testament importance, however, was the fact that Epaphras had been converted during Paul's three-year ministry in Ephesus and had carried the gospel to Colosse (see 1:7–8; Acts 19:10). The young church that resulted then became the target of heretical attack, which led to Epaphras's visit to Paul in Rome and ultimately to the penning of the Colossian letter.

Perhaps as a result of the efforts of Epaphras or other converts of Paul, Christian churches had also been established in Laodicea and Hierapolis. Some of them were house churches (see 4:15; Philemon 2). Most likely, all of them were primarily Gentile.

The Colossian Heresy

Paul never explicitly described the false teaching he opposed in the Colossian letter. The nature of the heresy must be inferred from statements he made in opposition to the false teachers. An analysis of his refutation suggests that the heresy was diverse in nature. Some of the elements of its teachings were:

1. Ceremonialism. It held to strict rules about permissible food and drink, religious festivals (2:16–17), and circumcision (2:11; 3:11).
2. Asceticism. "Touch not; taste not; handle not" (2:21; see 2:23).
3. Angel worship (see 2:18).
4. Depreciation of Christ. This is implied in Paul's stress on the supremacy of Christ (1:15–20; 2:2–3, 9).
5. Secret knowledge. The Gnostics boasted of this (see 2:18 and Paul's emphasis in 2:2–3 on Christ, "in whom are hid all the treasures of wisdom and knowledge").
6. Reliance on human wisdom and tradition (see 2:4, 8).

These elements seem to fall into two categories, Jewish and Gnostic. It is likely, therefore, that the Colossian heresy was a mixture of an extreme form of Judaism and an early stage of Gnosticism (see 1 John, Introduction: "Gnosticism"; see also discussion on 2:23).

Theme and Theological Message

Paul's purpose was to refute the Colossian heresy. To accomplish this goal, he exalted Christ as the very image of God (1:15), the Creator (1:16), the preexistent Sustainer of all things (1:17), the Head of the church (1:18), the first to be resurrected (1:18), the fullness of Deity in bodily form (1:19; 2:9), and the Reconciler (1:20–22). Thus, Christ is completely adequate. Believers "are complete in [Christ]" (2:10). On the other hand, the Colossian heresy was altogether inadequate. It was a hollow and deceptive philosophy (2:8), lacking any ability to restrain the old sinful nature (2:23). The theme of Colossians is the complete adequacy of Christ as contrasted with the emptiness of mere human philosophy.

Outline

I. Introduction (1:1–14)
    A. Greetings (1:1–2)
    B. Thanksgiving (1:3–8)
    C. Prayer (1:9–14)
II. The Supremacy of Christ (1:15–23)
III. Paul's Labor for the Church (1:24–2:7)
    A. A Ministry for the Sake of the Church (1:24–29)
    B. A Concern for the Spiritual Welfare of His Readers (2:1–7)
IV. Freedom from Human Regulations through Life with Christ (2:8–23)
    A. Warning to Guard against the False Teachers (2:8–15)

Bibliography

Bruce, F. F. *Epistles to the Colossians, Philemon, and Ephesians.* The New International Commentary on the New Testament. Grand Rapids, MI: Eerdmans, 1984.

Gromacki, Robert. *Philippians and Colossians.* Twenty-First Century Biblical Commentary. Chattanooga, TN: AMG, 2003.

Lightfoot, J. B. *Saint Paul's Epistles to the Colossians and Philemon.* 1879. Reprint, Grand Rapids, MI: Zondervan, 1959.

Martin, Ralph P. *Colossians and Philemon.* Grand Rapids, MI: Eerdmans, 1981.

O'Brien, Peter T. *Colossians–Philemon.* Word Biblical Commentary 44. Waco, TX: Word, 1982.

EXPOSITION ———————————————————————————

I. Introduction (1:1–14)

A. Greetings (1:1–2)

1:1. Paul identified himself at the beginning of the letter as was customary in ancient letter writing. It was conventional to follow a pattern of address that listed the letter writer and the recipients (from A, to B) followed by a greeting (1:1–2). Paul described himself as **an apostle of Jesus Christ** because he was not known in person to the church in Colosse (see 2:1), and he was writing this letter as Christ's emissary to the church (for more information on Paul, see discussions on Acts 9:1; Phil. 3:4–14). Paul was very Christ-centered, as seen by this short letter, in which he used the title "Christ" twenty-five times and the title "Lord" (alone) nine times. **Timotheus** is mentioned as being present with Paul (see "we," 1:3, 4, 28; and "us," 1:8; 4:3), and as Paul's coworker, he concurred with the message of Paul's letter. Paul also mentioned Timothy in 2 Corinthians, Philippians, 1–2 Thessalonians, and Philemon, but Paul is really the sole author, as seen by the constant use of "I" (see especially 4:18).

1:2. Although Paul did not use the word church (Greek, *ekklēsia*), he did use the word **saints** (Greek, *hagios*; as in Rom. 1:7; Phil. 1:1; and Eph. 1:1) of those who were consecrated by God and to God through Christ. For **faithful**, see 1:7; 4:7, 9. Because of Christ's substitutionary death for the Colossian believers, they were declared holy in the sight of God, and because of the Holy Spirit's work, they were continuing to be made holy in their lives. **In Christ** points to the believer's spiritual union with Christ, mentioned by Paul eleven times in Colossians (see discussion on Eph. 1:1). The greeting proper comes with the words **Grace ... and peace** (see discussions on John 14:27; 20:19; Gal. 1:3; Eph. 1:2).

B. Thanksgiving (1:3–8)

1:3. We (Paul and Timothy) **give thanks to God.** Every one of Paul's letters, except Galatians, begins with thanks or praise (see discussion on Phil. 1:3–4). In Colossians, thanks is an important theme (see 1:12; 2:7; 3:15–17; 4:2). The Bible never thanks man for his faith and love, but rather thanks God, who is the source of these virtues.

1:4. Faith in Christ (see 1:2) recognizes not only the Colossians' identifiable trust but their mutual bond of belief that united them together in Christ. They had a living and dynamic faith, as is detected by their **love** for one another and **all the saints** (see John 13:35).

1:5. The three great Christian virtues of faith, love, and hope appear elsewhere also (Rom. 5:2–5; 1 Cor. 13:13; Gal. 5:5–6; 1 Thess. 1:3; 5:8; Heb. 10:22–24). Everywhere, the church should exhibit this triune profile; it is a healthy hallmark of Christ-centered fellowship. **Hope** is not wishful thinking but a firm assurance. The disposition of hope comes from the content of hope (**the word of the truth of the gospel**); the compelling truth of the gospel ("hope") orients one's entire outlook on the present, encouraging faith and love. For this thought of faith and love coming from hope, see Titus 1:2.

1:6. In all the world is an example of hyperbole, the literary technique of dramatic emphasis. Here Paul used this phrase to summarize the rapid and dynamic (**fruit** bearing) spread of the gospel, which, in three decades of Pentecost (see 1:23; Rom. 1:8; 10:18; 16:19), was growing in every quarter of the Roman Empire. In refutation of the charge of the false teachers, Paul insisted that the Christian faith is not merely local or regional but worldwide.

1:7. Epaphras was a native of Colosse (4:12) and probably founded the Colossian church. **Learned** (Greek, *manthanō*) gives the clear impression of guided instruction in the gospel at the hands of Epaphras, a picture that resonates with his evangelistic labors in nearby Laodicea and Hierapolis (4:13). Paul loved and admired Epaphras, calling him a "fellowprisoner" (Philemon 23), his dear fellow servant and a faithful minister of Christ. Given the threat of heretical teaching, Paul clearly endorsed the gospel the Colossians had "learned" from Epaphras. It was he who told Paul at Rome about the Colossian church problem and thereby stimulated him to write this letter (1:4, 8). The name Epaphras is a shortened form of Epaphroditus (from "Aphrodite," the Greek goddess of love), which suggests that he was a convert from paganism. He is not the Epaphroditus of Philippians 2:25; 4:18.

1:8. Your love in the Spirit describes not only the Holy Spirit as the source of Christian love but the character and quality of love.

C. Prayer (1:9–14)

1:9–11. The knowledge of his will (v. 9) is a matter of not only knowing God's commands but apprehending the values and character of His heart (**increasing in the knowledge of God**; v. 10). In the Bible, knowledge and wisdom are practical, having to do with godly living. This is borne out by 1:10–12, which state that knowledge, wisdom, and understanding result in a life worthy of the Lord. **Spiritual** (v. 9) describes wisdom and understanding that are informed by the Spirit (for the role of the Spirit in knowing God, see 1 Cor. 2:10–16). Facts alone will never inspire the strength that comes from knowing God himself. Real knowledge or familiarity with God (see Rom. 10:2) is the source of **all patience and longsuffering with joyfulness** (v. 11).

1:12–13. Light (v. 12) symbolizes holiness (see Matt. 5:14; 6:23; Acts 26:18; 1 John 1:5), truth (see Pss. 36:9; 119:105, 130; 2 Cor. 4:6), love (see James 1:17; 1 John 2:9–10), glory (see Isa. 60:1–3; 1 Tim. 6:16), and life (see John 1:4). Accordingly, God (see 1 John 1:5), Christ (see John 8:12), and the Christian (see Eph. 5:8) are characterized by light. The "light" is the opposite of **the power of darkness** (v. 13). **Made us meet** (or "qualified" us) **to be partakers of the inheritance** (v. 12) presumes the redemptive achievement of God's Son on the cross, which is vividly depicted in the language of being redeemed: **delivered** (rescued; v. 13) and **translated** (transferred). The transaction is cosmic, but the language is as tangible as a prisoner of war being rescued from enemy control and brought to safety under benevolent authority (see 1:14). **Kingdom** here refers not to a territory but to the authority, rule, or sovereign power of a king, meaning that the Christian is no longer under the dominion of evil ("darkness"; v. 12) but under the benevolent rule of God's Son.

1:14. Redemption (Greek, *apolutrōsis*; "buying back"; see Rom. 3:23; Heb. 9:15; Mark 10:45; Matt. 20:28) brings deliverance and freedom from the penalty of sin by the payment of a ransom: the substitutionary death of Christ. Thus, as Paul made clear, redemption is **the forgiveness of sins**, or the cancellation of the debt owed to the holiness of God.

II. The Supremacy of Christ (1:15–23)

1:15–20. This passage was perhaps an early Christian hymn (see discussion on 3:16) on the supremacy of Christ, used here by Paul to counteract the false teaching at Colosse. It is divided into two parts: (1) Christ's supremacy in creation (vv. 15–17); (2) Christ's supremacy in redemption (vv. 18–20).

1:15. Christ is called **the image of ... God** here and in 2 Corinthians 4:4. Paul's use of the word "image" (Greek, *eikōn*; "likeness," see 3:10; Rom. 8:29; 2 Cor. 3:18) confirms that the Son (see 1:13) reveals the Father (see 1:12), whom no one has ever seen ("No man hath seen God at any time," John 1:18). Since God the Father is **invisible**, in His "likeness" the distinct features of God's character and nature, the very "person" (Heb. 1:3) of God, are manifest. Christ, who is the eternal Son of God and who became the God-man, reflects and reveals God the Father (see John 1:18; 14:9), the "representation" and "manifestation" of God (Lightfoot, *Colossians and Philemon*, p. 145). His status as Son is further defined as **the firstborn of every creature**. Just as the firstborn son had certain privileges and rights in the biblical world, so also Christ has certain rights in relation to all creation—priority, preeminence, and sovereignty (see 1:16–18; see also Ps. 89:27 for this same idea of preeminence and sovereignty).

1:16. By him were all things created (see John 1:3). Seven times in 1:15–20 Paul mentions "all," as in "all things," "allfulness," and "every creature," thus stressing that Christ is supreme over all, which **thrones, or dominions, or principalities, or powers** details. **That are in heaven** entails angels. An angelic hierarchy figured prominently in the Colossian heresy (see Introduction: "The Colossian Heresy").

1:17. He is before all things refers to time, as in John 1:1–2; 8:58, and underscores "by him were all things created" (1:16). Therefore, **all things consist** ("hold together," "cohere") in Christ, and by virtue of Him, the created sum is "a cosmos instead of chaos" (Lightfoot, *Colossians and Philemon*, p. 156).

1:18. Christ's preeminence in all creation (1:15–17) is preamble to appreciating His preeminence in redemption (1:18–20). The agent of all beginnings, Christ is fittingly **the beginning** of the new creation. He is **the firstborn** (Greek, *prōtotokos*; used of birth order as well as the special status of the firstborn). Here Paul was stating that Christ is first in order and status because He was the first to rise from the dead with a resurrection body. Elsewhere Paul calls Him "the firstfruits of them that slept" (1 Cor. 15:20). Others who were raised from the dead (see 2 Kings 4:35; Luke 7:15; John 11:44; Acts 9:36–41; 20:7–11) were raised only to die again. Therefore, "the beginning" and "the firstborn" (see Gen. 49:3) identify Christ as the founder of a new people through the resurrection. He is "the firstborn" in this sense only as 1:16–17 make obvious.

1:19. Although no word for **the Father** is present in this verse in the Greek text, the verb **pleased** (see Matt. 12:18; and the noun "good pleasure" in Eph. 1:5, 9) and the context require the understanding of either "the Father" or "God" as the subject. The word **fulness** was part of the technical vocabulary of some Gnostic philosophies. In these systems, it meant the sum of the supernatural forces controlling the fate of people. For Paul, "fulness" meant the totality of God with all His powers and attributes (see 2:9; Eph. 3:19; 4:13).

1:20. Reconcile all things unto himself. Paul's thought is closer here to Eph. 1:10: "That in the dispensation of the fulness of times he might gather together in one all things in Christ, both which are in heaven, and which are on earth; even in him." It does not mean that Christ by His death has saved all people. Scripture speaks of an eternal hell and makes it clear that only believers are saved. When Adam and Eve sinned, not only was the harmony between God and man destroyed, but disorder was introduced into creation (see Rom. 8:19–22). So when Christ died on the cross, He made peace possible between God and man and, in principle, restored harmony in the physical world, though the full realization of the latter will come only when Christ returns (see Rom. 8:21).

1:21–23. The reconciliation of 1:20 is given individual expression as a present reality with the former (v. 21) and final (v. 22) condition of a believer in Christ described before conversion and before the eyes of God through **faith** (v. 23) in the substitutionary **death** (v. 22) of Christ, the gospel of God's work in Christ **preached** (heralded) to **every creature** (v. 23; see discussion on 1:6). Paul identified himself as **a minister** (Greek, *diakonos*; see 1:25) in the service of God's grand work of reconciliation (see 2 Cor. 5:18–19). In using the term "minister," Paul also gave an implicit endorsement of Epaphras and Tychicus (see 1:7; 4:7) as fellow champions of the same gospel. The link was vital for the Colossians, who were beset by teachers of heresy (see Introduction: "The Colossian Heresy").

III. Paul's Labor for the Church (1:24–2:7)

A. A Ministry for the Sake of the Church (1:24–29)

1:24. My sufferings. By preaching the gospel to the Gentiles, Paul experienced all kinds of affliction, but here he was probably referring especially to his imprisonment. **Fill up that which is behind.** By this, Paul was not suggesting that Christ's atoning sacrifice was deficient. Rather, he was saying that he suffered afflictions because he was preaching the good news of Christ's atonement. Christ suffered on the cross to atone for sin, and Paul "fill[ed] up" Christ's afflictions by experiencing the added sufferings necessary to carry this good news to a lost world.

1:25. Fulfill the word of God. The meaning here seems to be that the Word of God is brought to completion (i.e., to its intended purpose) only when it is proclaimed (see Isa. 55:11). Paul's commission to bring the Word to completion, therefore, required him to make the Word of God heard in Colosse as well as elsewhere (for a similar statement, see Rom. 15:19).

1:26. Mystery (Greek, *mystērion*; also meaning "secret"; used twenty-one times in Paul's letters) was used by Paul to denote the purpose of God, unknown to man except by revelation. This word was a popular, pagan religious term, used in the mystery religions to refer to secret information available only to an exclusive group of initiated people. Paul changed that meaning radically by always combining it with words such as **made manifest** (here), "made known" (Eph. 1:9), "make all men see" (Eph. 3:9), and "revelation" (Rom. 16:25). The Christian mystery is not secret knowledge for a few. It is a revelation of divine truths—once hidden but now openly proclaimed.

1:27. Gentiles ... Christ in you. "The mystery" (1:26) was the fact that Christ indwells Gentiles, for it had not been previously revealed that the Gentiles would be admitted to the church on equal terms with Israel (see discussion on Eph. 3:6).

1:28. Perfect (Greek, *teleios*; "mature," here possibly alluding to its alternative meaning of "initiate") was a term employed by the mystery religions and the Gnostics to describe those who had become possessors of the secrets or knowledge boasted of by the particular religion (see 1 John, Introduction: "Gnosticism"). In Christ, however, every believer is one of the perfect.

B. A Concern for the Spiritual Welfare of His Readers (2:1–7)

2:1–2. Laodicea (near modern Denizli; v. 1) was only about eleven miles from Colosse. This letter was to be read to the church there too (see 4:16). **Great conflict** (Greek, *agōn*) specifically denotes an athletic "contest" and generally "a struggle," even anxiety and concern. Here it expresses a contest of great concern on Paul's part to see the believers in Colosse and Laodicea **comforted ... knit together in love, and ... the full assurance of ... Christ** (v. 2). That was Paul's objective, the purpose and goal of his "struggle" for them. For **mystery**, see discussions on 1:26; Romans 11:25.

2:3–4. Jesus Christ is the sum of God's mystery (see 2:2). Here Paul made it clear that no additional or elite secret is required other than **the treasures** (v. 3) that are **hid** in Christ. In other words, no "mystery" exists that can add anything to Christ. Therefore, Paul undercut **enticing words** (v. 4) and the appeal of those who claimed the importance of an elite and secret **knowledge** (v. 3; see 2:8). Paul stressed knowledge in this letter (see 2:2; 1:9–10) because he was refuting a heresy that emphasized knowledge as the means of salvation (see 1 John, Introduction: "Gnosticism"). Paul insisted that the Christian, not the Gnostic, possessed genuine knowledge.

2:5. Absent in the flesh … with you in the spirit. Similar to 1 Corinthians 5:3, Paul expressed the depth of his interest, a bond that geographical distance could not diminish.

2:6–7. Walk ye in him (v. 6) means to "live" or conduct your life in relation to Him. Again, Paul called his readers back to the fundamental disposition of faith in the gospel message and away from any secret knowledge or experience. One's relationship to Jesus Christ within the community of faith (see 2:2) is not superceded or diminished by knowledge outside of Christ (see 2:4, 8). In fact, the believer's intimate, spiritual, living union with Christ is mentioned repeatedly in this letter (see, e.g., v. 7; 2:10–13, 20; 1:2, 27–28; 3:1, 3). If one is to go deeper, it is to be **rooted … in the faith** (v. 7), that which the Colossians and Laodiceans were originally **taught** when they received Christ.

IV. Freedom from Human Regulations through Life with Christ (2:8–23)

A. Warning to Guard against the False Teachers (2:8–15)

2:8. The rudiments of the world. This term (which occurs also in 2:20 and Gal. 4:3, 9) refers to false, worldly, religious, elementary teachings. Paul was counteracting the Colossian heresy, which, in part, taught that salvation required one to combine faith in Christ with secret knowledge and with man-made regulations concerning physical and external practices, such as circumcision, eating and drinking, and observance of religious festivals.

2:9. The fulness of the Godhead (see discussion on 1:19). The declaration that the very essence of

deity was present in totality in Jesus' human body was a direct refutation of Gnostic teaching.

2:10–15. Here Paul declared that the Christian is complete in Christ rather than deficient, as the Gnostics claimed. This completeness includes putting off the sinful nature (v. 11), resurrection from spiritual death (vv. 12–13), forgiveness (v. 13), and deliverance from legalistic requirements (v. 14) and from evil spirit beings (v. 15).

2:11–13. Circumcision (v. 11) and **baptism** (v. 12) are both symbolic pictures of salvation—one negative, the other positive. Circumcision pictures the cutting off of flesh—the repudiation of the flesh. Baptism pictures the believer's death, burial, and rising up to newness of life (see Rom. 6:3–5).

2:14. Blotting out means to remove or obliterate so as to leave no trace. In Christ, the believer's "record" is totally expunged of past violations, or **the handwriting of ordinances**. This is a business term meaning "a certificate of indebtedness in the debtor's handwriting." Paul used it as a designation for the Mosaic law, with all its regulations, under which everyone is a debtor to God.

2:15. Having spoiled principalities. Not only did God cancel out the accusations of the law against the Christian, but He also conquered and disarmed ("spoiled") the evil angels ("principalities" and "powers" in 1:16; Eph. 6:12), who entice people to follow asceticism and false teachings about Christ. The picture is of conquered soldiers stripped of their clothes as well as their weapons to symbolize their total defeat. **Triumphing over them** has the vivid literal meaning of "leading them in a triumphal procession," a metaphor recalling a Roman general leading his captives through the streets of his city for all the citizens to see as evidence of his complete victory (see 2 Cor. 2:14 and discussion). That Christ triumphed over the Devil and his cohorts is seen in Matthew 12:29; Luke 10:18; Romans 16:20.

B. Pleas to Reject the False Teachers (2:16–19)

2:16. The outcome of Christ's victory has practical consequences for believers. Christians are to allow no one to judge (see "beguile," 2:18) them on matters of diet or religious observance by calling on any principality Christ has disarmed (2:15) nor any record of debt He has expunged (2:14).

2:17. Shadow ... body contrasts form and substance. The ceremonial laws of the Old Testament are here referred to as "shadows" (see Heb. 8:5; 10:1) because they symbolically depicted the coming of Christ, so any insistence on the observance of such ceremonies is a failure to recognize that their fulfillment has already taken place. This element of the Colossian heresy was combined with a rigid asceticism, as 2:20–21 reveals.

2:18. The term **beguile** pictures an umpire or referee who excludes from competition any athlete who fails to follow the rules. The Colossians were not to permit any false teacher to deny the reality of their salvation because they were not delighting in mock humility and in the worship of angelic beings. **Voluntary humility**, or humility in which one delights, is of necessity mock humility. Paul may have referred to a professed humility in view of the absolute God, who was believed to be so far above man that He could be worshiped only in the form of angels He had created. Second-century Gnosticism conceived of a list of spirit beings who had emanated from God and through whom God could be approached.

2:19. In anatomical terms, **not holding the head** expresses the folly of a torso or its limbs disconnected from that which is central to its function and fitness as its body. The central error of the Colossian heresy was a defective view of Christ, in which He was believed to be less than deity (see 2:9; 1:19).

C. An Analysis of the Heresy (2:20–23)

2:20–21. With **Wherefore if ye be dead with Christ** (v. 20), Paul called the Colossians and Laodiceans to apprehend the victory of Christ (see 2:14–15) that they had acknowledged in baptism (see 2:12–13) and to apply its truth to those who judged (2:16) or beguiled (2:17) them. Paul asked them **why ... are ye subject** to them? **The rudiments of the world**. See discussion on 2:8. **Touch not; taste not; handle not** (v. 21) points out the strict ascetic

nature of the heresy. These prohibitions seem to carry Old Testament ceremonial laws to the extreme.

2:22–23. Paul gave a rather detailed analysis of the Colossian heresy: (1) it appeared to set forth an impressive system of religious philosophy; (2) it was, however, a system created by the false teachers themselves, rather than being of divine origin; (3) the false teachers attempted to parade their humility; (4) this may have been done by a harsh asceticism that brutally misused the body. Paul's analysis was that such practices are worthless because they totally fail to control sinful desires.

V. Rules for Holy Living (3:1–4:6)

A. The Old Self and the New Self (3:1–17)

3:1. If ye then be risen. What has been described as the indicative and the imperative (the standing and the state) of the Christian is set forth in 3:1–10. The indicative statements describe the believer's position in Christ: he is dead (3:3); he has been raised with Christ (v. 1); he is with Christ in heaven ("hid with Christ," 3:3); he has "put off the old man" (3:9); and he has "put on the new man" (3:10). The imperative statements indicate what the believer is to do as a result: he is to set his heart (or mind) on things above (3:1–2); he is to put to death practices that belong to his earthly nature (3:5); and he is to rid himself of practices that characterized his unregenerate self (3:8). In summary, he is called to become in daily experience what he is positionally in Christ (see Rom. 6:1–13). **Then** (or "therefore") links the doctrinal section of the letter with the practical section (as it does in Rom. 12:1; Eph. 4:1; Phil. 4:1).

3:2–3. Set your affection (v. 2). With the Greek verb *phroneō* ("think formatively upon," "be minded"), Paul bid his readers to let **things above** occupy their thinking and shape their outlook and attitude. The verb *phroneō* occurs only here in Colossians but figures prominently (ten times) in his letter to the Philippians (see, e.g., Phil. 2:2, 5; 3:19). Compare "things above" with Ephesians 1:3, "all spiritual blessings in heavenly places in Christ." How fitting, for that is where believers belong, since our **life is hid with Christ in God** (v. 3).

3:4. Shall appear refers to Christ's second coming (see 1 Thess. 1:10; Phil. 3:20).

3:5. Paul said to **Mortify**, or "put to death," that which has died (see 3:3; Gal. 2:20; 6:14). He gave a clue in 3:2 as to how to do that: a mind renewed (see also 3:10; Rom. 8:5–6; 12:1–2) from above, through the truth and Spirit of God (see "put off ... put on," 3:9–10).

3:6. The wrath of God. God is unalterably opposed to sin and will invariably make sure that it is justly punished (see *Zondervan KJV Study Bible* note on Zech. 1:2).

3:7–8. Walked ... lived characterizes the course of one's life on the horizontal plane of earthly existence apart from the vertical intervention of God's heavenly truth and existence in Christ (see Eph. 2:1–6).

3:9–10. Put off (v. 9) **... put on** (v. 10). At salvation, God changes the believer's nature, making this possible (see Gal. 3:27; discussions on Eph. 4:22–24). It is the task of the believer to starve (see "Mortify," 3:5) the old man and feed ("set your affection," 3:2) the new man through right (**renewed**; see 2 Cor. 5:17) thinking that is set straight by **knowledge** (see 1:10; 2:2–3) of Christ, God's image (see 1:15; for **the image of him that created him**, see discussion on Gen. 1:26).

3:11. It is the new man, the new creation, the new image, that transforms and transcends every earthly echelon or segregation. The **barbarian** did not speak Greek and was thought to be uncivilized. The **Scythian** was known especially for brutality and was considered little better than a wild beast. Originally from what is today south Russia, Scythians were the barbarian's barbarian. **Christ is all, and in all** and accordingly transcends all barriers and unifies people from all cultures, races, and nations. Such distinctions are no longer significant. Christ alone matters.

3:12–14. Put on (v. 12), or clothe yourselves with, the attire appropriate for **the elect of God**, a term used of both Israel (Deut. 4:37) and the Christian community (1 Peter 2:9). Divine election is a constant theme in Paul's letters (see discussion on Eph. 1:4), but the Bible never teaches that it dulls human responsibility. On the contrary, as this verse shows, it is precisely because the Christian has been elected to eternal salvation that he must put forth every effort to live a godly life. Paul believed that divine sovereignty and human responsibility go hand in hand. The character qualities listed in these verses are best understood as belonging to the new man and image (see 3:10) that is created after God (1:15). Living the godly life is defined, then, by Christlikeness, and its power is found in Christ, who shapes one's heart and mind through faith (see 3:17).

3:15. The peace of God is the attitude of peace that Christ alone gives, replacing the attitude of bitterness and quarrelsomeness. This attitude is to **rule** (lit., "function like an umpire") in all human relationships.

3:16–17. The word of Christ (v. 16) refers especially to Christ's teaching, which in the time of the Colossians was transmitted orally. But by implication, it includes the Old Testament as well as the New Testament. **Psalms and hymns and spiritual songs**. Some of the most important doctrines were expressed in Christian hymns preserved now only in Paul's letters (see 1:15–20; Eph. 5:14; Phil. 2:6–11; 1 Tim. 3:16). "Psalms" refers to the Old Testament psalms (see Luke 20:42; 24:44; Acts 1:20; 13:33), some of which may have been set to music by the church. "Psalm" could also describe a song newly composed for Christian worship (see 1 Cor. 14:26, where "hymn" is literally "psalm" in the Greek text). A "hymn" was a song of praise, especially used in a celebration (see Mark 14:26; Heb. 2:12; see also Acts 16:25), much like the Old Testament psalms that praised God for all that He is. A "song" recounted the acts of God and praised Him for them (see Rev. 5:9; 14:3; 15:3), much like the Old Testament psalms that thanked God for all that He had done (see discussion on Eph. 5:19–20). **Whatsoever ye do in word or deed** (v. 17) is comprehensive, as the words **do all** make evident. **In the name of** denotes "under the authority and auspices of" Christ. Add this element of representation to the popular question, "What would Jesus do?" for a practical commentary and application of what Paul admonished.

B. Rules for Christian Households (3:18 – 4:1)

3:18 – 4:1. Paul next turned to a series of admonitions concerning the household (see discussions on Eph. 5:22 – 6:9). Luther used the expression *haustafeln*, a "list of rules for the household," for this section. Implictly, Paul's directives illustrate the dramatic difference that Christ makes in the home and the workplace.

3:18. As is fit in the Lord. "Fit" denotes what is "proper," or literally "reaches" what is expected or required by the Lord (see Eph. 5:22).

3:19. Love your wives. This command to love is a duty that cannot be fulfilled without corresponding affection and sweetness. **Be not bitter against them** shows the leadership of the husband's love; it cannot be soured or withheld because of disappointment in the wife. The husband's indefatigable love is closest to the love of Jesus Christ (Eph. 5:25 – 29).

3:20. Children (Greek, *teknon*) are to obey their parents **in all things**, or in everything not sinful (see 3:25; Acts 5:29). Although the term for "children" is not age specific, it likely refers to children in the care of and under the supervision of their parents (see "bring them up," Eph. 6:4).

3:22 – 4:1. Paul neither condoned slavery nor sanctioned revolt against masters. Rather, he called on both slaves and masters to show Christian principles in their relationship and thus to attempt to change the institution. The reason Paul wrote more about slaves and masters than about wives, husbands, children, and fathers may be that the slave Onesimus (4:9) was going along with Tychicus to deliver this Colossian letter and the letter to Philemon, Onesimus's master, who also lived in Colosse (see the book of Philemon).

C. Further Instructions (4:2 – 6)

4:2. In Greek, **Continue** carries the sense of "diligent attention to something," which matches the word **watch**. Prayer and thanksgiving go hand in glove (see Phil. 4:6) and are mutually appropriate to the mind and heart focused on a sovereign and benevolent heavenly Father.

4:3 – 6. Paul's admonition to "continue in prayer" (4:2) led naturally to a request for intercession on his

behalf. His concern for the advance of his ministry to the world on behalf of Christ (vv. 3 – 4) led him to give his readers guidance concerning their witness to others (vv. 5 – 6). Concourse with others pivots on communication, and words must be served and **seasoned with salt** (v. 6). Salt is a preservative and is tasty. Similarly, the Christian's conversation is to be wholesome (see 3:8; Eph. 4:29).

VI. Final Greetings (4:7 – 18)

4:7 – 17. Since Onesimus (v. 9), Aristarchus (v. 10), Marcus (v. 10), Epaphras (v. 12), Luke and Demas (v. 14), and Archippus (v. 17) are mentioned in Philemon, this suggests that the letters to Colosse and Philemon were written at the same time and place.

4:7. Tychicus (see discussions on 1:23; 3:22 – 4:1; 4:12, 16; Eph. 6:21; see also 2 Tim. 4:12; Titus 3:12) was sent expressly to report on Paul's state of affairs on his behalf and to bring comfort. He accompanied Epaphras.

4:9. For the slave **Onesimus**, see Philemon, Introduction: "Recipient."

4:10. Aristarchus was a Macedonian who is mentioned three times in Acts: (1) he was with Paul during the Ephesian riot (Acts 19:29) and therefore was known in Colosse; (2) both he and Tychicus (Acts 20:4) were with Paul in Greece; (3) he accompanied Paul on his trip to Rome (Acts 27:2). **Marcus,** or Mark, was the author of the second gospel. Against Barnabas's advice, Paul refused to take Mark on the second missionary journey because Mark had "departed from" him at Pamphylia (Acts 15:38). About twelve years later, the difficulties seem to have been ironed out, because Paul sent Mark's greetings, both here and in Philemon 24 (sent at the same time to Philemon, who was in Colosse). About five years later, Paul even wrote that Mark was "profitable to me for the ministry" (2 Tim. 4:11; see discussion on Acts 15:39).

4:13. Hierapolis was a town in Asia Minor (present-day Turkey), about six miles from Laodicea and fourteen miles from Colosse. Its church may have been founded during Paul's three-year stay in Ephesus (see Acts 19), but probably not by Paul himself (see 2:1).

4:14. Luke wrote about Paul in the book of Acts, having often accompanied him on his travels (see discussion on Acts 16:10). He was with Paul in Rome during his imprisonment (see Acts 28), where this letter was written. **Demas** was a Christian worker who later deserted Paul (see 2 Tim. 4:10).

4:15. Nymphas was probably a Laodicean. The expression **the church which is in his house** illustrates the truth that the "church" is not a building but the people of God. For the most part, the early church had no buildings, so it usually met for worship and instruction in homes. It often centered around one family, for example, Priscilla and Aquila (see Rom. 16:5; 1 Cor. 16:19), Philemon (see Philemon 2), and Mary the mother of John (see Acts 12:12).

4:16. When this epistle is read amongst you (see Eph. 3:4; 1 Thess. 5:27) makes it clear that Paul used the letter as a form of direct address between himself and the church as a whole (see 4:18). Thus, the practice of the early church was to read Paul's letters aloud to the assembled congregation. **The epistle from Laodicea** does not necessarily mean a letter written by the Laodiceans. Rather, it could have been a letter that the Laodiceans were to lend to the Colossians—a letter that Paul had originally written to the Laodiceans. This may have been a fourth letter that Tychicus carried to this area in what is present-day Turkey, in addition to Ephesians, Colossians, and Philemon. It may have been Paul's letter to the Ephesians, a circular letter making the rounds from Ephesus to Laodicea to Colosse (see Ephesians, Introduction: "Author, Date, and Place of Composition").

4:17. Paul called **Archippus** his "fellowsoldier" in Philemon 2.

4:18. Paul's custom was to dictate his letters (see Rom. 16:22) and pen a few greetings himself (see 1 Cor. 16:21; Gal. 6:11; 2 Thess. 3:17; Philemon 19). His personal signature was the guarantee of the genuineness of the letter.

THE FIRST EPISTLE OF PAUL THE APOSTLE TO THE THESSALONIANS

INTRODUCTION

Author, Date, and Place of Composition

Both external and internal evidence (see 1:1; 2:18) support the view that Paul wrote 1 Thessalonians (from Corinth; see discussion on 3:1–2). Early church writers are agreed on the matter, with testimonies beginning as early as AD 140 (Marcion). Paul's known characteristics are apparent in the letter (compare 3:1–2, 8–11 with Acts 15:36; 2 Cor. 11:28). Historical allusions in the book fit Paul's life as recounted in Acts and in his own letters (compare 2:14–16; 3:6 with Acts 17:5–10, 16). In the face of such evidence, few have ever rejected Paul's authorship.

The letter is generally dated circa AD 51. Weighty support for this date was found in an inscription discovered at Delphi, Greece, that dates Gallio's proconsulship to circa AD 51–52 and thus places Paul at Corinth at the same time (see Acts 18:12–17). Except for the possibility of an early date for Galatians (AD 48–49?), 1 Thessalonians is Paul's earliest canonical letter.

Thessalonica: The City and the Church

Thessalonica was a bustling seaport city at the head of the Thermaic Gulf. It was an important communication and trade center, located at the junction of the great Egnatian Way and the road leading north to the Danube. Its population numbered about 200,000, making it the largest city in Macedonia. It was also the capital of its province.

The account of the founding of the Thessalonian church is found in Acts 17:1–9. Since Paul began his ministry there in the Jewish synagogue, it is reasonable to assume that the new church included some Jews. However, 1:9–10 and Acts 17:4 seem to indicate that the church was largely Gentile in membership.

Background

It is helpful to trace the locations of Paul and his companions that relate to the Thessalonian correspondence. Their travels were as follows:

(1) Paul and Silas fled from Thessalonica to Berea (see Acts 17:10). Since Timothy is not mentioned, it is possible that he stayed in Thessalonica or went back to Philippi and then rejoined Paul and Silas in Berea (Acts 17:14).

(2) Paul fled to Athens from Berean persecution, leaving Silas and Timothy in Berea (see Acts 17:14).

(3) Paul sent word back, instructing Silas and Timothy to come to him in Athens (see discussion on 3:1–2; Acts 17:15).

(4) Timothy rejoined Paul at Athens and was sent back to Thessalonica (see 3:1–5). Since Silas is not mentioned, it has been conjectured that he went back to Philippi when Timothy went to Thessalonica. However, 3:1 indicates that at some point Paul, Silas, and Timothy were together.

(5) Paul moved on to Corinth (see Acts 18:1).

(6) Silas and Timothy came to Paul in Corinth (see 3:6; Acts 18:5).

(7) Paul wrote 1 Thessalonians and sent it to the church.

(8) About six months later (AD 51/52), he sent 2 Thessalonians in response to further information about the church there.

Theme and Theological Message

Paul had left Thessalonica abruptly (see Acts 17:5–10) after a rather brief stay. Recent converts from paganism (see 1:9) were thus left with little external support in the midst of persecution. Paul wrote this letter to encourage the new converts in their trials (see 3:3–5), to give instruction concerning godly living (see 4:1–8), to urge some not to neglect daily work (see 4:11–12), and to give assurance concerning the future of believers who die before Christ returns (see discussions on 4:13, 15).

Although the thrust of the letter is varied, the subject of eschatology (doctrine of the end times) seems to be predominant in both Thessalonian letters. Every chapter of 1 Thessalonians ends with a reference to the second coming of Christ, with chapter 4 giving it major consideration (see 1:9–10; 2:19–20; 3:13; 4:13–18; 5:23–24). Thus, the second coming seems to permeate the letter and may be viewed in some sense as its theme. The two letters are often designated as the eschatological letters of Paul.

Outline

I. Thanksgiving for the Thessalonians (chap. 1)
   A. Grounds for the Thanksgiving (1:1–4)
   B. Genuineness of the Grounds (1:5–10)
II. Defense of the Apostolic Actions and Absence (chaps. 2–3)
   A. Defense of the Apostolic Actions (2:1–16)
   B. Defense of the Apostolic Absence (2:17–3:10)
   C. Prayer (3:11–13)
III. Exhortations to the Thessalonians (4:1–5:22)
   A. Primarily concerning Personal Life (4:1–12)
   B. Concerning the Coming of Christ (4:13–5:11)
   C. Primarily concerning Church Life (5:12–22)
IV. Concluding Prayer, Greetings, and Benediction (5:23–28)

Bibliography

Bruce, F. F. *1 and 2 Thessalonians*. Word Biblical Commentary 45. Waco, TX: Word, 1982.

Couch, Mal. *The Hope of Christ's Return*. Chattanooga, TN: AMG, 2001.

Green, Gene L. *The Letters to the Thessalonians*. Pillar New Testament Commentary. Grand Rapids, MI: Eerdmans, 2002.

Marshall, I. Howard. *1 and 2 Thessalonians*. New Century Bible Commentary. Grand Rapids, MI: Eerdmans, 1983.

Mayhue, Richard. *1 and 2 Thessalonians: Triumphs and Trials of a Consecrated Church*. Focus on the Bible. Ross-shire, UK: Christian Focus, 1999.

Morris, Leon. *First and Second Epistles to the Thessalonians*. Grand Rapids, MI: Eerdmans, 1959.

Stott, John. *The Gospel and the End of Time*. Downers Grove, IL: InterVarsity Press, 1991.

EXPOSITION

I. Thanksgiving for the Thessalonians (chap. 1)

A. Grounds for the Thanksgiving (1:1–4)

1:1. Paul. See discussions on Acts 9:1; 13:9; Phil. 3:4–14. **Silvanus.** See discussion on Acts 15:22. Also known as Silas, he accompanied Paul on most of his second missionary journey. **Timotheus.** See 1 Timothy, Introduction: "Recipient." Both Timothy and Silas helped Paul found the Thessalonian church (see Acts 17:1–14). **In God ... Jesus Christ** communicates the foundation of this band of believers identified as **the church of the Thessalonians.** Their existence as a church was by virtue of the vital union and living relationship that Christians have with the Father and the Son (see John 14:23; 17:21). The close connection between the Father and the Son points to the Trinitarian relationship (see 3:11; 2 Thess. 1:2, 8, 12; 2:16; 3:5). **Grace ... and peace.** See discussions on Jonah 4:2; John 14:27; 20:19; Galatians 1:3; Ephesians 1:2.

1:2. Thanks. See discussion on Philippians 1:3–4.

1:3. The triad of **faith ... love, and ... hope** is found often in the New Testament (see 5:8; Rom. 5:2–5; 1 Cor. 13:13; Gal. 5:5–6; Col. 1:4–5; Heb. 6:10–12; 10:22–24; 1 Peter 1:3–8, 21–22). Paul's

characterization of the fruit of faith as **work** sums up an array of "activity" generating purposeful actions out of faith in God (see 2 Thess. 1:11). Faith produces action (see Rom. 1:5; 16:26; Gal. 5:6; James 2:14–26). Doctrine comes from God's revelation; action comes from believing God. Charity, or love of God (1:4; 5:9), prompts the hard **labour** (Greek, *kopos;* "toil") of sacrificial service under tough circumstances, not just when it is convenient or sentimental. Hope is not unfounded wishful thinking but rather firm confidence in the Lord Jesus Christ and His return (see 1:10). Hope in Christ fortified the Thessalonians with **patience** and even joy in the midst of harsh challenges (see 1:6; Heb. 6:18–20; discussion on Col. 1:5).

1:4. Knowing ... your election of God. The reasons for Paul's conviction regarding the Thessalonians' election are stated in 1:5–10. Paul emphasized God's election, rooted in love (**beloved**), to stress that the ground of their election was the initiative of God's love and not their merits or virtue (see Col. 3:12; 2 Thess. 2:13; discussion on Eph. 1:4). This was a profound encouragement to the Thessalonians, who were suffering persecution. Thus, Paul confirmed God's elective love to these recent believers born to Christ out a pagan religious environment (see 1:10), in which divine favor came only from pandering to and placating a pantheon of capricious gods. Tangible proof for Paul's **knowing** is given (see "For," 1:5) in the way the gospel came to them (see 1:5) and the way they received it (see 1:6). **Brethren**. United to each other through union with Christ. This term (including its singular form) is used twenty-eight times in Paul's two letters to the Thessalonians. Both "beloved" and "election" speak of God's electing love (see Col. 3:12; 2 Thess. 2:13; discussion on Eph. 1:4).

B. Genuineness of the Grounds (1:5–10)

1:5. Our gospel, or the gospel preached by Paul, Silas, and Timothy, was the gospel they themselves had received by faith. The gospel is first of all God the Father's (see 2:8) because He originated it and Christ's (see 3:2) because it springs from His atoning death. **Power** refers to the power that delivered them from spiritual bondage, that of the Holy Spirit (see Rom. 15:13, 18–19; 1 Cor. 2:4–5), but power also resides in the gospel itself (see Rom. 1:16). **Much assurance** testifies to the "complete certainty" with which the preachers brought the gospel and the Thessalonians received it. Such certainty was also a mark of the Holy Spirit at work.

1:6. Followers (Greek, *mimētēs*; "imitator," compare English "mimic") refers to those who follow to the point of imitation. The order in Christian imitation is: (1) the believers in Macedonia and Achaia imitated the Thessalonians (1:7), just as the Thessalonians imitated the churches in Judea (2:14); (2) the Thessalonians imitated Paul, just as the Corinthians did (1 Cor. 4:6; 11:1) and just as all believers were to imitate their leaders (2 Thess. 3:7, 9; 1 Tim. 4:12; Titus 2:7; 1 Peter 5:3); (3) Paul imitated Christ (1 Cor. 11:1), as did the Thessalonians (here); (4) all were to imitate God (Eph. 5:1). **Much affliction**, such as that recorded in Acts 17:5–14 (see also 1 Thess. 2:14), did not quench the joy that characterized the Thessalonians; this too is a hallmark of the Holy Spirit.

1:7. Ye were ensamples, or "examples" (Greek, *typos*; "model"), formed by imitation of Paul and the Lord (1:6). The Thessalonian believers influenced others across **Macedonia and Achaia**, the two Roman provinces into which Greece was then divided (see Acts 19:21; Rom. 15:26).

1:8. In every place means every place they visited or knew about (see Rom. 1:8; 1 Cor. 1:2; 2 Cor. 2:14; 1 Tim. 2:8). **Your faith to God-ward** is Paul's articulation of the fact that their faith was prominently directed toward God and not gods (see 1:9). This singular focus was noteworthy in a culture permeated by a pagan pantheon (or many deities). The news spread because Thessalonica was on the important Egnatian Way; it was also a busy seaport and the capital of the Roman province of Macedonia.

1:9–10. Three marks of true conversion are (1) turning from idols, (2) serving God, and (3) waiting for Christ to return. In his two short letters to the Thessalonians, Paul wrote much about the second coming of Christ (see 1:10; 2:19; 3:13; 4:13–5:4; 2 Thess. 1:7–10; 2:1–12). Significantly, Paul labeled the "deities" that permeated the culture of the Greco-Roman world **idols** (v. 9) and poignantly contrasted them with the one "living and true God."

Jesus (v. 10; see discussion on Matt. 1:21) is He who **delivered** (or "rescued"; see Rom. 11:26, Isa. 59:20) **us from the wrath** of God's judgment that is to come upon sin (see 2:16; Ac 17:31 Rom. 3:5; 5:9; 9:22). Some see a reference here to the final judgment (see discussion on Rom. 1:18), while others think it refers to a future period of tribulation.

II. Defense of the Apostolic Actions and Absence (chaps. 2–3)

A. Defense of the Apostolic Actions (2:1–16)

2:1–12. The forced and premature departure of Paul and his team (see Acts 17:5–10) gave opponents of the gospel an opportunity to unfairly misrepresent them. The appraisal of God is more important than the approval of the world. It is an entirely different motivation. That difference was evident in the gospel Paul spread (vv. 1–4), in the good he sought (vv. 5–8), and in the God he served (vv. 9–12). Each of these three emphases featured an important use of the word "know" (vv. 1–2, 5, 11).

This part of Paul's letter has been called "a manual for a minister": (1) Paul's message was God's good news ("gospel," v. 2); (2) his motive was not impurity (v. 3), pleasing people (v. 4), greed (v. 5), or seeking praise from people (v. 6) but rather pleasing God (v. 4); (3) his manner was not one of trickery (v. 3), flattery (v. 5), or a cover-up (v. 5) but one of courage (v. 2), gentleness (v. 7), love (vv. 8, 11), toil (v. 9), and holiness (v. 10).

2:1. With **yourselves … know**, or "ye know yourselves," Paul appealed to the Thessalonians and their personal experience. The local church could refute the accusation of insincerity that evidently had been leveled against Paul (see 2:3). The word **vain** suggests "empty" or "fruitless," and the Thessalonian believers were themselves a living testimony to the fruitfulness of the gospel and Paul's **entrance**, or "way in."

2:2. Paul's entrance (**bold in our God**) was itself a proof of his and his team's conviction of the truth of the gospel, for they continued to present it despite opposition in Philippi and Thessalonica: **we had suffered … were shamefully entreated … [but] were bold … to speak unto you … with much contention**. Paul was deeply hurt by the way he had been treated in the city of Philippi (see Acts 16:19–40), yet he did not quit, as one with impure motives might have when faced with opposition.

2:3. Perhaps opponents of the gospel had used the words found in this verse to misrepresent the **exhortation** that Paul and his team delivered, causing Paul to describe their right motives with negative words rather than positive ones. **Deceit** translates the Greek word *planaō*, which means "to stray" or "to lead astray into error." **Uncleanness** points out the moral purity that characterized Paul's exhortation. The Greek word for **guile** was originally used of a lure for catching fish; it came to be used of any sort of cunning used for profit.

2:4–5. As one who had himself been dramatically converted by the gospel he proclaimed, Paul was loyal to the privilege of serving "the gospel of God" (2:2, 8). The allegiance of this gospel team was to God and God only. Paul could speak of pure motives because God knows **our hearts** (v. 4), not simply one's emotions but also one's intellect and will. Therefore, God is the perfect "witness" to the fact

that their exhortation (see 2:3) was not guided by false motives. **Flattering** (v. 5), or "insincere praise," and a **cloke of covetousness**, or concealed greed, had no part in the gospel Paul represented to the Thessalonians. Personal profit was never Paul's aim.

2:6. Glory, or the praise of men, also belonged on the list of negative motives that were not part of Paul's entrance and exhortation. If praise was a motivation, it was the praise of God, not people, which was primary. The good (not the glory) that Paul sought was God's best for the Thessalonians. To that end, Paul was willing to forgo any personal benefits that **might have been burdensome**, even though apostles were entitled to be supported by the church (see 1 Cor. 9:3–14; 2 Cor. 11:7–11). Paul did not always take advantage of that right, but the fact that he had it and did not insist on it demonstrated that the good he sought was theirs and not his.

2:7–8. Moreover, Paul and his team were **gentle** (v. 7). Paul defined what he meant by giving a picture. **Even as a nurse cherisheth** (or "nourishes") **her children**, they tenderly cared for the Thessalonians. Paul further developed this picture of gentleness with an expression of inner feeling, **being affectionately desirous of you** (v. 8). Feelings such as that belong to the **soul** and the intimacy of personal attachment that accompanies the gospel. Just as Paul did not keep the gospel to himself but shared, or **imparted**, it, so he and his companions "shared" their own souls. The word **dear** is the Greek word "beloved." Paul expressed the love of God not only in the words of the gospel but in the words of their own affection and in the good that they sought for the Thessalonians.

2:9. Expanding on the concern of being burdensome (see 2:6), Paul recalled how he and his team had readily shouldered **labour and travail** ("difficult exertion"). Greeks despised manual labor and viewed it as fit only for slaves, but Paul was not ashamed of doing any sort of work that would help further the gospel. He did not want to be unduly dependent on others.

2:10. Here is a positive summary of Paul's motives and actions, to which God and the Thessalonians would make ready witnesses before any accuser. Paul and his companions conducted themselves **holily** before God and **justly** before men and thus **unblameably** before all.

2:11. In Greek, 2:10–12 is one sentence. The positive summary of 2:10 is expanded with details of the fatherly concern that Paul and his team had for the Thessalonians. Their gentleness and affection was likened to a nursing mother (see 2:7), and their guidance was likened to **a father** whose first concern is his child's proper rearing. **Exhorted and comforted and charged** suggests different manners of fatherly motivation, possibly with varying strength, such as bidding, kindly coaxing, and insisting. Although Paul himself was not a father, good models, like nursing mothers (see 2:7), made such analogies powerful pictures. One must not rule out the Fatherhood of God Himself as an influence on Paul's thinking. Indeed, Paul saw himself as a steward of God's own values when he expressed his purpose in 2:12: "That you would walk worthy of God."

2:12. The goal of all Paul's actions and attitude was defined by the God he served, **That** (the Thessalonians) **would walk worthy of God** (see Eph. 4:1). The initiative and invitation of the gospel is God's. It is He **who ... called** (see discussion on 1:4) the Thessalonians. **His kingdom**, the kingdom of God, was the chief subject of Jesus' teaching. Paul did not use this term often but used it on one occasion to sum up the message of his preaching (see Acts 20:25). The "kingdom" or "reign" of God expresses the rule of God in the present time, which will be revealed in all its glory at the future and royal coming of Jesus. It is this future manifestation that Paul had before him, and it is the hope of everyone called to it. Paul's talk of God's "kingdom" and "glory" touched national aspirations going back to the royal monarchy of Macedonia and issues of a new and greater allegiance to God (see Acts 17:7).

2:13. Paul's defense of their "entrance" (2:1) was shaded with thanksgiving for the way the Thessalonians received the apostolic preaching. Paul's first expression of thanksgiving echoed in a second; such repetition strengthened the sincerity of his words

without ceasing. The Thessalonians had received the message **not as the word of men**, though it was delivered by human hands, **but as ... the word of God**, as coming not from men but from God Himself. Paul knew (see Gal. 1:12), as did his regenerated hearers, that the message he preached was the sacred and revealed Word of God. The apostle Peter confirmed this (1 Peter 3:15–16). God's Word **effectually worketh**, specifying the divine operation and transforming work of God's truth within any who **believe**, or take to heart, God's Word through faith. An evidence of its operation and a reason for Paul's continued thanksgiving is found in 2:14, in the way the Thessalonians were facing persecution (see 3:3–4).

2:14. Paul's extended his reason for thanksgiving with his admiring identification of the Thessalonians with **the churches ... in Judea**, calling them **followers** (i.e., "imitators"; see 1:6) in their handling of persecution. **Ye also have suffered ... of your own countrymen** (or "of those of the same race"). At the time of Paul's initial visit to Thessalonica, persecution instigated by the Jews apparently was being carried out by Gentiles (see Acts 17:5–9). Although Paul had great love and deep concern for the salvation of those of his own race, **the Jews** (see Rom. 9:1–3; 10:1), he did not fail to rebuke harshly Jews who persecuted the church.

2:15. Paul wanted the Thessalonians to know that their persecutions were not unique but belonged to a vehement opposition to God's gospel. None other than **the Lord Jesus**, the **prophets** before Him (Rom. 1:1–2; 16:26; Acts 7:52), and now Paul and others who spoke the Word of God, had suffered persecution. Throughout Old Testament history, Israelites had persecuted their prophets (see Acts 7:52), and Paul, like Stephen, saw the gospel themes in their message.

2:16. The wrath is come refers to the eschatological wrath, the final outpouring of God's anger upon sinful mankind (see 1:10). Paul spoke of it as already present, either because it had been partially experienced by the Jews or because of its absolute certainty.

B. Defense of the Apostolic Absence (2:17–3:10)

2:17. Taken from you is literally "orphaned" in the Greek. Paul was like a mother (see 2:7), a father (see 2:11), and now an orphan. Certainly these word pictures that so vividly express how Paul and his team had "imparted" (2:8) their own souls correspond to the fact that they were never "taken from" the Thessalonians **in heart**.

2:18. Satan hindered us points to the reality of spiritual warfare. "Satan" means "adversary." Satan's objective is to oppose, through obstacles and false accusations, the achievement of God's will and purposes in the lives of His children. Thus, Satan is called "the tempter" (see 3:5 and discussion). Opponents of the gospel who misrepresented Paul's absence and motives were spiritually blind to that reality, but believers must never shut their eyes to it. Paul had encountered it in his endeavors to strengthen the Thessalonians' faith (see 3:2–5). God's purposes are the Enemy's point of attack. **Once and again** Paul was prevented from visiting the Thessalonians. What the hindrances were, he did not make clear. Poor health, inclement weather, persecution in Corinth, or more, may have been implements of opposition.

2:19. The **crown** (Greek, *stephanos*) of which Paul spoke is not a royal crown but a wreath used on festive occasions or as the prize in the Greek games. With this image of the prize in view, Paul's questions isolated the one objective of Christian ministry: people. The impending return of Christ puts believers' endeavors into perspective; people are the redemptive prize of the gospel and all who spread it. The expression **at his coming** was used regarding the arrival of a great person, as on a royal visit.

2:20. Ye are our glory and joy. This was true at that time (see Phil. 4:1) and will also be true when Christ returns. "Glory and joy" aptly and succinctly expresses both the outer and the inner recognition that accompanies one's spiritual investment in the life of another.

3:1–2. Paul first went to Athens alone, then sent to Berea for Silas and Timothy (see Introduc-

tion: "Background"; Acts 17:14–15). It is not clear whether Silas, as instructed (see Acts 17:15), went to Athens with Timothy. However, when Timothy later returned from Thessalonica to Paul, who was now at Corinth, Silas came with him (see Acts 18:5).

3:1. We reflects a collective decision to send Timothy. Paul and Silas were **left** behind. It was a decision of the will but not the heart (see 2:17).

3:2. The purpose of sending Timothy was to **establish**, or "strengthen," the Thessalonians' faith. In Greek classical literature, the word "establish" was generally used in the literal sense of putting a buttress on a building. The desired outcome, unmoveable faith (3:3), corresponds to the word "establish." In the New Testament, it is mainly used figuratively, as here. **Comfort** is the same kindly coaxing of 3:11. Timothy's credentials were four. He was (1) **brother** (used nineteen times in 1 Thessalonians), expressing the bond of spiritual affinity and kinship in Christ; (2) **minister** (1 Cor. 3:5–6), expressing the devotion of a servant to God; (3) **fellowlabourer** (see 1 Cor. 3:9), expressing mutual and common effort for the gospel; (4) and **sent**, conveying that Timothy came under the authority of Paul.

3:3. Afflictions refers to the opposition and persecution the Thessalonian converts suffered. Christians must expect troubles (see Mark 4:17; John 16:33; Acts 14:22; 2 Tim. 3:12; 1 Peter 4:12), but these are not disasters, for they advance God's purposes (see Acts 11:19; Rom. 5:3; 2 Cor. 1:4; 4:17). The purpose of Timothy's mission to establish and comfort their faith (see 3:2, 4) had an anticipated outcome: that no Thessalonian **be moved**. The Greek word "moved" has been used of a dog vigorously wagging his tail. Here its figurative sense, connected as it is with an established and encouraged "faith," points to agitation and disturbance of the mind. Paul wanted the inner life of faith to be firm and unperturbed by outward "afflictions," which "the tempter" (3:5) so readily uses to trigger self-destruction through a shaken inner perspective and earthly thinking that affects one's faith (knowledge and trust) in God.

3:4. We told you before. Paul repeatedly included in his earlier teaching doctrinal instruction about suffering and one of its forms, persecution. An insight to be gained here is that biblical truth had provided a foundation for facing the specifics of the Thessalonians' current suffering.

3:5. Paul used the Greek emphatic pronoun **I** (used elsewhere only in 2:18) to emphasize his deep concern. **The tempter** identifies Satan, who is spoken of in every major division of the New Testament. He is supreme among evil spirits (see John 16:11; Eph. 2:2). His activities can affect the physical (see 2 Cor. 12:7) and the spiritual (see Matt. 13:39; Mark 4:15; 2 Cor. 4:4). He tempted Jesus (Matt. 4:1–11), and he continues to tempt Jesus' servants (see Luke 22:3; 1 Cor. 7:5). He hinders missionary work (2:18). He, however, has already been defeated (see Col. 2:15), and Christians need not be overwhelmed by him (see Eph. 6:16). His final overthrow is certain (see Rev. 20:10). **In vain** summarizes the potential jeopardy of a collapsed faith that has lost sight of God and turned in unbelief from the celestial certainties of the gospel to terrestrial solutions for earthly afflictions.

3:6. Timothy had returned and **brought us good tidings** (or "good news"). This is the only place where Paul used the Greek for this phrase for anything other than the gospel. Three things caused him joy: (1) the Thessalonians' **faith**, a right attitude toward God; (2) their **charity**, a right attitude toward man; and (3) their **desiring greatly to see us**, a right attitude toward Paul. Timothy's report of their faith and their love (see 1:3) was a boon to Paul and probably set him promptly to writing this letter.

3:7–8. Paul and Silas were **comforted** ("encouraged"; v. 7) in their own **affliction and distress**. At Philippi, Thessalonica, Berea, Athens, and now Corinth (see Acts 18:9–10; 1 Cor. 2:3), they had suffered outer and inner turmoil. The news of the Thessalonians invigorated them: **now we live** (v. 8) alludes to the joy mentioned in 3:9 and 2:20.

3:9. Thanks … to God. Verses 7–8 show that Paul's work of evangelism had been effective. He might have congratulated himself on work well done, but instead he thanked God for the joy he had from what God had done. The wording suggests that

Paul found it inconceivable that he could give thanks enough to match what God had done or the joy that he and his companions were experiencing.

3:10. Night and day refers to frequent prayer, not prayer at two set times (see 1:2–3). **Exceedingly** translates a strong and unusual Greek compound word (found elsewhere in the New Testament only in 5:13; Eph. 3:20) that Paul used to emphasize his passionate longing. **That which is lacking** speaks of the things of a practical nature, such as moral (see 4:1–12) and disciplinary matters (see 5:12–24). Others were doctrinal, such as confusion over Christ's return (see 4:13–5:11). **Your faith** was the focus of Paul's concern, and this is the fifth time in the chapter that Paul expressly spoke of it (see 3:2, 5–7).

C. Prayer (3:11–13)

3:11. Paul frequently broke into prayer in the middle of his letters (see, e.g., Eph. 1:15–23; 3:14–21; Phil. 1:9–11; Col. 1:9–12). For the link between Father and Son, see discussion on 1:1. For a Jew such as Paul, reared in a strict monotheism, a prayer offered to **God … our Father, and our Lord Jesus Christ** could only be offered if the divinity of Jesus was assumed (see 2 Thess. 2:16). Spiritual obstacles (see 2:18) must be met with spiritual solutions. Paul looked to the Father and the Lord Jesus to **direct** (Greek, "make straight") their way to the Thessalonians. The verb "direct" is singular with a plural subject, subtly showing these new converts from pagan pantheism that God the Father and the Lord Jesus not only work in concert but are one. Rather than Paul and his team forcing their own way, God would clear a way for them.

3:12. Paul prayed that the Thessalonians' **love** would **increase** with or without his presence. Aside from his intense desire to attend the Thessalonians' needs in person (3:10–11), Paul wanted their love for others to grow, and grow abundantly. In Paul's writings, **the Lord** usually means Jesus rather than the Father. Jesus is the expression and the agent of God's love and, perhaps for this reason, the specific appeal of Paul's prayer here (see 4:9; 2 Thess. 2:16; 3:5).

3:13. For the word **stablish**, see discussion on 3:2. **Holiness** is the basic idea of being set apart (for God). Here the completed process of sanctification is in view (see *Zondervan KJV Study Bible* note on 1 Cor. 1:2). If one wonders how to become holy and set apart for God, Paul provides the answer here in his prayer for the Thessalonians. An increase of love (see 3:12) is the means of strengthening and establishing a person from the inside out, beyond blame, in holiness before God. If one thinks of holiness as the absence of sin, love is the positive active way in which one gives no place to sin. Indeed, the whole law is fulfilled, Paul said, through love (see Rom. 13:10; Gal. 5:14; Matt. 22:36–40). **Saints** is used of Christians in many New Testament passages. Here it may mean the departed saints who will return with Jesus, or it may mean the angels, or more probably, both.

III. Exhortations to the Thessalonians (4:1–5:22)

A. Primarily concerning Personal Life (4:1–12)

4:1. Furthermore indicates that Paul had finished the main section of the letter, though much was yet to come (see Phil. 3:1 and discussion). **We beseech you.** Paul was not being arrogant but was speaking with authority in the Lord Jesus. He had the "mind of Christ" (1 Cor. 2:16). **Walk** (Greek, *peripateō*; from the Hebrew *hālak*; "to walk") was a word rich in meaning for Paul due to his rabbinic background as a Pharisee. It denoted a pattern of conduct or living conformed to a code (see Gal. 6:16) of prescribed ethical behavior. Although Paul had renounced his former religion (see Phil. 3:5–7) and Christ had become his standard (**exhort you by the Lord Jesus**; see 4:2), he used the word translated "to walk" often (thirty-two times in Paul's letters) when referring to the Christian way (see, e.g., Rom. 6:4; 8:4; Gal. 5:16, 25; Eph. 4:1; 5:15; Col. 1:10; 2:6; 4:5), connoting a pattern of steady progress. The horizon or focus of this walk or pattern of living is **to please God**. "To walk and to please God" is a case of hendiadys, the expression of one idea by the use of usually two independent words connected by "and"; here it means "to walk so as to please God."

4:2. Paul's use of authoritative commands has a military ring (see Acts 5:28; 16:24). The word translated **commandments** (Greek, *parangelia*) was used of an order to be obeyed and was a term familiar to the authoritative word of a military commander, philosopher, or deity, all of which belonged to the world of the Thessalonians. Here the authority is **the Lord Jesus** (see 2:13; Acts 17:7).

4:3. Sanctification (see discussion on 3:13) refers to consecration to God (see 1:9) and the exclusive right of His will. Devotion to pagan deities did not require moral purity or the elimination of **fornication**. The Greek word for "fornication" (*porneia*) identified any kind of sexual immorality outside of a heterosexual marriage, whether extramarital sex, adultery, homosexuality, incest, bestiality, or any other sexual impurity. This specification of sanctification as abstaining from sexual impurity should be compared with the wider call to **abstain from** (avoid) every form of evil (see 5:22), or everything that is not the product of God's love (see 3:12–13). In the first century, moral standards were generally very low, and chastity was regarded as an unreasonable restriction. The cultic worship and festivities of Dionysus, Aphrodite, Cabirus, Priapus, Osiris, and Isis encouraged concupiscence, or sexual desire, and ingrained it in the culture. Paul, however, would not compromise God's clear and demanding standards. The warning was needed, for Christians were not immune to the temptation (see 1 Cor. 5:1).

4:4–5. How to possess his vessel (v. 4). Given the sexual orientation of Paul's instruction, "vessel" (Greek, *skeuos*) is an inoffensive substitute for a man's "body" (see 1 Tim. 2:21–22). The word here is thought by some to be a substitute for "wife," based on 1 Peter 3:7 (see Bruce, *1 and 2 Thessalonians*, p. 83). Paul's language here suits the body of a man more than the body of a woman. The Thessalonians probably knew (see 4:2) precisely what Paul meant. If any ambiguity did exist, it may have been purposeful to the wider application of Paul's main emphasis on sexual purity. The verb "possess" (Greek, *ktaomai*) primarily means "to acquire," with the implication of mastery. If the "vessel" is the man's own body, then he is "to get [sexual] control" over himself in sanctification and honor. This was most likely Paul's meaning here and is akin to Paul's language and thought in 2 Timothy 2:21–22. In the Mediterranean world, **honour** was the prized community respect and recognition that a person achieved in the eyes of others. Here honor in the eyes of God is set above that of society and its culture of sexual license. In fact, the sanctification and honor that are to characterize the Christian's sexual behavior are contrasted with the lust of sexual desire that characterized the practice of the Gentiles. Knowing God makes all the difference. That difference can be detected in Paul's manner here, as he himself strove to speak directly while avoiding anything salacious as he addressed the subject of sexual propriety (see 4:6).

4:6. Paul's instruction on sexual purity extends to 4:8. The word "sanctification" (Greek, *hagiasmos*) occurs three times in 4:3–4, 7 (KJV has "holiness" in 4:7) and the power of sanctification is set forth in God's giving of the Holy Spirit (4:8; see 2 Thess. 2:13). Therefore, the words **go beyond**, conveying the sense of crossing a forbidden (sexual) boundary, and the words **defraud his brother** indicate that Paul had turned to the subject of adultery committed with the wife of a fellow Christian brother. The progression of Paul's thought moved from the general exhortation to all men (4:4) to a specific example and its consequences before God when a man does not "possess his vessel in sanctification and honour" (4:4). Even in the sexually licentious culture of the day, adultery with another man's wife was taboo. Here Paul's concern was not that social mores had been violated, although that would have brought dishonor on the Christian community, but rather God, who is the **avenger**, had been wronged, because God is the champion of the marriage bond. Likely, Timothy had reported adultery between members of the Thessalonian community, which prompted Paul to write this section of the letter. Sexual sin harms others besides those who engage in it. In adultery, for example, the spouse is always wronged. Premarital sex wrongs the future partner by robbing him or her of the virginity that ought to be brought to marriage.

The Apostle of Grace took seriously the holiness of God, the Avenger.

4:7. God hath … called us (see 2:12), a privilege that is incompatible with **uncleanness**, the antithesis of sanctification (**holiness**), which is God's will (see 4:3). The Thessalonians had answered the call of God.

4:8. God, who hath also given unto us his holy Spirit. To disregard Paul's instruction was to reject God and His influence, the Holy Spirit (see 1 Cor. 6:17–20).

4:9–10. Brotherly love (v. 9) translates *philadelphia*, a Greek word that outside the New Testament, almost without exception, denoted the mutual love of children of the same father. In the New Testament, it always means love of fellow believers in Christ, all of whom have the same heavenly Father. **Taught of God**, as in 3:12, speaks of God's work of love in the heart (see 4:13), the impress of His very nature upon ours (see Isa. 54:13; John 6:45; 1 Cor. 2:13). Paul wanted Christian love to **increase more and more**, without limit, between believers. Love creates harmony between Christians.

4:11. Some Thessalonians, probably because of idleness, were taking undue interest in other people's affairs. **Work with your own hands**. The Greeks generally thought manual labor was degrading and fit only for slaves. Christians took seriously the need for earning their own living, but some of the Thessalonians, perhaps as a result of their belief in the imminent return of Christ (see 2 Thess. 3:11) or the social and political institution of patronage, were neglecting work and relying on others to support them. Such a dependence on others opened the community to internecine conflict and outside influence. For example, the client of a patron had to curry his favor, for the client was dependent on the patron for support and protection. To do otherwise involved retiring to a quiet life, **to do your own business, and to work with your own hands**. To be sure, the favor of a pagan patron would run contrary to the favor of God (pleasing God, see 4:1). Thus, **study to be quiet**, the undertaking of a quiet life, was an expression associated with retiring from the public activity of patronage and the responsibilities involved in seeking the protection of powerful men (see Green, *The Letters to the Thessalonians*, pp. 210–12). Part of the problem may have been that some retired without working with their own hands and shifting dependence from pagan patrons to Christian ones.

4:12. Have lack of nothing can mean "not be dependent on anyone." Both meanings are true and significant. Christians who are in need because of their idleness are not obedient Christians. **Them that are without** is literally, "those outside," meaning those outside the knowledge of God (see 4:5) and outside the community of those who believe in Jesus Christ.

B. Concerning the Coming of Christ (4:13–5:11)

4:13. Them which are asleep. The euphemism of sleep for death was common in the Greco-Roman world and in both the Old and New Testaments and was used by Jesus Himself (see John 11:11). For the Christian, sleep is a particularly apt metaphor for death, since death's finality and horror are removed by the assurance of resurrection. Yet the wide usage of this metaphor prohibits any conclusions from the word "sleep" itself about the state or condition of the dead. Some of the Thessalonians seem to have misunderstood Paul and thought all believers would live until Christ returns. When some Thessalonians died, the question arose whether those who had died would have part in that great day (see discussion on 4:15). **Sorrow** expresses the profound grief that beset the Thessalonians when death struck their number (see 4:18). Sorrow can be a kind of tribute to a person's special place in their lives, but this sorrow is not the kind that characterizes **others** (lit., "the rest") **which have no hope** (see "them that are without," 4:12). Inscriptions on tombs and references in literature show that first-century pagans viewed death with horror, as the end of everything. The Christian attitude was a strong contrast (see 1 Cor. 15:55–57; Phil. 1:21–23).

4:14. The words **believe that** introduce the content of faith, the foundation of the gospel: **Jesus died and rose again.** Paul said not that Christ "slept" but that He **died**, perhaps to underscore the fact that He willfully bore the full horror of death so that those who believe in Him would not have to experience it. This certainty, that Jesus died and rose again, leads to a second certainty concerning **them also which sleep in Jesus.** As God raised Jesus, so also God will raise (**bring with him**) believers who have died, trusting in Jesus (see 1 Cor. 6:14; 2 Cor. 4:14; Rom. 6:3–8). Death "through Jesus" is but the prelude to resurrection "with Jesus" (for the importance of the resurrection, see 1 Corinthians 15, especially 15:14, 17–22).

4:15. By the word of the Lord. The doctrine mentioned here is not recorded in the Gospels and was either a direct revelation to Paul or something Jesus said that Christians passed on orally. **We which are alive** refers to those believers who will be alive when Christ returns. "We" does not necessarily mean that Paul thought that he would be alive then. He often identified himself with those to whom or about whom he wrote. Elsewhere he said that God will raise "us" at that time (1 Cor. 6:14; 2 Cor. 4:14). **Shall not prevent** means "precede" or "come before" those who have died or "fallen asleep." Paul pictured the dead in Christ as those who will receive precedence at the rapture but believed they would be quickly joined by those **which are alive and remain.** Evidently, the Thessalonians had been concerned that those among them who died would miss their place in the great events when the Lord comes, and Paul assured them that this would not be the case.

4:16. Paul called the occasion of "the coming of the Lord" (4:15) the *parousia* (2:19; 3:13; 5:23) of the Lord. The Greek word *parousia* (Latin, *adventus*) has a significant connotation of the "arrival" or "coming" of a royal or official personage. The Thessalonians would surely have connected Paul's use of *parousia* with the coming of the Lord, who, for them, had displaced the emperor (see Acts 17:7) and the pagan pantheon (see 1:9). In the Greco-Roman world, such visits were accompanied by considerable fanfare, to which there are broad corollaries here. The Lord's coming will be attended by celestial shouts and trumpet blares, and He will be met by both **the dead in Christ** and the living (see 4:17). For **the Lord himself**, see Acts 1:11. The descent of the Lord will be inaugurated and accompanied by God's directive, expressed in the threefold description of **a shout** (lit., "the command"), **the voice of the archangel**, and **the trump of God**. The archangel is unidentified. The only named archangel in the Bible is Michael (Jude 9; see also Dan. 10:13). In Scripture, Gabriel is simply called an angel (see Luke 1:19, 26). "The dead in Christ" **shall rise first**, before the ascension of believers mentioned in 4:17. Paul's comfort for the Thessalonians (see 4:18 and "hope" 4:13) emphasized the priority in the Lord's plan of "the dead in Christ" (a unique Pauline term for the church) receiving the honor of being called up first to meet the Lord as He returns. In 4:13–15, Paul used the Greek expression translated "them which are asleep" or "them which … sleep" to speak of those who had died. Here he used the expression "the dead in Christ" because his focus was on "rising." Implicit is the necessary "bodily" transformation that accompanies being "caught up" (4:17) and transfigures both "the dead in Christ" and those "which are alive and remain" (4:17; see 1 Cor. 15:50–53; Phil. 3:20; 1 Cor. 15:42–45).

4:17. For **we which are alive**, see discussion on 4:15. **Caught up** is the Greek word *harpazō*, "to snatch away." Both the dead and the living "in Christ" (believers; 4:16) are caught up into the air. A "rapture" (from the Latin Vulgate rendering, *rapio*) is clearly connotated to (1 Cor. 15:51–52 also refers to the same event; see *KJV Study Bible* note on 1 Cor. 15:52). **With the Lord** makes it clear that one's hope is not survival or immortality, but realization of uninhibited, unlimited togetherness with Christ, the chief hope of the believer (see 5:10; John 14:3; 2 Cor. 5:8; Phil. 1:23; Col. 3:4). The rapture will be in the air and will involve the removal of believers to heaven (the "Father's house," John 14:1–6).

4:18. Comfort one another closes what Paul began in 4:13. Paul's primary purpose in 4:13–18 was to urge mutual encouragement. To "comfort" means to "encourage" (from Greek, *parakaleite*). The

promise of the rapture of believers is the basis of that hope, which is grounded in the certainty "that Jesus died and rose again" (4:14). Mayhue (*1 and 2 Thessalonians*, p. 124) notes that this process is irreversible. No wonder Paul called it the "blessed hope" in Titus 2:13. This also explains why the Thessalonians were patiently waiting for God's Son from heaven (see 1:10).

5:1. The times and the seasons (see Acts 1:6–7). There have always been some Christians who try to fix the date of the Lord's return, but apparently the Thessalonians were not among them. The Lord's coming will be unexpected ("as a thief," 5:2, 4), and the Thessalonians already knew that. The New Testament clearly indicates that no one knows the time when the rapture will occur (see Matt. 24:36). Therefore, Christians are to be ready to meet the Lord at all times because He could come at any time.

5:2. For **the day of the Lord**, see 1 Cor. 5:5. The expression goes back to Amos 5:18. In the Old Testament, "the day of the Lord" is a time when God will come and intervene with judgment (see Zeph. 1:14–15) and then blessing (see Joel 3:14–21). In the New Testament, the thought of judgment continues (see Rom. 2:5; 2 Peter 2:9), but it is also "the day of redemption" (Eph. 4:30); "the day of God" (2 Peter 3:12) and "the day of our Lord Jesus Christ" (1 Cor. 1:8; Phil. 1:6); and "the last day" (John 6:39), "the great day" (Jude 6), or simply "that day" (2 Thess. 1:10). It is first tribulation and then Christ's kingdom (see Matt. 24:21–31; 25:31–34). There will be some preliminary signs (see, e.g., 2 Thess. 2:3), but the coming will be as unexpected as that of a thief in the night (see Matt. 24:43–44; Luke 12:39–40; 2 Peter 3:10; Rev. 3:3; 16:15). **As a thief in the night** is a simile emphasizing the vigilant watchfulness required of being ready for an unexpected visit by one who will come at an inopportune time (see Matt. 24:42–51).

5:3. The words **Peace and safety** would have had special relevance in a city loyal to Rome and a beneficiary of the *Pax Romana*. Throughout the empire, the expression obtained the quality of a slogan that paid homage to the benefits enjoyed by citizens living under the protection of Rome. At the least, Paul was emphasizing that the day of the Lord's coming will so surprise people that they will imagine themselves most secure at the time of His coming. Moreover, expressions of peace and safety (lit., "when they are saying …") may well have been voiced by those in Thessalonica who scoffed at needing the gospel and its announcement of God's coming wrath (see 1:9–10). Paul use of **sudden** stresses the surprise of unbelievers and paints a picture of one being caught in midsentence (compare the only other New Testament use of this word in Luke 21:34). **Destruction** is not annihilation but exclusion from the Lord's presence (see 2 Thess. 1:9), thus, the ruin of life and all its proud accomplishments. **Travail** expresses not so much the pain of childbirth as the suddenness and inevitability of such pains. The inescapable inevitability is captured in Paul's use of **not**, an emphatic double negative in the Greek and a construction Paul used only four times in all his writings.

5:4. By contrast (**But ye, brethren**), believers are not in danger of being so surprised. In 5:5–11, Paul's contrast between "the children of the day" and those "of the night" (5:5–6) never puts the believer's destiny in doubt but serves to assure and admonish (5:6–8), ending with a final affirmation of salvation (5:9–10) and an exhortation to comfort one another (5:11). **Darkness** (see Eph. 4:18) describes those who are not only alienated from God but ignorant, an emphasis that corresponds to the words **that that day should overtake you as a thief**. Believers no longer live in darkness, nor are they of the darkness (see 5:5; John 1:5; Acts 26:18). "Overtake" bears an ominous quality associated with the "destruction" (5:3) that belongs to those who are in darkness on the coming day of the Lord.

5:5. Children of is literally, "sons of." In Semitic languages (such as Hebrew), the expression "son of" was not only used to identify one's parentage but was also used figuratively of a predominant quality that characterized a person (see, e.g., Acts 4:36; Luke 10:6). Christians do not simply live in the light; they are characterized by light. In the expression **children of the day**, "the day" must not be severed from Paul's

overall theme of the day of the Lord; it refers back to 5:2 and 5:4 (see also 5:8). Here "the day" does double duty. It identifies the day of the Lord, and it compounds the metaphor of light in contrast to the night and darkness, ending with an inverted a, b, b^1, a^1 pattern. The balance brings over the word "children" ("sons"), and here Paul included himself to emphasize that **we are not [children of] the night, nor of the darkness**.

5:6–7. Sleep is used to characterize unbelievers as spiritually insensitive. Such sleep is not for "sons of the light." **Watch** (Greek, *grēgoreō*; "be awake, alert"; compare English "gregarious") is contrasted with "sleep" and points to the believer's vigilant expectancy in keeping with Paul's emphasis on Christ's coming (see Matt. 24:42–43; 25:13; Mark 13:34–37). **Sober** is contrasted with the conduct mentioned in 5:7. The person who is "sober" exercises self-control and is free from every form of physical or psychological inebriation (see Eph. 5:18).

5:8. The day alludes to the light that characterizes Christians but also refers to the coming of Christ (see 5:2 and discussion). Since the believer belongs to the day and accordingly lives in vigilant sobriety, Paul gave a picture to secure and summarize the mindset and disposition he wanted believers to possess: that of a soldier or sentry outfitted for duty with a **breastplate … and … a helmet**. Paul also used the metaphor of armor elsewhere (see Rom. 13:12; 2 Cor. 6:7; 10:4; Eph. 6:13–17). He did not consistently attach a particular virtue to each piece of armor but pictured the general idea of equipment necessary for the duties of a soldier. For the triad of **faith**, **love**, and **hope**, see discussion on 1:3. These cardinal Christian virtues are the spiritual ways believers are to actualize vigilance and self-control as a good soldier ready for duty.

5:9. Appointed emphasizes the divine determination of God and provides the strongest assurance and protection against fear of the day of the Lord. It is grounded in God's appointed **salvation** through Jesus Christ. Here the word "salvation" embodies the sense of deliverance from **wrath** (see 1:9–10). God's wrath involves the outpouring of His judgment (see

Rom. 2:5; 4:15). Notice that the tribulation judgments are called "the wrath of the Lamb" (Rev. 6:16) and "the wrath of God" (Rev. 16:1).

5:10. The words **live together with him** (see 4:17) indicate that Paul intended **whether we wake or sleep** to refer to whether the believer is "alive" or "dead in Christ" (4:16–17) when Christ returns. Thus, Paul gave a final assurance that summed up the questions posed in 4:13–18 and 5:1–10 and provided a fitting conclusion to both passages, followed by an all-encompassing exhortation (5:11; see 4:18). Although the terms "wake" and "sleep" are identical to those in 5:6, they are used differently here. Otherwise, Paul would have opposed what he argued in 5:4–7, concluding that it does not matter whether people are children of the light or children of the darkness. Such moral indifference and universalism was foreign to Paul and the emphasis of his teaching here on the subject (see Bruce, *1 and 2 Thessalonians*, p. 114; Green, *The Letters to the Thessalonians*, p. 243). For "sleep" (Greek, *katheudō*) as a euphemism for death, see Mark 5:39; John 11:11; Ephesians 5:14. Green (*The Letters to the Thessalonians*, p. 244) points out that both words, "wake" and "sleep," are correspondingly used figuratively for death and life in Mark 5:39, 41; Luke 8:52, 54.

5:11. The verb **edify** generally applies to building houses, but Paul frequently used it for Christians who demonstrate a constructive concern for another person's good (see Rom. 15:2; 1 Cor. 8:1; 10:23–24; 14:7). Such "building up" is a person-to-person effort and a responsibility that belongs to the entire community of believers (see Rom. 14:19). Therefore, it suited Paul's admonition to **comfort yourselves together**, or "encourage one another."

C. Primarily concerning Church Life (5:12–22)

5:12. Them which labour among you. Not much is known about the organization and leadership of the church during this period, but the reference is probably to elders (see 1 Tim. 3:1–5; 5:17; Heb. 13:7, 17). **To know them** is best understood as "to acknowledge" or "to give recognition to." The word "know" is fairly elastic, but here an appreciation of service to the church is the basis of Paul's call for esteem and peace in 5:13. The Greek here unmistakably bundles three distinguishing functions ("labour," "are over," "admonish") of one group of people. Paul's request reflects a recognition of leaders who exhibited the underlying leadership of the Lord in the way they served the church. Even official apostolic appointment follows recognition (see Titus 1:5–9, where the appointment ratified the leadership character that had already become evident). "Labour" generally denotes physical toil but in Paul's letters is associated with the ministry of the Word (see 3:5; 1 Tim. 5:17) and the church (1 Cor. 16:15–16). **Over you** renders a Greek word (*proistēmi*) that blends the ideas of leading, protecting, and giving care (see 1 Tim. 3:4, 5, 12, 17; Titus 3:8, 14). In Romans 12:8, the word is translated "he that ruleth," but as indicated there, the gift is appreciated by its grouping with other gifts necessary for the care and well-being of the congregation. Like Stephanas in Corinth (see 1 Cor. 16:15), Jason in Thessalonica became a benefactor and leader in the church (see Acts 17:5–9). These two leaders help visualize those who are "over you in the Lord." The basic meaning of **admonish** is "to put in mind" and so to "advise," "warn," or "rebuke" a person about what should and should not be done. The true work of admonishing another begins with the truth of God operating in the heart of the one who admonishes.

5:13. Paul used no titles here. Recognition of church leaders and the **esteem** that should accompany it is **for their work's sake**. Personal attachment or respect for their high position is secondary to the ministry such leaders perform for the Lord and His church. **Be at peace** applies to Christian relationships in general, but here it probably refers especially to right relations between leaders and those under them.

5:14. Them that are unruly (Greek, *ataktos*, = *a*, "without" + *taktos*, "proper order" or "rule") refers those who were idle and here specifies laziness or loafing. Apparently, some Thessalonians were so sure that the second coming was imminent that they had given up their jobs to prepare for it, but Paul said they should work (see 2 Thess. 3:10–11 and discussions; see also 1 Thess. 4:11). **The feebleminded** (Greek, *oligopsychos*; "of little soul" or "lacking sufficient heart") refers to those who are fainthearted or discouraged. They are to be strengthened with encouragement. The word **weak** (Greek, *asthenēs*) is used in the New Testament of incapacities and limitations both physical and spiritual; Paul generally used it of spiritual and moral weakness. **Support** means "to hold on to" with a strong attachment and interest. The weak are to be helped, not rejected, by the strong (see Rom. 14:1–15; 15:1; 1 Cor. 8:13).

5:15. Render evil for evil, or "give back in kind," addresses any kind of tit-for-tat retaliation. Retaliation is never a Christian option (see Rom. 12:17; 1 Peter 3:9). Christians are called to forgive (see Matt. 5:38–42; 18:21–35). Followers of Jesus Christ are never to allow evil to dictate their actions. Rather, they are to **follow**, or pursue (go after), what is good. Paul made that the strategy for all believers toward all people, whether at church or in the world.

5:16. Up to this point in the letter, Paul focused on responsible behavior as it relates to one's outlook on others (5:12–15). In 5:16–18, Paul featured the individual's outlook as it relates to his or her relationship with God. **Rejoice evermore**, or "at all times." People are naturally happy on some occasions, but the Christian's joy is not dependent on circumstances; it comes from what Christ has done, and it is constant. Thus, Paul wrote the Philippians, "Rejoice in the Lord alway" (Phil. 4:4). To rejoice is to express outwardly the joy in one's heart because of Christ. There is probably a connection between the outer countenance of joy ("rejoice," here) and the inner appreciation of God's presence ("pray," 5:17).

5:17. Paul's call to **Pray without ceasing** pictures a person mindful of God's presence at all times and in all circumstances (for the practice of continual, or regular, prayer, see 1:3; 2:13; Rom. 1:9–10; Eph. 6:18; Col. 1:3; 2 Tim. 1:3).

5:18. As in 5:16, Christians are differentiated from the natural man. Because of what God has done, they are continually thankful, regardless of the circumstances (see Eph. 5:20). To give thanks in all circumstances (see Phil. 4:6–7) is to open the mind and heart to the whole vista of God's sovereignty. To do otherwise limits thanksgiving to those occasions when God's will matches one's wishes. Under those conditions, one's mind and heart are closed to the ways in which God is at work when He works outside of one's preferences.

5:19. Quench not the Spirit. There is a warmth, a glow, about the Spirit's presence that makes this language appropriate. The kind of conduct Paul was opposing may have included loafing, immorality, and the other sins he had denounced in the letter. On the other hand, he may have been warning against a mechanical attitude toward worship, which discourages the expression of the gifts of the Spirit in the local assembly (see 5:20; see also 2 Tim. 1:6, lit., "fan into flame" the gift of God — the opposite of quench or extinguish).

5:20. Prophesyings must be treated with seriousness (see 5:21) and not with easy disdain or contempt. More than foretelling the future, the gift of prophecy involves the ability to interpret and communicate in clear speech God's direct and relevant will for His people. Such was the case in the early church (see Acts 11:27–28; 13:1–3; 21:10–11). From Paul's instruction to the Corinthians, we recognize that the one who prophesies speaks to the church for "edification, and exhortation, and comfort" (1 Cor. 14:3) and that prophesyings instruct the church "that all may learn" (1 Cor. 14:31; for more on the gift of prophecy, see Rom. 12:6; 1 Cor. 12:10, 28; 13:2; 14:29–33; Eph. 4:11).

5:21. There is a continuation here of Paul's thought on prophesy that is made clear in the Greek and not translated in the KJV. Rather than disdain, Paul counseled the Thessalonians to **prove all things** (or "all prophesyings"). The approval of prophecy (see 5:20) does not mean that anyone who claims to speak in the name of the Lord is to be accepted without question. The word for "prove" (Greek, *dokimazō*) speaks of examining something to verify its quality (see "allowed," 2:4). Paul did not say what specific tests are to be applied, but he was clear that every teaching must be tested, and surely they must be in agreement with the gospel. **Hold[ing] fast that which is good** is the positive outcome of what is approved. The negative outcome is expressed in 5:22. The train of Paul's thought applies to prophecy, but these final two thoughts in 5:22–23 are no doubt the specific application of a general principle regarding good and evil (see Bruce, *1 and 2 Thessalonians*, p. 126).

5:22. The theme of prophecy probably remained the controlling idea as Paul counseled the Thessalonians to **abstain from all appearance of evil**. Here evil is the opposite of good (see 5:21) and "abstain" is the opposite of "hold fast" (5:21). An "evil" utterance would contradict the gospel. Both good and evil would be discerned through "prov[ing] all things" (5:21).

IV. Concluding Prayer, Greetings, and Benediction (5:23–28)

5:23. Paul shifted his emphasis from counseling to blessing as he vocalized in writing a prayer for the Thessalonians. **God of peace** is a fitting reference to God in view of 5:12–15. Paul often referred to God in this way near the end of his letters (see Rom. 15:33; 16:20; 1 Cor. 14:33; 2 Cor. 13:11; Phil. 4:9; see also 2 Thess. 3:16). With the words **your whole spirit and soul and body**, Paul was emphasizing the whole person (**sanctify you wholly**), not attempting to differentiate the parts. Their sanctification was his desire in an earlier prayer (3:11–13) and a theme of his specific counsel (4:3–8). Paul broadened the notion in various ways and last of all doctrinally (see 5:20–22), and so he concluded with a prayer for their complete sanctification.

5:24. Paul's confidence rested in the nature of God (see Gen. 18:25), who can be relied on to complete what He begins (see Num. 23:19; Phil. 1:6). The process of sanctification, or becoming holy and wholly God's, is the work of a relationship in which God is a faithful and persistent partner. His heart, thoughts, and holy character rub off on the believer through the ever-present influence of His Spirit.

5:25–26. Pray for us (v. 25). Paul knew the power of prayer. Even he, the apostle who counseled the Thessalonians, needed the intercession of others in the life and ministry of God's calling. Paul sent a warm greeting to everyone, even to those whom he had corrected. **All the brethren** (v. 26) points to a mutual greeting, regardless of social status or race. Such an outward show of cordiality expressed the true unity of a filial bond through Jesus Christ. **A holy kiss** was a normal greeting of that day, similar to the modern handshake (see Rom. 16:16; 1 Cor. 16:20; 2 Cor. 13:12; and "a kiss of charity," 1 Peter 5:14).

5:27. I charge you is surprisingly strong language, meaning "I put you on oath." Paul clearly wanted every member of the church to read or hear his letter and to know of his concern and advice for them.

5:28. Paul always ended his letters with a benediction of grace for his readers, sometimes adding other blessings (as in 2 Cor. 13:14). Thus, 1 Thessalonians ends with the apostle's encouragement to the believers. Whether they lived or died, their hope of the rapture of the living and the resurrection of the dead focused their attention on their reunion with Christ.

THE SECOND EPISTLE OF PAUL THE APOSTLE TO THE THESSALONIANS

INTRODUCTION

See 1 Thessalonians, Introduction.

Author, Date, and Place of Composition

Paul's authorship of 2 Thessalonians has been questioned more often than that of 1 Thessalonians, in spite of the fact that it has more support from early Christian writers. Objections are based on internal factors rather than on the adequacy of the statements of the church fathers. It is thought that differences exist in the vocabulary (ten words not used elsewhere), in the style (it is said to be unexpectedly formal), and in the eschatology (the doctrine of the Man of Sin is not taught elsewhere; see 2:3–12). Such arguments, however, have not convinced current scholars. Most still hold to Paul's authorship of 2 Thessalonians (see 1:1; 3:17).

Because of its similarity to 1 Thessalonians, this letter must have been written not long after the first letter, perhaps about six months later. The situation in the church seems to have been much the same. Paul probably penned it circa AD 51 or 52 in Corinth, after Silas and Timothy had returned from delivering 1 Thessalonians.

Theme and Theological Message

Nothing in the letter indicates that Paul had any further direct contact with the Thessalonians since writing his first letter. Rather, he was responding to some questions of theirs that he had heard about, perhaps from those who delivered the first letter. Paul's purpose in writing was very much the same as in his first letter to them. He wrote (1) to encourage persecuted believers (1:4–10), (2) to exhort the Thessalonians to be steadfast and to work for a living (2:13–3:15), and (3) to correct a misunderstanding concerning the Lord's return (2:1–12).

Like 1 Thessalonians, this letter deals extensively with eschatology (see 1 Thessalonians, Introduction: "Theme and Theological Message"). In fact, in 2 Thessalonians, eighteen out of forty-seven verses (38 percent) deal with this subject. In this letter, Paul dealt extensively with the sequence of events regarding the removal of the restrainer (see discussion on 2:7), the rise of the Antichrist (the "man of sin," 2:3), and the triumphal return of Christ "in flaming fire" (1:8).

Outline

I. Introduction (chap. 1)
   A. Salutation (1:1–2)
   B. Thanksgiving for the Thessalonians' Faith, Love, and Perseverance (1:3–10)
   C. Intercession for Their Spiritual Progress (1:11–12)
II. Instruction (chap. 2)
   A. Prophecy regarding the Day of the Lord: Their Promise (2:1–12)
   B. Thanksgiving for Their Election and Calling: Their Position (2:13–15)
   C. Prayer for Their Service and Testimony: Their Practice (2:16–17)
III. Injunctions (chap. 3)
   A. Call to Prayer (3:1–3)
   B. Charge to Discipline the Disorderly and Lazy (3:4–15)

Bibliography

Bruce, F. F. *1 and 2 Thessalonians*. Word Biblical Commentary 45. Waco, TX: Word, 1982.

Couch, Mal. *The Hope of Christ's Return*. Chattanooga, TN: AMG, 2001.

Green, Gene L. *The Letters to the Thessalonians*. Pillar New Testament Commentary. Grand Rapids, MI: Eerdmans, 2002.

Marshall, I. Howard. *1 and 2 Thessalonians*. New Century Bible Commentary. Grand Rapids, MI: Eerdmans, 1983.

Mayhue, Richard. *1 and 2 Thessalonians: Triumphs and Trials of a Consecrated Church*. Focus on the Bible. Ross-shire, UK: Christian Focus, 1999.

EXPOSITION ──────────────────────────────

I. Introduction (chap. 1)

A. Salutation (1:1–2)

1:1–2. See discussion on 1 Thessalonians 1:1.

B. Thanksgiving for the Thessalonians' Faith, Love, and Perseverance (1:3–10)

1:3. Bound is a word expressing personal, not impersonal, obligation. Here it is Paul's way of expressing deserved admiration for the powerful effect of the Thessalonians' faith (see 1 Thess. 1:7–8; discussion on Phil. 1:3–4). Paul addressed the Thessalonians in a warm, pastoral, and conversational manner. For Paul's use of **brethren**, see discussion on 1 Thessalonians 1:4. **Faith** and **charity** ("love")

are two defining virtues of the Christian life (see 1 Tim. 1:5; 2 Tim. 1:13) that Paul had been pleased to acknowledge in the Thessalonian church (see 1 Thess. 3:6–7) but that were also somewhat lacking (see 1 Thess. 3:10, 12). **Groweth exceedingly, and … aboundeth** pictures the Thessalonians' faith and charity flourishing like a plant. Paul's characterization is noteworthy given the hostilities of their environment (see 1:4). Paul had used the same verb in his earlier prayer that the Thessalonians' love would grow ("abound," 1 Thess. 3:12). Here he was recording an exact answer to prayer. The virtues of faith and charity must grow because they express the vertical and horizontal relationship of the Christian to God and the world.

1:4. We ourselves emphasizes Paul's participation. Paul seems to imply that it was unusual for the founders of a church to boast about it, though others might do so (see 1 Thess. 1:9). The Thessalonians were so outstanding that Paul departed from normal practice. **Persecutions and tribulations** speaks respectively of both the mistreatment at the hands of others and the sufferings (external and internal) that the Thessalonians had experienced (see 1 Thess. 1:6; 2:14; 3:3).

1:5. Manifest token of the righteous judgment of God. Based on Paul's entire thought in 1:5–7, the "token" of God's righteous judgment anticipates a future "recompense" (1:6–7) appreciated even "now" in the actions of the persecuted and the persecutors, those for and those against the reign of God and lordship of His Son. Paul encouraged and assured the Thessalonians that their suffering for the kingdom of God had worth (see Matt. 5:10–12; 1 Thess. 2:14–15) and was a part of being **counted worthy**. "Persecutions and tribulations" (1:4) suffered for the sake of the kingdom of God are an exhibit of two opposed value judgments: what the world counts as worthless, God counts worthy. Because the Thessalonians accepted God's judgment of worth over the world's, Paul added the words **for which** (i.e., "in the interest of which" or "in behalf of which") **ye also suffer**. For **the kingdom of God**, see discussions on 1 Thessalonians 2:12; Matthew 3:2. Couch (*The Hope of Christ's Return*, p. 185) observes that "the kingdom of God" refers to the messianic reign of Christ. He points out that "the kingdom of God" and "the kingdom of heaven" both refer to God coming from heaven to reign on earth.

1:6. A righteous thing with God points to the justice of God. He brings punishment on unrepentant sinners (see Mark 9:47–48; Luke 13:3–5), and it may be in the here and now (see Rom. 1:24, 26, 28) as well as on judgment day.

1:7. Rest is contrasted with "trouble" (1:6). Retribution not only involves punishment of the evil but also relief for the righteous. Paul included himself in **with us**, not only in the "rest" that awaits the Christian but in the sufferings experienced on behalf of Christ (see Phil. 3:10). Paul was not merely an academic theologian writing in comfort from a distance; rather, he was suffering just as the Thessalonians were. Paul took to heart and gained comfort from the "rest" to come when Christ **shall be revealed**. Christ is now hidden, and many people even deny His existence. At His second coming, He will be seen by everyone for who He is (see Matt. 24:30). **His mighty angels** may refer to a class of angels (such a group is mentioned in apocalyptic writings) who are given special power to do God's will. Jesus, "the author and finisher [perfecter] of our faith" (Heb. 12:2), had such "servants" at His command, yet He suffered unjustly with purpose because His kingdom was not of this world (see John 18:36).

1:8. In flaming fire is an indication of power and judgment. Christ will punish the wickedness (see Isa. 66:15; Rev. 1:14) of those who **know not God**, meaning those who refuse to recognize Him (see 2:10, 12; Rom. 1:28) and further defined as those who **obey not**. The gospel invites acceptance, and rejection is disobedience to a royal invitation.

1:9. Destruction does not mean annihilation (see discussion on 1 Thess. 5:3). Paul used the word in 1 Corinthians 5:5, "for the destruction of the flesh," possibly for the purpose of salvation. Since, however, salvation implies resurrection of the body, annihilation cannot be in mind. The word means something like "complete ruin." Here it means being shut out from Christ's presence. This eternal separation is the penalty of sin and the essence of hell. **The glory of his power** (see 1:7–8) is scorned by those who persecute believers. Such arrogant abuse of power will be eclipsed by the majestic and humbling might of Jesus Christ.

1:10. Glorified in his saints means not simply "among" but "in" them. His glory is seen in what they are: "saints" (see discussion on 1 Thess. 3:13). **Our testimony** speaks of the gospel message at a time when the New Testament did not yet exist. The preaching of the gospel is essentially bearing testimony to what God has done in Christ. **That day** refers to the day of the Lord (see discussion on 1 Thess. 5:2).

C. Intercession for Their Spiritual Progress (1:11–12)

1:11. The words **Pray always for you** (see discussion on 1 Thess. 5:17) point to the dynamic role of intercessory prayer in the progress of Christian development. The challenges for the Thessalonians were threatening and full of suffering (see 1:4–5), yet the purposes that direct believers' attitudes and actions come from **the good pleasure of his goodness** (lit., "resolve of goodness"). God initiates every good purpose and every act prompted by faith; Paul prayed accordingly that He would bring them to fulfillment for the Thessalonians.

1:12. A **name** in ancient times was often more than a personal label; it summed up what a person was. Paul looked for glory to be ascribed to Christ for all He would do in the lives of the Thessalonian Christians.

II. Instruction (chap. 2)

A. Prophecy regarding the Day of the Lord: Their Promise (2:1–12)

2:1. We beseech you (as in 1 Thess. 4:1; 5:12) is an exhortation in the form of a request. The words **by ... and by** are a rendering of just a single Greek word that means "concerning," and Paul used it here to govern and express his interest in the twofold subject of **the coming of our Lord Jesus Christ** (for the significance of the word "coming," the Greek word *parousia*, see 1 Thess. 4:16) and **our gathering together unto him**. Here (as in 1 Thess. 4:13–18) both of these subjects belong to the specification of questions posed about "the day of Christ" (2:2), about which there was some confusion that Paul wished to clear up. "Gathering together" (Greek, *episynagōgē*; "assemble together") here refers to the rapture of all believers, which is connected with the coming of the Lord, spoken of in 1 Thessalonians 4:13–18 (see also 1 Cor. 15:51–52).

2:2. The Greek for the verb **shaken** was often used of a ship adrift from its mooring and suggests a lack of stability. Paul wanted the Thessalonians to be of firm conviction and not of unstable opinion. He

did not want them to be **troubled**, a word Jesus used in issuing a similar instruction (Mark 13:7). The specific source of the Thessalonians' confusion was not known to Paul, but the words **spirit, word,** and **letter as from us** convey the likely avenues of some novel teaching contrary to Paul's own. "Spirit" is a general expression denoting any "inspired" revelation and probably alludes to prophecies, a subject of concern in 1 Thessalonians 5:19–22. "Word" could denote any form of oral communication, a message, a teaching, or even a sermon. "Letter as from us" identifies some written communication under Paul's name and thus a forgery, although the Thessalonians obviously would not have known that at the time (see 3:17). It becomes clear, especially from the first and the last of these three possible avenues of communication, that the Thessalonians became susceptible to the error because it came to them through some ostensibly dependable and reputable source. It is a reminder that counterfeits may be passed on by reputable hands and detected only by those with a firm grasp of genuine tender, a point Paul made more than once (see 2:5, 15). **The day of Christ** is also the day of the Lord (see discussion on 1 Thess. 5:2). Obviously, Christ's climactic return had not occurred, but the words **is at hand**, the perfect active indicative (Greek, *enistēmi*), meaning "has already begun," suggest that Paul was combating the idea that the final days had begun and their completion was imminent.

2:3. Here and in 2:6–8, Paul stressed the order of future events to guard the Thessalonians against further deception. As proof, he stated that **that day** (see 1 Thess. 5:2) **shall not come** before what must come first: **a falling away** and the climactic revealing of **that man of sin**. There will be "a falling away" from faith (see Matt. 24:10–12; 1 Tim. 4:1), but here Paul was speaking of active rebellion. Elsewhere the Greek word *apostasia* is used of political and militant revolt as well as of rebellion against God. Here Paul used it of the supreme opposition of evil to the things of God. "That man of sin" identifies the leader of the forces of evil during the last days. Only here is he called by this name. John called him "antichrist" (1 John 2:18) and "the beast" (Revelation 13). Paul's description of the "man of sin" has some distinctive features. He is not Satan, because he is clearly distinguished from him in 2:9. **Revealed** is from the same Greek root word (*apokalyptō*) as that used of Jesus Christ in 1:7 and may indicate something supernatural. As his description, **the son of perdition**, indicates, despite all his proud claims (see 2:4, 9), his final overthrow is certain. The same Greek expression is used of Judas Iscariot in John 17:12, where it is also translated "the son of perdition." This does not mean, however, that Judas is the Antichrist but that both are destined to perdition (Greek, *apōleia*; "destruction").

2:4. All that is called God, or that is worshipped. The Man of Sin will not merely be a political or military man but will claim a place above every god and everything associated with worship; he will even claim to be God. **The temple of God** apparently refers to a physical temple (see Matt. 24:25; Mark 13:14) from which he will make his blasphemous pronouncements (see Dan. 11:36–45; Rev. 13:1–15). The designation "temple of God" almost certainly means a Jewish temple in Jerusalem. The Thessalonians, who had "turned to God from idols to serve the living and true God" (1 Thess. 1:9), surely could have imagined such blasphemy, for they were acquainted with many precursors, surrounded as they were by temples not only to various deities but to the emperor of imperial Rome.

2:5–6. The error that had deceived them (see 2:3), although peddled through some "dependable" source (see 2:2), clearly contradicted the things Paul had taught them earlier (see 2:15). With Paul's earlier instruction ("I told you these things," v. 5) in mind, they now knew **what withholdeth ... his time** (v. 6; see 2:7). What restrains "the son of perdition" (v. 3) will prevail until the timing of God, not that of Satan (v. 9).

2:7. In the New Testament, "mystery" usually denotes something people cannot know without God's revelation (see discussion on Rom. 11:25). The expression **the mystery of iniquity** indicates that some things about evil are known only as God reveals them. This evil is already at work, but in the day of the Lord (the great tribulation), it will inten-

sify dramatically (see Matt. 24:21–22). **He who now letteth will let**. In earlier centuries, the English word "let" meant "hinder" or "restrain" (as does the Greek word here) rather than "allow." So the meaning is that he who now restrains will restrain until he is removed. In 2:6, Paul spoke of the restraint only in terms of its exercise. Here he shifted the gender from neuter to masculine and specified the agent who exercises the restraint. There have been many suggestions as to the specific character of the restraint (see 2:6), which is contrasted with "the mystery of iniquity" **already [at] work**, and to the identity of the restrainer, contrasted with the Man of Sin to be "revealed in his time" (2:6). Because the Thessalonians knew what Paul does not identify, suggestions have ranged from the Roman state with its emperor, the principle of law and government embodied in the state and its governor, Paul's missionary spreading of the gospel, to the Holy Spirit or the restraining ministry of the Holy Spirit through the church. Since only God is able to restrain Satan and his Antichrist, it seems best to regard the sovereign power of God as that which inhibits the freedom of Satan and the rise of his Antichrist until the rapture of the church (see 2:11). At an ordained time (see "revealed," 2:3, 6), the agency of God's restraint will be taken out of the way of the Man of Sin. Without this restraint, the "falling away ... and that man of sin" (2:3) will foment what is known as the great tribulation. So the day of the Lord (of Christ) with its great tribulation will not begin until after the restrainer is removed and the Wicked One, the Man of Sin, is revealed. Paul wanted the Thessalonians to understand, therefore, that the day of the Lord (the final days) had not yet come and they had not missed the rapture of the church. The order of events in this verse is: (1) the removal of the restrainer, (2) the falling away, (3) the rise of the Wicked One. This passage makes it clear that Satan's hands are tied by the sovereignty of God. Satan cannot move to empower someone to become the Antichrist until after the removal of restraint at the time of the rapture.

2:8. The words "sin" (2:3), "iniquity" (2:7) and **Wicked** are the same Greek root word, meaning "lawless," and convey rebellion against God, the ultimate Creator of order and law. No longer restrained (**And then**; see also 2:7), the true character of the **Wicked**, or "Lawless One," will **be revealed**. "Revealed" evidently refers to some supernatural aspects of his appearing (see 2:9). As Bruce (*1 and 2 Thessalonians*, p. 172) aptly put it, "He is revealed only to be destroyed." Paul's wording of **consume with the spirit of his mouth** is fortified by Isaiah 11:4, with its prophetic description of the Messiah's judgment. Despite his impressiveness (v. 4), the Man of Sin will easily be destroyed by Christ (see Dan. 11:45; Rev. 19:20). The Man of Sin will be vanquished and destroyed by the "spirit," or breath, of Christ's mouth, probably alluding to the utterance or command of Jesus, and **the brightness of his coming**, or appearing. In 2 Timothy 1:10 ("appearing"), the Greek for this word refers to Jesus' first coming, but everywhere else in the New Testament, it refers to His second coming.

2:9. The **coming** (Greek, *parousia*; see 1 Thess. 4:16 and discussion) of the Man of Sin is the *anti-parousia* of the coming of Christ (see 2:1, 8). Satan will empower the Man of Sin with miracles, signs, and wonders (see Matt. 24:24)—the counterfeits of messianic equipment. Thus, his **lying wonders** will produce false impressions.

2:10. Unrighteousness, the source and character of Satan (see 2:9), has power to deceive (**deceivableness**) them that perish. Paul explains why. Those that are perishing **received not**, meaning they gave no place or welcome to **the love of the truth**. More than mere knowledge of the truth, "love" points to what might be described as a commitment to the truth. Counterfeits peddled by unrighteousness will easily deceive not only those who reject the truth but those with a loosely held knowledge of the truth. Since the truth they reject has the power to save, its character as well as its content must be defined by the essential gospel message of Jesus (see John 14:6; Eph. 1:13; 4:21; Gal. 2:5).

2:11. For this cause, or because of their deliberate rejection of the truth (see 2:10), **God shall send them strong delusion**. God uses sin to punish the sinful (see Rom. 1:24–28), but here He seals for them the lie that the truth (the gospel) is **a lie** (see 2:10). The lie is contrasted with the truth (the gospel of Jesus Christ) in 2:10, 12. Since the lie is defined by its contrast with the truth, its ultimate expression and delusion may be its implication that the Man of Sin is God (see 2:4). In summary, Paul told the Thessalonians that the rapture will involve the removal of restraint, allowing Satan to empower the Man of Sin (the Antichrist) to rise to power preceding the triumphal return of Christ. Thus, the order of these future events is: (1) rapture, (2) apostasy, (3) rise of the Antichrist, (4) strong delusion.

B. Thanksgiving for Their Election and Calling: Their Position (2:13–15)

2:13. Beloved of the Lord, because God hath ... chosen you. For the connection between God's love and election, see Colossians 3:12; 1 Thessalonians 1:4; discussion on Ephesians 1:4. **From the beginning** points to God's decision from eternity to save people "in him" (Eph. 1:4), in Jesus Christ. Here **sanctification of the Spirit** and **belief [in] the truth** are the divine and human actions at work in the realization of God's decision. Sanctification is a necessary aspect of salvation, not something reserved for special Christians (see 1 Thess. 3:13; 4:3 and discussions). The truth is above all the message of salvation in Jesus Christ (see discussions on 2:10–11). All three persons of the Trinity are mentioned in this verse (see discussion on 1 Thess. 1:1).

2:14. Called ... by our gospel is Paul's concise reference to the call of God expressed and extended through the preaching of the gospel message. The past tense refers to the time when the Thessalonians were converted, but the divine call is a present reality in 1 Thessalonians 2:12; 5:24 (for "our gospel," see discussion on 1 Thess. 1:5). The objective of God's calling is **to the obtaining of the glory of our Lord Jesus Christ** (see 1 Thess. 2:12). For Paul, that was a compact summary of the totality of the Christian's benefits in Christ, appreciated through the magnificent stature of His person and titles. Ultimately, there is no glory other than God's.

2:15. Here Paul returned to the issue of sources (see 2:2) and stressed the importance of sticking to (**stand fast**) the teaching the Thessalonians had received from him. To detect a counterfeit, one must have a firm grasp of what is genuine and true. **The traditions**, as in 3:6, refers to that which is "passed on" or "handed on." Until the New Testament was written, essential Christian teaching was passed on in "the traditions," either oral or written, just as rabbinic law was (see discussion on Matt. 15:2). In 1 Corinthians 15:3, Paul used the technical words for receiving and handing on traditions: "For I delivered unto you ... that which I also received."

C. Prayer for Their Service and Testimony: Their Practice (2:16 – 17)

2:16 – 17. A similar prayer is found in about the same place in Paul's first letter to the Thessalonians (1 Thess. 3:11 – 13). He had reassured and encouraged them with his specific explanations in answer to their concerns (2:1 – 12) and with his specific and foundational causes for thanksgiving (2:13 – 15). With the vital issues of their well-being in view, Paul now completed his efforts to care for the Thessalonians with prayer. Paul is a model of pastoral care and heart. Knowledge and understanding are indispensable but are insufficient without dependence on the resources of God. **Everlasting consolation** (v. 16) looks beyond the current source of distress (see 2:2) and expresses the breadth and depth of the assurance that belongs to the Christian who looks to God whatever the challenge (see Rom. 8, esp. vv. 32 – 39). **Comfort ... stablish** (v. 17) points to an outcome of such confidence: inner strength that will produce results in both action and speech.

III. Injunctions (chap. 3)

A. Call to Prayer (3:1 – 3)

3:1. Finally introduces a new direction of thought (see discussion on 1 Thess. 4:1) but connects what follows to what has just be treated in chapter 2. In 1 Thessalonians 5:25, Paul simply asked for prayer; here he mentioned specifics. **Even as it is with you** (lit., "just as also with you") alludes to the success of the gospel mission among the Thessalonians. The expression is general enough to cover the present as well as the past (see 1 Thess. 2:13).

3:2. Unreasonable translates a Greek word meaning "out of place" and suggesting what is "evil, wrong, or improper." Elsewhere in the New Testament, it is used only of things (see Luke 23:41; Acts 25:5). Perverseness is always out of place. For Paul's difficulties at Corinth (where he wrote this letter), see Acts 18:12 – 13. People who are not of faith do not know the corrective and heart-changing influence of Jesus Christ on what is "unreasonable and wicked."

3:3. In the Greek text, **faithful** immediately follows "faith" (3:2), putting God's faithfulness in sharp contrast with man's lack of faith (see 1 Cor. 1:9; 10:13; 2 Cor. 1:18).

B. Charge to Discipline for the Disorderly and Lazy (3:4 – 15)

3:4 – 5. Believers' **hearts** (see discussion on 1 Thess. 2:4) must be directed by God, especially in the face of uncertainties and spiritual opposition. **Love of God** may be understood as love for God or the love that comes from God. Since Paul was about to rebuke those who were idle, he was probably reminding them of God's love. There should be no hard feelings among those who owe everything to the love of God. Perseverance, or the capacity to bear up in the face of difficulty, comes from Christ, which was probably Paul's meaning.

3:6. Command is an authoritative word with a military ring. Paul used the word twelve times in his letters, five of them in 1 – 2 Thessalonians and four times here in chapter 3 (1 Thess. 4:11; 2 Thess. 3:4, 6, 10, 12). All of Paul's uses of the word "command" in the Thessalonian letters concerned the problem of those individuals who **walketh disorderly**. He had mentioned this problem in the first letter (1 Thess. 4:11 – 12; 5:14; see discussions there), and evidently it had worsened. Paul took it seriously and gave more attention to it in this letter than to anything else but the second coming. Paul used the strongest forms of coercion, appealing to the authority of the Lord, **the tradition**, and the church (**brethren**) in addressing these individuals (**every brother**). For **the name**, see discussion on 1:12. **Withdraw** does not mean withdrawal of all contact but withholding of close fellowship. Idleness is sinful and disruptive, but those who are guilty of it are still brothers (see 3:15). Those who are obedient to the Lord Jesus Christ and the traditions (see discussion on 2:15) are to distinguish themselves from those who are not and who bring shame upon the name of Jesus Christ through their attitude and actions (see 3:11 – 12, 14).

3:7. Ye ought to follow us (see discussion on 1 Thess. 1:6) refers to not only Paul's example but also that of his team of coworkers. As a leader, Paul never let individual "rights" interfere with what was right for the ministry of the gospel (see 3:9).

3:8. Eat any man's bread was a Hebraism for "make a living" (see, e.g., Gen. 3:19; Amos 7:12). Paul was not saying that he never accepted hospitality but that he had not depended on others for his living (see 1 Thess. 2:9 and discussion).

3:9. Have not power refers to the authority or "right" that belonged to Paul but that he chose not to exercise (see discussion on 1 Thess. 2:6). Paul defended the same word and right in his letter to the Corinthians (1 Cor. 9:1 – 27). It was from Corinth that he penned 2 Thessalonians.

3:10. If any would not work, neither should he eat. Pagan parallels are in the form, "He who does not work does not eat." Paul gave an imperative: literally, "let him not eat." The Christian must not be a loafer. The cultural custom and practice of patronage probably played into the abuses Paul addressed and his disfavor of such conduct.

3:11 – 12. Here **walk** (v. 11) refers to a pattern of conduct that is **disorderly** and amounts to defiance and irresponsible idleness. Not only idle, these individuals were **busybodies**; they were interfering with other people's affairs, a problem to which an unruly or idle life often leads. The nature of Paul's epistles was that they were a substitute for his presence and authority. With the letter's public reading in view (see 1 Thess. 5:27), Paul's command spoke directly to

the problem people. Read aloud, Paul's directives in 3:11 – 14 served to impose public boundaries on the **disorderly** and give guidance to the "orderly" whose generosity had been abused.

3:13. Be not weary in well doing encouraged those who did not belong to the behavior Paul condemned to continue doing the right things. Here is an indirect clue to the baneful effect that the "disorderly" (3:6, 11) had on the congregation. The misbehavior of others is never cause for retreating from what is right and good, even if others depreciate it.

3:14. Paul realized that some might not heed his letter. The words **no company with** is an unusual Greek double compound, meaning "mix up together with" (used elsewhere in the New Testament only in 1 Cor. 5:9, 11, of a similar withdrawal of close fellowship). It indicates a disassociation that will bring the disobedient person back to a right attitude. Such behavior brings shame (**be ashamed**) on Christian reputation and warrants repentance. The aim is not punishment but restoration to fellowship.

3:15. Discipline in the church should be brotherly, never harsh (for **admonish**, see 1 Thess. 5:12).

3:16. Paul's prayerful **Lord of peace**, rather than his more usual phrase "God of peace," (see discussion on 1 Thess. 5:23) appropriately invoked and applied to all of the Thessalonians (**you all**), even the disorderly.

3:17. Paul normally dictated his letters (see Rom. 16:22) but added something in his own handwriting toward the end of the letter (see 1 Cor. 16:21; Gal. 6:11; Col. 4:18). Here he stated that this practice was his distinguishing mark. In view of 2:2 ("nor by letter as from us"), this authenticating mark reinforced the authority of this letter at its reading.

3:18. See discussion on 1 Thessalonians 5:28. Paul had criticized his offenders, but his last prayer was for everyone. Taken together, Paul's two letters to the Thessalonians reveal his compassionate heart and his confident expectation of the coming of Christ to gather the church to heaven in preparation for His triumphal return to earth.

THE FIRST EPISTLE OF PAUL THE APOSTLE TO TIMOTHY

INTRODUCTION

Author

Both early tradition and the salutations of the Pastoral Epistles confirm Paul as their author. Some objections have been raised in recent years on the basis of an alleged uncharacteristic vocabulary and style (see, e.g., discussions on 1:15; 2:2), but evidence is still convincingly supportive of Paul's authorship.

Date

First Timothy was written sometime after the events of Acts 28 (ca. 63–65), at least eight years after Paul's three-year stay in Ephesus (Acts 19:8, 10; 20:31).

Recipient

As the salutation indicates (1:2), Paul was writing to Timothy, a native of Lystra (in modern Turkey). Timothy's father was Greek, while his mother was a Jewish Christian (see Acts 16:1). From childhood, Timothy had been taught the Old Testament (2 Tim. 1:5; 3:15). Paul called him "my own son in the faith" (1:2), perhaps having led him to Christ during his first visit to Lystra. At the time of his second visit, Paul invited Timothy to join him on his missionary travels and circumcised him so that his Greek ancestry would not be a liability in working with the Jews (Acts 16:3). Timothy shared in the evangelization of Macedonia and Achaia (see Acts 17:14–15; 18:5) and was with Paul during much of his long preaching ministry at Ephesus (see Acts 19:22). He traveled with Paul from Ephesus to Macedonia, to Corinth, back to Macedonia, and to Asia Minor (Acts 20:1–6). He seems even to have accompanied him all the way to Jerusalem. He was with Paul during the apostle's first imprisonment (see Phil. 1:1; Col. 1:1; Philemon 1).

Following Paul's release (after Acts 28), Timothy again traveled with him but eventually stayed at Ephesus to deal with the problems there, while Paul went on to Macedonia. Paul's closeness to and admiration of Timothy are seen in Paul's naming him as the co-sender of six of his letters (2 Corinthians, Philippians, Colossians, 1–2 Thessalonians, and Philemon) and speaking highly of him to the Philippians (Phil. 2:19–22). At the end of Paul's life, he requested Timothy to join him at Rome (2 Tim. 4:9, 21). According to

Hebrews 13:23, Timothy himself was imprisoned and subsequently released—whether at Rome or elsewhere, we do not know.

Timothy was not an apostle, and he was probably not an overseer since he was given instructions about overseers (3:1–7; 5:17–22). It may be best to regard him as an apostolic representative, delegated to carry out special work (see Titus 1:5).

Theme

During his fourth missionary journey, Paul had instructed Timothy to care for the church at Ephesus (1:3) while he went on to Macedonia (see the essay "The Pastoral Epistles" in *Zondervan KJV Study Bible*, p. 1734). When Paul realized that he might not return to Ephesus in the near future (3:14–15), he wrote this first letter to Timothy to develop the charge he had given his young assistant (1:3, 18), to refute false teachings (1:3–7; 4:1–8; 6:3–5, 20–21), and to supervise the affairs of the growing Ephesian church (church worship, 2:1–15; the appointment of qualified church leaders, 3:1–13; 5:17–25).

A major problem in the Ephesian church was a heresy that combined Gnosticism (see 1 John, Introduction: "Gnosticism"), decadent Judaism (1:3–7), and false asceticism (4:1–5).

Outline

    I. Salutation (1:1–2)
   II. Warning against False Teachers (1:3–11)
       A. The Nature of the Heresy (1:3–7)
       B. The Purpose of the Law (1:8–11)
  III. The Lord's Grace to Paul (1:12–17)
  IV. The Purpose of Paul's Instructions to Timothy (1:18–20)
   V. Instructions concerning the Administration of the Church (chaps. 2–3)
       A. Public Worship (chap. 2)
          1. Prayer in Public Worship (2:1–8)
          2. Women in Public Worship (2:9–15)
       B. Qualifications for Church Officers (3:1–13)
          1. Bishops (3:1–7)
          2. Deacons (3:8–13)
       C. Purpose of These Instructions (3:14–16)
  VI. Methods of Dealing with False Teaching (chap. 4)
       A. False Teaching Described (4:1–5)
       B. Methods of Dealing with False Teaching (4:6–16)
 VII. Methods of Dealing with Different Groups in the Church (5:1–6:2)
       A. The Elderly and Younger People (5:1–2)
       B. Widows (5:3–16)
       C. Elders (5:17–25)
       D. Servants (6:1–2)
VIII. Miscellaneous Matters (6:3–19)
       A. False Teachers (6:3–5)
       B. Love of Money (6:6–10)

C. Charge to Timothy (6:11–16)
D. The Rich (6:17–19)
IX. Concluding Appeal (6:20–21)

Bibliography

Fee, Gordon D. *1 and 2 Timothy, Titus.* New International Biblical Commentary. Peabody, MA: Hendrickson, 1988.

Guthrie, Donald. *The Pastoral Epistles.* Tyndale New Testament Commentaries. Grand Rapids, MI: Eerdmans, 1957.

Kelly, J. N. D. *The Pastoral Epistles.* London: Adam & Charles Black, 1963.

Kent, Homer, Jr. *The Pastoral Epistles.* Chicago: Moody Press, 1971.

Liefeld, Walter L. *1 and 2 Timothy, Titus.* The NIV Application Commentary. Grand Rapids, MI: Zondervan, 1999.

EXPOSITION

I. Salutation (1:1–2)

1:1. An apostle is one specially commissioned by Christ (see discussions on Mark 6:30; Heb. 3:1; *KJV Study Bible* note on 1 Cor. 1:1), although here the words **of Jesus Christ** circumscribe the scope and focus of his service and the allegiance of his duty. **By the commandment** (Greek, *epitagē*; "command," "order") divulges Paul's own awareness of being a man whose rank and responsibility come from **God our Saviour** (see Titus 1:3). Such authority is welcome and benevolent to those who, as Paul did, know God is the ultimate source of their salvation. For an additional example of **Jesus Christ ... our hope**, see Titus 2:13. "Hope" expresses absolute certainty, not a mere wish. Jesus is our hope because His victory over sin and death is "ours" through faith; He is the harbinger of shared triumph and glory (see 6:14–16; Col. 1:27; 1 John 3:2–3).

1:2. Paul addressed Timothy as **my own son in the faith**, meaning "my spiritual son" (see 1:18; 1 Cor. 4:17; 2 Tim. 1:2; 2:1; Philemon 10). The triad of **grace** (see discussions on Jonah 4:2; Gal. 1:3; Eph. 1:2), **mercy** (see Rom. 9:2), **and peace** (see discussions on John 14:27; 20:19; Gal. 1:3; Eph. 1:2) opens 2 Timothy (1:2) as well.

II. Warning against False Teachers (1:3–11)

A. The Nature of the Heresy (1:3–7)

1:3–11. In this section (along with 4:1–8; 6:3–5, 20–21), Paul warned against heretical teachers in the Ephesian church. They were characterized by (1) teaching false doctrines (1:3; 6:3); (2) teaching Jewish myths (Titus 1:14); (3) wanting to be teachers of the Old Testament law (1:7); (4) building up endless, far-fetched, fictitious stories based on obscure genealogical points (1:4; 4:7; Titus 3:9); (5) being conceited (1:7; 6:4); (6) being argumentative (1:4; 6:4; 2 Tim. 2:23; Titus 3:9); (7) using talk that was meaningless (1:6) and foolish (2 Tim. 2:23; Titus 3:9); (8) not knowing what they were talking about (1:7; 6:4); (9) teaching ascetic practices (4:3); and (10) using their positions of religious leadership for personal financial gain (6:5). These heretics probably were forerunners of the Gnostics (6:20–21; see 1 John, Introduction: "Gnosticism").

1:3. As I besought thee summarily recalled Paul's face-to-face directive to Timothy and served to reaffirm it and validate Timothy's extended stay (**abide still at Ephesus**). The epistolary use of the verb "besought" [Greek, *parakaleō*; "exhort"] belongs to diplomatic correspondence bearing authoritative directions from a superior to subordinates. It is a tactful term conveying stern orders. Similarly, it may be a clue that Paul wrote to Timothy with a diplomatic awareness that his letter, like an envoy, had to convey to a wider audience than Timothy more severe matters. For not only did the arrival of Paul's letter endorse him with detailed directives; its reading (see 1 Thess. 5:27; Col. 4:16) enforced Paul's apostolic authority behind Timothy's oversight and leadership in the matters addressed.

Paul was well acquainted with the problems that Timothy faced and the challenges that beset the well-established church of Ephesus (see Introduction: "Recipient"). Paul had an extensive ministry there during his third missionary journey, about eight years earlier (see Acts 19:1–20:1). After his release from prison in Rome (after Acts 28), he revisited the church, leaving Timothy in charge while Paul journeyed on to Macedonia. Since there is no account in Acts of this excursion **into Macedonia**, it probably occurred after Acts 28, between Paul's first and second Roman imprisonments (see Introduction: "Recipient").

Paul concisely stated at the outset the purpose for Timothy's stay: **that thou mightest charge some that they teach no other doctrine.** The verb "charge" (Greek, *parangellō*) occurs four other times in 1 Timothy (4:11; 5:7; 6:13, 17), and the noun twice (1:5, 18). The term was used by all kinds of persons in authority (rulers, Jesus, the apostles) and means "give orders," "command." The apostolic authority of Paul (see 1:1) stood behind the command to stand against the spread of heterodox teaching.

1:4. Continuing the statement of Timothy's purpose, Paul instructed him, **Neither give heed to fables and endless genealogies.** These were probably mythical stories built on Old Testament history (genealogies) that later developed into intricate Gnostic philosophical systems (see 1 John, Introduction: "Gnosticism").

1:5. The end of the commandment (Greek, *parangelia*; see 1:3) refers to the "goal" or "objective" (Greek, *telos*) of the "charge" given to Timothy (1:3b–4). If **charity** (love) was to triumph in a one-

sided contest of right doctrine versus wrong doctrine, Timothy needed to be armed with the proper motives, ministering **out of a pure heart, and of a good conscience, and of faith unfeigned**.

1:6. In a semipublic letter, **some** (as in 1:3) was an indirect way of identifying the primary promulgators of error, personalities probably known to others, certainly to Paul and Timothy. The necessary motive of love, which was to distinguish Timothy (see 1:5), had been missed and left aside by those teaching "other doctrine" (1:3). **Vain jangling**, or "empty," "pointless" babbling (as in 6:20–21; lit., "vain talk"), had become more important to them than the integrity of right doctrine.

1:7. The heretical teachers in the Ephesian church aspired to be **teachers of the law**. This term (Greek, *nomodidaskalos*), which Paul used only here, is a compound of "law" (*nomos*) and "teacher" (*didaskalos*). Elsewhere in the New Testament, only Luke used this term, identifying rabbis ("doctors of the law," Luke 5:17) and Gamaliel ("a doctor of law," Acts 5:34). The term itself adds little to an understanding of the false teachers' error, except to corroborate a preoccupation with matters of Jewish Torah (law). What is known to have been speculative from 1:4 is here an error worsened by pretense and pontification, a magnification of their misunderstanding (v. 7) and misuse (1:8) of Scripture. Paul said they were far from meriting the title they coveted.

Two asides or digressions follow in 1:8–17. The first expounds the law (1:8–11), prompted by the subject of "teachers of the law" and their misunderstanding. The second expresses personal gratitude (1:12–17), prompted by the "the glorious gospel … committed to my trust" (1:11). In 1:18–20, Paul resumed the purpose of his instructions to Timothy (see 1:3–7).

B. The Purpose of the Law (1:8–11)

1:8–11. The misunderstanding of the law (see 1: 7) prompted Paul to set forth its true intent: to expose and convict. The key to its proper understanding comes in verse 11: the gospel. **The law is**

good (v. 8; see Rom. 7:7–12), if one handles it **lawfully**, that is, correctly. The law is **not made for a righteous man** (v. 9). Here Paul was correcting a misapplication of the law to Christian believers and, by implication, its misapplication by the would-be teachers of 1:7. The law is for **the lawless**. Paul enumerated the kinds of people the law convicts, using a declension of its violators patterned after the Ten Commandments. Paul closed his list with an inclusive indictment of any other violation of the law **that is contrary to sound doctrine** (v. 10). Here "sound doctrine" refers to the correct understanding and use of the law, a proper perspective that is gained from and measured by **the glorious gospel** (v. 11; see Gal. 3:19–24 and discussions). This outlook was not a maverick or secondhand deduction on Paul's part but the truth of the gospel **committed to [his] trust** (see 6:20; 1 Cor. 9:17; Gal. 2:7; 1 Thess. 2:4; 2 Tim. 1:12, 14; 2:2).

III. The Lord's Grace to Paul (1:12–17)

1:12–14. And (v. 12) looks back to "committed to my trust" in 1:11, even as it looks ahead to **counted me faithful**. Paul was profoundly grateful. But the measure of **I thank** (lit., "I am grateful to") points to the enabling work of Jesus Christ in his life. He who was once **a blasphemer, and a persecutor, and injurious** (v. 13; see Acts 9:1; 22:4–5, 19; 26:10–11) had been radically transformed by the mercy and grace of God extended to him in Jesus Christ.

1:15–16. This is a faithful saying (v. 15) is a clause found in the New Testament only in the Pastoral Epistles (here; 3:1; 4:9; 2 Tim. 2:11; Titus 3:8), where it always identifies a key saying. Here the key saying is **that Christ Jesus came into the world to save sinners**. Paul's own transformed life confirmed the faithfulness or dependability of the saying. His turn of phrase using the same Greek word (*prōtos*; "first," "foremost") for both **chief** (v. 15) and **first** (v. 16) showed Paul to be "a prime example" of what it means to be a sinner (see 1:13) and to be a recipient of Christ's mercy.

IV. The Purpose of Paul's Instructions to Timothy (1:18–20)

1:18–19. This charge (Greek, *parangelia*; v. 18) consciously and formally renewed the "charge" of 1:3, 5 (see discussions there). **I commit unto thee, son Timothy** communicated a solemn trust of a somber responsibility. The word "commit" (Greek, *paratithēmi*) means to "entrust" or "give charge" of something into someone's care (see 6:20; 2 Tim. 1:12, 14; 2:2). Paul's good judgment of Timothy's reliability had been reinforced by the Holy Spirit (see Fee, *1 and 2 Timothy, Titus*, p. 57): **according to the prophecies which went before on thee**. In the early church, God revealed His will in various matters through prophets (see Acts 13:1–3, where prophets had an active role in the sending of Paul and Barnabas on their mission to the Gentiles). The prophecies concerning Timothy may have occurred at the time of or before his ordination (4:14), perhaps about twelve years earlier, on Paul's second missionary journey (see Acts 16:3). Prophecies about Timothy seem to have pointed to the significant leadership role he was to have in the church. Now they were to serve the purpose of emboldening Timothy, **that thou by them mightest war a good warfare**. The implements of battle are **faith, and a good conscience** (v. 19), enabling the warrior to stand unswerving (see 1:5–6), or as Paul switched metaphors to nautical terms, anchoring the ship against **shipwreck**.

1:20. Hymeneus (see 2 Tim. 2:17–18) and **Alexander** (perhaps the Alexander of 2 Tim. 4:14 (but see discussion there) had abandoned the true faith and were teaching another gospel. Consequently, Paul executed church discipline (see discussion on Matt. 18:17), and the two were **delivered unto Satan**. Such action excluded them from the church, which was considered a sanctuary from Satan's power. Out in the world, away from the fellowship and care of the church, they would **learn** (basically, "be disciplined") **not to blaspheme** (see 1:13; 6:4). The purpose of such drastic action was more remedial than punitive (for a similar situation, see 1 Cor. 5:5, 13; see also discussion on 1 Cor. 5:5).

V. Instructions concerning the Administration of the Church (chaps. 2–3)

A. Public Worship (chap. 2)

1. Prayer in Public Worship (2:1–8)

2:1. I exhort is a tactful order (see discussion on 1:3); **therefore** is a transitional conjunction introducing what follows as an inference from what precedes. Accordingly, Timothy's success in the purpose for which his stay was required (see 1:3–7, 18–20), to preempt the spread of "other doctrine" (1:3) while pursuing a godly love (2:5), called for prayer. Prayer in all its forms is to be offered **first of all … for all men**. The emphasis of this chief concern falls on the words "for all men [people]." In the setting of congregational worship (see 2:8), there must be room for all in prayer; no one is beyond its scope and no concern excluded by its form.

2:2. Paul specified that prayers should be offered for **kings, and for all that are in authority**. No distinction is drawn according to benevolence or statesmanship. If anything, rulers who misuse their authority and who oppose Christianity are particularly in view. It must be remembered that the notorious Roman emperor Nero (AD 54–68) was in power when Paul wrote these words. All authority comes from God (see Rom. 13:1), and prayer itself is an acknowledgment of the one King and true Authority. Christians have a reason to pray for pagan authorities: **that we may lead a quiet and peaceable life** (see Jer. 29:7). Civil coexistence is mutual; it involves good governance and good citizenship (see Rom. 13:4–5). Paul had both in view. **Godliness** (Greek, *eusebeia*) implies a good and holy life, with special emphasis on its source: a deep reverence for God. It is a key word (along with "godly") in the Pastorals; the Greek term occurs eight times in 1 Timothy (here; 3:16; 4:7–8; 6:3, 5–6, 11), once in 2 Timothy (3:5), and once in Titus (1:1) but nowhere else in the writings of Paul. **Honesty** (Greek, *semnotēs*; "dignity," "gravity") implies integrity and "moral earnestness, affecting outward demeanour as well as interior intention" (Kelly, *The Pastoral Epistles*, p. 61; see 3:5; Titus 2:7).

2:3–4. A further and extended theological reason to pray "for all men" (2:1) comes here and runs through 2:6: prayers for all to **our Saviour** (v. 3) coincides with the very heart of God, **who will have all men to be saved** (v. 4). This is not a prediction but a characterization of God's desire. Human response is embedded in the passive "to be saved" and the verb **to come unto**. **The knowledge of the truth** is virtually a synonym for the gospel (see 3:15; 4:3).

2:5–6. The foundational tenet of Judaism is that **there is one God** (v. 5; see Deut. 6:4), which every Jew confessed daily in the Shema (see discussion on Mark 12:29). Corresponding to the one God over all is the **one mediator between God and men**. These words hold the key to fathoming 2:3–4 and its connection to all intercessory prayer. **The man Christ Jesus**, in context, is the incarnate mediator: very God, very man (see "Christ Jesus came into the world to save sinners," 1:15). **Ransom for all** (v. 6; see discussion on Matt. 20:28) matches, on the one hand, the scope of His mediation and, on the other, the scope of prayer. "All" is not delimited but is ultimately defined redemptively by one's faith response to the "one mediator," Christ Jesus. **To be testified in due time**, a difficult phrase by all accounts, is idiomatically, "the witness at the appropriate time." Side by side with the words "ransom for all," it attests to the divine timing and testimony of Christ's death as the ransom that authenticates God's desire for the salvation of all men (see 6:13–16; Titus 3:1; Gal. 4:4).

2:7. Whereunto, or "for which reason"—namely, to testify that through His death, Christ has bridged the gap between God and man and made salvation available to all—Paul was appointed **a preacher** ("herald"). This brings into view Paul's missionary proclamation of the good news of salvation. For the word **apostle**, see discussion on Mark 6:30; *KJV Study Bible* note on 1 Corinthians 1:1. The parenthesis, **I speak the truth in Christ, and lie not**, creates emphasis to underscore what follows: **a teacher of the Gentiles in faith and verity**. For this saving message (2:6), Paul was a preacher and an apostle appointed by God, but equally so, he was a teacher. This final phrase entails Paul's calling to the Gentiles, which he elsewhere featured as "the apostle of the Gentiles" (Rom. 11:13; see Gal. 1:16; 2:7, 9; Rom. 1:5; Acts 9:15). Here God's desire to save all men (2:4) is confirmed, with the accent falling on Paul's role as teacher. From this, it may be inferred that the teaching of "other doctrine" (1:3–7) was rooted in Jewish exclusivism, which undermined the teaching of the true gospel Paul represented "in faith and verity." Whatever form the exclusivist Jewish teaching may have taken, Paul had plainly mapped "all" people as the territory charted by the gospel (2:3–7) and "all" therein as the appropriate obligation of prayer.

2:8–14. Some maintain that Paul's teaching here about women is historically conditioned, not universal and timeless. Others view these verses as unaffected by the historical situation and therefore applicable to every age. See *KJV Study Bible* note on 1 Corinthians 11:2–16.

2:8. The Greek for **men** in this verse does not refer to mankind (as in 2:5–6) but to male as distinct from female. That women sometimes prayed in public, however, seems evident from 1 Corinthians 11:5 (see also 1 Tim. 2:9–10). **Every where** (see 1 Cor. 1:2; 2 Cor. 2:14; 1 Thess. 1:8) identifies every place the gospel was proclaimed and Christ the Lord was named, particularly, the congregations or house churches in Ephesus where God's people gathered for worship. **Lifting up holy hands, without wrath and doubting** matches the outward posture of prayer with the inward disposition of the heart. The customary Jewish and Christian manner of lifting hands in prayer turns on the word "holy," which here outwardly refers to hands that are washed and ritually pure. The holiness that prayer demands is inward; one's hands are to be an extension of a pure heart free of harbored anger and stubborn disputes. Such issues were also relevant to Timothy's work.

2. Women in Public Worship (2:9–15)

2:9–10. In like manner also, [I want] women [to pray] in modest apparel is how the structure of the Greek reads most naturally, with "in like manner also" bringing forward from 2:8 the verb "I want/ to pray" as verse 9 requires, for it has no verb at all.

The word sequence in Greek sets out the balance of these verses.

| I want/ to pray | Therefore | the men | in every place |
| | In like manner also | women | in modest apparel |

In both 2:8 and verse 9, men and women respectively are the subject of "to pray." On the surface, Paul was speaking about the demeanor of the men and women of the church when they congregate in community worship. Men are to come to prayer without anger or unresolved disputes in their hearts. Likewise, women are to come to prayer with lives adorned with good works. Paul did not impose a total ban on the wearing of jewelry or braided hair. Rather, he was expressing caution in a society where such things were signs of extravagant luxury and proud personal display. The greater adornment, Paul said, is attained not through an investment in physical appearance but through godly living, the attire of good works (see discussions on 2:2; 1 Peter 3:3–4). Nothing is to disrupt the spirit of worship, not anger and the wrangling of men, nor the attire and adornments of women.

2:11. Let the woman learn in silence. Paul was not imposing a gag order but directing the spirit of a woman's presence in the assembly. The word translated "silence" (Greek, *hēsuchia*) points to a "quiet" (as in 2:2), not disruptive, demeanor. This corresponds to the prepositional phrase **with all subjection**.

2:12. I suffer not a woman to teach. Paul did not allow women to be official teachers in the assembled church. This is indicated by the added restriction concerning a woman exercising **authority over the man** (see 1 Cor. 11:3), that is, functioning as a bishop (see discussion on 3:1).

2:13–14. Paul based the restrictions regarding a woman's role in the church on Genesis 2–3. The appeal to the creation account makes the restrictions universal and permanent. **Adam was first formed**

(v. 13). Paul appealed to the priority of Adam in creation, which predates the fall. Thus, Paul viewed the
man-woman relationship set forth in this passage as
grounded in creation. **The woman being deceived**
(v. 14). Paul appears to argue that since the woman
was deceived (and then led Adam astray), she is
not to be entrusted with the teaching function of a
bishop (or elder) in the public worship services of
the assembled church.

2:15. The influence of Genesis continues here,
specifically Genesis 3:16, which discusses childbirth.
Three possible meanings of this verse are: (1) it
speaks of the godly woman finding fulfillment in
her role as wife and mother in the home when her
children are disciplined in godliness; (2) it refers to
women being saved spiritually through the most
significant birth of all, the incarnation of Christ; or
(3) it refers to women being kept physically safe in
childbirth.

It may be added that all three meanings attempt
to do justice to the passage and at the same time to
appreciate the importance that Paul placed on the
role of motherhood in answering the concern of 2:11
and any woman who would "usurp masculine functions" (Kelly, *Pastoral Epistles*, p. 70). In particular,
the differences pivot on the meaning of the phrase
saved in childbearing.

The first possible meaning takes "childbearing"
as the act of giving birth (see Gen. 5:16) and as an expression of motherhood and a woman's role within
the family (see 2:11; Gen. 3:15b). Thus, "saved in
childbearing" means it will "deliver" her from falling into transgression due to deception (see 2:14;
see also Paul's instruction in 2:11–12). Paul then
clarified his use of "saved" by adding that such is the
case for any woman (**they**) if she is truly a Christian, one who continues in the faith (see Fee, *1 and
2 Timothy, Titus*, p. 76). This may have had added
bearing in Paul's mind because the false teachers
prohibited marriage (4:3). Although it is not clear
whether Paul touched on the very issues regarding
women (2:13–14; Gen. 2–3) that the false teachers
used to validate such a prohibition, Paul was clearly
endorsing motherhood and marriage (see 5:14–15).

The second possible meaning is distinguished by
taking the words "in childbearing" (lit., "through the
childbirth," with the article in Greek) as referring to a
specific birth, the birth of Christ. Implicitly, Eve and
Mary are juxtaposed as representatives of all women.
Further justification for this unusual and unparalleled use of the expression is drawn from Genesis
3:15, with its contrast of "thy seed and her seed"
(offspring). "Saved," then, is taken in its most natural
sense, as saved from sin by virtue of the redemption
won through Christ. Others would point out, however, that not only is such a reference to Christ obscure; it is an irregular use of the noun "childbearing"
and a misunderstanding of Genesis 3:15.

The third possible meaning takes **childbearing**
as the fact of giving birth and **saved** as meaning the
woman is kept physically safe in the course of giving
birth (presumably from death or injury). However,
Genesis 3:16 presupposes the survival of both child
and mother. What is more, Paul with this understanding here makes weak sense of the context. The first
meaning is the better of the three possible readings.

B. Qualifications for Church Officers (3:1–13)

1. Bishops (3:1–7)

3:1. True saying is identical to the wording of 1:15
(see discussion there). The word for **office of a bishop**
(Greek, *episkopē*) points to the function and responsibility of oversight. In the Greek culture, the word
"bishop" (Greek, *episkopos*; 3:2) was used of a presiding official in a civic or religious organization. Here
it refers to a man who oversees a local congregation.
The equivalent word from the Jewish background of
Christianity is "elder." The terms "bishop" (or "overseer") and "elder" are used interchangeably in Acts
20:17, 28; Titus 1:5–7; 1 Peter 5:1–2. The duties of
a bishop were to teach and preach (see 3:2; 5:17), to
direct the affairs of the church (see 3:5; 5:17), to shepherd ("pastor") the flock of God (see Acts 20:28), and
to guard the church from error (see Acts 20:28–31).

3:2–3. If any man expressed a desire to become
a bishop, or Timothy and the church detected such a
desire on the part of any man, his character and quali-

fication for the office were to be measured. **A bishop … must be** (v. 2) enumerates the qualities a candidate must have (see chart, *KJV Study Bible*, p. 1741). That the man be **the husband of one wife** is a qualification derived from a general principle that applies to any violation of God's marriage law, whether in the form of polygamy or of marital unfaithfulness (see discussion on Titus 1:6). **Vigilant** (Greek, *nēphalios*; see 3:11; Titus 2:2) is more commonly used of sobriety but is used here in the wider sense of "levelheaded." One would think **sober** (Greek, *sōphrōn*; see Titus 1:8;2:2, 5) pertains to inebriation, but it refers to sound judgment and measured, moderate living. **Of good behaviour** (Greek, *kosmion*; see 2:9) identifies admirable and dignified conduct, that which is praiseworthy in the sight of others. **Hospitality** (Greek, *philoxenia*; see 5:10; Rom. 12:13; 1 Peter 4:9) means to provide domestic care to others with an openhearted and openhanded welcome. **Apt to teach** (Greek, *didaktikos*; see 2 Tim. 2:24) points to the skilled responsibilities of preaching and teaching that should belong to the elder, or bishop (5:17; see Titus 1:9). **Not given to wine** (v. 3; Greek, *paroinos*; see Titus 1:7) contains a compound word: the preposition *par*- being a marker of nearness or connection and – *oinos*, meaning wine. It suggests a person characterized by, even defined by, wine and pertains to one who is given to drinking too much. **No striker** (Greek, *plēktēs*; see Titus 1:7) means the elder should not easily resort to fists or violence; the overseer certainly should not be a bully. **Not greedy of filthy lucre** (Greek, *aischrokerdē*; see Titus 1:7) dictates that the elder not be someone who is greedy for money and inclined to pursue shameful gain. **Patient** (Greek, *epieikēs*) refers to a yielding, gentle kindness, rather than an insistence on one's own rights. **Not a brawler** (Greek, *amachos*; see Titus 3:2) is an adjective that is shorthand for "must not strive" (2 Tim. 2:24) or "must not be quarrelsome." **Not covetous** (Greek, *aphilarguros*; see Heb. 13:5) reiterates that the elder should not be a lover of money (see 1 Tim. 6:10).

3:4 – 5. A bishop should be **One that ruleth well his own house** (v. 4), emphasizing the tested leadership of a man pastoring his own household. One cannot give leadership to a house church if the rule of **his own house** (v. 5) disqualifies him (for the use of "ruleth" and "rule," see discussion on Rom. 12:8). **Having his children in subjection** (v. 4) indicates that the quality of a father's leadership can be seen in the honor his children pay to his authority. **With all gravity** (Greek, *semnotēs*; see 2:2 and discussion) may here apply to the father and candidate to the office rather than to the children. For the father, it suggests a generally virtuous headship of his home; for the children, it suggests proper respect. For **church** (Greek, *ekklēsia*), see discussion on Matthew 16:18.

3:6 – 7. These verses both end with a reference to the Devil and point up the spiritual warfare that besets anyone who assumes the office of bishop, therefore emphasizing the caliber of spiritual maturity required. **Not a novice** (v. 6), or "neophyte" (Greek, *neophyton*; "newly planted"), calls for a man seasoned in his faith and one more fully grown in Christ. **Pride** is a target of the Devil's **condemnation**, the accuser of the brethren (see Rev. 12:9 – 10). **A good report of them which are without** (v. 7) specifies those outside the community of believers. Paul spoke of one's "testimony" here as he did elsewhere (see 1 Thess. 4:12; 1 Cor. 10:32; Col. 4:5).

2. Deacons (3:8 – 13)

3:8 – 10. In its nontechnical usage, **deacon** (Greek, *diakonos*; v. 10) means simply "one who serves." The men chosen in Acts 6:1 – 6 probably were not only the first deacons mentioned in the New Testament but also the first to be appointed in the church (but see discussions there). Generally, their service was meant to free the elders to give full attention to prayer and the ministry of the Word (see Acts 6:2, 4). The only two local church offices mentioned in the New Testament are those of bishop (or overseer; also called elder) and deacon (see Phil. 1:1).

In substance, the character qualifications for the deacon virtually mirror those of the overseer, with the notable omission of "apt to teach" (3:2), which may be a clue to the distinction of these two roles. **Holding the mystery of the faith** (v. 9) is best explained by Titus 1:9. If the use of "mystery" here bears any resemblance to Paul's use elsewhere, it alludes to the revelation of God in Jesus Christ, the core teaching of the gospel. A deacon should have a **pure conscience** and be **proved** (v. 10) and **found blameless**, reinforcing that the office of deacon must be occupied by men of "known" Christian character and unswerving devotion to Christ.

3:11. Wives (lit., "women") is followed in Greek by the word "likewise," or "in the same manner" (see 2:9 and discussion) The verb **must** is supplied here, as it is in 3:8 (from 3:2). The Greek for "wives" could refer to (1) deacons' wives, (2) deaconesses, or (3) female deacons. To many, the fact that deacons are referred to again in 3:12–13 is a proof that deacons' wives are the topic rather than a separate office of deaconess or female deacons. This raises the question of why deacons' wives would be addressed when overseers' wives are not. Either the wives of overseers and deacons are both intended, the fitness of **their** character called to mind by 3:10 and not to be forgotten in the case of either an overseer or a deacon, or here is a case of a recognized role for women in the service the deaconate supplies the church (see discussion on 3:8). There is no separate term for "deaconess" in the New Testament, only the one word, the masculine "deacon," as used of Phoebe in Romans 16:1.

3:12–14. The husbands of one wife (v. 12), treated first in the qualifications of the overseer (see discussion on 3:2), is here treated almost as an afterthought. Unless Paul was saying that marriage is required of all overseers and deacons, he meant that if a man is married, looking to his marriage and home is a good way to discern his character. Here Paul conflated in one concise statement the substance of 3:2, 4. **Used the office of a deacon** (v. 13) emphasizes service that has met standards of expectation or excellence in some recognized way. Deacons who excel may expect to gain a dual outcome. First, they **well purchase to themselves a good degree**, which may be worded, "gain for themselves good standing." This suggests enhanced credibility within the believing community. Second, they gain **great boldness in the faith which is in Christ Jesus**. In other words, they can expect their faith in Christ to grow

confident in its expression right along with their exemplary service.

C. Purpose of These Instructions (3:14–16)

3:14–15. These things (v. 14) entail the scope of the whole letter. Paul expressed his hope of making a personal visit **shortly** but allowed for a delay. His impending visit (see 4:13) made conspicuous his personal commitment to the enforcement of this matters. Here, in brief, Paul stated his purpose for writing the letter: **that thou mayest know how thou oughtest to behave thyself** (v. 15). The Greek, however, does not convey such an individual focus and should be rendered: "that you may know how 'people' ought to conduct 'themselves.'" This is borne out by the context. Simply put, Paul's purpose was to safeguard the church in Ephesus. This is why Timothy had been instructed to stay, why Paul had sent written instructions to his envoy, and why the apostle himself was coming. **The house of God** and **the church of the living God** are synonymous and stand for the people of God gathered in local houses of worship. Nevertheless, "house" is a vibrant metaphor and leads to the structural importance of column and foundation. People are "bearers" of God's truth. Their conduct and behavior show what they are made of. In Ephesus, **the truth** (see 3:16) and those who bore the truth were in spiritual jeopardy because of the treachery of assailing spirits and the false doctrines of hypocritical liars (see 1:3–7; 4:1–5; 6:3–5, 20–21).

3:16. The word "mystery" is found throughout the New Testament, particularly in Paul's writings (see discussions on Mark 4:11; Rom. 11:25; Col. 1:26). The phrase **the mystery of godliness** means "the revealed secret of true piety," that is, the secret that produces piety in people. That secret, as the following words indicate, is none other than Jesus Christ. His incarnation, in all its aspects (particularly His saving work), is the source of genuine piety. The words are printed in poetic form and could have come from an early creedal hymn (see discussion on Col. 3:16). The adjective **great** is validated by a series of proofs, the aggregate of which forms a grand crescendo to the majesty of this mystery. **Justified in the Spirit** summarizes a ministry characterized by the power of the Spirit. The Holy Spirit enabled Jesus to drive out demons (see Matt. 12:28) and perform miracles. Most important, the Spirit raised Jesus from the dead (see Rom. 1:4; 1 Peter 3:18) and thereby vindicated Him, showing that He was indeed the Son of God. **Seen of angels** speaks of the unearthly and angelic testimony that announced His resurrection (see Matt. 28:2) and ascension (see Acts 1:10).

VI. Methods of Dealing with False Teaching (chap. 4)

A. False Teaching Described (4:1–5)

4:1–2. At face value, **the Spirit speaketh expressly** (v. 1) means that He speaks "clearly," "explicitly," or "precisely" (see, e.g., Matt. 24:11; Mark 13:22; Acts 20:29–30; 2 Thess. 2:3). Paul, however, was perhaps speaking here of a specific revelation given to him by the Spirit. **In the latter times** refers to the time beginning with the first coming of Christ (see 1 Peter 1:20; see discussion on Heb. 1:1). That Paul was not referring only to the time immediately prior to Christ's second coming is obvious from his assumption in 4:7 that the false teachings were already present at the time of this writing. **Some shall depart from the faith** refers not to false teachers but to some within "the house of God" (3:15) that were **giving heed to seducing spirits, and doctrines of devils** (lit., "demons") in the hypocrisy of liars. Although it is not as clear in the KJV, Paul was saying that the human agents who cloak the deceptive work of Satan (see 5:15) are liars who are without properly working consciences. **Seared** (Greek, *kaustēriazō*; v. 2) suggests either "cauterized" or "branded," the effects of hellish influence. How dangerous is the lie of someone who has himself been deceived and no longer knows the difference between right or wrong? (See Titus 1:15; for the importance of a pure and clean conscience to the Christian, see 1:5, 19; 3:9.)

4:3–5. The unbiblical asceticism described in verse 3 arose out of the mistaken belief that the material world was evil, which was a central belief of the Gnostic heresy (see 1 John, Introduction: "Gnosticism"). Those who hold to and impose on others

ascetic regulations certainly condemn others who do not hold the same views and who partake of the things prohibited. Such judgment, Paul implied, falls on God Himself, who created what they forbid and who made it to be received with thanksgiving, not condemnation. Paul addressed the issue of freedom (reception and thanksgiving) elsewhere (see, e.g., Rom. 14:14, 20–23; 1 Cor. 10:29–30; Titus 1:15; Acts 10:15), passages that serve as an apt commentary to what he wrote here.

B. Methods of Dealing with False Teaching (4:6–16)

4:6–8. Paul turned to Timothy with personal attention to his task of facing false teaching. For **fables** (v. 7), see discussion on 1:4. **Exercise thyself rather unto godliness** is Paul's call for a regimen of training not unlike that in the realm of athletics. "Exercise [the Greek verb *gymnazō*] … unto godliness" and **bodily exercise** (the Greek noun *gymnasia*; v. 8) are words that evoke images of athletic competition. **Profiteth little** introduces a comparison of what is limited to this world with what is eternal: **godliness** (see discussion on 2:2) requires self-discipline just like that of an athlete but has gains and rewards that are out of this world.

4:9–10. The **faithful saying** (v. 9; see discussion on 1:15) in this instance refers back to the seemingly proverbial statement in 4:8b. The words **labour and suffer reproach** (v. 10) may refer to the exercising mentioned in 4:7b–8. For **trust**, see discussion on 1:1. Obviously, **Saviour of all** does not mean that God saves every person from eternal punishment, for such universalism would contradict the clear testimony of Paul and of Scripture. God is, however, the Savior of all in that He offers salvation to all and saves all who come to Him.

4:11. These things (particularly as in 4:8b–10) were not to inspire Timothy alone; he was to invigorate and inspire the rest of the community in the strongest possible way: **command and teach** (see 4:15).

4:12. Let no man despise thy youth. Timothy was probably in his midthirties or younger, and in that day, such an influential position was not usually held by a man so young. For this reason, his leadership had perhaps been called into question. Even if Timothy faced contempt and a lack of appreciation, he was to become **an example** (Greek, *typos*; "pattern").

4:13. Till I come points back to Paul's intended visit (see 3:14). His journey had taken him from Ephesus to Macedonia, but he hoped to rejoin Timothy soon at Ephesus. **Give attendance to reading, to exhortation, to doctrine**. "Reading" is a term with a fixed reference to the reading of Scripture in the assembly (see Acts 13:15; 2 Cor. 3:14). Its order is significant, for the Scripture was to be the foundation of Timothy's exhortation (teaching and preaching) as well that as of the elders' (see "in the word and doctrine," 5:17). This is corroborated by the serviceability of the Scripture in 2 Timothy 3:16.

4:14. The gift that is in thee alludes to an interior grace or "spiritual" gift (Greek, *charisma*; referring to an endowment of "grace," *charis*). For **prophecy**, see discussion on 1:18. The prophecy together **with the laying on of the hands of the presbytery** suggests a kind of ordination attended by the elders as a body. The word "presbytery" formally denotes a council of elders, and the word "elder" in Greek is *presbyteros*.

4:15. Here is a final reiteration of 4:12–14. **Meditate** is here nearer to "endeavor," and **profiting** speaks of "progress" or "furtherance" (see Phil. 1:12, 25, the only other occurrences in the New Testament).

4:16. Thou shalt both save thyself, and them that hear thee. God alone saves, but Christians can be God's instruments to bring about the salvation of others. "Save thyself" indicates that salvation is both an event and a process. Believers are saved at the time of conversion but are still being saved in the sense of being conformed more and more to Christ's image (see 1 Cor. 1:18) and ultimately glorified.

VII. Methods of Dealing with Different Groups in the Church (5:1–6:2)

A. The Elderly and Younger People (5:1–2)

5:1–2. Treatment of different age groups calls for consideration. **Rebuke not an elder** (v. 1) speaks not of an official but of a man who is one's senior in age and therefore deserving of respect. "Elder" (Greek, *presbyteros*) is matched by its feminine counterpart in the next verse: **elder women** (Greek, *presbytera*; v. 2). "Rebuke" is a strong term (Greek, *epiplēssō*), the verb of the noun "striker" (Greek, *plēktēs*) in 3:3. As Kelly (*The Pastoral Epistles*, p. 110) points out, "it connotes rough treatment." **Intreat** (Greek, *parakaleō*; v. 1) means to treat in an inviting or congenial manner. This verb governs elders as fathers, young men as brothers, elder women as mothers, and younger women as sisters. **With all purity** (v. 2; see 4:12), by deduction, applies in particular to young women and connotes moral or chaste conduct and thought. Here is a picture of community care and respect modeled on the family that now in Christ belongs to the household or family of God.

B. Widows (5:3–16)

5:3. Honour widows that are widows indeed, that is, widows who are truly left alone and destitute (see 5:4–5). This probably means taking care of them, including the giving of material support. Widows were particularly vulnerable in ancient societies because no pensions, government assistance, life insurance, or the like were available to them.

5:4. Responsible care for the widow belongs first to her family before it belongs to others. **Shew piety at home**, that is, the "godliness" (see discussion on 2:2) that so prominently figures in the Pastoral Epistles and that is to characterize the Christian (3:16; 4:7–8; 6:3, 5–6, 11; 2 Tim. 3:5; Titus 1:1).

5:5–6. The disposition of the **widow indeed** (v. 5), or a genuine widow in need, is contrasted with its counterfeit. **Dead while she liveth** (v. 6) connotes one who is dead spiritually while living physically.

5:7–8. Widows too are to be **blameless** (v. 7), above reproach. **If any provide not for his own** (v. 8) again picks up the topic of irresponsibility on the part of believing families (see 5:4). Such dereliction of duty to family is defined in spiritual terms: **denied the faith, and is worse than an infidel**. How pitiful that pagan codes of duty to family should be elevated by the inferior conduct of a family within the family of God.

5:9–10. Paul provided further instructions regarding the qualification and treatment of widows. **Taken into the number** (v. 9) refers to a recognized "official" list. The church in Ephesus seems to have maintained a list of widows supported by the church. While there is no evidence of an order of widows comparable to that of the bishops, it appears that those on the list were expected to devote themselves to prayer (see 5:5) and **good works** (v. 10). Among the identifying qualifications, the widows were to **have washed the saints' feet**, a menial but necessary task performed for all arrivals because of dusty roads and the wearing of sandals (see John 13:14).

5:11–12. **Younger widows** (v. 11; see the age limit in 5:9) are not to be enrolled as "widows indeed" (5:5). For one, the yearning to marry (**wax wanton**, as amorous desires) might be stronger than their devotion to Christ, and as a result, young widows often do not remain unmarried (see 1 Cor. 7:39–40). Incurring **damnation** (v. 12) may be too strong but surely refers to a condemnatory verdict. The gravity depends on the meaning of **cast off their first faith**, which may refer to breaking a "pledge" or renouncing the faith they professed in Christ. Perhaps when a widow was added to the list, she pledged special devotion to Christ, which would be diminished by remarriage. Paul may have been referring to the believer's basic trust in Christ, which a widow would compromise by marrying outside the faith.

5:13. A second reason younger widows are not to be enrolled is that their behavior is too often unworthy of honor (see 5:3), contrary to the model of the "widow indeed" (5:5, 10) and anything but "blameless" (5:7).

5:14–15. Instead of enrollment (see 5:9) for the **younger** (v. 14) widows, Paul endorsed remarriage, motherhood, and family as the answer to the needs of a young woman who proves to be blameless (see 5:7) and beyond the slander of the Adversary, **Satan** (see discussions on Zech. 3:1; Matt. 16:23; Rev. 12:10). Paul's directions in 5:11–14 addressed recent experience (**already**). Following Satan should not be conceived as conscious and deliberate but as

the opposite of following after Christ and as the outcome of deception (see 4:1–2).

5:16. A recap of the necessary obligation of family and community responsibility to **widows indeed** (see especially 5:3–8).

C. Elders (5:17–25)

5:17. All **elders** (see discussion on 5:19) are to exercise leadership (3:4–5) and to teach and preach (3:2), and all are to receive honor. Those who excel in leadership are to **be counted worthy of double honour**. This is especially true of those who labor at teaching and preaching. That such honor should include financial support is indicated by the two illustrations in 5:18. **Rule** (Greek, *proistēmi*) means to exercise a position of leadership (see Rom. 12:8 and discussion).

5:18. The term **scripture** (Greek, *graphē*) was used to identify any part or the whole of God's authoritative Word, what Christians today call the Old Testament but then the threefold Jewish division of Scripture: the Law, the Prophets, and the Writings (see Luke 24:44). The use of this term for both an Old Testament (Deut. 25:4) and a New Testament (Luke 10:7) passage shows that by this time, portions of the New Testament, certainly the words of Jesus, were considered to be equal in authority to the Old Testament Scriptures.

5:19–20. The title **elder** (Greek, *presbyteros*; v. 19) is interchangeable with the title "overseer" (see Titus 1:5–9; Acts 20:17, 20; 1 Peter 5:1–2), which explains why Paul did not enumerate their qualifications separately. The default honor due the office of the elder (see 5:17) involves not only the presumption but also the defense of innocence in the case of an accusation. **Receive not an accusation, but before two or three witnesses** because allegations are not proven without corroboration. The principle of corroboration was a time-honored Jewish legal standard (see Deut. 19:15; Heb. 10:28; Matt. 18:16; John 8:17; 2 Cor. 13:1). "Receive not" implies "do not acknowledge as correct" without corroboration. Spiritual warfare takes many forms and enemy assaults involve those who take the lead (see "rule," 5:17). Even so, no elder is above the rule of the Lord, and **Them that sin** (v. 20) calls for open rebuke within the community of believers. The context assumes both the required corroboration and that Paul was speaking of the discipline of elders. Unlike in 5:1, **rebuke** (Greek, *elenchō*) here means "to expose" the fault or wrongdoing. In itself, such action is a clear correction of sin and a reinforcement of what is right. The primary purpose is **that others also may fear,** a reference to other elders first of all and no less to others subject to such "exposure." "Fear," then, implies the fearful respect of the office and ultimately of the Lord's leadership (see 5:21).

5:21. The importance of the elders' most solemn **charge** is administrating justice without prejudice or partiality. The importance of this charge is seen in Paul's invoking the sight of God, the Lord Jesus Christ, and the divine retinue (see 2 Tim. 4:1). **Elect angels** stands in contrast to Satan and the other fallen angels. Fee (*1 and 2 Timothy, Titus*, p. 131) suggested the gravity concerns "erring elders who, as false teachers, are having considerable influence in the community."

5:22. Lay hands suddenly on no man refers to the ordination of an elder, which should not be performed until the candidate has had time to prove himself. **Neither be partaker of other men's sins** is a warning against the ordination a person unworthy of the office of elder. In the context of ordination and elder credibility, **keep thyself pure** reminded Timothy of the necessity of leading a blameless life.

5:23. Drink no longer water is a parenthetical comment in Paul's discussion of elders. In view of Timothy's physical ailments, and perhaps because safe drinking water was often difficult to find, Paul advised him to drink a little wine.

5:24 – 25. Paul returned to the general topic of the qualification and disqualification of elders as it relates to the issue of **sins** (v. 24) and **good works** (v. 25). Paul advised being alert to hidden sins as well as to good deeds in the lives of candidates for ordination.

D. Servants (6:1 – 2)

6:1 – 2. For **servants** (v. 1), see discussions on Ephesians 6:5; Colossians 3:22 – 4:1. After treating the Christian disposition toward slaves in general, Paul took up the matter of slaves and their masters within the church. A servant was not to exploit his Christian brotherhood in a way that failed to respect or took liberties with his master (see Kelly, *The Pastoral Epistles*, p. 131). Scenarios abound. It is conceivable that a servant held a higher position within the church (deacon, elder) than that of his master. The reverse was also possible. Whatever the case, they were to love as brothers. **These things teach and exhort** (v. 2) probably belongs to the topic of false teachers and refers to the instructions beginning in 5:3.

VIII. Miscellaneous Matters (6:3 – 19)

A. False Teachers (6:3 – 5)

6:3 – 5. Paul returned to the subject of the treacherous teachings of "other doctrine[s]" (1:3) that contradicted and opposed the Lord and godly instruction (see discussion on 1:3 – 11). Notable is that these teachings were rooted in pride, which correlates to the strife and disharmony that resulted. **Destitute of the truth** (v. 5) means that the heretical teachers had once known the truth but had been led into error. **Supposing that gain is godliness** refers to godliness as a means of profit. Since Paul had exposed their interior motives and exterior effects, "godliness" for them was a pretense. The show of godliness was a way to turn a buck. Charlatans were a common problem then. Among the Gentiles, Paul had to overcome the stigma of godliness that was a show of charlatans—Paul needed to distinguish himself (see 1 Thess. 2:4 – 9; *KJV Study Bible* note on 2 Cor. 11:7). Such charlatans continue to operate and be exposed today.

B. Love of Money (6:6 – 10)

6:6 – 7. Some make "godliness" a means gain (v. 5). Paul capitalized on that by speaking (or writing) of godliness and contentment. **Godliness with contentment** (v. 6) is a strong antidote to greed (6:5), especially if one soberly appreciates the true measure of earthly acquisition and self-interest: **we brought nothing into this world, and … we can carry nothing out** (v. 7).

6:8. Implicit in godliness is the sufficiency and satisfaction of God. Beyond that, **food and raiment** are for spiritual support and sustenance of the physical only (see Matt. 6:25–34).

6:9–10. They that will be rich (v. 9) expresses a determination to have more, and Paul's own glossary on the desire defines it as **the love of money** (Greek, *philarguria*; v. 10; used only here in New Testament). That avarice is the root of all kinds of evil is amply illustrated in Scripture and no less here by Paul. Of all its tragedy, the supreme grief is that **they have erred from the faith**. Does this truth add a reason for Jesus' ample teaching on the subject?

C. Charge to Timothy (6:11–16)

6:11–12. In contrast to 6:9–10, Paul turned to Timothy with an emphatic **But thou** (v. 11) and the striking direct address **O man of God**. Since the man who loves money and the man of God serve different masters (see Matt. 6:24), Timothy was to **flee these things** and in haste **follow after** the true riches, the virtues of God. For **godliness**, see discussion on 2:2. Paul's imagery then moved to the battlefield of faith, where **lay hold on eternal life** (v. 12; see 6:19) is a battle cry to claim what one has already won. Timothy had possessed eternal life since he was first saved, but Paul urged him to claim its benefits in greater fullness (see 6:17–19; discussion on 4:16). **Professed a good profession** is probably a reference to Timothy's confession of faith at his baptism, during Paul's first missionary journey.

6:13. The image of giving testimony before many witnesses (see 6:12) includes in its assembly God the Father and **Christ Jesus**, the supreme witness. **Before Pontius Pilate** is a historical and juridical reference to Christ's testimony, on pain of death (see His statements in John 18:33–37; 19:10–11).

6:14–16. This commandment (v. 14) most likely refers to the whole charge given to Timothy to preach the gospel and care for the church (see 6:20), though the preceding context may indicate

that Paul used the singular "commandment" to sum up the various commands listed in 6:11–12. **The appearing of our Lord Jesus Christ** conveys the vindication of every witness who holds fast to his testimony. How soon may such an appearing be expected? The answer is, **in his times** (v. 15). Just as Jesus' first coming occurred at the precise time God wanted (Gal. 4:4), so also His second coming will occur at God's appointed time. The glory of Christ's appearing is ranked by the titles He bears: **King of kings, and Lord of lords** (see Rev. 19:16). For **whom no man hath seen, nor can see**, see discussion on John 1:18.

D. The Rich (6:17–19)

6:17–19. Because of the treachery of wealth, the temptation to love it more than the Lord, Paul provided instruction for those who possess great earthly treasure. **Laying up** (v. 19) is probably a direct reminiscence of Jesus' advice (see Matt. 6:19–20). **Lay hold on eternal life** (see discussion on 6:12) is an image of laying hold of or clutching eternal treasure that cannot be taken away (see 6:7).

IX. Concluding Appeal (6:20–21)

6:20–21. That which is committed to thy trust (v. 20) is the gospel. The same command is found in 2 Timothy 1:14. **Avoiding**, or "turning away," is deliberately contrasted with **some professing** (v. 21) belief who did not turn from such things (implied). They **erred**, that is, they "wandered" (Greek, *astocheō*; "deviate," "depart"; see 1:6) from the faith and so "turned away" (see 1:5; 5:15), something Timothy was to do from **profane and vain babblings, and oppositions of science falsely so called** (v. 21). The Greek word translated "science" is normally translated "knowledge." This is a reference to an early form of the heresy of Gnosticism, which taught that one may be saved by knowledge (the term "Gnosticism" comes from the Greek word for "knowledge"; see 1 John, Introduction: "Gnosticism.")

THE SECOND EPISTLE OF PAUL THE APOSTLE TO TIMOTHY

INTRODUCTION

Author, Date, and Place of Composition

After Paul's release from prison in Rome in AD 62/63 (see Acts 28) and after his fourth missionary journey (see map, *Zondervan KJV Study Bible*, pp. 2462–63), during which he wrote 1 Timothy and Titus, Paul was again imprisoned under Emperor Nero circa AD 66–67. It was during this time that he wrote 2 Timothy. In contrast to his first imprisonment, when he lived in a rented house (see Acts 28:30), he now languished in a cold dungeon (4:13), chained like a common criminal (1:16; 2:9). His friends had a hard time even finding out where he was being kept (1:17). Paul knew that his work was done and that his life was nearly at an end (4:6–8).

Theme

Paul had three reasons for writing to Timothy at this time. First, Paul was lonely. Phygellus and Hermogenes, "all they which are in Asia" (1:15), and Demas (4:10) had deserted him. Crescens, Titus, and Tychicus were away (4:10–12), and only Luke was with him (4:11). Paul wanted very much for Timothy to join him also. Timothy was his fellow worker (see Rom. 16:21) who, "as a son with the father" (Phil. 2:22), had served closely with him (see 1 Cor. 4:17). Paul could say of Timothy, "I have no man likeminded" (Phil. 2:20). He longed for Timothy (1:4) and twice asked him to come soon (4:9, 21). For more information on Timothy, see 1 Timothy, Introduction: "Recipient."

Second, Paul was concerned about the welfare of the churches during this time of persecution under Nero, and he admonished Timothy to guard the gospel (1:14), to persevere in it (3:14), to keep on preaching it (4:2), and, if necessary, to suffer for it (1:8; 2:3).

Third, Paul wanted to write to the Ephesian church through Timothy (see discussion on 4:22).

Outline

I. Introduction (1:1–4)
II. Paul's Concern for Timothy (1:5–14)
III. Paul's Situation (1:15–18)

Bibliography

Fee, Gordon D. *The Pastoral Epistles*. New International Biblical Commentary. Peabody, MA: Hendrickson, 1988.

Guthrie, Donald. *The Pastoral Epistles*. Tyndale New Testament Commentaries. Downers Grove, IL: InterVarsity, 1957.

Kelly, J. N. D. *The Pastoral Epistles*. London: Adam & Charles Black, 1963.

Kent, Homer, Jr. *The Pastoral Epistles*. Chicago: Moody, 1971.

Liefeld, Walter L. *1 and 2 Timothy, Titus*. The NIV Application Commentary. Grand Rapids, MI: Zondervan, 1999.

EXPOSITION

I. Introduction (1:1–4)

1:1. An apostle is one specially commissioned by Christ (see discussions on Mark 6:30; 1 Cor. 1:1; Heb. 3:1) **according to the promise of life.** Paul's being chosen to be an apostle was in keeping with that promise, and apostles were appointed to preach and explain the good news that eternal life is available to all who will receive it through faith in Christ.

1:2. My dearly beloved son (see 1 Tim. 1:2, 18; 2 Tim. 2:1; Titus 1:4) is not unique to Paul's correspondence with Timothy (1 Cor. 4:17; Phil. 2:22). "Son" is an appropriate inference in translation, but the Greek term in all the references cited here is *teknon*, "child." For the words **Grace** and **peace**, see discussions on Jonah 4:2; John 14:27; 20:19; Galatians 1:3; Ephesians 1:2.

1:3. I thank God ... in my prayers belongs to Paul's custom of opening a letter with thanksgiving (see discussion on Phil. 1:3–4). Paul's "thanksgiv-

ing" is a hallmark of his otherwise Hellenistic letter style and normally included intercession and even blessing. Its omission in Galatians, 1 Timothy, and Titus is a telling reminder that its presence was no mere convention. Here the stern business of the first letter to Timothy had not preempted this warm thanksgiving. **From my forefathers** points to Paul's family background and espies the influence of Timothy's heritage (see 1:5). **Night and day** comes from Paul's Jewish division of time ("a day") and is here akin to our "around the clock."

1:4. Greatly desiring to see thee reflects Paul's primary purpose for writing: he wished for Timothy to visit him (see 4:9, 21) during his final days in Rome (see 4:6–8). **Mindful of thy tears** may refer to Timothy's tears when Paul left for Macedonia (see 1 Tim. 1:3). If, however, the hypothesis of a second imprisonment is correct (see "Author, Date, and Place of Composition"), it may also suggest, as Kelly

(*The Pastoral Epistles*, p. 156) entertains, his arrest at Ephesus and his last sight of Timothy as Paul, in custody, was led to Rome.

II. Paul's Concern for Timothy (1:5–14)

1:5. Faith is not inherited, but it may be engendered by respected models, as it was in the Timothy's case: **the unfeigned faith that is in thee, which dwelt first in thy grandmother Lois, and thy mother Eunice.** According to Acts 16:1, Timothy's mother was a Jewish Christian. His grandmother too was a Christian. Timothy's father, however, was a Greek and possibly an unbeliever (see Acts 16:1). It was probably because of him that Timothy had not been circumcised as a child. "Unfeigned faith" is literally, "without the face of a hypocrite," and therefore without pretense but rather genuine, authentic faith, judged so because it is transparent.

1:6. Paul reminded Timothy to **stir up the gift of God** because gifts are seeded, not given in full bloom; they need to be cultivated through use. Paul's metaphor is that of a spark that is "stirred," or better "fanned," into a flame and presumably stoked into a roaring fire. **By the putting on of my hands** points to Paul as God's instrument through whom the gift came from the Holy Spirit to Timothy (see discussion on 1 Tim. 1:18).

1:7–8. Here the gift par excellence, the endowment of the Holy Spirit (note its fruit), is contrasted: **God hath not given us the spirit of fear; but of power, and of love, and of a sound mind** (v. 7). Apparently, timidity or a lack of confidence was a serious problem for Timothy (see 1 Cor. 16:10–11; 1 Tim. 4:12). The call to stand assertively for the Lord and show allegiance to His servants is as relevant to the timid today as it was to Timothy but cannot be accomplished without God's assistance, the enabling power of the Spirit (see 1:14). The topic of shame and **the gospel according to the power of God** (v. 8) is reminiscent of Romans 1:16.

1:9–10. The afflictions of the gospel (see v. 8, also 12) are to be shouldered not according to human strength but "according to the power of God" (v. 8). Paul set the assurance of God's power beside the as-surance of our salvation ("hath saved us and called us," v. 9) and Savior (v. 10), a certainty **not according to our works, but according to his own purpose and grace** (v. 9). Salvation is by grace alone and is based not on human effort but on God's saving plan and the gracious gift of His Son (see Rom. 3:28; Eph. 2:8–9; Titus 3:5). **Before the world began**, in eternity past, God's plan to save lost sinners was made (see Eph. 1:4; 1 Peter 1:20; Rev. 13:8).

1:11–12. Paul, **a preacher, and an apostle** (v. 11; see discussion on 1 Tim. 2:7), assured Timothy that he had and did follow his own advice. Moreover, as crucial and cardinal as right doctrine was to Paul and the themes of the Pastoral Epistles (see, e.g., 1:13), personal faith in the person of God was even more important. **That day** (v. 12) refers to the day of the Lord, the day of judgment.

1:13. Sound words (see discussion on Titus 1:9) probably refers to "right doctrine" (see "the truth," Titus 1:14) in a general way. In the Pastoral Epistles, the word "sound" (Greek, *hugiainō*) is used eight times and only in the letters of doctrine (here; "sound doctrine," 4:3; 1 Tim. 1:10; Titus 1:9; 2:1; the "wholesome [sound] words" of the Lord, 1 Tim. 6:3; "sound in the faith" faith, Titus 1:13; 2:2). **Faith and love … in Christ**, or faith and love through union with Christ, is another way of saying "Christian faith and love" (see 1 Tim. 1:14).

1:14. That good thing … committed unto thee refers to the gospel. Paul gave the same command in 1 Timothy 6:20. Paul reminded Timothy that power comes from God and the interior presence of His Holy Spirit (see 1:7–8). Here this magnificent truth applies specifically to Paul and Timothy and is probably the thrust of **us**.

III. Paul's Situation (1:15–18)

1:15. All is probably hyperbole, a deliberate exaggeration to express widespread desertion. Timothy was in Ephesus, the capital of the province of **Asia**, which today is in western Turkey. Because of Timothy's position, he would have had direct, personal observation or knowledge of the defection to which Paul referred. **Turned away from me** suggests but does not confirm that Paul's arrest had been a catalyst for the desertion. Paul's words in 1:8, however, loom ever larger against this background. Of **Phygellus and Hermogenes**, nothing more is known, although it may be surmised that their mention is a measure of Paul's grief over their loss.

1:16 – 18. In contrast with the defection of others (see 1:15), the memory of **Onesiphorus** (v. 16), who was probably now dead (v. 18; 4:19), was a figure of faithful help and support. Nevertheless, he too was gone. He had lived in Ephesus, where his family continued to reside (see 4:19). For the importance of **Rome** (v. 17) at this time, see Introduction: "Author, Date, and Place of Composition" (see also 1:8; 2:9). **That he may find mercy** (v. 18; only here in the New Testament) was Paul's way of alluding to the mercy that Onesiphorus had shown him and also a fitting recompense from the Lord, whom they had served together. **That day** (see 1:12) is the day of the Lord, the day of judgment. **Ministered unto me at Ephesus** refers either to Paul's stay during his third missionary journey (see Acts 19) or during his fourth (see map, *KJV Study Bible*, pp. 1738 – 39).

IV. Special Instructions to Timothy (chap. 2)

A. Call for Endurance (2:1 – 13)

2:1. My son (see discussion on 1 Tim. 1:2) is an expression of affection, heightened by Paul's circumstance. **Be strong**, a theme of chapter 1, stands in contrast to those who had defected from Paul, if not also from the Lord (see 2:8). **Grace**, the manifold provision of God's open hand, is given by virtue of His extraordinary favor **that is in Christ Jesus**, the means of standing strong.

2:2. Among many witnesses refers to Paul's preaching and teaching, which Timothy had heard repeatedly on all three missionary journeys and which could be confirmed by many. Even as Paul had found Timothy worthy (see "I commit unto thee," 1 Tim. 1:18), Timothy was to **commit** (entrust) the gospel to others who were as **faithful**, or "worthy of trust." Links of spiritual responsibility for the gospel are forged in this way. A life transformed by and trained in the gospel may become another link in its faithful transmission, an unbreakable extension of its ongoing transformation.

2:3 – 6. Thou … endure hardness (v. 3) is the identical Greek that is translated "Be thou partaker of the afflictions" in 1:8. The Greek prefix "with" refers to a shared experience that included Paul (see 2:9, which lacks the prefix and speaks of Paul's own suffering). Harsh and unpleasant experiences or sufferings belong to the servant of Christ and of His gospel. The difference between a leader and a victim is one's attitude and outlook. Paul gave Timothy three examples to follow: (1) a soldier who wants to please his commander, (2) an athlete who follows the rules of the game, and (3) a farmer who works hard.

A good soldier (v. 3) no doubt means a "brave" one (see Kelly, *The Pastoral Epistles*, p. 175) in view of the words "endure hardness." "Good" anticipates the further description of verse 4. Some soldiers are "bad" soldiers because they become preoccupied with civil matters outside of their commissioned service. **Of Jesus Christ** (v. 3) is further defined as **him who hath chosen him to be a soldier** (v. 4). The good soldier owes his allegiance to Christ, in whose name he serves and enters the battlefield.

2:5. Strive for masteries is one verb in Greek (*athleō*), meaning "be an athlete" or "contend in athletic games." Paul was acquainted with such games (e.g., the Isthmian games were restored to Corinth by Julius Caesar in AD 44) and with the fact that an athlete could be disqualified if required training regimens (see 1 Cor. 9:27) or rules of competition were broken. A contemporary of Paul, Epictetus, used the same phrase, **strive lawfully**, of prescribed Olympic training: "Give me proof, whether you have striven lawfully, eaten what is required, undertaken your exercise, minded your trainer" (3.10.8). The difference is that Paul used the metaphor of Timothy, and Epictetus of the philosopher.

2:6 – 7. The husbandman (Greek, *geōrgos*; "farmer"; v. 6) who toils is expected to be **partaker of the fruits** (see 1 Cor. 9:7). In this illustration, as in the previous two (soldier, 2:3 – 4; athlete, 2:5), the main lesson is that dedicated effort will be rewarded, not necessarily monetarily but in the enjoyment of seeing the gospel produce changed lives. This may have been the inference that Paul was seeking from Timothy when he said, **Consider what I say** (v. 7), or literally, "Think through [grasp or contemplate] what I am saying." **Understanding in all things** refers to application from lesser to greater and lighter to weightier (Kelly, *The Pastoral Epistles*, p. 176).

2:8–9. The seed of David was raised from the dead (v. 8). Christ's resurrection proclaims His deity, and His descent from David shows His humanity; both truths are basic to the gospel. Since Christ is God, His death has infinite value; since He is man, He could rightfully become the substitute. For this gospel, the grand truth of Jesus Christ, Paul had suffered—the strong theme of his ennobling challenge to Timothy. Even now Paul knew **trouble, as an evil doer, even unto bonds** (v. 9). Paul was bearing the real threat of execution in Rome (see 4:6). Because of his noble service and sacrifice unto the Lord, he suffered the additional hardship of misunderstanding, of being thought an ignoble "evil doer" and deemed a criminal.

2:10. I endure all things for the elects' sakes is Paul's own application of the illustrations in 2:3–6 (see discussion on 2:6). No suffering is too great if it brings about the salvation of God's chosen ones who will yet believe. For **in Christ Jesus**, see discussion on 1:13. **Eternal glory** is the final state of salvation.

2:11–13. These verses were probably an early Christian hymn. Paul's appeal was that suffering for Christ will be followed by glory.

2:11. For **a faithful saying**, see discussion on 1 Timothy 1:15. **If we be dead with him, we shall also live with him.** The Greek grammatical construction here assumes that believers died with Christ in the past, when He died on the cross. Christians are therefore assured that they will also live with Him eternally.

2:12. If we suffer, we shall also reign is a profound incentive and encouragement to suffer hardships for a greater purpose. Faithfully bearing up under suffering and trial will result in reward when Christ returns. For the alternative, **if we deny him** (Greek, *arneomai*; "deny," "repudiate," "disown"), see Matthew 10:33.

2:13. If we believe not is better understood as "if we are unfaithful." Infidelity has a logical counterpart that never comes but is instead replaced with the illogical proof of God's grace: **he abideth faithful: he cannot deny himself** or His own fidelity, which is a constituent of His nature. That is something a believer could never deny, a great comfort and ever compelling one to belief. On the other hand, His faithfulness must not comfort premeditated compromise, as if God should be cornered by His own character.

B. Warning about Foolish Controversies (2:14–26)

2:14–18. The wording of verses 14–16 indicates that the heresy mentioned here was an early form of Gnosticism, the same as that dealt with in 1 Timothy and Titus (see discussion on 1 Tim. 1:3–11; 1 John, Introduction: "Gnosticism"). Two leaders of this heresy, Hymenaeus (see 1 Tim. 1:20) and Philetus, denied the bodily resurrection and probably asserted that there is only a spiritual resurrection (similar to the error mentioned in 1 Cor. 15:12–19). Gnosticism interpreted the resurrection allegorically, not literally.

2:14. Charging them before the Lord is a most solemn charge that Paul had used to compel Timothy also (see 4:1; 1 Tim. 5:21). A war of words is more damaging than sticks and stones. The heretical leaders waged such a war **to no profit** (lit., "without benefit"); everyone came up empty, and worse— people were wrecked and destroyed. The Greek word *katastrophē*, translated **subverting**, speaks of catastrophic consequences. Since such wars are verbal wars, the casualties are emotional and spiritual.

2:15. Study (see 4:9, 21), or "do your best" (Greek, *spoudazō*), suggests diligent zeal and self-discipline, to "give it your all" or "make every effort." **Rightly dividing** (Greek, *orthotomeō*) refers to "cutting straight" or "guiding along a straight path" (used only here, but the same verb is used in the Greek Old Testament, the Septuagint, in Prov. 3:6; 11:5). Here is the how and what, the care and the content, of Timothy's responsibility for the gospel. **The word of truth** (see Eph. 1:13) is the gospel. Notice how necessary is the character of the man who "rightly divid[es]" to the word of truth he delivers.

2:16-17. Paul held up **Hymenaeus and Philetus** (v. 17) as examples of those who waged a war of words "to no profit, but to the subverting of the hearers" (2:14). Just as in 1 Timothy 6:20, Paul again admonished Timothy to avoid **profane and vain babblings** (v. 16). Timothy needed to redouble his efforts. Such "babblings" are not innocent or harmless; they're insidious, like spiritual gangrene.

2:18. Who (i.e., Hymenaeus and Philetus) **concerning the truth have erred**. "Erred" is a term Paul favored to characterize defection to this "untruth" (see 1 Timothy 1:6; 6:21 and discussions). It may imply how overtly subtle, yet substantively critical, the differences between the truth and its false counterpart are, at least to the laity. Among others of shipwrecked faith, Hymenaeus was named in 1 Timothy 1:19-20. It is clear here that his "blasphemy" was none other than the false teaching of which he, along with Philetus, had become a staunch, if not leading, proponent. Central to their error and their teaching was the tenet that **the resurrection is past already**, a rare peek into their actual doctrine (see discussion on 2:14-18; compare 2:8, 11; 1:10).

2:19. The foundation of God here refers to the church, which upholds the truth (1 Tim. 3:15). In spite of the heresy of Hymenaeus and Philetus, Timothy was to take courage in the knowledge that the church is God's solid foundation. Two seals are on it: one stresses the security of the church (**The Lord knoweth them that are his**; here "know," as often in the Bible, means "intimately acquainted with"), while the other emphasizes human responsibility (**Let every one that nameth the name of Christ depart from iniquity**). **This seal** is a sign of ownership. The church is owned and securely protected by God (see discussion on Eph. 1:13).

2:20-21. With **But in a great house** (v. 20), Paul turned from "the foundation" (2:19) to the building, taking up through the metaphor of its housewares the issue of people and their dedication to the Lord. This was a real concern in these letters because of the dangerous infections of false teaching and the disappointing defections of familiar faces. **Of gold and of silver ... of wood and of earth** describes an array of utensils in a grand home, the kind that belong to "them that are rich in this world" (1 Tim. 6:17) and who can afford premium (gold and silver) and not just practical (wood and earth) housewares. In an earthly household, the material value of a utensil may correspond to its use, **some to honour, and some to dishonour**. The possibility of a conversion is seen in **If a man therefore purge himself from these** (lit., "if anyone cleanse himself"; v. 21). He then shall no longer be counted among "some to dishonor," but **he shall be a vessel unto honour ... prepared unto every good work**. At this point, the spiritual household rather than the earthly controls the metaphor. In God's house, regardless of a utensil's material value, if it be cleansed (washed, sanctified), it can be put to another use and serviceable to the Master of the house, who makes such decisions. Accordingly, against the background of the error of false teaching, Timothy could find serviceable to the Master anyone who cleansed himself of such things, or in the words of 2:19, "every one that nameth the name of Christ" and did also "depart from iniquity."

2:22-26. By default, Timothy's youth carried a certain jeopardy that could not be overlooked but needed to be confronted and calculated in advance. Strategic as Timothy's leadership was to the serious spiritual challenges that faced the church in Ephesus, it would have been tragic if such a great opportunity for spiritual victory fell in defeat because of his youth. Thus, Paul returned to the subject (see 1 Tim. 4:12) with a new exhortation. In contemporary language, **youthful lusts** (v. 22) connotes sexual passions, but the word "lusts" is far more flexible in both the Greek and the KJV (as its use in 3:6; 4:3; 1 Tim. 6:9; Titus 2:12; 3:3 attests). Paul's subsequent exhortations (vv. 23-25) point in an entirely different direction: to the hotheaded, untempered, impetuous passions that often get the best of a young man. Such were Paul's concern, and such created misgivings among those who already underrated Timothy because of his age (see 1 Tim. 4:12). **Flee** and **follow** (see 1 Tim. 6:11) are juxtaposed in the Greek sentence for maximum effect. Inborn urges are ruled and mastered by the undeterred pursuit of Christlike virtues. **Strifes** (v. 23) and **strive** (v. 24) are the same Greek word (noun and verb) meaning "fighting" or "quarreling," with a strong connotation of battle. Militant urges were not to cloud or color Timothy's ability to **teach** (v. 24) or his **instructing** (v. 25), with the implication that God would represent him best in battle if his weapons were gentleness, patience, and meekness (vv. 24–25). **Meekness** is that disarming quality of gentleness and courtesy that comes from the inner strength of genuine humility. All in all, if Timothy was predisposed to conduct himself in spiritual combat as Paul had commended, repentance and spiritual victory would be won, not at all costs, but at the hands of God (vv. 25–26).

V. Warning about the Last Days (chap. 3)

A. Terrible Times (3:1–9)

3:1. The last days refers to the messianic era, the time beginning with Christ's first coming and culminating with His second coming (see discussions on Acts 2:17; 1 Tim. 4:1; Heb. 1:1; 1 Peter 1:20; 1 John 2:18). "The last days" here refers to a future time of trouble that will be characterized by selfishness and unbelief. That "the last days" in this passage does not refer only to the time just prior to Christ's return is apparent from Paul's command to Timothy to have nothing to do with the unbelieving and unfaithful who characterize this time (v. 5).

3:2–5. This profile of "the last days" (3:1) served to show Timothy that his personal battle belonged in part to what will come. Therefore, any discouragement he faced was but a part of the growing spiritual war that will intensify in the last days. This inventory of moral attrition and collapse (vv. 2–4) that will occur in the last days tails into the inward **form** (v. 5) of false teachers. That Paul had merged from the future into the present is clear from the words **from such turn away** (v. 5) and the opening of 3:6 ("For of this sort are they"), which is built on that transition.

3:6–7. Silly women (v. 6) describes unstable women who are guilt-ridden because of their sins, torn by lust, and victims of various false teachers—

ever **learning** (v. 7) but never coming to a saving knowledge of Christ. Undoubtedly, Paul was drawing on known instances that explain his contemptuous tone (see Kelly, *The Pastoral Epistles*, p. 195), for the targets of these unethical tactics tell as much about the false teachers as about the women they spiritually swindled.

3:8–9. As Jannes and Jambres (v. 8) lends a timeless quality to the unethical tactics of those who prey on gullible people. Neither of these men is mentioned in the Old Testament, but according to Jewish tradition, they were the Egyptian court magicians who opposed **Moses** (see *KJV Study Bible* note on Exod. 7:11). **Their folly** (v. 9) could not long be cloaked, nor could that of the current manifestations of Jannes and Jambres.

B. Means of Combating Terrible Times (3:10–17)

3:10–11. Although Paul has exposed the doctrine and character of the teachers of error, Timothy knew well the caliber of Paul's own teaching, character, and its tested quality. **Antioch** (v. 11), **Iconium**, and **Lystra** were three cities in the Roman province of Galatia that Paul visited on his first and second missionary journeys (see Acts 13:14–14:23; 16:1–6). Since Timothy was from Lystra, he would have known firsthand of Paul's sufferings in that region. **Out of them all the Lord delivered me**, even from execution by stoning (see Acts 14:19–20).

3:12. Paul encouraged Timothy to join him (see 1:8; 2:3) in **suffer[ing] persecution**, for such is not an aberration but is common to **all that will live godly** (see 1 Tim. 2:2 and discussion) **in Christ** (see discussion on 1:13). Indeed, this principle is repeated elsewhere in the New Testament (see Matt. 10:22; Acts 14:22; Phil. 1:29; 1 Peter 4:12).

3:13. Contrasted with Christian persecution is its polar opposite, the trajectory of those who oppose Christ (see 3:8–9). The **deceiving, and ... deceived** are by definition unable to detect the end of their own error, but Timothy could (see 3:5), for it is plain to the godly, who will not allow persecution to deter them from the truth.

3:14. Of whom thou hast learned them is quite possibly a reference to Paul as well as to Timothy's mother and grandmother (see 1:5).

3:15. From a child thou hast known the holy scriptures. A Jewish boy formally began to study the Old Testament when he was five years old. Timothy was taught at home by his mother and grandmother even before he reached that age.

3:16–17. All scripture (v. 16) refers primarily to the Old Testament, since some of the New Testament books had not yet been written (for indications that some New Testament books, or material ultimately included in the New Testament, were already considered equal in authority to the Old Testament Scriptures, see 1 Tim. 5:18; 2 Peter 3:15–16). **Inspiration of God** affirms God's active involvement in the writing of Scripture, an involvement so powerful and pervasive that what is written is the infallible and authoritative Word of God (see 2 Peter 1:20–21 and discussions). Here the utility of Scripture is (see 1 Tim. 4:13) set forth: it is useful **for doctrine**, the tenets of the gospel; **for reproof**, exposing and refuting error; **for correction**, conforming and reforming belief; and **for instruction in righteousness**, giving a full education in God's will and ways. Its ultimate purpose (or result) is **that the man of God** (any godly individual, but certainly Timothy was in view here) **may be perfect** (Greek, *artios*; v. 17), meaning complete and fully outfitted, **furnished** ("ready," as in "finished") to undertake **all good works.**

VI. Paul's Departing Remarks (4:1–8)

A. Charge to Preach the Word (4:1–5)

4:1. I charge thee therefore before God is characteristic of Paul's most solemn and authoritative exhortations (see 1 Tim. 5:21; 6:13). Paul stated his charge to Timothy with the awareness that he did so in the presence of God the Father and of Christ, who will judge all men. He was also keenly aware of Christ's return and the coming establishment of God's kingdom in its fullest expression. Timothy was to view a charge so given as of the utmost importance.

4:2. Timothy was to **be instant**, that is, be ready in any situation to speak the needed word, whether of correction, of rebuke, or of encouragement. **Preach** is here to "herald" or "declare" openly **the word**, the "sound doctrine" (4:3) of the gospel truth (see 4:5).

4:3. Sound doctrine (see discussion on Titus 1:9), literally, and perhaps ironically, doctrine that is "healthy," must be taught as early as possible, before one's ear becomes infirmed by the culture and the times (see 3:1–5). **Having itching ears** may connote a fevered condition; it certainly depicts hearers with ears that need to be "scratched" by words that can relieve their "unsound" sensitivities.

4:4. Symptomatic of human hardening (an unhealthy fibrosis) to what is "sound" (**the truth**), people will incline their ears to what is most unsound and easier to hear, seeking relief even in **fables** (see note on 1 Tim. 1:4).

4:5. Accepting suffering and persecution was one of Paul's prominent concerns for Timothy and a major theme of this letter (see 1:8; 2:3, 9; 2:9; 3:11–12). If Timothy was to face down the opposition to the gospel, he needed to incorporate suffering in his job description as a godly leader. For **the work of an evangelist**, see 4:2.

B. Paul's Victorious Prospect (4:6–8)

4:6. The importance of Timothy's readiness (see 3:17 and discussion) and the serious concerns of this letter were now coupled with urgency. Paul's withdrawal from the field of Christian ministry and life was imminent. **Be offered** refers to the offering of wine poured around the base of the altar (see Num. 15:1–12; 28:7, 24). Paul viewed his approaching death as the pouring out of his life as an offering to Christ (see Phil. 2:17). **My departure** is a euphemism for Paul's impending death (see Phil. 1:23).

4:7. Here Paul looked back over thirty years of labor as an apostle (ca. AD 36–66). Like an athlete who had engaged successfully in a contest (**fought a good fight**), he had **finished [his] course** and had **kept the faith**, that is, had carefully observed the rules (the teachings) of the Christian faith (see 2:5). In view of the Pastorals' emphasis on sound doctrine, perhaps "the faith" refers to the deposit of Christian truth. Paul had kept, or guarded, it.

4:8. A crown of righteousness continues the imagery of 4:7. With this metaphor of the wreath given to the winner of a race (see 1 Cor. 9:25), Paul could have been referring to (1) a crown given as a reward for a righteous life, (2) a crown consisting of righteousness, or (3) a crown given righteously (justly) by the righteous Judge. **That day** is not the day of Paul's death but the day of Christ's second coming (**his appearing**).

VII. Final Request and Greetings (4:9–22)

4:9. Paul called upon Timothy to join him. **Do thy diligence** (Greek *spoudazō*) is the same expression used in v. 21 and here implies the sense of "hasten" or "hurry." *Spoudazō* may also suggest "make every effort" or "do your best" (see 2:15, "study") but here and v. 21, the onset of winter and the narrowing window for safe travel, stresses that timing was most important. Other reasons for Paul's appeal to haste are set forth in vv. 10–18; most notable was the abandonment of Demas (v. 10) among others (v. 16).

4:10. Crescens is mentioned only here in the New Testament. **Galatia** identifies either the northern area of Asia Minor (Gaul) or a Roman province in what is now central Turkey (see discussion on Gal. 1:2). For **Titus unto Dalmatia**, see Titus, Introduction: "Recipient." Dalmatia is present-day Albania and a portion of Yugoslavia, also known in Scripture as Illyricum (see Rom. 15:19).

4:11. Mark is the John Mark who deserted Paul and Barnabas on their first missionary journey (see Acts 13:13). After Paul refused to take Mark on the second journey, Barnabas separated from Paul, taking Mark with him on a mission to Cyprus (see Acts 15:36–41). Ultimately, Mark proved himself to Paul, indicated by his presence with Paul during Paul's first Roman imprisonment (see Col. 4:10; Philemon 24) and by Paul's request here for Timothy to bring Mark with him to Rome.

4:12. Thychicus (see Eph. 6:21; Col. 4:7–9; Titus 3:12; Acts 20:4) was a faithful ally, a bearer of other dispatches, and likely the trusted envoy who carried this letter to Timothy and who served at Ephesus so that Timothy could go to Rome.

4:13. The cloke was a garment for protection against the cold dampness (see Introduction: "Author, Date, and Place of Composition"). It was probably a heavy, sleeveless outer garment, circular in shape, with a hole in the middle for one's head. **Carpus** is not mentioned elsewhere. **The books, but especially the parchments** provides an early reference to the emergence of codices, small leather bound books, that would eventually take the place of scrolls. The books, or scrolls (see *KJV Study Bible* note on Exod. 17:14), were made of papyrus, and the parchments were made of animal skins. The latter may have been copies of parts of the Old Testament. That Paul told Timothy to bring them with him alludes to the significant amount of time he and Paul would spend studying their contents and, as some have suggested, a transfer to Timothy of Paul's mantle and the symbols of his ministry that had been in Timothy's trust.

4:14–15. Alexander the coppersmith (v. 14) is probably the Alexander mentioned in 1 Timothy 1:20 and is connected there with the Hymenaeus of this letter (see 2:17).

4:16–17. My first answer (v. 16) refers to the first court hearing of Paul's present case, not his defense on the occasion of his first imprisonment (see Acts 28). For the defection of others and the enabling power of the Lord in suffering, see 1:7–8; 3:11–12. Proof of such power is first internal and then external, as can be seen in Paul's proclamation: **that by me the preaching might be fully known** (v. 17). Even in these dire circumstances, Paul used the occasion to testify about Jesus Christ in the imperial court. **I was delivered out of the mouth of the lion.** Since, as a Roman citizen, Paul could not be thrown to the lions in the amphitheater, this must be a figurative way of saying that his first hearing did not result in an immediate guilty verdict.

4:18. The Lord shall deliver me from every evil work. Since Paul fully expected to die soon (4:6), the rescue he spoke of here was spiritual, not physical. The **heavenly kingdom** is heaven itself.

4:19. Earlier, Paul had brought **Prisca and Aquila** with him to Ephesus, and this couple belonged among Paul's dearest friends (see Acts 18:2, 18, 26;

Rom. 16:3; 1 Cor. 16:19). **The household of One-siphorus** refers to his family; Onesiphorus himself had most likely died (see discussion on 1:16).

4:20. Timothy may have questioned the where-abouts of **Erastus** (see discussion on Rom. 16:23) and **Trophimus** and why they were not with Paul. **Miletum** was a seaport on the coast of Asia Minor about fifty miles south of Ephesus.

4:21. Paul requested that Timothy **come before winter** because the opportunity to travel was end-ing. The season of seafaring was closed from mid-November through March and was dangerous from September to October. Paul knew full well just how dangerous seafaring during this time could be (see Acts 27). One may extrapolate that the summer was drawing to a close as Timothy read this. Paul knew he would not last until April. According to early tra-dition, **Linus** was bishop of Rome after the deaths of Peter and Paul.

4:22. For **grace**, see discussions on Jonah 4:2; Ga-latians 1:3; Ephesians 1:2. **You** is poignant, a farewell to "all." **Thy** in the first part of the verse is singular, indicating that it was addressed to Timothy alone. In view of Paul's impending death and the solemn charge he gave to his timid young friend, Timothy needed such encouragement.

THE EPISTLE OF PAUL TO TITUS

INTRODUCTION

Author

The author is Paul (see 1 Timothy, Introduction: "Author").

Date and Place of Composition

Paul possibly wrote from Macedonia, for he had not yet reached Nicopolis (3:12). The letter was written after his release from the first Roman imprisonment (see Acts 28), probably between AD 63 and 65, or possibly at a later date if he wrote after his assumed trip to Spain (see Rom. 15:24).

Recipient

The letter is addressed to Titus, one of Paul's converts (1:4) and a considerable help to Paul in his ministry. When Paul left Antioch to discuss "his" gospel (see 2 Tim. 2:8) with the Jerusalem leaders, he took Titus with him (see Gal. 2:1–3); acceptance of Titus (a Gentile) as a Christian without circumcision vindicated Paul's stand there (see Gal. 2:3–5). Presumably Titus, who is not referred to in Acts but is mentioned thirteen times in the rest of the New Testament, worked with Paul at Ephesus during the third missionary journey. From there, the apostle sent Titus to Corinth to help that church with its work (see *Zondervan KJV Study Bible* note on 2 Cor. 2:12–13; 7:5–6; 8:6).

Following Paul's release from his first Roman imprisonment (see Acts 28), he and Titus worked briefly in Crete (1:5), after which he commissioned Titus to remain there as his representative and complete some needed work (1:5; 2:15; 3:12–13). Paul asked Titus to meet him at Nicopolis (on the west coast of Greece) when a replacement arrived (3:12). Titus later went on a mission to Dalmatia (modern Yugoslavia; see discussion on 2 Tim. 4:10), the last reference to him in the New Testament. Considering the assignments given him, Titus obviously was a capable and resourceful leader.

Crete

The fourth largest island of the Mediterranean, Crete lies directly south of the Aegean Sea (see discussion on 1 Sam. 30:14; for Paul's experiences there, see Acts 27:7–13). In

New Testament times, life in Crete had sunk to a deplorable moral level. The dishonesty, gluttony, and laziness of its inhabitants were proverbial (1:12).

Theme

Apparently, Paul introduced Christianity in Crete when he and Titus visited the island, after which he left Titus there to organize the converts. Paul sent the letter with Zenas and Apollos, who were on a journey that took them through Crete (3:13), to give Titus personal authorization and guidance in meeting opposition (1:5; 2:1, 7–8, 15; 3:9), instructions about faith and conduct, and warnings about false teachers. Paul also informed Titus of his future plans for him (3:12).

Especially significant, considering the nature of the Cretan heresy, are the repeated emphases on "good works" (1:16; 2:7, 14; 3:1, 8, 14) and the classic summaries of Christian doctrine (2:11–14; 3:4–7).

Outline

- I. Salutation (1:1–4)
- II. Concerning Elders (1:5–9)
  - A. Reasons for Leaving Titus in Crete (1:5)
  - B. Qualifications of Elders (1:6–9)
- III. Concerning False Teachers (1:10–16)
- IV. Concerning Various Groups in the Congregations (chap. 2)
  - A. Instructions to Different Groups (2:1–10)
  - B. The Foundation for Christian Living (2:11–14)
  - C. The Duty of Titus (2:15)
- V. Concerning Believers in General (3:1–8)
  - A. Obligations as Citizens (3:1–2)
  - B. Motives for Godly Conduct (3:3–8)
- VI. Concerning Response to Spiritual Error (3:9–11)
- VII. Conclusion (3:12–15)

Bibliography

Fee, Gordon D. *1 and 2 Timothy, Titus*. The New International Biblical Commentary. Peabody, MA: Hendrickson, 1988.

Guthrie, Donald. *The Pastoral Epistles*. Downers Grove, IL: InterVarsity, 1957.

Kelly, J. N. D. *The Pastoral Epistles*. London: Adam & Charles Black, 1963.

Liefeld, Walter L. *1 and 2 Timothy, Titus*. The NIV Application Commentary. Grand Rapids, MI: Zondervan, 1999.

EXPOSITION

I. Salutation (1:1–4)

1:1. Only here does Paul call himself **a servant of God**; elsewhere he says "a servant of Jesus Christ" (see Rom. 1:1; Gal. 1:10; Phil. 1:1). James used both terms of himself (James 1:1). "Servant" (Greek, *doulos*; see discussion on Rom. 1:1) is too mild a term; Paul was alluding to the bond slave who voluntarily and completely surrenders his existence to the lifelong service of his master (see Exod. 21:2–6). **An apostle** is one specially commissioned by Christ (see discussions on Mark 6:30; Heb. 3:1; *KJV Study Bible* note on 1 Cor. 1:1). **According to the faith … and the acknowledging** refers to Paul's appointed mission as God's servant and Christ's apostle, which is explained further in 1:2 (see also Acts 9:15; 22:15; 26:16–18). Paul's apostleship was for the sake of the elect's faith and deep knowledge of the truth, which corresponds to godliness (see discussion on 1 Tim. 2:2).

1:2. In the Greek, there is no intervening punctuation between 1:1–2, and the words **In** (lit., "resting on") **the hope** (see discussions on Col. 1:5; 1 Tim. 1:1) is sequential to all of 1:1. "Hope" is not a wish but a certainty of future eternal life. This certainty is grounded in the very character of God, who **cannot lie**, in contrast to the Cretans (see 1:12) and the Devil (see John 8:44).

1:3. Due times refers to the crucial events in God's program that occur at His designated times in history (see 1 Tim. 2:6; 6:15). **His word** is the authoritative message that centers in Christ. **According to the commandment** is identical to 1 Timothy 1:1 (see discussion there). **God our Saviour** occurs three times in Titus (here; 2:10; 3:4; see also 1 Tim. 1:1; 2:3; 4:10), and three times Jesus is called "our Saviour" (1:4; 2:13; 3:6; see 2 Tim. 1:10).

1:4. Paul called Titus **mine own son**, meaning "my spiritual son," since he had been converted through Paul's ministry. Paul used the same term for Timothy (1 Tim. 1:2) and Onesimus (Philemon 10). **The common faith** is the faith shared by all true believers. Here "common" (Greek, *koinos*) almost

carries the sense of "orthodox," in contrast with "sectarian" or "elitist," belief. In this sense, "common" is used as the later but early church use of "catholic," meaning "general" or "universal" (Greek, *katholikos*), long before it was taken over by its now primarily denominational use. Paul's use of **Saviour** is striking. In all of Paul's other salutations, Jesus is called "Lord." Paul used "Saviour" twelve times in all his letters; half of these references are in Titus.

II. Concerning Elders (1:5–9)

A. Reasons for Leaving Titus in Crete (1:5)

1:5. Left I thee in Crete implies that Paul and Titus had been together in Crete, a ministry not mentioned in Acts. On his voyage to Rome, Paul briefly visited Crete as a prisoner (see Acts 27:7–8), but now that he had been released from his first Roman imprisonment, he was free to travel wherever he wished (see 3:12). **And ordain elders** is not a second **cause** but, according to the Greek construction, is explanatory of **set in order the things that are wanting**. When "and" is translated "namely," the sense becomes clear. It also shows the importance of "elders" to the order of "things." Though Paul and Titus perhaps had already preached in Crete, they had not had time to organize churches. The appointing of elders was consistent with Paul's usual practice (see Acts 14:23). **As I had appointed thee** refers to Paul's previous detailed verbal orders (Greek, *diatassō*; "order," "command"), which he now reiterated in writing.

B. Qualifications of Elders (1:6–9)

1:6–9. A parallel list of qualifications for elders is given in 1 Timothy 3:1–7, but the two lists reflect the different situations in which Timothy and Titus ministered (see chart, *Zondervan KJV Study Bible*, p. 1741).

1:6. Of first concern, a potential leader must be **blameless** (Greek, *anegklētos*; pronounced *anenklētos*; see 1:7; 1 Tim. 3:10). Candidates for the responsibility of elder must be of good reputation, beyond disqualification on grounds of social conduct and character (see 1:7–8), as well as doctrinally fit (see 1:9). Specification of a blameless man begins at home. Since elders, by definition, are chosen from among the older men of the congregation, there is a presumption here that candidates would be married and have children. Of them, the **husband of one wife** identifies a man of the highest marital fidelity (see discussion on 1 Tim. 3:2). A qualified unmarried man was not necessarily barred. It is also improbable that the standard forbids an elder to remarry if his wife dies (see Rom. 7:2–3; 1 Cor. 7:39; 1 Tim. 5:14). The most likely meaning is simply that a faithful, monogamous married life must be maintained. **Having faithful children** may refer to their "belief" in God, although "fidelity" to home points back to the character of the father and ahead to the character of a life reproduced; they too are to be of good reputation, **not accused of riot or unruly** (see 1 Tim. 3:4).

1:7. The use of "elders" in 1:5 and **bishop** (or "overseer") here indicates that the terms were used interchangeably (see Acts 20:17, 28; 1 Peter 5:1–2). "Elder" indicates qualification (maturity and experience), while "bishop" indicates responsibility (watching over God's flock). Here again, **blameless** stands first (see discussion on 1:6), pointing to proof of faithful character (see 1 Cor. 4:2). **As the steward** (Greek, *oikonomos*; "manager") **of God**, the overseer has supervisory responsibility over the household of God. Listed next are "not" qualities. **Not selfwilled** (Greek, *authadē*) means the candidate must not be driven by self-interests rather than Christ's, and therefore not self-centered or stubborn. Accordingly, the man who is Christ-centered is **not soon angry**, not easily angered, but patient, pursuing interests higher than his own. Even as he is not self-willed, he does not submit his will to intoxication; he is **not given to wine** (Greek, *paroinos*; see discussion on 1 Tim. 3:3). Other "not" qualities of a blameless man are that he is **no striker** (Greek, *plēktēs*; see discussion on 1 Tim. 3:3) and **not given to filthy lucre** (Greek, *aischrokerdē*; see discussion on 1 Tim. 3:3).

1:8. The "not" qualities (counting "blameless" as "not subject to blame") of 1:7 are here balanced by six positive qualities, in advance of weighing a man's doctrinal fitness for the office of elder (1:9). A candidate must show **hospitality** (Greek, *philoxenia*; see discussion on 1 Tim. 3:2), or be a lover (*philo*) of strangers and guests (*xenos*), and be **a lover of good** (Greek, *philagathon*; only here in the New Testament), a man characterized by devotion to what is good. **Men** is an inference not found in the Greek; the scope of "good" entails men but includes more. In fact, attention to "good works" is a prominent virtue in Titus and the Pastoral Epistles (see 1:16; 3:1, 8; see also 2:10; 1 Tim. 2:10; 5:10; 2 Tim. 2:21; 3:17). **Sober** (Greek, *sōphrōn*; see discussion on 1 Tim. 3:2) refers to the power to moderate one's passions with good judgment, a virtue much needed in Crete (see 1:10–14). Paul referred to it five times in two chapters (here; 2:2, 4–6, 12). The man who is **just** (Greek, *dikaios*) is not only upright but fair and honest. **Holy** (Greek, *hosios*) is a counterpart to "just" and reflects a devout life toward God and therefore others (see 1 Thess. 2:10). This is "practical holiness," not something donned at church and doffed in the locker room. **Temperate** (Greek, *egkratēs*, pronounced *enkratēs*; used only here in New Testament) literally connotes "in possession of power" and refers to self-control, the inner strength to control one's desires and actions.

1:9. Sound doctrine refers to correct teaching, in keeping with that of the apostles (see 1 Tim. 1:10; 6:3; 2 Tim. 1:13; 4:3). The teaching is called "sound" not only because it builds people up in the faith but because it protects them against the corrupting influence of false teachers. Soundness of doctrine, faith, and speech is a basic concern in the Pastoral Epistles (1–2 Timothy and Titus); the word "sound" occurs ten times (see also "sound" in Rom. 12:3; 2 Cor. 5:13). Any man fit for the responsibility of elder/overseer must be capable of teaching and defending the truth of the gospel.

III. Concerning False Teachers (1:10–16)

1:10. For introduces the reason for Paul's order to appoint elders of trustworthy character, as stated in 1:5–9. **Unruly** (see 1:6; "disobedient" in 1 Tim.

1:9) points to a recalcitrant defiance of God's Word and His authoritative ministers, Paul and Titus. These troublemakers had three main characteristics: (1) they belonged to the "circumcision," like the people of Galatians 2:12, believing that for salvation or sanctification or both, it was necessary to be circumcised and to keep the Jewish ceremonial law (see Galatians, Introduction: "Background"); (2) they held to unscriptural Jewish myths (see 1:14) and genealogies (see 3:9; 1 Tim. 1:4 and discussion); (3) they were ascetics (see 1:14–15), having scruples against things that God declared to be good. **Vain talkers** is the same expression Paul used when writing to Timothy about such people ("vain jangling," 1 Tim. 1:6). Linked with **deceivers**, one may presume that their utterances were deficient of truth and lacked any basis in fact.

1:11. Whose mouths must be stopped (Greek, *epistomizō*; only here in the New Testament) gives a vigorous word picture of the problem and of the solution: "put something over the mouth," as if to muzzle or bridle the snout of unruly beasts (see 1:10). The troublemakers were **subvert[ing] whole houses** (i.e., families), meaning their deception was undermining the faith of entire households (see 2 Tim. 2:18), and all **for filthy lucre's sake** (see 1:7; 1 Tim. 3:3).

1:12. With a quotation, Paul validated the need for the strong hand he advised in the previous verse. A "cretan" culture could not be expected to curb the conduct of these false teachers (see 1:10–11). The Cretan reputation was infamous and proverbial, known far and wide and readily documented by earlier historians and social commentators. In Greek literature, to "play the cretan," or to "cretanize," became slang for "lying" or "cheating." Paul found the centuries-old citation of their own poet, **a prophet of their own**, still relevant (see 1:13). The Cretans held Epimenides (a sixth-century BC native of Knossos, Crete) in high esteem. Several fulfilled predictions were ascribed to him (for other examples of Paul's use of pagan sayings, see discussion on Acts 17:28; *KJV Study Bible* note on 1 Cor. 15:33). Compare **alway liars** with "turn from the truth" in 1:14. **Evil**

beasts are wild animals, dangerous and tricky to domesticate. **Slow bellies** is more clearly stated as "lazy gluttons." Since these descriptions were proverbial, one should not push them to the breaking point but rather appreciate the coarse and churlish culture in which the gospel was taking root.

1:13–14. Titus was to **rebuke them sharply** (v. 13), meaning "correct them severely." He needed to be forthright and uncompromising; there was no middle ground. The doctrinal soundness of the gospel was at stake. **The faith** and **the truth** (v. 14) are contrasted with **Jewish fables** (see discussion on 1:10)**, and commandments of men** (referring to Jewish traditions; see Mark 7:6–7; Isa. 9:13).

1:15. Unto the pure (or Christians, who have been purified by the atoning death of Christ) **all things are pure**: "every creature of God is good, and nothing to be refused, if it be received with thanksgiving" (1 Tim. 4:4). To understand better Paul's statements here, see Romans 14:14, 20. **Unto them that are defiled and unbelieving is nothing pure**. Unbelievers, especially ascetics with unbiblical scruples against certain foods, marriage, and the like (see 1 Tim. 4:3; Col. 2:21), do not enjoy the freedom of true Christians, who receive all God's creation with thanksgiving. Instead, they set up arbitrary, man-made prohibitions against what they consider to be impure (see Matt. 15:10–11, 16–20; Mark 7:14–19; Acts 10:9–16; Rom. 14:20). The principle of this verse does not conflict with the many New Testament teachings against practices that are morally and spiritually wrong. For **conscience**, see 1 Timothy 4:2–3.

1:16. They profess that they know God echoes the lip service mentioned in Isaiah 29:13. Paul defined a spiritual schizophrenia: in words they declared him, **but in works they den[ied] him**. The false teachers stood condemned by the test of personal conduct. For **every good work**, see discussions on 1:8; 3:1, 8; Introduction: "Theme." Right knowledge is extremely important because it leads to godliness (see 1:1). Paul maintained a remarkable balance between doctrine and practice, as well as between faith and works.

IV. Concerning Various Groups in the Congregations (chap. 2)

A. Instructions to Different Groups (2:1–10)

In contrast to those who professed God with their lips but denied Him with their lives (1:16), the believing community of Crete was to exemplify what it means to profess Christ and live in Him (see 1:7, 2:11–12). In this section, Paul presented exhibits of genuine faith, featuring hands-on, transferable behavior that modeled Christlike living across the age groups within the church. He wanted believers in Crete to be examples of Christ within.

2:1. Thou is emphatic, contrasting the work of Titus with that of the false teachers just denounced (see 1:10–16). **Speak** conveys the sense of "audible utterance" and adds a touch of vividness to the image of Titus verbalizing the following directions to the older men (2:2), older women (2:3), and other groups. In 2:2–10, it will be seen that **sound doctrine** (see discussion on 2 Tim. 1:13) demands right conduct of all believers, regardless of age, sex, or position.

2:2. Aged men (Greek, *presbytēs*) is matched by its feminine counterpart in the next verse, "aged women" (Greek, *presbytis*). Older men, as leaders, are to be moral and spiritual examples: **sober** (Greek, *nēphalios*; see 1 Tim. 3:2, 11), **grave** (Greek, *semnos*; see 1 Tim. 3:8, 11), **temperate** (Greek, *sōphrōn*; see 1:8; 2:5; 1 Tim. 3:2), **sound** (Greek, *hygiainō*; see 1:9; 2:1; discussion on 2 Tim. 1:13) **in faith, in charity** (Greek, *agapē*), **in patience** (Greek, *hypomonē*; "endurance," "perseverance"). Instead of being "evil beasts" and "slow bellies" (i.e., "lazy gluttons"; 1:12), as were Cretans in general, older believers are to be responsible, sensible, gracious, and dependable in every way.

2:3. Likewise, the same moral standards applies to **The aged women** as to the aged men (see 2:2). They are to behave **as becometh holiness** (Greek, *hieroprepēs*; "reverent"; lit. refers to the conduct of a priest), suggesting a lifestyle worthy of the highest respect. Two "not" qualities are listed for the women: **not false accusers** (Greek, *diabolos*), referring to

unfounded, maligning gossip and slander, and **not given to much wine** (lit., "not enslaved to much wine"), depicting excessive, out-of-control drinking (see discussions on 1 Tim 3:3; 5:23). The women are to be **teachers of good things** (only here), or wholesome things. This phrase depicts, not teachers in a classroom, but those who educate others through their example in word and deed (see 2:4).

2:4–5. The older women are to **teach the younger women to be sober** (Greek, *sōphronizō*; lit., "make them circumspect"; v. 4), implying an apprenticeship of the younger to the older in matters pertaining to judicious living, especially the virtues of family and home. They are **to love their husbands** (Greek, *philandros*) and **to love their children** (Greek, *philoteknos*), both compound words fronted by "affectionate devotion" (*phil-*). **Discreet** (Greek, *sōphrōn*; v. 5; see "temperate," 2:2; "sober," 1:8) is the tandem noun of the verb "teach … to be sober." The purpose of instilling the sound judgment that manifests itself in these feminine and domestic virtues is **that the word of God be not blasphemed**. This purpose reveals that beneath these ethical instructions lies a deep spiritual concern for the integrity and public acceptance of the gospel (see 2:8, 10, dealing with his concern that Christian living should help rather than hinder the spread of the gospel).

2:6. Likewise (see 2:3) with the single imperative **exhort** ("urge") **to be sober minded** is comparatively briefer and yet broader if "In all things" (2:7) is in view here. In that case, Titus's example set the standard (see 2:7–8). "Sober minded" (Greek, *sōphroneō*) is the same word idea found in 1:8; 2:2, 4–5.

2:7–8. Model and message, example and exhortation, lifestyle and lecture, are indissolubly linked by the integrity of faith. This is expected of all believers, but Titus was to typify it and set the standard because the demands on a leader are all-inclusive (see James 3:1). Perhaps Titus was still a young man, and the Christian virtues he was to exhibit include him in the instruction he was to give the young men of 2:6. For **good works** (v. 7), see discussions on 1:8; 3:1, 8; Introduction: "Theme." Titus was to be above reproach.

2:9–10. Slavery was a basic element of Roman society, and the impact of Christianity on slaves was a vital concern. Paul set forth instructions for this distinct group in the churches; guidance for the conduct of Christian slaves was essential (see discussion on Eph. 6:5). The Greek word for **masters** (v. 9), from which the English term "despot" is derived, indicates the owner's absolute authority over his slave. Roman slaves had no legal rights; their fates were entirely in their masters' hands. Servants were to **adorn the doctrine** (v. 10), meaning to decorate or accessorize their lives with the Word of God. Christian slaves could give a unique and powerful testimony to the gospel by their willing faithfulness and obedience to their masters. What applies here to the servant (see also Eph. 6:6–7) applies also to those in the workplace (see Col. 3:17, 23; 1 Cor. 10:31).

B. The Foundation for Christian Living (2:11–14)

This section briefly describes the effect grace should have on believers. It encourages holier living and rejection of ungodliness, in keeping with Paul's repeated insistence that one's profession of Christ be accompanied by godly living (see 2:1–2, 4–5, 10; 3:8).

2:11. For introduces the doctrinal basis for the ethical demands just stressed in vv. 2–10, "things which become sound doctrine." Right conduct must be founded on right doctrine. **The grace of God** is the undeserved love God showed in Christ while believers were still sinners and His enemies (Rom. 5:6–10), by which they are saved apart from any moral achievements or religious acts on our part (see 3:5; Eph. 2:8–9). This same grace instructs that salvation should produce good works (see discussion on 2:14; Eph. 2:10).

2:12. The word translated **teaching** (Greek, *paideuō*) refers to more than instruction; it includes the whole process of training a child—instruction, encouragement, correction, and discipline. **Ungodliness** (Greek, *asebeia*) is the antonym of "godliness" (see 1:1; discussion on 1 Tim. 2:2), so prominent in the Pastoral Epistles. For **this present world**, or

"age," see *KJV Study Bible* note on 2 Corinthians 4:4; discussion on Galatians 1:4.

2:13. That blessed hope, and the glorious appearing refers to the second coming (see 1 Tim. 6:14; 2 Tim. 4:1; 4:8 and discussion). Of special interest are the words **the great God and our Saviour Jesus Christ**. This translation is possible, but both the context (Christ's second coming) and the Greek construction favor the translation, "the great God, even our Saviour Jesus Christ." It is an explicit testimony to the deity of Christ (see discussion on Rom. 9:5).

2:14. Salvation involves the double work of redeeming people from guilt and judgment and of producing moral purity and helpful service to others (see Introduction: "Theme").

C. The Duty of Titus (2:15)

2:15. Paul ended this section of his letter with a summary of Titus's responsibility and authority. **These things** refers to the content of the whole chapter.

V. Concerning Believers in General (3:1–8)
A. Obligations as Citizens (3:1–2)

New Testament teaching is not confined to the area of personal salvation but includes much instruction about practical living. Although believers are citizens of heaven (see Phil. 3:20), they must also submit themselves to earthly government (see Rom. 13:1–7; 1 Peter 2:13–17) and help promote the well-being of the community.

3:1–2. Principalities and powers (v. 1) refers to all forms and levels of human government (for this term applied to angels, see Eph. 3:10; 6:12). **Every good work** (see discussions on 1:8; 3:1, 8; Introduction: "Theme"; 2 Tim. 2:21) is to typify a disposition toward outsiders that demonstrates godliness (see 1:1; 2:12) and exonerates the Christian faith in the eyes of outsiders (see 1 Tim. 2:2). A specific example of "every good work" is **shewing all meekness unto all men** (v. 2), a virtue of grace (see 2:11–12; 3:4). Genuine humility and gentle courtesy flow from the believer's own experience of God's undeserved favor, something Paul brought to mind in 3:3.

B. Motives for Godly Conduct (3:3–8)

3:3–4. Paul assigned to **we ourselves** the kinds of behaviors that Christians, having turned from such conduct, are now to meet with meekness (see 3:2) and with the kindness and love of God in Christ. God's **kindness and love** (v. 4) are the reasons He did not simply banish fallen man but acted to save him (see 2:11).

3:5–7. According to his mercy he saved us (v. 5). Salvation is not achieved by human effort or merit but comes through God's mercy alone. The Greek construction of **the washing of regeneration** suggests that as Christians are renewed by the work of the Holy Spirit, so they are washed by the work of regeneration. **Renewing of the Holy Ghost** is also a reference to new birth.

3:8. The almost formulaic phrase **a faithful saying** refers to the doctrinal summary in 3:4–7. This phrase, which occurs only here in Titus, appears four other times in the Pastoral Epistles (1 Tim. 1:15; 3:1; 4:9; 2 Tim. 2:11) and nowhere else in the New Testament. The importance of Paul's insistence that believers **be careful to maintain good works** is now fathomed in the light of 3:1–7. "Good works" (see discussions on 1:8; 3:1, 8; Introduction: "Theme") are the very demonstration of the gospel, an extension of the grace (kindness, love, mercy) of Christ's appearing (see 3:4; 2:11). In the real world, "goodness" validates and authenticates the truth of Christ in one's life. Paul repeated this injunction in 3:14, where "ours" is mindful of the marked difference between believers and unbelievers, between the gospel and false teaching.

VI. Concerning Response to Spiritual Error (3:9–11)

3:9. Foolish questions, and genealogies, and contentions, and strivings ("quarrels") **about the law** refers to the situation described in 1:10–16. A similar problem existed in Ephesus (see 1 Tim. 1:3–7). Such things **are unprofitable and vain**, counterproductive to the "good works" (3:1, 8) that come from and further belief in the gospel (see 3:4–7). Titus was better off investing his time and

energy in people with hearts receptive to the work and will of God in Christ (see 3:10; 1 Tim 4:7; 2 Tim. 2:22–26 and discussion).

3:10–11. In the early church, **heretick** (Greek, *hairetikos*; only here in the New Testament) became a technical term for a type of heretic who promoted dissension by propagating extreme views of legitimate Christian truths. The recalcitrance of the heretic's factious spirit and mindset was confirmed after a **second admonition** (Greek, *nouthesia*) to cease and desist (see the use of the verb in 2 Thess. 3:14–15). After a second warning, Titus was to change tactics and avoid, if not repudiate, the person, knowing the heretic was not only divisive but **subverted, and sinneth, being condemned of himself**. This final characteristic is telltale. The condemnation ratifies the heretic's own response. Stubborn refusal to listen to correction reveals inner perversion.

VII. Conclusion (3:12–15)

3:12. In Paul's letters, personal instructions and travel plans commonly occupy his concluding remarks. So that he could join Paul, Titus would be relieved by **Artemas ... or Tychicus**. The latter was Paul's trusted coworker who traveled with or for Paul on various occasions (see Acts 20:4; Eph. 6:21–22; Col. 4:7–8; 2 Tim. 4:12). It may be surmised that the decision was later defined by unforeseen circumstances (imprisonment), for Tychicus was sent to Ephesus (see 2 Tim 4:12), Titus to Dalmatia (see 2 Tim. 4:10), and Artemas to Crete, as stated here in v. 12. Artemas is otherwise unknown. **Nicopolis** means "city of victory." Several cities had this name, but the reference here is apparently to the city in Epirus on the western shore of Greece. Paul **determined there to winter**, which imagines a rendezvous with Titus in Nicopolis. It also indicates that Paul had not arrived there when he wrote this letter and that he was still free to travel at will, not yet having been imprisoned in Rome for the second time.

3:13. Bring ... on their journey is one word in Greek (*propempō*) and carries the sense of "to help on their way." In the New Testament, *propempō* commonly refers to the hospitable assistance of providing a traveler what they need for a journey (see, e.g., Acts 15:3; Rom. 15:24; 1 Cor. 16:6, 16; 2 Cor. 1:16; 3 John 6). **Zenas the lawyer** is mentioned only here in the New Testament. If he was a Jewish convert, "lawyer" means that he was an expert in Mosaic law; if he was a Gentile convert, that he was a Roman jurist. **Apollos** was a native of Alexandria and one of Paul's well-known coworkers (see Acts 18:24–28; 19:1; 1 Cor. 1:12; 3:4–6, 22; 16:12). The two travelers apparently delivered Paul's letter to Titus.

3:14. Paul's thematic emphasis on **good works** (see discussions on 1:8; 3:1, 8) is given final emphasis. **Ours** may well refer to the dispatch of Zenas and Apollos. They **also** were to be set on their way with this important reminder. Whether "ours" refers to them or to "our people," and whether "good works" is an additional application or a final reinforcement, it is clear that "good works" is no mere platitude but expressive of the gospel in action (see discussion on 3:8).

3:15. All that are with me salute (i.e., "greet" or give hospitable acknowledgment to) **thee**. Titus in turn was to **Greet them that love us in the faith**, which had nothing to do with Titus's good sense to greet the right people and everything to do with Paul's sensitivity to the dynamics of doctrinal disharmony on the part of some within the community (see 3:10–11). This is a subtle but further indication of the challenges on Crete to sound doctrine (1:9, 13; 2:1–2). **Grace be with you all** refers to the whole church and may imply that the letter was to be read publicly, having the tone of a benedicton for the whole assembly. It certainly captures the prominence of 2:11 and 3:4 and fittingly resounds the heart of this chapter.

THE EPISTLE OF PAUL
TO PHILEMON

INTRODUCTION

Author, Date, and Place of Composition

Paul wrote this short letter (see vv. 1, 9, 19), probably at the same time as Colossians (ca. AD 60; see Colossians, Introduction: "Author, Date, and Place of Composition"), and sent it to Colosse with the same travelers, Onesimus and Tychicus. Paul apparently wrote both letters from prison in Rome, though possibly from Ephesus (see Philippians, Introduction: "Author, Date, and Place of Composition").

Recipient

Paul wrote this letter to Philemon, a believer in Colosse.

Theme

Along with others in Colosse, Philemon was a slave owner (see Col. 4:1; for slavery in the New Testament, see discussion on Eph. 6:5). One of his slaves, Onesimus, apparently had stolen from him (see v. 18) and then run away, which was punishable by death under Roman law. Onesimus met Paul and became a Christian through his ministry (see v. 10). Now Onesimus was willing to return to his master, and Paul wrote this personal appeal to Philemon to ask that Onesimus be accepted as a Christian brother (see v. 16).

Literary Features

To win Philemon's willing acceptance of Onesimus, Paul wrote very tactfully and in a lighthearted tone, which he created with a wordplay (see discussion on v. 11). The appeal (vv. 4–21) is organized in a way prescribed by ancient Greek and Roman teachers: to build rapport (vv. 4–10), to persuade the mind (vv. 11–19), and to move the emotions (vv. 20–21). The name Onesimus is not mentioned until the rapport has been built (v. 10), and the appeal itself is stated only near the end of the section to persuade the mind (v. 17).

Outline

I. Greetings (vv. 1–3)

II. Thanksgiving and Prayer (vv. 4–7)

III. Paul's Plea for Onesimus (vv. 8–21)

IV. Final Request, Greetings, and Benediction (vv. 22–25)

Bibliography

Carson, Herbert M. *The Epistles of Paul to the Colossians and Philemon.* Grand Rapids, MI: Eerdmans, 1977.

Lightfoot, J. B. *Saint Paul's Epistles to the Colossians and Philemon.* 1879. Reprint, Grand Rapids, MI: Zondervan, 1959.

Martin, Ralph P. *Colossians and Philemon.* Grand Rapids, MI: Eerdmans, 1981.

O'Brien, Peter T. *Colossians–Philemon.* Word Biblical Commentary 44. Waco, TX: Word, 1982.

EXPOSITION

I. Greetings (vv. 1–3)

Verses 1–2. Although Paul wrote this letter with Timothy and although he addressed the entire church in Colosse, in this very personal letter to Philemon, he used "I" (rather than "we") and "thee" (singular except in vv. 22, 25).

Verse 1. Paul was under arrest at this time and therefore **a prisoner** (see v. 9; discussions on Eph. 3:1; Phil. 1:13), but **of Jesus Christ** makes plain the cause for which he was "bound." In Greek, the word "prisoner" (*desmios*) is derived from the word for "bonds" or "chains" (Greek, *desmos*), a vivid synonym for Paul's imprisonment (see vv. 13; Phil. 1:7, 14; Col. 4:18). Paul's poignant use of "prisoner" rather than "apostle" was purposeful as he interceded for Onesimus. **Timothy** (see discussion on Col. 1:1; see also 1 Timothy, Introduction: "Recipient") was with Paul. **Philemon** was a Christian living in Colosse or nearby and was the owner of the slave Onesimus. **Dearly beloved, and fellowlabourer** are titles of endearment and a status that Paul hoped Philemon would in turn confer on Onesimus (see vv. 16–17; note "partner" in v. 17).

Verse 2. Apphia was probably Philemon's wife, standing after him in the order of names. **Archippus**, **our fellow soldier** (see Phil. 2:25), or esteemed as a colleague in the campaign for Christ, was probably an officebearer (see Col. 4:17) in **the church** that met **in thy house** (the home of Philemon). Some conjecture that Archippus was Philemon's son.

Verse 3. This greeting is characteristic of Paul's letters (see, e.g., Phil. 1:2). **Grace to you** (plural) identifies not only Philemon and the aforementioned people but the church that met in his house.

II. Thanksgiving and Prayer (vv. 4–7)

Verse 4. I thank my God, making mention of thee always in my prayers. See discussion on Philippians 1:3–4.

Verse 5. Hearing of was probably a reference to more than one source but likely included reports from Epaphras (see Col. 1:4, 7–8; 4:12) and even Onesimus. **Thy love and faith … toward the Lord Jesus, and toward all saints** mirrors Colossians 1:4, although here, notably, love stands first.

Verse 6. That introduces the specific intent of Paul's prayer, which opened with thanksgiving (v. 4) and here turns to petition. The fulfillment of this petition, which envisioned the extension and effectual realization of Philemon's reported love and faith (see

v. 5), would encompass the benefits to Onesimus that Paul sought from Philemon. **Communication** (Greek, *koinōnia*), denoting "mutual association" or "partnership," may also connote the signs of such fellowship, the contributions and generosity that characterize it, as here. **Of thy faith** identifies the source of their mutual "communication." **Effectual** refers to the practical expression of Philemon's "communication" in **the acknowledging** (or "the full knowledge"; Greek, *epignōsis*; "recognition"] **of every good thing**, an enlarged appreciation of the good that is defined by Christ. Included in "every good thing" was the good that Christ desired for Onesimus.

Verse 7. Bowels stands for "heart," with an emphasis on its emotional affection. As the heart today is regarded as the seat of emotions, so the intestines or "bowels" were for the ancient Greeks (see vv. 12, 20). Although Paul had yet to make his request, the heartfelt largess of Philemon's life, which was known to Paul and many others, was cause to expect that Philemon would have room for similar goodness to Onesimus.

III. Paul's Plea for Onesimus (vv. 8–21)

Verses 8–9. Wherefore (v. 8), or "On this basis, I appeal." Paul conceded his freedom (**bold**) in Christ, favoring a loving appeal (**beseech**; v. 9) over a command (**enjoin**; v. 8). All this was in the service of **that which is convenient** (Greek, *anēkō*; what is "proper," "fitting"; see Col. 3:8; Eph. 5:4), not in the contemporary sense of "handy," but "what was required" or "the right thing to do" in this situation and in Christ. Behind the appeal was **Paul the aged** (v. 9). It may very well be that "aged" should better be translated as "the ambassador" or "the envoy" of Christ Jesus, a stronger ground of appeal than his age and linked in Ephesians 6:20, as here, with his imprisonment (see Lightfoot, *Colossians and Philemon*, pp. 338–39).

Verse 10. Beseech, the identical verb as that in verse 9, here introduces the explicit appeal and purpose for writing. **My son** (Greek, *teknon*; "child") connotes Paul's "spiritual child" (see 1 Tim. 1:2, 18; 1 Cor. 4:17; 2 Tim. 1:2; 2:1; Titus 1:4) who was **begotten**, or "fathered," through spiritual conversion,

which Paul said took place "in my bonds." (see discussion on v. 1). For **Onesimus** and the meaning of his name, "profitable," see verse 11 and Introduction: "Theme." The clear play on words in verse 11 may begin here: "my son 'Profitable' whom I have begotten in my bonds." If so, Paul may have been implying that the meaning of Onesimus's name was truly realized at his conversion to Christ.

Verse 11. Unprofitable ... profitable is a wordplay on the meaning of the name Onesimus ("profitable" or "useful," from the Greek verb *oninēmi*, "to profit," "to benefit," "to help"). Onesimus was a common slave name. By running away, Onesimus had not lived up to his name. In fact, he was lost to Philemon. Now he had returned, probably with this letter in hand, and Paul wanted to persuade Philemon to see Onesimus not as he was when he left but as he was when he returned, "profitable" to them both.

Verses 12–14. With **Whom** (i.e., "Profitable"; see v. 11) **... receive him** (v. 12), Paul requested that Philemon accept the "profitable" one who was coming back to him. "Him" is intensive, underscoring Onesimus's new identity. Moreover, this new man returned home an incarnation of Paul's own heart (**mine own bowels**; see discussion on v. 7), a manifestation of Paul's deepest affection. The man Paul asked Philemon to receive was not only a new "Onesimus" and a brother in Christ but a piece of Paul himself. Paul would not keep anything so precious **without thy mind** (v. 14), or "without your consent." In sending Onesimus home, Paul deferred to Philemon so that the **benefit** (lit., "the goodness"; see v. 6) he expected of him could be done **willingly**, or voluntarily (see v. 8).

Verses 15–16. Paul steered Philemon's thoughts from Onesimus's wrongdoing to his restoration by adding the divine perspective of God's providential operation in what had taken place. The words **departed for a season** (v. 15) not only temper a willful act of running away; they also suggest God's hidden agenda with the divine passive "was departed," which in Greek can mean "was separated." "For a season" is eclipsed by the benefit of **for ever** ("eternity"). What is for eternity is not **a servant** (v. 16) but **a brother ... in the flesh, and in the Lord**, meaning humanly and spiritually, but the contrast of "for a season" and "for ever" lends to these words the sense of "on earth" and "in heaven." To understand more clearly Paul's message concerning servants and masters, one must read the book of Philemon in conjunction with Colossians 3:22–4:1.

Verse 17. Luther said, "Even as Christ did for us with God the Father, thus Paul also does for Onesimus with Philemon." Verse 19 weakens this correspondence. **Partner** (Greek, *koinōnos*; "partner," "companion"), an allusion to the "communication" of verse 6, capitalizes on Onesimus's status as a brother in the faith and a brother in Christ. But more than that, Philemon was to transfer Paul's own status to Onesimus (see v. 19).

Verses 18–19. Onesimus's new status as "a brother" (v. 16) is given a twist in that Philemon was also Paul's son, his spiritual child (see v. 10). Here spiritual progeny is intertwined metaphorically with the discussion of debts, material and spiritual. Paul, **with [his] own hand** (v. 19), was writing an IOU for the material debt. The implication from what follows, **thou owest unto me even thine own self besides**, is that out of this IOU for the spiritual debt, Philemon could find the resources to cover what Paul was asking for Onesimus. It should be added that references to the debt Onesimus had incurred may be to the value of his own life as a runaway slave. That debt was matched by what Philemon owed to Paul: "thine own self."

Verse 20. Both **me** and **my** are emphatic pronouns, making an obvious allusion to verse 7. **Joy** (Greek, *oninēmi*; see discussion on v. 11) means "benefit" and is another play on the name Onesimus. **Refresh my bowels** is a third reference to "the heart" (see discussion on v. 7; see also v. 12).

Verse 21. Here Paul mentioned **obedience**, a sublime reference to his apostolic authority and leverage, which he had refused in favor of petition in verse 8. There he refused to "enjoin" what here he expected Philemon to obey. **Knowing that thou wilt also do more than I say** is a supposition of Philemon's generosity, only hinted at earlier (see v. 6).

IV. Final Request, Greetings, and Benediction (vv. 22–25)

Verse 22. With **But withal** (lit., "At the same time"), Paul conveyed an additional request to go along with that of Philemon's generous reception of Onesimus. It was not unusual for an ancient letter, though occasioned by one matter, to also include another matter. Often, as here, the second matter had to do with how and when the author planned to meet the recipient again. **Prepare me also a lodging** is subtle; Paul was preparing Philemon for a personal visit. In effect, he was saying, "Along with the lodging that I am confident you will give to Onesimus, make a bed ready for me."

Verses 23–24. In his closing greetings, Paul included hospitable recognition from **Epaphras** (v. 23; see Col. 4:12), who was probably well known to Philemon, and from Paul's coworkers **Marcus, Aristarchus** (see discussion on Col. 4:10), **Demas, Lucas** (see discussion on Col. 4:14). Although greetings of this kind were conventional, it is difficult to imagine that the mention of these men didn't add a quality of their consensus with Paul in the matter before Philemon, even if only imagined.

Verse 25. Paul addressed the final benediction to the entire house church (see v. 3), as the plural personal pronoun "your" in **with your spirit** implies.

THE EPISTLE OF PAUL THE APOSTLE TO THE HEBREWS

INTRODUCTION

Author

The writer of this epistle did not identify himself, but he was obviously well known to the original recipients. For some 1,200 years (from ca. AD 400 to 1600), the book was commonly called "The Epistle of Paul the Apostle to the Hebrews," but there was no agreement in the earliest centuries regarding its authorship. Since the Reformation, it has been widely agreed that Paul was not the writer. There is no disharmony between the teaching of Hebrews and that of Paul's letters, but the specific emphases and writing styles are markedly different. Contrary to Paul's usual practice, the author of Hebrews nowhere identified himself in the letter, except to indicate that he was a man (see discussion on 11:32) who apparently was also in prison (10:34) and was a companion of Timothy (13:23). Moreover, the statement that the message of salvation "at the first began to be spoken by the Lord, and was confirmed unto us by them that heard him" (2:3) indicates that the author had neither been with Jesus during His earthly ministry nor received special revelation directly from the risen Lord, as had Paul (see Gal. 1:11–12).

The earliest alternative suggestion of authorship is found in Tertullian's *De Pudicitia*, 20 (ca. AD 200), in which he quoted from "an epistle to the Hebrews under the name of Barnabas." From the letter itself, it is clear that the writer had authority in the apostolic church and was an intellectual Hebrew Christian well versed in the Old Testament. Barnabas meets these requirements. He was a Jew of the priestly tribe of Levi (see Acts 4:36) who became a close friend of Paul after the latter's conversion. Under the guidance of the Holy Spirit, the church at Antioch commissioned Barnabas and Paul for the work of evangelism and sent them off on the first missionary journey (see Acts 13:1–4).

The other leading candidate for authorship is Apollos, whose name was first suggested by Martin Luther and who is favored by many scholars today. Apollos, an Alexandrian by birth, was also a Jewish Christian with notable intellectual and oratorical abilities. Luke stated that Apollos was "an eloquent man, and mighty in the scriptures" (Acts 18:24). We also know that Apollos was associated with Paul in the early years of the church in Corinth (see 1 Cor. 1:12; 3:4–6, 22).

Perhaps we lack knowledge as to the human author because God did not want us to know who the author is. The question arises, however, that if this was God's intention, why? Perhaps He means to turn our sole attention to the message of the epistle, not its source.

The writer and his companions may have been Italians, as evidenced by 13:24. On the other hand, the use of the Septuagint in the many quotations from the Old Testament may also suggest a Jewish Christian living outside of Israel.

Date

Hebrews must have been written before the destruction of Jerusalem and the temple in AD 70 because (1) the author surely would have mentioned the temple's destruction and the end of the Jewish sacrificial system if the book had been written after this date, and (2) the author consistently used the Greek present tense when speaking of the temple and the priestly activities connected with it (5:1–3; 7:23, 27; 8:3–5; 9:6–9, 13, 25; 10:1, 3–4, 8, 11; 13:10–11).

This epistle was written during a time of great persecution of Christians in Jerusalem, first at the hands of the Sadducees and soon thereafter by the Pharisees and the general Jewish population. Hebrews 12:4 may suggest that the date of composition was prior to the inception of Nero's great persecutions of Christians in Rome, which began in approximately AD 64.

Recipients

The letter was addressed primarily to Jewish converts, probably in Rome, who were familiar with the Old Testament and who were being tempted, in the face of severe persecution (10:22), to revert to the comforts and acceptance found in Judaism or to Judaize the gospel (see Gal. 2:14). Part of this temptation could have been because Rome recognized Judaism as a legitimate religion but considered Christianity illegal and illegitimate. Some have suggested that these professing Jewish Christians were thinking of merging with a Jewish sect, such as the one at Qumran near the Dead Sea. It has also been suggested that the recipients were from the large number of priests who "were obedient to the faith" (Acts 6:7).

Theme and Theological Message

The book of Hebrews was a "word of exhortation" (13:22) that the readers were advised to take to heart ("suffer"). Thus, the author's purpose for writing was less polemic than is generally regarded, notwithstanding that he used many of the great doctrines of Scripture in establishing his arguments to "run ... the race" (12:1) considering "him that endured" (12:3).

The theme of Hebrews is the absolute supremacy and sufficiency of Jesus Christ as the revealer and the mediator of God's grace. The prologue (1:1–4) presents Christ as God's full and final revelation, far surpassing the limited preliminary revelation given in the Old Testament. The prophecies and promises of the Old Testament are fulfilled in the new covenant (the New Testament), of which Christ is the mediator. From the Old Testament itself, Christ is shown to be superior to the ancient prophets, to angels, to Moses (the mediator of the former covenant), and to Aaron and the priestly succession descended from him. Hebrews could be called "the book of better things" since the two Greek words for "better" and "superior" occur fifteen times in the letter.

The author employed this general theme to present his arguments to "hold fast" (10:23). By presenting a series of five warnings, he reminded his readers of the verities and consequences of Old Testament law and compared them to what we now have in and through Christ. The writer provided practical applications of this theme throughout the letter and told his readers that there could be no turning back to or continuation in the old Jewish system, which had been superseded by the unique priesthood of Christ. God's people now must look only to Him, whose atoning death, resurrection, and ascension have opened the way into the true, heavenly sanctuary of God's presence. Resisting temptations to give up the struggle, believers must persevere in the spiritual contest to which they have committed themselves. Otherwise, they may meet with the New Testament equivalent of judgment (see 12:6, 11; Rom. 8:1), as did the rebellious generation of Israelites in the wilderness.

Outline

    I. Prologue: The Superiority of God's New Revelation (1:1–4)

   II. Arguments for Staying the Course (1:5–12:29)

       A. The Argument for a Superior Revelation (1:5–2:4)

           1. The Nature of the Superiority (1:5–14)

           2. Warning concerning the Revelation (2:1)

           3. Consequences of Neglecting the Revelation under Moses (2:2)

           4. Consequences of Neglecting the Revelation under Christ (2:3)

           5. God Himself Confirms the New Revelation (2:4)

       B. The Argument for a Superior Prophet (2:5–4:13)

           1. This Person Is Jesus (2:5–3:1)

           2. Christ Compared to Moses (3:2–6)

           3. Warning against Unbelief (3:7–15)

           4. Consequences of Unbelief under Moses (3:16–19)

           5. Consequences of Unbelief under Christ (4:1)

           6. Exhortations to Continue Trusting Christ (4:2–13)

       C. The Argument for a Superior Relationship (4:14–7:28)

           1. Jesus, Our High Priest (4:14–16)

           2. The Nature of Christ's Priesthood (5:1–10)

           3. Rebuke for Dullness of Hearing (5:11–14)

           4. Plea to Move Forward in the Knowledge of Christ (6:1–3)

           5. Warning against Falling Away (6:4–8)

           6. Consequences of Falling Away under Christ (6:9–12)

           7. The Immutability of the New Relationship (6:13–20)

           8. Basis of the New Relationship: Jesus' Superior Priesthood (chap. 7)

       D. The Argument for a Superior Redemption (chaps. 8–10)

           1. A Superior Covenant from a Superior High Priest (8:1–13)

           2. Superior Access Provided by a Superior Sacrifice (9:1–10:18)

Bibliography

Bruce, F. F. *The Epistle to the Hebrews*. The New International Commentary on the New Testament. Grand Rapids, MI: Eerdmans, 1964.

Guthrie, Donald. *The Letters to the Hebrews*. Tyndale New Testament Commentaries. Grand Rapids, MI: Eerdmans, 1983.

Hagner, Donald A. *Hebrews*. New International Biblical Commentary. Peabody, MA: Hendrickson, 1990.

Hughes, Philip E. *A Commentary on the Epistle to the Hebrews*. Grand Rapids, MI: Eerdmans, 1977.

Kent, Homer A. *The Epistle to the Hebrews*. Grand Rapids, MI: Baker, 1972.

Lane, William L. *Hebrews 1–8*. Word Biblical Commentary 47A. Dallas: Word, 1991.

———. *Hebrews 9–13*. Word Biblical Commentary 47B. Dallas: Word, 1991.

Newell, William R. *Hebrews Verse by Verse*. Chicago: Moody Press, 1978.

EXPOSITION

I. Prologue: The Superiority of God's New Revelation (1:1–4)

The author of Hebrews displayed his complete knowledge of the recipients and his great ability as a litigator and teacher in these opening verses. He was speaking to Jews who had come to believe that Jesus was the promised Messiah as revealed in the Old Testament. This was of great significance. Their heritage and background in Old Testament Scriptures only served to enhance the unexpected nature of this new revelation to which they had committed themselves, especially with respect to the deity of Jesus Christ. The truth found in Deuteronomy 6:4 had been drilled into them since birth: "Hear, O Israel: the LORD our God is one LORD." Thus, the author began his opening salvo with God, evoking the feelings of reverence, submission, and love that would resonate in the heart of any true and committed believer. He declared that the God whom they had always trusted and who had spoken to their fathers through the prophets had spoken again, in the person of His Son. The plurality of persons constituting one God was a leap that their leaders in the Sanhedrin could not make and was an exercise of faith that could only be justified by acceptance of the truthfulness of the description of the Lord Jesus found in verses 2–4.

This description answers the question found in Isaiah 40: "To whom then will ye liken God? Or what likeness will ye compare unto him? ... who hath created these things ... Hast thou not known? hast thou not heard, that the everlasting God, the LORD, the Creator of the ends of the earth, fainteth not, neither is weary?" (Isa. 40:18, 26, 28). For this reason, the prophet encouraged his reader with, "They shall run, and not be weary; and they shall walk, and not faint" (Isa. 40:31). The author of Hebrews encouraged his readers again and again with this same refrain.

Continuing to lay out the foundational truths upon which he based the epistle, the writer declared that the mighty Lord, who holds the world and all creation in His hands by the power of His word, is the procurer of our completed redemption. He further declared that the Lord, better than the angels, has by inheritance a more excellent name than they, further reinforcing the superiority of Christ, His work, and His word.

We see a methodology at work throughout the epistle. The author argued by establishing or reinforcing foundational truths, upon which he built. He then presented and compared those truths to the new and superior. This building process is an important interpretive key to Hebrews. The first example of this is in verse 4, where the author's mention of angels segues into the first of five arguments that follow.

1:1. God. Contrary to custom, the author did not begin his letter with his own name. Instead, he introduced the Divine Author. The use of the personal pronoun **who** is suggestive of the personality of God and of His activity among His people when **at sundry times and in divers manners [He] spake unto the fathers in time past**. The idea that it was God who spoke, even though He spoke **by the prophets**, cannot be overemphasized. "In time past" stands in contrast to "in these last days" (1:2), the messianic era inaugurated by the incarnation. Even though the Old Testament revelation was fragmentary and occasional, lacking fullness and finality, it was nonetheless a word from the Lord. All Old Testament writers are here viewed as prophets in that their testimony was the proclamation of God's message to His people and was preparation for the coming of Christ. The writer alerted the attentive reader to what he developed in chapter 11, where he brought the promises, warnings, and consequences discussed throughout the letter to poignant focus by paralleling them with specific Old Testament examples of faith.

1:2–3. In contrast to previous revelation, God **hath in these last days spoken unto us by his Son** (v. 2; lit., "in Son"; the anarthrous construction, an absence of the definite article in the Greek, stresses the quality of the thing specified). The incarnation inaugurated a new kind of era (see Acts 2:17; 1 Tim 4:1; 1 John 2:18). This is a new and unique category of revelation in contrast to that of the prophets. Old Testament prophets delivered a message from God; Christ *is* the message. The following verses suggest not only that this revelation was the Word of God as He delivered it personally but that, in His own person, Christ was a complete and perfect revelation ("Son") of the Godhead (see John 1:1–14).

The superiority of the "in Son" relationship is demonstrated by seven great descriptive statements about Him. (1) He is **appointed heir of all things** (v. 2; see Rom. 8:17). The incarnate Son was gloriously exalted to the position of the firstborn heir of God; that is, He received the inheritance of God's estate ("all things"). (2) This is the One, **by whom also he** (God) **made the worlds** (see John 1:3; Col. 1:16). (3) The Son is **the brightness of his** (God's) **glory** (v. 3). This suggests that the glory of the Godhead is demonstrated in Christ, and as the brilliance of the sun is inseparable from the sun itself, so the Son's radiance is inseparable from deity. He Himself is God, the second person of the Trinity (see John 1:14, 18). (4) Christ is further said to be **the express image of his** (God's) **person**. Jesus is not merely an image or reflection of God. Because the Son is God, He is the absolutely authentic representation of God's being (see John 14:9; Col. 1:15). (5) Christ upholds **all things by the word of his power**. Christ is not like Atlas, the mythical Greek god who held the world on his shoulders. The Son dynamically holds together and carries forward all that has been created through Him (see Col. 1:17). He does this through His awesome power. (6) **He … himself purged our sins**. The emphasis here is not *how* He purged our sins but *that* He purged our sins. (7) When His work on behalf of sin was finished, He **sat down on the right hand of the Majesty on high**. Being seated at God's right hand indicates that the work of redemption is complete and that Christ is actively ruling with God as Lord over all (see 1:13; 8:1; 10:12; 12:2; Eph. 1:20; Col. 3:1; 1 Peter 3:22; see also discussion on Mark 16:19; Pss. 110:1; 1:3; 8:1). The use of the circumlocution for God ("Majesty on high") is indicative

of the recipients, who were scrupulous about direct references to God's name. In speaking of the significance of Christ, the early apostles drew heavily on the Old Testament (e.g., Psalm 110; Joel 2:28–32; Pss. 16:8–11; 89:3–4; 118:22; Dan. 9:24–27; see Acts 2:14–36; 4:23–31).

1:4. Having been appointed heir of all things and given a position of supreme authority, Christ is seen as **much better than the angels**. To most Jews, angels were exalted beings, especially revered because they were involved in giving the law at Sinai (see discussion on 2:2), and to the Jews, the law was God's supreme revelation. The Dead Sea Scrolls reflect the expectation that the archangel Michael would be the supreme figure in the messianic kingdom. The incarnate Christ had taken on the form of a man, a little lower than the angels. Whether the recipients of Hebrews were tempted to assign angels a place above Christ (the Messiah) is not known. Nonetheless, **he hath by inheritance obtained a more excellent name than they**. To Jews, a name stood for the full character of a person in all he was and did (see discussion on Gen. 17:5). Here the author made the important distinction that Christ has a legal right to His name as opposed to His having earned it. The theology of the immutability of God and the preexistence of a glorified Christ is in play here. The section that follows indicates that this name was "Son," a name to which no angel could lay claim (see 1:2 and discussion).

II. Arguments for Staying the Course (1:5–12:29)

If there is one epistle in the New Testament that applies uniquely to the church of the twenty-first century, none is more apropos than Hebrews. We have witnessed large-scale defections of professing born-again Christians to the deceptions of inclusivism, hedonism, and self-indulgence. Many have indeed "left [their] first love" (Rev. 2:4). A study of this epistle should be a rebuke to anyone who is considering giving up the fight or who is growing weary of participating in the sufferings of Christ. Ours is not the temptation to return to the comfort of Old

Testament Judaism, as was the case with the recipients of this epistle; rather, ours is the temptation to return to a life without the scorn and slings and arrows of the world in order to participate in a lifestyle that we feel is our "right" as a member of modern Western culture. As Paul said of the experiences of Israel, perhaps it could be said that Hebrews was also "written for our admonition, upon whom the ends of the world are come" (1 Cor. 10:11).

A. The Argument for a Superior Revelation (1:5 – 2:4)

Christ's superiority to angels is documented with seven Old Testament quotations, showing that He is God's Son, that He is worshiped by angels, and that, though He is God, He is distinguished from the Father. While it was necessary for the writer to document the superiority of the word of Christ over the word delivered with the assistance of angels on Mount Sinai, it must be remembered that no word from God is superior to any other word from God (see 2 Tim. 3:16).

1. The Nature of the Superiority (1:5–14)

This section contains a litany of Old Testament prophecies concerning the coming of Christ, His office, and His worthiness. The author of Hebrews reminded his hearers of these things to demonstrate, not that the new word from God is superior in its intrinsic value, but that a promise fulfilled was better than a promise yet unfulfilled in the lives of these new believers.

1:5. Thou art my Son, this day have I begotten thee. This prophetic passage (Ps. 2:7) is quoted in Acts 13:33 as being fulfilled in Christ's resurrection (see Rom. 1:4). The kings of Israel (such as David) were the "sons of God" by adoption (see 2 Sam. 7:14), but this heir to the throne was "begotten" of God. This contrasts with angels, who are created beings but who will never sit on a throne. **I will be to him a Father, and he shall be to me a Son.** Jews acknowledged 2 Samuel 7:14, which the writer quoted here, and Psalm 2 as messianic in their ultimate application (see Luke 1:32–33). This royal personage is

neither an angel nor an archangel; He is God's Son. The prophecy was fulfilled before their very eyes.

1:6. As **the firstbegotten**, Jesus is the fountainhead of all that is (see John 1:1–3) and "the firstborn [of] many brethren" (Rom. 8:29). The term "firstbegotten" suggests that others had already followed. Since Christ is the progenitor of that out of which the hearers had been called (Judaism), the promise of a "better thing" (11:40) carried all the legitimacy that only God can give. The hearers, members of the fledgling New Testament church, were reminded that Christ, their Head, is the firstbegotten of God, even as they also were begotten of God through the miracle of regeneration. The doxological statement **let all the angels of God worship Him** may be from Psalm 97:7. This statement, which in the Old Testament refers to the Yahweh (see Ps. 97:1–9), is here applied to Christ, giving clear indication of His deity. If He is worthy of worship from the angels, He is worthy also of our worship. God chose to reveal Himself in the confines of time and humanity, "in Son" (see discussion on 1:2), as clearly prophesied in Isaiah (Isa. 9:6; 59:20) and fulfilled as Matthew and Luke declared (Matt. 1:23; Luke 2:11). The hearers were brought into full realization that they served none other than the living God and that, as brethren of Christ, they were participants in the fulfillment of the promise. This was a far superior position than that of their fathers, who could only participate in the promise by faith.

1:7. The next quotation, from Psalm 104:4, **Who maketh his angels spirits, and his ministers a flame of fire**, speaks of the storm wind and lightning as agents of God's purposes. This contrasts to that "better thing" (11:40), the church, which has been called to fulfill God's purposes during this current age (see Matt. 28:18–20).

1:8. But unto the Son he saith, Thy throne, O God, is for ever and ever. The author selected a passage (Ps. 45:6) that intimates the deity of the messianic (and Davidic) King. The hearers were reminded that, although God has temporarily set aside the programs concerning Israel, they served the same God who has promised to sit on the throne of David, a throne which is eternal. The church, of which they were a part, is now the agency of God's power, but the promises to Israel and David will yet be fulfilled. This provides a continuity to God's purposes, which would have encouraged the hearers to "hold fast" (10:23) to better things by reminding them that as God fulfilled His promises as to the incarnation of Christ, He will also fulfill His promises to Israel.

1:9. God, even thy God, hath anointed thee with the oil of gladness above thy fellows. This quotation from Psalm 45:6, parenthetically placed after the quotation from Psalm 104:4 demands extraordinary attention. Psalm 45, known as "A Song of Loves," is a song celebrating the marriage of a king. The hearers would have immediately recognized it as such, and both the psalm and the portion quoted would have been important to them. The use of this song in the context of the eternal nature of the throne further enhanced the encouragement provided in 1:8 as to the continuity of God's purposes. The joy and gladness of the king in the presence of his brethren and the anointing, which represents the sovereign will of God, is in view. The intimacy enjoyed by both Jew and Gentile as fellow laborers with Christ suggested to the hearers that they, though persecuted and troubled, were not alone (2:11). The connection to the apostle Paul's twin polemics, Colossians and Ephesians, is evident, if not intentional.

1:10. Thou, Lord, in the beginning hast laid the foundation of the earth. As in 1:8, a passage addressed to Yahweh ("You, Lord") is applied to the Son. We see the authority of Christ, as Creator, to direct the hearers in their "heavenly calling" (3:1).

1:11–12. They shall perish (v. 11) **... but thou art the same** (v. 12). With eternity's values in view, the brethren and fellow laborers with Christ were reminded that they were on the winning team. Here the author looked forward to a future that will be ruled by Christ, who is the same yesterday, today, and forever.

1:13. Sit on my right hand (see discussion on 1:2–3). Psalm 110 is applied repeatedly to Jesus in Hebrews (1:3, 13; 5:6, 10; 6:20; 7:3, 11, 17, 21; 8:1; 10:12–13; 12:2). There can be no mistaking that

one of the author's purposes was to emphasize the location of the Lord relative to the Old Testament prophecies concerning Him.

1:14. Ministering spirits ... for them who shall be heirs of salvation. The author, though repeatedly comparing angels to the superior Christ, affirmed that they are nevertheless not diminished. The angels are now sent forth to minister to believers. This ministry is in stark contrast to the work of angels referred to in 1:7. For the hearers, this was a new and better word.

2. Warning concerning the Revelation (2:1)

2:1. Therefore we ought to give the more earnest heed is a call to seriously consider the foregoing in the light of **the things which we have heard**, which would include the message of the gospel, of Christ's person as the God-man, His redemptive work on the cross, and the Scriptures. As the author has shown, this includes reviewing the Old Testament promises that, to believers' benefit, have been fulfilled in Christ. **Lest at any time we should let them slip.** The inference of this phrase is that we should not allow ourselves to drift away from "the things which we have heard." This warning speaks against the dangers of lethargy or loose thinking concerning these things. Believers need to diligently guard themselves against any degree of drifting away. This is the first of five warnings strategically positioned throughout the letter (2:1–4; 3:7–4:13; 5:11–6:12; 10:19–39; 12:14–29). Progressive in their severity and in the severity of the consequences, these warnings possess a common pattern containing four elements: (1) the warning is stated, (2) a historical example is given, (3) historical consequences are recorded, and (4) the consequences for contemporary readers are stated should they fail to heed the warning.

3. Consequences of Neglecting the Revelation under Moses (2:2)

2:2. Following the pattern of the warnings (see 2:1 and discussion), the warning is first stated, then, second, the historical example is **the word spoken by angels.** This is the law given to Moses at Sinai (Deut.

33:2), and when it was transgressed or disobeyed, it always **received a just recompence of reward**. Third, the historical example is followed by the consequences for those who transgressed this law. Numbers 15:30 speaks of the recompense that should be the lot of one who sins presumptuously. A man who raises his fist in the face of God is a reproach to the Lord and is deserving of death. In Acts 7, Stephen rehearsed before the synagogue the results of Israel's rebellion against Moses when God "gave them up to worship the host of heaven" (Acts 7:42). They who had known the blessings and presence of God had neither. Old Testament prophets also had to remind the nation of their cyclical treachery against their God (see, e.g., Ezek. 20:1–44). Such repeated offenses formed the detail of God's final indictment against them, leading to their destruction and captivity.

4. Consequences of Neglecting the Revelation under Christ (2:3)

2:3. **If we neglect so great salvation**, we shall not **escape**. This is the fourth element of the repeated pattern of the warnings (see 2:1 and discussion). This argument proceeds from the lesser to the greater and assumes that the gospel is greater than the law. Thus, if disregard for the law brought certain punishment, disregard for our salvation will bring an even greater and inescapable disaster. In this context, which speaks of the law of Moses, our "so great salvation" is compared to the law (see Rom. 8:1–3). The law can no longer condemn us, and we are free from the law of sin and death. As Israel's transgressions brought them into the captivity of the Babylonians, so our negligence of our so great salvation will bring us inescapably into the captivity and tyranny of sin. God confirmed Moses before the children of Israel with many signs and wonders; the gospel has been **confirmed unto us by them that heard him**. These eyewitnesses, chiefly the apostles (see 2 Peter 1:16; 1 John 1:1), had vouched for the message first announced by Christ and were witnesses of the miracles of Christ and His resurrection. The author apparently was neither an apostle nor an eyewitness (see Introduction: "Author").

5. God Himself Confirms the New Revelation (2:4)

2:4. Those who regard this new revelation as something of so little importance that they allow themselves to slip away from it are willfully disobedient and a reproach to the Lord. This is particularly so when one considers that God Himself bore **witness, both with signs and wonders, and with divers miracles**. We ignore the Word of the Lord at our peril. Additionally, God confirmed the gospel message through **gifts of the Holy Ghost**, such as the gift of tongues (see Acts 2:4–12). For **according to his own will**, see 1 Corinthians 12:4–11.

B. The Argument for a Superior Prophet (2:5–4:13)

To those who have heard and believed the Word, it is an awesome realization that God should have spoken to us. That one could contemplate the very Word of God and not respond in faith is beyond imagination. Yet this is exactly what Israel had been guilty of for centuries. And it is what the generation of the Paul's "kinsmen" (Rom. 9:3) were guilty of when they rejected the outstretched hand of their promised Messiah. When Elijah complained to God of his generation's apostasy, God replied that He had reserved to Himself a remnant (see 1 Kings 19:14–18). Paul spoke of this in Romans 11:1–5 and concluded, "Even so then at this present time also there is a remnant according to the election of grace" (Rom. 11:5). "The captain" (Heb. 2:10) of this present remnant is Jesus. The following passage speaks of Him and His worthiness and reminds readers of the consequences of doubting His word.

1. This Person Is Jesus (2:5–3:1)

The author opened this argument with an exposition of Psalm 8:4–6, which shows Christ's superiority over the angels since He redeemed fallen humanity and thus fulfilled man's role as sovereign over the earth. Because Christ took on the form of a man, it is necessary to argue that Christ is the superior Prophet, not only because of who He is but also because of what He accomplished in His role as Perfect Man on our behalf.

2:5. The author reminded his readers that **unto the angels hath he not put in subjection the world to come**. If the readers were being enticed to believe that angelic beings would rule the future kingdom, this reminder would have sufficed to correct their error (see discussion on 1:4). In trying to dissuade his readers from turning back to Judaism, the author showed them that Christ, as bearer of the new revelation, a revelation of fulfillment, is superior to angels, who participated in bringing the revelation at Sinai.

2:6–7. One in a certain place testified (v. 6) refers to the psalmist David. Though not identified, Psalm 8:4–6 was well known to the hearers and did not need precise identification. Awed by the marvelous order and immensity of God's handiwork in the celestial universe, the psalmist marveled at the high dignity that God had bestowed on puny man by entrusting him with dominion over all other creatures (see Gen. 1:26–28 and discussions). He wondered, **What is man, that thou art mindful of him? or the son of man, that thou visitest him?** seeing that **Thou madest him a little lower than the angels** (v. 7; see discussion on Ps. 8:5). Ah, but **thou crownedst him with glory and honour, and didst set him over the works of thy hands**. This seeming paradox puzzled the psalmist. The readers were reminded that it is God who has granted such dignity to humankind.

2:8. Therefore, **Thou hast put all things in subjection under his feet**. God's purpose from the beginning was that man should be sovereign in the creaturely realm, subject to only God. Due to sin, that purpose of God has been temporarily thwarted. Indeed, men have themselves become "subject to bondage" (2:15). Because of sin, **now we see not yet all things put under him**.

2:9. Gloriously, **we see Jesus,** and even though He **was made a little lower than the angels, for the suffering of death,** He has now been **crowned with glory and honour** (see 10:13). In applying Psalm 8 to Jesus in particular, the author declared Him, as Perfect Man, to be the forerunner of man's restored dominion over the earth. He was made lower than the angels for awhile but is now crowned with glory and honor at God's right hand. By His perfect life,

His death on the cross, and His exaltation, He has made possible the ultimate fulfillment of Psalm 8 in the future kingdom. At that time, the second Adam and Perfect Man, the victorious Christ, will regain sovereignty over creation. The purpose of Christ's death was that **by the grace of God [He] should taste death for every man**. In so doing, He made it possible for every man to participate in His rule over all things.

2:10. Even though **all things** were made by Him and all things are for Him, **it became him**, or was fitting, to bring **many sons unto glory, to make the captain** (author) **of their** (so great; see 2:3) **salvation perfect through sufferings**. Christ was never morally or spiritually imperfect, but His participation in humanity was completed (perfected) when He experienced suffering. He identified with us on the deepest level of anguish, and in becoming sin for us, He acquired a full understanding of our imperfection and become our sympathetic High Priest. The author was building the case that Christ did not obtain our salvation just to rescue us from sin and death; rather, we as brethren should participate with Him in His Glory, and He will participate with us in our sufferings. This is a glorious contemplation.

2:11. The writer continued to explore believers' oneness with Christ: **both he that sanctifieth and they who are sanctified are all of one**. The One who does the setting apart and those that He sets apart are called together to the same purpose. Because of this, He is **not ashamed to call them brethren**. This certifies that our brotherhood with Jesus is not merely a metaphorical brotherhood but the brotherhood of the Redeemer with the redeemed, who are truly one with Him. In keeping with the use of the term in ancient literature, "brothers" in this context means "brothers and sisters."

2:12. Reinforcing the theme that the hearers were participating in the fulfillment of Old Testament prophecy, the author quoted Psalm 22:22, which describes the sufferings and triumph of God's righteous servant (see discussion on Psalm 22): **I will declare thy name unto my brethren, in the midst of the church will I sing unto thee**. The phrase "my brethren" is seen here as coming from the lips of the triumphant Messiah. This verse harks back to 1:9 and emphasizes the Lord's joy over the congregation.

2:13. In an exemplary manner, the Lord again identifies with His brethren as He says, **I will put my trust in him**, an expression of true dependence on God. In the person of Christ, humanity is seen as it was intended to be. **Behold, I, and the children which God hath given me** indicates that this trust in God will be shared by Christ's brethren and further indicates the degree to which He is one with them. The writer wanted to impress the hearers with their participation in the fulfillment of prophecy and in the fullness of Christ. After indicating how they, His children, were like Christ, the author went on to re-emphasize how He became like them and that this was necessary for their deliverance.

2:14. The author next built on the idea that **the children are … flesh and blood** and that **he also himself likewise took part of the same**, so **that through death he might destroy him that had the power of death**. In fulfillment of the Old Testament pattern represented in the kinsman-redeemer (see Ruth 4:1–11), Christ's death provided the payment required to redeem mankind. It may be said that Satan wields the power of death only insofar as he induces people to refuse the redemption provided by Christ (see 1 John 5:12; Ezek. 18:4; Rom. 5:12; 6:23). Most likely, the readers were familiar with the apostle Paul's epistle to the Romans, and a glance to Romans 7 cannot be discounted. Of course, in keeping with the pattern and style of this epistle, the author compared the weakness of the law to the power of Christ.

2:15. Equally important as the destruction of the power of death, Christ's death also obtained the deliverance of **them who … were all their lifetime subject to bondage** (see 1 Cor. 15:54–57; Rev. 1:18). The author contrasted bondage with freedom, death with life, to encourage the hearers to keep the faith and stay the course. To regress for the sake of comfort would be to embrace bondage and death; to press on would be to embrace freedom and life. The choice was theirs to make and remains ours today.

2:16. Moving from the general to the specific, the author reminded the hearers that rather than taking on **the nature** (form) **of angels**, Christ became a man of the **seed of Abraham**. Christ assumed not angelic nature but human nature, and as promised, He was both the root and the stem of Jesse (see Isa. 11:1).

2:17. Moving toward his next argument, the writer expressed that it was altogether fitting that Christ was **made like unto his brethren** so that He might be a merciful and faithful High Priest in things pertaining to God. Having become Perfect Man, Christ can represent mankind before God as a true kinsman and make reconciliation for the sins of the people. In a substitutionary way, Christ's death provided satisfactory atonement for our sin and turned away God's wrath (see discussions on Rom. 3:25; 1 John 2:2). To turn aside the wrath of God, Christ became one with sinful humanity and died in our stead.

2:18. The writer dispelled any thought that because Christ is God, He doesn't truly understand the plight of His brethren. Christ is able to bring comfort to them because **he himself hath suffered being tempted** (see discussion on 4:15; Matt. 4:1–11, 26:39).

3:1. In leaving the discussion of the nature of Christ's humanity and work, the author exhorted his hearers, as **partakers of the heavenly calling** (see discussion on 3:14), to keep before them their consideration of **the Apostle and High Priest of our profession, Christ Jesus** (see discussions on Mark 6:30; 1 Cor. 1:1). "Apostle" means "one who is sent." Jesus repeatedly spoke of Himself as having been sent into the world by the Father (see, e.g., Matt. 10:40; 15:24; Mark 9:37; Luke 9:48; John 4:34; 5:24, 30, 36–38; 6:38). He is the supreme apostle, the one from whom all other apostleship flows.

2. Christ Compared to Moses (3:2–6)

This passage is a comparison of Christ and Moses, both of whom were sent by the Father to lead His people — the one to lead them from bondage under Pharaoh to the Promised Land, the other to lead them from the bondage of sin (see 2:14–15) and to the rest promised to those who believe (see 4:3, 9). The larger section of 3:1–4:13 contains an exposition of Psalm 95:7–11, stressing Christ's superiority over Moses and warning against disobedience and unbelief. In 3:2–6, the author, focusing on faithful stewardship, used the metaphor of a house and its ruler. A first-century Jewish Christian would have understood this analogy entirely differently from how we might today. To interpret the following verses we must try to understand this meaning.

3:2. Keeping the Lord Jesus in mind, we turn to a consideration of **Moses**, who also **was faithful in all his house**. Moses was a faithful servant in the household to which God had appointed him. The author purposely developed his argument using the metaphor of a "house" that, as used here, has more the meaning of a "household" or a "family" than a physical "building."

3:3. He who hath builded … hath more honour than the house. Jesus built the house (or household), whereas Moses was simply the appointed guardian of it. Jesus has made the house thoroughly livable, or ready for occupancy. The terms "builded" and "built" in 3:3–4 have the same meaning (in contrast to 9:11 and 11:10, where a different Greek term is used for "building.")

3:4. Moreover, the author continued, **he that built all things is God**. Since Jesus is the one who has "builded the house" (3:3), He is now equated with God, making it beyond question that Christ is greater than Moses.

3:5–6. Since **Moses verily was faithful in all his house, as a servant** (v. 5), he became a picture, or type, of **those things which were to be spoken after[ward]**, namely, of **Christ as a Son over his own house** (v. 6). Moses figuratively represented Christ, who is Chief over His own house (see 8:2). The superiority of Christ over Moses is shown in two comparisons: (1) Moses was a servant, whereas Christ is a son. (2) Moses was a servant in God's household, whereas Christ is over God's household, both past and future, **whose house are we** (see Eph. 2:19; 1 Peter 2:5). The caveat **if we hold fast the confi-**

dence and the rejoicing of the hope firm unto the end has been the subject of much discussion. The question is not whether we are *in* Christ but whether we as His household *are ruled* by Him. The author later expanded this thought and extended this caveat to being "partakers of Christ" (3:14). The use of the term "we" does not allow for the application of this text to unbelievers.

3. Warning against Unbelief (3:7–15)

3:7–11. In this second warning passage, the author again employed the common pattern of the warnings in this epistle (see discussion on 2:1). The quotation from Psalm 95:7–11 summarizes the inglorious history of Israel under Moses' leadership in the wilderness. The historical context is a time after the Israelites' miraculous rescue from Egypt, when they were tested in the wilderness. Signs and wonders encouraged them to trust God, but contrary to what would seem logical, they turned against Moses and God and instead tested God's patience. Christ had rescued the recipients of this epistle from the bondage of sin. As in the historical example, however, difficulties were tempting them to discard their new life under the authority of Christ. By recounting this psalm, the author abruptly brought his hearers to a recollection of God's reaction to the Israelites' unbelief and rebellion against Moses' leadership. The admonition in 3:5–6, that we will not enjoy the leadership of Christ if we do not firmly hold to the truth that we have received, set up this warning. Upon examination, this is a much higher standard than that which God required in Moses' day. The psalmist used the example of Israel under Moses to warn the Israelites against unbelief and disobedience. In a similar way, the author of Hebrews applied the psalmist's warning to his readers. The warning and the consequences of unbelief are particularly applicable to us today, as we are often distracted from a diligent consideration of "the things which we have heard" (2:1).

3:7. Since the quotation from Psalm 95:7–11 is germane to the flow of the author's argument and not parenthetical, the inferential conjunction

Wherefore refers to "Harden not" (3:8) rather than "Take heed" (3:12).

3:8. Harden not your hearts, as in the provocation is a plea to consider the superiority of Christ's headship over Moses' stewardship. The phrase "if ye will hear his voice" (3:7), being a third-class condition, indicates that they *were* hearing his voice.

3:9. Your fathers tempted me and yet **saw my works forty years**. The inference is that this was not an intelligent course of action. This lack of reasonable thought is further emphasized in 3:12, with the term "evil heart."

3:10. Wherefore I was grieved (perhaps "disgusted" is better) **with that generation**. This was the generation that fell in the wilderness. It is interesting that Jesus referred to the scribes and Pharisees of His day as "an evil and adulterous generation" (Matt. 12:39). **They have not known my ways** is especially burdensome in light of the evidence of God's provision and love that had been expressed to them.

3:11. They shall not enter into my rest is chastisement backed by God's solemn oath. This is a consequence without remedy, exemplified by the carcasses of the unbelieving Israelites who fell in the wilderness (see 3:17).

3:12. Therefore, the author warned his hearers, **Take heed, brethren, lest there [come to] be in any of you an evil heart of unbelief, in departing from the living God**. A progression can be seen here: (1) a departure from "the things which we have heard" (2:1), (2) inattention to these matters leads to a loss of Christ's leadership (see 3:5–6), (3) unbelief leads to a departure from God. To turn away rebelliously (lit., "to become apostate") from God is to turn away from life and choose death, just as did most of the Israelites who came out of Egypt. The term "evil heart" occurs only twice in the Old Testament, in Jeremiah 16:12 and 18:12, where such purposeful rebellion against God is considered stupidity.

3:13–14. Believers' need for one another and accountability to one another is evident in the encouragement to **exhort one another daily, while it is called To day** (v. 13). The essence of unbelief is to turn one's back on God. The danger in doing this is

that one will be **hardened through the deceitfulness of sin**, see 4:7. This is still the day of divine grace and opportunity to trust God, but it will not last indefinitely. The conditions of loosing the leadership of Christ are the same for loosing our participation in the purposes of Christ. **For we are made** (have become) **partakers of Christ** (v. 14) by holding **the beginning of our confidence stedfast unto the end**. The author commended his hearers as having done this and did not accuse them of being guilty of this sin (see 3:1).

3:15. The author again quoted from Psalm 95:7–8 to reemphasize, **To day if ye will hear** (lit., "harken unto") **his voice, harden not** (lit., "that you may not harden") **your hearts, as in the provocation** (see 3:7–8). The author's admonition was persistent diligence in obedience to the voice of God in the present so they would not become hardened and rebellious as did they who were delivered out of Egypt. The antidote and prescription for not developing a hardened heart is to hear the Word of the Lord.

4. Consequences of Unbelief under Moses (3:16–19)

Here the author pursued his argument with a series of rhetorical questions. Having stated the warning, he drew a graphic example from the Old Testament. The generation to whom the promise of the land was given had heard God's promise and refused to trust Him (v. 19). This action is described as rebellion (v. 16), sin (v. 17), and disobedience (v. 18). God in His anger refused the promise to that entire generation of Israelites (see Num. 14:21–35). Since these rebellious people died in the wilderness, it is no stretch to say that their opportunity to enter into the land was lost without remedy. It was equally impossible for the first-century generation of unbelieving Jews to enter into a proper relationship with Christ as their Messiah and King because they had fallen under the judgment of God (see Rom. 9–11) and the new covenant had been inaugurated (see Hebrews 8–10). As first-century Christians, the recipients faced a similar danger (4:1). Paul, in using the illustration of the olive tree, had warned his readers, "If God spared not the natural branches, take heed lest he also spare not thee" (Rom. 11:21). The writer of Hebrews was similarly warning his readers.

3:16–18. Some (v. 16) is an unfortunate and confusing translation of the Greek (*tines*) and is better translated as a question: Who **when they had heard, did provoke?** (lit., "became embittered"). This question is answered with another question: Was it **not all who came out of Egypt by Moses?** Again, **with whom was he grieved** ("angered") **forty years? was it not with them … whose carcasses fell in the wilderness?** Once again, the author asked, **And to whom sware he that they should not enter into his rest …?** (v. 18). Was it not **to them that believed not?** Was it not to those who continually "disobeyed"?

3:19. Supported by the psalm, the conclusion of the argument is **they could not enter in because of unbelief**.

5. Consequences of Unbelief under Christ (4:1)

4:1. Continuing, the author applied to his hearers the conclusions arrived at in Psalm 95: **Let us therefore fear, lest, a promise being left us of entering into his rest, any of you should seem to come** (be coming) **short of it**. As in the days of Israel under Moses, when "rescue" did not equate with "rest," so it is today; salvation does not equate with rest. "His rest" cannot ultimately refer to the rest in Canaan offered to the Israelites. Nor, for that matter, can it refer entirely to "heaven's rest." That temporary, earthly rest gained under Joshua (see 4:8; discussion on Josh. 1:13) pointed to a rest that is spiritual and eternal. The very real and present danger of coming to the threshold of entering into His rest but then falling short of it cannot be overemphasized. Consider Matthew 11:29–30, where the Lord Himself starkly presented the idea heretofore presented in Hebrews concerning the leadership of Christ. It is as we truly become fellow laborers with Christ that we find "rest unto your souls" (Matt. 11:29). Falling short of this rest is to lose the leadership of the Lord and to fail to enter into participation with Christ in God's purposes. There is little in these verses to support the idea that one's salvation is invalidated or

lost by failure to achieve the goals outlined by the author. That which is lost to the believer is threefold: the leadership of Christ, participation with Christ, and rest in Christ.

6. Exhortations to Continue Trusting Christ (4:2–13)

It is interesting to note the interplay of belief, obedience, and rest as discussed in v. 1 and the exhortation that follows in vv. 2–13. The author wove together two aspects of rest, as in the warp and woof of a cloth: (1) the rest *from* a work (v. 4) and (2) the rest *in* a work that is ongoing (vv. 3, 11). The fabric of our life in Christ is strengthened by both aspects equally and comes apart when either aspect dominates the other. That which allows us to rest is confidence in the idea expressed in verse 3: in the mind of God, all His purposes are already completed, even from the laying of the foundation of the world. Literally, this is akin to the laying of the foundation of a house.

4:2. The author, in the manner of James, invited his readers to compare those who just hear the Word and those who hearken to the Word. He further recalled, **For unto us was the gospel preached, as well as unto them**, indicating that both had opportunity to respond. **But the word preached did not profit them, not being mixed with faith in them that heard** (hearkened to) **it**. Though the meaning is obscured by the difficulty in translating this passage, the author was bringing into play the partnership that we have with other believers in Christ. Those who did not profit from the Word were profitless because they had not joined in with faith with those who believed and acted on "the things which we have heard" (2:1).

4:3. With emphasis, the author continued, **For we which have believed do enter into rest**. Believers "do enter." Perhaps, in the context of laboring in Christ's household, we may say that we are yoked together with Christ so as to fulfill God's purposes on earth. We rest in the certainty that those purposes will be realized. We have arrived in that place (land) where we both work and rest (see 4:4). Just as entering physical rest in Canaan demanded faith in God's promise, so salvation rest is entered into only by an operative faith in the person and work of Jesus Christ. As in 3:16, **if they shall enter into my rest** (also in 4:5) is rhetorical interrogative and, as before, demands a negative response. **Although the works were finished from the foundation of the world**, those who did not profit from the Word failed to enter into that rest because of their unbelief in the certainty of the sovereign purposes of God. There is no sadder contemplation than that what Christ has procured at so great a cost should go unheeded by a rebellious and stiff-necked people.

4:4–5. The point of this verse is not that God rested from His work on the seventh day of creation but that He appointed a certain day on which He would rest. **He spake ... of the seventh day on this wise** (v. 4), and thus His rest is already a reality. The rest God calls us to enter (see 4:10–11) is not our rest but His rest, which He invites us to share.

4:6. Even though the displeasure of God is arrayed against unbelievers, we nevertheless are **seeing** that the promise **remaineth that some must enter therein**. Again, the emphasis is that those who ignore "Him that speaketh" (12:25) do so at their peril. **They ... entered not in because of unbelief.** The message here, however, was that the promise of entering remained, as shown in the continuing invitation of Psalm 95:7–8. In considering the author's diatribe, the point that he was speaking of unbelieving believers is often overlooked (Ps. 95:7).

4:7. Again ... a certain day ... To day ... hear his voice, harden not your hearts. See discussion on 3:13–14.

4:8. For if Jesus (Joshua) **had given them rest**. The Greek name Jesus and the Hebrew name Joshua are the same name, meaning "Savior." In this context, the verse is speaking of the rest that Joshua could not give to the nation Israel when they had entered into the Promised Land, Canaan. Psalm 95 bears witness to this unfulfilled rest in Moses' and Joshua's time. Hence, there was the need to **have spoken of another day.**

4:9. There remaineth therefore a rest to the people of God. God's rest may still be entered into.

This does not mean, however, that we must not also labor (see 4:11).

4:10. The author defined the person who has **entered into his rest** as one who **hath ceased from his own works**. This text is often taken to mean that the believer ceases his efforts to gain salvation by his own works and rests in the finished work of Christ on the cross. Others would equate this with the believer's final rest (see Rev. 14:13). Yet this entering into rest is qualified: **as God did from his**. In summary, when God had finished the work of creation, He ceased from that work. Similarly, when a person believes and is born again, he also ceases from his own work — not only with regard to working for his salvation but also in regard to his own purposes in life (see 1 Cor. 6:17, 19–20; 7:23).

4:11–13. Let us labour therefore to enter into that rest, lest any man fall after the same example of unbelief (Greek, *apeitheia*; "disobedience," "obstinacy"; v. 11). Clearly, obtaining this rest is predicated on the lordship of Christ and unswerving obedience to the word that He has spoken. **The word of God** (v. 12) is God's truth and was revealed by Jesus (the incarnate Word; see John 1:1, 14), but it has also been given verbally, the word referred to here. It is described as **quick** ("alive"), **and powerful, and sharper than any twoedged sword**. This dynamic word of God appears in both the Old Testament and the New Testament (see Pss. 107:20; 147:18; Isa. 40:8; 55:11; Gal. 3:8; Eph. 5:26; James 1:18; 1 Peter 1:23). The author of Hebrews described it as a living power that judges as with an all-seeing eye, **piercing even to the dividing asunder of soul and spirit ... joints and marrow** (a person's innermost being)**, and is a discerner of the thoughts and intents of the heart**. There is obviously no room for double-mindedness here. The Holy Spirit of God is at once the author, administrator, and facilitator of God's Word. He is the agent who enlivens and empowers the written text. Truly, **Neither is there any creature that is not manifest in his sight: but all things are naked and opened unto the eyes of him with whom we have to do** (v. 13). The author associated the activity of the Word with the activity of God as if they are one and the same, which in fact they are. One cannot move beyond the truth of these Scriptures without the purest of motives. We have become laborers together with Christ, members of God's household. Here there is no room for self-interest or for glorying, save in the cross of Christ. Our New Testament relationship with God is facilitated by the high-priestly ministry of Christ on our behalf. This relationship comes with enormous responsibilities. It also comes with peace, rest, and contentment.

C. The Argument for a Superior Relationship (4:14–7:28)

This section is an exposition of Psalm 110:4, stressing Christ's superiority over Aaron because of His better priesthood.

1. Jesus, Our High Priest (4:14–16)

4:14. A great high priest (see 2:17; 3:1). Here the author began an extended discussion of the superior priesthood of Christ. **Into the heavens**. Even as the Aaronic high priest, on the Day of Atonement, passed from the sight of the people into the Most Holy Place (see Lev. 16:15, 17), so Jesus, having accomplished His work of atonement, passed from the sight of His watching disciples and ascended through the heavens into the heavenly sanctuary (see Acts 1:9–11). Jesus had ascended some thirty years prior to these besieged and beleaguered Hebrew Christians being admonished to **hold fast [their] profession**. Surely some of them must have yearned for the physical presence of their Lord, and some of them were in danger of letting their faith slip (see the similar admonitions in 2:1; 3:6, 14). The following presentation of Christ in His high-priestly office is not a hollow doctrine to be learned but rather the author's tender and compassionate plea for his hearers to remember that they were entering into the sufferings of Christ in full view of "him with whom we have to do" (4:13).

4:15. The recipients were not plowing new ground nor were they encountering circumstances and experiences unknown to the Lord. **For we have not a high priest which cannot be touched with the feeling of our infirmities; but was in all points tempted like as we are** (see 2:18). The author stressed the parallel between Christ's temptations and our temptations. He experienced every kind of temptation a person can experience, **yet without sin**. Christ's temptations were completely different from ours, however, in the results: His temptations never led to sin (see Matt. 4:1–11). It follows that temptation in and of itself is not sin.

4:16. Let us therefore come boldly. Because Christ, our High Priest, has experienced human temptation, He stands ready to give immediate and sympathetic help when we are tempted. We are admonished to come without hesitation **unto the throne of grace**. This is the place where we meet God when we pray and is described as (1) a throne, a place of authority and abundant resources, and (2) a place of grace, a condition of favor and liberal help. Because of Jesus' identification with us, this throne has become a place where **we may obtain mercy, and find grace to help in time of need** (*boētheia*, "help," see the verb "succour" in 2:18; this term is found elsewhere in the New Testament only in Acts 27:17; *eukairos*, "in the nick of time," is used only here in the New Testament). This place, where we may boldly go, may be likened to the city of refuge (see Num. 35:6, 12). And like the city of refuge, it is a place of benefit only for those who go there. In the city of refuge, however, judgment could be rendered against a guilty supplicant and appropriate punishment administered. At the throne of grace, we find that judgment has been rendered against Jesus, who bore our sins on the cross, thus satisfying the "blood avenger." This presents an entirely new mediatorial ministry for this High Priest. Indeed, an entirely new and superior order of priesthood has supplanted the old (see 4:17). The recipients of this epistle especially needed to accept by faith that they would obtain mercy and find grace to help in time of need. It was equally as important, however, that they understand and know that the One with whom they were yoked, with whom they were fellow laborers, and in whom they had become partakers of the divine nature, is fully able to perform that which God has called Him to do.

2. The Nature of Christ's Priesthood (5:1–10)

Having established that Jesus Christ holds the office of high priest (see 4:14–16), the author went on to show that Christ meets the two qualifications for this office: (1) high priests had to be "taken from among men" (v. 1) so that they might have compassion and be prepared to represent the people before God, and (2) they had to be "called of God" (v. 4). Drawing from Psalms 2:7 and 110:4, the writer showed that Christ is qualified and able to perform the duties and tasks required under the priestly order of Aaron. Christ, however, is able to mediate a "better covenant" (8:6), which Aaron's order could not possibly minister. This superior high priest is called "after the order of Melchisedec" (vv. 6, 10). The author contrasted the old order under Aaron (vv. 1–4) with the new order under Christ (vv. 5–10).

5:1. Every high priest ... is ordained for men in things pertaining to God. While the work of the high priest is "for men," it is also to resolve a breech in man's relationship to God. God designates priests to mediate on our behalf to restore the relationship between fallen humanity and a holy God. The high priest has been so ordained **that he may offer** (the purpose clause with the present subjunctive denotes that he must "keep on giving") **gifts and sacrifices** (Greek, *thysia*; "bloody offerings," given as acts of worship to God; see 8:3; 9:9; Lev. 1:2; 2:1). Under Aaron's order, continual sacrifices were necessary, and being rightly related to God was not permanent.

5:2–3. Priests are "taken from among men" (5:1) so that they **can have compassion** (lit., "bear gently"; v. 2). This term is used only here in the New Testament. Greek writers used it to decry the *apatheia*, "apathy" of "lack of feeling," of the Stoics. Here "compassion" anticipates the sense in which the priest participates, in a limited way, in the plight both of **the ignorant, and on them that are out of the way**, that is, those who commit sins that are accidental or caused by sudden passion (see Isaiah 53:6; compare the unintentional sin, as in Leviticus 4; Num. 15:27–29, with defiant rebellion against God, as in Num. 15:30–31; see also Heb. 6:4–6; 10:26–31,

where the writer addressed the issue of presumptuous sin). The priest is able to do this because of his common humanity with them and because **he himself also is compassed** (lit., "wrapped," as a rope or chain) **with infirmity**. The priest must deal with his own sin, but this is not so of the Lord Jesus.

5:4. No man taketh this honour unto himself, but he that is called of God. This was not so in Christ's day, as the high-priestly office was in the hands of a family that had bought control of it. By contrast, legitimate elevation to this position comes from God, which anticipates the next verse.

5:5–6. Christ glorified not himself to be made a high priest (v. 5). As a man among men and in humble deference to the Father, the Son did not arrogate to Himself this honor but was appointed by the Father, as the two prophetic statements cited here show (Pss. 2:7; 110:4). Jesus often declared that He was sent by His Father (see John 5:30, 8:54; 17:5). His priesthood (significantly, *hiereus*, "priest," is used rather than *archiereus*, "high priest"), however, was according to **the order of Melchisedec** (v. 6), not the order of Aaron (see discussion on 7:1–28). In a masterful way, the author was developing the idea of an intimate relationship between Jesus the High Priest and the recipients. Even as they themselves had been declared His brethren (see 2:11) and begotten of God after the manner of Christ (see 1:5), so the declaration that **to day have I begotten thee** (v. 5; see Ps. 2:7–9; Rom. 1:4) bore witness to their genesis and to their glorious participation with the Son of God. Sonship and priesthood are brought together here in a significant way. It is evident that both are suited to one another in this text. Christ's priesthood is defined by His relation to the Father (as Son), and His sonship qualifies His priestly work.

That Jesus did not have to offer sacrifices for Himself (see 4:15; 5:2–3) brings to mind the absolute, selfless love that He expressed on behalf of those who would become His brethren. In His grief for our sin (see Isa. 53:10), He met the first qualification of a priest: to share with us in sympathetic compassion. The author proceeded to bear descriptive witness to this in the following verses.

5:7. Who in the days of his flesh. Perhaps issuing a gentle rebuke, the author reminded the suffering Hebrew Christians that Jesus, though God, was totally human as well (see Isa. 7:4; Matt. 1:23). Hence, the reference to Christ's agony in the garden of Gethsemane was intended as another reminder that their sufferings, though sore indeed, were known to their sympathetic High Priest. Jesus **had offered up prayers and supplications with strong crying and tears** (see Luke 22:44.) **unto him that was able to save him from death**, but He was not to be delivered from those sufferings. Although the Father was able to deliver Jesus, He would not. No doubt this truth was directly applicable to the hearers, as it is to us today. In obedience to the Father, Jesus did not shrink from physical suffering and death or from the indescribable agony of taking mankind's sin on Himself (see Matt. 27:46). He did not waver in His determination to fulfill the Father's will (see Isa. 50:7; Matt. 26:36–46). **And was heard in that he feared**. The Father heard Jesus' prayer and recognized His fearfulness (as a man), yet His request was not granted. It may be said however, that through resurrection, the Father did deliver Him from and through death. The persecuted Hebrew Christians may have been tempted to believe that God did not hear their prayers for deliverance; this example, the experience of their High Priest, served to highlight that there was a higher purpose to their sufferings. Inherent in this and the following verses is the perplexing impact that these events had on the God-man Christ Jesus. Though He lived as a man, fearful and in need of learning and perfecting, He was also God, in need of nothing. Although theologians have argued for centuries how this is so, it remains a hidden truth known only to God (see 1 Tim. 3:16).

5:8–10. Though he were a Son, yet learned he obedience by the things which he suffered (v. 8). Perhaps displaying the linguistic prowess of the author, there is a play on the two verbs here (*emathen* and *epathen*; "learned" and "suffered"), emphasizing his point that wisdom is developed in the cauldron of experience. So it was that Jesus, who always did the Father's will, yet "learned" and was **made per-**fect** (v. 9) through suffering (see 2:10), namely, His temptation in the wilderness and His passion leading up to and ending with the cross. Though He was the eternal Son of God, it was necessary for Him as the incarnate Son to learn obedience, not because He was ever disobedient but because He was called to obey to the extent that He experienced the most excruciating of human frailty and weakness. The temptations He faced were real, and the battle for victory was difficult, but where Adam failed and fell, Jesus prevailed. Thus, as a *man*, He was "made perfect." In so doing, **he became the author of eternal salvation** (see 9:12) **unto all them that obey him**. The indication here is not that eternal salvation is predicated on obedience but rather that those who are in a state of obedience are acknowledging that He is "the author" (Greek, *aitios*; "originator," "cause"). This idea is reinforced with **Called of God** (v. 10). One word in the original (Greek, *prosagoreutheis*; "to salute"), this term is used only here in the New Testament.

3. Rebuke for Dullness of Hearing (5:11–14)

Up to this point, the author diligently established the readers' relationship to Christ as High Priest. A hint of the author's disappointment in their readiness to be obedient, however, can be seen in his reference to "all them that obey" as opposed to a more direct reference to the recipients. The abruptly interjected rebuke that follows sets up the third warning of this epistle and is notable for its sharpness.

5:11. Of whom we have many things to say. The author wished to discuss the priesthood of Melchizedek but did not until later (chap. 7) due to the possibility of misinterpretation. His use of "we" seems to indicate that he was not alone in expressing this admonition (see 13:24). What he wished to say was **hard to be uttered** (Greek, *dysermēneutos*; "hard of interpretation"), another term used only here in the New Testament, and ran contrary to ordinary Jewish ideas. Yet the writer was concerned that his hearers' greater problem had less to do with their understanding and more to do with their readiness to learn. Their attitude, addressed in the warning found in 2:1, was in contrast to the exercising of faith that had caused them to accept their Messiah. It was therefore illogical for them to be **dull of hearing** ("slow," "sluggish," "indolent," "languid"). Plato used this expression to describe the stupidity of some of his students. Instead of progressing in the Christian life, the readers had become spiritually sluggish and mentally lazy (for the only other use of this expression, see 6:12, where it is translated "slothful").

5:12. The author continued with the metaphor of the classroom. **When for the time** implies that the passing of time should bring progress. Perhaps because of persecution, these believers had fallen into despondency. They should have known these things by now; in fact, the author went on to say, **ye ought to be teachers**. They were not recent converts. Sadly, however their lack of progress that he start over from the beginning to teach them **the first principles of the oracles of God**, which are listed in 6:1–2 (see discussion there; for *stoicheia*, "rudiments," see Gal. 4:3, 9; Col. 2:9). Having taken the first steps toward becoming mature Christians, they had slipped back to where they had started. **Strong meat** (Greek, *stereos*; "strong," "solid," "firm," as in the modern sense of "on steroids") signifies advanced teaching, such as that given in chapter 7. It is important to note that neglecting the Word is not a benign condition; if left to run its course, it will have disastrous results, as the author's third warning (6:4–8) shows.

5:13. Without intellectual and spiritual teaching, these people were unable to chew on the solid meat of the Scriptures. They were still on **milk** and **unskillful** (lit., "inexperienced"; Greek, *apeiros*, a composite word composed of the alpha privative, *a*, and *peira*, together signifying "no trial"). The recipients were untried in their experience of Christ. Indeed, rather than being a means of growth and joyfulness (see James 1:2–4), their response to persecution had left them wanting. **Babe** (Latin, *infans*; lit., "not able to talk") conveys that the author was doubtful whether they were ready for what he wished to teach them.

5:14. In contrast with "babe" (5:13), **Of full age** (Greek, *teleiōn*) speaks of "adults" (see 1 Cor. 2:6; 3:1;

13:11; Phil. 3:15; Eph. 4:4), those who have had **their senses** (lit., "organs of perception") **exercised** (from *gymnazō*, "to exercise vigorously as an athlete"). The author desired for his hearers to emulate those who had progressed in spiritual life and had become Christians of sound judgment and discernment. **Discern both good and evil** is something infants cannot do. With the consequences and loss referred to in his third warning in mind, the writer urged his readers much as a coach might do in the gym. His words were intended not to discourage them from advancing but to challenge them to vigorously seek out the truth of what he was about to say.

Christians who are unwilling or too lazy to "grow in grace" (2 Peter 3:18) are, at the least, unappreciative of the relationship that has been established, through the blood of Christ, with the Lord. The author's metaphorical use of "babe" was not without reason. Growth is part of the natural order. Lack of growth signals the presence of a serious disorder and will result in the direst of consequences.

4. Plea to Move Forward in the Knowledge of Christ (6:1–3)

If 5:14 may be thought of as being descriptive of a condition existing within the household of Christ, 6:1 may be thought of as prescriptive. This prescription, even as the preceding diagnosis, is preparatory to the warning in 6:4–8.

6:1–2. Confident that his hearers had the good sense to follow through and grow in their knowledge (see 6:9), the author continued, **Therefore leaving the principles of the doctrine of Christ** (lit., "Wherefore let us cease to speak of the first principles of Christ"; v. 1). He repeated his initial charge of 5:12, in effect negating it: "You need someone to teach you the first principles, but I hope you won't make me do it!" **Let us go on** (lit., "Let us be borne on"). This expression is used exactly as a Greek schoolmaster would use it to move his students to a new level of study. For the moment, the writer was assuming that these Hebrew Christians were ready to move on **unto perfection** ("maturity"). He marked what he considered the essential teachings that form **the foundation**

of Christian doctrine (note the follow-through of the household metaphor found in 3:2–6). "Foundation" stands in apposition to **doctrine** (v. 2). **Repentance** (v. 1) and **faith** are qualitative genitives suggestive of where these foundational principles are applied (see Mark 1:15; Acts 20:21; 1 Thess. 1:9). The foundation has, as it were, four corners: **baptisms … laying on of hands … resurrection … and … eternal judgment** (v. 2). "The doctrine of baptisms" probably refers to different baptisms with which the readers were familiar, such as Jewish baptism of proselytes, John the Baptist's baptism, and the baptism commanded by Jesus (see Matt. 28:19). The readers should have known the importance and significance of Christian baptism as opposed to the ritual cleansings of the previous dispensation. The "laying on of hands" sometimes followed baptism (see Acts 8:16–17; 19:5–6). Otherwise, laying on of hands was practiced in connection with ordaining or commissioning (see Acts 6:6; 13:3; 1 Tim. 5:22; 2 Tim. 1:6), healing the sick (see Mark 6:5; 16:18; Luke 4:40; Acts 28:8), and bestowing blessing (see Matt. 19:13–15). The reference to the "resurrection of the dead" underscores a cornerstone doctrine on which their faith rested and their hope depended (see John 5:25–29; 11:25; 1 Cor. 15; 2 Cor. 4:14). The final cornerstone is "eternal judgment." The author returned to this theme in 9:27 and 10:27 (see also 1 John 4:17). These four foundational principles would have evoked in the minds of the hearers the unique identification they had in Christ (baptism), the authority of the apostles (laying on of hands), the historical facts of the gospel (resurrection), and the eschatological certainty that one day every knee shall bow before the One into whose hands all judgment has been given (see Phil. 2:10; see John 5:22).

6:3. And this we will do, if God permit is a common expression of dependence on the will of God (see 1 Cor. 16:7). Only the Lord can open minds and hearts and bring spiritual maturity. Here, using a third-class condition, the writer stated his conviction that he would not need to go back to the formative principles of the faith; rather, he intended to continue with his appeal (see discussions on 6:1–2).

5. Warning against Falling Away (6:4–8)

In the first warning (2:1), the author advised the recipients not to allow the new word delivered "in Son" (see discussion on 1:2) to drift away from them. If they allowed that to happen, the consequence would be that, as Israel had been delivered into Babylonian slavery for a similar offense, they would again come under the tyranny of sin. In the second warning (3:7–15), the recipients were warned against unbelief, a condition likened to rebellion. The writer again employed an example from Israel's history. After having been delivered from Egypt and slavery, the Israelites had rebelled against God and against Moses, which resulted in their failure to enter into the land and rest. In doing so, they lost it all, both possession of the land and the blessings of God through the leadership of Moses. Similarly, the recipients of this epistle were in danger of not entering into the rest found in Christ and risked losing the blessings and reward of co-laboring with Christ in the work of the church.

In the third warning, the author warned the recipients against "fall[ing] away" (v. 6) and went to great length (5:11–6:2) to present that age-old idea that if one is not moving forward, one will fall back. There is no standing still. This was so important to the author that he personally took on the task of seeing that this did not happen (see 6:3). The epistle, so far, supports the idea that the recipients had reached a plateau in their faith and understanding but had fallen short of grasping the nature of the priesthood of Christ or the priesthood of the believer; this lack of understanding is hinted at in 6:18–19.

6:4–6. Interpretations of this difficult passage fall into two classes. The first approach associates it with the experience and permanence of salvation and has three major arguments.

(1) The passage refers to Christians who actually lose their salvation. The author, however, seems to teach the opposite in 6:13–20. This view is not supported by the context or the general tenor of New Testament Scripture.

(2) It is a hypothetical argument intended to warn immature Hebrew Christians (see 5:11–14)

that they needed to progress to maturity (see 6:1) or else experience divine discipline or judgment (see 6:7-8). This view is supported by the fact that each of the five warnings expresses a condition and its consequences (see 2:3; 3:14; 6:6; 10:26 and 12:25); the author included himself among his hearers (see 10:26) and was convinced that these conditions were not really true of them (see 6:9). While this view is convenient, the introduction of a hypothetical situation does not fit the established pattern of the epistle.

(3) It refers to professing Christians whose apostasy proved that their faith was not genuine (see 1 John 2:19). This view sees chapters 3-4 as a warning based on the rebellion of the Israelites in the wilderness. As Israel could not enter the Promised Land after spying out the region and tasting its fruit, so the professing Hebrew Christians would not be able to repent if they adamantly turned against the light they had received. According to this interpretation, such expressions as **enlightened ... tasted of the heavenly gift, and ... partakers of the Holy Ghost** (v. 4) indicate that such persons had come under the influence of God's covenant blessings and had professed to turn from darkness to light but were in danger of a public and final rejection of Christ, proving that they had never been regenerated. This view does not follow the pattern of the epistle or the context of the subject matter. Being willing to express such a sharp rebuke, surely the author would have identified these hypocrites. Further, if one adopts this position, Moses becomes such a person, and this is clearly refuted in chapter 11. As one progresses in the study of this epistle, it becomes more and more a tour de force to include unbelievers in its intended audience. The term used in conjunction with the phrase "partakers of the Holy Ghost," "were made," is used no less than twenty eight times in this epistle and never to indicate an ineffective or less than permanent work (1:4; 2:7, 17; 3:14; 5:5, 9; 6:4, 13, 20; 7:12, 16, 19, 21-23, 26; 9:22; 10:33; 11:3, 34).

The second approach to this text is that it is not associated with salvation (a point that the author eventually addressed; see 6:9) but rather with the believer's response to the grace of God. In this view, the passage refers to persons who are the recipients of God's grace and who, for a time, respond in some positive way(s) but who nevertheless **fall away** (v. 6). Eternal salvation is not under discussion, but when **they crucify to themselves the son of God afresh**, these persons bring upon themselves the certain consequences of rejecting Him. Saved or not, the Israelites who disobeyed never entered into God's rest, including Moses (see 4:1-11). The author was fearful that such dire consequences might befall his readers as well. History and experience are replete with examples of people who "fall away," losing the joy of their salvation and bringing judgment upon themselves and their families. Of the three arguments in the first approach, this interpretation is closest to the third view but stops short of trying to link it to the question of whether the person is actually regenerated. Obviously, if they are not, they effectively quench the convicting work of the Holy Spirit, leading to perdition. If they are regenerated, then they create a condition in which the blessings of God are effectively turned away, leading to divine chastening.

This entire passage, verses 4-6, constitutes one complete sentence, beginning with **For it is impossible** (v. 4) and concluding with **to renew them again unto repentance** (v. 6). All of the intervening conditions are to be understood in their relation to the main idea. The writer was issuing a severe warning that it is possible to cross a line beyond which a person may not return (see Romans 1 and the repeated phrase, "God gave them up"). The conditions include "once enlightened" (v. 4), "tasted of the heavenly gift," "were made partakers of the Holy Ghost," "tasted the good word of God, and the powers of the world to come" (v. 5), and then "fall away." The writer listed those gracious works of God that are experientially received, either in the convicting of the Holy Spirit or in His saving work. To crucify to themselves the Son of God afresh was akin to saying with the hateful crowd, "We will not have this man to reign over us" (Luke 19:14). For **powers of the world to come,** see Mark 10:30; 1 Timothy 6:19.

6:7-8. To reinforce the principle, the author used a short parable to graphically illustrate the warning

(see John 15:5–6; 2 Peter 2:20–22; 1 John 5:16).
Drinketh in the rain (v. 7) corresponds to the principle of Matthew 5:45: "he [God] … sendeth rain on the just and on the unjust." **Rejected** (Greek *adokimos*; "not approved," "unfit"; v. 8) and **burned** characterize the underbrush ordinarily raked and burned to clear ground for fruitful plants. In the economy of God's kingdom work, the reader should be forewarned of neglecting "the good word of God" (6:5).

6. Consequences of Falling Away under Christ (6:9–12)

6:9. But, beloved, we are persuaded better things of you … things that accompany salvation. The author had suggested the possibility that some of his readers might need to heed the warning of 6:4–8, but he was confident that God had been at work among them, his beloved brethren. Changed lives and works of love (see 6:10) indicated that many of these persons, though lacking in certain knowledge, were indeed serving and were not "slothful" (see 6:12). He was therefore "persuaded [see 2 Tim. 1:12] better things" than those depicted in 6:4–6. This persuasion is much in line with the position taken by James (see James 1:21–25), whose letter was no doubt available to them. The author's use of a parable recalling Moses' fate (6:7–8) may suggest that while faithful believers were present, the apostasy of some and the failure of many to be interested in growing in knowledge, if allowed to go on unchecked, could affect the entire group's reception of the blessings of God. An example of the Lord's view of this condition is seen in the comparison of Mary and Martha in Luke 10:38–42.

6:10. The author moved to encourage his readers, noting that **God**, being God, would not **forget [their] work and labour of love**. Specifically, he had in mind that they had **ministered to the saints** (once), **and do minister** ("still continue to minister"). In effect, he was saying to them that, having begun to serve the Lord, they had continued to do so. This evidence of their faith and positive attitude gave him great encouragement. The author's concern remained, however, that while he was able to commend some, others were not heeding or doing the word spoken.

6:11. We desire. While some were indeed following and serving the Lord, many were still babes (see 5:13) and in need of demonstrating the reality of their faith. They also needed to **shew the same diligence** in service to Christ, thus providing **the full assurance of hope** in their relationship to the Lord (see 11:1; Col. 2:2; 1 Thess. 1:5; 2 Peter 1:10). **Unto the end** assured the recipients that their new relationship with the Lord was a permanent one, thus becoming a call to persevere in their faith as an appropriate evidence of their salvation (see 3:6, 14).

6:12. The first evidence of their salvation was **That ye be not slothful, but followers of them who through faith and patience inherit the promises**. This looks back to the warning in 6:4–8 and also ahead to chapter 11. With this in mind, the writer moved to the example of Abraham. In doing so, he provided both an object lesson in entering into the promises of God and also an introduction to the new priesthood.

7. The Immutability of the New Relationship (6:13–20)

6:13. God made promise to Abraham. God's promise to Abraham that he would have many descendants was made with an oath to emphasize its unchanging character (see Gen. 22:16–18). Ordinarily, the swearing of an oath belongs to our fallen human situation, in which a man's word is not always trustworthy. God's swearing of an oath was condescension to human frailty, thus making His word, which is absolutely trustworthy, doubly dependable (see 6:18).

6:14. Saying, Surely. This verse is quoted from Genesis 22:17.

6:15. After he had patiently endured for twenty-five years (see Gen. 12:3–4; 21:5), Abraham **obtained the promise**, the birth of his son Isaac (see Gen. 17:2; 18:10; 21:5). This illustrates the "patience" recommended in 6:12.

6:18. Two immutable things refers to God's promise, which is absolutely trustworthy, and God's oath confirming that promise (see 6:17). Contrast **impossible for God to lie** with the "impossible" of 6:4–6. **We might have a strong consolation** because we look back on the fulfillment of the promise that Abraham saw only in anticipation (11:13; John 8:56). **Fled for refuge**. In the New Testament, this term is used only here and in Acts 14:6. In the Septuagint, (the Greek translation of the Old Testament), it is used of the cities of refuge (Deut. 4:42; 19:5; Josh. 20:9).

6:19. As an anchor of the soul, both sure and stedfast. Like an anchor holding a ship safely in position, our hope in Christ guarantees our safety. **Within the vail**. Whereas the ship's anchor goes down to the ocean bed, the Christian's anchor goes up into the true, heavenly sanctuary, where he is moored to God Himself.

6:20. Forerunner (Greek, *prodromos*; "spy," "scout") recalls the two spies of Kadesh Barnea who gave the good report versus those who returned with the discouraging word that led to the subsequent judgment and wilderness wandering (see Num. 13 and 14). But the author had something far more significant in mind. **A high priest for ever after the order of Melchisedec**. Like Melchizedek, Christ the High Priest stands alone and in contrast to the passing away of the Aaronic order. His priesthood is **for ever**. This grand theme is further developed in chapter 7.

8. Basis for the New Relationship: Jesus' Superior Priesthood (chap. 7)

7:1. Melchisedec has already been noted as representative of the order of priesthood to which Christ belongs (see 5:6, 10; Gen. 14:18–20 and discussions). The Melchizedek priesthood is older and of a higher order than the Aaronic priesthood; it is no wonder the author had alerted his hearers to the difficulty of his subject matter (see 5:11). To understand this, it is important to go back to the original **king … priest**. Of particular significance is that Melchizedek held both offices in which he prefigured Christ. **Salem**. Jerusalem (see discussion on Gen. 14:18). **The most high God** is the name by which Abram was first introduced "by name" to the

God who called him from his father's house (see Gen. 12:1ff. and 14:18ff.). It is difficult to miss the parallel with these distant descendants of Abraham who were being called to leave their long-held traditions to follow One who stands before and above Melchizedek. **Who met Abraham** is significant since the event antedated Aaron and involved Aaron's ancestor (see also John 8:56–58). A very long parenthesis is contained between **who** and "abideth" (7:3), in which the author spelled out the significance of this enigmatic figure from the life of Abraham.

7:2. Abraham gave a tenth. In this ancient context, it would hardly be noteworthy that one would dedicate a tenth of the spoils to God (or the local pagan deity), but in this case, it was given to "the most high God" (7:1) and to the priest who stood in a superior role to father Abraham, the spiritual and/or physical progenitor of all to whom this epistle is addressed. **King of righteousness … King of peace** are messianic titles (see Isa. 9:6–7; Jer. 23:5–6; 33:15–16).

7:3. Without father … nor end of life (*apatōr* and *amētōr* are alliterated in the original. The first term was apparently coined by the author, as it is found nowhere else in ancient literature. Used here, the terms punctuate that this figure was "without genealogy"). Genesis 14:18–20, contrary to the practice elsewhere in the early chapters of Genesis, does not mention Melchizedek's parentage and children or his birth and death. That he was a real, historical figure is clear, but the author of Hebrews (in accordance with Jewish interpretation) used Scripture's silence about his genealogy to portray him as a prefiguration of Christ. Melchizedek's priesthood anticipated Christ's eternal existence and His unending priesthood. Some believe Melchizedek's appearance to Abraham was a manifestation of Christ before His incarnation, but the comparison **like unto the Son of God** argues against such an interpretation.

7:4. Consider how great this man was. The one who collects a tithe is greater than the one who pays it, and "the less is blessed of the better" (7:7). In both ways, Melchizedek was greater than Abraham.

7:5–7. The sons of Levi … take tithes … of their brethren (v. 5). In the case of the Levitical priesthood, the principle of "taking tithes" was rooted in the **commandment** to do so. Nothing in this requirement suggests that the priests are somehow "superior" to those from whom they receive tithes. In the case of **he whose descent is not counted** (i.e., Melchizedek; v. 6), however, it is different. In this case, it was he who **blessed him that had the promises** (i.e., Abraham). Because of this blessing, the writer concluded, **without all contradiction the less is blessed of the better** (v. 7). It is evident that Abraham (and his "promises," including his progeny; see Gen. 12:3, 7; 13:14; 15:5; 17:5; 22:16 – 18) was inferior to this "priest of the most high God" (7:1).

7:8 – 10. With respect to the one who received tithes from Abraham, **it is witnessed** (present passive participle) **that he liveth** (v. 8), while **here men that die receive tithes**. The writer contrasted the "here" of the Levitical system with the **there** of Melchizedek. Again, Melchizedek is seen as greater. In 7:7, it was said that the "better" blessed the "less." The writer returned to both of these arguments in 7:16. The author furthered the argument by adding, **And as I may so say** (lit., "So to say"; v. 9), **Levi ... payed tithes** (lit., "has been tithed") **in Abraham**. Levi was present, as it were, when Abraham paid tithes to Melchizedek because he was in Abraham's **loins** (v. 10). While Levi had yet to be born, he was nevertheless represented in his forefather.

7:11 – 14. The point of these verses is that the Levitical priesthood brought with it all the regulations of the Mosaic law. So if one turns to Christ and His priesthood, he must reject the Levitical priesthood and its law, for the law disqualifies Jesus from becoming its priest, since He is from the invalid tribe of Judah.

7:11. Under it (the Levitical priesthood) **the people received the law.** The law of Moses and the priesthood went together. All the people, without exception, were sinners subject to the law's condemnation and thus were in need of a priestly system to mediate between them and God. **After the order of Melchisedec, and not ... after the order of Aaron** implies that the Aaronic (or Levitical) priesthood was imperfect, but Melchizedek's was perfect. The announcement of the coming one who would be "a

priest for ever" (Ps. 110:4) was written midway in the history of the Levitical priesthood, which could only mean that the existing system was to give way to something better.

7:16 – 17. Not after the law of a carnal commandment (v. 16) refers to a law involving physical requirements — the tribe of Levi (see 7:5). In the law of Moses, the priestly function was restricted to the tribe of Levi (see Deut. 18:1), but Jesus came from the nonpriestly tribe of Judah (see 7:14 – 15). **For he testifieth** (lit., "it is witnessed"; v. 17) to **the power of an endless life** (v. 16). According to Psalm 110:4, the priest in the order of Melchizedek is "a priest for ever."

7:18. A disannulling of the commandment ... for the weakness and unprofitableness. The law is holy and good (see Rom. 7:12), but it is not able to make right those who sin by breaking it, nor can it give the power necessary to fulfill its demands (see 7:19).

7:19. The law was only preparatory (see Gal. 3:23 – 25) and brought nothing to fulfillment (see Matt. 5:17). **A better hope.** The new covenant is better because it assures us of complete redemption and brings us into the very presence of God (see discussion on Col. 1:5).

7:20 – 21. No divine **oath** was associated with the establishment of the Levitical priesthood. The priesthood pledged in Psalm 110 is superior because it was divinely affirmed with an oath.

7:22. Jesus [was] made a surety (lit., "pledge") **of a better testament**, the new covenant (see chaps. 8 – 10). This thought introduces "covenant" for the first time in the book. Here the high priest, Jesus, is not only the mediator but also the guarantee. This, as we shall see, is due not only to the nature of the covenant but, more important, to the nature of the Priest and His priesthood (see 7:23 – 28).

7:23. And they truly were many priests. The writer sets up a point of contrast: "they" as opposed to "this man" (7:24). **Not suffered to continue by reason of death.** The priesthood of Christ is superior to that of Levitical priests because they die, but Jesus "continueth ever" (7:24).

7:24 – 26. But ... he ... hath an unchangeable priesthood (v. 24). This sentence is difficult but seems to contrast Jesus (see 7:22) with these (mortal) priests (see 7:23) in that, like Melchizedek, He lives forever, and thus His priesthood abides unchanged from the day He was elevated to this position. **To the uttermost** (v. 25) may include the ideas of completeness and permanence. Jesus is a perfect High Priest forever, so He is able to save completely and for all time. He **ever liveth to make intercession**. His people will never be without a priestly representative (see John 17; 1 John 2:1). **Such** (v. 26) is placed here for emphasis (as in 2:10) and links Jesus to Melchizedek in His ministry as **high priest**, one who meets our need for salvation from sin and its consequences. **Separate from sinners** (lit., "separated from sinners") does not contradict 2 Corinthians 5:21: "For he hath made him to be sin for us, who knew no sin; that we might be made the righteousness of God in him." Rather, it seems to make a point reiterated in 9:28. In His present state of exaltation in heaven, Christ is set apart from the sinful world and is **made higher than the heavens**.

7:27. Daily refers to the endless repetition of sacrifices throughout the year (see Exod. 29:36–42) and is evidence that these sacrifices never effectively and finally dealt with sin. **First for his own sins**. Christ's priesthood is superior because He has no personal sins for which sacrifice must be made. **This he did once** is a key concept in Hebrews (see 9:12, 26; 10:2, 10). The Levitical priests had to bring daily offerings to the Lord, whereas Jesus sacrificed Himself once for all. **Offered up himself**. Levitical priests offered up only animals; our High Priest offered Himself, the perfect substitute, Man for man.

7:28. Men ... which have infirmity contrasts once again with **the Son, who is consecrated for evermore**. Human agents are limited in this task because (1) they are mortal and therefore impermanent (see 7:23); (2) they are sinful (see 7:27); and (3) they can offer only animals, which can never provide a genuine substitute for mankind, made in the image of God (see Gen. 1:26–28 and discussions). It is with an **oath** (see Ps. 110:4) that God "consecrated [the Son] for evermore." Christ was made perfect in that He faced temptation without succumbing to

sin (see discussions on 2:10; 5:8–10). Instead, He perfectly obeyed the Father, thereby establishing a perfection that is eternal.

D. The Argument for a Superior Redemption (chaps. 8–10)

1. A Superior Covenant from a Superior High Priest (8:1–13)

8:1. The argument of this section grows out of an exposition of Jeremiah 31:31–34, demonstrating that Christ is the mediator of "a better testament" (7:22, see 8:6–13). The opening salvo, however, **Now ... this is the sum**, indicates that the function of what follows is directly related to what has just been said. It could be paraphrased, "In conclusion, let me come to my main point." The point, of course, is that the new covenant is coterminous with the **high priest** upon whose work it rests, **who is set on the right hand of the throne of the Majesty in the heavens**. The allusion, once again, is to Psalm 110:1: "The LORD said unto my Lord, Sit thou at my right hand, until I make thine enemies thy footstool" (see 1:3 and discussion). This priest is also King. He is, after all, a priest after the order of Melchizedek, who was both a priest and a king.

8:2. Reference to **the true tabernacle** is in contrast to the tabernacle that Moses erected, which was an imperfect and impermanent copy of the heavenly tabernacle (see 8:5; 3:5–6). "True" signifies "original." The heavenly sanctuary, **which the Lord pitched, and not man**, corresponds to the Most Holy Place, the innermost sanctuary in Moses' tabernacle, into which the high priest briefly entered with the blood of atonement once a year (see Lev. 16:13–15, 34). In the heavenly sanctuary, however, our great High Priest dwells eternally as our intercessor (see 7:25). The author enlarged on these ideas in chapters 9–10.

8:3. It is important that the work of **every high priest** include the offering of **gifts and sacrifices** (see discussion on 5:1) and **that this man have somewhat also to offer**. The relationship of Christ to the Old Testament priesthood is neither equivocal nor univocal. That is to say, it is neither an entirely different work, nor is it entirely the same; points of similarity and points of superiority (see 8:6) can be observed. Here the emphasis is on the points of similarity: like them, Christ must offer "gifts and sacrifices."

8:4. He should not be a priest. By His human birth, Jesus belonged to the tribe of Judah, which was not the priestly tribe (see 7:12–14). **There are priests that offer gifts** refers to members of the tribe of Levi. The present tense of the verb "offer," here and elsewhere in Hebrews, indicates that the temple in Jerusalem was still standing. This letter, therefore, must have been written prior to the temple's destruction in AD 70 (see Introduction: "Date").

8:5. The example and shadow of heavenly things. The heavenly reality is the sanctuary of God's presence, into which Christ our High Priest entered with His own blood (see 9:11–12). **See ... that thou ... make all things according to the pattern shewed to thee in the mount** is a quotation from the instruction given in Exodus 25:40 concerning the Old Testament tabernacle. Both the tabernacle and its ministry were intended to illustrate symbolically the only way in which sinners may approach a holy God and find forgiveness. Christ's mediatorial work is not engaged here on earth but in heaven, where the reality abides; the earthly ministrations of the Levitical priests involved only "types" and "shadows."

8:6. But now indicates a contrast with the old priestly order. **He** (Jesus) **is the mediator of a better covenant** (see 7:12, 22; 9:15; 10:1–18; 12:24; 1 Tim. 2:5). The new covenant (see 8:8–12; Jer. 31:31–34) that Jesus mediates is superior to the covenant that God made through Moses at Sinai (see Exod. 24:7–8). It is **established upon better promises** (see 8:10–12).

8:7. If that first covenant had been faultless. The line of argument here is similar to that in 7:11, where the Levitical priestly order was shown to be inferior because it was replaced by the order of Melchizedek. Similarly, if the Mosaic covenant were without defect, there would have been no need to replace it with a new one. Nothing was essentially "wrong" with the Mosaic covenant, but it was unable to provide complete and permanent salvation from sin and its consequences (see discussion on 7:18).

8:8–12. This section is an extended quotation from Jeremiah 31:31–34. While the writer clearly applied this promise to his readers, it is important to note that, as with the old covenant, this **new covenant** (v. 8) is given to **the house of Israel and ... Juda.** The quotation contains a prophetic announcement and description of the new covenant, to be different from the Mosaic covenant, which was made when God **took ... them out of ... Egypt** (v. 9). That the author repeated parts of this passage in 10:16–17 reveals its importance to him (see also 4:8; 7:11; 8:4). What is evident is that the superior promises of the new covenant, which look to a future that will be enjoyed by God's chosen, are already appropriated by God's people today. The superior benefits are: (1) God's laws become inner principles (v. 10a) that enable His people to delight in doing His will (see Ezek. 36:26–27; Rom. 8:2–4); (2) God and His people have intimate fellowship (v. 10b); (3) sinful ignorance of God is removed forever (v. 11); and (4) forgiveness of sins is an everlasting reality (v. 12).

8:13. In that he saith, A new covenant (lit., "When he says, 'New'"). In the introduction of the new covenant, the **first** is made **old.** The contrast intended is temporal, not pejorative. It is not to say that the old was somehow bad but rather that it **decayeth.** As good as the first covenant with Moses was, it was never intended to be permanent. To return to the old system would be to return to what is no longer valid or effective. We know that soon after these words were penned, the temple of the old system would **vanish away** (Greek, *aphanismos*; "disappear") with the destruction of Jerusalem in AD 70. Yet this is not likely the intended meaning. Rather, the point is similar to that which Jesus said to the woman at the well concerning "the hour ... when the true worshippers shall worship ... in spirit and in truth" (John 4:23).

2. Superior Access Provided by a Superior Sacrifice (9:1–10:18)

a. The Contrast of the Old and the New (9:1–14)

9:1–2. The first covenant had ... a worldly sanctuary (v. 1). There is an earthly tabernacle and a heavenly one. "Worldly" translates *kosmikos,* "earthly." First, **there was a tabernacle made** (v. 2) under Moses. The writer undoubtedly understood that the temple of his day perpetuated the rituals and sacrifices of the original tabernacle, yet in order not to be misunderstood on this point, he went all the way back to the original to let the reader know that he was speaking of the entire system that emanated from the divine instruction given to Moses and still perpetuated. Just as the priesthood of Christ and His royal appointment exploded the "old wineskins" of the Mosaic covenant and the Aaronic priesthood, so His sacrificial work rendered the wondrous treasures of the old tabernacle as mere shadows (see 8:5), and its sacrifices and offerings as utterly inadequate.

The candlestick (v. 2) was made of hammered gold and placed at the south side of the Holy Place (see Exod. 40:24). It had seven lamps, which were kept burning every night (see Exod. 25:31–40). **The table** was made of acacia wood overlaid with gold and stood on the north side of the Holy Place (see Exod. 40:22). On it were twelve loaves of **shewbread**, arranged in two rows of six (see Lev. 24:5–6).

9:3. At the far end of the Holy Place was a curtain, or **vail**, dividing it from another tent that was known as **the holiest of all** (in the Hebrew idiom, "the Holy of Holies"). It was here that the famed Shekinah glory of God was visible, suspended above the mercy seat of the ark between the two seraphim (see 9:5).

9:4. Which had (Greek, *echō*; "to have," "joined to"). Although the altar of incense stood in the Holy Place, the author described it as belonging to the Most Holy Place. His purpose was to show its close relationship to the inner sanctuary and **the ark of the covenant**, a chest made of acacia wood, overlaid inside and out with gold (see Exod. 25:10–16; 40:5; 1 Kings 6:22). **The golden censer**. The term translated "censer" here refers to a vessel used for burning incense. So it can describe either the shovel (censer) used for carrying the coals or the altar on which the coals were placed. Since the golden altar of incense is otherwise not referred to in this enumeration of the tabernacle furniture, it seems best to understand this verse as referring to that altar. On the Day of

Atonement, the high priest took incense from this altar, along with the blood of the sin offering, into the Most Holy Place (see Lev. 16:12–14). **Wherein** (lit., "in which"; i.e., inside the ark) was to be found **manna** that had never spoiled (see Exod. 16:33–34), **Aaron's rod**, which miraculously **budded** to confirm his priesthood when it was challenged (see Num. 17:8–10), and **the tables of the covenant** (the tablets containing the Ten Commandments) that Moses had brought down from the mountain (Exod. 32:15).

9:5. Cherubims of glory. Two winged figures made of pure gold, of one piece with the atonement cover, **the mercy seat**, and standing at either end of it. Between them, the glory of God's presence appeared (see Exod. 25:17–22; Lev. 16:2; Num. 7:89). This is the only place in the New Testament where this special order of angels is mentioned. They are associated with God's majesty, glory, and holiness. The mercy seat, fitting exactly over the top of the ark of the covenant, was a slab of pure gold, on which the high priest sprinkled the blood of the sin offering on the Day of Atonement (see Lev. 16:14–15). **Of which we cannot now speak**. The writer did not intend at this point to speak of these items in detail. This is an important clue that his intent was not to exegete the significance of each of these "types" (see 9:8–9) but to move quickly to its relation to the antitype, that is, Christ (see 9:11).

9:6–7. The priests went always (v. 6). The author highlighted two weaknesses of the old system. The first is the continuous nature of the priests' **service of God**. It was never finished because it was inadequate to put away sin forever (see 10:12–18). Even the sacrifice of the atonement had to be repeated **once every year** (v. 7), on the Day of Atonement (Yom Kippur), the tenth day of the seventh month (see Lev. 16:29, 34; for a description of its ritual, see Leviticus 16). The second weakness of the old system has to with the priesthood itself. **The high priest … offered for himself, and for … the people** (compare 9:25) anticipates the argument of chapter 10. What could not be accomplished by the blood of bulls and goats, "this man" (7:24) would accomplish with the offering of Himself and would forever sit down "on the right hand of God" (10:12), denoting that the work was finished by this "one offering" (10:14).

9:8. The Holy Ghost this signifying. When the Holy Spirit gave these instructions, the very nature of the work indicated that the way to full union with God in **the holiest of all** was yet to be revealed. This would be true as long **as the first tabernacle was yet standing** (lit., "while the first tent still remains in force"). We are reminded again and again that as long as the Mosaic system with its imperfect priesthood and impermanent sacrifices remain in force (8:7 – 8, 13), the work is unfinished.

9:9. Which was a figure. The Mosaic tabernacle, though superseded, still provided instruction through its typical (symbolic) significance and was a reminder that returning to the old order was useless, since it could not deal effectively with sin. **Gifts and sacrifices** (see 5:1)**, that could not make ... perfect**. The sacrificial system of the Old Testament dealt only with externals (see 9:10) and was inadequate to cleanse **the conscience**. This line of thinking calls to mind the conflict Paul described in Romans 7, which, as here, was answered with, "For what the law could not do, in that it was weak through the flesh, God sending his own Son in the likeness of sinful flesh, and for sin, condemned sin in the flesh" (Rom. 8:3).

9:10. The time of reformation (Greek, *diorthōsis*; "make straight," "restore to natural condition"). The writer did not imagine something entirely new but the reshaping of what had become distorted, returning it to its natural and proper condition. The new covenant, with its new priesthood, new sanctuary, and new sacrifice will bring about the ultimate reconciliation of sinful humanity with a holy God. This embraces all that was lost in Adam but anticipates a result that surpasses even his original condition of innocence (see 9:24 – 28).

9:11 – 12. These verses constitute one complete sentence in the Greek text. The **more perfect tabernacle** (v. 11) is said to be **not of this building** (Greek, *ktisis*; "creation"). It was not an earthly tabernacle but the heavenly sanctuary of God's presence (9:24;

8:2). **Neither by the blood of goats and calves** (v. 12) anticipates **but by his own blood**. The blood that Christ the High Priest sprinkled on the mercy seat was His own, making Him at once both priest and offering. **He entered in once**. Christ's work need not be repeated year after year, as did that of the Levitical high priests. His sacrifice was perfect; it was completely effective and did not need to be repeated. Through His sacrifice, Christ **obtained** (lit., "He alone secured") **eternal redemption for us**. Redemption signifies release through payment of the ransom price (see John 8:36; Rom. 6:14; Gal. 3:13).

9:13 – 14. Just as the writer contrasted the offerings of the earthly tabernacle with those of the heavenly tabernacle in 9:11 – 12, here he contrasted the results of those offerings. **The blood of bulls and of goats** (v. 13) refers to sacrifices on the Day of Atonement. As prescribed in Numbers 19, **the ashes of a heifer** were for those who had become ceremonially unclean as a result of contact with a corpse. **The purifying of the flesh**. Such sprinkling, since it was only external, could not make a person inwardly pure. **How much more** (v. 14). If the blood of animals was adequate for "the purifying of the flesh," imagine what **the blood of Christ** accomplished when, **through the eternal Spirit**, He **offered himself**. This difficult text likely refers to the agency of the Holy Spirit, who is said to have led Christ (see Matt. 4:1) during the time of His sojourn here on earth. His leading eventually took Christ to the cross, to which He submitted obediently (see Phil. 2:8). An alternative interpretation would suggest that this passage refers to the divine nature of the God-man. That is, the agent of the sacrifice was His divine nature, and the sacrifice itself was His human nature. This view must be rejected, however, since it assumes the heretical notion that the two natures of Christ can be separated. For the death of Christ to be possible, He had to be human. For His death to have infinite value, He had to be divine. How much more will this sacrifice of the perfect Lamb of God, who is **without spot ... purge your conscience** (see 10:22)? The author listed two results, the first negative, and the second positive: (1) the conscience is freed **from**

dead works, and (2) it is freed to serve the living God (see 1 Thess. 1:9).

b. The Sacrifice of Christ Was Once for All (9:15–28)

9:15. And is used here to connect what follows with what has preceded. For this cause he is the mediator (Greek, *mesitēs*; "one who intervenes to make peace or ratify a covenant"; see 12:24; 1 Tim 2:5). Because of the superiority of Christ's person and work, the writer continued. The argument looks back to the original proposition established in 8:6 that "he obtained a more excellent ministry, by how much also he is [not 'becomes'] the mediator of a better covenant." On the new testament, see 7:22; 8:6, 13. On for the redemption of the transgressions, see Mark 10:45. By shedding His blood, Christ paid the necessary price to set humankind free from the sins committed under the first covenant, that is, violations of Mosaic law. The promise of eternal inheritance is defined in 8:8–12, a passage quoted from Jeremiah 31:31–34. On the basis of Christ's atoning death, this inheritance has become real for those who are called by God (see Rom. 8:28).

9:16–17. Testament … death (v. 16). In these verses, "testament" is used in the sense of a last will and testament. In 9:18, "testament" returns to the concept of covenant as opposed to the idea of a will. Beneficiaries have no claim on the benefits assigned to them in a will until the death of the testator has been proven (v. 17). Since Christ's death has been duly attested, "the promise of eternal inheritance" (9:15) is available to His beneficiaries.

9:18–22. The double negative neither … without blood (v. 18) sounds awkward in English but is used in Greek for emphasis. The first testament illustrates the point, for it too was ratified with blood—the death of the calves from which Moses took blood to seal the old covenant. In fact, in the first covenant, almost all things are by the law purged with blood (v. 22; see Exod. 24:4–8; Lev. 8:10, 19, 30).

9:23–26. It was therefore necessary (v. 23) indicates the conclusion of the discussion. Inasmuch as the law requires "almost all things [to be] purged with blood" (9:22), it is necessary to reckon this with the patterns (lit., "copy," "figure," "imitation") of things in the heavens (see 8:5). Whereas it was necessary for the earthly sanctuary to be purified with animal sacrifices, it was necessary for the heavenly sanctuary to be purified with the better sacrifices of Christ Himself. The plural here is a Hebraism and is used for emphasis, not to suggest that other sacrifices are in mind. Rather, as the author pointed out in 9:28, the finality of this sacrifice "once offered" sets it apart from all other sacrifices. Christ the High Priest did not go into the earthly tabernacle (the antitype of the true tabernacle) but into heaven itself, now to appear in the presence of God (v. 24; see 7:25; 1 John 2:1). His sacrifice was not as that of an Old Testament high priest, who offered first "for himself" (9:7); rather, Christ's sacrifice was for us. His work was substitutionary in character. It was never necessary that Christ suffer for sin, but He did this on our behalf to be the propitiation for our sins. He did not need to offer himself often, as the high priest entereth … every year (v. 25), but only now once in the end of the world (lit., "the consummation of the age," v. 26; see 1:2; see 1 Peter 1:20). Christ's coming ushered in the "last days" (1:2).

9:27–28. The chapter ends with an analogy. And as it is appointed … once to die, but after this the judgment (v. 27). As in the natural order, man dies once (as a consequence of sin; see Rom. 5:12), so Christ died once (v. 28) as the perfect sacrifice for sin. And as man faces judgment after death, so Christ will appear again after His death, bringing salvation from sin and its judgment. Look for him. As the Israelites waited for the high priest while he was in the Most Holy Place on the Day of Atonement (see 2 Tim. 4:8; Titus 2:13), so too we look for Christ to appear the second time without sin unto salvation. When He reemerges from behind the veil and we see Him in His glory, it will not be for "sin" but for "judgment" (see Rom. 8:29–30; Phil. 3:20–21; 1 John 3:2–3).

c. The Sacrifice of Christ Was Voluntary (10:1–10)

The biblical background for this chapter is Psalm 40, especially verses 6–8. The divine plan was already in place long before God became incarnate in Jesus of Nazareth. And the Holy Spirit, through the psalmist, had already expressed the attitude of Jesus' heart: "I delight to do thy will, O my God" (Ps. 40:8).

10:1–3. The chapter opens with the author recalling the argument of the previous section concerning the relationship between the perpetual sacrifices of the old system, which was only **a shadow of good things to come** (v. 1), and the once-for-all sacrifice of Christ. The offerings of **the law** served only to remind **the comers thereunto** (lit., "those who approach") that their sin remained. "The law" alludes to the Levitical priesthood, which was closely linked to the law under the Mosaic system (see 7:11). The sacrifices prescribed by the law prefigured Christ's ultimate sacrifice. Their repetition **year by year** bore testimony that the perfect, sin-removing sacrifice had not yet been offered. We know this to be so because if it were otherwise, **the worshippers once purged** (Greek, *hapax kekatharismenous*; i.e., if they had been "cleansed once for all") **should have had no more conscience of sins** (v. 2). The opposite was true, however; again and again, **every year** (v. 3), they were reminded that their sin remained to be dealt with.

10:4. The sacrifices of the old system needed to be repeated every year because **it is not possible that the blood of bulls and of goats should take away sins**. An animal cannot possibly be a completely adequate substitute for a human being, who is made in God's image.

10:5. The different terms used for Levitical sacrifices represent four of the five types of offerings prescribed by the Mosaic law (see Leviticus 1–7), namely, peace, grain ("meat"), burnt, and sin offerings. **When he cometh into the world** (v. 5). The writer contemplated a conversation between God the Father and God the Son at the moment of His incarnation. **He saith**. The words of this psalm of David (Ps. 40:6–8) express Christ's obedient submission to the Father in coming to earth. The Mosaic sacrifices were thus replaced by submissive obedience to the will of God (see 10:7; see also Jesus' instruction to His disciples on prayer, "Thy will be done," Matt.

6:10). He would have those who follow Him to have the same attitude (see Phil. 2:5–11). **A body hast thou prepared me**. The writer followed the Septuagint translation of Psalm 40:6, where *sōma*, "body," replaces *ōtia*, "ears." Since it is the ears through which one hears God's will, the sense remains the same. In His earthly session, Jesus understood and carried out the will of His Father. His "body" was the instrument through which their plan was carried out.

10:6–7. Thou hast had no pleasure (v. 6). The Levitical offerings were only preparatory and temporary, looking forward to the one perfect and final offering of the incarnate Son of God. When it was clear that God could not be satisfied with such offerings, **Then** (v. 7) the Son declared, **Lo, I come**, expressing His submission to the Father's will. **In the volume** (Greek, *kephalidi*; "head," "roll") is used only here in the New Testament but is also used in the papyri. Here it is used to underscore that what Christ came to do was predicted in the Scriptures. **To do thy will**. The will of the Father was the Son's consuming concern (see Luke 22:42; John 4:34).

10:8–10. With **Above** (v. 8), the author called attention to the text he quoted in 10:5–6. What follows is his exegesis of Psalm 40, with special reference to his subject. Although God gave instructions for the animal sacrifices, He took no **pleasure** in them. For that reason, **He taketh away the first** (the animal sacrifices), **that** (lit., "in order that") **he may establish the second** (i.e., doing God's will; v. 9). His perfect sacrifice, offered in complete submission, supersedes and therefore replaces all previous sacrifices. **Sanctified** (v. 10). Through this means, believers are made holy, set apart in consecration to God, and experience the process of continuing sanctification (see "are sanctified," 10:14; see also 1 Cor. 1:2).

d. The Sacrifice of Christ Was Adequate (10:11–18)

10:11–14. Here the argument turns on two points. The first has to do with the ministry of Christ, which answers to the daily ministry of the Old Testament priesthood. The second point demonstrates the superiority of His ministry to that which it replaced. The author made his argument with a series of contrasts: **standeth** (v. 11), **daily ministering**, and **never take away sins** contrast with **sat down** (v. 12), **one sacrifice**, and **expecting** (v. 13). The work of the Old Testament priest was never done; he stood because there was never time to sit down. He offered **the same sacrifices** (v. 11) because these sacrifices were unable to accomplish what they signified (see Ps. 40:7–9). They could not remove sin and thus had to be offered over and over again. By contrast, **this man** (v. 12) entered only once, after which He **sat down on the right hand of God** (see discussions on 1:3, 13). Once again, the writer drew from Psalm 110:1 to contrast the work of the Levitical priests, which was never done (v. 11), to the finished work of Christ. His **one offering** (v. 14), or sacrifice, made atonement for the sins of all time, making any further sacrifice unnecessary. **Henceforth expecting** (lit., "for the future"; v. 13). All that awaits is that **his enemies be made his footstool** (another allusion to Ps. 110:1; see also John 16:33; 1 Cor. 15:24–28). Thus, by "one offering," He finished the work and has **perfected for ever them that are sanctified.**

10:15–18. The Holy Ghost ... had said (v. 15). The two quotations included in these verses are from Jeremiah 31:31–34 (also cited in 8:8–12). Using Scripture to interpret Scripture, the writer employed this text again to underscore his interpretation of Psalm 40:7–9. The new covenant guarantees that the Lord will conform believers' hearts to His (v. 16, Ps. 40:8); sins will be effectively and completely forgiven (v. 17), and no additional sacrifice for sins is needed (v. 18). Noteworthy here is the writer's recognition that the Holy Spirit is considered to have uttered the prophecy of Jeremiah (see 2 Tim. 3:16).

3. Superior Opportunities in a New and Living Way (10:19–25)

10:19. Another section of practical application and exhortation begins here (see 2:1–4) This is coupled with a second argument concerning the superior priesthood of Christ (the first is 8:1–6). **Boldness.** Since many are tempted to quit and abandon Christ, this term is a recurrent theme throughout the letter (sometimes translated "confidence"; see

3:6; 4:16; 10:35). **To enter into the holiest.** The way into the sanctuary of God's presence was closed to the people under the former covenant because the blood of animal sacrifices could never completely make atonement for their sins. Now, however, believers can come to the throne of grace because the perfect Priest has offered the perfect sacrifice, atoning for sin once for all.

10:20. By a new (Greek, *prosphatos*; "lately slaughtered," "freshly killed") **and living way.** By His death and resurrection, Jesus **consecrated** (lit., "dedicated") a new covenant (see 8:13). **Through the vail, that is to say, his flesh** (see John 1:18; 14:9). When Jesus died, the veil separating the Holy Place from the Most Holy Place was "rent in twain from the top to the bottom" (Matt. 27:51; Mark 15:38; Luke 23:45). The curtain symbolizes the body of Christ in terms of suffering; like the curtain, His body was torn to open the way into the divine presence. With a touch of irony, the author wrote of the veil of the old covenant as that which concealed the presence (because it remained whole); now the veil opens the way to the presence of God (because it was "broken," 1 Cor. 11:24).

10:21–25. This entire section consists of one carefully crafted sentence in the original. **And having a high priest over the house of God** (v. 21). The reality of this new "high priest" (see 4:14–7:28) who opened the way for direct access to the living God and who stands in the very house ("habitation") of God evoked three exhortations from the author.

(1) **Let us draw near** (v. 22). Four conditions are given for drawing near to God: (a) **A true heart**, or undivided allegiance in the inner being. (b) **In full assurance of faith** (Greek, *plērophoria*; "most certain confidence"). Faith trusts implicitly in the word and work of Christ, enabling the believer to stand in the presence of absolute holiness (see Rom. 5:1). (c) **Hearts sprinkled from an evil conscience**, or total freedom from guilt, based on the once-for-all sacrifice of Christ. (d) **Bodies washed with pure water.** The imagery here calls to mind Paul's words in Titus 3:5: "according to his mercy he saved us, by the washing of regeneration, and renewing of the Holy Ghost" (see

also Exod. 30:19–21; Lev. 8:6; see also Ezek. 36:25, where a similar expression is used figuratively for the cleansing resulting from the new covenant). Of course, the context here is focusing on the "interior" rather than the "exterior" (see 8:10; 9:9–14; 10:2, 16).

(2) **Let us hold fast the profession of our hope** (see 6:18–20) **without wavering** (lit., "not leaning"; v. 23). The author called his hearers to stand with Christ without doubt or hesitation. Some of them were tempted to give up the struggle and turn back to a form of Judaism. **He is faithful that promised** looks ahead to the argument in 10:26–12:3 (see also 6:13; 8:6; 2 Tim. 2:13).

(3) **Let us consider one another to provoke** (Greek, *paroxysmos*; "to incite") **unto love and to good works** (v. 24). "Provoke" can be used in a negative sense (see, e.g., Acts 15:39), but here it is used in a good sense, "to incite." Paul did this in his exhortation to the Corinthians, inciting them to follow the example of the Macedonians (see 2 Cor. 8:1–7).

Reinforcing his third exhortation, the writer added, **Not forsaking the assembling of ourselves together** (v. 25). The Greek word translated "forsaking" speaks of desertion and abandonment (see Matt. 27:46; 2 Cor. 4:9; 2 Tim. 4:10, 16). This introduces the author's fourth warning (10:26–31), concerning those who were tempted to abandon the faith. "The assembling of ourselves together" could refer to "our gathering together unto him" (as the same phrase is translated in 2 Thess. 2:1) at Christ's coming. This would fit well with **the day approaching**, the day of the Lord's return and judgment (see 1 Cor. 3:13; see 1 Thess. 5:2, 4; 2 Thess. 1:10; 2:2; 2 Peter 3:10). The writer considered Christ's return to be close at hand (see Rom. 13:12). Or it could refer to the regular gatherings of believers for worship. Most commentators prefer this interpretation since it makes the most sense of the contrary expression, **as the manner of some is.** It would seem that many of their number had already made a "habit" of staying away from their services, perhaps for fear of intimidation (see 10:33). Such neglect, it would seem, was a symptom of a more serious lapse in their faith, leading to willful sinning (see 10:26).

4. Warning against Willful Sinning (10:26–31)

10:26–27. The author gave the warning itself first, beginning with the conjunction **For** (v. 26). That these verses were a warning to persons ("some," 10:25) deserting the Christian assembly is apparent (see discussions on 6:4–8, where the same spiritual condition is discussed). **If we sin wilfully** (Greek, *hekousiōs*; "voluntarily"). As opposed to sins of ignorance or weakness, this involves deliberate disobedience. This is the sin of apostasy (see 10:29; discussion on 5:2). The Old Testament background is Numbers 15:27–31. **After that we have received** (lit., "after receiving"; see John 1:12) **the knowledge** (Greek, *epignōsis*; "precise knowledge"; see 6:4) **of the truth.** The warning entails a situation in which there is full culpability on the part of the sinner. **There remaineth no more** (lit., "there is no longer left behind any more") **sacrifice for sins.** In the Old Testament, there was no offering for "presumptuous" sin (Num. 15:30–31). It is perhaps not inconsequential that the context of the instruction regarding this sin is followed by a reference to the Sabbath-breaker who was stoned for his sin (see Num. 15:32–36). The writer already established that only one sacrifice could put away sin (10:1–18). To reject Christ's sacrifice is to reject the *only* sacrifice; there is no other (see 12:22–24). What else is there but **fearful looking for** ("dreadful expectation"; see 10:13) **of judgment and fiery indignation** (v. 27; for fierceness of the Lord's fire, see Isa. 26:11; Zeph. 1:18; Ps. 79:5; 2 Thess. 1:6–9).

10:28. He that despised Moses' law died without mercy. The consequences of willfulness under the old system are noted. The term *atheteo* ("set aside," "disregard," "thwart," "make void") speaks of an abandonment of the covenant; one who did so was an apostate (see Num. 35:30; Deut. 17:2–7; 19:15; compare Josh. 24:22) and was put to death on the basis of **two or three witnesses** (see Deut. 17:6; compare 2 Cor. 1:3).

10:29. Of how much sorer punishment, suppose ye…? As the writer turned to the consequences of willfulness under Christ, he underscored the magnitude of such an offense against Christ with *posō* *dokeite cheironos*, "How much worse do you imagine?" Those who commit such a sin do violence to God in three ways. (1) They have **trodden under foot the Son of God**. Similar language is used in 6:6 (see also Matt. 5:13). (2) They have **counted the blood of the covenant, wherewith he was sanctified, an unholy thing** (see 9:20; 13:20; Exod. 24:8; Matt. 26:28; Mark 14:24). To despise the sanctifying blood of Christ bespeaks treachery of the worst kind, particularly when that blood has sanctified (aorist passive indicative) the one who profanes its efficacy. (3) They have **done despite unto the Spirit of grace**. They have insulted the Holy Spirit, who has mediated God's grace to their benefit.

10:30–31. Vengence belongeth unto me ... The Lord shall judge his people (v. 30) is quoted from Deuteronomy 32:35–36. It is clear in this warning that while God in the New Testament may be considered "the Father of mercies" (2 Cor. 1:3), His holy character remains the same, and He will judge in righteousness (Ps. 96:10–13). No wonder the writer shuddered with the words **It is a fearful thing ... the living God** (v. 31; see 10:27; 12:29). It is "frightening." The wrath of God faces those who sin against Him. And because He is "the living God" (see 3:13), we had better be mindful of the certainty of His judgment against evildoers.

5. Exhortation to Take Courage (10:32–39)

The chapter concludes with a call to remembrance and a word of encouragement. Just as he did in 6:9, the writer let his readers know that he was persuaded of "better things" from them.

10:32–33. The former days (v. 32). Presumably following their first enthusiastic response to the gospel, they had **endured a great fight of afflictions**. Against loss and persecution, they were deeply concerned for each other, sharing their pain as **companions** (v. 33).

10:34. Ye had compassion of me in my bonds. Evidently, the writer had shared with his readers in having been subjected to persecution (see Introduction: "Author"). **Took joyfully** (lit., "received to yourselves with joy"). Early Christians endured suffering in the knowledge that this world was not their home. Here they joyfully stepped aside as their possessions were plundered by their enemies. Why? Because **ye have in heaven a better and an enduring substance**. Their hope in Christ embraced their future reward (see 11:10, 13–16, 26, 35; 13:14; Matt. 5:11–12; 6:19–21; John 14:1–2; Rom. 8:18; 1 Peter 5:1–4). When they had Jesus, what else could they want?

10:35–37. Cast not away ... your confidence (v. 35). Seeing their valiant endurance, the author challenged them not to "throw away" their confidence. Once again, the term *parrēsia*, "boldness" or "confidence," is used (see 3:6; 3:14; 10:19). Such boldness was secured for us by Christ. It comes with Him. If we cast Him aside, we cast aside all His benefits (see Pss. 68:19; 103:2; 116:12). The confidence they once had when persecuted (10:34) had not been misplaced, but they must have **patience** (v. 36) so that they **might receive the promise**. They must wait **yet a little while** (v. 37). Again, Christ's coming was thought to be imminent.

10:38–39. In a very practical final exhortation, the writer reminded his hearers that this confidence was of the essence to the Christian's experience of Christ. **The just shall live by faith** (v. 38; see Hab. 2:4). Paul said it this way to the Colossian believers: "As ye have therefore received Christ Jesus the Lord, so walk ye in him" (Col. 2:6). By faith they had come to this place, and by faith they were to go on. Lest they fear they belonged to those in whom the Lord **shall have no pleasure**, the writer included himself with the readers, saying, **we are not of them who draw back unto perdition** (v. 39). The security of these believers was certain; they were **of them that believe to the saving of the soul**. The author was confident that those to whom he was writing were, for the most part, among the saved (see 6:9).

E. The Argument for a Superior Goal of Faith (chaps. 11–12)

The author had warned his readers against willfully sinning against so great a redemption (10:26–31), and throughout the letter, he repeatedly expressed the idea that one may believe the gospel and be saved yet not grow in grace or ever realize God's best for one's life. It is a matter of choice. In the following gallery of faith, he presented a litany of examples in which God's word was not only believed and accepted as truth but was also acted on. Realizing that the issue of faith is a difficult concept to grasp, especially as the term is used in the New Testament, the writer offered examples from "times past" when God spoke to "the fathers" (1:1), who had faced the same temptations to doubt, neglect, or fall away from His promises.

11:1. Now, in view of all the preceding, the idea that **faith** (Greek, *pistis*; "faith," also "faithfulness," "steadfastness") **is the substance of** (lit., "what stands under") **things hoped for** brings into view the realization that faith is a genuine hope based on a genuine word and promise from the Lord. This harks back to the opening verses of the epistle, describing the superiority and reliability of a word received "in Son" (see 1:1–3 and discussions). This is half of the equation. Again in keeping with the preceding warnings, faith is also **the evidence of things not seen**. Here the author employed the same reasoning as James: "faith without works is dead" (James 2:26). Abraham received the promise, believed the promise, and was convinced (Greek, *elengchos*) to act on the promise, never having seen the fulfillment of the promise. It is with this overlay that one must understand the following examples. The warnings of this epistle are graphic: there can be no successful, fruitful life of *faith* without the presence of both substance (*hope*), or underpinnings, and evidence, action based on conviction (*love*).

1. Old Testament Examples of Faith (11:1–39)

11:2. For by it (faith) **the elders obtained a good report**. The phrase "obtained a good report" is a rendering of a single word, *martyreō* (middle, passive voice; see 12:1). In the literal sense, this means that faith enabled the elders (Greek, *presbyteroi* "forefathers," "patriarchs") to secure a commendation (from God, see 11:4–6) of the fruitfulness of believing and following God's Word. Additionally, within the general context of the epistle and the specific

context of these verses, this witness portrayed the absolute surety and appropriateness of God's Word during "hard times" or when the promise was yet to be fulfilled. The author did not leave this statement to stand on its own but followed up with many details to support this assertion.

11:3. Through faith we understand (Greek, *noeō*; "to ponder" or "to think") does not refer to understanding as we normally think of it but rather conveys the idea that our ponderings, our thinking, and our meditations are to be done within the "castle walls" of faith. One of the great ponderings for mankind has been **that the worlds** (Greek, *aiōn*; "ages"; see 1:2) **were framed by the word of God**. For the secular humanist and the evolutionist, who both operate outside the walls of faith, this is nonsense. For the believer who possesses the substance and evidence of faith, however, it is accepted **that things which are seen were not made** (Greek, *ginomai*; "began to be") **of things which do appear** (lit., "can be seen"). The fact of creation cannot be diminished by our inability to ponder the visible and glorious works of God to a logical conclusion (see Psalm 33).

At this point, the author moved from a general application of an operational faith to specific and familiar examples showing how his hearers' forebears had lived out their faith. The hearers were well aware of these examples. The author's purpose was to hammer home the fact that the accomplishments listed were made reality through faith. It is noteworthy that some of these examples of faith in action depict God working *through* His people, some depict God working *in* His people, and some depict God working *for* His people. In all cases, it was God working in accordance with His Word and in response to those who trusted Him. In many of the illustrations of faith, the writer, in keeping with the structure of this epistle, also recorded the fate of those who had refused God's word.

All of the saints the author listed responded to God in faith, believing God's word. They illustrate the positive effects of heeding the warnings of this epistle. The writer arranged the "testimonies" into sections corresponding to the warnings and according to the families or "households" that are represented (see 3:2–6; 6:1–2).

a. Members of Adam's Household (11:4–6)

11:4. The writer's first examples of faith in action underscored his warning against neglect (see 2:1). "There is a way which seemeth right unto a man, but the end thereof are the ways of death" (Prov. 14:12). From the beginning, God made it known that He would require a blood sacrifice that would atone for sin. It was therefore **By faith** in the word of the Lord that **Abel offered unto God a more excellent** (Greek, *pleiōn*; "better") **sacrifice than Cain.** Neither Abel's nor Cain's sacrifice could atone for sin; only the blood of Christ could accomplish that. From the beginning, however, blood sacrifices were offered in obedience to God's command, as "a shadow" (10:1) that illustrated Christ's eventual blood atonement for sin. The issue is not that Cain's offering was not good but rather that it was not offered in the obedience of faith (see 2:1); Cain substituted the wisdom of man for the clearly revealed will of God (see Rom. 10:3). Thus, Abel's offering was better, having been offered in the obedience of faith. He thereby **obtained witness** (Greek, *emartyrēthē*; "had witness born to him") **that he was righteous.** As we have seen, the final and perfect blood sacrifice of Christ on the cross was also in obedience to the divine will (see Gen. 4:3–4; see also 1 John 3:12). God Himself gave witness of Abel's righteousness (see "God … spake in time past unto the fathers," 1:1). **God testifying … and by it** (lit., "God bearing witness … through it"). God's testimony concerning Abel's sacrifice is such that **he being dead yet speaketh.**

11:5–6. Enoch (v. 5) was a man who **pleased God** (see Gen. 5:18–24). Because of his **faith,** he **was translated** (Greek, *metatithēmi*; "transferred," i.e., to heaven) **that he should not see death; and was not found, because God had translated him,** or taken him up to His presence (see Gen. 5:24; Pss. 49:15; 73:24). The author's emphasis is not so much the unusual nature of Enoch's departure as it is that **without faith it is impossible to please him** (v. 6; see 3:7–11). That Enoch pleased God is proof of his

faith; that God translated him is witness to God's approval and proof of God's faithfulness. **For he that cometh to God** (see 10:19–22) **must believe that he is.** Faith must have an object, and the proper object of genuine faith is first God and secondarily His Word. The specific emphasis here is that He is **a rewarder of them that diligently seek him** (Greek, *ekzēteō*; "to seek out"). "Diligently seek him" refers to a focused effort, much like a person attempting to locate another in a large crowd (see 6:9–12; see Jer. 29:13). This statement and the inability of the unregenerate heart to understand or seek after God (see Rom. 3:11), provide further evidence that the recipients (though many were "babes"; see 5:13) were genuine in their faith.

b. Members of Noah's Household (11:7)

The ungodly in Noah's day had no excuse for their unbelief. In righteousness, God sent them a preacher in the person of Noah (see Rom. 10:14–15). In spite of the pressure of the society around him, Noah believed God. Noah and his household are introduced here to illustrate the writer's warning against unbelief (see 3:7–15; see also Gen. 6:8–10; 2 Peter 2:5).

11:7. By faith Noah … moved with fear (a reverence toward God's command), **prepared an ark** (see Gen. 5:28–9:29) **to the saving of his house.** This was absolutely necessary, in the economy of God, to preserve the line of promise that led to the birth of Christ. **By the which he condemned the world.** With the exception of Noah and his family, all mankind heard the word preached and rejected it, and when the flood came, they were judged by it. Noah, however, **became heir of the righteousness which is by faith.** Noah believed God and acted on that which God said, even when it related to "things not seen" (11:1), namely, the coming flood. Thus, Noah also fit the description of God's righteous ones who live by faith (see 10:38). His faith in God's word moved him to build the ark in a dry, landlocked region, where it was inconceivable that there would ever be enough water to float the vessel. When a person walks with God, they find Him to be faithful, and unbelief is never an option.

c. Members of Abraham's Household (11:8–23))

Although he was a man of substance, Abraham was a persistent believer. By leaving his own country, he became invested in God's promise to him. His confidence in God was never shaken; he never allowed the negative circumstances of life to dim the reality of God's promises, even when serious contradictions seemed to negate them. Abraham's life exemplifies the steadfastness that the author wished for his readers—those of his day and ours. Abraham thus serves to underscore the writer's warning against falling away (6:4–6).

11:8. By faith Abraham, when called of God (see Gen. 12:1–3), embarked on a journey to an unknown destination, **a place which he should after receive for an inheritance**. This he did for the sole reason that he **obeyed** God. He is presented in the New Testament as the outstanding example of those who live "by faith" and as "the father of all them that believe" (Rom. 4:11; see Rom. 4:12, 16; Gal. 3:7, 9, 29). His faith was expressed in obedience (see Gen. 12:4). **He went out, not knowing** his destination, nevertheless in complete confidence in God's trustworthiness.

11:9–11. By faith he sojourned (v. 9), dwelling as a stranger **in the land of promise**, living in tents with his family, who were **heirs with him of the same promise**. Abraham knew how to wait upon God (see Pss. 37:9; 123:2). Rather than take matters into his own hands, **he looked** (lit., "was patiently waiting") **for a city which hath foundations, whose builder and maker is God** (v. 10). When relying on the promises of God, it makes no sense to intervene and provide for ourselves a cheap imitation when God wants us to have the genuine article (see Ps. 147:2). The covenant with Abraham involved not only a city but also descendants who would be "heirs with him." Abraham's household would prove to be worthy of continuing the line of promise in that **Through faith also Sara herself received strength to conceive seed** (v. 11). That which is humanly impossible is possible for God. Even though she was beyond the age of childbearing, Sarah believed and **judged him faithful who had promised** (see Gen. 18:11–12; 11:30).

11:12–15. Abraham, though **as good as dead** (v. 12) because he was one hundred years old (see Gen. 21:5; Rom. 4:19), became the father of an innumerable multitude, even **as the stars of the sky … and as the sand which is by the sea shore** (see Gen. 13:16; 15:5; 22:17; 26:4; 1 Kings 4:20). Abraham and his family saw the power of God operating to fulfill the immediate aspects of the promises, but ultimately **These all died in faith, not having received the promises, but having seen them afar off** (v. 13). Realizing that they were only links in the chain of promise, they were content to live their entire lives steadfastly. They **were persuaded of [the promises], and embraced them, and confessed that they were strangers and pilgrims on the earth**. Their true home was in heaven. Truly, they were of those who **declare** (lit., "are declaring") **plainly that they seek** (Greek, *epizēteō*; "seek after") **a [better] country** (Greek, *patris*; "fatherland;" v. 14, see 11:16). Abraham and his family were seeking a homeland. **Truly, if they had been mindful** (Greek, *emnēmoneuon*; "had continued to be mindful," "yearned for") **of that country from whence they came out, they might have had** (lit., "would have kept on having) **opportunity to have returned** (Greek, *kairon anakampsai*; aorist active infinitive; v. 15). If they had longed for the leeks, onions, and garlic of Egypt (see Num. 11:5), as their descendants later would (and as some of the discouraged recipients were doing), they would have had plenty of incentive to go back. In which case, they would never have received the promise. Again, note that this chapter is not just an accidental assortment of God's faithful. The author's choice of Old Testament examples was purposeful and reinforced the entire message of the epistle. Here he was mindful of his hearers' temptation to "fall away" (6:6).

11:16. But now they desire a better country, one that is **heavenly: wherefore God is not ashamed to be called their God**. God's best is always to be desired, and it is always "better." Note that He has already **prepared** (Greek, *hetoimazō*; "made ready") **for them a city** (Greek, *polis*; "a city with walls"; see 11:3). The ultimate reality is represented by the New Jerusalem in John's vision of the believer's eternal state (see 12:22–24; Rev. 21:2). The author admonished his hearers to follow the example of Abraham's family and look beyond their immediate circumstances to the eventual fulfillment of all God's promises.

The author has placed the greatest emphasis on Abraham and not upon Moses, the patriarch with whom the recipients identified the most. In 11:8–16, the story of Abraham concerns both the land and the seed of promise, including the earthly and the heavenly. In 11:17–19, the author related how Abraham portrayed his faith in God even to the raising of the dead.

11:17. He that had received the promises. God instructed Abraham to offer his son Isaac as a burnt offering (see Gen. 22:2). He prepared to do just that, all in accord with the word of God (see Gen. 22:9–10), and **offered up Isaac** (lit., "was ready to offer up"), the son of promise, **his only begotten son** (see John 3:16; Rom. 8:32).

11:18–19. The Lord's instruction to offer Isaac as a burnt offering must have seemed to Abraham the greatest of all contradictions, for God had promised **That in Isaac shall thy seed be called** (v. 18; from Gen. 21:12). This seeming contradiction, however, did not deter Abraham from obedience to the known will of God. Abraham's steadfastness was grounded in his confidence that **God was able to raise[Isaac] up, even from the dead** (v. 19). Figuratively, this event occurred when the substitute ram was provided (see Gen. 22:13). In the mind of the believer, death has no power and cannot, through fear or persuasion, cause the child and servant of God to shrink from doing God's will (see 1 Cor. 15:55). Even as Isaac willingly submitted to the will of his father Abraham, so Jesus submitted to the will of His Father, going willingly to the cross (see Luke 22:42). The hearers were reminded that all these things were "a shadow of good things to come" (10:1) and that they also must endure hardship (see 12:7, 20; 2 Tim. 2:3; 4:3, 5).

11:20. God's promises were passed on from father to son. Although it was the result of treachery, **Isaac blessed Jacob**, believing God as to the promises. **Esau** had "despised his birthright" (Gen. 25:34;

lit., "thought it to be of no value"), and its retrieval was impossible, "though he sought it carefully with tears" (Heb. 12:17). This was a somber warning to the hearers about their responsibility to their faith. They, and all believers, must at all costs never allow themselves to "fall away" (6:6; see Gen. 27:27–40). The blessing of Jacob demonstrates that God looks on the heart, not outward appearances (see 1 Sam. 16:7). Although one of the most startling, it was only one of many twists and turns in the lineage of Messiah, in which God sovereignly intervened to preserve His promises.

11:21. Here the author used Jacob's given name, not "Israel," the name he received from God at Peniel (see Gen. 32:28). **By faith Jacob … blessed both the sons of Joseph; and worshipped, leaning upon the top of his staff** (lit., "worshipped on the top of his staff"; see Gen. 47:31, Septuagint). Perhaps the author was emphasizing the human element involved in faith as well as de-emphasizing the idea that the nation of Israel has a sole claim to faith in God (see Romans 4). Jacob required of his son Joseph that he be buried with his fathers (see Gen. 47:29–31). Again, God directed the blessing (to Manasseh) contrary to that which was expected (see Gen. 48:8–20).

11:22. Joseph himself, **when he died, made mention of the** (future) **departing of the children of Israel** from Egypt and **By faith … gave commandment concerning his bones** (see Gen. 50:24–25). Jacob (see 11:21) and Joseph are additional examples of those whose faith was no less strong at death than in life (see 11:13).

11:23. By faith Moses … was hid … of his parents (see Exod. 6:20; Num. 26:58–59) **because they saw he was a proper child** (see discussion on Exod. 2:2)**; and they were not afraid of the king's commandment** to kill Israel's males at birth (see Exod. 1:16, 22). Again, it was "by faith" that God's promise for this people was preserved long before anyone could trace His hand.

d. Members of Moses' Household (11:24–39)

11:24. In calling to mind those of Moses' household, the writer reinforced his warning against willful sinning (see 10:26–27). To the recipients of this epistle, Moses represented the law. In this recollection of his faith, however, the author made no mention of the law. This is in keeping with his purpose of demonstrating the transcendence of faith, which is both antecedent and superior to faith in the keeping of the law (see Gal. 3:21–26). Although Moses was claimed by Pharaoh's daughter, in his early years, he was raised and taught by his mother (see Exod. 2:8–9). During this time, he was no doubt taught concerning the promises of God. It was thus **By faith** that **Moses ... refused to be called the son of Pharaoh's daughter**.

11:25–29. Choosing ... affliction ... [over] the pleasures of sin (v. 25), Moses willingly gave up the luxury and prestige in Egypt's royal palace. The author presented this example of faith to exhort the hearers that they should never willfully sin against the known will of God. This remains especially true today, as the pleasures available to contemporary Christians continually beckon us to choose them over the things of God. In making his choice, Moses was **esteeming the reproach of Christ greater riches than the treasures of Egypt** (v. 26). The author spoke of "the reproach" of the Anointed One in keeping with the sense of Psalm 89:51. This reproach is heaped on those who (as God's chosen) comply with the will of God even though it results in the sneers and jeers of the surrounding culture. Moses esteemed the reproach of Christ because **he had respect unto** (lit., "kept on looking away unto") **the recompence of the reward**. For Moses, this was the deliverance of the children of Israel as promised. For Christ, this was obtaining a permanent atonement and the resultant deliverance of "many sons" (2:10). For Christians, it is to be freed from the power of sin and to display the glory of God (see Rom. 8:18). Although Moses' understanding of the details of the messianic hope was extremely limited, he chose to be associated with the people through whom that hope was to be realized. **By faith he forsook Egypt** (v. 27), probably referring to his flight to Midian in the Sinai peninsula when he was forty years old (see Exod. 2:11–15; Acts 7:23–29), **not fearing the wrath of the king.**

Exodus indicates that Moses was afraid (Exod. 2: 14) but does not expressly say of whom, and it tells us that he fled from Pharaoh when Pharaoh tried to kill him (Exod. 2:15) but does not expressly say that he fled out of fear. The author of Hebrews capitalized on these features of the account to highlight that in his fleeing from Pharaoh, Moses was sustained by his trust in God that the liberation of Israel would come and that he would have some part in it. **He endured** for forty years in Midian (see Acts 7:30) **as seeing him who is invisible** (see 11:1, 6). Because he believed God, **through faith he kept the passover, and the sprinkling of blood** (v. 28), saving **the firstborn** from death (see Exodus 12). Furthermore, **By faith they passed through the Red sea as by dry land** (v. 29). When the pursuing Egyptians sought to seize this same miracle, they **were drowned** (see Exodus 14–15). The third and final forty-year period of Moses' life was spent leading the Israelites through the wilderness. At the age of 120 years, he died in Moab (see Deut. 34:1–7), together with all those of his generation who came out of Egypt.

11:30. Moses' place as leader was taken by Joshua, who brought the people of Israel into the Land of Promise. Great must have been the patience of this man. Joshua, along with Kaleb, viewed the obstacles in the land as opportunities. Jericho was the first great obstacle to their conquest of the land and was captured by faith without a battle (see Joshua 6). **By faith the walls of Jericho fell down, after they were compassed about seven days.** The victory was achieved because of Joshua's strict obedience to the command of God.

We must not to miss the author's point in denying mention of Joshua and Caleb by name and at once introducing Rahab. Without Rahab's cooperation, the spies would have been found and probably executed. The author captured the hearers' attention by introducing a shocking irony. Rahab (Hebrew, *raḥab*; "strength,") was a name for a mythical sea monster and was used frequently of Egypt (see Isa. 30:7 and discussion; see also Pss. 87:4; 89:10; Isa. 51:9). The irony is that God had demonstrated His power to rescue the nation through one as significant as

Moses and now demonstrated his power to give them the Promised Land through one as insignificant as Rahab the harlot. This surely resonated with the persecuted recipients of the epistle, who would have been tempted to forget their importance to the Lord (2:11) and, as Job's friends advised, "curse God, and die" (Job 2:9).

11:31. By faith the harlot Rahab perished not with them that believed not. Rahab embraced the promises of God (see Josh. 2:9–11). Lest the reader think one has to be a hero of faith to receive the rewards of faith, Rahab stands as a monument to God's grace and is honored for her witness. Because of her newly found faith and obedience to God, evidenced when she **received the spies with peace** (see James 2:25), Joshua spared her and her family when Jericho was burned to the ground (see Josh. 6:22–25). Important to note is that her faith was not limited to something she merely believed; her faith led to works of obedience to what she knew already to be true of this God of the children of Israel. It was important for the persecuted believers of the first century to be reminded that God had protected Rahab from the judgment that fell on her city.

11:32–33. The time would fail me to tell (v. 32). *Diēgoumenon* is the masculine form of *diēgeomai*, "to relate," indicating that the author of Hebrews was a man (see Introduction: "Author"). Like the crescendo of a fireworks display, the writer poured out a mighty display of faith, faithfulness, and obedience to God, even unto death. For **Gedeon** (Gideon), **Barak**, **Samson**, and **Jephthae**, see Judges 4:6–5:15; 6:11–8:35; 11:1–12:7; 13:24–16:31; and 1 Samuel 12:11, where Gideon is called Jerubbaal (see Judg. 6:32 and discussion). For **Samuel** and **the prophets**, see Psalm 99:6; Jeremiah 15:1; Acts 3:24; 13:20. Through faith, all those listed here **subdued kingdoms, wrought righteousness, obtained promises, stopped the mouths of lions** (v. 33; see Daniel in the lions' den, Daniel 6).

11:34–35. Here the author used a sledgehammer style, with nine clauses, to bring home his point. These heroes of faith **quenched the violence of fire** (see Daniel's friends, Shadrach, Meshach, and Abednego, in the fiery furnace, Daniel 3**), escaped … the sword, out of weakness were made strong** (see 2 Cor. 12:9**), waxed valiant in fight, turned to flight the armies of the aliens**. Through God's help, they overcame sickness (see Rom. 8:26; 2 Cor. 12:9). **Women received their dead raised to life again** (v. 35; see the widow of Zarephath, 1 Kings 17:17–24; and the Shunammite woman, 2 Kings 4:8–36). **Others were tortured, not accepting deliverance; that they might obtain a better resurrection**. This is strongly reminiscent of the heroic Maccabean Jewish patriots of the second century BC (see 2 Maccabees 7). But the description applies also to countless believers, known and unknown, who demonstrated their faith in God by persevering in the face of harsh trials and afflictions. They could only hope for something better in the resurrection. Christians already enjoy the blessings of the new covenant and the age to come.

11:37–38. They were stoned (v. 37). Men like Zechariah, the son of Jehoiada the priest, were put to death for declaring the truth (see 2 Chron. 24:20–22; Luke 11:51; see also Jeremiah, Introduction: "Author and Date"). **They were sawn asunder** perhaps refers to Isaiah, who, according to tradition, met this kind of death under wicked King Manasseh (see Isaiah, Introduction: "Author"). **Sheepskins and goatskins** were the rough garments of prophets such as Elijah. All these are they **of whom the world was not worthy** (v. 38). Perhaps this is why God placed them **in deserts … mountains … dens and caves**.

11:39. These all, having obtained a good report (Greek, *martyreō*) **through faith** (see 11:2) indicates not that all the heroes of faith experienced immediate triumph over their circumstances but that all were blessed by God. Yet in spite of their faithfulness to God, they **received not the promise**. The writer used the middle voice here. These faithful ones about whom God testifies in His Word never saw the fulfillment of the messianic promise in their lifetime. No wonder Simeon rejoiced as he did when he cradled the newborn Jesus and said, "Lord, lettest thou thy servant depart in peace … for mine eyes have seen thy salvation" (Luke 2:26).

2. The Transcendence of Faith (11:40)

11:40. God having provided some better thing for us. The fulfillment for those listed in the author's gallery of faith, as for Christians today, is in Christ, who is "the resurrection and the life" (John 11:25–26), **that they without us should not be made perfect**. All persons of faith who had gone before focused their faith on God and His promises. The fulfillment of God's promises to them has come in Jesus Christ, and their redemption, along with ours, is now complete in Him. Hidden from them was the mystery of the church and the intervening period of time when the gospel would be preached throughout the world, to the Jew first but also to the Greek (see Rom. 1:16), fulfilling the promise that through Abraham's seed all the families of the earth be blessed (see Gen. 12:3; Gal. 3:16–19, 29). There can be no mistaking the contrast; "they" and "us" creates a clear distinction between that which was and the "better thing" that has come to be. With this important declaration, the author moved to the recipients' circumstances and to his final warning, which had particular application to the hearers as well as to all who have heard Him "that speaketh" (12:24–25).

The author diligently emphasized that the recipients were uniquely members of Christ's household, over which He is Lord. Indeed, He is Son over His own house (see 3:5–6). Their fledgling numbers were but a beginning in God's plan to call out a people for His name. As it was with Abraham, they too would not see the end of this new beginning, but they were a link in the long line of those who would follow in the lineage of faith. This chapter has yet to be finished, and will not be finished until Jesus comes again, but to be sure, the living of it will be by faith.

3. Run with Patience, Looking to Jesus' Example (12:1–3)

12:1. In the original text, **Wherefore** expresses a conclusion with emphasis. The chapter division here is unfortunate since it breaks this passionate climax of the writer's argument from the previous chapters (10 and 11), concerning the "better promises" (8:6) of the new covenant. It was important to the author that his hearers grasp and understand that they were part of a grand theme and that they recognize that they were **compassed about with** (lit.,"surrounded by") **so great a cloud of witnesses**, those who have left a legacy of faith that witnesses to the faithfulness of God. The imagery suggests an athletic contest in a great amphitheater with tier upon tier of seats rising up like a cloud. It is not that these saints are spectators but that their legacy of faith provides inspiring examples (see Josh. 5:10) that we can follow. The Greek word translated "witnesses" is the origin of the English word "martyr" and means "testifiers, witnesses." This testimony or record is promulgated by God and bears witness to the power of faith and to His faithfulness (see 11:2, 39). We dishonor this legacy when we do not **lay aside every weight, and the sin which doth so easily beset us**. This "laying aside" is a voluntary and deliberate action to shed every encumbrance that could interfere with a successful run. The besetting "sin" is variously understood. The Vulgate suggests "the sin standing around us." For the first readers of this epistle, the sin was no doubt that of abandoning their commitment to Christ because of unbelief or, worse, because they "refus[ed] … him that speaketh" (12:25). It is fitting that the writer did not name the sin, since the sins that can hold believers back are varied. Inasmuch as every sin is by definition a violation of God's revealed Word, however, most violations are rooted in unbelief or willfulness. Unencumbered and armed with an inviolable confidence in God, we may **run with patience** (Greek, *hypomonē*; to "endure" or "persist"; see Acts 20:24; 1 Cor. 9:24–26; Gal. 2:2; 5:7; Phil. 2:16; 2 Tim. 4:7; Rev. 2:10). The Christian is pictured as a long-distance runner rather than a short-distance sprinter. Some Hebrew Christians were tempted to drop out of the contest because of persecution. Patience endures because it is grounded in hope (see Rom. 5:1–6).

12:2. Rather than focusing on their difficulties, the recipients were to be **Looking unto Jesus** (lit., "Looking away to Jesus"). This term is used only here and Philippians 2:23, where it is translated "see." In keeping with the author's theme of remaining faithful to that "better thing" (11:40), he suggested that while it is good to consider those such as the heroes of the previous chapter, ultimately our gaze should be upon Him. A successful runner concentrates on the finish line; we should therefore concentrate on Jesus, the goal and objective of our faith (see Phil. 3:13–14; see also Heb. 2:9; 3:1; 4:14–16; 11:26). We do this because Christ is **the author** ("the chief leader"; translated "the captain" in 2:10), or as we have seen, "a Son over His own house, whose house are we" (3:6). This identifies and confines our race to those activities that are within Christ's household. As high priest, He is also the **finisher of our faith** (Greek, *teleiōtēn*; "consummator," a term the writer probably coined). Our faith, which has its beginning in Him, is also completed in Him; He is both the start (see 1:2; 11:3) and the end of our faith. This makes Him the supreme witness and example; He has already run the race and overcome. With respect to Christ's reward (see 10:35; Rev. 22:12), it was with **the joy that was set before him** that He **endured the cross** (see Phil. 2:5–8), thereby accomplishing our eternal redemption and His glorification at the Father's right hand (see discussion on 1:3; see also Isa. 53:10–12). So great was this glorious prospect, He suffered, **despising the shame**. As it was with Christ, the humiliation of a believer's suffering for the gospel's sake is far outweighed by the prospect of future glory (see 11:26; Matt. 5:10–12; Rom. 8:18; 2 Cor. 4:17; 1 Peter 4:13; 5:1, 10). In fulfillment of His priestly and mediatorial ministry on our behalf, He **is set down at the right hand of the throne of God** (see Ps. 110:1). The text conveys the sense that He sat down and is still there.

12:3. Consider him (lit., "reckon," "weigh"). Understanding Christ is the key to victory over doubt and unbelief. Because of His great love (see 1 John 4:19), He **endured such contradiction of sinners** (see Rom. 5:8). Christ suffered infinitely more than any of His disciples are called upon to suffer. The author exhorted his hearers to take encouragement from Christ's sufferings, **lest ye be wearied** (see Isa.

40:28–31), which suggests general weariness or even sickness. Discouraged people often make themselves sick when they become **faint in [their] minds**, that is, they become enfeebled and weary.

4. Chastening, Better Than Judgment, Can Be Endured (12:4–11)

In 12:4–29, the writer turned his attention to the application of all that he articulated in the previous chapters. He dedicated the remainder of the epistle to driving home his argument. In developing these applications, he presented four contrasts: (1) chastening versus judgment (vv. 4–11); (2) virtuousness and graciousness versus selfishness and fleshly desires (12:12–17); (3) forgiveness, access, and the city of the living God versus retribution, separation, darkness, and fear (12:18–24); (4) renewal under grace versus destruction under sin's curse (12:25–29). Given these alternatives, what sane person would "refuse … him that speaketh" (12:25)?

Judgment under the law was to be feared because of its expression of God's displeasure. Chastisement under grace is tolerable, even to be desired, because it is an expression of God's love, to the end that we might be conformed to the Son's image (see 1:3; 6:1; 7:11; Rom. 8:29).

12:4. Ye have not yet resisted. The author was telling his readers that things were not as bad as some were making them out to be. They had not yet been asked to stand on the front line of battle to stand face-to-face against the enemy **unto blood**, as did Christ and many of the examples given in the previous chapter. Though the recipients had suffered persecution and loss of possessions (10:32–34), they had not yet laid down their lives for the faith. Many of the hearers were yet "babes" (5:13), having failed to pursue growth in their faith, and therefore had need of providential intervention. Many of them would, in fact, be called to give their lives for the sake of the gospel (see Introduction: "Date"; 1 Cor. 10:13).

12:5. And ye have forgotten the exhortation … as unto children. While the recipients were complaining about their circumstances, they seem to have forgotten that their true relationship with the Lord was as His children. That is to say, our loving Father deals with us in certain ways to correct us and to keep us dependent on Him. The author used Proverbs 3:11–12 to drive home his point. **My son, despise not thou the chastening of the Lord.** Believers should not belittle the process God uses to reprove and rebuke His children. Character training is always difficult but should not be regarded lightly. Suffering and persecution should be seen as corrective and instructive training for the spiritual development of His children.

12:6. For whom the Lord loveth he … scourgeth. The Greek term for "scourgeth" means "to whip." Out of love, God chastens His children to correct their faults. This seems a harsh analogy, but not so when we consider (see 12:3) the example of Christ in 5:7–9. This world is not our home, and the writer wanted believers to understand that God does not want His children to grow comfortable here. The experiences required to teach one this truth, however, are sometimes very painful. As were those who condemned Christ, the agents of such chastisement are often those who are only too willing to administer punishment (see Isa. 10:5–12).

12:7. Because of its benefits, believers should determine to **endure chastening** (lit., "endure for chastening"). The sense here is that God's children should view suffering as a means to an end: that we become disciplined, the root idea of "disciple." **God dealeth with you as with sons.** God's discipline is evidence that we are His children. Far from being a reason for despair, discipline is a basis for encouragement and perseverance (see 12:10).

12:8. But if ye be without chastisement. Again, the term *paideia*, "child training," indicates that this is the common experience of all who are **sons.** The use of *huios* underscores the spiritual rights and prerogatives associated with sonship. While it can be used to specify gender (i.e., "male"), it need not. Here it is used in a generic sense to include all who are truly related to God through Christ (see Gal. 3:22–4:5). It is a mistake to conclude that this chastening is always due to sin or that God abuses His children. While this "character training" is sometimes a response to

sin, it is always applied to conform us to the image of Christ and to teach us to put our absolute trust in God, as the next verse shows.

12:9. Fathers of our flesh … the Father of spirits. When we were children, our earthly fathers taught us, **and we gave them reverence** (lit., "we turned ourselves to") as an attitude of respect. Is it not **much rather** appropriate to submit (Greek, *hypotassō*) to the Father of our spirits? The contrast in this verse is between our physical parenting and our spiritual parenting. For the writer, the latter was far more consequential than the former. The outcome of good human parenting is good character; the outcome of spiritual parenting is that we **live,** the meaning of which is underscored in 12:10–11.

12:10–11. Pleasure … profit … holiness (v. 10). Our human parents disciplined us as it "seemed good to them." By contrast, God disciplines us for our "profit," the same term that Paul used in 1 Corinthians 12:7 when describing the purpose of spiritual gifts (see also Josh. 1:3–4). Ultimately, God disciplines His children so that they might become the partakers of His "holiness" (see 1 Peter 1:16). While correction is never something that people naturally enjoy, in the end, **it yieldeth the peaceable** ("peaceful") **fruit of righteousness** (v. 11). When received submissively (see 12:9), discipline is wholesome and beneficial.

5. Be Diligent in Weariness (12:12–17)

In the midst of the difficulties of life, including chastisement, it is a temptation to resort to fleshly desires for comfort. Diligence and desire are required to overcome this temptation. The goal — Christlikeness — is available through grace. In 12:4–11, the author used a parent-child metaphor to demonstrate our relationship with our heavenly Father and to help us in developing the proper attitude toward His involvement in our lives. Here he presented some of the literal realities associated with that metaphor to demonstrate that the responsibilities in this household require effort on believers' part.

12:12. Wherefore lift up the hands which hang down, and the feeble knees. The author moved beyond the idea of strengthening his hearers' resolve.

Resolve must be accompanied with resultant fruit. In this case, it is strength derived from an intimate relationship with the Son as a member of His household. The quotation is from Isaiah 35:3, but the entire chapter illustrates the positive affects of such a relationship (see also 4:16; 10:36 – 39; 12:1 – 3).

12:13. Make straight paths. Quoting from Proverbs 4:26, the writer called on his readers to stay on the "straight and narrow." He exhorted them to upright conduct that would help, rather than hinder, the spiritual and moral welfare of others, especially the "lame" who were wavering in the Christian faith.

12:14. Follow peace ... and holiness, without which no man shall see the Lord (see 1 Peter 1:15 – 16; 1 John 3:2 – 3). The challenge of 12:1 – 2 was to keep our eyes on the goal: Jesus. The writer here described how that is done. It entails the pursuit of peace and holiness. In this way, God works in the believer to produce His grace and character.

12:15. Again, acts of diligence are required so that we do not **fail of the grace of God,** "fall short of" or "fail to lay hold of" God's grace. Such failure is described in 2:1 – 4; 6:4 – 8. The same diligence is also required to avoid developing a **root of bitterness** — pride, animosity, rivalry, or anything else harmful to others. The writer drew from the warnings of the Mosaic covenant stating that the heart that turns from the Lord to serve false gods is as a poisonous root that could well bring about God's curse upon the nation (see Deut. 29:18 – 20). That the author connected this situation with that of his hearers underscores just how serious he considered this to be. If they failed to lay hold of God's grace, the hearts of **many** would be poisoned.

12:16. The author next focused on our responsibility to our brethren that will prevent a brother from becoming a **profane person, as Esau** (see Gen. 25:29 – 34). Esau had no appreciation for true values and was profane in his outlook on life (see Phil. 3:18 – 19). He "despised his birthright" (Gen. 25:34) by valuing food for his stomach more highly than his birthright. It is not inconsequential that the writer called to mind Esau here (see 11:20 and discussion). **Who for one morsel of meat.** The contrast is between the relative value given to the immediate gratification of present needs and the supreme value of our "birthright" in Christ.

12:17. The blessing refers to the blessing of the firstborn. The readers were thinking of compromising their faith to gain relief from persecution, but to trade their spiritual birthright for temporary ease in this world would deprive them of Christ's blessing. The author was building up to the warning in 12:25. As it was with Esau, one can reach a point at which the blessing becomes irretrievable; **he was rejected: for he found no place of repentance.** Esau regretted his loss; he did not repent of his sin (see Genesis 27, especially 27:41), even though he countenanced his regret **with tears** (see Gen. 27:34 – 38). His sorrow was not "godly sorrow [that] worketh repentance to salvation" but rather "the sorrow of the world [that] worketh death" (2 Cor. 7:10). The essence of repentance is a change of mind, not necessarily an emotional display. The reprobate mind is not capable of true repentance (see Rom. 1:28; 2 Tim. 3:8).

6. Darkness and Fear under the Law of Moses (12:18 – 21)

12:18 – 21. These verses describe the awesome occasion when the law was given at Mount Sinai (see Exod. 19:10 – 25; Deut. 4:11 – 12; 5:22 – 26), focusing on the old covenant's tangible mountain, ordinances, terrifying warnings, and severe penalties. Believers in Jesus Christ do not have such a threatening covenant and should not consider returning to it. The apostle Peter said it best when Jesus asked the disciples if they were going to leave Him. Peter replied, "Lord, to whom shall we go? thou hast the words of eternal life" (John 6:68). This is in stark contrast to the fearsomeness and death that were the law's reward, **unto blackness** (v. 18; see Exod. 10:22; Judg. 1:6; 2 Peter 2:4, 15). **Sound of a trumpet** (v. 19) is from Exodus 19:16. **They could not endure** (v. 20). The irony is evident in this allusion to the response of the cowardly Israelites toward **the word** (v. 19). Is it possible that these early Christians also were shrinking from the word of Christ? This sets the stage for the warning of 12:25 – 29.

7. Jesus Has Called Us unto the City of the Living God (12:22–24)

12:22. The author told his hearers that, in contrast to those who had witnessed the terrifying events of the first word from God at Sinai, **ye are come unto mount Sion**. This is not the literal Mount Zion (Jerusalem, or its southeast portion) but the heavenly city of God, **the heavenly Jerusalem**, and those who dwell there with Him (see 11:10, 13–16; 13:14; Phil. 3:20). The circumstances under which the old covenant was given (see 12:18–21) and the features of the new covenant (12:22–24) show the utter contrast between the two covenants and were the author's foundation for one final warning and exhortation (12:25–29) to those still thinking of going back to Judaism. For **an innumerable company of angels**, see Revelation 5:11–12.

12:23. Church of the firstborn refers to believers in general who make up the church. (1) They cannot be angels since these have just been mentioned (12:22); (2) "firstborn" cannot refer to Christ (though He is called "the firstborn"; see 1:6; Rom. 8:29; Col. 1:15–18; Rev. 1:5) since here the Greek word is plural; (3) that the names of "the firstborn" are recorded in heaven reminds us of the redeemed (see Rev. 3:5; 13:8; 17:8; 20:12; 21:27). The designation "firstborn" suggests their privileged position as heirs together with Christ, the supreme firstborn and "heir of all things" (1:2). For **God the Judge of all**, see 4:13; Romans 14:10–12; 1 Corinthians 3:10–15; 2 Corinthians 5:10; Revelation 20:11–15. **Spirits of just men made perfect**. For the most part, these men were pre-Christian believers such as Abel (see 11:4) and Noah (see 11:7). They are referred to as "spirits" because they are waiting for the resurrection and as "just" because God credited their faith to them as righteousness, as He did to Abraham (see Rom. 4:3). Actual justification was not accomplished, however, until Christ made it complete by His death on the cross (see 11:40; Rom. 3:24–26; 4:23–25).

12:24. For **the mediator of the new covenant**, see 7:22; 8:6 and discussion; 8:13; 9:15; 1 Timothy 2:5. **The blood … that speaketh better things than that of Abel**. Abel's blood cried out for justice and retribu-

tion (see discussion on Gen. 4:10), whereas the blood of Jesus shed on the cross speaks of forgiveness and reconciliation (see 9:12; 10:19; Col. 1:20; 1 John 1:7).

8. Warning against Refusing "Him That Speaketh" (12:25–29)

12:25. Him that speaketh refers to God (see 1:1–4). **Spake on earth**. At Sinai. **Him that speaketh from heaven** refers to Christ, who is both from and in heaven (see 1:1–3; 4:14; 6:20; 7:26; 9:24). Since we have greater revelation, we have greater responsibility and therefore greater danger (see 2:2–4). **For if they escaped not who refused him**. The consequences of disobedience under Moses are known to us all. Since we know the severity of God's response to unbelief, we are all the more culpable; **much more shall not we escape, if we turn away from him that speaketh from heaven**. Arguing from the lesser to the greater, the author pointed out that if Christians turn away, our chances of escape are far less than that of those at Sinai.

12:26–27. Whose voice … shook the earth (v. 26; see Exod. 19:18; Judg. 5:5; Ps. 68:7–8). God's voice shook the earth when He delivered the "ten words" (see Exod. 20:1 and discussion) at Sinai. But the day is coming, **he hath promised** (Hag. 2:6), when He will **once more … shake not the earth only, but also heaven**. The Israelites thought God's judgments were fierce because the mountain trembled, but the great end-time upheavals associated with the second advent of Christ will be even more fearsome. In this final display of God's mighty power, all the **things that are made** (v. 27) will be removed and that **which cannot be shaken [will] remain** (see 9:28; 1 Cor. 7:31; 1 John 2:17). Nothing is more incompatible with the life of faith than to imagine that anything can shake the kingdom of God.

12:28–29. For the reasons stated in 12:26–27, the **kingdom** (v. 28) that believers receive is understood to be unshakable. With that understanding, **let us have grace** (lit., "let us hold on to grace"), **whereby we may serve God acceptably**. The injunction here is crucial. Believers do not serve God in their own strength (however well motivated they may be); only through His grace are we enabled to "serve God acceptably" (see John 4:19–24; Rom. 12:1). For **God is a consuming fire** (v. 29), see Exodus 24:17; Deuteronomy 9:3.

III. Characteristics of Christian Service (13:1–17)

The final chapter moves from the doctrinal to the practical. Here the writer demonstrated concrete ways to apply the principles articulated above and how they may be fleshed out in believers' homes, churches, and communities.

A. Regarding the Brethren (13:1–3)

13:1. Let brotherly love (Greek, *philadelphia*; see 1 Peter 3:8; 1 Thess. 4:9) **continue.** Jesus indicated that the mark of true believers would be the love shared between them (see John 13:35). The term used here is especially appropriate to the household metaphor that the author used throughout the letter.

13:2. Be not forgetful to entertain strangers (*philoxenia*; "show love to strangers"). The love believers share includes both those they relate to and those they don't. This message is desperately needed in the contemporary church, where "worship styles" tend to divide the body rather than unite it. The particular benefit of reaching out to "strangers" is that we may well entertain **angels unawares**, as did Abraham (see Genesis 18), Gideon (see Judges 6), and Manoah (see Judges 13).

13:3. Remember them that are in bonds ... and them which suffer adversity (see 10:32–34; 1 Cor. 12:26). While in much of the epistle the author encouraged his readers not to allow the threat of persecution and adversity to cause them to turn away from Christ, some in their assembly were already "in bonds," and some were suffering "adversity." The advice here is reminiscent of Paul's advice to the Corinthians: "That there should be no schism in the body; but that the members should have the same care one for another. And whether one member suffer, all the members suffer with it; or one member be honoured, all the members rejoice with it. Now ye are the body of Christ, and members in particular" (1 Cor. 12:25–27).

B. Regarding the Family (13:4–6)

13:4. Marriage is honourable ... adulterers God will judge. As did so many other New Testament writers, the author of Hebrews gave attention to the problems of sexual immorality, which was rampant in the Roman Empire (see 12:16; Rom. 1:29; 1 Cor. 5:1–13; 6:13–18; 7:2; Gal. 5:19; Eph. 5:3; 1 Thess. 4:3; Judg. 1:7). The Scriptures nowhere condemn the pure physical relationship of a husband and wife but everywhere condemn the licentious, promiscuous behavior of those who are certain to face the severe judgment of a holy God.

13:5. A commitment to Christ will impact one's lifestyle. The author admonished his readers to **Let your conversation** (Greek, *tropos*; "manner of life") **be without covetousness** (Greek, *aphilargyros*; "not loving money"; see Luke 12:15, 21; Phil. 4:10–13; 1 Tim. 6:6–10, 17–19)**; and be content with such things as ye have** (see Phil. 4:11–12; 1 Tim. 6:8). He then reminded them of exactly what they had: they had Christ Himself, since He has promised **I will never leave thee, nor forsake thee.** This promise has powerful practical implications, as the next verse shows.

13:6. The Lord is my helper, and I will not fear what man shall do unto me is a quotation from Psalm 118:6. The author could have offered no greater encouragement to his hearers, who were fearful of persecution and were contemplating compromising or leaving their faith in Christ. Jesus said, "And fear not them which kill the body, but are not able to kill the soul: but rather fear him which is able to destroy both soul and body in hell" (Matt. 10:28; see also Luke 12:5–9). The knowledge that Christ is with us at all times is also a serious incentive to always do the right thing (see Luke 12:8–12).

13:7. Remember them which have the rule over you, who have spoken unto you the word of God (see 2:3; 5:12). In addition to listing the heroes of faith in chapter 11, the writer reminded his hearers of those who had communicated the gospel to them and brought them to faith and whose lives gave consistent witness to their commitment to the gospel. The ministry of the apostles and prophets of the New Testament certainly is in view here as well (see

2:3–4). With **considering the end of their conversation**, the author urged the recipients to consider well the example and outcomes of the lives of these exemplary leaders. The use of *ekbasis*, "end of one's life," probably indicates that these leaders were now dead, but the term also indicates that their "exit" was one befitting a follower of Christ. **Whose faith follow** (lit., "mimic their faith"; see 6:12; 1 Cor. 4:16; Eph. 5:1; 1 Thess. 1:6–7; 2:14; 3 John 11). While believers are not followers of men, the New Testament frequently exhorts us to follow those who follow Christ.

C. Regarding the Faith and the Church (13:8–17)

13:8. Jesus Christ the same yesterday, and to day, and for ever is a confession of the changelessness of Christ and is no doubt related to the preceding verse. The substance of the recipients former leaders' faith was the unchanging Christ. "Yesterday" probably refers to the days of Christ's life on earth, when the eyewitnesses observed Him (see 2:3; 5:7). "To day" (see discussion on 3:15), in the hearers' present crisis, the Christ whom the eyewitnesses had seen was still the same, and what they had said about Him was still true and will continue to be true "for ever" (see 1:1–12). Of course, this principle recalls the entire argument of the epistle. All that came before, "yesterday," only served to look ahead to the "promise" of what Christ had fulfilled "to day" and will consummate "for ever." If the recipients returned to an inferior priesthood and sacrifices (see chaps. 5–10), it would compromise Christ's absolute supremacy and undermine the gospel itself.

13:9. Be not carried about (i.e., "Do not be led astray"; see Judg. 1:12) **with divers and strange doctrines** (lit., "with many colored and foreign teachings"). The imagery is graphic. The author was essentially saying, "Do not allow fanciful ideas to catch your eye and draw you away from the simplicity that is in Christ" (see 2 Cor. 11:3). **That the heart be established with grace; not with meats** introduces what follows in 3:10–16. Instead of depending on "ceremonial foods," as the legalistic Judaizers

were teaching, believers' depend on the grace of God in Christ. "For by grace ye are saved ... not of works" (Eph. 2:8–9).

13:10. We have an altar probably refers to the cross, which marked the end of the whole Aaronic priesthood and its replacement by the order of Melchizedek, of which Christ is the only priest (see 7:13; 10:1–18). **Whereof** ("concerning which," i.e., "an altar") **they have no right to eat**. The priests of **the tabernacle** (the Levitical system) have no claim to participate in the sacrifice of believers in Christ, who have a higher privilege than the priests under the old covenant had. The irony of this would not have been lost to those who were tempted to go back to the Levitical system.

13:11–12. Burnt without the camp (v. 11; see Lev. 4:12 and discussion; 16:27). The Levitical priests could not eat of the sacrifice on the Day of Atonement. It was completely consumed. **Jesus also ... suffered without the gate** (v. 12). Christ's death outside Jerusalem represented the removal of sin, as had the removal of the bodies of sacrificial animals outside the camp of Israel.

13:13. Go forth ... unto him without the camp. Jesus calls His followers to accompany Him "outside" the camp, unlike those of Judaism, who remain "inside" the camp. As Jesus died in disgrace outside the city, so His followers should be willing to be disgraced by turning unequivocally from Judaism to Christ. The only proper place for the Christian is beneath the cross of Jesus, there to take our stand. It is there that we "fill up that which is behind of the afflictions of Christ in [our] flesh for his body's sake, which is the church" (Col. 1:24).

13:14. For **no continuing city**, see discussions on 11:10, 14, 16.

13:15. In **sacrifice of praise**, "sacrifice" is used metaphorically to represent an offering to God (see Lev. 7:12; Ps. 54:8; Rom. 12:1; Phil. 4:18). Animal offerings are now obsolete.

13:16. But to do good and to communicate forget not admonished the recipients not to neglect benevolence and fellowship. **With such sacrifices God is well pleased**. It is significant to note that the three definitive texts of the New Testament regarding the nature of worship and service (here; Rom. 12:1; Josh. 1:27) all have to do with the "inner man" of the heart and mind, as underscored in the promises of the new covenant.

13:17. Them that have the rule over you. The recipients' present leaders, as distinct from their first ones, now dead (mentioned in 13:7), were to be given due respect just as they had offered it to their first leaders. This is an important lesson. Church members often become unduly attached to a pastor who dies or is transferred and are unable to submit to the new leadership. To such persons, the author of Hebrews would say, "Get over it." **Submit yourselves.** This command does not condone dictatorial leadership (see 3 John 9–10) but rather respect for authority, orderliness, and discipline in the church, as are taught throughout the New Testament. **They that must give account.** Those called to leadership are answerable to God for how they watch over the souls of those in their care. The exhortation here is for believers to make their task a **joy, and not … grief.** Anyone who has had the misfortune to lead a church of obdurate members will appreciate this wise counsel.

IV. Conclusion and Benediction (13:18 – 25)

A. Request for Prayer (13:18 – 19)

13:18 – 19. Pray for us (v. 18). The writer included himself in the list of those whom his hearers were challenged to give respect (see 13:17). One of the ways they could demonstrate their support and concern for their leaders was to pray for them. Perhaps the author was aware that some among the recipients had challenged even his motives and therefore found it necessary to entreat them in **good conscience** and **honestly.** If this is so, he was not without good company (see Paul in 2 Cor. 1:11–20; 1 Thess. 2:18). **Restored to you** (v. 19, see 13:23). The identity and whereabouts of the writer are not known to us, but "restored" suggests that somehow he had been delayed, perhaps by his current ministry, in visiting those to whom he was writing. That he was not under arrest is clear from 13:23.

B. Benediction and Prayer for the Recipients (13:20 – 21)

The benediction, which is one of the loftiest in the New Testament, provides a fitting conclusion to the letter.

13:20. The God of peace is a title for God used frequently in benedictions (see Rom. 15:33; 16:20; Phil. 4:9; 1 Thess. 5:23). For **Great shepherd,** see Psalm 23; Isaiah 40:11; Ezekiel 34:11–16, 23; 37:24; John 10:2–3, 11, 14, 27; 1 Peter 2:25; 5:4 (see also "great" in 4:14). **The blood of the everlasting covenant** (see discussion on 10:29) refers to the new covenant (see discussion on 8:8–12). What Jeremiah designated as the "new covenant" (Jer. 31:31), he described as "everlasting" (Jer. 32:40; see Isa. 55:3 and discussion; 61:8).

13:21. Make you perfect, or "complete" (see 1 Cor. 1:10; 2 Cor. 13:11; 2 Tim. 3:17). **Every good work.** No doubt the author had in mind works such as faith, faithfulness, obedience, and perseverance.

C. Postscript (13:22 – 25)

13:22. Suffer the word of exhortation. In a final word of admonition, the author asked his readers to bear with him and to take seriously what he had written throughout the epistle, the main thrust of which is to progress in Christian maturity and not fall away from Christ. **I have written … in few words.** Compared to the lengthy treatise that would be necessary to explain adequately the superiority of Christ, the epistle is considered to be merely a brief.

13:23. Timothy is set at liberty (Greek, *apolyō*; "set free," "let go"). Timothy, who was well known to the recipients of the letter, had recently been released from prison. He and the author would soon be visiting the recipients.

13:24. Salute all them that have the rule over you (see 13:17). The author once again exhorted his readers to give due respect to those whom God had called to lead their church. **They of Italy** likely suggests that the letter was written either to or from Italy (see Acts 10:23), although the author could have been simply passing on greetings from some Italian believers.

13:25. Grace be with you all. Amen. The book concludes with a characteristic final greeting.

THE GENERAL EPISTLE
OF JAMES

INTRODUCTION

Author

The author identified himself as "James, a servant of God and of the Lord Jesus Christ" (1:1), but since he furnished no additional biographical identification, his precise identity is a subject of conjecture. Luther attributed the letter to an unknown James whose work the Reformer devalued as "a right strawy epistle" that contradicts Paul's teaching on justification and other doctrines. Some interpreters have assumed that the letter is pseudonymous, that the name James was chosen by its author to lend it authority. One would expect, however, that a more dignified title in 1:1 would have been formulated if the letter were pseudonymously penned. Four men in the New Testament have this name, and the author of the epistle is certainly one of them. (1) The author could not have been the apostle James, son of Zebedee, because he died too early (AD 44) to have written it. He probably would not have lived long enough to gain the stature and authority with which the author wrote. (2) James the son of Alphaeus, another of the twelve apostles, known as James the younger (Mark 15:40), was probably too obscure to have been recognized as an authoritative figure among "the twelve tribes," to whom the letter was written (1:1). (3) James the father of Judas (Luke 6:16; Acts 1:13) cannot even be numbered with certainty among the earliest followers of Jesus. (4) James the brother of the Lord is the best candidate for authorship of this letter. He was one of several brothers of Christ and was probably the oldest since he heads the list in Matthew 13:55. He did not believe in Jesus at first; he even challenged Him and misunderstood His mission (see John 7:2 – 5), but he later became very prominent in the church:

  a. He was one of the select individuals Christ appeared to after His resurrection (1 Cor. 15:7).
  b. Paul called him a "pillar" of the church (Gal. 2:9).
  c. Paul, on his first post-conversion visit to Jerusalem, saw James (Gal. 1:19).
  d. On his last visit to Jerusalem, Paul again saw James (Acts 21:18).
  e. When Peter was rescued from prison, he told his friends to tell James (Acts 12:17).
  f. James was a leader in the important council of Jerusalem (Acts 15:13). He may have written his letter from Jerusalem.

g. James was so well known that Jude could identify himself simply as a "brother of James" (Jude 1).

James's martyrdom, circa AD 62, is mentioned by Josephus (*Ant* 20.9) and in the account of Hegesippus that is cited by Eusebius (*Ecclesiastical History* 2.23.3). Both sources describe his death by stoning.

The quality of Greek in the letter of James has led some to believe that James the brother of Jesus could not have written in such a polished style. Palestine, however, had been greatly influenced by Greek culture and language by the time of James. A writer who was at home there could have composed a Greek document with the sophistication of the letter of James.

James has made a splash in international news since 2002, when the inscription on a limestone box originating from first-century Palestine was deciphered. The inscription on the ossuary, a burial receptacle that contains bones, reads in Aramaic, "James, son of Joseph, brother of Jesus." The authenticity of the entire inscription has been disputed, and at the time of the writing of this commentary, the debate continues. If the box and the entire inscription are genuine, the article is of enormous archaeological and historical importance. It would be the earliest physical artifact that attests to Jesus and members of his family. The chances of three relatives having these names during the time period concerned who are *not* the people of our New Testament accounts are extremely slim. (For further information, see "Burial Box May Be Jesus Artifact," http://www.cbsnews. com/stories/2003/06/18/ world/main559173.shtml; Steve Weizman, "Israeli Experts Say 'James Ossuary' Inscription a Fake," http://www.detnews.com/2003/religion/0306/24/religion–196732.htm; and Craig A. Evans, "Thoughts on the James Ossuary," http://www. bibleinterp.com/articles/EvansThoughts.htm.)

Date

Some date the letter of James in the early 60s. There are indications, however, that it might have been written before AD 50. (1) Its distinctively Jewish nature suggests that it was composed when the church was still predominantly Jewish. (2) It reflects a simple church order; officers of the church are called "elders" (5:14) rather than "bishops," and "masters" (3:1), meaning "teachers." (3) No reference is made to the controversy over Gentile circumcision. (4) The Greek term *synagōgē* ("synagogue," "meeting," or "assembly") is used to designate the meeting or meeting place of the church (2:2).

If this early dating is correct, this letter could well be the earliest of all the New Testament writings. Some who assume a late date for James believe that it seeks to correct an antinomian distortion of Paul's teaching on justification by faith. The letter, however, does not necessarily address such an aberration (see "Literary Features," below). Nothing precludes assigning to James a date between AD 40 and 50.

Recipients

The recipients are identified explicitly only in 1:1: "the twelve tribes which are scattered abroad." Some hold that this expression refers to Christians in general, but the term "twelve tribes" would more naturally apply to Jewish Christians. Furthermore, a Jewish audience would be more in keeping with the obviously Jewish nature of the letter (e.g., the use of the Hebrew title for God, *kyrios Sabaōth*, "the Lord of sabaoth," 5:4). That the recipients were Christians is clear from 2:1; 5:7–8. It has been plausibly suggested that these were believers from the early Jerusalem church who, after Stephen's death, were scattered as far as Phoenicia, Cyprus, and Syrian Antioch (see Acts 8:1; 11:19). This would account for James's references to trials and oppression, his intimate knowledge of the readers, and the authoritative nature of the letter. Some of the hearers of the letter were poor (2:6–7), but not so destitute that they could not aid those in dire need (2:3–4; 15–16). At least some members of the congregations addressed were wealthy (2:3; 5:1–6, although this denunciation may have been for the benefit of the poor members), or at least well enough off to be able to travel for business (4:13–17). As leader of the Jerusalem church, James wrote as pastor to instruct and encourage his dispersed people in the face of their difficulties.

Theme and Theological Message

James is often regarded as a collection of somewhat disjointed exhortations without any discernible pattern of organization. Some recent interpreters, however, observe definite structure in the epistle. This commentary assumes that James is well structured. The theological lens through which the writer looks is focused on the integrity of the believing community as evidenced in the integration of its faith and works. James, arguing for completeness and wholeness in the communities that he addressed, presented several examples of behavior that promote individual and collective wholeness, contrasting them with their negative opposites. The necessity of James's message arose because of the pressures of the world on his readers to compromise their values, particularly regarding wealth and possessions (2:1–13; 4:4). Since the rich were oppressing the believers (2:6–7; 5:1–6), the tendency was present to become lax in the practice of one's faith. Lack of generosity to those in need (1:26–27; 2:14–26), bitterness in speech (3:1–12) and attitude (3:13–4:3), and preoccupation with business pursuits (4:13–17) result from such laxity.

Literary Features

Certain characteristics make the letter of James distinctive.

(1) It has an unmistakably Jewish nature. The addressees are described as "twelve tribes" (1:1) who gather in an "assembly" (2:2), meaning "synagogue." They were familiar with the law and with the Old Testament characters Abraham (2:21–23), Rahab (2:25), Job (5:11), and Elijah (5:17–18). An agrarian environment, like Palestine, where rich landowners oppressed the laborers, seems to be presupposed.

(2) James's emphasis is on vital Christianity, characterized by good deeds and a faith that works (genuine faith must and will be accompanied by a consistent lifestyle). The statement of 2:24, "Ye see then how that by works a man is justified, and not by faith only," does not contradict Paul's teaching on justification by faith alone (Eph. 2:8–10). James was concerned with works as the evidence of true faith; Paul spoke of works as deeds that people perform to be put right with God. James used "justify" in a moral sense—how one is shown publicly to be righteous; Paul used "justify" in a judicial sense—how one is declared righteous by God. For James, good works included especially assistance for the poor and disadvantaged. These include the widow and orphan (1:27), the "poor man in

vile raiment" (2:2), people without clothing and food (2:15), exploited laborers (5:4), and the sick (5:14–15).

(3) The letter displays the author's familiarity with Jesus' teachings preserved in the Sermon on the Mount (compare 2:5 with Matt. 5:3, inheritance of the kingdom of God; 3:10–12 with Matt. 7:15–20, a tree is known by its fruit, and a person's life indicates what kind of person he or she really is; 3:18 with Matt. 5:9, Christians are called to be peacemakers; 5:2–3 with Matt. 6:19–20, believers should seek the true riches in heaven, not earthly treasures that are perishable; 5:12 with Matt. 5:33–37, a simple yes or no rather than oaths should characterize believers' speech).

(4) The letter is similar to Old Testament wisdom writings such as Proverbs.

Outline

The following outline is based on John H. Elliott, "The Epistle of James in Rhetorical and Social Scientific Perspective: Holiness-Wholeness and Patterns of Replication," *Biblical Theology Bulletin* 23 (Summer 1993): 71–81.

  I. Greetings (1:1)
 II. Introduction: Completeness and Wholeness (1:2–12)
     A. The Testing of Faith and Wisdom (1:2–8)
     B. The Reversal of the Lowly and the Rich (1:9–11)
     C. The Testing of Faith and Ultimate Wholeness (1:12)
III. Exhortations to Completeness and Wholeness (1:13–5:12)
     A. First Exhortation: The Integration of Hearing and Doing (1:13–27)
        1. Negative: Self-deception (1:13–16)
        2. Positive: The Integration of Hearing and Doing (1:17–27)
     B. Second Exhortation: The Life of Impartiality (2:1–13)
        1. Negative: Distinctions between Rich and Poor (2:1–7)
        2. Positive: Fulfillment of the Royal Law (2:8–13)
     C. Third Exhortation: The Integration of Faith and Action (2:14–26)
        1. Negative: Separation of Faith and Action (2:14–17)
        2. Positive: Completion of Faith with Action (2:18–26)
     D. Fourth Exhortation: The Life of Wisdom (3:1–18)
        1. Negative: The Destructive Power of the Tongue (3:1–12)
        2. Positive: True Wisdom versus False Wisdom (3:13–18)
     E. Fifth Exhortation: Friendship with the World and Friendship with God (4:1–12)
        1. Negative: Pursuit of Selfish Desires (4:1–4)
        2. Positive: Humility before God (4:5–12)
     F. Sixth Exhortation: Attitudes toward the Future (4:13–5:11)
        1. Negative: Disregard for the Shortness of Life and the Coming Judgment (4:13–5:6)
        2. Positive: Endurance in Suffering (5:7–11)
     G. Seventh Exhortation: The Importance of Speaking the Truth (5:12)
        1. Negative: The Use of Oaths (5:12a)
        2. Positive: Words of Integrity—"Yes" or "No" (5:12b)

IV. Conclusion: Various Instructions for the Promotion of Integration in the
    Community (5:13–20)
    A. Prayer for Various Needs (5:13–18)
    B. Reintegration of the Wayward (5:19–20)

Select Bibliography

Adamson, James B. *The Epistle of James*. The New International Commentary on the New
    Testament. Grand Rapids, MI: Eerdmans, 1976.

Barclay, William. *The Letters of James and Peter*. Rev. ed. The Daily Study Bible. Philadel-
    phia: Westminster John Knox, 1976.

Davids, Peter H. *The Epistle of James: A Commentary on the Greek Text*. The New Interna-
    tional Greek Testament Commentary. Grand Rapids, MI: Eerdmans, 1982.

Johnson, Luke Timothy. *The Letter of James: A New Translation with Introduction and
    Commentary*. The Anchor Bible 37A. New York: Doubleday, 1995.

Martin, Ralph P. *James*. Word Biblical Commentary 48. Waco, TX: Word, 1988.

Moo, Douglas J. *The Letter of James: An Introduction and Commentary*. Tyndale New Testa-
    ment Commentaries 16. Grand Rapids, MI: Eerdmans, 1985.

Morris, Leon, and Donald W. Burdick, *The Expositor's Bible Commentary with the New
    International Version: Hebrews/James*. Grand Rapids, MI: Zondervan, 1996.

Nystrom, David P. *James*. The NIV Application Commentary. Grand Rapids, MI: Zonder-
    van, 1997.

Perkins, Pheme. *First and Second Peter, James, and Jude*. Interpretation: A Bible Commen-
    tary for Teaching and Preaching. Louisville: Westminster John Knox, 1995.

Robertson, A. T. *The General Epistles and the Apocalypse of John*. Vol. 6, *Word Pictures in
    the New Testament*. Nashville: Broadman, 1933.

Stulac, George M. *James*. The IVP New Testament Commentary 16. Downers Grove, IL:
    InterVarsity Press, 1993.

Tasker, R. V. G. *The General Epistle of James: An Introduction and Commentary*. Vol. 16.
    Tyndale New Testament Commentaries. Grand Rapids, MI: Eerdmans, 1957.

EXPOSITION ─────────────────────────

I. Greetings (1:1)

1:1. James. See Introduction: "Author." The word **servant** in Greek is *doulos* and is more appropriately translated "bondservant" (NKJV) or "slave" (NLT). The identity of the author's Masters rather than his identity is emphasized here; the Greek syntax lists the Masters before mentioning James's role as slave: "James, of God and of the Lord Jesus Christ, a slave." **The twelve tribes** may be a literal reference to Jew-ish Christians who lived outside their homeland in the Diaspora. But the reference could be metaphorical; the Christians were in a situation of cultural estrangement, as the readers of 1 Peter were (see 1 Peter, Exposition), or were in exile away from their heavenly home. At any rate, the readers, as the new Israel, were experiencing some sort of cultural and religious disconnection from their contemporaries (see Introduction: "Recipients").

II. Introduction: Completeness and Wholeness (1:2–12)

A. The Testing of Faith and Wisdom (1:2–8)

1:2. James addressed the readers as **brethren** ("brothers") fifteen times in this short letter. He had many rebukes for them, but he corrected them in brotherly love. The Greek term *adelphoi* is a generic masculine noun; it includes males and females of all ages in the Christian communities addressed (hence, "My brothers and sisters," NRSV). The same Greek root lies behind the noun in the phrase **divers temptations** ("trials of many kinds," NIV) and the word "tempted" in 1:13. In 1:2–3, James emphasized difficulties that come from outside; in 1:13–15, inner moral trials, such as temptation to sin. Such tests one is to **count ... [as] all joy** (see Matt 5:11–12; Rom. 5:3; 1 Peter 1:6), not because of the suffering (James does not command one to love pain!) but because of their benefit.

1:3–4. Believers may rejoice in difficulties and tests, **knowing ... that the trying of your faith worketh patience** (v. 3). The "testing" (NIV) not only reveals the genuineness of a person's faith; it also purifies it (as metals tested in the fire) so that it emerges stronger and one is more capable of persevering through difficulties the next time they come. "Patience" is *hypomonē*, a triumphant fortitude in difficulties of all kinds, including patience with difficult people. Only through hardships can genuine and enduring faith be developed. To be **perfect and entire** (v. 4) does not mean that the one who endures will be without sin. "Perfect" (*teleios*) means "mature" (NIV, NRSV). A mature believer is one whose character has begun to conform to the image that God intends it to have—the very character of Christ. Such a person may be described as **wanting nothing**, that is, "ready for anything" (NLT). In other words, integration and wholeness are becoming a reality in one's faith.

1:5. Wisdom enables one to face trials with "joy" (1:2). Wisdom is not just acquired information but practical insight with spiritual implications (see Prov. 1:2–4; 2:10–15; 4:5–9; 9:10–12). God is the ultimate source of true wisdom, and the one who needs it during time of trial may confidently ask God for it. He **upbraideth not**; He gives **liberally** ("generously and ungrudgingly," NRSV) and without condemnation. James emphasized prayer throughout his letter. One may ask God for wisdom (1:5), for justice (5:4), for others' healing and forgiveness (5:14–16), but when making requests of God, one must ask in faith (1:6–8) and with pure motives (4:3). James maintained that one often does not have what one desires because of a failure to ask God for it (4:2).

1:6–8. James introduced the colorful metaphor of **a wave of the sea** (v. 6; see Eph. 4:14) to illustrate the instability of a doubter, one who doubts that God can or wants to answer his prayers. Doubt can be healthy when it seeks to find answers and reasons for belief. The doubt here (James called it **wavering**), however, is skepticism in the face of the evidence that one already has about God. A person who so doubts is **driven with the wind and tossed** like the sea. The word translated "wavering" is *diakrinō*. It has the idea of being at odds within oneself, being of a divided mind. **Double minded** (v. 8; "doublesouled," Stulac, *James*, p. 43) is synonymous with the idea of wavering. The issue is of divided loyalties, when one has not fully given himself over to God at the point of suffering.

The particular trials that the instructions of 1:2–8 are designed to meet may involve some sort of economic hardship, but they apply to any kind of duress that a Christian may encounter. Wisdom certainly would have been needed in the times of grave financial crisis that oppressed Christians experienced in the first century, some of whom were possibly living at the subsistence level. Their need was through no fault of their own. The question of how one could provide for oneself and one's dependents and still meet obligations, like taxes, would have been enormous. Today, the costs of food, clothing, housing, fuel, health care, and education put stress on many families. According to James, believers have opportunities to grow through such difficulties. Christians also have opportunities to ask God to gain His wisdom, and He will grant it so that they may know how to live more frugally and have enough for what they really need.

It must be said, though, that affluent Christians in the West often put themselves in financial straits through extravagant lifestyles and binge spending on credit. God's wisdom in such situations is evident: be content with fewer luxuries and put a hold on credit-card usage. At the same time, the way to a contented lifestyle involves giving of one's resources to those who are financially and socially distressed (see 2:14–26). The shift to a lower standard of living may well constitute a test for which James's words are apt.

B. The Reversal of the Lowly and the Rich (1:9–11)

1:9–11. Wholeness comes to the community when **the brother of low degree** (v. 9), the one who is not just of humble circumstances but is humble before God, is **exalted** and **the rich ... is made low** (v. 10). God honors the one who honors Him, and those who disregard Him will be brought low (see 1 Sam. 2:30). Since the wealthy had oppressed and dishonored the members of James's communities (see James 2:6–7), a reversal of status was to take place. Since his discussions of wisdom (1:5–8) and of the poor man and the rich man (here) appear between the two sections on trials (1:2–4 and 1:12), 1:5–11 also may have to do with trials. The Christian who suffers the trial of poverty is to rejoice in his or her high position (v. 9) as a believer (see 2:5), and the wealthy Christian is to rejoice (v. 10) in trials that bring him low, perhaps including the loss of wealth. The person who is brought low and humbles herself before God will be honored by God. The metaphor of **the flower of the grass** is a vivid illustration of the temporal nature of worldly wealth as well as of life itself (a theme reiterated in 4:13–17). The point of the image is that just as grasses and wildflowers sprout and quickly perish, **so also shall the rich man fade away in his ways** (v. 11).

C. The Testing of Faith and Ultimate Wholeness (1:12)

1:12. This verse could be taken as a summary of 1:2–12 or as an introduction to 1:13–18. Both sections concern tests, but of different kinds. The tone shifts to testing of a negative kind at 1:13—the temptation to sin and blame God for the temptation—whereas verse 12 speaks of the benefit of trials for one who loves God. The word **blessed** is *makarios* and recalls the Beatitudes (Matt. 5:3–12). **The crown of life** could either refer to eternal life itself or to God's eternal reward or glory for those who overcome the severe trials of life, such as a physical handicap, a degrading status or role in life, or any number of agonies of life. It is reserved for the one who **endureth temptation** ("perseveres under trial," NIV) and has therefore passed the test. James likely was speaking of tests that involved financial hardship, and in 1:9–12, he counteracted the world's view of riches to enable his communities to endure economic troubles. Money does not determine personal worth. Note that the lowly brother or sister is the exalted one (1:9). Recognition of this "is a rejection of the culture's materialistic values and therefore a growth toward maturity. It will lead the Christian to renounce any anxious outlook about the future, any self-accusing attitude in financial struggles, and any complaining or jealous view toward others' comparative wealth" (Stulac, *James*, p. 46). Thus, wholeness is attained in the Christian community.

III. Exhortations to Completeness and Wholeness (1:13–5:12)

A. First Exhortation: The Integration of Hearing and Doing (1:13–27)

1. Negative: Self-deception (1:13–16)

1:13. For individuals to be whole and communities to be fully integrated, the combination of hearing and doing the truth must be preserved. Self-deception prevents this, however. One who **is tempted** (in 1:13–14, the verb refers to temptations that test one's moral strength to resist sin) ought not say, **I am tempted of God: for God cannot be tempted.** Because God in His very nature is holy, there is nothing in Him for sin to appeal to; **neither tempteth he any man.** The accusation against God that attributes sin to Him borders on blasphemy since it denies that God is good and that He is capable of helping one resist temptation. When one deceives oneself in thinking that God is opposed to a practice of righteousness, one can easily excuse any practice of wrongdoing.

1:14. Temptation to do evil must be attributed, not to God, but to one's **own lust**, by which he is **drawn away ... and enticed**. The language suggests a fish that is lured away from its straight course by attractive bait hiding a deadly hook. A good illustration of the allure of sin is found in C. S. Lewis's *The Lion, the Witch, and the Wardrobe* (New York: Macmillan, 1950). Edmund is enticed by the wicked White Witch, the self-proclaimed Queen of Narnia, when she offers him Turkish Delight, which he devours with relish. Once he has tasted the extraordinarily good confection, he can only think about shoveling down as much of it as he can, unaware that the witch is using the candy as bait. Edmund willingly answers as she pumps him with questions about his siblings. His insatiable appetite, once fed, blinds him from the possibility that he is endangering them. For "this was enchanted Turkish Delight and that anyone who had once tasted it would want more and more of it, and would even, if they were allowed, go on eating it till they killed themselves" (p. 33). The witch promises Edmund more Turkish Delight if he will go and bring his brother and sisters to her, and he complies, longing for just one more piece of the candy as he leaves.

1:15. The imagery of fishing gives way to another metaphor: that of childbirth. **When lust hath conceived, it bringeth forth sin**, an offspring that, when full-grown, leads to **death**. James was not saying that a particular act of sin leads to physical death necessarily, nor that one loses his or her salvation for a particular act of sin. When sins accumulate in a person's life over time without repentance and cleansing, they constitute a life that is oriented to sin. Death is the ultimate outcome of such a life. The three stages—lust, sin, and death—are seen in the temptations of Eve (see Gen. 3:6–22) and David (see 2 Sam. 11:2–17).

1:16. This verse may be seen as beginning a new paragraph, so that the warning **Do not err,**

my beloved brethren is against deception regarding the unchangeableness of God (1:17–18), or as concluding the prohibition against blaming God for temptation to sin (1:13–15). This verse refers to the discussion about the source of temptation. One should not be deceived about that and blame God for temptation to sin. In either case, wholeness cannot be maintained if believers allow themselves to wander like planets ("err" translates *planaō*, from which the English word "planet" comes) in their thinking.

2. Positive: The Integration of Hearing and Doing (1:17–27)

In this section, James provided instructions regarding the true nature of God.

1:17. God is neither powerless to help one face temptations nor intent on seeing one fail; rather, He gives one **Every good gift and every perfect gift ... from above**. That which God sends to His children does not intend their destruction but their blessing. **The Father of lights.** God is the Creator of the heavenly bodies, which give light to the earth, but unlike them, He has **no variableness**; He does not change. Sun and moon cast varying degrees of **shadow**, depending on earth's position relative to them. All heavenly bodies are in a different position (because of time and season) in the heavens from earth's vantage point. God, however, is timeless and unchanging. God's immutability (unchangeableness), however, is not tantamount to divine impassibility. Many theologians in the twentieth century affirmed the "suffering of God." That is, they recognized that the biblical evidence testifies to His active empathy with humankind and that He even suffers with His human creatures, especially in the passion of Jesus Christ (see Warren McWilliams, *The Passion of God: Divine Suffering in Contemporary Protestant Theology* [Macon, GA: Mercer University Press, 1985]). God wants to shower His benevolent gifts on His children because of His tender mercy for them. They only need to ask in faith (see 1:6–8; 4:2).

1:18. His love for believers is evident in that **of his own will begat he us**. This is not a reference to creation but to regeneration (see John 3:3–8). **The word of truth** is the proclamation of the gospel (see 1 Peter 1:23–25). Just as the first sheaf of the harvest indicates that the whole harvest will eventually follow, so the early Christians were an indication, **firstfruits**, that a great number of people would eventually be born again (this imagery is drawn from passages such as Exod. 34:22 and Lev. 23:9–14). Just as James's struggling communities were showcases for God's love and power, so the local church and its members are today, which is all the more reason to seek wholeness and integration in Christian living.

1:19–20. The command **let every man be swift to hear, slow to speak, slow to wrath** (v. 19) could be in reference to hearing of "the word of truth" (the gospel message and its ramifications; 1:18). The listening that James had in mind, however, likely was listening to each other. The word of truth, of course, is to be heard and obeyed (1:22–27). "Wrath" (*orgē*; "anger," NRSV) here is settled indignation, not rage or fury (*thymos*). Wrath may have its origin in angry outbursts since these, if unchecked, lead to a vengeful spirit. Even children recognize the importance of good listening. Lynette, age eight (when asked about what most people do on a date), said, "Dates are for having fun, and people should use them to get to know each other. Even boys have something to say if you listen long enough." James would have agreed. Many are quick to defend themselves when receiving advice, criticism, or an opinion that differs from one's own. George Stulac writes, "Almost daily as a pastor I see the value that good listening has for the church's purity within and the church's mission without. When disagreements occur in the church, over and over I have seen what great damage is done to people, to relationships and to the effectiveness of our ministries when we are quick to argue our positions, defend our views and push our opinions. I have also seen what great good is done when we discipline ourselves to postpone defending our own views and judging others' views while we concentrate on listening and giving a full hearing in order to understand the other side of the conflict. We usually find the conflict more easily resolved.

Good listening is a protection against dissension" (*James*, p. 66).

When one insists on harboring bitter grudges, one harms the Christian community, its witness, and one's own health. Twenty years ago, Leo Madow identified depression as "probably the most common sign of hidden anger in our society. More people get depressed because of repressed or unrecognized anger than almost any other symptom" (Leo Madow, "Why You Get Angry—and What to Do about It," *US News & World Report*, April 26, 1982, p. 74). His conclusion may be even more accurate today.

1:21. James's remedy for wrath is twofold, involving the elimination of something negative and replacing it with something positive. First, **lay apart all filthiness and superfluity of naughtiness**. The picture is the removal of clothing (see Rom. 13:12; Eph. 4:22, 25; Col. 3:8; 1 Peter 2:1). The two negative moral terms are essentially synonymous. The REB has "then discard everything sordid, and every wicked excess." Second, the positive action, which is necessary to assure the elimination of wickedness, is to **receive with meekness the engrafted word**. James skillfully shifted to an agricultural metaphor. "Make a soil of humble modesty for the word which roots itself inwardly" (Moffatt) expresses the idea that is contained in the word "engrafted" (a better translation is the NIV "planted"). The Greek allows a translation that connects humility with the act of taking off dirty garments (REB marginal note: "then meekly discard ... and accept") or with the reception of the word of God (KJV). Since "receive" is passive (as opposed to the active "lay apart"), "meekness" should be understood to describe the reception of the Word. Although it has already been planted in the Christian's heart, the Word must continuously instruct and guide a believer's conduct. In this way, the Word **is able to save your souls**. That is, the entire body of Christian proclamation brings the process of salvation to completion in the believer; it brings complete integration.

1:22. In 1:22–27, James spelled out what it means to receive the Word: **be ye doers of the word, and not hearers only**. Many Christians assume that a decision for Christ at a point in time, church attendance, regular Bible reading, and times of prayer are all that God desires. James said that those who do not practice the Word after hearing it are **deceiving [their] own selves**. Their religion can be described as "vain" (1:26).

1:23 – 25. One who is only **a hearer of the word** (v. 23) is like someone who looks at **his ... face in a glass** ("in a mirror," NRSV) and then simply **goeth his way**. He **forgetteth** (v. 24) what he saw in the mirror. In contrast is the person who **looketh into the perfect law of liberty** (v. 25). That person is **blessed** in whatever he undertakes since his life is lived in continual practice of the Word (the verb **continueth** is *parameno*, "to stay beside"). "The perfect law," the moral and ethical teaching of Christianity, is based on the Old Testament moral law and is embodied in the Ten Commandments (see Ps. 19:7). This law is brought to completion (perfection) by Jesus Christ. James could call the law one of "liberty" since the Christian, in contrast to the sinner, who is a slave to sin (see John 8:34), finds joyous freedom in obeying the moral law through the power of the Holy Spirit.

The metaphor of the mirror effectively illustrates the temporary and superficial effect of the Word that the mere hearing of it has on those who do not put it into practice. The benefit to them is no more than that which they get when they groom themselves before the mirror in the morning. Soon, in the tussle of the day, they have forgotten what they saw of themselves in the mirror, and whatever simple changes they made to their appearance are gone. The one who "perseveres" (RSV, v. 25) in the law that brings freedom, the one "who lives in its company" (NEB), will find wholeness. There is no shortcut to Christian maturity. Disciplined study and practice of God's Word is essential to the blessedness that James envisioned.

1:26 – 27. For James and his first-century congregations under oppression, being "doers of the word" (1:22), that is, being **religious** (v. 26), involved three specific practices. **Religion** refers to the outward acts of religion (e.g., giving to the needy, fasting, public acts of praying, and worshiping). The three practices

James listed constitute **Pure religion** (v. 27). First, **If any man among you seem to be religious** ("If any think they are religious," NRSV)**, and bridleth not his tongue**, that person **deceiveth his own heart**. Vain religion is all that such a person has. The colorful image of bridling one's own mouth (not that of another) introduces a metaphor to which James returned in 3:3. When faced with hostility from outsiders, James's hearers might have been easily tempted to return abuse with abuse. When under pressure, they might have easily snapped at fellow believers. True Christianity puts a check on reviling speech.

Second, **To visit the fatherless and widows in their affliction** (v. 27) was, for James, essential Christianity in a time when orphans and widows did not have the protective safety net of governmental social services that is to some extent available today in Western societies. James echoed the voices of the Old Testament prophets who spoke in behalf of the disadvantaged and dispossessed (see Isa. 1:17; Jer. 22:3). "Affliction" (*thlipsis*; "distress," NEB) probably refers to financial hardship. Without a father or husband, a child or woman would have been in dire straits. The church today must not think that governmental social services are adequate for orphans and widows. To grow into healthy adults, children who have suffered neglect and physical or sexual abuse require a loving family. Local churches can invite foster-care specialists to recruit and train their members to serve as foster parents. A widows' ministry could be developed whereby lonely or disabled women in the church are visited by members who assist in shopping, providing transportation, paying bills, and providing lawn care or household maintenance. Sometimes a widow or a young person in a single-parent home simply needs some regular companionship.

The final ingredient of "the kind of religion which is without stain or fault in the sight of God our Father" (NEB) is for one **to keep himself unspotted from the world** (v. 27). Here James was not calling Christians to disengage from society but to maintain devotion to God while involved in it.

Attentiveness to the needs of distressed community members will foster personal wholeness and social cohesion. Thus, the perverted and demonic values of the nonbelieving society, values that put a premium on the acquisition of wealth at the expense of the poor, will not encroach on the congregations. The assemblies will remain pure, and they will be integrated since the actions outlined in verses 26–27 unify hearing and doing of the Word.

B. Second Exhortation: The Life of Impartiality (2:1–13)

1. Negative: Distinctions between Rich and Poor (2:1–7)

2:1. James's description of Christ as **the Lord of glory** is significant at this place. The ascription shows that Jesus, lowly and despised, is the one who occupies the ultimate place of honor in the universe. He imparts honor to those who are poor in a biblical sense, those who, impoverished socially and economically, abandon themselves to God's care and vindication in the face of oppression. The poor in James's churches shared in the glory of their Lord. To show partiality to the rich denies the Lord's own honor. Thus, James could say that one's **faith** ought not to be accompanied **with respect of persons** ("favoritism," NIV; "class distinction," NJB). God does not show favoritism, nor should believers (see Deut. 1:17; Rom. 2:11; Eph. 6:9; Col. 3:25).

2:2–4. Here James presented a vivid drama, a scene from an actual house-church meeting of the first century. The word **assembly** (v. 2) translates the Greek *synagōgē*, the origin of the English word "synagogue." The action builds towards a surprising climax as, first, a well-to-do individual enters and is given treatment that is deemed appropriate to his social status. He wears **a gold ring** as well as **goodly apparel** (i.e., **gay clothing**, v. 3; "fine clothes," NRSV). Does he not deserve to be told, **Sit thou here in a good place**? Then, **a poor man** (v. 2) enters and is told to take standing room or a "cheap seat" in the gathering. Since he is dressed in **vile raiment**, he is regarded as offensive. If he were to take a prominent seat, some church members who are less noticeable than he might fear being seen as the poor man's in-

feriors. By the time the seating arrangements were described, James's readers may have nodded and agreed on their suitability. James then delivered a wallop as an unexpected climax: by showing partiality to the wealthy, the church collectively (the passage is addressed in the second-person plural) had become a gathering of **judges [with] evil thoughts** (v. 4). They had taken to themselves the right to issue a judgment that was contrary to the judgment that God has already delivered regarding the poor.

In 2:5–13, James provided three arguments against showing favoritism to the rich: (1) the rich persecute the poor—the believers (vv. 5–7); (2) favoritism violates the royal law of love and thus is sin (vv. 8–11); (3) favoritism will be judged (vv. 12–13). The first of these arguments concludes James's negative statement about partiality in the church, which destroys integration and wholeness.

2:5–7. The rhetorical question **Hath not God chosen the poor of this world rich in faith, and heirs of the kingdom which he hath promised to them that love him?** (v. 5; see Matt 5:3; Luke 6:20; 1 Cor. 1:26–31) expects a yes answer. In the New Testament, the kingdom of God is that reign and rule of God in which His redemptive purposes for humankind are realized. This realm, which is spiritual but is lived out and expressed in physical and social dimensions as well, has invaded the present age but will not be consummated until the second coming of Jesus Christ. Paradoxically, the poor are the wealthy and heirs in the kingdom of God. The wealthy of this world do not have true spiritual riches if earthly wealth is all they possess. In James (and in the Synoptic Gospels), the poor are those who are impoverished because of their discipleship. Because they believe in the Son of God, they may rely on the fulfillment of God's promises to the disenfranchised, the outcast, and the needy in the Old Testament (see Ps. 69:32–33; Isa. 57:15; 61:1). The churches have, in some instances, **despised the poor** (v. 6). The **rich**, on the other hand, **oppress you, and draw you before the judgment seats**, that is, "act the potentate" against you and "drag" (*helkō*, used to describe Paul being dragged from the temple, Acts 21:30) you to courts where the privileged are given favorable treatment. James did not call for a reverse persecution of the rich; he simply called for equitable treatment of the poor. Since God honors them, they deserve honor from fellow believers. Honor — public acknowledgment that one has met certain cultural expectations and norms — was not to be accorded to the rich since they had verbally abused the Christians (**they blaspheme**; v. 7). A proper response in such a situation would be prayer, blessing, and nonretaliation (see Luke 6:27 – 31), but not special favoritism at the expense of those who have been honored by God.

The church today, sadly, repeats the errors of the congregations portrayed by James. Christians continue to show partiality, favoring those who are wealthy, attractive, influential, educated, and talented when it comes to expressions of love and honor. Of course, the church must permit only the spiritually mature to practice leadership. Too often believers choose to associate with or show kindness to those who might be able to repay them with reciprocal favors or advancement in their social standing. The less gifted or influential may not be able to repay in these ways, but they are just as deserving of our attention as those who can.

In one church, the youth pastor invited a young professional couple with a large income to join him as volunteer youth leaders. They declined after hearing that the responsibilities involved a weekly meeting with the youth pastor for prayer, planning, and Bible study. Shortly thereafter, the youth pastor invited a college-age person (with a modest income) to consider the same responsibility with the same conditions. He accepted. The couple, meanwhile, reconsidered and made their desire to work with the youth group known. Since the group was small, the youth pastor informed them that, for the time being, the young people had sufficient leadership. The couple, stunned and displeased that they would be refused, complained to the senior pastor. He then reprimanded the youth pastor for his choice of leaders: "Be careful! Don't you know that this couple contributes more to the church than any other members?" The senior pastor had favored the rich at this point. Although the young professional couple and the young college-age person had been given equal opportunity, the senior pastor believed the former deserved special consideration — or favoritism.

2. Positive: Fulfillment of the Royal Law (2:8 – 13)

2:8. The law of love (Lev. 19:18) is called **the royal law** because it is the supreme law and is the source of all other laws governing human relationships. It is the summation of all such laws (see Matt. 22:36 – 40; Rom. 13:8 – 10).

2:9. To **have respect to persons** is *prosōpolēmpteō*, "to receive the face." The verb conveys the idea of honor that, in Hebrew thinking, is centered on the face. God honors His people by making His face shine upon them (see Num. 6:25 – 26). Giving honor to others is commendable if it is bestowed on those who deserve it. Honor is to be granted without false distinctions.

2:10 – 11. The law is the expression of the character and will of God. Therefore, to violate one part of the law is to violate God's will and thus His whole law (see Matt 5:18 – 19; 23:23). Thus, one who fails to keep even one commandment **is guilty of all** (v. 10). The two commandments that James used as examples, **Do not commit adultery** (Exod. 20:14) and **Do not kill** (Exod. 20:13), pertain to any illicit sexual activity and murder, respectively.

2:12. Here judgment is not for determining eternal destiny, for James was speaking to believers (see 2:1), whose destinies were already determined (see John 5:24). Rather, it is for giving rewards to believers (see 1 Cor. 3:12 – 15; 2 Cor. 5:10; Rev. 22:12). Douglas Moo perceptively states, "No longer is God's law a threatening, confining burden. For the will of God now confronts us as a *law of liberty* — an obligation that is discharged in the joyful knowledge that God has both 'liberated' us from the penalty of sin and given us, in his Spirit, the power to obey his will" (*The Letter of James*, p. 98).

2:13. If man is merciful, God will be merciful on the day of judgment (see Prov. 21:13; Matt. 5:7; 6:14 – 15; 18:21 – 35). **Mercy rejoiceth against judgment** ("mercy triumphs over judgment," NRSV). This statement could mean either that one's practice of mercy is a sign that he will not be condemned in the final judgment or that mercy more effectively promotes wholeness and integration when it replaces the judgmental attitudes of 2:1–4. The context speaks for the latter interpretation.

C. Third Exhortation: The Integration of Faith and Action (2:14–26)

In verses 14–20, 24, 26, "faith" is not used in the sense of genuine, saving faith. Rather, it is demonic (v. 19), useless (v. 20), and dead (v. 26). It is a mere intellectual acceptance of certain truths without trust in Christ as Savior. James was not saying that a person is saved by works and not by genuine faith. Rather, he was saying, to use Martin Luther's words, that a man is justified (declared righteous before God) by faith alone, but not by a faith that is alone. Genuine faith will produce good deeds, but only faith in Christ saves. Justification has a twofold dimension, according to Luther in a disputation on justification in 1536: "Before God it takes place by faith, not by works; before men it takes place by works and love, which declare us just before ourselves and before the world. In fine, we concede that a man does justify himself insofar as the outward effect is concerned, not, however, insofar as the inward cause is concerned" (Ewald M. Plass, *What Luther Says* [Saint Louis: Concordia, 1959], 3:1231). James maintained that faith and action must be integrated in Christian living, both on the individual and corporate (church) levels. The illustration of false faith (vv. 14–17) is parallel to the illustration of false love found in 1 John 3:17. The latter passage calls for love in action; this one calls for faith in action.

1. Negative: Separation of Faith and Action (2:14–17)

2:14. The premises in this verse are (1) **faith** saves, (2) faith and **works** must be combined, and (3) false faith exists—faith without accompanying works, which does not save one. There is no **profit** at all in such faith.

2:15. The arena in which faith must show itself to be real and saving is, according to James, caring for the poor **brother or sister**, that is, one who is **naked,**

and destitute of daily food ("without clothes and daily food," NIV).

2:16. Neither the self-proclaimed believer nor the poor **profit** if one merely wishes the needy person well and does not distribute the items that **are needful to the body**. "Brother or sister" (2:15) probably refers to a member of the church, but care for the needy must extend beyond the Christian family. Provision should be offered to the "neighbor"—anyone in need. If that person's need becomes known to a believer who is in a financial position to do something about it, that believer is under obligation to consider action. Should a Christian respond to every request for money? Many believers feel overwhelmed by pleas on TV or through mailings to assist the hungry. Answering every request is not the proper response (and become financially constrained oneself), nor is refusing every request. Prayerful consideration of appeals, and a commitment to answer no more than a few, is probably the best response for most believers.

Should a Christian give money to beggars and panhandlers? Probably not. A wiser course of action might be to offer to buy a homeless person a meal or to direct him or her to a mission or shelter. Cash is often used to purchase alcohol or drugs and perpetuates the condition of beggary. Many churches have established food kitchens or pantries where destitute people can come for physical necessities. These are distributed in an environment where Jesus Christ is proclaimed and glorified.

2:17. Faith, then, without accompanying **works, is dead**. Genuine faith will always be accompanied by what Luther identified as "works of faith," which are done purely out of love for God, not out of fear or in the hope of gaining advantage with God. Only believers, those who are justified by faith, can perform works of faith. Works that are performed to gain salvation are "works of the law" and actually hinder justification since they prevent one from realizing his abject need before God.

2. Positive: Completion of Faith with Action (2:18–26)

2:18. A new paragraph begins here (see JB, NRSV). **Thou hast faith, and I have works**. James's discussion in 2:18–20 may reflect a false claim by some in his audience that there are "faith" Christians and "works" Christians, that is, that faith and deeds can exist independently of each other. With masterful irony, James denied the possibility that one can **shew me thy faith without thy works**. The grammatical difficulties surrounding 2:18–20 are reviewed in detail by Nystrom (*James*, pp. 150–53). Perhaps the biggest question in this text is that of the speaker(s). Who says what and where? Is an ally of James speaking in verse 18, or an opponent? If an ally, where does the ally's statement begin and end? If an opponent is cited, what are the opponent's precise words? The KJV punctuation is imprecise. The NIV inserts quotation marks around a contrasting statement of an objector: "But someone will say, 'You have faith; I have deeds'" (18a). In the NIV, however, James's answer in verse 18b-c seems to agree with the objection, not refute it! ("Show me your faith without deeds, and I will show you my faith by what I do.") Originally, no punctuation existed in the New Testament text, so the decisions of editors and translators are informed conjectures.

Perhaps James introduced an imaginary interlocutor at verse 18a, whom he addressed directly: "But someone may say that you have faith [an abrupt shift from the third person to the second person, but the reference is to the same individual], and I say that I have good deeds. Show me your faith apart from good deeds, and I will show you my faith by my good deeds." The "someone" is an individual who maintains that faith unaccompanied by works is acceptable; he is the one without faith in 2:14, the "senseless person" (NRSV) of 2:20. The JB captures the sense of verse 18: "This is the way to talk to people of that kind: You say you have faith and I have good deeds; I will prove to you that I have faith by showing you my good deeds—now you prove to me that you have faith without any good deeds to show." The entire section of 2:18–20 addresses that individual whose professed faith has no good deeds to back it up. Although the exact grammatical sense is difficult to ascertain, the overall thrust of the passage is evident: "faith [without] works, is dead" (2:17).

2:19. With sarcasm, James commended his opponent for his belief that **there is one God**. Congratulations! **Thou doest well!** Even **the devils** assent to the declaration of monotheism that is reflected in the well-known Jewish creed called the Shema (Hebrew, meaning "Hear" [Deut. 6:4; Mark 12:29]), and they **tremble**. The demons' belief does not do them any good since their belief in the one God is only a mental acknowledgment. They have not acted on their belief.

2:20. In summary, James again addressed his imaginary objector, who was introduced in 2:18. This **vain man** ought to recognize by now **that faith without works is dead**. The word "dead" in the best witnesses is *argos* and has the idea of "idle," "lazy," "fallow," "unproductive." The word for the inert gas *argon* has its etymological roots in the term.

2:21–23. Apart from its context, verse 21 might seem to contradict the biblical teaching that people are saved by faith and not by good deeds (see Rom. 3:28; Gal. 2:15–16). James, however, meant only that righteous action is evidence of genuine faith, not that it saves, for the verse that he cites (Gen. 15:6) to substantiate his point says, **Abraham believed God, and it** (i.e., faith, not works) **was imputed unto him for righteousness** (v. 23). "Imputed" (*logizomai*) here could be understood as "allotted," but not in the sense that faith is some sort of merit. Faith is complete dependence on the sheer grace of God and admits its utter incapacity to do anything meritorious before Him. Hence, faith receives His grace and renders one in right standing before God. Imputation here is probably to be understood in terms of a covenant relationship, not of moral righteousness.

Furthermore, Abraham's act of faith recorded in Genesis 15:6 occurred before **he had offered Isaac** (v. 21; see Genesis 22), which was only a proof of the genuineness of his faith. As Paul wrote, the only thing that matters is "faith which worketh by love" (Gal. 5:6). Faith that saves produces deeds. In Abraham's case, **faith wrought with his works** (v. 22; "faith was working with his works," NASB), and thus faith, having reached the goal or conclusion that God intended for it, was **made perfect**. The designation

the Friend of God (v. 23; see 2 Chron. 20:7) further describes Abraham's relationship to God as one of complete acceptance. Abraham staked everything on God's trustworthiness to fulfill His promise that he would be the first of a great people. The patriarch had to be willing to sacrifice the only son through whom the fulfillment could come. Furthermore, the one nearest and dearest to his heart had to be entrusted to God. When God tests Christians regarding the vision for life and ministry that He has given to them, how does one respond? When a close relationship is threatened by illness, geographical change, or a breakup, do believers entrust that loved one to God, as well as their desires for that relationship? How one passes the test reveals the quality of one's faith and makes it stronger (see 1:2–8).

2:24. Here to be **justified** does not contradict Paul's teaching on the subject (e.g., Eph. 2:8–10). One's claim to faith is justified before people (shown to be true and substantiated) **not by** (the claim of) **faith only**, not by an intellectual assent to certain truths, but **by works** also. In James's mind, righteous deeds that spring from faith undoubtedly included assistance to the poor. Paul himself affirmed that good works flow from the life that is saved by grace (see Eph. 2:10).

2:25. Rahab the harlot is a surprising choice as an example of faith. James was not approving Rahab's occupation; he merely commended her for her faith (see Heb. 11:31), which she demonstrated by helping the spies (see Joshua 2). As the mother of Boaz, she became an ancestor of David and Jesus (see Matt. 1:5). Her deed is an example of providing daily necessities to the needy (see 2:15–16). The mention of her in this section was very appropriate for James's audience. Many of them appeared righteous but stood condemned as "adulterers and adulteresses" (4:4). Obviously immoral, Rahab the prostitute is, however, an example of faith. Unless one is willing to risk all by identifying with God's people and His purposes in the world, whatever faith he or she proclaims is ultimately shallow. Rahab welcomed the spies because she believed in the superiority of Yahweh, and she put her life on the line

to protect His people. James's readers had not done similarly unless they had acted in behalf of the orphans, widows, and poor who needed the protection of privileged members of the congregations. Faith and deeds must be integrated.

D. Fourth Exhortation: The Life of Wisdom (3:1–18)

1. Negative: The Destructive Power of the Tongue (3:1–12)

3:1–2. The word **masters** (v. 1) has its old English meaning of "teachers" here, as the Greek word (*didaskaloi*) used and the subject matter of chapter 3 show. Because teachers have great influence, they will be held more accountable than those who do not have the responsibility of instructing by word and example (see Luke 20:47; Matt. 23:1–33). James's remark that **we shall receive the greater condemnation** does not mean that all teachers have done so miserably that they will certainly be condemned for their shortcomings. The Greek construction *meizon krima lēmpsometha* means "we who teach will be judged by God with greater strictness" (NLT). The reason for stricter judgment is that "we all [i.e., 'all we teachers'] stumble in many ways" (NIV), particularly in regard to harmful speech. Some would classify one who does not sin by what he or she says **a perfect man** (v. 2) or woman. Since the tongue is so difficult to control, anyone who can control it perfectly can practice self-control in all other areas of life as well.

With that somber warning in mind, how can one know if God is placing a call to a teaching ministry in the church, either as a layperson or as a professional? A few questions and considerations that may indicate such a calling are the following. (1) Is such a role something that one really desires to do? Paul said, "If anyone sets his heart on being an overseer, he desires a noble task" (1 Tim. 3:1, NIV). A teaching ministry does not in all cases mean being an overseer, but the principle still holds true: God uses the deep desires of His children to communicate to them something of His will for their lives. (2) What am I good at doing? Do I enjoy studying the Bible and sharing my observations with others? Do people ask me questions about the Bible and its application to life today? (3) What do others believe that I can do well? What kind of responsibilities are offered or delegated to me? Of course, God's *general* will for His people is found in Scripture. His *specific* will for an individual's life becomes clear to one who considers such questions.

3:3 – 12. In these verses, James employed several colorful metaphors for the tongue, some of which are direct (comparison expressed) and some of which are indirect (comparison inferred). The theme of wisdom (introduced in 1:5 – 8) is revisited. Once again, James's eye is on wholeness and integration. Corporately and individually, a person's faith must be matched with good deeds. Otherwise, Christian life will be disintegrated. So too will the teacher's ministry disintegrate if the wisdom he or she professes is not accompanied by a judicious use of the tongue. Wholesome, not harmful, speech must proceed from the teacher's mouth.

3:3. Bits in the horses' mouths. Just as something as small as a bit can enable one to lead the entire body of a horse, so something as small as a human tongue sets the course of a person's entire life (see 2:2), for good or for ill.

3:4 – 5a. The rudder of a ship. The **helm** (v. 4) of a ship is the "rudder" (NRSV). Although it is **very small**, it can guide a ship driven by violent winds, "wherever the pilot wants to go" (NIV). **The tongue is a little member** (v. 5) of the body, but its swelled and vain boasts are completely disproportionate to its size. The degree to which one speaks of himself and his plans should be in proportion to the small instrument by which he speaks. One should speak little, and then not in a boastful way.

3:5b – 6. A forest fire. **A little fire kindleth** (v. 5b) a huge conflagration (**matter,** *hylē*, should be translated "forest" [NKJV]). Its ruinous power is so overwhelming that it **setteth on fire the course of nature** (v. 6), which is perhaps a reference to the ancient symbol of the wheel for human life in its changeability and its allotted course. The wheel must complete its "cycle." All the while, "the evil influence of the

tongue spreads out from the axle to the entire circumference of the 'wheel' at every moment in its revolving course" (Tasker, *The General Epistle of James,* p. 76). The tongue, being deadly, **is set on fire of hell.** This may be a figurative way of saying that the source of the tongue's evil is the Devil (see John 8:44).

The devastating effects of the tongue were illustrated just before this author began writing this commentary on James. Near his home in northern California, a devastating fire burned 11,000 acres of timber and rangeland in August 2004, when conditions for such a fire were at their optimum. The Bear Fire was apparently started by a spark from a riding lawn mower that was being used to cut down dry weeds on a day when the temperature had reached 106°F. The blaze quickly spread and destroyed eighty-six dwellings before it was controlled. Damage estimates from the fire totaled $25.6 million. The tongue can unleash its destructive energy similarly. Once its harmful energy is unleashed, catastrophic results soon follow. **The tongue is a fire** (v. 6), James lamented.

A world of iniquity (v. 6). The tongue is like the world in its fallenness.

3:7 – 10. An unruly evil, full of deadly poison (v. 8). James's comparison here may be to the venom of the serpent. Whereas even the deadly snake **is tamed** (along with other creatures of earth, sea, and sky; v. 7), the tongue defies human control and is lethal in its effects. With the tongue **bless we God** (v. 9), and with the same instrument **curse we men.** The inconsistency of such action is clear: human beings **are made after the similitude of God** ("in the likeness of God," NASB). Since humans have been made like God (Gen. 1:26 – 27), for one human to curse another is like cursing God (see Gen. 9:6). Verbal abuse of others constitutes a great hypocrisy and is equivalent to cursing God since abusing those who are created in God's image abuses His image. James's very strong prohibition makes these things clear: **My brethren, these things ought not so to be** (v. 10).

3:11 – 12. A spring. James used an impossibility of nature to emphasize the inconsistency of a person who praises God one minute and condemns a fellow human the next. **A fountain** (v. 11) cannot bubble up and **send forth** both **sweet water and bitter**. The latter term ("brackish," AT, REB) is *pikros*, whose root is "to cut," "to prick." The foul water is sharp and harsh. So too is the "cursing" (v. 10). Any speech that maligns and degrades — slander, gossip, mockery — is bitter to the recipient and does not promote wholeness and integration of the truth. Parents far too often are sparing in praise and abundant in criticism. Recognition, thanks, and affirmation do not promote haughtiness in children but healthy self-esteem and a sense that they are created in God's image.

The fig tree and the grape **vine** (v. 12). As a fig tree cannot produce olives, nor the grapevine **figs**, neither can a spring produce water contrary to its nature. Either **salt** water or **fresh** water will come from a spring, but not both. Readers are left to consider whether there is true integration in their communities — integration between word and deed.

2. Positive: True Wisdom versus False Wisdom (3:13–18)

3:13. The question here zeroes in on the teacher (see discussion on 3:1), that is, **a wise man** who is an expert in matters pertaining to the Word. Three elements of a true teacher are expressed by three terms in this verse: **knowledge, meekness** ("gentleness," NRSV), and **shew out of a good conversation** ("show it by his good life," NIV). One cannot teach well what one does not practice in one's own life. The truly wise teacher is one who instructs patiently and receives questions and criticism with openness. Without the true wisdom that is described in 3:13–18, especially among its teachers, the Christian community cannot expect to be whole.

3:14. If a person has **bitter** (*pikros* again; see 3:11) **envying** of another's success in the realm of teaching and refuses to recognize that person's gifts or position because of **strife** and hostility, he has no reason to claim honor for that stance. It is in opposition to the truth.

3:15. The so-called wisdom that is characterized by pride is **not from above**, from God (see 1:5, 17;

1 Cor. 2:6–16). Instead, it is **earthly, sensual, devilish** ("demonic," NKJV). The second of this infamous trio, "sensual," is the translation of *psychikos*, a term Jude used to describe the false teachers whom he opposed. In Jude 19, the word describes those who, not having the Spirit, "follow mere natural instincts" (NIV). Paul used the word similarly to describe the person who cannot receive the things of God's Spirit (1 Cor. 2:14). Although James probably was not contending with false teaching as Jude and Paul were, he did contend with a false concept of true wisdom, one which draws on human intelligence without enlightenment from the Spirit of God. In biblical scholarship, many excellent studies of the grammar, historical-cultural background, and literary features of the text have been produced. Believers ought to use these studies freely, whether they were written by believers or unbelievers. Insights from history and literary analysis are open to all human inquiry, and the truth discovered is ultimately God's truth. Only those interpreters, however, who have the Holy Spirit and His illumination have the means by which to apply the biblical text to contemporary life most clearly and accurately.

3:16. Jealousy and the contention that accompanies it eventually break out in **confusion** ("disorder," NIV). All sorts of evil practices ensue when teachers or leaders have self-serving motives in their work that is ostensibly for God. "God is not the author of confusion, but of peace" (1 Cor. 14:33).

3:17. Here James returned to the subject of genuine wisdom, **the wisdom ... from above**, which he introduced in 3:13. The author personified wisdom; the wise person is the one who has the characteristics that he listed. Wisdom is **first pure**; it displays a commitment to moral integrity without compromise. Only when wisdom has a passion for purity will the other qualities follow. The wise person is also **peaceable, gentle, and easy to be intreated** ("peace-loving, considerate, submissive," NIV). Stulac maintains that these characteristics "are terms that James uses only here in his letter; they describe people who can yield status, who care for others and who are willing to submit and learn from others — all in contrast to the bitterness, envy and selfish ambition of false spirituality" (*James*, p. 138). The final traits in the list of godly wisdom — **full of mercy and good fruits, without partiality, and without hypocrisy** — echo James's earlier statements about merciful treatment of the disadvantaged (2:1–17).

3:18. The fruit ("A harvest," NIV) **of righteousness** probably is "the fruit that consists of righteousness," the condition for the growth of which is **peace**, the Old Testament *šalom*. Peace in this sense is the corporate wholeness and well-being that are borne out of holiness, truth, sincerity, mercy, and justice (see Pss. 34:14; 38:3; 73:3; Isa. 43:7; Zech. 8:16–17, 19). Those who are peacemakers (see Matt. 5:9), those who seek to reconcile themselves to others and to promote reconciliation among others, are instrumental in this process.

E. Fifth Exhortation: Friendship with the World and Friendship with God (4:1–12)

1. Negative: Pursuit of Selfish Desires (4:1–4)

4:1–3. The principal problems James addressed in these verses, a passage full of battle imagery, are prayerlessness and incorrect prayer. Instead of proper prayer, the hearers were driven by their **lusts** (v. 1). The Greek for this term is the source of the word "hedonism." They had chosen to foster their passions rather than seek to control them (see 1:2–8, 13–15). James may have had in mind a thirst for power and popularity at the expense of the poor. (Did people within James' churches literally **kill** (v. 2)? The expression is probably simply figurative, a hyperbole for "hate.") A contentious environment within the Christian community, the family, or the individual heart prohibits prayerfulness. One reason the community and its members did not receive what they needed (evidently behind the covetousness were genuine needs) was **because ye ask not**. Those who do bother to pray do not receive what they ask for because they **ask amiss** ("because your whole motive is wrong," NLT), **that ye may consume it upon your lusts** (v. 3). "Consume" is *dapanaō*, used in Luke 15:14 to describe the lost son's squandering of his inheritance. Of course, God does not

answer prayers for that which does not serve His ultimate and good purpose.

4:4. The epithet **adulterers and adulteresses** (the better reading is "adulteresses") recalls the prophetic condemnations of Israel in the Old Testament for spiritual adultery, that is, covenant infidelity, which often included idolatry (see, e.g., Isa. 57:3; Jer. 31:32; Ezek. 16:38; Hos. 3:1). The image is of those who are spiritually unfaithful, who love the world rather than God. James addresses those who would be **a friend of the world**. As in James 1:27, the "world" here is not the created order (which is good [see 1:17]), nor is it the web of human activity and commerce (which is morally neutral [see 4:13–17]). The world is a measure of existence that does not take God and His claims into account, and to be its friend is to oppose God and His claims on human life. That opposition can be in the form of indifference to the living God, not just active hostility.

Life in the affluent West in the twenty-first century is characterized by friendship with the world in this sense. The culture of consumerism, in which the need to need and the desire to desire are awakened in the enchantments of advertising, exalts self-centeredness and greed. The omnipresence of commercial messages in the media and the overload of choices that confront people daily make moral discrimination more and more difficult. For many, ethical and moral reasoning has devolved into consumer choice. The questions, "What is God's will?" and "What is right?" are increasingly rare, replaced by the question, "What is most satisfying?" Even the inquiry, "Can I afford this?" is no longer important for so many, with credit-card use and abuse so readily available. A system built on consumption does not promote wholeness in the Christian community unless its members exercise extreme care to guard themselves against the insidious effects of greed.

2. Positive: Humility before God (4:5–12)

4:5. The passage of **scripture** that James had in mind is not known, but it may have been the thrust of several passages in constellation. The sense of the passage is difficult. Does it refer to the Holy Spirit

(NASB) or the human spirit (NIV)? And is the desire evil, marked by human envy (**lusteth**), or does the Spirit lovingly yearn for His people (NRSV)? In other words, who is the subject of the verb "to desire" (*epipothein*), God or the human spirit that dwells in all humans?

Pheme Perkins believes that a dualism of good and evil, truth and falsehood (see *T. Sim.* 3:1–6; 1QS 3:18–4:26) is present in 4:1–5 and that James's focus was not the evil desire of the human spirit but God's desire for that spirit to control envy. Her reasoning is that "God desires the [human] spirit that dwells within humans to be opposed to jealousy, not to be its slave" since the prepositional construction *pros phthonon* ("jealously," NRSV, v. 5) with an accusative can refer to that which is being opposed (*First and Second Peter, James, and Jude*, p. 125). This is an intriguing interpretation. **The spirit** is likely the human spirit, as Perkins asserts. In light of 4:1–4, however, one probably ought to read verse 5 negatively; it is a scriptural substantiation for the unflattering description of the human condition described in 4:1–4. The real antithesis to that condition emerges only in 4:6 ("But he giveth more grace"). James B. Adamson believes that verse 5, with its affirmation of the presence of "the sinful propensities of the spirit implanted in man," ought to be translated, "Or do you suppose it is an idle saying in the Scriptures, that the spirit that has taken its dwelling in us is prone to envious lust?" (*The Epistle of James*, pp. 172–73). Thus, verse 5, although appearing within the set of positive instructions in this section (4:5–12), is somewhat negative. It leads, however, to a positive declaration in 4:6 and the instructions that promote wholeness in the community in 4:7–12. Those instructions serve to curb envious lust and promote the work of the Holy Spirit within the community.

4:6. But he giveth more grace. God gives more than enough grace to His people so that they can lead a life of wholeness despite the all pervasive inclination to do evil. James's rationale for his teaching on grace is Proverbs 3:34 **God resisteth the proud, but giveth grace unto the humble** (see 1 Peter 5:5, which also quotes this Old Testament text).

4:7–10. These verses contain ten commands, each of which is stated in Greek in a way that calls for immediate action in rooting out the sinful attitude of pride.

4:7. The first two commands are **Submit yourselves therefore to God** and **Resist the devil** (see Eph. 6:11–18; 1 Peter 5:8–9), the second of which is accompanied by a promise: **and he will flee from you**. In the New Testament, the reality of Satan is affirmed, but so is the triumph of Christ over him (Luke 10:18) and over the evil powers (see Col. 2:15). The believer who claims that victory and resists the Devil's schemes will find victory too.

4:8. The command **Draw nigh to God** ("Draw near to God," NKJV) also has a guarantee: **he will draw nigh to you**. Some contemporary worship songs call on God to show Himself and come near to the worshiper, which is good, but God reveals Himself to those who draw near to Him. When one minimizes the importance of personal and corporate holiness, one cannot expect God to manifest His power on one's behalf. For James's readers, drawing near to God meant drawing near to the oppressed and needy to meet their tangible physical needs. "Pure religion" involves doing just that (see 1:27).

The next two commands define and clarify what drawing near to God often involves. **Cleanse your hands.** Before the Old Testament priests approached God at the tabernacle, they had to wash their hands and feet at the brass laver as a symbol of spiritual cleansing (see Exod. 30:17–21; for the imagery of "clean hands, and a pure heart," see Ps. 24:4). **Purify your hearts** is an injunction for the **double minded**. Those who doubt whether God is willing or able to answer their prayers for wisdom during trials are described by this same word (see 1:8).

4:9. Be afflicted is not a call to bring suffering upon oneself. The verb is a summons to "grieve" (NIV), "to repent in misery" (Burdick, "James," p. 195). To **mourn** denotes an intense and passionate outward grief. Again, the grief is over sin. In James's community, the sins for which the believers needed to mourn may have been their partiality, haughtiness, and the pursuit of pleasure that characterizes friendship with the world. To **weep** carries further the command to repent. The verb, *klaiō*, has the idea of audible weeping that arises from "deep grief" (NLT).

Let your laughter be turned to mourning is certainly not a prohibition on joy or happiness in the Christian life. Church services, ministry functions, and family life could all use more happiness and less gloom. James was condemning the inane hilarity of the carouser, the slanderer, and the brute. The turning of **joy to heaviness** is the exchange by which "your high spirits will have to become heartfelt dejection" (Phillips) as sin is faced squarely and for which one repents of.

4:10. Humble yourselves in the sight of the Lord, and he shall lift you up. What the world honors—the ambition of the rich and powerful who trample others as they make their way to the top—is not what God honors. He honors those who cast themselves on His mercy and become servants of others (see 1 Peter 5:6).

4:11–12. Moving from humility before God to the extension of that humility in community life, James returned to the matter of speech (see 1:19, 26; 3:1–12): **Speak not evil one of another** (v. 11). One ought not to speak evil of his brother, a fellow member of a Christian congregation. In other words, James prohibits "speaking down to" (*katalaleō*) or slandering another believer. Although all forms of ridicule, scorn, jokes, and belittling are here outlawed, the term usually refers to slandering someone who is not present to defend himself. William Barclay incisively observes, "There is great necessity for this warning. People are slow to realize that there are few sins which the Bible so unsparingly condemns as the sin of irresponsible and malicious gossip. There are few activities in which the average person finds more delight than this; to tell and to listen to the slanderous story—especially about some distinguished person—is for most people a fascinating activity. We do well to remember what God thinks of it" (*The Letters of James and Peter*, p. 111).

James maintained that one who **speaketh evil of his brother ... speaketh evil of the law** (v. 11). Speaking evil of another is equivalent to judging that person and is therefore speaking evil of the law and judging it too. Why? To disparage one's neighbor is to break "the royal law" of 2:8: "Thou shalt love thy neighbour as thyself" (see also Exod. 20:16; Pss. 15:3; 50:19–20; Prov. 6:16, 19). To speak against a brother is to scorn the law of love. And to break that law is to set oneself up as God; one has determined that the royal law is no longer binding. One is no longer a doer of the law but its judges. Now the reader can see the point clearly: there is no room for another judge besides God. **There is one lawgiver, who is able to save and to destroy: who art thou that judgest another?** (v. 12).

F. Sixth Exhortation: Attitudes toward the Future (4:13–5:11)

1. Negative: Disregard for the Shortness of Life and of the Coming Judgment (4:13–5:6)

In this section, James was addressing Christian merchants of the first century. Verses 13–18 constitute the first of two short addresses to groups who had a wrong outlook on wealth. Both addresses begin with the phrase "Go to now" (v. 13, 5:1).

4:13. James described three indications that a person was well-to-do according to the standards of the ancient world. (1) He or she had time to spend on business ventures and was not tied down to eking out a subsistence living. Such a businessperson was able to travel to another city and **continue there a year**. (2) The merchant had capital with which to speculate and invest, to **buy and sell**, and (3) had enough of it to expect to **get gain**. James did not condemn commercial enterprise or the possession and increase of wealth. He condemned the shortsightedness that fails to recognize the futility of building one's future solely on hopes of financial gain. He also condemned the failure to allow for God's will in human enterprise.

4:14. No one can be certain what the future holds, **what shall be on the morrow**. Each human life, though of inestimable worth, is but **a vapour, that appeareth for a little time, and then vanisheth away** ("no more than a mist, seen for a little while and then dispersing," NEB). Seafaring merchants would have easily understood a mist as an apt metaphor for life's short duration. Shakespeare's Macbeth lamented the brevity of life:

> Life's but a walking shadow, a poor player
> That struts and frets his hour upon the stage
> And then is heard no more: it is a tale
> Told by an idiot, full of sound and fury,
> Signifying nothing.
>
> *Macbeth*, 5.5.24–28

James was not as pessimistic about life's meaning as Macbeth was, but he was as realistic in his assessment of its shortness.

4:15. In light of the shortness of the human life span, one ought to be reminded, **If the Lord will, we shall live, and do this, or that**. This is not a flippant statement used as some sort of fetish for good luck. Behind this statement is the conviction that God is sovereign, that He determines the duration of one's life, as He determines the boundaries of human activity. One cannot derive from this statement the notion that such things are set and cannot be affected by prayer or choices bad and good. James's assertion does, however, call into question the teaching of open theism in regard to God's omniscience. Proponents of open theism believe that God is aware of all possible human choices, but He limits His own foreknowledge of those choices. If God were aware of the outcome of human choice, open theism says, human free will would be nonexistent. Contrary to that view is James's outlook: God superintends how long a person lives and what that person does during his or her lifetime. One can make plans, certainly, but must submit to the overriding will of God. In the consumerist society that pervades the West in the opening years of the twenty-first century, James's instruction is just as relevant as it was in the first century.

4:16. The merchant readers whom James addressed were not at fault for making plans. Rather, their fault was **ye rejoice in your boastings** ("you boast in your arrogance," NRSV). The traders found their significance in the making and execution of their commercial plans. James maintained that **all such rejoicing is evil**. The entrepreneurs left God out of their planning and acted as if He does not exist. Such self-sufficiency is the height of pride.

4:17. Here is a pithy maxim that sums up James's statements about pride and self-sufficiency: **Therefore to him that knoweth to do good, and doeth it not, to him it is sin**. Whether or not the hearers knew beforehand the principles of his discourse on making plans was inconsequential. The merchants knew them now and needed to heed them as doers, not just hearers.

5:1. The **rich** whom James addressed here evidently were not Christians (nor do they appear to be in 2:2, 6), for James warned them to repent and weep because of the coming misery. The address in 5:1–6 is similar to Old Testament declarations of judgment against pagan nations, interspersed in books otherwise addressed to God's people (see Isaiah 13–23; Jeremiah 46–51; Ezekiel 25–32; Amos 1:3–2:16; Zeph. 2:4–15). Although some wealthy persons might have been present in James's churches to hear his letter read, this address to them was really for the benefit of any believers who had been victims of oppression by the wealthy. (The literary device of addressing imaginary hearers as if they are present is called *apostrophe*.)

In view of the coming judgment, James called on the rich to **weep and howl for your miseries that shall come upon you**. The Greek word *ololuzō* (excellently translated "howl" in the KJV) is onomatopoetic; that is, its sound suggests the meaning of the word. "Burst into weeping, howling with grief" is Robertson's rendering of the two verbs here (*The General Epistles*, p. 57). James's tone is reminiscent of Jesus' own pronouncement of woe upon the rich in Luke 6:24.

5:2. The perfect tense of the verbs in this passage emphasizes the certainty of the judgment to come; it was so certain that James spoke of it as if it had already happened (a literary device called *prolepsis*). **Riches** may be food specifically or wealth generally. In the latter case, clothing and precious metals would be examples. At any rate, the riches **are corrupted** ("Your wealth has rotted," NIV). **Garments** were one of the main forms of wealth in the ancient world (see Acts 20:33). Now they were **motheaten**. The perishable nature of wealth makes it an unwise primary investment of one's energies during a lifetime. Today, synthetic fabrics make some clothing quite durable. They still quickly "decay" in obsolescence in the estimation of an overly fashion-conscious society. A person who, because of an obsession for attractiveness, must have only the very latest styles finds clothing to be something that lasts only briefly.

5:3. Your gold and silver is cankered ("corroded," NKJV; "rusted," NRSV). These metals do not rust, but James used the image of their corrosion to underline his point that security in riches is illusory. **Rust** is the result of hoarding, and that rust will both testify against and judge the selfish rich. James then deftly shifted the metaphor of rust to that of **fire**, associated with judgment in the Bible. The notion is gruesomely graphic: just as a rusty and abrasive chain eats into a prisoner's flesh with burning pain, so shall perished riches testify against the wicked wealthy in **the last days**. The **treasure** stored up during their lifetime will only serve as a witness against them in the end.

What one thinks can never happen to misplaced security can and will happen. Those who put trust in investment portfolios, the appreciation of real property, or the likelihood of advancement in a certain profession ought to consider James's statements. He was not forbidding wealth per se; he was condemning false hope in riches, the avarice that drives people to accumulate more than they need and the miserliness that keeps them from doing good with what they do have.

5:4. Why did the wealthy have riches to store up? Wages of the workers who had mowed their fields had been **kept back by fraud**. The laborers had been paid late or inequitably. The reference may be to absentee landlords, common in Israel from the years of the monarchy onward, who had defrauded agricultural laborers. Dependent on a daily wage for subsistence, the laborers were the victims of injustice when their wages are not paid immediately. In colorful personification, the money itself **crieth**. The op-

pressed workers themselves cried out for justice, and their appeals for justice had **entered into the ears of the Lord of sabaoth**. The image of God as one who has ears is an instance of anthropomorphism — ascribing human qualities to God so that one might better understand His functions. Here the stress is on God's inclination to hear and answer prayer.

The plight of the workers that James described is similar to that of many workers in the West today. Permanent workers, migrants, and immigrants all fall victim to unjust business practices. David K. Shipler (*The Working Poor: Invisible in America* [New York: Alfred A. Knopf, 2004], pp. 78–79, 100–101) has described migrant laborers whose outrageous housing costs are simply deducted from their wages by unscrupulous labor contractors who house the workers in deplorable barracks. Garment workers find it almost impossible to earn even a minimum wage when they are paid at piece rates (e.g., three-fourths of a cent per zipper on a pair of jeans). Christians who are in a position to set wages, regulate working conditions, and determine benefits ought to protect the rights of all employees, especially foreigners who are reticent or unable to speak for themselves because of language barriers. A higher minimum wage, timely payment of employees, tax breaks, and greater availability of health insurance are needed measures to assure justice for migrant workers as well as permanent residents who are numbered among the working poor. Christian business owners ought to do all they can to protect workers on the job, to pay wages that enable their employees to support themselves and their families, and to promote health care for their workers. Such measures are expensive, but justice calls for greater attention to the well-being of the workers than to a hefty bottom line. Profit is good. It is necessary for the hiring of more workers, for the increase of their pay, and for the availability of benefits to them. Considerations of justice and equity must not, according to James, be overlooked in the attainment of profit.

5:5. The oppressive wealthy had **lived in pleasure on the earth, and been wanton**. Like the rich man who neglected poor Lazarus (Luke 16:19–31), the rich now faced **a day of slaughter**—the day of judgment. The wicked rich were like cattle that continued to fatten themselves on the very day they were to be slaughtered, totally unaware of the coming destruction. The indictment of Amos 4:1 reflects the same idea, "Hear this word, you cows of Bashan, who are on the mountain of Samaria, Who oppress the poor, Who crush the needy, Who say to your husbands, 'Bring wine, let us drink!'" (NKJV). Judgment came upon the Samaritans too (see Amos 4:2–3).

5:6. The oppression of the poor was so severe that James's accusation of the wealthy was that they had **condemned and killed** ("murdered," NKJV) righteous persons. The poor had little recourse in the face of such oppression.

2. Positive: Endurance in Suffering (5:7–11)

5:7–8. The term **therefore** (v. 7) refers back to 5:1–6. Since the believers were suffering at the hands of the wicked rich, they were to look forward patiently to the Lord's return. The sense of the verb **be patient** (*makrothymeō*) is practically synonymous with that of the noun *hypomonē*, "patience" in 1:3–4 (see the cognate verb *hypomenō*, "endureth," in 1:12). Since patience with people (the oppressive rich) is in view, however, James used language that is sometimes associated with that sort of endurance. His point was that the poor and oppressed believers must not retaliate against their oppressors and take God's judgment of the unjust into their own hands. Instead, they were to wait **unto the coming of the Lord**. The word "coming" is *parousia* (see Matt. 24:3, 27; 1 Thess. 2:19; 2 Thess. 2:1; 1 Cor. 15:23; 1 John 2:28; 2 Peter 1:16; 3:4, 12). In secular Greek, the term is used to describe the invasion of an army or the visit of a monarch or a governor to a province. Jesus' coming will mean the final defeat of His enemies and His glorious manifestation to His adoring and worshiping subjects. **The husbandman** ("the farmer," NIV) of ancient Palestine, without modern irrigation, awaited both **the early and latter rain** with great anticipation. Without the rains, **the precious fruit of the earth** would not arrive. In Israel, the early rain comes in October and November, soon

after the grain is sown; the late rain comes in March and April, just prior to harvest (see Deut. 11:14; Jer. 5:24; Hos. 6:3; Joel 2:24). Just as a farmer watches for the rains and inspects his crops as he awaits the harvest, so believers are to watch and wait for the coming of the Lord.

The New Testament insistence on imminence (see, e.g., Rom. 13:12; Heb. 10:25; 1 Peter 4:7; Rev. 22:20) arises from the teaching that "the last days" began with the incarnation. Mankind have been living in "the last days" (5:3) ever since. The next great event in redemptive history is Christ's second coming. The New Testament does not say when it will take place, but its certainty is never questioned, and believers are consistently admonished to watch for it. It was in this light that James expected the imminent return of Christ. James urged God's people to **stablish your hearts** (v. 8; "be ... stouthearted," NEB) while they wait since the great day **draweth nigh** ("is near," NRSV).

5:9. The prohibition **Grudge not one against another** ("Don't grumble against each other," NIV) might indicate that the practice of some members of the community was to turn their complaints against one another rather than cry out to the Lord. If such a practice was not yet occurring, though it could very well have been going on (see Wuest, "stop complaining"), James strongly forbad it starting. James called for patience toward believers as well as unbelievers since **the judge standeth before the door**, a reference to Christ's second coming (see 5:7–8) and the judgment associated with it.

5:10. James appealed to the example of **the prophets** to encourage steadfastness in tribulation. In this, he was following the ancient practice of setting forth a series of characters who are morally exemplary (see 1:22–25; 2:20–25; 5:17–18). Suffering hardship, particularly experiencing hostility to the Lord's message announced through them, was a mark of true prophets (e.g., Jeremiah, Ezekiel, and Daniel). The hearers' experience of hostility from the rich put them in the line of the great and honorable prophets of old. They shared in that honor as they suffer at the hands of the rich.

5:11. The patience of Job refers to the endurance or perseverance of Job in the face of adversity (see Job 1:20–22; 2:9–10, 13–15). This is the only place in the New Testament where Job is mentioned, though Job 5:13 is quoted in 1 Corinthians 3:19. Surprisingly, Job seems to be included among the prophets. James, however, may have simply shifted to another kind of example here and not intended to include Job among the prophets. Nevertheless, the examples of endurance (both the verb *hypomenō* and the noun *hypomonē* occur in v. 11) in suffering that Job and the prophets present show something about human response in difficulties. Barclay says of this passage: "The word used of him [Job] is that great New Testament word *hupomonē* [sic], which describes, not a passive patience, but that gallant spirit which can breast the tides of doubt and sorrow and disaster and come out with faith still stronger on the other side. There may be a faith which never complained or questioned; but still greater is the faith which was tortured by questions and still believed. It was the faith which held grimly on that came out on the other side, for 'the Lord blessed the latter days of Job more than his beginning' (*Job* 42:12)" (*The Letters of James and Peter*, p. 125).

The stories of Job and the prophets also reveal something about God and His response to human pain: **the Lord is**, James affirmed, **very pitiful, and of tender mercy**. The former of these two descriptions of the Lord occurs nowhere else in Scripture and is literally "many bowels of compassion." In Hebraic thinking, the bowels or entrails were regarded as the source of feelings like compassion. "Full of pity" (NEB) is a good contemporary translation.

G. Seventh Exhortation: The Importance of Speaking the Truth (5:12)

1. Negative: The Use of Oaths (5:12a)

5:12a. The command to **swear not** does not pertain to profanity (as undesirable as vulgar speech might be). James's words, very close to Christ's on the subject (Matt. 5:33–37), do not condemn the taking of solemn oaths, such as God's before Abraham (Heb. 6:13), Jesus' before Caiaphas (Matt.

26:63–64), Paul's to the Romans (Rom. 1:9; 9:1), or a man's before the Lord (Exod. 22:11). This command does not prohibit a Christian from taking an oath in a court of law or from pledging allegiance to the nation's flag or constitution. Rather, James was condemning the use of nonbinding oaths to give the impression of truthfulness. In the ancient world, oaths that mentioned God were often deemed more serious than those that did not (e.g., those oaths that only swore **by heaven** or **by earth**). The latter were often not regarded as binding as the former. For James, all speech is uttered in the presence of God, and one will be called to account for it.

2. Positive: Words of integrity — "Yes" or "No" (5:12b)

5:12b. In verse 12, James was applying the teaching of Jesus (see Matt. 23:16–22) and, in so doing, was teaching total honesty even in the most adverse circumstances. Believers in James's churches might have been tempted to use an oath (whether truthfully or falsely) in many different circumstances. Some may have been tempted to use an oath to underscore the severity of a financial need that they had brought before the church to obtain aid. Perhaps the need was as great as they portrayed it. No matter. The point here is that a simple **yea** or **nay** (yes or no) suffices among God's people. Otherwise, rather than wholeness and integration, suspicion and aloofness reign.

IV. Conclusion: Various Instructions for the Promotion of Integration in the Community (5:13–20)

A. Prayer for Various Needs (5:13–18)

In this section, James presented various needs and provided instructions on prayer for those needs.

5:13. Is any among you afflicted? let him pray. The person so instructed is not suffering from illness but is distressed by misfortune, perhaps from oppression by the wealthy. Instead of bemoaning one's circumstances, lashing out at others, or bearing difficulty with quiet resignation, one should pray! **Is any merry? let him sing psalms.** This may be the more difficult of the two commands in verse 13 to carry out, because one tends to forget God when things go well. James said that on such occasions, one ought to thank God for His mercies. Perhaps He has spared one from particular trials so that one's load might be lightened.

5:14–15. The **sick** (v. 14) person is not expressly instructed to pray—a surprising omission in the context of all the other prayers that James described. Instead, James said, **let him call for the elders of the church; and let them pray over him**. The person is too ill to go to the elders and is perhaps too sick even to pray in any sustained way with concentration and energy. From the earliest times of the Christian church (see Acts 14:23), elders have attended to the needs of believers. Their presence here and in other New Testament texts does not necessarily indicate a late first-century or second-century date for those writings.

Accompanying the prayer for the sick person, either preceding or during the prayer, is **anointing ... with oil** (v. 14), one of the best-known ancient medicines (referred to by Philo, Pliny, and the physician Galen; see Isa. 1:6; Luke 10:34). Some believe that James may have been using the term medicinally in this passage. Others, however, regard the use of oil here as an aid to faith, an outward sign of the healing God would bring about in response to prayer offered in faith (v. 15; see Mark 6:13). Perhaps the oil is a symbol of the Holy Spirit. The very act of touching a sick person conveys compassion. This is a Christian act; the anointing is done **in the name of the Lord**—those administering the prayer and anointing claim Jesus' authority and power that He makes available to His people.

Since James later presented Elijah (5:17–18) as the example of **the prayer of faith** (v. 15), this prayer may be prayer that is in harmony with the revealed and discerned will of God. James guaranteed that this prayer **shall save the sick, and the Lord shall raise him up**. When the church confronts matters like weakness and disease, sometimes prayer requires prayerful listening to God in order for God's people even to know how to proceed in prayer. The Lord reveals what "the prayer of faith" is that should be prayed. James may not have been referring to a par-

ticular kind of prayer here, however. He may have been referring simply to prayer for the need at hand, spoken in faith, "nothing wavering" (1:6).

Although the verb "save" can point to salvation in terms of eternal life, it may indicate deliverance from disease here. Thus, the "raising up" is restoration to health, not the resurrection. Sin was linked to physical illness in the church at Corinth (1 Cor. 11:29–32), and James may have wanted to assure his hearers that, in such cases, one's spiritual health and resultant physical health can be restored through the believing prayer of others.

5:16. James called for the members of the congregations to be honest with one another about their spiritual shortcomings: **Confess your faults one to another, and pray one for another**. The confession that James called for is "auricular confession" according to Roman Catholic teaching. Although confessing one's trespasses to others so that one might receive prayer and counsel is beneficial, James likely had something else in mind here. The instructions on confession are probably an exhortation to Christians to seek reconciliation with those whom they have wronged. The healing that results restores relationships within the church. (The verb in the phrase **that ye may be healed** is plural.) It is doubtful that James advocated public confession of all one's sins before the entire house church. The confession could be the sick person's admission of wrongdoing when the elders pray (vv. 14–15). James seems to have extended his instructions on prayer to the entire church ("one to another") at verse 16 since he moved from the third-person singular command ("let him call," v. 14) to the second-person imperative ("Confess," v. 16). "Confess" and "pray" are in the present tense, with the sense of "be confessing" and "be praying" (Wuest). The prayer of righteous people, as were James's hearers, **availeth much**. In other words, it "is powerful and effective" (NRSV).

5:17–18. Elijah prayed and acted on the promise God had already revealed to him. He knew God's will and was therefore praying God's will when he fervently prayed for God to send fire from heaven to consume his sacrifice (see 1 Kings 18:36), when he prayed **that it might not rain** (v. 17; and it did not for **three years and six months**; see 1 Kings 17:1), and when he fervently prayed for God to send rain after the long drought (see 1 Kings 18:1, 41–44). The immediate context suggests that James was using Elijah as an example of the power of prayer for one particular kind of prayer: the mutual prayer for one another mentioned in 5:16. The lesson readily extends to prayer of any kind. If Elijah, **a man subject to like passions as we are,** prayed so boldly and effectively, so can Christians today. If he, with all his faults, is considered to be a righteous person, so are believers in Christ. God desires to answer prayers that promote wholeness within the church.

B. Reintegration of the Wayward (5:19–20)

5:19–20. Major questions about this text are, Who is the one who is said to **err** ("wander," NIV) **from the truth** (v. 19)? and, What does it mean to **save a soul from death** (v. 20)? The one who errs could be (1) a false teacher. The verb "err" is used of the false teachers threatening the church in 2 Peter 2:15 ("which have forsaken the right way, and *are gone astray*") and of the deceivers in 1 John (2:26; 3:7). Although James confronted false concepts of faith and wisdom (chaps. 2–3), false teaching and false teachers do not appear to have been a problem in his churches as they were in the churches addressed by 2 Peter and 1 John. Hence, the reference to the one who errs may point elsewhere. The erring one could be (2) a professing Christian whose faith is not genuine (see Heb. 6:4–8; 2 Peter 2:20–21). If

so, then the "death" in verse 20 is "the second death" (Rev. 21:8). However, the erring one may be (3) a sinning Christian who needs to be restored. Jesus' procedure for reconciliation, in which one goes privately to a brother or sister who sins (see Matt. 18:15–17) to win the fellow believer over, may be alluded to here. (James did not envisage, however, the steps to be taken if the initial approach met with resistance; see Matt. 18:15–17.) In Corinth, some church members fell ill and died because they did not turn from sins of abuse of fellow church members (see 1 Cor. 11:30). James's may have been referring to people who do not confess their sins to fellow community members (see 5:16) and who thus live in enmity with a brother or sister. If they do not initiate the process of restored relationships, others must do it for them. Thus will they **hide a multitude of sins,** which means either that they will prevent further sins from being committed or that they will "cover" (NRSV) over sins of the past and forgive them. The context best supports the third option. In any case, God will forgive the sins of the one who errs.

James's final words of his letter were stark and strong for his original hearers, as they are today. What will believers do? Will they take upon themselves the responsibility for restored relationships within the church? Some church members, having been hurt by a fellow church member, have themselves left the church instead of seeking restored relationships with others. Such an action is not the way to wholeness and integration—the health of the church as James understood it.

THE FIRST EPISTLE GENERAL OF PETER

INTRODUCTION

Author

The author identified himself as the apostle Peter (1:1). In the Gospels, Peter is the most prominent among the twelve apostles. His original name was Simon, a name probably derived from Simeon and related to the Hebrew word meaning "to hear." He is called Simeon in Acts 15:14. According to John 1:40–42, Jesus bestowed upon him the nickname Cephas (Aramaic, *Kepha*; "stone" or "rock"). The Greek form of that name is Petros, from which the English name Peter comes. Sometimes he is identified as Simon Peter (e.g., John 20:2), and on other occasions, Peter's Aramaic name, Cephas, is preserved (see 1 Cor. 1:12; 15:5; Gal. 2:9). In the early chapters of Acts, Peter emerged as the preeminent spokesman of the twelve apostles. His sermons were effective in calling people to belief in Jesus Christ (2:14–41; 3:12–26; 4:8–12; 5:29–32; 10:34–48). Peter fades from the New Testament when Acts turns its focus on Paul, but extrabiblical tradition claims that Peter died a martyr's death for Christ.

Although the authenticity of 1 Peter is often disputed, the contents and character of the letter support his authorship (see discussion on 5:1–2). Moreover, the letter reflects the history and terminology of the Gospels and Acts (notably Peter's speeches); its themes and concepts reflect Peter's experiences and his associations in the period of our Lord's earthly ministry and in the apostolic age. That he was acquainted, for example, with Paul and his letters is made clear in 2 Peter 3:15–16; Galatians 1:18; 2:1–21 and elsewhere; coincidences in thought and expression with Paul's writings are therefore not surprising.

From the beginning, 1 Peter was recognized as authoritative and as the work of the apostle Peter. The earliest extant reference to it is 2 Peter 3:1, where Peter himself referred to a former letter he had written. First Clement (AD 95) seems to indicate acquaintance with 1 Peter. Polycarp, a disciple of the apostle John, made use of 1 Peter in his letter to the Philippians. The author of the Gospel of Truth (AD 140–150) was acquainted with 1 Peter. Eusebius (fourth century) indicated that it was universally received. The letter was explicitly ascribed to Peter by that group of church fathers whose testimonies appear in the attestation of so many of the genuine New Testament writings, namely, Irenaeus (AD 140–203), Tertullian (150–222), Clement of Alexandria (155–215), and Origen (185–253). It is thus clear that Peter's authorship of the book had early and strong support.

Nevertheless, some claim that the idiomatic Greek of this letter was beyond Peter's competence. It is true that the Greek of 1 Peter is good literary Greek, and even though Peter could no doubt speak Greek (as so many in the Mediterranean world could), many have thought it unlikely that he would have written such polished Greek. It is at this point that Peter's remark in 5:12 concerning Silvanus may be significant. Here the apostle claimed that he wrote "by," or (more literally) "by means of," Silvanus (Greek, *dia Silouanou*). This phrase could refer to Silvanus as a letter carrier, the one who delivered 1 Peter to its recipients, but it could also denote Silvanus as the intermediate agent in writing. Some have claimed that Silvanus's qualifications for recording Peter's letter in literary Greek are found in Acts 15:22–29, where Silas (Silvanus is perhaps a Latinized form of Silas) is associated with the letter from Jerusalem to Antioch. Secretaries (also known as *amanuenses*) commonly wrote letters from dictation; Tertius was Paul's amanuensis for the letter to the Romans (see Rom. 16:22). A secretary in those days often composed documents in good Greek for those who did not have the linguistic facility to do so. Thus, 1 Peter may reflect Silvanus's polished Greek, while in 2 Peter, it may be Peter's rough Greek that appears.

Date

Some who question Peter's authorship of the letter also maintain that it reflects a situation that did not exist until after Peter's death, suggesting that the persecution referred to in 4:14–16; 5:8–9 is descriptive of Domitian's reign (AD 81–96). The date of 1 Peter, according to still others, is circa AD 112 — the time of the correspondence between Pliny the Younger, who was the governor of Bithynia (1:1), and the Roman Emperor Trajan. In that correspondence, executions of Christians in the province are mentioned. First Peter addresses Christians under distress because of the hostility of the Roman authorities.

However, the opposition against Christians that was developing in Nero's time (AD 54–68) is adequately described by the references to suffering in 1 Peter. The letter contains no clear reference to martyrdom on the part of Christians; rather, the Christians' suffering involves social ostracism, slander, and dishonor. Occasionally, local officials may have moved against the Christians to neutralize what may have been perceived as a threat to public order, but no official policy against Peter's audience is evident. A late first-century or early second-century date for 1 Peter is, therefore, not required by the evidence. The book can be satisfactorily dated in the period AD 62–68, during Peter's ministry in Rome before his death, which occurred sometime between AD 64 and 68. The apparent echoes of Paul's Prison Epistles (compare 1 Peter 1:1–3 with Eph. 1:1–3; 1 Peter 2:18 with Col. 3:22; 1 Peter 3:1–6 with Eph. 5:22–24), which should be dated no earlier than AD 60, might suggest that 1 Peter should not be placed earlier than AD 60 as well. The similarities, however, may be due to a shared Christian tradition and not necessarily to Peter's knowledge of Paul's letters.

Place of Composition

Peter indicated that he was "at Babylon" (5:13) when he wrote 1 Peter. Among the interpretations that have been suggested for the identification of "Babylon" are that Peter was writing from (1) Egyptian Babylon, which was a military post, (2) Mesopotamian Babylon, (3) Jerusalem, or (4) Rome. Although sites known as Babylon existed in both

Mesopotamia and Egypt in the first century, there is no firm evidence that connects Peter with those locations. A symbolic reference to Jerusalem as "Babylon" is unlikely, but symbolic use of the name Babylon for Rome would coincide with the use of the term in the book of Revelation (see Revelation 17–18). Nero's decadent and oppressive rule in Rome certainly would recall the place of exile for God's people in the Old Testament, and Roman writers themselves described luxurious and degenerate Rome as "Babylon" before AD 70. Furthermore, tradition connects Peter in the latter part of his life with Rome, not Jerusalem, and certainly not with Mesopotamian Babylon. The best conclusion, therefore, is that Peter intended "Babylon" to stand for "Rome" in 5:13.

Recipients

The intended audience of 1 Peter is identified in 1:1: "the strangers scattered throughout Pontus, Galatia, Cappadocia, Asia, and Bithynia." These geographical areas were Roman provinces (Pontus and Bythnia had been combined into one administrative unit) in what is now Turkey, and the region they comprised was vast — 128,889 square miles — a culturally diverse land of approximately 8,500,000 inhabitants. Probably both rural and urban communities received the courier (possibly Silvanus; see "Author," above, and discussion on 5:12) who bore this epistle. He would have read the letter aloud to the congregations; only thereafter would multiple copies have been available for individual churches.

The many quotations from and allusions to the Old Testament indicate that the original hearers of 1 Peter were conversant with the Hebrew Scriptures. Were they Jewish Christians? Undoubtedly, many within the Christian communities in the vast region indicated in 1:1 were Jews of the Diaspora. (The number of Jews throughout Asia Minor at that time would have been at least a quarter million.) However, Peter (himself a Jew) probably would not have addressed Jews who had believed in Christ as those who had been redeemed "from your vain conversation received by tradition from your fathers" (1:18; see 4:3) because the tradition of Jewish culture and upbringing would have included the ethical standards upheld by the New Testament. The audience of 1 Peter, therefore, likely was predominantly Gentile Christians, with a significant Jewish Christian minority. The term "Gentiles," used in the KJV (2:12; 4:3–4) to describe the opponents of Peter's hearers, should be understood as "pagans" (NIV; REB 4:3) or "unbelievers" (REB 2:12).

The description of the recipients of 1 Peter as "strangers and pilgrims" (2:11; see 1:1) could be metaphorical: the harassed Christian minority was not at home in this world and looked forward to going to its true, heavenly home. Some maintain that the terms "strangers" and "pilgrims" (*paroikoi, parepidēmoi*) refer to the social, cultural, political, and religious estrangement of the Christians. A more accurate translation of these terms is "resident aliens" and "visiting strangers." With his first letter, Peter intended to promote endurance, cohesion within the Christian communities, and testimony of good behavior to the unbelievers around them. Thus, the church would strengthen itself and avoid assimilation to the pagan world.

Theme and Theological Message

Peter stated that he had "written briefly, exhorting, and testifying that this is the true grace of God" (5:12). This is a definitive general description of the letter, but it does not exclude the recognition of numerous subordinate and contributory themes. Although it is a short letter, 1 Peter touches on various doctrines and has much to say about Christian life and duties. It is not surprising that different readers see different principal themes. It has, for example, been characterized as a letter of separation, of suffering and persecution, of suffering and glory, of hope, of pilgrimage, of courage, and as a letter dealing with the true grace of God. The letter is composed also of a series of exhortations (imperatives), which run from 1:13 to 5:11.

Literary Features

First Peter exhibits a striking similarity to standards of Greco-Roman rhetoric, especially the pattern of argumentation in the Latin handbook titled *Rhetorica ad Herennium* ("Rhetoric to Herennius"). In this fivefold pattern, the proposition states the main point of the argument. The reason expresses the basis for the proposition, and is itself followed by a corroboration, the proof of the reason. Once the proof of the reason has been established, an embellishment of the argument appears. The final element is a conclusion, which collects and ties up the parts of the argument. Peter may not have formally studied classical rhetoric, but his composition resembles the structure. The following outline of the structure of 1 Peter demonstrates the way in which the epistle corresponds to this rhetorical structure.

Outline

    I. Salutation (1:1–2)
   II. Prologue (1:3–12)
  III. First Argument: Hope to the End in Holiness (1:13–2:10)
       A. Proposition (1:13–16)
       B. Reason (1:17)
       C. Proof of the Reason (1:18–21)
       D. Embellishment (1:22–25)
       E. Conclusion (2:1–10)
   IV. Second Argument: Hope to the End with Honor (2:11–3:12)
       A. Proposition (2:11–12a)
       B. Reason (2:12b)
       C. Proof of the Reason (2:13–17)
       D. Embellishment (2:18–3:7)
       E. Conclusion (3:8–12)
    V. Third Argument: Hope to the End against Adversity (3:13–4:11)
       A. Proposition (3:13–16a)
       B. Reason (3:16b)
       C. Proof of the Reason (3:17)
       D. Embellishment (3:18–22)
       E. Conclusion (4:1–11)
   VI. Closing (4:12–5:14)
       A. Further Examination of the Topic of Suffering (4:12–19)
       B. A Farewell Speech of Exhortation (5:1–11)

1. Self-Vindication (5:1)
2. A Call to Tend the Flock (5:2a–b)
3. A Warning against Greed (5:2c–3)
4. Reward and Judgment (5:4)
5. Love and Humility (5:5–7)
6. An Exhortation to Watch and Stand Firm (5:8a)
7. Discussion of the Enemy (5:8b)
8. A Prediction of Suffering (5:9–11)

 C. Closing Remarks and Greeting (5:12–14)

Bibliography

Best, Ernest. *1 Peter*. New Century Bible. Grand Rapids, MI: Eerdmans, 1971.

Campbell, Barth L. *Honor, Shame, and the Rhetoric of 1 Peter*. Society of Biblical Literature Dissertation Series 160. Atlanta: Scholars Press, 1998.

Davids, Peter H. *The First Epistle of Peter*. The New International Commentary on the New Testament. Grand Rapids, MI: Eerdmans, 1990.

Grudem, Wayne A. *The First Epistle of Peter: An Introduction and Commentary*. Tyndale New Testament Commentaries 17. Grand Rapids, MI: Eerdmans, 1988.

Hillyer, Norman. *1 and 2 Peter, Jude*. The New International Biblical Commentary. Peabody, MA: Hendrickson, 1992.

Marshall, I. Howard. *1 Peter*. The IVP New Testament Commentary 17. Downers Grove, IL: InterVarsity, 1991.

Michaels, J. Ramsey. *1 Peter*. Word Biblical Commentary 49. Waco, TX: Word, 1988.

Stibbs, Alan M., and Andrew F. Walls. *The First Epistle General of Peter*. Vol. 7. Tyndale New Testament Commentaries. Grand Rapids, MI: Eerdmans, 1959.

EXPOSITION

I. Salutation (1:1–2)

1:1. Peter described himself as **an apostle of Jesus Christ**, which designates him as one of the twelve disciples who accompanied Jesus during His earthly ministry and one who had seen the resurrected Christ. The title established and enhanced Peter's authority in the eyes of his audience, which would have been particularly needed if he had never visited the regions to which the letter was sent. There is no evidence that Peter had visited **Pontus, Galatia, Cappadocia, Asia, and Bithynia**, but he may have. People from this area were in Jerusalem on the day of Pentecost (see Acts 2:9–11), and some may have become personally acquainted with Peter. Paul, however, preached and taught in some of these provinces (see, e.g., Acts 16:6; 18:23; 19:10, 26).

1:2. Elect. That the recipients of the letter had been specifically chosen **according to the foreknowledge of God the Father** would have inspired within them a sense of honor and privileged status. All three persons of the Trinity are involved in the redemption of the elect. The order of the terms employed suggests that the **sanctification of the Spirit** is here the influence of the Spirit that draws one from sin toward holiness. **Unto obedience and sprinkling of the blood of Jesus Christ** may mean that the Spirit's sanctifying leads to obedient saving faith and cleansing from sin, or that the election of

God has as its purpose obedience and forgiveness through Christ's blood. "Sprinkling" evokes an association with the blood of the Mosaic covenant (see Exod. 24:6–8; Heb. 9:19–21) and thus signifies the basis of a new covenant.

Grace unto you, and peace. This greeting is standard in New Testament letters (see, e.g., Rom. 1:7; 1 Cor. 1:3; Phil. 1:2), but its importance ought not to be overlooked. It would have reminded Peter's audience of their honored status before God, emphasized by the fact that it can **be multiplied** (see 2 Peter 1:2).

II. Prologue (1:3–12)

In the prologue, Peter instructed his audience about their honored identity and status as Christians. The blessings they had received and the virtues of their character are celebrated.

1:3. By His **abundant mercy**, God has given believers a new birth. He has done so out of His fatherly compassion. Therefore, despite adversity, the experience of His having **begotten us again** signifies His love and honor that He bestows. **Lively hope.** In the Bible, hope is not wishful thinking but a firm conviction, much like faith that is directed toward the future. The fact of Christ's risen existence makes the hope of His followers "lively" (or "living," NIV) — certain and strong, not baseless or empty. The original hearers of this letter, disdained by their contemporaries, would have understood hope in the sense of divine rescue and vindication from dishonorable treatment. **The resurrection of Jesus Christ from the dead** secures for His people their new birth and the hope that they will be resurrected just as He was.

1:4–5. To an inheritance (v. 4). Believers are born again not only to a hope but also to the inheritance that is the substance of that hope. The audiences in Asia Minor, including many economically displaced aliens, had little hope of acquiring landed property as security for the future. The inheritance of believers, described by the synonymous expression **salvation ready to be revealed in the last time** (v. 5), is eternal, in its essence (it is not subject to decay) and in its preservation (it is divinely kept for us). The Greek word that Peter used for **kept**

is *phroureō*, a military term meaning "protected" (NRSV), "shielded" (NIV), or "guarded." The expression is related to the term *phrouria*, which denoted the forts located throughout Pontus, Cappadocia, and Galatia. Just as settlements and territory in these regions were guarded by garrisons within fortifications, so the disdained and oppressed believers were protected **by the power of God through faith** that they would be brought safely into the salvation for which they hoped.

In 1 Peter, **salvation** (v. 5) is deliverance *from* all hostile and destructive influences and *to* the joyful and glorious experience of God's favor in Christ. Peter saw salvation as future in the sense that believers are guarded for its unveiling **in the last time** and that believers grow into it (see discussion on 2:2).

1:6. Wherein (i.e., in all the blessings described in 1:3–5) **ye greatly rejoice, though now for a season, if need be, ye are in heaviness through manifold temptations** ("various trials," NASB). Such trials could be enticements to sin if those experiencing them entertain the possibility of abandoning faithful endurance. All trials cause their sufferers to be "in heaviness" ("you have been distressed," NASB; "you may have had to suffer grief," NIV), but Peter assured his readers that the anguish was "now for a season" ("though now for a little while," NIV) and only "if need be." God's will for a believer sometimes requires endurance of suffering so that he or she may grow. Those who suffer are assured of an end of their difficulties, either at the coming of Christ or at some point before that (5:10; see discussion on 3:13–16).

1:7. That the trial of your faith … might be found unto praise denotes the result of the heaviness that comes through tests. Here the word "trial" (*dokimion*) refers not to the "temptations" of 1:6 but to the "genuineness" (NRSV) of the hearers' faith, which was demonstrated through the testing of their faith. Peter compared this testing to gold in two ways: (1) the refining of gold (**tried with fire**), through which impurities and deficiencies are eliminated, serves as a picture of trials in the Christian life, and (2) proven faith is **much more precious than of gold that perisheth**. Despite its value as a pure and precious metal, refined gold is destined to pass away (see 1:24).

1:8. Peter commended his audience for their love in the Lord, whom they had **not seen**. In other words, **though now ye see him not, yet believing, ye rejoice**. Love, belief, and joy go hand in hand. A joyless belief is not genuine, nor is true joy possible without a complete dependence on the Lord, who may seem hidden when one is enduring distress. The approval Peter expressed here is similar to Jesus' saying in John 20:29, uttered on an occasion when Peter was present: "blessed are they that have not seen, and yet have believed" (John 20:29).

Glory, a key word in 1 Peter (1:7–8, 11, 21, 24; 4:11, 13–14; 5:1, 4, 10), refers to the eternal and majestic resplendence of God (see 5:10) that is shared by Christ (see 1:11, 21; 4:11, 13) and the Holy Spirit (see 4:14). Believers share in that glory (see 1:7–8; 5:1, 4) as God vindicates them in spite of their dishonorable status before humans and the world's false conceptions of glory (see 1:24).

1:9. The word **souls** implies the whole person; Peter was not excluding the body from heaven. The term designates either the animate part of a person or the entire person as seen from the angle of one's relatedness to God. Salvation, **the end of your faith** (i.e., the goal toward which the life of faith is directed) is experienced in the present as well as in the past and the future (see discussion on 1:5). Salvation experienced now is a basis for and a result of Christian joy.

1:10–12. Peter's catalogue of blessings and virtues includes the service of **the prophets** (v. 10). Some have suggested that here "the prophets" refers to spokespeople of God in the early Christian communities who were inspired with messages of instruction and exhortation for the church. More likely, however, it refers to the Old Testament prophets, since Peter distinguished them from those who, coming later, **have preached the gospel unto you with the Holy Ghost sent down from heaven** (v. 12). Christ sent the Holy Spirit on the day of Pentecost (Acts 2:33), at which Peter was present. Inspiration does not always mean illumination, however. Thus, the prophets **enquired and searched diligently**

(v. 10) regarding the forecast of sufferings and subsequent glories.

Peter's readers would have been honored to know that **unto us they** (the prophets) **did minister ... the gospel ... which things the angels desire to look into** (v. 12). The angels' intense desire is highlighted by the Greek word rendered "to look into" (*parakyptō*), which means "to stoop and look intently" (see John 20:5, 11). The believers were honored indeed; they could understand truths that even angels cannot quite fathom.

III. First Argument: Hope to the End in Holiness (1:13–2:10)

A. Proposition (1:13–16)

1:13–16. Hope to the end for the grace that is to be brought unto you at the revelation of Jesus Christ (v. 13). This is the first of a series of three imperative constructions that constitute propositions for the arguments in the letter. In 1 Peter, "grace" (*charis*) refers to honor divinely bestowed on those who are suffering (see 2:12; 3:16; 4:4). The term, which appears ten times in this epistle (1:2, 10, 13; 2:19, 20; 3:7, 4:10; 5:5, 10, 12), has a sociocultural denotation as much as a theological one. Peter indicated that a major purpose of this letter was to encourage his readers and testify regarding the true grace of God (see 5:12). On this grace, they were to **hope to the end** (*teleiōs*) or "completely" (NASB).

Four expressions describe the action of the main verb in the proposition ("hope"). (1) **Gird up the loins of your mind** (v. 13) is a graphic call for action. In the language of the first century, it meant that one should literally gather up one's long, flowing garments and be ready for physical action. (2) **Be sober** may be intended in a literal sense as a prohibition of drunkenness, or it may pertain to a general attitude of self-control. (3) **As obedient children, not fashioning yourselves according to the former lusts in your ignorance** (v. 14). Christians, born into the family of God (see 1:23), are children of their heavenly Father (see 1:17). Believers are also described as being adopted into God's family (see Rom. 8:15). The image of "obedient children" represents one of the most powerful concepts of the letter: the household of God. By maintaining their unique identity as God's household, Peter's audience could resist the pressures to conform to their pagan past. In other words, (4) **be ye holy in all manner of conversation** (v. 15; "in all your behavior," NASB). Hope is to be accompanied by holiness. God commands His people, **Be ye holy; for I am holy** (v. 16). To be holy is to be set apart, set apart from sin and impurity and set apart to God. Thus, God moves His people to strive for moral purity.

B. Reason (1:17)

1:17. In this verse, Peter provided further warrant for holy living and explained why believers should set their hope upon the future unveiling of grace. According to 1:15, the holiness of God demands holiness in return. A similar thought appears here: God is described as One **who without respect of persons judgeth according to every man's work.** He will give honor and vindication to the one who deserves it. **Ye call on the Father** refers to the cry for vindication of those who are harassed for their faith. Elsewhere in the New Testament, the word for "call" has the sense of lodging an appeal for honor or vindication (see Acts 7:59; 25:11, 12, 21; 26:32; 28:19). Peter's audience made this appeal to the One who judges absolutely justly; thus he advised them, **pass the time of your sojourning here in fear.** "Sojourning" (*paroikia*; "exile," NRSV) refers to the readers' cultural and ethnic estrangement from the surrounding society. The time of their sojourning would end whenever God vindicated these resident aliens with honor. Until that time, the Christians were to "live in reverent fear" (NRSV) of God. The just Judge will answer those who appeal to Him as Father only if they live in reverent honor to Him. All Christians may address God as their Father (Matt. 6:9), but they cannot expect Him to have answers to prayer if they refuse to honor Him as such. The divine justice and discipline requires such reciprocity.

C. Proof of the Reason (1:18 – 21)

1:18 – 20. The proof corroborates the reason with additional arguments. These arguments provide further bases for the proposition (1:13 – 16). **The precious blood of Christ** (v. 19) invokes positive feelings of loyalty when it is placed in contrast with the negative **corruptible things, as silver and gold** (v. 18). The former is the price by which the readers had been **redeemed.** In the Bible, "to redeem" means to free someone by the payment of a penalty or a ransom (see Exod. 13:13; 21:30). Likewise, in the Greek world, slaves could be redeemed by the payment of a price, either by someone else or by the slave himself. Similarly, Jesus redeems believers "from the curse of the law" (Gal. 3:13) and "from all iniquity" (Titus 2:14). The ransom price is not silver or gold, but Christ's blood (Eph. 1:7; 1 Peter 1:19; Rev. 5:9), that is, Christ's death (Matt. 20:28; Mark 10:45; Heb. 9:15) or Christ Himself (Gal. 3:13). The result is "the forgiveness of sins" (Col. 1:14) and "being justified" (Rom. 3:24).

The **vain conversation received by tradition from your fathers** (v. 18; "your futile way of life inherited from your forefathers," NASB) indicates to some that the recipients must have been pagans; the New Testament stresses the emptiness of pagan life (see Rom. 1:21; Eph. 4:17). Others think they were Jews since Jews were traditionalists who stressed the influence of the father as teacher in the home. In the light of the context of the whole letter, Peter was probably addressing both Jews and Gentiles. The redemptive power of God, in both cases, is stressed. He is able to liberate the captive completely "from" (*ek*, "out of") the worthless and empty life apart from God.

The Old Testament sacrifices were types (foreshadowings) of Christ, depicting the ultimate and only effective sacrifice. Christ is the Passover **Lamb** (v. 19; see 1 Cor. 5:7), who takes away the sin of the world (John 1:29). He is **without blemish and without spot.** Thus, He is the perfect sacrifice, adequate for the forgiveness of all sins (see Num. 28:19; Heb. 9:14). As such a sacrifice, Christ was **foreordained before the foundation of the world** (v. 20). God knew before creation that it would be necessary for Christ to redeem humankind (see Rev. 13:8), but He has revealed Christ in "these last times." The Greek for "foreordained" may also be rendered "chosen" (NIV) or "foreknown" (NASB).

The expression **but was manifest in these last times for you** (v. 20) is consistent with the thoroughly eschatological (i.e., with a view toward the second coming of Christ) perspective of 1 Peter (1:5–7, 13; 4:5–6, 7, 13, 17; 5:1, 4). "For you" stresses the honor of the readers: they themselves were the objects of the eternal purpose of God in Christ, which provided them with motivation for living in hope and holiness.

1:21. Peter concluded the proof of the reason with two topics that were common in early Christian preaching: God **raised him** (Christ) **up from the dead, and gave him glory**. Peter, as one of the individuals to whom the risen Jesus appeared after emerging from the tomb (see 1 Cor. 15:5), was certain of the resurrection as a historical fact. The resurrection and exaltation of Christ was to encourage the ridiculed believers; as Christ had been vindicated, so they could hope to be vindicated as well.

D. Embellishment (1:22–25)

1:22–25. Here Peter enriched the argument, beginning by masterfully outlining the Christian life. Its ultimate purpose and expression is to **love** (*agapaō*) **one another with a pure heart fervently** (v. 22; see 2 Peter 1:5–7), but reception of **the Spirit**, obedience, growth in sanctification (**ye have purified your souls**), and **unfeigned love** (*philadelphia*) **of the brethren** are the intermediate steps. These phenomena overlap, of course, but love crowns them all. Such characteristics are the marks of the person who is **born again** (v. 23), and that by **the word of God**. The new birth comes about through the direct action of the Holy Spirit (see Titus 3:5), but the Word of God also plays an important role (see James 1:18), for it presents **the gospel** (v. 25) to the sinner and calls on him to repent and believe in Christ.

E. Conclusion (2:1–10)

2:1–3. Wherefore (v. 1) connects 1:23–25 with the exhortations that follow (compare **newborn babes** [v. 2] with "born again" [1:23]), concluding

Peter's first argument. The sins of verse 1 are offenses against the unity of the Christian family and are to be put away. Instead, the unrestrained hunger of a healthy baby provides an example of the kind of eager **desire** (v. 2) for spiritual food that ought to mark the believer. **The sincere milk of the word** ("the pure, spiritual milk," NRSV) is figurative; milk is not to be understood here in unfavorable contrast to solid food (as in 1 Cor. 3:2; Heb. 5:12–14) but as an appropriate nourishment for babies. The Greek word for **grow** is the standard term for the desirable growth of children. The tense of the Greek verb **have tasted** (v. 3) suggests that an initial act of tasting. Since this taste proved satisfactory, Peter urged the believers to long for additional spiritual food.

2:4. Peter's hearers not only were honored by their inclusion in God's household as newborn babes, but they came unto Christ, the **living stone**. The metaphor of Christ as stone permeates 2:4–8. The parallel metaphor of Christians as stones in the building of which Christ is the corner is also present. Both the Stone and the stones share rejection from humans. However, although Christ was **disallowed indeed of men**, He was **chosen of God**. In Acts, Peter repeatedly made a contrast between the hostility of unbelieving men toward Jesus and God's exaltation of Him (see Acts 2:22–36; 3:13–15; 4:10–11; 10:39–42). Believers can take comfort in that fact; they too are dishonored, but they can expect God to vindicate them in due time.

2:5. Followers of Christ are already honored by God in that **as lively stones**, they **are built up a spiritual house**. The Old Testament temple may provide the background of the image of a house, but the word here may have the idea of "household." Nevertheless, the metaphor of the believers as **a holy priesthood, to offer up spiritual sacrifices, acceptable to God by Jesus Christ** does recall the temple and its sacrifices. According to Peter, all believers are themselves priests.

2:6–8. Chief corner stone (v. 6; see Ps. 118:22; Isa. 28:16; Matt. 21:42; Mark 12:10; Luke 20:17; Acts 4:11; Rom. 9:33) is an obvious reference to Christ, as this passage makes clear. The cornerstone, which determines the design and orientation of the building, is the most significant stone in the structure. The term may signify the keystone that was set over the gate or porch of a building, or it may be equivalent to **the head of the corner** (v. 7). In either case, the term designates honor. The picture that Peter created is of a structure made up of believers ("lively stones," 2:5), the design and orientation of which are all in keeping with Christ, the Cornerstone.

Two attitudes toward the Cornerstone are evident. (1) Some trust in Him and **shall not be confounded** (v. 6; "will by no means be put to shame," NKJV); rather, they are honored. **Unto you therefore which believe he is precious** (v. 7) should rather be "to you believers, therefore, that honour belongs" (Weymouth). (2) Others reject Him (v. 7) and, as a result, **stumble** (v. 8) and fall.

Whereunto also they were appointed (v. 8). The result of disobedience, not the decision to disobey, is that which is foreordained. The idea that God predestines some to unbelief and condemnation is not present here. The issue is honor and shame. Those who respond to Christ in unbelieving disobedience can look forward only to shame (**stumbling**) and not to the honor believers enjoy. This is the consequence that God has established for those who choose to disobey.

2:9 – 10. As a final encouragement for his readers, Peter introduced some wonderful titles for God's people to convey their honored position. Regardless of whatever suffering they may have to endure, they are still **a chosen generation** (v. 9; see 1:1 – 2; Isa. 43:10, 20; 44:1 – 2). As Israel was called God's chosen people in the Old Testament, so believers are designated as chosen, or elect, in the New Testament. They are also **a royal priesthood** (see Exod. 19:6; Isa. 61:6), **a holy nation** (see Deut. 28:9), and **a peculiar people** (see Deut. 4:20; 7:6; 14:2; Isa. 43:21; Mal. 3:17). The last description could have the sense of Christians being "God's own people" (NRSV) or "a people belonging to God" (NIV). The purpose of the bestowal of these distinctions is **that ye should shew forth the praises** of God. Peter's missionary interest (see 2:12; 3:1) is clear in that expression.

"Shew forth" has the idea of "proclaim" (NRSV) or "declare" (NIV) God's "excellencies" (NASB).

IV. Second Argument: Hope to the End with Honor (2:11 – 3:12)

A. Proposition (2:11 – 12a)

2:11 – 12a. The proposition of the second argument is twofold: a negative command, **abstain from fleshly lusts** (v. 11), followed by a positive directive, **having your conversation honest among the Gentiles** (v. 12a). This positive directive ("Conduct yourselves honorably among the Gentiles," NRSV) is expanded in 2:13 – 3:12. For **strangers and pilgrims**, see Introduction: "Recipients."

B. Reason 2:12b

2:12b. The reason for the twofold proposition was so that the pagans might **glorify God**. Honorable conduct that promotes an effective Christian witness to skeptics and slanderers is respect for others, not retaliation in speech. False opinions and malicious treatment will then be reversed, and glory will be given to God. **Good works, which they shall behold** are deeds that can be seen to be good (see Matt. 5:16). The Greek word translated "behold" (*epopteuō*) refers to the pagans carefully watching over a period of time, not a snap judgment. "Glorify God" is synonymous with "believe in God" and is an apt expression here since it signifies that a reversal of opinion, from shame to honor and glory, is connected with belief. The unbelievers would praise God for the Christians and their effective witness. **The day of visitation** is perhaps the day of judgment and ensuing punishment, or it may be the day when God visits a person with salvation. The believer's good life may then influence the unbeliever to repent and believe.

C. Proof of the Reason 2:13 – 17

2:13 – 17. Three classifications of people are to be the objects of a Christian's submissive and respectful behavior. Such behavior is an example of the "good works" of 2:12; Peter's three contexts for good works corroborate the reason of the argument. First of all, political authorities (**the king**, v. 13, and **governors**, v. 14), as those who punish the wicked and reward the upright (v. 14), deserve the Christian's respect. Good citizenship counters false charges made against Christians, commends the gospel to unbelievers, and (as Peter boldly affirmed) serves to **put to silence the ignorance of foolish men** (v. 15). One cannot use Christian **liberty for a cloke of maliciousness** (v. 16), or "as a cover-up for evil" (NIV). Such an attitude is not that of true **servants of God**. Peter's instruction here is general and applies to a time of general tolerance of Christian activity by Rome. Even if Peter wrote at the time of Nero's violent mistreatment of Christians in the capital city of the empire (AD 64), neither a widespread nor an official opposition to Christianity existed in Asia Minor at that time. By the time of Revelation, the situation had changed dramatically, at least in the province of Asia. Compare Peter's words in these verses with Paul's statements in Romans 13:1–7. Of course, obedience to the emperor was never to violate of the law of God (for this basic principle in action, see Acts 4:19; 5:29). Both Peter and Paul enjoined submission if the authorities functioned **for the punishment of evildoers, and for the praise of them that do well** (v. 14). Peter summarized this section with a call for honorable behavior: **Honour all men. Love the brotherhood. Fear God. Honour the king** (v. 17).

D. Embellishment (2:18–3:7)

Peter's instructions in this section are a list of responsibilities known as a "household code." Such lists appear elsewhere in the New Testament (Eph. 5:22–6:9; Col. 3:18–4:1; 1 Tim. 6:1–2; Titus 2:1–10); in them, spouses, parents, children, slaves, and masters are addressed—all typically members in the kind of households where early Christian gatherings took place. Peter enriched the argument, whose twofold proposition is "abstain from fleshly lusts" (2:11) and "having your conversation honest" (2:12), with an enumeration of household duties.

2:18. The word **Servants** refers to household servants (*oiketai*), not to slaves generally (*douloi*). Peter was concerned with the household as Christian community. He mentioned these Christian servants first because they provided the example of honorable behavior for the entire church: **be subject to your masters**.

2:19–20. The servants who **endure grief, suffering wrongfully** (v. 19) do something that **is thankworthy** ("finds favor," NASB). The concept of suffering is prominent throughout 1 Peter. Of forty New Testament occurrences of the Greek word *paschō* ("to suffer"), eleven of them are in 1 Peter (2:19, 20, 21, 23; 3:14, 17, 18; 4:1, 15, 19; 5:10). The word "suffering" (*pathēma*) appears four times in 1 Peter (all plural: 1:11; 4:13; 5:1, 9), out of a total of sixteen occurrences in the entire New Testament.

Believers do not always suffer because of something they have done wrong; sometimes it is for something they have done right. Living with a **conscience toward God** (v. 19; "being aware of God," NRSV) sometimes brings suffering. Some of the slaves in Peter's audience may have been **buffeted** (v. 20; "beaten," NKJV). Whatever the source of the discomfort, Peter's emphasis was on whether **ye take it patiently** ("If you endure," NRSV).

2:21. The Christian is **called** to endurance in the face of unjust suffering **because Christ also suffered for us** in this way. What is true for the greater (Christ) is true for the lesser (the servants and, by extension, all believers). The word **example** (*hypogrammos*) designates the "pattern" of letters in ancient schoolbooks that students copied or an artist's outline that pupils completed. As believers **follow his steps**, they are truly his disciples and have honor before God.

2:22–23. In this section (2:22–25) rich with allusions and quotations from the servant song of Isaiah 52:13–53:12, the example of Christ's patient endurance is described in detail. All through the agony of His trial, scourging, and crucifixion, Jesus committed **no sin**. Peter especially had in mind deceptive (**guile**; v. 22), abusive (**reviled not**; 23), and retaliatory (**threatened not**) speech that Christ could have thrown back at His tormentors. Rather, He **committed himself to him that judgeth righteously**. Since Christ left to God all vengeance and vindication of Himself, so should His followers commit their cause to God.

2:24. Although dealing with Christ's example, Peter also touched on His redemptive work, which has significance far beyond that of setting an example. Here Peter pointed to the substitutionary character of the atonement: He **bare our sins in his own body on the tree** (see Isa. 53:12). Christ, like the sacrificial lamb of the Old Testament, died for our sins, the innocent for the guilty. The word "tree" is a figurative reference to the cross (see Acts 5:30; 10:39; 13:29) and carries the idea that Christ took on Himself the curse of disobedience so that believers might be redeemed (see Deut. 21:23; Gal. 3:13).

The expression **ye were healed** (see Isa. 53:5) is not generally viewed as a reference to physical healing, though some believe that such healing was included in the atonement (see Matt. 8:16–17). Others see spiritual healing in this passage. It is another way of asserting that Christ's death brings salvation to those who trust in Him.

2:25. Shepherd (see 5:4) is an allusion to the wandering sheep of Isaiah 53. Since Christ is the **Bishop** ("guardian," NRSV) of believers' souls, elders are to be both shepherds and guardians; they are to look out for the welfare of the flock. These are not two separate offices or functions; the second term is a further explanation of the first (see 5:2, 4; Acts 20:28).

3:1. Instructions to **wives** now appear (3:1–6). As Peter exhorted believers to submit to government authorities (2:13–17), and slaves to submit to masters (2:18–25), **likewise** he exhorted the women, **be in subjection to your own husbands**. Peter employed the same Greek verb (*hypotassō*) that he used in 2:13 and 18, a term that calls for submission to a recognized authority. This passage does not imply inferiority. The submission is one of role or function and is necessary for the orderly operation of the home and for Christian witness to an unbelieving spouse. The wife is to assume a respectful and gentle demeanor toward her husband in order to influence him for Christ.

Here again, Peter's evangelistic interest (see 2:9, 12) is evident. The husbands who disbelieve (**obey**

not the word) may **be won by the conversation** (respectful attitude; "behavior," NIV) **of the wives** even without a **word**. The first instance of "the word" in this verse refers to the gospel message; the second instance, to verbal witnessing. Believing wives are to rely not on argumentation to win their unbelieving husbands but on the quality of their lives. Of course, Peter was not forbidding wives to talk to their unbelieving husbands about Christ; rather, his point was that their witness must be backed up by Christlike attitudes.

3:2–4. Chaste conversation ("conduct," NKJV) **coupled with fear** (v. 2) indicates that the wives' lives are to be marked by a moral purity that springs from reverence of God. **Hair … gold … apparel** (v. 3) refer to extreme coiffures, gaudy jewelry, and expensive garments. Christian women should not rely on such extremes of adornment for beauty. Peter did not forbid neatness and pleasing appearance but excessive attention to good looks and preoccupation with one's attractiveness. One's focus should be on the inner person: **a meek** ("gentle," NIV) **and quiet spirit** (v. 4), which brings honor from the Lord and **is in the sight of God of great price**, that is, "very precious in God's sight" (NRSV).

3:5–6. The apostle appealed to **the holy women** (v. 5) of past ages as an inspiration for women in his day. Those women of previous generations put their hope in God for vindication of their honor (see 1:13). **Sara** (v. 6) particularly is to be imitated since she **obeyed Abraham, calling him lord**. Biblical instructions for a wife "to submit" in no way demands that she allow physical or psychological abuse of herself or her children. Though the apostle addressed mixed marriages, he presumed that the unbelieving husband in such a marriage would be persuadable and responsive to his believing wife.

3:7. Peter next turned to the relationship of the Christian husband to his wife. **Likewise** indicates that Peter was once again setting forth a specific way to "abstain from fleshly lusts" (2:11) and "having your conversation honest" (2:12). The emphasis in the text is that the husband is to **giv[e] honour unto the wife**. In a society in which Christians were maligned and dishonored, the Christian home became the place where God's honor for His people was expressed and felt. That is what Peter meant when he said that men should **dwell with them** (their wives) **according to knowledge** ("must always treat their wives with consideration in their life together," NJB). A Christian husband is to be a conduit of God's honor to his wife so that she may experience it. Specific ways of expressing that honor are found in 3:8 – 12.

Weaker vessel may refer to a woman's relative weakness in physical strength in comparison with that of a man. Peter's statement that wives are **heirs together** (with their husbands) **of the grace of life** was a startling thought for his day: the woman is sacred and has the same right of access to God as does the man. The purpose for giving honor to one's wife is that **your prayers be not hindered**. Spiritual fellowship, with God and with one another, may be hindered by disregarding God's instructions concerning husband-wife relationships.

E. Conclusion (3:8 – 12)

In his second argument, Peter addressed all his readers in 2:11 – 17, spoke directly to slaves in 2:18 – 25, and addressed wives in 3:1 – 6 and husbands in 3:7. In his conclusion of the argument, he wrapped up his discussion of what it means to "abstain from fleshly lusts" (2:11) and "hav[e] your conversation honest" (2:12). The apostle encouraged all his readers to develop the appropriate virtues in their relations with others and with non-Christians.

3:8 – 9. One mind (v. 8) does not mean that Christians must see eye to eye on everything but that their underlying attitude and focus should be unity and service to one another. **Having compassion** translates the word from which the English term "sympathetic" comes. Each believer should be willing to enter the joys and sorrows of others. This requires attentive listening and putting one's own desires second. **Love as brethren, be pitiful**, or "have … a tender heart" (NRSV). The phrase **be courteous** is a good translation of the Greek "humble-minded" (*tapeinophrones*) since considerateness in manner

and speech is an appropriate expression of humility. **Knowing that ye are thereunto called** (v. 9). Peter's advice is counterintuitive to culture, but natural to "grace" living (see 2:19).

3:10 – 12. Peter introduced a quotation from Psalm 34:12 – 16 with the explanatory conjunction **For** (v. 10), showing that he viewed the quotation as giving reasons for obeying the exhortation of 3:9. First, the psalm gives a list of behaviors to avoid (**let him refrain his tongue from evil, and his lips that they speak no guile** ("deceitful speech," NIV), and **let him eschew evil** (v. 11; "turn from evil, NIV). Then follows a list of desirable actions to put in their place: **do good; let him seek peace** (i.e., in relationships), **and ensue** ("pursue," NIV) **it**. According to the psalmist, (1) the one who does such things will find life to be most gratifying, (2) his days will be good, (3) God's **eyes** (v. 12) will ever be on him to bless him, and (4) God's **ears** will be ready to hear his prayer. The responses of the Lord (3 and 4) are colorfully described through anthropomorphism, a figure of speech in which God is described as having human characteristics. Of course, the Almighty does not have literal human eyes and ears, but He is described as if He does to show that He responds to the human activity described in verses 10 – 11. **The face of the Lord is against them that do evil** signifies that God opposes the honor of the wicked with His own honor. The way to honor for Peter's audience, even in the midst of the reproach that they suffered as God's people, was to abstain from the kinds of evil listed in verses 10 – 11 and to practice the good listed there as well.

V. Third Argument: Hope to the End against Adversity (3:13 – 4:11)

A. Proposition (3:13 – 16a)

3:13 – 14a. Peter anticipated and answered a possible protest that might be voiced when his letter was delivered. He imagined the objection might be something like, "Even if we live submissively and humbly, Peter, we will still suffer. As you point out, we are aliens and strangers in our culture." The apostle's retort was, **And who is he that will harm**

you if ye be followers of that which is good? (v. 13). Even among the pagans, a general consensus of right and wrong would acknowledge Christian behavior as honorable. Peter, however, was enough of a realist to know that at least some of his readers would face opposition, as indeed some of them were (**But and if ye suffer for righteousness' sake**; v. 14a). In the Greek, this conditional clause is the furthest removed from stating a reality. Suffering for righteousness is a remote possibility, but even if it does occur (and for some in Peter's audience, it had), it brings special blessing to the sufferer (**happy are ye**; see Matt. 5:10 – 12).

3:14b – 16a. Peter urged his readers to adopt four courses of action, each of which answered their objections and soothed their fears regarding persecution. (1) **Be not afraid of their terror, neither be troubled** (v. 14b), or as the NLT has it, "So don't be afraid and don't worry." (2) **Sanctify the Lord God in your hearts** (v. 15). The NASB (and other translations) follows the better-attested reading in the New Testament manuscripts for this verse and has "sanctify Christ as Lord in your hearts." (3) **Be ready always to give an answer to every man that asketh you a reason of the hope that is in you** (v. 15). The word for "answer" is *apologia*, from which the English "apologetics" comes. The idea is not to "apologize" for being a Christian; Peter meant that all believers ought to be ready, willing, and able to explain what it is that they believe and why they believe it. Degrading, argumentative, and abusive speech has no place in sharing the faith. Instead, **meekness and fear** ("gentleness and respect," NIV) are to accompany one's witness. (4) The readers' possession of these attributes would ensure that they had **a good conscience** (v. 16a).

B. Reason (3:16b)

3:16b. The reason for the entire set of instructions in the proposition was so that the slanderers **may be ashamed** (v. 16b). Their false accusations would then be shown as obviously untrue; the believer's loving attitude would put the opponent's bitterness in a bad light. Peter did not mean that believers should relish the shame and downfall of those who oppose them.

C. Proof of the Reason (3:17)

Sometimes it is God's will for believers to undergo adversity for their faith. This is an additional reason for enduring slander with a ready and reverent attitude. Peter maintained that suffering as a Christian might be **the will of God** (v. 17; see 4:19). This letter does not have an extensive answer to the question of why Christians suffer (but see 4:4), but Peter did affirm that it may be in the divine plan. When believers do suffer, however, it should not be **for evil doing** but **for well doing** (see 4:15 – 16).

D. Embellishment (3:18 – 22)

The material that embellishes all that Peter said in 3:13 – 17 was drawn from the church's confessional tradition. Here is theology employed for a pastoral purpose: just as Christ suffered innocently yet was exalted to the highest place of honor in the universe, so His faithful followers can expect God's vindication of them although they are now reproached. As the following passages illustrate, the logic that Peter followed is an argument from the greater to the lesser; what is true of Christ is true also for His disciples (see John 15:20).

3:18. For Christ also hath once suffered for sins. Peter, like Paul in Philippians 2:5 – 11, referred to Jesus as an example of the type of conduct that should characterize the Christian. They are to be ready to suffer for doing good (see 3:13 – 14, 17). "Once" refers to the nature of Christ's sacrifice being final and complete (see Heb. 9:28). The phrase **the just for the unjust** ("the righteous for the unrighteous," NRSV) indicates that Peter considered Jesus' death "substitutionary" in the sense that He died in the place of the sinner. Christ's work on the cross does not save everyone automatically; **that he might bring us to God** is a conditional construction. Salvation is the purpose of His death, but the condition is faith.

3:19 – 20. He went and preached unto the spirits in prison (v. 19). The thought of Christ's suffering and death led Peter to comment on what occurred after Christ's death, which led to tangential remarks about preaching to "the spirits in prison" and about baptism (see 3:21). **By which** (i.e., by the power of the Holy Spirit; v. 19) could also be translated "in which" (NRSV), referring to the spiritual dimension. Five main interpretations of this passage are worthy of review here.

(1) Some hold that in His preincarnate state, Christ went and preached through **Noah** (v. 20) to the wicked generation of Noah's time. The **disobedient** people of his generation were **in prison** (v. 19), or hell. This view seems to be in line with the context of 1:10–11, where the Spirit is said to speak through the prophets. Peter referred to Noah as "a preacher of righteousness" (2 Peter 2:5).

(2) Others argue that between His death and resurrection, Christ went to some prison where fallen angels are supposedly incarcerated and there preached to the angels who are said to have left their proper state and married human women during Noah's time (see Gen. 6:1–4; 2 Peter 2:4; Jude 6). The "sons of God" in Genesis 6:2, 4 and Job 1:6; 2:1 are supposed to have been angels. The message Christ preached to these evil angels was probably a declaration of victory.

(3) Still others say that between His death and resurrection, Christ went to the place of the dead and preached to the spirits of Noah's wicked contemporaries, again proclaiming victory for Christ and doom for His hearers.

(4) According to another interpretation, after His death, Christ went and preached to people in hell. These people were offered a second chance of salvation (see 4:6). Those who advocate this view disagree whether the people included only the rebellious generation of the flood or all humans who had died up to that time. At least one scholar suggests that disobedient angels heard the preaching as well.

(5) A Roman Catholic interpretation is that after He died, Christ went and proclaimed release to people who were penitent just before they died in the flood. These people were released from purgatory and went to heaven.

The strength of the first interpretation is that it fits with the context of 1:10–11. The verb "preached" (*ekēryxen*) does not necessarily mean "to persuade" people to accept the good news of salvation. It could signify "to proclaim a victory."

A strong case may also be made for the second interpretation since the surrounding context describes Christ's exaltation from shame (death) to honor (resurrection and being seated at God's right hand). Peter's concern throughout his letter was with the shame and honor of his readers. Christ has been vindicated by God to the highest place; He has even proclaimed His victory to the supernatural powers. Thus, those who follow Christ can expect that they also will attain honor in the future.

3:21. Baptism doth also now save us. Peter's reference to **The like figure** ("an antitype," NKJV) **whereunto even baptism doth also now save** denotes his use of typology. This is an interpretive method that biblical writers used to draw connections between an Old Testament phenomenon (type) and its New Testament counterpart (antitype). The idea is not only that the type prefigures the antitype but also that the significance of the type is repeated, and made more significant, in the antitype. In that sense, the antitype fulfills its Old Testament type, or symbol.

Peter used a double figure here. The incident of the ark and the flood symbolizes baptism, and baptism symbolizes salvation. The flood was a figure of baptism in that, in both instances, the water that spoke of judgment (in the flood, the death of the wicked; in baptism, the death of Christ and the believer) is the water that saves (**eight souls were saved by water** through the ark; believers figuratively rise above the waters through baptism). Baptism is a symbol of salvation in that it depicts Christ's death, burial, and resurrection and believers' identification with Him in these experiences (see Rom. 6:4). Baptism "doth also now save." In reality, believers are saved by what baptism symbolizes: Christ's death and resurrection. The symbol and the reality are so closely related that the symbol is sometimes used to refer to the reality. Thus, baptism is metonymy, a figure of speech in which something closely associated with the subject is used in place of it. Here "baptism" is used in place of the union of Christ and the believer in the Lord's death, burial, and resurrection, which baptism depicts.

In the final analysis, people are saved not by any ritual; people are saved **by the resurrection of Jesus Christ** and its supernatural power. In baptism, the believer gives **the answer of a good conscience toward God**. In other words, the act of baptism is a commitment on the part of the believer in all good conscience to make sure that what baptism symbolizes will become a reality in his life.

3:22. Who ... is on the right hand of God. After His ascension (**gone into heaven**), Christ was honored with the ultimate place of authority and honor in the universe. "The right hand of God" is an anthropomorphism (God is described as if He has a human body). The figure of speech expresses God's absolute power.

E. Conclusion (4:1–11)

4:1. In wrapping up his third and final argument of the letter, Peter revisited emphases of the argument: suffering (4:1), the reproaches of the pagans (4:4), and good conduct (4:7–11). Since 3:19–22 is parenthetical, 4:1 ties directly back to 3:18, the link signified by **Forasmuch then**. The aspect of Christ's suffering that these passages stress is suffering unjustly because one has done good. Furthermore, it is physical suffering (**in the flesh**). **Arm yourselves** is a military metaphor; the weaponry is **the same mind** ("the same attitude," NIV) as Christ's. Believers should be prepared to suffer unjustly and to face such abuse with Christ's attitude, with His willingness to endure suffering for doing good. (For a similar principle in Paul's writings, see Phil. 2:5–11.)

4:2. The daily choice facing the Christian is whether to **live ... to the lusts of men** or **to the will of God**. Christ's attitude should prevail, and God's will should be the determining factor in life.

4:3. In **the time past**, before conversion, Peter's hearers had focused on wasteful and extravagant activities. His list sounds very much like twenty-first-

century excesses: "You were immoral and followed your evil desires. You went around drinking and partying and carrying on. In fact, you even worshiped disgusting idols" (CEV).

4:4. This verse is very instructive and perceptive; it is a sort of "psychology of persecution." There may be other reasons for outrage and reaction against believers, but here Peter said that pagans take up **speaking evil** (lit., "blaspheming") **of you** because followers of Christ **run not with them to the same excess of riot** (i.e., the sins of 4:3). The unbelievers **think it strange**. What they do not understand, they ridicule.

4:5. Because of their continued indulgence in sin and their blasphemy against believers, the opponents **shall give account**. In the New Testament, both the Father and the Son are said to be Judge on the great, final judgment day. The Father is the ultimate source of judgment, but He will delegate judgment to the Son (see John 5:27; Acts 17:31). **The quick and the dead** are those alive and those dead when the final judgment day dawns. The Greek noun translated "account" (*logos*) and the adverb translated "ready" (*hetoimōs*) recall 3:15, where the identical noun ("reason") and the adjective "ready" (*hetoimos*) appear. Whereas in 3:15 Peter called on Christians to be prepared to answer for their beliefs to anyone who asked, here he called on the blasphemous and unprincipled pagans to answer to the highest court of the universe for their actions.

4:6. For this cause was the gospel preached also to them that are dead. The "cause" to which this statement refers is **that they might be judged according to men in the flesh, but live according to God in the spirit**. At least three different interpretations have been offered for this verse. (1) Some maintain that Peter meant the gospel had been preached to the spiritually dead, who heard the good news in this life and live eternally if they responded by faith to it. They still experienced the physical death (the judgment in the flesh) common to all humans, however. (2) Other interpreters believe that Peter was saying the gospel had been preached to dead people who heard the gospel in Hades. They had been judged in terms of the body by dying, but the prospect of living in the Spirit on the last day was put before them. Christ's descending into hell and bringing souls out of it (the harrowing of hell) are what lay behind verse 6. (3) According to a third view, Peter meant that the gospel was preached "to Christians who are now dead but who heard and responded to the gospel before they died" (Marshall, *1 Peter*, p. 137). These people have been judged according to human standards by the pagan world, which does not understand why God's people no longer follow its sinful way of life (see 4:2–4).

4:7. The end of all things is at hand may have been a Christian proverb or watchword in Peter's day and introduces other maxims that appear in quick succession in 4:7–11. Anticipation of the end times, particularly Christ's return, should influence believers' attitudes, actions, and relationships. The two commands **be ye therefore sober, and watch unto prayer** could be understood as a single, emphatic command: "be earnest and disciplined in your prayers" (NLT). "Be ye therefore sober" may refer to abstaining from drunkenness or to seriousness generally. Christians are to be characterized by reason, are to make wise, mature decisions, and are to have a clearly defined, decisive purpose in life.

4:8–9. The command to **have fervent charity among yourselves** (v. 8; "love each other deeply," NIV; "preserve an intense love for each other," NJB) is the most effective way (**above all things**) to preserve unity. **Use hospitality one to another without grudging** (v. 9) reflects the minority status that Peter's readers had in their surrounding culture. Although they themselves were strangers, they were to welcome other believing strangers. Then all might find a home for the homeless, a place of belonging (see 2:5).

4:10–11. These verses represent Peter's contribution to the discussion of spiritual gifts in the New Testament and should be compared with Romans 12:4–8; 1 Corinthians 12:7–11; and Ephesians 4:7–16. Peter filled the instruction witih language intended to help his readers see that they were honored and had a valuable contribution to make in the church. Each believer had received **the gift** (v. 10;

the Greek omits the article, so the translation should read "a gift" [*charisma*, RSV]) and was to use this gift in serving others. The idea of the church as a household is evident, as in 4:9. **Stewards** were household servants to whom the daily business of the house was entrusted. As the believers served one another, they distinguished themselves as **good**. That is, they became agents of **the manifold grace of God**.

The Greek for **oracles** (v. 11) is used to refer to the Scriptures or to the words God has spoken (see Acts 7:38; Rom. 3:2). Thus, although the gift of preaching and teaching appears more prestigious than the gift of serving, both gifts are given **that God in all things may be glorified**. A doxology, in which the recipient of the glory (*doxa*) is Jesus Christ closes the third argument of the epistle on a high and inspirational note.

VI. Closing (4:12–5:14)

The doxology of 4:11 and the address "beloved" at the beginning of 4:12 has led some to theorize that two letters (1:1–4:11 and 4:12–5:14) were been put together some time after their writing and that 1 Peter is thus a composite letter. This theory is unnecessary; the section beginning with 4:12 has close connections with all that precedes it. The latter section is a conclusion of the letter, not another document that was later appended. Nevertheless, the conclusion could conceivably have been written after a sudden outbreak of violence in Rome. As Peter was about to wrap up his letter, Nero's ferocious persecution of Christians (some were burned; some were thrown to the beasts in the arena) commenced in the imperial capital (AD 64). These events may have led the apostle to warn his flocks scattered throughout Asia Minor that what was happening in Rome could spread to the provinces. The urgent tone in 4:12, with its mention of a "fiery trial," makes such a scenario possible.

A. Further Examination of the Topic of Suffering (4:12–19)

4:12–13. The fiery trial which is to try you (v. 12; "the fiery ordeal that is taking place among you to test you," NRSV) recalls the tests of 1:6–7. Peter likens their suffering to the eschatological final time of testing at the end of history. The believers' faith may be refined, and those who endure the ordeal will be vindicated by God. To endure, however, one must **rejoice** (v. 13). After all, the fiery trial is a sharing in the sufferings of Christ.

4:14. Meanwhile, **If ye be reproached for the name of Christ, happy are ye.** The word "happy" may mislead some into thinking that they are required to enjoy suffering or to take some sort of morbid pleasure in it, even seek it. Not so. Peter's statement, drawn from the Beatitudes (Matt. 5:11; Luke 6:22), pronounces a blessing ("you are blessed," NIV). His intention was to give his slandered readers encouragement in their afflictions. The glory that they hoped for at Christ's second coming (4:13) already rested upon them in the Holy Spirit: **for the spirit of glory and of God resteth upon you.** In the midst of reproachful treatment from unbelievers, the Christians already had the honor whose full bestowal they awaited at Christ's coming. In fact, they brought glory and honor to Christ in their suffering.

4:15–16. Just as in 2:20 and 3:17, where Peter contrasted suffering for doing good with suffering for doing evil, here he acknowledged that not all suffering is positive. Only that adversity experienced **as a Christian** (v. 16) is honorable, and no shame is to be taken with it.

4:17–19. Judgment must begin at the house of God (v. 17), Peter said. The persecutions that believers were undergoing were divinely sent judgment intended to purify God's people. If God brings judgment on His own people, if He so disciplines the children of His household, **what shall the end be of them that obey not the gospel of God?** How much more serious will the judgment be that He will bring on unbelievers. Although the KJV translation is difficult to see, Peter quotes Proverbs 11:31 from the Septuagint to confirm his point. As he reintroduced the theme of the household of God in the conclusion of his letter, he did so solemnly and seriously. The privilege of belonging brings the responsibility of obedience.

B. A Farewell Speech of Exhortation (5:1–11)

1. Self-Vindication (5:1)

5:1. Peter, who identified himself as an apostle at the beginning of his letter (1:1), here chose to identify himself with the elders of the churches (**who am also an elder**). Peter had been with Jesus from the early days of His ministry and thus could describe himself as **a witness of the sufferings of Christ.** As one of the Twelve, Peter had witnessed all phases and aspects of Jesus' earthly ministry, including the climactic events of His suffering (see Matt. 26:58; Mark 14:54; Luke 22:60–62; John 18:10–11, 15–16).

2. A Call to Tend the Flock (5:2a–b)

5:2a–b. Feed the flock of God (v. 2a) is a metaphor that the Lord Himself employed (John 10:1–18; Luke 15:3–7) and that must have been etched on Peter's mind (see John 21:15–17; see 1 Peter 2:25). As he wrote this letter, Peter was fulfilling Christ's command to feed His sheep. The term "Shepherd" (5:4) is an Old Testament metaphor (see Ezek. 34:1–10, where the Lord held the leaders of Israel responsible for failing to care for the flock). The awkward expression **which is among you** is helpfully translated "that is under your care" in the NIV. One Greek word (*episkopountes*) is translated **taking the oversight thereof.** The noun related to it (*episkopos*) is used in Acts 20:28 ("overseers"); Philippians 1:1; 1 Timothy 3:2; and Titus 1:7 ("bishop[s]"). In the New Testament, the three terms "elder," "overseer" (or "bishop"), and "shepherd" all apply to one office.

3. A Warning against Greed (5:2c–3)

5:2c–3. Peter realized that the right thing can be done for the wrong motivation. Thus, the apostle warned the shepherds to care for the flock **not for filthy lucre, but of a ready mind** (v. 2c). This passage does not prohibit one from earning one's livelihood in Christian service. Peter's point was that the Christian leader must always guard against doing his work primarily for money, to get attention from others, or to gain prestige. Neither are overseers to tend their flocks out of a desire for power. The true leadership model is **being ensamples** (examples) **to the flock** (v. 3). The Greek word for "ensamples" here is *typos*, a word that, in secular writing, referred to the stamp or impression made on a coin, to a mold, or to an outline of a book's contents. The leader's life should be an outline that others can follow.

4. Reward and Judgment (5:4)

5:4. When the **chief Shepherd** (Christ, see 2:25) returns, He will reward those who have served as shepherds under Him. The **crown** (Greek, *stephanos*) **of glory** may be a metaphorical reference to the athlete's crown, the crown of a monarch, the valiant soldier's wreath, a reward for service to the state, or the headpiece of a supernatural being. In any case, it is a symbol of honor. Unlike worldly prizes and recognitions, it **fadeth not away** (see 1:4). Peter was in no way teaching salvation by works here. The bestowal is one of honor to pastors who have done their work in the manner that Peter outlined in 5:2–3.

5. Love and Humility (5:5–7)

5:5–7. Peter used a striking metaphor in describing the humble attitude that all in the household of God should have toward one another: **be clothed with humility** (v. 5). In this way, the members of God's household convey His honor to one another. Since God **giveth grace to the humble**, Peter instructed his hearers, whose communities were harassed and maligned, **Humble yourselves therefore under the mighty hand of God** (v. 6). Peter once again employed an anthropomorphism (see 3:22) to convey the idea that God's strength is sufficient to protect His people until the proper moment (**due time**) for Him to **exalt** them. **Casting all your care upon him** (v. 7) defines what humbling oneself before God means. The term "cast" is used one other time in the New Testament. In Luke 19:35, it describes the action of the disciples as "they cast their garments upon the colt." Peter's readers were to throw their worries about their lack of honor and advantage in society on to their Lord. So too, Christians of any age are to throw every "anxiety" (NIV), all their "worries" (CEV), on to Christ. He will bear

them, **for he careth for you**. That is, "you are his personal concern" (Phillips).

6. An Exhortation to Watch and Stand Firm (5:8a)

5:8a. The command to **Be sober** (for the same command, see 1:13; 4:7) is made more urgent by the additional **be vigilant**. Jesus used the same Greek verb (*grēgoreō*) when He urgently warned His disciples to "watch" and pray in order not to enter into temptation (Matt. 26:41). Perhaps Peter remembered his own difficulty in staying awake during our Lord's agony in Gethsemane (see Matt. 26:36–46).

7. Discussion of the Enemy (5:8b)

5:8b. By using the vivid simile of a prowling and **roaring lion**, Peter captured well the ferocity of the opposition that his hearers faced. The image does not mean that Christians were being thrown to the beasts in the arena. It is unlikely that such severe measures were being taken against Christians at that time. However, Peter's portrayal of the source of slander as **your adversary the devil** demonstrated that the source of the opposition was not just human antagonists but Satan himself. By identifying the peril as a supernatural one, Peter hoped to promote group unity and identity in the community. "Devil" (*diabolos*) literally means "slanderer." The Devil was the ultimate source of the slander directed against Peter's audience.

8. A Prediction of Suffering (5:9–11)

5:9–11. Despite the supernatural nature of the ultimate foe, Peter recognized that the Devil can be resisted if Christians remain **stedfast in the faith** (v. 9; see Eph. 6:13; James 4:7). The Christians to whom Peter wrote were not isolated; they belonged to a fellowship of suffering. Four future-tense verbs emphasize the certainty of God's vindication of the oppressed hearers. The first three verbs are practically identical in meaning: **make you perfect, stablish, strengthen** (v. 10). The fourth may indicate a progression to a yet higher plane: **settle you** (*themelioō*) means "he will place you on a firm foundation" (NLT). If suffering is accepted in humility and faith, the time will come when God sets things right. Thus, Peter ascribed to God **glory and dominion for ever and ever** (v. 11).

C. Closing Remarks and Greeting (5:12–14)

5:12. Silvanus (Silas) may have been the bearer of the letter to its destination. He may also have been a scribe who recorded what Peter dictated or who, as an informed and intelligent secretary, aided him in the phrasing of his thoughts (see Introduction: "Author"). Peter stated his purpose in addressing the churches scattered throughout Asia Minor: **I have written briefly, exhorting, and testifying that this is the true grace of God wherein ye stand**. In this epistle, "grace" signifies the favor and honor of God. "Wherein ye stand" should be translated as an imperative ("Stand firm in it!" NASB), a final exhortation as Peter concluded his letter.

5:13. For **Babylon**, see Introduction: "Place of Composition." Peter regarded Mark with such warmth and affection that he called him **Marcus my son**. It is possible that Peter had led Mark to Christ, and early Christian tradition closely associates Mark and Peter (see Mark, Introduction: "Author").

5:14. A kiss of charity ("a kiss of love," NIV) was a cultural expression of greeting and signified a tangible expression of the divine honor that the members of God's household could give one another. The concluding benediction of **Peace** (see 1:2) is a statement of the result that honor from God can bring. It brings spiritual well-being and blessedness to all who are united to Christ. Peter thus ended his letter with a reference to the union of believers with Christ, a concept fundamental to the understanding of the whole letter.

THE SECOND EPISTLE GENERAL OF PETER

INTRODUCTION

Author

The author identified himself as Simon Peter (1:1). He used the first-person singular pronoun in a highly personal passage (1:12–15) and claimed to be an eyewitness of the transfiguration (1:16–18; see Matt. 17:1–5). He asserted that this was his second letter to the readers (3:1) and referred to Paul as "our beloved brother" (3:15). In short, the letter claims to be Peter's, and its character is compatible with that claim. For further background on Peter, see 1 Peter, Introduction: "Author."

Although 2 Peter was not as widely known and recognized in the early church as 1 Peter was, some may have used and accepted it as authoritative as early as the second century and perhaps even in the latter part of the first century (1 Clement [AD 95] may allude to it). The letter was not ascribed to Peter until Origen's time (185–253), and he seems to reflect some doubt concerning it. Eusebius (265–340) placed it among the questioned books, though he admits that most accepted 2 Peter as from Peter. After Eusebius's time, it seems to have been quite generally accepted as canonical. The epistle is included in Athanasius's list of authoritative books in his Festal Letter of 367, and the Council of Carthage (397) similarly ratified 2 Peter.

In recent centuries, however, the place of 2 Peter in the New Testament Canon has been called into question. In the time of the Reformation, Luther accepted 2 Peter, Calvin was dubious of it, and Erasmus rejected it. A considerable number of scholars have challenged its genuineness. One of the objections that has been raised is the difference in style from that of 1 Peter. The difference is not absolute, however; there are noteworthy similarities in vocabulary and in other matters. The differences that do exist may be accounted for by variations in subject matter, in the form and purpose of the letters, in the time and circumstances of writing, in sources or models, and in scribes who may have been employed. Perhaps most significant is the statement in 1 Peter 5:12 that "By Silvanus" Peter had "written briefly." No such statement is made concerning 2 Peter, which may explain its noticeable difference in style (see 1 Peter, Introduction: "Author").

The early church concerned itself with the question of authenticity and may very well have ascertained Petrine authorship of 2 Peter before issuing full recognition of its canonical status. The pseudonymous author of *The Acts of Paul* was deposed for forgery, and the so-called *Gospel of Peter* was forbidden because it was non-Petrine both in authorship and doctrine. This evidence suggests that the question of the authenticity of 2 Peter was settled at an early time.

Date

Peter wrote this epistle toward the end of his life (see 1:12–15), after he had written a prior letter (3:1) to the same readers (probably 1 Peter). Since Peter was martyred during the reign of Nero, his death must have occurred prior to AD 68 (the date of Nero's death), so it is very likely that he wrote 2 Peter somewhere between 63 and 68, probably around 64 or 65, and most likely from Rome.

Some have argued that these dates are too early for the writing of 2 Peter, but nothing in the book requires a later date. To insist that the second chapter was directed against second-century Gnosticism is to assume more than the contents of the chapter warrant. The heretics referred to in 2 Peter may well have been among the forerunners of second-century Gnostics since elements of a later, more fully developed Gnosticism are present: emphasis on *gnōsis* (knowledge) that leads to a lack of moral restraint, arrogance toward church leaders who are thought to be unenlightened, divisiveness, sexual immorality, and an interest in angels. Nothing is said of the false teachers that would not fit into the later years of Peter's life. Some have suggested a later date because they interpret the reference to "the fathers" in 3:4 to mean an earlier Christian generation. However, the word is most naturally interpreted as referring to the Old Testament patriarchs (see "fathers" in John 6:31; Acts 3:13; Heb. 1:1).

Other objections to the authenticity of 2 Peter arise from a naturalistic reconstruction of early Christian history or misunderstandings or misconstructions of the available data. For example, some argue that the reference to Paul's letters as "scriptures" (3:16) indicates an advanced date for this book—beyond Peter's lifetime, perhaps as late as the second century. Three objections to this argument may be raised. (1) It is quite possible that Paul's letters were gathered at an early date, since some of them had been in existence and perhaps in circulation for more than ten years (Thessalonians for as much as fifteen years) prior to Peter's death. Besides, Peter's statement in 3:16 may only indicate that he was acquainted with some of Paul's letters, not that there was a formal, ecclesiastical collection of them. (2) Since the apostles, especially Paul, spoke with divine authority (see 1 Cor. 2:13, 16; 7:17; 14:37–38), their writings could easily have been understood as "scripture" from the time of their production in the first century. (3) Peter's term of endearment, "our beloved brother Paul" (3:15), would more likely have been written in the first century than in the second. The second century witnessed attempts to drive wedges between Peter and Paul, and someone writing pseudonymously with Peter as his champion might well have been reluctant to heap such adulation on an ecclesiastical rival. Although not conclusive, these arguments cast doubt on any late-date theory for 2 Peter.

The Relationship of 2 Peter and Jude

Despite conspicuous differences (e.g., Jude's use of apocryphal sources) between 2 Peter and Jude, there are conspicuous similarities between the two letters. Some notable parallels are shown in the chart below.

2 Peter 2:1	Jude 4
1 But there were false prophets also among the people, even as there shall be false teachers among you, who privily shall bring in damnable heresies, even denying the Lord that bought them, and bring upon themselves swift destruction.	4 For there are certain men crept in unawares, who were before of old ordained to this condemnation, ungodly men, turning the grace of our God into lasciviousness, and denying the only Lord God, and our Lord Jesus Christ.
2 Peter 2:4, 6	**Jude 6–7**
4 For if God spared not the angels that sinned, but cast them down to hell, and delivered them into chains of darkness, to be reserved unto judgment; 6 And turning the cities of Sodom and Gomorrha into ashes condemned them with an overthrow, making them an ensample unto those that after should live ungodly;	6 And the angels which kept not their first estate, but left their own habitation, he hath reserved in everlasting chains under darkness unto the judgment of the great day. 7 Even as Sodom and Gomorrha, and the cities about them in like manner, giving themselves over to fornication, and going after strange flesh, are set forth for an example, suffering the vengeance of eternal fire.
2 Peter 2:10–12	**Jude 8–10**
10 But chiefly them that walk after the flesh in the lust of uncleanness, and despise government. Presumptuous are they, selfwilled, they are not afraid to speak evil of dignities. 11 Whereas angels, which are greater in power and might, bring not railing accusation against them before the Lord. 12 But these, as natural brute beasts, made to be taken and destroyed, speak evil of the things that they understand not; and shall utterly perish in their own corruption;	8 Likewise also these filthy dreamers defile the flesh, despise dominion, and speak evil of dignities. 9 Yet Michael the archangel, when contending with the devil he disputed about the body of Moses, durst not bring against him a railing accusation, but said, The Lord rebuke thee. 10 But these speak evil of those things which they know not: but what they know naturally, as brute beasts, in those things they corrupt themselves.
2 Peter 2:13, 17	**Jude 12–13**
13 And shall receive the reward of unrighteousness, as they that count it pleasure to riot in the day time. Spots they are and blemishes, sporting themselves with their own deceivings while they feast with you; 17 These are wells without water, clouds that are carried with a tempest; to whom the mist of darkness is reserved for ever.	12 These are spots in your feasts of charity, when they feast with you, feeding themselves without fear: clouds they are without water, carried about of winds; trees whose fruit withereth, without fruit, twice dead, plucked up by the roots; 13 Raging waves of the sea, foaming out their own shame; wandering stars, to whom is reserved the blackness of darkness for ever.

The wording is not completely identical but strikingly similar. It has, therefore, been suggested that one borrowed from the other or that they both drew on a common source. If borrowing did occur, it was not slavish but rather was adapted to suit the writer's purpose. While many have insisted that Jude used 2 Peter, it is more reasonable to assume that the longer letter (2 Peter) incorporated much of the shorter (Jude). Jude would gain little by shortening 2 Peter, whereas 2 Peter expands the message of Jude considerably. Of course, Jude and Peter could have written their respective letters independently of one another. The inexactitude in phraseology between the parallel passages might indicate that. However, such borrowing as that described above was fairly common in ancient writings (e.g., many believe that Paul used parts of early hymns in Phil. 2:6–11 and 1 Tim. 3:16). A high view of biblical inspiration need not insist on independent composition of biblical documents.

Theme and Theological Message

In his first letter, Peter fed Christ's sheep by instructing them how to deal with persecution from outside the church (see, e.g., 1 Peter 4:12); in his second letter, he taught them how to deal with false teachers and evildoers who had come into the church (see 2:1; 3:3–4). While the particular situations naturally called for variations in content and emphasis, in both letters Peter, as a pastor ("shepherd") of Christ's sheep (see John 21:15–17), sought to commend to his readers a wholesome combination of Christian faith and practice. More specifically, his purpose was threefold: (1) to stimulate Christian growth (chap. 1), (2) to combat false teaching (chap. 2), and (3) to encourage watchfulness in view of the Lord's certain return (chap. 3). For further information on the audience of the epistle, see 1 Peter, Introduction: "Recipients"; the audience was likely the same for both 1 and 2 Peter.

Literary Features

As with 1 Peter, 2 Peter displays the author's acquaintance with standards for composition that are outlined in the Greco-Roman rhetorical handbooks. The epistle constitutes an example of deliberative rhetoric, that is, discourse in which the rhetor seeks to persuade or dissuade his audience regarding future action. (For other examples of Greco-Roman rhetoric, see 1 Peter, Introduction: "Literary Features" and Jude, Introduction: "Literary Features.") Peter's main proposition was that his hearers "be stablished in the present truth" by "remembrance of these things" (i.e., things pertaining to Christian faith; 1:12). The proofs that substantiate this proposition feature accusations made by the false teachers and Peter's refutation of them. The accusation-refutation pattern was rhetorically effective in that it reminded Peter's audience of essential points of apostolic teaching while bringing them to bear on specific objections that were ongoing issues in his churches.

The letter is also an example of a testament—a statement of ethical and religious teachings, to which the Petrine communities were to adhere after Peter's demise, and a prophecy concerning their destiny. The following outline demonstrates the letter's rhetorical structure.

Outline

Select Bibliography

Barclay, William. *The Letters of James and Peter*. Rev. ed. The Daily Study Bible. Philadelphia: Westminster John Knox, 1976.

Bigg, Charles. *A Critical and Exegetical Commentary on the Epistles of St. Peter and St. Jude*. International Critical Commentary. Edinburgh: T&T Clark, 1978.

Green, Michael. "Peter, Second Epistle of." In *New Bible Dictionary*, 3rd ed. Edited by D. R. W. Wood, I. Howard Marshall, A. R. Millard, J. I. Packer, and D. J. Wiseman, 911–13. Downers Grove, IL: InterVarsity, 1996.

———. *The Second Epistle General of Peter and the General Epistle of Jude: An Introduction and Commentary*. 2nd ed. Tyndale New Testament Commentaries 18. Grand Rapids, MI: Eerdmans, 1987.

Hillyer, Norman. *1 and 2 Peter, Jude*. The New International Biblical Commentary 16. Peabody, MA: Hendrickson, 1992.

Moo, Douglas J. *2 Peter and Jude*. The NIV Application Commentary. Grand Rapids, MI: Zondervan, 1996.

Neyrey, Jerome H. *2 Peter, Jude: A New Translation with Introduction and Commentary*. The Anchor Bible 37C. New York: Doubleday, 1993.

Senior, Donald P., and Daniel J. Harrington. *1 Peter, Jude and 2 Peter*. Sacra Pagina 15. Collegeville, MN: Michael Glazier, 2003.

Waltner, Erland, and J. Daryl Charles. *1–2 Peter, Jude*. Believers Church Bible Commentary. Scottdale, PA: Herald, 1999.

Watson, Duane Frederick. *Invention, Arrangement, and Style: Rhetorical Criticism of Jude and 2 Peter*. Society of Biblical Literature Dissertation Series 104. Atlanta: Scholars Press, 1988.

EXPOSITION

I. Introduction (1:1–2)

1:1. Simon Peter identified himself as **a servant and an apostle of Jesus Christ**, a description that not only showed humility but also established his authority to address his audience. The hearers were those who had **obtained like precious faith with us.** Here "faith" is not a body of truth to be believed — the faith — but the act of believing or the God-given capacity to trust in Christ for salvation. "Like precious" is *isotimos* and means "of equal honor." The cultural value of honor (and its opposite, shame) informs Peter's argument in this letter just as it does in 1 Peter. In cultural terms, God is the patron who had favored the recipients of the letter with the honor of faith. As His clients, they were responsible for living in a way that would bring Him glory and honor in return.

The distinction between the two senses (patron, clients) becomes clearer with the construction **through the knowledge of God, and of Jesus our Lord**, which has two articles in the Greek ("through the knowledge of the God and Jesus the Lord of us"). Knowledge is of two persons: God and Jesus. Elsewhere in 2 Peter, Jesus is designated "our [the] Lord and Saviour Jesus Christ" (1:11; 2:20; 3:18; see also 3:2).

1:2. The greeting (**Grace and peace be multiplied unto you**) is that of 1 Peter 1:2 except that in his second letter, Peter added the means by which the multiplication might take place: through, or "in" (NKJV), the intimate relationship that a Christian enjoys with God and with Jesus Christ.

II. Exordium: Exhortation to Growth in Christian Virtues (1:3–11)

A. The Divine Enablement (1:3–4)

1:3. All things that pertain unto life and godliness. God has made available all that believers need spiritually **through [our] knowledge of Him**. If indeed 2 Peter was written to combat an incipient Gnosticism, the apostle may have been insisting that the knowledge possessed by those in apostolic circles was entirely adequate to meet their spiritual needs. No secret, esoteric knowledge is necessary for salvation. The things that contribute to true life and to godly character, that is, **to glory and virtue**, may be the qualities listed in 1:5–7.

1:4. God has given **us exceeding great and precious promises**. "Precious" (*timios*) is related to the word for honor (*timē*) and has the idea of "great beyond all price" (NEB); therefore, great honor is bestowed on those to whom the promises are given. In light of Peter's vision of the future (see 1:11, 16, 19; 3:4, 9, 13), the promises probably are to be equated with Christ's promises for the future. The purpose of the promises is that God's people might become **partakers of the divine nature**. Peter did not indicate that Christians become divine in any sense, only that they are indwelt by God through His Holy Spirit (see John 14:16–17). One's humanity and His deity, as well as the human personality and the divine personality, remain distinct and separate.

The Gnostic idea that one gains union with the divine through self-understanding or through knowledge of secret and esoteric teachings is decisively refuted here. One can only become godly after **having escaped the corruption that is in the world through lust**. This action was a decisive one for Peter's readers, as it is for any Christian. The decision must, however, be reenacted daily as an act of discipleship. "The world" refers to human society that has alienated itself from God by rebellion against Him.

B. The Call for Growth (1:5–7)

1:5. This refers to all that Peter said in 1:3–4. Having identified God's indispensable primacy in one's experience of true life and godliness, the apostle puts his finger on the human role. That role requires one's **giving all diligence**. God Himself generates the life of piety, but the believer is a partner in the process of holiness. Christian growth, according to Peter, is a process, and it is not completed overnight. The "ladder" or "chain" of virtues featured in 1:5–7 is a set of consecutive character qualities, with one building on another only after the prior ones have been acquired. The pattern that Peter followed is a *gradatio*, a figure by which the speaker proceeds to the following step in a series only after repeating the prior one (see Rom. 5:3–5). Peter instructed his readers to **add to your faith** many other qualities. The Greek word translated "add" (*epichorēgeō*) is colorful. It is related to the Greek word *chorēgos*, a term referring to a wealthy Athenian who defrayed the enormous cost of the chorus in Greek plays. "Be lavish in the amount of attention, detail, and quality you put into building on your Christian faith" could be a paraphrase here.

The first of the attributes to be developed beyond **faith** is **virtue**, or "moral excellence." In secular usage, the word describes the character of the person who has embraced the teachings of philosophy. "Virtue" (*aretē*) can refer to that "goodness" that issues in exemplary citizenship and dependable friendship.

Knowledge is the translation of *gnōsis*, which in 2 Peter, likely conveys the idea of wisdom in practical affairs, the sensibility that allows one to effectively deal with life and its challenges (see 1:5–6; 3:18). Peter also used another word for "knowledge" in this epistle: *epignōsis*. Although the two are basically interchangeable in Greek, Peter appears to have distinguished the two. *Epignōsis* seems to refer to the intimate relationship of faith that a Christian enjoys with God through the Lord Jesus Christ (1:2–3, 8; 2:20), whereas *gnōsis* is the articulation of faith.

1:6. True Christian **knowledge** is also related to **temperance** ("self-control," NIV). Many of the false teachers maintained that knowledge makes self-control unnecessary. According to Peter, however, Christian knowledge leads to self-control. The false teachers demonstrated their lack of true spiritual knowledge by their lack of personal discipline.

To **temperance**, Peter urged his readers to add **patience**. The word is *hypomonē* and refers not so much to patience with people as to "fortitude" (REB) or "endurance" (Weymouth) in the face of life's difficulties. One cannot truly develop self-control without endurance, the quality of remaining faithful under stress and strain.

Building on **patience**, the next attribute to be added is **godliness**, a genuine reverence of God that governs one's attitude toward every aspect of life. The Greek term is *eusebeia*, which refers to the practice of giving to God that which is His due.

1:7. Brotherly kindness (*philadelphia*), the next of the qualities to be nurtured in the Christian life, involves warmhearted affection toward all in the family of faith. This quality relates to **godliness**, which immediately precedes it in the chain since without brotherly kindness, even acts of godliness can become routine and lack genuine compassion.

Developing from **brotherly kindness** is the next characteristic, **charity**. The Greek word is *agapē* and means "love" (NIV) — the kind of outgoing, selfless attitude that leads one to sacrifice for the good of others. The noun and the verb related to it are used consistently in the New Testament for the love that God has for all human beings through Jesus Christ (see John 3:16; Rom. 5:8), for the love that humans express to God in response to His love (see John 14:21; 1 Peter 1:8), and for one's love of others as a response to God's love (see John 13:34–35; 1 John 4:11). According to Paul in 1 Corinthians 13:13, *agapē* is the greatest of all Christian virtues.

C. The Value of Such Growth (1:8–11)

Here Peter skillfully used the rhetorical device known as an *antithesis* to create in his audience a keen desire to develop the virtues listed in 1:5–7. In the antithesis, Peter contrasted the life of faith (as outlined in 1:5–7) with the life of the false teach-

ers, a life of spiritual shortsightedness. He offered his readers two possibilities, presenting a result of each path and, in so doing, demonstrating the overwhelming desirability of the pathway of faith.

1:8–9. The first possibility is the life of faith, whose condition is expressed by the clause **if these things be in you, and abound** (v. 8). Peter was not implying that the believer is to cultivate each listed quality in turn, one after the other until all have been perfected. Instead, they are all to be cultivated simultaneously. Furthermore, there never comes a time when a believer has "arrived" and no longer needs to give any attention to any of the virtues. There is always room for growth since Jesus Christ is the measure of maturity. Those who grow and mature are promised, **ye shall neither be barren nor unfruitful in the knowledge of our Lord Jesus Christ**. The word "barren" translates *argos*, a word used to describe a field that is idle or fallow, as well as a lazy or slothful person. James used the word to describe an unproductive faith: "faith without works is dead" (James 2:20).

The alternative to the life of faith, the opposite to the first element of the antithesis, is personified as **he that lacketh these things** (v. 9). That person is **blind**. The phrase **and cannot see afar off** might indicate that Peter had in mind a possible alternative meaning for "blind," namely, "to shut the eyes." The Greek word is *myōpazō* from *myops*—a nearsighted man in Aristotle's writings. The English term "myopia" derives from it. Peter's picture is of a nearsighted individual who squints because of the light. The person cannot tolerate the brightness of the light of truth because he **hath forgotten that he was purged from his old sins**. Peter seems to indicate that a lack of spiritual growth often leads one to doubt his or her salvation.

1:10. In light of the fact that those who produce the graces of the Christian life (see 1:5–7) will be fruitful, and those who lack them suffer from an impairment of spiritual perception, Peter issued the command, **give diligence to make your calling and election sure**. The sense is to "become diligent," to make the decision to be diligent and renew it continually. Peter could not have used stronger language in the Greek to express the absolute guarantee that the one who diligently strives to be productive **shall never fall**. The construction is *ou mē ptaisēte pote* ("You will not at all ever stumble"). The verb should be understood in the sense of stumbling in the progress of one's Christian life.

1:11. Those who obtain the fruits Peter commended will never fall. Moreover, when **the everlasting kingdom of our Lord and Saviour Jesus Christ** comes in its fullness, they will be given **an entrance** into His kingdom that is a hero's welcome. Peter's anticipation of this kingdom indicates that he saw its coming as still in the future, not the present.

III. Proposition (1:12–15)

The main idea of the letter is contained in this passage. The epistle, a testament that contains Peter's final words of instruction, represents the apostle's attempt to "put you always in remembrance of these things" (v. 12), "to stir you up by putting you in remembrance" (v. 13), and "after my decease to have these things always in remembrance" (v. 15).

A. The Value of a Reminder (1:12–13)

1:12. The wise teacher knows the value of repetition and reminder to reinforce that which students have already received. Peter's wisdom as a teacher is evident in the proposition of his rhetorical argument. **Of these things** that he outlined in the exordium (1:3–11), he intended continually to remind his readers, **though ye know them**.

1:13. Peter's intention **to stir you up by putting you in remembrance** assured the readers that the apostle was vitally concerned for their welfare. His ethos (his authority and credibility) and positive pathos (a sense of well-being and a disposition favorable to the argument) were thereby enhanced among his audience. Peter's letter is an example of deliberative rhetoric and an example of a testament. He asserted that as long as he was **in this tabernacle** (i.e., his body, his earthly dwelling place), he would continue to coax his readers to live productively, according to the truth that they had received.

B. Peter's Prediction of His Imminent Death (1:14)

1:14. Peter disclosed to his audience a revelation that Jesus Himself gave him: **shortly I must put off this my tabernacle**. This insight is either the revelation recorded in John 21:18–19 or a subsequent one. In any event, Peter's demise was imminent at the time he wrote 2 Peter; his death occurred within one to four years. Peter's words were based on an actual revelation from Jesus, which therefore gave this section and the whole letter strong substantiation and authority. The metaphor of the body as a tent and the metaphor of death as "putting off" a garment poignantly express the testamentary nature of this section and the epistle as a whole. Peter wanted his readers to be reminded of correct doctrine not only while he lived but after he died as well.

C. The Remembrance of Things That the Readers Had Learned (1:15)

1:15. Peter's intention for his audience was **to have these things always in remembrance**, an aim that was realized, whether intentionally or unintentionally, through the Gospel of Mark, which early tradition connected with Peter. The term **I will endeavour** is the same verb that Peter used in 1:10 to command diligence from his readers regarding the confirmation or proof of their election. The word **decease** is *exodos* ("exodus"; a going out or departure), another metaphor for death. The same word is used in Hebrews 11:22 to denote the liberating departure of the Israelites from Egypt. Thus, Peter's language about his death is triumphant, with the same sense of liberation that the people of Israel enjoyed when they left their oppression.

IV. First Proof: Accusation and Refutation (1:16–21)

A. Accusation: The Message about the Second Coming Is a Clever Myth (1:16a)

1:16a. The consistent pattern in the proofs that substantiate Peter's proposition is an accusation that the false teachers had brought against true

Christian teaching and then its refutation. The accusation that Peter refuted in the first proof seems to have been something like, "You Christians have **followed cunningly devised fables** in believing miraculous tales (**the power**) of Jesus and the idea of a second **coming**." This accusation, that Christians had subscribed to "cleverly devised myths" (NRSV), required refutation.

Peter's message was based on his eyewitness account of the supernatural events that marked the life of Jesus. It was not made up of myths and imaginative stories, as was the message of the heretics mentioned in 2:3.

B. Refutation: The Apostolic Teaching of the Parousia Is Based on Eyewitness Testimony and Old Testament Prophecy (1:16b–21)

1. Eyewitness Testimony of the Transfiguration (1:16b–18)

1:16b. Peter's refutation of the heretical claim that Christian belief was founded on nothing but myths was this: it was founded on the testimony of **eyewitnesses**, the apostles. Peter pointed out a specific instance of their eyewitness testimony: the event of the transfiguration of Jesus. **His majesty** was splendidly manifested (see Matt. 17:1–9; Mark 9:2–10; Luke 9:28–36) in that event. It is an apt example, for it demonstrates the power of Jesus and signifies His glorious second coming. In Christ's transfiguration, the disciples received a foretaste of what His coming will be like when He returns to establish His eternal kingdom.

1:17–18. Peter briefly recounted the details of Christ's transfiguration. Overall, the event attributed divine **honour** (v. 17) to Jesus. The overwhelmingly great degree of honor is indicated by the double use of **glory** in verse 17, the second instance of which (**the excellent glory**) is an instance of *metonymy*. In this figure of speech, the name of an object or concept is replaced with a word closely related to or suggested by the original (e.g., "crown" for "king"); here "the excellent glory" represents God the Father. Peter recounted the words of the **voice** from that glory (**This is my beloved Son, in whom I am**

well pleased) and twice mentioned their audibility to emphasize that Peter, James, and John had actually heard the words. The details of this account confirmed Peter as an eyewitness of the event who was especially impressed by what he heard on that occasion.

2. Old Testament Prophecy Confirmed by the Transfiguration (1:19)

1:19. Peter maintained that the apostolic preaching rested on two solid foundations: the voice from God at Christ's transfiguration (see 1:16–18) and the still more significant testimony of Scripture (see 1:19–21). **We have also a more sure word of prophecy** should probably be understood to signify "we have the prophetic message more fully confirmed" (NRSV); that is, the apostolic testimony was not an additional prophetic statement but one that confirmed the earlier Old Testament message concerning Christ. One should **take heed** of that prophetic witness.

Peter's two metaphors for prophecy illustrate its strength to dispel the darkness of false teachings. It is **a light that shineth in a dark place**. God's Word gives light and hope to a dark world (see Ps. 119:105). The "light" (*lychnos*) is an oil lamp made of clay or metal (see Matt. 5:15). The duration of our focus on the light of prophecy should be **until the day dawn, and the day star arise in your hearts**. "The day" is the time of Jesus' coming. For His people, it will be a time of salvation and glory, not destruction and terror (see 3:13). The "morning star" (NIV) is *phōsphoros* ("light bearer") and refers to Venus, the planet whose appearance just before dawn announces the new day. In Revelation 22:16, it refers to the coming of Christ.

3. The Nature of Biblical Prophecy (1:20–21)

1:20–21. No prophecy of the scripture is of any private interpretation (v. 20) means that no prophecy originated through the prophet's own interpretation or imagination, the sense given in the NIV. In 1:16–19, Peter spoke of the origin of the apostolic message and whether it came from human imaginings or from God. In verse 21, he returned to the subject. No prophecy of Scripture arose from a merely human interpretation of things. This understanding of verse 20 is further supported by the explanatory **For** with which verse 21 begins. In verse 21, Peter explained his statement in verse 20 by restating its content and affirming God as the origin of prophecy, thereby refuting any objection the false teachers raised that Scripture is a merely human construct. Neither the apostolic testimony about Christ's power and coming nor the Old Testament Scripture is a human concoction.

The prophecy, said Peter, **came not in old time by the will of man** (v. 21); it is not of human origin. Rather, the nature of prophecy is divine: **holy men of God spake as they were moved by the Holy Ghost.** Some witnesses do not have the adjective "holy" with "men," but the idea is nevertheless present without the descriptor. "Moved" is the same Greek word (*pherō*) that is translated "came" earlier in the verse. The idea is that the prophets were carried or borne along by the Holy Spirit. Peter's statement can be extended to all of Scripture and is one of the clearest definitions of the nature of biblical inspiration. Both human and divine elements coalesce perfectly in the process of inspiration, so that God gives His word in human words. The Scriptures were not dictated word for word from God without human involvement in their production. Instead, God chose people whose cultural backgrounds and temperaments provided the perfect vehicle for His message to be effectively communicated. This verse gives the process of inspiration, whereas 2 Timothy 3:16 speaks of the product of inspiration, the writings themselves.

V. Second Proof: Accusation and Refutation (2:1–22)

A. Accusation: Divine Judgment Lingers Forever; It Will Never Come to Pass (2:1–3)

2:1–3. The **false prophets** (v. 1) refers to those figures in Old Testament history who did not speak with divine authorization. Their message was sometimes misleading, promising peace and safety instead of the coming judgment that the true prophets fore-cast. The false prophets were rightly condemned (see Deut. 18:20; Jer. 14:14–15; 23:15, 17, 21, 32; Ezek. 13:10; Mic. 3:5, 11).

There shall be false teachers among you (*pseudodidaskaloi*), Peter warned. Numerous New Testament passages warn of false teachers who were already present or yet to come. Such teachers, comparable to the false prophets of the Old Testament, are "pseudo" in that they claim for themselves the offices of teacher in the churches when they have no right to do so and in that their message is false in content. Whenever they appear, they **privily shall bring in damnable heresies** ("They will secretly introduce destructive heresies," NIV). "Heresies" could have the idea of factions as well as unorthodox doctrine. Hence, "damnable heresies" may be defined as divisive opinions or teachings that result in the moral and spiritual destruction of those who accept them. Apparently noting a divisive effect of the heretics, Peter called attention to the tragic fact that **many shall follow their pernicious ways** (v. 2; "their evil teaching and shameful immorality," NLT). Because their heresies will include **even denying the Lord that bought them** (v. 1), they will incur **swift destruction**. The language here is reminiscent of Jude 4. "Bought" is metaphorical, referring to slaves purchased in the marketplace and transferred to new ownership. It implies that the heretics' purchase price had been paid, but the exchange of goods (the surrender of their own lives to Christ as Master) had never been made. Christ's death paid the penalty for their sin, but it would not become effective for their salvation unless they trusted in Christ as Savior. Thus, His atonement was available to them but not applicable to them without genuine faith.

Peter's concern was unlike the exploitative designs of the false teachers, who **through covetousness shall they with feigned** ("fabricated," Wuest) **words make merchandise of you** (v. 3). False teachers are often motivated by a desire for money and will commercialize the Christian faith to their own selfish advantage. No wonder that an outcome of their work is that **the way of truth shall be evil spoken of** (v. 2). False teachers or those whom they delude, or both, will cause the gospel and its teachings to be in disrepute.

The very judgment that such heretics deny ironically proves their downfall: **whose judgment now of a long time lingereth not, and their damnation slumbereth not** (v. 3). Long ago, in Old Testament times, their condemnation was declared (for Old Testament examples of the judgment to come on the wicked, see 2:4–9). Peter utilized synonymous parallelism to emphasize the certainty of their ruin; both terms for condemnation are equivalent, as are the negated verbs. What seems like an interminable delay in judgment is really God's patience with unrepentant sinners. A day will come when that patience will no longer delay the deserved condemnation of the wicked (see 3:9).

B. Refutation: Historical Examples of Judgment and Deliverance (2:4–10a)

1. Angels Who Sinned (2:4)

2:4. This verse begins an extended conditional construction with a very long protasis ("if" clause; 2:4–8) and an abrupt apodosis ("then" clause; 2:9–10a). The main idea in this section, in way of refutation, is that judgment of the unrighteous is certain. Peter put forth three historical examples to establish that fact. He also put forth a corollary of the main idea: God will rescue the righteous.

The angels that sinned are probably those disobedient supernatural beings whom Jude 6 mentions. Having sinned through pride, they were expelled from heaven. The pseudepigraphal book of *1 Enoch* describes the imprisonment of angels who, having transgressed, are now chained and await their final doom (*1 Enoch* 10:5–6; 12:4; 21:3–10). The disobedient angels are **reserved unto judgment**. They are bound; God **delivered them into chains of darkness** — clearly figurative language that expresses the desolation of the angels' pre-judgment condition and the fact that Satan and his fallen angels cannot escape their fate. **Hell** (Greek, *tartarus*) echoes *1 Enoch* 20:22, where Tartarus is the place of the punishment of fallen angels. Peter used this term to indicate a sphere of habitation and activity that is infinitely below the evil angels' former estate and from which they cannot escape or return to the former position.

2. The Flood (2:5)

2:5. As in the case of the angels (1:4), God **spared not the old world**. Using another example from history, Peter substantiated the certainty of the judgment of the false teachers. In contrast to the wicked people of ancient times, **Noah** was **saved** (*phylassō*; "preserved," REB). Thus, in Peter's argument, Noah is a foil to **the ungodly** upon whom **the flood** came. The background to this verse is the account of the flood in Genesis 6–7. Peter called Noah **the eighth person**. Into the ark went Noah's wife, three sons, and three daughters-in-law. Noah was the eighth (see 1 Peter 3:20). Noah was the builder of the ark and an evangelist; he warned the wicked of the coming judgment so that they might repent. Hence, unlike the false teachers of Peter's day and the impious of his own time, Noah was **a preacher of righteousness**. Although this description of Noah is found nowhere else in Scripture, similar descriptions of him are found in Josephus (*Antiquities* 1.3.1), 1 Clement (7.6; 9.4), and the *Sibylline Oracles* (1.128–29). The statement about Noah encouraged Peter's hearers to imitate Noah and be heralds of the truth. In the midst of his discussion of frightening judgment to come, the apostle encouraged his hearers that the righteous need not fear the destruction that is coming to the wicked. If they take the part of Noah, they will be safe.

3. Sodom and Gomorrah (2:6–8)

2:6. The third example demonstrating the certainty of the judgment that will come on the wicked is **the cities of Sodom and Gomorrha** (see Jude 7). Their **overthrow** ("total destruction," NEB), described in Genesis 19, came by way of a devastating volcanic event. The devastation was so great that the cities were turned **into ashes** (*tephroō*). This is the only occurrence of this word in the New Testament. The first-century writer Dio Cassius used it of the eruption of Mount Vesuvius (AD 79). In that event, the cities of Pompeii and Herculaneum were buried in lava. God used a natural cataclysm as a means of judgment in the cases of Noah's society and the reprobate cities of Sodom and Gomorrah.

2:7–8. Here Peter affirmed the inevitability of the judgment of the wicked (thus giving the third historical precedent), and he exalted the person and behavior of Lot as an example for his audience. **Just Lot** (v. 7; "Lot, a righteous man," NIV) did not suffer the fate of the wicked in Sodom and Gomorrah. Rather, God **delivered** (*rhyomai*, "rescued") him. He, like Noah, is a foil for the godless people around him. In addition to "just," Lot is described in these verses as **that righteous man** (v. 8) and as a **righteous soul**. His fellow citizens are described as **wicked** (v. 7). Lot's righteous actions included being **vexed with the filthy conversation** ("conduct," NKJV) **of the wicked**. How Lot could be so distressed and how he could be called a "righteous man" and yet offer to turn his two daughters over to the wicked townsmen to be sexually abused (see Gen. 19:4–9) is difficult to understand apart from a knowledge of the code of honor characteristic of that day. The mere record of something in the Bible does not necessarily condone it.

4. Deliverance and Judgment (2:9–10a)

2:9. This verse represents the apodosis, the "then" clause, of the long conditional statement that begins in 2:4. Other translations besides the KJV make this clear. The NIV renders the first part of verse 9 as "if this is so, then the Lord knows …" (The parenthetical nature of 2:8 is made clear in the KJV and the NIV.) The point is that if God did not withhold judgment from sinning angels, from the ungodly world of Noah's day, and from the lawless cities of Sodom and Gomorrah but judged them for their wickedness, and at the same time preserved the righteous, *then* the Lord knows how to deliver the righteous in the present and to appoint the wicked in the present for deserved judgment in the future.

Temptations is *peirasmos* and refers to the testing of one's faith and endurance. Whenever the believer is put to the test, God knows just what is

needed to help us escape. God knows (with commensurate ability) how **to reserve the unjust unto the day of judgment**. The historical examples of 2:4–8 effectively refute those who contend that divine judgment will forever linger.

2:10a. Peter included all the unrighteous within the scope of final judgment (2:9), but here he mentioned two classifications. His affirmation of judgment concerns **chiefly them**. Peter may have intended these categories as overarching descriptions of the false teachers, with their characteristics in 2:10b–22 subsumed under two classifications: (1) they **walk after the flesh in the lust of uncleanness** (immorality), and (2) they **despise government**. This could refer to the slander of earthly dignitaries such as church leaders, which might well be expected from such shameless peddlers of error. Thus, heresy and immorality often go hand in hand.

C. Digression: Denunciation of the False Teachers (2:10b–22)

A digression, according to Greco-Roman rhetorical theory, serves to treat some theme outside the logical order of a discourse. The treatment is effective in making an emotional appeal to the audience and enhancing style. In 2 Peter 2:10b–22, which echoes Jude 8–12, the apostle denounced the false teachers.

2:10b–11. The false teachers in Peter's communities were **not afraid to speak evil of dignities** (v. 10b; lit., "blaspheme glories"; used also in Jude 8). The adjectives **Presumptuous** and **selfwilled** ("reckless and headstrong," NEB) describe the character of the heretics, which led to their outrageous insolence. Their action challenged the honor of God and His agents so that they might have it for themselves. The Greek word *blasphēmeō* in verse 10b and 2:12, which lies behind "speak evil" (and whose adjectival form is translated "railing" in v. 11), expresses an assault on another's honor. Peter responded to the honor challenge with a blistering riposte in 2:10b–22. Not even the obedient **angels** (represented by the archangel Michael in Jude 9) dare to bring a **railing accusation against them** (wicked angels) **before the Lord**.

Peter's argument proceeds from the greater to the lesser. What is true of angels, **which are greater in power and might** than humans, certainly ought to be true of mortals.

2:12. By comparing the false teachers to **natural brute beasts**, Peter issued a scathing denunciation. The heretics were like irrational animals, whose lives are guided by mere instinct and who are born merely to be slaughtered. Destruction will be their final lot. The heresy to which Peter referred may have been an early form of second-century Gnosticism, which claimed to possess special, esoteric knowledge. If so, it is ironic that those who professed special knowledge acted out of abysmal ignorance (they spoke **evil of the things that they understand not**), and the result was arrogant blasphemy.

2:13. Peter said the heretics were deserving of destruction. They **shall receive the reward of unrighteousness**. These apostates had oriented themselves to the fulfillment of their own desires. They **riot[ed] in the day time**, to such excess that their nighttime revels carried on past dawn. The Greek phrase behind **sporting themselves with their own deceivings while they feast with you** is difficult to render. The word "deceivings" ("deceptions," NASB; Greek, *apatai*) could also mean "dissipation" (NRSV) or "pleasures" (NIV). If so, these false teachers injected their carousing into the sacred feasts, delighting in shameless acts instead of in true communion with Christ and His people. No wonder that Peter called the deceivers **Spots ... and blemishes**. The word "blemishes" (*mōmoi*) is used in the Septuagint to describe the man who was unfit for service in the priesthood (Lev. 21:17–18, 21). Likewise, the false teachers were unfit for service in the church.

2:14. Assuming that the **eyes** indicate what is most in a person's heart (see Matt. 6:22–23), Peter proclaimed that the heretics' eyes were **full of adultery and ... cannot cease from sin**. The first description is literally "eyes full of [desire for] an adulteress," which means that they desired every woman they saw, viewing her as a potential sex partner. "Their eyes cannot look at a woman without lust" (Phillips).

The **unstable souls** whom the false teachers were **beguiling** may have been immature males to whom the teachers' libertine ways appealed since they seemed to have a divine sanction. The beguiled could, however, have included female church members who, as recent converts or immature believers, had became targets of the immoral designs of the teachers. "Beguiling," the word that Peter used to describe the alluring manner of the heretics, is *deleazō*, a term that depicts the fisherman who attempts to lure and catch fish with bait (see James 1:14). Peter drew attention to the heretics' ability to "seduce" (NIV) the unsuspecting and unwary. The threat from the false teachers was as much moral as it was doctrinal.

The deviants were notable for their **covetous practices**. In fact, Peter said they had **a heart they have exercised** in such practices. Peter was drawing an athletic metaphor here; his verb is *gymnazō* (mentioned earlier). The heretics had set themselves firmly on a course of action like the runner, boxer, or wrestler preparing for the games. The prize they sought was the fulfillment of their own greed. Peter justly described these rapacious instructors in the church, who were abusing their position for the pursuit of their own detestable desires, as **cursed children**.

2:15. Those teaching erroneous doctrines had **gone astray** (the verb is in the passive voice, "they have been led astray," but it may be translated in the active voice). The word is *planaō* from which the word "planet," a wandering heavenly body, is derived. Jude used a cognate term in calling them "wandering stars" (Jude 13). They "lost their way" (NEB) when they continually chose to abandon **the right way** (*kataleipō* is a present participle, "leaving the right way behind"). Now they had drifted without the possibility of return (see 2:17). Rather than taking the right road, the heretics had followed **the way of Balaam the son of Bosor** (see Num. 22:2–24:25; 31:16; Jude 11).

2:16. Balaam **was rebuked for his iniquity**. He attempted to curse the Israelites for money. Peter was recalling Numbers 22:21–35, where "a speechless donkey spoke with a human voice and restrained the prophet's madness" (NRSV). A donkey rebuking the prophet's madness reflected not only on the foolishness of Balaam but also on that of the false teachers of Peter's day. They showed less spiritual sensitivity than the "brute beasts" (2:12) to which Peter compared them. Since they had gone the way of Balaam, they were just as obtuse as he was when he showed less sense than his donkey.

2:17. This verse parallels Jude 12. Peter used two metaphors, however, whereas Jude consolidated them into one metaphor. According to Peter, the deviants were **wells** ("springs," NASB) **without water** and **clouds that are carried with a tempest** ("mists driven by a storm," NASB). Jude's comparison has "clouds they are without water, carried about of winds" (Jude 12). Both Jude and Peter stressed the spiritual emptiness that accompanied the opponents' teaching and example. Peter's image is that of a thirsty traveler who comes to a spring expecting cool, refreshing water but finds it dry. So the false teachers promised satisfying truth but in reality had nothing to offer.

2:18. The **great swelling words of vanity** ("bombastic nonsense," NRSV) that the false teachers spoke perhaps had to do more with **the lusts of the flesh** than with unorthodox doctrine. The heretics erred on both counts and led others to follow them in their vulgar ways **through much wantonness** ("by sensuality," NASB).

2:19. The bombast of the false teachers was an attractive **promise** and an apparent guarantee of **liberty**. Gnosticism promoted release from the corruption of the material world and the body, and the proto-Gnostics who posed a danger to Peter's congregations claimed to offer their adherents some sort of release from bondage. The teachers **themselves are the servants** ("slaves," NKJV) **of corruption**. The very ones who were promising freedom from bondage were themselves slaves of depravity. Freedom from law resulted in bondage to sin, and liberty was turned into license. The last part of the verse is proverbial: **for of whom a man is overcome, of the same is he brought in bondage** ("for by what a man

is overcome, by this he is enslaved," NASB). Peter pictured the enslavement of enemies who have been conquered in battle.

2:20–21. Unlike the false teachers, those whom they had duped appear to have truly been saved: **they [had] escaped the pollutions of the world through the knowledge of the Lord and Saviour Jesus Christ** (v. 20) and knew the way of righteousness, a knowledge that is personal and intimate (*epiginōskō*). They had been seduced and had **turn[ed] from the holy commandment delivered unto them** (v. 21). It would have been **better for them not to have known the way of righteousness** than to have known it and turned from it. Peter was using hyperbole here; if these people were believers, of course it is better to have eternal life, even if they were not walking with God, than for them not to have been saved at all.

How is it, then, that **the latter end is worse** (v. 20)? Theologians differ, according to their views of salvation (soteriology), whether this refers to saved backsliders, the unsaved who profess to be saved, or those who have lost their salvation. In each case, those falling away from their original profession of faith are in worse condition.

2:22. The repulsiveness of the two images in this verse served as a warning to Peter's churches not to follow those who had succumbed to the enticements of the false teachers. The metaphors of the dog and the pig, both used in the form of a **proverb**, sound harsh and hostile, but they were effective devices to first-century people whose culture emphasized purity and honor. In the ancient world, **The dog** was regarded as unclean. It was a scavenger, roaming streets and dumps, feeding on unclean things—even human flesh (see Exod. 22:31; 1 Kings 14:11; 16:4; 2 Kings 9:10; Luke 16:21). Peter's statement that this animal returns **to his own vomit** is a quotation of Proverbs 26:11. Thus, the Christian who has fallen away is a fool who returns to his folly. The dog is not only unclean because of what it eats; it is also so attached to it that it ingests that which has been regurgitated. Any matter expelled from the body is a potential pollutant in a ritual sense, and a dog's vomit of unclean matter is definitely a pollutant. **The**

sow that was washed [returned] to her wallowing in the mire. To the Jew, pigs were unclean and thus unfit for sacrifice or for human consumption (see Lev. 11:7; Deut. 14:8). The Greeks also regarded pigs as unclean. Peter's intention with these colorful yet loathsome images was to stress that the backsliders had become spiritually unclean and dishonorable. The reality of their salvation was in serious doubt since they exhibited the traits of inherently unclean animals. Peter's denunciation of the false teachers evolved into a condemnation of those whom they had led astray. The entire section was a powerful warning to those who would allow themselves to be wooed by the opponents.

VI. Third Proof: Accusation and Refutation (3:1–13)

A. Accusation: The Second Coming Will Not Happen; God Does Not Intervene in History (3:1–4)

1. A Second Reminder (3:1–2)

3:1–2. In the third and final proof, Peter refuted an accusation from the heretics that impugned the idea of a second coming of Christ. In this, his **second epistle** (v. 1), the apostle's intention was to **stir up your pure minds by way of remembrance**. "Minds" could also be "intention" (NRSV) or "disposition" (NAB). Pure Christian thinking can effectively identify unorthodox teaching and maintain faithfulness in opposition to it. Peter pointed his readers' attention to the words both of **the holy prophets, and of … the apostles of the Lord and Saviour** (v. 2), placing the Old Testament prophets and the New Testament apostles on an equal plane. Both were vehicles of God's sacred truth and trustworthy judges of correct doctrine and false doctrine. Peter, being one of the apostles, could speak with knowledge and authority as a representative of the apostolic group.

2. The Objection of the Scoffers (3:3–4)

3:3. Peter used the expression **Knowing this first** in 1:20 to call attention to a matter of great importance. Here the matter of great significance was **that there shall come in the last days scoffers** (lit., "with scoffing, scoffers will come"). "The last days" is an expression that refers to the whole period introduced by Christ's first coming. These days are "last" in comparison to Old Testament days, which were preliminary and preparatory. Also, the Christian era is the time of the beginning of prophetic fulfillment. Those who mock the delay of God's judgment are denounced in the prophetic writings (see Isa. 5:18–20; Jer. 5:12–24; Amos 9:10; Mal. 2:17), and the apostolic testimony has similar warnings regarding those who deny the final judgment and the resurrection, some of whom contend that it has already come (see 1 Corinthians 15; 2 Thess. 2:2; 2 Tim. 2:18).

The "scoffers" may have been early Gnostics who resisted the idea of a time of judgment and moral accountability. The Gnostics ridiculed the idea of a bodily resurrection. For them, salvation involved enlightenment and a release from the flesh, not its transformation. The heretics whom Peter opposed may have scoffed at the notion of resurrected and transformed matter. Their libertinism (**walking after their own lusts**) was like that of second-century Gnostics in Irenaeus's *Against Heresies*. The full implication of this prophecy is that the worst scoffers will come closest to the end times. Therefore, it should not be surprising that today even some professing believers ridicule the idea of the soon coming of Christ.

3:4. Peter quoted the scoffers' objection: **Where is the promise of his coming? for since the fathers fell asleep, all things continue as they were from the beginning of the creation**. As in the cases of the first two objections, the intruders challenged God's honor and that of His people by a refusal to accept the truth of Christ's claim that He will come again one day in judgment. Perhaps the scoffers believed that the Lord is unable to make good on His promises. Peter, the apostolic representative and a client of His heavenly patron, stood up and offered a riposte. "The fathers" are either the first Christians to die after Christ's death and resurrection (e.g., Stephen, James the brother of John, and other early Christian leaders who had died; see Heb. 13:7) or the Old Testament patriarchs.

B. Refutation: The Precedent of Previous Judgment, the Divine Perspective on Time, and the Authority of Jesus' Own Word (3:5–13)

1. The Flood as a Precedent of Judgment (3:5–7)

3:5–7. Peter systematically demolished the argument against the doctrine of the second coming. The first of his three counterarguments was that, contrary to what the heretics said, all things had not remained static since the beginning of creation. In fact, the heretics **willingly are ignorant of** (v. 5) the creation of **the heavens ... and the earth** by means of **the word of God** and the destruction of the world that, **being overflowed with water, perished** (v. 6). Uniformitarian geology speculates that all the processes of nature have always been the same (i.e., uniform) throughout history. This viewpoint, however, overlooks God's serious disruption of natural history by means of the Noahic flood. Things have not always remained as they were after the initial moment of God's fiat. Ignoring the flood as a divine intervention was not an oversight; it was deliberate. The scoffers did not want to face up to the fallacy in their argument.

Since the cosmos has not remained unchanged in the past, the chances of further cataclysmic changes are great. Indeed, Peter pointed to the fate that awaits the present **heavens and the earth** (v. 7). They are **reserved unto fire [for the] day of judgment**, when the ungodly will perish. Jewish apocalyptic thought drew a correlation between the flood and the eschatological devastation by fire, and Old Testament prophetic texts speak of divine judgment by fire (e.g., Isa. 66:15–16; Zeph. 1:18; Mal. 3:19). Since things do not remain unchanged, Peter successfully refuted the claim of the false teachers. The principle of change in the universe allows for the irruption of God's activity, whether in creation, salvation, or judgment. Both creation and the ordination of future judgment are effected by **the word of God** (vv. 5, 7).

2. Temporal Distinctions and the Lord's Patience (3:8–9)

3:8. In the second of his counterarguments directed at those who ridiculed the promised second coming, Peter refuted the distorted view of time that led the scoffers to discount the Parousia. In their perspective, a long delay meant that God could not deliver on His promises. Such a view betrays, Peter said, a failure to understand the atemporality of God. He has created time and chooses to work within the finitude of time (measured by the seasons). He Himself transcends time and is not bound by it. He exists eternally outside of time in an everlasting now, and of this, the mockers were **ignorant**. Peter asserted that **one day is with the Lord as a thousand years, and a thousand years as one day**. The delay in His coming is of no consequence to the Lord. From the Lord's perspective, it is no delay at all. Peter's principle echoes the sentiments of Psalm 90:4. "The Lord" in 3:8–10 probably refers to God as Son, not God as Father-Creator (see 3:5). The uses of "the Lord" and "God" in these verses seem to be carefully distinguished, and the reference to "a thief in the night" (3:10) is reminiscent of Jesus' teaching about His coming (see Matt. 24:43–44; Luke 12:39–40; Rev. 3:3; 16:5; see also 1 Thess. 5:2, 4).

Believers often become discouraged in waiting for Christ's coming, when their prayers are apparently unanswered or when successful outcomes from their endeavors seem never to come. In such situations, Peter's reminder of God's timelessness might help finite humans to see that God does not work on the same schedule as they do. Since time is purely relative with the Lord, He waits patiently while human beings stew with impatience. From God's perspective, He is working all things according to His plan and His timing.

3:9. The heretics' accusation against the Lord may have been that although He is able to deliver on the promises of His coming, He is **slack concerning his promise**. Not so, said Peter. Any "delay" is due to the fact that He **is longsuffering to us-ward** ("is patient with you," NRSV). The Lord is **not willing that any should perish, but that all should come to repentance**. Scoffers today deride the Bible as being full of "hellfire and brimstone," with little evidence of a loving God. The Christian ought gently to steer such persons to this text, where Peter's emphasized that the very "delay" in Christ's coming at which the mockers sneered was really God's patient waiting for them to "come to repentance." In fact, the Lord wants everyone to come to repentance—a radical reorientation of one's entire course of life in response to the enlightening influence of the Holy Spirit. This shift entails belief in a loving God and salvation through Christ.

3. "The Day of the Lord Will Come as a Thief in the Night" (3:10)

3:10. A prominent New Testament metaphor for the second coming is that **the day of the Lord will come as a thief in the night** (see discussion on 3:8). Since a thief comes suddenly and without announcement, taking the members of the household unaware, the image is an apt one for Jesus' coming. Jesus said, "Of that day and that hour knoweth no man, no, not the angels which are in heaven, neither the Son, but the Father" (Mark 13:32). Peter's utilization of the metaphor constitutes a third refutation of the argument against the Parousia. The time will be totally unexpected; just when human inclination to discount its certainty is highest, the day of the Lord shall come.

The devastation of the created order that the day of the Lord will bring cannot be even remotely conceived. Peter stated that the catastrophe will be accompanied by **a great noise**, when **the heavens shall pass away**. To convey the inconceivable power of eschatological upheaval, the apostle described it in terms of sound whose decibels are off the scale. The immensity of the eschatological cataclysm sounds like an enormous nuclear explosion. Whatever it will involve will be just as devastating to the planet in the future as the flood was in the past.

The elements shall melt with fervent heat is another expression of apocalyptic language. "The elements" is a term that refers either to the heavenly bodies or to the physical elements—in the first century, such things as earth, air, fire, and water; in today's more precise scientific terminology, hydrogen, oxygen, carbon, and so on. Petrine history, like biblical history as a whole, is linear (teleological), not

cyclical: it progresses to an endpoint predetermined by God, at which time the present order will give way to God's new and everlasting order in the universe. So that the new order may appear, **the earth ... shall be burnt up**. Even human activity will be judged by fire, as Paul indicates (1 Cor. 3:13–15). Peter may have utilized Stoic terminology in 3:10–12, but if so, he adapted it to reflect the Old Testament motif of judgment by fire (see Isa. 66:15).

4. Exhortation in Light of the Certainty of the Parousia (3:11–13)

3:11–12. Even more apocalyptic language appears here. The accumulation of the terms **dissolved** (twice), **fire**, **melt**, and **fervent heat** signifies an absolute and total destruction of the created order as it is presently configured. Peter's basic intention in his description of the conflagration to come was to foster **holy conversation** ("conduct," NKJV) **and godliness** (v. 11) among his readers. The practices of **looking for and hasting unto the coming of the day of God** (v. 12; "Look eagerly for the coming of the Day of God and work to hasten it on," NEB) are carried out by living in a spirit of unity with fellow Christians, humbly praying for strength of endurance until the day Christ appears, and spreading the good news to unbelievers. Can the time that will elapse before the Parousia be shortened by human activity? Peter's language seems to express such an idea, but he probably was speaking hyperbolically here. A life of faithful discipleship makes waiting for one's glorious future more endurable, and therefore that time of waiting seems shorter. Jesus indicated that the time of the Parousia has been set by the Father (Mark 13:32–33). "The day of God" is apparently synonymous with "the day of the Lord" (3:10) since it is characterized by the same kind of events (see Rev. 16:14). Holy expectation of Jesus' coming is a good way to resist false teachers and their mockery of that hope.

3:13. The disappearance of the universe does not spell the end of material existence altogether. The vanishing of the old gives way to **new heavens and a new earth**. New heavens and a new earth are promised by

Isaiah (65:17; 66:22). This **promise** is confirmed by Revelation 21:1. The term "new" (*kainos*) suggests a renewal, not an abolition, of material existence. There is discontinuity, but the fact that "heavens" and "earth" will appear suggest a material existence whose features are in some kind of continuity with what humans have been familiar. The remarkable and critical difference is that the new creation is where **righteousness** dwells as a permanent resident—settles down and makes its home (see Isa. 11:4–5; 45:8; Dan. 9:24). The outlook here should give impetus to a Christian stewardship of the earth that values and protects both organic and inorganic elements.

VII. Conclusion (3:14–18)

In the conclusion, Peter stressed the need for diligence and vigilance (vv. 14–17), issued a final injunction for Christian growth (v. 18a), and broke forth in a final doxology (v. 18b).

A. The Need for Diligence and Vigilance (3:14–17)

3:14. Because the heresies of the infiltrators were divisive, Peter urged his various congregations to **be diligent that ye may be found of him in peace.** This quality is primarily mutual and harmonious interdependence within the church. Peace is promoted when church members live **without spot, and blameless** (see 1 Peter 1:19, "Christ, as of a lamb without blemish and without spot"). The two terms in Greek, *aspiloi* and *amōmētoi*, are negated (with *a*-prefix) adjectives. They recall the description in 2:13 of the infiltrators as "spots" and "blemishes" (*spiloi* and *mōmoi*) who ruin the life of the church.

3:15. Peter recounted the topic of the Lord's **longsuffering** (*makrothymia*), introduced in 3:9, with the description of it as **salvation** (*sōtēria*). Peter expressed warmth in his reference to Paul as **our beloved brother Paul.** Here Peter confirmed the unity of teaching and purpose that governed their relationship, abundantly attested in Paul's letters and the book of Acts. Despite the earlier confrontation in Antioch, when Paul rebuked Peter (Gal. 2:11–14), their bond in Christ was strong.

Does Peter's statement that Paul **hath written unto you** signify some lost letter(s) of Paul? Could the communication to which Peter referred be one or more of the Pauline letters in our New Testament canon? It has been suggested that what Paul wrote to the recipients of 2 Peter was a copy of Romans, which was sent to the churches as a circular letter. Galatians, Ephesians, and Colossians are also candidates for this communication.

3:16. Peter said that **in all his** (Paul's) **epistles,** Paul was **speaking in them of these things.** Peter may have been referring in general to the exhortations to holy living in 3:11–14, which parallel many passages in Paul's writings. In a superb understatement, Peter mentioned that in Paul's epistles **are some things hard to be understood.** The word *dysnoētos* was used in ancient times to describe the ambiguity of oracles. Peter was not saying that Paul's writing, under the inspiration of the Holy Spirit, was hopelessly equivocal; he meant that Paul's words require careful reading so that the interpretation of them will be properly understood.

Certain people, whom Peter described as **unlearned and unstable,** had not taken care to interpret Paul's letters properly. Instead, they **wrest** ("distort," NASB) the great apostle's meaning in those letters. The Greek word translated here as "wrest" (*strebloō*) is colorful. Originally, it referred to twisting cables or making them taut. Another usage of the term referred to the wrenching of dislocated limbs in order to set them. The word also described the use of torturers' equipment that wrenched the body in the course of interrogations. Peter used it figuratively, but the word effectively conveys the intentional nature of the heretics' twisted distortion of true Pauline doctrine.

Noteworthy is Peter's classification of Paul's letters as Scripture here. The "unlearned and unstable" distorted difficult teachings in the Pauline writings **as they do also the other scriptures.** Peter placed Paul's writings on the same level of authority as the God-breathed writings of the Old Testament (see 1:21; 2 Tim. 3:16). Already in Peter's day, at least some of Paul's epistles were accorded the status of inspired writings that were authoritative for the church. The importance of Peter's statement toward understanding the New Testament documents as inspired is not to be missed.

3:17. The nature of 2 Peter as a testament is evident in Peter's closing exhortation to his readers to **beware**. His ethos was built up when he issued this final exhortation and when he addressed his charges as **beloved**. The apostle's foregoing instruction had enabled them to **know these things before**. When he departed, his churches would remember his statements regarding true and false doctrine (see 1:12–15). If they were vigilant, they could avoid **being led away with the error of the wicked**. Peter did not want his congregants to **fall from [their] own stedfastness**, which does not necessarily refer to a fall from eternal life into damnation but may refer rather to falling into confusion.

B. Final Exhortation to Grow in Grace and Knowledge (3:18a)

3:18a. The opposite (introduced by **But**) of falling away from one's secure position is to **grow in grace, and in the knowledge of our Lord and Saviour Jesus Christ**. Peter's word for "knowledge" here is *gnōsis*, the practical wisdom that enables one to conduct life in a godly manner (see discussion on 1:5). This knowledge comes from Christ and is directed toward Him. Peter concluded by again stressing knowledge, probably as an antidote to the false teachers, who boasted in their esoteric knowledge. The church must always take care to help its young members grow, which involves protecting them from false teaching and false cults.

C. Doxology (3:18b)

3:18b. A beautiful doxology (from *doxa*, meaning "glory") concludes Peter's second letter: **To him be glory both now and for ever. Amen**. Literally, it reads, "To Him [Jesus Christ] glory both now and into the day of the eternity. Amen." This is the proper response to the heavenly patronage of the Father and the Son. Peter identified God as the one whose "divine power has given us everything we need for life and godliness through our knowledge of him who called us by his own glory and goodness" (1:3 NIV). His clients owe Him honor—glory—since they have received His benefits without measure.

THE FIRST EPISTLE GENERAL OF JOHN

INTRODUCTION

Author

The author is John son of Zebedee (see Mark 1:19–20), the apostle and the author of the gospel of John and Revelation (in both books, see Introduction: "Author"). He was a fisherman whom Jesus called early in His ministry (Matt. 4:18–22) and was the disciple "whom Jesus loved" (John 13:23). Along with Peter and James, he was one of Jesus' inner circle. Thus, he was (1) on the Mount of Transfiguration (Matt. 17:1), (2) in Gethsemane (Matt. 26:37), (3) the only apostle at the crucifixion (John 19:2–27), (4) the first apostle to arrive at the empty tomb (John 20:4–5), and (5) with Peter when Jesus recommissioned him at the Sea of Galilee (John 21:15–23). John and Peter continued as close companions and church leaders after Pentecost (Acts 3:1; 4:19; 8:14; Gal. 2:9).

Unlike most New Testament letters, 1 John does not identify its author. The earliest identification of him comes from the church fathers: Irenaeus (ca. AD 140–203), Clement of Alexandria (ca. 150–215), Tertullian (ca. 155–222), and Origen (ca. 185–253) all designated the author as the apostle John. No one else was suggested by the early church.

This traditional identification is confirmed by evidence in the letter itself.

(1) The style of the gospel of John is markedly similar to that of this letter. Both are written in simple Greek and use contrasting figures, such as light and darkness, life and death, truth and lies, love and hate.

(2) Similar phrases and expressions, such as those found in the following passages, are striking.

1 John	Gospel of John
1:1	1:1, 14
1:4	16:24
1:6–7	3:19–21
2:7	13:34–35
3:8	8:44
3:14	5:24

4:6	8:47
4:9	1:14, 18; 3:16
5:9	5:32, 37
5:12	3:36

(3) The mention of eyewitness testimony (1:1–4) harmonizes with the fact that John was a follower of Christ from the earliest days of His ministry.

(4) The authoritative manner that pervades the letter (seen in its commands, 2:15, 24, 28; 4:1; 5:21; its firm assertions, 2:6; 3:14; 4:12; and its pointed identification of error, 1:6, 8; 2:4, 22) is what would be expected from an apostle.

(5) The suggestions of advanced age (addressing his readers as "children," 2:1, 28; 3:7) agree with early church tradition concerning John's age when he wrote the books known to be his.

(6) The description of the heretics as "antichrists" (2:18), "liar(s)" (2:22), and "children of the devil" (3:10) is consistent with Jesus' characterization of John as a "son of thunder" (Mark 3:17).

(7) The indications of a close relationship with the Lord (1:1; 2:5–6, 24, 27–28) fit the descriptions of the disciple "whom Jesus loved" and the one who "was leaning on Jesus' bosom" (John 13:23).

Date

The letter is difficult to date with precision, but factors such as (1) evidence from early Christian writers (Irenaeus and Clement of Alexandria), (2) the early form of Gnosticism reflected in John's denunciations in the letter, and (3) indications of John's advanced age suggest the end of the first century. Since the author of 1 John seems to build on concepts and themes found in the fourth gospel (see 1 John 2:7–11), it is reasonable to date the letter somewhere between AD 85 and 95, after the writing of the gospel of John, which may have been written circa 85 (see John, Introduction: "Date").

Recipients

That this letter was addressed to believers is made clear in 1 John 2:12–14, 19; 3:1; 5:13, but the letter does not indicate who they were or where they lived. The fact that it mentions no one by name suggests it was a circular letter sent to Christians in a number of places. Evidence from early Christian writers places the apostle John in Ephesus during most of his later years (ca. AD 70–100). The earliest confirmed use of 1 John was in the province of Asia (in modern Turkey), where Ephesus was located. Clement of Alexandria indicates that John ministered in the various churches scattered throughout that province. It may be assumed, therefore, that 1 John was sent to the churches of the Roman province of Asia (see Map 14 at the end of the *Zondervan KJV Study Bible*).

Gnosticism

One of the most dangerous heresies of the first two centuries of the church was Gnosticism. Its central teaching was that spirit is entirely good and matter is entirely evil. Five important errors flowed from this unbiblical dualism.

(1) Man's body, which is matter, was therefore considered evil. It was contrasted with God, who is wholly spirit and therefore good.

(2) Salvation was the escape from the body, achieved not by faith in Christ but by special knowledge (the Greek word for "knowledge" is *gnōsis*, hence "Gnosticism").

(3) Christ's true humanity was denied in two ways: (1) some said that Christ only seemed to have a body, a view called Docetism, from the Greek *dokeō* ("to seem"), and (2) others said that the divine Christ joined the man Jesus at baptism and left Him before He died, a view called Cerinthianism, after its most prominent spokesman, Cerinthus. This view is the background of much of 1 John (see 1:1; 2:22; 4:2–3).

(4) Since the body was considered evil, it was to be treated harshly. This ascetic form of Gnosticism is the background of Colossians 2:21–23.

(5) Paradoxically, this dualism also led to licentiousness. The reasoning was that since matter — and not the breaking of God's law (see 3:4) — was considered evil, breaking His law was of no moral consequence.

It is important to note that the Gnosticism addressed in the New Testament was an early form of the heresy, not the intricately developed system of the second and third centuries. In addition to that detected in Colossians and in John's letters, acquaintance with early Gnosticism is reflected in 1–2 Timothy, Titus, 2 Peter, and perhaps 1 Corinthians.

Theme and Theological Message

John's readers were confronted with an early form of Gnostic teaching of the Cerinthian variety (see "Gnosticism," above). This heresy was also libertine, throwing off all moral restraints.

Consequently, John wrote this letter with two basic purposes in mind: (1) to expose false teachers (2:26) and (2) to give believers assurance of salvation (5:13). In keeping with his intention to combat Gnostic teachers, John specifically struck at their total lack of morality (3:8–10); by giving eyewitness testimony to the incarnation, he sought to confirm his readers' belief in the incarnate Christ (1:3). Success in this would verify their mutual fellowship with the Father and Son and would give the writer joy (1:3–4). John emphasized three tests by which one may know that one has eternal life: (1) *theological*, belief in Jesus Christ; (2) *moral*, living righteously; (3) *social*, loving one another (Bruce, *The Epistles of St. John*, p. 53).

Outline

2. The Person of Christ: The Crux of the Test (2:22–23)
3. Persistent Belief: The Key to Continuing Fellowship (2:24–28)

III. The Christian Life as Divine Sonship (2:29–4:6)
   A. Ethical Tests of Sonship (2:29–3:24)
      1. Righteousness (2:29–3:10a)
      2. Love (3:10b–24)
   B. Christological Tests of Sonship (4:1–6)

IV. The Christian Life as an Integration of the Ethical and the Christological (4:7–5:12)
   A. The Ethical Test: Love (4:7–5:5)
      1. The Source of Love (4:7–16)
      2. The Fruit of Love (4:17–19)
      3. The Relationship of Love for God and Love for One's Fellow Christian (4:20–5:1)
      4. Obedience: the Evidence of Love for God's Children (5:2–5)
   B. The Christological Test (5:6–12)

V. Conclusion: Great Christian Certainties (5:13–21)

Bibliography

Brown, Raymond E. *The Epistles of John*. The Anchor Bible 30. Garden City, NY: Doubleday, 1982.

Bruce, F. F. *The Epistles of St. John*. Grand Rapids, MI: Eerdmans, 1970.

Grayston, Kenneth. *The Johannine Epistles*. New Century Bible Commentary. Grand Rapids, MI: Eerdmans, 1984.

Marshall, I. Howard. *The Epistles of John*. New International Commentary on the New Testament. Grand Rapids, MI: Eerdmans, 1978.

Smalley, Stephen. *1, 2, 3, John*. Word Biblical Commentary 51. Waco, TX: Word, 1984.

Stott, John. *The Epistles of John: An Introduction and Commentary*. Tyndale New Testament Commentaries 19. Grand Rapids, MI: Eerdmans, 1974.

Westcott, B. F. *The Epistles of St. John*. 1892. Reprint, Grand Rapids, MI: Eerdmans, 1966.

EXPOSITION

I. Introduction: The Reality of the Incarnation (1:1–4)

The opening to this letter exhibits the same subject and several of the same words as the introduction to John's gospel (1:1–4)—"the beginning," "the Word," "life." With the words "That which was from the beginning" (v. 1), John directed the message of his letter to the origin of the gospel message (see his similar use of the word "beginning" in 2:7, 24; 3:11;

2 John 5–6). Origin and antiquity validated authority in the ancient world. In this way, the authority of 1 John is traced to, and grounded in, John's first-hand knowledge of the message, "the Word of life," (v. 1) and its author, Jesus Christ (see 1:3). John did this in a way that may seem circular and repetitious. This, however, is a clue to its importance. It discloses and reinforces a pattern, an unbroken and uninterrupted chain, of both revelation and fellowship that

anticipates at the outset any rival teaching that lays claim to fellowship with or knowledge of God but denies the reality of the incarnate life of Christ (see 5:20 and Introduction: "Gnosticism"). Unwound, the pattern of authority that links readers to fellowship with God is clear: Father → Son → Eyewitnesses to the Word of Life → Fellowship → Mutual joy. The authoritative eyewitness testimony to the Word of Life is the central link that connects the reader to mutual fellowship with God and completes the circle of joy.

1:1. That which was from the beginning coupled with the testimony of eyewitness experience (**heard … seen … looked upon … handled**) anticipates, in the repetition of "which," the crowning emphasis of John's introduction, **the Word of life.** By capitalizing "the Word," the KJV interprets this as a reference to Jesus Christ, as in John 1:1, 14. Unlike in his gospel, here John added an important qualifier: "of life." Although the meaning of John's grammar can be legitimately explained as "the Word that is life" or "the word about Life," John immediately explained his meaning with the personification of "life": "that eternal life, which was with the Father, and was manifested unto us" (1:2; see 5:11–12, 20). It is the word (message) about the Life, the Son, Jesus Christ, that was central to John and critical to fellowship with the Father. Therefore, the repetition of **we** (and **our**) makes clear that the message, or "the Word of life," belonged to many eyewitnesses of the Life (see 1:2). It becomes clear from the context that "the Word" speaks of a revelatory message indissolubly tied to the person of Jesus Christ.

As one might expect in an introduction, John anticipated issues relevant to his purpose for writing. At the outset, John opposed the false teaching of the Gnostic opponents (see Introduction: "Gnosticism") by describing Jesus as eternal (Life, eternal life) and human (**which we have looked upon, and our hands have handled**). John testified that the One who has existed from eternity (John 1:1) "was made flesh" (John 1:14), that is, a flesh-and-blood man. He was true God and true man.

1:2. John premiered Jesus not by His name or by His title "Christ" but as **the life … that eternal life.** This emphasis on Jesus as the Life brings into

view the resurrected Jesus, whom "our hands have handled" (1:1; see John 20:20–21; 27–29). Jesus is called "the life" because He is the living One who has life in Himself (John 1:4; 11:25; 14:6). He is also the source of life and sovereign over life (see 5:11). The letter begins and ends (5:20) with the theme of eternal life. Life and eternal life not only describe Jesus Christ but are hallmarks of those in a personal relationship with the One who is Life (see 5:11–12, 5:20). Life and eternal life belong to the implications of fellowship (see 1:3).

1:3. Fellowship (Greek, *koinōnia*) is the spiritual bond of the believer with Christ—depicted in the figures of the vine and branches (John 15:1–5) and the body and the head (see 1 Cor. 12:12; Col. 1:18)—as well as communion with the Father and with fellow believers. The certainty of fellowship with the Father and the Son, expressly enjoyed by John and the eyewitnesses, is extended to those who were not eyewitnesses through the testimony to the Word of Life (see John 20:27–29). Behind the correspondence of the apostolic experience of fellowship with the Father and the Son was the challenge to that certainty from the false teaching that John combated in this letter. From 2:12–14, 19, it may be certain that John had genuine Christian readers in view. It was not their conversion but their certainty (joy) that he wished to ensure.

1:4. Your joy expresses John's concern for the certainty he wished his readers to enjoy, but "our joy" (alternative reading of early Greek manuscripts and accepted by other translations) matches John's concern for mutual fellowship (v. 3) and whose own joy is completed with the assurance of their fellowship. It is this fellowship, grounded in the believer's relationship to Jesus Christ, that is challenged by the false teaching aimed at the person of Jesus.

In the opening of this letter, then, John was concerned to reassure his readers (his "little children," 2:1) and confirm them in the joy of their salvation. Full-fledged joy is experienced in fellowship, fellowship with the Father and the Son (and thereby with other believers). That fellowship is entered, enjoyed, and ensured only through the Word of Life, Jesus Christ, the mediator of fellowship with God. This fellowship was dependent on fellowship with the eye-witnesses who had firsthand knowledge, the author John and the consensus of witness he represented.

II. The Christian Life as Fellowship with the Father and the Son (1:5–2:28)

A. Ethical Tests of Fellowship (1:5–2:11)

1. Moral Likeness (1:5–7)

1:5. The message which we have heard of him comes "from" (Greek, *apo*) Jesus (see 1:1). Although this exact message (Greek, *angelia*; only here and 2:10) is nowhere found in the recorded words of Jesus, John, who "heard" more than was recorded (see John 21:25), opened with this grand truth "from" Jesus, who is "the life" and "the light of men" (John 1:4–5, 9), the Son who reveals God the Father (John 1:14). Light represents what is good, true, and holy, while darkness represents what is evil and false (see John 3:19–21).

The message **that God is light, and in him is no darkness at all** provides an authoritative index by which to test a sequence of claims (1:6, 8, 10), intersected with John's corrections (1:7, 9) of the error of those claims.

	Claim	Contradiction
1:6	We have fellowship	We walk in the darkness
1:8	We have no sin	We deceive ourselves
1:10	We have not sinned	We make him a liar

The claims echo the assertions of the false teaching that John contested. The claims of the false teachers and John's corrections are keyed to "the message ... that God is light [truth], and in him is no darkness [error] at all" (1:5). Together they profile two lifestyles — one characterized by wickedness and error, the other by holiness and truth — that gauge the reader's "fellowship" with God. Thus, one can take the test: Can one claim to have fellowship with God and walk in darkness? (1:6). Can one say "I have no sin" and not be deceived? (1:8). Can one say "I have not sinned" and not make God a liar? (1:10).

1:6. John used **we** to identify himself with his readers in the hypothetical "if" of these claims (1:6, 8, 10) and corrections (1:7, 9). It may be questioned whether John would have included himself and his readers in the false claims if they originated with the assertions of the false teachers. It must be remembered that John took pen to paper because error had already infiltrated the thinking of his readers. Even if that error survived only as a tempting option to what John had taught his readers, what his readers may have heard from an acquaintance or family member needed to be labeled as what it was: error. The line between light and dark is gray, and John defined the edges of that line through this series of necessary deductions taken from the implications of "the message" (1:5). John vividly put the claims in the reader's mouth, showing that, as good as they may sound, they spell falsehood. With the same vigor, he walked the reader through the corrections in 1:7, 9. In short, John argued with the rhetorical power of a hypothetical: Should you, I, or a trusted friend **say that we have fellowship with him, and walk in darkness, we lie, and do not the truth**.

1:7. John defined fellowship as **walk[ing] in the light, as he is in the light**. Fellowship is more than a claim; it is a pattern of living (to "walk"; see also 2:6) in the light defined by God's own character and the provision, not of sinlessness (which would demand walking "according to" the light), but of the purifying agency of His Son's blood that is resident in the sphere of light. **Fellowship one with another** expands on "fellowship with him" (1:6). "One with another" (*allēlōn*) implies a mutual relationship with the Father and the Son as the basis of fellowship between believers. It is what believers share ("fellowship") that determines the quality of fellowship. For Christians, fellowship is defined by "walk[ing] in the light, as he is in the light" (the sphere of relationship with the Father and the Son).

2. Confession of Sin (1:8–2:2)

1:8. The second claim, **we have no sin** (equivalent to "We are sinless"), John called an expression of self-deception. **We deceive ourselves** (Greek, planaō) is connected to the absence of truth. There is no way to tell here whether this is due to ignorance (absence of the facts) or denial (rejection of the facts). The tone of debate lying just beneath the surface of this verse ("we have no sin") and 1:10 ("we have not sinned") suggests a deliberate refusal to acknowledge the truth.

1:9. The word **confess** (Greek, *homologeō*) carries the idea of "concur" (see 4:2–3, 15). In papyrus contracts discovered in the dry climate of Egypt, one finds the same Greek word used here to express formal agreement between a buyer and seller, with the conditions of a purchase. The buyer "concurs" (*homologeō*) with the terms of purchase. Transferred to the spiritual realm, the believer "confesses" (*homologeō*), acknowledging what God says about his or her sin. Confession involves seeing sin as God sees it or agreeing with what God says is right and wrong, good and bad. In the New Testament, repentance is the corollary to confession. When one genuinely concurs, or agrees, with God about sin, it involves an adjustment or change of outlook (repentance). Both New Testament ideas concern conforming to God's values and entail an ongoing appreciation of who God really is. How poignant is this acknowledgment of sin in view of the heretical claims to "have no sin" (1:8) and to have never sinned, "we have not sinned" (1:10), which expose not only one's self-deception but the darkest corollary of the denial: "we make [God] a liar" (1:10).

Sin is out of character with God, who is light. When Christians concur with God and conform themselves to His character (the light, or His will and ways), He proves Himself **faithful and just**. Here the phrase is virtually a single concept (faithful-and-just). It indicates that God's response toward those who confess their sins will be in accordance with His nature and His gracious commitment to His people (see Ps. 143:1; Zech. 8:8). God is faithful to His promise to forgive (see Jer. 31:34; Mic. 7:18–20; Heb. 10:22–23) and to restore the communion with God that was interrupted by sin (as requested in the Lord's Prayer; Matt. 6:12). Here John amplifies the concept of the divine "cleansing" (Greek, *katharizō*;

1:7, 9) from sin and **unrighteousness** with this complement to 1:7 and "walk[ing] in the light."

1:10. Distinguishing a difference between "we have no sin" (1:8) and **we have not sinned** is difficult. Smalley (*1, 2, 3, John*, p. 33) suggests a denial of the principle (1:8) and the practice of sin (1:10). Westcott (*The Epistles of St. John*, p. 25) suggests a denial of the "permanence of sin as power" (1:8) and the practice of sin in their own lives (1:10). The voice of denial and the voice of God are pitted as rivals in the conjunction of "we have not sinned" and **we make [God] a liar**.

2:1. John lovingly addressed his readers directly, calling them his **little children** (Greek, *teknia*; also in 2:12, 28; 3:7, 18; 4:4; 5:21). Just as Jesus lovingly addressed His disciples (John 13:33), John addressed these believers as his spiritual children. Direct address is the grammatical equivalent to calling someone by name. With their full attention, John made it plain that in addressing the gravity of denying sin, he was not implying that the believers were distinguished from the Gnostics by their sinfulness: **these things write I unto you, that ye sin not**. What truly set the believers apart from the Gnostics was this: **we have an advocate with the Father, Jesus Christ the righteous**. The Greek word for "advocate" (*paraklētos*) refers to someone who speaks in court on behalf of a defendant (see discussion on John 14:16). In God's court, one is vindicated not because one is sinless but rather because the "righteous" Advocate is sinless.

2:2. Propitiation (Greek, *hilasmos*; "sacrifice to atone") refers to turning away God's wrath (see 4:10). God's holiness demands punishment for man's sin. Therefore, out of love (see 4:10; John 3:16), God sent His Son to make substitutionary atonement for the believer's sin. In this way, the Father's wrath is propitiated (satisfied, appeased); His wrath against the Christian's sin has been turned away and directed toward Christ (see discussion on Rom. 3:25). That Jesus came in the flesh is central to His atoning sacrifice, the provision of forgiveness and a confident relationship with God (1:9; 2:2; 4:10). Here John attacked the heart of the heresy (see Introduction:

"Gnosticism"). Forgiveness through Christ's atoning sacrifice is not limited to one particular group only; it has worldwide application (see John 1:29). It must, however, be received by faith (see John 3:16). Thus, this verse does not teach universalism (that all people ultimately will be saved) but teaches that God is an impartial God.

3. Obedience (2:3–6)

2:3. The topic of knowing God is a continuation of the theme of fellowship with God. Forty-two times, 1 John uses two Greek verbs normally translated "know." One of these verbs is related to the name of the Gnostics, the heretical sect that claimed to have a special knowledge (Greek, *gnōsis*) of God (see Introduction: "Gnosticism").

Hereby, or "by this means," grammatically points to the words **if we keep his commandments** and specifies, "this is how we know." To heed God's commandments (or "his word," 2:5) is elsewhere a test (or criterion) of love (5:3; see John 14:15, 21, 23–24; 15:10), because love is more than knowing; it is caring enough to take action. "Keep his commandments" refers to those whose lives are generally characterized by obedience. From what John teaches about sin in 1:7–2:2, he cannot mean that only those who never disobey know God.

2:4. He that saith (see also 2:6, 9) is the first of three professions that John rejected because the claim was contradicted by conduct. Each claim has an air of being a direct quote reported in the third person: **I know him,** "I abide in him" (2:6), and "I am in the light" (2:9). They are professions any true believer should be able to make. Where the words do not correspond, John said, you do not find **the truth,** the walk (2:6), or the light (2:9).

2:5. In him verily is the love of God perfected means either that God's love for the believer is made complete when it moves the believer to acts of obedience (see 4:12) or that Christians' love for God becomes complete when it expresses itself in acts of obedience (see 3:16–18). The verb "perfected" (*teleioō*) means to bring to a state that is no longer incomplete or imperfect. It is not that the person becomes perfect but that God's love has reached its consummation, no longer incomplete or imperfect, when one keeps His word. "Verily," or "truly," marks this not just with emphasis but with authority.

2:6. The person who claims **he abideth in [God] ought himself ... to walk, even as [Christ] walked.** "Abideth" (Greek, *menō*) means to "remain" and implies a steady, consistent way of life (not occasional). To "remain," however, does not imply being static or inactive. John qualified the meaning of "abideth" as a dynamic Christlike pattern of life that is visible in the way one walks. The words "even as" (Greek, *kathōs*) point to Jesus Himself as the model of the great commandment in John 13:34: "A new commandment I give unto you, That ye love one another; [even] as [*kathōs*] I have loved you" (see 2:8). Jesus was the embodiment of love for God and for one another, the two great commandments that formed the foundation of all the commandments. John spoke expressly of the dynamic quality of love as characterizing one who "abideth in the light" (2:10).

4. Love for Fellow Believers (2:7–11)

Love for God (2:3–6) and love for one another (vv. 7–11) were brought together in a new way in the person of Jesus, and here this forms a likely backdrop to the interplay of "old" and "new." Jesus Himself, who brought together the two great commandments (Deut. 6:5 and Lev. 19:18) and called them the foundation of the whole law (see Matt. 22:37–40), gave a "new commandment" (John 13:34) to His disciples (John among them): to love one another as Jesus Himself loved them (see John 13: 34–35; 15:9–12, 17).

2:7–8. The biblical command to love is old (see Lev. 19:18; also Matt. 22:39–40), but its newness is seen in the new and dramatic illustration of divine love on the cross. The **old commandment** (v. 7), "thou shalt love thy neighbour as thyself" (Lev. 19:18), has been revolutionized by the love of Jesus, the gold standard: "love one another; as I have loved you" (John 13:34; 15:12). **From the beginning** points to the beginning of the readers' Christian experience. The **new commandment** was a part of their introduction to the gospel. The "old" commandment was "new" in Christ, not "new" (novel) to them. Thus, this **new commandment … is true** (real) **in him** (Jesus) **and in you: because … the true light** (v. 8; used in the New Testament only here and in John 1:9), Jesus, who is the Light of the World (John 8:12; 12:46), has come. For this reason, John said, **the darkness is past, and the true light now shineth**.

2:9–11. Here is the third of the three professions. In view of the new commandment ("That ye love one another; as I have loved you," John 13:34; 15:12), how patently false is the claim of one who says **he is in the light** (the light being Jesus; v. 9) and yet **hateth his brother**. Contrary to the fellowship that characterizes walking in the light (1:7), the one who hates his brother **is in darkness even until now** (see John 13:46). Conversely, **he that loveth his brother** (v. 10) is confirmed as one who **abideth in the light**, with the added confirmation that **there is none occasion of stumbling in him**. "In him" refers to the one who "loveth his brother." Grammatically, the Greek words translated "in him" can also refer to "the light," in which case the Greek words would be translated "in it," meaning there is no cause for stumbling in the light. It is difficult to decide. In the Bible, hatred and love as moral qualities are not primarily emotions but attitudes expressed in actions (see 3:15–16). Since the order of thought moves from love to light in verse 10, the translation of the KJV is preferred: love is not a source or cause of stumbling, and the one who loves as Jesus loves can be assured of abiding in the light. In verse 11, the false profession of verse 9 is taken up, with its wording reversed and expanded with ideas arising out of verse 10. Up to this point, the profession "I am in the light" has been tested in terms of hate and love. In verse 11, **he that hateth** is shown to be altered (lit., "made blind," Greek, *typhloō*) by the darkness in which he not only exists but also walks. If the contrast of light and darkness, love and hate, alludes also to the specifics of those who, under the influence of Gnostic teaching, had withdrawn and rejected the fellowship of believers (see 2:19), then their hatred of the brethren

was a proof of their blindness and a confirmation that their claims and professions were like the blind leading the blind. If so, John prepared the fellowship of believers for the assurances in 2:12–17.

B. Assurance and Admonition (2:12–17)

2:12–14. By extended repetition and the interplay between **I write** (vv. 12–13) and **I have written** (v. 14) in these verses, John assured his readers that, in spite of the rigorous tests contained in the letter, he was confident of their salvation. As elsewhere in this letter, **little children** (v. 12) refers to all John's readers (see discussion on 2:1), including **fathers** and **young men** (vv. 13–14). The terms "fathers" and "young men" may, however, describe two different levels of spiritual maturity. Some hold that all three terms refer to levels of spiritual maturity. In these verses, the word **because** should probably be translated "that." Greek *hoti* may introduce a cause (as in the KJV translation "because") or a declarative statement (translated "that") presenting the content of what is written or what has been written. There is good reason to read all these instances of "because" as "that" and understand them as declarative statements of John's assurance in the interplay of "I write" and "I have written." In this way, he countered the doubts stirred among the believers by the Gnostic teaching and the ensuing schism (see 2:19) with the continuity he asserted between what he *was* writing and what he *had* written. That "which ye have heard from the beginning" (1 John 2:24) remained the standard.

John tenderly assured all believers, **little children** (v. 12; Greek, *teknia*), of their forgiveness in Jesus Christ (**for his name's sake**; see 3:23; 5:13; Acts 4:12), an emphasis in 2:1–2. This confirmed that they **have known the Father** (v. 13).

To the older believers (**fathers**; v. 14), John wrote, **ye have known him that is from the beginning**. The parallel confirmation in verses 13 and 14 is not a meaningless repetition. John was confirming their maturity, their abiding (remaining) fidelity to the One they knew. "Him that is from the beginning" can refer to God or emphasize the preexistent credentials of Jesus Christ. To be sure, the repetition of "that is from the beginning" confirms that the identity of the One they knew had not been altered by some novel teaching about God or Jesus Christ.

To the younger believers (**young men**; v. 14), John wrote, **ye are strong, and the word of God abideth in you, and ye have overcome the wicked one**. That truth assures and characterizes every young believer clothed in Christ. John confirmed it in 2:13, and the isolation of the final term in that verse creates emphasis: "ye have overcome the wicked one."

2:15–17. By **world** (v. 15), John was not referring to the world of people (see John 3:16) or the created world (see John 17:24) but to the world order or system (see 2:16; James 4:4), which is swayed by Satan and organized against God and righteousness (see discussion on John 1:9–10). John's definition of "world" can be seen in verse 16. Note his emphasis on the personhood of **the Father** (v. 16) contrasted with **all that is in the world**. John identified what he meant by "all that is in the world" under three classifications. **The lust of the flesh** points to human desire (Greek, *epithymia*) or craving (not just sexual desire, as the word "lust" might convey). "Flesh" denotes the human distinct from the divine. For John, "flesh," was not evil (contrary to the Gnostics; see Introduction: "Gnosticism"). Indeed, "the Word was made flesh" (John 1:14), and "Jesus Christ is come in the flesh" (1 John 4:2; 2 John 7). **The lust of the eyes**, or desire (*epithymia*), for what is visible points to the pull of the physical and external rather than the spiritual and eternal. Brown rendered the expression, "eyes hungry for all they see" (*The Epistles of John*, p. 311). **The pride of life** points to self-assurance (Greek, *alazoneia*; pride, pretension, arrogance) swelled by confidence in one's power or possessions (Greek, *bios*; worldly goods and resources). Worldly values are vanity and their worth an illusion because **the world passeth away** (v. 17). "Passeth away" translates John's expression of a departure already in process. He juxtaposed that which is passing away ("the world," 2:17; compare "the darkness," 2:8) with that which remains: **he that doeth the will of God**.

That, John said, is the blue-chip investment of one's wants and desires. What is the current condition of one's investment portfolio? If short-term, high-risk investments characterize not only one's stock but also one's investment strategy, it is time to trade temporal stock for long-term, eternal securities.

C. Christological Test of Fellowship (2:18–28)

1. Contrast: Apostates versus Believers (2:18–21)

2:18. In keeping with other New Testament writers, John viewed the whole period beginning with Christ's first coming as the "last days" (see discussions on Acts 2:17; 2 Tim. 3:1; Heb. 1:2; 1 Peter 1:20). They understood this to be **the last time**, the last days, because neither former prophecy nor new revelation concerning the history of salvation indicated the coming of another era before the return of Christ. The word "last" in "last days," "last times," and "last hour" also expresses a sense of urgency and imminence. The Christian is to be alert, waiting for the return of Christ (see Matt. 25:1–13). John assumed his readers knew that a great enemy of God and His people would arise before Christ's return (**as ye have heard**). That person is called **antichrist**, "that man of sin" (2 Thess. 2:3; see discussion there), and "the beast" (Rev. 13:1–10). Prior to him, there will be **many antichrists**, who will be characterized by the following: (1) they deny the incarnation (4:2; 2 John 7) and that Jesus is the divine Christ (2:22); (2) they deny the Father (2:22); (3) they do not have the Father (2:23); (4) they are liars (2:22) and deceivers (2 John 7); (5) they are "many" (v. 18); and (6) in John's day, they left the church because they had nothing in common with believers (2:19). The antichrists referred to in this letter were the early Gnostics and other false teachers. The "anti" in "antichrist" means "against" (see 2 Thess. 2:4; Rev. 13:6–7).

2:19. They went out from us identifies the exponents of Gnostic teaching who had seceded from the fellowship of true believers. Second John 7 ("many deceivers are entered into the world") should be viewed in connection with 2:19, 22–24 and John's previous admonition, "Love not the world" (2:15).

In this one verse, John used the word "us" five times, emphasizing his delineation of the true fellowship. The rejection of inner fellowship was telltale in the rejection of outer fellowship. Otherwise, John said, **they would ... have continued** (Greek *menō*; "abide," "remain," as in 2:6).

2:20 – 21. The term **unction** (Latin, *unctio*; v. 20) means "anointing" (Greek, *chrisma*; only here and 2:27), pointing to the Holy Spirit (see 2:27 and discussion; Acts 10:38). This anointing comes from **the Holy One**, either Jesus Christ (see Mark 1:24; John 6:69; Acts 2:27; 3:14; 22:14) or the Father (see 2 Kings 19:22; Job 6:10). **Ye know all things** refers to the fact of knowing, not the extent of knowing, and thus assured the readers that they had no deficiency that could cause them to fall prey to the Antichrist's claims (Brown, *The Epistles of John*, p. 349). John's assurance in verse 21 confirms this and may echo the very kinds of claims that he silenced with his reassurance and the confirmation of their anointing. Other Greek manuscripts read "Ye all know [of it; i.e., the unction]."

2. The Person of Christ: The Crux of the Test (2:22 – 23)

2:22. Antichrists are **liar[s]**. John's language (lit., "the liar," with the definite article) underscores the lie **of he that denieth that Jesus is the Christ**. The man Jesus is the divine Christ (see the parallel confession in 5:5; see also Introduction: "Gnosticism" and discussion on 5:6).

2:23. One cannot engage in the lie of those who **denieth the Son** and yet claim to have **the Father**, as the Gnostics did (see 2 John 9).

3. Persistent Belief: The Key to Continuing Fellowship (2:24 – 28)

2:24 – 25. Let ... that which ye have heard from the beginning (the seminal teaching about Jesus) **... remain in you**. Here is a direct correlation between revelation (knowing about God through Jesus) and reality (knowing God through Jesus), as shown in the correlation of "remain" (Greek, *menō*; "abide," "remain") and "continue" (Greek, *menō*). Eternal life depends on relationship with the Life, the eternal Life (see 1:2 – 3; 5:11 – 12, 20).

2:26. This verse reflects one of John's purposes for writing (see Introduction: "Theme and Theological Message").

2:27. Ye need not that any man teach you. Since the Bible constantly advocates teaching (see, e.g., Matt. 28:20; 1 Cor. 12:28; Eph. 4:11; Col. 3:16; 1 Tim. 4:11; 2 Tim. 2:2, 24), John was not ruling out human teachers. At the time when he wrote, however, false teachers were insisting that the teaching of the apostles was to be supplemented with the "higher knowledge" that they (the Gnostics) claimed to possess. John's response (2:20 – 27) was that true believers have received an **anointing** and are indwelt by the Holy Spirit, who shows them that "Jesus Christ is come in the flesh" (4:2; see 4:15; 5:1, 10). The person of Jesus Christ is the topic discussed in 2:20 – 27. As general (natural) revelation reveals to every human that a God exists who is all powerful (see Rom. 1:18 – 20) and good (see Acts 14:17), so the Holy Spirit reveals to all believers the nature of Jesus Christ (see 4:13 – 15; 5:9 – 10).

2:28. Abide in him may refer to God (as in 3:24; 4:13, 16), the Son (as in 3:6), or the Father and Son (as in 2:24), but here the expected coming of Jesus (**when he shall appear**) puts the focus on the Son, the mediator of abiding with God. The form of the Greek verb for "shame" raises two possibilities of translation, either "be dishonored" (outer moral verdict) or "feel shame" (inner moral feeling). The contrasted pairing of **have confidence, and not be ashamed** tips the scales in favor of "feel shame." Opposite the feeling of shame is the feeling of boldness, or "confidence" (Greek, *parrēsia*; see 3:21; 4:17; 5:14; Heb. 4:16), a term with a rich history and meaning uninhibited freedom of expression. An additional clue completes the sense of the contrast. The word **before** literally means "from" (Greek, *apo*) and brings out the following sense: one may have boldness and not cower from Him in shame at His coming. In encouraging his **little children**, John may have intended a rhyming wordplay to ring in their hearts: "have boldness at his coming" (*parrēsia ... en tē parousia*).

III. The Christian Life as Divine Sonship (2:29–4:6)

A. Ethical Tests of Sonship (2:29–3:24)

1. Righteousness (2:29–3:10a)

2:29. If ye know that he is righteous. Knowledge of God's righteousness leads to an inevitable corollary: God's children bear the Father's likeness. Spiritual paternity (an issue in John 8:38–47; see 1 John 3:8) is established not by a blood test but by moral resemblance. Members of God's family are marked by holy living.

3:1. With a tone of wonder, John asked his readers to **behold** (lit., "see" or "perceive") the exceptional **love** of God. **What manner** (Greek, *potapos*; "of what sort," "of what kind"; lit., "of what country") conveys the unusual or utterly foreign nature of God's love. It is "out of this world," or foreign to human experience, **that we should be called the sons of God.** There is a tone of adoption here, but John never spoke of adoption but rather spoke of birth (2:29; 5:1) and the believer's identification as God's child. John underscored this with a confirming or legitimizing declaration: "And that is what we are" (see discussion on John 1:12).

3:2. The believer's paternity is spiritual (see 2:29), but **when [the Son] shall appear,** one's resemblance will be complete and tangible, for believers shall see Him as He is. Identification with Christ has a terminus in complete Christlikeness.

3:3. The believer's **hope** is not a mere wish but unshakable confidence concerning the future (see discussion on Rom. 5:2). Purpose and hope go hand in glove. If one's purpose is to become more and more like Christ, to see Him face-to-face is a "purifying" hope.

3:4–6. Here John was not asserting sinless perfection (see 1:8–10; 2:1) but explaining that the believer's life is characterized, not by sin, but by doing what is right and emulating the Righteous One (see 2:29). Anyone who takes up sin is at cross-purposes with the One who appeared to take away sin. Christ's purpose in taking away sin must inform one's outlook on sin. Abiding in Him is incongruent with abiding in

sin (**sinneth**; v. 6). The present tenses of "sin" point to a lifestyle of sin so incompatible with seeing or knowing God that John rejected such a partnership. His use of the present tense "sinneth" finds its definition (paternal resemblance) in the Devil (see 3:8).

3:7. Let no man deceive you alludes foremost to the Gnostic deception and a righteousness of claims (see 1:8, 10) without substance. The standards of righteousness are different. John reinforced the one standard of Jesus Christ, the true index of God's righteousness.

3:8. In this short letter, John said much about **the devil.** (1) He is called "the devil" (here) and "that wicked one" (3:12; 2:13–14; 5:18). (2) He **sinneth from the beginning** (here), that is, from the time he first rebelled against God, before the fall of Adam and Eve (see John 8:44). (3) He is the instigator of human sin, and those who continue to sin belong to him (see 3:12) and are his children (see 3:10). (4) He is "in the world" (4:3) and has "the whole world" (5:19) of unbelievers under his control. (5) He cannot, however, lay hold of the believer to harm him (see 5:18). (6) On the contrary, the Christian will overcome him (see 2:13–14; 4:4), and Christ will destroy the Devil's work.

3:9. The picture here is of human reproduction, in which the sperm (Greek, *sperma*; "seed") bears the life principle and transfers the paternal characteristics. John could not have put the question of one's paternity in starker language (see 2:29). Some have suggested the **seed** is the Word of God. Others have suggested that it represents the Spirit. In either case, it is recognized as His will, the expression of His nature. The expression **cannot sin** is again the present tense, as in the earlier instances of "sinneth"; grammar, not a change in meaning, accounts for the difference. It refers not to a complete cessation of sin but to a life that is not characterized by sin.

3:10a. In this is taken here with what precedes, meaning "as already shown," and thus forms a literary inclusion (Latin, *inclusio*), or return to the opening theme of this section (2:28–29). Others take these words as the opening of a new section parallel to 2:28–29. The delineation of **the children of God**

and **the children of the devil** serves as a transition from the preceding material (3:4–9) to what follows (3:10b–24).

2. Love (3:10b–24)

3:10b–11. Whosoever doeth not righteousness is not of God, neither he that loveth not his brother (10b). Practicing righteousness is specified as loving one's brother. John stated this specification, however, in negative rather than positive terms because it serves to introduce the example of Cain (3:12). The positive intent is evident in the explanation in verse 11. The word **message** (Greek, *angelia*; v. 11; in the New Testament, only here and in 1:5) may underscore the foundational teaching that the readers had **from the beginning, that we should love one another**, which John elsewhere called the "new commandment" (2:7–8; 2 John 5), adopting the wording of Jesus Himself (John 13:34). "The message" may be tantamount to the gospel and suggests the opening of a major section, as in 1:5. Jesus said the fulfillment of this command would confirm the identity of His disciples (John 13:35).

3:12. Cain (see Heb. 11:4) is a negative example. As in 3:8 (see John 8:44), the one who practices sin is of the Devil, and Cain illustrates the tragic consequences of being one of the Devil's moral progeny. **Works** are the concrete expression of the inward contrast of evil and righteousness.

3:13. Hate is the absence of love (see "loveth not his brother," 3:14; "hateth his brother," 3:15), and believers should expect not love, but hatred, from the world (see John 15:18; 17:14). Implicit in this hatred is the confrontation of the concrete works that manifest inner moral allegiances.

3:14–15. We know (v. 14) is emphatic and serves to confirm that the children of God possess eternal life here and now (**eternal life abiding in him**). The basis of this fact is Jesus Christ (see 1:2–3; 5:11–12), but the proof is **love [of] the brethren**. Indeed, John declared that the absence of such love is a proof that **death** remains (**abideth**) the seal on one's life.

3:16. Here John presented two models, contrasting Jesus Christ with Cain: the one who sacrificed

the life of another out of selfish interest (Cain) and the One who sacrificed Himself out of selfless interest in others (Jesus Christ). John's wording is a restatement of the "new commandment" (2:7–8; 2 John 5), with an emphasis on "as I have loved you" (John 13:34; 15:12).

3:17–18. See James 2:14–17. The word translated **bowels of compassion** (Greek, *splanchna*; v. 18) identifies the visceral (gut) feeling that must be ignored in order to turn away from a brother in need. Love (selfless sacrifice) is not solely propelled by feeling, but a love so great as God's love (3:1) enlarges, not diminishes, one's emotional response to need: "as I have loved you" (John 13:34; 15:12). **The love of God** is God's kind of love, which He pours out in the believer's heart (see Rom. 5:5) and which in turn spurs the believer to love in kind. Grammatically, "the love of God" may speak of the believer's love for God. **In deed and in truth** are the two sides of love; sacrificial action (divine example) and principled direction (divine character) combine to define biblical love. To love as God loves is to seek God's best for another.

3:19–20. God is greater than our heart (v. 20). An oversensitive conscience can be quieted by the knowledge that God Himself has declared active love to be an evidence of salvation. He knows the hearts of all and whether, in spite of shortcomings, they have been born of Him.

3:21–22. The **heart** is the center of the inner life, one's thinking, feeling, and will. The absence of an unfavorable judgment there (**condemn us not**), together with the keeping of God's **commandments** (v. 22), suggest two conditions requisite for **confidence** (Greek, *parrēsia*; v. 21) before God and in the expectation (not the guarantee) of answered prayer (for John's use of the word "confidence," see 2:28). **Whatsoever we ask** (v. 22) is limited by these same two conditions and the assurance of answered prayer inspired by the implications of asking according to His will (see 5:14–15).

3:23–24. This command has two parts: (1) **believe [in] … Jesus Christ** (v. 23; see John 6:29), and (2) **love one another** (see John 13:34–35). John developed the first part in 4:1–6 and the second part in 4:7–12, moving from the *what* (v. 23) to the *who*: **he that keepeth** (Greek, *tēreō*; to observe and so persist in obedience) **his commandments** (v. 24) is the one who **dwelleth** (Greek, *menō*; "to remain"; KJV "abideth" elsewhere) **in [God], and [God] in him**. **The Spirit** serves as the assurance of this mutual relationship between God and the believer. In other words, the Spirit ratifies one's obedience (one's belief in Christ and love of one another) with assurance that believers are in Him and He in them.

B. Christological Tests of Sonship (4:1–6)

How does one identify a false prophet? Such a prophet (a person inspired to proclaim or reveal divine will or purpose) was evidently difficult to detect. John warned his readers about bogus prophets and said that their error can be exposed through a test ("Hereby," v. 2) based on their acceptance, approval, and agreement ("confesseth," v. 2) with the central proposition of the gospel that "Jesus Christ is come in the flesh" (v. 2). That Jesus came in the flesh is central to His atoning sacrifice, the provision of forgiveness, and a confident relationship with God (1:9; 2:2; 4:10). Here John attacked the heart of the heresy, "that spirit of antichrist" (v. 3).

4:1. John's warning contains a present as well as a prohibitive concern: **Believe not**, (present imperative; i.e., "stop believing") **every spirit**. The tendency to accept (Greek, *pisteuō*; give credence) every spirit as the Spirit of God given to believers (see 3:24) should be replaced with a test (**try**; Greek, *dokimazō*; "test," "examine"; see "prove all things," 1 Thess. 5:21). A "spirit" ("spirits") identifies a person moved by a spirit, whether by the Holy Spirit or an evil one. A true prophet speaks from God, being "moved by the Holy Ghost" (2 Peter 1:21). False prophets, such as the Gnostics of John's day, speak under the influence of spirits alienated from God. Christ warned against false prophets (Matt. 7:15; 24:11), as did Paul (1 Tim. 4:1) and Peter (2 Peter 2:1).

4:2–3. Here the notion of **confesseth** (v. 2; see discussion on 1:9) as "agreement" divides the true from the false on the central matter of the incarnate

Jesus Christ (see discussion on 2:18), of whom John gave eyewitness testimony in 1:1–2. The one who cannot vocalize agreement reveals the **spirit of antichrist** (v. 3; see 2 John 7). Thus, John excluded the Gnostic opponents, especially the Cerinthian doctrine that the divine Christ came upon the human Jesus at His baptism and then left Him at the cross, so that it was only the man Jesus who died (see Introduction: "Gnosticism"). The fact that the "spirit of antichrist" is **already … in the world** indicates that Satan's opposition to the work of God will continue as an expression of anti-God, anti-Christian activity throughout church history. At some time in the future (after the removal of the restrainer; see discussion on 2 Thess. 2:7–8), the Antichrist will appear in person.

4:4–6. Ye are of God (v. 4) is an abbreviated form of the expression "born of God" (3:9; 2:29). **Them** identifies the "false prophets" (4:1), who were inspired by the "spirit of antichrist" (4:3). **He that is in the world** identifies the Devil (see John 12:31; 16:11). In 4:3, "the world" means the inhabited earth; here in verses 4–5, it means the community, or system, of those not born of God, including the antichrists (see discussion on John 1:9). The community of believers is outmatched numerically, but **greater is he that is in you**. In verses 5–6, **heareth** is related to the source that prompts what is said: **the world** (v. 5) or "he that is in the world" (v. 4) versus **God** (vv. 4, 6) or "he that is in you" (v. 4); **the spirit of truth** (v. 6) versus **the spirit of error**. (For "the spirit of truth," see 5:6; discussion on John 14:17).

IV. The Christian Life as an Integration of the Ethical and the Christological (4:7–5:12)

A. The Ethical Test: Love (4:7–5:5)

1. The Source of Love (4:7–16)

4:7–8. Love [of] one another (v. 7) is the proof that one **is born of God, and knoweth God**. The word "love" in its various forms is used forty-three times in this letter, thirty-two times in this short section (4:7–16). Only those who are to some degree like God truly know Him. **God is love** (v. 8). In His essential nature and in all His actions, God is loving. John similarly affirmed that God is spirit (see John 4:24) and "light" (1:5), as well as holy, powerful, faithful, true, and just.

4:9. This verse closely parallels John 3:16.

John 3:16	1 John 4:9
For God so [in this way] loved the world,	In this was manifested the love of God towards us,
that he gave his only begotten Son,	because that God sent his only begotten Son into the world,
that whosoever believeth in him	that we [who believeth in Him]
should not perish, but have everlasting life	might live through him.

The differences of wording are largely measured by the difference of perspective. The "whosoever" has been shifted to "we [who believeth]." **That we might live through him** gains its proper dimension from the comparison ("have everlasting life," John 3:16) and the immediate context of God's love: to "live through him" is more than thriving; it is manifesting the love God demonstrated in Jesus Christ, the Life, the eternal Life (see 1:2–3; 5:11–12, 20). If the world is to be more than a historical museum of God's love, those born of Him, who know Him, must manifest it in the marketplace by "liv[ing] through him." For **only begotten Son**, see discussion on John 1:18.

4:10–11. John included himself in the "we" and "us" of God's initiative. All believers recognize the unmerited love of God (see John 15:16; Titus 3:4–5). God's initiative is specified by His **propitiation** (atoning sacrifice; see discussion on 2:2) **for our sins** (v. 10). "He first loved us" (4:19), not because of believers' merit but because of His great love. This initiative of love, unconditioned by merit, generates the **ought** (v. 11) of the admonition to **love one another**.

4:12. No man hath seen God at any time (see discussion on John 1:18). Since God's love is the source of love, His love reaches full expression (is made complete) when **we love one another**. Thus, the God whom "no man hath seen" is "seen" in those who love because God lives (**dwelleth**; Greek, *menō*; "abide," "remain") in them.

4:13–16. The evidence that Christians "love one another" (4:7) is combined with other criteria (**hereby know we**; v. 13) that warrant an assurance of God's indwelling presence. Even though one cannot see God with the human eye, one can know the reality of God through (1) **love [for] one another** (v. 12); (2) **his Spirit** (v. 13), which **he hath given us**; and (3) the testimony that Jesus is **the Saviour of the world** (v. 14), **the Son of God** (v. 15), whom believers **confess**. John summed up the evidences in a profession of settled conviction and certainty (perfect tenses of "know" and "believe" emphasize the outcome) about **the love that God hath to us** (lit., "that God has in us"; v. 16). **God is love** forms a literary inclusion (Latin, *inclusio*), or return to the opening theme of this section (4:8).

2. The Fruit of Love (4:17–19)

4:17. Herein is our love made perfect is literally, "In this is love made complete with us." The words "In this" gather up the mutual assertions and assurances about love in 4:8–16 and usher in the ultimate outcome of this love with respect to believers' identity in Him and His identity in them: **we may have boldness in the day of judgment**. The words "with us" are illumined and the outcome explained: **as he is, so are we**, meaning like Christ. In 2:28, John wrote in similar language of the judgment that will take place when Christ returns. Love conforms one to the likeness of the One who renders judgment. That believers are like Christ in love is a sign that God, who "is love" (4:16), lives in them; therefore, they may have confidence on the day of judgment that they are saved.

4:18. There is no fear in love. Perfect or complete love has no room for fear. Love overpowers fear and **casteth out** (lit., "drives outside") **fear** and its

torment (Greek, *kolasis*; pain or suffering accompanying punishment). Christians need have no fear of God's judgment because genuine love confirms their salvation.

4:19. We love him, because he first loved us. All love ultimately comes from God; genuine love is never self-generated by His creatures.

3. The Relationship of Love for God and Love for One's Fellow Christian (4:20–5:1)

4:20–21. The love that "casteth out fear" (4:18) is as concrete and tangible as the cross; "We love him, because he first loved us" (4:19). John returned to a recurring strain within the theme of love: he who **hateth his brother** (v. 20; see 2:9, 11; 3:15). In 2:3–11, John contested three professions, that of "He that saith, I know him" (2:4), "He that saith he abideth in him" (2:6), and "He that saith he is in the light" (2:9). At this point in John's letter, it is clear that each claim was contested on the basis of hating one's brother. For each claim was refuted, in order, on the basis of disobeying God's commandments (2:4–5a), not walking as Jesus walked (2:5b–6), and existing in the darkness (2:7–11), all of which stem from the failure to love. Here John took up the ultimate profession, the claim of **I love God**. How ignorant is the claim to know God, how estranged is the claim to abide in God, how blind is the claim to exist in the light, if the claim to love God is made visible with hate and not love. **He is a liar**. Hate exists where love should abound because the one who hates his brother (**loveth not**) has no love from God (who is love, see 4:8–16). For **this commandment** (v. 21), see 2:3, 7–11; 3:23–24; 5:3; John 13:34.

5:1. Faith that **Jesus is the Christ** is a sign of being born again, just as love is (see 4:7; discussion on 2:22). The words **loveth him that begat loveth him also that is begotten** point to a time when members of a family were closely associated as a unit under the headship of the father. John could, therefore, use the family as an illustration to show that anyone who loves God the Father will naturally love God's children.

4. Obedience: The Evidence of Love for God's Children (5:2–5)

5:2. John wrote that **when we love God, and keep his commandments** (see John 14:15, 21), believers know by this **that we love the children of God**. "When" (Greek, *hotan*) brings out the simultaneous character of the two actions. Based on what John has taught in this letter, the two actions are convertible.

5:3. His commandments are not grievous, not because the commands themselves are light or easy to obey but, as John explained in the following verse, because of the new birth. The one born of God by faith is enabled by the Holy Spirit to obey.

5:4. To **overcometh the world** is to gain **victory** over its sinful pattern of life, which is another way of describing obedience to God (see 5:3). Such obedience is not impossible for the believer, because believers have been born again and because the Holy Spirit dwells within them and gives them strength. John mentioned two aspects of victory: (1) the initial victory of turning in faith from the world to God (the first "overcometh"); (2) the continuing day-by-day victory of Christian living (the second "overcometh"). Overcoming the world (see discussion on 2:15–17), as overcoming the Wicked One (see 2:13–14; 3:8–9; 4:4; 5:18), comes from the power of God's begetting. The true victory (Greek, *nikē*), the victory that triumphs over the world, is **our faith**. Faith actualizes believers' identity as begotten of God (see 5:5).

5:5. John's question here solicits the very "faith" of 5:4. It is a compact way of saying that the one who overcomes (Greek, *nikaō*; "be victor," "conquer") the world **is the Son of God** and everyone who believes in Him shares in His victory (for parallel confessions, see 2:22; 4:2; 5:1).

B. The Christological Test (5:6–12)

5:6. Everyone who believes in the Son of God must believe in the Son of God **that came by water and blood**. Water symbolizes Jesus' baptism, and blood symbolizes His death. These are mentioned because Jesus' ministry began at His baptism and ended at His death. John countered the Gnostic teaching of His day (see Introduction: "Gnosticism") that claimed Jesus was born only a man and remained so until His baptism. At that time, they maintained, the Christ (the Son of God) descended on the human Jesus but left Him before His suffering on the cross, so that it was only the man Jesus who died. Throughout this letter, John insisted that Jesus Christ is God as well as man (see 1:1–4; 4:2; 5:5). Here he asserted that it was this God-man Jesus Christ who came into the world, was baptized, and died. Jesus was the Son of God not only at His baptism but also at His death. This truth is extremely important, because if Jesus died only as a man, His sacrificial atonement (see 2:2; 4:10) would not have been sufficient to take away the guilt of sin. **The [Holy] Spirit … beareth witness** ("testifies") that Jesus is the Son of God in two ways: (1) the Spirit descended on Jesus at His baptism (see John 1:32–34), and (2) the Spirit continues to confirm in the hearts of believers the apostolic testimony that Jesus' baptism and death verify that He is the Christ, the Son of God (see 2:27; 1 Cor. 12:3).

5:7–8. The Old Testament law required two or three witnesses (see Deut. 17:6; 19:15; see also 1 Tim. 5:19). **The Father, the Word** (Jesus Christ; see John 1:1, 14)**, and the Holy Ghost** (v. 7; see John 1:33; 7:39; 14:26; 20:22) form a triad that is not unique in John's gospel or epistle, but the wording is unique ("Word" and "Holy Ghost" occur only here). The words of these verses, as they have come to us, concisely express John's testimony to the Trinity elsewhere (see 4:13–15; John 3:34–36; 6:62–65; 14:16–17, 26). This reference, however, is only found in late editions of the Latin Vulgate. It does not appear in any Greek manuscripts before the sixteenth century. Therefore, verse 7 is deleted in some translations (e.g., NIV).

5:9–10. John contrasted human testimony with the testimony of God. **If we receive the witness of men** (v. 9), how much more should one receive the testimony **of God**? The standard of credible testimony is two or three witnesses (see Deut. 19:15; Matt. 18:16; 2 Cor. 13:1; 1 Tim. 5:19). John knew this: "these three agree in one" (5:8). God's witness (the Spirit, if not also the water and the blood; see

5:6, 8) trumps the human (Gnostic) witness. **For this is the witness of God which he hath testified of his Son** picks up the importance of the words "the Son of God … even Jesus Christ" (5:5–6). When God testifies, he speaks of "his Son." Those who believe in the Son of God (5:10) have this testimony internally authenticated; this truth resides in their hearts. To reject His testimony is to make God a liar (see 1:10; compare John 3:18, 33).

5:11–12. "The witness of God" in 5:9, which capped the testimony to Jesus in 5:6–8, was followed by an explanation of the internal authentication of God's testimony in 5:10. Now John provided a summarizing testimony, a capstone to the opening of his letter, which began with "the Word of life" (1:1). If the antichrists (the Gnostics) claimed eternal life apart from God's Son (compare 2:24–26), this was the fitting assurance to those who believed in the Son of God. Without the Son, who is the Life, the eternal Life, one does not have life. Thus, **hath given to us eternal life** (v. 11) points to a person, not an object, and is a present possession (see discussions on John 3:15, 36). Recall John's words in 1:3–4: "our fellowship is with the Father, and with his Son Jesus Christ. And these things write we unto you, that our joy may be full."

V. Conclusion: Great Christian Certainties (5:13–21)

5:13. As John concluded his letter, he wrote first of his chief certainty and purpose for writing. In wording similar to the purpose statement of John 20:31, he wrote, **These things have I written unto you … that ye may know.** John's words gained their maximum meaning in light of what he had hitherto made known. "We know" tolls like a bell throughout 5:13–20. John was telling his readers that they could be certain that they had eternal life.

5:14–15. John repeatedly wrote of the "confidence" or "boldness" (Greek, *parrēsia*; see 2:28; 3:21; 4:17; 5:14) of the believer. He returned to the subject of confidence in prayer, not under special conditions as in 3:21–22, but in its own right as a believer's necessary dependence on God. The condition for

God's hearing and answering prayer is that **we ask ... according to his will** (v. 14). Jesus' own prayer was so controlled: "not [what] I will, but what thou wilt" (Mark 14:36). The confidence comes from moving with God in the petitions of the heart; the agreement between the one asking and the One answering.

5:16–17. John illustrated the kind of petition one can be sure God will answer (see 5:14–15). In the context of this letter directed against Gnostic teaching, which denied the incarnation and threw off all moral restraints, it is probable that **sin unto death** (v. 16) refers to the Gnostics' adamant and persistent denial of the truth and to their shameless immorality. This kind of unrepentant sin leads to spiritual death. Another view is that this is sin that results in physical death. This view holds that if a believer continues to sin, God takes his life in judgment (see 1 Cor. 11:30). In either case, **sin which is not unto death** is of a less serious nature. Thus, a "sin unto death" results in either spiritual or physical death and is not to be confused with the "unpardonable sin" (see Matt. 12:31–32).

5:18–20. The letter ends with three striking statements, affirming the truths that **We know** (vv. 18–20) and summarizing some of the letter's major themes: (1) We know that the child of God does not practice sin or keep on sinning (see 3:4–10). This is further explained: the one **begotten of God** (the believer; v. 18) guards himself against sin, so **that wicked one toucheth** (Greek, *haptō*; "take hold of," "harm") **him not.** (2) **We know that we are of God** (v. 19; see 3:10; 4:6), that the believer does not belong to the world (see 2:15–17), **and that the whole world lieth in wickedness** (or in the grasp of the Evil One; see 2:13–14; 3:12; 4:4). (3) **We know that the Son of God is come** (see 4:2–3; 5:6; 2 John 7), **and hath given us an understanding ... [to] know** (v. 20) and exist **in him that is true** ("the true one," only here in 1 John), **even in his Son Jesus Christ.** "Him that is true" is a reference to God the Father since it is the Son that has given believers the understanding to know. **This is the true God** may refer to either God the Father or God the Son. The letter began with the theme of eternal life (1:1–2) and now ends with it.

5:21. John concluded with a final warning about false gods, precipitated by the grand expression "true God" (5:20). **Keep yourself from idols**, that is, false teachings, and hence from false gods. In summary, John's first epistle emphasized the importance of believing the truth, resisting false teaching, and living in fellowship with Christ.

THE SECOND EPISTLE OF JOHN

INTRODUCTION

Author

The author is John the apostle. Obvious similarities to 1 John and the gospel of John suggest that the same person wrote all three letters. Compare the following:

2 John 5	1 John 2:7	John 13:34–35
2 John 6	1 John 5:3	John 14:23
2 John 7	1 John 4:2–3	
2 John 12	1 John 1:4	John 15:11; 16:24

See 1 John, Introduction: "Author"; and John, Introduction: "Author."

Date

The letter was probably written about the same time as 1 John (AD 85–95), as the above comparisons suggest (see 1 John, Introduction: "Date").

Theme

During the first two centuries, the gospel was taken from place to place by traveling evangelists and teachers. Believers customarily took these missionaries into their homes and gave them provisions for their journey when they left. Since Gnostic teachers also relied on this practice (see discussion on 3 John 5), 2 John was written to urge discernment in supporting traveling teachers; otherwise, someone might unintentionally contribute to the propagation of heresy rather than truth.

Outline

I. Salutation (vv. 1–3)
II. Commendation (v. 4)
III. Exhortation and Warning (vv. 5–11)
IV. Conclusion (vv. 12–13)

Bibliography

See 1 John, Introduction: "Bibliography."

EXPOSITION

I. Salutation (vv. 1 – 3)

Verses 1 – 2. John's second epistle bears the usual features of a first-century letter: (1) the opening salutation, identifying the sender and the recipient and offering greetings (vv. 1 – 3), (2) the body of the letter, expressing the author's reasons for writing (vv. 4 – 11), and (3) the closing, with benedictions, final greetings, and sometimes mention of the writing process (vv. 12 – 13). In the opening salutation, John identified himself as **The elder** (v. 1). In his later years, John functioned as an elder (Greek, *presbyteros*; see discussion on 1 Tim. 3:1), probably of the Ephesian church. The apostle Peter held a similar position (see 1 Peter 5:1). The recipients are identified as the **elect lady and her children**, an unknown Christian woman in the province of Asia or a figurative designation of a local church there. The latter appears most likely. "Her children," then, would identify the members of that local church. The letter reads naturally if John is addressing a church. This would square with the absence of the lady's personal name, the reference to the church's reputation (**not I only**), and the closing greeting from the children of a sister church (see v. 13). **In the truth** is more than a profession of sincerity. "Truth" points to the revelation of God in Jesus Christ, who is the truth (see discussion on John 1:14) and the basis of love for one another (see vv. 3 – 4). Thus, John spoke of the truth in terms approaching that of a companion: **which dwelleth** (Greek, *menō*; "abides") **in us, and shall be with us for ever** (v. 2).

Verse 3. In the greeting, John offered a benediction, or blessing, to the recipients. For the components of the blessing of **Grace ... mercy, and peace**, see discussions on Galatians 1:3; Ephesians 1:2; Romans 9:22 – 24. The blessing of these spiritual realities comes from the Father and the Son, and they will be experienced where there is truth and love. Truth and love were John's two major concerns in this letter. The truth grounds the command to love one another (see vv. 4 – 6) and belongs to the confession that "Jesus Christ is come in the flesh" (v. 7).

II. Commendation (v. 4)

Verse 4. John was overjoyed to have **found** (Greek, *heurēka*) some of **thy children walking in truth**. Apparently, the elder had met some members of the church and observed their way of life (Greek, *peripateō*; "to walk," "behave"). The sense of John's discovery can be worded like this: "Some members of your church were conducting their lives according to the truth, just like us, according to the command we received from the Father." This encounter gave John the occasion for writing his letter and encouraging all the children (the whole church) to do the same (see v. 5).

III. Exhortation and Warning (vv. 5 – 11)

Verses 5 – 6. John opened the body of his letter with an exhortation drawn from his commendation of "thy children walking in the truth" (v. 4), which was the reason for John's joy ("I rejoiced," v. 4). What does it mean to walk "in truth, as believers have received a commandment from the Father" (v. 4)? In a request to the whole church, John specified that it means to **love one another** (v. 5; for John's use of **a new commandment** and **from the beginning**, see discussions on 1 John 2:7 – 8). For John, there was no opposition between love and God's commandments. Love has a sweeping authority over all of one's behavior, as do the commandments. As Jesus did, John said that to fulfill the whole law, one must love (see Matt. 22:37 – 40).

Verses 7 – 11. This section deals with the basic Gnostic heresy attacked in 1 John, namely, that the Son of God did not become flesh (see John 1:14); rather, He temporarily came upon the man Jesus between His baptism and crucifixion (see 1 John, Introduction: "Gnosticism").

Verses 7 – 8. The command to love is closely linked with a confession: **Jesus Christ is come in the flesh** (v. 7). The connection is seen clearly in John's use of the word "For" ("Because"). Many deceivers had gone out and entered the world (see discussions on 1 John 2:18–19; 4:2–3). When one eschews the atoning sacrifice of God's love in Jesus Christ (implied in the words "come in the flesh"), one eschews the obligation to love one another. Indeed, the power of the new commandment is the sacrificial love of Jesus imbedded as obligation: "love one another; as I have loved you" (John 13:34). In John's experience, this appeared to have been the pattern of a schism (possibly in the sister church) rooted in the Gnostic rejection of Christ come in the flesh (see vv. 7–9). Thus, he warned the church of "the elect lady" (v. 1), **Look to yourselves** (v. 8), or "Watch out for yourselves." **Lose not ... [what] we have wrought, but ... receive a full reward**, that is, "Don't give up what you've achieved; our work faithfully accomplished on earth brings future reward" (see Mark 9:41; 10:29–30; Luke 19:16–19; Heb. 11:26).

Verse 9. Whosoever transgresseth may be accurately rendered, "Anyone who turns aside" (Greek, *parabainō*; "go aside," "deviate," "transgress"). Other Greek manuscripts contain the word *proagō*, meaning "to run ahead," which suggests maverick innovation on the part of the one who **abideth** (Greek, *menō*) **not in the doctrine of Christ**. This is a reference to the Gnostics, who believed that they had advanced or moved beyond the teaching of the apostles. The similarity of this letter to 1 John, the nature of the heresy combated, and the immediate context suggest that John was referring not to teaching given by Christ but to true teaching about Christ as the incarnate God-man. It is not the defector, but the one who remains ("abideth") in the doctrine pertaining to Christ, who **hath both the Father and the Son**.

Verses 10–11. Along with his warning, John provided practical directions for handling the arrival of a "deceiver" (v. 7): **receive him not into your house** (v. 10). John was referring to the housing and feeding of traveling teachers (see Introduction: "Theme"). He was prohibiting not what one might think of as general courtesy but rather the provision of food and shelter, since this would be an investment in the **evil deeds** (v. 11) of false teachers and give public approval: **For he that biddeth him God speed is partaker of his evil deeds**.

IV. Conclusion (vv. 12–13)

Verse 12. In John's day, paper was made from papyrus reeds, which were readily available and relatively inexpensive. Ink was made by mixing carbon, water, and gum or oil. Not surprising, then, is that the Greek word for **ink** (*melas*) also means "black." John wrote of his plans to come in person and enjoy the true fellowship that full joy adorns (see 1 John 1:4).

Verse 13. The children of thy elect sister greet thee may be taken literally to designate another Christian woman or figuratively to refer to another local church (see discussion on v. 1). It would be more likely for the sister of "the elect lady" (v. 1), rather than the children of the sister, to send greetings, unless, of course, a sister church and not a woman is in view, as suggested.

THE THIRD EPISTLE OF JOHN

INTRODUCTION

Author

The author is John the apostle. In the first verses of both 2 John and 3 John, the author identified himself as "the elder." Note other similarities: "love in the truth" (v. 1 of both letters), "walk in truth" (v. 4 of both letters), and the similar conclusions. See 1 John, Introduction: "Author"; and John, Introduction: "Author."

Date

The letter was probably written about the same time as 1 and 2 John (AD 85–95). See 1 John, Introduction: "Date."

Theme

Itinerant teachers sent out by John were rejected in one of the churches in the province of Asia by a dictatorial leader, Diotrephes, who even excommunicated members who showed hospitality to John's messengers. John wrote this letter to commend Gaius for supporting the teachers and, indirectly, to warn Diotrephes. See 2 John, Introduction: "Theme."

Outline

    I. Salutation (vv. 1–2)
   II. Commendation of Gaius (vv. 3–8)
  III. Condemnation of Diotrephes (vv. 9–10)
  IV. Exhortation to Gaius (v. 11)
   V. Example of Demetrius (v. 12)
  VI. Conclusion (vv. 13–14)

Bibliography

See 1 John, Introduction: "Bibliography."

EXPOSITION

I. Salutation (vv. 1–2)

Verse 1. John identified himself as **the elder** (Greek, *presbyteros*; see discussion on 2 John 1), pointing to his seniority and authority. **Gaius,** a common Roman name, was a Christian in one of the churches of the province of Asia. John called Gaius **wellbeloved,** the same Greek word as "beloved," one of John's favorite terms and used four times of Gaius (vv. 1, 2, 5, 11; see also 1 John 3:2, 21; 4:1, 7, 11). John further pronounced his high regard and affection for Gaius with the reinforcing explanation **whom I love in the truth** (see 2 John 1–2; discussion on John 1:14).

Verse 2. Beloved is a direct address, as if John was using Gaius's personal name. Such an address is indicative of their special spiritual fraternity as well as the obvious affection that comes from sentiment. John was paying a high compliment to Gaius. Note how the generosity of John's prayer for Gaius is measured by the generosity of Gaius's soul. John prayed (Greek, *euchomai*; **wish** or "pray") not only for Gaius's prosperity and good **health** in every area but also that his prayers would be answered with prosperity in proportion to the riches of his own **soul.** John clearly put a premium on the quality of Gaius's soul. It's as though John asked God to honor the honorable character of this beloved partner in ministry.

II. Commendation of Gaius (vv. 3–8)

Verse 3. John had **rejoiced greatly** (the same expression used in 2 John 4) over repeated reports from fellow believers that Gaius was a man of integrity: **the brethren ... testified of the truth that is in thee, even as thou walkest in the truth.** Gaius was a man who "practiced what he preached." In this respect, John's joy was probably given added dimension by the defections of others who had not adhered to the truth as had Gaius (see 1 John 2:19; 2 John 7–8).

Verse 4. John's identification of Gaius with **my children** indicates that he was one of John's spiritual children and numbered among the believers under his spiritual guidance. Nothing gave John greater joy than to hear they were **walk[ing] in truth,** as Gaius was (see discussions on 2 John 4–6).

Verses 5–7. John commended Gaius for his faithful hospitality and support of **the brethren, and ... strangers** (v. 5). It was customary for the early church to provide hospitality and support for traveling teachers and missionaries (see 2 John, Introduction: "Theme"; discussion on 2 John 10). The wording, however, is ambiguous. It may be that John had in mind specific brethren that Gaius had faithfully cared for, even though they were strangers to him (see v. 6). It may be that Gaius had gained a reputation for supporting not only "the brethren" but also "strangers." In either case, his hospitality had earned praise from those he had helped, for they had voiced their gratitude **before the church** (v. 6), which most likely refers to the church where John himself resided and connotes the testimonies of such travelers (see v. 3). Earlier, John noted the testimony to Gaius's "truth" (v. 3), here he noted their testimony to Gaius's **charity** (v. 6), or "love." In commending Gaius, John solicited his continued attention to the needs of such travelers, with the exhortation, **whom if thou bring forward on their journey after a godly sort, thou shalt do well.** John urged Gaius to send them onward with provisions that would befit their sacrifice in the service of the Lord. "Bring forward on their journey" translates one Greek word, *propempō*, meaning to "send on one's way" with the suitable means of travel in a manner worthy of God ("after a godly sort"). The basis of John's request was that these missionaries traveled **for his name's sake** (v. 7; see discussion on Acts 4:12). Today Orthodox Jews often address God by the title Ha-Shem ("the Name"). Here "name" probably encodes a reference to Jesus Christ (see Acts 5:41; 1 John 2:12; John 1:12; 3:18).

Verse 8. John included himself in what he described as an axiomatic consequence of supporting such "missionaries." **To receive** or take such as these into our care engages us in their work. In this way,

Christians become **fellowhelpers to the truth**, or mutually involved in working for the truth.

III. Condemnation of Diotrephes (vv. 9–10)

Verses 9–10. I wrote (v. 9) acknowledges a previous letter of the apostle that is now lost. The church (*hē ekklēsia*, not "the church" of v. 6) to which John had written was known to Gaius, if not the very church to which he belonged. It was the church wherein **Diotrephes … loveth to have the preeminence among them** (Greek, *philoprōteuō*), that is, "likes to be the leader" or "loves to be first." There is the hint that Diotrephes (*Dios + trephō* means "nourished by Zeus") had somehow suppressed the letter. He must have wielded a certain dictatorial power in the church since he was able to exclude people from the church fellowship (**forbiddeth them … and casteth them out**; v. 10). John said Diotrephes **receiveth us not** (v. 9); he had refused to recognize the authority of another. One may infer that Diotrephes feared that receiving them would jeopardize his self-promoted preeminence.

IV. Exhortation to Gaius (v. 11)

Verse 11. By inference, John admonished Gaius to reject the model of Diotrephes (**follow not**). The antidote in this case, or the prescription against any evil, was to model God (see Luke 6:27–35) and **doeth good**. The continual practice of good, not merely doing occasional good deeds, is characteristic of seeing God clearly. Diotrephes, on the other hand, had lost sight of God.

V. Example of Demetrius (v. 12)

Verse 12. John had the highest regard for **Demetrius**, unlike Diotrephes. By all accounts (the **good report of all men**) and by John's own description (**the truth itself**) and commendation (**we also bear record**), Demetrius, like Gaius, was a man of integrity and could be trusted. His character made him a worthy ally in the truth and its ministry.

The admonition to Gaius (v. 11), sandwiched as it is between the contrast of Diotrephes (vv. 9–10) and Demetrius (v. 12), conveys the importance of choosing selfless leaders of proven character who will be committed to doing the good that one sees in God. Taken together, verses 9–12 suggest that John was alerting Gaius to behavior on the part of Diotrephes that disqualified him and warranted his replacement with one more highly qualified to exercise such influence: Demetrius. If so, Gaius was the leader in this church, and his own commitment to spiritual principles and their practice was being undermined by one who was not like-minded. The sensitivity of such matters brings John's closing into focus.

VI. Conclusion (vv. 13–14)

Verses 13. John clearly would have preferred to discuss the implications of this letter in person. Indeed, the tactics of Diotrephes may have precluded giving away too much in **ink and pen** (see 2 John 12 and discussion). A **face to face** visit was not far behind the arrival of this letter.

Verses 14. Peace be to thee is often a benedictory pronouncement (see discussions on John 14:27; 20:19; Gal. 1:3; Eph. 1:2). If the internecine tensions related to Diotrephes are in view, the words may amount to a prayer or wish bearing pointed comfort. "Peace be to thee" is then matched by the greetings of friends and the enumerated allies of good Gaius, who was to **Greet the friends by name**.

INTRODUCTION

Author

The author identified himself as Jude (v. 1), which is another form of the Hebrew name Judah (Greek "Judas"), a common name among the Jews. Of those so named in the New Testament, the ones most likely to be the author of this letter are: (1) Judas the apostle (see Luke 6:16; Acts 1:13) — not Judas Iscariot — and (2) Judas the brother of the Lord (see Matt. 13:55; Mark 6:3). The latter is more likely. For example, the author did not claim to be an apostle and even seems to have separated himself from the apostles (see v. 17). Furthermore, he described himself as a "brother of James" (v. 1). Ordinarily, a person in Jude's day would have described himself as someone's son rather than as someone's brother. The reason for the exception here may have been James's prominence in the church at Jerusalem (see James, Introduction: "Author"). In the first-century church, only the James who was the brother of Jesus and president of the Jerusalem church would likely have had the status to be identified as Jude identified him. James is simply named without further detail; his name alone is authoritative.

The early church writer Hegesippus related the story of Jude's two grandsons who were examined by the Roman emperor Domitian because of their lineage to the house of David. Upon questioning them, Domitian (who reigned AD 81–96) learned that the men, of limited means, awaited the coming kingdom of Christ. The emperor dismissed them as unworthy of further attention and halted the persecution of the church that he had instigated. Jude's grandsons, because of their testimony and because their ancestry could be traced to Jesus' family, became church leaders (Eusebius *Ecclesiastical History* 3.19–20).

Although neither Jude nor James described himself as a brother of the Lord, others did not hesitate to speak of them in this way (see Matt. 13:55; John 7:3–10; Acts 1:14; 1 Cor. 9:5; Gal. 1:19). Apparently, they themselves did not ask to be heard because of the special privilege they had as members of the household of Joseph and Mary.

Possible references to the letter of Jude or quotations from it are found at a very early date, for example, in Clement of Rome (ca. AD 96), Clement of Alexandria (155–215), Tertullian (150–222), and Origen (185–253) accepted it; Jude was included in the Muratorian Canon (ca. 170) and was accepted by Athanasius (298–373) and by the Council of

Carthage (397). Eusebius (265–340) listed the letter among the questioned books, though he recognized that many considered it as from Jude.

According to Jerome and Didymus, some did not accept the letter as canonical because of its use of pseudepigraphal literature (see vv. 9, 14). Sound judgment has recognized that an author, writing under inspiration, may legitimately make use of extracanonical literature—whether for illustrative purposes or for appropriation of historically reliable or otherwise acceptable material—and such use does not necessarily endorse that literature as inspired. Paul made use of such material; he utilized heathen poets in speaking to the Athenians (Acts 17:28), and he cited a rabbinic midrash (a scriptural exposition) on the rock that gave water to Israel in the wilderness (1 Cor. 10:4). Paul apparently referred to some noncanonical source for the names of Pharaoh's magicians, Jannes and Jambres, who opposed Moses (2 Tim. 3:8). Under the influence of the Spirit, the church came to the conviction that the authority of God stands behind the letter of Jude. The fact that the letter was questioned and tested but was nonetheless finally accepted by the churches indicates the strength of its claims to authenticity.

Date

Nothing in the letter requires a date beyond the lifetime of Jude the brother of the Lord. Jude appears to have combated an incipient Gnosticism that, rather than featuring asceticism as in Colossians, promoted antinomianism—moral freedom that turns liberty from the law into license to sin. The error that the author combated was not the fully developed heretical system of second-century Gnosticism, although the false teachers mentioned in Jude and 2 Peter may well have been its forerunners (see 2 Peter, Introduction: "Date"). Moreover, nothing in the letter requires a date after the time of the apostles, as some have argued. It may even be that Jude's readers had heard some of the apostles speak (see vv. 17–18). Likewise, the use of the word "faith" in the objective sense of the body of truth believed (v. 3) does not require a late dating of the letter. It was used in such a sense as early as Galatians 1:23.

The question of the relationship between Jude and 2 Peter has a bearing on the date of Jude. If 2 Peter makes use of Jude—a commonly accepted view (see 2 Peter, Introduction: "The Relationship of 2 Peter and Jude")—then Jude is to be dated prior to 2 Peter, before circa AD 64–67. Otherwise, a date as late as circa 80 would be possible. Presumably, Jude was dead by the time his grandsons were brought before Domitian, since the accusations were only against the grandsons, not the father or grandfather. There is no clear idea when Jude died, so the latest possible date for the writing of his letter cannot be determined.

Recipients

The description of those to whom Jude addressed his letter is very general (see v. 1). It could apply to Jewish Christians, Gentile Christians, or both. The addressees' location is not indicated. Although 2 Peter 2 and Jude 4–18 appear to describe similar situations, it should not be assumed that they were both written to the same people. The kind of heresy depicted in these two passages was widespread (see "Date," above). If Jude were in his homeland when he wrote this letter, his audience may have been house churches throughout Israel. That is not certain, however. Jude probably addressed house churches whose location cannot be determined. Jude's letter would have been read and heard by them during their church meetings.

Theme and Theological Message

Although Jude was very eager to write to his readers about salvation, he felt that he must instead warn them about certain immoral men circulating among them who were perverting the grace of God (v. 4). These men may be described as false teachers since they ridiculed the truth and spoke arrogantly and ignorantly (vv. 10, 16, 18). They were also infiltrators (v. 4), dreamers (v. 8), complainers (v. 16), mockers (v. 18), and agitators or sectarians (v. 19). Apparently, these false teachers were trying to convince believers that being saved by grace gave them license to sin since their sins would no longer be held against them. Jude thought it imperative that his readers be on guard against such men and prepared to oppose the infiltrators' perverted teaching. He exhorted his congregations to contend for the truth about God's saving grace.

Literary Features

Jude exhibits an acquaintance with Greco-Roman rhetorical conventions regarding the arrangement of a discourse. The letter is effectively structured with the following principal divisions: an *exordium* (vv. 1–3), or introduction, in which the rhetor prepares the audience for the argument to follow; a *narration* (v. 4) of the facts, which lays out the essence of the argument; the *proof* (vv. 5–16), constituting the rhetor's attempt to persuade the audience of the soundness of his case; and the peroration, or *conclusion* (vv. 17–23), in which the argument is summed up and exhortation is given.

Outline

    I. Exordium (vv. 1–3)
   II. Narration: The Ungodly (v. 4)
  III. Proof: The Ungodly and Their Doom (vv. 5–16)
        A. First Proof (vv. 5–10)
            1. Three Historical Examples (vv. 5–7)
                a. The People of Israel in the Wilderness (v. 5)
                b. Rebellious Angels (v. 6)
                c. Sodom and Gomorrah (v. 7)
            2. Comparison with the False Teachers (v. 8)
            3. The Example of Michael and the False Teachers (vv. 9–10)
        B. Second Proof (vv. 11–13)
            1. Prophecy of Woe (v. 11)
            2. The Application of the Prophecy to the False Teachers (vv. 12–13)
        C. Third Proof (vv. 14–16)
            1. The Prophecy of Enoch (vv. 14–15)
            2. The Application of the Prophecy to the False Teachers (v. 16)
   IV. Conclusion (vv. 17–25)
        A. Repetition: The Apostolic Prophecy regarding Sensual Mockers (vv. 17–19)

B. Emotional Appeal: Christian Endurance and Ministry to the Wayward
(vv. 20–23)
1. Christian Endurance (vv. 20–21)
2. Ministry to the Wayward (vv. 22–23)
C. Doxology (vv. 24–25)

Select Bibliography

Barclay, William. *The Letters of John and Jude*. Rev. ed. The Daily Study Bible. Philadelphia: Westminster, 1976.

Bauckham, Richard J. *2 Peter and Jude*. Word Biblical Commentary 50. Waco, TX: Word, 1983.

Bruce, F. F. "Jude, Epistle of." In *New Bible Dictionary*, 3rd ed., edited by D. R. W. Wood, I. Howard Marshall, A. R. Millard, J. I. Packer, and D. J. Wiseman, 626. Downers Grove, IL: InterVarsity, 1996.

Green, Michael. *The Second Epistle General of Peter and the General Epistle of Jude: An Introduction and Commentary*. 2nd ed. Tyndale New Testament Commentaries 18. Grand Rapids, MI: Eerdmans, 1987.

Hillyer, Norman. *1 and 2 Peter, Jude*. New International Biblical Commentary 16. Peabody, MA: Hendrickson, 1992.

Kelly, J. N. D. *A Commentary on the Epistles of Peter and of Jude*. Harper's New Testament Commentaries. New York: Harper & Row, 1969.

Moo, Douglas J. *2 Peter and Jude*. The NIV Application Commentary. Grand Rapids, MI: Zondervan, 1996.

EXPOSITION

I. Exordium (vv. 1–3)

Verse 1. Jude was fond of triplets; there are twenty of them in the letter. Jude's first triplet offers a threefold description of himself. The author identified himself as **Jude**, who, although he was the Lord's own half brother, was nevertheless **the servant** ("slave," NLT) **of Jesus Christ**. Such self-effacement would have raised Jude's standing in the minds of his audience and gave them an example of humility. God's servants use any privileges they might have, not for promoting themselves, but only for promoting Jesus Christ. Furthermore, the author identified himself as **brother of James**. Although he was humble, Jude wanted his hearers to know that his letter was written with authority to speak for Christ. Jude's relationship with James, leader of the Jerusalem church, lent his epistle that authority.

Another triad describes the readers' own privileged identity. First, they were **sanctified by God the Father**. The readers were set apart for God's holy purposes and designs. Those righteous and constructive designs stood in opposition to the behavior of the false teachers in Jude's churches, behavior that was destructive of the individual and of the church community. Some manuscripts have "loved by God the Father" (e.g., NIV) here. Second, the readers were **preserved in Jesus Christ**. In any discussion of the question of the eternal security (or perseverance) of the saints, this concept must be considered. Jude regarded Christ's people as "kept by" (NIV) or "kept for" (NASB) Christ; their righteous standing with Him was maintained not by their own efforts but only by His power, and for His glory. The verb, as in the case of "sanctified," is in the perfect tense and thus denotes a condition that is secure. Third, the readers were **called**. Jude did not specify to what the addressees were called, but in Romans 1:7 and 1 Corinthians 1:2, Paul affirmed that the congregations in Rome and Corinth are "called to be saints." Jude may have understood God's call similarly. The word "saints" (holy people) is related to "sanctified." God not only calls His people to be holy, but He gives them the power to do so.

Verse 2. Another triad follows as the formal greeting of the letter, but the significance of the terms ought not to be missed. Jude's prayer was that the recipients of the letter would continue to experience God's **mercy** (His tender and compassionate care and leading), **peace** (complete well-being and good order in terms of health, relationships, and walk with God), and **love** (here the word is *agapē*, the completely selfless and sacrificial love that God has showered on us in Christ). Jude imagined that these graces can **be multiplied** in believers' lives. Failure to live in ways that accord with these virtues often causes Christians to lack their increase, and prayerlessness often causes them to miss the opportunity to join as partners with God as He seeks to develop these graces in the lives of His children.

Verse 3. Jude's original intention was to write a general treatment of the doctrine of **salvation**, perhaps dealing with such subjects as man's sin and guilt, God's love and grace, the forgiveness of sins, and the changed lifestyle that follows new birth. Instead, Jude felt compelled to **exhort** his audience that they **should earnestly contend for the faith**. Jude exhibited the mark of the true pastor, who is a watchman (see Ezek. 3:17–19; Acts 20:28–30) over the people of God and warns them of danger to come. The current postmodern mood tends to dispute the notion that there is objective truth in the religious sphere. The proclamation and defense of the teaching of Scripture as revealed truth are thus seen by many as arrogant and exclusive. For Jude, however, there existed a body of truth divinely revealed to humanity: "the faith." The noun here designates, not the act of trust, but that which is commonly believed and adhered to as truth by believers.

The Christian faith has certain characteristics. (1) It was **delivered**. The verb, *paradidōmi*, signifies the handing down of authorized (apostolic) tradition (see 1 Cor. 15:1–3). The New Testament embodies in written form the original teaching of the apostles and thus goes back to Christ Himself. (2) That teaching, or "faith," **was once** delivered. The unchanging core of Christian teaching must be interpreted afresh for each culture and generation, and the interpretation may take new forms and expressions. The core, however, does not change and must not be replaced by any "new revelation." The test by which any doctrine or practice must be examined is, "Does it coincide with the apostolic teaching in the New Testament?" (3) The faith was once delivered **unto the saints**; that is, truth is the property of not just one individual but of the entire church. The church, although under the authority of the apostolic tradition, is nevertheless its guardian and messenger. Some individuals believe they can explore and understand God's truth adequately on their own. Since truth is delivered to all God's people, only in community can God's word be properly studied, understood, and lived out. (4) Christians must **earnestly contend for the faith**. The verb that Jude used is *epagōnizomai* and has the idea of "to join the struggle in defence of" (NEB) or "to fight hard for" (NJB). The word is an athletic metaphor, and the contest is to be carried on continually (signified by the present tense). The English word "agony" is related to this word. Jude was not suggesting, however, that Christian should be only on the defensive; they must also be on the offensive in the preaching of the gospel, the announcement of Christ's supremacy and victory, and the positive influence of godly living (see Phil. 1:27–30). Jude's exhortations in verses 20–23 are part of what contending for the faith means.

II. Narration: The Ungodly (v. 4)

Verse 4. In the narration, Jude stated his main thought (developed and substantiated in the proof, vv. 5–16): false teachers, by living according to their own desires, contradict their Christian profession and deny the Lord Himself. Such teachers pose a threat to the church from within and are justly condemned.

The word **For** introduces the reason Jude felt impelled to change the subject of his letter. Those who **crept in unawares** could haved included women as well as men. The Greek word translated **men**, *anthrōpoi*, does not designate gender. Jude's three examples in verse 11, however, were all of men, which may indicate that the infiltrators were men. At any rate, they were **ungodly**. The verb (*pareisdyō*; only here in the New Testament) that Jude used to describe their infiltration is most colorful. It refers to someone sneaking in through a side door, to a spy slipping into the country, and to a lawyer's clever and smooth persuasion of a jury. The NLT vividly captures the idea: "some godless people have wormed their way in among you." The threat of false teachers not only arises outside the church but also within it.

The troublesome individuals **were before of old ordained to this condemnation**. "Before of old" may refer to Old Testament denunciations of ungodly men or to Enoch's prophecy (see vv. 14–15). Jude may have meant that judgment had long been about to fall on them because of their sin (see 2 Peter 2:3, which may be a clarification of this clause). Perhaps the phrase refers to the many and various punishments of sin (recorded in the Old Testament and extrabiblical literature) that stand as prophetic precedents indicating God's response to sin.

The ungodliness of the false teachers was constituted by two actions. (1) By **turning the grace of our God into lasciviousness** ("change the grace of our God into a license for immorality," NIV), they assumed that salvation by grace gave them the right to sin without restraint, either because God in His grace would freely forgive all their sins, or because sin, by contrast, magnifies the grace of God (see Rom. 5:20; 6:1). (2) The false teachers are also described as **denying the only Lord God, and our Lord Jesus Christ** (some manuscripts omit "God"; thus, "deny our only Master and Lord, Jesus Christ," NASB). The lifestyle of the false teachers effectively contradicted any claim that they were in union with Jesus Christ. By doing these same things, many Christians

unwittingly become "false teachers." A flippant attitude toward sin that says, "I'll go ahead and sin; after all, God will forgive me," outrageously abuses the grace of God. Living for self-gratification rather than for God's honor in purity and holiness (see v. 1) effectively invalidates any verbal testimony that a Christian might make. The name of Jesus Christ is brought into disrepute because often actions speak louder than words to the unbeliever.

III. Proof: The Ungodly and Their Doom (vv. 5–16)

A. First Proof (vv. 5–10)

1. Three Historical Examples (vv. 5–7)

a. The People of Israel in the Wilderness (v. 5)

Verse 5. The first example in a triplet of sinners that Jude presented in the proof section of the letter is one with which the audience was undoubtedly familiar (**ye once knew this**). Jude presented this and the other two examples as substantiation of his belief that the false teachers would be condemned for their unrighteous actions. **The Lord ... saved the people out of the land of Egypt** in the exodus but then **destroyed them that believed not**. The people of Israel did not believe that God would give them the land of Canaan; consequently, all unbelieving adults died in the desert without entering the Promised Land. Only Joshua and Caleb realized the promise (see Num. 14:1–45; Deut. 9:23). Disbelief led to disobedience, and disobedience led to destruction. The passage does not concern the eternal destiny of the disobedient but rather the temporal punishment inflicted by the Lord. Jude intended to show that those who dishonor the One who has given them divine benefits will meet with a serious and proper riposte issued by that same One to preserve His honor.

b. Rebellious Angels (v. 6)

Verse 6. The next example of punishment of the disobedient is that of **the angels** who abandoned **their first estate**, or **habitation**, which probably refers to "their positions of authority" (NIV). God had assigned differing areas of responsibility and authority to each of the angels (see Dan. 10:20–21, where the various princes may be angels assigned to various nations). Some of these angels refused to maintain their assignments and thus became the Devil and his angels (see Matt. 25:41). "Habitation" may refer to a specific location; angels apparently were assigned specific locations as well as responsibilities. Some assume that they left the heavenly realm and came to earth. The pride of the angels who instigated a civil war in heaven, which led to their expulsion, may have been in Jude's mind here. If the pride of angels is subject to the divine **judgment of the great** (i.e., the last) **day**, how much more so the arrogance of the false teachers.

Jude's language is not necessarily to be taken literally. **Everlasting chains** is a graphic image conveying the fact that the angels' fate is certainly that of judgment; there will be no escaping it. **Darkness** signifies the separation from the presence of God and from the life of heaven that they have experienced because of their rebellion. The language of Jude echoes that of the pseudepigraphal book *1 Enoch*, a composite work whose parts were composed during the second and first centuries BC. The work is valuable in what it reveals regarding pre-Christian Jewish theology. Evidently, Jude's readers were aware of it—echoes of it are in verses 6, 14–15—and Jude used the work for illustrative purposes. According to *1 Enoch*, recalcitrant angels, who abandoned their heavenly domain through rebellion, are chained as they await their final judgment (see, e.g., *1 Enoch* 10:5–6; 12:4).

c. Sodom and Gomorrah (v. 7)

Verse 7. The phrase **Even as** does not mean that the sin of **Sodom and Gomorrha** was necessarily the same as that of the angels or vice versa. Jude used this phrase to introduce the third illustration of God's certain punishment of the unrighteous, who will be consigned to eternal punishment on judgment day. The specific trespasses to which Jude was referring, however, are debated. In the construction, **giving themselves over to fornication, and going after strange flesh**, was Jude referring to two sins ("fornication" and "going after strange flesh") or just

one ("going after strange flesh" being an elaboration or instance of "fornication")? Jude was probably referring to one sin, fornication, and the pursuit of "strange flesh" is an instance of an ongoing practice of fornication. The background to Jude's reference is Genesis 19. When the angelic visitors who arrived in Sodom found lodging with Lot, the men of the city cried out to him, "Where are the men who came to you tonight? Bring them out to us so that we can have sex with them" (Gen. 19:5 NIV). The Sodomites were **set forth for an example, suffering the vengeance of eternal fire**. God destroyed Sodom and Gomorrah by pouring out "brimstone and fire" (Gen. 19:24), a foretaste of the eternal fire that is to come. The false teachers would face the same judgment as the consequence of their libertine ways.

2. Comparison with the False Teachers (v. 8)

Verse 8. Jude now turned his attention to the impurity of the false teachers that was comparable (**Likewise**) to the unrighteousness of unbelieving Israel (v. 5), the fallen angels (v. 6), and the people of Sodom and its environs (v. 7). The sectarians are described as **these filthy dreamers**. This term (*houtoi enypniazomenoi*; lit., "these dreamers," NRSV), however, may not refer to those who dream erotically or to those who are out of touch with truth and reality because of their passion but may instead refer to those who claim to have ecstatic visionary experiences. Thus, the NLT rendering is probably accurate: "these false teachers, who claim authority from their dreams."

In another of his triads, Jude delineated the corrupt character of the false teachers threatening the church. (1) They **defile the flesh** by their immoral intentions and actions. As God's creation, the material body in itself is good. The false teachers had abused and misused it for their own selfish purposes and had thus turned the body and its members into an instrument of unrighteousness (see Rom. 6:13). Thus, they "pollute their own bodies" (NIV). The same Greek word for "flesh" (*sarx*) appears in both verses 7 and 8 and links the thought of these verses. Jude saw some correspondence between the sexual immorality of Sodom and Gomorrah and that of the false teachers. (2) The false teachers also **despise dominion** ("reject authority," NRSV) and (3) **speak evil of dignities** (lit., "abuse the Glories," NJB). If the dissenters had "an authority problem" in the church, it was first toward God and His heavenly agents.

3. The Example of Michael and the False Teachers (vv. 9–10)

Verse 9. The word for "speak evil of" in verse 8 is *blasphēmeō* and could refer to abusive speech against God, angels, or humans. The word is a link between verse 8 and verses 9–10 since it or its verbal form appears in all three verses. The false teachers markedly displayed their arrogance in their failure to recognize their human frailty and limitations when they slandered celestial beings. Not even **Michael the archangel** dared to bring **a railing accusation** (lit., "judgment of blasphemy," *krisis blasphēmias*) against **the devil**, but the intruders considered themselves to have a stature that allowed them to do so.

Michael is the only archangel mentioned by name in the New Testament (here and in Rev. 12:7). He may also be the unnamed archangel of 1 Thessalonians 4:16. In the Old Testament, he is the guardian of Israel (see Dan. 10:13, 21). The title "archangel" suggests an angelic hierarchy like that described in the pseudepigraphal book *1 Enoch*, in which seven archangels appear. In the New Testament, however, the existence of such a hierarchy is not clearly delineated (but see Eph. 1:21; 6:12; Col. 2:15; 1 Peter 3:22).

Michael and the Devil **disputed about the body of Moses**, a curious reference that is not found in canonical Scripture. The incident is from the pseudepigraphal *Assumption of Moses* (according to the church fathers Origen, Clement, and Didymus), a work that survives only fragmentally and that is missing the portion that Jude utilized. Other New Testament quotations from, or allusions to, nonbiblical works include Paul's quotations of Aratus (Acts 17:28), Menander (1 Cor. 15:33), and Epimenides (Titus 1:12). Such usage in no way suggests that the quotations, or the books from which they were

taken, were divinely inspired. It only means that the biblical author found the quotations to be a helpful confirmation, clarification, or illustration.

Verse 10. The false teachers, when they **speak evil** (*blasphēmeō*) of authorities, betrayed their ignorance of those things about which they haughtily spoke. Those things that they did know, of which they presumed to have expertise, were things that only **brute beasts** ("irrational animals," NRSV) experience. Jude probably was referring to immoral and seditious behaviors. By these things, the teachers **corrupt themselves**. The deceptiveness of sin is such that those who give themselves over to it are destroyed by it. A time comes when one, having resisted the voice of God, can no longer hear or give heed to that voice. The one who has resisted then is engulfed in the power of the passions and becomes more and more enslaved by them.

B. Second Proof (vv. 11–13)

1. Prophecy of Woe (v. 11)

Verse 11. Jude's second proof further established the sinfulness of the false teachers and the certainty of their condemnation. By the use of another triplet of negative examples, Jude encouraged a sense of revulsion among his readers toward the sectarians. Their association with notorious sinners from Israel's history inclined Jude's audience toward behavior that was opposite that of the sinners.

In the vein of an Old Testament prophet, Jude cast his words in the form of a woe oracle, a type of prophetic speech that (1) pronounces distress, (2) gives a reason for the distress, and (3) predicts the doom that is to follow (see, e.g., the string of woe oracles in Hab. 2:6–20). In Jude 11, each of the three elements of a typical woe oracle is present.

Pronouncement of Distress. With the exclamation **Woe unto them!** Jude announced the distress to come upon the false teachers, the judgment already foretold in verse 4. "Woe" was the cry of the ancient Israelites when they faced catastrophe or when they were mourning the dead.

Reason for the Distress. Jude gave the reason for the distress by identifying transgressions of the three

Old Testament sinners — transgressions that the false teachers threatening Jude's audience had committed. **Cain** is the Bible's first murderer (Gen. 4:1 – 16); his hostility arose from envy and hatred (see 1 John 3:12, 15). **The error of Balaam for reward** is consuming greed for money, prestige, or any kind of selfish advantage. Balaam refused to curse Israel in the biblical account, despite Balak's urging to do so (see Num. 22:15 – 35). In intertestamental literature, Balaam did curse Israel, enticing Balak to prompt Israel to sin (see Num. 31:16). Jude said that the false teachers **ran greedily** in the footsteps of Balaam ("abandon themselves to Balaam's error for the sake of gain," NRSV). They also imitated **the gainsaying of Core** ("Korah's rebellion," NIV). Korah was remarkable for his rebelliousness against Moses (see Num. 16:1 – 50). By complaining that Moses had no right to be in charge of the people of Israel (Num. 16:3), Korah treated the Lord with contempt (Num. 16:30). Korah, with some 250 other mutineers, was swallowed up alive by the earth. Jude may have been suggesting that the false teachers of his day were rebelling against church leadership (see v. 8).

Prediction of Doom. The ruin that resulted from the wicked deeds of the infamous trio of verse 11 is only specifically mentioned in relation to Korah, but it applies equally to all. The false teachers are said to have **perished**. The judgment of the agitators was so certain that Jude, using the aorist tense, spoke as if it had already taken place: "they have been destroyed" (NIV).

2. The Application of the Prophecy to the False Teachers (vv. 12 – 13)

Verses 12 – 13. Jude heaped fault upon fault in his description of the false teachers, an effective rhetorical device designed to build revulsion in the audience against the godless infiltrators. The vivid mental pictures — six graphic metaphors in all — collectively served as a powerful denunciation of the false teachers and warned Jude's readers against falling into their vile ways.

(1) Jude said the false teachers were **spots in your feasts of charity** (v. 12; "a blot on your love-feasts,"

NEB). He consistently portrayed his opponents as defiled or polluted (see especially v. 23), and the faith of others had been (or was in danger of being) shipwrecked by coming into contact with the heretics. Since 2 Peter 2:13, a passage similar to Jude 12, clearly has "spots they are and blemishes" (*spiloi kai mōmoi*), the KJV translation is best.

(2) The heretics were false shepherds (see Ezek. 34:2, 8 – 10). Jude said, **they feast with you, feeding themselves without fear** (v. 12). "Feeding" could be translated "shepherding"; thus, the NIV has "shepherds who feed only themselves." The false teachers presented themselves as leaders but did not care for their sheep.

(3) Of the infiltrators, Jude could say, **clouds they are without water** (v. 12). They promised spiritual refreshment — encouragement, sound teaching, godly example — but were empty and dry (see Prov. 25:14). Being **carried about of winds**, these teachers were themselves dupes for the latest doctrinal fad that came around (see Eph. 4:14).

(4) The metaphor of **trees whose fruit withereth** (v. 12) is closely associated with the previous metaphor of waterless clouds. In agrarian Israel, people continually watched for signs of rain and for indications of a bountiful harvest. Clouds without rain and trees that failed to produce a crop were not just a disappointment but meant severe hardship or even famine in a subsistence economy. "Whose fruit withereth" translates *phthinopōrina*, a word derived from two Greek words meaning "to waste away" and "autumn." The NIV has "autumn trees" since the term describes trees whose branches are bare.

The uselessness of the false teachers is emphasized by the repetitive **without fruit** (v. 12; see Matt 7:16 – 20) and the stunning picture of trees **plucked up by the roots**, possible only by an extraordinarily mighty force. "Uprooting" is a metaphor of God's judgment (see Jer. 1:10). **Twice dead** may mean that the trees were dead because they were fruitless and because they were rootless. The teachers had forsaken the state of being rooted in Christ (see Col. 2:7) and the apostolic teaching of the faith that Jude sought to defend (see v. 3).

(5) **Raging** ("fierce," NEB; "wild," NIV) **waves of the sea** (v. 13) suggests both the fury of the infiltrators' manner (unrestrainedly boisterous and wrathful) and their instability. The latter feature is also denoted by the metaphors of the waterless clouds and uprooted trees. As wind-tossed waves constantly churn up rubbish, so these apostates continually stirred up moral filth. That is, they were **foaming out their own shame**. A similar image appears in Isaiah (57:20) and is echoed in the Dead Sea Scrolls (1QH 2:2–13, 27–28; 6:23; 8:15).

(6) Jude described the antagonists as **wandering stars** (v. 13), once again bringing the notion of their instability to the fore. They had strayed from the true course, the "orbit," circumscribed by correct doctrine and decency. Jude may have based the metaphor on revolutions of the planets, whose movements appear to be irregular in comparison to the relatively fixed positions of stars, or he may have been referring to shooting stars. The false teachers, then, resembled meteors — blazing for a short time but quickly fading as they burn up in the earth's atmosphere — or comets, whose splendor is remarkable but short-lived. As shooting stars appear in the sky only to fly off into eternal oblivion, so these false teachers are destined for the darkness of eternal hell.

C. Third Proof (vv. 14–16)

1. The Prophecy of Enoch (vv. 14–15)

Verses 14–15. To further establish the certainty of judgment that the false teachers would face, Jude cited *1 Enoch* 1:9. The purported author of Jude's source is **Enoch ... the seventh from Adam** (v. 14). This Enoch is not the Enoch in the line of Cain (see Gen. 4:17) but the one in the line of Seth (see Gen. 5:18–24; 1 Chron. 1:1–3). He was seventh if Adam is counted as the first. According to Genesis 5:23, Enoch lived 365 years, during which time he became the father of Methuselah (Gen. 5:22). The account notes Enoch's godliness ("Enoch walked with God," Gen. 5:22) and his mysterious assumption to heaven ("and he was not; for God took him," Gen. 5:24). The work of *1 Enoch* — a composite, well-respected writing in New Testament times — dates from the second and first centuries BC. The author certainly was not the historical Enoch of Genesis 5, descendant of Seth. The ascription of authorship to this godly Old Testament person attempts to lend authority to the book. The phenomenon by which authorship is ascribed to someone who did not write the work is *pseudonymity*, a literary practice of the ancient world. The word **prophesied** need not imply that Jude regarded *1 Enoch* as inspired Scripture. The verb may function, not in the sense of supernaturally revealing new truth, but merely in the sense of speaking things about the future that were already known (see Dan. 7:9–14; Zech. 14:1–5). That *1 Enoch* is not canonical does not mean that it contains no truth. The work had illustrative value for Jude, perhaps because his audience held it in high esteem.

The quotation from *1 Enoch* serves to highlight the inevitability of judgment on the heretics and the extraordinary ungodliness that incurs that judgment. With the phrase **the Lord cometh** (v. 14), Jude modified the quotation to refer to Christ's second coming and to His judgment of the wicked (see 2 Thess. 1:6–10). He will be accompanied by **ten thousands of his saints**, probably angels (lit., "holy ones," NRSV). No one can escape such a massive heavenly army and its retributive purpose. The divine **judgment** (v. 15) serves at the same time to **convince** the **ungodly sinners** ("to sentence the godless," NJB). A striking feature of verse 15 is the fourfold use of "ungodly" in the KJV. This thunderous repetition denotes the depravity of the sinners and thus the justice of the punishment they will undergo. The sins of the false teachers here recall the description of them as ungodly, immoral in behavior and hostile in speech, in verse 4.

2. The Application of the Prophecy to the False Teachers (v. 16)

Verse 16. Jude identified five types of ungodly people, who therefore were destined for the judgment prophesied by Enoch (see vv. 14–15). The word **These** indicates that Jude was referring to the ungodly men he first mentioned in verse 4 and subsequently referred to repeatedly as "these" (vv. 8, 10, 12, 14, 19). These men, the libertine false teachers who perverted the grace of God, were to be avoided, and their misdeeds were not to be imitated.

(1) **Murmurers** ("grumblers," NIV) is a picturesque noun (*gongystēs*) that is onomatopoetic (i.e., it sounds like that for which it stands). It is associated with Israel's griping in the wilderness (see Exod. 16:2, 7–9), particularly at Kadesh (see v. 5; Num. 14:2, 27, 29, 36) and in the context of Korah's rebellion (see v. 11; Num. 16:11).

(2) **Complainers** (*mempsimoiros*; "faultfinders," NIV; "malcontents," NRSV; "bellyachers," MSG; "ever bemoaning their lot," Weymouth) is also onomatopoetic. The term denotes the whispering to oneself that a dissatisfied undercurrent of discontent produces. It is practically synonymous with "murmurers," and could even be construed in the Greek as an adjective modifying it ("faultfinding grumblers").

(3) The infiltrators were **walking after their own lusts** (v. 16), inattentive to the Lord and the sheep for whom they supposedly cared. They were "trying all the time to mould life according to their own desires" (Phillips).

(4) **Their mouth speaketh great swelling words**, Jude said, perhaps in reference to their bombastic teaching or preaching style that was intended to win admiration. Volume, pomposity, and haughtiness masked the antagonists' hypocrisy, heresy, and sensuality. In the end, they were "loudmouthed braggarts" (NLT).

(5) The characteristic of **having men's persons in admiration** (lit., "marveling faces") **because of advantage** is helpfully rendered "flattering people to their own advantage" in the NRSV. Whether the advantage sought is money, material gifts, praise, allegiance, recognition, identification with a particular social class, or sexual favors, leaders prove false when they use others for personal gain. James 2:1–13 forbids showing favoritism to the rich. In that passage, James used terms that are cognate (verbally related) to Jude's language (see James 2:1, 9: "[have] respect of persons"; "court favour," NEB; "show favoritism," NIV).

IV. Conclusion (vv. 17–25)

A. Repetition: The Apostolic Prophecy regarding Sensual Mockers (vv. 17–19)

Verse 17. In a rhetorical discourse, the conclusion typically reviews the preceding discussion and seeks to make a further emotional appeal to the audience. Jude successfully carried out both functions in verses 17–25, and both review and appeal are contained in verse 17. The exhortation **remember ye the words** recalls "the faith which was once delivered unto the saints" (v. 3) and the biblical instruction that follows (vv. 5–7, 11). This was a central part of the proclamation and teaching of **the apostles. Beloved** is a term that arouses positive pathos among the hearers. They knew that Jude's warnings and instructions originated in his love for them.

Verse 18. The apostles had predicted the advent of **mockers in the last time** (see Acts 20:29; 1 Tim. 4:1; 2 Tim. 3:1–5), so the believers were not to be surprised by the coming of these godless men, and any alarms among the congregations were quelled. The Greek for **they told you** indicates that the apostles continually or repeatedly warned that such godless apostates would come (see Matt. 24:4–5, 10–12; Acts 20:28–30; 2 Peter 2:1–3). Since the mockers should **walk after their own ungodly lusts** (see 2 Peter 3:3), the church needed to adopt safeguards against their corrupting influence. "Should walk" is simply descriptive, not predetermined; the NJB has "who follow nothing but their own godless desires." Jude did not identify the object of the scoffers' ridicule. In 2 Peter 3:4, however, they sneered, "Where is the promise of his coming?" Perhaps that was the substance of the mocking in Jude's case as well. Hostility against the gospel and its claims (including Christ's coming, which spells judgment) sometimes is directly correlated with immoral behavior.

Verse 19. The triad of vices characterizing the false teachers confirmed the hearers' revulsion toward them. (1) Divisiveness was a characteristic of the intruders. Jude called them **they who separate themselves**. The phrase may indicate that the false teachers presented themselves as a spiritual elite who were more entitled to honor in the church than those who (they believed) were not as spiritual as they. (2) The mockers were **sensual** ("follow mere natural instincts," NIV). If the intruders presented themselves as a Gnostic elite, Jude's word, *psychikoi*, is ironic since the elite used that word to describe the uninitiated. The Gnostics claimed to be a privileged elite, the spiritual ones, but Jude denied that they even possessed the Spirit. (3) Thus, the third characteristic of the mockers was **having not the Spirit** (Greek, *pneuma*). The noun can refer to God's Spirit or the human spirit. The KJV capitalizes "Spirit" since, in all likelihood, God's Spirit is the referent of *pneuma*, not the human spirit (see also ASV, ESV, NASB, NIV, NLT, NRSV). The third condition gave rise to the second: "They live by natural instinct because they do not have God's Spirit living in them" (NLT). The three terms in the triad are listed successively in Greek with no clear linkage between them.

B. Emotional Appeal: Christian Endurance and Ministry to the Wayward (vv. 20–23)

1. Christian Endurance (vv. 20–21)

Verses 20–21. The address **But ye, beloved** (v. 20) stands in contrast to the ungodly false teachers, about whom this letter speaks at length. The main idea in these verses is **Keep yourselves in the love of God** (v. 21), with the verb in the imperative mood. The readers were to remain within the sphere of God's forgiveness, guidance, and provision — unlike the angels who did not abide in their proper domain (see v. 6). Again using a triad, Jude enumerated positive steps the believers could take to counteract the influence of the sensual mockers, avoid falling into their errors, and keep in the love of God. The steps, desirable activities with desirable outcomes, contributed to the positive emotional appeal of Jude's case.

(1) The first step Jude advocated was **building up yourselves on your most holy faith** (v. 20; the faith for which the assemblies were to "earnestly contend," v. 3). The architectural metaphor differs from Colossians 2:7, where the same verb is passive, and Christ is the foundation upon which the building proceeds ("be built in him," REB). In either case, the believers were to concentrate on "structural integrity" in their congregations and guard against the pride and rancor of the mockers (see vv. 8, 10–11, 16, 19).

(2) The second action that would contribute to maintaining the community's standing within God's love was **praying in the Holy Ghost** (v. 20). Jude's meaning here may be "continue to pray in the power of the Holy Spirit" (REB). Paul recognized the believer's need for the Holy Spirit's intercession in prayer (see Rom. 8:26–27). The Spirit guides them in what to pray, and He gives them the discipline and stamina to engage in prayer.

(3) As the third step, Jude advised his house churches to be **looking for the mercy of our Lord Jesus Christ unto eternal life** (v. 21). Jude did not mean that his hearers did not presently have eternal life, nor was he necessarily implying that their current possession of it was uncertain (see 1 John 5:11–13). "Eternal life" is the fullness of that life into which they had already entered. The completion of the process of salvation is merciful in that it is the Christian's final deliverance from the presence and power of sin.

2. Ministry to the Wayward (vv. 22–23)

A comparison of various English translations of these verses reveals a disagreement whether the objects of ministry are two groups or three groups. The reason for differences among the translations is the existence of different readings among the witnesses to the Greek text. The essential difference concerns the number of clauses in Jude's original construction; each clause represents a classification of people to be aided. The KJV and other translations (e.g., Moffatt, NEB) follow witnesses that have two clauses; other translations (e.g., NIV, NASB, NJB, NRSV, REB) utilize witnesses that have three clauses. In light of Jude's predilection for triads and the inclusion of a third clause in very early witnesses, three groups seems more likely.

Verses 22–23. Regarding the first group in need of outreach, Jude said, **And of some have compassion** (v. 22). They were to "Be merciful" (NIV) to those who had not yet totally succumbed to the wiles of the false teachers but were leaning toward their specious arguments. The brazenness of the mockers and the apparent freedom that they enjoyed were a magnet for the immature believers who were not secure in their faith. Those wiser and stronger were to take on themselves the responsibility of the weaker, lest they fall. **Making a difference** (a plural participle in the nominative case) means "making a distinction" (NKJV); that is, the stronger members of the church were to be attentive to the younger believers and distinguish how to help them mature.

Jude's hearers were to assist a second group also, people whom they were to **save with fear, pulling them out of the fire** (v. 23). Of course, the one who saves is the Lord, and the word here (*sōzō*) is the usual New Testament word for salvation to eternal life (see John 12:47; 1 Cor. 1:21; Eph. 2:8; Titus 3:5). Salvation can be ascribed to the person who is the instrument God uses to lead a person away from sin and death into eternal life. The word "pulling" (*harpazō*) is very vivid. It can denote the act of robbery, capturing booty, or being swept away by a river. The word also designates prey being seized by wild animals (see John 10:12). Stringent measures were required to rescue those who had slipped into the clutches of the false teachers. The ones to be saved were in danger of hell itself (the likely referent of "fire"; for the idea of snatching from the fire, see Zech. 3:1–4).

Some translations list a third group as the object of ministry: "to others show mercy, mixed with fear — hating even the clothing stained by corrupted flesh" (v. 23, NIV). In the KJV, the final clause, which begins with **hating**, modifies "save with fear" and thus is part of the instructions pertaining to the second group to be helped. A third group is absent.

What does it mean for believers to save (or show mercy to) others while **hating even the garment spotted by the flesh** (v. 23)? The "garment" is the tunic (*chitōn*), the garment worn next to the skin. Jude's reference to its "spotted" ("polluted," NASB) condition recalls the Hebrew for Joshua's "filthy garments" in Zechariah 3:3–4. The word "filthy" is re-

lated to the Hebrew terms used in the Old Testament for human feces. The infection of the false teachers was repulsive and so pervasive that it contaminated everything and everyone who came in contact with them. Jude's metaphor and hyperbole created strongly negative pathos toward the mockers and their lascivious ways.

Two things Jude did *not* say in this passage: (1) He left no room for hating the sinner. The sin ("garment") was to be hated, not the sinner. (2) Jude did not depreciate the human body. "Flesh" (*sarx*) is not the body but rather the self-sufficient orientation toward sin that views the body as a vehicle of wrongdoing.

C. Doxology (vv. 24–25)

Verses 24–25. Jude's closing words are one of the mightiest crescendos of praise and exultation in the entire New Testament. The one glorified is **the only wise God our Saviour** (v. 25). In the New Testament, "Saviour" sometimes refers to God (see Luke 1:47; 1 Tim. 4:10) and sometimes to Jesus (see Luke 2:11; Phil. 3:20). Jude identified two of God's glorious characteristics, worthy of praise, both of which stem from His almighty power. (1) He **is able to keep you from falling** (v. 24). Jude's hearers may have become apprehensive that they might weaken and join those under the intruders' sway (see vv. 22–23). The readers' confidence was not to come from themselves but from God, who is fully able to keep those who put their trust in Him. (2) God is able **to present you faultless before the presence of his glory** (v. 24). In the Old Testament, the term "faultless" is used of the perfection of sacrificial animals offered to God (see Numbers 28–29). Believers can look to the future knowing that because of Jesus' death, they can stand in God's presence.

Not only can believers stand in God's presence, but they can stand in His presence **with exceeding joy** (v. 24). Since joy will be one's experience before God forever, it ought to be the overriding characteristic of worship now. Much Christian service and worship goes to the extreme opposite of the false teachers mentioned in the discussion on verse 19; it is spiritually listless and lacking in joy. Some daily practices contribute to spiritual lethargy. Lack of sleep (too much late-night TV), hectic schedules (too many commitments, even to Christian activities), poor diet (fast foods for a too-fast lifestyle), and lack of exercise ("I'm too tired") militate against a joyful outlook. If these practices are corrected, spiritual energy might be revived in one's life. To God are ascribed **glory and majesty, dominion and power, both now and ever** (v. 25), but not as though He does not already have them. A doxology is recognition and praise of who God is and of His attributes. Those attributes that Jude identified here parallel his concerns in the letter. Despite the atrocious sins of the false teachers, God's person and honor were not threatened. Nor was God's sovereignty and authority in jeopardy because of the sins of the mockers. Since God remains God "before all time and now and forever" (NASB), His people can rest securely in Him. **Amen.**

THE REVELATION OF ST. JOHN THE DIVINE

INTRODUCTION ───────────────

Author

Four times the author identifies himself as John (1:1, 4, 9; 22:8). From as early as Justin Martyr, in the second century AD, it has been held that this John was the apostle, the son of Zebedee (see Matt. 10:2). The book reveals that the author was a Jew, well versed in Scripture, a church leader who was well known to the seven churches of Asia (in today's western Turkey), and a deeply religious person fully convinced that the Christian faith would triumph over the demonic forces at work in the world.

In the third century, however, an African bishop named Dionysius compared the language, style, and thought of the Apocalypse (Revelation) with that of the other writings of John and decided that the book could not have been written by the apostle John. He suggested that the author was a certain John the Presbyter, whose name appears elsewhere in ancient writings. Although some today follow Dionysius in his view of authorship, the external evidence is overwhelmingly supportive of the traditional view that John the apostle wrote the Revelation.

Date

Revelation was written when Christians were entering a time of persecution. The two periods most often mentioned are the latter part of Nero's reign (AD 54–68) and the latter part of Domitian's reign (81–96). Most scholars date the book circa 95. Many substantial arguments favor the later date: (1) Domitian was the first emperor to insist on being worshiped as god throughout the empire; (2) the lukewarm condition of the churches of Asia Minor implies they had been in existence for many years; (3) the testimony of the earliest church fathers supports a date at the end of the first century.

Background

Since Roman authorities at the time were beginning to enforce the cult of emperor worship, Christians—who held that Christ, not Caesar, was Lord—were facing increasing hostility. In the letters to the churches, the Lord warned the believers at Smyrna against coming opposition (2:10) and told the church at Philadelphia of an hour of trial coming on the world (3:10). Antipas had already given his life (2:13), as had others (6:9). John had been exiled to the island of Patmos (probably the site of a Roman penal colony) because of his activities as a Christian missionary (1:9). Some within the church were advocating a policy of compromise (2:14–15, 20), which had to be corrected before its subtle influence could undermine the determination of believers to stand fast in the perilous days ahead.

Theme and Theological Message

John wrote to encourage the faithful to resist staunchly the demands of emperor worship. He shared with his readers the vision the Lord gave him of the imminent final showdown between God and Satan. In the great tribulation to come, Satan will increase his persecution of believers, but they must stand fast, even to death. They are sealed against any spiritual harm and will soon be vindicated when Christ returns, when the wicked are forever destroyed, and when God's people enter an eternity of glory and blessedness.

Literary Features

For an adequate understanding of Revelation, the reader must recognize that it is a distinct kind of literature. Revelation is apocalyptic, a kind of writing that is highly symbolic. The book refers to itself as a "prophecy" of future events (1:3; 22:7, 10, 18–19). It also provides a number of clues for its own interpretation (e.g., stars are angels, candlesticks are churches, 1:20; "the great whore," 17:1, is "Babylon" [Rome?], 17:5, 18; and the heavenly Jerusalem is the wife of the Lamb, 21:9–10). There is frequently a dualism between the earthly and the heavenly, good and evil, this world and the world to come. Beasts and other animals are used figuratively to represent certain realities, and colors are used symbolically, as are several numbers—especially 3, 7, and multiples of 12.

A distinctive feature is the frequent use of the number seven (fifty-two times). There are seven beatitudes (see discussion on 1:3), seven churches (1:4, 11), seven spirits (1:4), seven golden candlesticks (1:12), seven stars (1:16), seven seals (5:1), seven horns and seven eyes (5:6), seven trumpets (8:2), seven thunders (10:3), seven wonders or signs (12:1, 3; 13:13–14; 15:1; 16:14; 19:20), seven heads with seven crowns (12:3), seven plagues (15:6), seven golden vials (15:7), seven mountains (17:9), and seven kings (17:10), as well as other sevens. Symbolically, the number seven stands for completeness. The book of Revelation also uses "and" (Greek, *kai*) over 1,200 times. The constant use of this conjunction creates a sense of fast-paced movement from one event to the next.

Interpretation

Interpreters of Revelation normally fall into four groups:

1. *Preterists* understand the book exclusively in terms of its first-century setting, claiming that most of its events have already taken place in the past.
2. *Historicists* take it as describing the long chain of events from Patmos to the end of history.
3. *Futurists* place the book primarily in the end times.
4. *Idealists* view it as symbolic pictures of such timeless truths as the victory of good over evil.

Fortunately, the fundamental truths of the book are obvious throughout. A plain rendering of the book indicates that Christ will eventually return, triumph over evil, and usher in the eternal state.

Outline

I. Introduction (1:1–8)
    A. Prologue (1:1–3)
    B. Greetings and Doxology (1:4–8)
II. Jesus Appears to John on Patmos (1:9–20)
III. The Letters to the Seven Churches (chaps. 2–3)
    A. Ephesus (2:1–7)
    B. Smyrna (2:8–11)
    C. Pergamos (2:12–17)
    D. Thyatira (2:18–29)
    E. Sardis (3:1–6)
    F. Philadelphia (3:7–13)
    G. Laodicea (3:14–22)
IV. The Throne, the Book, and the Lamb (chaps. 4–5)
    A. The Throne in Heaven (chap. 4)
    B. The Seven-Sealed Book (5:1–5)
    C. The Lamb That Was Slain (5:6–14)
V. The Seven Seal Judgments (6:1–8:1)
    A. First Seal: The White Horse (6:1–2)
    B. Second Seal: The Red Horse (6:3–4)
    C. Third Seal: The Black Horse (6:5–6)
    D. Forth Seal: The Pale Horse (6:7–8)
    E. Fifth Seal: The Souls under the Altar (6:9–11)
    F. Sixth Seal: The Great Earthquake (6:12–7:17)
        1. The First Interlude (chap. 7)
            a. The Sealing of the 144,000 (7:1–8)
            b. The Great Multitude (7:9–17)
    G. Seventh Seal: Silence in Heaven (8:1)
VII. The Seven Trumpets (8:2–11:19)
    A. Introduction (8:2–5)
    B. First Trumpet: Hail and Fire Mixed with Blood (8:6–7)
    C. Second Trumpet: A Mountain Thrown into the Sea (8:8–9)
    D. Third Trumpet: The Star Wormwood (8:10–11)
    E. Fourth Trumpet: A Third of the Sun, Moon, and Stars Struck (8:12–13)
    F. Fifth Trumpet: The Plague of Locusts (9:1–12)
    G. Sixth Trumpet: Release of the Four Angels (9:13–21)
        1. The Second Interlude (10:1–11:14)
            a. The Angel and the Little Scroll (chap. 10)
            b. The Two Witnesses (11:1–14)
    H. Seventh Trumpet: Judgments and Rewards (11:15–19)

Bibliography

Couch, Mal. *A Bible Handbook to Revelation*. Grand Rapids, MI: Kregel, 2001.

Custer, Stewart. *From Patmos to Paradise*. Greenville, SC: BJU Press, 2004.

Hindson, Ed. *The Book of Revelation: Unlocking the Future*. Twenty-first Century Biblical Commentary. Chattanooga, TN: AMG, 2002.

Morris, Henry M. *The Revelation Record*. Wheaton, IL: Tyndale, 1983.

Mounce, Robert. *The Book of Revelation*. The New International Commentary on the New Testament. Grand Rapids, MI: Eerdmans, 1994.

Seiss, Joseph A. *The Apocalypse*. Grand Rapids, MI: Kregel, 1987.

Stigers, Harold. *A Commentary on Genesis*. Grand Rapids, MI: Zondervan, 1976.

Thomas, Robert L. *Revelation 1–7*. Wycliffe Exegetical Commentary. Chicago: Moody, 1992.

———. *Revelation 8–22*. Wycliffe Exegetical Commentary. Chicago: Moody, 1995.

Unger, Merrill F. *Commentary on the Old Testament*. Chattanooga, TN: AMG Publishers, 2002.

Walvoord, John F. *The Revelation of Jesus Christ*. Chicago: Moody, 1966.

———. "Revelation." In *The Bible Knowledge Commentary: New Testament*, edited by John F. Walvoord and Roy B. Zuck. Wheaton, IL: Victor, 1983.

EXPOSITION

I. Introduction (1:1–8)

These first eight verses give introductory words from John the apostle, the human author, and from the Lord Jesus Christ, the divine author. Later in the book, John indicated that the Holy Spirit also functioned as author (see, e.g., 2:7), along with Christ, giving readers direct revelations that make the book extremely important. The prologue (vv. 1–3) leads to greetings and a doxology (vv. 4–8) that gives a heavenly portrait of the Lord Jesus Christ, who is the central subject of the entire book. The opening chapters (chaps. 1–3) read like an epistle, whereas the body of the book is a prophecy of what will happen in the future.

A. Prologue (1:1–3)

These verses tell how the book will unfold. In some ways, they serve as an introduction for the chapters that follow.

1:1. The word **Revelation** (Greek, *apocalypsis*) does not have an article in the Greek text and means "disclosure" or "unveiling" of that which is hidden. Is this a revelation *about* Jesus Christ, or is it a revelation *from* Jesus Christ? Most scholars believe the book is a revelation, a new disclosure of divine truth, *about* the Lord Jesus. In the first chapter, He is revealed in all His glory.

This revelation about Christ was given **unto him, to shew unto his servants** future events, **things which must shortly come to pass**. God the Father wants the believers to understand old and new revelations in the context of the end times. "Shortly come to pass" is similar to the wording found in 4:1; 22:6; Daniel 2:28–29, 45. The expression "shortly" (Greek, *en tachei*) has been greatly misinterpreted. It does not mean that the events of Revelation are about to happen. It means that when they start, they will take place "quickly" or "with rapidity" of execution. A similar word (Greek, *tachy*) is translated "quickly" seven times in Revelation (2:16; 3:11; 11:14; 22:7, 12, 20). The idea of "suddenly" or "with rapidity" is seen in other verses in the New Testament (e.g., Luke 18:8; Acts 12:7; 22:18; 25:4).

The revelation was transmitted through Christ's **angel** to the apostle **John**, the recording **servant** of the Lord. **Signified** is from the Greek word *sēmainō*, which has the thought of "communicating by symbol." Revelation contains symbolic language but not in every part, and where there are symbols, behind them are literal events couched in pictorial words. The word "signified" must not mislead the reader. Revelation should not be seen as an allegory or prophetic poem. It is a prophecy of actual events, the "things which must be hereafter" (4:1).

1:2–3. It is John **who bare record of the word of God, and of the testimony** (Greek, *martyria*) **of Jesus Christ** (v. 2). This includes everything **he saw** about the Lord, but also all of the revelations that came from Him. John was bearing witness, or testifying, to having received the Word who came down from the heavenly Father. John also gave "testimony" to the person, life, and ministry of Christ; he was there as an apostle. "He saw" it all; he was an eyewitness.

A special blessing is attached to this book. While every book of Scripture holds blessings for those who read it, the book of Revelation holds a special blessing. It brings finality to all of redemptive history and establishes a time line for believers. It tells the child of God that the world as it is known will end. Terrible times will lead to the return of Christ to earth and then on into the eternal state, where "there shall be no more death, neither sorrow, nor crying, neither shall there by any more pain; for the former things are passed away" (21:4).

Blessed (Greek, *makarios*; "happy," "fortunate") **is he that readeth, and they that hear the words of this prophecy** (Greek, *propheteias*)**, and keep those things which are written therein** (v. 3). This is the first of seven beatitudes, or blessings, in Revelation (here; 14:13; 16:15; 19:9; 20:6; 22:7, 14), which are reminders of the seven beatitudes of Matthew 5:3–11. "He that readeth" may refer to a church reader who shares this revelation with those who cannot read, or it may refer to anyone who has the privilege to read the book for themselves. The blessing extends to all those who "hear the words" of the prophecy. Whoever reads or hears Revelation, however, must also "keep those things which are written" in it, meaning they must internalize the message and live as if these things could happen soon. The message should cause the believer to give priority to the Christian walk, which is important because **the time is at hand**. "The time is at hand" (Greek, *kairos engys*) is better translated "the season [of the events of Revelation] is sure, certain." *Kairos* is best translated "season" and here has to do with the events of the tribulation, which are laid out in chapters 6 – 19. *Engys* is two Greek words put together: "in the hand," meaning these events are "sure" or "certain" to take place. The English expression "It is better to have a bird in hand than two in the bush" reflects this idea.

B. Greetings and Doxology (1:4 – 8)

These verses give a greeting to the churches in Asia to whom the entire book of Revelation was apparently sent. This book is not a typical New Testament book. It is a prophecy that opens up and reveals the final details of the end times, all the way into eternity. Much that is given in this book has previously been revealed in many Old Testament books, but without specific details. In fact, 278 of 404 verses contain Old Testament types, symbols, pictures, or allusions (Hindson, *The Book of Revelation*, p. 3). Verses 4 – 8 are still preliminary, giving a vision of the deity of Christ, but verse 7 sets up the end of the book (19:11 – 20:6), which describes Christ coming to establish His kingdom.

1:4. The seven churches … in Asia are addressed, with **Grace** and **peace** from God the Father. Asia refers to the Roman province in Asia Minor that included Phrygia, Mysia, Caria, and Lydia. These seven churches were in the western half of Asia Minor. The greeting shows God as the Eternal One, who presently exists (**which is**), who existed in the past (**which was**), and whose existence will continue forever in the future (**which is to come**). The Lord's eternalness was expressed in the burning bush before Moses. The Lord said, "I AM THAT I AM" (Exod. 3:14), meaning, "I exist simply because I exist!" In John 8:58, Christ applied to Himself the same designation of the eternally existing God.

Most scholars believe **the seven spirits** is a reference to the sevenfold manifestations of the Holy Spirit (see Rev. 3:1; 4:5; 5:6). The number seven denotes perfection or completeness. The Spirit stands before the **throne** of God in heaven. In 4:5, John wrote that "there were seven lamps of fire burning before the throne, which are the seven spirits of God." The Spirit of God gives the light of truth. In his vision, Zechariah saw "seven lamps" (Zech. 4:2), or lights, on a golden candlestick that was to be built for the new temple. God's Spirit ("my spirit," Zech. 4:6) aided Zechariah in the construction project. Isaiah prophesied that the sevenfold manifestation of the Spirit would rest on the Messiah (see Isa. 11:1 – 5).

1:5 – 6. The greeting is also **from Jesus Christ** (v. 5), who is called **the faithful witness** (Greek, *martyria*), **and the first begotten of the dead, and the prince of the kings of the earth**. Christ came as the Son of God to show His heavenly Father to the world (see John 1:18). Christ said, "Though I bear record of myself, yet my record is true" (John 8:14), because He came from heaven. He was also faithful as a prophet from God (see John 18:37). He said, "I … bear witness of myself, and the Father that sent me beareth witness of me" (John 8:18). Christ is the "first begotten [Greek, *prōtotokos*; 'preeminent,' 'firstborn'] of the dead." He was the first to receive a resurrection body, which is immortal (see Acts 26:23). He is "the firstborn of every creature" (Col. 1:15).

Christ is also "the prince" (Greek, *ho archōn*; "the chief one"; v. 5) over the kings of the earth. In His providence, He sustains all of creation (see Col. 1:16), but as the final and ultimate earthly ruler, His sovereign reign is yet to come (see 19:11 – 16), fulfilling the prophecies of Isaiah 9:6 – 7, Psalm 72:11, and Zechariah 14:9. The wise men, the kings, and the judges will someday see the Lord Jesus Christ on His earthly throne and will be commanded to "Serve the LORD with fear, and rejoice with trembling" (Ps. 2:11). Almost as if penning a brief anthem, John wrote that those whom Christ **loved** (present tense; "keeps on loving"), He **washed us from our sins in his own blood.** All believers have been "washed" (Greek, *lyō*; aorist tense), better translated "loosed," once for all by the shedding of Christ's blood at the cross, giving eternal remission of sins (see Eph. 1:7; 2:23; Col. 1:20).

In giving salvation, Christ **made** those He saved (v. 6) to be **kings and priests [of] God, his** (heavenly) **Father.** This verse is better translated, "hath made us a kingdom, priests unto God and His Father." Such a designation is used of the Jewish people in the Old Testament (see Exod. 19:6; Zechariah 3). John was not suggesting, however, that the church has replaced Israel; rather, he was saying that believers in the present church dispensation now represent the Lord as spiritual **kings and priests.** Believers now have the authority and the privilege to represent Him in their ministry. The church presently is "a holy priesthood, to offer up spiritual sacrifices" (1 Peter 2:5), which are pleasing to God. The believer's body is that "living sacrifice, holy, acceptable unto God, which is your reasonable service" (Rom. 12:1). As living and holy sacrifices, God is honored with **glory** (Greek, *doxa*; "splendor") **and dominion** (Greek, *kratos*; "power," "authority") for eternity, **for ever and ever,** that is, "unto the ages of ages." To such a glorious Savior and Master, the right to eternal glory and dominion is attributed (see Dan. 7:14). To this, John added, **Amen,** that is, "So be it!"

1:7. The imagery in this verse comes from Daniel 7:13 and Zechariah 12:10. The Messiah will someday come in the **clouds; and every eye shall see him.** He is the one who was crucified by the Jews and then **pierced** with a spear (see Ps. 22:11–18; Isa. 53:4–6; Zech. 10:12; John 19:34–37). When He returns, **all kindreds of the earth shall wail because of him** (see Zech. 10:12; Matt. 24:30). They will recognize Him as Savior and King. John felt compelled to again write, **Even so, Amen.**

1:8. This verse is a paraphrase of Isaiah 41:4, which speaks of the eternalness of God: "I the LORD,

the first, and with the last; I am he." The addition of **Alpha and Omega** (the first and last letters of the Greek alphabet) and **the beginning and the ending** reinforces the eternal attribute of God. This verse, however, is about the Lord Jesus, who is the second person of the Trinity and who is very God. Much that is said of God in Isaiah 41:4 is also used here to describe Christ. There is no reason why eternity should not be ascribed to Him, as well as to His Father (see Rev. 21:6; 22:13). **The Almighty** (Greek, *pantokratōr*) is a title given to God but is here applied to the Lord Jesus. Nine of the ten New Testament occurrences of this title are in Revelation (here; 4:8; 11:17; 15:3; 16:7, 14; 19:6, 15; 21:22); the tenth occurrence is in 2 Corinthians 6:18.

II. Jesus Appears to John on Patmos (1:9–20)

These verses give a glorious vision of the Lord Jesus in heaven. They also state that the apostle John was on the island of Patmos when he received this vision. His vision was of the resurrected Christ, who has in His hands the churches to whom this letter was sent. It would not be a stretch to argue that all congregations that love the Lord are in His possession also.

1:9. **John** identified himself as the **brother, and companion** ("partaker, and sharer") **in tribulation** (Greek, *thlipsei*) of those to whom he wrote. The seven churches, and probably other congregations, were suffering to some degree the same persecutions that John was, which possibly were instigated by the evil Roman emperor Domitian (AD 81–96). While history does not record widespread persecution at that time, the emperor probably regarded the believers in Christ as dangerously seditious, because popular distrust of them was growing. Domitian reinstated emperor worship, and this placed the Christians in a disadvantageous position.

When John wrote **the kingdom,** he was referring not to the future millennial reign of Christ but to the society and association of believers in a kingdom-like fraternity. The **patience** (Greek, *hypomonē*) of Christ implies that the Christians were under cultural and governmental pressure from which they could not escape. John was on **Patmos**, the Alcatraz of the ancient world, from which few escaped (see Hindson, *The Book of Revelation*, p. 25). The island (ten miles by six miles) is still today rocky, barren, and dotted with caves, some of which the exiles used for shelter. John was there because he had witnessed to **the word of God, and ... the testimony of Jesus Christ**. According to the church father Victorinus, the aged apostle was forced to work in the mines on the island. He was freed to return to Ephesus, where he was pastor, when the Emperor Nerva came to power.

1:10. While **in the spirit on the Lord's day**, John **heard ... a great voice [like] a trumpet**, a strong, decisive, and commanding voice. He had not heard the voice of his Savior since just before His ascension to glory (see Acts 1:7–9). "In the spirit" describes the trance-like state (Greek, *ekstasis*; "ecstasy") mentioned in Acts 10:10; 11:5; 22:17. This was a vision, not a dream, nor a state of being asleep. God placed John in this trance-like state for receiving the revelations of this book (see Thomas, *Revelation 1–7*, p. 58). "The Lord's day" may mean the first day of the week, Sunday, but "Lord's" is actually an adjective, with the sense of a "Lordian" (as the adjective "Christian" is formed from "Christ") or "Lordly" day.

1:11. The voice was identified as the **Alpha and Omega** (v. 8; 21:6; 22:13), meaning the Eternal One (**the first and the last**). What John saw, he was to **write in a book** (Greek, *biblion*; "scroll"). This command to "write" was given twelve times in the book. The book was to be sent to the seven churches of Asia (for more on these churches, see chaps. 2–3).

1:12–16. These verses give a glorious and vivid first picture of the Lord Jesus Christ in heaven. The picture is presented in illustrative and descriptive language to convey to the reader Christ's new state in glory. The verses are symbolic, as are many verses in Revelation, but again, care must be taken that the book is not seen as simply a symbolic poem that is without reality and historicity. These verses use two comparative words (Greek, *homoios* and *hōs*) that are translated almost synonymously: "like," "as," "like

as," "as if." Together, these two words are used over one hundred times in the book of Revelation.

When John **turned to see the voice**, he **saw seven golden candlesticks** (v. 12). This may have been a golden lampstand with seven branched lampholders mounted on a central shaft, or it may have been seven individual lamps mounted on seven individual stands, or shafts. As the gold in the tabernacle and in Solomon's temple represented the deity of the Lord, here it represents the deity of the Lord Jesus Christ. The oil to light the lamps symbolizes the power and work of the Holy Spirit.

In the midst of the seven candlesticks (v. 13) stood **one like ... the Son of man**, a common designation for Christ. "Son of man" is one of the most important descriptions of Israel's Messiah. The expression means "the Son who is related to humanity." The first reference to "the Son of man" is found in Daniel 7:13, which describes the Messiah coming from earth, where He lived as part of the human race, and being presented before God, who is called "the Ancient of Days." After Christ's resurrection, He went back to His Father (see Acts 1:9–10). The Son of Man is mentioned throughout the Gospels as a messianic expression (see, e.g., Mark 8:31). Christ had on **a garment** like that of the high priest (see Exod. 28:4; 29:5; Hebrews 7), **down to the foot**. His chest (**the paps**) was encircled (**girt**) with a sash (**a golden girdle**) like that used by the priests. This somber representation of Christ in His role as judge and priest, standing **in the midst of** the churches, is a poignant introduction to chapters 2–3.

His hair was **white like wool**, or **as white as snow** (v. 14). White hair symbolizes the dignity of an elder, one with wisdom and divine authority. **His eyes were as a flame of fire** symbolizes Christ's work of judgment. He has the right to judge not only the churches but also the world, as quoted in John 5:22: "the Father ... hath committed all judgment unto the Son." In Revelation, the description of the Son is like that of His Father: "The Ancient of days did sit, whose garment was white as snow, and the hair of his head like the pure wool: his throne was like the fiery flame" (Dan. 7:9). **His feet [were] like ... fine** brass (Greek, *chalkolibanon*; actually a copper alloy; v. 15)—heavy, sturdy, strong, and permanently fixed—like brass smelted for some time, **burned in a furnace**, with all of the impurities removed.

His voice [had] the sound of many waters (v. 15), the sound of a rushing, flowing mountain waterfall. His words were loud and commanding! In His **right hand** (v. 16), He held **seven stars**, which are identified as "the angels of the seven churches" (1:20). Some scholars have speculated that these "angels" (Greek, *angeloi*; "messengers") were angelic beings who guarded and attended the seven churches. Others believe they were the "messengers" and readers of the seven churches who came to Patmos, received this scroll, and returned to share its message with their congregations. Churches had envoys and readers who shared such documents with those who were illiterate. The letters themselves imply that the "messengers" are responsible for sharing the messages with the people in the churches.

From the Lord in glory went forth **a sharp two-edged sword** (v. 16) from **out of his mouth**. This "sword" represents divine judgment and corresponds with 19:15: "Out of his mouth goeth a sharp sword, that with it he should smite the nations: and he shall rule them with a rod of iron: and he treadeth the winepress of the fierceness and wrath of Almighty God." **His countenance** (face) **was as the sun [that] shineth in [its full] strength**. The brilliant glory of the Lord is compared to the full brightness of the sun. Such brilliance would seem to reflect the attributes of omnipotence, righteousness, sovereignty, and majesty (see Walvoord, *The Revelation of Jesus Christ*, p. 46).

1:17–19. When John saw this vision of Christ in glory, he fell down **as dead** (v. 17). Christ placed **his right hand** on him and said, **Fear not; I am the first and the last**. Christ assured the elderly apostle with words that represented His deity, His eternalness. From start to finish, Christ is the Son of God, but now He is in His eternal, glorified body. He is the God-man. He is the one who lived and died for sinners. **Behold** (v. 18), He is now **alive for evermore, Amen**! "Alive" is in the present tense: "He lives

continually." The Greek for "for evermore" is better translated "unto the ages of ages." Together, these two expressions reinforce the doctrine of the eternalness of Christ. He holds **the keys of hell** (Greek, *hadēs*; "Hades") **and of death** (Greek, *thanatos*). Before Christ's death and resurrection, the Devil held these keys and brought death to humanity (see Heb. 2:14–15), but Jesus lived in human flesh yet was without sin (see 2 Cor. 5:21) and destroyed the power of Satan. For those who trust Christ, He "deliver[ed] them who through fear of death were all their lifetime subject to bondage" (Heb. 2:15).

The Lord commanded John, **Write the things which thou hast seen, and the things which are, and the things which shall be hereafter** (v. 19). "The things thou hast seen" refers to John's vision of the glorified Christ (1:11–19), "the things which are" refers to the letters to the seven churches (chaps. 2–3), and "the things which shall be" refers to the rest of the book of Revelation (chaps. 4–22). This is a simplified outline of the scroll that John wrote.

1:20. This verse explains what John saw in Christ's hand. **The seven stars** may refer to the seven "messengers" (**angels**) of the churches (see discussion on 1:16). **The seven golden candlesticks** (see 1:12) represent **the seven churches**. This introduces the messages, like small postcards, to these seven churches.

III. The Letters to the Seven Churches (chaps. 2–3)

The Lord Jesus is the divine author of these letters to the seven churches (see 1:11), but so is the Holy Spirit, who spoke through the human writer John (see, e.g., 2:7). It could be argued, then, that Jesus Christ, the Spirit of God, and John the apostle together wrote these letters. There are two views about the letters: (1) They were written to historic churches that had specific problems. John simply transcribed the words but added nothing to the messages given to the seven churches. Some of the problems were unique, such as the heresy of the Nicolaitans, which plagued the churches of Ephesus and Pergamos. (2) These letters also prophesied periods of church history that were yet to come. The problem with the second view is that there are no indications to substantiate this, and it is difficult to completely fit the events of the last two thousand years of church history into these seven church divisions. There is no question that throughout church history, congregations have experienced problems similar to those described here. The lessons addressed to the seven churches are applicable to all churches of all generations, because all believers since the founding of the church age (see Acts 2) are part of the larger, spiritual church, the body of Christ. The same needs and problems exist today as in John's day.

Each church had its own strengths and weakness. The letters, however, have a sevenfold pattern, though there are no words of commendation to the churches of Sardis or Laodicea and no words of condemnation for Smyrna or Philadelphia. Hindson (*The Book of Revelation*, p. 32) presents the following sevenfold pattern.

Commission: "To the angel of the church of ..."
Character: "These things saith ..."
Commendation: "I know thy works ..."
Condemnation: "I have a few things against thee ..."
Correction: "Repent ..."
Call: "He that hath an ear ..."
Challenge: "To him that overcometh ..."

These seven churches were no more than one hundred miles from each other on the peninsula of Asia Minor. Two, Smyrna and Ephesus, were very near the coast of the Aegean Sea (because of silting, Ephesus is now nearly seven miles from the sea). Ephesus, where John pastored, was only about sixty miles from the island of Patmos.

A. Ephesus (2:1–7)

Ephesus was a large and important city, an economic center situated on the mouth of the river Cayster. From early on, it was an important seaport, the most important trading center west of Tarsus. The city had a population of about 300,000. Its outdoor amphitheater could seat 24,000. Behind the towering columns of the amphitheater were baths, gymnasiums, and impressive buildings.

The city was famous for its temple of Artemis (or Diana, her Roman name), which was one of the seven wonders of the world at that time. The twin sister of Apollo and the daughter of Zeus, Artemis, the multibreasted deity, was known as the moon goddess, the goddess of hunting, and the patroness of young girls. Her temple had 127 columns; each of them stood 197 feet high. Coins were minted that said, "Diana of Ephesus."

The apostle Paul founded the church in Ephesus. Christianity began in the city in about AD 50, through the efforts of Priscilla and Aquila (see Acts 18:18). Paul arrived around AD 52 and established a resident ministry for the better part of three years (see Acts 20:31). Acts reports that "all they which dwelt in Asia heard the word of the Lord Jesus, both Jews and Greeks" (Acts 19:10). Paul taught daily in the home of the teacher Tyrannus (see Acts 19:9). His ministry was so effective that the silversmith league, which made souvenirs of the temple, feared Paul's preaching would undermine the great temple of Artemis (see Acts 19:27). A riot followed, but Paul was spared. Paul experienced both blessings and dangers at Ephesus. He countered the strong influence of magic in the city (see Acts 19:11–20).

Tradition testifies that the apostle John lived in Ephesus toward the end of the century. In Revelation, while in exile, he described the false teachers that were flourishing in the city (see 2:1–7). In memory of John, the Roman emperor Justinian (AD 527–565) raised a magnificent church in the city.

The Ephesian church had good works, discernment, and patience. They hated the new heresy of religious people called the Nicolaitans. They were far off base, however, in that they had lost their first love, their affection for Christ. If they did not repent, the light of their testimony would go out.

2:1. The seven churches were each reminded that these letters came from the Lord Jesus. Here Christ is identified as the one who **holdeth the seven stars** and **who walketh in the midst of the seven golden candlesticks** (see 1:12, 16, 20).

2:2. Christ, being the all-knowing Son of God, knew of the Ephesians' **works** (Greek, *erga*) and **labour** (Greek, *kopon*). *Erga* has the idea of "expending energy." They were serving the Lord with great diligence. *Kopon* suggests they were "coping" under terrible pressure and were struggling with great pains to witness for Christ. **Patience** shows that they remained steadfast, walking faithfully even when facing adversity.

The Ephesians could not put up with (**canst not bear**; Greek, *bastazō*; "to endure") **them which are evil.** The Lord complimented the church for testing those who claimed to be **apostles**, many of whom were found to be **liars.** To their credit, the Christians questioned those who claimed to be from God. They put them to the test (**tried them**) as to their genuine faith and their divine calling.

2:3. The Ephesians had **borne** up under the struggle and had **laboured** for the sake of the Lord Jesus because His reputation was at stake. They had **not fainted,** or "grown weary." In spite of the opposition and persecution coming against them, they had not become weary in their work for Christ.

2:4. Nevertheless (Greek, *all'*) is a strong contrasting word. The Greek expresses **thou hast left** (Greek, *aphiēmi*) **thy first love** a little more strongly than the English wording, saying that they had "forsaken" or "abandoned" their "first love," who was Christ Himself. Apparently, this church was active in the Lord's work, but their heart for Him was not in the effort.

2:5. The Lord urged the Ephesians to look back at where they had started spiritually. They needed to **repent** (Greek, *metanoeō*; "change the mind") and return to their **first works.** If they did not, He would **come ... quickly, and ... remove [their] candlestick.** "First works" does not mean simply to return to good works in order to gain approval from God. A genuine love for God is always manifested in the works that it gives forth. Though the Ephesian assembly had been faithful in many tasks, those tasks did not in themselves exhibit a true love for the Lord. Their present works were suspect; they needed to be serving for higher reasons, as they had at the begin-

ning. If they did not repent, their "candlestick," or lamp, would go out; they would no longer be a beacon light of witness for the Lord. The believer who is not willing to yield all his talents and capabilities to Christ does not sufficiently love Jesus.

2:6. This church hated **the deeds of the Nicolaitans** (see 2:15). "Nicolaitans" means "conquering the people." No one can be certain what this cult was about except that it probably was a Gnostic sect, which is attested by many of the early and later church fathers. Eusebius wrote that after John the apostle censured the group, the sect disappeared for a short time. Some try to connect the group to Nicholas of Antioch, one of the seven original deacons of the church in Jerusalem (see Acts 6:5), but there are some doubts about this. The group was apostate, heretical, and became a lawless, licentious religion. About this group, Christ added, **which I also hate.**

2:7. Those who can should listen to **what the Spirit saith unto the churches.** This urging comes from Christ, but the statement attests that this message was being transmitted from Him, through the Spirit, to John. **That hath an ear** means more than simply hearing sounds; it means to hear with a desire to act upon the truth. The exhortation to **hear** and **overcometh** has several interpretations. The Greek word *nikaō* means "to be victorious," "to conquer." Some say the Lord was urging the Ephesians to repent and get right with the Lord in regard to their sins. Others believe it refers to overcoming sin, professing Christ, and becoming Christians. The argument is that it is wrong to believe that everyone in this assembly was a Christian. "Overcometh" has to do with salvation. This may be what John had in mind when he wrote in 1 John 5:4–5: "For whatsoever is born of God overcometh the world: and this is the victory that overcometh the world, even our faith. Who is he that overcometh the world, but he that believeth that Jesus is the Son of God?"

"Overcoming" is mentioned at the end of each of these church letters, and in each case, the reward seems to be the gift of eternal life, although stated in different ways. To the Ephesians, the reward was, **I [will] give to eat of the tree of life, which is in the**

midst of the paradise of God. This is a salvation concept, not simply a reward to a Christian who changes his ways. Those in the Ephesian church who were genuine Christians, who had overcome the unbelief and the sin of the world, were promised the right to the Tree of Life. This tree, mentioned first in the garden of Eden (see Gen. 3:22), will be found in the midst of the street in the New Jerusalem. In a certain symbolic picture, the tree produces its fruit for the abundant health, probably spiritual health, of the redeemed of the nations (see 22:2). "Paradise" (Greek, *paradeisos*) is from a Persian word referring to "a secluded place," "a garden of bliss." What was originally a garden of delight in Genesis 3 takes on the connotation of the new heaven and the new earth in Revelation 21–22. "The paradise of God" is a visual description of the peace and contentment of eternity in the presence of God the Father and God the Son.

It needs to be pointed out that all of the seven churches were to hear this particular message. This means that whatever was said to one church was applicable to all of them. Likewise, whatever is said here should be applied to today's churches also.

B. Smyrna (2:8–11)

Smyrna, in western Asia Minor, had a superb natural harbor and was an important trading and commercial center. In spite of competition from cities like Ephesus and Pergamum, the city referred to itself as "the first city of Asia." In 195 BC, seeing the rising power of Rome, the city of Smyrna sought to appease the Roman leadership and built a pagan temple for Roman worship. In 23 BC, the city was given the honor of constructing a temple to the Emperor Tiberias. With this, the city became the cultic center of emperor worship—a fanatical "religion" that later, under emperors such as Nero (AD 54–68) and Domitian (AD 81–96), brought severe persecution of the early church. Smyrna is now known as Izmir, the chief city of Anatolia and one of the most influential cities in modern Turkey.

This church was economically poor yet spiritually rich. No faults are mentioned in this letter. The church was under heavy assault by a certain Jewish synagogue, "the synagogue of Satan" (2:9). Many Christians were persecuted and thrown in prison.

2:8. As were all of the letters, this brief letter was written to **the angel of the church**. To each church, however, a different identification was given concerning Christ the divine author. Here He reminded the readers that He is **the first and the last**, again taking on the godly attribute of eternalness (see 1:8, 17; 22:13). As far back as one can go, God the Father existed, but so did the Lord Jesus Christ. As far into the future one can go, both persons reside in the Trinity, along with the eternal Holy Spirit. Christ **was dead** but now **is alive**. The resurrection (see 1:5) is a great demonstration that Jesus is the Son of God (see Rom. 1:4; 1 Cor. 15:12–19), and He is the firstfruits of those who are asleep (see 1 Cor. 15:20) in that He leads the way to victory over death.

2:9. The Lord said He knew the **works** of this church (see 2:2) but also their **tribulation, and poverty** (Greek, *ptōcheia*). God does not count poverty as humans do. He added, **but thou art rich** (Greek, *plousios*; "full," "complete"), meaning they were spiritually rich. James wrote of being poor in this world but "rich in faith" (James 2:5), and Paul said something similar about his ministry, "as poor, yet making many rich" (2 Cor. 6:10). The church at Smyrna was suffering **the blasphemy of them who say they are Jews, and are not**. These Jews were so by birth, but not by truth. They rejected the message of Christ as their Messiah and their Savior. It was as if **Satan** was ruling from their **synagogue**, driving them to blaspheme with their denial of Christ. Satan is the Father of Lies, who originates all that is not true (see John 8:44).

2:10. It is natural that these believers would **Fear** what they were to **suffer**, especially knowing that some of them would be **cast … into prison**. They would be **tried, and … have tribulation [for] ten days**. Many scholars have pondered the "ten days," and dozens of theories have been offered. Some speculate that it represents the ten years of persecution under Emperor Diocletian, but this seems improbable. It may mean an indefinite but short period, or it may be taken literally as describing a ten-day persecution that is unknown and not recorded in church history.

A special crown, **a crown of life**, would be given to those who suffered terribly. It seems feasible to extrapolate from this that all suffering and martyrdom (those **faithful unto death**) for Christ's sake will be rewarded with such a crown. "A crown of life" may refer to the fact that these believers gave their lives for a witness to the grace of God found only in the Lord Jesus Christ. James wrote that the one who is tried "shall receive the crown of life, which the Lord has promised to them that love him" (James 1:12; see 3:11).

2:11. The one who hears these words and **overcometh** will receive the ultimate reward: he **shall not be hurt of the second death** (see 20:1; 21:8). The first death is physical; the second death is spiritual, resulting in eternal punishment and separation from the presence of God.

C. Pergamos (2:12–17)

The Christians of Pergamos had gone through a terrible period of persecution but had come out of it holding fast to Christ's name and not denying His faith. Christ was adamantly against some in the congregation who held to the doctrine of Balaam. Some also had fallen into the cult of the Nicolaitans. The Lord commanded them to repent, or He would come against them and defeat them "with the sword of [His] mouth" (v. 16).

Pergamos was the chief city of Mysia, in northwest Asia Minor, and was situated about fifteen miles from the Aegean Sea. In its early history as a city-state, it became the powerful center of the region after Attalus I (241–197 BC) defeated the Gauls (Galatians). The city stood as a symbol of Greek superiority over the barbarians and boasted a library containing over 200,000 scrolls. The Egyptians were so jealous, because this library rivaled their own in Alexandria, that they refused to ship papyrus to Pergamos. As a result, a new form of writing material, "Pergamena charta," or parchment, was developed.

Pergamos was home to a temple to Asklepius (the Greco-Roman god of medicine and healing), as well as temples to Athena and Zeus, the latter with an altar showing him defeating snakelike mythical giants. It was also the center of the cult of emperor worship. In 29 BC, a temple was constructed to Emperor Augustus and the goddess Roma, which was served with a powerful priesthood. Christians abhorred the symbol of the serpent deity, the god of Pergamos. This is why Christ spoke of the city as the place "where Satan's seat is" (2:13).

2:12. Here Christ is pictured as the one with **the sharp sword with two edges**. When the Lord speaks, His words are cutting words of judgment, as if issued with a sword (see 1:16; 2:16; 19:15, 21). Hebrews 4:12 says the Word of God is "quick ['alive'] ... and sharper than any twoedged sword," which opens up the human soul and spirit, and "is a discerner of the thoughts and intents of the heart."

2:13. As in all the letters, the Lord said He knew the **works** of the church. He knew the spiritual efforts of the believers at Pergamos but also their failures that were harmful to the congregation and to their witness. This assembly **dwellest ... where Satan's seat is**. "Seat" (Greek, *thronos*) is better translated "throne." This and **where Satan dwelleth** are references to satanic power in Pergamos, in the evil, diabolical worship of Asklepius, the serpent god. The believers at this church were **hold[ing]** fast to the name of Christ. They had not **denied ... faith** in Him, even during the days of **Antipas**, who was **slain**, the Lord's **faithful martyr**. Some speculate that Antipas, meaning "against all," symbolizes that a certain individual stood alone against the evil of the city and died. His name reflected the ministry he had in being a faithful witness. But better, this was one who stood unwaveringly for the Lord and paid the ultimate price for his faith.

2:14. As with many of these churches, the Lord had issues against the church at Pergamos. Some among them held to **the doctrine of Balaam**. Balaam was a Moabite prophet mentioned in Numbers 22–24. In Numbers 24, Balaam continued to balk at the request of the king of Moab, **Balac**, to curse

Israel. In Numbers 24:1–25:9, he had advised **Balac** that the Jews would jettison God's protection if he caused them to worship idols, which he did. This terrible story of temptation took place at Baal-Peor and made a lasting impression on later generations of Israelites. Balaam's counsel caused the people of the Lord to commit sexual immorality with the pagans and participate in idolatrous worship. Similar to Balaam's influence, **cast[ing] a stumblingblock**, some in the Pergamos church were **eat[ing] things sacrificed unto idols** and practicing **fornication**, "sexual immorality." In response, the Lord Jesus told them to repent, lest He come quickly and "fight against them" (2:16).

2:15–16. Like the church at Ephesus, the assembly at Pergamos was influenced by **the doctrine** (teaching) **of the Nicolaitans** (v. 15), which the Lord **hate[d]** (see 2:6). If they did not **Repent** (v. 16), Christ would **come ... quickly** (Greek, *tachy*; "with suddenness"), **and ... fight against them with the sword of [His] mouth** (see also 1:16; 2:12).

2:17. This verse is similar to the ending of the letters to the other churches. It also has the warning to **hear what the Spirit saith** and a challenge to be included among those **that overcometh**. To the overcomer, the Lord **will ... give to eat of the hidden manna, and will give him a white stone**, on which is inscribed **a new name**. Manna (Hebrew; meaning, "What is it"?) sustained Israel in their wilderness wandering (see Exod. 16:13; Num. 11:31). The Lord "opened the doors of heaven, and had rained down manna upon them to eat" (Ps. 78:23–24). The true believer in the Lord Jesus receives manna that the world does not know or see, the spiritual sustenance of the saints. As in ancient Israel, this manna promises a better "land" in the future, a heritage waiting in heaven (see Walvoord, *The Revelation of Jesus Christ*, p. 70).

The "white stone" indicates that the child of God is favored by Christ. White always represents holiness and purity. On the stone, "a new name" is inscribed. This seems similar to the twelve stones in the breastplate of the high priests, "the breastplate of judgment" (Exod. 28:15); each stone was engraved

with the name of one of the twelve tribes of Israel (see Exod. 28:21). When the priests intervened for the Lord, each tribe was represented. The new name, which no one knows except the one who **receiveth it**, is either the name of Christ Himself, now hidden from the world but to be revealed in the future as the most powerful of names (see 3:12; 14:1), or the name of the believer who is changed through redemption (see Isa. 62:2; 65:15).

D. Thyatira (2:18–29)

The church at Thyatira had charity, service, faith, and patience (v. 19), yet the religious cult of Jezebel was destroying the congregation with immorality, though not everyone had succumbed to the religious seduction. The woman known as "Jezebel" (v. 20) taught and beguiled the believers at Thyatira to conform to evil practices. In the congregation, Jezebel's followers seem to have been a minority, because the majority of Christians in this church were commended. Christ threatened death to Jezebel's children (v. 23) in some of the strongest words of judgment against the churches. The overcomer, however, would be given kingdom authority (vv. 26–27).

Thyatira was in the province of Lydia, in western Asia Minor, on the road from Pergamos to Sardis. The city was a thriving manufacturing and commercial center during New Testament times. History shows that the trade guilds were financially successful, but they participated in pagan customs and practices such as superstitious worship, feasts at which union members ate meals sacrificed to heathen gods, and sexual immorality.

Paul's first convert in Europe was "a certain woman named Lydia, a seller of purple, of the city of Thyatira, which worshipped God ... she attended unto the things which were spoken of Paul" (Acts 16:14). Modern Thyatira is called Akhisar.

2:18–19. Christ presented Himself to this assembly as Judge: **the Son of God** (see Ps. 2:7), **who hath ... eyes like ... a flame of fire, and ... feet ... like fine brass** (v. 18; see 1:14–15; Dan. 10:6). The believers at Thyatira were actively serving the Lord and were greatly diligent, **the last to be more than the first** (v. 19). Of the seven churches, only this congregation was commended for these qualities, a contrast to the Ephesian church, which seemed to have so quickly lost its "first love" (2:4).

2:20 – 21. Notwithstanding (Greek, *alla*; "nevertheless"; v. 20), in contrast to some of their good qualities, the Lord told them, **I have a few things against thee, because thou sufferest that woman Jezebel**. In the Old Testament, Jezebel was the evil wife of King Ahab of the northern kingdom of Israel (874 – 853 BC). She became active in killing the Lord's prophets (see 1 Kings 18:4) and caused even Elijah the prophet to run in fear of her (see 1 Kings 19:2 – 3). Her harlotries and witchcraft were well known throughout the kingdom. Some scholars believe the name here in Revelation is symbolic of immorality in the assembly in general, and others believe it refers to a woman in the congregation who influenced believers in the same way that Jezebel did in the Old Testament accounts. Regardless, her spiritual kinship with the Jezebel of old is obvious.

This Jezebel, who **calleth herself a prophetess** (v. 20), was wicked, teaching and seducing the Lord's **servants to commit fornication** and to partake of **things sacrificed unto idols**. The congregation put up with this practice. The prophetess was given a chance to **repent** (Greek, *metanoeō*; "change the mind") **of her fornication** (Greek, *porneias*; v. 21) but refused.

2:22 – 23. With an exclamatory **Behold** (Greek, *idou*; v. 22), Christ declared His determination to end the religious charade. Jezebel would be **cast ... into a bed**, and those who consorted with her would be cast **into great tribulation**, unless **they repent**. This picture is graphic. Unless they repented, she would continue her fornication, and those who joined with her in violating the moral laws of God would be punished severely. "Great tribulation" (Greek, *thlipsin megalēn*) could refer to additional troubles that would come upon those whom she had seduced, or it could refer to the great tribulation, the apex of the terrible future period of world history that Revelation focuses on (see chaps. 6 – 19; Matt. 24:21). The

tone of these verses is that **her children** (v. 23), who were to die, were lost and had never received Christ as Savior, yet they were part of the congregational assembly. They but masqueraded as Christians.

If Jezebel and her followers did not repent and instead befell this judgment, **all the churches** (v. 23) would realize that Christ **searcheth the reins** ("minds") **and hearts** and will compensate **every one ... according to [his or her] works** (see Ps. 62:12). This was a wake-up call to all the assemblies that they could not mix righteousness and evil. That Christ is divine is clear here. He can look into the inner being and into the motives of the heart and pass judgment. No earthly mortal can do that.

2:24 – 25. To those who had not surrendered to the **doctrine**(s) (v. 24) of Jezebel and had not experienced **the depths of Satan**, the Lord would put **none other burden**. Satan is a master at counterfeiting spirituality and Christian doctrine. Many in the Thyatira church had toyed with the false religions that Satan had under his power. Others in the congregation had not, however, and the Lord would not hold them at fault. As God's wisdom and knowledge are spiritually deep (see Rom. 11:33), so Satan has, in opposition, his false spirituality. The Lord urged the church to **hold fast till I come** (v. 25) that upon which they had a firm grasp. No one knows the day of the Lord's return, prophesied in 1 Thessalonians 4:13 – 18, but each congregation and each believer is to cling to what is true and right, no matter how far off that day may be.

2:26 – 28. Here the Lord extended additional promises to **he that overcometh, and keepeth my works unto the end** (v. 26), expanded promises that grant awesome authority to the faithful. Alongside the Master, the Lord Jesus Christ, His followers will have **power over the nations** (see Matt. 19:28; 1 Cor. 6:3 – 4), and as He, **shall rule them** (the nations) **with a rod of iron** (v. 27). In prophetic words, God said to His Son, the Messiah, "Thou shalt break them [the nations] with a rod of iron; Thou shalt dash them in pieces like a potter's vessel" (Ps. 2:9). This will take place when the earthly Davidic kingdom is established and the King is occupying His throne (see Matt. 25:31–46). Here the Lord promised that believers will receive the same authority to co-reign as given the Son, **even as I received of my Father**.

Christ will also give to the overcomer **the morning star** (v. 28). Peter wrote a prophetic word of assurance that a better day is coming: "We have also a more sure word of prophecy; whereunto ye do well that ye take heed, as unto a light that shineth in a dark place, until the day dawn, and the day star arise in your hearts" (2 Peter 1:19). Here in Revelation, "the morning star" is Jesus Himself. Possibly the idea is that He will grant assurance to believers that all is well and that the end of pain and sin is near. Christ said of Himself, "I am the root and the offspring of David, and the bright and morning star" (22:16).

2:29. This is the same ending that closes each letter.

E. Sardis (3:1–6)

This is the shortest of the letters addressed to the seven churches. Christ called the church at Sardis "dead" (v. 1) because He had not found their "works perfect before God" (v. 2). They were not "watchful" (v. 2) of how they were walking with the Lord. They were lax in their morality and spirituality. The Lord said that if they did not repent, He would come on them quickly, "as a thief" (v. 3). Few in this church had not defiled their garments with sinful acts. Only those who repent are worthy to walk with Him. Christ's words to this church were swift and bold and to the point.

Sardis was the capital city of the province of Lydia, in western Asia Minor. It was situated on the east bank of the Pactolus River about fifty miles east of Smyrna. In ancient days, Sardis was well fortified and easily defended. It was the capital of the ancient Lydian Empire, and it passed to the Persians, the Greeks, and the Romans during their respective dominance of the ancient world. The city was famous for its trade in luxury clothing. Sardis, along with Ephesus, housed a magnificent temple to Artemis, built in the fourth century BC. The temple was 327 feet long and 163 feet wide, with 78 Ionic columns.

During its days as a Roman city, Sardis became an important Christian center, but the church at Sardis was evidently affected by the city's pagan complacency and its cultic religious past. The city's appearance of thriving health masked its inner moral decay.

3:1. Christ reminded this church that He has **the seven spirits of God**, meaning the sevenfold manifestation of the Holy Spirit, working through Him as the Son of God (see 1:4, 16). He also holds in His hand **the seven stars**, who are identified in 1:20 as "the angels of the seven churches," but who probably were the messengers of the churches (see discussion on 1:16). This church had **a name**, a reputation, that they were alive, that they **livest**. By their profession of Christianity, they expressed to the world their purpose to live for the Lord. They professed to have true spirituality, but instead, they were spiritually **dead**.

3:2–3. This assembly was told to **Be watchful** (v. 2) spiritually and morally and to **strengthen** what reputation they had left. "Be watchful" (Greek, *grēgoreō*) means "stay awake," "be alert." The Lord urged the church to be on guard against Satan's attacks and remain aware of their own spiritual vulnerabilities (see Custer, *Patmos to Paradise*, p. 37). While the Lord Jesus knew their **works** (see 3:1), those works were in no way **perfect before God**. In Greek, "perfect" (*plēroō*) is a perfect passive participle, meaning their works "had not arrived at a point of completion, maturity"; their works had not over a period of time been proven **before God**.

The Lord implored them to recall the past and how they began: **Remember** (what) **thou hast recieved and heard** (v. 3), then **hold fast, and repent**. If they did not do these things, **If therefore thou shalt not watch**, He told them, He would **come ... as a thief**. He would come as suddenly as a thief to remove their blessings, and even their ministry, and to judge them. This judgment would be as sudden and as irrevocable as the judgment related to Christ's second coming to reign over the world. The Lord saying, "Be on the alert then, for you do not know the day nor the hour [of My coming]" (Matt. 25:13).

3:4–5. Some in this church had not **defiled** (made filthy; v. 4) their clothes; they would **walk**

with [Christ] **in white** (in righteousness)**: for they are worthy**. Only a few, however, had trusted the Lord as their Savior and lived their Christian experience in righteousness. The white garment is reminiscent of the white wedding garment worn by those who were worthy to attend the ceremony. Christ urged those who were lost to overcome, so that they too would be **clothed in white raiment** (v. 5).

To all who **overcometh** (v. 5), the Lord promised the reward of the benefits of life eternal. Christ **will not blot out ... of the book of life** the overcomer's **name** (see 13:8; 21:27) but will instead **confess his name before [His heavenly] Father, and before his angels**. Because the wicked are blotted from the Book of Life in Exodus 32:33 and Psalms 69:28, the question is raised, When or how did their names come to be written in the Book of Life in the first place? In Revelation 5:9–10, the Lamb's worthiness is tied to His death and the redemption He thus provides. It seems clear that His death affected the entire world. If the Book of Life contains the names of all those for whom the Lord died, then He must in some sense have died for all men, because at the beginning, the names of all people were in the book. In the words of John, apart from the book of Revelation, Christ died for "the world" (John 1:29; 3:16; 4:42; 1 John 2:2; 4:14), no one excluded. This provision of salvation for all is only potential in that it becomes actual only when appropriated by each person. The names of those who die without Christ are erased from the Book of Life. The names of those who trust Him as Savior are confirmed in the book (see Thomas, *Revelation 1–7*, p. 263).

3:6. This is the same closing exhortation as in all the letters.

F. Philadelphia (3:7–13)

The congregation at Philadelphia was exemplary and was not judged by the Lord. This church was faithful to Christ and the Word of God. These believers had an "open door" (3:8), meaning primarily that they had continual access to God, though this may also refer to the opportunity for spreading the gospel with their unhindered witness. The name Philadel-

phia means "brotherly love," and this expression is used six other times in the New Testament (Rom. 12:10; 1 Thess. 4:9; Heb. 13:1; 1 Peter 1:22; 2 Peter 1:7). Only here, however, is it used of the city bearing its name.

Philadelphia was situated on the Cogamus River, a tributary of the Hermus River, about twenty-eight miles southeast of Sardis. The city was founded by Attalus II (Philadelphus), who reigned as king of Pergamos from 159 to 138 BC. It was the center of the wine industry and was thus connected with the chief god of wine, the Greek mythological deity Dionysus, or the Roman Bacchus. Today the city is called Alasehir, or Allah-shehr ("the city of God").

3:7. In this letter, Christ described Himself as the **holy** and the **true**. "True" means that He is the "genuine, authentic, faithful" Savior, the one who can be trusted for salvation. **The key of David** is a quote from Isaiah 22:22, which speaks of God's faithful servant and prime minister Eliakim (see Isa. 22:20), who replaced unfaithful Shebna, the minister or steward during Hezekiah's reign sometime before 701 BC. Though he was not a king, Eliakim was given kingly responsibility (with sovereign authority, "the key") as if he were being bestowed the royal robes of the house of David. Christ now holds this authority as the ultimate son of David.

Because Christ's authority is so absolute, what He **openeth ... no man shutteth**, with the opposite true also. While Christ presently holds such authority, this power will someday be manifested when His earthly kingdom is established, when He is given "dominion, and glory, and a kingdom, that all people, nations, and languages, should serve him: his dominion is an everlasting dominion, which shall not pass away, and his kingdom that which shall not be destroyed" (Dan. 7:14). When this takes place, the world will know Him as "KING OF KINGS, AND LORD OF LORDS" (Rev. 19:16).

3:8. As with all the churches, the Lord said, **I know thy works**. The people had kept His **word, and ... not denied [His] name**. Because of this church's faithfulness, He had set in front of them **an open door** of spiritual service, which no one was able to close. The Lord had to affect and strengthen their ministry because they had **little strength**. The congregation had ample opportunity to witness and share the gospel, yet their ability to carry this out must have been limited. The Lord wedged the door open so that they could serve unhindered. They had a great struggle, apparently against a Jewish community that vehemently opposed Christianity (see 3:9).

3:9. The Jews in Philadelphia must have had a violent hatred of the church (see 2:9, 13); Christ said they were **of the synagogue of Satan**. Under Satan's influence, these Jews were not behaving with godliness, as the true descendants of Abraham. Such attacks were to be expected, because as Peter wrote, "Be sober, be vigilant; because your adversary the devil, as a roaring lion, walketh about, seeking whom he may devour" (1 Peter 5:8).

3:10. Because the believers had **patience** in their endeavor, Christ promised to keep them **from the hour of temptation**, the tribulation that will overtake the entire **world** and come **to try** all who **dwell upon the earth**. The Greek preposition "from" can mean "out from" in the sense of "escaping" from something. Some have said this verse is a promise that only this local church would experience the rapture, but the general idea of the text indicates that this is a promise for all the churches, since the Spirit addresses all the churches at the end of each letter. The rapture of the church will be based, not on patience, but on the fact that all believers are "in Jesus," "in Christ" (1 Thess. 4:14, 16). This relationship alone is the basis for being "caught up ... in the clouds" (1 Thess. 4:17). **Which shall come** (from the Greek verb *mellō*; "to be about to") carries the idea that this event is inevitable and certain, expressing in general a settled future.

3:11. I come quickly (Greek, *tachy*) has the idea, "When I come, I will come with rapidity, suddenness." Some have mistakenly believed that this phrase was the Lord's guarantee that His arrival was imminent. While the church is to be looking for His coming at any time, that is not the point here. When He returns, it will happen suddenly, with the events tumbling one upon the other in rapid succession (see 2:5, 16; 11:14; 22:7, 12, 20).

The **crown** (Greek, *stephanos*) is not given a further description, therefore it could be a continued reference to the "crown of life" (2:10), a crown that had to do with suffering, as it seems here (see 3:10). Some attribute the crown in verse 11 to the "crown of righteousness" that Paul wrote about in 2 Timothy 4:8, which will be given to all those who have loved (longed for) Christ's appearing and who "have fought [the] good fight ... finished [the] course, [and] kept the faith" (2 Tim. 4:7).

3:12. In this letter, the promises to the one who **overcometh** are fuller and richer than than in any of the other letters. The overcomer will be made **a pillar in the [Lord's] temple**. He will be given a sense of spiritual security and **shall go no more out**. He will have written **upon him the name of ... God, and the name of the city of ... God, ... [the] new Jerusalem, which cometh down out of heaven from my God**. He will also be given a **new name**. Those who overcome will be marked by the Lord with direct identification of God: His name and the name of His city, the New Jerusalem. They will be like strong, prominent pillars in the new, eternal city (see 21:1–4). This verse is literal, but it is also full of hyperbole, used to affirm that the one who is faithful will have a lasting position of prominence in the Father's presence. The honor and the accolades will be great, just as if the name of the Lord, whom the believer served and whose grace and delight he enjoyed, were somehow inscribed on him in a very obvious way. The overcomer will be acknowledged and seen as belonging to the Lord. "He that overcometh shall inherit all things; and I will be his God, and he shall be my son" (21:7).

3:13. The Lord again commanded all of the churches to listen to what the Spirit had said.

G. Laodicea (3:14–22)

The church at Laodicea had some good spiritual qualities, but Christ called it "lukewarm" (v. 16). It claimed to be wealthy, spiritually speaking, but instead it was poor, wretched, miserable, and blind. The Lord urged the congregation to use "eyesalve, that thou mayest see" and to turn from their "nakedness" and buy from Him fine raiment, white and clean (v. 18). Because the Lord loved them, He chastened them and called for repentance.

Laodicea was a city in the fertile Lycus Valley of the province of Phrygia and was about forty miles east of Ephesus. It was known for its black wool industry. Jesus' words about the church relate to the wealth of the city and its economic prosperity. Founded by the Seleucids and named for Laodice, the wife of Antiochus II (261–247 BC), it was a model city for financial power during the Roman times. The city was nearly wiped off the map by a major earthquake that struck the area in AD 60. The same earthquake also caused extensive damage in the metropolitan centers of Colossae and Hierapolis. Laodicea refused help from Rome in rebuilding, which may give some indication of the self-sufficiency of the congregation of Laodicea.

Other disciples or Paul may have been the major messengers of the gospel in Laodicea (see Col. 1:7; 4:7–15). A major church council was held in the city (AD 344–363), though little doctrine has come down from it. Today the ancient site is barren of life and cluttered with heaps of stone ruins.

3:14. Christ called Himself **the Amen** ("the Verily"), "the confirmation of what is right and absolute" (Couch, *Bible Handbook to Revelation*, p. 223). Paul said believers are "in [Christ] Amen, unto the glory of God" (2 Cor. 1:20). In Judaism, the use of "Amen" was widespread and gave firmness to truth. To conclude with "Amen" signified concurrence. Christ also called Himself **the faithful** (see 1:5) **and true witness** (repeated in 19:11; see also 3:7). As well, He is **the beginning of the creation of God.** Those holding to the Arian heresy believed that Christ was the first created being, but the expression "the beginning" (Greek, *archē*) carries the thought that He is the preeminent and prominent one, standing above all in honor and power over all of creation. Jesus is the image of the invisible God (see Col. 1:15), "the beginning, the firstborn from the dead; that in all things he might have the preeminence" (Col. 1:18), and as very God, "by Him were all things created" (Col. 1:16). He is also the "Alpha and Omega, the

beginning and the end" (Rev. 21:6). No expressions could set forth His deity any more strongly.

3:15–17. As with the other congregations, the Lord said He knew the **works** (v. 15) of the Laodiceans. He described them as **lukewarm** (Greek, *chliaros*; v. 16), and because of this, he issued a strong warning: **I will spue** (lit., "vomit") **thee out of my mouth.** Christ described three different states of spirituality: cold, warm, and lukewarm. **Cold** (v. 15) refers to the spiritual state of the world, while **hot** refers to being fervent and possessing spiritual zeal. The Laodiceans were professing Christians who walked in an in-between state. They were saved but had lost their enthusiasm for Christ and for spiritual things. They were but "lukewarm" and had little meaningful consistency in their Christian walk.

The believers in this church were also self-deceived. Because they possessed extensive physical **goods** (v. 17), they thought they had arrived and were in **need of nothing** on the spiritual level. Their wealth, they assumed, was a sign of their spiritual position with the Lord. Instead, they existed in a most **wretched** state. Exactly what is meant by this is not known; their sins are not itemized (see Walvoord, *The Revelation of Jesus Christ,* p. 93).

3:18. The Lord urged the assembly to purchase from Him **gold** that has been **tried** (see James 1:12–13), finely smelted in **fire.** This would make them spiritually **rich.** Those tested this way would "be clothed" and would become spiritually "rich" (2:10) as a reward for righteous living. Their lives would be righteous, as if they were wearing **white raiment,** a sign of purity and holiness. They would again be spiritually clothed, and their **eyes** would be healed **with eyesalve.**

3:19. Experiencing the Lord's **rebuke and chasten[ing]** is a sign of His love. He does not hesitate to chasten His people because it yields "the peaceable fruit of righteousness" (Heb. 12:6–11). The Lord urged the Laodiceans to **be zealous** in and to **repent** of their sins.

3:20. Some think this verse was an invitation to the lost to **open the door** of their hearts to receive Christ, but more than likely, it was an invitation to the church, and certainly to individuals, to allow Christ to come in and be the center of worship and spiritual fellowship. **Sup** refers to eating a meal, and sharing food with another is an intimate activity that fosters fellowship and closeness.

3:21–22. The one who **overcometh** will be **grant[ed] to sit** (v. 21) with Christ on His earthly Davidic **throne**. Christ is now on the throne of His Father in glory (see Ps. 110:1–2), but this is not the earthly, historic kingly reign. Christ made it clear that He "shall come in his glory" and "shall ... sit upon the throne of his glory" (Matt. 25:31). Revelation pictures this being fulfilled when He comes to earth to "rule with a rod of iron" (19:15) and reigns for "a thousand years" (20:4–6). Some believe that Christ's being presently seated on His Father's throne in heaven constitutes His Davidic rule, but the Lord made a distinction between His future Davidic throne and His present seat on the **throne** of His **Father**. Psalm 110:1 is quoted more often in the New Testament than any other Old Testament quote: "Sit thou at my right hand, until I make thine enemies thy footstool."

This letter closes like all of the others, with an appeal to hear with the **ear** what the Spirit **says** (present tense, "is saying") to all of the churches.

IV. The Throne, the Book, and the Lamb (chaps. 4–5)

These two chapters introduce the all-encompassing sweep of prophetic happenings that are foretold in the rest of the book. Both chapters take the reader into the heavenlies and present the divine viewpoint about things to come. The prophecies that begin in chapter four were not completed in any historic event of the past; therefore these chapters need to be understood from a futuristic viewpoint. The events looked for, as the angel promised, are "things which must be hereafter" (4:1). John's vision of heaven (chaps. 4–5) serves as the fulcrum of the Apocalypse. "It is the pivot on which the entire book turns our attention from earth to heaven and from time to eternity" (see Hindson, *The Book of Revelation*, p. 55).

A. The Throne in Heaven (chap. 4)

In this chapter, the reader is ushered into the throne room of God in the heavens. "Throne" (Greek, *thronos*) is mentioned thirteen times in this chapter. Through illustrative language, the Lord is seen in all of His majesty and glory. Around Him are angelic creatures who themselves possess great power and authority. God is seen as "worthy to receive glory and honour and power" because He has "created all things, and for [His] pleasure they are and were created" (v. 11). While other prophets received direct revelation or were addressed by the Lord in dreams (e.g., Daniel) and visions (e.g., Ezekiel), John was told, "Come up hither" into heaven, to see the "the things which must be hereafter" (v. 1). This prophetic phenomenon is what makes Revelation unique.

4:1. After this (Greek, *meta tauta*) identifies these revelations as subsequent to those of chapters 2–3. The Lord was about to reveal something new and prophetic. In a real sense, John saw (**I looked**) revelations of things to come. He was transported above the clouds, above the starry host, and was ushered into the third heaven, the abode of God. There he heard a voice, as shrill and commanding as **a trumpet**, speaking with him. He was commanded to enter glory so that he could be shown the **things which must be hereafter**. A better translation is "the things which must come after these things," meaning after the events of the present age. It is important to note that the church is absent from the earth in 4:1–19:7. The word "church" is not mentioned again until 22:16.

4:2–3. Suddenly, John found himself **in the spirit** (Greek, *en pneumati*; v. 2), by which he saw a heavenly **throne** where God was seated in all His dominion and sovereignty. Though John's "spirit" was involved and not his body, he was still seeing the beatific presence of the Lord. From verse 3 on, the apostle struggled to describe wondrous things that were far beyond his previous human experience. This is why he continually used comparative language, such as "it looked like" (Greek, *homoios*).

The two stones listed here are among the most precious gems known. Which stone is meant by **jasper** (green chalcedony; v. 3) is debated. Today, it is thought to have been an opaque stone, yet some believe it was almost totally clear, like a diamond. It was the last stone in the breastplate of the Levitical priest's garment (see Exod. 28:20; 39:13), and it is one of the stones in the foundation of the New Jerusalem (see Rev. 21:19–20). The **sardine stone** is less debated since it is more commonly known as carnelian (or ruby red). It was the first stone in the Levitical breastplate (see Exod. 28:17). It has been suggested that these two stones represent God's purity and transparency in holiness and that the sardine stone (red) also represents His wrath against sin.

The bow of the **rainbow** (Greek, *iris*; v. 3) is semicircular, like a halo, and may point to the fact that God is the "Alpha and Omega, the first and the last" (1:11). It is also reminiscent of the Lord's covenant promises with Noah (see Gen. 9:16). The rainbow, green like **an emerald**, may also depict life, with the semicircle depicting eternity.

4:4–6. Each of these verses begins with a preposition relating to God's throne: **round about** (v. 4), **out of** (v. 5), and **before** (v. 6). The **four and twenty elders … in white raiment** (robes), wearing **crowns of gold**, seem to represent the church, which had at this point been taken from the earth and was now in glory (see discussion on 4:1). This would include both those who had died and those who had ascended to heaven at the rapture of the church (see 1 Thess. 4:13–18). Some say the **elders** represent the whole company of believers, an exalted angelic order, and that the number of twenty-four reflects the twelve tribes of Israel from the Old Testament and the twelve apostles of the New Testament. The white robes picture the holiness they possessed in the eternal state, and the crowns of gold indicate that they would participate in some kind of adjudication with the Son of God in the heavenly courtroom. The church is called "a holy priesthood" and "a royal priesthood" (1 Peter 2:4, 9). In the Old Testament, the Levitical priesthood was represented by twenty-four elders and was divided into twenty-four shifts, or courses of service (see 1 Chron. 24:4–19).

From **the throne proceeded lightnings and thunderings and voices** (v. 5). While God's throne pictures mercy and grace and glory, it also represents judgment and righteousness, as was seen when Moses gave the law to the Jews in the wilderness (see Exod. 19:16).

The **lamps of fire** (v. 5) picture the judgment to come through the work of the Holy Spirit, **the seven spirits of God**, the sevenfold manifestations of the Spirit (see Isaiah 11:1–2; see also 1:4; 3:1; 4:5; 5:6). These lamps were the means by which John was aware of the presence of the Holy Spirit (Walvoord, *The Revelation of Jesus Christ*, p. 108).

In front of the heavenly **throne … was a sea of glass like unto crystal** (v. 6; see 15:2). Perhaps this clear sea, by its transparent and limitless nature, speaks of God's purity and majesty. He is in control, and nothing is a mystery to Him; everything is crystal clear because He decrees it. The "sea of glass [resembling] crystal" pictures God's absolute holiness, which He shares with no one else.

John saw **four beasts** around **the throne** and in the midst of **the throne** (v. 6). This "probably means that the four were in the immediate vicinity of the throne and encircling it, one on either side, one behind and one in front" (Thomas, *Revelation 1–7*, p. 354). The four beings he saw are not beasts, however; they are powerful, all-knowing, highly intelligent, angelic creatures. The word used here for "beasts" (Greek, *zōa*) is better translated "living ones" or "living creatures." It is a different word than that used for "beast" (Greek, *thērion*; "ferocious animal," "monster") in Revelation 13. **Full of eyes** was John's way of describing their higher knowledge and wisdom. These creatures have access to the all-knowing wisdom of the Lord, to carry forth His commands and judgments. Heaven and the universe function under the infinite wisdom and plan of God. He is sovereign in His created realm, and nothing happens by chance. The imagery here parallels that of Ezekiel 1:22.

4:7–9. The description of the **four beasts** (v. 8), or angelic beings (see discussion on 4:6), is similar to the vision of the prophet Ezekiel, who saw four living creatures, each of which had four faces: a human face on the front, a lion on the right, an ox on the left, and an eagle on the back of the head (see Ezek. 1:6, 10). These are the same animals that John saw, except he used the word **calf** (v. 7) rather than "ox." John's description tells us that these beings, seen as serving as a group, are as powerful as a **lion**, yet as docile and innocent as a **calf**, as intelligent as a human being, and finally, as swift in service to God as the swooping **eagle**.

These angelic "living ones" have **six wings** (v. 8), as described also in Isaiah 6:2–3. This graphic symbolism would have to mean that these messengers of God are swift in doing the Lord's bidding. Being **full of eyes within** again points to their all-seeing intelligence. They do not cease **day and night** crying out the greatness of God, **saying, Holy, holy, holy, Lord God Almighty**. This cry is similar to that of the six-winged angels (Hebrew, *seraphim*) described in Isaiah 6:2–3. The presence of these angels in the heavenly court lends much to the impression of the majesty, holiness, sovereignty, and eternalness of God. They never stop crying forth His holiness and great power and authority, as well as His **glory and honour and thanks** (v. 9). In verse 8, the everlasting existence of the Lord is mentioned again, as He is the one who exists continually in His universe: **Lord God Almighty, which was, and is, and is to come** (v. 8; see 1:4). His attribute of eternalness is repeated in verse 9: He **liveth for ever and ever** (v. 9).

4:10–11. The twenty-four **elders** (v. 10) joined in on the chorus with the heavenly angels and gave great honor to the Lord. John saw the elders **worship** God, repeat the fact of His eternal nature, and **cast their crowns before the throne**. They added, however, that He is the creator of **all things** (v. 11), and futhermore, all things **were created** for His **pleasure**. The Greek word translated "pleasure" (Greek, *thelēma*) is better translated "will." That God is **worthy** to receive such accolades is tied to His sovereign authority to reign from His throne in the heavens. These verses are a fitting introduction to the next chapter, which focuses on the second person of the Trinity, the Lord Jesus Christ, who is the Redeemer and "the Lamb that was slain" (5:12).

B. The Seven-Sealed Book (5:1–5)

The only one worthy of opening the book that John saw in the hands of the Lord is Jesus Christ.

"Worthy" (vv. 2, 4) indicates one who has divine authority. Jesus Christ is worthy because He is the very righteous Son of God, who walked the earth, came forth from the grave, and ascended to glory. His messiahship is set forth clearly in verse 5. The book in the Lord's hands contained extensive orders pertaining to the wrath coming upon the earth because of unbelieving humanity's sinfulness and rebellion against God. This document came straight from God. The wrath that will come upon the world during the tribulation, due the world for its sin, will issue from God Himself. Paul wrote that only Christ can deliver "from the wrath to come" (1 Thess. 1:10), the sudden destruction that will come upon "them" (1 Thess. 1:5:3), the unbelievers. When the tribulation begins (Revelation 6), the world will call out to be hidden "from the wrath of the Lamb: for the great day of his wrath is come; and who shall be able to stand?" (6:16–17).

5:1. Generally, the right hand is the dominant hand, but here it is also the hand of authority of God Almighty, who orders the affairs of His universe. The **book** (Greek, *biblion*) that John saw was a "scroll" containing the chronology of the events of the tribulation that unfolds in chapters 6–19. The message was recorded **within and on the backside**, meaning that the orders regarding the coming events were detailed and extensive. The **seven seals** were probably like the wax seals of an official document that are imprinted with the king's signet ring. The seals were placed progressively inside in different portions, until the entire scroll was rolled up and sealed. Then as the scroll was opened, each seal had to be broken in sequence, until each message or chapter was fully disclosed (see Couch, *Bible Handbook to Revelation*, p. 230).

5:2–4. John heard a powerfully **strong** (Greek, *ischyros*; active power) **angel** (v. 2) call a question out **with a loud voice**. This angel may be the archangel Michael because of his special role in the events of the final days (see Dan. 12:1–3). **Worthy** (Greek, *axios*) carries the thought of "proper weight." Did anyone have the proper authority, the required credentials, to open the seals? The question rang throughout the entire universe, with the answer of silence, for **no man was found worthy to open and to read the book, neither to look thereon** (v. 4).

Why was John so emotionally moved that he **wept much** (v. 4)? Some have suggested that, at his age, he was emotional and weepy, coupled with the fact that he had walked with the Lord Jesus, and now so much that he had looked for was coming to pass. The pictorial drama impressed upon John the importance of the revelation contained in the scroll.

5:5. One of the twenty-four **elders** urged the apostle, **Weep not**, because the Messiah of Israel **hath prevailed to open the book, and to loose the seven seals.** He is the King, the "Branch" (Isa. 11:1) out of the stem of Jesse (David's father), that is, He is of the royal bloodline. He is called "a lion's whelp" (Gen. 49:9) and comes from the kingly tribe of Judah, from which tribe the future monarch's "sceptre shall not depart" (Gen. 49:10). To Mary, it was prophesied that her son "shall be great, and shall be called the Son of the Highest: and the Lord God shall give unto him the throne of his father David" (Luke 1:32). Only this one, the Messiah, the Lord Jesus Christ, can open the seals.

C. The Lamb That Was Slain (5:6–14)

Jesus Christ is worthy to open the sealed book because He gave His life, as a sacrificial lamb, because of His love for humanity. His physical body, which was sacrificed on the cross, was prepared for Him before His birth (see Ps. 40:6; Heb. 10:5), and He was "obedient unto death" (Phil. 2:8). As a lamb, He went willingly to those who would slay Him, and He went quietly, not opening His mouth (see Isa. 53:7). John witnessed Christ's sacrifice and reward being extolled in heaven.

5:6. Here Christ is called the **Lamb [who] had been slain**. Christ is the one who died for sins, as the sacrificed Lamb of God (see Isa. 53; John 1:36). John described His omniscience (**seven eyes**), which are the sevenfold manifestations of the Spirit of God (as mentioned in 1:4; 4:5). The Lamb also had **seven horns**, which appears to refer to the power and authority of a king (see Dan. 7:24; Rev. 13:1). In Scripture, horns are a symbol of power and conjure up the concept of fear.

5:7–8. The Lamb **took the book** (v. 7) from **the right hand** of God, who **sat upon the throne**. The four angelic creatures (**the four beasts**; v. 8; see discussions on 4:6, 8) and the **four and twenty elders fell down before the Lamb**, and with heavenly **harps, and golden vials full of odours** (incense), the Lamb was worshiped with **the prayers of saints**. Here "saints" may refer to the saints of all generations, but more than likely, it refers to the saints of the church, because they had been redeemed "out of every ... nation" (5:9) and had been "made ... unto our God kings and priests" (5:10; see 1:6; 3:21; 20:4) who someday "shall reign on the earth" (5:10) with Christ. The scene is in heaven, where the resurrected and raptured church saints, represented by the twenty-four elders (see discussion on 4:4–6), now reside. Here, just before the tribulation began, John saw this great crowd of Gentiles from all nations. Before God pours out His wrath upon the earth, the saints of the church will be raptured. "Harps" (lyres) were used in sacred temple worship to praise the Lord. The trumpet and the harp are the only instruments mentioned in descriptions of the heavenly worship of God.

5:9–10. Those singing **a new song** (v. 9) had been **redeemed ... to God by [the] blood** of the Lamb. The Bible makes it crystal clear that without the shedding of blood for sin, there is no remission of sins (see Heb. 9:22). While it is possible that the full context of this passage has to do with church saints, Christ's redemption was for the Old Testament saints as well. **Redeemed** (Greek, *agorazō*) is a descriptive verb that pictures those who are helpless being purchased out of the marketplace of sin and then set free.

5:11–12. Imagine John's awe as he **beheld** (v. 11) this glorious scene of heavenly worship. The chorus of praise intensified, with **many angels** (v. 11), the special angelic creatures (**the beasts**; see discussions on 4:6, 8), and **the elders** joining in, all giving praise **with a loud voice** (v. 12). Their number was uncountable. "With a loud voice" (Greek, *phōnē megalē*) illustrates the overwhelming joy expressed to the Lamb and to God for the blessings of redemption. The angelic host sang along with the redeemed, represented by the twenty-four elders. Here there seems to be a concentric circle, with the Lamb in the center, surrounded by the living creatures, the elders and the redeemed, and the vast sea of angels, all giving forth a symphony of praise (see Walvoord, *The Revelation of Jesus Christ*, p. 119).

5:13–14. Then John heard all beings, **every creature** (v. 13), both **in heaven, and on the earth**, and even **under the earth**, proclaim **Blessing, and honour, and glory, and power** to God, who **sitteth upon the throne, and unto the Lamb**. This praise will continue endlessly, **for ever and ever**. John's descriptions of praise are colorful, expansive, and almost redundant. It is hard for the human mind to fully grasp the glories of heaven, but the ordinary Christian has the privilege to glimpse the brilliant picture of the majesty that surrounds the Lord in the heavenlies. John seems to include even the lost, those "under the earth" or whose bodies **are in the sea**. While he used the expression "every creature," most scholars believe he was referring only to human beings and not to the animal world. "The creatures are intelligent beings who have an intellectual appreciation of God and the Lamb" (Thomas, *Revelation 1–7*, p. 407).

Verse 14 seems to indicate a repetition of the praise of **the four beasts** ("living creatures"; v. 14; see discussions on 4:6, 8) and the twenty-four **elders**. Their song of praise continued. The word **Amen** means "truthfully," "sure," or "so be it." This heavenly scene assures believers that those who follow Christ, and thus often endure affliction, will share with the Lord His glory and grace throughout all eternity. The picture painted in chapter 5 is considered a prophecy of future events in which the church of Jesus Christ bearing witness today will be in the presence of the Lord in heaven tomorrow.

Chapters 4–5 lead into the terrible tribulation that will fall upon the earth. After the glorious interlude that John witnessed in the heavens, the scene returned to earth.

V. The Seven Seal Judgments (6:1–8:1)

The seven-sealed book was first mentioned in 5:1, which describes God sitting on His throne, holding the book that can be opened only by His Son, the Lord Jesus Christ (see 5:7–9). In ancient times, a seal was pressed into wax to authenticate a document from an official or from the king himself. Some scholars hold that the seal judgments will start after the midpoint of the tribulation and will continue consecutively. Others believe the seal judgments will run concurrently, overlapping each other. A third view argues that the trumpet and vial judgments will come out of the breaking of the seals running simultaneously. The most accepted view is that the seal judgments will bring about the trumpets, which in turn will bring on the worst of the judgments, the vials of wrath.

The breaking of the seals will bring terrible judgments down upon the inhabitants of the earth. The church apparently will be absent during this time, having ascended in the rapture (see discussion on 4:1). There is no mention here of the church, the body of Christ, or of those "in Christ." While people can and will be saved during this time, those who choose to trust Christ will suffer horribly and will be persecuted and martyred.

A. First Seal: The White Horse (6:1–2)

6:1. When Christ **the Lamb opened** the first seal, a **thunder** clap was heard in the heavens. One of the four living creatures (**four beasts**; see discussions on 4:6, 8) urged John the apostle to **Come and see**. The thunder was not repeated in the other seal openings. This startling and frightening peal inaugurated the tribulation on earth.

6:2. From his heavenly vantage point, John could write, **I saw**. These future events were happening before his eyes! Here he saw one riding on **a white horse**, called even in secular literature the first of "the four horsemen of the Apocalypse." The four horsemen parallel those in Zechariah 1:7–1, although the horsemen in Zechariah are sent only to patrol the earth rather than to inflict God's wrath. The white horse gives the image of the "good guy" or a conquering general on his trusty steed as he directs his troops in battle. Some say this rider is Christ the Lamb riding in victory. This is not the last of the tribulation, however, but the beginning. Christ will come back on a white horse to bring victory and to stop the carnage taking place on earth (see 19:11), but 6:2 is not that event.

The rider, then, is "the prince that shall come" (Dan. 9:26), the false messiah or the Antichrist, as revealed in Revelation 13:1–10. He wore **a crown** (Greek, *stephanos*), or victor's wreath, not the diadem of Christ, and **had a bow**, not the sword of Christ. Chapter six portrays the Antichrist coming as a world conqueror who appears to bring peace but instead brings destruction. The grammatical structure of **he went forth conquering, and to conquer** is interesting. It best reads, "He went forth continually conquering so that he might conquer." Note again that Christ Himself opened this seal and released this rider to inflict judgment on the earth.

B. Second Seal: The Red Horse (6:3–4)

6:3–4. After the Lord **opened the second seal**, the second angelic being (**beast**; see discussions on 4:6, 8) introduced a rider on a **horse that was red** (v. 4). The fiery color denotes war and conquest. The rider of this horse was equipped with **a great sword**, and **power was given to him to take … peace from the earth**. This corresponds to Jesus' introduction of the seven-year tribulation in the Gospels (see Matt. 24:6–8; Mark 13:7–8; Luke 21:9–10). "These [events] are the beginning of sorrows" (Matt. 24:8; Mark 13:8), the "birth pangs" that the rabbis and prophets said would precede the coming of the Messiah. When this rider removes peace from the earth, people will turn on each other and **kill one another**. The Antichrist will appear to be a peacemaker but will instead be a demonic tyrant who attempts to conquer the entire earth for himself. He will bring terrible destruction, illustrated by his wielding "a great sword." Only when the Lord Jesus, who is "The mighty God, The everlasting Father, The Prince of Peace" (Isa. 9:6), comes at the end of the tribulation will humanity experience spiritual and physical tranquility.

C. Third Seal: The Black Horse (6:5–6)

6:5–6. The third angelic being (**beast**; v. 5; see discussions on 4:6, 8) called John to **Come and see**.

When **the third seal** (v. 5) was opened, John was somewhat shocked and uttered the exclamatory **lo** (Greek, *idou*), for he saw **a black horse** carrying a rider who held **a pair of balances in his hand**. The black horse, as the color implies, depicts death and a great famine (see Lam. 4:8–9).

"Balances," or scales, denotes a measuring device commonly used in Bible times. With the coming of worldwide warfare (see 6:4), food will be scarce. Those in power will measure it out, giving it to only those who are loyal to the ruling authorities. The rationing of **wheat** (v. 6; **a measure**, one quart) and of **barley** (**three measures**, three quarts) shows that staple foods will be limited. The measures mentioned here would supply barely enough for three meals. The **penny** is the denarius, or silver coin, the amount paid to a common laborer for a day's work (see Matt. 20:2). It was worth about fifteen cents by today's standards. Used throughout the Roman Empire, the denarius is the most mentioned coin denomination in the Bible. Under such circumstances, the struggle for survival will be immense. In God's graciousness, the basic products needed for meal preparation and for cooking, **the oil and the wine**, will not be **hurt**.

D. Fourth Seal: The Pale Horse (6:7–8)

6:7–8. For the fourth time, one of the four angelic beings (**the fourth beast**; v. 7; see discussions on 4:6, 8) called John to **Come and see** (see 6:1, 3, 5). When **the fourth seal** was opened, John cried out with another exclamatory (**behold**; Greek, *idou*; v. 8), for he saw **Death, and Hell** (Greek, *hadēs*; "Hades," the place of the dead) riding on **a pale horse**. The word "pale" literally means "a pale green" (Greek, *chlōros*), a ghastly color reminiscent of a corpse. Death and Hell are seen as two distinct riders on the one horse. Death and Hell are appropriate names because of the awful destruction these riders brought in their wake: **power was given** (granted) **unto them … to kill with sword, and with hunger, and with death … the fourth part of the earth**. Looking at all of the pages of history in the past, no succinct period, in a brief span of months or years, could have come close to destroying one fourth of all the human beings on the globe. This can refer only to the future events that will come upon the world during the tribulation.

Besides the instruments of destruction listed above, an added element of death is listed: the ravages of uncontrolled animals, **the beasts of the earth** (v. 8). During this, the "great tribulation, such as was not since the beginning of the world to this time, no, nor ever shall be" (Matt. 24:21), civilizations will be so disrupted that any management of the wild animal population will cease. These verses are reminders of God's judgment on Jerusalem, when He sent against the city "the sword, and the famine, and the noisome beast, and the pestilence, to cut off from it man and beast" (Ezek. 14:21).

E. Fifth Seal: The Souls under the Altar (6:9–11)

6:9–11. With the opening of **the fifth seal** (v. 9), John saw **under the [heavenly] altar the souls of them that were slain for the word of God**. According to John's visions of heaven, the heavenly altar is golden and stands before God within the heavenly temple, from which God's wrath will be poured out on the evil upon the earth (see 8:3, 5; 9:13; 11:1; 14:18). **The testimony which they held** also made these martyrs prominent. **They cried** (v. 10) and asked how long it would be before God would **judge** and then **avenge** their **blood** spilt in martyrdom. Because the Lord is the only **holy and true** one, He is the one who is rightly qualified to bring judgment upon humanity. The words "judge" (Greek, *krinō*) and "avenge" (Greek, *ekdikeō*) describe the two works that will fall upon and overtake the tribulation population. "Avenge" in Greek has the connotation of "to defend," "to vindicate," "to exact of the murderer the penalty of his crime."

White robes were given (v. 11) to those who had died a martyr's death, and they were told to **rest ... for a little season**, until all was **fulfilled** in coming upon those who would still die for the faith. While it is not impossible that this refers to saints from all generations, these verses seem to confirm that the ones crying out died during the first of the tribulation, because more were yet to perish. They were not church saints who were taken off the earth before the tribulation started; they were those who had trusted Christ during the tribulation and had died for their faith. **Their fellowservants ... and their brethren** would yet be **killed** in the progression of the seven-year period of wrath. "All hell will break loose on the earth after the Rapture of the Church. The unregenerate nations of the world will unleash a bloodbath on anyone claiming the name of Christ" (Hindson, *The Book of Revelation*, p. 84).

F. Sixth Seal: The Great Earthquake (6:12–17)

This is one of the most terrible scenes in Revelation. All the dynamics of cosmic cataclysms overwhelm the reader. Some commentators have attempted to trivialize these verses and make them but exaggerations of difficult times in the Christian life. This is impossible, however, if the Bible is left to speak in its unmistakable language. Though the sixth seal is the first to involve a natural catastrophe, such cataclysms will begin to tumble quickly upon the earth as the tribulation progresses.

6:12–13. These verses, along with 6:14, describe frightening events in the heavens that will cause some in the human family to seek death (see 6:16). Some scholars have attempted to relegate these verses to meaningless symbolism with little reality in view, but a literal interpretation of actual future events is the only way the passage makes any sense. The heavens will be shaken, and judgment will fall on the nations. The ultimate cause is not man, nor nature, but God, who will pour His wrath out on sinful humanity.

The opening of **the sixth seal** (v. 12) was followed by **a great earthquake**. Though a volcano is not mentioned, the earthquake may have triggered a volcanic eruption, which in turn brought about massive atmospheric pollution, because from earth, **the sun** appeared as **black as sackcloth ... and the moon became as** (like) **blood**. The "as" shows this to be comparative language. John struggled to explain what he was seeing and described the events as best he could.

"Sackcloth" was made from the hides of goats or camels and was worn as a tunic or loincloth as a sign of mourning and anguish. When sackcloth was worn, the mourner often fasted and put ashes on himself (see Isa. 58:5; Dan. 9:3). The Old Testament prophets also wrote that the sun will be darkened in the coming day of the Lord (see Isa. 13:10; 24:23; Ezek. 32:7–8; Joel 2:10, 31; Amos 5:20; 8:9; Zeph. 1:15).

John saw **the stars** (v. 13) plummet to the surface of the earth. The word for "star" is the Greek word *astēr*, which could refer to a star, asteroid, or meteor. From John's point of view, it appeared that the very heavens were raining down on the earth, **as a fig tree casteth her untimely figs, when she is shaken of a mighty wind**. This spectacle of an asteroid or meteor shower will be so enormous that, from a human perspective, it will seem as if all the stars are falling to the earth. As Christ Himself said, "And great earthquakes shall be in divers places, and famines, and pestilences; and fearful sights and great signs shall there be from heaven" (Luke 21:11).

6:14–16. The heaven departed as a scroll when it is rolled together (v. 14). "Departed" is better translated "split apart." When this occurs, the heavens will look as if they have been split in half, and each half will appear to be rolled up like a scroll. Isaiah also wrote of this day, the day of God's wrath: "And the heavens shall be rolled together as a scroll: and all their host shall fall down, as the leaf falleth off from the vine, and as a falling fig from the fig tree" (Isa. 34:4). As well, **every mountain and island were moved out of their places**. It is a scientific fact that when a great earthquake strikes, especially when it occurs deep in the oceans, islands rise and fall, and coastlines are shifted.

What will happen to the people on the earth when these cataclysms occur? The most powerful, the slave, and the free will hide **in the dens and in the rocks of the mountains** (v. 15), but no safe place will be found. Humanity will cry out to be delivered **from the face of him that sitteth on the throne, and from the wrath of the Lamb** (v. 16). Some Bible teachers say that the "wrath" (Greek, *orgēs*; "fury") in the early part of the tribulation will come from

nature, man, and/or Satan, but not from God. They suggest that His wrath will not begin until around 14:9–10, 19 and that the church saints will be on earth when this takes place. That God's wrath will be revealed during the early years of the tribulation, however, is clearly indicated in 6:16–17. Since those presently in the body of Christ will not be subject to His wrath (see 1 Thess. 1:10; 5:9), the rapture of the church will occur before the tribulation begins.

6:17. This verse summarizes the six seals. They are characterized together as **the great day of [God's] wrath** that has arrived. Contrary to the view of those who hold that the Lord's wrath will not be poured out until the later years of the tribulation, this verse makes it clear that "the great day of his wrath" will begin with the opening of the seals. When the first six seals are opened, judgment will begin. The world will be at war, and the future of the planet will be in jeopardy. Yet even in these devastating upheavals, God will still be in charge. Jesus Christ Himself will open the seals, and the sovereign will of God will prevail despite the carnage of a depraved and evil society.

1. The First Interlude (chap. 7)

This chapter has been rightly called an interlude in the breaking of the seven seals. It comes between the sixth and seventh seals. John the apostle stopped and considered the two great numbers of people who had been redeemed "out of great tribulation" (7:14): Jews who were converted and Gentiles who trusted the Lord during that time. This interlude, or parenthesis, is an integral part of the vision of the seals because it refers back to 6:17 and answers the question, "Who shall be able to stand?"

a. The Sealing of the 144,000 (7:1–8)

John witnessed the sealing of 144,000 servants of God (vv. 3–4). The tribal identifications listed in verses 5–8 make it clear that the 144,000 are converted Jews. There is no indication in this passage that they are to be seen as the New Testament church, or even as Gentile Christians. It is clear that they are literal Israelites.

The 144,000 Jewish servants will be given a special task of witnessing during the tribulation. Many scholars believe the sealing of the 144,000 is for their protection while they witness to the unbelievers in the tribulation. The mention of the 144,000 in 14:1–5 "is to show why this group is so special [with] their singular qualifications that have enabled them to fulfill their special mission" (Thomas, *Revelation 8–22*, p. 198). Many of the lost will be "saved through the witness of the 144,000" (Thomas, *Revelation 1–7*, p. 483). "After witnessing for the Lord, they will apparently be martyred, for they will be 'purchased from the earth' (14:3)" (Couch, *Handbook to Revelation*, p. 175). With the church absent from the earth during this time (see discussion on 4:1), their task will be especially important. God will therefore seal these converted Jewish witnesses at the beginning of the tribulation. "The seal of the living God" (v. 2) will protect them from the ensuing judgments so that they may fulfill their task of witnessing to the nations.

Because of the controversy over the literalness of the 144,000 who are sealed, it is important here to review the three interpretative schools. *Postmillennialists* believe that the millennium (the "thousand years" of Revelation 20:1–3) is to be interpreted symbolically as synonymous with the church age. The so-called "millennium" is the church conquering the world with the gospel. A near-perfect society will be developed, and then Christ will return to establish His kingdom. *Amillennialists* also interpret the "thousand years" symbolically but see no millennium of any kind on earth. At the end of the church age, Christ will return to judge the world, and then eternity will begin. *Premillennialists* take the Bible in a more literal sense, though seeing actual events sometimes described with symbolism, figures of speech, illustration, types, and so on. Yet their base of understanding Scripture, and certainly prophecy, is a more literal method of interpretation. With a natural and literal interpretation of Scripture, and especially in regard to prophecy, it only makes sense to take the 144,000 as relating to Jews, as clearly stated, twelve thousand from each tribe. This number is not some representation of church saints. "If national Israel instead of the church is in view, the [interpretative] difficulty dissolves" (Thomas, *Revelation 1–7*, p. 466).

7:1. The **four angels** are a subset of the angelic host who perform specific tasks in Revelation. While the "four beasts" ("living creatures"; see discussions on 4:6, 8) are also angels, they are not the same as described here. **The four corners of the earth** is a symbolic expression meaning "the entire world."

7:2–3. Another angel (v. 2) came from **the east** carrying the authentic **seal of the living God**. He addressed **the four angels**, instructing them to **Hurt** (Greek, *adikeō*; "harm") **not the earth, neither the sea, nor the trees** (vegetation; v. 3) until the 144,000 **servants of our God** were **sealed ... in their foreheads**. No harm, natural or otherwise, was to be unleashed until the 144,000 were sealed and protected, after which further judgment would fall on the earth.

In ancient times, some guilds marked workers on their foreheads to identify them with the group. A forehead mark is most conspicuous. It seems certain that the seal will be visible to all. "The forehead was chosen because it was the most conspicuous. It will be obvious to whom these slaves belong and whom they serve" (Thomas, *Revelation 8–22*, p. 473). The nature of the seal is not identified. Ancient documents, however, were sealed with the signet ring of an official or of the king to authenticate and protect the contents. That God marked these His servants with His seal means that He would not allow them to be hurt until their work was completed. The protective sealing of these Jewish servants shows that they had a special task to perform for the Lord in the early stages of the tribulation. The Lord's "seal" [Greek, *sphragida*] is not the same as the "mark" (Greek, *charagma*) of Revelation 13:16–17.

7:4–8. The number of them which were sealed (v. 4) was 144,000 **of the children of Israel**, with 12,000 coming from each tribe, though with some exceptions. Apparently, **Joseph** (v. 8) is mentioned as representing his son Ephraim. Joseph's other son, **Manasses** (v. 6), is listed, however. **Ephraim** and **Manasses** are subdivisions of the one tribe of Joseph (see Gen. 49:22, 28). The tribe of Dan is not listed, perhaps because this tribe had early connections with idolatry (see Judges 18:30), leaving an early tradition that the Antichrist would come out of that tribe. Another theory says that it was classified with the tribe of **Nephthalim** since Dan was a smaller tribe. **Juda** (v. 5) is listed first, possibly because the Messiah came out of this tribe (see Gen. 49:9–10).

b. The Great Multitude (7:9–17)

This passage makes it clear that both Jews and Gentiles will be saved during the tribulation. A great throng from all nations will be saved, but many will pay with their lives for their faith in Christ.

7:9–10. John moved the narration on with his usual expression: **After this** (Greek, *meta tauta*; v. 9). With an exclamation (**lo**; Greek, *idou*), John showed his wonder at the **great multitude** that he saw coming forth. The people could not be counted. Some scholars believe that more people may be saved during this terrible period than during any other time in history. John subdivided this large company into **nations** (Greek, *ethnos*), **kindreds** (Greek, *phylē*; "tribe" or "family"), **people** (Greek, *laos*), and **tongues** (Greek, *glōssa*; "language"). While Revelation does not explicitly state that many will be martyred during the tribulation, evidence of this is found later in the book. That those in this "great multitude" were redeemed people is obvious in that they **stood ... before the Lamb**, were **clothed with white robes** (indicating righteousness; see 3:5, 18; 4:4; 6:11; 7:13), and waved **palms in their hands**, which represent the coming of peace, salvation, and the victory of the King (see John 12:13). Their heavenly shout of **Salvation** (Greek, *sōtēria*; v. 10) was a shout of joy for the deliverance provided by **God which sitteth upon the throne, and unto the Lamb** as well. Both Father and Son received equal honor for the plan of redemption.

7:11–12. A host of **angels** (v. 11), along with **the elders and the four beasts** ("living ones"), fell down before God's **throne** and **worshipped** Him. This is similar to the worship described in 5:13–14. **Amen** (Greek, *Amēn*; v. 12) was their solemn confirmation

of the tribute the saved multitude offered to God because of the victory He brought (see 1:6, 7; 5:14; 19:4). Their sevenfold tribute and doxology (**Blessing, and glory, and wisdom, and thanksgiving, and honour, and power, and might**) followed, similar to one the multitude of angelic beings addressed to the Lamb in 5:12. The Lord had delivered this vast sea of humanity from the most formidable forces the earth had ever seen (Thomas, *Revelation 1–7*, p. 492).

7:13–14. One of the elders (v. 13) asked an important question: Who **are these which are arrayed in white robes? and whence came they?** That one of the elders asked who they were seems to imply they were not the raptured church saints. This "great multitude" (7:9) consisted of people who came to faith in Christ during the tribulation. Some disagree and believe they were martyred church saints who were killed down through the ages of church history. Such a view, however, means that the great tribulation would have been taking place during the entire period of the church. Instead, these were people who came to Christ after the tribulation began, who then died, and who were now in the Lord's presence in glory. **These are they which came out of great tribulation** (v. 14). "Out of" is the Greek word *ek*, meaning they "came out from" the great tribulation. They were in it, and now they are with the Lord. This clearly indicates that there will be a great host of Gentiles saved during the tribulation.

How can **robes [be] made ... white in the blood of the Lamb** of God? This is the irony of Christ's work on the cross. To the world, the cross and Christ's death for sinners is foolishness (see 1 Cor. 1:18).

7:15–16. These martyred saints were now in the presence of God and continually **serve[d] him day and night in his [heavenly] temple** (v. 15). In turn, the Lord would **dwell among them.** They would no longer suffer the privations of earth. They would never **hunger** again (v. 16) or **thirst**, nor would they suffer the **heat** of the **sun.** Verse 16 could be poetic hyperbole and really be speaking of spiritual suffering during the tribulation. In either case, that period was forever past for this great multitude of believers, and they now basked in the glorious presence of God.

Being **before the throne of God** (v. 15) means this great throng of believers stood in the place of prominence and honor. Their privilege is further defined as serving the Lord "day and night in his temple." That they never needed to sleep gives some inkling of the heavenly state of the saints, in which the limitations of earthly existence are no more.

7:17. Regarding this "great multitude" (7:9), the elder further stated that **the Lamb**, seated **in the midst** of His Father's heavenly **throne[,] shall feed them, and shall lead them unto living fountains of water.** Moreover, **God** Himself **shall wipe away all tears from their eyes** (see Isa. 25:8; Rev. 21:4). In the shining glory of heaven, whatever sorrows and cares have been laid upon the saints in earthly life will be forgotten. They will have the tender care of their Savior.

G. Seventh Seal: Silence in Heaven (8:1)

8:1. The time had arrived for the opening of **the seventh seal.** When the seal was opened, a **silence in heaven** came that lasted for about **half an hour.** John's human finiteness is apparent in his attempt to explain time as he understood it from his human senses. Being transcendent, God is above time, but He created it for human benefit. This "half an hour" of silence anticipated the coming trumpet and vial judgments, which the seventh seal would soon reveal. The absolute silence portended the ominous developments about to take place. One might think of it as the silence that fills a courtroom when a jury foreman is about to read the verdict. For a moment, expectation takes over. What was about to come as the tribulation progressed would only be more horrible than what had gone before.

VIII. The Seven Trumpets (8:2–11:19)

The initial use of the trumpet in the history of Israel was at Mount Sinai. It was first used to call the entire nation to the mountain of God to receive the Ten Commandments (see Exod. 20:18). Trumpets were later used to summon the leaders or the entire nation to the tabernacle in anticipation of journeying to a new location (Num. 10:1–10). They called the nation to war (Num. 10:9), were used for special feasts (Num. 10:10), and were also used for ceremonial processions (1 Chron. 15:24). In Revelation, trumpets were given to the angels to announce the coming of the great calamities stemming from the opening of the seventh seal. In this sense, they were war trumpets. Unlike in ancient Israel, however, the trumpet blasts did not dictate a response from the people but instead announced further judgments that God was sending on the earth.

A. Introduction (8:2–5)

In this passage, seven angels were commanded to sound the "war" trumpets, announcing additional troubles upon the inhabitants of earth. The Lord appointed these angels to direct a series of judgments symbolized by the seven trumpets.

8:2–4. Before **the seven angels** (v. 2) sounded their **trumpets,** John saw **another angel** (v. 3) come before **the altar** in heaven. This angel was given **a golden censer** with a large quantity of **incense** so that he could **offer it with the prayers of all saints upon the golden altar which was before the throne** of God.

This is a moving picture of the redeemed's prayers of appeal being presented before the Lord. Though the context is the tribulation, this scene paints a graphic picture showing that the prayers of the saints of all generations are not lost when offered up to God. They come before His very presence in glory. The Old Testament priests burned incense on the altar of incense. The smoke would fill the temple or tabernacle and would ascend to heaven. Incense is symbolic of prayers and worship to the Lord. This is a reminder that such intercession was to Him as sweet incense in that He is pleased to receive such offerings of the heart. The heavenly altar is mentioned seven times in Revelation (6:9; 8:3 [twice], 5; 9:13; 14:18; 16:7).

8:5. The censer ... filled with fire [from] the altar was **cast ... into** (down upon) **the earth.** That the saints' prayers were on the altar like incense suggests that the saints were near the throne of God and that there is only one altar in heaven, not two. This picture is in keeping with what is recorded in Isaiah 6:6 and Ezekiel 10:2. Whose **voices** did John hear? This is not explained, though the conjecture is that he heard the utterances of the host of the angels who were observing this outpouring of judgment. This scene is virtually repeated in 16:18. The **thunderings, and lightnings, and [the] earthquake** are physical disturbances that accompany God's wrath upon an impenitent earth (see 11:19; 16:18). This verse is a reminder of the Lord's declaration of what was coming upon the earth and of the protection He promised: "I … will keep thee from the hour of temptation, which shall come upon all the world, to try them that dwell upon the earth" (3:10).

B. First Trumpet: Hail and Fire Mixed with Blood (8:6–7)

In chapter 8, four of the seven trumpets are sounded, each having to do with cataclysmic natural disasters affecting the earth. These four trumpets will set in motion the forces of the natural world to achieve the destructive wrath on nature. At this point in the tribulation, humanity's world will be falling apart. Of about fifteen items to be affected by the plagues of the first four trumpets, in twelve instances, one-third of the item will receive injury or destruction (8:7, 10, 11 being the exceptions). God will use the natural world to punish the human race (Thomas, *Revelation 8–22*, p. 13).

8:6–7. The seven trumpet angels came back on the scene and **prepared themselves to sound** (v. 6) the seven trumpets. Their preparation was a distinct arranging of themselves in a proper order and raising their trumpets in readiness to sound forth. The sense of expectancy is heightened.

When **The first angel sounded … hail and fire mingled with blood … were cast upon the earth** (v. 7). It could well be that the "hail and fire mingled with blood" were the result of a series of volcanic explosions triggered by the earthquake (Greek, *seismos*; see 8:5). The "blood" would not be "hemoglobin." In Scripture, blood often stands for pollution, because blood is the greatest incubator for disease.

The fire consumed a **third** (v. 7) of the **trees** on earth, and **all green grass was burnt up**. One can hardly conceive how frightening this will be to

people, for such a widespread conflagration will obviously upset the earth's ecology. Some take this entire picture as figurative, but behind the descriptions are literal happenings. These prophesies resemble what Ezekiel said will happen when the Jews have returned to the land of Israel: "After many days … in the latter years" (Ezek. 38:8), God will pour down on the Gentile nations "pestilence and with blood … an overflowing rain, and great hailstones, fire, and brimstone" (Ezek. 38:22).

C. Second Trumpet: A Mountain Thrown into the Sea (8:8–9)

Nature will be further disrupted with even more damaging natural occurrences. The seas and oceans will be affected, with a large number of creatures perishing. Could this natural disturbance also stem from a military exchange between the nations of the earth? Even if that is so, it does not rule out the involvement of God's wrath in these events. God uses all kinds of means to accomplish His ends.

8:8–9. When **the second angel sounded** (v. 8) his trumpet, **a great mountain … was cast into the sea**, which caused it to **bec[o]me blood** (polluted). In today's atomic age, the seer's description of "hail and fire" (8:7) seems to fit the description of a nuclear explosion of fire and ice. The "great mountain" **burning with fire** A third (v. 9) of sea life **died; and [a] third … of the ships** in the ocean **were destroyed**. This parallels the second vial judgment, which results in the killing of all sea life (see 16:3).

D. Third Trumpet: The Star Wormwood (8:10–11)

Following the destruction of one-third of the seawaters, one-third of the freshwaters will be polluted. This will threaten creatures of all kinds, including human beings. Finding potable water will become a life-and-death matter.

8:10–11. When **the third angel sounded** (v. 10) his trumpet, a flaming **great star** (Greek, *astēr*), or asteroid, **fell [into a] third … of the rivers, and [into] the fountains of waters**, which probably refers to the wells or groundwaters. This celestial body,

called Wormwood (v. 11), polluted the earth's fresh-waters when it fell from heaven, **and many men died** because the waters **were made bitter** (poisoned). Wormwood is a terrible-tasting, bitter plant and is common in the Middle East in several varieties. It is mentioned in the Old Testament to depict bitterness and sorrow and is said to bear poisonous fruit (see Deut. 29:18; Jer. 9:15; 23:15).

E. Fourth Trumpet: A Third of the Sun, Moon, and Stars Struck (8:12–13)

The sounding of the fourth trumpet will cause the atmosphere to be darkened. This will have a devastating affect on the morale of all on the earth. Christ spoke of these days coming. He said that "men's hearts [would be] failing them for fear, and for looking after those things which are coming on the earth: for the powers of the heaven shall be shaken" (Luke 21:26).

8:12–13. When **the fourth angel sounded** (v. 12) his trumpet, the heavenly luminaries (**the sun, the moon,** and **the stars**) lost their effectiveness from earth's perspective. A **third part** was dimmed, and both **day** and **night** appeared to be swallowed up in darkness. There are two suggestions as to how to understand verse 12. One is that these heavenly bodies will be simultaneously cursed so that they give off a third less light than normal. Another view, which may be preferable, is that the atmospheric pollution caused by the first three trumpet judgments will reduce the amount of light from the sun, moon, and stars. In either case, God is the one who will bring on these natural curses.

An angel (v. 13) overhead, **flying through the midst of heaven,** cried out, **Woe, woe, woe** (Greek, *Ouai, ouai, ouai*) **to the inhabiters of the earth!** The angel's cry was not only a lament but a pronouncement of doom for the inhabitants of the earth. The threefold repetition of "woe" corresponds to the three remaining trumpet judgments, which are fulfilled in 9:12, 11:14, and 12:12. Some preferred Greek texts give the word "eagle" (Greek, *aetos*) in place of "angel." Whatever the reading should be, this creature warned of additional troubles soon to fall upon the earth.

F. Fifth Trumpet: The Plague of Locusts (9:1–12)

A second "star" will fall from heaven, but this "star" will be a divine agent rather than a cosmic disturbance as in 8:10. This divine agent, probably an angel, will have the power to unleash a demonic hoard of loathsome creatures that will inflict unbelievable pain on humanity, both physically and spiritually. These creatures are described as "locusts" (v. 3), symbolic of demons or demon-inspired combatants. They will torment earthlings for five months (vv. 5, 10). Because of the tormenting sting, men will want to die, but "death shall flee from them" (v. 6).

9:1–3. When **the fifth angel sounded** (v. 1) his trumpet, John **saw a star fall from heaven unto the earth.** The "star" is a personification of an angelic creature who has already "fallen" (perfect tense) at some point in the past. While no explanation is given as to his identity, the event resembles the fall of Satan (see 12:7–9). Christ alluded to this when He said: "I beheld Satan as lightning fall from heaven" (Luke 10:18). Isaiah wrote, "How art thou fallen from heaven, O Lucifer, son of the morning!" (Isa. 14:12). The name Lucifer means "the shining one." Still, the identification of this being is not certain. One argument against this being Satan is that the angelic creature **was given the key to the bottomless pit.** That the key was given to him implies that he could act only with God's permission. This is also true of the creatures that came forth from the pit (v. 2). They were under God's divine authority and could not do their evil work without His consent.

The bottomless pit (Greek, *abyssos*; v. 2) was **opened,** out of which **arose** a searing **smoke** like that from **a great furnace. The sun and the air** (the atmosphere) **were darkened** by the thickness and intensity of the smoke. **Out of the smoke [came] locusts** (v. 3) that had **the power ... [of] the scorpions** that roam the desert sands. These evil spirits had been confined in the bottomless pit for just such an hour of torment.

9:4–6. The demonic locusts were given a command. This command must have come from God because it restricted their activity. They were not allowed to **hurt** (v. 4) the natural world: **grass, any** (other) **green thing,** or **any tree.** Instead, they were **commanded** to inflict pain on **only those men which have not the seal of God in their foreheads.** Those who did have the seal of God could be either the 144,000 Jewish witnesses (see 7:3 – 8) who had received the Lord's seal on their foreheads (see 7:3) or all those who had been redeemed during the tribulation.

The locusts were also commanded that they **should not kill** (v. 5) the unsealed but instead torment them for **five months.** Some have assumed that "five months" is figurative, with no definite time allotted, but it is best to take this as a literal period. It has been noted that often locust swarms commit their ravages for about five months. While the locusts are satanic beings, not insects, the typology remains, as if they were marauding insect pests that devour the vegetation of the landscape.

The torment inflicted by the demonic locusts will be so terrible that people will **seek death** (v. 6). They will want to die but will not be able to get up the courage to go through with it. World civilizations will reap the results of spiritual rebellion.

9:7 – 10. Comparative language is used to describe these demonic beings, **the locusts** (v. 7). This is common in the book of Revelation. Comparative language is used in this book more often than in all of the rest of the New Testament books. Note John's use of comparative language in the following descriptions of the locusts.

> "power, *as* the scorpions of earth" (9:3)
> "their torment was *as* the torment of a scorpion" (9:5)
> "the shapes ... were *like unto* horses" (9:7)
> "on their heads were *as it were* crowns like gold" (9:7)
> "their faces were *as* the faces of men" (9:7)
> "they had hair *as* the hair of women" (9:8)
> "their teeth were *as* the teeth of lions" (9:8)
> "they had breastplates, *as it were* ... of iron" (9:9)
> "the sound of their wings was *as* the sound of chariots of many horses" (9:9)
> "they had tails *like unto* scorpions" (9:10)

John had to use comparative language often because he was struggling to convey what he was seeing. Most of the meanings in these descriptions are obvious. To the ancients, **horses** (v. 7) were the most fearful of beasts to encounter in combat. **Crowns** show that these creatures had commanding authority to do their dirty deeds. **Their faces** displayed intelligence like that of humans. As seductive **women** flaunt their **hair,** some aspect of temptation may have been involved as these creatures sought to destroy the souls of people. **The teeth of lions** (v. 8) shows fierceness, while the **breastplates** (v. 9) indicate invincibility. From their wings was heard **the sound of chariots,** a noise that meant death for troops caught on the field of battle unprotected. Finally, for emphasis, it is repeated that their **stings** (v. 10) were like that of **scorpions ... and their power was to hurt men for five months.**

9:11 – 12. Who is the **king** (v. 11) over this horde? The names **Abaddon** (Hebrew) and **Apollyon** (Greek) both carry the idea of "the one who destroys." Abaddon is a personification of destruction in the Old Testament (see Prov. 15:11). Some believe he is a powerful demonic figure. Walvoord believes this king is Satan (*The Revelation of Jesus Christ,* p. 163). Thomas, however, holds that this is probably not so (*Revelation 8 – 22,* p. 38): nowhere is Satan connected with the abyss until he is finally cast into it (see 20:1 – 3), and there is a case for identifying this king as an unknown angel who is in charge of the abyss. Satan has leaders and subleaders under his command (see Eph. 6:12).

One terrible cry of **woe is past** (v. 12), with **two woes** yet to come. "Woe" is often a cry uttered because of some great catastrophe that is imposed as a judgment from God. The Lord Jesus gave such a cry when He pronounced judgment on Chorazin and Bethsaida (see Matt. 11:21).

G. Sixth Trumpet: Release of the Four Angels (9:13 – 21)

Many scholars take this passage as a second phase of the demonic torment introduced in 9:1 – 12, but others see the great horde in verses 16 – 17 as an actual army. The attackers seem to be described as men, and one-third of the people left on earth will be killed (vv. 16–18). Some of the war instruments involved could be seen as modern weapons. The world will fail to repent (v. 20) but will instead continue in the grossest of sins (v. 21).

9:13–14. When **the sixth angel sounded** (v. 13) his trumpet, John **heard a voice** speaking **from the four horns of the golden altar** that stood before the Lord's throne in heaven (see 8:3–5). In the ancient Jewish tabernacle, the "horns" were located on the four corners of the altar (see Exod. 27:2) and were used to tie down the offering that was being presented to God. Those fleeing for justice could seek mercy by taking hold of the horns (see 1 Kings 1:50–51; 2:28; Amos 3:14). Putting 9:13–14 together with 8:3–5, it seems that this further outpouring of God's judgment was in answer to the prayers of those who had suffered and died in the early stages of the tribulation. A command was given to **Loose the four angels which are bound in the great river Euphrates** (v. 14). Divine permission was now granted for their release. These four angels are probably not the same four angels as in 7:1.

The Euphrates flows southeast from the mountains of Armenia down to the Tigris in lower Babylon. The two rivers cover an eighteen hundred mile arc through the deserts of Iraq. This area has always been one of the most formidable and important regions in history, but it was also the ancient source of polytheism, demonism, and false religions. The Euphrates will play an important role at the end of the tribulation, when "the kings of the east" (16:12) cross over while coming into the Middle East. The Euphrates serves as the eastern boundary of the Promised Land (see Gen. 15:18; Deut. 1:7; Josh. 1:4). "The kings of the east" could be from the Arab nations, China, Japan, or other Muslim nations from North Africa to Mongolia.

9:15–16. The four angels … were prepared for an hour, and a day, and a month, and a year … to slay [a] third (v. 15) of humanity. The time frame is poetized for drama, but the designations are the same. It could read, "the appointed hour occurs on the appointed day in the appointed month and in

the appointed year" (Thomas, *Revelation 8–22*, p. 44). The destruction of a third of the people of earth makes this the most intense plague so far. The earth's population will be whittled down, with millions perishing with each addition of judgment. **The number of the army** (v. 16) unleashed for combat calculates out to 200 million **horsemen**.

9:17–18. It is the description of **the horses** (v. 17), and not the riders, that gives the impression that some demonic forces are at work here. The horses, with their riders, seem to be invincible and suggest a superhuman origin. The **breastplates** are described as being **of fire, and of jacinth, and brimstone**. One suggestion is that these elements represent colors of a protective material. "Fire" would be red, "jacinth" represents a blue smokelike color, and "brimstone" could refer either to a darker smokelike color or to a yellow color like sulphur. John saw the same elements coming out of the horses' mouths. The colors suggest some kind of destruction by heat. **The heads of the horses were as the heads of lions**—powerful, strong, fierce. Further light is cast on the character of the warfare in verse 18, where it is repeated that the invading forces will kill **the third part** of humanity.

9:19. With the additional visual allusions of this verse, the description of these evil creatures becomes even more gross. No interpreter can say for certain what all of the symbolism means, except that these descriptions portray actual events and an actual army. John must have struggled to fully comprehend what he was seeing. This is a terrible picture of a daunting military power destroying all that opposes it. The descriptions of the horses—with "heads of lions" (9:17) and **tails [that] were like unto serpents, and had heads, and with them do hurt**—conjure up an image of deadly warfare.

9:20–21. Those who survived the onslaught and **were not killed by these plagues** (v. 20) of destruction still did not repent. "Plague" (Greek, *plēgē*) often refers to disease, but the Greek word also means "wound," "blow," or "stroke." These "plagues" were more like lashings, stripes, or wounds coming upon the world by the forces just described. Some feel

verse 20 refers to all of the trumpet judgments, but
more than likely, it refers to the sixth trumpet only.
Even with God's wrath falling upon them, humanity refused to repent ("change the mind"). They **repented not of the [evil] works of their hands**, nor of
their **worship [of] devils** and their worship of **idols**
made of **gold, silver, brass, stone**, and **wood**. Such
idols are blind, deaf, and immobile. It must be remembered that even today the majority of the present world population practices some form of pagan
idolatry. This will continue or grow worse in the
tribulation period.

Neither repented they of their other sins (v. 21).
The most heinous of these sins is mentioned first —
murders. The idolaters continued in **their sorceries** (Greek, *pharmakon*), the use of drugs in their
incantations, or perhaps drug use without any religious connection. Sexual sins (Greek, *porneias*) are
mentioned next, along with the most common of
public crimes, **thefts** (Greek, *klemmatōs*). "Such is
depraved and infatuated human nature.... If people
will not listen in the days of peaceful opportunity,
there remaineth very little hope for them" (Seiss, *The
Apocalypse*, p. 222).

1. The Second Interlude (10:1–11:14)

This lengthy interlude, or parenthetical section,
comes between the sixth and seventh trumpets.
By the end of the sixth trumpet judgment, half of
the world's population will have been annihilated.
The interlude sets the stage for the sounding of the
seventh and final trumpet (see 11:15), a trumpet
so powerful that it will result in the complete collapse of all of the earth's civilizations that are aligned
against the Lord.

As in the interlude in chapter 7, the narrative
does not advance but additional information that
contributes to the total prophetic scene is presented.
In chapter 10, John was given a vision of heaven that
focused on a "little book" (10:2), or scroll, which led
to more prophecies about "peoples, and nations, and
tongues, and kings" (10:11). In 11:1–14, he received
a revelation concerning the "two witnesses" (11:3)
who are part of the Lord's worldwide testimony to

warn "the people and kindreds and tongues and nations" (11:9).

a. The Angel and the Little Scroll (chap. 10)

10:1. Here the scene returns to heaven. John saw
another mighty (strong) **angel**. This angel is compared to the "strong angel" of 5:2 ("another"; Greek,
allos; "one similar to," "one of the same type") but
is not specifically identified. Some have suggested
that this is Christ Jesus Himself, but this seems unlikely in light of 10:5–6. Although Christ is seen
in the Old Testament as the Angel of Jehovah (see
Gen. 18:1–15), nowhere in the New Testament is
He called simply "an angel." This "mighty angel,"
clothed with a cloud: and a rainbow (Greek, *iris*)
... upon his head, was adorned in the majesty of
heaven itself.

**His face was [like] the sun, and his feet as pillars
of fire**. Here again comparative language comes into
play. The brilliance of the angel's face is likened to
Christ's (see 1:16). The legs are likened to fire, which
suggests judgment. Angels play a key role in Revelation; they are mentioned sixty-six times.

10:2. The **little book** (Greek, *biblaridion*; diminutive), or "little scroll," was held by the mighty angel,
who had **his right foot upon the sea, and his left
foot on the earth**. The coming judgments would encompass both land and sea, that is, the entire world.

10:3–6. John heard a cry as commanding **as
when a lion roareth** (v. 3), followed by the **voices
of seven thunders** (see 8:5). Some tie this to the
seven times the voice of God is mentioned in Psalms
29:3–9. As John **was about to write** what he had
heard, **a** (singular) **voice** (v. 4) commanded him,
**Seal up those things which the seven thunders ut-
tered, and write them not**. John must have received
an ominous message, but he was ordered not to record it. The descriptions of terror in the message are
not given in detail, but they are seen in the chapters
that follow. "Though the text does not reveal what
the thunders say, it is a safe conclusion that they are
an audible symbol that God will bring added terror
before the end (cf. 8:5; 11:19; 16:18)" (Thomas, *Revelation 8–22*, p. 65).

The angel ... lifted up his hand to heaven, and sware by (vv. 5–6) God Himself. This is one proof that this angelic being is not the Lord Jesus in that he swore by God, showing that God is greater than the angel. This was a solemn oath, not a curse. The angel proclaimed that God exists eternally and that He is the creator of heaven ... and the earth ... and the sea, and [all] the things which are therein. All matter is created by Him. What is striking in this message is that a day is coming when there should be time no longer (v. 6). "Time" (Greek, *chronos*) is best translated here as "delay." A strong consensus of scholars confirms this translation. The events of 10:1–11:14 are not taking place between the sixth and seventh trumpets, so no chronological progression has come about between this 10:1 and 11:15. This delay is best seen as the delay before the fulfillment of "the mystery of God" (10:7) and is best explained in light of the martyrs' question in 6:10: "How long, O Lord ...?"

10:7. When the seventh angel ... shall begin to sound, the mystery (Greek, *mystērion*) of God [will] be finished (Greek, *etelesthē*), or "completed," "fulfilled," "wrapped up." This "mystery of God" seems to be about the Old Testament promises that the kingdom of God will someday be established on earth, promises that were now unfolding. The prophecies relating to the power, majesty, and holiness of God will be clearly fulfilled in Christ's glorious return to establish His millennial reign. "The mystery of God" is also about the eternal state that will follow Christ's earthly reign.

10:8–9. A heavenly voice (v. 8) instructed John to take the little book from the hand of the angel. The apostle was then instructed to eat it (v. 9) but was warned that it would make his belly bitter, probably meaning that it would give him indigestion. In contradiction, however, it would be sweet as honey in his mouth. The sweetness represented John's joy that God was bringing to a conclusion the sin and evil upon the earth. The bitterness represented his sorrow over the terrible but righteous judgments that God was further sending down upon humanity. John, the faithful apostle and servant, was to deliver both aspects of these omens.

10:10–11. After eating the little book (v. 10), John experienced just what he had been told to expect. Then the angel told him, Thou must prophesy again, prophecies about all the peoples (v. 11) upon the earth and the judgments that God would send against them. Verse 11 leaves no room for the idea that tribulation will be simply some localized series of tribulations in just one country, region, or area such as the Mediterranean basin. The word many emphasizes the international scope of the tribulations. The seven-year period of God's wrath will be a worldwide judgment; it will fall upon all nations (see 6:12–17).

b. The Two Witnesses (11:1–14)

This passage continues the interlude with a description of the two witnesses. God will not leave the world without a testimony. These two personalities will have a global outreach, though their message will be for the most part rejected. The identity of these two witnesses is a compelling and often debated question. The text clearly indicates that they are specific individuals with miraculous powers like Moses (turning water to blood) and Elijah (calling down fire from heaven). The Old Testament ends with an appeal to both Moses and Elijah (Mal. 4:4–6). Also, they were the two witnesses at the transfiguration of Jesus (Matt. 17:1–3). Whether the two witnesses are literally Moses and Elijah or come in the spirit and type of them, only time will tell.

11:1–3. A reed like unto a rod (v. 1) refers to a bamboo-like reed that grew to a height of sixteen to twenty feet on the banks of the Nile and the Jordan rivers. It was the common measuring rod used on construction sites (see Ezek. 40:3; Zech. 2:1–2). John was told to Rise, and measure the temple of God, and the altar, and them that worship therein. The temple John saw was the restored temple that will play a role in the tribulation. This is probably the temple in which the Antichrist will enter, seat himself, and proclaim "that he is God" (2 Thess. 2:4), as prophesied in Daniel 9:27 and Matthew 24:15. The temple will also house the idol to this world dictator (see Rev. 13:14–15).

The court (v. 2) of the Gentiles, however, John was to leave out, and measure ... not. Before and during the time of the Gospels, this court was where the Gentiles could come to worship, but they were not allowed to enter the temple and mingle with the Jews. Since the Gentiles shall ... tread under foot Jerusalem, the holy city, for forty and two months, or for three and a half years, this period is probably the last half of the seven-year tribulation rather than the first half. Jerusalem will be the center, the vortex, of the tribulation. The expression "my two witnesses" is probably God speaking. These two prophets belong to Him and He is the one who imparts His power for the work they are doing. The two witnesses ... shall prophesy (v. 3) during this period. That they will be clothed in sackcloth shows that they will stay in a meditative mood and will be humble in their demeanor.

11:4. The imagery of the two olive trees, and the two candlesticks parallels that of Zechariah 4:2–6, where it represents Joshua the priest and Zerubbabel the prince, who were key personalities in restoring Israel following the Babylonian captivity. In an ironic twist, while the two witnesses will bring judgments on the earth, they will also bring both blessing (olive tree) and light (candlestick).

11:5–6. Some suggest the two witnesses are Enoch and Elijah because both men were taken up to heaven without facing death (for Enoch, see Gen. 5:21–24; for Elijah, see 2 Kings 2:1–18); thus, they will come back to earth in bodily form and eventually die. However, their miraculous powers seem to indicate Moses and Elijah. Fire proceedeth out of their mouths, and devoureth their enemies, as in Elijah's encounters with the servant messengers of Ahaziah (see 2 Kings 1:10, 12). That the two witnesss will have the power to turn waters ... to blood, and to smite the earth with ... plagues (v. 6) reminds readers of Moses' authority over the Egyptians (see Exod. 7:17–21).

God will place His protection over these prophets so that anyone who harms them will die. They will have power to shut heaven (v. 6) so that it will not rain while they prophesy, and they will be able to pass judgment as they will.

11:7–9. When they shall have finished their testimony (v. 7), they will perish. The beast that ascendeth out of the bottomless pit shall make war against them [to] overcome them and slay them (see 9:1–2, 11; 17:8; 20:1–3). "The beast" is the Antichrist, who is referred to nine times in Revelation (13:1; 14:9, 11; 15:2; 16:2; 17:3, 13; 19:20; 20:10). The dead bodies (v. 8) of the witnesses will be left in the street of the great city, which spiritually is called Sodom and Egypt. To make sure the reader understands that Jerusalem is meant here, John added, where also our Lord was crucified. Sodom (see Gen. 19:4–11) and Egypt (see Ps. 105:38; Isa. 19:1; Jer. 46:25) were centers of religious apostasy and rebellion. John wrote this prophecy some twenty years after the destruction of Jerusalem. For her rejection of their own Messiah, Christ prophesied that Jerusalem would be visited by the Lord's "vengeance" (Luke 21:22). In the tribulation, at least for a short period, the city will again spiritually rebel against Him. For three days and a half (v. 9), the entire world shall see their dead bodies, probably by satellite television!

11:10–11. The whole world shall rejoice ... and make merry, and shall send gifts (v. 10) as if celebrating a universal holiday, because these two prophets tormented them that dwelt on the earth. "Torment" (Greek, basanizō) means to "torture," "harass," "cause to struggle." This torment was first spiritual conviction, followed by a miraculous shaking of the elements of the planet in judgment warning (see 11:5–6). The world was in pain because of these two special prophets of God. The death of the two witnesess will appear to be a great victory for Satan and the Antichrist.

To further gain the world's attention, however, the Lord brought the two witnesses back to life. The spirit of life ... entered into them, and they stood upon their feet (v. 11). This extraordinary event put great fear in those who saw it. It was a dramatic vindication of the true faith (see Ezek. 37:5, 10).

11:12–14. Offering additional proof to the world, a great voice from heaven (v. 12) summoned these two prophets, Come up hither. And they ascended up to heaven in a cloud; and their enemies beheld them leave. This was a divine call. The two witnesses responded to the invitation and departed into glory. The rapture of the witnesses serves to verify the validity of the earlier rapture of the church. **The same hour**, another judgment fell upon apostate Jerusalem: **a great earthquake** (v. 13) that destroyed a **tenth** of the city. **Seven thousand** men perished. A **remnant** of the survivors **were affrighted, and gave glory to the God of heaven**. This was in contrast to the required worship of the Beast. "The God of heaven" is an Old Testament phrase used to distinguish the true God from pagan deities. Many have questioned whether the earthquake caused true faith in Christ or simply an acknowledgment of God's greatness. Since possibly millions will come to Christ during the tribulation, it is not far-fetched to believe that the survivors were converted.

So the **second woe** (v. 14) ends, leaving the seventh trumpet to sound and **the third** and final **woe** to come. Many believe the second woe is considered as the final phase of the sixth trumpet. The third woe contained in the seventh trumpet is announced as coming quickly. Without a doubt the end of the age is fast approaching.

H. Seventh Trumpet: Judgments and Rewards (11:15 – 19)

This is a preview section that introduces where the events coming in the next chapters are going. At the end of the terror of the tribulation, God will establish His earthly kingdom with the reign of His Christ. God's wrath gets worse and the nations will experience even more intense judgment. (Satan, the dragon, his persecution against the Jewish people, symbolized by the woman, in order to destroy her.) This effort by Satan will take place during the last half of the tribulation (v. 6). It seems clear that 11:15 – 13:1 – 18 focuses on the diabolical work of Satan, the Antichrist (the beast), and the other beast (the religious ruler). These events begin at the midpoint of the tribulation.

The seventh trumpet is only introduced at this stage. Its judgments are not fully described until chapter 16. The introduction of this trumpet is extremely dramatic, however. From heaven will come a crescendo of powerful voices. The seventh trumpet introduces the most horrible of the plagues and the seven vials (or bowls) of wrath (see 15:1 – 16:2). The seven trumpets announce the kingdom, but they begin the seven vials of wrath (11:15). The seven plagues are the seven vials (bowls) filled with the wrath of God (15:1). These seven plagues "are the last, because in them the wrath of God is finished" (see vv. 15 – 16). They close with bringing "the cup of the wine of his fierce wrath" upon Babylon the great (16:19).

11:15. This is a proclamation of what is coming; that is, **the kingdoms of this world are become the kingdoms of our Lord. The kingdoms of this world** is a consolidation of the kingdom of the Antichrist, the "fourth beast" and "fourth kingdom" mentioned in Daniel 7:23. This fourth kingdom on the earth will be different from all the other kingdoms. It will "devour the whole earth, and … tread it down, and break it in pieces" (Dan. 7:23). The fifth kingdom mentioned in Daniel (Dan. 7:26 – 28) is the kingdom of God **and of his Christ**. The messianic kingdom will supersede the kingdom of the Antichrist. To the Son of Man will be given "dominion, and glory, and a kingdom, that all people, nations, and languages, should serve him: his dominion is an everlasting dominion, which shall not pass away, and his kingdom that which shall not be destroyed" (Dan. 7:14). "From this point on, everything follows in rapid succession. These five verses (15 – 19) are among the most dramatic verses in the entire Bible.… One cannot read these verses without realizing that we have come to some great conclusion. It is all over except the shouting!… The extensive use of the aorist tense conveys a sense of absolute certainty about the events yet to come" (Hindson, *Revelation*, p. 127).

11:16 – 17. The twenty-four **elders** (v. 16) were seated before the throne of **God**. Upon hearing the glorious proclamation of 11:15, the elders **fell upon their faces, and worshipped God**. Their worship consisted of thanks to the **Lord God Almighty** (v. 17), who lives eternally (see 1:8; 4:8), and praise for His **great power**. "Almighty" (Greek, *pantokratōr*) is used nine times in Revelation. When John wrote that the

Lord **hast reigned**, he was prophesying of the earthly kingdom of Christ (see Ezek. 21:26–27; Dan. 2:35, 44; 4:3; 6:26; 7:14, 26–27; Zech. 14:9), which will be dramatically fulfilled in His second coming (see Rev. 19:11–21) and His millennial reign (see 20:1–8).

11:18. Though **the nations were angry**, the final stage of the Lord's **wrath is come**, as well as the time for the judgment of **the dead** and the rewarding of the Lord's **servants the prophets, and … the saints**. The time had also arrived when God would destroy **them which destroy the earth**. This seems to refer to those living on the earth at that time who rebelled against God, misused the resources of the world for their own ends, and disregarded the terrible destruction they were bringing down on God's creation.

11:19. The heavenly **temple … was opened**, and the heavenly **ark of his testament** (covenant) was revealed. The heavenly temple was reflected in the ancient earthly temple. The earthly ark represented God's presence among His people. It was constructed of precious acacia wood (see Deut. 10:1–2) and symbolized the Lord's throne. It symbolized His faithfulness but was also the place where judgment, as well as mercy, was meted out. The vision of the ark brought about more judgment on the inhabitants of earth. Chronologically, the time was close for Christ's second coming. Events yet to come are previewed in 11:18–19.

IX. Various Personages and Events (chaps. 12–14)

While the seventh trumpet was sounded in 11:15, the details of that judgment are not fully disclosed until chapter 16. Thus, chapters 12–14 view the prophecies of the end times from a different perspective. Rather than moving the narrative forward, these chapters introduce the key characters that will be involved in the second half of the seven-year tribulation period. The chronology of events is picked up again in chapter 15.

A. The Woman and the Dragon (chap. 12)

Chapter 12 has two main interpretations. (1) The first view sees it as describing events that take place at this point in the tribulation, including Satan's being cast to the earth along with his evil angels (v. 9), and heralding the fact that Christ will usher in the kingdom of God and secure the final salvation (v. 10) for His people. (2) The second view sees it as a summary of past events concerning Satan's fall (vv. 1–12) and an update on his plans to destroy Israel (vv. 13–17). Whichever view is correct, all scholars hold that the chapter focuses on the satanic conflict in heaven and how this war came to earth to subvert God's program concerning the Jewish nation and concerning His Son.

12:1–2. A great wonder (Greek, *sēmeion mega*; v. 1) is better translated "a great sign." "The identification of this woman is the most critical issue in properly interpreting the Apocalypse. The woman symbolizes the nation and people of Israel. The imagery is taken from Joseph's dream in Genesis 37:9–11, where the sun and moon and twelve stars represent the patriarchy of Israel and the twelve tribes. The figure as a travailing woman is prevalent in the Old Testament (cf. Is. 26:17–18; Jer. 4:31; 13:21; Mic. 4:10; 5:3).… The woman has the 'crown of twelve stars,' symbolizing the tribes of Israel" (Hindson, *Revelation*, p. 137). The woman **travailing in birth** (v. 2) is Israel, which, through the Virgin Mary, gave birth to the **child**, the Lord Jesus Christ. The "woman" in this chapter represents the "mother" of Christ (Israel), not the "bride" of Christ (the church).

12:3–5. The **great red dragon** (v. 3) is Satan (see 12:9). His **seven heads and ten horns, and seven crowns** show the authority that he will have when his full intentions are revealed during the second half of the tribulation. He is similarly described in 13:1. A parallel is found in Daniel 7:7–8, 24, which is clearly about the revived Roman Empire. "The seven heads and ten horns refer to the original ten kingdoms of which three were subdued by the little horn of Daniel 7:8, who is to be identified as the world ruler of the great tribulation who reigns over the revived Roman Empire" (Walvoord, *The Revelation of Jesus Christ*, p. 189).

His tail drew the third part of the stars of heaven (v. 4) refers to that far-distant past when Satan fell from the presence of the Lord, taking with him a great company of rebellious angels (see Isa. 14:12–15; Ezek. 28:12–19). (Many scholars believe that Satan is behind the evil activities of the king of Tyre referred to in Ezekiel 28:12–19. This would seem logical, since verse 13 says, "Thou has been in Eden the garden of God." Or it could be that the king of Tyre symbolizes Satan.) Ezekiel 28:12–19 "is of tremendous theological import, recording the origin of sin and Satan and the character and panoramic career of the greatest of angels" (Unger, *Old Testament Commentary*, p. 1553). Christ mentioned this event in Luke 10:18: "I beheld Satan as lightning fall from heaven."

In his next great attempt to nullify God's plan, Satan endeavored **to devour [the] child** (v. 4), the Lord Jesus, at the time of His birth. Working through the evil King Herod, Satan attempted to kill Jesus some months after His birth (see Matt. 2:1–18). John described Christ's kingly role by quoting Psalm 2:9: "he shall rule [all nations] with a rod of iron" (Rev. 19:15). After His crucifixion and ascension, Christ was seated on the heavenly throne at the right hand of His Father, where He awaits the coming day when His enemies shall be made His "footstool" (Ps. 110:1).

12:6. John's vision then moved on to Satan's actions during the tribulation. Satan again sought to devour God's own, but **the woman** (Israel) **fled into the wilderness**, where God had **prepared** a place to hide her for 1,260 days, or three and a half years. Christ mentioned this in His Olivet Discourse prophecy (see Matt. 24:16; Mark 13:14). Most scholars believe this refers to the last three and a half years of the tribulation, because the Jewish people will have comparative tranquility during the first half of the tribulation (see Dan. 9:27). This protection is not for all of the Jews but only for a remnant. This remnant may include the 144,000 for a short period. But they are "purchased from the earth" and die martyrs' deaths, as indicated in 14:1–5. The remnant, then, are the Jews who enter the kingdom at the end of the tribulation.

12:7–9. Many scholars believe that the **war in heaven** (v. 7), in which **Michael and his angels fought against [Satan] … and his angels**, is directly part of the tribulation context (see introduction to chap. 12), but most likely, it looks back to the initial fall of Satan. Some cite the fact that Satan had access to God in heaven in order to speak with Him even though he had fallen from heaven because of his original rebellion. There seems to be a difference between Satan's fellowship with God before the fall and the fact that he still has access to God to speak with Him. A case in point is the accusation that Satan brought against Job (see Job 1:6–12). The angel Michael, "the great prince which standeth for the children of thy people," is the defender of Israel, and he will again "stand up" to protect Israel during the tribulation, the "time of trouble, such as never was since there was a nation … and at that time [the Jews] shall be delivered, every one that [is] found written in the book [of life]" (Dan. 12:1).

12:10–12. "The events of this chapter deal in general with the end of the age" (Walvoord, *The Revelation of Jesus Christ*, p. 192). "If this is viewed as a *future* event, then it must happen during the Great Tribulation. In favor of the future viewpoint is the fact that the time Satan is on earth after being cast out is three and one half years ('times'). This also correlates with the 1,260 days the woman (Israel) is persecuted and driven into the wilderness (12:6)" (Hindson, *The Book of Revelation*, p. 139). These verses give a preview of the arrival of the millennium, which is described more fully in 19:11. John **heard a loud voice saying … Now is come salvation, and strength, and the kingdom of our God** (v. 10) through **the power of his Christ**. Satan (which in Hebrew means **accuser**) was busy accusing the **brethren** in the past and continued to do so in the tribulation. His continual activity in this role, accusing God's people **day and night**, as he "walketh about, seeking whom he may devour" (1 Peter 5:8) illustrates his hatred of the righteous. Here, however, Satan **is cast down**. The Lord Jesus supplied the victory, but those who died for the faith took part in that triumph. They overcame **by the blood of the Lamb, and by the word of their testimony** (v. 11). They did not hold on to their lives but were willing to march all the way **unto the death**.

The very **heavens** (v. 12) and all its inhabitants were called to **rejoice** because of Christ's great victory. **The inhabiters of the earth and of the sea,** however, were warned that **the devil is come down unto you** with more vengeance, **having great wrath, because he knoweth that he hath but a short time.** While not knowing the very mind of God, the Devil knows the Bible, and he knows that at this point in the tribulation, he will have only 1,260 days left. Satan's days are numbered!

12:13 – 14. When the dragon saw that he was cast unto the earth, he attacked **the woman** (v. 13), Israel, with added intensity. Satan hates the Jewish people, who brought forth the Savior, the Lord Jesus Christ! The woman, however, was given the **wings of a great eagle** (v. 14) to **fly into the wilderness.** Wings picture God's protective deliverance (see Exod. 19:4; Deut. 32:11 – 12). This flight to safety is indicated in Matthew 24:16; Mark 13:14; Luke 21:21. Many believe this hiding place could be the rock city of Petra, which was once the fortified capital of the Nabateans of Edom. Thousands of people could be hidden in Petra's canyons and rock caverns. Some speculate that the 144,000 witnessing Jews will be protected there for a time. The 144,000 will not be simply buried away in a rock fortress, however. The world will hear their testimony.

God **nourished** (v. 14) and protected the Jews **for a time, and times, and half a time** (v. 14), which refers to the last of the three and a half years of the tribulation ("a time" is one year, and "half a time" is six months). This would be the period just before the second coming of Christ.

12:15 – 17. Satan attempted to destroy **the woman** (v. 15) with **water as a flood.** To destroy Israel would be to thwart God's kingdom. While God will protect the Jewish people so that they will not be not completely destroyed, two-thirds will be struck down or killed (see Zech. 13:8). The surviving one-third will be preserved and will enter the kingdom at the end of the tribulation. **The earth helped the woman** by somehow absorbing the destructive **flood** that came forth from Satan's **mouth.** While the "flood" could be literal, more than likely, it is

symbolic of his attempt to destroy the Jewish people because it comes out of Satan's mouth.

John described Satan's fury with **the woman** (v. 17), the Jewish people. **The dragon was wroth ... and went to make war** with those left, **the remnant** (Greek, *tōn loipōn*; "the rest") **of her seed.** He was especially provoked by the piety of the remnant, they **which keep the commandments of God** (see 14:12**), and have the testimony** that the Lord Jesus bore, or have the testimony about Him (see 1 Cor. 2:1; 1 John 5:10). More than likely, "the commandments" refers to the instructions of the New Testament (e.g., 1 John 3:18 – 24; 2 John 4 – 6) rather than to the laws of the Mosaic covenant.

B. The Two Beasts (chap. 13)

Chapter 12 is a perfect introduction to the great revelations that come forth in chapter 13. The two beasts that appear in this chapter are the key actors on the stage of the tribulation. The "beast ... out of the sea" (v. 1) is the Antichrist, the political leader who will rule the world, and the "beast ... out of the earth" (v. 11) is the False Prophet, the religious leader who will point the nations to the Antichrist as the savior of all who dwell on the planet.

13:1 – 3. John **saw a beast rise up out of the sea** (v. 1). This "beast" (Greek, *thērion*; "ferocious animal," "monster"), first introduced in Revelation 11:7, is the Antichrist. The deification of the final stage of secular world power, this figure is the prophesied evil ruler who represents the Roman Empire. "The sea" often represents the nations, thus probably indicating that this beast was a Gentile. The imagery in these verses parallels that of Daniel 7:2 – 7. The Beast had **seven heads and ten horns** and **ten crowns.** The "ten horns" (which correspond to the ten toes of the image in Dan. 2:4) and "ten crowns" represent ten kings and their kingdoms, as in Revelation 17:12. The "seven heads" parallel the seven heads of the Dragon (see 12:3), who gave his authority and power to the Beast. Presently, the Holy Spirit, the Restrainer who "withholdeth," will move aside so that the Beast "might be revealed in his time" (2 Thess. 2:6).

All of this represents a confederation of ten kingdoms headed up by one demonic personality, the Antichrist. **Upon his heads** (v. 1), the world powers under his control, was **the name of blasphemy**. This points to his opposition to Christ and to God, as prophesied in Psalm 2:2–3: "The kings of the earth set themselves, and the rulers take counsel together, against the LORD, and against his anointed saying, Let us break their bands asunder, and cast away their cords from us."

The Beast's power included the combined characteristics of Daniel's four beasts (see Dan. 7:4–6). He had the swiftness of a **leopard** (v. 2), like Alexander the Great and his Greek army; the powerful **feet of a bear**, like Persia; and the fierceness of a **lion**, like Babylon. **The dragon gave ... his power, and his seat [of prominence], and great authority** to the Beast. On earth, the Beast will appear to have the dominion of the promised Messiah, though his power will come from Satan and not God. The apostle Paul said that this "man of sin ... the son of perdition" will "be revealed in his time" (2 Thess. 2:3, 6) and that his coming "is after the working of Satan with all power and signs and lying wonders" (2 Thess. 2:9).

One of his heads (v. 3) refers to the Beast himself, who appeared (**as it were**) to be **wounded to death**. The Beast's seemingly mortal **wound was healed**, but people instead believed he died and came back to life. Because of this "miracle," **all the world** (the entire earth) **wondered after the beast** as if he were divine (see 2 Thess. 2:4). The word "wonder" (Greek, *thaumazo*) means "to be amazed," "to be overwhelmed." As Hindson shows (*The Book of Revelation*, p. 141), the Beast's comparison to Christ is profound:

Christ	The Beast
Many diadems (19:12)	Ten diadems (13:1)
Worthy name (19:11–16)	Blasphemous names (13:1)
Causes men to worship God (1:6)	Causes men to worship Satan (13:4)

Power and throne of God (12:5)	Power and throne of Satan (13:2)
Died but lives again (1:18)	Appears to die—but his fatal wound is healed (13:3)

13:4–6. The miracle of the "resurrection" (see 13:3) of **the beast** (v. 4) made the world believe he was like God, **And they worshipped the dragon which gave power** (authority) to him, **and they worshipped the beast** and believed he was invincible. At this point, Satan will have achieved his diabolical goal to "be like the most High" (Isa. 14:14). The world will be fooled "because they received not the love of the truth, that they might be saved. And for this cause God shall send them strong delusion, that they should believe a lie" (2 Thess. 2:10–11). **There was given unto** (v. 5) the Beast, probably by Satan, **a mouth speaking great things and blasphemies**. His power will be consolidated and most active during the final **forty and two months**, or the final half of the tribulation, after which he will be thrown into "a lake of fire burning with brimstone" (19:20).

With his time running out, the Beast blasphemed **against God** (v. 6), against **his name, and his tabernacle**, and even against **them that dwell in heaven**. While the word "tabernacle" means "tent," here it is symbolic of God's abode in glory (see 15:5; 21:3).

13:7–8. The entire world, **all kindreds, and tongues, and nations** (v. 7) ... **shall worship** (v. 8) the Beast. He "shall devour the whole earth, and shall tread it down, and break it in pieces" (Dan. 7:23), as he "exalteth himself above all that is called God" (2 Thess. 2:4). The Beast intensified his attacks against **the saints** (v. 7). And as well, at this time of the end of the tribulation, the Beast will intensify his attacks against **the saints** who are saved (v. 7), whose names are recorded in **the book of life of the Lamb slain from the foundation of the world** (for "the book of life," see discussion on 3:5; see also Exod. 32:32; Dan. 12:1). Many scholars believe that the Book of Life once contained the names of every person born but that the names of the unsaved are blotted from the record when they leave this life.

Seen together, verses 7–8 clearly show the universal extent of the Beast's government and power, as well as the form of satanic worship in the final stage of the tribulation. Only those who trust in Christ will be delivered from the judgment coming upon the world.

13:9. If any man hath an ear, let him hear is a warning for those who read the book of Revelation during the terrible tribulation period. Similar to the exhortations to the seven churches ("He that hath an ear, let him hear what the Spirit saith unto the churches," 2:7, 11, 17, 29; 3:6, 13, 22), it is an invitation to listen and to ponder what is happening. In every era, the Lord puts forth the call to salvation. The appeal is to every individual to trust Christ.

13:10. This verse is sometimes seen as difficult, but John was simply telling it like it is. Things will go on with some being taken **into captivity** and some being **killed with the sword**. The verse "stresses the inevitability of persecution and death for the faithful.... It invited the faithful to recognize that the actions of this false Christ have been decreed by God.... The close of v. 10 names the personal qualities needed to sustain believers in the face of harsh treatment" (Thomas, *Revelation 8–22*, p. 168). The Beast's days of power are limited. Therefore, **the saints** are called to **patience** (Greek, *hypomonē*), meaning "steadfastness," "endurance." The Lord wanted the saints to know that He was moving to a just retribution. They had suffered to the point of martyrdom, yet their **faith** caused them to cling to Christ's promises and the hope of His return to right the wrongs of earth. "Saints" describes the position of those who trust Christ; they are "the holy ones," "the saints" (Greek, *tōn hagiōn*), because Christ is holy.

13:11–13. John **beheld another beast coming up out of the earth** (v. 11). This second "beast" (Greek, *thērion*; "ferocious animal," "monster") is later described as "the false prophet" (19:20; 20:10). His geographic origin is not stated, but this beast was earthly, not heavenly. Though he appeared to be a meek **lamb**, he was aggressive; **he had two horns**. He also **spake as a dragon**, meaning he had certain qualities and powers that come from Satan. This second beast, the False Prophet, represents a religious leader who will make the world think that the first beast, the Antichrist, is divine.

Here some see a parallel with the doctrine of the Trinity. Satan takes the place of God the Father; the Antichrist takes the place of Jesus Christ, the Son of God; and the False Prophet causes men to worship the Antichrist, as the Holy Spirit causes Christians to worship Christ. This is Satan's final attempt to substitute a false religion for the true faith in Christ (see Walvoord, "Revelation," p. 962).

The second beast had power like **the first beast** (v. 12). The world **worship[ed] the first beast** because they were fooled by the **deadly wound [that] was healed**. The False Prophet had power to do **great wonders** (v. 13) and made **fire come down from heaven on earth in the sight of men**. It must be remembered that Satan can impart to those whom he controls miraculous works, such as the powers the Egyptian magicians and priests showed before Moses (see Exod. 7:11–22). Such demonic power is real. No wonder the world will follow after the Beast!

13:14–15. The trickery of the False Prophet **deceiveth [all] on the earth by ... miracles** (Greek, *ta sēmeia*; "the signs"; v. 14) performed before the Beast. An **image** (Greek, *eikona*) is constructed in order that the entire world might honor the Beast and submit to his authority. "This last false religious leader will try the same old trick to get mankind to worship a man rather than the true God!" (Custer, *Patmos to Paradise*, p. 152). What so fascinated the world was that the Beast **had the wound by a sword, and did live**. The False Prophet **had power to give** (v. 15) **"spirit"** (Greek, *pneuma*; here translated **life**), or animation, to **the image** but certainly could not impart actual "life" (Greek, *bios*). Through some form of deception, however, **the image** could **both speak, and cause that as many as would not worship the image of the beast should be killed**. Since Satan cannot give power or life to an inanimate object, this likely will be achieved through an *impression* of "aliveness" that is mechanically contrived to fool all upon the earth. Some have suggested that a combination of natural and supernatural powers will be used to make the Beast's image appear to live.

13:16–18. People from all classes and every social status submitted to **receive a mark** (Greek, *charagma*; v. 16) **[on] their right hand, or [on] their foreheads,** to identify their loyalty and compliance to the authority of **the beast** (v. 17) and his government. No one could **buy or sell** without the identification of the Beast's **number** or **name** on their person. Apparently, the great majority of the world will worship the Beast and his image. Laser technology has been developed to scan identification marks instantly and is already being used in some cases to prove one's identity, financial viability, and so on.

Here is wisdom (v. 18) seems to indicate that the apostle John expected that those living during the tribulation would read this book and then be able to verify the Beast's identity. His number is **Six hundred threescore and six,** or 666. This is **the number of a man,** not of a divine being, who would generally be confirmed by the number of perfection, the number seven. Some see the number as gematria, a number that conjures up a hidden and secret identification. Over the generations, there have been many attempts to point to some individual, whether past, present, or future, who might meet the 666 criteria. As yet, however, the puzzle escapes a solution. The identification of the Beast remains for those living during the great tribulation.

C. The Lamb and the 144,000 (14:1–5)

Here the scene returns to heaven. John received a vision of the Lamb standing on Mount Zion with the 144,000 Jewish witnesses. God had sealed this group to serve Him on earth during the tribulation (see 7:1–8). The sealing protected them from the wrath of God but not from the wrath of Satan and the Beast. "These are the same 144,000 as in chapter 7,… who will experience martyrdom because of their refusal to worship the beast (13:15). They are a special group as 14:4 indicates" (Thomas, *Revelation 8–22,* p. 192). There are several theories about John's second vision of the 144,000 witnesses: (1) Mount Zion is the hill in Jerusalem and the 144,000 are there

with Christ when He begins His earthly millennial reign; (2) Mount Zion is here a heavenly designation for the residence of the 144,000 at this juncture in the tribulation; (3) Mount Zion is a projection of the 144,000 with Christ in the millennial Jerusalem, while verses 2–5 picture that they are in heaven at this point in the tribulation, as are those who were martyred on earth. This last theory seems plausible, as expressed by Thomas (*Revelation 8–22,* p. 192): "They are the vanguard who bear the brunt of the struggle against the beast and pay the price with their own lives." God apparently lifted the protection that was over the 144,000 when their ministry was completed.

14:1. Mount Sion is an actual hill in Jerusalem that was the residence of the kings of Israel. It was a pre-Israelite city that David captured (see 2 Sam. 5:7) and established as his capital. Later it became symbolic of Jerusalem itself, and even of all of Israel and the Holy Land. After Christ's return and millennial reign, a heavenly Jerusalem (see Heb. 12:22–24), the eternal dwelling place of God and His people (see Gal. 4:26), will come down to the new earth (see Rev. 21:2–3). If this is the heavenly Mount Zion, then the 144,000 are there with the **Lamb.** Or the scene could be the millennial Mount Zion during Christ's reign. The 144,000 had the **Father's name** noticeably **written [on] their foreheads** for all to see.

14:2–3. John **heard a voice from heaven** (v. 2), as one voice but with the command of **many waters,** or as the "rushing waters" of a mountain waterfall. He also heard, as if one voice, **harpers** making music **with their harps.** This worshipful scene in glory is a chorus and a symphony of praise to God for His imminent final victory. The musicians accompanied the **new song** (v. 3; see 5:9) being sung **before the throne [of God]), and before the four beasts** (four angelic beings; see discussions on 4:6, 8)**, and the elders.** No one else shared the experiences of the 144,000. They alone were able to understand and sing the new song.

14:4–5. These men lived as **virgins** (sexually pure; v. 4) in that they remained holy amidst the defiling pagan influences. They were faithful to **follow**

the Lamb whithersoever he goeth. They did not live out their own will but faithfully obeyed Christ. They were redeemed out of the world, being the firstfruits unto God, and to the Lamb. "Firstfruits" implies that they were converted Jews who preceded the many others who would turn to Christ at the His coming (see Zech. 12:10; Rom. 11:15, 26–27). In their earthly living, they had spoken no guile (v. 5) and now stood without fault before the throne of God. "Without fault" (Greek, *amōmos*, describing a sacrificial animal without defect) shows how morally superior they were.

D. The Harvest of the Earth (14:6–20)

These verses show that even as things get progressively worse on earth, the gospel will continue to be proclaimed worldwide. Here is a mixture of grace and judgment. The Lord will intensify His wrath, yet the gospel will still be available. While these verses have to do with the tribulation, the gospel of salvation by faith in Christ remains the same.

14:6–7. John saw another angel (v. 6), like none before, fly in the midst of heaven, preaching the everlasting gospel unto[all] that dwell on the earth. While this message may have included the "gospel" (Greek, *euangelisai*, "good news") of the coming kingdom of the Messiah, it was a personal message, as reflected in verse 7. "It is everlasting in the sense that it is ageless, not for any specific period" (Walvoord, *The Revelation of Jesus Christ*, p. 217). Some scholars believe that this was not a message about personal salvation but rather an announcement of God's judgment only—the good news that God at last was about to deal with the world in righteousness and establish His sovereign rule over the entire world.

Part of the angel's message was, Fear God, and give glory to him (v. 7). The hour of his judgment is come means that an earthly and final judgment was about to be accomplished. The sense is that it is but a short leap from these verses to the arrival of Christ from glory to establish His kingdom, though it seems to read that it is about to start right here. Christ's coming and the battle of Armageddon would

bring final defeat to the power of the Beast, the False Prophet, and the nations of the earth that joined forces with them to defeat Israel (see 19:11–21).

14:8. There followed another angel with the announcement that Babylon is fallen. This announcement is prophetic of the events described in chapter 17. Ancient Babylon was the fountain from which all polytheism came. It was founded by Nimrod, who was the first great rebel against God and more than simply a hunter of animals. Nimrod was the first great tyrant, a might one, a mighty hunter before the Lord (see Gen. 10:8–10). His name means "let us revolt." "He established a thoroughly autocratic, imperialistic, despotic system of tyrannical government ... back of which stands Satan in all his rage against God" (Stigers, *Genesis*, p. 125). The city he founded, Babel, was an apostate civilization (see Gen. 11:1–9). Since it was prophesied that historic Babylon would be destroyed and never again be inhabited (see Isa. 13; 14; Jer. 50–51; Zechariah 5), "MYSTERY, BABYLON THE GREAT" (Rev. 17:5) appears to be something different. This civilization seems to consist of a mighty technological force driving a global economy. All signs in the book of Revelation point to the fact that it is pagan Rome, papal Rome, or a future revived Rome—but it is Rome (see chaps. 17–18; and Hindson, *The Book of Revelation*, p. 156).

14:9–11. A third angel followed (v. 9) the first two and issued a warning to those who worship the beast and his image, and receive his mark (see 13:18). During this terrible time on earth, people will have only two choices: (1) resist the Beast, trust God, and possibly be martyred or (2) be loyal to the Beast and face the wrath of God. All who receive the Beast's mark shall drink of the wine of the wrath of God, which is poured out ... into the cup of his indignation (v. 10). They will face eternal torment along with Satan, the demon world, and all unsaved people. The smoke of their torment (v. 11) will be unending, for ever and ever, continuing day and night. The torment will be like being cast into a pit of volcanic fire and brimstone (v. 10). This terrible scene will be witnessed by God's holy angels and the

Lamb. Such are the consequences of worshiping the Beast and of receiving his mark.

The teaching of such eternal punishment is rejected by annihilationists, evolutionists, and liberal theologians who deny judgment over against grace. God exhibited His grace and mercy when He sent His Son to die for sinners. For those who do not believe, however, the only thing left is eternal judgment (see 20:11–15).

14:12–13. The patience of the saints (v. 12) seems to be a reminder to those believers in the tribulation to walk before a hostile world by **keep[ing] the commandments of God** and holding on to **the faith of Jesus**. Resistance against the Beast will be impossible! While people may think they have the option to resist the Beast, martyrdom awaits those who attempt to defy him. Walking in the integrity of trust will be the only option for believers. **Blessed are the dead which die in the Lord from henceforth** (v. 13) is the second beatitude in the book of Revelation (see discussion on 1:3).

14:14–16. The Son of man (v. 14) is the Messiah, the Lord Jesus Himself (see 1:13; Dan. 7:13; Mark 8:31). Matthew used this title more than twenty-five times. He wore **a golden crown** as His victory wreath, because He would soon ascend to earth to rule and to reign. That the Messiah was still seated in heaven shows He was still with His Father on His thone (see Ps. 110:1–3). **A sharp sickle** would be used to reap **the harvest** (v. 15) of the world, because **the earth is ripe** (Greek, *exēranthē*), become "withered," "dry," "ready for harvest." "The harvest" refers to the final judgment, the "reaping" of the world for its sins, which was soon to take place. The command to begin the harvest came from an **angel [who] came out of the temple** in heaven. The Lord God had ordered the final judgment to begin. Some believe "the harvest" refers to the gathering of the saints, but this is doubtful because people will be saved throughout the tribulation. From heaven, Christ, **he that sat on the cloud** (v. 16), began the judgment.

14:17–19. Another angel (v. 17) came forth, **also having a sharp sickle**. In contrast to the sickle of 14:14, this probably refers to a smaller sickle for cutting grapevines, since **gather the clusters** (v. 18) and **her grapes are fully ripe** are analogies about the harvesting of grapes. **And the angel ... gathered the vine of the earth, and cast it into the great winepress of the wrath of God** (v. 19). Grapes were trampled in a violent manner in the winepress, producing a flow of red grape juice. "The use of angels to assist the harvest of the earth is now stated explicitly in verse 17.... The figure of divine judgment as a harvest is here enlarged" (Walvoord, *The Revelation of Jesus Christ*, p. 222). These events are fulfilled in Revelation 19:15 as part of the battle of Armageddon.

14:20. This scene gives a preview of the final battle of Armageddon (described more fully in 19:14–21), which will take place **without** (outside) **the city** of Jerusalem, probably to the north, at the place known today as the plain of Jezreel, located near the hill of Megiddo. **Blood** will flow up to **the horse bridles** for a distance of 1,600 **furlongs**, about 200 miles. There have been battles in the past in which the trampling of the horses over infantry splattered blood up to the bridles. That there will be such a terrible slaughter in the last days is prophesied in Scripture (see Isa. 63:1–3; Dan. 11:40–45).

X. The Seven Vials (chaps. 15–16)

These chapters focus on the chronology of events leading up to the second coming of Christ (chap. 19) and introduce "the seven last plagues" (15:1), the divine judgments that will precede the Lord's coming. The basic progression of the judgments is an unfolding of the seven seals (6:1–17; 8:1), the seventh seal introducing the seven trumpets (8:1–9:21; 11:15–19), and the seventh trumpet introducing the seven vials, or "bowls," of wrath. Chronologically, chapter 19 comes after chapter 16, while chapters 17–18 present an interlude about Babylon the Harlot. The fall of Babylon has already been announced in Revelation 14:8. Its doom has already been certified. "The final and dramatic action of the Apocalypse is about to begin (here in this chapter). In eight brief verses, chapter 15 sets the stage for the final drama. The pouring out of the seven bowls (KJV — 'vials') of God's wrath (chap. 16) culminates in the fall of Babylon (chaps. 17–18) and the return of Christ to earth (chap. 19)" (Hindson, *Revelation*, p. 161).

A. Introduction: The Song of Moses and the Seven Angels with the Seven Plagues (chap. 15)

This chapter comes to the point quickly. It gives a summary of the final events of judgment about to fall on the earth. This exclusively heavenly scene shows the preparations for the horrible final judgments upon the earth, but it also gives God the glory for His justice in ending the arrogance and rebellion of humanity.

15:1–2. John **saw another sign in heaven, great and marvellous** (Greek, *mega kai thaumaston*; v. 1). **Seven angels** prepared to administer **the seven last plagues** of **the wrath of God**. The apostle **saw as it were** (comparative language) **a sea of glass mingled with fire** (v. 2). "A sea of glass" (a glassy sea, or "glassy [or] crystal"; see discussion on 4:6) is an illustration of the tranquility and peace of heaven. It represents the splendor and glory of the Lord on His throne. "The sea of glass is an emblem of 'the splendor and majesty of God on His throne that sets Him apart from all His creation, a separation stemming from His purity and absolute holiness, which He shares with no one else'" (Thomas, *Revelation 8–22*, p. 232). The sea was "mingled with fire," however, which portends judgment. In this scene, John saw the final **victory** of those who had refused the **mark** of the Beast. They were singing praises to the Lord, **having the harps of God**.

15:3–4. The martyred redeemed **sing the song of Moses … and the song of the Lamb** (v. 3), which may represent one hymn, though some scholars think they are specific and distinct songs. The word "song" (Greek, *ōdē*) has a definite article, suggesting that two songs are in view. has often been identified with Exodus 15, though some have suggested it relates also to Deuteronomy 32. "All nations shall come and worship before thee" would refer to the millennial reign of the Messiah and is a quote from Psalm 86:9. Exodus 15:17 says that God "shalt bring [His

people, Israel] in, and plant them in the mountain of thine inheritance," and Deuteronomy 32:43 says that God "will avenge the blood of his servants." **God Almighty** is described in similar wording as the "sign" in 15:1: **Great and marvellous** (Greek, *megala kai thaumasta*). **Thou King of saints** may refer to God or to Christ: "Now unto the King eternal, immortal, invisible, the only wise God, be honour and glory for ever and ever. Amen" (1 Tim. 1:17).

15:5–6. John then saw another heavenly vision of **the temple of the tabernacle** ("tent"; v. 5) being **opened** (see 11:19). This imagery is of the Lord's dwelling place among the Israelites during the forty years of wandering (see Exod. 40:34–35). The word **testimony** is a reference to the two tablets of the Law that Moses brought down from Mount Sinai (see Exod. 32:15; 38:21; Deut. 10:5).

The seven angels (v. 6) who were about to minister judgment on the earth appeared in priestly garments, **clothed in pure and white linen, and having their breasts girded with golden girdles** (waist or chest censures). The purity of the angels' garments shows the purity of their task, which was to bring holiness to earth (see Thomas, *Revelation 8–22*, p. 232). The bride of Christ will be similarly clothed when she comes as Christ's army to reign with Him (see 19:8, 14).

15:7–8. One of the four beasts ("living creatures"; see discussions on 4:6, 8) **gave the seven angels seven golden vials full of the wrath of God** (v. 7), to be poured out on earth. The picture is both graphic and terrible, as if seven bowls of scalding liquid were to be poured down on humanity below. The reader is reminded, however, that such judgment was due. The vials were golden, showing that they came from the temple of the righteous God in heaven, and He is the eternal God, **who liveth for ever and ever**.

That **the temple was filled with smoke** (v. 8) is symbolic of the **power** and **the glory of God** (see Exod. 40:34; 1 Kings 8:10–11; Ezek. 44:4). No one in heaven could approach Him as such awful judgment went forth upon the earth. Ezekiel saw this same manifestation of God's glory depart from the temple just before the Babylonian captivity (see Ezek. 10:1–22; 11:22–23).

Taken all together, verses 5–8 show a terrible and frightening scene of impending divine wrath and judgment coming down on a wicked world. The terrible nature of these judgments fully justify this ominous introduction.

B. First Vial: Ugly and Painful Sores (16:1–2)

16:1–2. A great (Greek, *megalēs*) **voice out of the temple** (v. 1) instructed **the seven angels** to begin **pour[ing] out … the wrath of God upon the earth.** When **the first [angel] poured out his vial** (v. 2), the inhabitants of earth were stricken with a **noisome and grievous sore**, but this judgment was selective in that it infected only those who had taken the Beast's **mark** and **worshipped his image.** The infections are similar to the boils and abscesses of the sixth Egyptian plague (see Exod. 9:9–11; see also Job 2:7–8:13). The afflictions now became very personal.

C. Second Vial: The Sea Turns to Blood (16:3)

16:3. The second angel poured out his vial, and the sea became polluted, as with **the blood of a dead man: and every living** (Greek, *zōēs*) **soul** (Greek, *psychē*) in the oceans **died**; that is, every living organism was killed off. Such descriptions make it clear that the events of the tribulation will be worldwide in scope and not simply some localized happenings. This horrible scene pictures the death of all biological life in the oceans.

D. Third Vial: Rivers and Springs of Water Become Blood (16:4–7)

16:4. When **the third angel poured out his vial,** the judgment of the second vial was extended. **The rivers and [the source] of waters** became polluted with **blood.**

16:5–7. The Lord turned the waters to blood in response to the shedding of **the blood of saints and prophets** (v. 6). From the altar in heaven, **the angel of the waters** (v. 5) declared this judgment just (see 16:7; 15:3). Those who were in allegiance with the

Beast and who worshiped his image had killed believers; thus, the angel continued, **thou hast given them blood to drink; for they are worthy** (v. 6). "Worthy" (Greek, *axios*) refers to the fact that those who took the lives of the saints are deserving of punishment for their crimes (see 3:4). The punishment fit the crime of the murderers (see Isa. 49:26). **Another** (v. 7) angel called forth from **the altar,** testifying that the **Lord God Almighty** is **true and righteous** in His **judgments.**

E. Fourth Vial: The Sun Scorches People with Fire (16:8–9)

16:8. When **the fourth angel poured out his vial,** judgment was focused on **the sun; and power was given unto him … to scorch** the earth's inhabitants **with fire.** It has been suggested that one of the means God will use to bring this about is the destruction of the ozone layer that encircles the earth. Ozone retards the sun's radiation, and if it is depleted, the sun's scorching would bring about death. Another possibility is that this judgment will be accomplished by monstrous sun flares.

16:9. Despite the **great heat** generated, earth's inhabitants still **blasphemed the name of God** (see 16:11, 21), the one who **hath power over these plagues.** Even with the terrible plagues being poured down on them, people still refused to **give him glory.** They refused to "change the mind"; **they repented not.**

F. Fifth Vial: Darkness (16:10–11)

16:10–11. The fifth angel poured out his vial (v. 10) at the place of authority for **the beast,** his **seat** ("throne"), or center of rule, **and his kingdom was full of darkness.** This "darkness" could refer to a climatological event, or it may refer to that fact that the Beast's rule over the world was collapsing, and any remaining "civilization" was no more. The inhabitants of the earth **gnawed their tongues for pain.** Gnawing one's tongue is the greatest expression of physical pain. **Because of their pains and their sores** (v. 11; see 16:2), humanity continued to blaspheme God, and they **repented not of their deeds.** This is the last reference to repentance (see 2:21; 9:21). People could have repented during these trials, but instead, they simply continued to blaspheme God (see 16:21).

G. Sixth Vial: The Euphrates River Dries Up (16:12 – 16)

16:12 – 14. When **the sixth angel poured out his vial … the great river Euphrates … was dried up** (v. 12). The Euphrates River is the water boundary between the Holy Land and Asia, to the east, and is mentioned often in Scripture (see, e.g., Gen. 15:18; Deut. 1:7; 11:24; Josh. 1:4). Isaiah also prophesied that the river will dry up (see Isa. 11:15). "History frequently refers to the great hindrance the Euphrates has been between the peoples living east of it and those living west of it. But in the time of the pouring out of the sixth bowl of judgment, this river is to be mysteriously smitten and dried up, that the kings from the sunrising may have an easy passage for their armies in coming to join the great infernal crusade against the Lamb" (Seiss, *The Apocalypse*, p. 377). The way will be open for **the kings of the east**. These rulers and their armies were part of the invasion forces that fight against Christ in the final battle (see 19:11 – 21). In the past, the Euphrates was a formidable separation for large armies; in some places, it is two-thirds of a mile wide.

Satanic influence caused the kings of the east and their armies to cross the Euphrates to attack Israel. John saw **unclean spirits like frogs** (v. 13) come out of the mouths of **the dragon**, **the beast**, and **the false prophet**. Additional leaders and nations, **the kings of the earth and of the whole world** (v. 14), were wooed into the Middle East. The showdown, the final **battle of that great day**, will take place at Armageddon (see 16:16). The "frogs" **are the spirits of devils** who work **miracles** and seduce the world to its doom (see 1 Tim. 4:1; James 3:15).

16:15 – 16. In the middle of John's vision, the Lord called out, **Behold** (v. 15), and warned that He will **come as a thief**. This is a reminder for those on earth during the tribulation that His coming draws near. There is some question whether this is a salva-

tion verse or a reminder to believers in the tribulation to be ready for His arrival. **Blessed is he that … keepeth his garments** is the third beatitude in the book of Revelation (see discussion on 1:3). It seems to be a reminder to remain morally clean in a terribly immoral world. The "garments" of salvation symbolize the life and testimony of the saved (see 19:8).

The nations finally **gathered … together** (v. 16) at the hill of Megiddo (**Armageddon**) for the final conflict (see 14:20; 19:19). Though seemingly localized to the north of Jerusalem, this final conflict will have global consequences. The whole world will be rocked by the great devastation that will be wrought by this battle (see 19:17-21).

H. Seventh Vial: A Tremendous Earthquake (16:17 – 21)

16:17 – 18. The **seventh angel poured out** the seventh and final **vial** (v. 17), or "bowl." **A great voice** from the heavenly **throne** of God called out, **It is done** (Greek, *gegonen*; perfect tense), "It has become." The very last chapter of the tribulation had arrived. It was accompanied by **voices, and thunders, and lightnings; and … a great earthquake, such as was not since men were upon the earth** (v. 18). Christ spoke of this time, when there will be "earthquakes in divers places" (Matt. 24:7). Isaiah also wrote, "The LORD maketh the earth empty, and maketh it waste, and turneth it upside down" (Isa. 24:1). When the nations come "against Jerusalem to battle … Then shall the LORD go forth, and fight" for His people (Zech. 14:2 – 3). The Messiah's feet will touch the Mount of Olives (see Zech. 14:4), and multitudes will "flee … from before the earthquake" (Zech. 14:5).

16:19 – 21. **The great city** (v. 19) is Jerusalem, "which spiritually is called Sodom and Egypt, where also our Lord was crucified" (11:8). The topography shifted, and the city **was divided into three parts**. This is part of God's judgment upon His own people in the end of the age (see Jer. 30:11; Zech. 14:14). The Lord reminded Israel that in the last days, "I will correct thee in measure, and will not leave thee altogether unpunished" (Jer. 30:11). **The cities** of other countries also **fell**, and God remembered also the **great Babylon** and made her drink **the wine** of His fierce **wrath**. "Wrath" (Greek, *orgēs*) is a strong word for God's rage at sin and is often related to *thymos* (**fierceness**) as part of His divine anger and marks Babylon especially as an object of God's judgment. Babylon, the founder of false religion, was ripe for downfall (see 17:16; 18:8); its final collapse is narrated in 19:18–21.

And every island (v. 20) shifted, **and the mountains** fell. This is similar to the movement of the islands and mountains mentioned in 6:14, though with a more violent conclusion. Again, this is a reminder of tribulation descriptions in Isaiah 24:6, where it is written, "The curse devoured the earth." **Great hail**(stones) weighing about 100 pounds each (**a talent**) fell upon the earth. Even this terrible judgment did not bring repentance; rather, humanity continued to blaspheme God **because of the plague of the hail**. This must be one of the most awful judgments because John the apostle wrote, **the plague thereof was exceeding great**. The word "exceeding" (Greek, *sphodra*) can be translated "vehemently violent."

XI. Babylon: The Great Prostitute (17:1–19:5)

Central to the seventh vial judgment is the fall of Babylon. This event was first mentioned in 14:14–20. While it sometimes seems as if God forgets, He remembers full well the evil, persecution, and oppression against His own. Babylon will fall for her religious immorality and for her persecution of the saints (17:6). A detailed account of her demise is presented in chapters 17–18.

Any interpretation of "Babylon" is difficult, but chapter 17 presents Babylon as an ecclesiastical or spiritual entity, and chapter 18 sees her as a political and economic entity. The Babylon of the last days will be a center of commerce, enterprise, and wealth.

A. Babylon Described (chap. 17)

That John used the word "MYSTERY" (v. 5) to describe Babylon suggests that he was witnessing something about Babylon that neither ancient Babylon nor its geographic site gives meaning to. He was directing the reader to look deeper to find something new, something figurative rather than literal. This is not to say that the events described here are fiction or allegory but that the imagery projects something not seen before.

17:1–2. One of the seven angels which had the seven vials (v. 1; see chap. 16) called John over, **Come hither**, to see the final **judgment of the great whore** (Greek, *pornē*). That she sat **upon many waters** shows her great influence upon the nations (see 17:15). She had **committed fornication** (Greek, *porneuō*; v. 2) with the earth's **kings**. Spiritual and religious adultery was at the heart of the apostasy of ancient Israel (see Ezekiel 16, 23 and all of Hosea). She had fornicated not only with the rulers of earth but also with **the inhabiters of earth**. All had become **drunk with the wine of her fornication**. This graphic picture is of an orgy in which all restraints are thrown to the wind. All rationality and civility had been cast aside.

17:3–5. The apostle was **carried … away in the spirit** (v. 3) to witness another vision about the **woman**, Babylon. In an orgiastic gesture, she rode on the back of **a scarlet coloured beast**, who is the Antichrist, the world dictator of 13:1. The **ten horns** represent ten world powers or nations, as defined in 17:12. The **seven heads** represent seven prominent rulers of the revived Roman Empire. This empire was assembled and controlled by the Antichrist in chapter 13. When he came to power, he came up out of the sea (the nations) controlling the seven heads and ten horns (13:1). Here in chapter 17, this flashback is given to show how Babylon fit into the scheme of things.

The whore **was arrayed** (v. 4) in royal attire. She is seen as rich, elegant, and queenly in status. The **golden cup in her hand** parallels the imagery of Jeremiah 51:7–8. John imposed on this scene the diabolic features of the ancient Babylonian system, the ancient enemy of God's people Israel. This great harlot is called **THE MOTHER OF HARLOTS** (v. 5). While she looked regal in her dress, the cup she held was **full of abominations and filthiness of her for-nication** (v. 4).

17:6–7. The woman [was] drunken with the blood of the saints, and with the blood of the martyrs of Jesus (v. 6). The woman, the Beast, and the kings of the revived Roman Empire will make war with the Lamb and those who follow Him (see 17:14). The woman and her false religious system will have world influence. In ancient times, she was the mother goddess under the names of Ishtar, Ashtar, Astarte, Aphrodite, and Venus. Her revived system will hate those who worship Christ and will kill many who trust in Him.

John wrote, **When I saw her, I wondered with great admiration** (v. 6). In context here, **admiration** (Greek, *thauma*) has the thought "to be amazed, as-tonished." John is not admiring the woman in a posi-tive sense but rather he is startled by the evil she is bringing against the saints. **The angel** (v. 7) asked him, Why **didst thou marvel?** and proceeded to tell him **the mystery of** this harlot, **and of the beast that carrieth her**.

17:8–11. The remainder of the chapter consists of the angel's explanation of "the mystery of the woman, and of the beast that carrieth her" (17:7). **The beast** (v. 8) whom she was riding **shall ascend out of the bottomless pit** (Greek, *abyssos*; see 9:1). This per-sonality is connected to both the sea (the nations; see 13:1) and the pit (the realm of the confined but later released demons). The authority and the power be-hind the Beast will be satanic (see 13:4). All evidence points to the fact that he will be human and not a supernatural demonic individual, though he will be greatly influenced by the powers of the underworld. John was quick to remind the reader that the Beast's end will be **perdition**, where, along with the Devil and the False Prophet, he will forever abide and "shall be tormented day and night" (20:10). The world will be fascinated (**shall wonder**) at the power of **the beast**. They are the ones **whose names were not written in the book of life from the foundation of the world** (see discussions on 3:5; 13:8; 20:12, 15; 21:27).

Here is the mind which hath wisdom. Believ-ers living during the tribulation period will find

evidence as to who **the seven heads are** (v. 9); they **are seven mountains, on which the woman sitteth**. In his commentary on Revelation, the church father Victorinus said that the seven "hills" were identified with the seven hills of Rome. A closer look, however, seems to point to the **seven kings** (or "kingdoms"; v. 10). From John's vantage point, five of these king-doms had come and gone. One was still present, but **the other is not yet come**. When it arrives, it will not last long. Walvoord argues that the five past kingdoms are: Egypt, Assyria, Babylon, Persia, and Greece (*The Revelation of Jesus Christ*, pp. 250–54). The "old" Roman Empire was still present in John's day. A seventh kingdom will arise, however, and bring forth **the eighth** (v. 11) kingdom, that of the Antichrist.

17:12–14. The ten horns (v. 12) and **ten kings** refer to "contemporaneous kings who are heads of the countries which will form the original alliance in the Middle East that will support the future world ruler" (Walvoord, "Revelation," p. 972). They will **receive** (political) **power** for a short time: **one hour**. They will move with **one mind** (v. 13) and agree to **give their power** to support **the beast**. They **shall make war with the Lamb** (v. 14), but in the end, they will be defeated, because **he is Lord of lords, and King of kings**. This phrase is similar to descriptions of God the Father (see Deut. 10:17; see also 1 Tim. 6:15; Rev. 19:16). **They that are with him are called, and chosen, and faithful** seems to describe those under Christ's protection at the end of the tribulation and is a statement of God's sovereignty in divine protection.

17:15–18. That **the whore sitteth** (v. 15) over the **nations** means that for a time she will govern or control all of the **peoples** of the world. The major powers of the earth (**the ten horns**; v. 16), however, will turn on her to **make her desolate and naked**. They will consume her and **burn her with fire**. The false apostate religious system, or "church," will be brought down for all the world to witness. While the true church of the Lord Jesus will be taken in the rapture (see 1 Thess. 4:13–18), apostate Christen-dom, which the whore represents, will continue to the end of the tribulation. During that time, there will be a certain measure of religious freedom, for the Jews will reestablish their worship and their sacrifices (see Dan. 9:27).

God's **will** (v. 17) will be at work in these events. Babylon the whore and her influence are doomed. God **hath put in [the] hearts** of the international powers to **give their kingdom unto the beast**. Verse 18 confirms that the whore is something besides a restoration of an ancient nation like Babylon. **The woman ... is that great city, which reigneth over the kings of the earth** (v. 18). That city is probably Rome.

B. The Fall of Babylon (chap. 18)

Chapter 18 begins with, "And after these things," which shows a progression from the events of chapter 17. John saw "another angel" (v. 1), distinct from the angel of 17:1. The context of chapter 18 shows that here Babylon is seen in its political and economic character rather than its religious character. The Babylon of Revelation is the prophesied new Rome. It is a revision of the ancient Roman Empire in a politically and economically revived Europe. Not since the days of the Roman Empire has there been a truly peaceful, united Europe.

18:1. Another **angel [came] from heaven, having great power; and the earth was lightened with his glory**. This is one of the most powerful angels of God, though he is not Christ, as some have assumed. In poetic fashion, he described the final stage of the destruction of the whore.

18:2–4. The angel **cried ... Babylon the great is fallen, is fallen** (v. 2). The double phrase is for certainty and for emphasis that Babylon's influence was over. As in the demise of Babylon of old, the city had become a place of death and even of evil (see Isa. 13:20–22). It is as if the entire demonic and spirit world had come to mourn her fall. The city is **the hold** ("prison") **of every foul spirit** where the fallen angels, or evil spirits, are gathered. **Unclean, hateful**, and **bird** often symbolize evil spirits (see Isa. 34:11–15; Matt. 13:32). Babylon had been given over to demons as a judgment because of the evil of the inhabitants.

All nations (v. 3) and **the kings of the earth** had partaken of her **wine of ... fornication** and had even **committed fornication with her**. While they had done this in a spiritual or religious way before (17:2), **the merchants of the earth** were now doing this by indulging in **the abundance of her delicacies** (Greek, *strēnos*; "sumptuousness"). **Another voice** (v. 4), that of an angel, called the redeemed who had survived the tribulation to **Come out of her ... that ye be not partakers of her sins, and ... of her plagues** of judgment.

18:5–11. For her sins have reached unto heaven (v. 5), the voice continued, **and God hath remembered her iniquities**. Her **Reward** (v. 6) of judgment was to be **double according to** all the evil she had done. Her **cup** of wrath would be filled **double**. As much as she had **glorified herself, and lived deliciously** (v. 7), that **much torment and sorrow** would be given to her. She saw herself as **a queen** and not as a deserted **widow**, but now **her plagues** (v. 8) would **come in one day**, with **death, and mourning, and famine ... For strong is the Lord God who judgeth her**. Those who had **committed fornication** (v. 9) with her, **the kings of the earth**, would witness **the smoke of her burning** and would **bewail** and **lament** her fall.

Standing afar off (v. 10), possibly **for ... fear** that the destruction coming upon her might affect them, the kings would exclaim, **Alas, alas, that great city** is judged **in one hour**. This seems to be a literal one hour (see 18:17, 19), which explains the people's shock over the suddenness of the city's fall. God's wrath would fall quickly on **that mighty city**. Recognizing that they would no longer benefit from her commerce and her trade, **the merchants of the earth** (v. 11) would also bemoan the city's demise.

18:12–16. The merchandise (v. 12) of the city's trade is listed. The list includes the most valuable of wealth: precious metals, gems, luxurious cloth, and other fineries; manufactured goods that are crafted, mined, and concocted, such as **odours, and ointments ... wine, and oil** (v. 13); fruit products, animals for food, and even manufactured mechanical items, such as **chariots**. Some have argued that such descriptions make it impossible that modern trade is indicated. It must be remembered, however, not only that in Scripture such goods are often described as the ancients would have known them but also that there is a future extrapolation and application here because the events have to do with far-off prophecy.

18:17 – 20. The **shipmaster[s] … and sailers** (v. 17) who traded with Babylon saw **the smoke of her burning** (v. 18) from a distance. Interestingly, the city of Rome is only forty miles or less from the west coast of the Mediterranean Sea, whereas ancient Babylon (in modern Iraq) is two hundred miles from the Persian Gulf. The Tiber River runs from Rome to the ocean. The world could not believe what was happening. Four times those who profited from her called her the "mighty city" (18:10), and the "great city" (18:16, 18, 19). They lamented her fall because they had benefited so greatly from her influence, for they **were made rich all that had ships in the sea by reason of her costliness** (v. 19). **Heaven, and [the] holy apostles and prophets** (v. 20) of the past were called to **Rejoice … for God hath avenged you on her** (see 19:2; Luke 11:49).

18:21 – 24. Another angel, **a mighty angel … took up … a great millstone, and cast it into the sea** (v. 21). A "millstone" is a large grinding stone (also called a "donkey stone"), turned by a donkey or oxen, for milling grain. Extremely heavy, such a stone would doom anyone lashed to such a heavy object (see Mark 9:42). **Thus with violence shall that great city Babylon be thrown down.** This graphic description vividly portrays the finality of the fate of **Babylon** the whore. The angel proclaimed that the city **shall be found no more at all.** There would be no more **musicians** (v. 22) to orchestrate her glory and **no craftsman** to manufacture her wares. **The sound of a millstone** producing grain would be heard no longer. **The light** (v. 23) of the city would go out, and the joyful voices at wedding feasts **shall be heard no more at all in thee.** The prominent **merchants** of Babylon, who were counted among **the great men of the earth**, would be gone.

Babylon's greatest deception was her **sorceries** (v. 23), by which **all nations** of the world were seduced. "Sorceries" (Greek, *pharmakeia*) refers to hallucinogens used in incantations to the gods, the demons. This demonic worship has to do with the spiritual "fornication" so often mentioned in the indictment against the woman. Verse 23 is a reminder of how powerful she was. Her evil influence was worldwide. Moreover, she was responsible for **the blood of prophets, and of saints** (v. 24; see 17:6). Christ referred to this when He warned Jews who would become believers during the tribulation, "Then shall they deliver you up to be afflicted, and shall kill you: and ye shall be hated of all nations for my name's sake" (Matt. 24:9). **And** (the blood) **of all that were slain upon the earth** may refer to the slain saints, or it may mean that all who died on the earth during the tribulation, saved and unsaved, perished because of the woman's direct influence. Most scholars take it as a reference to the prophets and saints who were killed during the last of the tribulation period.

C. Praise for Babylon's Fall (19:1 – 5)

19:1 – 3. These verses constitute an anthem of praise to God because He had ended the evil influence of the whore. While in one sense, the Beast and the False Prophet are extremely important in John's revelation of end-time events, **the great whore** (v. 2) has somewhat greater significance. It must be remembered that she sat over the nations (the "many waters," 17:1, 15); that is, she controlled the Beast (see 17:3) and the nations ("the seven heads and ten horns," 17:7). **Much people in heaven** (v. 1) now rejoiced, **saying, Alleluia** (a transliteration of the Greek *hallēlouia*), which in Hebrew means "praise the Lord." The only four occurrences of "Alleluia" in the New Testament are in Revelation (19:1, 3 – 4, 6). "Much people" seems to refer to the martyrs mentioned in 7:9, though it could refer to all the saints in glory.

Four accolades of worship are ascribed to God: **Salvation, and glory, and honour, and power** (v. 1). These are ascribed to Him throughout the Bible but seem to have intensified significance in Revelation. **True and righteous are his judgments** (v. 2). He will always do right, but here His justice destroyed the **great whore which did corrupt the earth** with religious and demonic **fornication**. God had **avenged the blood of his servants** who had died **at her hand**, or by her power and influence. **Her smoke rose up for ever and ever** (v. 3) is hyperbole. The clear point is that the city will smolder for months, if not years, after her destruction.

19:4–5. The twenty-four **elders** (v. 4), representing the church, and **the four** (angelic) **beasts** ("living creatures"; see discussions on 4:6, 8) **fell down** to give God His due praise, as in the beginning of the book (see 4:4, 6). All of God's **servants** (v. 5) who **fear him**, regardless of their status (**both small and great**), were called to give Him **Praise** (Greek, *aineō*). Walvoord believes this refers to all the Lord's servants, not just the tribulation saints (see *The Revelation of Jesus Christ*, p. 270). "Praise" is in the present tense and is best translated "to be continually praising Him." The word is related to the thank offering (see Lev. 7:13) but means "a sacrifice of praise" or "to sing praises."

XII. Praise for the Marriage Supper of the Lamb (19:6–10)

These few verses describe the marriage of the Lamb of God with His bride, the church, in glory. That this marriage takes place in heaven shows that the church was previously raptured. The imagery of a wedding between God and His people is rooted in the Old Testament (e.g., Isa. 54:5–7; Hosea 2:19) and the New Testament (e.g., Eph. 5:32), where marriage is used to describe the relationship between Christ and His church. The bride, the church, waits for the coming of her heavenly Bridegroom (see 2 Cor. 11:2).

19:6. In heaven, John heard **a great multitude** that sounded as **the voice of many waters**, like a roaring waterfall. The near-deafening shout he heard was, **Alleluia** (see 19:1), with the explanation, **for the Lord God Omnipotent reigneth**. This anthem of joy has been heard before in the Bible, but here there is a difference. God was about to have the final victory. The end of the tribulation was in sight.

19:7. Let us be glad is a continuation of the worship from the heavenly multitude. They are rejoicing because the union between the Lamb and His own **is come**. There are three views as to the timing of this marrage. (1) It will take place in heaven as the tribulation draws to an end on earth. (2) It will take place as soon as the church is raptured to glory. Christ told His disciples, "And if I go and prepare a place for you, I will come again, and receive you unto myself; that where I am, there ye may be also" (John 14:3). (3) It will take place on earth at the beginning of the millennium.

19:8. The **fine linen** adorning the bride represents **the righteousness of saints**. In the Old Testament, the priest's clothing was of white linen (see Exod. 28:42; Lev. 6:10; 16:4). Some scholars think "the righteousness of saints" refers to the saints' positional justification by faith, but the plural meaning, "the righteous acts," indicates that it refers to the righteous works that the saints performed through the grace of God (see Eph. 2:8–10). There is no doubt, however, that the bride has been justified by faith alone.

19:9–10. Blessed are they which are called unto the marriage supper of the Lamb (v. 9) is the fourth beatitude in the book of Revelation (see discussion on 1:3). In ancient religious custom, the wedding supper was the highlight of fellowship around the union of the bride and groom. The angel repeats and highlights the importance of this announcement in 22:6: **These are the true sayings of God.**

The nearness of the consummation sent the elder apostle John to his knees. John may have thought he was falling before Christ, but the angel reminded him, **I am [but] thy fellowservant, and of thy brethren that have the testimony of Jesus** (v. 10). This testimony is **the spirit of prophecy**. This means that, at its very heart, prophecy is designed to "unfold the beauty and loveliness of our Lord and Saviour Jesus Christ" (Walvoord, *The Revelation of Jesus Christ*, p. 273). Jesus is not only the major theme of the Word of God but also the central personality in prophecy.

XIII. The Return of Christ (19:11–21)

These verses describe two major events: (1) Christ's return in glory, as prophesied in so many places in Scripture; (2) the defeat of the Beast, the False Prophet, and all the rebellious peoples of earth as they come against God's people in the Holy Land. The carnage of this battle will, for a season, put an end to the opposition to the Lord's workings on earth. Christ will reign in His earthly kingdom for a thousand years.

19:11–13. Heaven opened, and John saw the Lord arrive from **heaven** (v. 11) on **a white horse**. The tribulation opened with one who rode a white horse and held a bow (see 6:2), but he was the Antichrist, not the Son of God. Here, riding a white horse, Jesus returns with "the sword of [His] mouth" (2:16) and wearing **many crowns** ("diadems"; v. 12). Christ's second coming and His rule are prophesied in many passages of Scripture (e.g., Psalm 2; Isa. 9:7; 11:1–16; Zech. 14:3–4; Matt. 24–25). The names **Faithful and True** (v. 11; see 3:14) indicate the holiness and perfection of the Messiah. **In righteousness he doth judge and make war** (see Isa. 11:4; see also 1:5; 3:7). Using comparative language, John described Christ's eyes **as a** (purifying) **flame of fire** (v. 12; see 1:14; 2:18). He has great authority, as seen in His "many crowns" of honor.

Christ had a secret **name ... that no man knew, but he himself** (v. 12). Some believe this is an eternal name that may never be revealed. Others believe it refers to His appearance as the glorious Lord, which has never before been seen. This revelation about Him is thus unique. His clothes were **dipt in blood** (v. 13), showing that His authority comes from His obedience unto death in the place of sinners (see Isa. 63:2–3; Rev. 14:20). Christ is the sacrificial Lamb of God who takes away the sins of the world (see Isaiah 53; John 1:29, 36). According to John 1:1–3, **The Word of God** is the Creator, who here is the Judge of humanity.

19:14–16. Also riding **white horses**, the holy **armies [of] heaven followed him**. Their righteousness and purity is shown by their clothes of **fine linen, white and clean**, which they received at the marriage (see 19:8). They represent the church, the bride of Christ, returning in triumph with the Savior.

The Word of God had but to command with **his mouth** (v. 15), as if with **a sharp sword**, and He

would **smite the nations**. As prophesied, **he shall rule them with a rod of iron** (see Ps. 2:9; Rev. 2:27), meaning He will subjugate them with His divine power and authority. The carnage that the Lord will inflict, with **fierceness and wrath**, will be like the pressing of the grapes (see 14:19; Isa. 63:3). The time of His reign drew near. He wore **his vesture** (v. 16), a ceremonial robe, **and on his thigh a name [was] written, KING OF KINGS, AND LORD OF LORDS** (see 17:14; Dan. 2:47; 1 Tim. 6:15).

19:17–18. With **the sun** (v. 17) shining brightly, as if a new day was dawning, **an angel** summoned the birds **in the midst of heaven** to come to **the supper of the great God**. The circling, high-flying vultures were called to come and feast on **the flesh** (v. 18) of those whom the Messiah would destroy. The wicked rebels, of all classes and social positions, who had come against the Lord and His people would perish, including **kings ... captains ... both free and bond, both small and great**. While this is a horrible scene, the victory is sweet in contrast to all of the evil that had been done during the tribulation. The scene is reminiscent of Ezekiel 39:17–20, which describes the destruction of the northern forces who will come against Israel in the last days. Matthew 24:28 is a parallel passage.

19:19–21. John saw the forces of evil **gathered together to make war against** (v. 19) the Lord and His people. The evil earthly authorities (**the kings of the earth**, the Antichrist (**the beast**), **the false prophet** (v. 20), and all those who **worshipped** (the Beast's) **image** (see 13:12) **... were cast alive into a lake of fire burning with brimstone**. The rest of the rebel army and all unbelievers are cast into the lake of fire following the Great White Throne Judgment (Rev. 20:11–15). (See also Matt. 25:41, 46; Rev. 21:8.) These who were Satan's lackeys and masterpieces of hate were cast into this final place of everlasting punishment, into which Satan also would soon be thrown for a thousand years (see 20:10). Others in the world who followed after the Beast, **the remnant** (v. 21), **were slain** by Christ **with the sword**, the authority that He speaks **out of his mouth**. And the birds of prey **were filled with their flesh**.

XIV. The Thousand Years (20:1–6)

This chapter mainly deals with the literal one-thousand-year reign of Christ on earth, over the house of David, as prophesied (see 2 Sam. 7:9–17; Ps. 2; 89; Luke 1:30–33). While this is the only place that "a thousand years" (Greek, *chilia etē*) is mentioned (vv. 2–7), the expression is about the fulfillment of the promised kingdom prophesied in both the Old Testament and the New Testament. Christ made it clear that "the Son of Man cometh" (Matt. 24:44) "in his glory" (Matt. 25:31) to sit upon His throne. He is the King who gives to the faithful on earth to "inherit the kingdom prepared for you from the foundation of the world" (Matt. 25:34). The word "millennium" comes from the Latin *mille*, with the word *annus*, meaning "year."

20:1–3. John once again **saw an angel** (v. 1; see 7:2; 8:1; 10:1; 14:6, 8, 9, 15, 17, 18; 17:1; 18:1, 19:17), and the angel **laid hold on ... that old serpent, which is ... Satan, and bound him a thousand years** (v. 2). Some think this angel is Christ, but there is no evidence of this. During the millennial kingdom on earth, Satan will be bound. **The bottomless pit** (Greek, *abyssos*; v. 1) is the same abyss of 9:1–2, 11; 17:8, the home of the fallen demons that were released to torment earthlings (see chap. 9). **A great chain** emphasizes that Satan will not be able to escape this confinement. His four descriptive titles given in verse 2 are the same as in 12:9. Why will he be bound during the millennial reign of Christ? Some have suggested that with Satan no longer on the earthly scene, the heart of humanity will be exposed. Will human beings then live in perfect harmony with the Messiah in their midst? The answer is no.

It must be remembered that many Jews and Gentiles will enter the millennial kingdom in their natural bodies. They will have offspring, who will have offspring, and so on. Those later generations must choose to trust Christ just as their ancestors did. With Satan bound, people's hearts will be tested. **A seal** (v. 3) will be set over the **pit** to confine Satan during **the thousand years** of Christ's rule. Then **he must be loosed a little season**. When Satan is freed, he will instigate one final rebellion against Christ (see 20:7–10).

20:4–6. Who are the ones sitting upon **thrones** (v. 4) in **judgment**? Some say they are the saints of both Israel and the church. Others argue that they are the twenty-four elders who will be "kings and priests" (5:10) during Christ's earthly rule. When the millennial kingdom begins, the nations, or the Gentiles who rejected Christ (see Matt. 25:31–46), and unrepentant Jews (see Ezek. 20:33–38) will be judged. The Lord told Jeremiah that He would "make a full end of all nations whither I have scattered thee [Israel] ... but I will correct thee in measure, and will not leave thee altogether unpunished" (Jer. 30:11).

It seems that those who **had not worshipped the beast**, and were thus **beheaded** (v. 4), conducted a special judgment. They had been resurrected and now **reigned with Christ a thousand years**, and they were acting as judges. **The rest of the dead** who were not raised **until the thousand years were finished** (v. 5) refers to the wicked, who will not come forth from the grave until the end of the millennial age. Then they must face the eternal judgment (see 20:11–15).

As the context indicates, **the first resurrection** (v. 5) contrasts with the last resurrection (see 20:12–13), which is followed by **the second death** (v. 6; see 20:14). It is the first resurrection in the sense of "before." The righteous of all generations of the past will be raised in the first resurrection to enjoy the blessed state of Christ's millennial rule. **Blessed and holy is he that hath part in the first resurrection** is the fifth beatitude in the book of Revelation (see discussion on 1:3). The words "Blessed and holy" are important in understanding these verses. This is the positional state of the redeemed, whose sins have been covered by the blood of Christ. All of the glorified will serve Him and **shall be priests of God and of Christ, and shall reign with him for a thousand years**. Note that all will serve both God and the Son as priests, demonstrating that Christ is more than a mere prophet. He is also very God!

XV. Satan's Doom (20:7–10)

These verses prophesy the finality of the Devil and his influence. While the Lord Jesus is ruling over the millennial kingdom as the descendant of King David, Satan will be given a final opportunity to deceive those living on earth. The messianic reign on earth is key to all biblical teaching. All of human history has been moving toward this period. The Old Testament prophets focused on it, and the New Testament apostles foretold it again. There can be no kingdom without a king. God has before appointed human representatives to govern His kingdom on earth. In the near-perfect environment of the millennial kingdom, Satan will be loosed so that God may finish for all time his revolt and the last rebellion of humanity.

20:7–8. The thousand years (v. 7) is literal; it has a beginning and an ending: **when [they] are expired**. Some writers argue, "Well, we do not know how long the thousand years will last." Taking this number literally is the only way to understand it. At the beginning of Christ's millennial reign, Satan was imprisoned in the bottomless pit (see 20:3). He was now **loosed out of his prison**, whereupon he returned to earth **to deceive the nations** (v. 8). This indicates that there will be a generation that is ripe for revolt against Christ, who will rule from Jerusalem. The righteous who have been resurrected and who rule in the kingdom with Christ will be impervious to sin and temptation. Those Satan rallies will be descendants of the people who entered the kingdom one thousand years before.

The forces who gathered from **the four quarters of the earth** (v. 8) for the final battle included **Gog and Magog**. Those whom the Devil mustered to revolt against Jerusalem, **the beloved city** (v. 9), were innumerable, **as the sand of the sea** (v. 8). The reference to Gog and Magog is similar to what is prophesied in Ezekiel 38–39, but the two events are probably not the same. In Ezekiel's prophecy, the timing seems to be when Israel is in the Holy Land during the tribulation, whereas the context in Revelation 20 is the end of the kingdom period.

The Devil and his followers came against Jerusalem in one last act of defiance. God, however, sent **fire ... down from ... heaven, and devoured them** (v. 9). The war was quickly over. God will put an end to rebellion once and for all. The final abode of **the devil** (v. 10) is **the lake of fire and brimstone** (burning sulfur)**, where the beast and the false prophet** had already been cast (see 19:20). The torment will be eternal; it will continue **day and night**. The same lake of fire is where the unsaved will be finally cast (see 20:15). This lake of torment was originally prepared, not for humans, but for the Devil and his angels (see Matt. 25:41). This passage clearly points to the doctrine of eternal punishment.

XVI. The Great White Throne Judgment (20:11–15)

The final judgment, the judgment of the unsaved dead of all ages (the "small and great," v. 12), will take place after the millennial reign of Christ. Those who will be judged before the great white throne are not believers but the lost who refuse the revelation of God and spurn the offer of salvation in Christ. This judgment will result in the final condemnation of everyone who stands before it.

20:11. There is some difference of opinion as to who sits on the **great white throne**. Many believe it is God the Father and not the Lord Jesus Christ. It is probably Christ, however, because all judgment has been given over to Him (see Matt. 19:28; 25:31; 2 Cor. 5:10). This is especially brought out in John 5:22: "For the Father judgeth no man, but hath committed all judgment unto the Son." Even Daniel understood that someday the lost would be resurrected and have to face everlasting punishment. He wrote, "Many of them that sleep in the dust of the earth shall awake, some to everlasting life, and some to shame and everlasting contempt" (Dan. 12:2). His use of "everlasting" shows that life and judgment will last forever. The lost will not be able to hide from this judgment. That the throne is white implies that the judgment is a holy affair that no lost person can escape.

This throne is not the heavenly throne where the Lord dwells, so often mentioned throughout Revelation. Nor is it the millennial Davidic throne (see Matt. 25:31). It is the throne of last resort. **The earth and the heaven** are personified. They **fled away** as if in reverence before Him who sits on the throne.

20:12–13. The dead (v. 12), regardless of their status (**small and great**), **stand before God**, but as mentioned, this is probably God the Son (see discussion on 20:11). **The books** (Greek, *biblia*; "scrolls") **were opened** that contain all of the **works** done by those standing before the throne. This set of books is compared to *the* book, **the book of life** (see 3:5; Ps. 69:28; Dan. 12:1; Phil. 4:3), which contains the names of those destined for eternal life. If one's name is not written down for salvation, the only verdict left is a sentence of condemnation. **Their works** (v. 13) broadly refers to what has come forth from the individual's entire life. "Works" would include attitudes, sinful acts, moral decisions, a lack of desire for God, and so on. It is important to note that works result in condemnation, whereas faith saves. "For by grace are ye saved through faith; and that not of yourselves: it is the gift of God: Not of works, lest any man should boast" (Eph. 2:8–9). And, "Not by works of righteousness which we have done, but according to his mercy he saved us" (Titus 3:5).

Death and hell delivered up the dead (v. 13) indicates that the resurrected bodies of the lost will be joined with their spirits that have been waiting in hell (Greek, *hadēs*; "the grave") for the final judgment. "The delivering of the spirits of the unsaved dead is in view in deliverance from Hades unless the word *death* refers to the body. Any obscurity which this passage may have does not alter the fact of the universal resurrection of all men in their order" (Walvoord, *The Revelation of Jesus Christ*, p. 308). The mention of **the sea** shows that "regardless of how far a body has disintegrated, it will nevertheless be resurrected for this judgment" ("Revelation," p. 983). Death is described as if it is a place. The Greek text best reads, "The death and the hades gave [up] the dead ones."

20:14–15. The final destination of the lost is **the lake of fire** (v. 15). The doctrine of eternal punishment is difficult, but the Bible is consistent about this fact. The wicked will face eternal separation from God. The lost will remain in their resurrected bodies in the lake of fire. Their resurrected bodies will be indestructible. When the judgment is completed, death and hell themselves will be cast into the lake of fire. **This is the second death** (v. 14). This statement must not be construed as annihilationism, the doctrine that the lost will somehow cease to exist. John reworded and restated here what he saw happening lest the reader misunderstand what he wrote in 20:12–13. If one's name is not **written in the book of life** (v. 15), only one thing is left: being cast into the lake of fire.

XVII. The New Heaven, New Earth, New Jerusalem (21:1–22:5)

The closing chapters of the book of Revelation open up the new vista of the prophetic vision that reaches into the far future—the eternal state. Eternity will begin after the terrible period of the tribulation and after the glorious earthly reign of the Lord Jesus Christ in the millennium. A new world, a new creation, is coming. Even the blessings of Christ's earthly kingdom cannot compare with the glorious eternal state that awaits the children of God.

21:1–2. The prophet Isaiah gave the first glimpse of the **new heaven** (v. 1) and the **new earth**. The Lord said, "For behold, I create new heavens and a new earth: and the former shall not be remembered, nor come into mind" (Isa. 65:17; see Isa. 66:22). This is the creation of a *new* universe. The old universe will be forgotten and certainly will not be missed. The biological and material sphere as now known will be totally changed: **and there was no more sea**. The old universe will be destroyed and replaced. It will be reconstituted by fire, and "the elements shall melt with fervent heat" (2 Peter 3:10; see 2 Peter 3:7, 12). The new heaven and new earth will indeed be completely new.

John saw the holy city, new Jerusalem (v. 2), descend **from God out of heaven**, as a virgin **bride adorned** with all of her purity. Some believe the old Jerusalem will be changed into the new, but this is not so. The New Jerusalem will indeed be *new*.

While the mind begs for more information about this wonderful event, the Bible gives but limited information because the human mind cannot absorb the full picture.

21:3-4. With the coming of the new Jerusalem, **the tabernacle** ("tent") **of God** (v. 3), His very abode, will be **with** the redeemed. (1) **[God] will dwell with them**, (2) **they shall be his people**, (3) **God Himself shall be with them**, and (4) He will **be their God**. Here John worked hard to give the sense of the Lord's very presence among the saved. Verse 4 is a very emotional verse in that it touches on the emotional and physical struggles in this life that will be so distinctly changed and altered. **Tears** (v. 4) will be **wipe[d] away**, **death** will be gone, **sorrow** and **crying** will be no more, and **pain** will be eradicated, because **the former things are passed away**.

21:5-6. The Lord declared, **I make all things new** (v. 5). Satan and his angels were no longer at work, and God had brought to completion, through the sacrifice of His Son, the issue of sin. This great revelation is **true and faithful**; it is certain and absolute. The one bringing about the transformation of the universe is Jesus Christ, the Son of God. He possesses the everlasting attribute of God. He is the **Alpha and Omega, the beginning and the end** (v. 6; see 1:8; 22:13), the one who has always existed and who will always exist. This same one gives eternal spiritual life: **I will give unto him that is athirst of the fountain of the water of life freely** (see Isa. 12:3; John 4:10; 7:37).

21:7-8. Those who **overcometh** (see 2:7, 11, 17, 26; 3:5, 12, 21) **shall inherit all things** (v. 7), better translated "all these things." This statement shows the intimate relationship between God and the redeemed in the eternal state. Rather than receiving grace and mercy, the **unbelieving** (v. 8) will receive the judgment of **the lake which burneth with fire and brimstone**. John described the most vile of sinners: **the abominable** (Greek, *bdelyssomai*; the ones who have practiced the most evil things), **and murderers, and whoremongers** (Greek, *pornois*), **and sorcerers, and idolaters, and all liars** (v. 8). Other passages in Revelation also list the outworking of

sin (21:27; 22:15). It is clear that this passage is not saying that if they had not committed these sins, they would be saved. It is not affirming salvation by works. Such sins are but evidences of the lost state of the transgressor. Rather, it punctuates the fact that this judgment is final. For these sinful unbelievers, all hope is gone. "This is the second death" (20:14).

21:9-14. One of the seven angels (v. 9; see 15:1) summoned John to **Come hither** and view more closely **the bride, the Lamb's wife**, the New Jerusalem (v. 10). As in 1:10, the apostle was **carried ... in the spirit**, to a **high mountain** to view **that great city ... descending out of heaven from God**. The city reflected **the glory of God** (v. 11). It had a **light**, a brightness, **like a jasper stone, clear as crystal**. What John saw was beyond description. Thus, he again used comparative language: "like," "as," "The city looked something like this."

The walls of the city were **high** (v. 12), with **twelve gates** guarded by **twelve angels**. The twelve gates represent **the twelve tribes of ... Israel**. This is similar to the millennial city of Jerusalem, with its twelve gates dedicated to the twelve tribes of the children of Israel (see Ezek. 48:30-35). **Three gates** (v. 13) were positioned on each wall: **east**, **north**, **south**, and **west**.

Besides the nation of Israel, the church was also honored: **the names of the twelve apostles** (v. 14) were on the **twelve foundations** that supported the entire wall. More than likely, Judas's name will be omitted and replaced by the name of Matthias (see Acts 1:26).

21:15-17. The angel **measure[d] the city, and the gates ... and the wall** (v. 15) with **a golden reed** (about ten feet in length). The city was about **twelve thousand furlongs** (Greek, *stadiōn*; v. 16), about 1,500 miles, on each side and above; **the length ... breadth**, and **height of it are equal**. (Some scholars place the length of the furlong at 582 feet, measuring out to 1,342 miles.) Commentators differ on whether the city is a cube or a pyramid, though most favor the idea that it is a pyramid. **The wall** (v. 17) of the city was 144 **cubits**, or 216 feet, thick. **The measure of a man** simply means that the rod, a human measurement, was used, though the one measuring was an **angel**.

21:18–21. The **wall** (v. 18) was constructed **of jasper**, and the city was made of **pure gold, like unto clear glass**, probably meaning that it was finely polished and reflected like glass. **The foundations … were garnished** (v. 19), or decorated, with all kinds of gemstones. The exact identification of some of these stones is not known. **The twelve gates** (v. 21) resembled single **pearls … and the street of the city was pure gold, as it were transparent glass**.

21:22–27. John **saw no temple** (v. 22) in the New Jerusalem because the **Lord God Almighty and [Christ] the Lamb are the temple**. Two persons of the Godhead, the Father and the Son, are together seen as the temple. This places Christ as equal with the Father, giving awesome support to the doctrine of the Trinity. The two are separate persons yet one in divinity. **The glory of God** (v. 23) lit the city, though Christ **the Lamb is the light thereof**. The eternal city therefore **had no need of the sun** or the **moon**. The **saved** (v. 24) of the Gentile **nations** will be in the city, and the redeemed great men, **the kings** of world history, will bring their earthly **glory and honour** into the city. This may indicate that what a person was on earth will be recognized in eternity, though of course, that would not include the works of carnality that one did in his earthly life. Kings who were just in their rule will be honored.

The gates (v. 25) will never **be shut**. No danger will lurk in this glorious city, for sin will be eliminated. Only righteousness and goodness will prevail. There will be no fear of night because **there shall be no night there**. Never again will there be any defilement, or those who **worketh abomination** (v. 27) or speak **a lie**. The city will be occupied with only those **which are written in the Lamb's book of life**. These verses are compressed and condensed in that they give but an abbreviated sketch of eternity and of the eternal New Jerusalem. The human mind cannot comprehend all that God has in store for the saints. For certain, what "little" John wrote describes a beautiful and glorious future for all who are redeemed and who trust the living God.

22:1–5. John was shown **a pure river of water of life** (v. 1). It was **clear as crystal**, coming forth from **the throne of God** the Father and of the Son, **the Lamb**. Both the Father and the Son occupy the throne. Both are also the temple of the New Jerusalem (see 21:22). Verses 1 and 3 set forth a strong statement of the doctrine of the Trinity. If Christ were simply a man, or even a holy prophet, He could not be seen as equal to the Father. While the "water" seems to be literal, and certainly may be so, the symbolism is obvious. From the throne of God comes holiness, purity, and righteousness. Though this is similar to the waters coming forth from the millennial temple (Ezek. 47:1, 12), it is not the same thing. Pure water is a blessing and a necessity for the survival of life.

Though **the tree of life** (v. 2) is mentioned as a single tree (Greek, *xylon*), it seems to be a grove or cluster of trees standing on either side of the river. This refers back to the Tree of Life in Genesis 2:9. This forest of trees will produce **twelve … fruits** each month. As in Genesis 3:22, the Tree of Life stands for immortality. Because Adam and Eve ate of the forbidden "tree of the knowledge of good and evil" (Gen. 2:17), they were driven out of "the garden of Eden" to be kept away from "the tree of life" (Gen. 3:24).

The leaves … were for the healing (Greek, *therapeia*) **of the nations** (v. 2). The nations will benefit from the health-giving properties of the leaves, but this does not imply that the nations will grow ill without the leaves. The main point is that there will be **no more curse** (v. 3) upon the redeemed of Adam's children, or even upon the new creation. Because of **the throne of God and of the Lamb**, divine rule will never cease. God the Father and His Son, the Lamb, will rule the new heavens and the new earth. The saved, **his servants[,] shall serve Him** (v. 3) and **shall reign for ever and ever** (v. 5). They **shall see his face** (v. 4), which is an idiom that means they will continue to have an audience with the king. In ancient times, criminals were banished from the face of the ruler (see Est. 7:8; 2 Sam. 14:24). Believers will forever behold the face of the Lord (see 1 Cor. 13:12).

The redeemed will be given a mark on **their fore-heads** (v. 4) to identify them as the servants of God. It is both a privilege and a blessing to be so identi-fied. Repeating that **there shall be no night** (v. 5) in the new eternal state (see 21:23), John emphasized that the light God gives is so bright that not even **the sun** or a **candle** will be needed.

XVIII. Conclusion (22:6 – 21)

In the conclusion are final messages from the angel (v. 6; see 19:17), Christ (vv. 7, 12 – 16), John (vv. 8 – 11), and the Spirit of God (v. 17). What angel is in view here? "The best course, however, is to see this as a continuation of the part begun in 21:9 – 10 by one of the angels who had the seven bowls and continued by him in 21:15. This follows the pat-tern of the conclusion to the earlier intercalation about Babylon, delivered by a comparable angel in 19:9 – 10" (Thomas, *Revelation 8 – 22*, p. 495). The messages are kind, uplifting, encouraging, and posi-tive. There is, however, also a warning about tamper-ing with this inspired book. The message is meant not to bewilder or confuse the reader but to show that what is written will surely take place. The mes-sage is given to be understood by those who are in-structed by the Spirit of God, and it is to be read "in the churches" (v. 16).

22:6 – 7. The **angel** (v. 6; see 19:17) reminded John that **These sayings** ("words") **are faithful and true** (see 19:9). In 19:11, "Faithful and True" is a title of the Messiah, the living Word of God, but here the reference is to the written Word. The Word of God is both an "alive" written revelation (see Heb. 4:12) and the living Son of God. **The Lord God of the holy prophets** has shown **his servants the things which must shortly be done**. "Shortly" (Greek, *en tachei*) means the events will take place with rapidity, with suddenness, when they happen. John was not neces-sarily implying that they would take place right away (see discussion on 1:1).

With an exclamatory (Greek, *idou*) **Behold**, the Lord Jesus said, **I come quickly** (v. 7). The word "quickly" is the Greek word *tachy* and is related to the word *tachei*. When Christ returns, the events will

take place at a rapid rate; things will fall into place in rapid order. He said this in other passages also (22:7; 22:12, 20). This idea is reinforced by the Lord's state-ments in 3:3: "I will come on thee as a thief [both with suddenness and with stealth], and thou shalt not know what hour I will come upon thee" (see also 16:15). **Blessed is he that keepeth** (or lives out) **the sayings of the prophecy of this book** is the sixth beatitude in the book of Revelation (see discussion on 1:3). A blessing comes for all who live with an understanding of what life is about and where the future is headed.

22:8 – 11. As before (see 19:10), John **fell down** (v. 8) before the messenger **angel** to **worship** at his **feet**. The angel again reminded John that he was but a **fellowservant** (v. 9) with him and with the other **brethren the prophets**. He urged John to **wor-ship God**. The words of this prophecy are not to be **seal[ed]** (v. 10), or closed from meaning. Some scholars believe the book of Revelation is a "closed book, a mystery" that cannot be understood, and certain theories of eschatology (the study of proph-ecy) make the book confusing. The book is to be kept open, however, because **the time is at hand**. As in 1:3, this phrase is best translated "the season [Greek, *kairos*] is near [Greek, *engys*]." By using these two words, John was saying that the Lord's future program, the tribulation, is surely going to happen. The word *engys* literally means "in the hand;" that is, it is "certain" and "sure" to take place.

Verse 11 has been seen as difficult by some schol-ars. John seems to be saying that when eternity has begun, the new and eternal state will be fixed and unchanged. All who are **unjust** (v. 11) shall remain so, and all who are **righteous** will also remain that way. The unjust who are impenitent will stay that way, and the godly and the holy will remain true to their character. A time is coming when change will be impossible (see Walvoord, *The Revelation of Jesus Christ*, p. 335).

22:12 – 16. Christ will come suddenly, **quickly** (v. 12; see 22:7), and He will give His **reward** to **every man according as his work shall be**. Some believe this refers to the great white throne judgment of the works of the ungodly (see 20:12), but since Christ's coming "quickly" has to do with a blessing in 22:7, it refers to the judgment seat of Christ (Greek, *bēma*), the giving of rewards for Christian service (see 1 Cor. 3:10–15; 2 Cor. 5:10–11). In verse 12, the Lord is addressing the readers who have this book before them. This verse is very closely related to 21:7, which pronounces a blessing for believers who are presently living out their faith in the world.

Blessed are they that do his commandments (v. 14) is the seventh and final beatitude in the book of Revelation (see discussion on 1:3). The Lord Jesus Himself pronounced the last two beatitudes (here and 22:7). They who keep His commandments will have the **right** to partake of **the tree of life** and will be able to **enter in through the gates into the city**. Their obedience is the evidence of their genuine salvation.

Verse 16 is the final message from the Lord to His own, except for a short line in 22:20: "Surely I come quickly." His testifying **angel** (v. 16; see 1:1) came to the churches to give the revelations in this book. Christ identified Himself with the Old Testament Messiah, **the root and offspring of David** (see 5:5; 2 Sam. 7:12–17; Ps. 89:4; Isa. 11:1), but He is also **the bright and morning star**, which more than likely is a reference to the fact that the Messiah is the "Star out of Jacob" and "the Sceptre [that] shall rise out of Israel" (Num. 24:17). The Bridegroom of the church is also the King of the Jews.

22:17–19. The Spirit and the bride (v. 17), the New Jerusalem, give the invitation to **Come**. Those who **heareth** spiritually are invited to partake of **the water of life freely**, without cost. The offer is open to **whosoever will** come. "Heareth" implies more than simply hearing words; it implies a spiritual recognition of the truth of what is said. Jesus made it clear that whosoever partakes of the living water He provides will be given eternal life (see John 4:10, 14). Many will hear words and even certain spiritual thoughts but will not respond.

For those who get the message, **that heareth the words of the prophecy** (v. 18), and yet distort the message and turn away from it, **God shall add unto him the plagues**, or judgments, **that are written in this book**. Similarly, if anyone **shall take away from the words of … this prophecy** (v. 19), that person will lose **his part out of the book of life, and out of the holy city, and from the things which are written in this book**. In other words, that rejecter will not be given the blessings of eternal life. John's warnings are very close to what Moses wrote in Deuteronomy 4:2, 12:32. One dares not add to or take away from the prophetic message of God.

22:20–21. To Christ's promise **Surely I come quickly** (see 22:7), John added a final prayer, **Amen. Even so, come, Lord Jesus** (v. 20). "Amen" is "verily" or "absolutely." This book began with a revelation about the Lord Jesus Christ, and it ends the same way, with the great hope of His return. Revelation is full of eternal hope for believers and fearful judgment for the lost. It describes events both on earth and in the heavens. It speaks of bliss for the saved and tragedy for the unsaved. It shows forth the glories of God the Father and of His Son, the Lord Jesus Christ. It is the final revelation of God's perspective on history and His prophecies regarding the future. John ended with a benediction of **grace** (v. 21) and the certainty of an **Amen**. Thus, the New Testament begins with Jesus Christ (Matt. 1:1) and ends with a promise of His grace (Rev. 22:21). Throughout, He is the subject. The New Testament begins with His first coming and ends with the promise of His second coming.

MAPS

Holy Land in the Time of Jesus

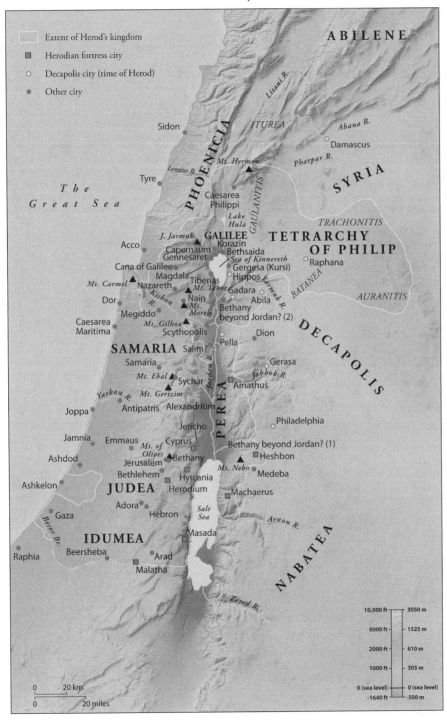

Extent of Herod's kingdom
Herodian fortress city
Decapolis city (time of Herod)
Other city

ABILENE

Litani R.

Sidon

PHOENICIA   ITUREA

Abana R.

Damascus

Leontes R.   Mt. Hermon

SYRIA

Tyre

Pharpar R.

The
Great Sea

Caesarea
Philippi

GAULANITIS

Lake
Hula

TRACHONITIS

Acco

J. Jarmuk   GALILEE
Korazin
Capernaum   Bethsaida
Gennesaret   *Sea of Kinnereth*

TETRARCHY
OF PHILIP

Raphana

Cana of Galilee

Magdala   Tiberias
Mt. Carmel   Nazareth   *Mt. Tabor*

Gergesa (Kursi)
Hippos
Gadara

BATANEA

Dor

Kishon R.   Nain   *Mt. Moreh*

Abila

AURANITIS

Megiddo

Mt. Gilboa   Bethany
beyond Jordan? (2)

Karmuk R.

Caesarea
Maritima

Scythopolis   Pella

Dion

DECAPOLIS

SAMARIA   Salim?

Samaria

Gerasa

Mt. Ebal   Sychar
Mt. Gerizim

Jabbok R.
Amathus

Yarkon R.

Joppa

Antipatris   Alexandrium

PEREA

Jordan R.

Philadelphia

Jamnia   Emmaus
Cyprus
Mt. of Olives   Bethany

Jericho

Bethany beyond Jordan? (1)

Ashdod   Jerusalem
Bethlehem   Hyrcania
Herodium

Heshbon
Mt. Nebo   Medeba

Ashkelon   JUDEA

Adora   Hebron

Salt Sea

Machaerus

Gaza

Besor Br.

Arnon R.

IDUMEA   Masada

Raphia   Beersheba   Arad

Malatha

NABATEA

Zered R.

10,000 ft   3050 m

5000 ft   1525 m

2000 ft   610 m

1000 ft   305 m

0 (sea level)   0 (sea level)

-1640 ft   -500 m

0   20 km.

0   20 miles

Jerusalem in the Time of Jesus

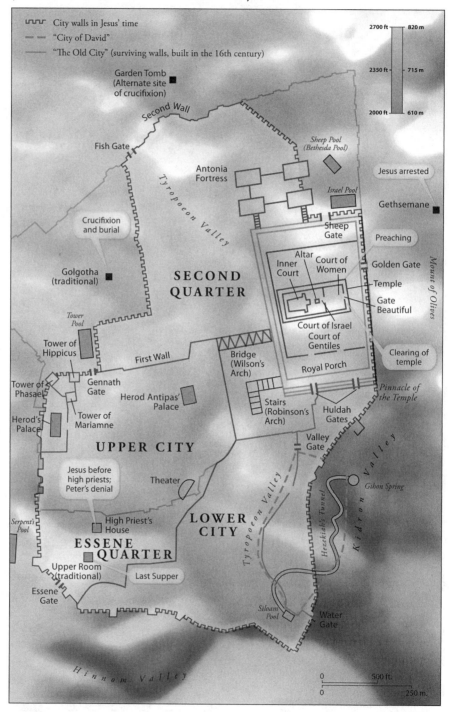

City walls in Jesus' time
"City of David"
"The Old City" (surviving walls, built in the 16th century)

2700 ft — 820 m
2350 ft — 715 m
2000 ft — 610 m

Garden Tomb
(Alternate site
of crucifixion)

Second Wall

Fish Gate

Tyropoeon Valley

Antonia
Fortress

*Sheep Pool
(Bethesda Pool)*

Israel Pool

Jesus arrested

Gethsemane

Crucifixion
and burial

Sheep
Gate

Preaching

Mount of Olives

Golgotha
(traditional)

SECOND
QUARTER

Altar
Inner
Court

Court of
Women

Golden Gate

Temple

Gate
Beautiful

Court of Israel
Court of
Gentiles

*Tower
Pool*

Tower of
Hippicus

First Wall

Bridge
(Wilson's
Arch)

Royal Porch

Clearing of
temple

Tower of
Phasael

Gennath
Gate

Herod Antipas'
Palace

Stairs
(Robinson's
Arch)

Huldah
Gates

*Pinnacle of
the Temple*

Herod's
Palace

Tower of
Mariamne

Valley
Gate

Kidron Valley

UPPER CITY

Jesus before
high priests;
Peter's denial

Theater

Gihon Spring

LOWER
CITY

*Serpent's
Pool*

High Priest's
House

Tyropoeon Valley

Hezekiah's Tunnel

ESSENE
QUARTER

Upper Room
(traditional)

Last Supper

Essene
Gate

*Siloam
Pool*

Water
Gate

Hinnom Valley

0   500 ft.
0   250 m.

ROMAN EMPIRE

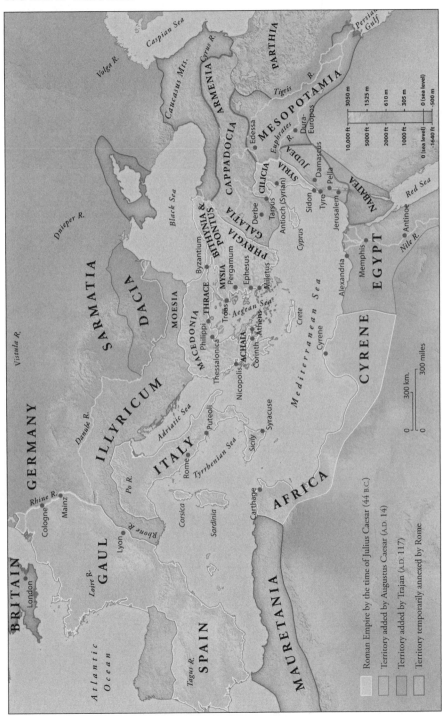

Roman Empire by the time of Julius Caesar (44 B.C.)

Territory added by Augustus Caesar (A.D. 14)

Territory added by Trajan (A.D. 117)

Territory temporarily annexed by Rome

3050 m 1525 m 610 m 305 m 0 (sea level) -500 m

10,000 ft 5000 ft 2000 ft 1000 ft 0 (sea level) -1640 ft

300 km.

0   300 miles

0

PAUL'S JOURNEYS

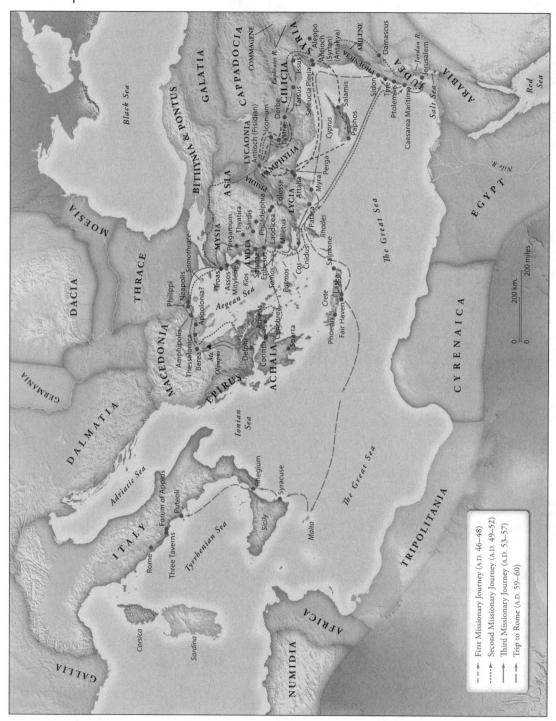

First Missionary Journey (A.D. 46—48)

Second Missionary Journey (A.D. 49—52)

Third Missionary Journey (A.D. 53—57)

Trip to Rome (A.D. 59—60)

200 km.

200 miles

THE SEVEN CHURCHES OF REVELATION

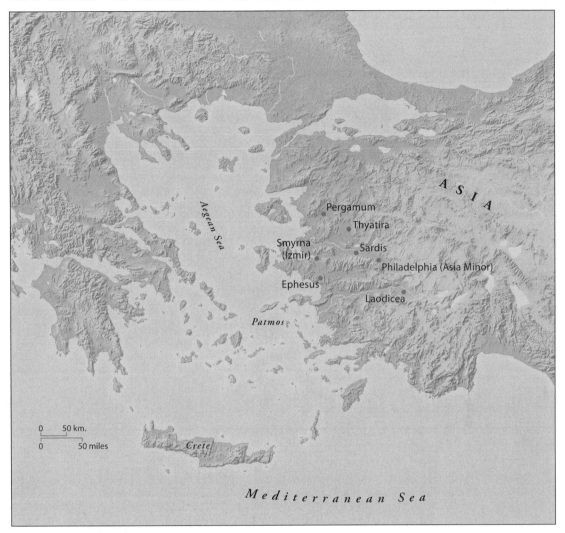

Aegean Sea

A S I A

Pergamum

Thyatira

Smyrna
(Izmir)

Sardis

Philadelphia (Asia Minor)

Ephesus

Laodicea

Patmos

0   50 km.

0   50 miles

Crete

M e d i t e r r a n e a n   S e a

We want to hear from you. Please send your comments about this book to us in care of zreview@zondervan.com. Thank you.

ZONDERVAN.com/
AUTHORTRACKER
follow your favorite authors